# JavaFX

## Rich Client

## Programming on the

# NetBeans Platform

# JavaFX

## Rich Client Programming on the NetBeans Platform

Gail Anderson • Paul Anderson

Addison-Wesley

Saddle River, NJ • Boston • Indianapolis • San Francisco
New York • Toronto • Montreal • London • Munich • Paris • Madrid
Capetown • Sydney • Tokyo • Singapore • Mexico City

For information about buying this title in bulk quantities, or for special sales opportunities (which may include electronic versions; custom cover designs; and content particular to your business, training goals, marketing focus, or branding interests), please contact our corporate sales department at corpsales@pearsoned.com or (800) 382-3419.

For government sales inquiries, please contact governmentsales@pearsoned.com.

For questions about sales outside the U.S., please contact international@pearsoned.com.

Visit us on the Web: informit.com/aw

Library of Congress Control Number: 2014947363



ISBN-13: 978-0-321-92771-2
ISBN-10: 0-321-92771-0
Text printed in the United States on recycled paper at RR Donnelley in Crawfordsville, Indiana.
First printing, September 2014

# Contents

# Foreword

"The NetBeans Platform abides," is what the Dude in the *Big Lebowski* might have said, had he known about the NetBeans Platform at all, which he probably did, somehow. Over the years, an incredibly wide range of applications have been built on top of the application framework that is the NetBeans Platform, from air defense systems at NATO to medical applications at Stanford, from military software at Northrop Grumman to software development tools at Oracle. . . and hundreds, probably thousands, of other applications in between.

Even whilst the uninitiated queried the relevance of the NetBeans Platform—at first challenging NetBeans Platform users with "what about the browser?" and then a few years later with "what about mobile devices?"—those using the NetBeans Platform have always known its applicability to the niche in which it fits so well. There will always be a need to put together modular applications that run on the desktop, and cross-platform portability will always be a predominant concern, making Java in combination with the NetBeans Platform a uniquely well-suited environment for serious application developers.

There certainly is something deeply intellectual about working with the NetBeans Platform. Once you're out of the woods of the initial learning experience, you will discover that you're not only figuring out how to construct a puzzle out of a disparate set of pieces, but that the pieces themselves are objects that you're constructing. There's a meta-level of enjoyment that is a strangely distinct feature of progressing in your understanding of the NetBeans Platform and all it provides.

Moreover, as this book shows throughout, what Swing and JavaFX have in common is that they're UI toolkits, not application frameworks. Neither of these toolkits provides any infrastructure to connect the pieces together. The NetBeans Platform is an application framework for both toolkits, either separately or together. In fact, as you will quickly learn in this book, the NetBeans Platform is a meeting point that unites the stability and depth of experience that Swing developers bring to the table together with the innovation and the rich content that the JavaFX world provides.

I wish you a lot of fun as you acquire new knowledge with the NetBeans Platform, while learning how to create meaningful applications in Java.

**Geertjan Wielenga**
NetBeans Product Manager

# Preface

The NetBeans Platform provides a rich client framework to build desktop applications in Java and JavaFX. Its design has a certain symmetry and elegance. As you use its many APIs, each new feature learned will become familiar. You'll learn that this familiarity, coupled with code and design reuse, is a good trait.

Simply stated, the NetBeans Platform will save you years in building and maintaining application framework code. Even the simplest NetBeans Platform application has amazing features. And the platform's best feature is that as users change and technology and requirements evolve, your application can evolve, too.

## Our Approach

This book takes a holistic approach to presenting the NetBeans Platform. We begin with the basic Java architectural tenets of event notification, JavaBeans property support, and UI responsiveness with background tasks. As we build upon these Java basics, we present the NetBeans Platform APIs and features in the context of small sample applications. For example, you will learn how the Nodes API, Action framework, Lookup API, and modular architecture all contribute to the overall design of a CRUD-based database application. Our examples are relatively small and familiar, so you can spend more time learning the NetBeans Platform APIs and not our application business logic.

We wanted to write a book that pulls together many of the excellent NetBeans Platform tutorials and documentation so that you don't have to search for examples. To that end, we provide you with a lot of sample code including screen shots and step-by-step instructions to help you on your journey.

And finally, this book is not just about the NetBeans Platform. With this text, we want to encourage Swing programmers out there to take the plunge with JavaFX. If you want to leverage the ease and beauty of JavaFX, the NetBeans Platform can help you transition from a Swing UI to a JavaFX UI as you develop applications. In fact, the modular architecture of the NetBeans Platform is a great vehicle for easing into JavaFX. Pinpoint your requirements that fit well with JavaFX and start there. Do your visualization requirements include charts or perhaps 3D? Maybe you'd simply like to have stunning effects, such as linear gradients, drop shadows, or animations. Pick and choose all you want, but know that you'll still have the underpinnings of a modular, well-designed NetBeans Platform application.

## About the Examples

You can download the source for the reference application (described briefly in "FamilyTreeApp Reference Application" on page 10) at `https://java.net/projects/nbfamilytreeapp`. You can download the remaining examples and projects described in this book at `http://www.asgteach.com/NetBeansPlatformBook/`.

## Notational Conventions

We've applied a rather light hand with font conventions in an attempt to keep the page uncluttered. Here are the conventions we follow.

| Element | Font Example |
|---|---|
| Java/JavaFX class | ChildFactory, AbstractNode, Shape, Circle |
| code | `Rectangle rectangle =`<br>`    new Rectangle(200, 100, Color.BLUE);`<br>`rectangle.setEffect(new DropShadow());` |
| URL | `http://netbeans.org` |
| file name | Person.java, PersonEditor.fxml |
| key combinations | **Ctrl+Space** |
| NetBeans menu selections | **New \| Window** |
| code within text | The animation affects the `opacity` property . . . |
| code highlighting (to show modified or relevant portions) | `Rectangle rectangle =`<br>`    new Rectangle(200, 100, Color.BLUE);`<br>**`rectangle.setArcWidth(30);`**<br>**`rectangle.setArcHeight(30);`**<br>`rectangle.setEffect(new DropShadow());` |

## Acknowledgments

First, we'd like to thank Geertjan Wielenga, without whose involvement, this book would not have been written. Geertjan provided both technical and philosophical support and introduced us to the vast NetBeans Community.

We'd also like to thank our readers. John Kimball provided much valuable feedback that especially shaped our early chapters. Both Mike Kelly and Stephen Voynar participated in reading early versions of the chapters.

Greg Doench, our editor at Pearson Technology Group, is a good friend and was a valuable part of this project. In fact, Greg has guided us through many book projects. Thank you as well to Elizabeth Ryan at Addison-Wesley, who oversaw the book's production. Her attention to detail and keen eye kept the project on track with a fast-paced production schedule. Our copy editor, Geneil Breeze, performed an amazing feat in making our manuscript as consistent as possible.

The NetBeans Platform has always had a strong, active community of software developers and technical writers. We'd especially like to thank the many members of the NetBeans Community who influenced and helped us in our NetBeans Platform journey, mostly without realizing it. Certain names appear over and over, contributing technical solutions to a myriad of questions asked by the community at large. We'd like to thank and recognize Jaroslav Tulach, Geertjan Wielenga, Toni Epple, Sven Reimers, Tim Boudreau, Tom Wheeler, Jesse Glick, Timon Veenstra, Sean Phillips, and many others who have contributed to the NetBeans Platform body of knowledge.

We'd like to give a shout out to Sharat Chander, who has given us opportunities to meet and mingle with Java experts at home and internationally.

In the JavaFX world, we'd like to thank those who are constantly sharing their knowledge to further the acceptance of JavaFX. Stephen Chin, Jonathan Giles, Richard Bair, Brian Goetz, Jim Weaver, Gerrit Grunwald, and Carl Dea have all contributed to our understanding of the finer points of JavaFX. And finally, we'd like to thank Adam Bien, who has been a strong advocate and an early adopter of JavaFX for real-world applications.

**Gail and Paul Anderson**
Anderson Software Group, Inc.
`www.asgteach.com`

# About the Authors

**Gail Anderson** and **Paul Anderson** are well-known authors, having published books on a wide range of Java technologies, including Enterprise JavaBean Components, Java Studio Creator Field Guide, and Essential JavaFX. In addition, Paul is the author of *JavaFX Programming LiveLessons* and *Java Reflection LiveLessons* training videos. Paul and Gail are frequent speakers at JavaOne and cofounders of the Anderson Software Group, Inc., a leading provider of software training courses in Java and JavaFX.

# 1

# A Tour of the NetBeans Platform

Welcome to JavaFX Rich Client Programming on the NetBeans Platform.

Swing and JavaFX both have sophisticated component libraries for creating rich client applications. While Swing is stable and well-entrenched, the newer JavaFX API offers an improved rich media solution. However, both libraries lack a framework. That is, both lack an out-of-the-box solution with a window management system and modular framework that sophisticated desktop applications require.

This chapter is a big picture description of what the NetBeans Platform offers application developers and an executive summary of what you can expect to learn in the rest of the book. We also show you how JavaFX fits into the world of modular desktop application development.

## What You Will Learn

- How Swing and JavaFX fit into the NetBeans Platform programming model.
- The main NetBeans Platform systems and APIs.
- Where to find detailed information in this book about the different NetBeans Platform systems.
- Examples of why you might want to incorporate JavaFX into your NetBeans Platform application.
- Where to find the latest JDK software, NetBeans software, and examples for this book.

## 1.1 Background Basics

Let's begin our tour of the NetBeans Platform by looking at the Java technology used by application developers. The NetBeans Platform makes use of fundamental Java architecture principles. Before we show you the NetBeans Platform, Chapter 2 takes a brief tour of some of the background basics Java programmers use to create desktop applications. These include

- JavaBeans and JavaBeans Properties.
- Property Change Events and Listeners.
- Swing basics and common Swing components.
- Swing component events and listeners.
- Logging.
- Background threads and thread safety to keep the UI responsive.

In exploring these topics, we'll build a small desktop Swing application. Later in the book, we break this application into cohesive modules and port it to the NetBeans Platform.

### JavaFX Integration

The NetBeans Platform is built with Swing, a well-established single-threaded GUI system in the Java world. JavaFX is a newer GUI system (also single threaded) that offers significant improvements and features.

JavaFX is based on a scene graph model that is different than models used with Java 2D or Swing. With JavaFX, you define objects in terms of a scene graph hierarchy and specify transforms to position these objects relative to one another. Animation is easy to achieve with transforms and effects.

JavaFX is bundled with the JDK and is accessible in NetBeans Platform applications. The modular nature of the NetBeans Platform lets you pick and choose which parts of your application are best fits for JavaFX.

Chapter 3 introduces JavaFX and provides a first look at this relatively new technology. In Chapter 4, we show you how to build desktop applications with JavaFX. You'll learn how to use observable collections and create JavaFX properties. We also port the Swing application introduced in Chapter 2 to JavaFX. If you have a background in Swing, this chapter shows you how to migrate to JavaFX.

After you learn how to create a basic NetBeans Platform application in Chapter 5, we'll show you how to integrate JavaFX content into NetBeans Platform applications.

We discuss how to structure modules that contain JavaFX and how to make sure you access JavaFX scene graph structures on the JavaFX Application Thread and Swing components on the Event Dispatch Thread (EDT). These communication strategies are necessary whenever you integrate JavaFX content in NetBeans Platform windows.

We'll also provide an example application that uses the JavaFX Charts package in Chapter 15 and a reference application (briefly described in this chapter).

## 1.2 The NetBeans Platform: The Big Picture

Now let's give you a big-picture description of the NetBeans Platform and describe several of its major systems and APIs. Along with the description of each part, we'll also tell you where you can find more information on these topics in this book. This, then, is the executive summary. If you're considering developing an application based on the NetBeans Platform, the following descriptions will give you a general idea of your application's architecture and what the NetBeans Platform offers.

### Module System API

Perhaps the most important feature of the NetBeans Platform is the module system, which provides a way to divide your application into cohesive parts. The NetBeans Platform includes a Runtime Container that manages all of the modules in your application. These modules include those contributed by the NetBeans Platform and ones that you create yourself. The module system helps you build loosely-coupled applications that can evolve without breaking. Specifically, the module system

- Provides a way to break up an application into cohesive parts.
- Lets you specify dependencies between modules so these dependencies are deliberate and non-cyclical. This helps keep your modules loosely coupled.
- Lets you add and remove features without breaking your application.

Modules are basically JAR files, but they include meta information that enables the Runtime Container to manage them. When a module uses classes contained in another module, you must explicitly set a dependency on that module. Furthermore, the packages that contain these classes must be declared public. The Runtime Container makes sure any packages in a dependency declaration are available. In this way, you can break up applications into cohesive parts with explicit contracts between modules. This approach lets you design applications with high cohesion and low coupling.

Chapter 5 discusses the Module System and shows you how to break up a Swing application into modules. You'll learn how to port the example presented in Chapter 2 and create a modular NetBeans Platform application.

All modules have a life cycle, which you can hook into via annotations. Thus, you can execute code when a module starts, shuts down, and when the window system initializes. See "Module Life Cycle Annotations" on page 242 for the module life cycle hooks and "Using @OnShowing" on page 374 for the window system initialization hook.

### And What About OSGi Bundles?

The OSGi Framework is an industry standard supported by the OSGi Alliance and described by JSR-291. The OSGi Framework provides a modular runtime environment. An OSGi bundle is comparable to a NetBeans Platform module. You can add dependencies between OSGi bundles and NetBeans Platform modules. Furthermore, the NetBeans Platform has been extended to support OSGi bundles in the following ways.

- Using the Add New Module wizard, you can create new modules that are OSGi bundles in your NetBeans Platform application, as shown in Figure 1.1.

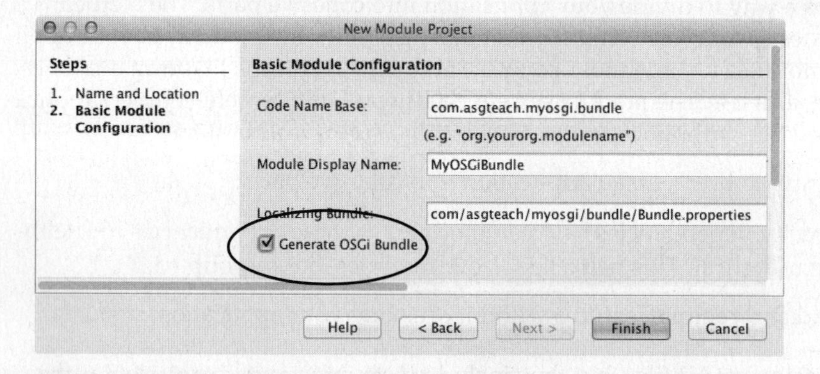


Figure 1.1 Create an OSGi bundle in your NetBeans Platform application

- You can add existing OSGi bundles to your NetBeans Platform application—`https://platform.netbeans.org/tutorials/nbm-osgi-quickstart.html` (shows how to integrate OSGi bundles into a NetBeans Platform application).
- You can build an OSGi-only application by executing NetBeans module code natively as OSGi bundles—`http://wiki.netbeans.org/NetBeansInOSGi`.

## Lookup API

Module systems let you break up your application into loosely coupled parts. These modules must have, however, a way to communicate with each other. This is where you use the Lookup API, as described in the following two related scenarios.

1. In client modules you look up service providers based on an interface or abstract class. The Lookup API returns one or more service providers. The client module must explicitly declare a dependency on the module that defines the interface/abstract class, but no dependencies are required on any service provider modules. With dynamically installed modules, applications have the ability to acquire new features and evolve without breaking.
2. NetBeans Platform objects (such as windows) implement context sensitivity with Lookups. A Lookup is basically a map where the key is an interface, abstract class, or class. The value is an implementation of the interface, an extension of the super class, or a class object.

   When a window puts an object in its Lookup, the window instantly acquires the capability that object implements. Another module can listen for the presence of a particular capability in an exposed Lookup and invoke that capability.

   Neither the window nor the interested listener has any direct dependencies. There are only dependencies on the module that defines the interface or class represented by the key.

"Registering a Service Provider" on page 214 shows how to use service providers as described above. "Configuring a Window for Selection" on page 219 shows how a window uses a Lookup. "Context-Aware Actions" on page 428 describes how Lookup dynamically enables and disables actions. Furthermore, "Implement Openable and SavablePersonCapability" on page 500 describes the power of capabilities and module communication. Context sensitivity can also apply to selection management, which we explore in "Creating a Selection History Feature" on page 332.

## Window System API

Desktop applications need windows to display components and a GUI to let users interact with the application. The NetBeans Platform Window System lets modules create and manipulate application windows.

The Window System provides default behaviors for windows, which you can optionally limit. The default behaviors include opening, closing, floating, docking, minimizing, maximizing, acquiring focus, and moving to different locations. You can also persist the state of each window between restarts and reset the windows to their default state and position.

The NetBeans IDE has a wizard to create and configure application windows. The NetBeans Platform window extends the TopComponent class. TopComponent itself extends JComponent, and therefore is a Swing container. You can create UI content using the NetBeans IDE Matisse designer. Additionally, you can integrate JavaFX content into a TopComponent with the JFXPanel control. Using FXML markup, you build JavaFX content with the stand-alone Scene Builder application.[1]

The NetBeans Platform also includes a Window Manager that manages all of your application's windows. You can access this Window Manager for programmatic window control.

We discuss the NetBeans Platform Window System in Chapter 8 and JavaFX integration with a NetBeans Platform application window in Chapter 6.

As an example, Figure 1.2 shows the SmartPhoneDataApp from Chapter 15 with windows both docked and floating (separately or in a group). All floating windows can be moved independently, possibly for displaying in a separate monitor. This application uses the JavaFX Charts API and a Swing JTable together.

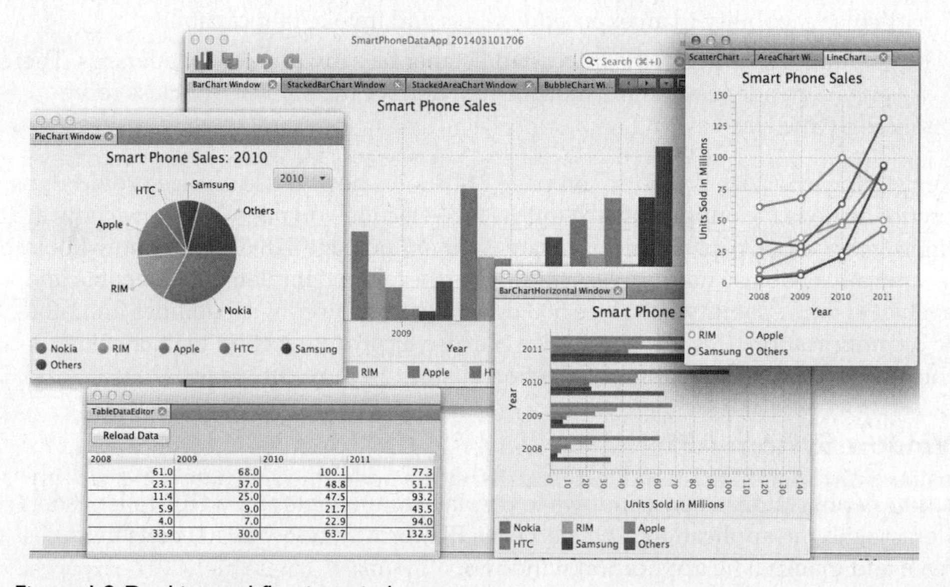


Figure 1.2 Docking and floating windows

1. You can download Scene Builder for free at www.oracle.com.

## File System API

The File System is part of the basic runtime system of a NetBeans Platform application and provides a hierarchical view of configuration information. The File System is made up of folders, files, and data and lets you access a file system in the traditional sense. That is, you can create, read, update, and delete files and folders within the user's local file system. Each application also stores configuration information in a special file system called the System File System. Here you find folders with names like "Actions" and "Menu Bar" that in turn contain subfolders like "Edit" or "File." Each of these folders in turn contains files that describe objects through attributes.

Any module can modify the System FileSystem and contribute data or configuration information to the application with a module configuration file, known as the Layer file. When an application runs, all module configuration data is merged into a single configuration.

Importantly, this means that the File System provides a mechanism by which modules can communicate with each other. The File System complements the Lookup API discussed earlier for inter-module communication. That is, one module can register folders and files in a module configuration file that other modules can access without creating dependencies.

We discuss the File System API in Chapter 13, which includes file-oriented operations, installing and accessing files in modules, and accessing and modifying artifacts in the application's configuration. We show you how to include the Favorites window in a NetBeans Platform application to access the local file system within the UI. "Using the Layer File for Inter-Module Communication" on page 665 uses the File System and Layer file for communication between modules in a NetBeans Platform application.

## Nodes and Explorer Views

The Nodes API and Explorer and Property Sheet API go together. In a NetBeans Platform application, nodes provide a model for your business objects. Nodes wrap the business object and have a Lookup. Furthermore, nodes have a context menu with actions that users can invoke.

The Explorer Manager is a controller class that manages a node hierarchy. Explorer Views are Swing-based UI components that display a node hierarchy by accessing an Explorer Manager. You add Explorer Views to NetBeans windows. The NetBeans Platform provides several different Explorer Views with different looks (tree, table-based, icon, property-based, master-detail). Explorer Views are interchangeable because they use the same node-based model.

Finally, because nodes and Explorer Managers both implement selection management, selected nodes and their wrapped objects become available to other modules transparently and without defining dependencies on the modules with Explorer Views. Architecturally, these APIs support the NetBeans Platform concepts of loosely-coupled modules.

We show you how to use nodes, Explorer Views and Property Sheets, and the Explorer Manager in Chapter 7 ("Nodes and Explorer Views").

## But Wait . . . There's More

The APIs and systems we've described in the previous section constitute the central parts of all NetBeans Platform applications. But there are additional modules and APIs in the NetBeans Platform.

### Action Framework

An application performs work with menu, toolbar, or keyboard shortcut selections. Chapter 9 introduces the NetBeans Platform Action framework. Because the Action framework registers actions through configuration (with annotations), you'll learn how to easily add and remove actions to an application. The framework also lets you dynamically enable and disable actions and customize behavior based on selectable context.

### CRUD-Based Applications

Chapter 10 explores the concepts of capabilities within the Action framework to create context-aware actions. The example builds a CRUD-based application with a database for persistence. We apply the concepts introduced in Chapter 2 to keep the UI responsive using background threads.

### Dialogs and Wizards

Chapter 11 explores the NetBeans Platform Dialogs API that lets you create, display, and obtain input from dialogs. You can build custom dialogs with Swing or even integrate JavaFX in a dialog panel.

The Wizard framework lets you create multi-step processes within your application that users invoke to build application artifacts. The NetBeans IDE uses the Wizard framework for many of its tasks, such as creating projects, windows, files, RESTful web clients, and so forth. You can use JavaFX with visual wizard panels, as well. Chapter 12 discusses the Wizard framework.

## Data System API

The Data System API is an important bridge between nodes and files. The Data System lets you integrate new file types into your application. Chapter 14 shows you how to create a new file type, use the NetBeans Platform text editor in an application, and integrate the NetBeans Platform XML editor. We also discuss creating editors with MultiView elements, using both the Visual Library API and JavaFX to build synchronized views in a MultiView editor.

## JavaFX Charts

Chapter 15 shows how to build a NetBeans Platform application with JavaFX Charts to visualize data. Long missing from Swing-based applications, JavaFX provides an integrated Chart package with many supported chart types, as shown in Figure 1.3. This example application shows you how to print a TopComponent window, save a chart window (or any window with JavaFX content) to a PNG format file, use binding to keep JavaFX content synchronized, and add special effects (such as animating a pie slice).

We apply the design concepts discussed earlier to make the application highly modularized. You can remove any of the Chart modules or easily add modules.

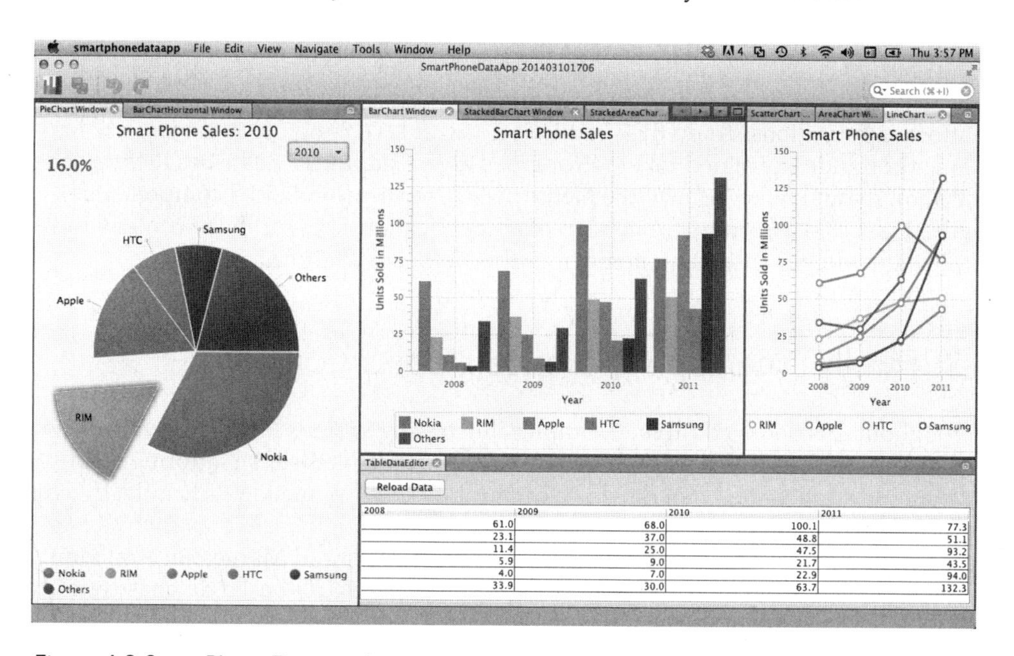


Figure 1.3 SmartPhoneData application with JavaFX Charts

### Using Web Services

Chapter 16 explores creating a RESTful web service client within a NetBeans Platform application. Additionally, the application has a JavaFX-based UI for its windows and uses the JavaFX concurrency framework for background services. This example application applies the concepts presented in Chapter 4 (JavaFX background threads), Chapter 6 (JavaFX integration), and Chapter 15 (JavaFX Charts) to create a web service client application.

### Branding, Distribution, and Update

Branding helps you customize your application. Chapter 17 shows you how to configure your application's title, name, and splash screen (or have no splash screen at all). Chapter 17 also discusses how to distribute your application and make updates available to users. Importantly, "Enable Updates of Your Application" on page 857 shows how to integrate the NetBeans Platform Plugin UI into your application. "Create an Update Center" on page 858 explains how to build an update center. We also show you how to dynamically add and remove plugins (modules) in a running application. You can customize any of the text in a NetBeans Platform module (see "Branding and Resource Bundles" on page 854).

### Internationalization and Localization

The NetBeans Platform supports internationalization and localization of NetBeans Platform applications. To do this, you isolate target text using the `@Messages` annotation and provide translated text in Properties files. Chapter 17 describes these steps and shows you how to localize the NetBeans Platform-provided UI components. Figure 1.4 shows a Portuguese version of an application with localized content and a localized menu bar and menu items from the NetBeans Platform.

## 1.3 FamilyTreeApp Reference Application

Throughout this book, you'll see examples illustrating various NetBeans Platform features. As we researched how to create a book about the NetBeans Platform, we built an example application. This reference application lets you manage a Family Tree by documenting relationships among family members through life events such as marriage, birth, divorce, and death. We embraced the Homer and Marge Simpson family of the popular TV show for our example and created a CRUD-based database application called FamilyTreeApp.

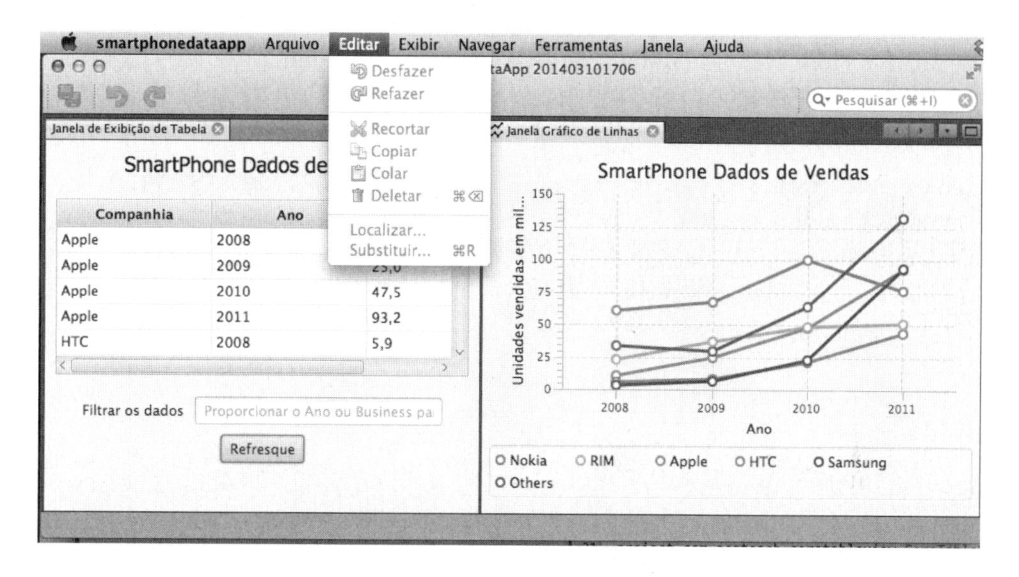


Figure 1.4 SmartPhoneDataApp with localized NetBeans Platform modules

You can find the source for this application at `https://java.net/projects/nbfamilytreeapp`. This project illustrates many of the features of a modular NetBeans Platform application. The examples we present in this book, however, have been greatly simplified from this application to concentrate on specific NetBeans Platform features.

Nevertheless, this reference application provided many of the insights we gained, especially integrating JavaFX into NetBeans Platform applications. We wanted to explore not only best practices for designing modular desktop applications with the NetBeans Platform, but how to best incorporate JavaFX for a great look and added functionality. We encourage our readers to access the NetBeans Platform FamilyTreeApp to explore a well-developed example.

## FamilyTreeApp and JavaFX

Let's show you a few NetBeans Platform / JavaFX features illustrated in this application. Figure 1.5 shows the application running. The left window is an Explorer View providing a list of Persons and their Events. The right window is a similar Explorer View, providing a list of only Persons. Both of these windows use the NetBeans Platform Explorer Views and Nodes API. (Chapter 7 describes this important topic.) You can select nodes (Person or Event objects), expand nodes, and right click to see a context menu. A double click opens the selected object for editing.

The FamilyTreeApp includes a Welcome window, which is a great place to incorporate JavaFX. Here, we use a radial gradient for the background, put drop shadows around the question marks, and initiate a fade animation when the user clicks anywhere in the window's background.

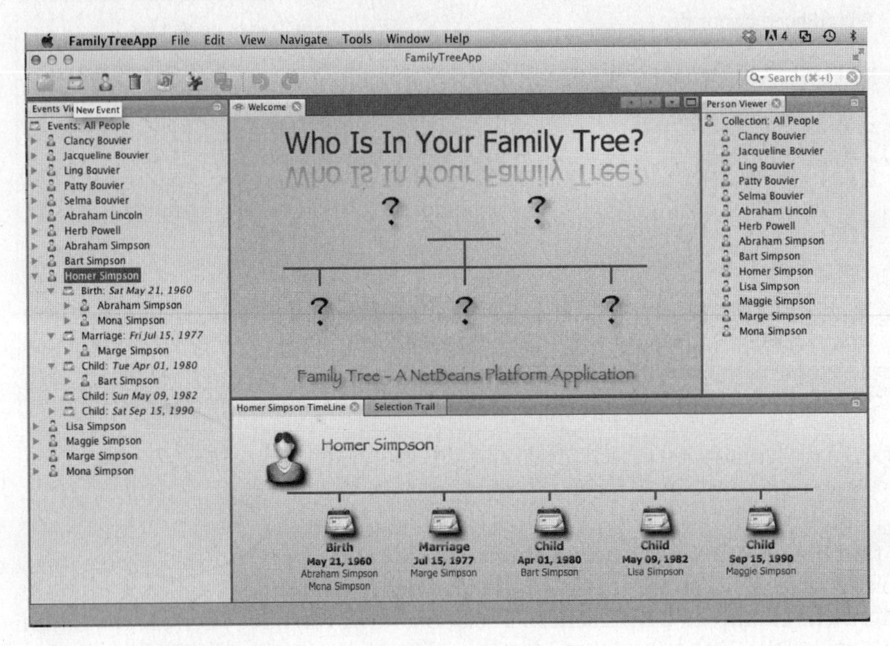


Figure 1.5 FamilyTreeApp

The Person Timeline window (shown in the lower portion in Figure 1.5 and in Figure 1.6) displays the selected person's events chronologically. Each event fades in sequentially using animation. The Timeline window displays changes through the powerful NetBeans Platform selection mechanism and updates a person's event details with property change listeners.

We also installed roll-over animations to scale up events as the user passes over an event with the mouse. (The last event is scaled up in Figure 1.6). This technique is not just eye candy. The scale-up animation is useful during presentations to highlight an artifact within a window.

We've used JavaFX to build the Person Editor, shown in Figure 1.7, creating the JavaFX content using Scene Builder (see "Scene Builder and FXML" on page 155). We added a linear gradient to the background, a drop shadow on the image, and JavaFX controls for textfields, radio buttons, and the text area.

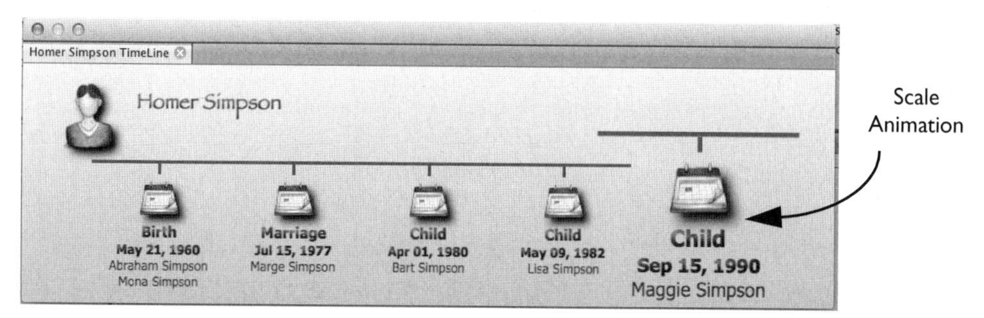


Figure 1.6 FamilyTreeApp—Person Timeline window

Figure 1.7 Using JavaFX with the Person Editor

Similarly, Figure 1.8 shows the Event Editor, which uses JavaFX for the UI controls. Here, we also used Scene Builder to create the UI.

The NetBeans Platform provides a powerful and flexible Wizard framework that lets you create multi-step processes for building application artifacts (projects, data objects, special files). You can implement each visual Wizard panel with JavaFX, as shown in Figure 1.9. The panel (with JavaFX content) is incorporated into the Swing-based Wizard panel. (Chapter 12 covers wizards.)

You can similarly use JavaFX with the NetBeans Platform dialogs or incorporate the JavaFX File Chooser, Color Picker, or Date Picker controls into your application. Figure 1.10 shows the JavaFX File Chooser control, which implements the FamilyTree-App Add Picture action.

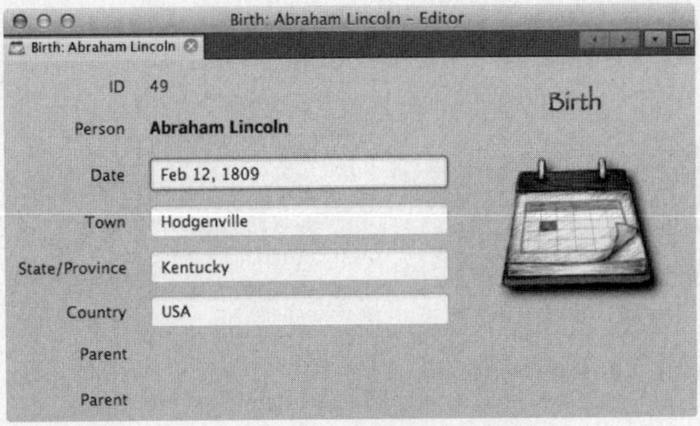

Figure 1.8 Using JavaFX with the Event Editor

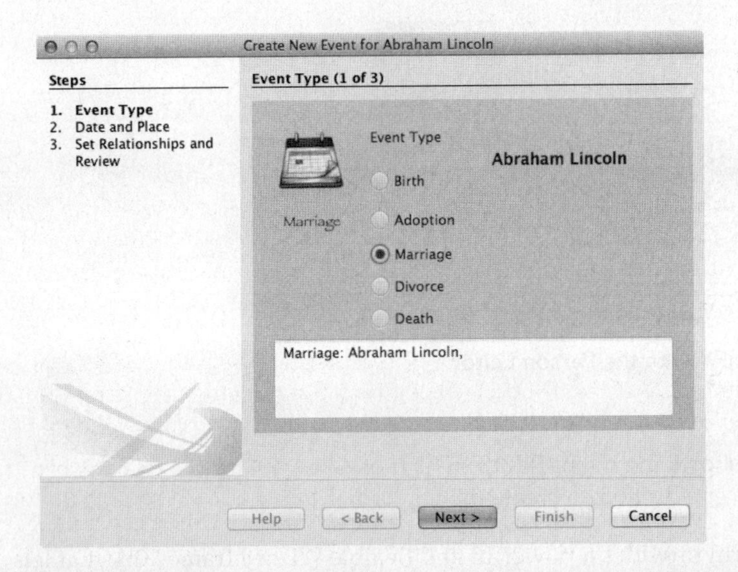


Figure 1.9 Using JavaFX with a New Event wizard

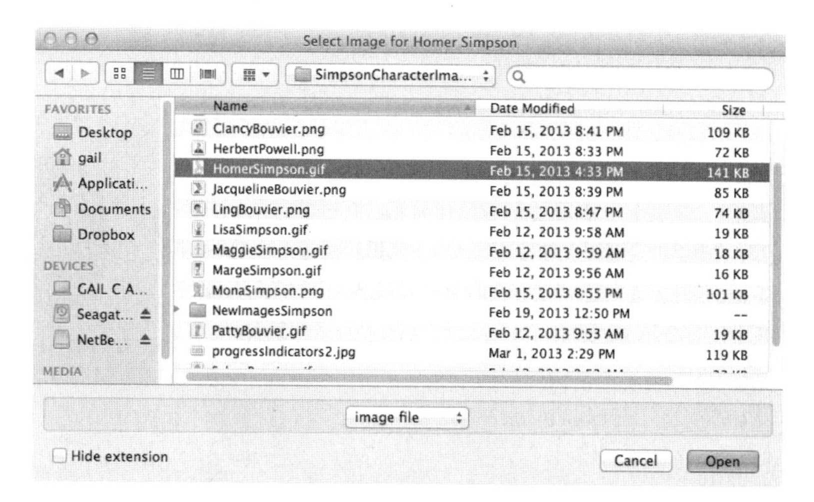


Figure 1.10 Using the JavaFX File Chooser control

## JavaFX 3D Integration Possibilities

You can incorporate JavaFX 3D content into NetBeans Platform applications. As JavaFX evolves and graphics processing units (GPUs) become faster and more advanced, 3D will no longer be a specialized visualization technique but a common look in many applications.

You use JavaFX 3D by creating a JavaFX Scene with Depth Buffering capabilities (also called Z-buffering) and a perspective camera. This sets up the underlying hardware pipelines to transform pixels into the proper perspective. As an example, Figure 1.11 shows several JavaFX (2D) shapes with different Z values (in 3D, the Z value provides depth to an otherwise two-dimensional XY coordinate system). This is a floating window from a NetBeans Platform application. (The source for this example is available in the book's download bundle.) The shapes in Figure 1.11 overlap, but you can't really discern their relative depth.

However, as you rotate the enclosing group, as shown in the second image, you see their relative depth. This rendering is only possible with a perspective camera and 3D capabilities.

Of course, these are 2D shapes being manipulated within a 3D space. A more compelling example shows actual 3D shapes, such Box, Cylinder, and Sphere primitives. Figure 1.12 shows a second window (and module) added to the ThreeDee example application with a rotating cube built with the Box primitive. Although we don't spe-

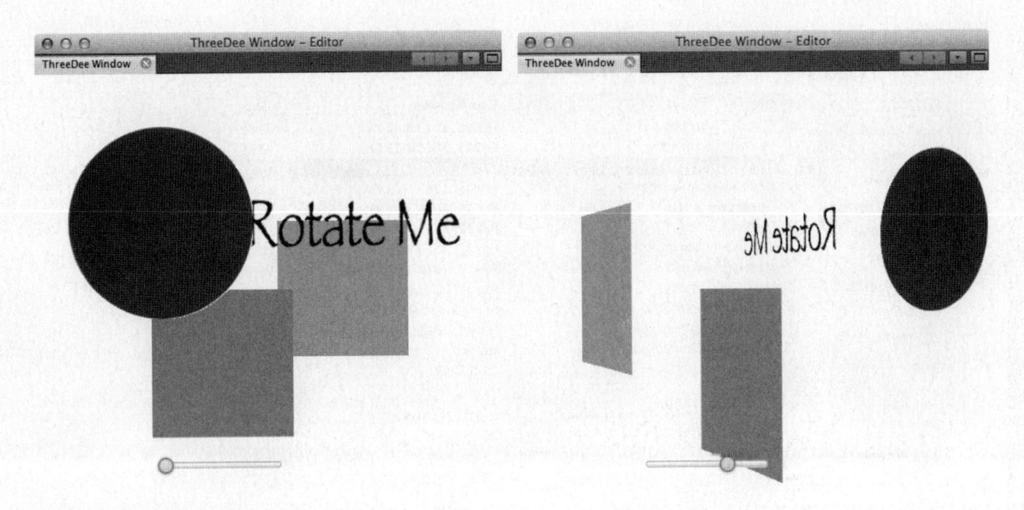


Figure 1.11 JavaFX provides 3D capabilities

cifically cover 3D in this book, you can still leverage all of the best of JavaFX capabilities in your NetBeans Platform applications, including 3D.

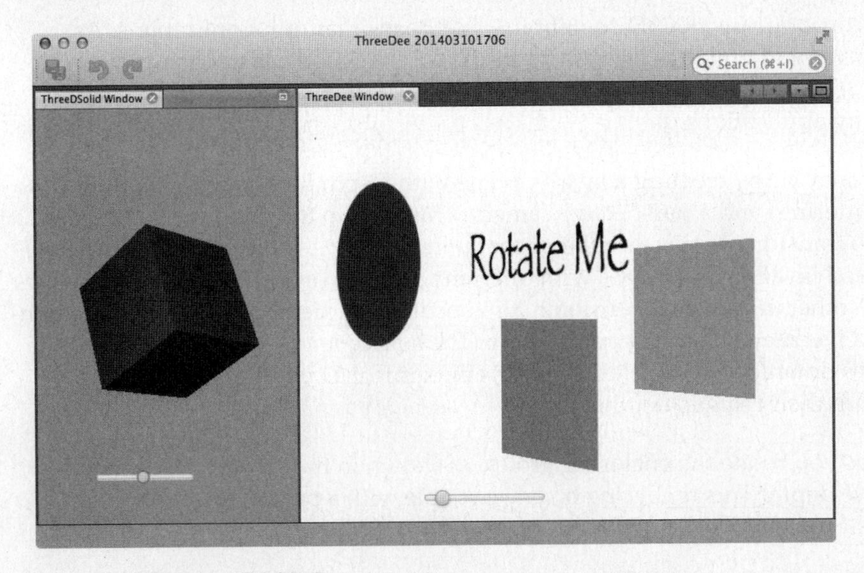


Figure 1.12 The JavaFX 3D Box primitive

## 1.4 Documentation

While you're developing NetBeans Platform applications, you'll want access to the NetBeans Platform API documentation. The APIs are available online at `http://bits.netbeans.org/dev/javadoc/`, but you can also install them in the IDE, as follows.

1. From the NetBeans IDE top-level menu, select **Tools | PlugIns**.
2. NetBeans displays the PlugIns dialog. Select the **Available PlugIns** tab.
3. In the list of PlugIns, select **NetBeans API Documentation**, as shown in Figure 1.13, and click **Install**.

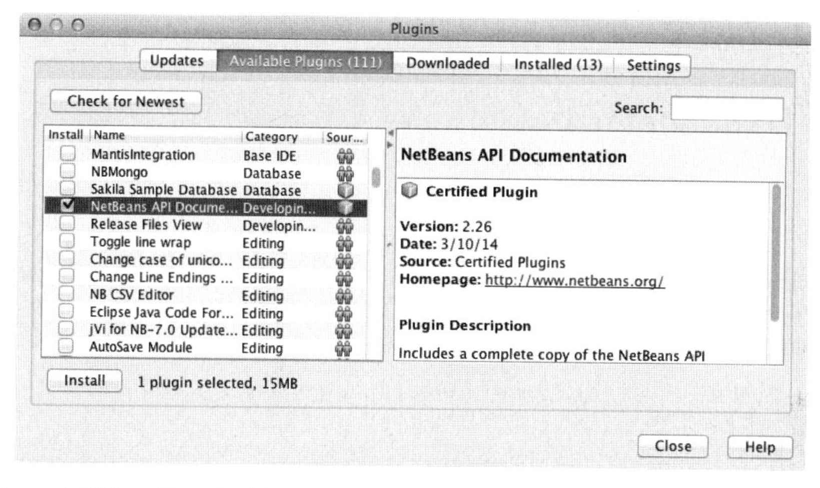


Figure 1.13 Installing the NetBeans Platform API documentation

4. NetBeans runs the installer, which will download the selected Plugin and install it.

After restarting the IDE, you'll have access to the NetBeans API Documentation. For example, you can select a Java class in the NetBeans Platform API, right click, and select **Show Javadoc** to display the relevant documentation in your browser.

## 1.5 How to Get Java and the NetBeans Platform Software

Download the latest JDK at `http://www.oracle.com/technetwork/java/javase/downloads/index.html`. Note that the JDK includes JavaFX.

When you download the NetBeans IDE software, you automatically receive all of the modules you'll need to build a NetBeans Platform application. Download the Net-

Beans IDE at `https://netbeans.org/downloads/`. If you select a language other than English, the localized property files for the officially supported languages are included. Also, note that you can add or remove software bundles later using the IDE's Plugin Manager (**Tools | Plugins**).

## 1.6 Example Software Bundle

You can download the source for the reference application (described above in "FamilyTreeApp Reference Application" on page 10) at `https://java.net/projects/nbfamilytreeapp`. You can download the remaining examples and projects described in this book at `http://www.asgteach.com/NetBeansPlatformBook/`.

## 1.7 Key Point Summary

The NetBeans Platform offers a rich desktop programming environment that supports building complex, modular applications.

We've described the main features of the NetBeans Platform application framework and provided you with a road map to begin your exploration of this framework. We hope you enjoy your journey.

# 2

# Background Basics

The Swing graphical user interface, JavaBeans, and JavaBean properties are all central to using the NetBeans Platform. You manipulate Swing components and any business objects that you create with listeners, events, and event handlers. Broadly speaking, these concepts are vital in having objects in an application communicate with each other. This chapter describes techniques for this type of communication, so that when you see them later in a NetBeans Platform application, you'll understand their purpose and structure.

We begin with JavaBeans, JavaBean properties, and property change events. In building an application, you typically define business objects (or *model objects*) with JavaBeans and access their data with JavaBean properties. Methods that manipulate business objects make sure these application objects remain consistent with your business logic. We'll also briefly show you lambda expressions, an important Java 8 language feature that we use in our code examples.

After introducing JavaBeans, properties, and property change handlers, we'll show examples that give you a broad overview of Swing as a graphical user interface. We'll explore examples that handle user input events and keep track of changes to model data. This ensures that the view (graphical user interface) and model are always consistent. We'll also introduce the standard Java Logging facility.

We finish this background chapter by discussing thread safety and threading techniques as they relate to Swing-based applications. Because Swing uses a single-threaded model, dedicated background threads should perform long-running tasks within Swing applications. In this case, thread safety is crucial. We'll discuss making objects thread safe and how to launch background threads in Swing.

### What You Will Learn

- Create JavaBeans and JavaBean properties.
- Use bound properties and property change listeners.
- Replace anonymous inner classes with lambda expressions.
- Understand Swing basics.
- Use common Swing components.
- Create UI forms with the Swing form designer.
- Incorporate Swing component events and listeners into your application.
- Use the Java logging facility.
- Understand concurrency in Swing.

## 2.1 JavaBeans and Properties

Let's begin our review of background basics with JavaBeans. A JavaBean is a Java class that encapsulates data as class fields. You access the class data through methods that set values (called *setters*) and get or read values (called *getters*). When the methods that access the JavaBean class fields follow well-defined naming conventions we call these fields *properties*.

We begin with class Person,[1] which has fields that hold information for each Person object we create. The naming convention for property names includes an initial lowercase letter, no special symbols, and camel casing for obvious compound words. Listing 2.1 shows class Person with its private fields and constructors. Note that each Person object has an incremented `id` value.

**Listing 2.1 Person.java**

```
package com.asgteach.familytree.model;

import java.io.Serializable;
import java.util.Objects;
```

1. After we fully describe class Person, we'll show you how to build a Java application with the NetBeans IDE that uses Person.

```
public final class Person implements Serializable {

    private final long id;
    private String firstname;
    private String middlename;
    private String lastname;
    private String suffix;
    private Person.Gender gender;
    private String notes;

    private static long count = 0;

    public enum Gender {
        MALE, FEMALE, UNKNOWN
    }

    public Person() {
        this("", "", Gender.UNKNOWN);
    }

    public Person(String first, String last, Person.Gender gender) {
        this.firstname = first;
        this.middlename = "";
        this.lastname = last;
        this.suffix = "";
        this.gender = gender;
        this.id = count++;
    }

    public Person(Person person) {
        this.firstname = person.getFirstname();
        this.middlename = person.getMiddlename();
        this.lastname = person.getLastname();
        this.suffix = person.getSuffix();
        this.gender = person.getGender();
        this.notes = person.getNotes();
        this.id = person.getId();
    }
}
```

Class Person has three constructors: a constructor that creates default values for the fields, a constructor for specifying `firstname`, `lastname`, and `gender`, and a *copy constructor* that creates a new Person object that is a copy of its parameter.

Property fields are private with getters and setters to manipulate them. We'll create getters and setters for each field, except for the read-only `id` field, which needs only a getter.

### Generating Getters and Setters

*Once you define private fields within a class, NetBeans (and other IDEs) can generate setters and/or getters for you, since these methods follow well-known naming conventions.*

To be recognized as a property method, each getter method name includes the prefix "get" followed by the property name with an initial capital letter. A getter's return type is the same as the field's type. A boolean property typically uses the prefix "is," although you can optionally use the prefix "get." For example, here is a getter for boolean property `manager`.

```
private boolean manager = true;
. . .
// getter for manager
public boolean isManager() {
    return manager;
}
```

### Properties and Getters

*Not all getters necessarily correspond to a field with the same name. For example, suppose a Person class has private integer* `age`*. We can write a boolean getter called* `isTeenager()` *as follows.*

```
private int age;

// getter for age
public int getAge() {
    return age;
}
. . .
public boolean isTeenager() {
    return (age >= 13 && age <= 19) ? true : false;
}
```

*The class includes boolean (read-only) property* `teenager`*, but the class does not have a field called* `teenager`*. Instead, the getter returns a boolean computed from the* `age` *property.*

Setters include the prefix "set," return void, and include a single parameter whose type matches the property's type. Listing 2.2 shows the getter and setter methods for class Person.

**Listing 2.2 Person Getters and Setters**

```
    public String getNotes() {
        return notes;
    }
```

```
    public void setNotes(String notes) {
        this.notes = notes;
    }

    public String getFirstname() {
        return firstname;
    }

    public void setFirstname(String firstname) {
        this.firstname = firstname;
    }

    public Person.Gender getGender() {
        return gender;
    }

    public void setGender(Person.Gender gender) {
        this.gender = gender;
    }

    public String getLastname() {
        return lastname;
    }

    public void setLastname(String lastname) {
        this.lastname = lastname;
    }

    public String getMiddlename() {
        return middlename;
    }

    public void setMiddlename(String middlename) {
        this.middlename = middlename;
    }

    public String getSuffix() {
        return suffix;
    }

    public void setSuffix(String suffix) {
        this.suffix = suffix;
    }

    public long getId() {
        return id;
    }
```

There are three additional methods you should override for a JavaBean class: `toString()`, `equals()`, and `hashCode()`. These methods all have default implementations provided by Object, so you'll get the defaults if you don't provide your own implementations.

Always override `toString()` to provide a more meaningful value than the default. (The default value is the class name, followed by "@" and the unsigned hexadecimal value of the hash code. For example, without overriding `toString()`, the Person class `toString()` method returns

```
com.asgteach.familytree.model.Person@123
```

which is not very useful.)

Methods `equals()` and `hashCode()` are crucial for correct behavior of your JavaBean in determining equality. You should always override both methods. Method `hashCode()` is used in Java collection classes that need to compute hash codes. Both `hashCode()` and `equals()` should rely on the same fields for their implementations.

NetBeans and other IDEs can also generate implementations for `equals()` and `hashCode()`. You specify which field(s) participate in the implementation. For class Person, we use field `id`. Two Person objects are equal if their `id` fields are equal; none of the other fields affect equality. This means you can have two Person objects with the same `firstname` and `lastname` fields that will be unequal if their `id`s are not equal. Similarly, two Person objects with equal `id`s will be equal even if their `lastname` fields (for example) are not equal.

**Correct equals() and hashCode() Generation**

*If you use an IDE to generate code for these methods, make sure you specify the same fields for* `equals()` *code generation as you do for* `hashCode()` *code generation.*

Listing 2.3 shows methods `equals()`, `hashCode()`, and `toString()` for class Person.

**Listing 2.3 Methods equals(), hashCode(), and toString() for Class Person**

```
// Class Person
 @Override
 public int hashCode() {
     int hash = 3;
     hash = 97 * hash + Objects.hashCode(this.id);
     return hash;
 }

 @Override
 public boolean equals(Object obj) {
     if (obj == null) {
         return false;
     }
```

```
        if (getClass() != obj.getClass()) {
            return false;
        }
        final Person other = (Person) obj;
        return Objects.equals(this.id, other.id);
    }

    @Override
    public String toString() {
        StringBuilder sb = new StringBuilder();
        if (!firstname.isEmpty()) {
            sb.append(firstname);
        }
        if (!middlename.isEmpty()) {
            sb.append(" ").append(middlename);
        }
        if (!lastname.isEmpty()) {
            sb.append(" ").append(lastname);
        }
        if (!suffix.isEmpty()) {
            sb.append(" ").append(suffix);
        }
        return sb.toString();
    }
```

## Creating a Java Application

We now have a simple JavaBean object with properties. Let's create a Java application that uses class Person. Use the following steps.[2]

1. From the NetBeans IDE top-level menu bar, select **File | New Project**. NetBeans displays the Choose Project dialog. Under Categories select **Java** and under Projects select **Java Application**, as shown in Figure 2.1. Click **Next**.
2. NetBeans displays the Name and Location dialog. For Project Name, specify **PersonAppBasic**. For Project Location, click **Browse** and navigate to the desired project location. Accept the defaults on the remaining fields and click **Finish**, as shown in Figure 2.2.

NetBeans builds a Java application project for you and brings up PersonAppBasic.java in the Java editor. Next, we'll add the Person class to the project and replace the code in the empty main method.

2. In this chapter we're providing background information. We introduce creating a NetBeans Platform application in Chapter 5.

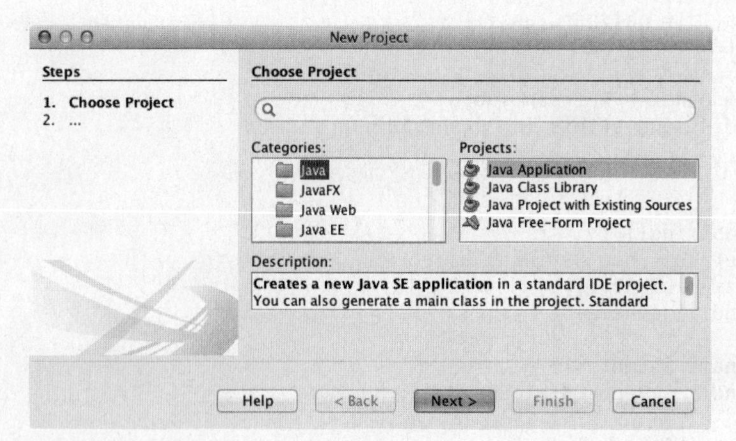


Figure 2.1 Creating a new Java Application with the NetBeans IDE

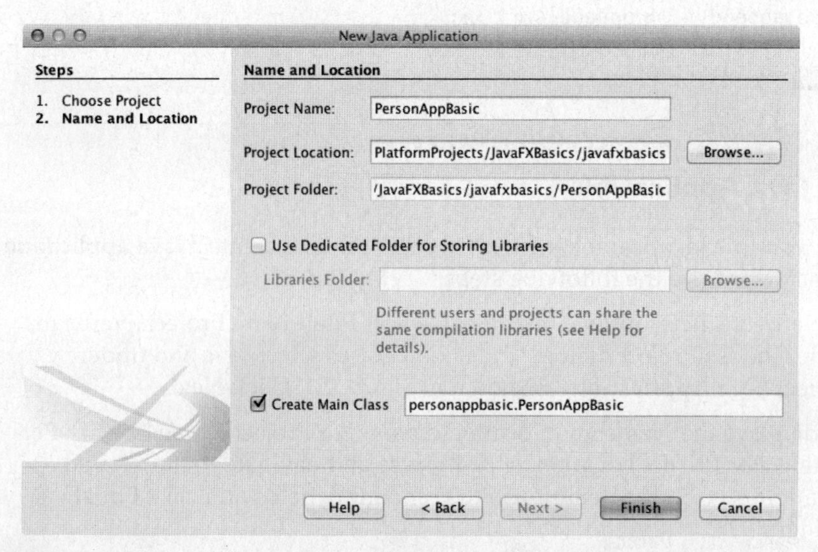


Figure 2.2 New Java Application: specifying the Name and Location

## Add Person.java to Project PersonAppBasic

Follow these steps to create class Person.java.

1. Expand project PersonAppBasic, right click on Source Packages, and select **New | Java Class...** as shown in Figure 2.3.

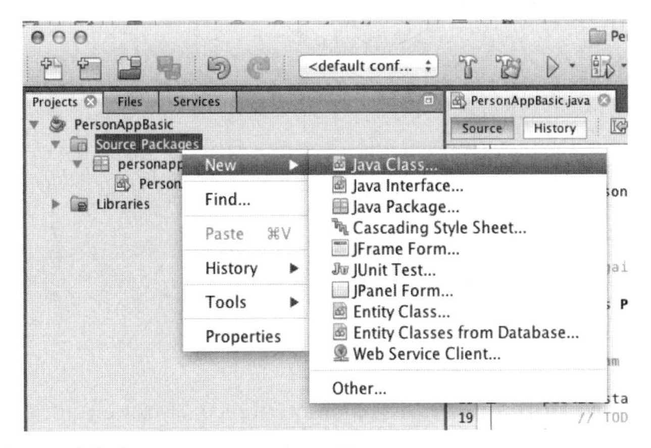


Figure 2.3 Creating a new Java Class

2. NetBeans displays the Name and Location dialog. For Class Name specify **Person** and for Package specify **`com.asgteach.familytree.model`**, as shown in Figure 2.4. Click **Finish**.

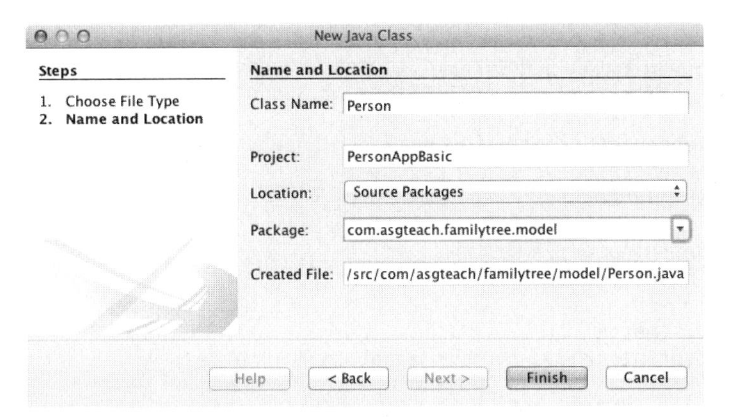


Figure 2.4 Creating class Person

NetBeans creates class Person.java in package `com.asgteach.familytree.model`, as shown in the Projects view in Figure 2.5. Insert the Java code for class Person (using copy/paste or edit), as indicated in Listing 2.1 through Listing 2.3.

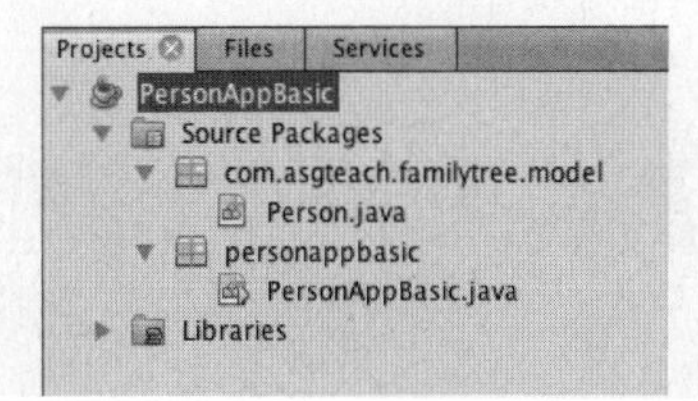


Figure 2.5 Projects view for project PersonAppBasic

## Program PersonAppBasic

Listing 2.4 shows program PersonAppBasic with two Person objects. After creating the objects `homer` and `marge`, we modify their properties (`middlename` and `suffix`) using appropriate setters. Because the Person class overrides `toString()`, we can show useful output with print statements. We can also compare Person objects with `equals()`.

**Listing 2.4 Program PersonAppBasic**

```
public class PersonAppBasic {
    public static void main(String[] args) {

        Person homer = new Person("Homer", "Simpson", Gender.MALE);
        Person marge = new Person("Marge", "Simpson", Gender.FEMALE);

        homer.setMiddlename("Chester");
        marge.setMiddlename("Louise");
        homer.setSuffix("Junior");

        System.out.println(homer);
        System.out.println(marge);

        if (homer.equals(marge)) {
            System.out.println(homer + " is equal to " + marge);
        } else {
            System.out.println(homer + " is not equal to " + marge);
        }
    }
}
```

```
Output:
Homer Chester Simpson Junior
Marge Louise Simpson
Homer Chester Simpson Junior is not equal to Marge Louise Simpson
```

## Bound Properties

Bound properties use the well-known Publish-Subscribe pattern to let interested parties know when property values change. This technique is useful for communicating changes among participants in an application.

We will show two approaches for notifying interested parties (listeners) of changes. The first approach is a fine-grained notification. Each setter fires a property change event to its listeners when invoked, since a setter changes its property's value. The second approach uses a more coarse-grained notification, where interested listeners respond to overall changes to an object, rather than specific property changes. We'll discuss the second approach in the next section.

Here are the modifications to class Person to create bound properties.

1. Add property change support using convenience class PropertyChangeSupport from package `java.beans`.
2. Provide methods `addPropertyChangeListener()` and `removePropertyChangeListener()` so that interested classes can add and remove themselves as listeners.
3. Provide convenience method `getPropertyChangeSupport()` to register a Person as the event source for property change events. (Method `getPropertyChangeSupport()` enables safe registration without an unsafe "leaking this" reference.)
4. Create public static Strings for each bound property so that publishers and subscribers have a consistent way to identify property names.
5. Modify the setters of bound properties to fire a property change event to all registered listeners.

Listing 2.5 shows the modifications (in bold) to class Person to create bound properties for `firstname`, `middlename`, `lastname`, `suffix`, `notes`, and `gender`.

The first step creates a PropertyChangeSupport reference and sets it to null. Next, we create static final Strings for each property name so publishers and subscribers (listeners) can access these Strings instead of the property names directly. (This also lets you use your IDE's code completion mechanism when accessing the Strings.) Lastly, the `getPropertyChangeSupport()` method creates a PropertyChangeSupport object the first time it's invoked. This method is used to add and remove listeners and fire property change events in the setters.

### PropertyChangeSupport Thread Safety and Behavior

*A PropertyChangeSupport instance is thread safe. (We discuss thread safety and PropertyChangeSupport in more detail. See "Concurrency and Thread Safety" on page 68.) Further-*

*more, PropertyChangeSupport does not fire a property change event if the property's old value and new value are the same and non-null.*

---

**Listing 2.5 Adding Bound Properties to class Person**

```
package com.asgteach.familytree.model;

import java.beans.PropertyChangeListener;
import java.beans.PropertyChangeSupport;
import java.io.Serializable;
import java.util.Objects;

public final class Person implements Serializable {

    private final long id;
    private String firstname;
    private String middlename;
    private String lastname;
    private String suffix;
    private Person.Gender gender;
    private String notes;
    private PropertyChangeSupport propChangeSupport = null;

    // Property names
    public static final String PROP_FIRST = "firstname";
    public static final String PROP_MIDDLE = "middlename";
    public static final String PROP_LAST = "lastname";
    public static final String PROP_SUFFIX = "suffix";
    public static final String PROP_GENDER = "gender";
    public static final String PROP_NOTES = "notes";

    private static long count = 0;

    public enum Gender {
        MALE, FEMALE, UNKNOWN
    }

    . . . constructors unchanged . . .

   // Convenience method to make sure object is fully constructed
   // before passing to PropertyChangeSupport constructor
   // (see "Leaking 'this'" on page 32).

    private PropertyChangeSupport getPropertyChangeSupport() {
        if (this.propChangeSupport == null) {
            this.propChangeSupport = new PropertyChangeSupport(this);
        }
        return this.propChangeSupport;
    }
```

```
    public void addPropertyChangeListener(PropertyChangeListener listener) {
        getPropertyChangeSupport().addPropertyChangeListener(listener);
    }

    public void removePropertyChangeListener(PropertyChangeListener listener) {
        getPropertyChangeSupport().removePropertyChangeListener(listener);
    }

. . . getters unchanged . . .

    public void setNotes(String notes) {
        String oldNotes = this.notes;
        this.notes = notes;
      // oldNotes is oldValue and notes is newValue
        getPropertyChangeSupport().firePropertyChange(
            PROP_NOTES, oldNotes, notes);
    }

    public void setFirstname(String firstname) {
        String oldFirst = this.firstname;
        this.firstname = firstname;
        getPropertyChangeSupport().firePropertyChange(
            PROP_FIRST, oldFirst, firstname);
    }

    public void setGender(Person.Gender gender) {
        Person.Gender oldGender = this.gender;
        this.gender = gender;
        getPropertyChangeSupport().firePropertyChange(
            PROP_GENDER, oldGender, gender);
    }

    public void setLastname(String lastname) {
        String oldLast = this.lastname;
        this.lastname = lastname;
        getPropertyChangeSupport().firePropertyChange(
            PROP_LAST, oldLast, lastname);
    }

    public void setMiddlename(String middlename) {
        String oldMiddle = this.middlename;
        this.middlename = middlename;
        getPropertyChangeSupport().firePropertyChange(
            PROP_MIDDLE, oldMiddle, middlename);
    }

    public void setSuffix(String suffix) {
        String oldSuffix = this.suffix;
        this.suffix = suffix;
```

```
        getPropertyChangeSupport().firePropertyChange(
            PROP_SUFFIX, oldSuffix, suffix);
    }

    . . . unchanged code omitted . . .
}
```

### Leaking 'this'

*Don't do this:*

```
private PropertyChangeSupport propChangeSupport =
                new PropertyChangeSupport(this);
```

*Such a construct allows the* `this` *reference to escape when it is not yet properly constructed, creating an object that isn't thread safe.*

Project PersonAppBound uses property change support, as shown in Listing 2.6. After creating two Person objects, the program supplies a property change listener and event handler. This property change listener accesses the property name and the event source (the object that fired the property change event). You can also access the property change event's old value with `getOldValue()` and new value with `getNewValue()`. (See "Lambda Expressions" on page 38 to see how this listener can be simplified.)

**Listing 2.6 Program PersonAppBound**

```
public class PersonAppBound {

    public static void main(String[] args) {
        Person homer = new Person("Homer", "Simpson", Gender.MALE);
        Person marge = new Person("Marge", "Simpson", Gender.FEMALE);

        // create a property change listener
        final PropertyChangeListener pcl = new PropertyChangeListener() {
            @Override
            public void propertyChange(PropertyChangeEvent evt) {
                System.out.println("Property " + evt.getPropertyName()
                        + " changed for " + evt.getSource());
            }
        };

        homer.addPropertyChangeListener(pcl);
        marge.addPropertyChangeListener(pcl);

        homer.setMiddlename("Chester");
        marge.setMiddlename("Louise");
```

```
        homer.setSuffix("Junior");
        homer.setLastname("Jones");

        System.out.println(homer);
        System.out.println(marge);
        // old and new value same, no property change event generated
        homer.setMiddlename("Chester");

        homer.removePropertyChangeListener(pcl);
        marge.removePropertyChangeListener(pcl);
    }
}
```

```
Output:
Property middlename changed for Homer Chester Simpson
Property middlename changed for Marge Louise Simpson
Property suffix changed for Homer Chester Simpson Junior
Property lastname changed for Homer Chester Jones Junior
Homer Chester Jones Junior
Marge Louise Simpson
```

Optionally, you can also supply methods to add and remove listeners that are only interested in changes to a specific property, as shown in Listing 2.7. These methods support single-property listeners. When using this add/remove listener pair, listeners will only be notified when the specified property is changed.

**Listing 2.7 Single Property Listener Support**

```
    public void addPropertyChangeListener(String propertyName,
                                PropertyChangeListener listener) {
        getPropertyChangeSupport().addPropertyChangeListener(
                propertyName, listener);
    }

    public void removePropertyChangeListener(String propertyName,
                                PropertyChangeListener listener) {
        getPropertyChangeSupport().removePropertyChangeListener(
                propertyName, listener);
    }
```

## Coarse-Grained Notification for JavaBean Objects

CRUD is an acronym for Create, Read, Update, Delete and refers to database-type applications with some sort of persistent store. In a typical CRUD application, you may not care if a particular property has changed. Instead, you may be interested when an object is created, updated, or deleted. In this case, you need some type of manager class that keeps track of your objects. This manager class may simply store objects in memory or it may write objects to a persistent store.

Let's design a manager class that uses property change support to notify listeners when Person objects are updated, added, or removed. We call this manager class FamilyTreeManager. This is an example of the coarse-grained notification approach we mentioned previously. We'll retain the code support for a Person's bound properties. However, changes to a Person's properties will not generate property change events because we do not register any listeners.

Listing 2.8 shows the FamilyTreeManager class. We could use a database to store Person objects here, but to simplify our example we use a hash map instead.[3] The FamilyTreeManager has property change support similar to the property change support you've seen in class Person. FamilyTreeManager provides methods for adding, updating, and deleting Person objects. Each of these actions modifies the underlying collection, stores and updates copies of the Person object, and notifies listeners via property change support when changes occur. Note that `firePropertyChange()` uses null for the old value and Person for the new value as arguments. This makes sure the property change fires, since the old and new values are different. Public static Strings define property names. Both `addPerson()` and `updatePerson()` make local copies of the Person argument before modifying the map. A local copy ensures the stored Person object can be modified only through the FamilyTreeManager's modifier methods.

FamilyTreeManager provides method `getAllPeople()` to return a copy of all Person objects stored (as a list), without any kind of sorted ordering.

FamilyTreeManager is a singleton, so users of this class obtain a FamilyTreeManager object through the static factory method `getInstance()`.

**Singletons**

*A singleton class guarantees only one instance of that class object exists. This is typically achieved with a static factory method as shown in Listing 2.8. However, you'll discover the NetBeans Platform provides a better way to obtain singleton objects (see "Global Lookup" on page 218).*

3. We show a database implementation in Chapter 10 (see "Using CRUD with a Database" on page 501).

**Listing 2.8 FamilyTreeManager**

```
public class FamilyTreeManager {

    private final Map<Long, Person> personMap = new HashMap<>();
    private PropertyChangeSupport propChangeSupport = null;

    // FamilyTreeManager property change names
    public static final String PROP_PERSON_DESTROYED = "removePerson";
    public static final String PROP_PERSON_ADDED = "addPerson";
    public static final String PROP_PERSON_UPDATED = "updatePerson";

    private static FamilyTreeManager instance = null;

    protected FamilyTreeManager() {
        // Exists only to defeat instantiation.
    }

    public static FamilyTreeManager getInstance() {
        if (instance == null) {
            instance = new FamilyTreeManager();
            instance.propChangeSupport = new PropertyChangeSupport(instance);
        }
        return instance;
    }

    public void addPropertyChangeListener(PropertyChangeListener listener) {
        this.propChangeSupport.addPropertyChangeListener(listener);
    }

    public void removePropertyChangeListener(PropertyChangeListener listener) {
        this.propChangeSupport.removePropertyChangeListener(listener);
    }

    public void addPerson(Person p) {
        Person person = new Person(p);
        personMap.put(person.getId(), person);
        this.propChangeSupport.firePropertyChange(
                    PROP_PERSON_ADDED, null, person);
    }

    public void updatePerson(Person p) {
        Person person = new Person(p);
        personMap.put(person.getId(), person);
        this.propChangeSupport.firePropertyChange(
                PROP_PERSON_UPDATED, null, person);
    }

    public void deletePerson(Person p) {
        Person person = personMap.remove(p.getId());
```

```
        if (person != null) {
            this.propChangeSupport.firePropertyChange(
               PROP_PERSON_DESTROYED, null, person);
        }
    }

    public List<Person> getAllPeople() {
        List<Person> copyList = new ArrayList<>();
        for (Person p : personMap.values()) {
            // Make a copy of Person
            copyList.add(new Person(p));
        }
        return copyList;
    }
}
```

Unlike class Person, FamilyTreeManager does not need a private method `getPropertyChangeSupport()` (see Listing 2.5 on page 30). Instead, FamilyTreeManager uses a static factory method and can therefore supply the fully constructed instance object to the PropertyChangeSupport constructor.

Program PersonAppCoarse uses the FamilyTreeManager, as shown in Listing 2.9. This program defines a property change listener with a `propertyChange()` event handler. Next, it instantiates a FamilyTreeManager object and adds the previously defined property change listener. The program creates Person objects, adds them to the FamilyTreeManager store, and modifies and updates the Person objects. It then deletes one of the Person objects (`marge`) and displays the modified collection.

The output shows the results of the `propertyChange()` event handler calls, as well as the output from the `getAllPeople()` method.

**Listing 2.9 Program PersonAppCoarse**

```
public class PersonAppCoarse {

    public static void main(String[] args) {
        // Define a property change listener
        final PropertyChangeListener pcl = new PropertyChangeListener() {
            @Override
            public void propertyChange(PropertyChangeEvent evt) {
                System.out.println(evt.getPropertyName()
                        + " for " + evt.getNewValue());
            }
        };

        FamilyTreeManager ftm = FamilyTreeManager.getInstance();
        ftm.addPropertyChangeListener(pcl);
```

```
        Person homer = new Person("Homer", "Simpson", Person.Gender.MALE);
        Person marge = new Person("Marge", "Simpson", Person.Gender.FEMALE);
        ftm.addPerson(homer);
        ftm.addPerson(marge);

        System.out.println(ftm.getAllPeople());

        homer.setMiddlename("Chester");
        homer.setSuffix("Junior");
        ftm.updatePerson(homer);

        marge.setMiddlename("Louise");
        marge.setLastname("Bouvier-Simpson");

        ftm.updatePerson(marge);
        System.out.println(ftm.getAllPeople());

        ftm.deletePerson(marge);
        System.out.println(ftm.getAllPeople());
        // delete marge again
        ftm.deletePerson(marge);
        ftm.removePropertyChangeListener(pcl);
    }
}
```

```
Output:
addPerson for Homer Simpson
addPerson for Marge Simpson
[Homer Simpson, Marge Simpson]
updatePerson for Homer Chester Simpson Junior
updatePerson for Marge Louise Bouvier-Simpson
[Homer Chester Simpson Junior, Marge Louise Bouvier-Simpson]
removePerson for Marge Louise Bouvier-Simpson
[Homer Chester Simpson Junior]
```

In summary, this program has the following features:

- The overridden methods `toString()`, `hashCode()`, and `equals()` in class Person let you use Person objects in hash maps and display their data with print statements.
- FamilyTreeManager implements property change support for operations that modify its underlying store.
- FamilyTreeManager is implemented as a singleton.
- FamilyTreeManager makes sure that Person objects stored in its collection are only updated with `addPerson()`, `updatePerson()`, and `deletePerson()`. It also copies the Person collection before returning objects to the caller.

- The application defines a property change listener and `propertyChange()` event handler and adds this listener to the FamilyTreeManager.

## 2.2 Lambda Expressions

Java 8 has acquired a major language innovation: lambda expressions. Because lambdas are significant, let's take a quick detour and show you how lambda expressions help reduce boilerplate code.

What is a lambda? A lambda is an anonymous method. Like a method, it has a parameter list, return type, and function body. However, unlike "regular" methods, the compiler can infer many of these characteristics so you don't need to completely specify them. You can use lambdas in place of an anonymous inner class when that class has a single abstract method. Interfaces with a single abstract method are called *functional interfaces*. Let's look at a few examples.

### Lambda Expressions with Functional Interfaces

The program shown in Listing 2.9 on page 36 implements a property change listener as an anonymous inner class. Interface PropertyChangeListener has one abstract method `propertyChange()` that returns `void` and has one parameter, PropertyChangeEvent. To override this method with an anonymous inner class, you use

```
// Define a property change listener
final PropertyChangeListener pcl = new PropertyChangeListener() {
    @Override
    public void propertyChange(PropertyChangeEvent evt) {
        System.out.println(evt.getPropertyName()
                + " for " + evt.getNewValue());
    }
};
```

This anonymous inner class can be converted to a lambda expression as follows.

```
final PropertyChangeListener pcl = (PropertyChangeEvent evt) -> {
    System.out.println(evt.getPropertyName()
            + " for " + evt.getNewValue());
};
```

Because PropertyChangeListener is a functional interface, the compiler can infer that the lambda expression defines void method `propertyChange()` with parameter type PropertyChangeEvent. You can further reduce code by omitting the parameter type and, if the method body is a single line of code, the surrounding braces. In fact, you can reduce this code even further when you use the lambda expression with the FamilyTreeManager `addPropertyChangeListener()` method, as follows.

```
ftm.addPropertyChangeListener(evt ->
        System.out.println(evt.getPropertyName()
                + " for " + evt.getNewValue()));
```

If you only need to print the PropertyChangeEvent argument (instead of using `getPropertyName()` and `getNewValue()`), you can use a *method reference*. In this case, the compiler supplies the PropertyChangeEvent argument to `System.out.println()` for you.

```
 // method reference
ftm.addPropertyChangeListener(System.out::println);
```

Another common functional interface is Runnable. The following pre-Java 8 code instantiates a Swing form (class PersonJFrame), wraps it in a Runnable, and invokes the code on the Swing thread with `SwingUtilities.invokeLater()`. (We discuss SwingUtilities in more detail in "Swing Basics" on page 40.)

```
/* Create and display the form */
SwingUtilities.invokeLater(new Runnable() {
    public void run() {
        PersonJFrame.newInstance().setVisible(true);
    }
});
```

With lambda expressions, this code reduces to the following.

```
/* Create and display the form */
SwingUtilities.invokeLater(() -> {
    PersonJFrame.newInstance().setVisible(true);
});
```

Since method `run()` has no parameters, the empty parentheses act as a placeholder. The braces in this example are optional, since the method body is a single statement.

In general, we use lambda expressions in our code examples instead of anonymous inner classes.

## Functional Data Structures

Java 8 also has *streams* or functional data structures. These are data structures with functional interfaces. Let's develop an example so when you see streams and lambdas in our code examples, you'll recognize them.

The following example is FamilyTreeManager method `getAllPeople()` as shown previously in Listing 2.8 on page 35. This method uses a for loop (an external iterator) to copy each element in the map and add it to an array list.

```
public List<Person> getAllPeople() {
    List<Person> copyList = new ArrayList<>();
    for (Person p : personMap.values()) {
        // Make a copy of Person
        copyList.add(new Person(p));
    }
    return copyList;
}
```

The Java 8 Stream interface `forEach()` method provides an internal iterator. The verbose form explicitly instantiates an anonymous inner class with functional interface Consumer, as shown here with the `getAllPeople()` method.

```
public List<Person> getAllPeople() {
    List<Person> copyList = new ArrayList<>();
    personMap.values().forEach(new Consumer<Person>() {
        public void accept(Person p) {
            copyList.add(new Person(p));
        }
    });
    return copyList;
}
```

Because Consumer is a functional interface, we can replace the anonymous inner class with a lambda expression, as follows.

```
public List<Person> getAllPeople() {
    List<Person> copyList = new ArrayList<>();
    // Use lambda expression
    personMap.values().forEach(p -> copyList.add(new Person(p)));
    return copyList;
}
```

Functional data structures (streams) let you use a declarative style of programming. When you want to apply multiple operations on a stream of data, your code becomes more clear. This style also lends itself to easier parallelization.

Our example uses only method `forEach()` with lambdas, which in itself lets us write more concise code. Other methods (which you can chain together) include `filter()` (you provide a criterion with a lambda expression), `map()` (transform an element to a different type), `findFirst()`, or `reduce()` (you provide a criterion).

## 2.3 Swing Basics

Let's continue our exploration of background basics by examining the Swing graphical user interface (GUI). Swing is part of the Java standard and provides a set of lightweight components based on the JavaBeans model. Knowledge of Swing is important because the NetBeans Platform is based on the Swing GUI. In this section, we'll introduce these topics.

- Swing threading model
- Java Logging facility
- Swing components and the GUI Form Designer
- Loose-coupling when responding to changes in the model and view

These topics help developers create GUI-based programs that are correct, maintainable, and easily ported to the NetBeans Platform.

We'll explore each of these concepts with a Swing application called PersonSwingApp. Let's begin by porting a version of the Person application to Swing; that is, we'll use the same Person and FamilyTreeManager classes and provide a GUI to display and edit Person objects. We'll use the NetBeans GUI Builder to compose the look of the application.

Our program will initialize several Person objects and display these in a Swing tree component called JTree. Swing components require a model to hold data that is displayed. Here we'll use the default model for JTree, called DefaultMutableTreeNode (a JTree model that lets you make modifications to the nodes in the tree).

A JTree provides a selection mechanism, either single selection or multi-selection. We'll use single selection and display the selected node (Person) in an adjacent panel that lets users edit fields. After editing is complete, the user clicks an Update button to save the changes. (That is, the edited Person object is saved to an in-memory store.)

Figure 2.6 shows this application running. On the left you see a JTree component with its top node People and five child nodes. The node for Marge Simpson is selected and Marge Simpson's properties are displayed in the right-hand panel. This editing panel uses text field components (JTextField) for the `firstname`, `middlename`, `lastname`, and `suffix` Person properties. A radio button group includes radio buttons (JRadioButton) to select gender. A text area (JTextArea) holds property `notes` and text labels are displayed with JLabel components.

Below this editing area is an Update button (JButton) that the user clicks to update a selected Person object.

## Creating a GUI-Form Project

Let's begin by creating a project with the NetBeans IDE. Follow these steps to create a project and a JFrame (Swing) container.

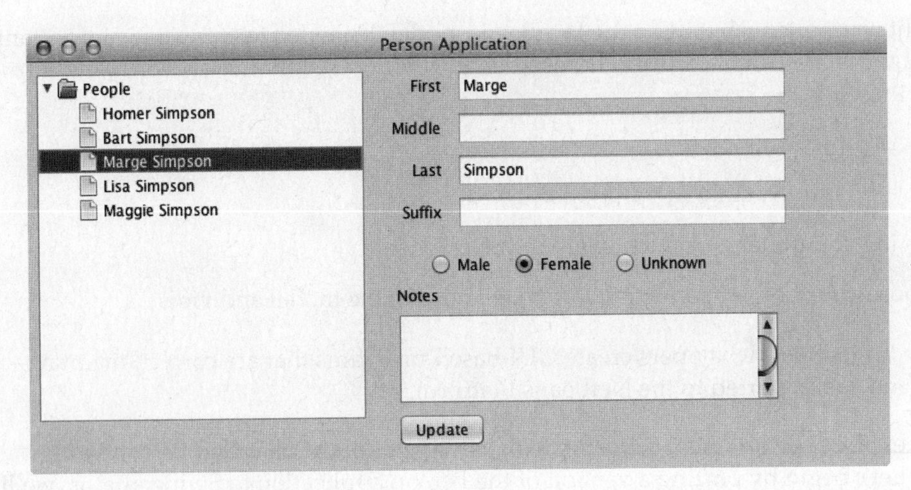


Figure 2.6 PersonSwingApp running

1. From the NetBeans IDE top-level menu bar, select **File | New Project**. NetBeans displays the Choose Project dialog. Under Categories select **Java** and under Projects select **Java Application**. Click **Next**.
2. NetBeans displays the Name and Location dialog. For Project Name, specify **PersonSwingApp**. For Project Location, click **Browse** and navigate to the desired project location. Uncheck **Create Main Class** as shown in Figure 2.7 and click **Finish**.

NetBeans creates an empty Java Application project. You now must add a JFrame container to your project in order to build a Swing-based GUI.

## Add a JFrame Container

Follow these steps to add a JFrame container to project PersonSwingApp.

1. From the Projects view window, expand project node PersonSwingApp.

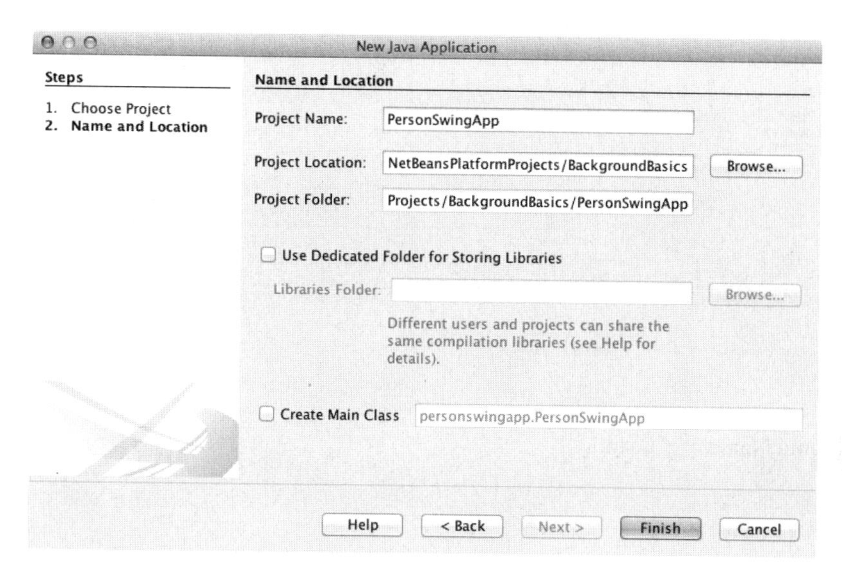


Figure 2.7 New Java Application with Swing

2. Right click on Source Packages and select **New | JFrame Form...** from the context menu, as shown in Figure 2.8.

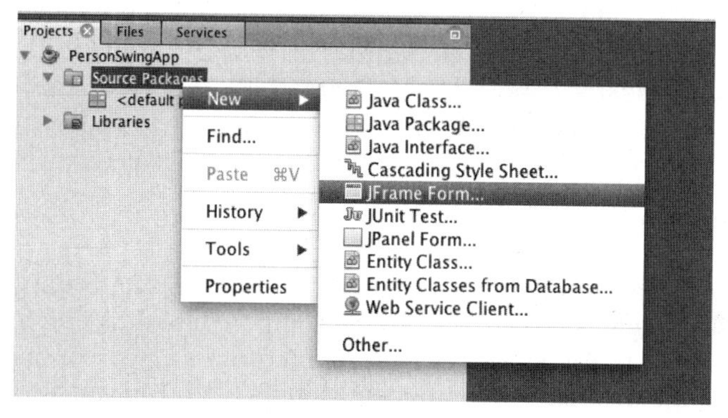


Figure 2.8 Creating a new JFrame Form

3. NetBeans displays a Name and Location dialog. For Class Name, specify **Person-JFrame** and for Package, specify **personswingapp**, as shown in Figure 2.9. Click **Finish**.

NetBeans creates class PersonJFrame.java and brings up the form in the GUI Builder.

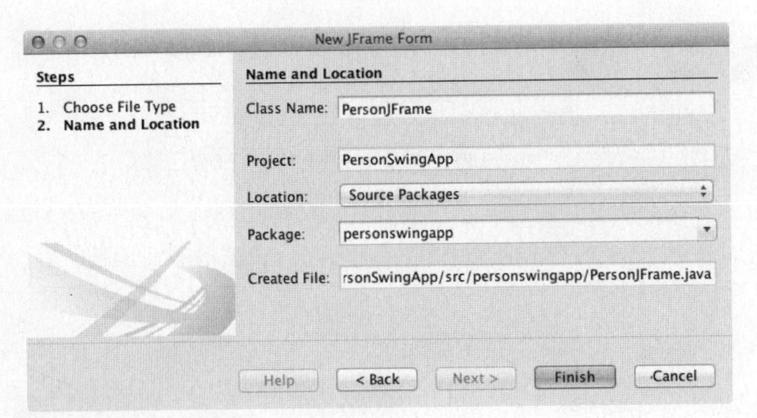


Figure 2.9 JFrame Name and Location

## Swing Form Designer

The NetBeans IDE Swing Form Designer is an easy way to design the look of your application. You drag and drop components from the Swing component palette onto the form designer. You can align multiple components using right-justified, center alignment, or left-justified. Alternatively, you can align them using column-wise or row-wise placement.

Figure 2.10 shows the entire form with the components placed. Note that the text field opposite label First is selected (highlighted on the form). This in turn highlights the text field in the Component Navigator window (`firstTextField` as shown on the left in Figure 2.11) and brings up the component's Property Editor (as shown on the right in Figure 2.11) .

The Swing Component palette is shown in Figure 2.12.

The form designer generates Java code that instantiates the components and configures their properties. It also generates code to lay out the components according to your placement. You cannot edit the generated code, but you can configure component properties by invoking setters after the component is initialized. You can also provide custom code with the Property Editor.

Listing 2.10 on page 46 shows a portion of the generated code that instantiates and initializes the Swing components for our application.

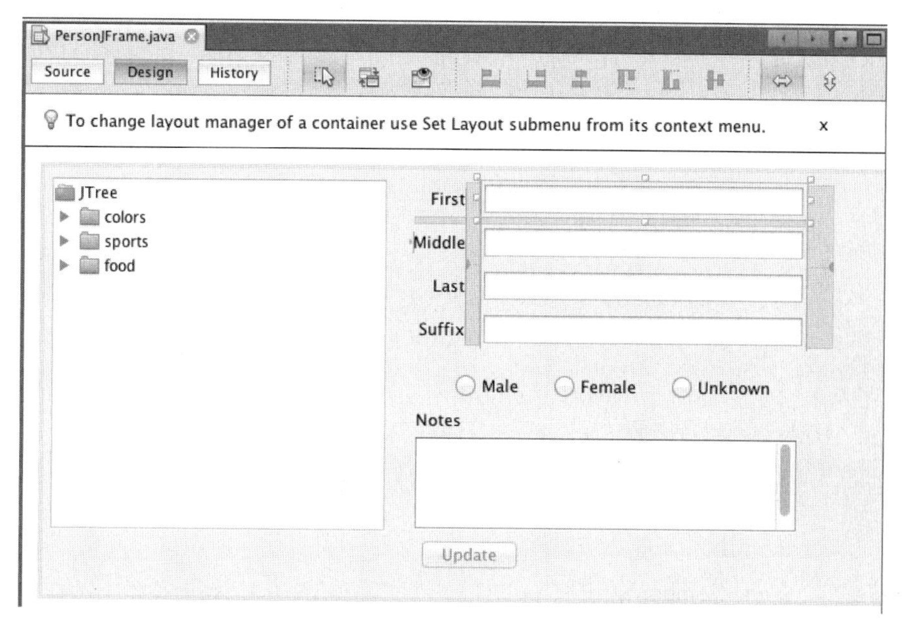


Figure 2.10 NetBeans Form Designer

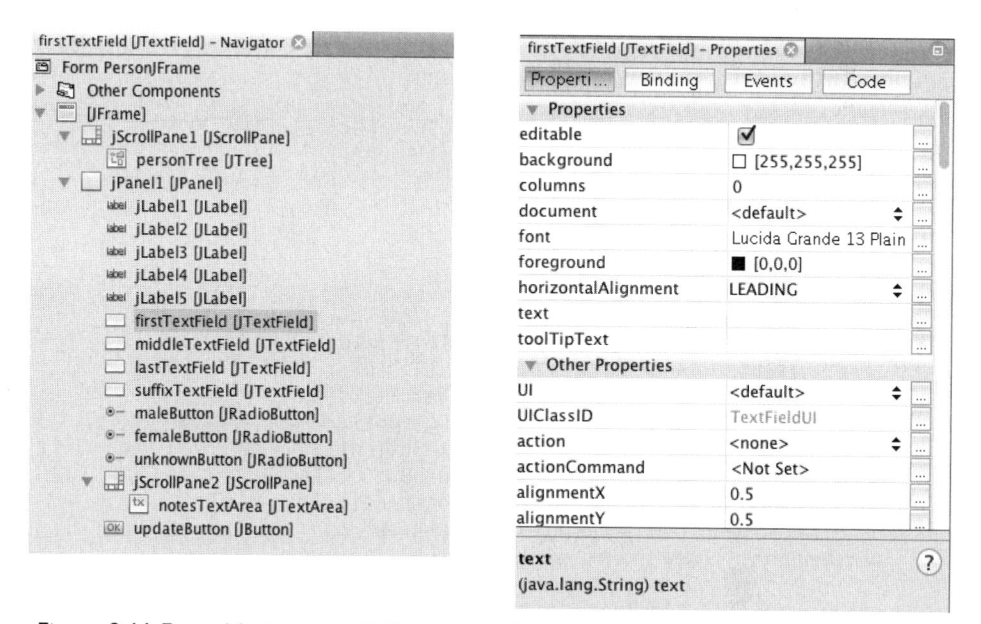


Figure 2.11 Form Navigator and Component Property Editor

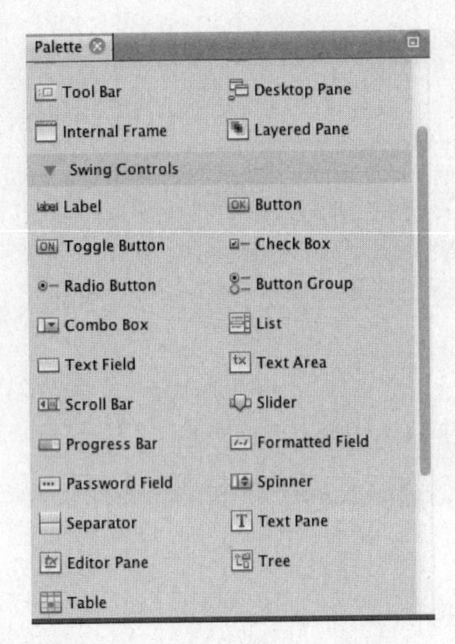


Figure 2.12 Swing Component Palette

**Listing 2.10 Form Designer Generated Code**

```
// invoked from the constructor
private void initComponents() {

     genderButtonGroup = new javax.swing.ButtonGroup();
     jScrollPane1 = new javax.swing.JScrollPane();
     personTree = new JTree(top);
     jPanel1 = new javax.swing.JPanel();

     jLabel4 = new javax.swing.JLabel();
     jLabel5 = new javax.swing.JLabel();
     firstTextField = new javax.swing.JTextField();
     middleTextField = new javax.swing.JTextField();
     lastTextField = new javax.swing.JTextField();
     suffixTextField = new javax.swing.JTextField();
     maleButton = new javax.swing.JRadioButton();
     femaleButton = new javax.swing.JRadioButton();
     unknownButton = new javax.swing.JRadioButton();
     jScrollPane2 = new javax.swing.JScrollPane();
     notesTextArea = new javax.swing.JTextArea();
     updateButton = new javax.swing.JButton();

 . . . more code to instantiate components and configure layout . . .
 }
```

Each component placed on the form requires its own variable, as shown in Listing 2.11. The Property Editor lets you specify an alternate name for the variable. Like the code that initializes the components, you cannot edit these component variable declarations directly. Here, we supply meaningful names to all variables that we subsequently access programmatically. We didn't bother to rename the JLabel components, since they hold text that doesn't change and we don't write code to access them.

**Listing 2.11 Swing Component Variable Declarations**

```
// Variables declaration - do not modify
    private javax.swing.JRadioButton femaleButton;
    private javax.swing.JTextField firstTextField;
    private javax.swing.ButtonGroup genderButtonGroup;
    private javax.swing.JLabel jLabel1;
    private javax.swing.JLabel jLabel2;
    . . . code omitted . . .
    private javax.swing.JTextField suffixTextField;
    private javax.swing.JRadioButton unknownButton;
    private javax.swing.JButton updateButton;
    // End of variables declaration
```

### Working with the NetBeans GUI Form Designer

*For more information on working with the NetBeans GUI Form Designer, see this tutorial on the NetBeans IDE web site:*

`https://netbeans.org/kb/docs/java/quickstart-gui.html`

## Program Structure

Figure 2.13 shows the project structure in the NetBeans IDE. Classes FamilyTreeManager and Person are located in package `com.asgteach.familytree.model` and class PersonJFrame (the main application class) is located in package `personswingapp`.

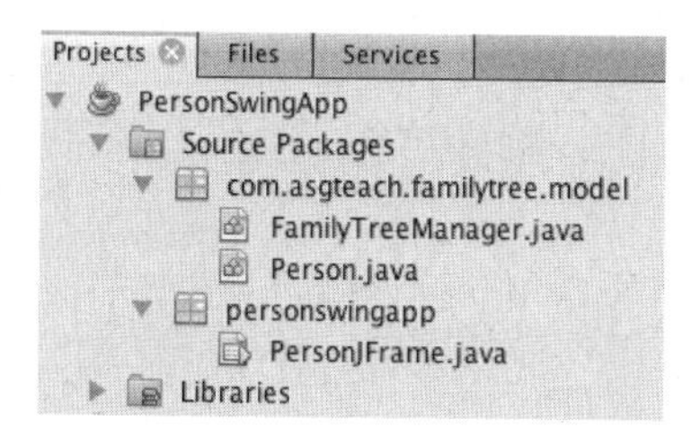


Figure 2.13 PersonSwingApp project structure

Before we start throwing methods and variables at you, let's look at the overall program structure of our main class, PersonJFrame, as shown in Listing 2.12. This class extends JFrame, which is a top-level Swing window.

Next, we define fields or class variables. Variable `top` is a DefaultMutableTreeNode, which is the root of the JTree model data. Variable `ftm` is the FamilyTreeManager object (which we initialize with the static factory method `getInstance()`). Field `thePerson` contains the currently selected Person. Finally, field `logger` defines a Logger object (see "Java Logging Facility" on page 51).

The `main()` method calls factory method `newInstance()`, which invokes the private constructor. This creates the JFrame window and makes it visible (see "Single-Threaded Model" on page 49 for more on `invokeLater()`). The Swing Form Designer generates code in `initComponents()` as well as field declarations for components. This code is not editable in the IDE. Any customized code for the Swing components must follow method `initComponents()` in the constructor.

We also provide the following three listener classes for program event handling: ActionListener, to respond to Update button clicks, PropertyChangeListener for property change events, and TreeSelectionListener for tree selection changes. We describe these listeners in detail later in this chapter.

**Listing 2.12 Overall Program Structure**

```
public class PersonJFrame extends javax.swing.JFrame {

    // Class variables
    private final DefaultMutableTreeNode top =
            new DefaultMutableTreeNode("People");
    private final FamilyTreeManager ftm = FamilyTreeManager.getInstance();
    private Person thePerson = null;
    private static final Logger logger =
            Logger.getLogger(PersonJFrame.class.getName());

    // private constructor
    private PersonJFrame() { . . .}

    // factory method
    public static PersonJFrame newInstance() { . . . }

    // initialize components (generated)
    private void initComponents() {
      . . .
    }
```

```
    public static void main(String args[]) {
        /* Create and display the form */
        SwingUtilities.invokeLater(()->
                PersonJFrame.newInstance().setVisible(true));
    }

    // Define listeners
    // ActionListener for Update button
    private final ActionListener updateListener = (ActionEvent e) -> { . . . };

    // PropertyChangeListener for FamilyTreeManager
    private final PropertyChangeListener familyTreeListener =
         (PropertyChangeEvent evt) -> { . . . };

    // TreeSelectionListener for JTree
    private final TreeSelectionListener treeSelectionListener =
         (TreeSelectionEvent e) -> { . . . };

   // Variables declaration - do not modify
   // (generated)
    private javax.swing.JRadioButton femaleButton;
    private javax.swing.JTextField firstTextField;
   . . .
}
```

Let's now examine the code in `main()` and explain why we start up our application in a separate thread.

## Single-Threaded Model

Swing component objects are not thread safe. Thread safety is achieved by performing all Swing-related operations on a single thread, called the Event Dispatch Thread or EDT. As it turns out, most GUI frameworks are single threaded because it's difficult to implement components efficiently while accounting for thread safety issues. Therefore, all GUI operations must be performed in the EDT. Normally, this is not an issue; events occur and are handled in the EDT. Components, in turn, are accessed and updated in the EDT. You only have to worry about executing within the EDT if, during execution of a background thread, you need to access the GUI. We'll cover this scenario later in the chapter.

To help you work with the EDT, Swing has utility method `invokeLater()`, which guarantees that its `run()` method executes in the EDT. We use `invokeLater()` to set up our Swing application from `main()`, as shown in Listing 2.13. (We can use a lambda expression here since Runnable is a functional interface.)

**Listing 2.13 Swing Application main()**

```
public static void main(String args[]) {

    /* Create and display the form */
    SwingUtilities.invokeLater(()->
            PersonJFrame.newInstance().setVisible(true));
}
```

Note that the initial thread, that is, the thread that creates and begins executing your application, is *not* the EDT. The above lambda expression instantiates the PersonJFrame object with the static `newInstance()` method and makes the window frame visible. We use the `newInstance()` factory method here so that later we can configure listeners in a thread-safe way.

Listing 2.14 shows the code for the constructor and methods `configureListeners()` and `newInstance()`. Method `configureListeners()` is invoked by `newInstance()` after the constructor returns.

**Listing 2.14 Constructing PersonJFrame**

```
private PersonJFrame() {                    // constructor
    // Configure Logger
    . . . code omitted . . .

    buildData();
    initComponents();               // generated by the form builder
    personTree.getSelectionModel().setSelectionMode(
            TreeSelectionModel.SINGLE_TREE_SELECTION);
    createNodes(top);
}

private void configureListeners() {
    // Listeners are registered after constructor returns
    // for thread safety
    ftm.addPropertyChangeListener(familyTreeListener);
    personTree.addTreeSelectionListener(treeSelectionListener);
    updateButton.addActionListener(updateListener);
}

public static PersonJFrame newInstance() {
    PersonJFrame pjf = new PersonJFrame();
    pjf.configureListeners();
    return pjf;
}
```

Take another look at the PersonJFrame constructor (Listing 2.14). The constructor invokes method `buildData()` to initialize our Person objects, and `initComponents()`, a generated method that initializes the Swing components. After `initComponents()` completes we configure the Swing component JTree. This provides the tree view in our application and is discussed in more detail later (see "JTree" on page 58).

Listing 2.15 shows the code for `buildData()`. (We also log the collection returned by FamilyTreeManager's `getAllPeople()`.)

**Listing 2.15 Method buildData()**

```
// Add Person objects to FamilyTreeManager
 private void buildData() {
     ftm.addPerson(new Person("Homer", "Simpson", Person.Gender.MALE));
     ftm.addPerson(new Person("Marge", "Simpson", Person.Gender.FEMALE));
     ftm.addPerson(new Person("Bart", "Simpson", Person.Gender.MALE));
     ftm.addPerson(new Person("Lisa", "Simpson", Person.Gender.FEMALE));
     ftm.addPerson(new Person("Maggie", "Simpson", Person.Gender.FEMALE));
     logger.log(Level.FINE, ftm.getAllPeople().toString());
 }
```

## Java Logging Facility

Listing 2.12 on page 48 instantiates a Logger object in the PersonJFrame.java class as follows.

```
private static final Logger logger =
            Logger.getLogger(PersonJFrame.class.getName());
```

A logging facility, especially in large, complex applications, is helpful in generating messages with relevant information during debugging and testing phases. At later stages of program development, you can remove this output since it often clutters the console and is probably not meaningful to the user. By assigning different levels to logging output, you can control which log records appear on the console. Furthermore, you can direct logging to a file, filter records, and format log records.

Table 2.1 shows the logging levels, from highest to lowest. By default the standard logging facility sends all log messages of level `INFO` and higher to the console. Thus, any debugging-type log messages should be at level `CONFIG` or lower.

**TABLE 2.1 Java Logging Levels**

| Logging Level | Description |
|---|---|
| SEVERE | Highest |
| WARNING | |
| INFO | Default threshold level for console output |

**TABLE 2.1 Java Logging Levels** *(Continued)*

| Logging Level | Description |
|---|---|
| CONFIG | |
| FINE | |
| FINER | |
| FINEST | Lowest |

To see log messages at levels lower than the standard threshold of `INFO`, you need to set both the logging level and the log handler level. You can also add additional handlers. For example, the logging API provides a FileHandler that sends log messages to a file.

Our example application configures two handlers in the constructor, as shown in Listing 2.16. One handler (`handler`) directs log messages of `FINE` or higher to the console. A second handler (`fileHandler`) writes log messages to a default file (`javaN.log` in the user's home directory).

**Listing 2.16 Java Logging and Handler Configuration**

```
public class PersonJFrame extends javax.swing.JFrame {

   . . . other class variables . . .
   private PersonJFrame() {
        // Configure Logger: set its level to FINE
        // (default threshold level is CONFIG)
        logger.setLevel(Level.FINE);
        // Define a handler to display messages on the console
        // Set level to FINE
        Handler handler = new ConsoleHandler();
        handler.setLevel(Level.FINE);
        logger.addHandler(handler);

        // Define a second handler to write messages to a file
        try {
            FileHandler fileHandler = new FileHandler();
            // records sent to file javaN.log in user's home directory
            fileHandler.setLevel(Level.FINE);
            logger.addHandler(fileHandler);
            logger.log(Level.FINE, "Created File Handler");
        } catch (IOException | SecurityException ex) {
            logger.log(Level.SEVERE, "Couldn't create FileHandler", ex);
        }
        . . . code omitted . . .
   }
}
```

You can also build log messages with parameters. Here `{0}` is a placeholder for variable `node` in this log message.

```
logger.log(Level.FINE, "Node updated: {0}", node);
```

We have several log statements throughout our program. As Listing 2.16 shows, log messages are also useful in catch handlers. (Catch handler log messages will typically be level `SEVERE` or `WARNING`.)

Listing 2.17 shows messages that appear in the File Handler's log file for our application. All levels here are `FINE` and the message text is bold for clarity.

**Listing 2.17 Log File Output (XML format)**

```
<?xml version="1.0" encoding="UTF-8" standalone="no"?>
<!DOCTYPE log SYSTEM "logger.dtd">
<log>
<record>
  <date>2013-05-18T09:29:16</date>
  <millis>1368894556261</millis>
  <sequence>0</sequence>
  <logger>personswingapp.PersonJFrame</logger>
  <level>FINE</level>
  <class>personswingapp.PersonJFrame</class>
  <method>&lt;init&gt;</method>
  <thread>13</thread>
  <message>Created File Handler</message>
</record>
<record>
  <date>2013-05-18T09:29:16</date>
  <millis>1368894556362</millis>
  <sequence>1</sequence>
  <logger>personswingapp.PersonJFrame</logger>
  <level>FINE</level>
  <class>personswingapp.PersonJFrame</class>
  <method>buildData</method>
  <thread>13</thread>
  <message>
   [Homer Simpson, Bart Simpson, Marge Simpson, Lisa Simpson, Maggie Simpson]
  </message>
</record>
<record>
  <date>2013-05-18T09:29:26</date>
  <millis>1368894566117</millis>
  <sequence>2</sequence>
  <logger>personswingapp.PersonJFrame</logger>
  <level>FINE</level>
  <class>personswingapp.PersonJFrame$4</class>
  <method>valueChanged</method>
```

```
  <thread>13</thread>
  <message>Bart Simpson selected</message>
</record>
<record>
  <date>2013-05-18T09:29:31</date>
  <millis>1368894571564</millis>
  <sequence>3</sequence>
  <logger>personswingapp.PersonJFrame</logger>
  <level>FINE</level>
  <class>personswingapp.PersonJFrame$3</class>
  <method>propertyChange</method>
  <thread>13</thread>
  <message>Node updated: Bart Seymour Simpson</message>
</record>
</log>
```

Listing 2.18 shows the same messages as they appear on the console (again, each message text is bold).

**Listing 2.18 Logging Messages on the Console**

```
run:
May 18, 2013 9:29:16 AM personswingapp.PersonJFrame <init>
FINE: Created File Handler
May 18, 2013 9:29:16 AM personswingapp.PersonJFrame buildData
FINE: [Homer Simpson, Bart Simpson, Marge Simpson, Lisa Simpson, Maggie Simp-
son]
May 18, 2013 9:29:26 AM personswingapp.PersonJFrame$4 valueChanged
FINE: Bart Simpson selected
May 18, 2013 9:29:31 AM personswingapp.PersonJFrame$3 propertyChange
FINE: Node updated: Bart Seymour Simpson
```

## Using Swing Components

A discussion of the Swing components and all their APIs would fill an entire book. Our goal here is to familiarize you with some frequently used components (specifically, those that appear in our example program). Swing also has layout components that handle the arrangement of components within a window. The advantage of using the Swing Form Designer, however, is that you can use a drag-and-drop editor to arrange your components.

Figure 2.14 shows a partial class hierarchy of Swing components. Note that most components descend from JComponent, which includes many methods that control appearance, such as font, background color, foreground color, border, and opacity.

Our program uses JLabel components to hold static text and JTextField components to edit text.

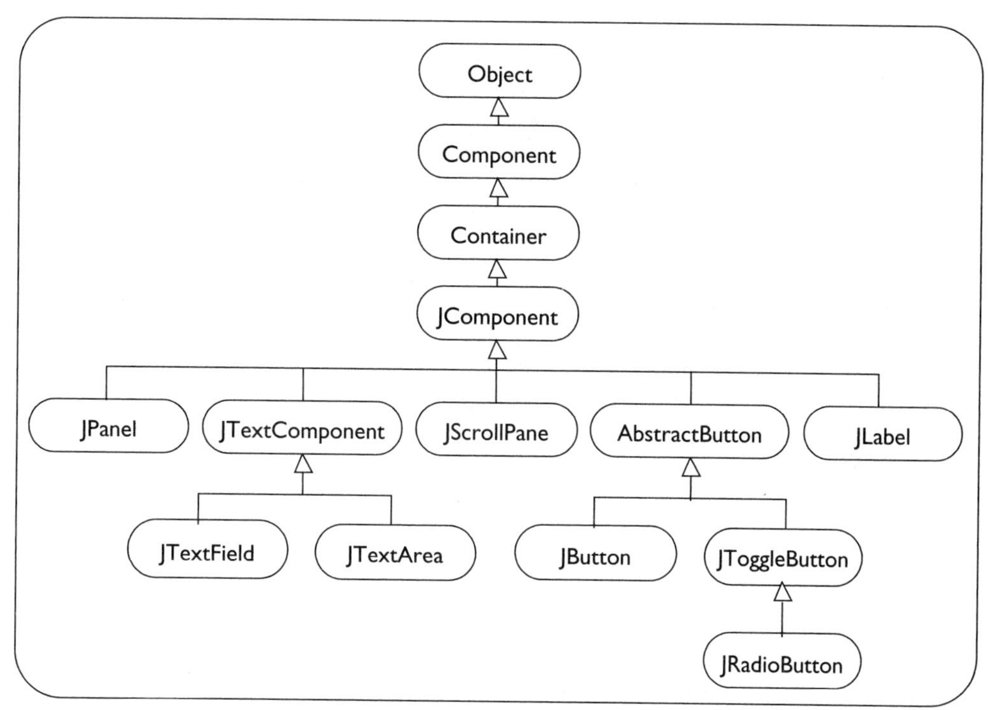


Figure 2.14 Swing Component Hierarchy (Partial)

## JLabel

JLabel holds text that users don't edit, although you can change the text programmatically. Here's the code that defines a JLabel that displays "First."

```
javax.swing.JLabel jLabel1 = new javax.swing.JLabel();
jLabel1.setText("First");
```

JLabel components can be more nuanced than the above code indicates. You can use both images (icons) and text with labels, format label text with HTML, and configure their appearance with JComponent methods `setFont()`, `setForeground()`, `setBorder()`, `setOpaque()`, and `setBackground()`. You can also connect a label with another component (such as a JTextField) that lets the associated component affect the label's appearance. For this purpose, use method `setLabelFor()` to associate a label with another component.

We use JLabel to display the static text in our Swing application, as shown in Figure 2.6 on page 42.

### JTextField

JTextField lets users edit text within a single-line field. Use method `setText()` to write a text field's text and `getText()` to read its contents. If the user hits the Enter or Return key, JTextField generates an Action event. The underlying model for JTextField is Document, which lets you listen for insert, delete, and replace edit operations. For our current example, however, we don't respond to any events and simply use `getText()` and `setText()` to keep our model data synchronized with the text fields.

Here's the code for the text field that holds the Person property `firstname` and sets its value from a Person object (`thePerson`).

```
JTextField firstTextField = new javax.swing.JTextField();
firstTextField.setText(thePerson.getFirstname());
```

And here's the code to update a Person object (`thePerson`) from the text field.

```
thePerson.setFirstname(firstTextField.getText());
```

### JTextArea

While JTextField is useful for single-line input, JTextArea lets you provide multi-line input. We use JTextArea to edit the Person `notes` property and let the user provide multi-line input. Similar to JTextField, use `setText()` to write the text and `getText()` to read the text area's text.

```
JTextArea notesTextArea = new javax.swing.JTextArea();

// set the text in the text area
notesTextArea.setText(thePerson.getNotes());

// get the text from the text area
thePerson.setNotes(notesTextArea.getText());
```

### JRadioButton

JRadioButtons provide an on/off toggle. Radio buttons placed together in a radio button group provide mutually exclusive behavior. This means only one radio button can be selected at once. When you select a different radio button, the other radio buttons in the same group automatically turn "off." We use this mutually exclusive behavior to determine a person's gender. The value can be only one of male, female, or unknown.

Here's the code that defines the three gender radio buttons, the gender radio button group, and the code that initializes them. The ButtonGroup component provides mutually exclusive behavior for the radio button components.

```
// Define the ButtonGroup
 ButtonGroup genderButtonGroup = new javax.swing.ButtonGroup();

// Define the three JRadioButtons
 JRadioButton maleButton = new javax.swing.JRadioButton();
 JRadioButton femaleButton = new javax.swing.JRadioButton();
 JRadioButton unknownButton = new javax.swing.JRadioButton();

// Add the radiobuttons to the ButtonGroup
 genderButtonGroup.add(maleButton);
 maleButton.setText("Male");

 genderButtonGroup.add(femaleButton);
 femaleButton.setText("Female");

 genderButtonGroup.add(unknownButton);
 unknownButton.setText("Unknown");
```

The `setSelected()` and `isSelected()` methods set and query a JRadioButton. Here, we set the radio buttons from a Person object's gender property.

```
if (thePerson.getGender().equals(Gender.MALE)) {
    maleButton.setSelected(true);
} else if (thePerson.getGender().equals(Gender.FEMALE)) {
    femaleButton.setSelected(true);
} else if (thePerson.getGender().equals(Gender.UNKNOWN)) {
    unknownButton.setSelected(true);
}
```

### JButton

JButton components provide a graphic that is "pushed" when the user clicks the button. You create buttons with a text label or an icon label (image) or both. Buttons can be programmatically enabled and disabled, and you typically define an action event handler to process button clicks. Here is how we use the Update button in our example program.

```
// Create a JButton with text "Update"
JButton updateButton = new javax.swing.JButton("Update");

// we begin with the update button disabled
updateButton.setEnabled(false);

// later we enable the button
updateButton.setEnabled(true);

// define an action event handler that is invoked
// when the button is clicked
```

```
updateButton.addActionListener((ActionEvent e) -> {
        // do something
});
```

## JTree

The JTree component displays hierarchical information. JTree provides graphical handles that let you expand tree nodes as well as compress them. The tree displays data from a model. We use Swing's default model in our example program, which consists of a root or top node and children nodes. Children nodes can themselves have child nodes, or they can be "leaf" nodes (no children).

The hierarchy in our example is very simple. The top node is a String ("People") with five child nodes, which are all leaf nodes. Each child node is a Person object. The JTree uses an object's `toString()` method for display. Here's the code to construct the JTree model and the JTree.

```
// Define the top node
DefaultMutableTreeNode top =
        new DefaultMutableTreeNode("People");

// Create the JTree with node top
JTree personTree = new JTree(top);

// Set the selection model to single (that is, not multi-select)
personTree.getSelectionModel().setSelectionMode(
            TreeSelectionModel.SINGLE_TREE_SELECTION);

// Build the JTree model using FamilyTreeManager getAllPeople()
ftm.getAllPeople().forEach(p -> top.add(new DefaultMutableTreeNode(p)));
```

Here's how to access the selected node.

```
// Get the selected node
DefaultMutableTreeNode node = (DefaultMutableTreeNode)
            personTree.getLastSelectedPathComponent();
```

You can access the object in a node with method `getUserObject()`. Here we check to make sure the selected node is a "leaf" node, since all the Person objects (in our example) are stored in leaf nodes.

```
if (node == null) {
    // no node is selected
} else if (node.isLeaf()) {
    // it's a child node, so we know it's a Person object
    // get the node's user object
    Person person = (Person) node.getUserObject();
    // do something with person
```

```
    } else {
        // it's not a leaf node, so it must be the top node
    }
```

## Event Handlers and Loose Coupling

Now that we've described our model data and view (the Swing components), let's examine how the program interacts. Based on user interactions, we have three different kinds of events and three event handlers to process these events.

Our program begins with the JTree component collapsed (showing only the top node People) and the Update button disabled. When the user expands the JTree, the rest of the nodes appear showing Person objects for Homer, Marge, Bart, Lisa, and Maggie. The user can now select one of these nodes or even the top node. Figure 2.15 shows the sequence of a collapsed JTree component, an expanded JTree component, and finally the JTree component with node Bart Simpson selected.

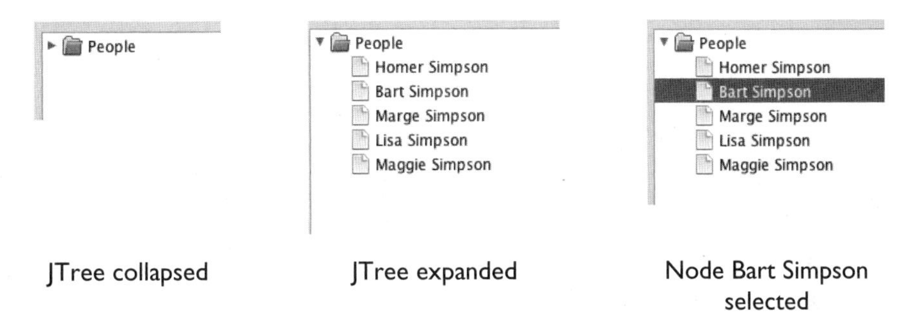


Figure 2.15 JTree component behavior

When the user selects a Person node, the Update button is enabled and the Person's data appear in the Edit area. More precisely, when the user selects a node, the TreeSelection event handler is invoked, as shown in Listing 2.19.

In the event handler lambda expression, we get the selected node and if it's null, disable the Update button and return.

If the node is a leaf node, the user has selected a Person object (such as Bart Simpson in Figure 2.15). We grab the selected Person object and invoke method `editPerson()`, which in turn calls `updateForm()`.

Method `updateForm()` copies the Person properties to the appropriate text fields, radio buttons, and text area for editing. The method also enables the Update button. Now the user can edit and update the Person object.

**Listing 2.19 Handling JTree Selection Changes**

```
// TreeSelectionListener for JTree
private final TreeSelectionListener treeSelectionListener =
            (TreeSelectionEvent e) -> {
    DefaultMutableTreeNode node = (DefaultMutableTreeNode)
            personTree.getLastSelectedPathComponent();
    if (node == null) {
        updateButton.setEnabled(false);
        return;
    }
    if (node.isLeaf()) {
        Person person = (Person) node.getUserObject();
        logger.log(Level.FINE, "{0} selected", person);
        editPerson(person);
    } else {
        updateButton.setEnabled(false);
    }
};

private void editPerson(Person person) {
    thePerson = person;
    updateForm();
}

private void updateForm() {
    firstTextField.setText(thePerson.getFirstname());
    middleTextField.setText(thePerson.getMiddlename());
    lastTextField.setText(thePerson.getLastname());
    suffixTextField.setText(thePerson.getSuffix());
    if (thePerson.getGender().equals(Gender.MALE)) {
        maleButton.setSelected(true);
    } else if (thePerson.getGender().equals(Gender.FEMALE)) {
        femaleButton.setSelected(true);
    } else if (thePerson.getGender().equals(Gender.UNKNOWN)) {
        unknownButton.setSelected(true);
    }
    notesTextArea.setText(thePerson.getNotes());
    updateButton.setEnabled(true);
}
```

Figure 2.16 shows the application as the user edits Bart Simpson fields. Note that the Update button is enabled and several fields have been modified.

When the user clicks the Update button, the button's action event handler is invoked. Listing 2.20 shows this method. We gather all of the information in the text fields, radio buttons, and notes text area and update our Person object. We then use the FamilyTreeManager to update the Person object in the FamilyTreeManager store.

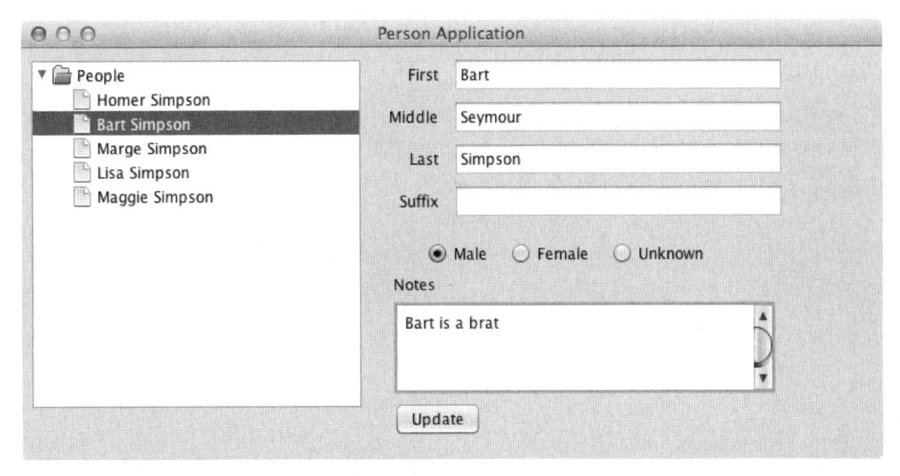


Figure 2.16 Editing Person Bart Simpson

**Listing 2.20 Handle Update Button**

```
// ActionListener for Update button
private final ActionListener updateListener = (ActionEvent e) -> {
    updateModel();
    ftm.updatePerson(thePerson);
};

// Get all the data from the components
private void updateModel() {
    thePerson.setFirstname(firstTextField.getText());
    thePerson.setMiddlename(middleTextField.getText());
    thePerson.setLastname(lastTextField.getText());
    thePerson.setSuffix(suffixTextField.getText());
    if (maleButton.isSelected()) {
        thePerson.setGender(Gender.MALE);
    } else if (femaleButton.isSelected()) {
        thePerson.setGender(Gender.FEMALE);
    } else if (unknownButton.isSelected()) {
        thePerson.setGender(Gender.UNKNOWN);
    }
    thePerson.setNotes(notesTextArea.getText());
}
```

After the Update button's action handler finishes, the edited Person (in this case Bart Simpson) is saved in the FamilyTreeManager store. As a result, the JTree component updates its view and shows the modified Bart Simpson, as shown in Figure 2.17.

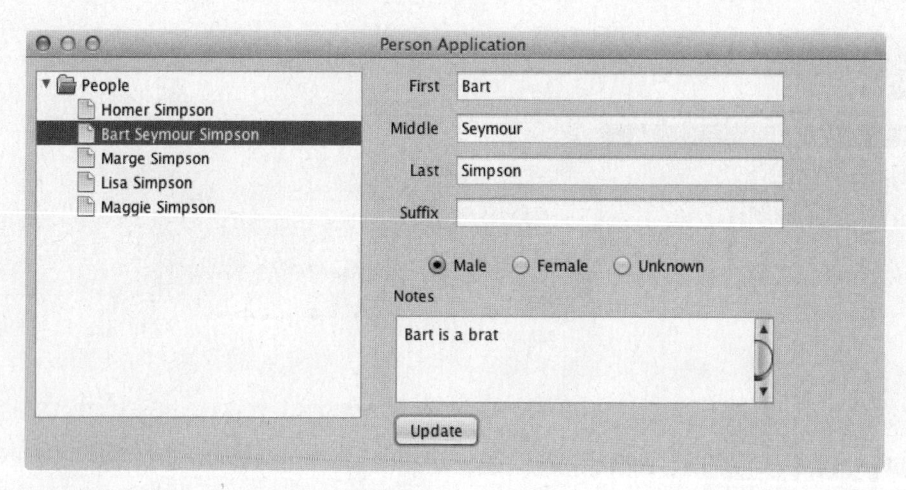


Figure 2.17 Updating the JTree model

How the JTree correctly displays the underlying Person model is perhaps the most important architectural take-away from this chapter. The JTree component updates its model because we've defined a property change listener that listens for changes to the FamilyTreeManager. While we *could have* put the JTree model update code inside the Update button's event handler (see Listing 2.20), this would be wrong! Why? Because the JTree model should not be coupled with the Update button's code. The JTree model's only job is to make itself consistent with the FamilyTreeManager's Person objects. How the Person objects are modified (via an Update button or from some other as yet undefined action) should not be relevant.

Indeed, as you begin using the NetBeans Platform, you'll see that it's possible for one (independently executing) module to modify model data and a separate module to reflect these changes. The editing code is not aware of the display code and vice versa. This makes the modules loosely coupled. Making modifications to the editing code (for example, replacing the Update button with a Save menu item) should not affect the code that displays the data. Thus, property change events are a powerful mechanism for communicating among otherwise non-connected objects.

Here, both the Update button and the JTree model are dependent on the FamilyTreeManager, but neither of these is dependent on each other.

Listing 2.21 shows the FamilyTreeManager property change listener. The method gets the updated Person object from the PropertyChangeEvent and searches the JTree model to find the target node. Method `setUserObject()` updates the JTree model and method `nodeChanged()` lets the JTree model know which node has been updated so that the JTree component can refresh itself.

Not only does the Update button event handler have no code to update the JTree model, the property change listener in Listing 2.21 has no code that deals with any of the components (text fields, radio buttons, and text area) that provide the Update button with new property values for Person. As you can see, event handlers help keep your code loosely coupled.

**Listing 2.21 PropertyChangeListener for FamilyTreeManager**

```
private final PropertyChangeListener familyTreeListener =
                (PropertyChangeEvent evt) -> {
    if (evt.getNewValue() != null && evt.getPropertyName().equals(
                        FamilyTreeManager.PROP_PERSON_UPDATED)) {
        Person person = (Person) evt.getNewValue();
        DefaultTreeModel model = (DefaultTreeModel) personTree.getModel();
        for (int i = 0; i < model.getChildCount(top); i++) {
            DefaultMutableTreeNode node = (DefaultMutableTreeNode)
                            model.getChild(top, i);
            if (person.equals(node.getUserObject())) {
                node.setUserObject(person);
                // Let the model know we made a change
                model.nodeChanged(node);
                logger.log(Level.FINE, "Node updated: {0}", node);
                break;
            }
        }
    }
};
```

## 2.4 Improving the User Experience

The application we showed you in the previous section is very basic. When the user selects different Person nodes, the Update button is enabled, even if the user has not actually made edits to the Person. Furthermore, if the user selects the top node ("People"), the previously selected Person still appears in the Editing panel.

In this section, we'll make improvements to the user interface and in the process discover more useful features of the Swing GUI and its components. We'll make the following changes to the application.

- Enable the Update button only after the user makes at least one edit to the Person displayed in the Editing panel. (Why update the Person if you haven't made any edits?)
- After the user clicks the Update button to save changes, disable the Update button (until the user makes further edits).

- If the user selects a different Person in the JTree component, disable the Update button (even if changes have been made to the currently displayed Person).
- If the user selects the top node, clear the Editing form and disable the Update button. This provides the expected feedback to the user.

Figure 2.18 shows the Editing panel when the user first selects a Person from the JTree component (here the user selects Bart Simpson, shown on the left side). The Update button is initially disabled, but after the user makes the first edit, the Update button becomes enabled (as shown on the right side).

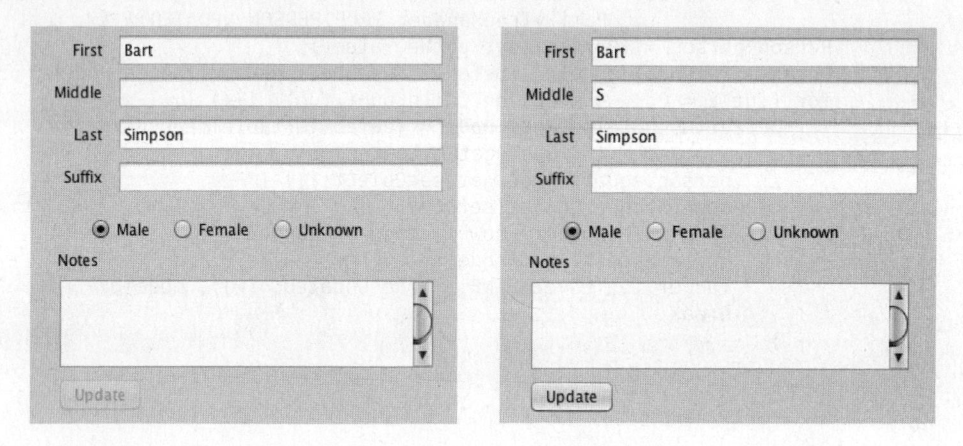


**Figure 2.18** The Update button is enabled after the first user edit

These improvements require that we listen for changes in the text fields and the text area as soon as the first keystroke is detected. We don't care what edits the user makes, only that a change has occurred.

We must also listen for selection changes in the radio buttons and enable the Update button when a change occurs.

To do all this requires additional event handlers for these listeners. We need a method to clear the form, and we must make sure that we don't start listening for changes before the Editing panel is fully initialized with all of its values.

Let's begin with a boolean class variable called `changeOK` to regulate when we listen for changes, as shown in Listing 2.22.

**Listing 2.22 New PersonJFrame Class Variables**

```
public class PersonJFrame extends javax.swing.JFrame {

    private final DefaultMutableTreeNode top =
            new DefaultMutableTreeNode("People");
    private final FamilyTreeManager ftm = FamilyTreeManager.getInstance();
    Person thePerson = null;
    private static final Logger logger =
            Logger.getLogger(PersonJFrame.class.getName());
    private boolean changeOK = false;
. . . code omitted . . .
```

Next, we provide code that clears the Editing panel, as shown in Listing 2.23. This code disables the Update button, sets boolean `changeOK` to `false`, and sets all the text fields and text area to empty strings. We set the `selected` property of all the radio buttons to `false` and call `clearSelection()` on the radio button group.

**Listing 2.23 Method clearForm()**

```
    private void clearForm() {
        updateButton.setEnabled(false);
        changeOK = false;
        firstTextField.setText("");
        middleTextField.setText("");
        lastTextField.setText("");
        suffixTextField.setText("");
        maleButton.setSelected(false);
        femaleButton.setSelected(false);
        unknownButton.setSelected(false);
        genderButtonGroup.clearSelection();
        notesTextArea.setText("");
    }
```

Once the user selects a Person to edit, we initialize the Editing panel using method `updateForm()`. The changes include code that disables the Update button and toggles the `changeOK` boolean. Listing 2.24 shows the new `updateForm()` method with the changes shown in bold.

**Listing 2.24 Method updateForm()**

```
    private void updateForm() {
        changeOK = false;
        updateButton.setEnabled(false);
        firstTextField.setText(thePerson.getFirstname());
        middleTextField.setText(thePerson.getMiddlename());
        lastTextField.setText(thePerson.getLastname());
        suffixTextField.setText(thePerson.getSuffix());
```

```
        if (thePerson.getGender().equals(Gender.MALE)) {
            maleButton.setSelected(true);
        } else if (thePerson.getGender().equals(Gender.FEMALE)) {
            femaleButton.setSelected(true);
        } else if (thePerson.getGender().equals(Gender.UNKNOWN)) {
            unknownButton.setSelected(true);
        }
        notesTextArea.setText(thePerson.getNotes());
        changeOK = true;
    }
```

The Editing panel is now ready to detect changes. When any of the listener event handlers are invoked, these methods make a call to the `modify()` method, which enables the Update button (see Listing 2.25).

**Listing 2.25 Method modify()**

```
    private void modify() {
        updateButton.setEnabled(true);
    }
```

We make a similar change to method `updateModel()`, as shown in Listing 2.26.

**Listing 2.26 Method updateModel()**

```
    private void updateModel() {
        if (!changeOK) {
            return;
        }
        updateButton.setEnabled(false);
        thePerson.setFirstname(firstTextField.getText());
        . . . code unchanged . . .
    }
```

Now let's show you the new listeners. First, in order to detect changes to the underlying text in text-based components (such as JTextField and JTextArea), you write DocumentListeners and add these listeners to the underlying Documents of text-based components.

**JTextComponent**

*Note that both JTextField and JTextArea derive from abstract class JTextComponent (see Figure 2.14 on page 55). JTextComponents provide an underlying model called Document to manipulate text. You use DocumentListeners to respond to changes in the Document model.*

Listing 2.27 shows the DocumentListener we use to detect changes in the underlying text for the text-based components. DocumentListeners must provide implementations for methods `insertUpdate()`, `removeUpdate()`, and `changeUpdate()` to handle insertions, deletions, and changes to the underlying Document model. In each of these event handlers, we make sure that the Editing panel is ready to listen for changes before we call method `modify()`.

**Listing 2.27 DocumentListener for Text Components**

```
// DocumentListener for text fields and text area
private DocumentListener docListener = new DocumentListener() {
    @Override
    public void insertUpdate(DocumentEvent evt) {
        if (changeOK) {
            modify();
        }
    }

    @Override
    public void removeUpdate(DocumentEvent evt) {
        if (changeOK) {
            modify();
        }
    }

    @Override
    public void changedUpdate(DocumentEvent evt) {
        if (changeOK) {
            modify();
        }
    }
};
```

Changes to the radio button selection status is detected with ActionListeners. Listing 2.28 shows the ActionListener we use for the radio buttons.

**Listing 2.28 ActionListener for Radio Buttons**

```
// ActionListener for Radio Buttons
private final ActionListener radioButtonListener = (ActionEvent e) -> {
    if (changeOK) {
        modify();
    }
};
```

The final change includes adding these new listeners to the respective components. We add listeners to the components in method `configureListeners()`. Here's the modified `configureListeners()` method, as shown in Listing 2.29. The changes are shown in bold. Note that we attach the listener to the text components' Document model using text component method `getDocument()`.

**Listing 2.29 Method configureListeners()**

```
private void configureListeners() {
    // Listeners are registered after constructor returns
    // for thread safety
    ftm.addPropertyChangeListener(familyTreeListener);
    personTree.addTreeSelectionListener(treeSelectionListener);
    updateButton.addActionListener(updateListener);

    // add document listeners to text fields, text area
    firstTextField.getDocument().addDocumentListener(this.docListener);
    middleTextField.getDocument().addDocumentListener(this.docListener);
    lastTextField.getDocument().addDocumentListener(this.docListener);
    suffixTextField.getDocument().addDocumentListener(this.docListener);
    notesTextArea.getDocument().addDocumentListener(this.docListener);

    // add action listeners to radiobuttons
    maleButton.addActionListener(this.radioButtonListener);
    femaleButton.addActionListener(this.radioButtonListener);
    unknownButton.addActionListener(this.radioButtonListener);
}
```

Our Swing application (called PersonSwingAppEnhancedUI) now has a nicely responsive UI, and the Update button is enabled only when it makes sense to save changes to the underlying model.

## 2.5 Concurrency and Thread Safety

Before we demonstrate how concurrency works with Swing and make modifications to our Swing application to support execution of background threads, let's discuss concurrency and thread safety. Some thread safety issues are a result of using Swing (which is not thread safe) in a multi-threaded execution environment, and others are basic concurrency principles that apply even when you're not using Swing. Let's discuss these issues now. After we prepare our application to run safely in a multi-threaded environment, we'll modify the code so that the Update button event handler code runs in a background thread.

### Thread-Safe Objects

If your execution environment is multi-threaded, then you need to use objects that are thread safe. An excellent reference on thread safety is *Java Concurrency in Practice* by

Brian Goetz (Addison-Wesley, 2006) as well as *Effective Java, Second Edition* by Joshua Bloch (Addison-Wesley, 2008).

Thread safety can be achieved several ways. You can work with immutable objects, for instance, or mutable objects that are thread safe. You can also achieve thread safety with objects that are contained within a call stack frame or in a single thread (this is how Swing works).

Both Person and FamilyTreeManager require scrutiny to use them in a multi-threaded environment. Let's begin with Person, which is a mutable object. To achieve thread safety with Person objects, we'll use thread containment. That is, we will only invoke setters on a Person object in the EDT. Any Person object used on a background thread will be an exclusive copy. We'll show you this code when we describe the update action, which will now execute on a background thread.

Let's discuss the changes required to make the FamilyTreeManager class thread safe.

### SwingPropertyChangeSupport

Since we have a multi-threaded Swing application, we want to make sure property change events fire on the EDT (because their event handlers access Swing components). To do this, we'll replace PropertyChangeSupport with SwingPropertyChangeSupport and call its constructor with `true` as the second argument. With this modification, SwingPropertyChangeSupport ensures that property change events fire on the EDT. We use SwingPropertyChangeSupport with the FamilyTreeManager class.

### ConcurrentHashMap

We use thread-safe ConcurrentHashMap instead of HashMap (HashMap is not thread safe). Next, we use `synchronized` with static factory method `getInstance()`. (Since method `getInstance()` is static, the lock is on the class.) This method needs to be synchronized because of the check and set, which is not atomic.

### Synchronized Methods

We provide synchronization for the three FamilyTreeManager modifier methods: `addPerson()`, `updatePerson()`, and `deletePerson()`. The `firePropertyChange()` method is outside the synchronize block since we're using SwingPropertyChangeSupport, which fires property change events on the Swing EDT. Method `getAllPeople()` is also synchronized. It performs a deep copy of the map, creating an ArrayList to return to the caller. Listing 2.30 shows the changes to class FamilyTreeManager in bold.

**Listing 2.30 Thread-Safe FamilyTreeManager**

```
public class FamilyTreeManager {

    private final ConcurrentMap<Long, Person> personMap =
            new ConcurrentHashMap<>();
     // PropertyChangeSupport and SwingPropertyChangeSupport are thread safe
    private SwingPropertyChangeSupport propChangeSupport = null;
    // FamilyTreeManager property change names
    public static final String PROP_PERSON_DESTROYED = "removePerson";
    public static final String PROP_PERSON_ADDED = "addPerson";
    public static final String PROP_PERSON_UPDATED = "updatePerson";
    private static FamilyTreeManager instance = null;

    protected FamilyTreeManager() {
        // Exists only to defeat instantiation.
    }

    // Thread-safe lazy initialization
    public synchronized static FamilyTreeManager getInstance() {
        if (instance == null) {
            instance = new FamilyTreeManager();
            instance.propChangeSupport =
                    new SwingPropertyChangeSupport(instance, true);
        }
        return instance;
    }

    public void addPropertyChangeListener(PropertyChangeListener listener) {
        this.propChangeSupport.addPropertyChangeListener(listener);
    }

    public void removePropertyChangeListener(PropertyChangeListener listener) {
        this.propChangeSupport.removePropertyChangeListener(listener);
    }

    public void addPerson(Person p) {
        Person person;
        synchronized (this) {
            person = new Person(p);
            personMap.put(person.getId(), person);
        }
        this.propChangeSupport.firePropertyChange(
                        PROP_PERSON_ADDED, null, person);
    }

    public void updatePerson(Person p) {
        Person person;
        synchronized (this) {
            person = new Person(p);
            personMap.put(person.getId(), person);
        }
```

```
        this.propChangeSupport.firePropertyChange(
                        PROP_PERSON_UPDATED, null, person);
    }

    public void deletePerson(Person p) {
        Person person;
        synchronized (this) {
            person = personMap.remove(p.getId());
            if (person == null) {
                return;
            }
        }
        this.propChangeSupport.firePropertyChange(
                        PROP_PERSON_DESTROYED, null, person);
    }

    public synchronized List<Person> getAllPeople() {
        List<Person> copyList = new ArrayList<>();
        personMap.values().forEach(p -> copyList.add(new Person(p)));
        return copyList;
    }
}
```

## Adding Listeners and Thread Safety

A common mistake with thread safety is to use reference `this` as an argument to a method inside a constructor. This creates a leaking "this" reference, because the reference is not fully initialized until after the constructor returns. There are various techniques to fix this problem. In the FamilyTreeManager class, for example, the static factory method `getInstance()` invokes the constructor first. It then provides the returned reference (`instance`) for the PropertyChangeSupport instantiation as follows.

```
. . .
    // thread safe
    instance = new FamilyTreeManager();
    instance.propChangeSupport = new PropertyChangeSupport(instance);
. . .
```

Similarly, in our Swing application, we use a static `newInstance()` method to call the PersonJFrame constructor and then set the listeners after the constructor is fully initialized. Listing 2.31 shows the code for PersonSwingApp, a Swing program that safely configures listeners.

**Listing 2.31 PersonSwingApp class PersonJFrame**

```
public class PersonJFrame extends javax.swing.JFrame {
    . . .
    private PersonJFrame() {            // constructor
        // Configure Logger
            . . . code omitted . . .
        buildData();
        initComponents();
        personTree.getSelectionModel().setSelectionMode(
                TreeSelectionModel.SINGLE_TREE_SELECTION);
        createNodes(top);
    }

    private void configureListeners() {
        // Listeners are registered after constructor returns
        // for thread safety
        ftm.addPropertyChangeListener(familyTreeListener);
        personTree.addTreeSelectionListener(treeSelectionListener);
        updateButton.addActionListener(updateListener);
    }

    public static PersonJFrame newInstance() {
        PersonJFrame pjf = new PersonJFrame();  // call the constructor
        pjf.configureListeners();               // safely configure listeners
        return pjf;
    }
      . . . code omitted . . .
}
```

Another thread-safe technique to add listeners is callback methods; that is, methods invoked by a caller after the object is constructed. For example, in the NetBeans Platform you typically add listeners in the TopComponent life cycle method `componentOpened()` and remove listeners in method `componentClosed()`. (See "Window System Life Cycle Management" on page 369.)

## Concurrency in Swing

Because you typically create background tasks in Swing applications to execute long-running tasks, Swing provides several static methods to manage threads, all callable with SwingUtilities.

- `invokeLater()`

  ```
  public static void invokeLater(Runnable doRun)
  ```

  Executes `doRun.run()` asynchronously on the EDT. This happens after all pending AWT/Swing events have been processed.

- `invokeAndWait()`

```
public static void invokeAndWait(Runnable doRun)
                    throws InterruptedException,
                           InvocationTargetException
```

Executes `doRun.run()` synchronously on the EDT. This call blocks until all pending AWT events have been processed and `doRun.run()` returns. Be very careful using this method, since a block can potentially cause a deadlock.

- `isEventDispatchThread()`

```
public static boolean isEventDispatchThread()
```

Returns `true` if the current thread is the event dispatching thread. Use this method when you need to execute code on the EDT, but you could be executing in a background thread.

## 2.6 Swing Background Tasks

Let's now turn our attention to background threads in Swing applications that execute potentially long-running tasks. Since Swing uses a single-threaded model, it's important that event handlers execute quickly. While an event handler is executing (always on the EDT), the EDT is not processing subsequent user input. If an event handler results in a long-running task, the UI will temporarily freeze since no processing of user input can occur until the task finishes. Project PersonSwingAppMultiThread takes our example Swing application and executes the Update button in a background thread.

### Introducing SwingWorker

Long-running tasks should run in background threads. Swing provides a helper class to launch background threads called SwingWorker. Listing 2.32 shows how to use SwingWorker to save updated Person objects in a background thread.

#### Testing Background Threads

*To simulate a long-running task, we'll use* `Thread.sleep()` *in method* `doInBackground()`. *This technique helps test how long-running background threads affect your application.*

Listing 2.32 shows the Update button's modified event handler, which is invoked on the EDT. Before leaving the EDT, you execute any code that updates or accesses GUI components. Here, we invoke `updateModel()`, which synchronizes the Person (model) object with the Swing component text fields, radio buttons, and text area. We then make a copy of the Person object, field `thePerson`.

**Concurrency Tip**

---

*Making a copy of* `thePerson` *is crucial for correct behavior. Without a copy in the background thread, the wrong Person object might be saved if the user selects a different Person in the JTree component. In general, don't access mutable class fields in background threads without first making a copy.*

---

Generic class SwingWorker provides two parameterized types. The first type (Person) is the return type for methods `doInBackground()` and `get()`. The object returned by `doInBackground()` is accessible with `get()` when the background task completes. The second parameterized type applies to periodically published values. This is useful when long-running tasks publish partial results. Here, we use Void, since we don't publish partial results. See "Monitoring SwingWorker Status" on page 76 for an example of SwingWorker that publishes periodic results.

Put code inside method `doInBackground()` that should execute in a background thread. Here we call `ftm.updatePerson()` to save the modified Person object with the FamilyTreeManager.

**Concurrency and Property Change Events**

---

*Recall that method* `updatePerson()` *fires a property change event to FamilyTreeManager property change listeners. Because we're invoking* `updatePerson()` *in a background thread, we use SwingPropertyChangeSupport to fire the property change event on the EDT* (*see "SwingPropertyChangeSupport" on page 69*).

---

To start the background thread, invoke the SwingWorker `execute()` method. This schedules the thread for execution and immediately returns. We've also overridden the `done()` method, which is invoked on the EDT after the background task completes. This method is where you place code to update or refresh the GUI. Method `get()` blocks until the background task completes. However, if you call `get()` within method `done()`, no block occurs since the background task has finished.

**Listing 2.32 Program PersonSwingAppMultiThread—Using SwingWorker**

---

```
    // ActionListener for Update button
    private final ActionListener updateListener = (ActionEvent e) -> {
        // first update the model from the UI
        updateModel();
```

```
        // copy Person for background thread
        final Person person = new Person(thePerson);
        SwingWorker<Person, Void> worker = new SwingWorker<Person, Void>() {
            @Override
            public Person doInBackground() {
                // Simulate a long running process
                try {
                    Thread.sleep(3000);

                } catch (InterruptedException e) {
                    logger.log(Level.WARNING, null, e);
                }
                // save in background thread
                logger.log(Level.FINE, "calling ftm for person {0}", person);
                ftm.updatePerson(person);
                // only if interested in accessing person after
                // background thread finishes; otherwise, return null
                return person;
            }

            // invoked after background thread finishes
            @Override
            protected void done() {
                try {
                    if (!isCancelled()) {
                      logger.log(Level.FINE, "Done! Saving person {0}", get());
                    }
                } catch (InterruptedException | ExecutionException ex) {
                    Logger.getLogger(PersonJFrame.class.getName())
                              .log(Level.SEVERE, null, ex);
                }
            }
        };
        // invoke background thread
        worker.execute();
    };
```

### SwingWorker Tip

*SwingWorker is designed to be executed only once. Executing a SwingWorker object more than once has no effect; it will not result in invoking the* `doInBackground()` *method again.*

With Family Tree updates executing in a background thread, our new PersonSwing-AppMultiThread application lets you interact with the user interface while updates are running. For example, it's now possible to select different Person objects in the JTree, edit the Person displayed in the Editing pane, and even update a newly edited Person object. (Method `Thread.sleep()` helps test these concurrency scenarios.)

## Monitoring SwingWorker Status

Class SwingWorker provides several callback methods to monitor background tasks. You can make intermediate results available with `publish()`, set the progress of a task with `setProgress()`, and safely update the GUI with `process()`. This section shows you how to use these methods.

To illustrate, let's add a Process All button to our application that performs a background task on the FamilyTreeManager collection of Person objects. We'll show you how to publish partial results and synchronize partial completion with a progress bar.

Application PersonSwingAppSwingWorker includes a Process All button, a progress bar, and a status text area. The processing converts (copies of) each Person's name to all uppercase. Figure 2.19 shows how the new user interface appears with the Process All button, progress bar, and status text area all below the JTree component.

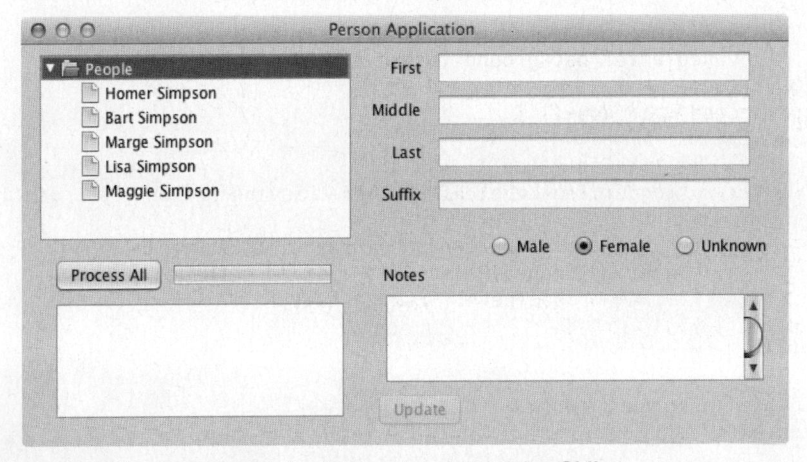


Figure 2.19 Incorporating a background task into the GUI

### JProgressBar

We use the Swing Form Designer to place a progress bar on our form. The default constructor sets the minimum to 0 and the maximum to 100, with a horizontal orientation and no progress String displayed indicating percent complete. The `setProgress()` method updates the progress. You can also use a progress bar to reflect an indeterminate-length task with method `setIndeterminate(true)`.

```
private javax.swing.JProgressBar progressBar;
progressBar = new javax.swing.JProgressBar();
. . .
```

```
// reset progress to 0
progressBar.setProgress(0);
. . .
// currentProgress is current value, maxProgress is finished value
// convert currentProgress to percentage for progressBar range 0 to 100
progressBar.setProgress(100 * currentProgress / maxProgress);
```

**Built-In Progress Indicator**

*The NetBeans Platform provides an easy-to-use progress indicator for actions that execute in background threads. This means you don't have to create a progress bar yourself and add it to the Swing form. (See "Progress Indicator" on page 518 for an example.)*

Figure 2.20 shows the Process All background task running. Partial results appear in the text area, and the progress bar indicates the task is 60 percent complete. The Process All button is disabled during execution to prevent more than one Process All background task from running at the same time.

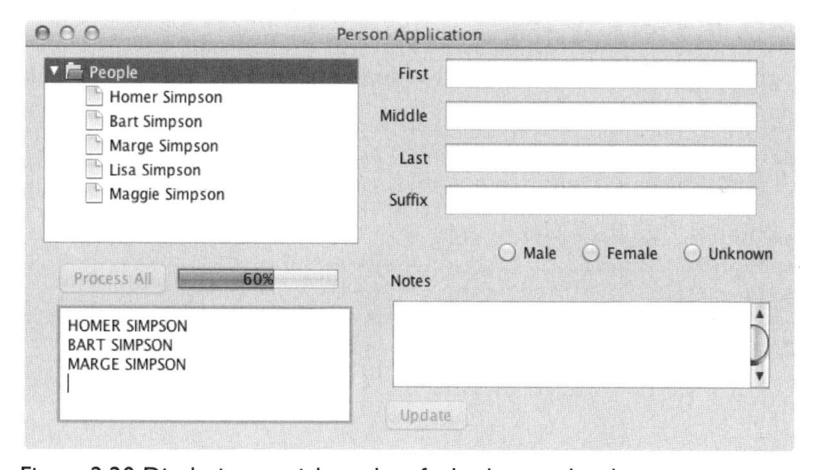


Figure 2.20 Displaying partial results of a background task

Listing 2.33 shows the Process All action listener. As in the previous example, we first configure the GUI on the EDT. Here, we disable the Process All button, configure the progress bar, and get a collection of Person objects from the FamilyTreeManager.

In this example, the first parameterized type for SwingWorker is `Collection<Person>`. This type specifies the return type for methods `doInBackground()` and `get()`. The second parameterized type (Person) specifies the type of partial results published.

Method doInBackground() processes the list one Person at a time and publishes the processed Person object with method publish(). Method publish() makes its argument available to method process(), which is invoked on the EDT. This enables safe updates of the GUI with partial results.

Method doInBackground() invokes setProgress(), which causes a property change event to fire to registered listeners. We define a property change listener; the property change event handler updates the progress bar. (The property change event handler is called on the EDT so you can safely update the GUI.)

Method doInBackground() returns the processed Person list, which becomes available using method get(). As in the previous example, we override method done() to call get(). Recall that done() is invoked on the EDT when the background task completes. Method done() is also a convenient place to reset GUI components. Here, we re-enable the Process All button, reset the status text area, and reset the progress bar.

Because the Process All event handler spawns a background thread, the application's GUI remains responsive during the thread's execution.

**Listing 2.33 Program PersonSwingAppSwingWorker—Monitoring SwingWorker**

```
// ActionListener for Process All button
private final ActionListener processAllListener = (ActionEvent e) -> {
    // get list of people from ftm
    final Collection<Person> processList = ftm.getAllPeople();
    processAllButton.setEnabled(false);
    progressBar.setValue(0);
    progressBar.setStringPainted(true);
    logger.log(Level.FINE, "Process All requested for {0}", processList);
    SwingWorker<Collection<Person>, Person> worker =
            new SwingWorker<Collection<Person>, Person>() {
        final int count = processList.size();

        @Override
        public Collection<Person> doInBackground() {
            int i = 0;
            for (Person person : processList) {
                try {
                    // do something with each person
                    doProcess(person);
                  logger.log(Level.FINE, "Processing person {0}", person);
                    publish(person);    // make available to process()
                    setProgress(100 * (++i) / count);
                    // simulate a long-running task
                    Thread.sleep(500);
```

```
                } catch (InterruptedException e) {
                    logger.log(Level.WARNING, null, e);
                }
            }
            return processList;
        }

        private void doProcess(Person p) {
            p.setFirstname(p.getFirstname().toUpperCase());
            p.setMiddlename(p.getMiddlename().toUpperCase());
            p.setLastname(p.getLastname().toUpperCase());
            p.setSuffix(p.getSuffix().toUpperCase());
        }

        @Override
        protected void done() {
            try {
                if (!isCancelled()) {
                    logger.log(Level.FINE, "Done! processing all {0}",
                            get());
                }
            } catch (InterruptedException | ExecutionException ex) {
                Logger.getLogger(PersonJFrame.class.getName())
                        .log(Level.SEVERE, null, ex);
            }
            // reset any GUI elements
            progressBar.setValue(0);
            progressBar.setStringPainted(false);
            statusTextArea.setText("");
            processAllButton.setEnabled(true);
        }

        @Override
        protected void process(List<Person> chunks) {
            chunks.stream().forEach((p) -> {
                statusTextArea.append(p + "\n");
            });
        }
    };
    worker.addPropertyChangeListener((PropertyChangeEvent evt) -> {
        if ("progress".equals(evt.getPropertyName())) {
            progressBar.setValue((Integer) evt.getNewValue());
        }
    });
    worker.execute();
};
```

## 2.7 Key Point Summary

This chapter covers basic concepts used repeatedly in both Swing and NetBeans Platform applications. The approach encourages loosely-coupled designs by building model objects with JavaBeans properties and property change support. Here are the key points in this chapter.

- Use JavaBeans and JavaBean properties to store model data.
- Provide getters for readable properties and setters for writable properties.
- Provide property change support for bound properties.
- Provide implementations for `toString()`, `equals()`, and `hashCode()` for model objects.
- Provide a singleton "manager" class for coarse-grained property change support models.
- To reduce boilerplate code, use lambda expressions for functional interfaces, such as event listeners and Runnable.
- Swing is a well-established GUI framework with a single-threaded model. Swing components are not thread safe and must be accessed only on the Event Dispatch Thread (EDT).
- Use `SwingUtilities.invokeLater()` to execute code on the EDT.
- The NetBeans IDE Form Designer helps you design and configure Swing components with drag and drop on forms.
- Choose Swing components from the Form Designer's Swing Component Palette.
- Java has a standard logging facility that helps you configure which messages appear on the console. You can also log messages to other destinations, such as files.
- Use JTextField for single-line text editing and JTextArea for multi-line text editing.
- Use JLabel to display text labels, JButton to represent a graphic action, and JRadioButton for mutually exclusive choices.
- The Swing JTree component lets you display hierarchical data and provides a user selection event.
- Swing components generate one or more specific events, which you can listen for and respond to with corresponding event handlers.
- Writing listeners and event handlers for specific events (property change events, tree selection events, action events) helps your application remain loosely coupled.

- Use DocumentListeners to detect editing events for text-based Swing components.
- JRadioButtons generate action events for selection changes.
- Execute potentially long-running tasks in background threads. Use helper class SwingWorker to create the background thread and manage the communication between the background thread and the EDT.
- When building multi-threaded applications, pay attention to mutable objects that can be accessed concurrently and use them in a thread-safe way.

## What's Next?

Perhaps you noticed that we did not implement user actions to add or delete Persons in our Swing example programs. Once you have a Swing desktop application with several actions, you'll typically want to use a menu bar with menu items. We didn't add this functionality to these programs (yet) because this is exactly one of the many features the NetBeans Platform provides: a built-in menu bar, toolbar, and action framework.

We'll be exploring how to do all this and more in upcoming chapters. But first, let's take a slight detour and examine the new Java GUI: JavaFX.

# 3

# Introduction to JavaFX

Swing has been around for a long time and some very powerful applications and frameworks are written with this library. One of those powerful applications is the NetBeans IDE, and one of those powerful frameworks is the NetBeans Platform. Just because these applications and frameworks are based on Swing, however, doesn't mean you can't or shouldn't use JavaFX. Indeed, we hope that the material in this book will help you incorporate JavaFX into your NetBeans Platform applications, and by doing so, create rich client applications that both perform well and are beautiful.

We begin with a nice, gentle introduction to JavaFX. But rest assured, we ramp up the material quickly in this chapter. Obviously, we can't cover everything you need to know about JavaFX here, but like the previous chapter's presentation of Swing, we want to give you enough so that you'll be comfortable reading and using JavaFX code in desktop applications.

In this chapter, you'll learn the basics of JavaFX, its structure, and the philosophy of how JavaFX constructs a GUI. You'll learn about different coding styles and discover the styles that best suit you and your development team. In the next chapter, we'll show you how JavaFX fits into the world of desktop application development. We'll also lay the groundwork for using JavaFX with the NetBeans Platform.

## What You Will Learn

- Understand JavaFX basics.
- Build JavaFX programs and use JavaFX APIs.

- Build a scene graph with shapes, controls, and layout.
- Use FXML and controller classes.
- Incorporate CSS files into your JavaFX designs.
- Apply JavaFX animation and event handling.
- Understand JavaFX properties, observables, InvalidationListeners, and ChangeListeners.
- Understand and apply JavaFX binding.

## 3.1 What Is JavaFX?

If the NetBeans Platform is written with Swing for its GUI and I already know Swing, why should I learn and use JavaFX? This is a good question. Here are several reasons why.

- JavaFX provides a *rich* graphical user interface. While you can certainly provide rich content with Swing, JavaFX has the structure and APIs specifically for animation, 2D and 3D geometry, charts, special effects, color gradients, graphical controls, and easy manipulation of media, including audio, video, and images. The bottom line: you can create rich content a whole lot easier using JavaFX than with Swing and Java2D.
- JavaFX graphics rendering takes advantage of hardware-accelerated capabilities. This makes rendering graphics and animation perform well.
- You can embed JavaFX content within Swing panels with JFXPanel. The magic of this specialized Swing component lets you create sophisticated NetBeans Platform applications *and* include JavaFX rich content in your application windows. Furthermore, you can start using JavaFX without throwing away existing Swing applications.

### A Bit of History

JavaFX began as a declarative scripting language (JavaFX Script) that was built on top of Java. While developers enjoyed the ease of a declarative script, it was difficult to integrate JavaFX Script with existing Swing applications. Furthermore, JavaFX Script required learning a new language.

JavaFX 2.0 was released in 2011 and is based on Java APIs. With Java 7, JavaFX is included in the standard release, and beginning with Java 8, which includes 3D capabilities with JavaFX 8, all JavaFX libraries (JAR files) are included in the standard classpath. This means that JavaFX is now part of the Java standard when you download the Java Development Kit (JDK).

While you can certainly use JavaFX APIs in the traditional Java coding style, JavaFX also provides FXML, a declarative XML markup language that describes the graphical components in your application. Scene Builder is a stand-alone application that generates FXML markup. With Scene Builder, you drag-and-drop controls and shapes to design the UI in a visual editor. These coding options make it easier to construct complicated UIs and work with user experience designers. You can also style your JavaFX application with CSS, a standard that is used and known by many designers. We'll introduce FXML in this chapter and further explore FXML and Scene Builder in the next chapter.

## The Scene Graph Metaphor

JavaFX programs with a graphical user interface define a *stage* and a *scene* within that stage. The stage represents the top-level container for all JavaFX objects; that is, the content area for the application's window frame. The central metaphor in JavaFX for specifying graphics and user interface controls is a *scene graph*. A scene defines a hierarchical node structure that contains all of the scene's elements. Nodes are graphical objects, such as geometric shapes (Circle, Rectangle, Text), UI controls (Button, TreeView, TextField, ImageView), layout panes (StackPane, AnchorPane), and 3D objects. Nodes can be containers (parent nodes) that in turn hold more nodes, letting you group nodes together. The scene graph is a strict hierarchical structure: you cannot add the same node instance to the graph more than once. Figure 3.1 shows the hierarchical structure of a JavaFX scene graph.

Parent nodes are nodes that contain other nodes, called *children*. A child node with no children nodes is a *leaf node*. With parent nodes, you can include Panes (layout containers) and Controls (buttons, table views, tree views, text fields, and so forth). You add a node to a parent with

```
myParent.getChildren().add(childNode);
```

or

```
myParent.getChildren().addAll(childNode1, childNode2);
```

The power of the JavaFX scene graph is that, not only do you define the visual aspect of your application in a hierarchical structure, but you can manipulate the scene by modifying node properties. And, if you manipulate a node property over time, you achieve animation. For example, moving a node means changing that node's `translateX` and `translateY` properties over time (and `translateZ` if you're working in 3D). Or, fading a node means changing that node's `opacity` property over time. JavaFX properties are similar to the JavaBean properties we've already presented, but JavaFX prop-

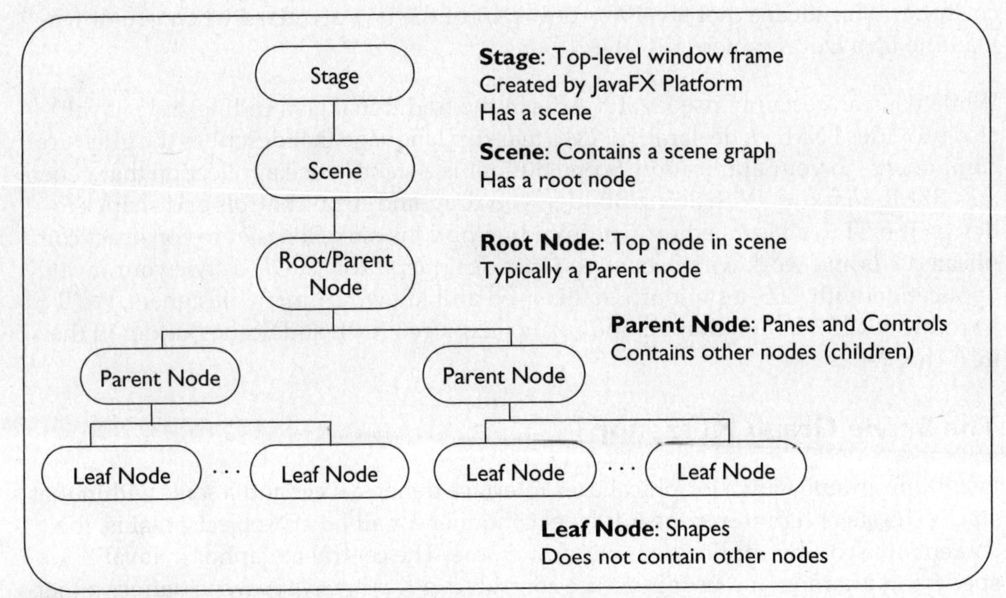


Figure 3.1 The JavaFX stage and scene

erties are much more powerful. Applying these transformations to a node generally propagates to any of the node's children as well.

## Single-Threaded Model

Like Swing, JavaFX uses a single-threaded model. The JavaFX scene graph must be manipulated in the JavaFX Application Thread, a separate thread from Swing's Event Dispatch Thread.[1] Like Swing, working with a single-threaded UI is mostly transparent: events are sent and received on the JavaFX Application Thread. And like Swing, threading issues arise when you create tasks to execute on a background thread. The solutions to these common programming scenarios are similar.

How do JavaFX and Swing code co-exist? Will you be writing intertwined graphical spaghetti code? No, not at all. In this chapter you'll learn about JavaFX without any Swing. Then when you learn how to integrate JavaFX into a NetBeans Platform application window, you'll see how to keep the JavaFX code separate, cohesive, and highly modular. Both the NetBeans Platform architecture and JavaFX program structure make it easy to add and maintain JavaFX rich content.

1. There is experimental support in JDK 8 for making the EDT and JavaFX Application Thread (FXT) the same thread. Currently, this is not the default behavior. To run with a single EDT-FXT thread, supply runtime VM option `-Djavafx.embed.singleThread=true`.

## 3.2 Building JavaFX Programs

Let's begin with a simple, graphical example of JavaFX shown Figure 3.2. This application consists of a rounded rectangle geometric shape and a text node. The rectangle has a drop shadow effect and the text node includes a "reflection" effect. The top-level node is a layout node (a StackPane) that stacks and centers its children nodes on top of each other. Let's show you one way to build this program.

Figure 3.2 MyRectangleApp running

Figure 3.3 shows a diagram of the (partial) JavaFX class hierarchy for the Rectangle, Text, and StackPane classes used in the MyRectangleApp application. Rectangle, Text, and Circle (which we'll use in a later example) are all subclasses of Shape, whereas StackPane is a subclass of Parent, a type of node that manages child nodes.

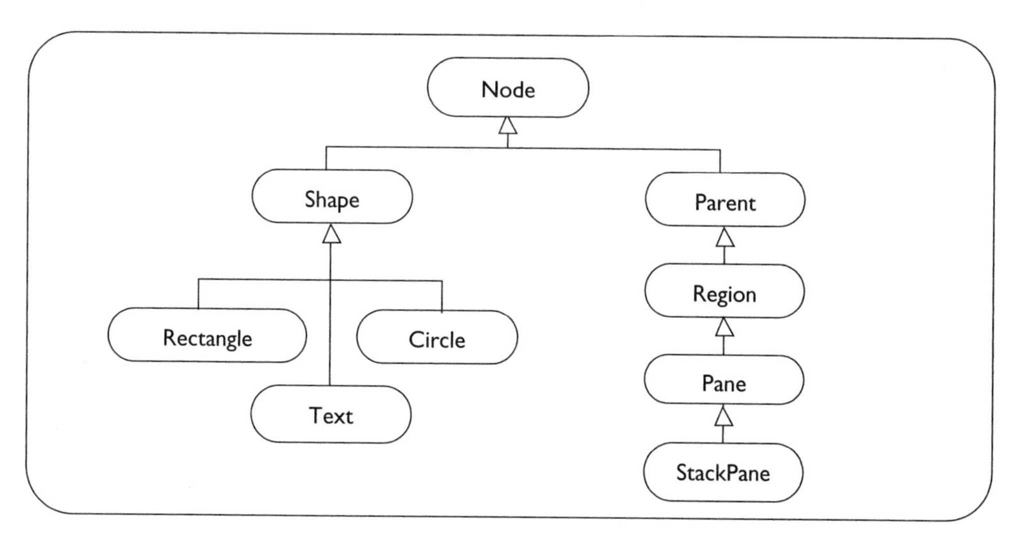


Figure 3.3 JavaFX node class hierarchy (partial) used in MyRectangleApp

## Creating a JavaFX Application

To build the MyRectangleApp application with the NetBeans IDE, use these steps.

1. In the NetBeans IDE, select **File | New Project**. NetBeans displays the Choose Project dialog. Under Categories, select **JavaFX** and under Projects, select **JavaFX Application**, as shown in Figure 3.4. Click **Next**.

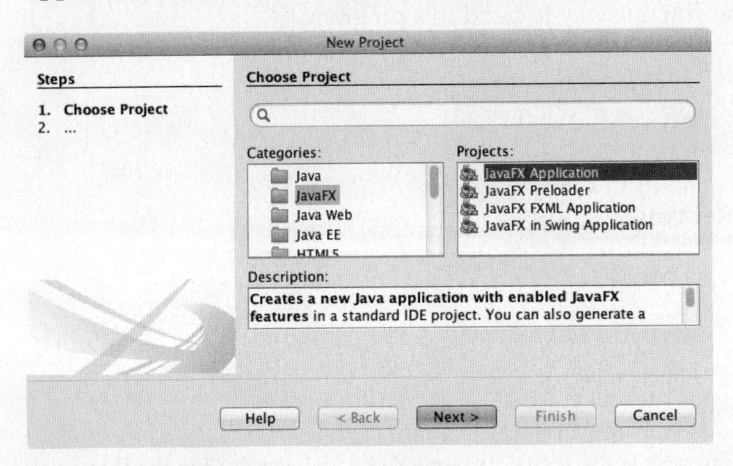


Figure 3.4 Creating a new JavaFX Application

2. NetBeans displays the Name and Location dialog. Specify **MyRectangleApp** for the Project Name. Click **Browse** and navigate to the desired project location. Accept the defaults on the remaining fields and click **Finish**, as shown in Figure 3.5.

NetBeans builds a "starter" Hello World project for you with a Button and event handler. Figure 3.6 shows the project's structure, Java file MyRectangleApp.java in package `myrectangleapp`. NetBeans brings MyRectangleApp.java up in the Java editor. Let's replace the code in the `start()` method to build the application shown in Figure 3.2 on page 87.

## Java APIs

JavaFX, like Swing, lets you create objects and configure them with setters. Here's an example with a Rectangle shape.

```
Rectangle rectangle = new Rectangle(200, 100, Color.CORNSILK);
rectangle.setArcWidth(30);
rectangle.setArcHeight(30);
rectangle.setEffect(new DropShadow(10, 5, 5, Color.GRAY));
```

Figure 3.5 New JavaFX application: Name and Location dialog

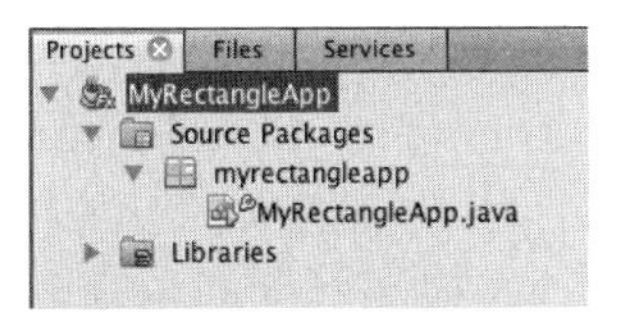


Figure 3.6 MyRectangleApp Projects view

This code example creates a Rectangle with width 200, height 100, and color `Color.CORNSILK`. The setters configure the `arcWidth` and `arcHeight` properties (giving the rectangle a rounded appearance) and add a gray drop shadow effect.

Similarly, we create a Text object initialized with the text "My Rectangle." The setters configure the Text's `font` and `effect` properties with Font and Reflection objects, respectively.

```
Text text = new Text("My Rectangle");
text.setFont(new Font("Verdana Bold", 18));
text.setEffect(new Reflection());
```

The layout control is a StackPane for the top-level node. Here we use the StackPane's default configuration, which centers its children, and specify a preferred height and width. Note that StackPane keeps its children centered when you resize the window. You add nodes to a layout control (a Pane) with `getChildren().add()` for a single node and getChildren().addAll() for multiple nodes, as shown here. (The getChildren() method returns a JavaFX Collection.)

```
StackPane stackPane = new StackPane();
stackPane.setPrefHeight(200);
stackPane.setPrefWidth(400);
stackPane.getChildren().addAll(rectangle, text);
```

Since the rectangle is added to the StackPane first, it appears behind the text node, which is on top. Adding these nodes in the reverse order would hide the text node behind the rectangle.

JavaFX has other layout controls including HBox (horizontal box), VBox (vertical box), GridPane, FlowPane, AnchorPane, and more.

### Import and JavaFX

*Be sure you specify the correct package for any import statements. Some JavaFX classes (such as Rectangle) have the same name as their AWT or Swing counterparts. All JavaFX classes are part of package* javafx.

Listing 3.1 shows the complete source for program MyRectangleApp.

**Listing 3.1 MyRectangleApp.java**

```
package myrectangleapp;

import javafx.application.Application;
import javafx.scene.Scene;
import javafx.scene.effect.DropShadow;
import javafx.scene.layout.StackPane;
import javafx.scene.paint.Color;
import javafx.scene.shape.Rectangle;
import javafx.scene.text.Font;
import javafx.scene.text.Text;
import javafx.stage.Stage;

public class MyRectangleApp extends Application {

    @Override
    public void start(Stage primaryStage) {

        Rectangle rectangle = new Rectangle(200, 100, Color.CORNSILK);
        rectangle.setArcWidth(30);
        rectangle.setArcHeight(30);
        rectangle.setEffect(new DropShadow(10, 5, 5, Color.GRAY));
```

```
        Text text = new Text("My Rectangle");
        text.setFont(new Font("Verdana Bold", 18));
        text.setEffect(new Reflection());

        StackPane stackPane = new StackPane();
        stackPane.setPrefHeight(200);
        stackPane.setPrefWidth(400);
        stackPane.getChildren().addAll(rectangle, text);

        final Scene scene = new Scene(stackPane, Color.LIGHTBLUE);
        primaryStage.setTitle("My Rectangle App");

        primaryStage.setScene(scene);
        primaryStage.show();
    }

    // main() is invoked when running the JavaFX application from NetBeans
    // but is ignored when launched through JavaFX deployment (packaging)2
    public static void main(String[] args) {
        launch(args);
    }
}
```

Figure 3.7 depicts the scene graph for program MyRectangleApp. Stage is the top-level window and is created by the JavaFX Platform. Every Stage has a Scene which contains a root node. In our example, the StackPane is the root node and its children include the Rectangle and the Text nodes. Note that StackPane is a parent node and Rectangle and Text are leaf nodes.

## Using CSS

We're not quite finished with our example. Figure 3.8 shows the same program with a linear gradient added to the rectangle. Originally, we built the rectangle with fill color `Color.CORNSILK`. Now let's use CSS to configure the rectangle's `fill` property with a linear gradient that gradually transforms from a light orange to a dark orange in a rich-looking fill, as shown in Figure 3.8.

(You'll have to trust our description or run the program, since the book's black and white print medium lacks color.)

2. The NetBeans IDE packages your JavaFX Application for you when you Build and Run a JavaFX project. You can package a JavaFX application yourself using command line tool **`javafxpackager`**, which is found in the `bin` directory of your JavaFX SDK installation.

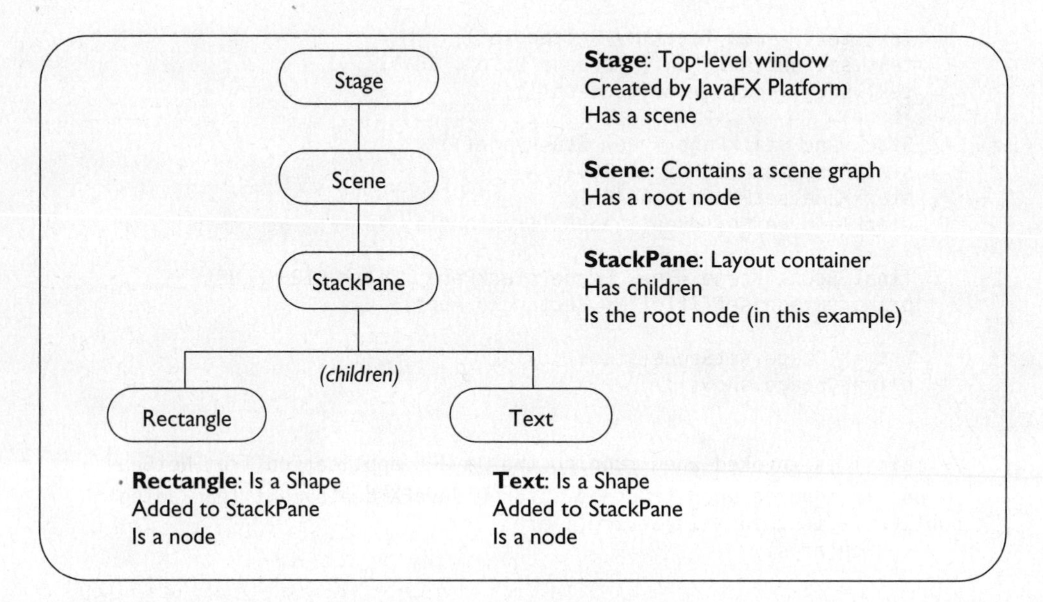


Figure 3.7 The JavaFX scene graph for MyRectangleApp

Figure 3.8 Applying a linear gradient

To create this linear gradient, we apply a CSS style with the `setStyle()` method. This CSS specifies style element `-fx-fill`, which is the JavaFX-specific CSS style for a Shape's `fill` property.

```
rectangle.setStyle("-fx-fill: "
    + "linear-gradient(#ffd65b, #e68400),"
    + "linear-gradient(#ffef84, #f2ba44),"
    + "linear-gradient(#ffea6a, #efaa22),"
    + "linear-gradient(#ffe657 0%, #f8c202 50%, #eea10b 100%),"
    + "linear-gradient(from 0% 0% to 15% 50%, "
    + "rgba(255,255,255,0.9), rgba(255,255,255,0));");
```

This style defines five linear gradient elements.[3]

**JavaFX and CSS**

---

*There are other ways to apply CSS to nodes. One of the most common is importing a CSS file. Indeed, all JavaFX controls have standard styles that you can access in the runtime JAR file jfxrt.jar. The default JavaFX CSS style in JavaFX 8 is Modena, found in file modena.css. We'll show you how to apply a CSS file to your JavaFX scene shortly.*

---

The ability to style nodes with CSS is an important feature that allows graphic designers to participate in styling the look of a program. You can replace any or all of the styles in the JavaFX default CSS file and add your own on top of the default styles.

## Creating a JavaFX FXML Application

A helpful structural tool with JavaFX is to specify JavaFX scene graph nodes with FXML. FXML is an XML markup language that fits nicely with the hierarchical nature of a scene graph. FXML helps you visualize scene graph structures and lends itself to easier modification that can otherwise be tedious with Java code.

FXML typically requires three files: the program's main Java file, the FXML file, and a Java controller class for the FXML file. The main Java class uses an FXML Loader to create the Stage and Scene. The FXML Loader reads the FXML file and builds the scene graph. The controller class provides JavaFX node initialization code and accesses the scene graph programmatically to create dynamic content or handle events.

Let's redo our previous application and show you how to use FXML. You can create a JavaFX FXML Application with the NetBeans IDE using these steps.

1. From the top-level menu, select **File | New Project**. NetBeans displays the Choose Project dialog. Under Categories, select **JavaFX** and under Projects, select **JavaFX FXML Application**, as shown in Figure 3.9. Click **Next**.
2. NetBeans displays the Name and Location dialog. Provide **MyRectangleFXApp** for the Project Name, click **Browse** to select the desired location, and specify **MyRectangleFX** for the FXML document name, as shown in Figure 3.10. Click **Finish**.

---

3. We borrowed this awesome five-part linear gradient from Jasper Potts' style "Shiny Orange" published on `fxexperience.com` (December 20, 2011).

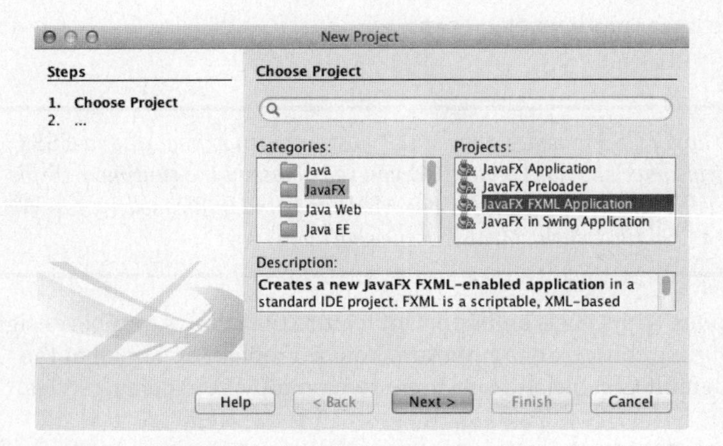


Figure 3.9 Creating a JavaFX FXML application project

NetBeans creates a project consisting of three source files: MyRectangleFXApp.java (the main program), MyRectangleFX.fxml (the FXML document), and MyRectangleFXController.java (the controller class).

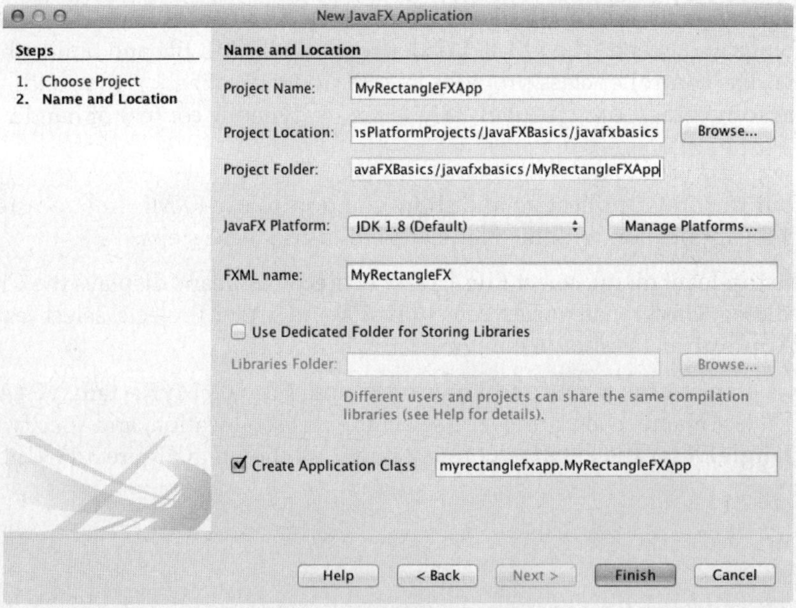

Figure 3.10 Specifying the project and FXML file name

Listing 3.2 shows the structure of the new main program. Note that the FXML Loader reads in the FXML file, MyRectangleFX.fxml, and builds the scene graph.

**Listing 3.2 MyRectangleFXApp.java**

```
package myrectanglefxapp;

import javafx.application.Application;
import javafx.fxml.FXMLLoader;
import javafx.scene.Parent;
import javafx.scene.Scene;
import javafx.scene.paint.Color;
import javafx.stage.Stage;

public class MyRectangleFXApp extends Application {

    @Override
    public void start(Stage stage) throws Exception {
        Parent root = FXMLLoader.load(getClass().getResource(
                          "MyRectangleFX.fxml"));
        Scene scene = new Scene(root, Color.LIGHTBLUE);
        stage.setScene(scene);
        stage.show();
    }

    public static void main(String[] args) {
        launch(args);
    }
}
```

Figure 3.11 shows the structure of a JavaFX FXML Application. Execution begins with the main program, which invokes the FXML Loader. The FXML Loader parses the FXML document, instantiates the objects, and builds the scene graph. After building the scene graph, the FXML Loader instantiates the controller class and invokes the controller's `initialize()` method.

Now let's look at the FXML markup for this application, as shown in Listing 3.3. Each FXML file is associated with a controller class, specified with the `fx:controller` attribute (marked in bold). With XML markup, you see that the structure of the FXML matches the hierarchical layout depicted in Figure 3.7 on page 92 (that is, starting with the root node, StackPane). The StackPane is the top node and its children are the Rectangle and Text nodes. The Rectangle's properties are configured with property names and values that are converted to the correct types. The `style` property matches element `-fx-fill` we showed you earlier. (Fortunately, you can break up strings across lines in CSS.)

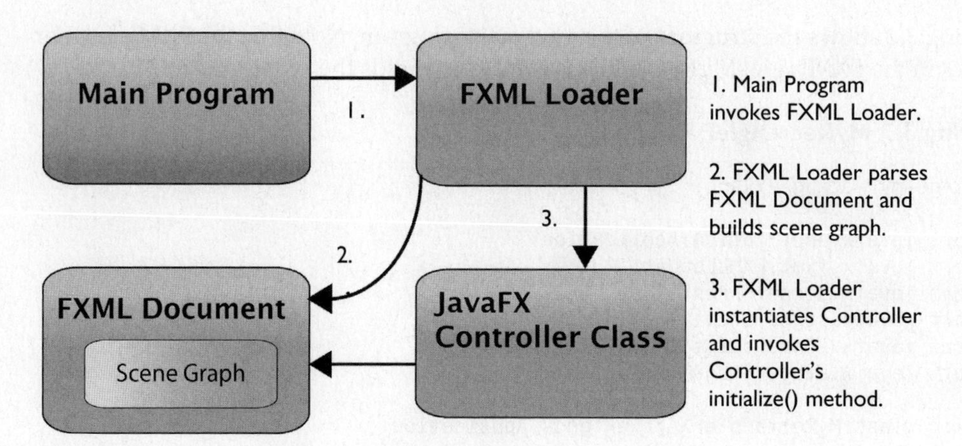


Figure 3.11 Structure of a JavaFX FXML Application

Both the Rectangle and Text elements have their `effect` properties configured. The Rectangle has a drop shadow and the Text element has a reflection effect.

### Object Creation with FXML

*Each element that you specify in the FXML file is instantiated. Thus, you will not have Java code that creates the StackPane, Rectangle, Text, Font, DropShadow, or Reflection objects. The FXML Loader creates these objects for you.*

**Listing 3.3 MyRectangleFX.fxml**

```
<?xml version="1.0" encoding="UTF-8"?>

<?import java.lang.*?>
<?import java.util.*?>
<?import javafx.scene.*?>
<?import javafx.scene.control.*?>
<?import javafx.scene.layout.*?>
<?import javafx.scene.shape.*?>
<?import javafx.scene.text.*?>
<?import javafx.scene.effect.*?>

<StackPane id="StackPane" prefHeight="200" prefWidth="400"
           xmlns:fx="http://javafx.com/fxml"
           fx:controller="myrectanglefxapp.MyRectangleFXController">
    <children>
        <Rectangle fx:id="rectangle" width="200" height="100"
                   arcWidth="30" arcHeight="30"
                   style="-fx-fill: linear-gradient(#ffd65b, #e68400),
```

```
            linear-gradient(#ffef84, #f2ba44),
            linear-gradient(#ffea6a, #efaa22),
            linear-gradient(#ffe657 0%, #f8c202 50%, #eea10b 100%),
            linear-gradient(from 0% 0% to 15% 50%, rgba(255,255,255,0.9),
            rgba(255,255,255,0));" >
            <effect>
                <DropShadow color="GRAY" offsetX="5.0" offsetY="5.0" />
            </effect>
        </Rectangle>
        <Text text="My Rectangle">
            <effect>
                <Reflection />
            </effect>
            <font>
                <Font name="Verdana Bold" size="18.0" />
            </font>
        </Text>
    </children>
</StackPane>
```

To access FXML elements from the controller class, give them an `fx-id` tag. Here, we've assigned the Rectangle element `fx:id="rectangle"` (marked in bold). This references a class variable that you declare in the controller class.

**FXML and Controller Class**

*Name the controller class the same name as the FXML file with Controller appended to it. This is not required but helps identify the link between the FXML file and its controller class.*

Now let's show you the controller class. Listing 3.4 displays the source for MyRectangleFXController.java.

Annotation `@FXML` marks variable `rectangle` as an FXML-defined object. The `initialize()` method is invoked after the scene graph is built and typically includes any required initialization code. Here we configure two additional Rectangle properties, `strokeWidth` and `stroke`. While we could have configured these properties in the FXML file, Listing 3.4 shows you how to access FXML-defined elements in the controller class.

### Listing 3.4 MyRectangleFXController

```
package myrectanglefxapp;

import java.net.URL;
import java.util.ResourceBundle;
import javafx.fxml.FXML;
import javafx.fxml.Initializable;
```

```
import javafx.scene.paint.Color;
import javafx.scene.shape.Rectangle;

public class MyRectangleFXController implements Initializable {

    @FXML
    private Rectangle rectangle;

    @Override
    public void initialize(URL url, ResourceBundle rb) {
        rectangle.setStrokeWidth(5.0);
        rectangle.setStroke(Color.GOLDENROD);
    }
}
```

The controller class also includes event handlers (we'll add an event handler when we show you animation). Figure 3.12 shows MyRectangleFXApp running with the Rectangle's `stroke` and `strokeWidth` properties configured.

Figure 3.12 Rectangle's customized stroke and strokeWidth properties

## CSS Files

Instead of specifying the hideously long linear gradient style in the FXML file (see Listing 3.3 on page 96), let's hide this code in a CSS file and apply it to the scene graph.

You can specify a CSS file either directly in the FXML file or in the main program. To specify a CSS file in the main program, add a call to `scene.getStylesheets()`, as shown in Listing 3.5.

**Listing 3.5 Adding a CSS Style Sheet in the Main Program**

```
package myrectanglefxapp;

import javafx.application.Application;
```

```
import javafx.fxml.FXMLLoader;
import javafx.scene.Parent;
import javafx.scene.Scene;
import javafx.scene.paint.Color;
import javafx.stage.Stage;

public class MyRectangleFXApp extends Application {

    @Override
    public void start(Stage stage) throws Exception {
        Parent root = FXMLLoader.load(getClass().getResource(
                "MyRectangleFX.fxml"));
        Scene scene = new Scene(root, Color.LIGHTBLUE);
        scene.getStylesheets().add("myrectanglefxapp/MyCSS.css");
        stage.setScene(scene);
        stage.show();
    }

    public static void main(String[] args) {
        launch(args);
    }
}
```

It's also possible to specify the style sheet in FXML, as shown in Listing 3.6. Note that you must include `java.net.*` to define element `URL`.

### Listing 3.6 MyRectangleFX.fxml—Adding a Style Sheet

```
<?import java.lang.*?>
<?import java.net.*?>
<?import java.util.*?>
<?import javafx.scene.*?>
<?import javafx.scene.control.*?>
<?import javafx.scene.layout.*?>
<?import javafx.scene.shape.*?>
<?import javafx.scene.text.*?>
<?import javafx.scene.effect.*?>

<StackPane id="StackPane" fx:id="stackpane" prefHeight="200" prefWidth="400"
          xmlns:fx="http://javafx.com/fxml"
          fx:controller="myrectanglefxapp.MyRectangleFXController">
    <stylesheets>
        <URL value="@MyCSS.css" />
    </stylesheets>
    <children>
        <Rectangle id="myrectangle" fx:id="rectangle" width="200" height="100"
                   arcWidth="30" arcHeight="30"
                   onMouseClicked="#handleMouseClick" />
```

```
            <Text text="My Rectangle">
                <effect>
                    <Reflection />
                </effect>
                <font>
                    <Font name="Verdana Bold" size="18.0" />
                </font>
            </Text>
        </children>
</StackPane>
```

Before we show you the MyCSS.css file, take a look at the Rectangle element in Listing 3.6. It's much shorter now since the FXML no longer includes the `style` or `effect` property values. The FXML does, however, contain a property `id` value. This `id` attribute identifies the node for the CSS style definition.

We've also defined an event handler for a mouse clicked event in the Rectangle FXML (`#handleMouseClick`). The `onMouseClicked` attribute lets you wire an event handler with an FXML component. The mouse clicked event handler is invoked when the user clicks inside the Rectangle. (We'll show you the updated controller class in the next section.)

Finally, as shown in Listing 3.6, we modified the StackPane to include element `fx:id="stackpane"` so we can refer to the StackPane in the controller code.

Listing 3.7 shows the CSS file MyCSS.css, which defines a style specifically for the component with `id` "myrectangle."

**Listing 3.7 MyCSS.css**

```
#myrectangle {
    -fx-fill:
        linear-gradient(#ffd65b, #e68400),
        linear-gradient(#ffef84, #f2ba44),
        linear-gradient(#ffea6a, #efaa22),
        linear-gradient(#ffe657 0%, #f8c202 50%, #eea10b 100%),
        linear-gradient(from 0% 0% to 15% 50%, rgba(255,255,255,0.9),
         rgba(255,255,255,0));
    -fx-effect: dropshadow( three-pass-box , gray , 10 , 0 , 5.0 , 5.0 );
}
```

## Animation

You don't actually think we'd introduce JavaFX and not show some animation, do you? As it turns out, animation with JavaFX is easy when you use the high-level animation APIs called *transitions*.

For our example, let's rotate the Rectangle node 180 degrees (and back to 0) twice. The animation begins when the user clicks inside the rectangle. Figure 3.13 shows the rectangle during the transition (on the right). We rotate both the Rectangle and the Text.

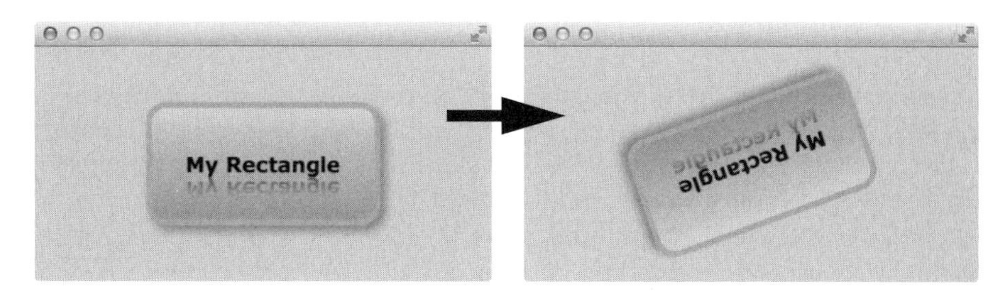


Figure 3.13 The Rectangle node rotates with a rotation animation

Each JavaFX Transition type controls one or more Node (or Shape) properties, as listed in Table 3.1. The RotateTransition controls a node's `rotate` property. The FadeTransition controls a node's `opacity` property. The TranslateTransition controls a node's `translateX` and `translateY` properties (and `translateZ` if you're working in 3D). Other transitions include PathTransition (animates a node along a Path), FillTransition (animates a shape's `fill` property), StrokeTransition (animates a shape's `stroke` property), and ScaleTransition (grows or shrinks a node over time).

**TABLE 3.1 JavaFX Transitions**

| Transition | Affected Property(ies) | Applies to |
|---|---|---|
| RotateTransition | `rotate` (0 to 360) | Node |
| FadeTransition | `opacity` (0 to 1) | Node |
| TranslateTransition | `translateX`, `translateY`, `translateZ` | Node |
| ScaleTransition | `scaleX`, `scaleY`, `scaleZ` | Node |
| PathTransition | `translateX`, `translateY`, `rotate` | Node |
| FillTransition | `fill` (color) | Shape |
| StrokeTransition | `stroke` (color) | Shape |

You can play multiple transitions in parallel (ParallelTransition) or sequentially (SequentialTransition). It's also possible to control timing between two sequential transitions with a pause (PauseTransition), configure a delay before a transition begins (with Transition method `setDelay()`), or define an action at the completion of a Transition (with Transition action event handler property `onFinished`).

You start a transition with method play() or playFromStart(). Method play() initiates a transition at its current time; method playFromStart() starts the transition at time 0. Other methods include stop() and pause(). You can query a transition's status with getStatus(), which returns one of the Animation.Status enum values RUNNING, PAUSED, or STOPPED.

Since transitions are specialized, you configure each one slightly differently. However, all transitions support the common properties duration, autoReverse, cycleCount, onFinished, currentTime, and either node or shape (for Shape-specific transitions Fill-Transition and StrokeTransition).

Listing 3.8 shows the modifications to the controller class to implement the Rotate-Transition and mouse click event handler. We instantiate the RotateTransition rt inside method initialize(). In order to rotate *both* the Rectangle and the Text together, we specify a rotation for the parent StackPane node, which then rotates its children together (the Rectangle and the Text). Then, inside the event handler we initiate the animation with method play().

The @FXML annotation applies to variables stackpane and rectangle, as well as method handleMouseClick(), in order to correctly wire these objects to the FXML markup.

**Listing 3.8 MyRectangleFXController.java—RotateTransition**

```
package myrectanglefxapp;

import java.net.URL;
import java.util.ResourceBundle;
import javafx.fxml.FXML;
import javafx.fxml.Initializable;
import javafx.scene.input.MouseEvent;
import javafx.scene.paint.Color;
import javafx.scene.shape.Rectangle;
import javafx.util.Duration;

public class MyRectangleFXController implements Initializable {

    private RotateTransition rt;

    @FXML
    private Rectangle rectangle;
    @FXML
    private StackPane stackpane;

    @FXML
    private void handleMouseClick(MouseEvent evt) {
        rt.play();
    }
```

```
    @Override
    public void initialize(URL url, ResourceBundle rb) {
        rectangle.setStrokeWidth(5.0);
        rectangle.setStroke(Color.GOLDENROD);
        // Create and configure RotateTransition rt
        rt = new RotateTransition(Duration.millis(3000), stackpane);
        rt.setToAngle(180);
        rt.setFromAngle(0);
        rt.setAutoReverse(true);
        rt.setCycleCount(4);
    }
}
```

The RotateTransition lets you specify either a "to" angle or "by" angle value. If you omit a starting position (property `fromAngle`), the rotation uses the node's current `rotation` property value as the starting rotation angle. Here we set `autoReverse` to true, which makes the StackPane rotate from angle 0 to 180 and then back again. We set cycle count to four to repeat the back and forth animation twice (back and forth counts as two cycles).

## 3.3 JavaFX Properties

The previous sections make frequent references to JavaFX properties. We said that JavaFX properties are similar to JavaBean properties, but JavaFX properties are *much more powerful*. Clearly, JavaFX properties have considerable significance in JavaFX applications. In fact, JavaFX properties are perhaps the most significant feature in JavaFX. In this section, we'll explore JavaFX properties in detail and show you how to use them.

### What Is a JavaFX Property?

At the heart of JavaFX is its scene graph, a structure that includes (perhaps many) nodes. The JavaFX rendering engine displays these nodes and ultimately what you see depends on the properties of these nodes.

Properties are oh-so-important. They make a Circle red or a Rectangle 200 pixels wide. They determine the gradient for a fill color or whether or not a text node includes reflection or a drop shadow effect. You manipulate nodes with layout controls—which are themselves nodes—by setting properties such as spacing or alignment. When your application includes animation, JavaFX updates a node's properties over time—perhaps a node's position, its rotation, or its opacity. In the previous sections, you've seen how our example applications are affected by the properties that the code manipulates.

The previous chapter describes how JavaBean properties support encapsulation and a well-defined naming convention. You can create read-write properties, read-only properties, and immutable properties. We also show how to create bound properties—properties that fire property change events to registered listeners. Let's learn how these concepts apply to JavaFX properties.

JavaFX properties support the same naming conventions as JavaBeans properties. For example, the radius of a Circle (a JavaFX Shape) is determined by its `radius` property. Here, we manipulate the `radius` property with setters and getters.

```
Circle circle1 = new Circle(10.5);
System.out.println("Circle1 radius = " + circle1.getRadius());
circle1.setRadius(20.5);
System.out.println("Circle1 radius = " + circle1.getRadius());
```

This displays the following output.

```
Circle1 radius = 10.5
Circle1 radius = 20.5
```

You access a JavaFX property with *property getter* method. A property getter consists of the property name followed by the word "Property." Thus, to access the JavaFX `radius` property for `circle1` we use the `radiusProperty()` method. Here, we print the `radius` property

```
System.out.println(circle1.radiusProperty());
```

which displays

```
DoubleProperty [bean: Circle[centerX=0.0, centerY=0.0, radius=20.5,
      fill=0x000000ff], name: radius, value: 20.5]
```

Typically, each JavaFX property holds metadata, including its value, the property name, and the bean that contains it. We can access this metadata individually with property methods `getValue()`, `getName()`, and `getBean()`, as shown in Listing 3.9. You can also access a property's value with `get()`.

**Listing 3.9 Accessing JavaFX Property Metadata**

```
System.out.println("circle1 radius property value: "
      + circle1.radiusProperty().getValue());
System.out.println("circle1 radius property name: "
      + circle1.radiusProperty().getName());
System.out.println("circle1 radius property bean: "
      + circle1.radiusProperty().getBean());
System.out.println("circle1 radius property value: "
      + circle1.radiusProperty().get());
```

```
Output:
circle1 radius property value: 20.5
circle1 radius property name: radius
circle1 radius property bean: Circle@243e0b62
circle1 radius property value: 20.5
```

## Using Listeners with Observable Properties

All JavaFX properties are Observable. This means that when a property's value becomes invalid or changes, the property notifies its registered InvalidationListeners or ChangeListeners. (There are differences between invalidation and change, which we'll discuss shortly.) You register listeners directly with a JavaFX property. Let's show you how this works by registering an InvalidationListener with a Circle's `radius` property. Since our example does not build a scene graph, we'll create a plain Java application (called **MyInvalidationListener**) using these steps.

1. From the top-level menu in the NetBeans IDE, select **File | New Project**. NetBeans displays the Choose Project dialog. Under Categories, select **Java** and under Projects, select **Java Application**, as shown in Figure 3.14. Click **Next**.

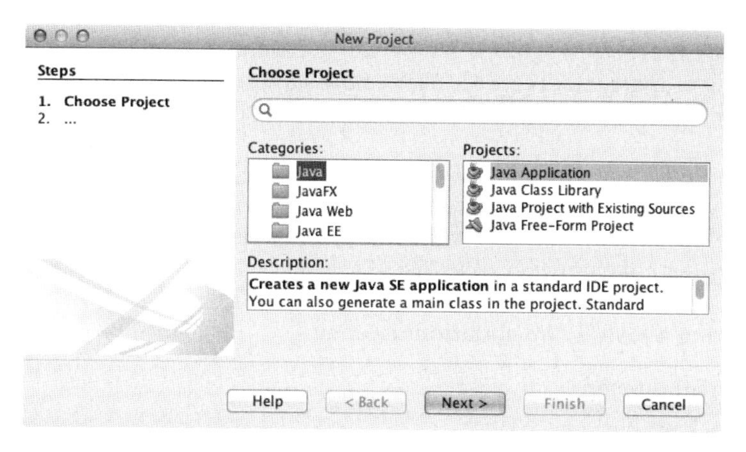


Figure 3.14 Create a Java Application when you don't need a JavaFX scene graph

2. NetBeans displays the Name and Location dialog. Provide **MyInvalidation-Listener** for the Project Name, and click **Browse** to select the desired location, as shown in Figure 3.15. Click **Finish**.

### Using InvalidationListeners

Listing 3.10 creates two Circle objects and registers an InvalidationListener with the `radius` property of `circle2`. Inside the event handler, the `invalidated()` method sets

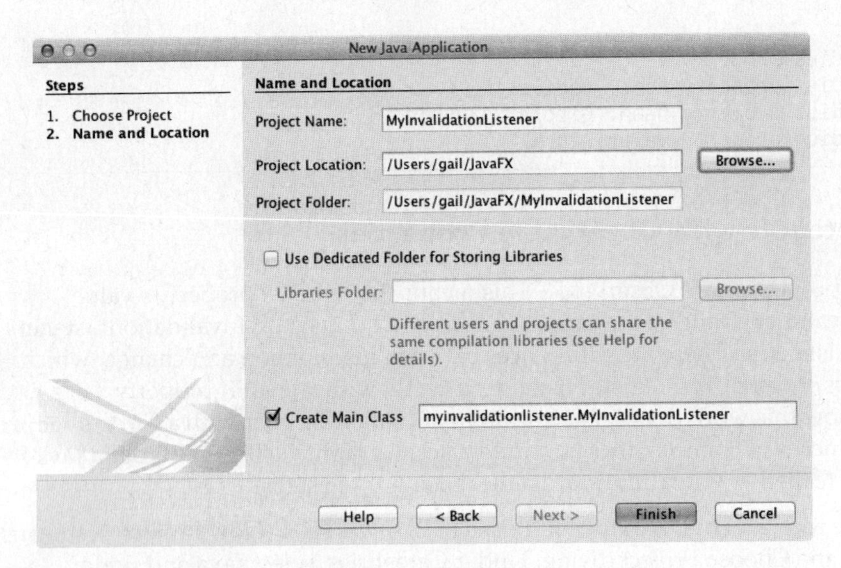


Figure 3.15 Specify the project's name and location

the `radius` property of `circle1` with `circle2`'s new value. Essentially, we are saying "make sure the `radius` property of `circle1` is always the same as the `radius` property of `circle2`."

A registered InvalidationListener is notified when the current value is no longer valid.[4] Invalidation events supply the observable value, which is the JavaFX property including the metadata. If you don't need to access the previous value, listening for invalidation events instead of change events (discussed next) can be more efficient.

**Listing 3.10 Registering a JavaFX InvalidationListener**

```
package myinvalidationlistener;

import javafx.beans.InvalidationListener;
import javafx.beans.Observable;
import javafx.scene.shape.Circle;
```

4. You can also use a lambda expression in place of the anonymous inner class in Listing 3.10. However, here we're leaving in the InvalidationListener with the `invalidated()` method for clarity. Later in the chapter we'll show you how to use lambda expressions.

```
public class MyInvalidationListener {

    public static void main(String[] args) {

        // Define some circles
        final Circle circle1 = new Circle(10.5);
        final Circle circle2 = new Circle(15.5);

        // Add an invalidation listener to circle2's radius property
        circle2.radiusProperty().addListener(new InvalidationListener() {
            @Override
            public void invalidated(Observable o) {
                System.out.println("Invalidation detected for " + o);
                circle1.setRadius(circle2.getRadius());
            }
        });

        System.out.println("Circle1: " + circle1.getRadius());
        System.out.println("Circle2: " + circle2.getRadius());
        circle2.setRadius(20.5);
        System.out.println("Circle1: " + circle1.getRadius());
        System.out.println("Circle2: " + circle2.getRadius());
    }
}
```

---

```
Output:
Circle1: 10.5
Circle2: 15.5
Invalidation detected for DoubleProperty [bean: Circle[centerX=0.0,
centerY=0.0, radius=20.5, fill=0x000000ff], name: radius, value: 20.5]
Circle1: 20.5
Circle2: 20.5
```

---

The output shows the original radius values for both Circles (10.5 and 15.5), the invalidation event handler output, and the updated `radius` property for both Circles. The `getRadius()` method displays the value of the `radius` property. You can also use `radiusProperty().get()` or `radiusProperty().getValue()`, but the traditionally named `getRadius()` is more familiar and more efficient.

Note that with InvalidationListeners, you must cast the non-generic `Observable o` to `ObservableValue<Number>` to access the new value in the event handler.

```
System.out.println("new value = " +
        ((ObservableValue<Number>) o).getValue().doubleValue());
```

## Using ChangeListeners

Listing 3.11 shows the same program with a ChangeListener instead of an InvalidationListener attached to `circle2`'s radius property (project **MyChangeListener**). ChangeListener is generic and you override the `changed()` method.

The event handler's signature includes the generic observable value (`ov`), the observable value's old value (`oldValue`), and the observable value's new value (`newValue`). The new and old values are the property values (here, Number objects) without the JavaFX property metadata. Inside the `changed()` method, we set `circle1`'s `radius` property with the `setRadius(newValue.doubleValue())` method. Because ChangeListeners are generic, you can access the event handler parameters without type casts.

**Listing 3.11 Registering a JavaFX Property ChangeListener**

```
package mychangelistener;

import javafx.beans.value.ChangeListener;
import javafx.beans.value.ObservableValue;
import javafx.scene.shape.Circle;
public class MyChangeListener  {

    public static void main(String[] args) {

        // Define some circles
        final Circle circle1 = new Circle(10.5);
        final Circle circle2 = new Circle(15.5);

        // Use change listener to track changes to circle2's radius property
      circle2.radiusProperty().addListener(new ChangeListener<Number>() {

            @Override
            public void changed(ObservableValue<? extends Number> ov,
                        Number oldValue, Number newValue) {
                System.out.println("Change detected for " + ov);
                circle1.setRadius(newValue.doubleValue());
            }
        });

        System.out.println("Circle1: " + circle1.getRadius());
        System.out.println("Circle2: " + circle2.getRadius());
        circle2.setRadius(20.5);
        System.out.println("Circle1: " + circle1.getRadius());
        System.out.println("Circle2: " + circle2.getRadius());
    }
}
```

```
Output:
Circle1: 10.5
Circle2: 15.5
Change detected for DoubleProperty [bean: Circle[centerX=0.0, centerY=0.0,
radius=20.5, fill=0x000000ff], name: radius, value: 20.5]
Circle1: 20.5
Circle2: 20.5
```

The output of the MyChangeListener program is similar to the InvalidationListener output in Listing 3.10.[5] Note that ChangeListeners make it possible to access the old value of a changed property and generics mean casting is not needed.

## Read-Only Properties

JavaFX also supports read-only properties. Although you cannot modify read-only properties directly with setters, the value of a read-only property can change. A typical use of a read-only property is with a bean that maintains a property's value internally. For example, the `currentTime` property of an Animation object (a Transition or a Timeline) is read only. You can read its value with `getCurrentTime()` and access the property with `currentTimeProperty()`, but you can't update its value with a setter.

Since read-only properties change and are observable, you can listen for change and invalidation events, just as you can with read-write properties. You can also use read-only (as well as read-write) JavaFX properties in binding expressions, which we discuss next.

## Binding

There may be situations where you need to define a ChangeListener and register it with an object's property to monitor its old and new values. However, in many cases, the reason you'd like to track property changes is to update another object with a new value (as we did in Listing 3.10 on page 106 and Listing 3.11 on page 108).

A JavaFX feature called *binding* addresses this use case. Because JavaFX properties are observable, they can participate in binding expressions. Binding means that you specify a JavaFX property as *dependent* on another JavaFX property's value. Binding expressions can be simple, or they can involve many properties in a cascade of property updates initiated perhaps by just one property changing its value (a program's butterfly effect). Binding is a powerful feature in JavaFX that lets you succinctly express dependencies among object properties in applications without defining or registering listeners. Let's look at some examples.

5. Again, a lambda expression can replace the anonymous inner class in Listing 3.11. We're leaving in the ChangeListener with its `changed()` method here for clarity.

### Unidirectional Binding

To bind one JavaFX property to another, use method `bind()` with a JavaFX property.

```
circle1.radiusProperty().bind(circle2.radiusProperty());
```

This binding expression states that `circle1`'s `radius` property will always have the same value as `circle2`'s `radius` property. We say that `circle1`'s `radius` property is *dependent* on `circle2`'s `radius` property. This binding is one way; only `circle1`'s `radius` property updates when `circle2`'s `radius` property changes and not vice versa.

Binding expressions include an *implicit assignment*. That is, when we bind the `circle1` `radius` property to `circle2`'s `radius` property, the update to `circle1`'s `radius` property occurs when the `bind()` method is invoked.

When you bind a property, you cannot change that property's value with a setter.

```
circle1.setRadius(someValue);                // can't do this
```

There are some restrictions with binding. Attempting to define a circular binding results in a stack overflow. Attempting to set a bound property results in a runtime exception.

```
java.lang.RuntimeException: A bound value cannot be set.
```

Let's show you an example program with binding now. Listing 3.12 defines two Circle objects, `circle1` and `circle2`. This time, instead of an InvalidationListener or ChangeListener that tracks changes to `circle2` and then updates `circle1`, we *bind* `circle1`'s `radius` property to `circle2`'s `radius` property.

**Listing 3.12 Unidirectional Bind—MyBind.java**

```
package asgteach.bindings;

import javafx.scene.shape.Circle;

public class MyBind {

    public static void main(String[] args) {
        Circle circle1 = new Circle(10.5);
        Circle circle2 = new Circle(15.5);
        System.out.println("Circle1: " + circle1.getRadius());
        System.out.println("Circle2: " + circle2.getRadius());
        // Bind circle1 radius to circle2 radius
        circle1.radiusProperty().bind(circle2.radiusProperty());
        if (circle1.radiusProperty().isBound()) {
            System.out.println("Circle1 radiusProperty is bound");
        }
```

```
        // Radius properties are now the same
        System.out.println("Circle1: " + circle1.getRadius());
        System.out.println("Circle2: " + circle2.getRadius());

        // Both radius properties will now update
        circle2.setRadius(20.5);
        System.out.println("Circle1: " + circle1.getRadius());
        System.out.println("Circle2: " + circle2.getRadius());

        // circle1 radius no longer bound to circle2 radius
        circle1.radiusProperty().unbind();
        if (!circle1.radiusProperty().isBound()) {
            System.out.println("Circle1 radiusProperty is unbound");
        }

        // Radius properties are now no longer the same
        circle2.setRadius(30.5);
        System.out.println("Circle1: " + circle1.getRadius());
        System.out.println("Circle2: " + circle2.getRadius());
    }
}
```

```
Output:
Circle1: 10.5
Circle2: 15.5
Circle1 radiusProperty is bound
Circle1: 15.5
Circle2: 15.5
Circle1: 20.5
Circle2: 20.5
Circle1 radiusProperty is unbound
Circle1: 20.5
Circle2: 30.5
```

In this example, the Circle objects are initialized with different values, which are displayed. We then bind `circle1`'s `radius` property to `circle2`'s `radius` property and display the radius values again. With the bind's implicit assignment, the circle radius values are now the same (15.5). When the setter changes `circle2`'s `radius` to 20.5, `circle1`'s `radius` updates.

The `isBound()` method checks if a JavaFX property is bound and the `unbind()` method removes the binding on a JavaFX property. Note that after unbinding `circle1`'s `radius` property, updating `circle2`'s radius no longer affects the radius for `circle1`.

### Bidirectional Binding

Bidirectional binding lets you specify a binding with two JavaFX properties that update in both directions. Whenever either property changes, the other property updates. Note that setters for both properties always work with bidirectional binding (after all, you have to update the values somehow).

Bidirectional binding is particularly suited for keeping UI view components synchronized with model data. If the model changes, the view automatically refreshes. And if the user inputs new data in a form, the model updates.

### Bidirectional Binding Is Not Symmetrical

*Initially, both properties take on the value of the property specified in* `bindBidirectional()` *method's argument. Thus, bidirectional binding is not symmetrical; the order that you specify the binding affects the bound properties' initial value.*

Listing 3.13 shows how to use JavaFX property method `bindBidirectional()`. After objects `circle1` and `circle2` have their `radius` properties bound, both properties acquire value 15.5 (`circle2`'s `radius` property value), and a change to either one updates the other. Note that setters update the `radius` property values.

You can also unbind the properties with method `unbindBidirectional()`.

**Listing 3.13 Bidirectional Binding—MyBindBidirectional.java**

```
package asgteach.bindings;
import javafx.scene.shape.Circle;

public class MyBindBidirectional {

    public static void main(String[] args) {
        Circle circle1 = new Circle(10.5);
        Circle circle2 = new Circle(15.5);

        // circle1 takes on value of circle2 radius
        circle1.radiusProperty().bindBidirectional(circle2.radiusProperty());
        System.out.println("Circle1: " + circle1.getRadius());
        System.out.println("Circle2: " + circle2.getRadius());

        circle2.setRadius(20.5);
        // Both circles are now 20.5
        System.out.println("Circle1: " + circle1.getRadius());
        System.out.println("Circle2: " + circle2.getRadius());

        circle1.setRadius(30.5);
        // Both circles are now 30.5
        System.out.println("Circle1: " + circle1.getRadius());
```

```
        System.out.println("Circle2: " + circle2.getRadius());

        circle1.radiusProperty().unbindBidirectional(circle2.radiusProperty());
    }
}
```

```
Output:
Circle1: 15.5
Circle2: 15.5
Circle1: 20.5
Circle2: 20.5
Circle1: 30.5
Circle2: 30.5
```

### Fluent API and Bindings API

Method `bind()` works well with JavaFX properties that are the same type. You bind one property to a second property. When the second property changes, the first one's value gets updated automatically.

However, in many cases, a property's value will be dependent on another property that you have to manipulate in some way. Or, a property's value may need to update when more than one property changes. JavaFX has a Fluent API that helps you construct binding expressions for these more complicated relationships.

The Fluent API includes methods for common arithmetic operations, such as `add()`, `subtract()`, `divide()`, and `multiply()`, boolean expressions, `negate()`, and conversion to String with `asString()`. You can use these Fluent API methods with binding expressions. Their arguments are other properties or non-JavaFX property values.

Here's an example that displays a temperature in both Celsius and Fahrenheit using the conversion formula in a binding expression for the Fahrenheit label.

```
// Suppose you had a "temperature" object
Temperature myTemperature = new Temperature(0);

// Create two labels
Label labelF = new Label();
Label labelC = new Label();

// Bind the labelC textProperty to the Temperature celsiusProperty
labelC.textProperty().bind(myTemperature.celsiusProperty().asString()
          .concat(" C"));
```

```
// Bind the labelF textProperty to the Temperature celsiusProperty
// using F = 9/5 C + 32
labelF.textProperty().bind(myTemperature.celsiusProperty().multiply(9)
          .divide(5).add(32)
          .asString().concat(" F"));
```

Another common use for binding is enabling and disabling a control based on some condition. Here we bind the `disable` property of a button based on the status of an animation. If the animation is running, the button is disabled.

```
// Bind button's disableProperty to myTransition running or not
startButton.disableProperty().bind(myTransition.statusProperty()
          .isEqualTo(Animation.Status.RUNNING));
```

The Bindings API offers additional flexibility in building binding expressions. The Bindings class has static methods that let you manipulate observable values. For example, here's how to implement the Fahrenheit temperature conversion using the Bindings API.

```
labelF.textProperty().bind(
        Bindings.format(" %1.1f F",
        Bindings.add(
        Bindings.divide(
        Bindings.multiply(9, myTemperature.celsiusProperty()),
            5), 32)));
```

Because the Bindings API requires that you build your expression "inside-out," the expression may not be as readable as the Fluent API. However, the Bindings methods are useful, particularly for formatting the result of binding expressions. The above `Bindings.format()` gives you the same flexibility as `java.util.Formatter` for creating a format String. You can also combine the Bindings API with the Fluent API.

Let's look at another example of using the Fluent API. Figure 3.16 shows an application with a Rectangle. As you resize the window, the Rectangle grows and shrinks. The opacity of the Rectangle also changes when you resize. As the window gets larger, the rectangle gets more opaque, making it appear brighter since less of the dark background is visible through a less-transparent rectangle.

Listing 3.14 shows the code for this application (project **MyFluentBind**). Constructors create the drop shadow, stack pane, and rectangle, and setters configure them. To provide dynamic resizing of the rectangle, we bind the rectangle's `width` property to the scene's `width` property divided by two. Similarly, we bind the rectangle's `height` property to the scene's `height` property divided by two. (Dividing by two keeps the rectangle centered in the window.)

The rectangle's opacity is a bit trickier. The `opacity` property is a double between 0 and 1, with 1 being fully opaque and 0 being completely transparent (invisible). So we

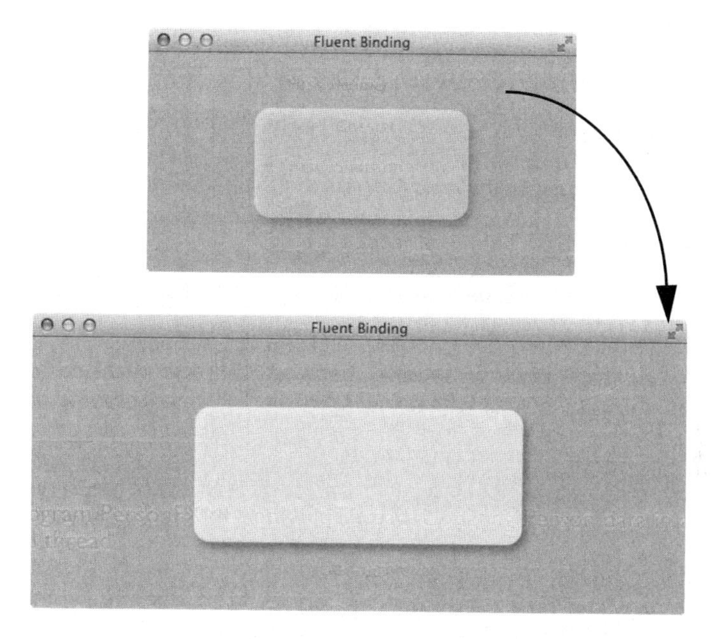


Figure 3.16 The Rectangle's dimensions and fill color change with window resizing

rather arbitrarily add the scene's height and width together and divide by 1000 to keep the opacity within the target range of 0 and 1. This makes the opacity change as the rectangle resizes.

**Listing 3.14 Fluent API—MyFluentBind.java**

```
package asgteach.bindings;
import javafx.application.Application;
import javafx.geometry.Pos;
import javafx.scene.Scene;
import javafx.scene.effect.DropShadow;
import javafx.scene.layout.StackPane;
import javafx.scene.paint.Color;
import javafx.scene.shape.Rectangle;
import javafx.stage.Stage;

public class MyFluentBind extends Application {

    @Override
    public void start(Stage stage) {

        DropShadow dropShadow = new DropShadow(10.0,
                        Color.rgb(150, 50, 50, .688));
        dropShadow.setOffsetX(4);
        dropShadow.setOffsetY(6);
```

```
        StackPane stackPane = new StackPane();
        stackPane.setAlignment(Pos.CENTER);
        stackPane.setEffect(dropShadow);

        Rectangle rectangle = new Rectangle(100, 50, Color.LEMONCHIFFON);
        rectangle.setArcWidth(30);
        rectangle.setArcHeight(30);

        stackPane.getChildren().add(rectangle);

        Scene scene = new Scene(stackPane, 400, 200, Color.LIGHTSKYBLUE);
        stage.setTitle("Fluent Binding");

        rectangle.widthProperty().bind(scene.widthProperty().divide(2));
        rectangle.heightProperty().bind(scene.heightProperty().divide(2));

        rectangle.opacityProperty().bind(
              scene.widthProperty().add(scene.heightProperty())
                        .divide(1000));

        stage.setScene(scene);
        stage.show();
    }

    public static void main(String[] args) {
        launch();
    }
}
```

## Custom Binding

When the Fluent API or Bindings API does not apply to your application, you can create a custom binding object. With custom binding, you specify two items:

- the JavaFX property dependencies
- how to compute the desired value.

Let's rewrite the previous example and create a custom binding object.

First, here is the binding expression presented earlier for the rectangle's `opacity` property.

```
rectangle.opacityProperty().bind(
      scene.widthProperty().add(scene.heightProperty())
                .divide(1000));
```

The binding has two JavaFX property dependencies: the scene's `width` and `height` properties.

Next, determine how to compute the value with this binding expression. Without using the Fluent API or the Bindings API, the computation (which results in a double value) is

```
double myComputedValue = (scene.getWidth() + scene.getHeight()) / 1000;
```

That is, the opacity's value is a double that is the sum of the scene's width and height divided by 1000.

For this example, the custom binding object is type DoubleBinding. You specify the JavaFX property dependencies as arguments in the binding object's anonymous constructor using `super.bind()`. The overridden `computeValue()` method returns the desired value (here, a double). The `computeValue()` method is invoked whenever any of the properties listed as dependencies change. Here's what our custom binding object looks like.

```
DoubleBinding opacityBinding = new DoubleBinding() {
    {
        // Specify the dependencies with super.bind()
        super.bind(scene.widthProperty(), scene.heightProperty());
    }
    @Override
    protected double computeValue() {
        // Return the computed value
        return (scene.getWidth() + scene.getHeight()) / 1000;
    }
};
```

For StringBinding, `computeValue()` returns a String. For IntegerBinding, `computeValue()` returns an integer, and so forth.

To specify this custom binding object with the Rectangle's `opacity` property, use

```
rectangle.opacityProperty().bind(opacityBinding);
```

Now let's show you another custom binding example. Figure 3.17 shows a similar JavaFX application with a rectangle whose size and opacity change as the window resizes. This time, we make sure that the opacity is never greater than 1.0 and we display the opacity in a text node inside the rectangle. The text is formatted and includes "opacity = " in front of the value.

Listing 3.15 shows the code for this program (project **MyCustomBind**). The same code creates the drop shadow, rectangle, and stack pane as in the previous example. The rectangle's `height` and `width` properties use the same Fluent API binding expression. Now method `computeValue()` returns a double for the opacity and makes sure its value isn't greater than 1.0.

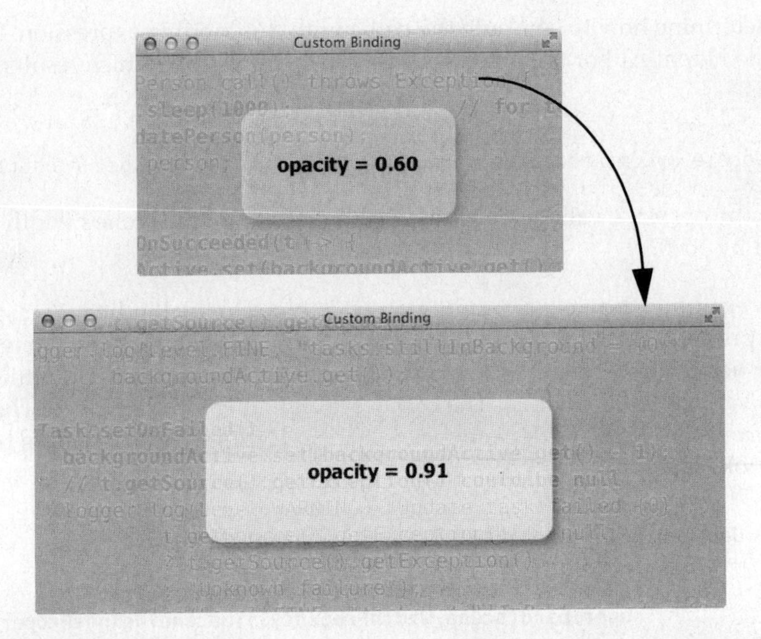


Figure 3.17 The Rectangle displays its changing opacity value in a Text component

The text label's text property combines the custom binding object opacityBinding with method Bindings.format() to provide the desired formatting of the text.

**Listing 3.15 Custom Binding Example—MyCustomBind.java**

```
public class MyCustomBind extends Application {

    @Override
    public void start(Stage stage) {

        . . . code omitted to build the Rectangle, StackPane
              and DropShadow . . .

        Text text = new Text();
        text.setFont(Font.font("Tahoma", FontWeight.BOLD, 18));

        stackPane.getChildren().addAll(rectangle, text);

        final Scene scene = new Scene(stackPane, 400, 200, Color.LIGHTSKYBLUE);
        stage.setTitle("Custom Binding");

        rectangle.widthProperty().bind(scene.widthProperty().divide(2));
        rectangle.heightProperty().bind(scene.heightProperty().divide(2));
```

```
        DoubleBinding opacityBinding = new DoubleBinding() {
            {
                // List the dependencies with super.bind()
                super.bind(scene.widthProperty(), scene.heightProperty());
            }
            @Override
            protected double computeValue() {
               // Return the computed value
               double opacity = (scene.getWidth() + scene.getHeight()) / 1000;
               return (opacity > 1.0) ? 1.0 : opacity;
            }
        };
        rectangle.opacityProperty().bind(opacityBinding);
        text.textProperty().bind((Bindings.format(
                        "opacity = %.2f", opacityBinding)));

        stage.setScene(scene);
        stage.show();
    }

    public static void main(String[] args) {
        launch();
    }
}
```

How do you create binding objects that return compute values that are not one of the standard types? In this situation, use ObjectBinding with generics. For example, Listing 3.16 shows a custom binding definition that returns a darker Color based on the `fill` property of a Rectangle. The binding object is type ObjectBinding<Color> and the `computeValue()` return type is Color. (The cast here is necessary because a Shape's `fill` property is a Paint object, which can be a Color, ImagePattern, LinearGradient, or RadialGradient.)

#### Listing 3.16 ObjectBinding with Generics

```
        ObjectBinding<Color> colorBinding = new ObjectBinding<Color>() {
            {
                super.bind(rectangle.fillProperty());
            }

            @Override
            protected Color computeValue() {
                if (rectangle.getFill() instanceof Color) {
                    return ((Color)rectangle.getFill()).darker();
                } else {
                    return Color.GRAY;
                }
            }
        };
```

## 3.4 Putting It All Together

Our final example in this chapter applies what you've learned about properties, binding, change listeners, and layout controls to create a program that simulates a race track with one car. As the car travels along the track, a lap counter updates each time the car passes the starting point. Figure 3.18 shows this program running at two points in time.

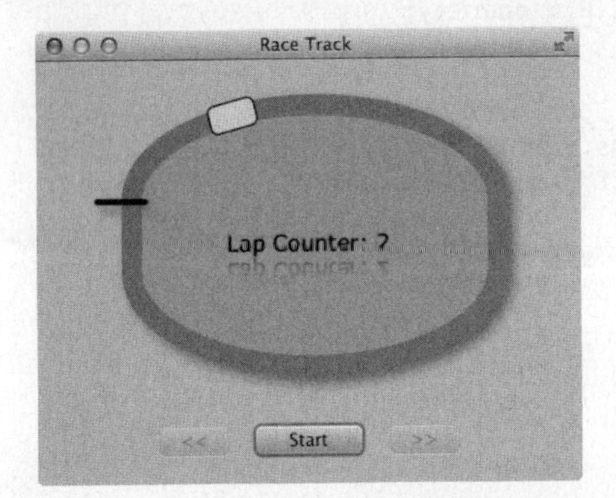


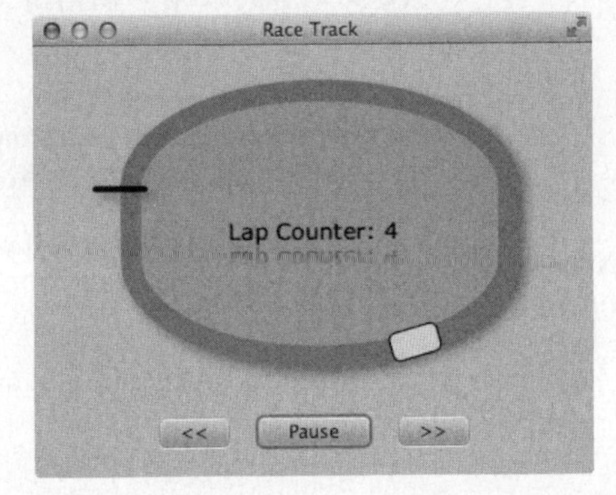


**Figure 3.18** A Race Track with PathTransition and Lap Counter

This example pulls together several important concepts from this chapter: binding properties to keep values synchronized as the program runs; using a change listener to track changes in a property; and writing button event handlers that control the execution of the program. We'll also show you how to organize nodes in a Group to keep items in their relative coordinate positions while still maintaining the layout's overall positioning. We've shown you a RotateTransition example; now we'll show you how to use PathTransition for the race track.

The program includes a Start/Pause button to start and pause the animation. Once you start, the speed up and slow down buttons alter the car's travel rate. When the animation is paused (as shown in the left side figure), the Start/Pause button displays Start and the slower/faster buttons are disabled. When the animation is running (the right side), the Start/Pause button displays Pause and the slower/faster buttons are enabled.

We'll implement the animation with PathTransition, a high-level Transition that animates a node along a JavaFX Path. Path is a Shape consisting of Path elements, where each element can be any one of several geometric objects, such as LineTo, ArcTo, QuadraticCurveTo, and CubicCurveTo. In our example, we build an oval track by combining Path elements MoveTo (the starting point), ArcTo, LineTo, and ClosePath (a specialized Path element that provides a LineTo from the current Path element point to the starting point).

Our race car is a rounded Rectangle and a Text node displays the current lap count. We implement this example using FXML. An associated controller class defines the buttons' action event handlers, binding, and the PathTransition.

Figure 3.19 shows the scene graph structure. The top-level node is a VBox, which keeps its children (a StackPane and an HBox) in vertical alignment and centered. The StackPane also centers its child Group and Text nodes. The Group, in turn, consists of the Path, the track's starting Line, and the race car (a Rectangle). These three nodes use the Group's local coordinate system for their relative placement.

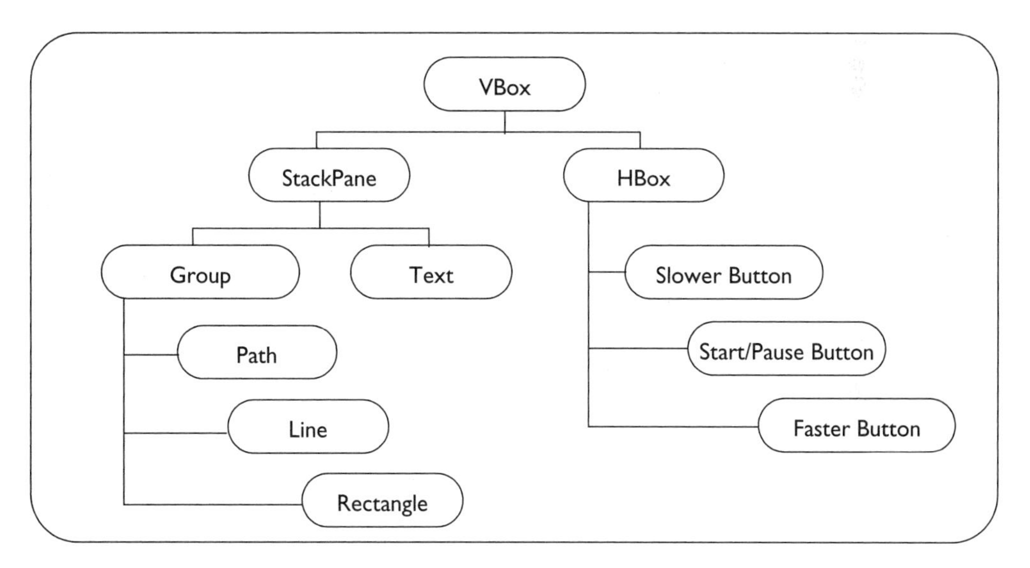


Figure 3.19 Scene graph hierarchy for project RaceTrackFXApp

The HBox maintains its children in a horizontal alignment. If you resize the JavaFX application window frame, these components all remain centered.

Listing 3.17 shows the FXML markup for the VBox, StackPane, Group, Text, and HBox nodes (we'll show you the other nodes next). The scene graph hierarchy from Figure 3.19 matches the FXML elements shown in RaceTrack.fxml. The top node, VBox, specifies the controller class with attribute `fx:controller`. Note that we also supply an `fx:id="text"` attribute with the Text node. This lets the Controller class access the Text object in Java controller code.

**Listing 3.17 RaceTrack.fxml**

```
<?xml version="1.0" encoding="UTF-8"?>

<?import java.lang.*?>
<?import java.util.*?>
<?import javafx.scene.*?>
<?import javafx.scene.control.*?>
<?import javafx.scene.layout.*?>
<?import javafx.scene.shape.*?>
<?import javafx.scene.text.*?>
<?import javafx.scene.effect.*?>

<VBox id="VBox" prefHeight="300" prefWidth="400" spacing="20"
        alignment="CENTER" style="-fx-background-color: lightblue;"
        xmlns:fx="http://javafx.com/fxml"
        fx:controller="racetrackfxapp.RaceTrackController">
    <children>
        <StackPane >
            <children>
                <Group>
                    <children>
                        (See Listing 3.18)
                    </children>
                </Group>
                <Text fx:id="text" >
                    <font><Font name="Verdana" size="16" /></font>
                    <effect><Reflection /></effect>
                </Text>
            </children>
        </StackPane>
        <HBox spacing="20" alignment="CENTER"  >
                        (See Listing 3.19)
        </HBox>
    </children>
</VBox>
```

Listing 3.18 shows the FXML for the Group's children: the Path, Line, and Rectangle nodes. The Path node includes the elements that form the oval RaceTrack: MoveTo, ArcTo, LineTo, and ClosePath. The Line node marks the starting line on the track. The Rectangle node represents the "race car." Nodes Path and Rectangle also have `fx:id` attributes defined for Controller access. Both the Path and Line nodes define a DropShadow effect.

**Listing 3.18 Path, Line, and Rectangle Nodes**

```
<Group>
   <children>
      <Path fx:id="path" stroke="DARKGOLDENROD"
         strokeWidth="15" fill="orange" >
```

```
      <effect>
         <DropShadow fx:id="dropshadow" radius="10"
                offsetX="5" offsetY="5" color="GRAY" />
      </effect>
      <elements>
         <MoveTo x="0" y="0"  />
         <ArcTo radiusX="100" radiusY="50" sweepFlag="true" x="270" y="0" />
         <LineTo x="270" y="50" />
         <ArcTo radiusX="100" radiusY="50" sweepFlag="true" x="0" y="50" />
         <ClosePath />
      </elements>
   </Path>
   <Line startX="-25" startY="0" endX="10" endY="0" strokeWidth="4"
      stroke="BLUE" strokeLineCap="ROUND" effect="$dropshadow" />
   <Rectangle fx:id="rectangle" x="-15" y="0" width="35" height="20"
      fill="YELLOW" arcWidth="10" arcHeight="10"
      stroke="BLACK" rotate="90" />
  </children>
</Group>
```

Listing 3.19 shows the FXML for the three Button nodes that appear in the HBox layout pane. All three buttons include `fx:id` attributes because they participate in binding expressions within the Controller class. The `onAction` attribute specifies the action event handler defined for each button. These event handlers control the PathTransition's animation. The startPauseButton configures property `prefWidth`. This makes the button maintain a constant size as the button's text changes between "Start" and "Pause."

**Listing 3.19 HBox and Button Nodes**

```
<HBox spacing="20" alignment="CENTER"  >
  <Button fx:id="slowerButton" onAction="#slowerAction"  />
  <Button fx:id="startPauseButton" prefWidth="80"
     onAction="#startPauseAction"   />
  <Button fx:id="fasterButton" onAction="#fasterAction" />
</HBox>
```

Now that the UI is completely described with FXML, let's examine the Controller class, class RaceTrackController, as shown in Listing 3.20 through Listing 3.23. The `@FXML` annotations mark each variable created in the FXML that the Controller class needs to access. Recall that the FXML Loader is responsible for instantiating these objects, so you won't see any Java code that creates them.

The `initialize()` method is invoked by the FXML Loader after the scene graph objects are instantiated. Here we perform additional scene graph configuration. Specifically, we instantiate the PathTransition (the animation object responsible for moving the "car" along the RaceTrack path). This high-level animation applies to a node (here, a Rectangle). The orientation property (OrientationType.ORTHOGONAL_TO-_TANGENT) keeps the rectangle correctly oriented as it moves along the path. We set the duration, cycle count, and interpolator, making the cycle count INDEFINITE. The animation rate remains constant with Interpolator.LINEAR.

**Listing 3.20 RaceTrackController.java**

```
package racetrackfxapp;

import java.net.URL;
import java.util.ResourceBundle;
import javafx.animation.Animation;
import javafx.animation.Interpolator;
import javafx.animation.PathTransition;
import javafx.beans.binding.When;
import javafx.beans.property.IntegerProperty;
import javafx.beans.property.SimpleIntegerProperty;
import javafx.beans.value.ObservableValue;
import javafx.event.ActionEvent;
import javafx.fxml.FXML;
import javafx.fxml.Initializable;
import javafx.scene.control.Button;
import javafx.scene.shape.Path;
import javafx.scene.shape.Rectangle;
import javafx.scene.text.Text;
import javafx.util.Duration;

public class RaceTrackController implements Initializable {

    // Objects defined in the FXML
    @FXML
    private Rectangle rectangle;
    @FXML
    private Path path;
    @FXML
    private Text text;
    @FXML
    private Button startPauseButton;
    @FXML
    private Button slowerButton;
    @FXML
    private Button fasterButton;
    private PathTransition pathTransition;

    @Override
    public void initialize(URL url, ResourceBundle rb) {

        // Create the PathTransition
        pathTransition = new PathTransition(Duration.seconds(6),
            path, rectangle);
```

```
        pathTransition.setOrientation(
            PathTransition.OrientationType.ORTHOGONAL_TO_TANGENT);
        pathTransition.setCycleCount(Animation.INDEFINITE);
        pathTransition.setInterpolator(Interpolator.LINEAR);
      . . .
      additional code from method initialize() shown in Listing 3.21,
      Listing 3.22, and Listing 3.23
      . . .
    }
}
```

Listing 3.21 shows how the Lap Counter works. Here, we create a JavaFX property called `lapCounterProperty` by instantiating SimpleIntegerProperty, an implementation of abstract class IntegerProperty. We need a JavaFX property here because we use it in a binding expression. (We discuss creating your own JavaFX properties in detail in the next chapter; see "Creating JavaFX Properties" on page 132.)

Next, we create a ChangeListener (with a lambda expression) and attach it to the PathTransition's `currentTime` property. We count laps by noticing when the animation's `currentTime` property old value is greater than its new value. This happens when one lap completes and the next lap begins. We then increment `lapCounterProperty`.

We create a binding expression to display the Lap Counter in the Text component. We bind the Text's `text` property to the `lapCounterProperty`, using the Fluent API to convert the integer to a String and provide the formatting.

Note that the ChangeListener method is invoked frequently—each time the current time changes. However, inside the listener method, we only update `lapCounterProperty` once per lap, ensuring that the Text node's `text` property only updates once a lap. This two-step arrangement makes the related binding with the Text node an efficient way to keep the UI synchronized.

### Listing 3.21 Configuring the Lap Counter Binding

```
// We count laps by noticing when the currentTimeProperty changes and the
// oldValue is greater than the newValue, which is only true once per lap
// We then increment the lapCounterProperty
final IntegerProperty lapCounterProperty = new SimpleIntegerProperty(0);
pathTransition.currentTimeProperty().addListener(
      (ObservableValue<? extends Duration> ov,
      Duration oldValue, Duration newValue) -> {
         if (oldValue.greaterThan(newValue)) {
            lapCounterProperty.set(lapCounterProperty.get() + 1);
         }
});
// Bind the text's textProperty to the lapCounterProperty and format it
text.textProperty().bind(lapCounterProperty.asString("Lap Counter: %s"));
```

The Start/Pause button lets you start and pause the animation, as shown in Listing 3.22. The `@FXML` annotations before the action event handlers make the FXML Loader wire the Start/Pause button's `onAction` property with the proper event handler. This invokes the handler when the user clicks the button. If the animation is running, method `pause()` pauses it. Otherwise, the animation is currently paused and the `play()` method either starts or resumes the animation at its current point.

The button's text is controlled with binding object When, the beginning point of a ternary binding expression. Class When takes a boolean condition that returns the value in method `then()` if the condition is true or the value in method `otherwise()` if it's false. For the Start/Pause button, we set its text to "Pause" if the animation is running; otherwise, we set the text to "Start."

**Listing 3.22 Start/Pause Button**

```
    @FXML
    private void startPauseAction(ActionEvent event) {
        if (pathTransition.getStatus() == Animation.Status.RUNNING) {
            pathTransition.pause();
        } else {
            pathTransition.play();
        }
    }
. . .
        startPauseButton.textProperty().bind(
            new When(pathTransition.statusProperty()
                .isEqualTo(Animation.Status.RUNNING))
                    .then("Pause").otherwise("Start"));
```

Listing 3.23 shows the faster/slower button handler code. Both buttons' action event handlers (annotated with `@FXML` to wire them to the respective Buttons defined in the FXML file) manipulate the animation's `rate` property. We specify a maximum rate of 7.0 (seven times the default rate) and a minimum rate of .3. Each time the user clicks the faster or slower button the rate changes up or down by .3. We set the new rate by accessing the transition's `currentRate` property. The `printf()` statements let you see the changed rates for each button click.

The faster/slower buttons are disabled when the animation is not running. This is accomplished with binding expressions that check the animation's status. Finally, the controller sets the text of the faster/slower buttons.

**Listing 3.23 Faster and Slower Buttons**

```
    // Constants to control the transition's rate changes
    final double maxRate = 7.0;
    final double minRate = .3;
    final double rateDelta = .3;
```

```
    @FXML
    private void slowerAction(ActionEvent event) {
        double currentRate = pathTransition.getRate();
        if (currentRate <= minRate) {
            return;
        }
        pathTransition.setRate(currentRate - rateDelta);
        System.out.printf("slower rate = %.2f\n", pathTransition.getRate());
    }

    @FXML
    private void fasterAction(ActionEvent event) {
        double currentRate = pathTransition.getRate();
        if (currentRate >= maxRate) {
            return;
        }
        pathTransition.setRate(currentRate + rateDelta);
        System.out.printf("faster rate = %.2f\n", pathTransition.getRate());
    }
. . .
        fasterButton.disableProperty().bind(pathTransition.statusProperty()
                .isNotEqualTo(Animation.Status.RUNNING));
        slowerButton.disableProperty().bind(pathTransition.statusProperty()
                .isNotEqualTo(Animation.Status.RUNNING));

        fasterButton.setText(" >> ");
        slowerButton.setText(" << ");
```

A key point with this example is that JavaFX properties and bindings let you write much less code. To enable and disable the buttons without binding, you would need to create a change listener, attach it to the animation's status property, and write an event handler that updates the button's disable property. You would also need a similar change listener to control the Start/Pause button's text property. Binding expressions (including custom binding objects) are much more concise and less error prone than listeners that configure property dependencies such as these.

However, at times you will need a ChangeListener or InvalidationListener, as we show in this example to implement the lap counter.

This example also shows how FXML markup helps you visualize the structure of the scene graph that you're building. Working with FXML, as opposed to only Java APIs, makes it easier to modify scene graphs. We've also built this example using only APIs (see project RaceTrack in the book's download). We encourage you to compare the two projects. We think you'll find the FXML version easier to understand.

## 3.5 Key Point Summary

This chapter introduces JavaFX and shows you how to write JavaFX programs that display and manipulate scene graph objects. Here are the key points in this chapter.

- JavaFX provides a rich graphical user interface. Its hierarchical scene graph lets you easily configure rich content and provide visually pleasing effects such as gradients, drop shadows, and reflection.
- JavaFX graphics take advantage of hardware-accelerated graphics capabilities for rendering and animation that performs well.
- You can embed JavaFX content within a Swing panel. This lets you use JavaFX without throwing away Swing applications. (See "The Magic of JFXPanel" on page 259.)
- Like Swing, JavaFX uses a single-threaded execution environment.
- You use Java APIs and/or FXML markup with a controller class to create JavaFX content.
- FXML is an XML markup language that lets you specify scene graph content. The hierarchical form of FXML lets you visualize the scene graph structure more easily than with Java APIs. FXML also helps you keep visual content separate from controller code (such as event handlers).
- You configure FXML scene graph nodes using property names and values that convert to the correct types.
- The FXML controller class lets you provide JavaFX node initialization code, dynamic content, and event handlers.
- CSS lets you style JavaFX nodes. You can configure the `style` property on nodes individually, or provide style sheets for styling an entire application.
- You can specify CSS files either in the main program or in the FXML markup.
- JavaFX provides high-level transitions that let you specify many common animations. This includes movement, rotation, fading in or out, scaling, color changes for `fill` or `stroke` properties, and movement along a path.
- JavaFX properties are a significant feature in JavaFX. JavaFX properties are observable and provide similar naming conventions to JavaBeans properties.
- JavaFX properties can be read-write, read-only, or immutable.
- You can attach a ChangeListener or InvalidationListener to any JavaFX property.

- Bindings are more concise and less error-prone than listeners. Bindings are a powerful mechanism that keep application variables synchronized.
- You can create bindings between JavaFX properties that specify a dependency of one property on another. Bindings can be unidirectional or bidirectional.
- Use the Fluent API and Bindings API to specify more complicated binding expressions with one or more properties.
- You can create custom binding objects that specify property dependencies and how to compute the binding's return value.

## What's Next?

With this introduction to JavaFX, you are now ready to learn how to use JavaFX effectively in a desktop application. The approach for these next examples will be similar to the examples we've presented previously with Swing.

# 4

# Working with JavaFX

The previous chapter shows you how to create JavaFX applications with simple controls and shapes. We also show you examples with animation. Chapter 3 is mostly about getting comfortable with JavaFX. With the chapter's examples, you learned how to use the JavaFX scene graph, manipulate JavaFX properties with binding expressions, and create custom binding objects.

In this chapter we move on to desktop applications that use JavaFX for the UI. There really is no "typical" desktop application. But desktop applications all present a UI to the user and let the user manipulate model objects through UI controls. This includes selection controls, button clicks, and editing with text input controls.

Chapter 2 presents a small Swing application that emphasizes loose coupling among event handlers and model objects. These concepts are no less important with JavaFX. This chapter shows you how to build a similar application with JavaFX. You'll also discover how to manipulate model objects using JavaFX UI controls.

## What You Will Learn

- Create JavaFX properties.
- Use ChangeListeners and observable collections.
- Explore Scene Builder and create a JavaFX UI.
- Incorporate JavaFX controls, events, and listeners into JavaFX applications.
- Create background tasks in JavaFX that safely update the UI.

## 4.1 Creating JavaFX Properties

The previous chapter showed you JavaFX properties in action with ChangeListeners, InvalidationListeners, and most importantly binding expressions and custom binding objects. Binding shows how powerful JavaFX properties are. Now let's show you how to create and use JavaFX properties in model classes.[1]

We start with the Person class from Chapter 2 (see Listing 2.5 on page 30). Recall that Person has JavaBeans properties, including several String properties, an immutable long property (`id`), and a Person.Gender property (`gender`). We're now going to create JavaFX properties for these values. Listing 4.1 shows a straightforward implementation for JavaFX property `firstname`.

To construct a StringProperty (an abstract type), we use SimpleStringProperty, which provides an implementation of a JavaFX StringProperty that wraps a String value. The property's constructor has three arguments: a reference to the containing bean, the name of the property, and the initial value of the property. (The initial value is optional.) The first two values let you invoke `getBean()` for the containing bean and `getName()` for the property name, as shown in Listing 3.9 on page 104.

The property's setter and getter methods forward their calls to the JavaFX property's setter and getter. Method `firstnameProperty()` returns the created JavaFX property. This arrangement follows the naming convention for traditional JavaBeans while still providing access to the JavaFX property. Remember, you only need to access a JavaFX property when creating a binding expression or attaching a listener.

**Listing 4.1 Person JavaFX Property firstname—Simple Implementation**

```
public class Person implements Serializable {

    private final StringProperty firstname =
            new SimpleStringProperty(this, "firstname", "");

    public String getFirstname() {
        return firstname.get();
    }

    public void setFirstname(String firstname) {
        this.firstname.set(firstname);
    }
```

1. We show you how to add JavaFX properties to JPA-annotated entity classes in Chapter 16. See "Entity Classes and JavaFX Properties" on page 807.

```
    public final StringProperty firstnameProperty() {
        return firstname;
    }
. . . code omitted for other properties . . .
}
```

## JavaFX Properties with Lazy Evaluation

Before we discuss the other JavaFX properties for class Person, let's show you another way to implement the JavaFX property `firstname`. Consider if you had a JavaFX bean with many JavaFX properties and your application creates many of these objects. Each JavaFX property is itself an Object and therefore the number of Objects created could become large. (For example, the JavaFX node hierarchy consists of classes with many JavaFX properties, and JavaFX applications potentially create many scene graph nodes.)

An alternate implementation delays the creation of the JavaFX property until you attach a listener or use the property in a binding expression. In other words, the JavaFX property is not created until the user invokes the `firstnameProperty()` method. Simply changing the property's value does not create the JavaFX property. To achieve this lazy instantiation, you create a shadow field to hold the value until the JavaFX property is needed. Listing 4.2 shows the approach.

The setter and getter first make sure the JavaFX property is not null before using it. Otherwise, you get and set the value using shadow field `_firstname`. Method `firstnameProperty()` creates the JavaFX property if it does not yet exist. Therefore, the JavaFX property is only created if method `firstnameProperty()` is invoked.

**Listing 4.2 Person JavaFX Property firstname—Alternate Implementation**

```
    private StringProperty firstname;
    private String _firstname = "";          // shadow field

    public String getFirstname() {
        return (firstname != null) ? firstname.get() : _firstname;
    }

    public void setFirstname(String newFirstname) {
        if (firstname != null) {
            firstname.set(newFirstname);
        } else {
            _firstname = newFirstname;
        }
    }
```

```
    public final StringProperty firstnameProperty() {
        if (firstname == null) {
            firstname = new SimpleStringProperty(this, "firstname", _firstname);
        }
        return firstname;
    }
```

Consider using this alternate implementation when your model class has a large number of properties.[2]

## Object Properties

JavaFX provides property implementations for primitive property types and the String class. You've already seen SimpleStringProperty for abstract StringProperty. There is also SimpleIntegerProperty for abstract IntegerProperty, SimpleDouble-Property for abstract DoubleProperty, and so on. For other types, use SimpleObject-Property with generics. For example, a Color property uses SimpleObjectProperty-<Color> for abstract ObjectProperty<Color>.

Listing 4.3 shows how to implement the Person `gender` property using SimpleObject-Property<Person.Gender> and ObjectProperty<Person.Gender>, which wraps a Person.Gender value. Here, we use the non-lazy implementation that we showed you for property `firstname` in Listing 4.1 on page 132. The constructor sets a reference to the containing bean (`this`), the property name (`"gender"`), and an initial value (`Gender.UNKNOWN`). The setter and getter forward calls to the JavaFX property's setter and getter. The `genderProperty()` method returns the JavaFX property when the user needs to create a binding expression or attach a listener.

**Listing 4.3 Person JavaFX Property gender**

```
. . .
    public enum Gender {
        MALE, FEMALE, UNKNOWN
    }

    private final ObjectProperty<Person.Gender> gender =
            new SimpleObjectProperty<>(this, "gender", Gender.UNKNOWN);

    public Person.Gender getGender() {
        return gender.get();
    }
```

2. We don't use lazy evaluation with class Person because Person includes a computed property that requires eager JavaFX property evaluations. See "Computed Properties" on page 135.

```
public void setGender(Person.Gender gender) {
    this.gender.set(gender);
}

public final ObjectProperty<Person.Gender> genderProperty() {
    return gender;
}
```

## Immutable Properties

Recall that property `id` in our Person class is immutable. In this case, there is no need to create a JavaFX property. The JavaFX properties are specifically designed to track changes in the property's value, which can't happen with immutable.

You can easily use the value of an immutable property to update another property. Here's an example that sets the text of a label to the value of the `id` property.

```
myLabel.setText(myPerson.getId());
```

If you have a property that depends on the value of the `id` property, you can still use `getId()` in a binding expression with the Fluent API.

**Immutable Properties**

*Even though it's pointless to observe immutable properties, you could provide a JavaFX property implementation for property* `id` *(for completeness). In this case, you should use the "lazy creation" approach described in Listing 4.2 on page 133.*

## Computed Properties

Listing 4.4 shows the implementation of Person method `toString()` from Chapter 2. This returns a nicely formatted String that depends on properties `firstname`, `middlename`, `lastname`, and `suffix` and excludes them if the values are empty.

**Listing 4.4 Conventional JavaBean toString() Method for Person**

```
@Override
public String toString() {
    StringBuilder sb = new StringBuilder();
    if (!firstname.isEmpty()) {
        sb.append(firstname);
    }
    if (!middlename.isEmpty()) {
        sb.append(" ").append(middlename);
    }
```

```
        if (!lastname.isEmpty()) {
            sb.append(" ").append(lastname);
        }
        if (!suffix.isEmpty()) {
            sb.append(" ").append(suffix);
        }
        return sb.toString();
    }
```

Let's create a read-only property in JavaFX that computes its value based on these same properties. Like `toString()`, we'll use StringBuilder to build a nicely formatted String and only include the values if they are not empty. We call this computed String-Property `fullname`.

Since we want method `getFullname()` to always return the most up-to-date value, we create a custom binding to keep property `fullname` synchronized with the rest of the properties upon which it depends. Listing 4.5 shows this custom binding object.

Using `super.bind()`, the anonymous constructor sets the property dependencies: `firstname`, `middlename`, `lastname`, and `suffix`. Method `computeValue()` builds the String, which looks very similar to the `toString()` implementation in Listing 4.4.

**Listing 4.5 Custom Binding Object for Property fullname**

```
public class Person implements Serializable {
. . .
    private final StringBinding fullNameBinding = new StringBinding() {
        {
            super.bind(firstname, middlename, lastname, suffix);
        }

        @Override
        protected String computeValue() {
            StringBuilder sb = new StringBuilder();
            if (!firstname.get().isEmpty()) {
                sb.append(firstname.get());
            }
            if (!middlename.get().isEmpty()) {
                sb.append(" ").append(middlename.get());
            }
            if (!lastname.get().isEmpty()) {
                sb.append(" ").append(lastname.get());
            }
```

```
            if (!suffix.get().isEmpty()) {
                sb.append(" ").append(suffix.get());
            }
            return sb.toString();
        }
    };
}
```

Listing 4.6 shows our implementation of property `fullname`. Note that it is fully observable and its value can change, but there is no setter. We return a ReadOnlyStringProperty for method `fullnameProperty()`. This prevents users of the property from changing its value.

JavaFX provides wrapper classes that implement read-only JavaFX properties. When you use a wrapper class, two properties are created: one is read only and the other can be modified. The wrapper class keeps these properties synchronized for you.

Listing 4.6 shows the Person constructors that set the binding for property `fullname`. With this binding, any changes to properties `firstname`, `middlename`, `lastname`, or `suffix` update property `fullname`. If a user binds to property `fullname`, changes will propagate to the user's binding, too.

Method `toString()` now becomes trivial. It returns the `fullname` property value for the Person.

**Listing 4.6 Person JavaFX Property fullname**

```
. . .
    private final ReadOnlyStringWrapper fullname =
            new ReadOnlyStringWrapper(this, "fullname");

    public final ReadOnlyStringProperty fullnameProperty() {
        return fullname.getReadOnlyProperty();
    }

    public final String getFullname() {
        return fullname.get();
    }

    public Person() {
        this("", "", Gender.UNKNOWN);
    }
```

```
    public Person(String first, String last, Person.Gender gender) {
        this.firstname.set(first);
        this.lastname.set(last);
        this.gender.set(gender);
        this.id = count++;
        this.fullname.bind(fullNameBinding);
    }

    public Person(Person person) {
        this.firstname.set(person.getFirstname());
        this.middlename.set(person.getMiddlename());
        this.lastname.set(person.getLastname());
        this.suffix.set(person.getSuffix());
        this.gender.set(person.getGender());
        this.notes.set(person.getNotes());
        this.id = person.getId();
        this.fullname.bind(fullNameBinding);
    }

    @Override
    public String toString() {
        return fullname.get();
    }
. . .
```

Note that if you have a read-only JavaFX property whose value is maintained internally rather than computed, you would use the same read-only wrapper approach. If the property is not computed, you would not need to bind its value.

## Methods equals() and hashCode()

The previous version of class Person based `equals()` and `hashCode()` solely on property `id` (see Listing 2.3 on page 24). This lets you use `equals()` on objects that perhaps have different values for the name properties but equal `id`'s. We're going to take a different approach now and make sure that two Person objects are equal only if all of their properties are equal. We're making this change to take advantage of the JavaFX observable collection classes, which we discuss in the next section.

Listing 4.7 shows the updated `equals()` and `hashCode()` methods for class Person. The computed property `fullname` necessarily includes all of its dependent properties, so we just need to include properties `id`, `notes`, and `gender` to the computation as well.

**Listing 4.7 Person equals() and hashCode() Methods**

```
public class Person implements Serializable {

. . . code omitted . . .
```

```
    @Override
    public int hashCode() {
        int hash = 3;
        hash = 97 * hash + Objects.hashCode(this.id)
                + Objects.hashCode(this.fullname.get())
                + Objects.hashCode(this.notes.get())
                + Objects.hashCode(this.gender.get());
        return hash;
    }

    @Override
    public boolean equals(Object obj) {
        if (obj == null || getClass() != obj.getClass()) {
            return false;
        }
        final Person other = (Person) obj;
        return Objects.equals(this.id, other.id)
                && Objects.equals(this.fullname.get(), other.fullname.get())
                && Objects.equals(this.notes.get(), other.notes.get())
                && Objects.equals(this.gender.get(), other.gender.get());
    }
}
```

## 4.2 Using JavaFX Properties in a JavaFX Application

Now let's create a JavaFX application that uses binding with a Person object to show how JavaFX properties are observable. Figure 4.1 shows program **PersonFXAppBound** program running. A label (the component at the top) is bound to Person `marge` with

```
margeLabel.textProperty().bind(marge.fullnameProperty());
```

The Change button modifies Person `marge`, resulting in the updated label (right side). The Reset button resets the Person `marge` to its original setting, as shown on the left side.

### Creating a JavaFX FXML Application

We structure this application with FXML. To build this application using the NetBeans IDE, following these steps.

1. From the top-level menu, select **File | New Project . . . .**
2. From the Choose Project dialog, select **JavaFX** under Categories and **JavaFX FXML Application** under Projects, as shown in Figure 4.2. Click **Next**.

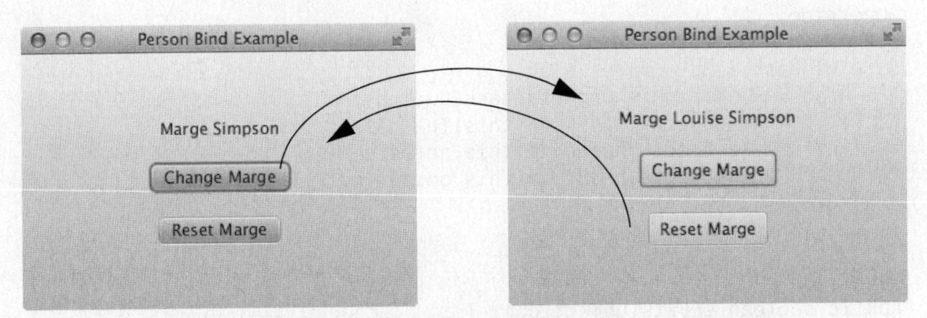


Figure 4.1 Program PersonFXAppBound: Binding the label's text will keep it synchronized with the underlying model

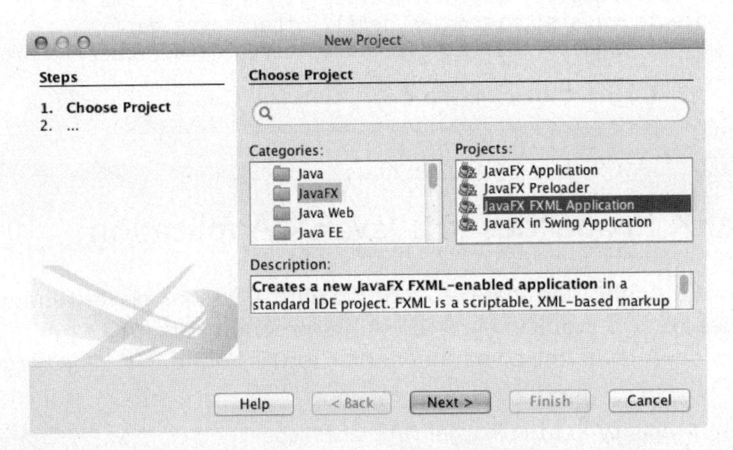


Figure 4.2 JavaFX FXML Application in the New Project wizard

3. In the Name and Location dialog, specify **PersonFXAppBound** for the Project Name and **PersonFXBound** for the FXML name. Make sure the JavaFX Platform is (at least) JDK 1.8. Accept the defaults for the remaining fields and click **Finish**, as shown in Figure 4.3.

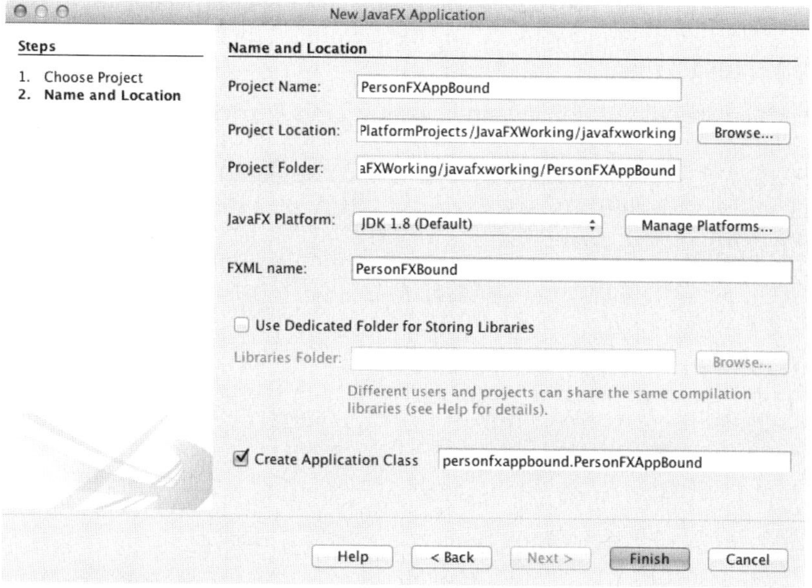

Figure 4.3 New JavaFX Project Name and Location dialog

NetBeans creates a JavaFX Application project. Expand node **Source Packages** and **personfxappbound** to view the three files created for this application: PersonFXApp-Bound.java (the main application class), PersonFXBound.fxml (the FXML file), and PersonFXBoundController.java (the controller class), as shown in Figure 4.4.

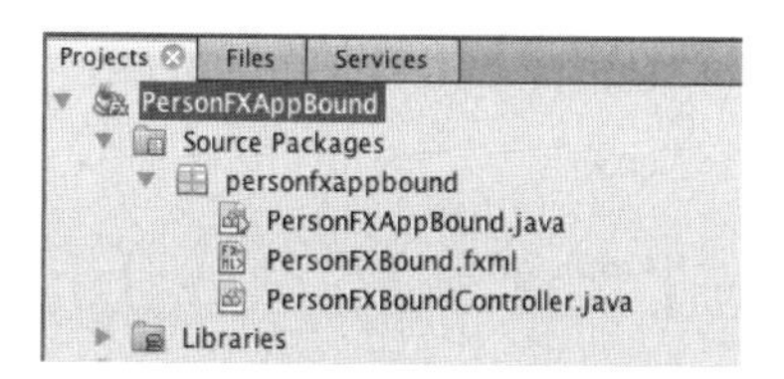


Figure 4.4 Project PersonFXAppBound shown in the Projects view

## Add Person.java to Application PersonFXAppBound

You'll now create class Person.java in its own package and supply code, as follows.

1. In project PersonFXAppBound, right click on node **Source Packages** and select **New | Java Class** from the context menu.

2. NetBeans displays the New Java Class Name and Location dialog. Specify **Person** for Class Name and **com.asgteach.familytree.model** for Package, as shown in Figure 4.5. Click **Finish**.
3. NetBeans creates file Person.java in package com.asgteach.familytree.model.

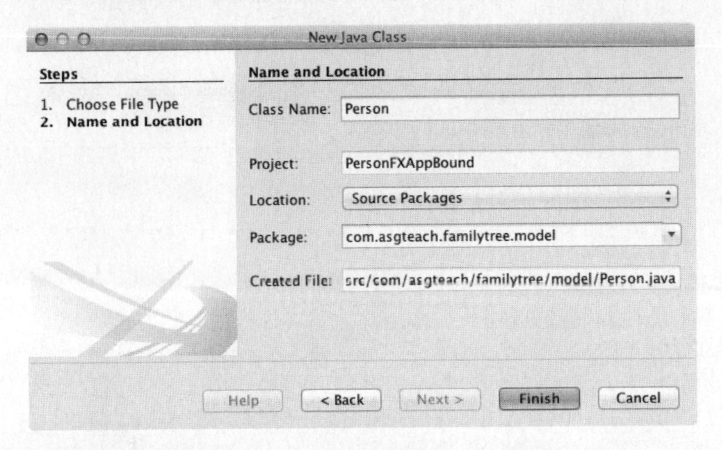


Figure 4.5 New Java Class Name and Location dialog

4. Use the code for Person.java as discussed in the previous section and shown here in Listing 4.8.

**Listing 4.8 Class Person.java**

```
public class Person implements Serializable {

    private final long id;
    private final StringProperty firstname =
            new SimpleStringProperty(this, "firstname", "");
    private final StringProperty middlename =
            new SimpleStringProperty(this, "middlename", "");
    private final StringProperty lastname =
            new SimpleStringProperty(this, "lastname", "");
    private final StringProperty suffix =
            new SimpleStringProperty(this, "suffix", "");
    private final ObjectProperty<Person.Gender> gender =
            new SimpleObjectProperty<>(this, "gender", Gender.UNKNOWN);
    private final StringProperty notes =
            new SimpleStringProperty(this, "notes", "");

    private final StringBinding fullNameBinding = new StringBinding() {
        {
            super.bind(firstname, middlename, lastname, suffix);
        }
```

```
        @Override
        protected String computeValue() {
            StringBuilder sb = new StringBuilder();
            if (!firstname.get().isEmpty()) {
                sb.append(firstname.get());
            }
            if (!middlename.get().isEmpty()) {
                sb.append(" ").append(middlename.get());
            }
            if (!lastname.get().isEmpty()) {
                sb.append(" ").append(lastname.get());
            }
            if (!suffix.get().isEmpty()) {
                sb.append(" ").append(suffix.get());
            }
            return sb.toString();
        }
    };
    private final ReadOnlyStringWrapper fullname =
            new ReadOnlyStringWrapper(this, "fullname");
    private static long count = 0;

    public enum Gender {
        MALE, FEMALE, UNKNOWN
    }

    public Person() {
        this("", "", Gender.UNKNOWN);
    }

    public Person(String first, String last, Person.Gender gender) {
        this.firstname.set(first);
        this.lastname.set(last);
        this.gender.set(gender);
        this.id = count++;
        this.fullname.bind(fullNameBinding);
    }

    public Person(Person person) {
        this.firstname.set(person.getFirstname());
        this.middlename.set(person.getMiddlename());
        this.lastname.set(person.getLastname());
        this.suffix.set(person.getSuffix());
        this.gender.set(person.getGender());
        this.notes.set(person.getNotes());
        this.id = person.getId();
        this.fullname.bind(fullNameBinding);
    }
```

```
public final long getId() {
    return id;
}

public final ReadOnlyStringProperty fullnameProperty() {
    return fullname.getReadOnlyProperty();
}

public final String getFullname() {
    return fullname.get();
}

public String getNotes() {
    return notes.get();
}

public void setNotes(String notes) {
    this.notes.set(notes);
}

public final StringProperty notesProperty() {
    return notes;
}

public String getFirstname() {
    return firstname.get();
}

public void setFirstname(String firstname) {
    this.firstname.set(firstname);
}

public final StringProperty firstnameProperty() {
    return firstname;
}

public Person.Gender getGender() {
    return gender.get();
}

public void setGender(Person.Gender gender) {
    this.gender.set(gender);
}

public final ObjectProperty<Person.Gender> genderProperty() {
    return gender;
}
```

```
public String getLastname() {
    return lastname.get();
}

public void setLastname(String lastname) {
    this.lastname.set(lastname);
}

public final StringProperty lastnameProperty() {
    return lastname;
}

public String getMiddlename() {
    return middlename.get();
}

public void setMiddlename(String middlename) {
    this.middlename.set(middlename);
}

public final StringProperty middlenameProperty() {
    return middlename;
}

public String getSuffix() {
    return suffix.get();
}

public void setSuffix(String suffix) {
    this.suffix.set(suffix);
}

public final StringProperty suffixProperty() {
    return suffix;
}

@Override
public int hashCode() {
    int hash = 3;
    hash = 97 * hash + Objects.hashCode(this.id)
            + Objects.hashCode(this.fullname.get())
            + Objects.hashCode(this.notes.get())
            + Objects.hashCode(this.gender.get());
    return hash;
}

@Override
public boolean equals(Object obj) {
    if (obj == null || getClass() != obj.getClass()) {
        return false;
    }
```

```
        final Person other = (Person) obj;
        return Objects.equals(this.id, other.id)
                && Objects.equals(this.fullname.get(), other.fullname.get())
                && Objects.equals(this.notes.get(), other.notes.get())
                && Objects.equals(this.gender.get(), other.gender.get());
    }

    @Override
    public String toString() {
        return fullname.get();
    }
}
```

### FXML Markup

Listing 4.9 shows the FXML for this application, which uses a vertical box (VBox) to hold three controls: a Label and two Buttons.

The VBox is the top or root node. We specify the controller class name (PersonFX-BoundController), the preferred width and height, and a linear gradient for the VBox's background color. The alignment is centered and we specify a 20-pixel spacing between children nodes.

The VBox has three children. Label is the first (so it appears at the top). We provide an `fx:id` value so we can reference the label in the Java controller code. Next, we define two buttons. For each one, we specify the `text` and `onAction` properties. The `onAction` property references a method that is defined in the controller.

**Listing 4.9 PersonFXBound.fxml**

```
<?xml version="1.0" encoding="UTF-8"?>

<?import java.lang.*?>
<?import java.util.*?>
<?import javafx.scene.*?>
<?import javafx.scene.control.*?>
<?import javafx.scene.layout.*?>

<VBox id="VBox" prefHeight="200" prefWidth="320"
              xmlns:fx="http://javafx.com/fxml"
              fx:controller="personfxappbound.PersonFXBoundController"
              alignment="CENTER" spacing="20"
              style="-fx-background-color:
                     linear-gradient(aliceblue, lightblue);">
    <Label fx:id="margeLabel" />
    <Button text="Change Marge"
                   onAction="#changeButtonAction" />
```

```
    <Button text="Reset Marge"
                    onAction="#resetButtonAction" />
</VBox>
```

## Controller Class

Controller class PersonFXBoundController is shown in Listing 4.10. Annotation `@FXML` identifies the scene graph object created in FXML (Label `margeLabel`) as well as the two action methods referenced in the FXML (`resetButtonAction()` and `changeButtonAction()`). The controller creates one Person object (`marge`).

Method `initialize()` is invoked after the scene graph is created. Here we specify that the label's `text` property is bound to the `fullname` property of Person `marge`.

Both button action methods modify the `middlename` property of Person `marge`. The binding keeps the label synchronized with the updated `fullname` property.

**Listing 4.10 PersonFXBoundController.java**

```
package personfxappbound;

import com.asgteach.familytree.model.Person;
import java.net.URL;
import java.util.ResourceBundle;
import javafx.event.ActionEvent;
import javafx.fxml.FXML;
import javafx.fxml.Initializable;
import javafx.scene.control.Label;

public class PersonFXBoundController implements Initializable {

    @FXML
    private Label margeLabel;

    final Person marge = new Person("Marge", "Simpson", Person.Gender.FEMALE);

    @FXML
    private void changeButtonAction(ActionEvent event) {
        marge.setMiddlename("Louise");
    }

    @FXML
    private void resetButtonAction(ActionEvent event) {
        marge.setMiddlename("");
    }
```

```
    @Override
    public void initialize(URL url, ResourceBundle rb) {
        // margeLabel uses binding to keep the textfield synchronized
        // with Person marge
        margeLabel.textProperty().bind(marge.fullnameProperty());
    }
}
```

### JavaFX Application Code

Listing 4.11 shows the Java application code that reads the FXML, starts the JavaFX Application Thread, and instantiates the scene graph.

**Listing 4.11 PersonFXAppBound.java**

```
package personfxappbound;

import javafx.application.Application;
import javafx.fxml.FXMLLoader;
import javafx.scene.Parent;
import javafx.scene.Scene;
import javafx.stage.Stage;

public class PersonFXAppBound extends Application {

    @Override
    public void start(Stage stage) throws Exception {
        Parent root = FXMLLoader.load(getClass()
                        .getResource("PersonFXBound.fxml"));
        Scene scene = new Scene(root);
        stage.setScene(scene);
        stage.setTitle("Person Bind Example");
        stage.show();
    }

    public static void main(String[] args) {
        launch(args);
    }
}
```

## 4.3 Observable Collections

The examples so far deal only with observable variables. JavaFX also has observable collections that let you observe when changes are made as you add to, remove from, or update a collection. You react to changes by attaching change listeners or invalidation listeners to these collections.

Significantly, collections signal change events by using the item's `equals()` method. If you replace one item with another, no change event is fired if the two items are equal. Thus, we need to make sure that a modified Person object with perhaps just an updated `notes` property or `middlename` property generates a change event. (This is why the Person class `equals()` verifies that all Person properties are equal, as shown in Listing 4.7 on page 138.)

Listing 4.12 shows the FamilyTreeManager class implemented with JavaFX collections. We create an observable map using static method `observableHashMap()`. FXCollections provides static methods that return observable versions of the same collection types as `java.util.Collections`.

The FamilyTreeManager forwards methods `addPerson()`, `updatePerson()`, and `deletePerson()` to the underlying observable map. Method `getAllPeople()` returns an ArrayList with copies of the Person items from the observable map using functional operations (see "Functional Data Structures" on page 39 for more information). To encapsulate the implementation of FamilyTreeManager as much as possible, we provide `addListener()` and `removeListener()` methods and forward these to the underlying observable map.

#### Listing 4.12 FamilyTreeManager—Using ObservableMap

```
package com.asgteach.familytree.model;

import javafx.collections.FXCollections;
import javafx.collections.ObservableMap;

public class FamilyTreeManager {

    private final ObservableMap<Long, Person> observableMap =
                                    FXCollections.observableHashMap();
    private static FamilyTreeManager instance = null;

    protected FamilyTreeManager() {
        // Singleton class: prevent direct instantiation
    }

    public static FamilyTreeManager getInstance() {
        if (instance == null) {
            instance = new FamilyTreeManager();
        }
        return instance;
    }

    public void addListener(
                MapChangeListener<? super Long, ? super Person> ml) {
        observableMap.addListener(ml);
    }
```

```
    public void removeListener(
                MapChangeListener<? super Long, ? super Person> ml) {
        observableMap.removeListener(ml);
    }

    public void addListener(InvalidationListener il) {
        observableMap.addListener(il);
    }

    public void removeListener(InvalidationListener il) {
        observableMap.removeListener(il);
    }

    public void addPerson(Person p) {
        Person person = new Person(p);
        observableMap.put(person.getId(), person);
    }

    public void updatePerson(Person p) {
        Person person = new Person(p);
        observableMap.put(person.getId(), person);
    }

    public void deletePerson(Person p) {
        observableMap.remove(p.getId());
    }

    public List<Person> getAllPeople() {
        List<Person> copyList = new ArrayList<>();
        observableMap.values().stream().forEach((p) ->
            copyList.add(new Person(p)));
        return copyList;
    }
}
```

Let's show you how to use the FamilyTreeManager in program PersonFXAppCoarse. Since this program does not create a JavaFX scene graph, we create a standard Java application using the following steps.

1. Select **File | New Project** from the NetBeans top-level menu. Select **Java** under Categories and **Java Application** under Projects.
2. NetBeans displays the Name and Location dialog. Specify **PersonFXAppCoarse** for Project Name and accept the defaults for the remaining fields, as shown in Figure 4.6. Click **Finish**.
3. Create package **com.asgteach.familytree.model** and add files Person.java (as shown in Listing 4.8 on page 142) and FamilyTreeManager.java (as shown in Listing 4.12 on page 149).

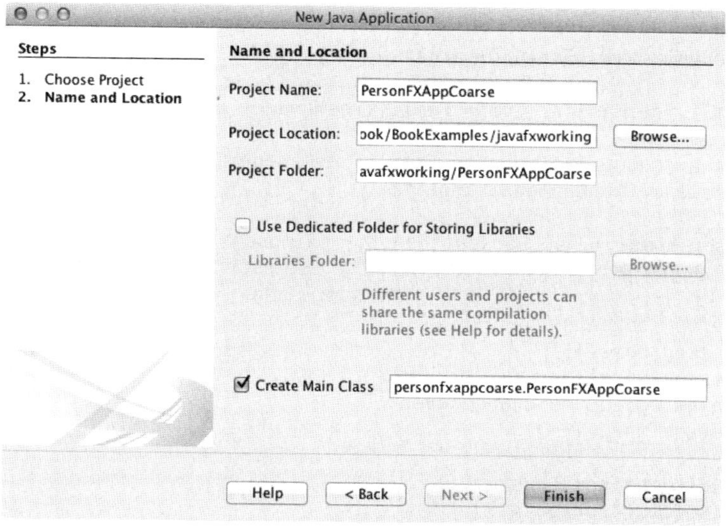

Figure 4.6 New Java Application, Name and Location dialog

The main program, class PersonFXAppCoarse.java, is shown in Listing 4.13. This program manipulates Person objects with the FamilyTreeManager.

After obtaining the singleton FamilyTreeManager object, we add listener `mapChangeListener`. The program then creates two Person objects (`homer` and `marge`) and adds them to the FamilyTreeManager with `addPerson()`. Because we attach a change listener, the `addPerson()` generates change events. To test the behavior of the observable map, the program invokes `addPerson()` again with `marge` and no change event is fired.

Next, the program modifies both Person objects and invokes method `updatePerson()`. Again we observe change events.

Finally, Person `marge` is removed with `deletePerson()` twice. The first remove generates a change event and the second remove does not.

**Listing 4.13 PersonFXAppCoarse—ObservableMap in Action**

```
package personfxapp;

import com.asgteach.familytree.model.FamilyTreeManager;
import com.asgteach.familytree.model.Person;
import javafx.collections.MapChangeListener;
```

```
public class PersonFXApp {

    public static void main(String[] args) {

        final FamilyTreeManager ftm = FamilyTreeManager.getInstance();

        // Attach a change listener to FamilyTreeManager
        ftm.addListener(mapChangeListener);

        final Person homer = new Person("Homer", "Simpson", Person.Gender.MALE);
        final Person marge = new Person("Marge", "Simpson",
                                        Person.Gender.FEMALE);
        // Add Person objects
        ftm.addPerson(homer);
        ftm.addPerson(marge);
        // add marge again, no change event
        ftm.addPerson(marge);

        homer.setMiddlename("Chester");
        homer.setSuffix("Junior");
        // Update homer
        ftm.updatePerson(homer);
        marge.setMiddlename("Louise");
        marge.setLastname("Bouvier-Simpson");
        // Update marge
        ftm.updatePerson(marge);
        ftm.deletePerson(marge);
        // delete marge again, no change event
        ftm.deletePerson(marge);
    }
. . . mapChangeListener shown in Listing 4.14 . . .
}
```

Listing 4.14 shows the MapChangeListener for this program. The change event (type `MapChangeListener.Change<Long, Person>`) includes boolean methods `wasAdded()` and `wasRemoved()`. Both of these methods return `true` when the map is updated. You can access the new value with `getValueAdded()` and the removed or replaced value with `getValueRemoved()`. Method `getValueRemoved()` returns null when an object is added, and `getValueAdded()` returns null when an object is removed. Method `getMap()` returns the updated map.

**Listing 4.14 MapChangeListener for FamilyTreeManager**

```
    // MapChangeListener<Long, Person> for FamilyTreeManager
    private static final MapChangeListener<Long, Person> mapChangeListener =
                (change) -> {
        if (change.wasAdded() && change.wasRemoved()) {
            System.out.println("\tUPDATED");
```

```
        } else if (change.wasAdded()) {
            System.out.println("\tADDED");
        } else if (change.wasRemoved()) {
            System.out.println("\tREMOVED");
        }
        System.out.println("\tmap = " + change.getMap());
        System.out.println("\t\t" + change.getValueAdded()
                + " was added [" + change.getKey() + "].");
        System.out.println("\t\t" + change.getValueRemoved()
                + " was removed [" + change.getKey() + "].");
    };
```

Listing 4.15 shows the console output after running program **PersonFXAppCoarse**. Tracking the changes, you see that Person `homer` is added, Person `marge` is added, Person `homer` is updated, Person `marge` is updated, and lastly Person `marge` is removed. Note that the second add for Person `marge` is not observed as well as the second removal of Person `marge`.

**Listing 4.15 Program PersonFXAppCoarse Output**

```
Output:
   ADDED
   map = {0=Homer Simpson}
      Homer Simpson was added [0].
      null was removed [0].
   ADDED
   map = {0=Homer Simpson, 1=Marge Simpson}
      Marge Simpson was added [1].
      null was removed [1].
   UPDATED
   map = {0=Homer Chester Simpson Junior, 1=Marge Simpson}
      Homer Chester Simpson Junior was added [0].
      Homer Simpson was removed [0].
   UPDATED
   map = {0=Homer Chester Simpson Junior, 1=Marge Louise Bouvier-Simpson}
      Marge Louise Bouvier-Simpson was added [1].
      Marge Simpson was removed [1].
   REMOVED
   map = {0=Homer Chester Simpson Junior}
      null was added [1].
      Marge Louise Bouvier-Simpson was removed [1].
```

## 4.4 JavaFX Applications

We are now ready to build a JavaFX application with the Person and FamilyTreeManager classes using JavaFX properties and observable collections. This is the JavaFX equivalent of the Swing program presented in Chapter 2 (program PersonSwingApp-EnhancedUI described in "Improving the User Experience" on page 63). In this JavaFX example, we display Person objects from the FamilyTreeManager in the left side of the application using the JavaFX TreeView control. Users edit the selected Person object with the form on the right side. The Update button is only enabled when the user makes modifications using the UI controls. The Person editor form is cleared when the user clicks on the top (root) node of the TreeView.

Figure 4.7 shows the JavaFX version of this application (project **PersonFXMLApp-EnhancedUI**) running with the user making edits to Person Lisa Simpson.

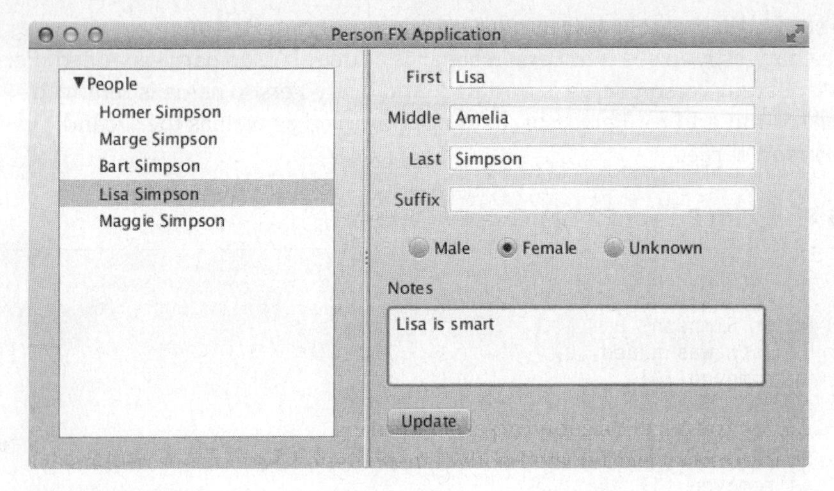


Figure 4.7 Program PersonFXMLAppEnhancedUI: Editing Person Lisa Simpson

## Program Structure

Use the NetBeans IDE to create a new JavaFX FXML Application, as described previously (see "Creating a JavaFX FXML Application" on page 139). Figure 4.8 shows the project structure of this application in the NetBeans IDE. Like the Swing programs you've seen, the FamilyTreeManager and Person source files are in the package `com.asgteach.familytree.model`. Since the application code is structured for FXML, you see three source files: the FXML (PersonFXML.fxml), the controller class (PersonFXMLController), and the main application code (PersonFXMLApp), all in package `personfxmlapp`.

Before we examine the FXML and controller class, let's look at the main application code as shown in Listing 4.16. Here you see the now-familiar code that reads and loads the scene graph from the FXML file and configures and shows the stage, the main window for JavaFX applications.

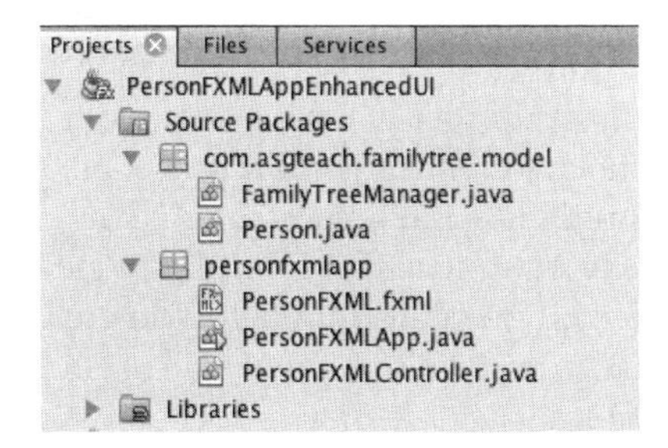


Figure 4.8 PersonFXMLAppEnhancedUI project structure

### Listing 4.16 PersonFXMLApp JavaFX Application

```
package personfxmlapp;

import javafx.application.Application;
import javafx.fxml.FXMLLoader;
import javafx.scene.Parent;
import javafx.scene.Scene;
import javafx.stage.Stage;

public class PersonFXMLApp extends Application {

    @Override
    public void start(Stage stage) throws Exception {
        Parent root = FXMLLoader.load(getClass().getResource(
                                     "PersonFXML.fxml"));

        Scene scene = new Scene(root);
        stage.setTitle("Person FX Application");
        stage.setScene(scene);
        stage.show();
    }

    public static void main(String[] args) {
        launch(args);
    }
}
```

## Scene Builder and FXML

So far we've built our FXML markup by manually editing the FXML and configuring the properties of the JavaFX controls we need. This works great for simple JavaFX scene graphs. However, the more controls you add, the more difficult this approach becomes. It's much nicer to have a visual editor to help you with the layout and generate the FXML markup for you.

Scene Builder is a stand-alone application that lets you create a JavaFX scene. Similar to the Swing Form Designer, you place controls on the design area through drag and drop and use context menus and property sheets to configure the controls. Scene Builder is written in JavaFX so you have some nice UI graphics that help you create your application's design.

Once you download and install Scene Builder,[3] NetBeans automatically brings it up when you open an FXML file (via **Open** or **double-click**). If you don't want to have Scene Builder edit your FXML, just open the FXML file with **Edit**.

Figure 4.9 shows the Scene Builder layout designer where you visually place and position controls. Here you see the controls we use for the PersonFXMLApp-EnhancedUI application. Note that the text field opposite label First is highlighted.

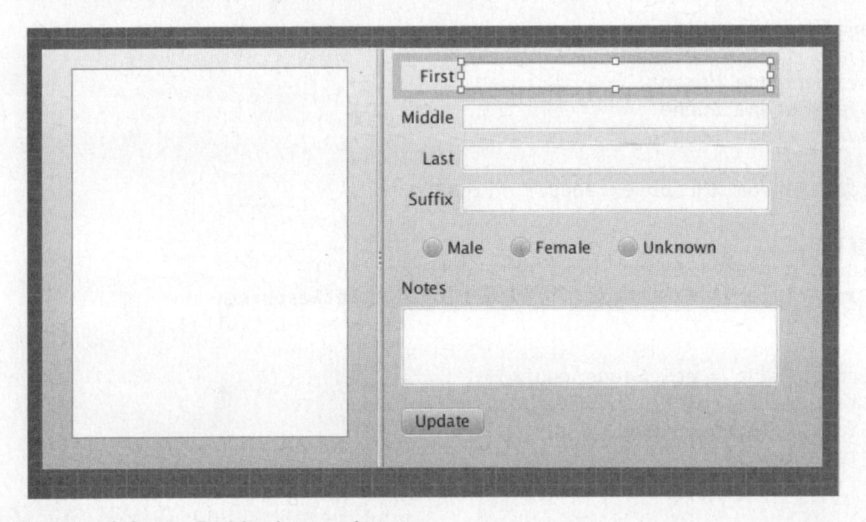


**Figure 4.9 Scene Builder layout designer**

Figure 4.10 shows the Scene Builder Hierarchy that displays an expandable/collapsible tree of your scene graph as well as the Inspector that lets you inspect and configure the controls in your design. The same text field that is highlighted in the design view is also highlighted in the Hierarchy.

3. You can download Scene Builder for free at `www.oracle.com`.

The Inspector is divided into three categories: Properties (collapsed), Layout (which is currently shown), and Code (not shown in this view). The Inspector is handy for specifying the FXML references from your controller class and for configuring other node properties.

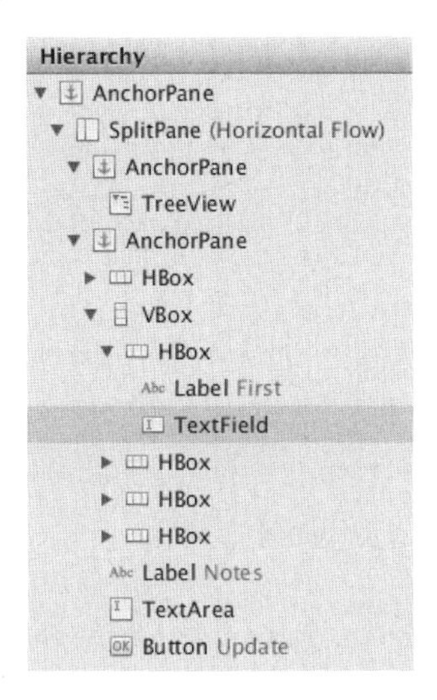


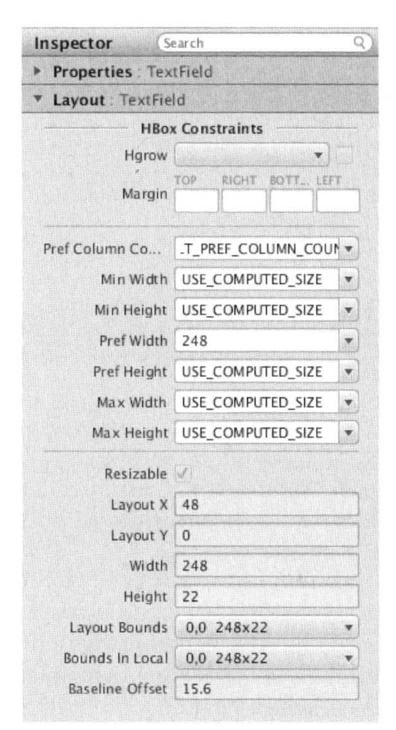


Figure 4.10 Scene Builder Hierarchy and Inspector controls

Figure 4.11 shows the Scene Builder Library selector. You use the Library selector to add basic controls, pop-up controls, containers, menu content, shapes, charts, and miscellaneous items to your layout design. The Library selector has a search mechanism that helps you quickly find and select the component you need.

There is a tie between an FXML file and its controller class. Scene Builder reads the designated controller class and provides references in drop down menus that are marked with the `@FXML` annotation in the controller class. Scene Builder does not modify the controller class.

However, you can use the FXML file's **Make Controller** menu item to synchronize the controller code with FXML edits. After saving the FXML file in Scene Builder, select the Make Controller menu item in NetBeans. NetBeans will add or remove @FXML

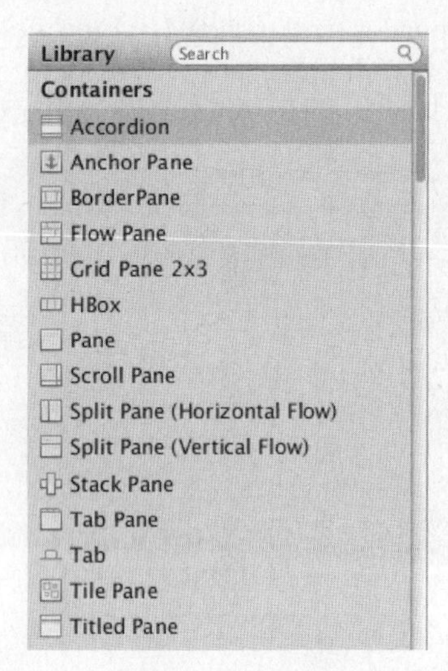


Figure 4.11 Scene Builder Library for searching and selecting JavaFX controls

annotated fields and methods in the controller class. As you gain experience working with Scene Builder, you'll discover the work flow that's right for you.

Remember, Scene Builder generates FXML code, not Java. Let's look at the FXML Scene Builder generated for our sample application, shown in Listing 4.17. First, you'll see that Scene Builder generates very readable FXML. Secondly, Scene Builder favors layout container AnchorPane, which lets you specify how its contained children should behave when the window is resized.

The main window for the application uses an AnchorPane that contains a SplitPane control. The SplitPane (with a left side and a right side) has an AnchorPane for each side. The TreeView control is on the left side and the right side holds the form for editing a Person. This includes a VBox with multiple HBox controls (one for each label and text field), an HBox to hold the radio buttons, a text area for the notes, and an Update button.

The SplitPane control has a linear gradient configured for its `background` property. The TreeView control is configured for a specific size (properties `prefHeight` and `prefWidth`), and the AnchorPane settings resize the TreeView dynamically to maintain its configured anchors.

Each radio button belongs to the same toggle group (providing the mutual exclusion behavior on selection), and its action event references method `genderSelectionAction()`, which is defined in the controller class. Note that the first radio button creates the toggle group, but the second and third radio buttons use the notation

```
toggleGroup="$genderToggleGroup"
```

which references the already-created toggle group.

Each text field and associated label appears in an HBox. The text field has an `fx:id` (so the controller class can reference it) and an `onKeyReleased` key event reference for the `handleKeyAction()` event handler, defined in the controller class.

The text area has a similar configuration as the text fields, with an `fx:id` and an `onKeyReleased` key event reference. You'll recognize (from the Swing applications in Chapter 2) that these event handlers detect when a user edits Person properties and subsequently enable the Update button.

Finally, the Update button has text "Update," an `fx:id` reference, and an action event reference for the `updateButtonAction()` event handler.

**Listing 4.17 Scene Builder Generated FXML**

```
<?import java.lang.*?>
<?import java.util.*?>
<?import javafx.scene.*?>
<?import javafx.scene.control.*?>
<?import javafx.scene.layout.*?>

<AnchorPane id="AnchorPane" prefHeight="328.0" prefWidth="630.0"
   xmlns:fx="http://javafx.com/fxml"
   fx:controller="personfxmlapp.PersonFXMLController">
  <children>
    <SplitPane dividerPositions="0.43630573248407645" focusTraversable="true"
      prefHeight="328.0" prefWidth="630.0"
      style="-fx-background-color:  linear-gradient(aliceblue, lightblue);"
      AnchorPane.bottomAnchor="0.0"
      AnchorPane.leftAnchor="0.0"
      AnchorPane.rightAnchor="0.0"
      AnchorPane.topAnchor="0.0">
      <items>
        <AnchorPane minHeight="0.0" minWidth="0.0"
            prefHeight="340.0" prefWidth="257.0">
          <children>
            <TreeView fx:id="personTreeView" prefHeight="289.0"
            prefWidth="225.0" AnchorPane.bottomAnchor="23.0"
            AnchorPane.leftAnchor="23.0" AnchorPane.rightAnchor="23.0"
            AnchorPane.topAnchor="14.0" />
          </children>
        </AnchorPane>
        <AnchorPane minHeight="0.0" minWidth="0.0" prefHeight="326.0"
            prefWidth="351.9998779296875">
          <children>
```

```
            <HBox id="HBox" alignment="CENTER_RIGHT" layoutX="31.0"
               layoutY="147.0" spacing="20.0">
              <children>
                <RadioButton fx:id="maleRadioButton"
                     onAction="#genderSelectionAction" text="Male">
                  <toggleGroup>
                    <ToggleGroup fx:id="genderToggleGroup" />
                  </toggleGroup>
                </RadioButton>
                <RadioButton fx:id="femaleRadioButton"
                  onAction="#genderSelectionAction" text="Female"
                  toggleGroup="$genderToggleGroup" />
                <RadioButton fx:id="unknownRadioButton"
                  onAction="#genderSelectionAction" text="Unknown"
                  toggleGroup="$genderToggleGroup" />
              </children>
            </HBox>
            <VBox id="VBox" alignment="TOP_CENTER" layoutX="14.0"
                  layoutY="10.0" spacing="10.0">
              <children>
                <HBox id="HBox" alignment="CENTER_RIGHT" spacing="5.0">
                  <children>
                    <Label text="First" />
                    <TextField fx:id="firstnameTextField"
                     onKeyReleased="#handleKeyAction" prefWidth="248.0" />
                  </children>
                </HBox>

              . . . other <HBox> elements for the rest of the text fields . . .

              </children>
            </VBox>
            <Label layoutX="14.0" layoutY="178.0" text="Notes" />
            <TextArea fx:id="notesTextArea" layoutX="14.0" layoutY="201.0"
               onKeyReleased="#handleKeyAction" prefHeight="62.0"
               prefWidth="303.0" wrapText="true" />
            <Button fx:id="updateButton" layoutX="14.0" layoutY="280.0"
            mnemonicParsing="false" onAction="#updateButtonAction"
            text="Update" />
          </children>
        </AnchorPane>
      </items>
    </SplitPane>
  </children>
</AnchorPane>
```

## JavaFX Controls

Before we examine the controller class, let's look at a partial hierarchy of the JavaFX controls, shown in Figure 4.12 and Figure 4.13. Node extends Object, Parent extends

Node, and Control extends Parent. We don't use most of these controls in our application, but the diagrams let you see how the TextField, Label, TextArea, RadioButton, Button, and TreeView controls fit into the JavaFX Control class hierarchy.

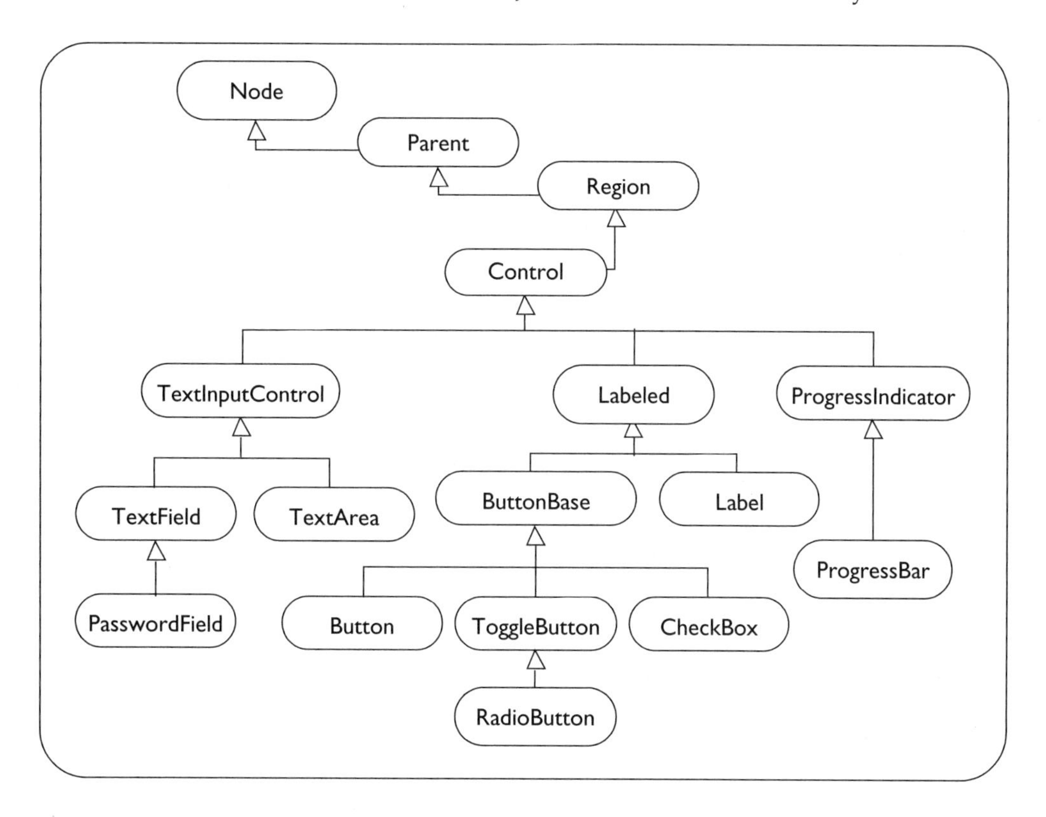


Figure 4.12 JavaFX controls hierarchy (partial)

Labeled is a superclass of Label, CheckBox, and other button controls. Many of the controls in Figure 4.13 are generic, with <T> denoting the type of item contained within the control. JavaFX controls are manipulated with their JavaFX properties and you can attach listeners to these properties or use them in binding expressions. We'll show you examples of binding properties and attaching listeners with controls in this section.

Let's look at some of the controls we use in our JavaFX application.

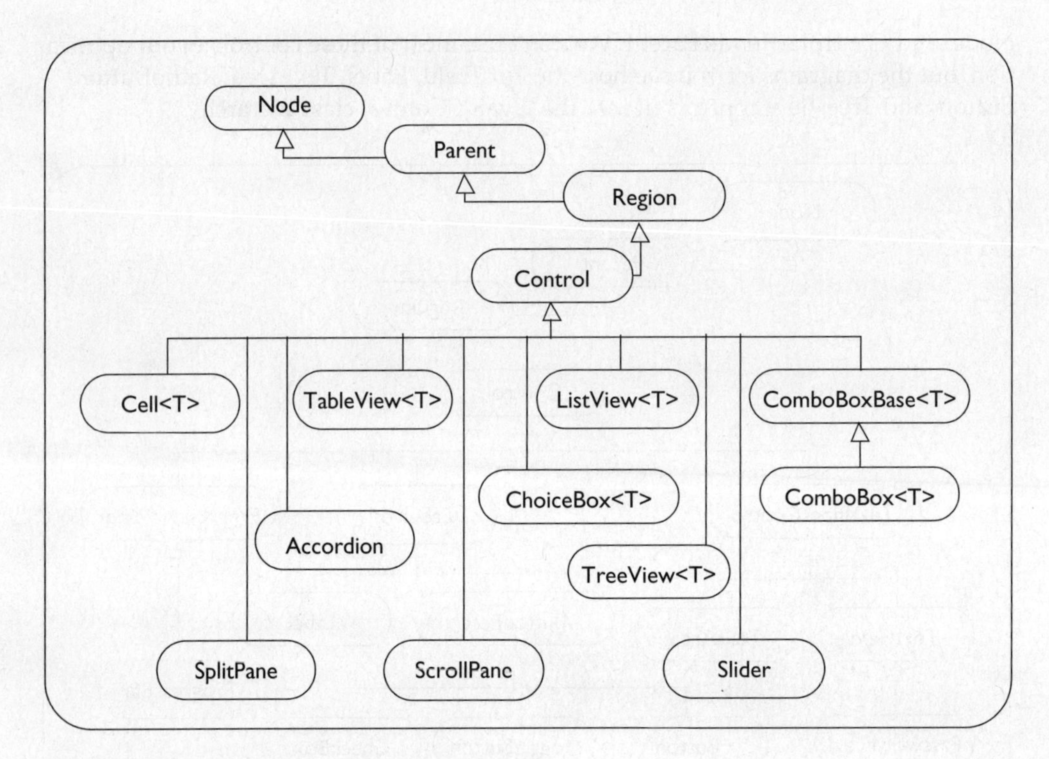


Figure 4.13 JavaFX controls hierarchy (partial)

### Label

Like Swing's JLabel, Label holds non-editable text. Label can display text, images, or both. If the text does not fit in the label, the label uses ellipsis to indicate truncated text. In our example, we define all the Label controls in FXML and do not need to reference them in the controller class. Here's how to create a Label in Java code.

```
Label mylabel = new Label("First");
```

### TextField

The TextField control lets users edit a single line of text. We define a key released event handler for all of the text fields and configure a bidirectional binding between the text field and its corresponding Person property. Here, for example, is the binding for the text field that edits the `firstname` Person property referenced by `person`.

```
firstnameTextField.textProperty()
            .bindBidirectional(person.firstnameProperty());
```

Because the binding is bidirectional, a change to either the `text` property in the TextField control or the `firstname` property in the Person object updates the corresponding property.

### TextArea

We use a TextArea control to edit the Person `notes` property. The TextArea control lets users edit multi-line text. Similar to the TextField, we configure a key released event handler and specify bidirectional binding. Here is the binding expression we use for the TextArea.

```
notesTextArea.textProperty().bindBidirectional(person.notesProperty());
```

TextArea also has a built-in context menu that helps you edit text, as shown in Figure 4.14.

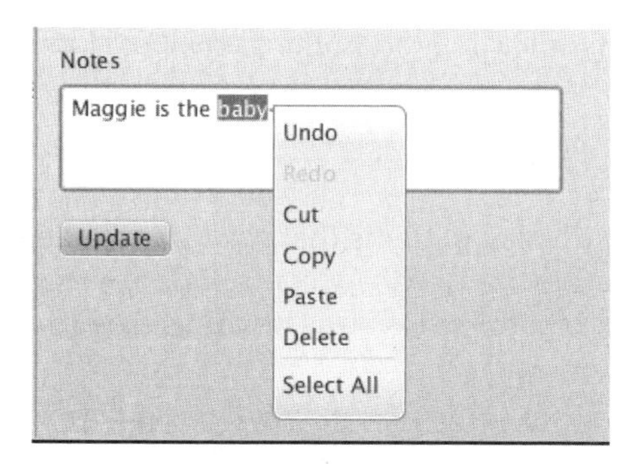


Figure 4.14 TextArea built-in context menu

### RadioButton

RadioButton is a Labeled control that's similar to Swing's JRadioButton. You specify a toggle group when radio buttons must be mutually exclusive. Here is the FXML that sets up a toggle group and adds three radio buttons to it. For each radio button, we specify an `fx:id` reference and method `genderSelectionAction()`, the action event handler implemented in the controller class.

```
<RadioButton fx:id="maleRadioButton"
        onAction="#genderSelectionAction" text="Male">
  <toggleGroup>
    <ToggleGroup fx:id="genderToggleGroup" />
  </toggleGroup>
</RadioButton>
```

```
            <RadioButton fx:id="femaleRadioButton"
                    onAction="#genderSelectionAction" text="Female"
                    toggleGroup="$genderToggleGroup" />
            <RadioButton fx:id="unknownRadioButton"
                    onAction="#genderSelectionAction" text="Unknown"
                    toggleGroup="$genderToggleGroup" />
```

### Button

Button is a Labeled control that presents a "pushed" graphic when clicked and invokes an action event handler if one is configured. Here's the FXML we use to define the Update button.

```
<Button fx:id="updateButton" layoutX="14.0" layoutY="280.0"
        onAction="#updateButtonAction" text="Update" />
```

Property `fx:id` is the reference name of the button in the controller class. Method `updateButtonAction()` is the button's action handler defined in the controller class.

### TreeView

The TreeView control presents a hierarchical display of items that can be expanded and collapsed. Here's the FXML we use to define the TreeView control. Configuring the AnchorPane setting enables the TreeView control to resize as its containing layout control resizes.

```
<TreeView fx:id="personTreeView" prefHeight="289.0" prefWidth="225.0"
     AnchorPane.bottomAnchor="23.0" AnchorPane.leftAnchor="23.0"
     AnchorPane.rightAnchor="23.0" AnchorPane.topAnchor="14.0" />
```

The items are displayed with TreeItem<Person>, which we build in the controller class. First, we create a "People" root node and then build the rest of the TreeItem objects. Next, we set the root node of the TreeView with `setRoot()` and specify that the root node should be expanded initially. FamilyTreeManager method `getAllPeople()` returns a list, which we use to build the TreeItems for the TreeView.

```
TreeItem<Person> rootNode = new TreeItem<>(new Person(
        "People", "", Person.Gender.UNKNOWN));

// Populate the TreeView control
ftm.getAllPeople().stream().forEach((p) -> {
    root.getChildren().add(new TreeItem<>(p));
});
```

```
        personTreeView.setRoot(rootNode);
        personTreeView.getRoot().setExpanded(true);
```

## JavaFX Controller Class

Recall that our application lets users select a Person item from the left-side TreeView UI control (see Figure 4.7 on page 154). When a Person is selected, that Person appears in the Person form editor on the right side. The Update button remains disabled until the user edits the Person.

Upon finishing editing, the user updates the application with new values for the Person by clicking the Update button. The FamilyTreeManager updates the application, and the TreeView displays the new values (if any) of the just-edited Person item.

Users can also select the top node (the root node), in which case the Person form editor clears and the Update button is disabled. Any edits made in the Person form editor are lost if the user selects a new item without saving the changes.

Let's look at the controller class now. This class provides method `initialize()` to configure the scene graph. The controller class is also responsible for defining the event handlers, change listeners, and other support code that implements the behavior we just described.

Listing 4.18 shows the controller class's declaration section, where we define any objects created in the FXML file that are accessed here in the controller class. Recall that the FXML loader is responsible for instantiating these objects, so you won't see any code that creates them.

We also create a Logger object (see "Java Logging Facility" on page 51 for a description) and a FamilyTreeManager instance. There are also several class variables here. Variable `thePerson` holds the currently selected Person from the TreeView control. Variable `genderBinding` is a custom binding object that keeps the Person gender property synchronized with the form editor. The `changeOK` boolean keeps track of when the application should listen for user edits. BooleanProperty `enableUpdateProperty` (a JavaFX property) controls the Update button's disable property with binding.

**Tip**

---

*We could just manually control the Update button's* `disable` *property. However, having a separate property lets us configure different artifacts or controls later, especially if we no longer use the Update button.*

---

**Listing 4.18 PersonFXMLController—Controller Class**

```
public class PersonFXMLController implements Initializable {

    @FXML
    private TextField firstnameTextField;
    @FXML
    private TextField middlenameTextField;
    @FXML
    private TextField lastnameTextField;
    @FXML
    private TextField suffixTextField;
    @FXML
    private RadioButton maleRadioButton;
    @FXML
    private RadioButton femaleRadioButton;
    @FXML
    private RadioButton unknownRadioButton;
    @FXML
    private TextArea notesTextArea;
    @FXML
    private TreeView<Person> personTreeView;
    @FXML
    private Button updateButton;
    private static final Logger logger = Logger.getLogger(
                    PersonFXMLController.class.getName());
    private final FamilyTreeManager ftm = FamilyTreeManager.getInstance();
    private Person thePerson = null;
    private ObjectBinding<Person.Gender> genderBinding;
    private boolean changeOK = false;
    private BooleanProperty enableUpdateProperty;
```

Listing 4.19 shows the controller's `initialize()` method. This method configures the Logger object, instantiates the `enableUpdateProperty`, binds the Update button to the inverse of the `enableUpdateProperty` (with `.not()`, see "Fluent API and Bindings API" on page 113), and defines the custom binding object for the `gender` property. Method `buildData()` (shown next) populates the FamilyTreeManager with Person objects. We then build and configure the TreeView control. Note that we also attach a listener to the `selection` property of the TreeView's underlying model.

**Listing 4.19 Controller Class initialize() Method**

```
    @Override
    public void initialize(URL url, ResourceBundle rb) {
        // Change level to Level.INFO to reduce console messages
        logger.setLevel(Level.FINE);
        Handler handler = new ConsoleHandler();
        handler.setLevel(Level.FINE);
        logger.addHandler(handler);
```

```
        try {
            FileHandler fileHandler = new FileHandler();
            // records sent to file javaN.log in user's home directory
            fileHandler.setLevel(Level.FINE);
            logger.addHandler(fileHandler);
            logger.log(Level.FINE, "Created File Handler");
        } catch (IOException | SecurityException ex) {
            logger.log(Level.SEVERE, "Couldn't create FileHandler", ex);
        }

        enableUpdateProperty = new SimpleBooleanProperty(
                  this, "enableUpdate", false);
        updateButton.disableProperty().bind(enableUpdateProperty.not());

        // the radio button custom binding
        genderBinding = new ObjectBinding<Person.Gender>() {
            {
                super.bind(maleRadioButton.selectedProperty(),
                        femaleRadioButton.selectedProperty(),
                        unknownRadioButton.selectedProperty());
            }

            @Override
            protected Person.Gender computeValue() {
                if (maleRadioButton.isSelected()) {
                    return Person.Gender.MALE;
                } else if (femaleRadioButton.isSelected()) {
                    return Person.Gender.FEMALE;
                } else {
                    return Person.Gender.UNKNOWN;
                }
            }
        };

        buildData();
        TreeItem<Person> rootNode = new TreeItem<>(
                    new Person("People", "", Person.Gender.UNKNOWN));
        buildTreeView(rootNode);
        personTreeView.setRoot(rootNode);
        personTreeView.getRoot().setExpanded(true);
        personTreeView.getSelectionModel().selectedItemProperty()
                    .addListener(treeSelectionListener);
    }
```

Listing 4.20 shows the code for private methods `buildData()` and `buildTreeView()`. The `buildData()` method adds Person objects for Homer, Marge, Bart, Lisa, and Maggie to the FamilyTreeManager. The `buildTreeView()` method fetches Person objects from the FamilyTreeManager to create each TreeItem<Person> object, adding the item to the root node. Note that we also attach a listener to the FamilyTreeManager (its underlying observable map).

**Listing 4.20 Methods buildData() and buildTreeView()**

```
private void buildData() {
    ftm.addPerson(new Person("Homer", "Simpson", Person.Gender.MALE));
    ftm.addPerson(new Person("Marge", "Simpson", Person.Gender.FEMALE));
    ftm.addPerson(new Person("Bart", "Simpson", Person.Gender.MALE));
    ftm.addPerson(new Person("Lisa", "Simpson", Person.Gender.FEMALE));
    ftm.addPerson(new Person("Maggie", "Simpson", Person.Gender.FEMALE));
    logger.log(Level.FINE, ftm.getAllPeople().toString());
}

private void buildTreeView(TreeItem<Person> root) {
    // listen for changes to the familytreemanager's map
    ftm.addListener(familyTreeListener);
    // Populate the TreeView control
    ftm.getAllPeople().stream().forEach((p) -> {
        root.getChildren().add(new TreeItem<>(p));
    });
}
```

## TreeView Selection Listener

This JavaFX application includes several listeners that react to changes much like the Swing version (see Listing 2.19 on page 60 and Listing 2.21 on page 63). First, we have the TreeView selection change listener, which we attach to the `selection` property of the TreeView model as follows. This listener is invoked when the user selects a different item in the TreeView.

```
personTreeView.getSelectionModel().selectedItemProperty()
                .addListener(treeSelectionListener);
```

Recall that ChangeListeners use generics so that observable values passed in the change event handler can be accessed without type casting. Listing 4.21 shows the code for the tree selection change listener. When a user selects a different Person item, the application performs the following tasks. Specifically, the change listener

- sets the `enableUpdateProperty` to false (which, because of binding, disables the Update button)
- disallows edits in the Person form editor until a new Person is displayed
- clears the Person editing form and returns if the new selection is either the root TreeView item or null (returned when the user collapses the tree view and a leaf node is selected)
- makes a copy of the selected Person object and configures its bindings. This populates the Person form editor with the newly selected Person's data. The gender

property is a bit tricky, since its type is a Person.Gender enum that corresponds to separate radio buttons.

Once the Person form editor and class variable `thePerson` are configured, the listener sets boolean `changeOK` to true, which allows the user to make edits in the Person form editor. The Update button remains disabled.

#### Listing 4.21 ChangeListener for TreeView Model Selection Property

```
// TreeView selected item event handler
private final ChangeListener<TreeItem<Person>> treeSelectionListener =
        (ov, oldValue, newValue) -> {
    TreeItem<Person> treeItem = newValue;
    logger.log(Level.FINE, "selected item = {0}", treeItem);
    enableUpdateProperty.set(false);
    changeOK = false;
    if (treeItem == null || treeItem.equals(personTreeView.getRoot())) {
        clearForm();
        return;
    }
    // set thePerson to the selected treeItem value
    thePerson = new Person(treeItem.getValue());
    logger.log(Level.FINE, "selected person = {0}", thePerson);
    configureEditPanelBindings(thePerson);
    // set the gender from Person, then configure the genderBinding
    if (thePerson.getGender().equals(Person.Gender.MALE)) {
        maleRadioButton.setSelected(true);
    } else if (thePerson.getGender().equals(Person.Gender.FEMALE)) {
        femaleRadioButton.setSelected(true);
    } else {
        unknownRadioButton.setSelected(true);
    }
    thePerson.genderProperty().bind(genderBinding);
    changeOK = true;
};
```

Listing 4.22 shows methods `configureEditPanelBindings()` and `clearForm()`. Method `configureEditPanelBindings()` is interesting and deserves a closer look. Note that although `bindBidirectional()` appears to be symmetric, it is not. That is, when you bind bidirectionally with

```
a.bindBidirectional(b);
```

property `a` takes on the value of property `b` initially. From then on, the binding is symmetric, where `b` will take on `a`'s value if `a` changes and `a` will take on `b`'s value if `b` changes. With this in mind, note that in method `configureEditPanelBindings()`, the UI controls invoke the `bindBidirectional()` method for several properties. This is how we initially configure the UI controls with the Person's property values and subsequently update the Person's properties with user edits.

Method `clearForm()` provides a straightforward clearing of the UI controls.

**Listing 4.22 Configure Bindings and Clear Person Form Editor**

```
private void configureEditPanelBindings(Person p) {
    firstnameTextField.textProperty()
            .bindBidirectional(p.firstnameProperty());
    middlenameTextField.textProperty()
            .bindBidirectional(p.middlenameProperty());
    lastnameTextField.textProperty()
            .bindBidirectional(p.lastnameProperty());
    suffixTextField.textProperty().bindBidirectional(p.suffixProperty());
    notesTextArea.textProperty().bindBidirectional(p.notesProperty());
}

private void clearForm() {
    firstnameTextField.setText("");
    middlenameTextField.setText("");
    lastnameTextField.setText("");
    suffixTextField.setText("");
    notesTextArea.setText("");
    maleRadioButton.setSelected(false);
    femaleRadioButton.setSelected(false);
    unknownRadioButton.setSelected(false);
}
```

We detect when the user makes changes by listening for key released events with the text field and text area controls. Here is the FXML for the TextField control for editing Person property `firstname`, where property `onKeyReleased` is set to method `handleKeyAction()`.

```
<TextField fx:id="firstnameTextField"
        onKeyReleased="#handleKeyAction" prefWidth="248.0" />
```

Similarly, here is the FXML for the RadioButton control where property `onAction` is set to method `genderSelectionAction()`. A radio button selection change invokes the `onAction` event handler.

```
<RadioButton fx:id="femaleRadioButton"
        onAction="#genderSelectionAction" text="Female"
        toggleGroup="$genderToggleGroup" />
```

Listing 4.23 shows the code for both event handlers. The `@FXML` annotation makes these method names accessible from the FXML markup. Once the user makes a change (either by releasing a key in the text input controls or by making a selection change with the radio buttons), the handlers set the `enableUpdateProperty` to true. Because of binding, this enables the Update button.

**Listing 4.23 Control onKeyReleased and RadioButton Selection Handlers**

```
@FXML
private void handleKeyAction(KeyEvent ke) {
    if (changeOK) {
        enableUpdateProperty.set(true);
    }
}

@FXML
private void genderSelectionAction(ActionEvent event) {
    if (changeOK) {
        enableUpdateProperty.set(true);
    }
}
```

Listing 4.24 shows the Update button event handler. Note that class variable `thePerson` is kept in sync with the editing controls thanks to the bidirectional binding and the custom binding object for the radio button controls. We set the `enableUpdateProperty` to false and update the Person in the FamilyTreeManager with `updatePerson()`.

**Listing 4.24 Update Button Action Event Handler**

```
@FXML
private void updateButtonAction(ActionEvent event) {
    enableUpdateProperty.set(false);
    ftm.updatePerson(thePerson);
}
```

## MapChangeListener

FamilyTreeManager method `updatePerson()` updates the FamilyTreeManager's observable map with the new Person data. Because we have a listener attached to the FamilyTreeManager observable map, the listener's event handler is invoked when an update occurs. The event handler method includes the new value. The change listener replaces the Person in the TreeView that corresponds to this new value. Note that we now must compare Person objects using `getId()`. Person method `equals()` won't work, since this method compares all Person properties. Listing 4.25 shows the code.

**Listing 4.25 MapChangeListener for FamilyTreeManager's Map**

```
// MapChangeListener when underlying FamilyTreeManager changes
private final MapChangeListener<Long, Person> familyTreeListener =
                                      (change) -> {
  if (change.getValueAdded() != null) {
     logger.log(Level.FINE, "changed value = {0}", change.getValueAdded());
```

```
            // Find the treeitem that this matches and replace it
            for (TreeItem<Person> node : personTreeView.getRoot().getChildren()) {
                if (change.getKey().equals(node.getValue().getId())) {
                    // an update returns the new value in getValueAdded()
                    node.setValue(change.getValueAdded());
                    return;
                }
            }
        }
    };
```

The above change listener uses TreeView method `getRoot().getChildren()` to loop through the items in the TreeView. A MapChangeListener change event includes methods `getKey()` (the key of the Person object that is changed), `getValueAdded()` (the Person object that is added), and `getValueRemoved()` (the Person object that is removed). When an object is replaced, `getValueAdded()` is the new value and `getValueRemoved()` is the old value. Here, we don't access the old value, but we make sure that the new value is non-null before attempting to perform the replacement.

### A Word About Loose Coupling

Note that this small JavaFX application follows the same principles of loose coupling that we described for the Swing example application (see "Event Handlers and Loose Coupling" on page 59). Specifically, the TreeView UI control is not accessed from the Update button event handler, even though the button event handler knows that a Person object displayed in the TreeView is about to change. Also, the FamilyTreeManager and Person are purely model objects and have no dependencies on any of the UI controls.

JavaFX bidirectional binding provides a convenient way to keep the model object (here Person) in sync with UI controls that let the user change the model's properties.

Program PersonFXMLAppEnhancedUI provides a functional equivalent of the Swing program PersonSwingAppEnchancedUI.

## 4.5 Concurrency and Thread Safety

JavaFX, like Swing, is a single-threaded GUI. All changes to the scene graph must occur on the JavaFX Application Thread. This means that if you have a long-running background task, you should execute that task in a separate thread so that your UI remains responsive. "Swing Background Tasks" on page 73 shows you how to do this with Swing using helper class SwingWorker. Let's apply these same principles of concurrency and thread safety to our JavaFX example.

## Concurrency in JavaFX

The JavaFX Platform class has several static methods to help you with multi-threaded applications: `runLater()` and `isFXApplicationThread()`.

### Platform.runLater()

The static `runLater()` method submits a Runnable to be executed at some unspecified time in the future. This is similar to the `SwingUtilities.invokeLater()`, where other UI events already scheduled may occur first. Use `runLater()` from a background thread to execute code that updates the JavaFX scene graph.

### Platform.isFXApplicationThread()

The static `isFXApplicationThread()` method returns true if the calling thread is the JavaFX Application Thread. Use this method when you want to execute code that updates the JavaFX scene graph and you may or may not be in a background thread.

## Observable Properties and Thread Safety

A general thread safety issue with JavaFX is that you should not update observable values in a background thread that are bound to or affect properties in the scene graph. Observable values include JavaFX properties that you can bind to, as well as properties that you can attach listeners to. With listeners, however, you can take precautions and place code that updates the scene graph in a `Platform.runLater()` Runnable. With binding, however, you must ensure that updates to properties occur on the JavaFX Application Thread if property changes affect the scene graph.

For class Person and its many JavaFX properties that can be bound to JavaFX UI controls, we ensure thread safety with thread containment. That is, we only update Person objects in the JavaFX Application Thread. Furthermore, when we use a Person object in a background thread, we always make a thread-safe local copy of it first.

Making the JavaFX version of the FamilyTreeManager thread safe is interesting. First, a caller can attach a change listener to the observable map. If map modifications occur on a background thread, the change event will fire on the background thread. In the Swing version, we address this issue by using SwingPropertyChangeSupport. This helper class configures the change support object to fire property change events on the EDT.

With JavaFX, we'll take the opposite approach with the FamilyTreeManager code. That is, we put the burden on the caller and require the listener to process any change events in the JavaFX Application Thread. We check to see if the method is invoked on the JavaFX Application Thread and process the change by invoking `Platform.runLater()`. This ensures that any change to the scene graph is performed on the JavaFX Application Thread. Listing 4.26 shows the modified MapChangeListener method in the PersonFXMLController class.

**Listing 4.26 Modified MapChangeListener**

```
// MapChangeListener when underlying FamilyTreeManager changes
// Check to see if on FXT, if not call Platform.runLater()
private final MapChangeListener<Long, Person> familyTreeListener =
                                                 change -> {
     if (Platform.isFxApplicationThread()) {
          logger.log(Level.FINE, "Is JavaFX Application Thread");
          updateTree(change);
     } else {
          logger.log(Level.FINE, "Is BACKGROUND Thread");
          Platform.runLater(()-> updateTree(change));
     }
};

private void updateTree(MapChangeListener.Change<? extends Long,
                                         ? extends Person> change) {
     if (change.getValueAdded() != null) {
          // Find the treeitem that this matches and replace it
          for (TreeItem<Person> node :
                              personTreeView.getRoot().getChildren()) {
               if (change.getKey().equals(node.getValue().getId())) {
                    // an update returns the new value in getValueAdded()
                    node.setValue(change.getValueAdded());
                    return;
               }
          }
     }
}
```

Listing 4.27 shows the thread-safe JavaFX version of FamilyTreeManager, which follows many of the steps we showed you in the Swing version from Chapter 2. The observable map uses a ConcurrentHashMap as its underlying collection. Method `getInstance()` and the add and remove listener methods are also synchronized.

In the methods that make changes to the map, we first make a copy of Person. Method `getAllPeople()` also makes copies of each Person item as it populates a list. These methods are synchronized.

**Listing 4.27 Thread-Safe FamilyTreeManager**

```
package com.asgteach.familytree.model;

import java.util.ArrayList;
import java.util.List;
import java.util.concurrent.ConcurrentHashMap;
import javafx.beans.InvalidationListener;
import javafx.collections.FXCollections;
import javafx.collections.MapChangeListener;
import javafx.collections.ObservableMap;

public class FamilyTreeManager {
    private final ObservableMap<Long, Person> observableMap =
         FXCollections.observableMap(new ConcurrentHashMap<Long, Person>());
    private static FamilyTreeManager instance = null;

    protected FamilyTreeManager() { }

    // Thread-safe lazy initialization
    public synchronized static FamilyTreeManager getInstance() {
        if (instance == null) {
            instance = new FamilyTreeManager();
        }
        return instance;
    }

    public synchronized void addListener(
            MapChangeListener<? super Long, ? super Person> ml) {
        observableMap.addListener(ml);
    }

    public synchronized void removeListener(
            MapChangeListener<? super Long, ? super Person> ml) {
        observableMap.removeListener(ml);
    }

    public synchronized void addListener(InvalidationListener il) {
        observableMap.addListener(il);
    }

    public synchronized void removeListener(InvalidationListener il) {
        observableMap.removeListener(il);
    }

    public synchronized void addPerson(Person p) {
        final Person person = new Person(p);
        observableMap.put(person.getId(), person);
    }
```

```
    public void updatePerson(Person p) {
        // both addPerson and updatePerson use observableMap.put()
        addPerson(p);
    }

    public synchronized void deletePerson(Person p) {
        final Person person = new Person(p);
        observableMap.remove(person.getId());
    }

    public synchronized List<Person> getAllPeople() {
        List<Person> copyList = new ArrayList<>();
        observableMap.values().stream().forEach((p)
                -> copyList.add(new Person(p)));
        return copyList;
    }
}
```

## 4.6 JavaFX Background Tasks

JavaFX has a concurrency package, `javafx.concurrent`, with classes that let you create background tasks and safely monitor a task's progress, state, and results. The JavaFX concurrency package consists of two main classes, Task and Service, that both implement the Worker interface. A Task is not reusable but a Service is. Let's examine the Task class and learn how to invoke it in a background thread in our JavaFX Family-Tree application.

### Worker and Task

Both the Task and Service classes implement the Worker interface with common JavaFX properties and a well-defined life cycle. We only use Task in our examples, but Service also implements the Worker interface and shares this life cycle behavior and properties. A Task object's life cycle is defined by Worker.State values shown in Table 4.1. A Worker always begins its life cycle in state `READY`. It then transitions to `SCHEDULED` and then `RUNNING`. It stays in state `RUNNING` until it either completes or is cancelled. After completion the state is one of `SUCCEEDED`, `FAILED`, or `CANCELLED`.

**TABLE 4.1 Worker.State Values**

| State | Description |
|---|---|
| `READY` | The only beginning valid state for a task. |
| `SCHEDULED` | After `READY` and before `RUNNING` (`running == true`). |
| `RUNNING` | During normal execution (`running == true`). |

**TABLE 4.1 Worker.State Values** *(Continued)*

| State | Description |
|---|---|
| `SUCCEEDED` | The task completed normally. ReadOnlyObjectProperty<V> `value` is accessible. |
| `FAILED` | An exception occurred during execution. ReadOnlyObject-Property<Exception> `exception` contains the exception. |
| `CANCELLED` | The task was cancelled. |

A Task object maintains several read-only JavaFX properties that you can safely observe from the JavaFX Application Thread. These properties let you monitor the state of a task and access a value upon successful completion or access a task's progress as it is running. Table 4.2 describes these JavaFX properties.

**TABLE 4.2 Worker Read-Only JavaFX Properties**

| JavaFX Property | Description |
|---|---|
| `ReadOnlyObjectProperty<Throwable> exception` | The Exception that caused the task to fail. This is set when status is `FAILED`. |
| `ReadOnlyStringProperty message` | A string message updated by the task. |
| `ReadOnlyDoubleProperty progress` | Current progress. Either -1 (indeterminate) or a value between 0 and 1, inclusive where 1 is 100 percent complete. |
| `ReadOnlyBooleanProperty running` | The task is either `SCHEDULED` or `RUNNING`. |
| `ReadOnlyObjectProperty <Worker.State> state` | The state of the task (one of Worker.State enums). |
| `ReadOnlyStringProperty title` | A string representing the title (which can change as the task proceeds). |
| `ReadOnlyDoubleProperty totalWork` | A double representing the total work to be completed by the task (between -1 and `Long.MAX_VALUE`). |
| `ReadOnlyObjectProperty<V> value` | The value returned by the task with a `SUCCESSFUL` state. |
| `ReadOnlyDoubleProperty workDone` | Either -1 (indeterminate) or a value between 0 and `totalWork`, inclusive. |

A Task must provide the `call()` method, which is invoked in a background thread. Method `call()` returns a value of its generic type. In addition, you can define callback methods that correspond to the various completion states of the Task in order to process the results depending on the Task's outcome.

The Task class also provides several methods you can invoke from any thread to update Task properties, as shown in Table 4.3. Note that the update may not happen immediately, and several update calls may be coalesced to reduce event notifications.

**TABLE 4.3 Thread-Safe Task Update Methods**

| Method | Description |
|---|---|
| `protected void updateProgress( long workDone, long max)` | Updates the `workDone`, `totalWork`, and `progress` properties |
| `protected void updateProgress( double workDone, double max)` | Updates the `workDone`, `totalWork`, and `progress` properties |
| `protected void updateMessage( String message)` | Updates the `message` property |
| `protected void updateTitle( String title)` | Updates the `title` property |
| `protected void updateValue( V value)` | Updates the `value` property |

With a general description of the JavaFX Task, let's modify the JavaFX FamilyTree application from the previous section and create a background task to update edited Person items in the FamilyTreeManager. We call this application project **PersonFXMLAppMultiThread**.

Since the program updates the Person in the FamilyTreeManager in a background task, we'll add a progress indicator to the scene graph to show that work is being done. Figure 4.15 shows this application running with the added progress indicator visible.

## ProgressIndicator

A JavaFX progress indicator control is a circular display that reflects either a percent complete (using a pie-shaped fill for partial completions) or a rotating, dashed circular graphic for indeterminate tasks. The default constructor creates an indeterminate indicator. To create a progress indicator that displays a percentage of completion, specify a starting value for the `progress` property in the constructor (or in the FXML markup).

Typically, progress indicators are visible only during the execution of a background task. When the task finishes, the indicator becomes invisible again. In this application, we control the progress indicator's visibility with binding.

To have a progress indicator reflect the completion progress of a task, bind the progress indicator `progress` property to the `progress` status of the background task. For example, the following code creates a progress indicator that reflects the comple-

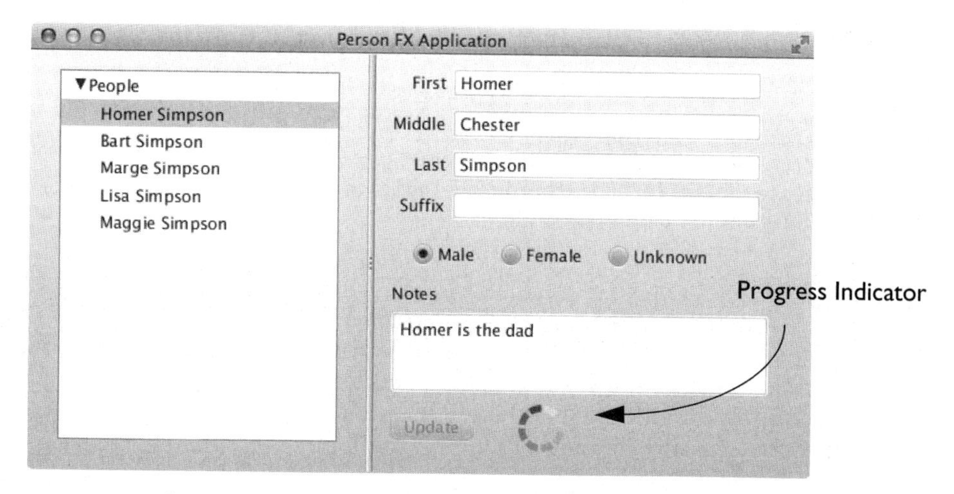


Figure 4.15 Program PersonFXMLAppMultiThread: Updating Person data in a background thread

tion of a background task called `myTask`. During the execution of this task, you invoke the Task `updateProgress()` method as needed. This method, described in Table 4.3, updates the task's `progress`, `workDone`, and `totalWork` properties in the JavaFX Application Thread, allowing you to safely bind to the `progress` property.

```
ProgressIndicator myProgressIndicator = new ProgressIndicator(0.0);
. . .
// Begin a Background Task
. . .
Task<Void> myTask = new Task<Void>() { . . . };

myProgressIndicator.progressProperty().bind(myTask.progressProperty());
new Thread(myTask).start();

// End a background task
```

Listing 4.28 shows the updated FXML file with the progress indicator added to the scene graph. We use the default constructor, which configures the progress indicator as indeterminate.

**Listing 4.28 Add a ProgressIndicator to Scene Graph**

```
<children>
    . . .
   <Button fx:id="updateButton" layoutX="14.0" layoutY="280.0"
         onAction="#updateButtonAction" text="Update" />
   <ProgressIndicator fx:id="updateProgressIndicator" layoutX="117.0"
         layoutY="272.0" />
</children>
      . . .
```

Most of the changes required to implement the background task are in the Controller class. First, Listing 4.29 shows the changes made to the class declarations and the `initialize()` method. We provide an `@FXML` annotation for the progress indicator to control its visibility. We also add an IntegerProperty counter (`backgroundActive`) that reflects how many background tasks are currently active. We bind the progress indicator's visibility to this property, using the Fluent API method `greaterThan(0)`. Since we increment property `backgroundActive` when a background task starts and decrement it when the task completes, the progress indicator remains visible only when a background task is active.

**Integer Counter and Thread Safety**

*Note that we always access property* `backgroundActive` *on the JavaFX Application Thread. This means that we can safely update and bind to this property.*

**Listing 4.29 Changes to Controller Class: Declarations and initialize()**

```
. . .
    @FXML
    private Button updateButton;
    @FXML
    private ProgressIndicator updateProgressIndicator;
    private static final Logger logger = Logger.getLogger(
            PersonFXMLController.class.getName());
    private final FamilyTreeManager ftm = FamilyTreeManager.getInstance();
    private Person thePerson = null;
    private ObjectBinding<Person.Gender> genderBinding;
    private boolean changeOK = false;
    private BooleanProperty enableUpdateProperty;
    private IntegerProperty backgroundActive = new SimpleIntegerProperty(0);
  . . .
```

```
@Override
public void initialize(URL url, ResourceBundle rb) {
   . . .

    updateProgressIndicator.visibleProperty()
                       .bind(backgroundActive.greaterThan(0));
   . . .
}
```

The big change, of course, happens with the Update button's action event handler, method `updateButtonAction()`, shown in Listing 4.30. Before the Task is started the event handler must configure a few variables on the JavaFX Application Thread. First, the event handler makes a local copy of class field `thePerson`. If another Update button click occurs before this task is finished, the subsequent task will have its own copy of the Person object. Second, we disable the Update button (until further edits are made either to this Person or to another Person). Third, we increment the `backgroundActive` property.

Because we use an indeterminate progress indicator, the Task has very little work to do. It implements method `call()` to invoke the FamilyTreeManager `updatePerson()` method.

We create callback methods for a successful completion (`setOnSucceeded`) and a failed completion (`setOnFailed`). These methods are always invoked on the JavaFX Application Thread after the Task completes, so you can perform scene graph modifications here. We decrement property `backgroundActive`. Because of binding, this makes the progress indicator invisible if `backgroundActive's` new value is less than 1.

After the Task is fully defined, we start the background thread with

```
new Thread(updateTask).start();
```

Note that, as in the Swing examples, we artificially make this a long-running task by including a call to `Thread.sleep()` in the background thread (in method `call()`). Method `call()` returns the updated Person object, which we access within the `onSucceeded` property's method. The `onFailed` property's method accesses the Exception object (which could be null).

**Listing 4.30 Method updateButtonAction()**

```
@FXML
private void updateButtonAction(ActionEvent event) {
    // update the family tree manager on a background thread
    final Person person = new Person(thePerson);
    enableUpdateProperty.set(false);
    backgroundActive.set(backgroundActive.get() + 1);
```

```
Task<Person> updateTask = new Task<Person>() {
    @Override
    protected Person call() throws Exception {
        Thread.sleep(1000);            // for test only
        ftm.updatePerson(person);
        return person;
    }
};
updateTask.setOnSucceeded(t -> {
    backgroundActive.set(backgroundActive.get() - 1);
    logger.log(Level.FINE, "Update task finished: {0}",
            t.getSource().getValue());
    logger.log(Level.FINE, "tasks stillInBackground = {0}",
            backgroundActive.get());
});
updateTask.setOnFailed(t -> {
        backgroundActive.set(backgroundActive.get() - 1);
        // t.getSource().getException() could be null
        logger.log(Level.WARNING, "Update task failed {0}",
                t.getSource().getException() != null
                ? t.getSource().getException()
                : "Unknown failure");
        logger.log(Level.FINE, "tasks stillInBackground = {0}",
                backgroundActive.get());
});
new Thread(updateTask).start();
}
```

To show you how all this works, let's run application **PersonFXMLAppMultiThread** and edit Person Bart. Here are the log messages produced when we click the Update button to save the changes. As shown, the MapChangeListener event handler is invoked on the background thread (see Listing 4.26 on page 174).

```
Dec 04, 2013 10:05:35 AM personfxmlapp.PersonFXMLController lambda$6
FINE: selected person = Bart Simpson
Dec 04, 2013 10:06:08 AM personfxmlapp.PersonFXMLController lambda$4
FINE: Is BACKGROUND Thread
Dec 04, 2013 10:06:08 AM personfxmlapp.PersonFXMLController updateTree
FINE: changed value = Bart Seymour Simpson
Dec 04, 2013 10:06:08 AM personfxmlapp.PersonFXMLController lambda$1
FINE: Update task finished: Bart Seymour Simpson
```

## 4.7 Monitoring Background Tasks

Now let's show you several examples that provide periodic or partial results to the main JavaFX Application Thread. These example programs let users initiate a background task that converts the FamilyTreeManager's Person items to all uppercase. The UI displays each Person when it completes the conversion, and a label shows the current Person being processed. These examples all show you how to safely update the JavaFX UI during execution of a background task.

We discuss several approaches that provide partial results to the main JavaFX Application Thread from a background task, as follows.

- Program **PersonFXMLAppFXWorker** invokes thread-safe method `updateValue()` to provide intermediate or partial results. We use binding with the task's `valueProperty()` to safely update the UI.
- Program **PersonFXMLAppFXWorker2** defines a read-only property and updates this property (safely) during execution of the background task. This approach is convenient when the task updates an observable collection. The program shows how easy it is to use an observable collection with a control such as TableView.
- Program **PersonFXMLAppFXWorker3** updates the JavaFX scene graph (safely) during execution of the background task. This approach is useful when a long-running background task produces data used to create nodes in the UI.

Let's show you each of these approaches.

## Using Method updateValue()

Figure 4.16 shows application **PersonFXMLAppFXWorker** running. Note that the UI is active while the background task is running and the user can select and edit Person items concurrently. Here you see both the uppercase conversion task running, as well as the background task that updates a Person to the FamilyTreeManager. (The uppercase conversion does not save the uppercase Person items; it's just busywork!)

Before examining the background task code, let's first show you the UI controls we add to the JavaFX scene graph.

### ProgressBar

The progress bar provides a horizontal bar, which, like the progress indicator, can also be indeterminate. In this example, however, we use a progress bar that indicates percent complete by updating its `progress` property. The `progress` property is a double value between 0 (0 percent complete) and 1 (100 percent complete).

We add a text area, label, progress bar, and button to the scene graph. Listing 4.31 shows the FXML markup generated by Scene Builder to add these UI controls. The Process All button and the progress bar are maintained by an HBox layout control for horizontal placement. The Label and TextArea are placed above and below the HBox component.

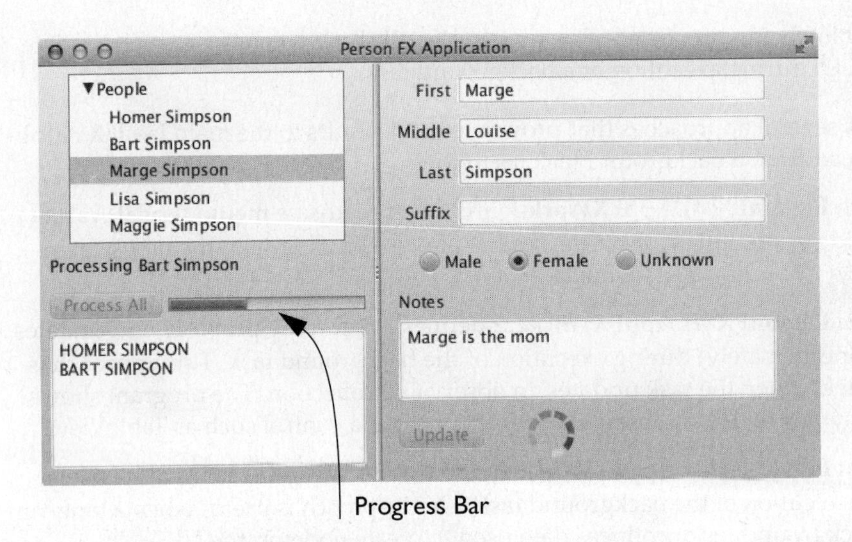


Figure 4.16 Program PersonFXMLAppFXWorker: Running a background task with partial results displayed in UI

**Listing 4.31 Add Controls to FXML**

```
<HBox id="HBox" alignment="CENTER" layoutX="7.0" layoutY="176.0" spacing="5.0">
  <children>
    <Button fx:id="processAllButton"
          onAction="#processAllButtonAction" text="Process All" />
    <ProgressBar fx:id="progressBar" prefWidth="161.0" progress="0.0" />
  </children>
</HBox>
<TextArea fx:id="statusTextArea" editable="false" layoutX="7.0"
    layoutY="208.0" prefHeight="106.0" prefWidth="257.0" wrapText="true" />
<Label fx:id="statusMessage" layoutX="7.0" layoutY="147.0" />
```

## Safely Updating the UI

Table 4.3 on page 178 lists the Task methods you can safely invoke from a background thread. These methods make Task update the appropriate JavaFX properties on the JavaFX Application Thread. This lets you safely bind your UI controls to any of these properties or use them in binding expressions. You'll see that we invoke `updateMessage()`, `updateProgress()`, and `updateValue()` in method `call()` to keep the Task properties synchronized with the task's progress.

## Extending Task

Our previous example uses class Task directly. Here we extend Task in order to encapsulate several class variables, as shown in Listing 4.32. Class ProcessAllTask extends class Task with `<String>` for Task's generic type. This means that method `call()` returns String, method `getValue()` returns String, `valueProperty()` returns a read-only String JavaFX property, and method `updateValue()` requires a String parameter. Here, String property `value` holds the constructed names transformed to uppercase letters.

The ProcessAllTask constructor takes an ObservableList<Person> and stores it in ProcessAllTask class variable `processList`. Class variable `buildList` is the StringBuilder object we use to construct the transformed names.

Method `call()` is invoked in a background thread. This method loops through `processList`, processing each Person, invoking `updateMessage()` with the current Person, appending the transformed name to `buildList`, and invoking `updateProgress()` with the current work done and the total work to be done. Property `value` is updated with thread-safe `updateValue()`.

The code that converts a Person's names to all uppercase is contained in method `doProcess()`. The call to `Thread.sleep()` helps test the responsiveness of the UI with a long-running background task. Method `call()` returns the completed String of transformed names.

**Listing 4.32 ProcessAllTask**

```
private class ProcessAllTask extends Task<String> {

    private final ObservableList<Person> processList;
    private final StringBuilder buildList = new StringBuilder();

    public ProcessAllTask(final ObservableList<Person> processList) {
        this.processList = processList;
    }

    @Override
    protected String call() throws Exception {
        logger.log(Level.FINE, "Begin processing");
        final int taskMaxCount = processList.size();
        logger.log(Level.FINE, "processing list: {0}", processList);
        int taskProgress = 0;
        for (final Person person : processList) {
            if (isCancelled()) {
                break;
            }
            // do something to each person
            updateMessage("Processing " + person);
            logger.log(Level.FINE, "processing: {0}", person);
```

```
                doProcess(person);
                buildList.append(person.toString()).append("\n");
                // Update value property with new buildList
                updateValue(buildList.toString());
                updateProgress(100 * (++taskProgress) / taskMaxCount, 100);
                Thread.sleep(500);
            }
            // return the final built String result
            return buildList.toString();
        }

        // Called on the background thread
        private void doProcess(Person p) {
            p.setFirstname(p.getFirstname().toUpperCase());
            p.setMiddlename(p.getMiddlename().toUpperCase());
            p.setLastname(p.getLastname().toUpperCase());
            p.setSuffix(p.getSuffix().toUpperCase());
        }
    }
```

Listing 4.33 shows the Process All button's action event handler that initiates the background task. The handler instantiates ProcessAllTask with a list of Person items. Then, it sets up the bindings between the UI controls and the ProcessAllTask properties that are monitored. The event handler also creates callback methods that are invoked on the JavaFX Application Thread when the background task completes (either successfully, with a failure, or with a cancellation). Finally, the event handler starts the task in a new background thread.

The event handler sets up the bindings by binding the UI control progress bar to the task's `progress` property. It also binds the UI Label control to the task's `message` property, which displays the currently processed Person. Lastly, the event handler binds the UI TextArea control to the task's `value` property.

The callback methods log the results of the Task and reset the UI controls (method `resetUI()` is shown next).

**Listing 4.33 Method processAllButtonAction()**

```
    @FXML
    private void processAllButtonAction(ActionEvent event) {
        logger.log(Level.FINE, "Process All Button");
        // only one task to run at a time so disable the button
        processAllButton.setDisable(true);
        // create the task with a list
        final ProcessAllTask processTask = new ProcessAllTask(
                FXCollections.observableArrayList(ftm.getAllPeople()));
        // configure the UI
        progressBar.progressProperty().bind(processTask.progressProperty());
```

```
        statusMessage.textProperty().bind(processTask.messageProperty());
        statusTextArea.textProperty().bind(processTask.valueProperty());

        // set up handlers for success and failure
        processTask.setOnSucceeded(t -> {
            logger.log(Level.FINE, "Process All task finished: {0}",
                    t.getSource().getValue());
            resetUI();
        });
        processTask.setOnFailed(t -> {
            // t.getSource().getException() could be null
            logger.log(Level.WARNING, "Update task failed {0}",
                    t.getSource().getException() != null
                    ? t.getSource().getException()
                    : "Unknown failure");
            resetUI();
        });
        processTask.setOnCancelled(t -> {
            logger.log(Level.FINE, "Process All task cancelled.");
            resetUI();
        });
        // start the task in a background thread
        new Thread(processTask).start();
    }
```

Listing 4.34 shows how to reset the UI. Note that we must unbind the UI controls before resetting their text properties. Method `resetUI()` also re-enables the Process All button.

**Listing 4.34 Method resetUI()**

```
    // reset the UI
    private void resetUI() {
        statusTextArea.textProperty().unbind();
        statusTextArea.setText("");
        progressBar.progressProperty().unbind();
        progressBar.setProgress(0);
        statusMessage.textProperty().unbind();
        statusMessage.setText("");
        processAllButton.setDisable(false);
    }
```

## Updating a Read-Only JavaFX Property

Our next example is a slight variation of the previous example. Figure 4.17 shows application **PersonFXMLAppFXWorker2** running, which uses a read-only observable list property to publish partial results. We then configure a TableView control with this observable list, automatically displaying partial results. Because the task does not use a thread-safe method to publish partial results, it must wrap updates in a Runnable and invoke `Platform.runLater()`.

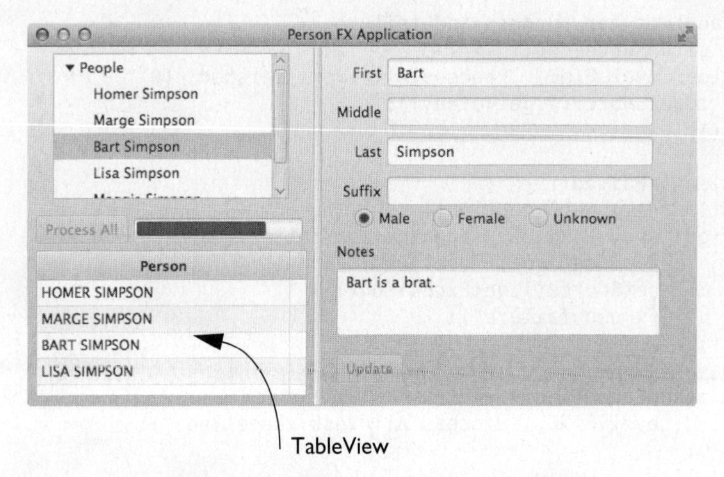


Figure 4.17 Program PersonFXMLAppFXWorker2: Running a background task with partial results displayed in UI

## Publishing Partial Results

As Figure 4.17 indicates, we add controls to the UI with FXML. We include the Process All button, a progress bar, and a TableView control with a single column, as shown in Listing 4.35.

**Listing 4.35 Add Controls to FXML**

```
<HBox id="HBox" alignment="CENTER" layoutX="7.0" layoutY="153.0" spacing="5.0">
   <children>
      <Button fx:id="processAllButton" mnemonicParsing="false"
               onAction="#processAllButtonAction" text="Process All" />
      <ProgressBar fx:id="progressBar" prefWidth="161.0" progress="0.0" />
   </children>
</HBox>
<TableView fx:id="nameDisplay" layoutX="7.0" layoutY="185.0" prefWidth="257.0"
      maxHeight="-Infinity" maxWidth="-Infinity" minHeight="-Infinity"
      minWidth="-Infinity" prefHeight="132.99990000000253" >
   <columns>
      <TableColumn prefWidth="240.0" text="Person" fx:id="personColumn" />
   </columns>
</TableView>
```

Listing 4.36 shows the ProcessAllTask for this example. This time we extend Task defined with generic ObservableList<Person>. Furthermore, we use a ReadOnly-ObjectWrapper to create a read-only JavaFX property (see "Read-Only Properties" on page 109 for a discussion) and provide two public methods to access the property: `getPartialResults()` and `partialResultsProperty()`. You'll see that ProcessAllTask maintains this read-only property on the JavaFX Application Thread, making its access by code that updates the UI thread safe.

Method `call()` is invoked on the background thread. It processes the list of Person objects passed in the constructor. As it adds Person objects to `partialResults` observable list, it invokes `Platform.runLater()`.

**Listing 4.36 ProcessAllTask**

```
private class ProcessAllTask extends Task<ObservableList<Person>> {

    private final ObservableList<Person> processList;

    private final ReadOnlyObjectWrapper<ObservableList<Person>>
     partialResults = new ReadOnlyObjectWrapper<>(this, "partialResults",
                   FXCollections.observableArrayList(new ArrayList<>()));

    public final ObservableList getPartialResults() {
        return partialResults.get();
    }

    public final ReadOnlyObjectProperty<ObservableList<Person>>
                         partialResultsProperty() {
        return partialResults.getReadOnlyProperty();
    }

    public ProcessAllTask(final ObservableList<Person> processList) {
        this.processList = processList;
    }

    @Override
    protected ObservableList<Person> call() throws Exception {
        logger.log(Level.FINE, "Begin processing");

        final int taskMaxCount = processList.size();
        logger.log(Level.FINE, "processing list: {0}", processList);
        int taskProgress = 0;
        for (final Person person : processList) {
            if (isCancelled()) {
                break;
            }
            // do something to each person
            logger.log(Level.FINE, "processing: {0}", person);
            doProcess(person);
```

```
                // Update the property on the FX thread
                Platform.runLater(() -> {
                    partialResults.get().add(person);
                });
                updateProgress(100 * (++taskProgress) / taskMaxCount, 100);
                Thread.sleep(500);
            }
            return partialResults.get();
        }

        // Called on the background thread
        private void doProcess(Person p) {
            p.setFirstname(p.getFirstname().toUpperCase());
            p.setMiddlename(p.getMiddlename().toUpperCase());
            p.setLastname(p.getLastname().toUpperCase());
            p.setSuffix(p.getSuffix().toUpperCase());
        }
    }
```

Listing 4.37 shows the code to handle the Process All button. Here, you see the power of observable lists, where we set TableView method `setItems()` to an observable list. As the list changes, the TableView control automatically refreshes. TableColumn method `setCellValueFactory()` specifies that the column's cell data is created from the Person object's `fullname` property.

Not apparent in the screen shot shown in Figure 4.17 on page 188, the ProcessAll Task completion callback methods invoke method `resetUI()`. This fades out the TableView control. When the fade animation completes, the Process All button is enabled. (See "Animation" on page 100 for more details on Transitions.)

**Listing 4.37 Process All Button**

```
    @FXML
    private void processAllButtonAction(ActionEvent event) {
        logger.log(Level.FINE, "Process All Button");
        // only one task to run at a time so disable the button
        processAllButton.setDisable(true);
        // create the task with a list
        final ProcessAllTask processTask = new ProcessAllTask(
                FXCollections.observableArrayList(ftm.getAllPeople()));
        // configure the UI
        progressBar.progressProperty().bind(processTask.progressProperty());
        personColumn.setCellValueFactory(
            new PropertyValueFactory<>("fullname"));
        nameDisplay.setOpacity(1);
        nameDisplay.setItems(processTask.getPartialResults());
```

```
        // set up handlers for success and failure
        processTask.setOnSucceeded(t -> {
            logger.log(Level.FINE, "Process All task finished: {0}",
                    t.getSource().getValue());
            resetUI();
        });
        processTask.setOnFailed(t -> {
            // t.getSource().getException() could be null
            logger.log(Level.WARNING, "Update task failed {0}",
                    t.getSource().getException() != null
                    ? t.getSource().getException()
                    : "Unknown failure");
            resetUI();
        });
        processTask.setOnCancelled(t -> {
            logger.log(Level.FINE, "Process All task cancelled.");
            resetUI();
        });
        // start the task in a background thread
        new Thread(processTask).start();
    }

    // reset the UI
    private void resetUI() {
        FadeTransition ft = new FadeTransition(Duration.millis(1500),
                        nameDisplay);
        ft.setToValue(0);
        ft.setDelay(Duration.millis(2000));
        ft.setOnFinished(a -> {
            processAllButton.setDisable(false);
        });
        ft.play();
        progressBar.progressProperty().unbind();
        progressBar.setProgress(0);
    }
```

## Updating the JavaFX Scene Graph from a Background Task

The previous example updates a read-only property in the background task. You can also safely update the JavaFX scene graph from a background task as long as you wrap any update code in a Runnable and invoke `Platform.runLater()`. Application **PersonFXMLAppFXWorker3** is an example of a background task that creates scene graph content within a background task. Figure 4.18 shows this application running. As each Person is processed, its name is added to the scene graph as a Text control with a Drop Shadow effect, and it fades in using a FadeTransition. When the background task completes, the list of names (Text controls) fades out and the Process All button is re-enabled.

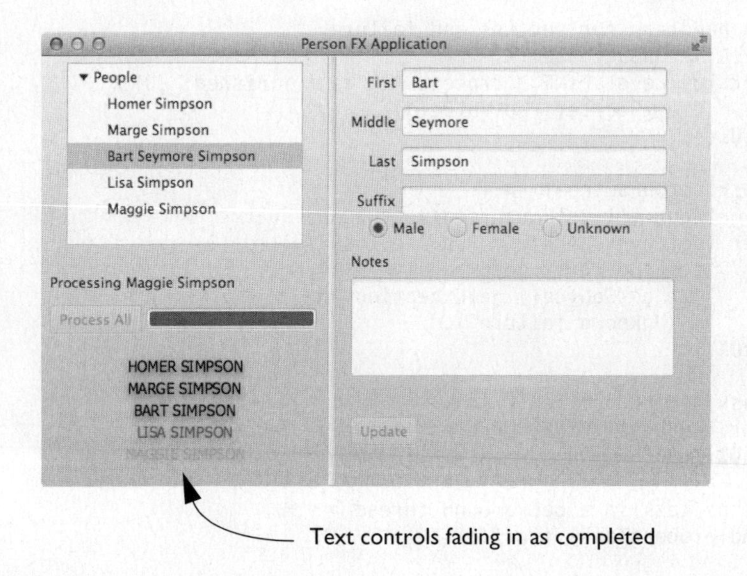


Figure 4.18 Program PersonFXMLAppFXWorker3: Running a background task with partial results displayed in UI

To build the UI for this background task, we add a Label, Button, Progress Bar, and TilePane layout to the scene graph, as shown in Listing 4.38. You've seen these same controls previously, except we now use a TilePane layout control to display the Text shapes that hold each name. The TilePane includes a drop shadow effect.

**Listing 4.38 FXML Controls for Background Task UI**

```
<HBox id="HBox" alignment="CENTER" layoutX="7.0" layoutY="226.0" spacing="5.0">
   <children>
      <Button fx:id="processAllButton" mnemonicParsing="false"
            onAction="#processAllButtonAction" text="Process All" />
      <ProgressBar fx:id="progressBar" prefWidth="161.0" progress="0.0" />
   </children>
</HBox>
<Label fx:id="statusMessage" layoutX="7.0" layoutY="197.0" />
<TilePane fx:id="nameDisplay" alignment="TOP_CENTER" hgap="50.0" layoutX="7.0"
      layoutY="268.0" prefHeight="109.0" prefWidth="257.0" vgap="3.0">
   <effect>
      <DropShadow color="#666666" offsetY="3.0" />
   </effect>
   <padding>
      <Insets top="5.0" />
   </padding>
</TilePane>
```

Listing 4.39 shows class ProcessAllTask. Note that in this example we specify `<Void>` for the generic type, since the Task does not return anything. As before, we pass in the Person list with the constructor.

The `call()` method sets a loop to process each person. It updates the message and invokes helper method `makeText()` to create and configure the Text. It builds a FadeTransition and sets the fade transition's "to" value to 1 (making the animation fade in the Text node). All the configuration code occurs on the background thread. Not until we add content to the scene graph must we invoke `Platform.runLater()`, as shown in Listing 4.39.

**Listing 4.39 Class ProcessAllTask**

```
private class ProcessAllTask extends Task<Void> {

    private final ObservableList<Person> processList;

    public ProcessAllTask(final ObservableList<Person> processList) {
        this.processList = processList;
    }

    @Override
    protected Void call() throws Exception {
        logger.log(Level.FINE, "Begin processing");

        final int taskMaxCount = processList.size();
        logger.log(Level.FINE, "processing list: {0}", processList);
        int taskProgress = 0;
        for (final Person person : processList) {
            if (isCancelled()) {
                break;
            }
            // do something to each person
            updateMessage("Processing " + person);
            logger.log(Level.FINE, "processing: {0}", person);
            doProcess(person);
            final Text t = makeText(person);
            FadeTransition ft = new FadeTransition(
                                Duration.millis(1500), t);
            ft.setToValue(1);
            // Update scene graph on JavaFX Application Thread
            Platform.runLater(() -> {
                nameDisplay.getChildren().add(t);
                ft.play();
            });
            updateProgress(100 * (++taskProgress) / taskMaxCount, 100);
            Thread.sleep(500);
        }
        return null; // because of <Void>
    }
```

```
    // Called on the background thread
    private void doProcess(Person p) {
        p.setFirstname(p.getFirstname().toUpperCase());
        p.setMiddlename(p.getMiddlename().toUpperCase());
        p.setLastname(p.getLastname().toUpperCase());
        p.setSuffix(p.getSuffix().toUpperCase());
    }

    private Text makeText(Person p) {
        final Text t = new Text(p.toString());
        t.setFill(Color.NAVY);
        t.setFont(Font.font("Tahoma", FontWeight.THIN, 14));
        t.setOpacity(0);
        return t;
    }
}
```

Listing 4.40 shows the code to handle the Process All Button event handler. As before, we instantiate ProcessAllTask with the list of Person objects and bind the Task progress and text properties to UI controls. The completion callback methods reset the UI. This time when we reset the UI, we fade out the TilePane control. When the fade finishes, we clear the TilePane control, enable the Process All Button, and return the (now empty) TilePane to opaque.

**Listing 4.40 Process All Button**

```
@FXML
private void processAllButtonAction(ActionEvent event) {
    logger.log(Level.FINE, "Process All Button");
    // only one task to run at a time so disable the button
    processAllButton.setDisable(true);
    // create the task with a list
    final ProcessAllTask processTask = new ProcessAllTask(
            FXCollections.observableArrayList(ftm.getAllPeople()));
    // configure the UI
    progressBar.progressProperty().bind(processTask.progressProperty());
    statusMessage.textProperty().bind(processTask.messageProperty());

    // set up handlers for success and failure
    processTask.setOnSucceeded(t -> {
        logger.log(Level.FINE, "Process All task finished: {0}",
                t.getSource().getValue());
        resetUI();
    });
```

```
        processTask.setOnFailed(t -> {
            // t.getSource().getException() could be null
            logger.log(Level.WARNING, "Update task failed {0}",
                    t.getSource().getException() != null
                    ? t.getSource().getException()
                    : "Unknown failure");
            resetUI();
        });
        processTask.setOnCancelled(t -> {
            logger.log(Level.FINE, "Process All task cancelled.");
            resetUI();
        });
        // start the task in a background thread
        new Thread(processTask).start();
    }

    // reset the UI
    private void resetUI() {
        FadeTransition ft = new FadeTransition(
                        Duration.millis(1500), nameDisplay);
        ft.setToValue(0);
        ft.setDelay(Duration.millis(2000));
        ft.setOnFinished(a -> {
            nameDisplay.getChildren().clear();
            processAllButton.setDisable(false);
            nameDisplay.setOpacity(1);
        });
        ft.play();
        progressBar.progressProperty().unbind();
        progressBar.setProgress(0);
        statusMessage.textProperty().unbind();
        statusMessage.setText("");
    }
```

## 4.8 Key Point Summary

This chapter explores ways to use JavaFX in desktop applications, where users are presented with model data and make changes to the data. We address creating model classes with JavaFX properties and using observable collections. We show typical JavaFX controls to build a UI, such as TreeView, TextField, RadioButton, Label, TextArea, and Button. We create listeners to respond to changes and use binding expressions to keep model data synchronized with UI controls. Finally, we show how to create background tasks with JavaFX, paying attention to thread safety and updating the scene graph only on the JavaFX Application Thread.

Here are the key points in this chapter.

- JavaFX provides implementations for the abstract JavaFX property classes that wrap the type's value. For example, SimpleStringProperty implements StringProperty and wraps a String value, SimpleIntegerProperty implements IntegerProperty and wraps Integer, and so forth.
- Use SimpleObjectProperty<T> to provide an implementation of a JavaFX property that wraps an Object of type T. We use SimpleObjectProperty<Person.Gender> to create a JavaFX property that wraps a Person.Gender enum value.
- Consider implementing JavaFX properties with lazy evaluation. This strategy prevents instantiation of the JavaFX property until a listener is attached or binding is applied.
- Immutable values don't require JavaFX property implementations.
- JavaFX computed properties use binding expressions to keep the computed value in sync with the properties upon which it depends.
- JavaFX provides read-only property wrappers to implement JavaFX read-only properties. When you use a wrapper class, two synchronized properties are created. One is exposed and read only. The other can be modified and is encapsulated in the model class.
- When you create a read-only JavaFX property, expose public methods for the read-only property and the getter, but not the setter.
- When model classes have JavaFX properties, use binding to keep the model and UI synchronized.
- JavaFX provides observable collections. Class FXCollections includes static methods that return observable versions of the same collection types available with `java.util.Collections`.
- Observable collections let you respond to changes by attaching change and invalidation listeners to the collection. InvalidationListener is type neutral, and the ChangeListener type depends on the underlying collection type.
- We use ObservableMap<Long, Person> in the FamilyTreeManager to maintain the collection of Person items.
- MapChangeListener lets you respond to changes in an observable map. You can determine if the change was an addition, update, or removal, and you can access the old and new values.
- Scene Builder is a stand-alone application that generates FXML. You place controls on the design area using drag and drop and configure controls with context menus and property sheets.

- JavaFX controls generate one or more events, which you can listen for and respond to with event handlers.
- You can attach a ChangeListener to the selection property of a TreeView model to listen for selection changes.
- Use bidirectional binding to keep the UI and model objects synchronized.
- JavaFX is a single-threaded UI. Put long-running tasks in a background thread to keep the UI responsive.
- JavaFX Tasks let you execute long-running code in a background thread and safely update the UI. Background tasks include status properties that you can safely bind to with UI control variables.
- In general, you should not update observable values in a background thread.
- To publish partial results with a background task, use thread safe Task method `updateValue()` or wrap any updates to public properties or the scene graph in a Runnable and execute with `Platform.runLater()`.

# 5

# A Taste of Modularity

With the background basics of Swing covered, it's time to explore the NetBeans Platform application architecture. In this chapter, you'll learn how to build a modular application that uses the NetBeans Platform Window System and leverages NetBeans Platform techniques to keep modules loosely coupled.

### What You Will Learn

- Understand the NetBeans module system.
- Create a NetBeans Platform application and add modules to it.
- Port a Swing application to the NetBeans Platform.
- Create windows for a NetBeans Platform application.
- Use Lookup to discover service providers.
- Use Lookup to share objects between modules.

## 5.1 Modular Architecture

Even though the applications in Chapter 2 are basic, they follow a loosely-coupled design. That is, a user event that changes model data generates a property change event and lets interested subscribers respond. Similarly, when a user selects a different Person to edit, a selection listener lets subscribers know the user selected a new object. These mechanisms keep event-processing code isolated from property change and selection events. However, the applications we presented in Chapter 2 are themselves monolithic, and we encapsulate functionality using Java class visibility. As you add more features to applications like these, it becomes difficult to isolate the different parts of the application, and the dependencies become more entangled.

Not only does the NetBeans Platform provide a wide range of features (window system, action framework, menu bar and toolbar, and so forth), but the NetBeans Platform also provides an architectural framework for your application. That is, the NetBeans Platform provides an execution environment that supports a module system called the *Runtime Container.* The Runtime Container consists of the minimum modules required to load and execute your application.

## Modules

Modules are the basic building blocks of the NetBeans Platform. A module is a collection of functionally related classes stored in a JAR file along with metadata. The metadata provides information to the Runtime Container about the module, such as the module's name, version information, dependencies, and a list of its public packages, if any.

The NetBeans Platform Runtime Container enforces the encapsulation of modules. This keeps applications loosely coupled and avoids accidental dependencies. Specifically, in order to use or access code in another module (say, Module B accesses classes in Module A), two conditions must be met, as shown in Figure 5.1.

1. You must put Module A classes in a public package and assign a version number.
2. Module B must declare a dependency on a specified version of Module A.

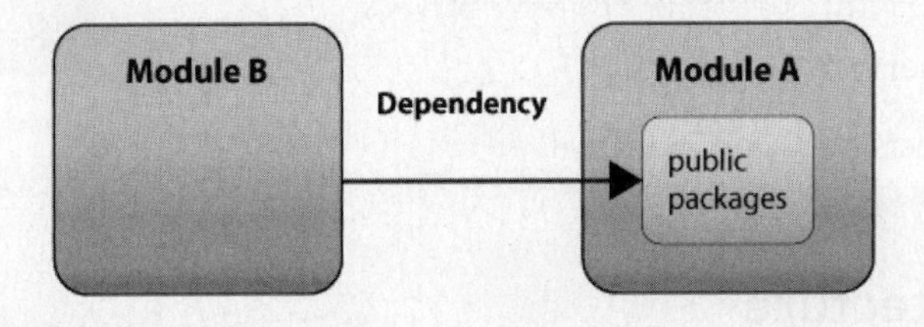


Figure 5.1 Setting a dependency on Module A

This arrangement keeps dependencies between modules deliberate, documented, and enforced by the Runtime Container.

### NetBeans Runtime Container

The NetBeans Runtime Container consists of the following six modules, as shown in Figure 5.2.

- Bootstrap—executes initially and loads and executes the Startup module.
- Startup—contains the Main method of the application and initializes the module system and the virtual file system.
- Module System API—manages modules, enforces module visibility and dependencies, and provides access to module life cycle methods.
- Utilities API—provides general utility classes.
- File System API—provides a virtual file system for your application.
- Lookup API—provides a mechanism for finding and loading classes that is loosely coupled and allows modules to communicate with each other.

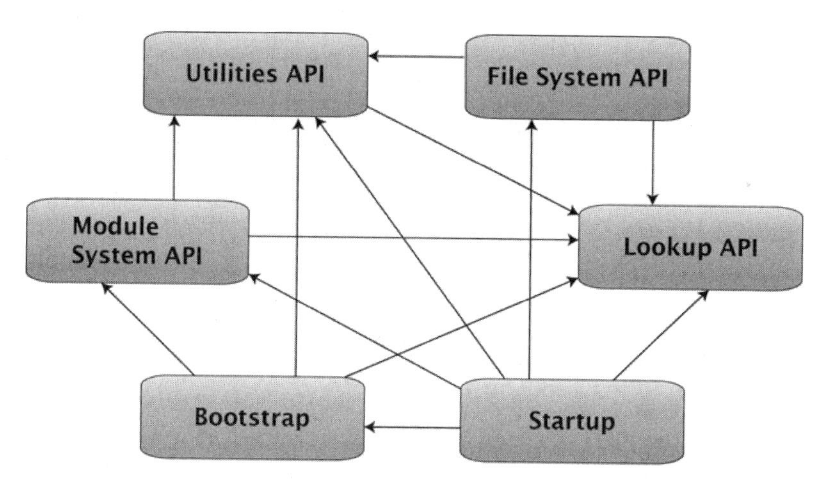


Figure 5.2 NetBeans Platform Runtime Container

Note that a NetBeans Platform application can run with just these modules, but your application will lack a GUI and many other useful features.

To show you the NetBeans Platform architecture, including its module system and communication mechanism, let's port the Swing application presented in Chapter 2, PersonSwingAppEnhancedUI (see "Improving the User Experience" on page 63). The application's basic functionality will remain unchanged, but the end result is a modular application with very specific dependencies. Furthermore, due to its modular structure, you'll see how to add features (in later chapters) without the fear of breaking code. And with the NetBeans Platform, we automatically get a fully functional window system, menu bar, and toolbar.

Figure 5.3 shows our complete NetBeans Platform application running (FamilyTreeApp). While this application is very similar to the Swing version, there are key differences.

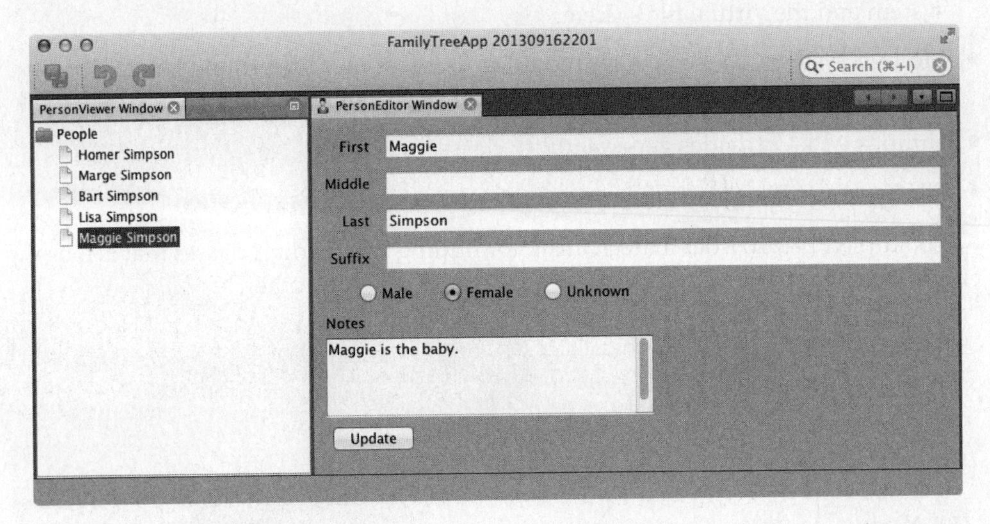


Figure 5.3 FamilyTreeApp running

- The application has a toolbar and menu bar (the menu bar uses the native operating system's menu bar, so it does not appear in the screen shot).
- The PersonViewer window (on the left) and the PersonEditor window (on the right) are both independently detachable and resizable windows.
- The application is divided into modules.
- The FamilyTreeManager is now a service, and the class that implements this service is in its own module.
- Each of the windows is implemented by separate modules.
- When you select a Person in the PersonViewer window, the selected Person is displayed in the PersonEditor window. This communication requires no dependency between the two windows, only a mutual dependency on the NetBeans Lookup module.

- The Person and FamilyTreeManager classes are in the same module (FamilyTree-Model). This package is public so that other modules can declare a dependency on it.

We'll show you exactly how to build this application and along the way, we'll describe two very important features of the NetBeans Platform: Modules and Lookup.

## 5.2 Creating a NetBeans Platform Application

A NetBeans Platform application project consists of a top-level structure containing one or more modules. When you use the New Project wizard to create a NetBeans Platform application, your application includes the Runtime Container. This application also contains additional modules needed to support the window system, actions, menu, and other features.

Follow these steps to create your NetBeans Platform application project with the NetBeans IDE.

1. From the NetBeans IDE top-level menu bar, select **File | New Project**. The NetBeans New Project wizard pops up the Choose Project dialog.
2. Under Categories select **NetBeans Modules** and under Projects select **NetBeans Platform Application**, as shown in Figure 5.4. Select **Next**. This is how you create a top-level NetBeans Platform Application to which you can then add your own modules.

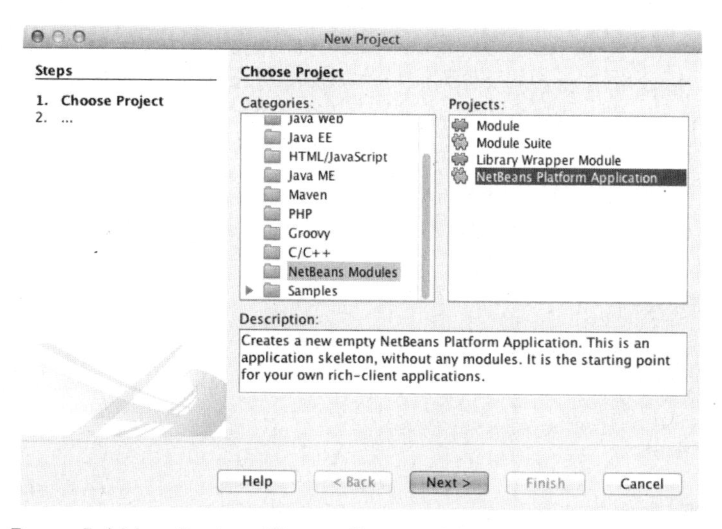


Figure 5.4 New Project Choose Project dialog

3. NetBeans now displays the Name and Location dialog. Provide the Project Name **FamilyTreeApp** and click **Browse** to select a Project Location directory. Accept the defaults for the remaining fields and click **Finish**, as shown in Figure 5.5.

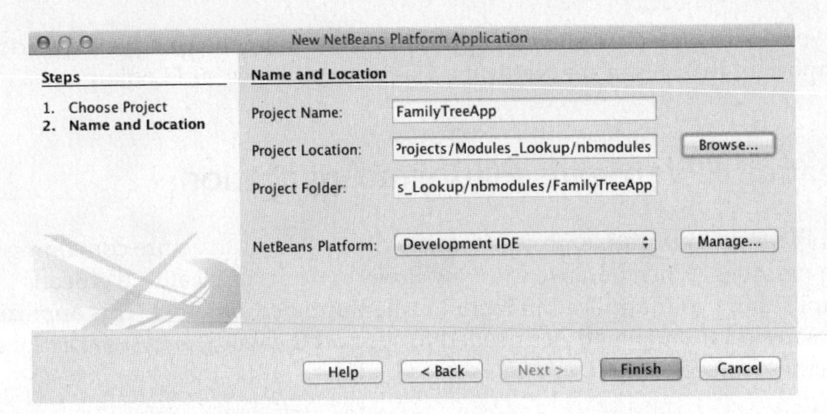


Figure 5.5 New Project Name and Location dialog

NetBeans creates your NetBeans Platform application project with the modules necessary to include a menu bar, toolbar, and empty window system. Let's examine the project structure and a few of the artifacts before we add functionality to this program.

## NetBeans Platform Project

Figure 5.6 shows project FamilyTreeApp in the Projects view. It has no user-created modules (the Modules node is empty). The metadata associated with the application appears under the Important Files node. These files include a Build Script (file build.xml), the Project Properties (file project.properties), NetBeans Platform Config (file platform.properties), and Per-user NetBeans Platform Config (file platform-private.properties).

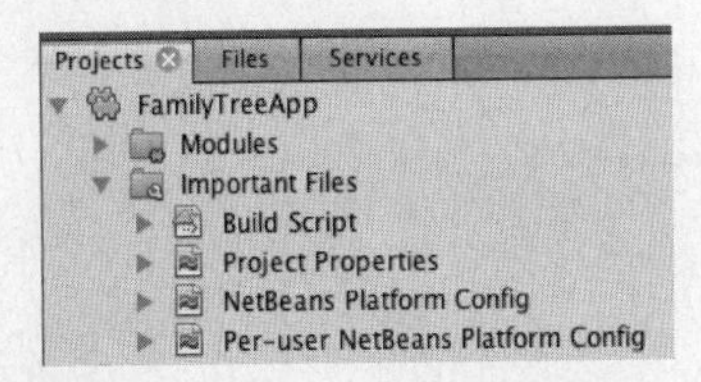


Figure 5.6 FamilyTreeApp Projects view

- An Ant build script is automatically generated for your project in file nbproject/build-impl.xml. You can customize this script by editing the Build Script (file build.xml) under Important Files.
- File Project Properties (file project.properties) describes the modules in your NetBeans Platform application as well as your application's name. Listing 5.1 shows this file before you create any new modules for your application.

**Listing 5.1 Project Properties (project.properties)**

```
app.name=${branding.token}
app.title=FamilyTreeApp
modules=
```

- Listing 5.2 shows the NetBeans Platform Config file (file platform.properties), which describes the collection of modules (a *cluster*) that is automatically included in your application. The standard cluster for NetBeans Platform applications is called **platform**.

  This configuration also includes property `branding.token` (used in the Project Properties file) and the list of disabled modules from the platform cluster. Since these modules are not frequently used, they are disabled to minimize your application's footprint.

**Listing 5.2 NetBeans Platform Config (platform.properties)**

```
branding.token=FamilyTreeApp
cluster.path=\
    ${nbplatform.active.dir}/platform
disabled.modules=\
    org.jdesktop.layout,\
    org.netbeans.api.visual,\
    org.netbeans.core.execution,\
    org.netbeans.libs.jsr223,\
    org.netbeans.modules.autoupdate.cli,\
    org.netbeans.modules.autoupdate.services,\
    org.netbeans.modules.autoupdate.ui,\
    org.netbeans.modules.core.kit,\
    org.netbeans.modules.favorites,\
    org.netbeans.modules.templates,\
    org.openide.compat,\
    org.openide.execution,\
    org.openide.options,\
    org.openide.util.enumerations
nbplatform.active=default
```

The project's Properties dialog lets you examine and change a project's settings. Let's look at the Properties dialog now.

To examine your application's various properties, select the application's project node in the Projects window, right click, and select **Properties** from the context menu. NetBeans displays a Project Properties dialog. Under Categories select **Libraries**. NetBeans displays the Libraries dialog, as shown in Figure 5.7.

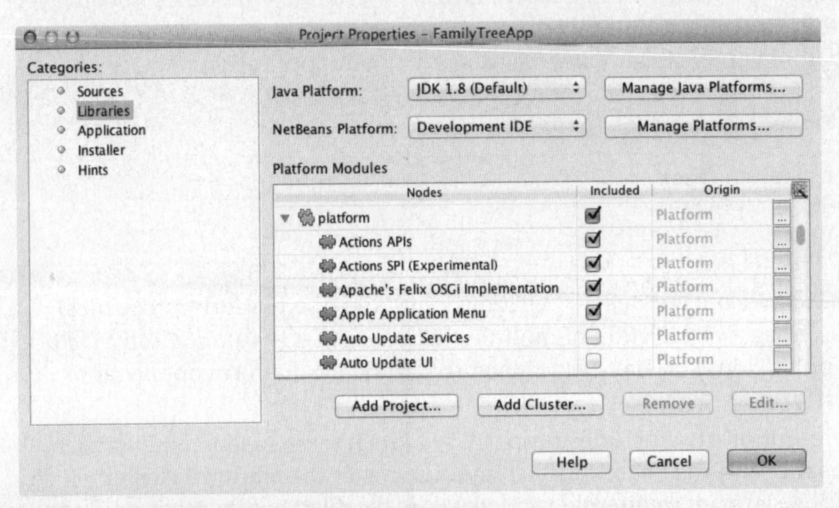


Figure 5.7 FamilyTreeApp Project Properties

The list of clusters available appears under heading Nodes. You see all clusters are excluded except cluster **platform**. If you expand the platform cluster, you'll see the modules included in this cluster. As you scroll down, module names appear that are included in your application, as well as additional available modules that are excluded. These excluded modules are the ones listed in the NetBeans Platform Config file (Listing 5.2).

You can also add additional projects or clusters to your application using the Add Project or Add Cluster buttons. Dismiss this dialog now by clicking **OK**.

- The Per-user NetBeans Platform Config file (platform-private.properties) lets you configure build properties that apply only to the local machine or to a specific user. This file is not typically checked into a source repository.

Although you have not yet added any modules of your own, your project contains NetBeans Platform modules that let you run this (not very interesting) application. Select the project in the Projects view and click the green chevron on the toolbar to run FamilyTreeApp. Figure 5.8 shows the application running. Note that the application includes a top-level menu bar, a toolbar, an application title, a search window, a main window area that is empty, and a status line. All of the icons in the toolbar are disabled (Save All, Undo, and Redo), but the menu bar includes many active menu items.

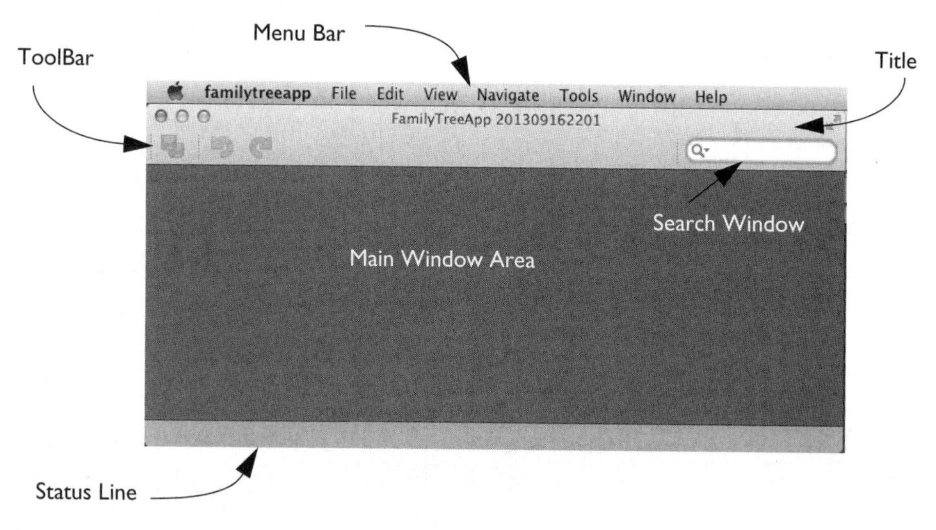


Figure 5.8 A bare-bones FamilyTreeApp running

The top-level menu bar has several useful features that you can select. Menu item View configures additional icons in the toolbar, such as the clipboard icons (copy, cut, and paste) and lets you view the IDE output log. Menu item Window opens and closes a Property Window or an Output Window. Most selections under menu item File are disabled except for Page Setup. Many artifacts come pre-configured, and with minimal effort on your part, you can incorporate these items in your application. We will show you how to do this in upcoming chapters.

Figure 5.9 shows the same application running with additional configurations, all performed with the menu bar. Here, we enabled a web browser to display the Anderson Software Group home page (**Window | Web | Web Browser**), configured the clipboard icons (**View | Toolbars | Clipboard**), enabled the IDE Output window (**View | IDE Log**), and opened a Properties window (**Window | IDE Tools | Properties**).

If you performed any of the above configurations, you can return to the default configurations as follows. First, exit the application. Next, right click on project **FamilyTreeApp** and select **Clean** from the context menu. The next time you run the application, the NetBeans Platform will use the default settings.

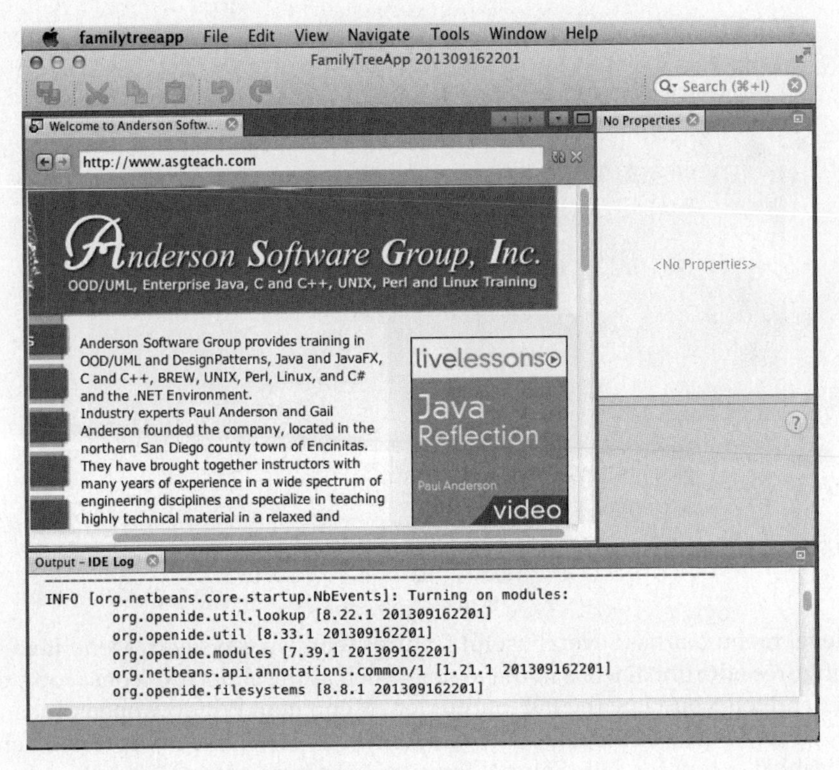


Figure 5.9 FamilyTreeApp with additional windows and toolbar icons configured

## 5.3 Creating Modules

With the bare bones structure of a NetBeans Platform Application created, it's time to add modules and functionality to the FamilyTreeApp application. To do this, we'll add four modules, as follows.

- Module FamilyTreeModel—This module contains class Person.java (our model), and a FamilyTreeManager interface. This interface includes all of the Family-TreeManager public methods from the Swing version of our application declared as abstract methods.
- Module FamilyTreeManagerImpl—This module contains the implementation of the FamilyTreeManager interface and registers itself as a service provider for the application.

- Module PersonViewer—This module includes a NetBeans Platform TopComponent (window) to display the Person objects from the FamilyTreeManager in a window. We discuss TopComponents in detail in Chapter 8.
- Module PersonEditor—This module also includes a NetBeans Platform TopComponent. Here, we display detailed information about the selected Person in a window that the user can edit and save to the FamilyTreeManager.

Figure 5.10 shows these four modules and the dependencies they form together in application FamilyTreeApp.

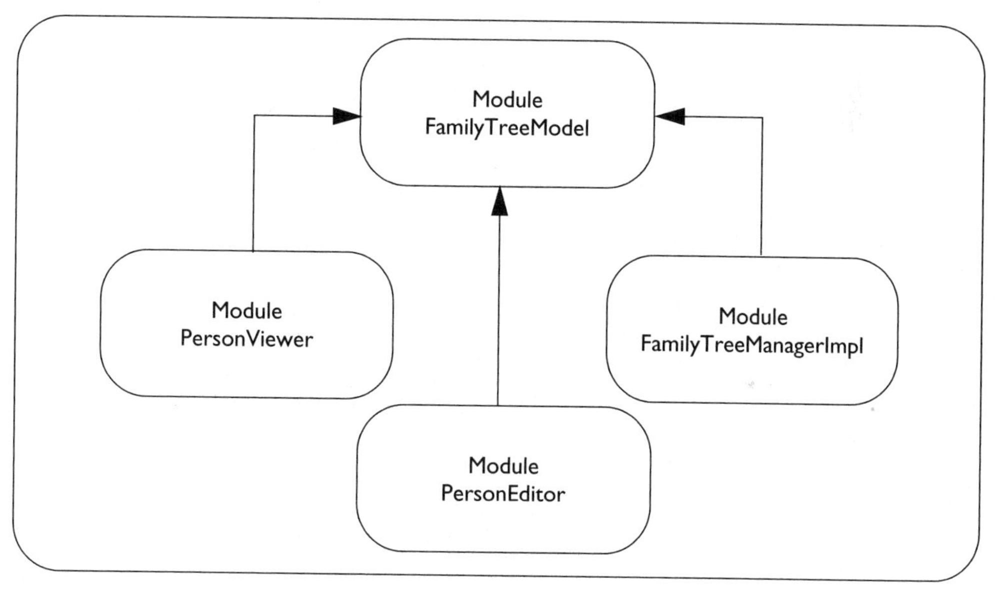


Figure 5.10 Added modules and their dependencies

## Creating a NetBeans Module

To create a module for a NetBeans Platform application, follow these steps. Here we create module **FamilyTreeModel**.

1. Right click on the **Modules** node in project FamilyTreeApp and choose **Add New...** as shown in Figure 5.11. NetBeans begins the New Module Project wizard.

Figure 5.11 Add a new module to FamilyTreeApp application

2. NetBeans displays the Name and Location dialog. Specify **FamilyTreeModel** for the Project Name. Accept the defaults for Project Location and Project Folder and click **Next**, as shown in Figure 5.12.

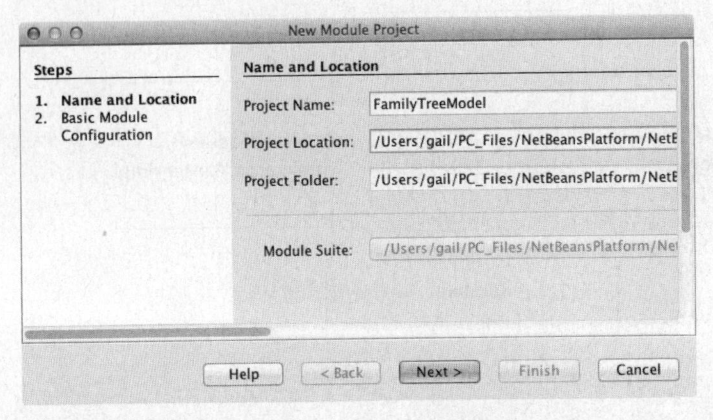


Figure 5.12 New module Name and Location dialog

3. NetBeans displays the Basic Module Configuration dialog. Specify **com.asgteach.familytree.model** for the Code Name Base. Accept the defaults for the Module Display Name (FamilyTreeModel) and Localizing Bundle (com/asgteach/familytree/model/Bundle.properties) and leave Generate OSGi Bundle unchecked, as shown in Figure 5.13. Click **Finish**.

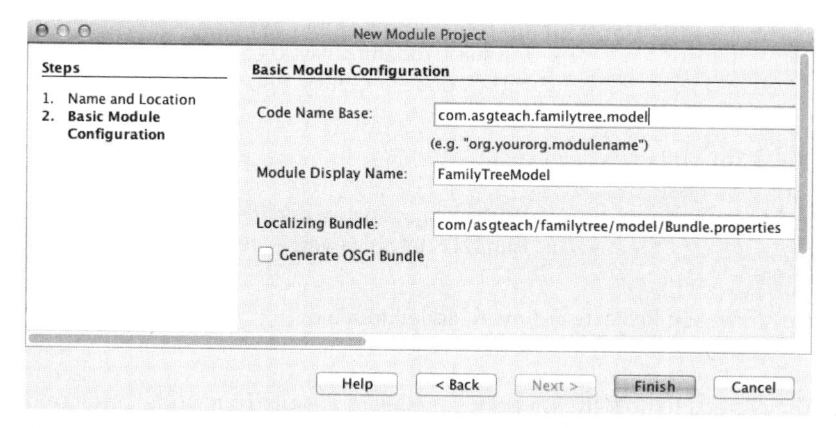


Figure 5.13 New module Basic Module Configuration dialog

### Creating Additional Modules

The FamilyTreeApp application now contains one user-added module called FamilyTreeModel. Before we add code to this module, repeat the above steps and add three more modules: FamilyTreeManagerImpl, PersonViewer, and PersonEditor, as follows.

1. New Module **FamilyTreeManagerImpl**, code name base **com.asgteach.familytree.manager.impl**, and display name **FamilyTreeManagerImpl**.
2. New Module **PersonViewer**, code name base **com.asgteach.familytree.personviewer**, and display name **PersonViewer**.
3. New Module **PersonEditor**, code name base **com.asgteach.familytree.personeditor**, and display name **PersonEditor**.

Figure 5.14 shows the Projects view for application FamilyTreeApp. When you expand the Modules node, you see the four newly-added modules. You also see new projects for each module. Note that when you work with these module projects, you select the project name outside the FamilyTreeApp project, not the module name under the Modules node, as indicated in Figure 5.14.

## 5.4 Configuring a Module with Public Packages

The FamilyTreeModel module contains the model for our application. This includes class Person.java and interface FamilyTreeManager. As shown previously (see Figure 5.10 on page 209), this module will be used by the other modules in our appli-

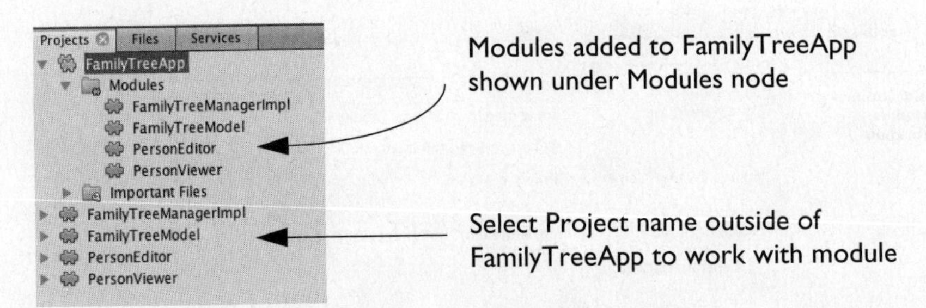


Figure 5.14 FamilyTreeApp Projects view with added modules

cation. Follow these steps to add the Java source files to FamilyTreeModel and configure them so that these classes can be accessed by other modules.

1. Select project **FamilyTreeModel** in the Projects view (be sure to select the project name, not the module name under Modules).
2. Expand the project name and **Source Packages** node. You will see package name **com.asgteach.familytree.model**.
3. As a starting point, use the code from project PersonSwingAppEnhancedUI and copy both Person.java and FamilyTreeManager.java to package **com.asgteach.familytree.model**. Class Person.java is unchanged. (Listing 2.5 on page 30 shows the version of Person.java used in project PersonSwingAppEnhancedUI.)
4. Modify class FamilyTreeManager so that it is an interface and all methods are abstract. Do not include static method `getInstance()` or the constructor. (You'll see soon why we don't need these anymore.) Remove all class variables except the property names (static final Strings). Listing 5.3 shows the new FamilyTreeManager interface.

**Listing 5.3 Interface FamilyTreeManager**

```
package com.asgteach.familytree.model;

import java.beans.PropertyChangeListener;
import java.util.List;

public interface FamilyTreeManager {

    // FamilyTreeManager property change names
    public static final String PROP_PERSON_DESTROYED = "removePerson";
    public static final String PROP_PERSON_ADDED = "addPerson";
    public static final String PROP_PERSON_UPDATED = "updatePerson";

    public void addPropertyChangeListener(PropertyChangeListener listener);

    public void removePropertyChangeListener(PropertyChangeListener listener);
```

```
    public void addPerson(Person p);

    public void updatePerson(Person p);

    public void deletePerson(Person p);

    public List<Person> getAllPeople();
}
```

---

Module FamilyTreeModel now has code for Person and the FamilyTreeManager interface, but we want other modules to reference these classes. Therefore, we must declare the package **com.asgteach.familytree.model** in this module as public, as illustrated in Figure 5.1 on page 200 (FamilyTreeModel is "Module A"). Let's do this now.

1. In the Projects view, select project **FamilyTreeModel**, right click, and select **Properties** from the context menu.
2. Under Categories, select **API Versioning**.
3. In the panel, click the checkbox to specify that package com.asgteach.familytree.model is **Public**, as shown in Figure 5.15. Accept the default for Specification Version 1.0. Click **OK**.

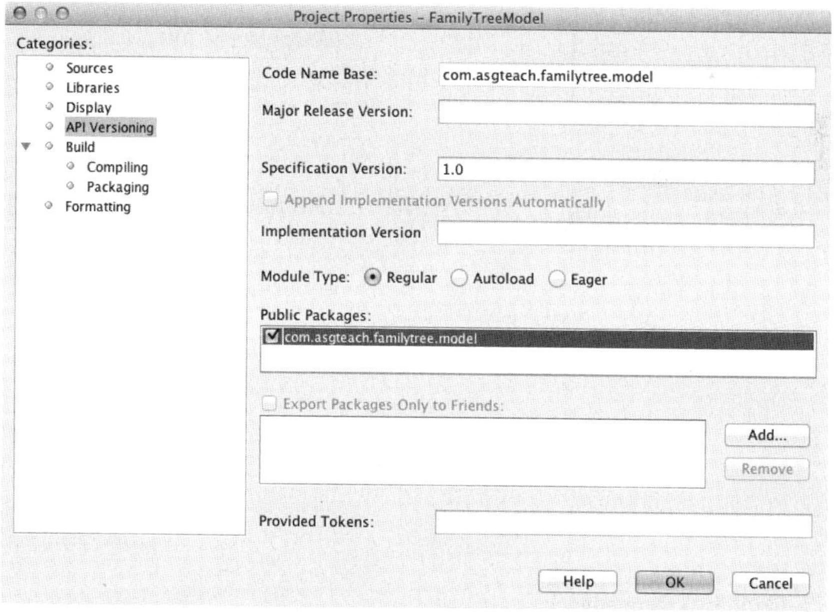

Project Properties - FamilyTreeModel

Categories:
- Sources
- Libraries
- Display
- API Versioning
- Build
  - Compiling
  - Packaging
- Formatting

Code Name Base: com.asgteach.familytree.model
Major Release Version:
Specification Version: 1.0
Append Implementation Versions Automatically
Implementation Version
Module Type: Regular Autoload Eager
Public Packages:
com.asgteach.familytree.model
Export Packages Only to Friends:
Add...
Remove
Provided Tokens:
Help OK Cancel

Figure 5.15 API Versioning: Specify Public Packages

Note that this is the first of two required steps in the NetBeans Platform for one module to access a class in another module. We'll show you the second step next.

## 5.5 Registering a Service Provider

The FamilyTreeManagerImpl module contains the code that implements interface FamilyTreeManager. Furthermore, it registers itself as a Service Provider for service FamilyTreeManager. The NetBeans Platform Lookup module makes services available in an application's Global Lookup, which means other modules can "look up" Services based on a class type. You register a service provider with annotation @ServiceProvider.

Because the FamilyTreeManagerImpl module provides an implementation for interface FamilyTreeManager and FamilyTreeManager is in a separate module, you must declare a dependency on module FamilyTreeModel to access classes Person and FamilyTreeManager. This is the second step required in creating module dependencies. Furthermore, in order to register the FamilyTreeManager implementation as a service, you must also declare a dependency on the Lookup API module. Follow these steps to declare module dependencies.

1. In project FamilyTreeManagerImpl, right click the **Libraries** node and select **Add Module Dependency . . .** as shown in Figure 5.16. NetBeans displays the Add Module Dependency dialog.

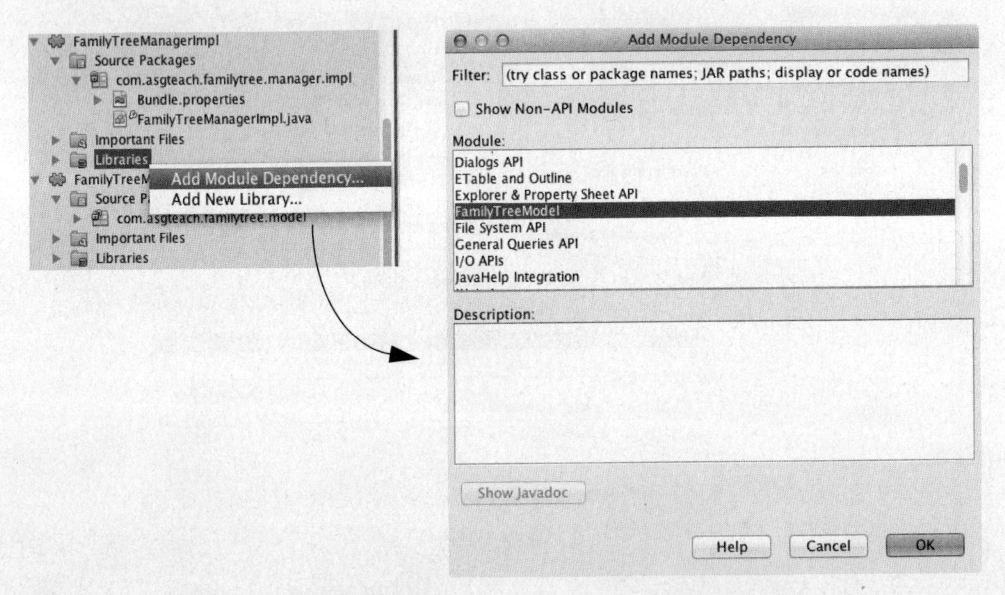


Figure 5.16 Add Module Dependency

2. In the list of modules, select both **FamilyTreeModel** and **Lookup API**. Click **OK**. NetBeans adds both FamilyTreeModel and Lookup API to FamilyTreeManager-

Impl's list of dependencies. When you expand the Libraries node, you'll see these modules listed, as shown in Figure 5.17.

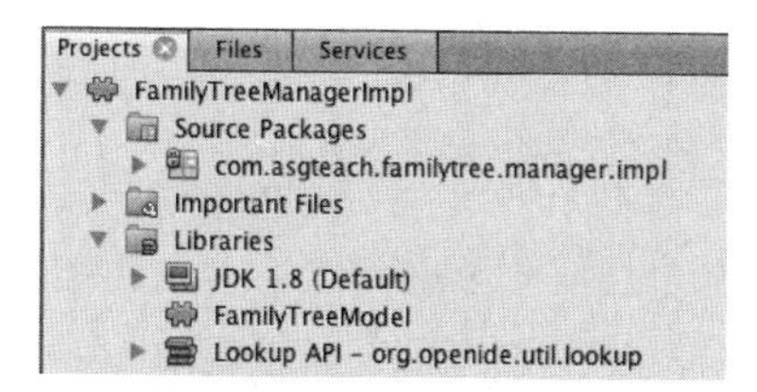


Figure 5.17 After adding module dependencies

When you add a module dependency, NetBeans updates the module's metadata so that the Runtime Container can enforce the declared dependencies. You can view a module's metadata as follows. Expand the **Important Files** node and double click **Project Metadata** (file project.xml). Listing 5.4 shows the project metadata for the FamilyTreeManagerImpl module after adding the module dependencies for the FamilyTreeModel and Lookup API modules. Note that a runtime dependency exists for specification version 1.0 for FamilyTreeModel and specification version 8.22.1 for Lookup API (your Lookup API specification version number may be different).

**Listing 5.4 Project Metadata for Module FamilyTreeManagerImpl**

```
<?xml version="1.0" encoding="UTF-8"?>
<project xmlns="http://www.netbeans.org/ns/project/1">
    <type>org.netbeans.modules.apisupport.project</type>
    <configuration>
        <data xmlns="http://www.netbeans.org/ns/nb-module-project/3">
            <code-name-base>com.asgteach.familytree.manager.impl
                                    </code-name-base>
            <suite-component/>
            <module-dependencies>
                <dependency>
                    <code-name-base>com.asgteach.familytree.model
                                    </code-name-base>
                    <build-prerequisite/>
                    <compile-dependency/>
                    <run-dependency>
                        <specification-version>1.0</specification-version>
                    </run-dependency>
                </dependency>
                <dependency>
                    <code-name-base>org.openide.util.lookup</code-name-base>
                    <build-prerequisite/>
                    <compile-dependency/>
```

```
                    <run-dependency>
                        <specification-version>8.22.1</specification-version>
                    </run-dependency>
                </dependency>
            </module-dependencies>
            <public-packages/>
        </data>
    </configuration>
</project>
```

Now add the implementation class for interface FamilyTreeManager to the FamilyTreeManagerImpl module. The NetBeans IDE helps out quite a bit with this.

1. In project FamilyTreeManagerImpl, expand the **Source Packages** node.
2. Select package **com.asgteach.familytree.manager.impl**, right click, and select **New** then **Java Class** from the context menus.
3. In the New Java Class dialog, provide **FamilyTreeManagerImpl** for Class Name and click **Finish**. You'll now see file FamilyTreeManagerImpl.java under the selected package name and the file opens in the Java editor.
4. Edit the Java class so that it implements FamilyTreeManager. Fix imports (right click and select **Fix Imports** from the context menu).
5. Let NetBeans generate override method stubs for all of the abstract methods in interface FamilyTreeManager. (Click the icon in the left margin and select **Implement all abstract methods** from the displayed menu as shown in Figure 5.18.)

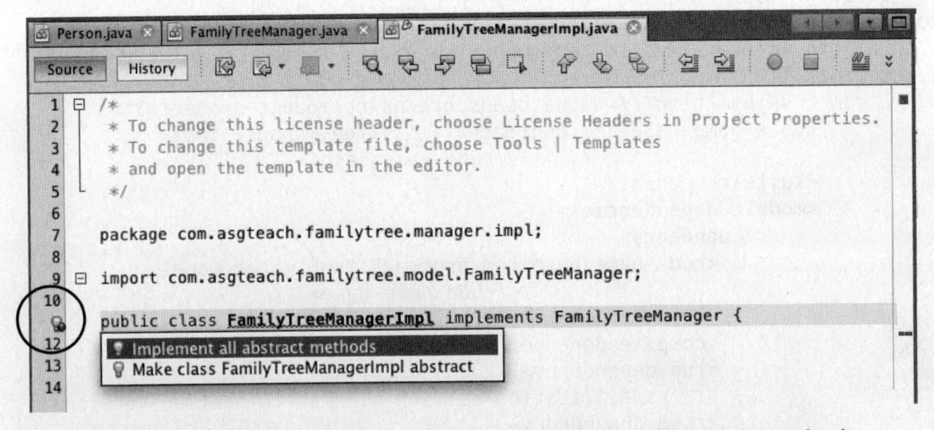


Figure 5.18 Tell NetBeans to generate implementations for all abstract methods

6. Copy the method bodies as well as any class variables and private methods from the FamilyTreeManager class in project PersonSwingAppEnhancedUI.

7. Add private method `getPropertyChangeSupport()` and invoke this method in all the methods that require accessing class variable `propChangeSupport`, as shown in Listing 5.5.
8. Add annotation @ServiceProvider to class FamilyTreeManagerImpl. Listing 5.5 shows the entire class.

### Listing 5.5 Class FamilyTreeManagerImpl.java

```
package com.asgteach.familytree.manager.impl;

import com.asgteach.familytree.model.FamilyTreeManager;
import com.asgteach.familytree.model.Person;
import java.beans.PropertyChangeListener;
import java.beans.PropertyChangeSupport;
import java.util.ArrayList;
import java.util.HashMap;
import java.util.List;
import java.util.Map;
import org.openide.util.lookup.ServiceProvider;

@ServiceProvider(service = FamilyTreeManager.class)
public class FamilyTreeManagerImpl implements FamilyTreeManager {
    private final Map<Long, Person> personMap = new HashMap<>();
    private PropertyChangeSupport propChangeSupport = null;

    private PropertyChangeSupport getPropertyChangeSupport() {
        if (this.propChangeSupport == null) {
            this.propChangeSupport = new PropertyChangeSupport(this);
        }
        return this.propChangeSupport;
    }
    @Override
    public void addPropertyChangeListener(PropertyChangeListener listener) {
        getPropertyChangeSupport().addPropertyChangeListener(listener);
    }

    @Override
    public void removePropertyChangeListener(PropertyChangeListener listener) {
        getPropertyChangeSupport().removePropertyChangeListener(listener);
    }

    @Override
    public void addPerson(Person p) {
        Person person = new Person(p);
        personMap.put(person.getId(), person);
        getPropertyChangeSupport().firePropertyChange(
                    FamilyTreeManager.PROP_PERSON_ADDED, null, person);
    }
```

```
    @Override
    public void updatePerson(Person p) {
        Person person = new Person(p);
        personMap.put(person.getId(), person);
        getPropertyChangeSupport().firePropertyChange(
                    FamilyTreeManager.PROP_PERSON_UPDATED, null, person);
    }

    @Override
    public void deletePerson(Person p) {
        Person person = personMap.remove(p.getId());
        if (person != null) {
            getPropertyChangeSupport().firePropertyChange(
                    FamilyTreeManager.PROP_PERSON_DESTROYED, null, person);
        }
    }

    @Override
    public List<Person> getAllPeople() {
        List<Person> copyList = new ArrayList<>();
        personMap.values().stream().forEach((p) -> {
            copyList.add(new Person(p));
        });
        return copyList;
    };
}
```

Note that the FamilyTreeManagerImpl class provides a HashMap to manage Person objects and fires property change events when Person objects are added to, updated, or deleted from the map. Clients can become listeners with the `addPropertyChangeListener()` method and remove themselves as listeners with the `removePropertyChangeListener()` method. This is the same behavior you saw with the Swing version of this program.

Annotation @ServiceProvider puts an instance of this class into the application's Global Lookup so that other modules can find and use it. This automatically provides a singleton object for our application, so we no longer need to provide code to create a singleton instance. We'll show you how client modules find and use this service provider when we add code to modules PersonViewer and PersonEditor.

## Global Lookup

The Global Lookup is an application-wide repository for modules to discover and provide services. This allows the separation of the service interface (FamilyTreeManager) and the service provider (FamilyTreeManagerImpl). A client module can thus use a service without being aware of or dependent on its implementation. This supports loose coupling between modules. Annotation @ServiceProvider lets you register an implementation as a service provider for an interface. The service interface is also known as an extension point of the interface's module (here, FamilyTreeModel).

The class that is annotated with @ServiceProvider must implement the interface for which it is providing the service. Furthermore, the class must be public and include a public no-argument constructor (or no constructor, as with class FamilyTreeManager-Impl). A module that uses this service *does not* declare a dependency on the provider's module (FamilyTreeManagerImpl). Instead, the client declares a dependency on the module that contains the service interface (FamilyTreeModel). We discuss the Lookup API in more detail in "Lookup API" on page 224.

## 5.6 Configuring a Window for Selection

Application FamilyTreeApp (see Figure 5.3 on page 202) has two windows. The left-side window provides a list of Person objects, which we implement in the Person-Viewer module. As described earlier, when a user selects a Person in the Person-Viewer window, the selected Person is displayed in the PersonEditor window, the right-side window.

### NetBeans Platform Windows

*A window in a NetBeans Platform application is provided by class TopComponent, the main display component that is automatically integrated into the NetBeans Platform Window System. We'll defer details on the Window System and Window Manager to Chapter 8 ("Net-Beans Platform Window System"). For now, we'll show you how to create a TopComponent and add Swing components to it.*

In this section, we'll show you how to create a NetBeans Platform window, add Swing components, and make the Person object selected by the user available to other modules in the application. Let's begin by configuring module PersonViewer so that it can access classes Person and FamilyTreeManager.

As indicated in Figure 5.10 on page 209, module PersonViewer must declare a dependency on module FamilyTreeModel, as follows.

1. In project PersonViewer, right click the **Libraries** node and select **Add Module Dependency . . . .** NetBeans displays the Add Module Dependency dialog.
2. In the list of modules, select **FamilyTreeModel**. Click **OK**. NetBeans adds Family-TreeModel to PersonViewer's list of dependencies. When you expand the Libraries node, you'll see this module listed.

Now let's add a window to the PersonViewer module with the following steps.

1. Expand project PersonViewer and Source Packages. Right click on package name **com.asgteach.familytree.personviwer** and select **New | Other** from the context menu.
2. NetBeans displays the Choose File Type dialog. Select **Module Development** under Categories and **Window** under File Type, as shown in Figure 5.19. Click **Next**.

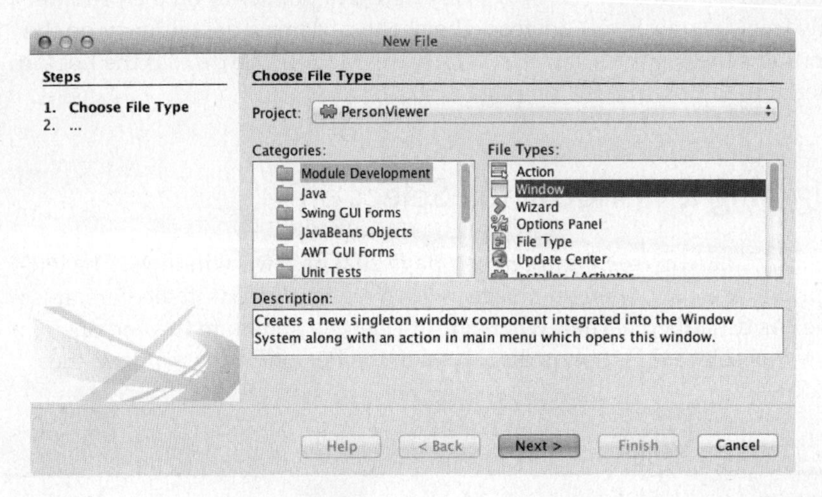


Figure 5.19 Adding a new window

3. NetBeans displays the Basic Settings dialog. For Window Position, select **explorer** from the drop down control and check the box **Open on Application Start**. This window position setting determines where the window will appear in your application's frame. This selection also influences window behavior.

   Leave the other checkboxes unchecked (these options limit the window's behaviors). Click **Next** as shown in Figure 5.20.

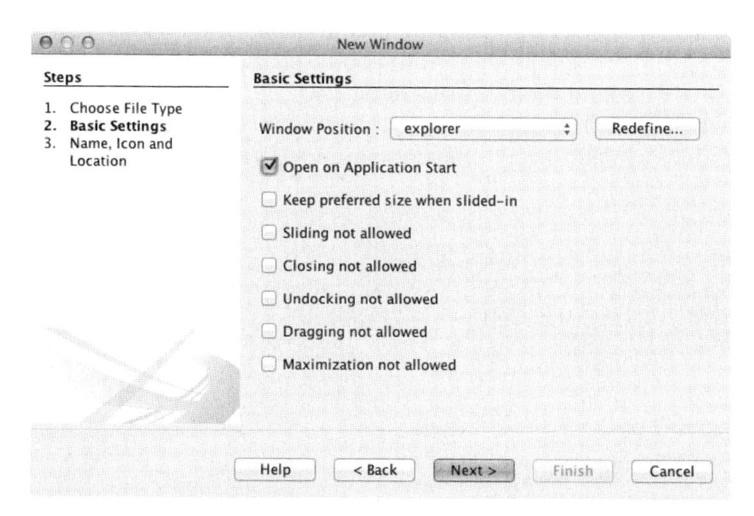


Figure 5.20 Basic Settings dialog for a new window

4. NetBeans displays the Name, Icon and Location dialog. Provide **PersonViewer** for the Class Name Prefix. Leave the Icon blank and accept the defaults for the rest, as shown in Figure 5.21. Click **Finish**.

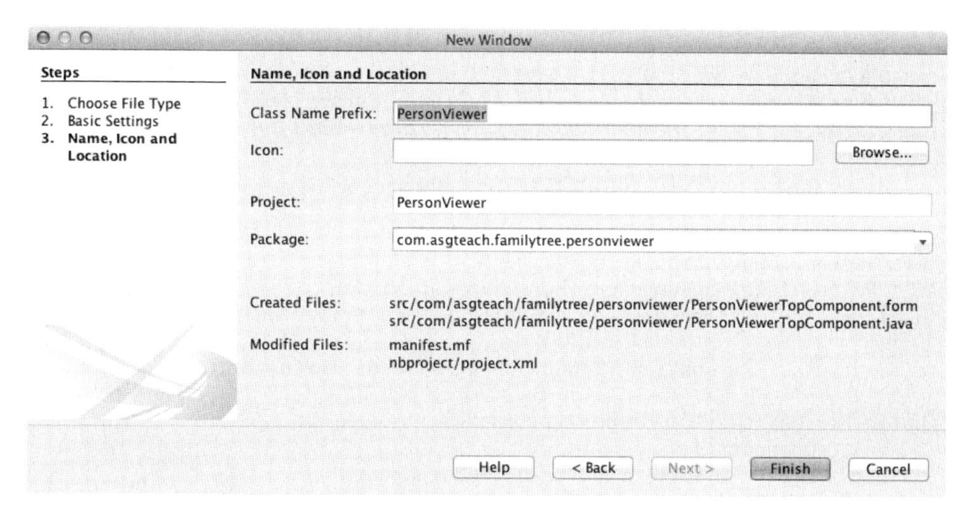


Figure 5.21 Name, Icon and Location dialog for a new window

NetBeans creates class PersonViewerTopComponent and brings the class up in the Swing Design View. If you click the Source button, you'll see the generated code, as shown in Listing 5.6. If you expand the Libraries node under project PersonViewer, you'll also see that the New Window wizard added dependencies for the following NetBeans Platform modules, in addition to the dependency already configured for FamilyTreeModel.

```
Lookup API
Settings API
UI Utilities API
Utilities API
Window System API
```

**Listing 5.6 PersonViewerTopComponent.java**

```
package com.asgteach.familytree.personviewer;

. . . import statements omitted . . .

@ConvertAsProperties(
        dtd = "-//com.asgteach.familytree.personviewer//PersonViewer//EN",
        autostore = false)
@TopComponent.Description(
        preferredID = "PersonViewerTopComponent",
        //iconBase="SET/PATH/TO/ICON/HERE",
        persistenceType = TopComponent.PERSISTENCE_ALWAYS)
@TopComponent.Registration(mode = "explorer", openAtStartup = true)
@ActionID(category = "Window",
      id = "com.asgteach.familytree.personviewer.PersonViewerTopComponent")
@ActionReference(path = "Menu/Window" /*, position = 333 */)
@TopComponent.OpenActionRegistration(
        displayName = "#CTL_PersonViewerAction",
        preferredID = "PersonViewerTopComponent")
@Messages({
    "CTL_PersonViewerAction=PersonViewer",
    "CTL_PersonViewerTopComponent=PersonViewer Window",
    "HINT_PersonViewerTopComponent=This is a PersonViewer window"
})
public final class PersonViewerTopComponent extends TopComponent {

    public PersonViewerTopComponent() {
        initComponents();
        setName(Bundle.CTL_PersonViewerTopComponent());
        setToolTipText(Bundle.HINT_PersonViewerTopComponent());
    }

. . . form designer code omitted . . .
```

```
    @Override
    public void componentOpened() {
        // TODO add custom code on component opening
    }

    @Override
    public void componentClosed() {
        // TODO add custom code on component closing
    }

    void writeProperties(java.util.Properties p) {
        // better to version settings since initial version as advocated at
        // http://wiki.apidesign.org/wiki/PropertyFiles
        p.setProperty("version", "1.0");
        // TODO store your settings
    }
    void readProperties(java.util.Properties p) {
        String version = p.getProperty("version");
        // TODO read your settings according to their version
    }
}
```

## Porting Swing UI Code to a TopComponent

Because TopComponent is a subtype of JComponent in Swing, we can port our Swing layout code from project PersonSwingAppEnhancedUI, as follows.

1. Open project **PersonSwingAppEnhancedUI** in NetBeans and expand the project node, **Source Packages**, and package **personswingapp**. Open **PersonJFrame.java** in the editor.

2. Click the **Design** tab to open the Swing Design View.

3. Right click inside the left panel that contains the JTree and select **Copy** from the context menu.

4. Return to project PersonViewer and make sure PersonViewerTopComponent.java is open in the Swing Form Designer. Paste the copied contents into the Form Designer. You may see the following message.

   ```
   Copied or inserted - not placed in layout yet.
   Move the component via mouse to place it.
   ```

5. Move the newly pasted component using the mouse to place the copied components in the layout.

6. Expand (grow) the component (grab the handles on the JTree component and drag them to the parent panel's edge) so that it takes up the entire window, as shown in Figure 5.22. There will be red lines in the source code, indicating compilation errors. You will fix these shortly.

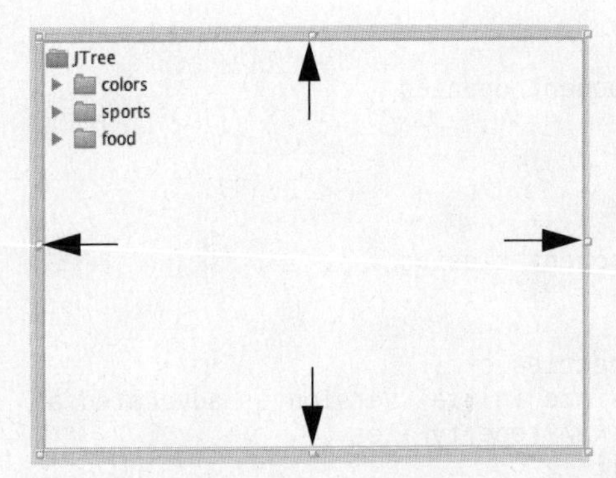


Figure 5.22 PersonViewerTopComponent.java Design View

You still need to add configuration code to PersonViewerTopComponent.java. Some of the code can be copied over directly from PersonJFrame.java. Before you do that, it's time to explain how the Lookup API lets you discover and use service providers. We'll also show you how Lookup allows modules to communicate with each other.

## Lookup API

Lookups are one of the most powerful features of the NetBeans Platform. Lookups can be application wide (called the "Global Lookup") or attached to objects within an application. For example, all TopComponents have a Lookup. Let's see how you can use Lookups to leverage loosely-coupled communication strategies.

In the previous section we used annotation @ServiceProvider to register a service provider in the application's Global Lookup. A Lookup is a map where the keys are class types and the values are class type instances. Lookups allow modules to communicate with each other by querying an object's Lookup. They are also type safe. You can use Lookups to discover service providers, but you can also discover arbitrary objects—not just service providers. You will see examples of both types of Lookups in this chapter as we configure the FamilyTreeApp application.

### Lookup as a Service Provider

Before you can use a Lookup, you must obtain it somehow. The Global Lookup that maintains all registered service providers is accessible with static method `Lookup.getDefault()`. Use the `lookup()` method to discover a service provider for a particular service interface. For the FamilyTreeApp application, you need a service provider for interface FamilyTreeManager. Here is how you obtain this service provider.

```
FamilyTreeManager ftm =
          Lookup.getDefault().lookup(FamilyTreeManager.class);
if (ftm == null) {
    logger.log(Level.SEVERE, "Cannot get FamilyTreeManager object");
    LifecycleManager.getDefault().exit();
}
 // do something with ftm
```

Note that this code assumes the service provider is registered elsewhere via the @ServiceProvider annotation. With a successful return value, `ftm` holds a reference to a FamilyTreeManagerImpl instance, provided by the Lookup API. This client code has no dependency on the FamilyTreeManagerImpl module. Indeed, you can later provide another implementation without any changes to this client code. We only need a dependency on the FamilyTreeModel module, which includes interface FamilyTreeManager.

**Lookup Tip**

*You should check the* `lookup()` *method's return value against null. In this example, if the return value is null, we exit the application with the NetBeans Platform LifecycleManager method* `exit()`.

### Lookup as an Object Repository

You've seen how Lookup can help you discover and obtain instances of service providers. In the FamilyTreeApp application, we also need a way to communicate the selected Person object to the PersonEditor when the user selects a different node in the JTree UI control. In the Swing version of this program, the TreeSelectionListener directly updates the Swing UI controls (see Listing 2.19 on page 60). In the NetBeans Platform application, however, the PersonEditor code and its UI controls are in their own, separate module. The PersonViewer module (which has the JTree component) must somehow make its selection available to the PersonEditor module. Furthermore, we want to maintain a loosely-coupled architecture, so we don't want to make either module dependent on the other. Using Lookups is the answer.

Lookups have been described as a data structure or a "bag of things." Importantly, Lookups help share objects, so that the bag of things can be discovered and accessed by other modules. Again, just like Lookups for service providers, object-sharing Lookups store objects in a map with class types as keys and instances as a set of values. Furthermore, Lookups are observable. That is, you can attach listeners to the result of a Lookup discovery. When a class or TopComponent puts something different into its Lookup, you can listen for this change and grab the new object (or objects) in the Lookup listener's event handler.

This is exactly how the PersonViewerTopComponent makes the user's Tree selection object available to any interested modules. The current Tree selection is placed in the TopComponent's Lookup.

As it turns out, TopComponents already have a Lookup, and TopComponents implement Lookup.Provider, an interface that lets others ask for its Lookup with method `getLookup()`.

Here are the steps required to add and remove content to a TopComponent's Lookup.

1. First, create the content holder with convenience class InstanceContent.

```
private final InstanceContent instanceContent = new InstanceContent();
```

2. Next, create a Lookup to hold the InstanceContent and associate this Lookup with the TopComponent's Lookup. This lets you use the TopComponent Lookup.Provider method `getLookup()` to access the Lookup. Class AbstractLookup extends Lookup and provides a default way to store class object and type pairs in the Lookup. You typically place this code in the TopComponent's constructor.

```
public PersonViewerTopComponent() {
    . . .
    associateLookup(new AbstractLookup(instanceContent));
}
```

3. Now you can add, remove, or search for objects of a certain type in `instanceContent`. For example, in a TreeSelectionListener, add the selected item using InstanceContent method `set()`.

```
        // Put person in this TopComponent's Lookup
        instanceContent.set(Collections.singleton(person), null);
```

   Similarly, if you want to remove this Person object from the Lookup, search for it and then remove it, as follows. (The PersonViewer TopComponent removes the Person object from the Lookup when the user selects the top node "People.")

```
        // Search for a person object in this TopComponent's Lookup
        // and remove if it's present
        Person person = getLookup().lookup(Person.class);
        if (person != null) {
            instanceContent.remove(person);
        }
```

   The NetBeans Platform provides additional features that are sensitive to what's in a TopComponent's Lookup. We explore these in more detail in Chapter 10 (see "Implementing Update" on page 488).

## Configuring the TopComponent

With an understanding of Lookups, let's finish configuring the PersonViewer TopComponent. We'll add class variables, configure the constructor code, and add code to the TopComponent's life cycle methods. We'll also write a TreeSelectionListener (to put the selected Person in the TopComponent's Lookup) and a PropertyChangeListener (to update the displayed Person objects when they change). These listener methods are similar to the ones you've seen already in the Swing version of this program. But here we will take advantage of the NetBeans Platform features that promote modularity and loose coupling.

We'll add this code starting from the top (class variables). You will encounter compilation errors when the source file is in intermediate states, but these will all be fixed when you are finished.

### Configure Class Variables and Constructor

1. Add the following class variables and constructor code to PersonViewerTopComponent.java (as shown in Listing 5.7 in bold). These same class variables are used in the Swing version of this program, except for `treeModel` and `instanceContent`. We previously described `instanceContent`. Variable `treeModel` provides access to JTree's model and lets you automatically expand the JTree hierarchy. We show this code later in Listing 5.11 on page 231.

**Listing 5.7 PersonViewerTopComponent—Class Variables and Constructor**

```
public final class PersonViewerTopComponent extends TopComponent {

    private FamilyTreeManager ftm;
    private final DefaultMutableTreeNode top =
            new DefaultMutableTreeNode("People");
    private final DefaultTreeModel treeModel = new DefaultTreeModel(top);
    private static final Logger logger = Logger.getLogger(
                        PersonViewerTopComponent.class.getName());
    private final InstanceContent instanceContent = new InstanceContent();

    public PersonViewerTopComponent() {
        initComponents();
        setName(Bundle.CTL_PersonViewerTopComponent());
        setToolTipText(Bundle.HINT_PersonViewerTopComponent());
        associateLookup(new AbstractLookup(instanceContent));
    }
```

2. Because we defined a model for the JTree component, its constructor requires different instantiation code. This is done in the Design View. Click tab **Design** to bring up the Design View.

3. From the Design canvas, select the **JTree** component. In the Properties window, click tab **Code**. As shown in Figure 5.23, specify property **Custom Creation Code** as

```
new JTree(treeModel)
```

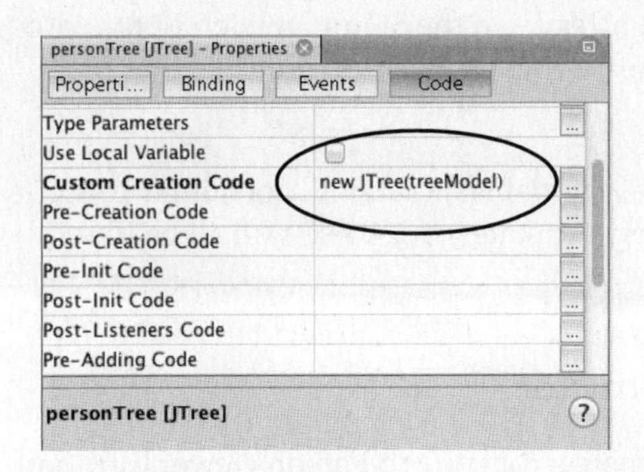


Figure 5.23 JTree Properties window—Custom Creation Code under tab Code

When finished, click the **Source** tab to return to the Java Editor.

## Add Listeners

As in the Swing version of the program, this module has a PropertyChangeListener to respond to changes generated from the FamilyTreeManager and a TreeSelectionListener to respond to the user's selections.

1. Add the PropertyChangeListener code to PersonViewerTopComponent to listen for changes to the FamilyTreeManager, as shown in Listing 5.8. This code is unchanged from the Swing version of the program.

**Listing 5.8 PropertyChangeListener for FamilyTreeManager**

```
   // PropertyChangeListener for FamilyTreeManager
   private final PropertyChangeListener familyTreeListener =
                              (PropertyChangeEvent evt) -> {
     if (evt.getPropertyName().equals(FamilyTreeManager.PROP_PERSON_UPDATED)
              && evt.getNewValue() != null) {
          Person person = (Person) evt.getNewValue();
          DefaultTreeModel model = (DefaultTreeModel) personTree.getModel();
          for (int i = 0; i < model.getChildCount(top); i++) {
              DefaultMutableTreeNode node =
                          (DefaultMutableTreeNode) model.getChild(top, i);
```

```
                if (person.equals(node.getUserObject())) {
                    node.setUserObject(person);
                    // Let the model know we made a change
                    model.nodeChanged(node);
                    logger.log(Level.FINE, "Node updated: {0}", node);
                    break;
                }
            }
        }
    };
```

2. Add the TreeSelectionListener to PersonViewerTopComponent to respond to changes in the selected JTree node, as shown in Listing 5.9.

   Note that in this code, we check to make sure the selected JTree node is a leaf node, which means the user selected a Person. If the selected node is not a leaf node, we remove the previously added Person object from the Lookup, if one is present. This lets us implement the ability to clear the PersonEditor forms when no Person object is selected. We show you the code to detect an empty Lookup result when we describe the PersonEditorTopComponent module in the next section.

**Listing 5.9 TreeSelectionListener Uses TopComponent's Lookup**

```
    // TreeSelectionListener for JTree
    private final TreeSelectionListener treeSelectionListener =
                                        (TreeSelectionEvent e) -> {
        DefaultMutableTreeNode node = (DefaultMutableTreeNode)
                personTree.getLastSelectedPathComponent();
        if (node == null) {
            return;
        }
        if (node.isLeaf()) {
            Person person = (Person) node.getUserObject();
            logger.log(Level.INFO, "{0} selected", person);
            // Put person in this TopComponent's Lookup
            instanceContent.set(Collections.singleton(person), null);
        } else {
            logger.log(Level.INFO, "{0} selected", node.getUserObject());
            Person person = getLookup().lookup(Person.class);
            if (person != null) {
                instanceContent.remove(person);
            }
        }
    };
```

**InstanceContent Tip**

*Note that in Listing 5.9, method* `instanceContent.set()` *resets the Lookup to the singleton Person object. To remove a Person object currently in the Lookup, use* `lookup(Person.class)` *to find a Person object and* `instanceContent.remove()` *to remove it.*

## Configure TopComponent Life Cycle Methods

Configure the TopComponent life cycle methods `componentOpened()` and `componentClosed()` as shown in Listing 5.10. (You typically add listeners in method `componentOpened()` and remove them in method `componentClosed()`. TopComponent life cycle methods are discussed in "Window System Life Cycle Management" on page 369.)

In method `componentOpened()`, we obtain an instance of service provider FamilyTreeManager using the application's Global Lookup, as explained earlier. Then, using code you've seen previously in the Swing application version, we invoke `buildData()` to instantiate several Person objects and register a property change listener with the FamilyTreeManager service provider.

Method `createNodes()` builds the JTree data structure. We also register a tree selection listener with JTree `personTree`. Method `componentClosed()` removes the registered listeners.

**Listing 5.10 TopComponent componentOpened() and componentClosed()**

```
@Override
public void componentOpened() {
    ftm = Lookup.getDefault().lookup(FamilyTreeManager.class);
    if (ftm == null) {
        logger.log(Level.SEVERE, "Cannot get FamilyTreeManager object");
        LifecycleManager.getDefault().exit();
    }
    buildData();
    ftm.addPropertyChangeListener(familyTreeListener);
    personTree.getSelectionModel().setSelectionMode(
            TreeSelectionModel.SINGLE_TREE_SELECTION);
    createNodes();
    personTree.addTreeSelectionListener(treeSelectionListener);
}

@Override
public void componentClosed() {
    personTree.removeTreeSelectionListener(treeSelectionListener);
    ftm.removePropertyChangeListener(familyTreeListener);
}
```

### Adding Helper Methods

Add the code for methods `buildData()` and `createNodes()`, as shown in Listing 5.11. Note that `buildData()` is unchanged from PersonJFrame.java, but `createNodes()` now contains extra code to expand the JTree with method `scrollPathToVisible()`. Since this method requires a TreePath argument, we use DefaultTreeModel `treeModel` to obtain the path. Class variable `treeModel` is defined in Listing 5.7 on page 227.

**Listing 5.11 Methods buildData() and createNodes()**

```
private void buildData() {
    ftm.addPerson(new Person("Homer", "Simpson", Person.Gender.MALE));
    ftm.addPerson(new Person("Marge", "Simpson", Person.Gender.FEMALE));
    ftm.addPerson(new Person("Bart", "Simpson", Person.Gender.MALE));
    ftm.addPerson(new Person("Lisa", "Simpson", Person.Gender.FEMALE));
    ftm.addPerson(new Person("Maggie", "Simpson", Person.Gender.FEMALE));
    logger.log(Level.FINE, ftm.getAllPeople().toString());
}

private void createNodes() {
    ftm.getAllPeople().stream().forEach((p) -> {
        top.add(new DefaultMutableTreeNode(p));
    });
    // Expand the tree
    if (top.getChildCount() != 0) {
        TreeNode[] nodes = treeModel.getPathToRoot(top.getLastChild());
        TreePath path = new TreePath(nodes);
        personTree.scrollPathToVisible(path);
    }
}
```

With these changes, you can now build and run the FamilyTreeApp application. Only the PersonViewer window appears, populated with Person objects, as shown in Figure 5.24. You can select different Person objects in the JTree component to test the TreeSelectionListener.

## 5.7 Configuring a Window with Form Editing

The PersonEditor module provides code to implement the right-side window of the FamilyTreeApp application from Figure 5.3 on page 202. Since PersonEditor has a window, we create a TopComponent for this. Also, we declare a dependency on the FamilyTreeModel module to access Person and FamilyTreeManager. We'll begin with the same steps we used to build the PersonViewer module.

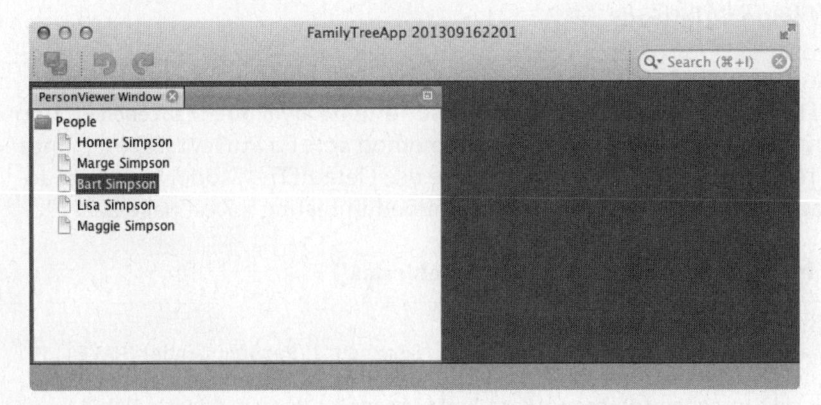


Figure 5.24 PersonViewer window populated with Person objects

## Set Module Dependency

Set the module dependency, as follows.

1. In project PersonEditor, right click the **Libraries** node and select **Add Module Dependency . . . .** NetBeans displays the Add Module Dependency dialog.
2. In the list of modules, select **FamilyTreeModel**. Click **OK**. NetBeans adds FamilyTreeModel to PersonEditor's list of dependencies. When you expand the Libraries node, you'll see the module listed.

## Create a Window

Create a window (TopComponent) in module PersonEditor.

1. Expand project PersonEditor and Source Packages. Right click on package name **com.asgteach.familytree.personeditor** and select **New | Other** from the context menu (or select **New | Window** if the choice is available and skip the next step).
2. NetBeans displays the Choose File Type dialog. Select **Module Development** under Categories and **Window** under File Type. Click **Next**.
3. NetBeans displays the Basic Settings dialog. For Window Position, select **editor** from the drop down control and check the box **Open on Application Start**. Position editor creates a large window for your application. Leave the other checkboxes unchecked. Click **Next**.
4. NetBeans displays the Name, Icon and Location dialog. Provide **PersonEditor** for the Class Name Prefix. Editor windows display icons (if one is provided) on their tab. For Icon, optionally provide a suitable 16 x 16 GIF or PNG graphic. (You can

use file personIcon.png found in the download bundle for this book.) Click **Finish**, as shown in Figure 5.25.

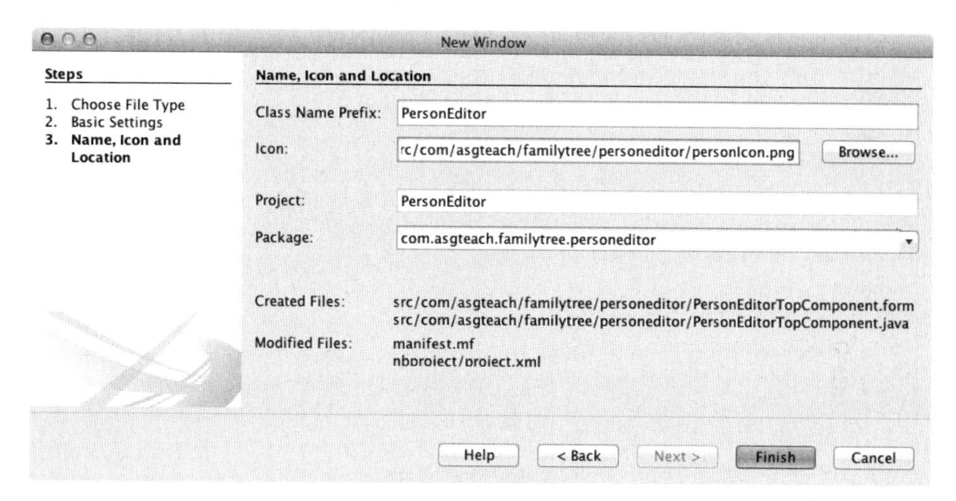


Figure 5.25 Name, Icon and Location dialog for new editor window

## Configure PersonEditorTopComponent UI

NetBeans creates class PersonEditorTopComponent and brings the class up in the Swing Design View. Once again, you can copy and paste the components from project PersonSwingAppEnhancedUI to create the UI form for editing Person objects. Use these steps to create the UI form for PersonEditorTopComponent.

1. Select the UI components for editing as well as the Update button from PersonJFrame.java and paste the components into the Design View of PersonEditorTopComponent.
2. Move the newly pasted components using the mouse to place the copied components in the layout.
3. Resize the panel that contains the components so that it takes up the entire space of the form. Figure 5.26 shows the UI components in PersonEditorTopComponent's Design View.

For mutually exclusive behavior, add the radio buttons to the same ButtonGroup with the following steps.

1. Add a ButtonGroup from the Swing Controls palette to the form. You'll see the ButtonGroup appear in the Navigator View under Other Components.

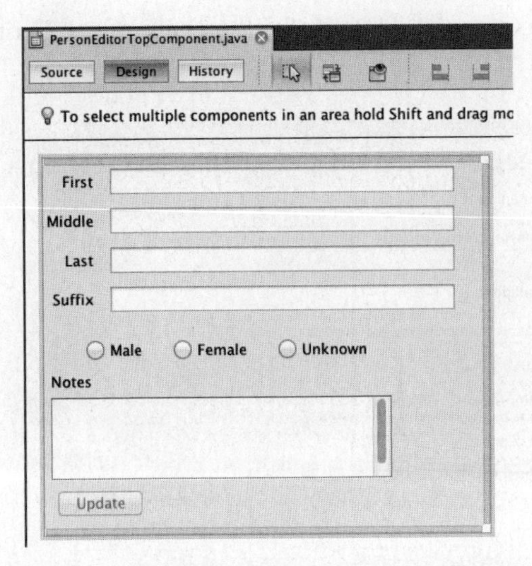


Figure 5.26 PersonEditorTopComponent Design View

2. Right click on the ButtonGroup in the Navigator View and choose **Change Variable Name** from the context menu. Use variable name **genderButtonGroup**.
3. Right click on the Male radio button in the Design View and select **Properties** from the context menu. Select **genderButtonGroup** in the drop down for property **buttonGroup**, as shown in Figure 5.27. Click **Close**.

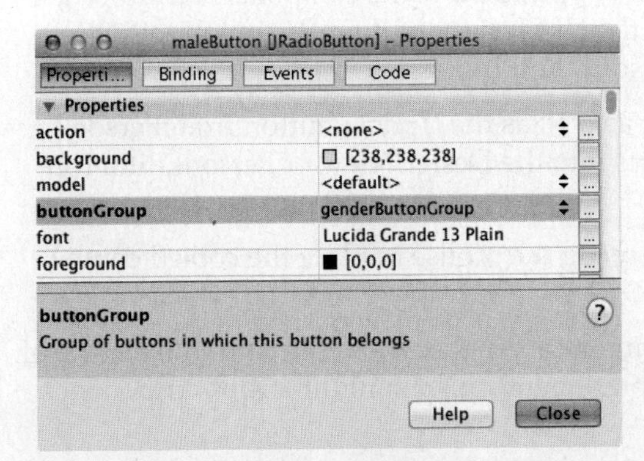


Figure 5.27 maleButton JRadioButton Properties dialog

4. Repeat this step for the Female and Unknown radio buttons so that all three radio buttons belong to the same ButtonGroup.

### Add Code to PersonEditorTopComponent

You'll now add code to PersonEditorTopComponent.java. You'll see that we can reuse much of the code from PersonJFrame.java to process user input. (We are still using project PersonSwingAppEnhancedUI described in "Improving the User Experience" on page 63 as our Swing porting reference.)

1. Select the **Source** button to return to the Java editor for PersonEditorTopComponent.java.
2. Add the following class variables, as shown in Listing 5.12. We add class variable `lookupResult` in order to attach a listener to a Lookup.Result object for Person objects. The remaining class variables are the same ones used in PersonJFrame.java. The constructor is unchanged from the generated code.

**Listing 5.12 PersonEditorTopComponent—Class Variables and Constructor**

```
public final class PersonEditorTopComponent extends TopComponent {

    private FamilyTreeManager ftm;
    private Person thePerson = null;
    private static final Logger logger = Logger.getLogger(
            PersonEditorTopComponent.class.getName());
    private boolean changeOK = false;
    private Lookup.Result<Person> lookupResult = null;

    public PersonEditorTopComponent() {
        initComponents();
        setName(Bundle.CTL_PersonEditorTopComponent());
        setToolTipText(Bundle.HINT_PersonEditorTopComponent());

    }
```

3. As shown in Listing 5.13, add method `configureListeners()` from PersonJFrame.java, but do not include the code to configure the PropertyChangeListener or TreeSelectionListener. (These listeners are now in the PersonViewer module.)

**Listing 5.13 Method configureListeners()**

```
    private void configureListeners() {
        // add action listener to Update button
        updateButton.addActionListener(updateListener);
        // add document listeners to textfields, textarea
        firstTextField.getDocument().addDocumentListener(docListener);
        middleTextField.getDocument().addDocumentListener(docListener);
        lastTextField.getDocument().addDocumentListener(docListener);
        suffixTextField.getDocument().addDocumentListener(docListener);
        notesTextArea.getDocument().addDocumentListener(docListener);
```

```
        // add action listeners to radiobuttons
        maleButton.addActionListener(radioButtonListener);
        femaleButton.addActionListener(radioButtonListener);
        unknownButton.addActionListener(radioButtonListener);
    }
```

4. Add helper methods `updateForm()`, `clearForm()`, `updateModel()`, and `modify()` unchanged from PersonJFrame.java, as shown in Listing 5.14.

**Listing 5.14 Code Ported Unchanged from PersonJFrame.java**

```
    private void updateForm() {
        See Listing 2.24 on page 65.
    }

    private void clearForm() {
        See Listing 2.23 on page 65.
    }

    private void updateModel() {
        See Listing 2.26 on page 66.
    }
    private void modify() {
        See Listing 2.25 on page 66.
    }
```

5. Add action and document listeners unchanged as shown in Listing 5.15. These include the DocumentListener (to detect editing changes), ActionListener (to detect radio button changes), and a second ActionListener (for the Update button's event handler).

**Listing 5.15 Listeners from PersonJFrame.java**

```
    // Define listeners
    // DocumentListener for text fields and text area
    private final DocumentListener docListener = new DocumentListener() {

        @Override
        public void insertUpdate(DocumentEvent evt) {
            if (changeOK) {
                modify();
            }
        }

        @Override
        public void removeUpdate(DocumentEvent evt) {
            if (changeOK) {
                modify();
            }
        }
```

```
        @Override
        public void changedUpdate(DocumentEvent evt) {
            if (changeOK) {
                modify();
            }
        }
    };

    // ActionListener for Radio Buttons
    private final ActionListener radioButtonListener = (ActionEvent e) -> {
        if (changeOK) {
            modify();
        }
    };

    // ActionListener for Update button
    private final ActionListener updateListener = (ActionEvent e) -> {
        updateModel();
        ftm.updatePerson(thePerson);
    };
```

### Configure TopComponent Life Cycle Methods

The TopComponent life cycle `componentOpened()` method lets you configure a TopComponent when it opens.

PersonEditorTopComponent requires access to the FamilyTreeManager service provider, which we obtain using the application's Global Lookup. This code is the same that we used in PersonViewerTopComponent. Note that we obtain the same instance, since Lookup returns a singleton for service providers.

After we invoke method `configureListeners()`, we obtain the PersonViewerTopComponent's Lookup. In the same way that static method `Lookup.getDefault()` provides the default Lookup, we use `WindowManager.getDefault()` to obtain the default Window Manager. The Window Manager manages all the application's TopComponents. We can find a particular TopComponent using WindowManager method `findTopComponent()`. (See Table 8.1, "Window Manager Useful Methods," on page 352 for a description of useful Window Manager methods.) Argument "PersonViewerTopComponent" is the TopComponent's `preferredID` property as shown in the TopComponent annotations in Listing 5.6 on page 222.

With a reference to the TopComponent, we obtain its Lookup with method `getLookup()` and register a LookupListener on its Lookup.Result. The LookupListener's `resultChanged()` method is invoked whenever PersonViewerTopComponent's Lookup changes with an addition or removal of a Person.class object.

Why do we invoke the `checkLookup()` method in `componentOpened()`? The user can close the PersonEditor window. When the window re-opens, you want to make sure that whatever is currently selected in the PersonViewer also appears in the editor. Since the user can make selection changes while the PersonEditor window is closed, it's necessary to invoke the `checkLookup()` method in `componentOpened()` and not wait for a LookupListener event to update the PersonEditor window.

Method `componentClosed()` removes the LookupListener.

- Add the following code to the TopComponent life cycle methods `componentOpened()` and `componentClosed()`, as shown in Listing 5.16.

**Listing 5.16 TopComponent componentOpened() and componentClosed()**

```
@Override
public void componentOpened() {
    ftm = Lookup.getDefault().lookup(FamilyTreeManager.class);
    if (ftm == null) {
        logger.log(Level.SEVERE, "Cannot get FamilyTreeManager object");
        LifecycleManager.getDefault().exit();
    }
    configureListeners();
    // Listen for Person objects in the PersonViewerTopComponent Lookup
    TopComponent tc = WindowManager.getDefault().findTopComponent(
            "PersonViewerTopComponent");
    if (tc != null) {
        lookupResult = tc.getLookup().lookupResult(Person.class);
        checkLookup();
        lookupResult.addLookupListener(lookupListener);
    }
}

@Override
public void componentClosed() {
    lookupResult.removeLookupListener(lookupListener);
}
```

### Add the LookupListener

Listing 5.17 shows the LookupListener code. Lookup inner class Lookup.Result method `allInstances()` returns a collection of Person objects currently in the Lookup. Recall that in the TreeSelectionListener, we put the selected Person object in the TopComponent's Lookup (when the user selects a Person). If the user selects the top node, we remove the Person object from the Lookup, if one is present. Thus, in the LookupListener, if a new Person is present in the Lookup, we update the UI form with the Person's data. Otherwise, the Lookup is empty, so we clear the UI form. This behavior matches the behavior of the Swing version of this program (project PersonSwingApp-EnhancedUI).

- Add the following LookupListener code to the PersonEditor TopComponent, as shown in Listing 5.17.

**Listing 5.17 LookupListener**

```
// LookupListener to detect changes in PersonViewer's Lookup
LookupListener lookupListener = (LookupEvent le) -> checkLookup();

private void checkLookup()  {
    Collection<? extends Person> allPeople = lookupResult.allInstances();
    if (!allPeople.isEmpty()) {
        thePerson = allPeople.iterator().next();
        logger.log(Level.FINE, "{0} selected", thePerson);
        updateForm();
    } else {
        logger.log(Level.FINE, "No selection");
        clearForm();
    }
}
```

Figure 5.28 shows application FamilyTreeApp running with both windows undocked. Like the Swing version of this application, you can select different Person objects in the left PersonViewer window, edit the selected Person in the right Person-Editor window, and save your changes with the Update button. You can also undock either window, resize or maximize it, and re-dock it. You can use the top level Window menu to open and close either window. Furthermore, because the program is modular and uses the Lookup API for discovering service providers and inter-module communication, the application is well designed and loosely coupled.

## Another Look at Lookup

The handshaking between the TreeSelectionListener in module PersonViewer (Listing 5.9 on page 229) and the LookupListener in module PersonEditor (Listing 5.17 on page 239) is a straightforward solution for the use case of editing the selected Person object and clearing the form when the user selects the top node. However, the PersonEditorTopComponent depends on the PersonViewerTopComponent, if for no other reason than it must know the PersonViewerTopComponent's `preferredID` string when invoking method `findTopComponent()`.

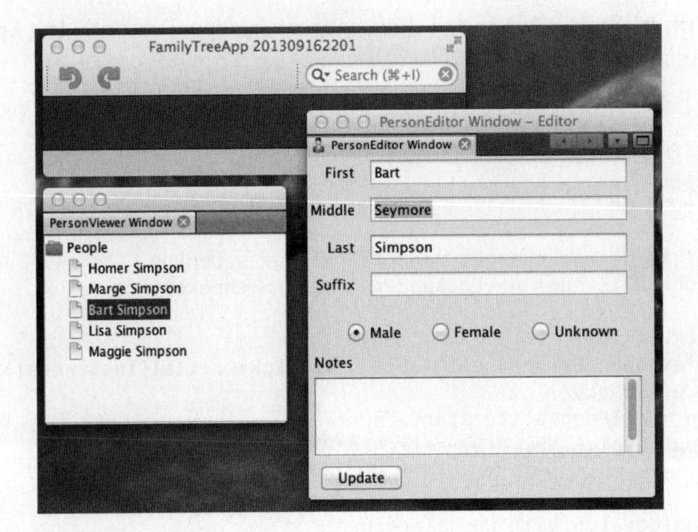


Figure 5.28 FamilyTreeApp running with windows undocked (floating)

## Tracking Global Selection

A more general solution lets us track the Global Selection Lookup, a Lookup of the TopComponent that currently has focus. When you make a selection in the PersonViewer window, the PersonViewerTopComponent has focus and the contents of its Lookup are available in the Global Selection Lookup. You access this Lookup with

```
private Lookup.Result<Person> lookupResult = null;
. . .

    // Listen for Person objects in the Global Selection Lookup
    lookupResult = Utilities.actionsGlobalContext()
            .lookupResult (Person.class);
    lookupResult.addLookupListener(lookupListener);
```

Now, whenever a Person object is added to or removed from the Global Selection Lookup, the LookupListener (`lookupListener`) is invoked. This removes the dependency on the PersonViewerTopComponent's name.

There is just one problem. When the user clicks inside the PersonEditorTopComponent's form to begin editing, the form clears because the Person object is no longer in the Global Selection Lookup. Because PersonEditorTopComponent has focus, its (empty) Lookup is now the Global Selection Lookup.

One way to solve this problem is to ignore the Global Selection Lookup when PersonEditorTopComponent has focus. Here is the modified LookupListener, as shown in Listing 5.18. As described in Chapter 8, the TopComponent registry keeps track of the application's TopComponents. The registry returns the TopComponent that has focus with method `getActivated()`. If the TopComponent with focus is the PersonEditorTopComponent (`this`), then the result change is ignored.

**Listing 5.18 LookupListener That Ignores Its Own TopComponent**

```
// LookupListener to detect changes in PersonViewer's Lookup
LookupListener lookupListener = (LookupEvent le) -> checkLookup();

private void checkLookup()  {
    Collection<? extends Person> allPeople = lookupResult.allInstances();

    // Make sure that the TopComponent with focus isn't this one
    TopComponent tc = TopComponent.getRegistry().getActivated();
    if (tc != null && tc.equals(this)) {
        logger.log(Level.FINER, "PersonEditorTopComponent has focus.");
        return;
    }
    if (!allPeople.isEmpty()) {
        thePerson = allPeople.iterator().next();
        logger.log(Level.FINE, "{0} selected", thePerson);
        updateForm();
    } else {
        logger.log(Level.FINE, "No selection");
        clearForm();
    }
}
```

Listing 5.19 shows the modified `componentOpened()` code that now uses the more general Global Selection Lookup instead of the PersonViewerTopComponent's Lookup.

**Listing 5.19 Method componentOpened()**

```
@Override
public void componentOpened() {
    ftm = Lookup.getDefault().lookup(FamilyTreeManager.class);
    if (ftm == null) {
        logger.log(Level.SEVERE, "Cannot get FamilyTreeManager object");
        LifecycleManager.getDefault().exit();
    }
    configureListeners();

    // Listen for Person objects in the Global Selection Lookup
    lookupResult = Utilities.actionsGlobalContext()
           .lookupResult (Person.class);
```

```
        lookupResult.addLookupListener(lookupListener);
        checkLookup();
    }
```

We've just scratched the surface on the Lookup API. In upcoming chapters you will see how to use the Global Selection Lookup together with the Nodes API to handle object selection. Stay tuned!

## 5.8 Module Life Cycle Annotations

The Module System API lets you build classes with specific methods that are invoked when your application starts as well as when your application shuts down. You use annotation `@OnStart` for the startup and `@OnStop` for the shutdown process. Note that these Runnables are executed in a background thread. If you need to execute UI code, you must be in the EDT. (See "Custom Login Dialog" on page 539 for an example.) If a module needs to invoke code after the UI is initialized, the Window System includes the `@OnShowing` annotation. (See "Using @OnShowing" on page 374.)

Let's show you how to use `@OnStart` by moving the FamilyTreeManager data initialization out of the TopComponent and into one of these special classes invoked during application startup. We'll build this startup code in module FamilyTreeModel in its own private package, making it easier to add and remove TopComponent modules without being concerned about where we initialize our test data.

We'll also add shutdown code with the `@OnStop` annotation to show you how you can customize your module or application shutdown process.

### Using @OnStart

To install startup code in module FamilyTreeModel, we define a class that implements Runnable annotated with `@OnStart`. The system invokes the `run()` method of such a Runnable as soon as possible during startup. If more than one module has an `@OnStart` Runnable, the system runs them in parallel to minimize the startup time of the application. The following steps create a module's `@OnStart` Runnable. Here, we add the `@OnStart` Runnable to the FamilyTreeModel module in a private package.

1. The `@OnStart` annotation requires a dependency on the Module System API, Lookup requires the Lookup API, and LifecycleManager requires Utilities API. Add all of these dependencies to the FamilyTreeModel module. (Select the **Libraries** node, right click, and select **Add Module Dependency . . .** from the context menu. In the Add Module Dependencies dialog, select **Lookup API**, **Module System API**, and **Utilities API** from the list of modules. Click **OK**.)

2. In the FamilyTreeModel project **Source Packages** node, right click on the package name, and add a new package called **data** to **com.asgteach.familytree.model**.
3. Right click on package **data** and select **New | Java Class . . . .**
4. NetBeans displays the New Java Class dialog. For Class Name, specify **DataInstaller** (any name is fine) and click **Finish**. NetBeans adds DataInstaller.java to package **com.asgteach.familytree.model.data**.
5. Add the following code to DataInstaller.java to initialize the FamilyTreeManager with test data. The `run()` method is invoked during startup. Listing 5.20 shows the added code.

**Listing 5.20 Module FamilyTreeModel—DataInstaller Class**

```
package com.asgteach.familytree.model.data;
. . . imports omitted . . .
@OnStart
public final class DataInstaller implements Runnable {
    private static final Logger logger = Logger.getLogger(
                                          DataInstaller.class.getName());

    @Override
    public void run() {
        FamilyTreeManager ftm = Lookup.getDefault().lookup(
                                          FamilyTreeManager.class);
        if (ftm == null) {
            logger.log(Level.SEVERE, "Cannot get FamilyTreeManager object");
            LifecycleManager.getDefault().exit();
        }
        populateMap(ftm);
    }

    private void populateMap(FamilyTreeManager ftm) {
        ftm.addPerson(new Person("Homer", "Simpson", Person.Gender.MALE));
        ftm.addPerson(new Person("Marge", "Simpson", Person.Gender.FEMALE));
        ftm.addPerson(new Person("Bart", "Simpson", Person.Gender.MALE));
        ftm.addPerson(new Person("Lisa", "Simpson", Person.Gender.FEMALE));
        ftm.addPerson(new Person("Maggie", "Simpson", Person.Gender.FEMALE));
        logger.log(Level.INFO, "Map populated: {0}", ftm.getAllPeople());
    }
}
```

## Using @OnStop

The `@OnStop` annotation can be applied to both a Runnable or a Callable. The Callable implementation includes the Boolean `call()` method. If the `call()` method returns true, then the system proceeds with shutdown. If you don't provide an `@OnStop` Callable, then permission is implicitly granted. If the shutdown is approved, all registered

`@OnStop` Runnables are invoked to perform any module or system cleanup code. The Runnables are invoked in parallel, and their execution will finish before the shutdown process completes.

For an example, add a class called DataRemover to the same module and package as the DataInstaller class. Listing 5.21 shows the code that removes the test data from the FamilyTreeManager data store when the application quits. (This doesn't do anything useful here, but you see the form for `@OnStop` Runnables.)

**Listing 5.21 FamilyTreeModel—DataRemover Class**

```
package com.asgteach.familytree.model.data;
. . . imports omitted . . .
@OnStop
public final class DataRemover implements Runnable {
    private static final Logger logger = Logger.getLogger(
                                        DataRemover.class.getName());

    @Override
    public void run() {
        FamilyTreeManager ftm = Lookup.getDefault().lookup(
                                        FamilyTreeManager.class);
        if (ftm != null) {
            ftm.getAllPeople().stream().forEach((p) -> {
                logger.log(Level.INFO, "Removing {0}.", p);
                ftm.deletePerson(p);
            });
        }
    }
}
```

## 5.9 What We Know So Far

The application that we built—that you built—does many things right. We've divided the application's functionality into loosely-coupled modules. Our model (Person and FamilyTreeManager) is in a public package in its own module. The other three modules declare dependencies on this FamilyTreeModel module. Furthermore, we provide an implementation of FamilyTreeManager as a service in a separate module. With Lookups and service providers, we can easily provide alternate implementations without changing client code.

We display the application's artifacts in separate windows: a PersonViewer window displays a tree view of Person objects and a PersonEditor window provides UI controls for editing Person data. There is no direct dependency between these two modules. This is a good first example of a modular NetBeans Platform application.

TopComponents use the NetBeans Platform window system and Lookup provides a loosely-coupled architecture for both service providers and inter-module communication.

But let's take a critical look at what we have so far, if for no other reason than to point to features in our application that don't quite conform to the "NetBeans Platform" way of doing things (yet). We'd also like to remind you that we want to introduce the NetBeans Platform gradually by building on the work we've done both in this chapter and the previous chapters.

Here's a brief summary of why the application we've built so far is not yet complete.

- The Update button doesn't use the NetBeans Platform action framework. Although button event handlers are a convenient way to port a Swing application, NetBeans Platform applications use the top-level menu bar, the toolbar, and perhaps a right-click context sensitive menu to perform such actions as saving Person data. We cover the action framework in Chapter 9.
- The NetBeans Platform includes a Presentation Layer for displaying hierarchical data: the Nodes API. Wrapping your model data in nodes lets you add different behaviors to selectable, visual objects. Importantly, nodes also have a Lookup. You've learned how to add objects to a TopComponent's Lookup. In the same way, you can add objects to a node's Lookup, including capabilities which let you dynamically implement node-specific behaviors. We discuss nodes in Chapter 7.
- Explorer Views display your model data using nodes. The NetBeans Platform has multiple Explorer Views that are interchangeable, since they all work with nodes. We discuss Explorer Views in Chapter 7 as well.
- Using a selection to "open" a Person for editing is not a typical user experience. It is better to open a target with a deliberate action, such as a double click, a selection in a context menu, or a selection in a menu or toolbar. We will discuss this common use case when we cover the Action framework in Chapter 9.
- Finally, in the next chapter, we'll show you how to add JavaFX content to windows to leverage the improvements offered by this UI.

## 5.10 Key Point Summary

In this chapter you built your first NetBeans Platform application by porting a Swing application from Chapter 2. In the process, you learned about two important features of the NetBeans Platform: Modularity and Lookup.

Here are the key points in this chapter.

- The NetBeans Platform provides an execution environment that includes a Runtime Container and a module system.
- The Runtime Container is responsible for loading the modules and classes in your application, providing the Main method, and executing your application.
- Modules are the basic building blocks of the NetBeans Platform. A module is a JAR file with related classes and metadata that describe a module's dependencies and public packages.
- A module can only access code from other modules when that code is in a public package and when the module specifically declares a dependency on the module that contains the public package. This enforces loose coupling between modules and prevents accidental dependencies. The Runtime Container enforces the declared dependencies.
- NetBeans Platform applications include default modules that provide (among other features) the menu and toolbar framework, the window system, the modular system, and inter-module communication.
- When porting a Swing application, place each major UI area in its own window and in its own module. This is a guideline only; let your application's GUI and logic determine how to modularize your application.
- TopComponents are windows that use the NetBeans Platform window system.
- Put service interfaces in public packages to make them accessible by other modules.
- Create a service provider implementation with annotation @ServiceProvider. You typically put service providers in their own modules.
- The Lookup API maintains an application-wide directory of available service providers (the Global Lookup). Use static method `Lookup.getDefault().lookup()` to discover a service provider. The discovery of service providers with Lookup is type safe and keeps your code loosely coupled.
- Use the Lookup API to share objects between modules. One module can place objects in a Lookup and another module can access objects of a specified type in a Lookup.
- TopComponents implement Lookup.Provider. Use InstanceContent to create a container for objects that can be added or removed. Use AbstractLookup to create a default implementation of Lookup.
- The TopComponent method `associateLookup()` designates a Lookup as the TopComponent's Lookup.

- Obtain a TopComponent's Lookup using TopComponent method `getLookup()`. Obtain a reference to a TopComponent with the Window Manager method `findTopComponent()` using a TopComponent's `preferredID` string as the argument.
- A LookupListener's event handler responds to changes in one or more Lookups in a type safe way. In application FamilyTreeApp, we use Lookups and LookupListener to make the selected Person object accessible to the PersonEditor module without module dependencies.
- The Global Selection Lookup provides the Lookup of the TopComponent that has focus. You can listen for the addition or removal of specific object types in the Global Selection Lookup. This lets you track a user's selection actions without creating dependencies on specific TopComponents.
- Use the `@OnStart` and `@OnStop` annotations to implement startup or shutdown code in your application.

## What's Next?

Let's now turn our attention back to JavaFX and see how we can leverage the improved functionality of JavaFX UI controls with JavaFX integration in a NetBeans Platform application.

# 6

# JavaFX Integration

In this chapter, we'll explore how to use JavaFX within a NetBeans Platform application. We'll first create a basic one-window NetBeans Platform application with JavaFX content. This will show you the minimum steps required to add JavaFX to your NetBeans Platform application.

Next, we'll port a JavaFX program from Chapter 4. We'll show you how to structure a multi-window NetBeans Platform application that follows the guidelines discussed in Chapter 5, taking advantage of the same NetBeans Platform features. This includes modularizing your application, using service providers, creating modules with public packages, and relying on Lookups and change events to keep your application loosely coupled. The discussion of this example assumes you have read Chapter 5.

We'll also show you communication strategies you can use to keep your JavaFX UI code isolated and separate from your Swing UI code.

## What You Will Learn

- Integrate JavaFX into a NetBeans Platform application.
- Add JavaFX content to a Swing UI.
- Structure JavaFX with FXML and controller class in the context of a NetBeans Platform application.
- Use Lookup to discover service providers and share objects between modules.

- Communicate between a TopComponent Swing window and its embedded JavaFX scene graph.

## 6.1 JavaFX and the NetBeans Platform

Let's begin by porting an example program from Chapter 3, project MyRectangleCSS-App in the book's download bundle. This single-window JavaFX application is described in "Creating a JavaFX FXML Application" on page 93, "CSS Files" on page 98, and "Animation" on page 100. Figure 6.1 shows the application running during a transition that rotates the rectangle and text elements. Recall that this program uses FXML to describe the scene graph and associated controller class to specify event handlers and any additional configuration. The main program invokes the FXML Loader to instantiate the elements in the scene graph and the controller class.

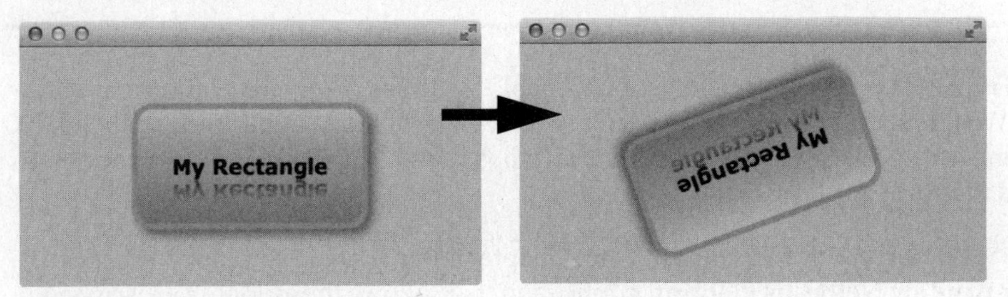


Figure 6.1 The Rectangle node rotates with a rotation animation

Figure 6.2 shows this program running as a NetBeans Platform application with the rectangle and text elements during rotation. Although similar, the NetBeans Platform application has a top-level menu and toolbar, a fully floating/docking resizable window, and the ability to open and close the FXDemo window via the Window menu.

Here are the general steps to build a NetBeans Platform application with JavaFX content.

1. Create a NetBeans Platform Application project.
2. Create a new module in the application.
3. Add a window (TopComponent) to the module.
4. Add JavaFX content to the TopComponent using Swing component JFXPanel.

There is flexibility with the final step. You can, for example, add JavaFX elements directly to the JFXPanel in the TopComponent class. Alternatively, you can use FXML with an FXML controller class. The FXML approach has several advantages.

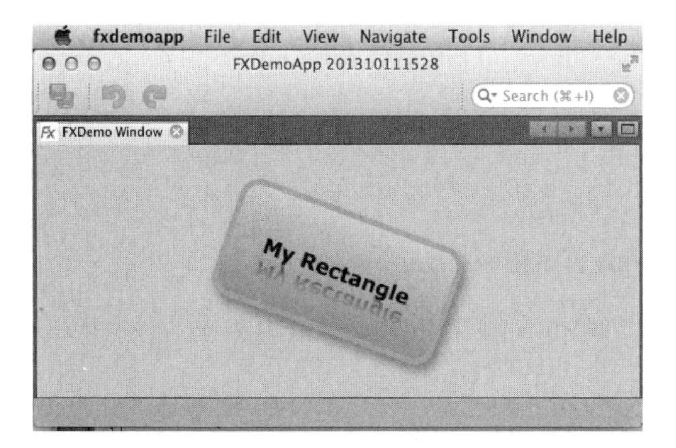


Figure 6.2 FXDemoApp NetBeans Platform application running

- You can use Scene Builder and FXML to build and edit your scene graph.
- FXML (with or without Scene Builder) helps you better visualize your scene graph. FXML also makes it easier to edit scene graph elements, since you don't have to configure them with Java APIs.
- The JavaFX code is separate and isolated from the TopComponent Swing code. Since you are integrating two different GUI APIs in a single application, your code will be much easier to read and maintain with FXML.
- If you already have an FXML document and controller class, it is straightforward to port this code to a NetBeans module.

For these reasons, we will use the FXML approach.

## Java 8 and JavaFX 8 Enhancements

Beginning with Java 8, JavaFX is fully integrated into the JDK and the JavaFX runtime libraries are included in the standard Java classpath. This means you don't have to do anything special to access JavaFX classes in NetBeans Platform applications. Prior to Java 8, however, you had to perform these additional steps.

1. Create a library wrapper for the JavaFX runtime JAR file, `jfxrt.jar`, and add it to your NetBeans Platform project. A library wrapper is a NetBeans module with all of the JAR file's packages declared public.
2. Declare a dependency on the wrapped library module with any module that contains JavaFX.

We show how to create and add a library wrapper to a NetBeans Platform project in Chapter 12 (see "Prepare to Use the Validation Library" on page 578). The JavaFX runtime is part of the JDK in Java 7 and can be found in subdirectory `jre/lib`. Note that these steps are only necessary if you're running Java 7 or earlier.

Let's begin our JavaFX integration by creating a NetBeans Platform application.

## Create a NetBeans Platform Application

Follow these steps to create your NetBeans Platform application project with the NetBeans IDE.

1. From the NetBeans IDE top-level menu bar, select **File | New Project**. The NetBeans New Project wizard pops up the Choose Project dialog.
2. Under Categories select **NetBeans Modules** and under Projects select **NetBeans Platform Application**, as shown in Figure 6.3. Select **Next**.

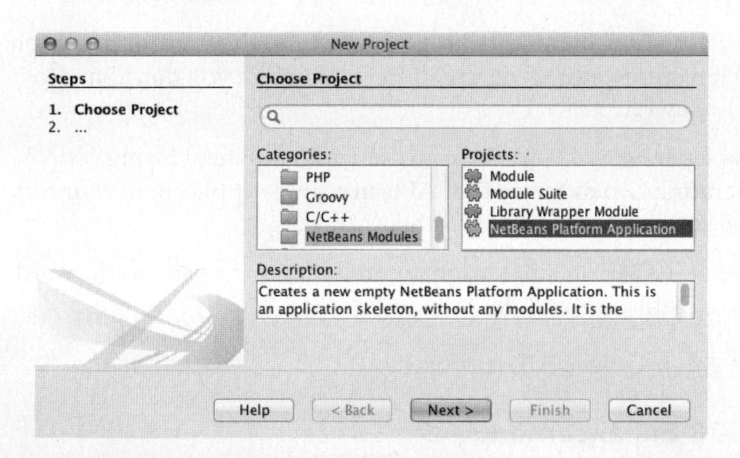


Figure 6.3 New Project Choose Project dialog

3. NetBeans displays the Name and Location dialog. Provide the Project Name **FXDemoApp** and click **Browse** to select a Project Location directory. Accept the defaults for the remaining fields, as shown in Figure 6.4. Click **Finish**.

NetBeans creates a basic NetBeans Platform application with no user modules added. Figure 6.5 shows the Projects view for the newly created FXDemoApp application.

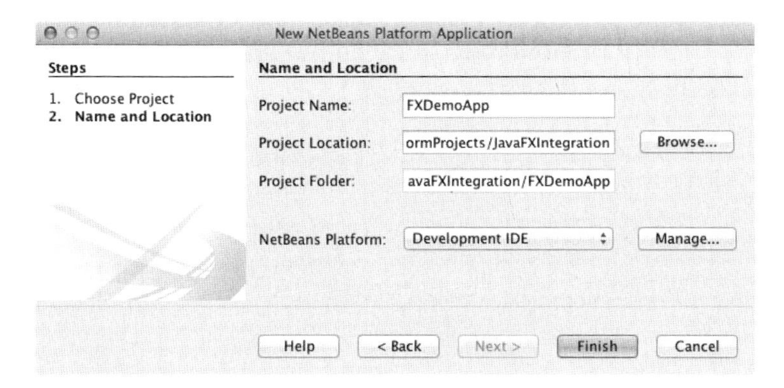


Figure 6.4 New Project Name and Location dialog

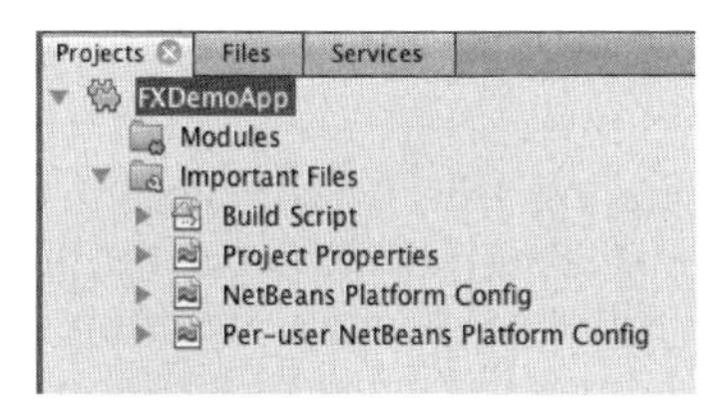


Figure 6.5 FXDemoApp Projects view

## Create a NetBeans Module

You'll now create a module for the application's window.

1. Right click on the **Modules** node in project FXDemoApp and choose **Add New**... as shown in Figure 6.6. NetBeans begins the New Module Project wizard.

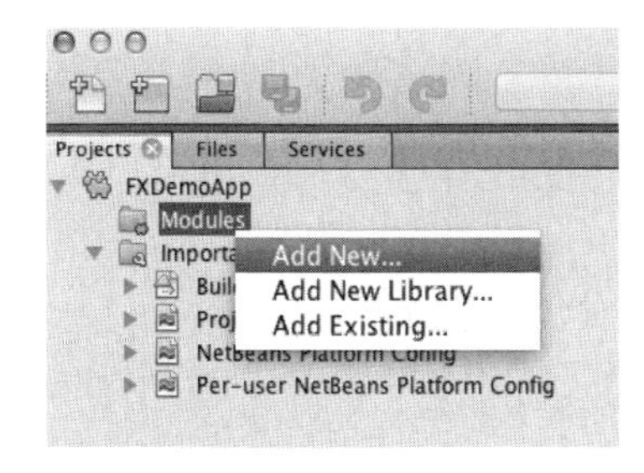


Figure 6.6 Add a new module to FXDemoApp

2. NetBeans displays the Name and Location dialog. Specify **FXDemoModule** for the Project Name. Accept the defaults for Project Location and Project Folder and click **Next**, as shown in Figure 6.7.

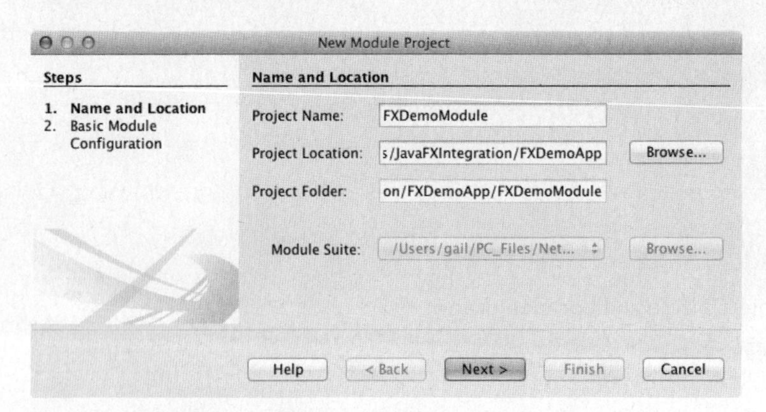


Figure 6.7 New module Name and Location dialog

3. NetBeans displays the Basic Module Configuration dialog. Specify **com.asgteach.fxdemomodule** for the Code Name Base. Accept the defaults for the Module Display Name (FXDemoModule) and Localizing Bundle (com/asgteach/fxdemomodule/Bundle.properties) and leave Generate OSGi Bundle unchecked, as shown in Figure 6.8. Click **Finish**.

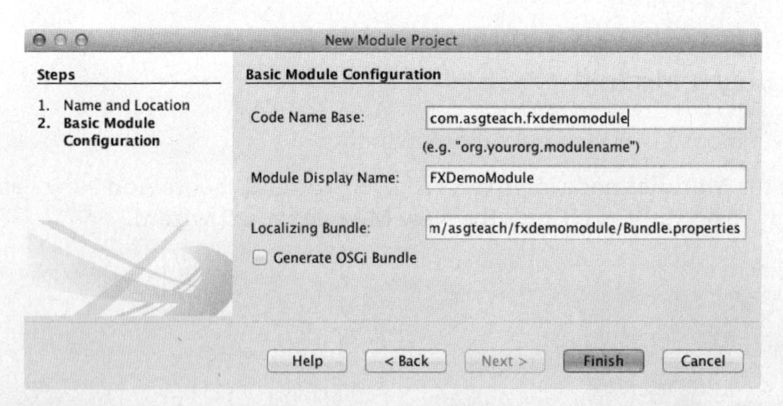


Figure 6.8 New module Basic Module Configuration dialog

NetBeans creates project FXDemoModule for your newly created module.

## Add a Window to the Module

Our FXDemoApp application has a single window. To add a TopComponent to the module, follow these steps.

1. Expand the FXDemoModule project and Source Packages nodes. Right click on package name **com.asgteach.fxdemomodule** and select **New | Other** from the context menu (or select **New | Window** if the choice is available and skip the next step).
2. NetBeans displays the Choose File Type dialog. Select **Module Development** under Categories and **Window** under File Type. Click **Next**.
3. NetBeans displays the Basic Settings dialog. For Window Position, select **editor** from the drop down control and check the box **Open on Application Start**. Position editor creates a large window for your application. Leave the other checkboxes unchecked. Click **Next**.
4. NetBeans displays the Name, Icon, and Location dialog. Provide **FXDemo** for the Class Name Prefix. Editor windows display icons on their tab (if you provide one). For Icon, optionally provide a suitable 16 x 16 GIF or PNG graphic, as shown in Figure 6.9. (You can use file **javafx_logo_color16.png** found in the download bundle for this book.) Click **Finish**.

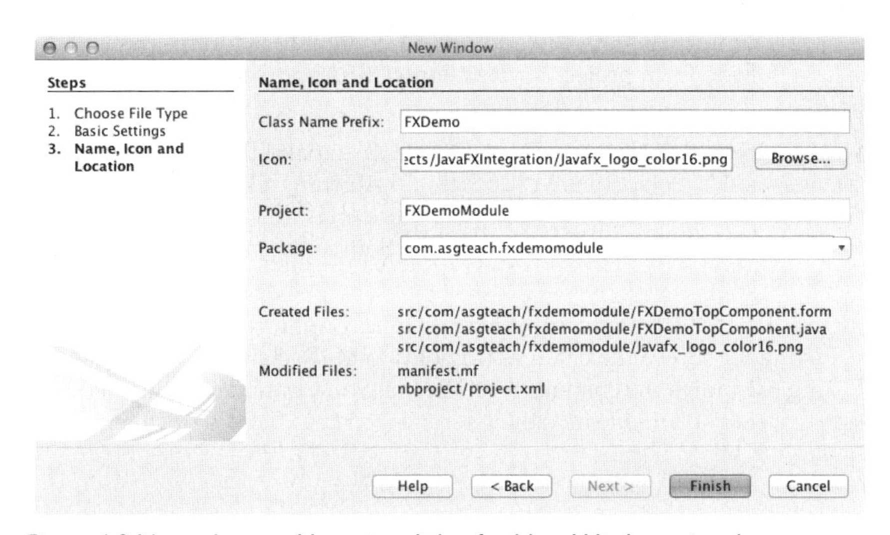


Figure 6.9 Name, Icon and Location dialog for New Window wizard

NetBeans creates file FXDemoTopComponent.java and brings it up in the Swing Form Designer. Click **Source** to bring up the Java Editor in the IDE.

Although you haven't added any JavaFX content to the window yet, you can run the application. Select project **FXDemoApp**, right click, and select **Run** in the context menu. The NetBeans Platform application runs with a single (blank) editor-style window, as shown in Figure 6.10.

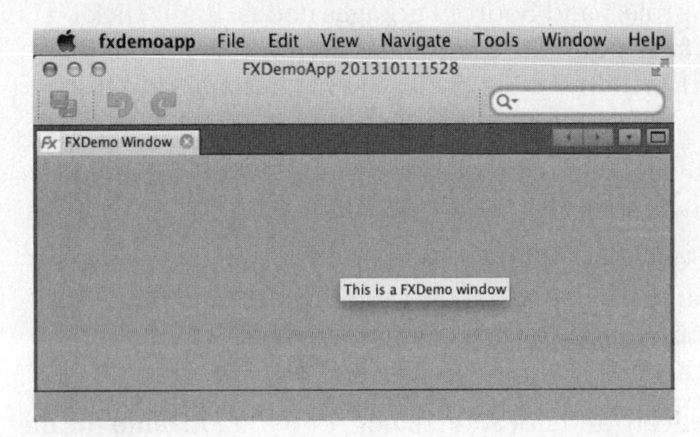


Figure 6.10 FXDemoApp running with a blank FXDemo window

## Add JavaFX Content to the TopComponent

The JFXPanel Swing component lets you add JavaFX content to a TopComponent. We'll use the JavaFX code from project **MyRectangleCSSApp** to configure our TopComponent.

1. Open project **MyRectangleCSSApp** from Chapter 3. Expand the project and the Source Packages nodes. Select files **MyCSS.css**, **MyRectangleFX.fxml**, and **MyRectangleFXController.java**, as shown in Figure 6.11. Copy these three files to package **com.asgteach.fxdemomodule** under the Source Packages node in project FXDemoModule.
2. Make changes to the FXML and controller class to account for the different package name. Listing 6.1 shows the changes (in bold) to MyRectangleFXController.java. Listing 6.2 shows the changes to MyRectangleFX.fxml. You don't need to edit the `<stylesheets>` element since the reference to MyCSS.css is unchanged.

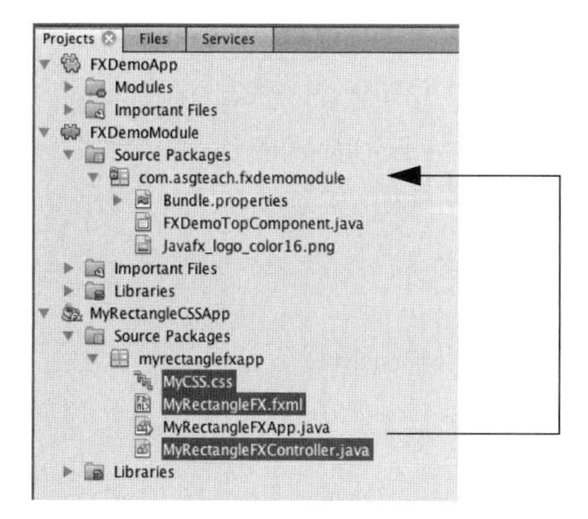


Figure 6.11 Copy CSS file, FXML file, and controller class

### Listing 6.1 MyRectangleFXController.java

```
package com.asgteach.fxdemomodule;

. . . import statements omitted . . .

public class MyRectangleFXController implements Initializable {

. . . unchanged code omitted . . .
}
```

### Listing 6.2 MyRectangleFX.fxml

```
<StackPane id="StackPane" fx:id="stackpane"
           xmlns:fx="http://javafx.com/fxml"
           fx:controller="com.asgteach.fxdemomodule.MyRectangleFXController">
    <stylesheets>
        <URL value="@MyCSS.css" />
    </stylesheets>
    <children>
  . . . unchanged code omitted . . .
    </children>
</StackPane>
```

3. Add the following code to the TopComponent, file FXDemoTopComponent.java, as shown in Listing 6.3. This code creates the JFXPanel and adds the scene and FXML-defined scene graph to the JFXPanel component. The added code is in bold.

**Listing 6.3 FXDemoTopComponent.java**

```
. . . topcomponent annotations and import statements omitted . . .

public final class FXDemoTopComponent extends TopComponent {

    private static JFXPanel fxPanel;

    public FXDemoTopComponent() {
        initComponents();
        setName(Bundle.CTL_FXDemoTopComponent());
        setToolTipText(Bundle.HINT_FXDemoTopComponent());
        setLayout(new BorderLayout());
        init();
    }

    private void init() {
        fxPanel = new JFXPanel();
        add(fxPanel, BorderLayout.CENTER);
        Platform.setImplicitExit(false);
        Platform.runLater(() -> createScene());
    }

    private void createScene() {
        try {
            Parent root = FXMLLoader.load(getClass().getResource(
                            "MyRectangleFX.fxml"));
            Scene scene = new Scene(root, Color.LIGHTBLUE);
            fxPanel.setScene(scene);
        } catch (IOException ex) {
            Exceptions.printStackTrace(ex);
        }
    }
. . . unchanged code omitted . . .
}
```

Creating JavaFX content in a NetBeans Platform TopComponent requires several actions as shown in Listing 6.3 and further described here.

- Create a Swing BorderLayout component and add it to the TopComponent's layout. BorderLayout will keep the resizing behavior consistent with a top-level JavaFX Stage (window frame).

**Adding JavaFX Content Tip**

*If you forget the* `setLayout(new BorderLayout())` *statement, you won't see any JavaFX content in your NetBeans Platform window.*

- Instantiate the JFXPanel component and add it to the TopComponent's layout with `Border.CENTER`. This keeps the JavaFX content centered in the window.
- When the first JFXPanel object is created, it implicitly initializes the JavaFX runtime (the JavaFX Application Thread). When the final JFXPanel is destroyed, the JavaFX runtime exits. With `Platform.setExplicitExit(false)`, the JavaFX Application Thread does not exit after the last JavaFX content window closes. This setting is necessary to close and then re-open JavaFX-enabled windows.
- Wrap the code that creates the JavaFX content in a runnable (or use a lambda expression) and invoke it with `Platform.runLater()`. TopComponent code executes on the Swing EDT, whereas JavaFX code that creates and manipulates the scene graph must execute on the JavaFX Application Thread.[1]
- The code in `createScene()` is analogous to the code in a JavaFX application's `start()` method (for example, as shown in Listing 3.2 on page 95). In both methods, you invoke the FXML Loader to load the scene graph and create and set the root for the scene. The `start()` method sets the Stage's scene, whereas `createScene()` sets the scene in the JFXPanel component.

With these modifications, FXDemoApp is ready to run. Note that the animation initiated by a mouse click inside the rectangle works exactly the same as the JavaFX-only application. Also note that we made no modifications (other than changing the package name) to either the FXML or the controller class!

## The Magic of JFXPanel

The JFXPanel component is a Swing JComponent specifically implemented to embed JavaFX content in a Swing application. JFXPanel starts up the JavaFX runtime for you. It also transparently forwards all input (mouse, key) and focus events to the JavaFX runtime. This transparent handling of user input allows the FXDemoApp application to run with minimal changes from the ported JavaFX program.

The JFXPanel component allows both Swing and JavaFX to run concurrently. You therefore must pay attention to code that manipulates Swing components from the JavaFX environment and code that manipulates the JavaFX scene graph from the Swing environment. To manipulate the Swing UI from JavaFX, you wrap the code in a

1. As noted in Chapter 3, there is experimental support in JDK 8 for making the EDT and JavaFX Application Thread (FXT) the same thread. Currently, this is not the default behavior. To run with a single EDT-FXT thread, supply runtime VM option **`-Djavafx.embed.singleThread=true`**. Since this feature is experimental, we show you how to use JavaFX and Swing in the default configuration (two separate threads).

Runnable and use `SwingUtilities.invokeLater()` (lambdas help reduce boilerplate code here).

```
SwingUtilities.invokeLater(() -> {
        // Change Swing UI
});
```

Conversely, to manipulate the JavaFX UI from Swing, wrap the code in a Runnable and call `Platform.runLater()`.

```
Platform.runLater(() -> {
        // Change JavaFX UI
});
```

The communication requirements, however, can be more involved. In the next section we'll examine the strategies to communicate between Swing and JavaFX from an architectural point of view and in the context of a NetBeans Platform application.

## SwingNode

SwingNode is the counterpart to JFXPanel and lets you install Swing content into a JavaFX scene graph. When you use SwingNode you'll have to pay attention to EDT / JavaFX Application Thread issues. Since SwingNode is part of JavaFX, you instantiate and manipulate it just like any other JavaFX node. However, when you install Swing content, you must execute on the EDT.

Let's show you how to use SwingNode with a Swing JButton component in our demo application, FXDemoApp. Listing 6.4 shows the modified FXML file with SwingNode added to the StackPane. We set the `fx:id` attribute to access the SwingNode in the controller class, and the `translateY` property places the SwingNode above the Text.

**Listing 6.4 MyRectangleFX.fxml—Add SwingNode**

```
<StackPane id="StackPane" fx:id="stackpane"
        xmlns:fx="http://javafx.com/fxml"
        fx:controller="com.asgteach.fxdemomodule.MyRectangleFXController">
    <stylesheets>
        <URL value="@MyCSS.css" />
    </stylesheets>
    <children>
        . . . unchanged code omitted . . .
        <SwingNode fx:id="swingNode" translateY="-30"  />
    </children>
</StackPane>
```

Listing 6.5 shows you how to install Swing content into SwingNode with `SwingUtilities.invokeLater()`. We add a Swing ActionListener to the `clickButton` JButton component. The event handler is invoked on the EDT. However, because we manipulate the JavaFX scene graph in the handler, we must then use `Platform.runLater()`.

**Listing 6.5 MyRectangleFXController.java—Using SwingNode**

```
public class MyRectangleFXController implements Initializable {

    @FXML
    private Rectangle rectangle;
    @FXML
    private StackPane stackpane;
    @FXML
    private SwingNode swingNode;
    private RotateTransition rt;
    private JButton clickButton;

    @Override
    public void initialize(URL url, ResourceBundle rb) {
        . . . unchanged code omitted
        createAndSetSwingContent(swingNode);
    }
    private void createAndSetSwingContent(final SwingNode swingNode) {
        SwingUtilities.invokeLater(() -> {
            swingNode.setContent(clickButton = new JButton("Click me!"));
            clickButton.addActionListener((ActionEvent e) -> {
                Platform.runLater(() -> rt.play());
            });
        });
    }
}
```

Figure 6.12 shows the rotating Rectangle, Text, and SwingNode, activated when the user clicks the Swing JButton.[2]

## 6.2 Communication Strategies

Depending on your NetBeans Platform application, there will be various requirements for communication between the TopComponent (which is tightly integrated into the NetBeans Platform framework and window system) and the JavaFX scene

2. SwingNode is a great way to add custom Swing components to the JavaFX scene graph. However, we recommend keeping the JavaFX and Swing elements as isolated as possible. See the section on "Communication Strategies" on this page for a discussion.

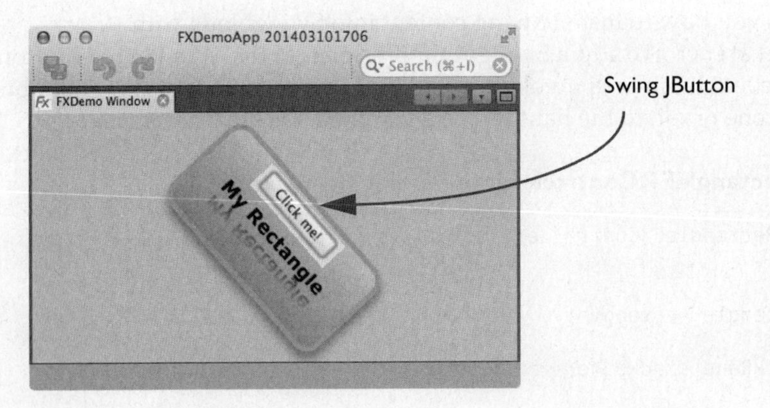


Figure 6.12 Using SwingNode in a JavaFX scene graph

graph and controller code. The simplest application requires no communication at all between the TopComponent and JavaFX code. In this case, the JFXPanel transparently forwards all input and focus events to the scene graph. The NetBeans Platform window with JavaFX content behaves like a stand-alone JavaFX program. This is the situation with the FXDemoApp program and its FXDemoTopComponent. As shown in Listing 6.3 on page 258, the TopComponent invokes the FXML Loader and builds the scene graph, and like a wind-up toy, lets the JavaFX code just "run."

However, to take advantage of the NetBeans Platform APIs, you'll need a more flexible structure. Any manipulation of the scene graph by the TopComponent should be controlled, deliberate, and well-documented. Public methods (that you write) in the JavaFX controller class provide this access. The TopComponent thus needs access to the controller instance.

Similarly, to maintain its isolation, the controller class should not invoke any methods in its TopComponent class. Instead, any communication from the JavaFX environment is implemented with property change events generated by the JavaFX controller. As we've seen from Chapter 2 (see "Event Handlers and Loose Coupling" on page 59), event handlers provide a powerful mechanism for communicating state change and maintaining loose coupling. We want the JavaFX code to be as independent as possible from its TopComponent.

Thus, the overriding goal is that the JavaFX scene graph and its controller should be encapsulated, as illustrated in Figure 6.13. The TopComponent communicates directly with the NetBeans Platform framework and is managed by the NetBeans Platform window system. The TopComponent invokes the FXML Loader and builds the scene graph. The FXML Loader instantiates the controller class. Any further manipulation of the scene graph goes through the controller's public methods.

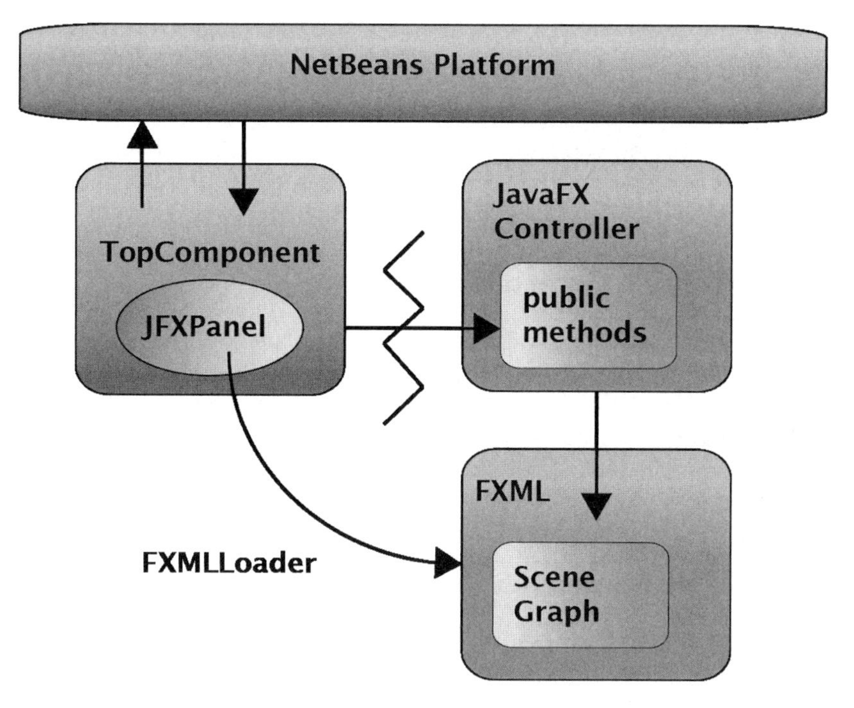


Figure 6.13 JavaFX in TopComponent communication graph

We can characterize a TopComponent with JavaFX content and its communication requirements as follows.

- Self-contained events—All events that occur in the JavaFX scene graph are self contained and no communication with the TopComponent is required. In the FXDemoApp application, for example, the user generates mouse click events, which initiates a rotation transition. Since the handler is in the controller class, no further communication is required.
- One-way communication—The TopComponent must initiate a change in the JavaFX scene graph (perhaps due to a user-selected top-level menu item). Any action that affects the JavaFX scene graph must occur on the JavaFX Application Thread. Thus, the TopComponent must call `Platform.runLater()` to invoke the controller method.

  If the controller method returns a value or reference, the TopComponent should wait for the controller method to complete. The Concurrent Library's CountDownLatch provides a safe and straightforward way to do this.
- Two-way communication—In addition to having the TopComponent manipulate the JavaFX scene graph, the JavaFX environment must communicate state change

back to the TopComponent. In this situation, PropertyChange events fired to interested listeners provide a workable approach that keeps the JavaFX environment isolated from its TopComponent.

Note that we are not saying you should never access the NetBeans Platform APIs from JavaFX controller code. As you will see in our example application, the powerful Global Lookup can be accessed directly from JavaFX code.

## Accessing the JavaFX Controller Instance

To access public methods in the JavaFX controller class, the TopComponent must access the controller instance. Listing 6.6 shows how to do this. Here, we separately instantiate the FXMLLoader so that we can access the associated controller with FXMLLoader method `getController()`. This approach lets you build the JavaFX scene graph in TopComponents that require access to the JavaFX controller instance.

**Listing 6.6 Build the JavaFX Scene Graph with Controller Access**

```
public final class MyFXTopComponent extends TopComponent {

    private static JFXPanel fxPanel;
    private MyFXController controller;

    public PersonFXEditorTopComponent() {
        initComponents();
        setName(Bundle.CTL_PersonFXEditorTopComponent());
        setToolTipText(Bundle.HINT_PersonFXEditorTopComponent());
        setLayout(new BorderLayout());

        init();
    }

    private void init() {
        fxPanel = new JFXPanel();
        add(fxPanel, BorderLayout.CENTER);
        Platform.setImplicitExit(false);
        Platform.runLater(() -> createScene());
    }

    private void createScene() {
        try {
            URL location = getClass().getResource("MyFX.fxml");
            FXMLLoader fxmlLoader = new FXMLLoader();
            fxmlLoader.setLocation(location);
            fxmlLoader.setBuilderFactory(new JavaFXBuilderFactory());
```

```
            Parent root = (Parent) fxmlLoader.load(location.openStream());
            Scene scene = new Scene(root);
            fxPanel.setScene(scene);
            controller = (MyFXController) fxmlLoader.getController();
        } catch (IOException ex) {
            Exceptions.printStackTrace(ex);
        }
    }
. . . other TopComponent code omitted . . .
}
```

The next section uses these communication strategies to port a different JavaFX application to the NetBeans Platform.

## 6.3 Integrating with the NetBeans Platform

Let's now convert a JavaFX program that is a more typical desktop application to the NetBeans Platform. We'll port project PersonFXMLAppEnhancedUI, the JavaFX version of the Swing application we converted to the NetBeans Platform in Chapter 5. (Project PersonFXMLAppEnhancedUI is described in detail in Chapter 4. See "JavaFX Applications" on page 153.) As we build this application, we'll use the same NetBeans Platform features you've seen previously. This includes breaking up an application into modules, creating windows with TopComponents, using Global Lookup and Service Providers, and having event listeners that respond to changes in data and user selection events.

Figure 6.14 shows the FamilyTreeFXApp project running as a JavaFX NetBeans Platform application with two windows. The left window (PersonFXViewer) displays Person objects using a JavaFX TreeView control. When the user selects a Person in the TreeView control, the selected Person object is displayed in the right window (the PersonFXEditor window). The user saves edits by clicking the Update button. Selecting the top item clears the controls in the PersonFXEditor window.

Here are the general steps to build this application. Note that we leverage the same NetBeans Platform features used in project FamilyTreeApp described in Chapter 5.

- Create a NetBeans Platform application called FamilyTreeFXApp.
- Create module FamilyTreeFXModel (for the Person class and FamilyTreeManager interface) and configure this module with public packages so that other modules can declare a dependency on this module.
- Create module FamiyTreeManagerFXImpl, set a dependency on module FamilyTreeFXModel, and implement FamilyTreeManager as a service provider.

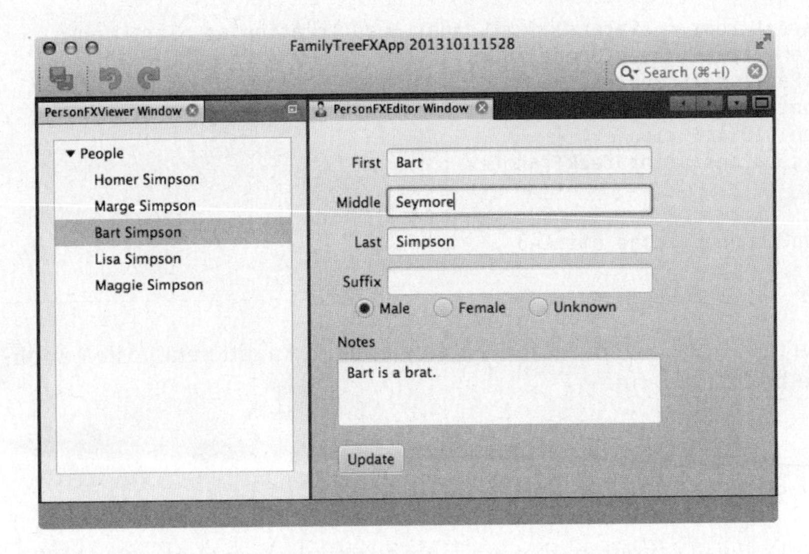


**Figure 6.14 FamilyTreeFXApp running**

- Create module PersonFXViewer for the left window. Set a dependency on the FamilyTreeFXModel module. Build a TopComponent and configure the window to hold a JavaFX TreeView control to display Person elements stored in the Family-TreeManager. Use FXML and a controller class.

  Module PersonFXViewer accesses the FamilyTreeManager service provider through the Global Lookup. The JavaFX controller code listens for changes to the FamilyTreeManager so that the Person items in the JavaFX TreeView control will be current with the FamilyTreeManager's data store.

  The JavaFX TreeView control's selection listener uses InstanceContent to publish selection changes through the TopComponent's Lookup. This makes the selection accessible to the PersonFXEditor module.

- Create module PersonFXEditor for the right window. Set a dependency on the FamilyTreeFXModel module. Build a TopComponent and configure the window to display a form (using JavaFX controls) to edit Person items and an Update button to save changes to the FamilyTreeManager. Use FXML and a controller class.

  Module PersonFXEditor accesses the FamilyTreeManager service provider through the Global Lookup.

  The PersonFXEditor's TopComponent implements a LookupListener that responds to changes in the PersonFXViewerTopComponent's Lookup. The listener invokes a JavaFX controller method to react to selection changes and update the JavaFX Person form.

Figure 6.15 shows the four modules and their dependencies for the FamilyTreeFXApp project. (The JavaFX version has the same module structure as the Swing / NetBeans Platform version shown in Figure 5.10 on page 209.)

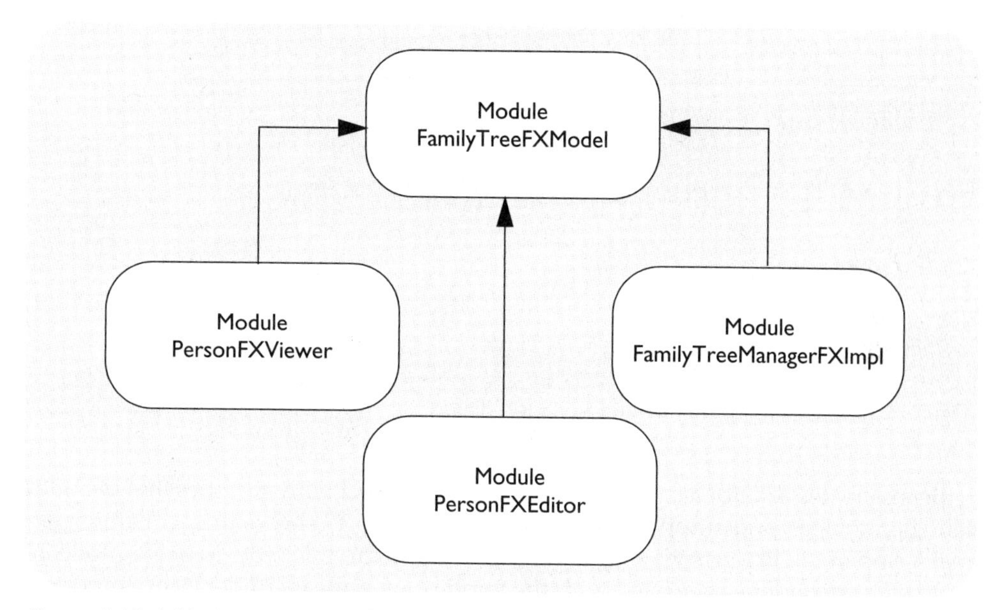


Figure 6.15 Added modules and their dependencies

These steps are analogous to the steps we followed to create the Swing version of this NetBeans Platform application. As we proceed through these steps, we'll concentrate on the JavaFX code and the communication required between NetBeans Platform APIs and JavaFX code. You will see that structuring the JavaFX code with FXML makes this communication clearer than using only JavaFX API code.

## Create a NetBeans Platform Application

Here are the steps to create the FamilyTreeFXApp NetBeans Platform application.

1. From the NetBeans IDE top-level menu bar, select **File | New Project**. The Net-Beans New Project wizard pops up the Choose Project dialog.
2. Under Categories select **NetBeans Modules** and under Projects select **NetBeans Platform Application**. Select **Next**.

3. NetBeans now displays the Name and Location dialog. Provide the Project Name **FamilyTreeFXApp** and click **Browse** to select a Project Location directory. Accept the defaults for the remaining fields and click **Finish**, as shown in Figure 6.16.

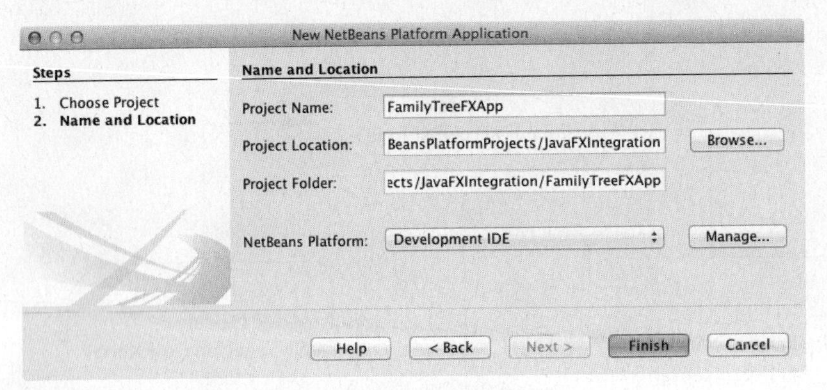


Figure 6.16 New Project Name and Location dialog

NetBeans creates a NetBeans Platform application project with modules that include a menu bar, toolbar, and empty window system. Figure 6.17 shows project FamilyTreeFXApp in the Projects view with no user-created modules (the Modules node is empty). The metadata associated with the application appears under node Important Files.

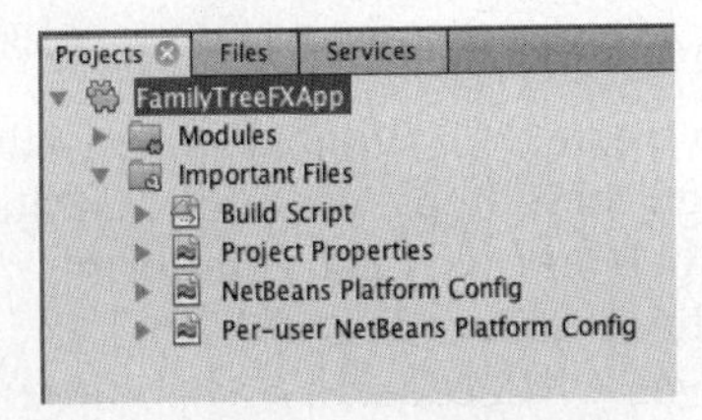


Figure 6.17 FamilyTreeFXApp Projects view

## Create NetBeans Platform Modules

Next, create a new NetBeans module for the FamilyTreeManager interface and Person class, as follows.

1. Right click on the **Modules** node in project FamilyTreeFXApp and choose **Add New...** . NetBeans begins the New Module Project wizard.
2. NetBeans displays the Name and Location dialog. Specify **FamilyTreeFXModel** for the Project Name. Accept the defaults for Project Location and Project Folder and click **Next**.

3. NetBeans displays the Basic Module Configuration dialog. Specify **com.asgteach.familytreefx.model** for the Code Name Base. Accept the defaults for the Module Display Name (FamilyTreeFXModel) and Localizing Bundle (com/asgteach/familytreefx/model/Bundle.properties) and leave Generate OSGi Bundle unchecked, as shown in Figure 6.18. Click **Finish**.

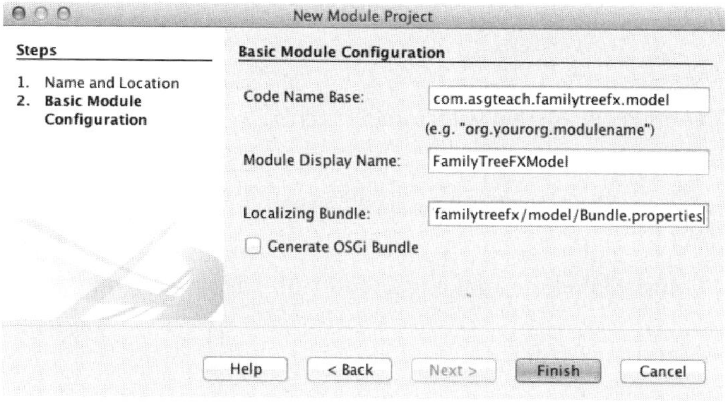

Figure 6.18 Basic Configuration dialog for module FamilyTreeFXModel

The FamilyTreeFXApp application now contains one user-added module called FamilyTreeFXModel. Repeat the above steps and add three more modules: FamilyTreeManagerFXImpl, PersonFXViewer, and PersonFXEditor, as follows.

1. New Module **FamilyTreeManagerFXImpl**, code name base **com.asgteach.familytree.managerfx.impl**, and display name **FamilyTreeManagerFXImpl**.
2. New Module **PersonFXViewer**, code name base **com.asgteach.familytree.personfxviewer**, and display name **PersonFXViewer**.
3. New Module **PersonFXEditor**, code name base **com.asgteach.familytree.personfxeditor**, and display name **PersonFXEditor**.

Figure 6.19 shows the Projects view for application FamilyTreeFXApp with its four modules. You also see new projects for each module. Recall that when you work with these module projects, you select the project name outside the FamilyTreeFXApp project, not the module name under the Modules node.

## Configure a Module with Public Packages

Now let's add code and configure module FamilyTreeFXModel.

1. Begin by copying files Person.java and FamilyTreeManager.java from project **PersonFXMLAppEnhancedUI** to package **com.asgteach.familytreefx.model**

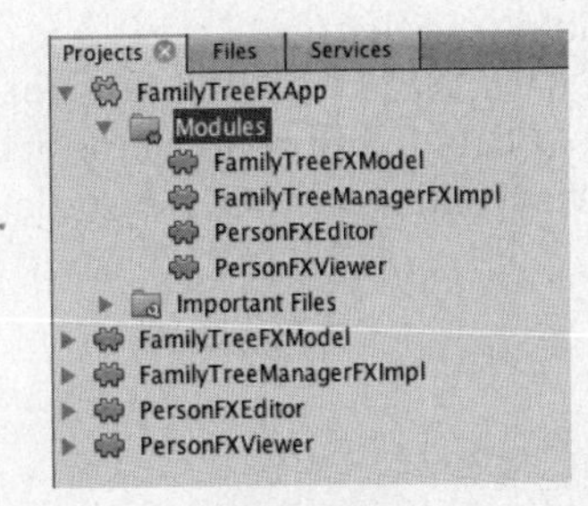


Figure 6.19 FamilyTreeFXApp Projects view with added modules

under Source Packages (use Refactor Copy). Class Person.java is unchanged (see Listing 4.8 on page 142).

2. Modify FamilyTreeManager.java and make it an interface, as shown in Listing 6.7.

**Listing 6.7 FamilyTreeManager Interface**

```
package com.asgteach.familytreefx.model;

import java.util.List;
import javafx.beans.InvalidationListener;
import javafx.collections.MapChangeListener;

public interface FamilyTreeManager {

    public void addListener(
         MapChangeListener<? super Long, ? super Person> ml);

    public void removeListener(
         MapChangeListener<? super Long, ? super Person> ml);

    public void addListener(InvalidationListener il);

    public void removeListener(InvalidationListener il);

    public void addPerson(Person p);

    public void updatePerson(Person p);

    public void deletePerson(Person p);

    public List<Person> getAllPeople();
}
```

3. Since we want other modules to access the code in this module, we declare package com.asgteach.familytreefx.model public. In the Projects view, select project **FamilyTreeFXModel**, right click, and select **Properties** from the context menu.

4. Under Categories, select **API Versioning**.
5. Under Public Packages, select the checkbox to specify that package com.asgteach.familytreefx.model is **Public**, as shown in Figure 6.20. Accept the default for Specification Version 1.0. Click **OK**.

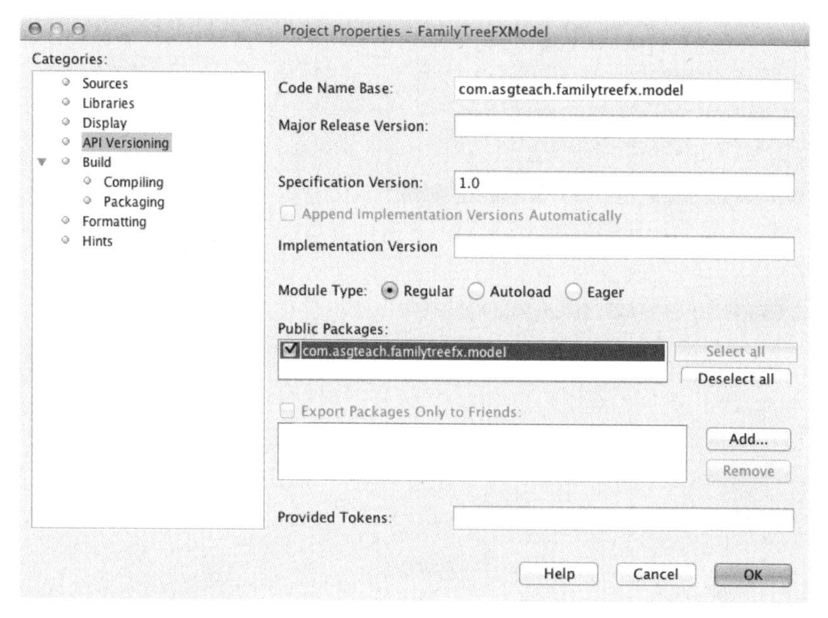


Figure 6.20 API Versioning: Specify Public Packages

## Register a Service Provider

The FamilyTreeManagerFXImpl module contains the code that implements interface FamilyTreeManager. Furthermore, it registers itself as a Service Provider for service FamilyTreeManager. You register a service provider with annotation @Service-Provider.

### Declare Module Dependencies

You must declare a dependency on module FamilyTreeFXModel to access classes Person and FamilyTreeManager. A dependency on the Lookup API module is also necessary to use annotation @ServiceProvider. Follow these steps to declare the module dependencies.

1. In project FamilyTreeManagerFXImpl, right click node **Libraries** and select **Add Module Dependency . . .** . NetBeans displays the Add Module Dependency dialog.
2. In the list of modules, select both **FamilyTreeFXModel** and **Lookup API** as shown in Figure 6.21. Click **OK**.

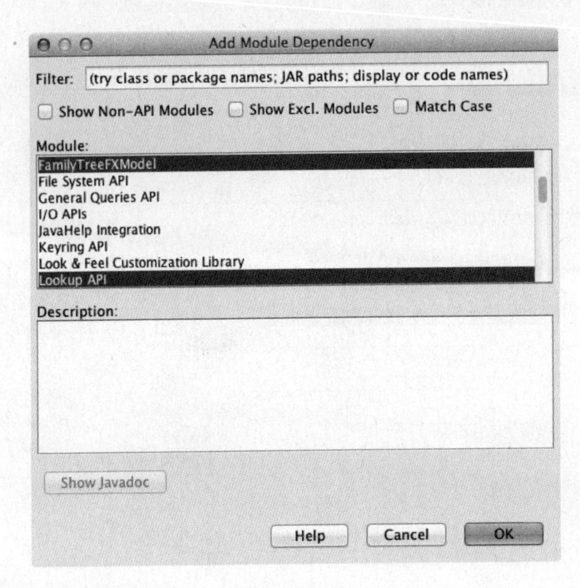


Figure 6.21 Add Module Dependency

3. NetBeans adds both FamilyTreeFXModel and Lookup API to FamilyTreeManagerFXImpl's list of dependencies. When you expand the Libraries node, you'll see these modules listed, as shown in Figure 6.22.

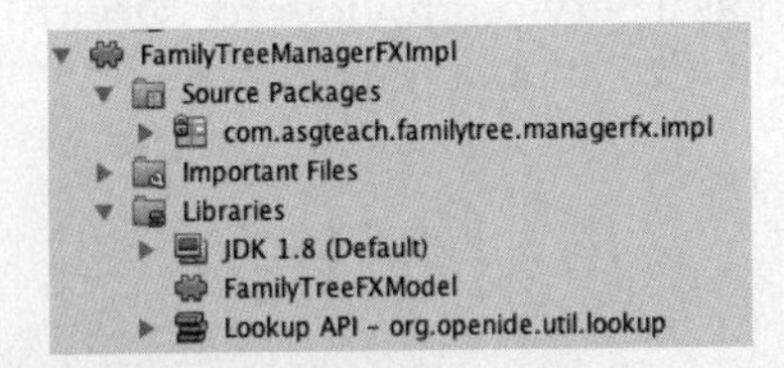


Figure 6.22 After adding module dependencies

## Create Implementation Class

Now add the implementation class for interface FamilyTreeManager, as follows.

1. In project FamilyTreeManagerFXImpl, expand node **Source Packages**.
2. Select package **com.asgteach.familytree.managerfx.impl**, right click, and select **New** then **Java Class** from the context menu.
3. In the New Java Class dialog, provide **FamilyTreeManagerFXImpl** for Class Name and click **Finish**. You'll now see file FamilyTreeManagerFXImpl.java under the selected package name and the file opens in the Java editor.
4. Edit the Java class so that it implements FamilyTreeManager. Fix imports (right click and select **Fix Imports** from the context menu).
5. Let NetBeans generate override method stubs for all of the abstract methods in interface FamilyTreeManager.
6. Copy the method bodies as well as class variable `observableMap` from the Family-TreeManager class in project PersonFXMLAppEnhancedUI (see Listing 4.12 on page 149). Do not include either the constructor or the `getInstance()` method.
7. Add annotation **@ServiceProvider** to class FamilyTreeManagerFXImpl. Listing 6.8 shows the code for the entire class.

**Listing 6.8 Class FamilyTreeManagerFXImpl.java**

```
package com.asgteach.familytree.managerfx.impl;

import com.asgteach.familytreefx.model.FamilyTreeManager;
import com.asgteach.familytreefx.model.Person;
import java.util.ArrayList;
import java.util.List;
import javafx.beans.InvalidationListener;
import javafx.collections.FXCollections;
import javafx.collections.MapChangeListener;
import javafx.collections.ObservableMap;
import org.openide.util.lookup.ServiceProvider;

@ServiceProvider(service = FamilyTreeManager.class)
public class FamilyTreeManagerFXImpl implements FamilyTreeManager {

    private final ObservableMap<Long, Person> observableMap =
          FXCollections.observableHashMap();

    @Override
    public void addListener(MapChangeListener<? super Long,
                                ? super Person> ml) {
        observableMap.addListener(ml);
    }
```

```
    @Override
    public void removeListener(MapChangeListener<? super Long,
                              ? super Person> ml) {
        observableMap.removeListener(ml);
    }

    @Override
    public void addListener(InvalidationListener il) {
        observableMap.addListener(il);
    }

    @Override
    public void removeListener(InvalidationListener il) {
        observableMap.removeListener(il);
    }

    @Override
    public void addPerson(Person p) {
        Person person = new Person(p);
        observableMap.put(person.getId(), person);
    }

    @Override
    public void updatePerson(Person p) {
        Person person = new Person(p);
        observableMap.put(person.getId(), person);
    }

    @Override
    public void deletePerson(Person p) {
        observableMap.remove(p.getId());
    }

    @Override
    public List<Person> getAllPeople() {
        List<Person> copyList = new ArrayList<>();
        observableMap.values().stream().forEach((p) ->
            copyList.add(new Person(p)));
        return copyList;
    }
}
```

Annotation @ServiceProvider puts an instance of this class into the application's Global Lookup so that other modules can find and use it. This automatically provides a singleton object for our application. Modules PersonFXViewer and PersonFXEditor will find and use this service provider to interact with the FamilyTreeManager.

## Configure a Window with JavaFX for Selection

Application FamilyTreeFXApp (see Figure 6.14 on page 266) has two windows. The left window provides a list of Person objects, which we implement in the PersonFX-Viewer module. As described earlier, when a user selects a Person in the PersonFX-Viewer window, the selected Person is displayed in the PersonFXEditor window, the right window.

As indicated in Figure 6.15 on page 267, module PersonFXViewer must declare a dependency on module FamilyTreeFXModel. Follow the steps in "Declare Module Dependencies" on page 271. Set a dependency on the FamilyTreeFXModel module.

We'll now add a window (TopComponent) to module PersonFXViewer with the following steps.

1. Expand project PersonFXViewer and Source Packages. Right click on package name **com.asgteach.familytree.personfxviwer** and select **New | Other** from the context menu (or select **New | Window** if the choice is available and skip the next step).
2. NetBeans displays the Choose File Type dialog. Select **Module Development** under Categories and **Window** under File Type. Click **Next**.
3. NetBeans displays the Basic Settings dialog. For Window Position, select **explorer** from the drop down control and check the box **Open on Application Start**. The explorer position makes the window appear on the left side of the application window frame.
4. Leave the other checkboxes unchecked and click **Next** as shown in Figure 6.23.
5. NetBeans displays the Name, Icon and Location dialog. Provide **PersonFXViewer** for the Class Name Prefix. Leave the Icon blank and accept the defaults for the rest, as shown in Figure 6.24. Click **Finish**.

NetBeans creates PersonFXViewerTopComponent.java and brings the class up in the Design View. Click **Source** to switch to the Java editor.

### Add FXML and Controller Code

As a starting point, copy the FXML document and Controller class from project PersonFXMLAppEnhancedUI with the following steps. Note that after you copy these files, you'll retain the code for the JavaFX TreeView control (the left window) and you'll strip out the code for the Person editor (the right window). When you configure the PersonFXEditor module on page 283, you'll use these same files but strip out the code for the JavaFX TreeView control and retain the code for the Person editor.

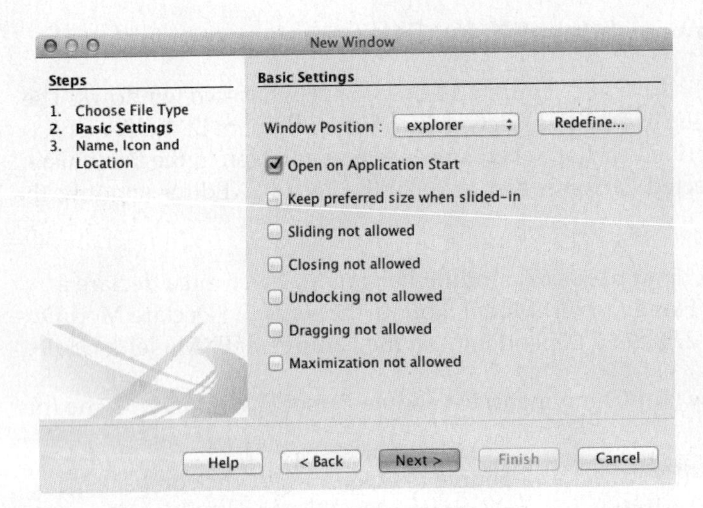


Figure 6.23 Basic Settings dialog for a new window

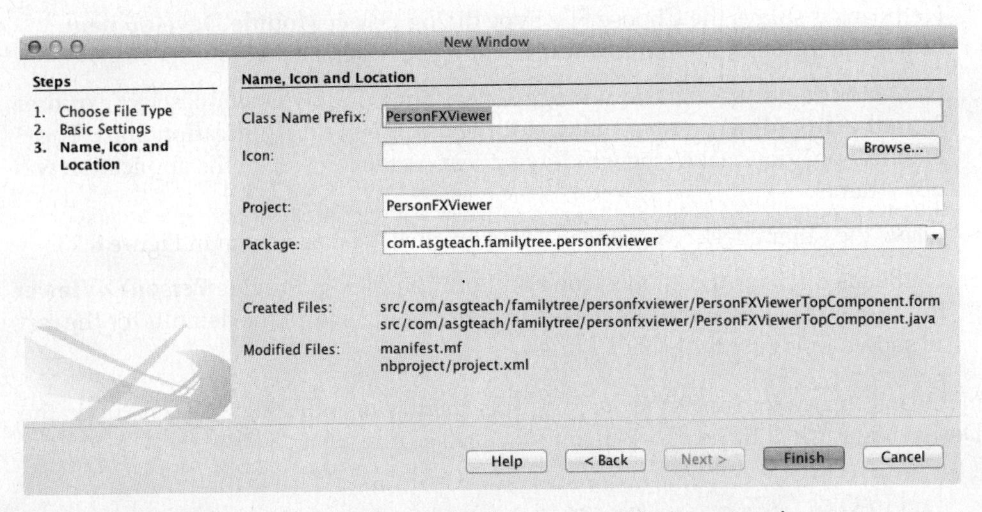


Figure 6.24 Name, Icon and Location dialog for the new Window wizard

1. In project PersonFXMLAppEnhancedUI, expand the **Source Packages** node and copy file **PersonFXML.fxml** to project **PersonFXViewer | Source Packages** under package **com.asgteach.familytree.personfxviewer**.
2. Rename the FXML file to **PersonFXViewer.fxml**.

3. Copy file **PersonFXMLController.java** to the same package in project PersonFX-Viewer.
4. Rename (refactor) the file to **PersonFXViewerController.java**.
5. Make sure the class name is **PersonFXViewerController** and its package name is correct, as shown in Listing 6.9. Fix imports so that the import statements for FamilyTreeManager and Person are correct. We'll make additional changes after configuring the FXML file.

**Listing 6.9 PersonFXViewerController.java**

```
package com.asgteach.familytree.personfxviewer;

import com.asgteach.familytreefx.model.FamilyTreeManager;
import com.asgteach.familytreefx.model.Person;
. . . other import statements omitted . . .

public class PersonFXViewerController implements Initializable {
   . . . code omitted . . .
}
```

### Configure the FXML

Using either Scene Builder or the NetBeans FXML editor, remove the FXML declarations that refer to the Person form editor controls in the right window. Edit the controller class attribute so that it refers to PersonFXViewerController. Listing 6.10 shows the updated FXML. Note that the top-level AnchorPane contains a single control, the TreeView, which is anchored as described by its FXML attributes.

**Listing 6.10 PersonFXViewer.fxml**

```
<?xml version="1.0" encoding="UTF-8"?>

<?import java.lang.*?>
<?import java.util.*?>
<?import javafx.scene.*?>
<?import javafx.scene.control.*?>
<?import javafx.scene.layout.*?>

<AnchorPane id="AnchorPane"  xmlns:fx="http://javafx.com/fxml"
      fx:controller=
         "com.asgteach.familytree.personfxviewer.PersonFXViewerController">
  <children>
    <TreeView fx:id="personTreeView" AnchorPane.bottomAnchor="25.0"
         AnchorPane.leftAnchor="14.0"
         AnchorPane.rightAnchor="14.0"
         AnchorPane.topAnchor="14.0" />
```

```
  </children>
</AnchorPane>
```

## Configure the JavaFX Controller

In the NetBeans Platform version of this application, the Controller class has the following responsibilities.

- Obtain an instance of FamilyTreeManager from the Global Lookup to display Person objects in the TreeView control.
- Implement a listener to respond to changes in the FamilyTreeManager's map of Person objects.
- Implement a TreeSelectionListener and publish the current selection in the TopComponent's Lookup.

Listing 6.11 shows the JavaFX controller's class variables and the `initialize()`, `buildData()`, and `buildTreeView()` methods where we populate the TreeView control with Person objects from the FamilyTreeManager and other variables.

We instantiate an InstanceContent object, which will contain the selected Person. The TopComponent publishes the contents of InstanceContent in its Lookup as described in "Lookup as an Object Repository" on page 225. We keep track of the selected Person with class variable `selectedPerson`.

The Global Lookup returns an instance of the FamilyTreeManager, which we assign to class variable `ftm`.

**Listing 6.11 PersonFXViewerController.java—Class Variables and initialize()**

```
public class PersonFXViewerController implements Initializable {

    @FXML
    private TreeView<Person> personTreeView;
    private static final Logger logger =
        Logger.getLogger(PersonFXViewerController.class.getName());
    private FamilyTreeManager ftm = null;
    private final InstanceContent instanceContent = new InstanceContent();
    private Person selectedPerson = null;

    @Override
    public void initialize(URL url, ResourceBundle rb) {
        // Change level to Level.INFO to reduce console messages
        logger.setLevel(Level.FINE);
        Handler handler = new ConsoleHandler();
```

```
        handler.setLevel(Level.FINE);
        logger.addHandler(handler);
        try {
            FileHandler fileHandler = new FileHandler();
            // records sent to file javaN.log in user's home directory
            fileHandler.setLevel(Level.FINE);
            logger.addHandler(fileHandler);
            logger.log(Level.FINE, "Created File Handler");
        } catch (IOException | SecurityException ex) {
            logger.log(Level.SEVERE, "Couldn't create FileHandler", ex);
        }
        ftm = Lookup.getDefault().lookup(FamilyTreeManager.class);
        if (ftm == null) {
            logger.log(Level.SEVERE, "Cannot get FamilyTreeManager object");
            LifecycleManager.getDefault().exit();
        }

        buildData();
        ftm.addListener(familyTreeListener);
        // Create a root node and populate the TreeView control
        TreeItem<Person> rootNode =
            new TreeItem<>(new Person("People", "", Person.Gender.UNKNOWN));
        buildTreeView(rootNode);
        // Configure the TreeView control
        personTreeView.setRoot(rootNode);
        personTreeView.getRoot().setExpanded(true);
        personTreeView.getSelectionModel().selectedItemProperty()
                .addListener(treeSelectionListener);
    }

    private void buildData() {
        ftm.addPerson(new Person("Homer", "Simpson", Person.Gender.MALE));
        ftm.addPerson(new Person("Marge", "Simpson", Person.Gender.FEMALE));
        ftm.addPerson(new Person("Bart", "Simpson", Person.Gender.MALE));
        ftm.addPerson(new Person("Lisa", "Simpson", Person.Gender.FEMALE));
        ftm.addPerson(new Person("Maggie", "Simpson", Person.Gender.FEMALE));
        logger.log(Level.FINE, ftm.getAllPeople().toString());
    }

    private void buildTreeView(TreeItem<Person> root) {
        // listen for changes to the familytreemanager's map
        ftm.addListener(familyTreeListener);
        // Populate the TreeView control
        ftm.getAllPeople().stream().forEach((p) -> {
            root.getChildren().add(new TreeItem<>(p));
        });
    }
. . . code omitted . . .
}
```

Listing 6.12 shows the MapChangeListener that responds to changes in the FamilyTreeManager's map of Person objects. This code is unchanged from the JavaFX-only version of the application.

**Listing 6.12 MapChangeListener**

```
// MapChangeListener when underlying FamilyTreeManager changes
private final MapChangeListener<Long, Person> familyTreeListener =
                                    (change) -> {
    if (change.getValueAdded() != null) {
        logger.log(Level.FINE, "changed value = {0}",
                change.getValueAdded());
        // Find the treeitem that this matches and replace it
        for (TreeItem<Person> node :
                            personTreeView.getRoot().getChildren()) {
            if (change.getKey().equals(node.getValue().getId())) {
                // an update returns the new value in getValueAdded()
                node.setValue(change.getValueAdded());
                return;
            }
        }
    }
};
```

Listing 6.13 shows the TreeSelectionListener, which updates class variable `instanceContent` depending on the TreeView control's selected item. The previously selected Person (stored in class variable `selectedPerson`) is removed from the InstanceContent if the user selects the top root node. Otherwise, the newly selected Person is saved to class variable `selectedPerson` and replaces whatever was previously in InstanceContent.

The public method `getInstanceContent()` returns class variable `instanceContent`. This method is invoked from the TopComponent's constructor to associate this InstanceContent object with the TopComponent's Lookup, publishing it within the running NetBeans Platform application.

**Listing 6.13 TreeSelectionListener and InstanceContent**

```
// TreeView selected item event handler
private final ChangeListener<TreeItem<Person>> treeSelectionListener =
        (ov, oldValue, newValue) -> {
    TreeItem<Person> treeItem = newValue;
    logger.log(Level.FINE, "selected item = {0}", treeItem);
    if (treeItem == null || treeItem.equals(personTreeView.getRoot())) {
        instanceContent.remove(selectedPerson);
        return;
    }
```

```
        // set selectedPerson to the selected treeItem value
        selectedPerson = new Person(treeItem.getValue());
        logger.log(Level.FINE, "selected person = {0}", selectedPerson);
      instanceContent.set(Collections.singleton(selectedPerson), null);
    };

    // called from TopComponent constructor
    public InstanceContent getInstanceContent() {
        return instanceContent;
    }
```

## Configure the TopComponent

Let's now turn our attention to the TopComponent. The constructor builds the JavaFX scene graph and obtains a reference to the JavaFX controller class. After building the scene graph, the TopComponent associates the controller's InstanceContent object with the TopComponent's Lookup. Because the TopComponent invokes a controller method in the constructor (here, the controller method `getInstanceContent()`), it must wait for completion of the `createScene()` method, which builds the scene graph and instantiates the controller. We use the Concurrency Library CountDownLatch for the wait. Furthermore, the TopComponent `associateLookup()` method must be invoked on the Swing EDT.[3] Listing 6.14 shows this code.

**Listing 6.14 PersonFXViewerTopComponent**

```
package com.asgteach.familytree.personfxviewer;

. . . import statements and TopComponent annotations omitted . . .

public final class PersonFXViewerTopComponent extends TopComponent {

    private static JFXPanel fxPanel;
    private PersonFXViewerController controller;
    private static final Logger logger = Logger.getLogger(
                         PersonFXViewerTopComponent.class.getName());

    public PersonFXViewerTopComponent() {
        initComponents();
        setName(Bundle.CTL_PersonFXViewerTopComponent());
        setToolTipText(Bundle.HINT_PersonFXViewerTopComponent());
        setLayout(new BorderLayout());
        init();
    }
```

3. Invoking controller method `getInstanceContent()` on the EDT is safe, since it does not access or modify the JavaFX scene graph.

```
    private void init() {
        fxPanel = new JFXPanel();
        add(fxPanel, BorderLayout.CENTER);
        Platform.setImplicitExit(false);

        // we need to wait for createScene() to finish
        final CountDownLatch latch = new CountDownLatch(1);

        Platform.runLater(() -> {
            try {
                createScene();
            } finally {
                latch.countDown();
            }
        });

        try {
            latch.await(); // wait for createScene() to finish
            // get the InstanceContent from the controller
            associateLookup(new AbstractLookup(
                        controller.getInstanceContent()));
        } catch (InterruptedException ex) {
            logger.log(Level.SEVERE, "JavaFX initialization interrupted");
            LifecycleManager.getDefault().exit();
        }
    }

    private void createScene() {
        try {
            URL location = getClass().getResource("PersonFXViewer.fxml");
            FXMLLoader fxmlLoader = new FXMLLoader();
            fxmlLoader.setLocation(location);
            fxmlLoader.setBuilderFactory(new JavaFXBuilderFactory());

            Parent root = (Parent) fxmlLoader.load(location.openStream());
            Scene scene = new Scene(root);
            fxPanel.setScene(scene);
            controller = (PersonFXViewerController) fxmlLoader.getController();
        } catch (IOException ex) {
            Exceptions.printStackTrace(ex);
        }
    }
. . . code omitted . . .
}
```

At this point, you can now run the FamilyTreeFXApp application. The PersonFX-Viewer window appears, as shown in Figure 6.25, and selection changes are logged.

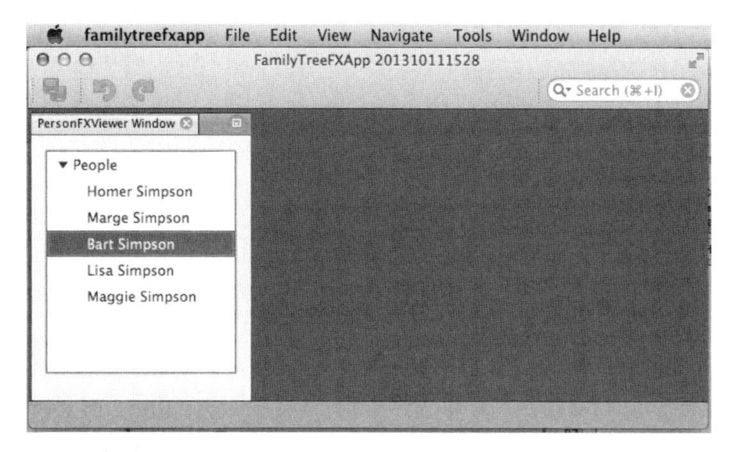


Figure 6.25 PersonFXViewer window populated with Person objects

## Configure a Window with JavaFX for Form Editing

Module PersonFXEditor implements the right window in the FamilyTreeFXApp application. You configure this module in a similar way to the PersonFXViewer module, as follows.

1. Set a dependency on module FamilyTreeFXModel so that module PersonFXEditor can access classes Person and FamilyTreeManager.
2. Add a window (TopComponent) to module PersonFXEditor. In the Basics Setting dialog, select **editor** from the window position drop down control and select the checkbox **Open on Application Start**. In the Name and Location dialog, provide **PersonFXEditor** for the Class Name Prefix. For Icon, optionally provide a 16 x 16 GIF or PNG graphic. (You can use file personIcon.png found in the download bundle for this book.) Click **Finish** to complete the New Window wizard, which creates file PersonFXEditorTopComponent.java.
3. From project PersonFXMLAppEnhancedUI, copy files **PersonFXML.fxml** and **PersonFXMLController.java** to project **PersonFXEditor | Source Packages** under package **com.asgteach.familytree.personfxeditor**.
4. Rename the FXML file to **PersonFXEditor.fxml**.
5. Rename the controller class to **PersonFXEditorController.java**.
6. Edit the controller class so that its class name is **PersonFXEditorController** and its package name is correct, as shown in Listing 6.15. Fix imports so that the import statements for FamilyTreeManager and Person are correct. We'll make additional changes to this controller class after configuring the FXML file.

**Listing 6.15 PersonFXEditorController.java**

```
package com.asgteach.familytree.personfxeditor;

import com.asgteach.familytreefx.model.FamilyTreeManager;
import com.asgteach.familytreefx.model.Person;
   . . . other import statements omitted . . .

public class PersonFXEditorController implements Initializable {
   . . . code omitted . . .
}
```

## Configure the FXML

Edit the FXML file and remove the FXML declarations that describe the TreeView control in the left window. Edit the controller class attribute so that it refers to PersonFXEditorController, as shown in Listing 6.16.

**Listing 6.16 PersonFXEditor.fxml**

```
<?xml version="1.0" encoding="UTF-8"?>

<?import java.lang.*?>
<?import java.util.*?>
<?import javafx.scene.*?>
<?import javafx.scene.control.*?>
<?import javafx.scene.layout.*?>

<AnchorPane id="AnchorPane"
   style="-fx-background-color: linear-gradient(aliceblue, lightblue);"
   xmlns:fx="http://javafx.com/fxml"
   fx:controller=
      "com.asgteach.familytree.personfxeditor.PersonFXEditorController">
  <children>

      . . . fxml for Person Editor form unchanged from
            project PersonFXMLAppEnhancedUI
            (See Listing 4.17 on page 159) . . .


  </children>
</AnchorPane>
```

## Configure the JavaFX Controller

The JavaFX controller class for module PersonFXEditor has the following responsibilities.

- Obtain an instance of FamilyTreeManager from the Global Lookup to update the edited Person object.
- Implement event handlers to process user input from the text field controls, the radio buttons, and the text area control. This code is unchanged from the JavaFX-only version.
- Implement the Update Button event handler, which invokes the FamilyTreeManager `updatePerson()` method. This is also unchanged.
- Replace the TreeSelectionListener with public method `doUpdate()`, which displays its Person argument in the Person editor form (or clears the form when no Person is available). The TopComponent invokes this method in its LookupListener event handler.

Listing 6.17 shows the updated controller code with the modified code shown in bold.

**Listing 6.17 PersonFXEditorController.java**

```
public class PersonFXEditorController implements Initializable {

   . . . unchanged code omitted . . .

    private FamilyTreeManager ftm = null;
    private Person thePerson = null;
    private ObjectBinding<Person.Gender> genderBinding;
    private boolean changeOK = false;
    private BooleanProperty enableUpdateProperty;

   . . . unchanged code omitted . . .

    // This is invoked from the LookupListener in the TopComponent
    public void doUpdate(Collection<? extends Person> people) {
        enableUpdateProperty.set(false);
        changeOK = false;
        if (people.isEmpty()) {
            logger.log(Level.FINE, "No selection");
            clearForm();
            return;
        }
        thePerson = people.iterator().next();
        logger.log(Level.FINE, "{0} selected", thePerson);
        configureEditPanelBindings(thePerson);
        // set the gender from Person, then configure the genderBinding
        if (thePerson.getGender().equals(Person.Gender.MALE)) {
            maleRadioButton.setSelected(true);
        } else if (thePerson.getGender().equals(Person.Gender.FEMALE)) {
            femaleRadioButton.setSelected(true);
```

```
        } else {
            unknownRadioButton.setSelected(true);
        }
        thePerson.genderProperty().bind(genderBinding);
        changeOK = true;
    }

    @Override
    public void initialize(URL url, ResourceBundle rb) {

         . . . unchanged code omitted . . .

        ftm = Lookup.getDefault().lookup(FamilyTreeManager.class);
        if (ftm == null) {
            logger.log(Level.SEVERE, "Cannot get FamilyTreeManager object");
            LifecycleManager.getDefault().exit();
        }
         . . . unchanged code omitted . . .
    }
}
```

## Configure the TopComponent

Listing 6.18 shows the TopComponent code, which has two main responsibilities. One, it builds the JavaFX scene graph, saving the controller reference in a class variable. Two, it implements a LookupListener and adds it to the Lookup.Result<Person> `lookupResult` class variable. The `lookupResult` variable stores the Lookup that contains Person objects from the Global Selection Lookup. The listener is invoked when the Lookup.Result changes. See "Configure TopComponent Life Cycle Methods" on page 230 for a detailed explanation of how the LookupListener reacts to selection changes in the PersonFXViewer window.

The LookupListener invokes the `checkLookup()` method. Here, we must make sure we're executing on the JavaFX Application Thread. If not, we use `Platform.runLater()` to invoke the JavaFX controller method `doUpdate()` with the Lookup results. The `doUpdate()` method updates the Person editor form in the JavaFX scene graph.[4]

4. Since we invoke the `checkLookup()` method both in the LookupListener and in the Top-Component life cycle method `componentOpened()`, we make sure that we always call the JavaFX controller method `doUpdate()` on the JavaFX Application Thread.

**Listing 6.18 PersonFXEditorTopComponent.java**

```
public final class PersonFXEditorTopComponent extends TopComponent {

    private static JFXPanel fxPanel;
    private Lookup.Result<Person> lookupResult = null;
    private PersonFXEditorController controller;
    private static final Logger logger =
      Logger.getLogger(PersonFXEditorTopComponent.class.getName());

    public PersonFXEditorTopComponent() {
        initComponents();
        setName(Bundle.CTL_PersonFXEditorTopComponent());
        setToolTipText(Bundle.HINT_PersonFXEditorTopComponent());
        setLayout(new BorderLayout());
        init();
    }

    private void init() {
        fxPanel = new JFXPanel();
        add(fxPanel, BorderLayout.CENTER);
        Platform.setImplicitExit(false);
        Platform.runLater(() -> createScene());
    }

    private void createScene() {
        try {
            URL location = getClass().getResource("PersonFXEditor.fxml");
            FXMLLoader fxmlLoader = new FXMLLoader();
            fxmlLoader.setLocation(location);
            fxmlLoader.setBuilderFactory(new JavaFXBuilderFactory());

            Parent root = (Parent) fxmlLoader.load(location.openStream());
            Scene scene = new Scene(root);
            fxPanel.setScene(scene);
            controller = (PersonFXEditorController) fxmlLoader.getController();
        } catch (IOException ex) {
            Exceptions.printStackTrace(ex);
        }
    }

    // LookupListener to detect changes in Global Selection Lookup
    LookupListener lookupListener = (LookupEvent le) -> checkLookup();

    private void checkLookup() {
        TopComponent tc = TopComponent.getRegistry().getActivated();
        if (tc != null && tc.equals(this)) {
            logger.log(Level.INFO, "PersonFXEditorTopComponent has focus.");
            return;
        }
```

```
        Collection<? extends Person> allPeople = lookupResult.allInstances();
        if (Platform.isFxApplicationThread()) {
            System.out.println("Already in JavaFX Application Thread");
            controller.doUpdate(allPeople);
        } else {
            System.out.println("NOT in JavaFX Application Thread");
            Platform.runLater(() -> controller.doUpdate(allPeople));
        }
    }

    @Override
    public void componentOpened() {
        // Listen for Person objects in the Global Selection Lookup
        lookupResult = Utilities.actionsGlobalContext()
                .lookupResult (Person.class);
        lookupResult.addLookupListener(lookupListener);
        checkLookup();
    }

    @Override
    public void componentClosed() {
        lookupResult.removeLookupListener(lookupListener);
    }

. . . code omitted . . .
}
```

Figure 6.26 shows the FamilyTreeFXApp NetBeans Platform application running with both windows detached.

As you select different Person items in the TreeView control, the Person details appear in the PersonFXEditor form. Also, if you close the PersonFXEditor window and then select different items in the TreeView, the currently selected Person appears in the PersonFXEditor when you re-open it. (This use case is handled in the PersonFXEditor-TopComponent `componentOpened()` method.) Furthermore, you can close both windows and then re-open them. The call to `Platform.setImplicitExit(false)` makes sure that the JavaFX runtime does not exit.

The FamilyTreeFXApp application not only shows how to build a NetBeans Platform application with JavaFX content, but it leverages the important NetBeans Platform features of modularity and Lookup to achieve the architectural advantages we describe in Chapter 5.

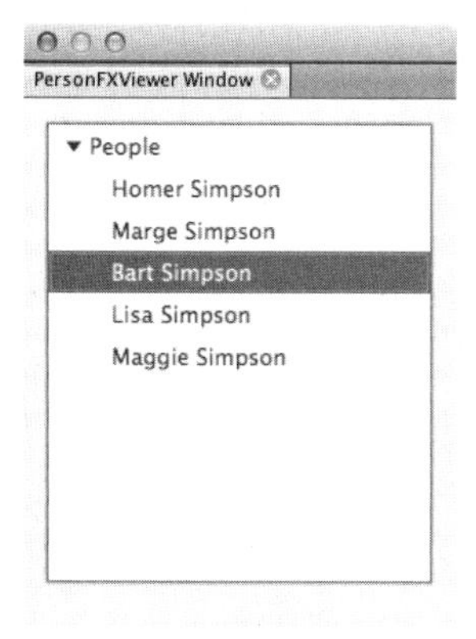


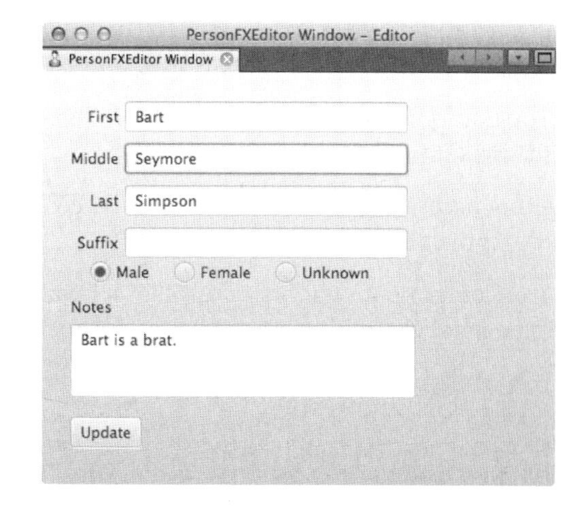


Figure 6.26 FamilyTreeFXApp running with windows detached (floating)

## 6.4 Key Point Summary

In the previous chapter, you learned how to build a well-designed, loosely-coupled NetBeans Platform application that is modular and uses the Lookup API for discovering service providers and inter-module communication. In this chapter, we use the same features (modules and Lookup) to build a NetBeans Platform application with JavaFX content. Here, we concentrate on the issues of JavaFX integration. In particular, we discuss the interaction between the Swing EDT and JavaFX Application threads, the mechanics of embedding JavaFX within the JFXPanel component, and the communication strategies between the Swing TopComponent code and the JavaFX scene graph.

Here are the key points in this chapter.

- You embed JavaFX content into a NetBeans Platform application by adding a scene graph to the Swing JFXPanel component.
- You place JavaFX content in a TopComponent (window).
- It is straightforward to copy an FXML document and controller class into a NetBeans module with a TopComponent with only minor modifications.
- The TopComponent constructor instantiates the JFXPanel component and then invokes the FXML Loader to build the scene graph.
- The JFXPanel implicitly initializes the JavaFX runtime.

- Use `Platform.setExplicitExit(false)` to prevent the JavaFX runtime from exiting when the last window with JavaFX content closes.
- The TopComponent wraps the code that creates the JavaFX content in a Runnable and invokes it with `Platform.runLater()`.
- Code that accesses or manipulates the JavaFX scene graph must execute on the JavaFX Application Thread.
- The TopComponent code that creates the JavaFX scene graph is analogous to the code in a JavaFX application's `start()` method.
- The JFXPanel transparently forwards all input and focus events to the JavaFX runtime.
- SwingNode is a JavaFX control that lets you install Swing content into a JavaFX scene graph.
- Communication strategies between a TopComponent and embedded JavaFX scene graph content can be characterized as self contained, one way, one way with waiting, and two way.
- Provide public methods in the JavaFX controller class when the TopComponent must access or modify the JavaFX scene graph.
- Use the Concurrency Library CountDownLatch when the TopComponent must wait for a JavaFX controller method to complete.
- JavaFX-enabled windows that provide selection events put selected items in a Lookup container (InstanceContent) that the TopComponent then publishes.
- JavaFX-enabled NetBeans Platform applications use service providers, listeners, and listener events to provide a modular and loosely-coupled design. This is the same approach you use with NetBeans Platform applications with just Swing-based windows.

# 7

# Nodes and Explorer Views

Most applications require a user to select objects from among many displayed in a window. Fortunately, the NetBeans Platform lets you easily organize your business objects, display them in a window, and manipulate them. In this chapter you'll learn how to use the Nodes API to organize your business objects. You'll also learn how to use Explorer Views to display objects and use the Explorer Manager to control the process.

## What You Will Learn

- Create a node hierarchy that reflects the structure of business objects.
- Take advantage of node property support, the Properties window, and other components to display and edit business object properties.
- Make user selections available in the Global Selection Lookup.
- Create alternate states of a node hierarchy with FilterNode.
- Select and use the appropriate Explorer View for your presentation requirements.
- Display your business data in table form with business object properties as columns.
- Create a Selection History module that displays a running list of users' selections.

## 7.1 The NetBeans Model View Controller

In Chapter 5 (see "What We Know So Far" on page 244) we suggested that the Nodes API makes selection management and display of business objects easier and more flexible. In this chapter, we'll show you how by introducing the Nodes API, Explorer Views, and a TopComponent's Explorer Manager.

NetBeans nodes wrap application business objects. In the context of the Model View Controller pattern, nodes are the Model. Nodes have a hierarchical structure with a root node at the top, and every node includes a child container. A leaf node's child container has the special designation Children.LEAF. To display a node hierarchy, NetBeans provides several Explorer Views, which are Swing components that work with nodes as their model. One or more Explorer View components constitute the View. NetBeans also has an Explorer Manager to manipulate the view and model as a Controller. Figure 7.1 shows the relationship among these three components.

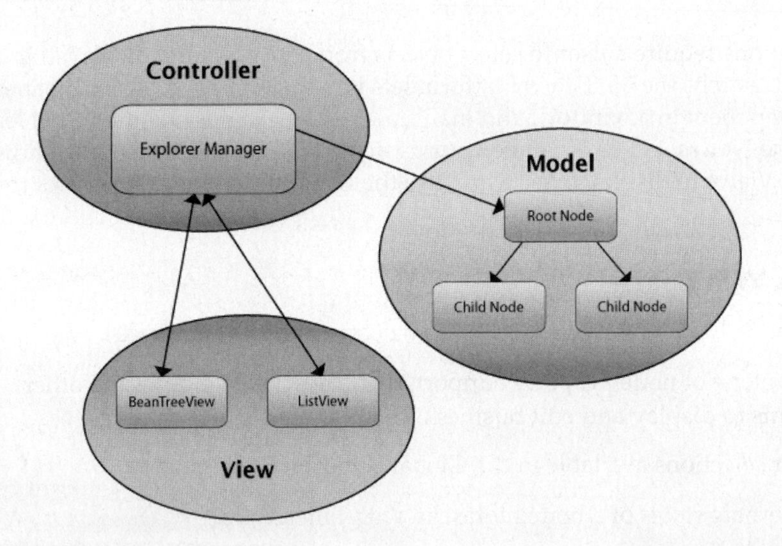


Figure 7.1 NetBeans Model View Controller pattern for displaying hierarchical data

You do not directly connect the Explorer Views to the Explorer Manager. Instead, you set the root node of the Explorer Manager (called the Root Context) to the root node of your node hierarchy. The Explorer Views access the Explorer Manager by searching the component tree to find the first component that implements ExplorerManager.Provider. Explorer Views use this provider to access the Explorer Manager and its node hierarchy. You don't write any code for this. All Explorer Views look for an Explorer Manager provider and take care of finding the node hierarchy. Furthermore, you can have multiple Explorer Views that display the same node hierarchy and share the same Explorer Manager.

All Explorer Views share the following behaviors.

- Display a node hierarchy.
- Respond to user selections.
- Respond to changes in the node hierarchy.
- Find their controller (their Explorer Manager) by searching the component tree for the first component that implements ExplorerManger.Provider. They access the node hierarchy through the Explorer Manager.

Why is this design approach significant to the NetBeans Platform application developer?

- Since all Explorer Views use the same model (nodes), your node hierarchy works with all of them. This means if you want to change the look from a tree view to an icon view or a table view, you only have to change the Explorer View component (one or two lines of code).
- You can use more than one Explorer View with the same node hierarchy by using the same Explorer Manager. This lets you display the same node hierarchy with different views.
- With a single line of code, you can tell the Explorer Manager to put all node selections (single or multi-selection) in the TopComponent's Lookup.

In this chapter, we'll show you how to use the Explorer Manager, Explorer Views, and Nodes API to present and manage hierarchical data. We'll provide multiple examples to show different node types as well as different Explorer Views. As an example, Figure 7.2 shows the FamilyTreeApp just after the user has finished updating Person Bart. This version of the application is based on the FamilyTreeApp presented in Chapter 5. The left window, however, displays its data using the Nodes and Explorer API instead of the Swing JTree component. No changes were made to the Person Editor module.

## 7.2 Nodes

Let's begin with the Nodes API. Nodes wrap a business object and create a hierarchical structure. They provide a configurable display for a business object. Nodes have a Lookup, which generally holds the wrapped object. Nodes also have a context, that is, a set of Actions that can be dynamically enabled and disabled. With its Lookup, nodes have a set of dynamically configurable capabilities. In this chapter, however, we'll

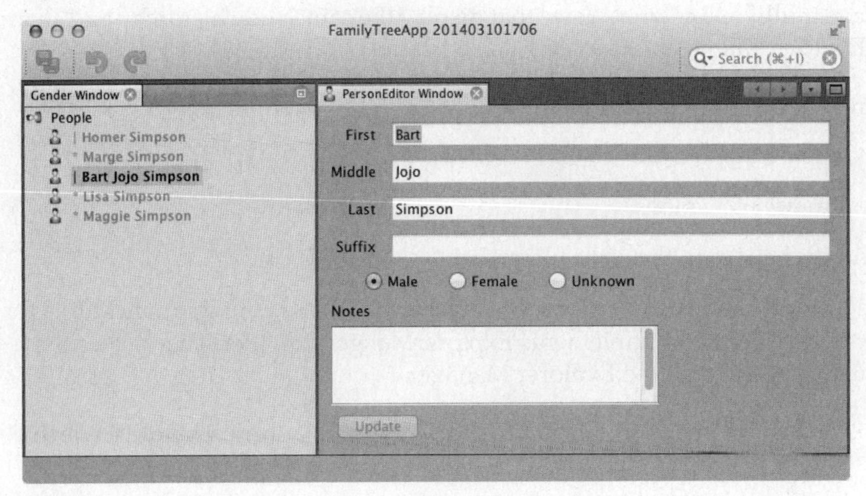


Figure 7.2 FamilyTreeApp running using Nodes and Explorer Views

limit ourselves to building node hierarchies and describing how nodes interact with the Explorer Manager and Explorer Views. We discuss the Action framework and capabilities in Chapter 9.

The Nodes API offers several implementations of super class Node. AbstractNode (which is not abstract) provides a general-purpose implementation of the Node class. BeanNode uses introspection to provide JavaBean property support of its wrapped object. When using BeanNode, you'll see other component features enabled that let you inspect and modify the wrapped object. IndexedNode lets you sort lists of data, although you can achieve list sorting and reordering with AbstractNode and Bean-Node as well. FilterNode is used in conjunction with an already-created node hierarchy that helps you display a subset of nodes based on one or more criteria. We'll show you how to use AbstractNode, BeanNode, and FilterNode in this chapter. We discuss DataNode in Chapter 14 (see "Using DataNode and Lookup" on page 677).

Figure 7.3 shows the Node class hierarchy.

All nodes include a child container with class Node.Children. When you create a node, you also specify how to create its children. If the node is a leaf node (no children), you use the special designation Children.LEAF. The Nodes API includes several options for creating child nodes. However, the recommended approach is to extend ChildFactory<T>, where T is the type of your wrapped business object. This means that when you create a node with children, you provide a ChildFactory.

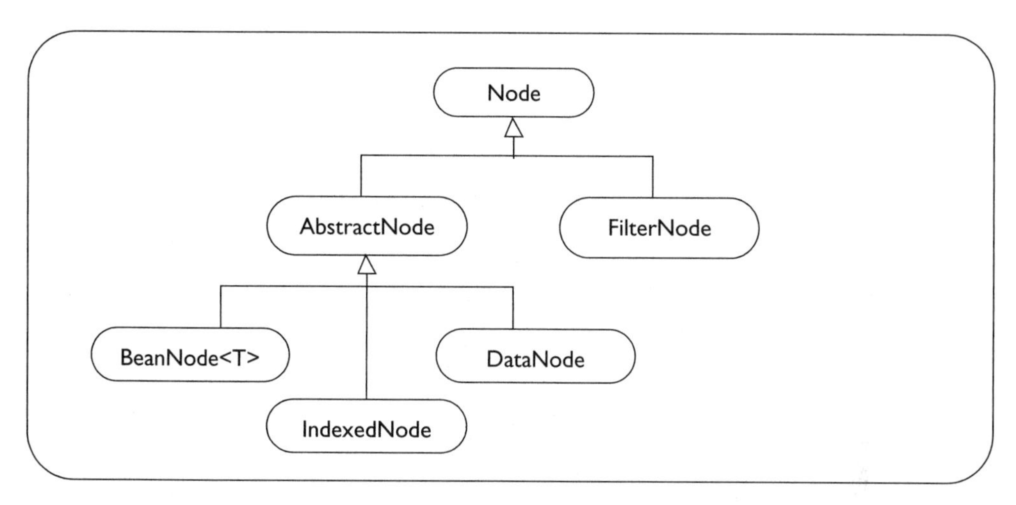


Figure 7.3 NetBeans node hierarchy

## NodeListener and PropertyChangeListener

Nodes also support the standard Java Event Model and fire change events. Nodes support both NodeListener and PropertyChangeListener. NodeListener support covers changes in the node itself, such as node destroyed, children added, children removed, children reordered, and name, display name, icon and short description changes. PropertyChangeListener support applies to changes to the node's underlying Property Sets. (We discuss a node's Property Sets later in the chapter.) When a node hierarchy changes because children are added or removed, the listening Explorer Views respond to these node events and subsequently update the view. All this happens quietly behind the scenes, but you can listen for node events yourself when updates to the underlying model require some action. We will discuss node events further as we explore building a multi-level node hierarchy.

## Building a Node Hierarchy

Let's show you how to build a single-level node hierarchy by replacing the PersonViewer module in the FamilyTreeApp application from Chapter 5 (see Figure 5.3 on page 202). In this example, we'll create a window that displays Person objects from the FamilyTreeManager. The new module will use nodes and Explorer Views, as shown in Figure 7.2. Once again you'll see the advantages of using modules when building an application.

## Create Module GenderViewer

Remove the PersonViewer module from the FamilyTreeApp application and create a new module using these steps.

1. In the Projects view, expand **FamilyTreeApp | Modules** node. Right-click on module PersonViewer. From the context menu, select **Remove**. This removes the PersonViewer module from the application.

**Benefits of Modules**

*Interestingly, the FamilyTreeApp runs without the PersonViewer module, although the PersonEditor window has nothing to display or edit.*

2. Select the Modules node in the FamilyTreeApp project, right-click, and select **Add New . . .** from the context menu. NetBeans displays the Name and Location dialog for the New Project wizard.
3. For Project Name, specify **GenderViewer** and accept the defaults for the remaining fields. Click **Next**.
4. NetBeans displays the Basic Module Configuration dialog. Specify **com.asgteach.familytree.genderviewer** for the Code Name Base and accept the defaults for the remaining fields. Click **Finish**. NetBeans creates project GenderViewer in the FamilyTreeApp application.

## Create a TopComponent

The GenderViewer module requires a TopComponent to display its content.

1. In the Projects view, expand project GenderViewer Source node and right click on node **com.asgteach.familytree.genderviewer**. Select **New | Window . . .** from its context menu.
2. NetBeans displays the Basic Settings dialog of the New Window wizard. Select **explorer** in the Window Position drop down menu and check **Open on Application Start**. Click **Next**.
3. NetBeans displays the Name, Icon and Location dialog. Specify **Gender** for Class Name Prefix, leave the Icon field blank, and accept the defaults for the remaining fields. Click **Finish**.

NetBeans creates the GenderTopComponent class and brings it up in the Design view. Create a BorderLayout to use with the TopComponent.

1. In the Design view, select the TopComponent in the Navigator window.

2. Right click and select **Set Layout | BorderLayout** in the context menu, as shown in Figure 7.4.

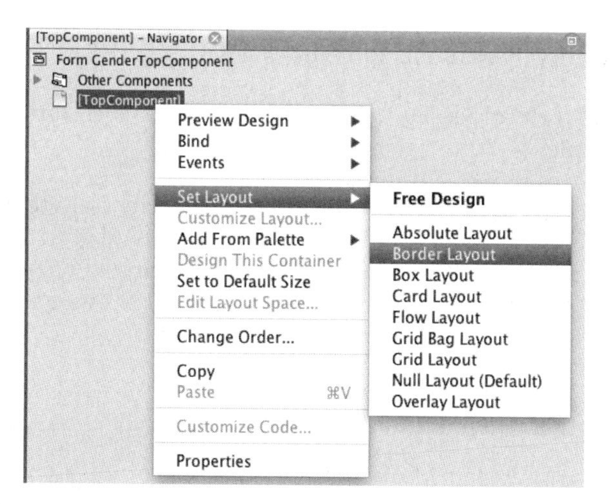


Figure 7.4 Set the TopComponent's layout to BorderLayout

## Create PersonNode Class

Now let's create the Java classes we need to build our node hierarchy. Figure 7.5 shows the Gender window (detached) with the Person nodes that appear under the root node People. Here we display special symbols in front of a person's name to indicate gender. We use | for Gender.MALE, * for Gender.FEMALE, and ? for Gender.UNKNOWN.

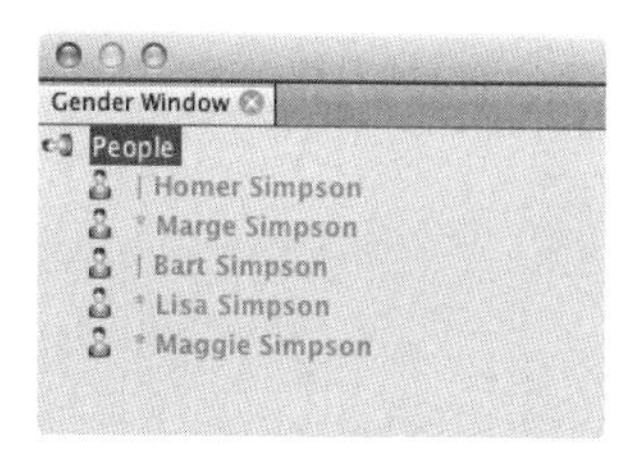


Figure 7.5 People node hierarchy with Gender symbols

In order to access the NetBeans Nodes API and the Explorer and Property Sheet API with the Gender window, you'll need to set dependencies. You'll also set a dependency on the FamilyTreeModel module to access both Person and FamilyTree-Manager.

1. In the NetBeans Projects view, right click on the **Libraries** node of project GenderViewer. In the context menu, select **Add Module Dependency**.
2. NetBeans displays the Add Module Dependency dialog. Select modules **Explorer and Property Sheet API**, **FamilyTreeModel**, and **Nodes API**. Click **OK**.

NetBeans adds a dependency to these modules, adding the libraries to the Libraries node in the GenderViewer module.

Now let's build the node classes for the Gender window node hierarchy from the bottom up. That is, we'll first build class PersonNode, a node that extends AbstractNode and implements PropertyChangeListener. This is a leaf node that wraps a Person object, and its children designation will be Children.LEAF. Listing 7.1 shows PersonNode.java.

**Listing 7.1 PersonNode.java**

```
@NbBundle.Messages({
    "HINT_PersonNode=Person"
})
public class PersonNode extends AbstractNode
                                 implements PropertyChangeListener {

    public PersonNode(Person person) {
        super(Children.LEAF, Lookups.singleton(person));
        setIconBaseWithExtension(
            "com/asgteach/familytree/genderviewer/resources/personIcon.png");
        setName(String.valueOf(person.getId()));
        setDisplayName(person.toString());
        setShortDescription(Bundle.HINT_PersonNode());
    }

    @Override
    public String getHtmlDisplayName() {
        Person person = getLookup().lookup(Person.class);
        StringBuilder sb = new StringBuilder();
        if (person == null) {
            return null;
        }
        sb.append("<font color='#5588FF'><b>");
        switch (person.getGender()) {
            case MALE:
                sb.append("| ");
                break;
            case FEMALE:
                sb.append("* ");
                break;
```

```
            case UNKNOWN:
                sb.append("? ");
                break;
        }
        sb.append(person.toString()).append("</b></font>");
        return sb.toString();
    }

    @Override
    public void propertyChange(PropertyChangeEvent evt) {
        fireDisplayNameChange(null, getDisplayName());
    }
}
```

The PersonNode constructor takes a Person object. The call to `super()` provides Children.LEAF for the children designation and a Lookup for the Person object. The Explorer Manager uses a node's Lookup to manage the selection behavior. (Nodes implement Lookup.Provider.)

The constructor sets the node's icon with `setIconBaseWithExtension()`. This loads not only file personIcon.png, but personIconOpen.png, personIcon32.png, and personIconOpen32.png, if present. (Icon files ending in 32 are larger than the standard 16 x 16 icon file.) Those that include Open are used when a node is opened (or expanded). If these extra icon files don't exist, NetBeans uses the same icon file for all states of the node. If you don't provide an icon file, NetBeans uses a generic "document" icon.

The `setName()` method provides a name for the node. In general, you don't change a node's name after setting it. Here, we use the Person `getId()` method converted to a String.

Nodes also have a human-friendly display name (set with `setDisplayName()`). The Explorer Views use this (along with the node's icon) to display the node. Additionally, the Explorer View invokes a node's `getHtmlDisplayName()` method, if provided. As its name implies, you can use a subset of HTML codes to alter the font color and style. Here we use a blue font color and specify bold (`<b>`), as well as provide the gender symbols.

The `setShortDescription()` method sets a node's tooltip.

The property change listener is invoked with changes to the wrapped Person object, which invokes the `fireDisplayNameChange()` method in the event handler. (We add the listener to the Person object in the PersonChildFactory class, shown in Listing 7.2.)

Why do we explicitly fire a display name change event instead of updating the name directly with the `setDisplayName()` method? The answer to this question is a subtle reflection on how property change events work in general.

A property change event does not fire if the old value and new value are non-null and equal. Here, we're forcing a NodeListener property change event so that the view will correctly update the node's display name. When you change the gender of a Person object without changing any other Person properties that affect the name, the `setDisplayName()` method will not fire a property change event. The `getDisplayName()` method relies only on the Person `toString()` method. However, the `getHtmlDisplayName()` depends on the Person `gender` property as well. Thus, the displayNameChange event forces the Explorer View to refresh the node's changed (HTML) display name when only the `gender` property changes.

### Create ChildFactory for Person

Next, we specify how to create the collection of PersonNodes. To do this, we extend ChildFactory<Person> and provide code to build the nodes. Here we'll need to access the FamilyTreeManager to get the list of Person objects.

1. Right click on the package name under **Source Packages** for the GenderViewer module and select **New | Java Class** from the context menu. Provide name **PersonChildFactory**.
2. NetBeans creates the class and brings it up in the Java Editor. Modify the class so that it extends **`ChildFactory<Person>`**. Fix Imports.
3. Use the NetBeans hints in the left column and select **Implement all abstract methods for this class**. NetBeans generates protected method `createKeys()`.
4. You also override the protected `createNodeForKey()` method. Use the IDE **Insert Code** context menu to create a stub for this method.

Listing 7.2 shows the code for the PersonChildFactory class.

**Listing 7.2 PersonChildFactory.java**

```
public class PersonChildFactory extends ChildFactory<Person> {

    private final FamilyTreeManager ftm;
    private static final Logger logger = Logger.getLogger(
                                PersonChildFactory.class.getName());

    public PersonChildFactory() {
        this.ftm = Lookup.getDefault().lookup(FamilyTreeManager.class);
        if (ftm == null) {
            logger.log(Level.SEVERE, "Cannot get FamilyTreeManager object");
```

```
            LifecycleManager.getDefault().exit();
        }
        ftm.addPropertyChangeListener(familyTreeListener);
    }

    @Override
    protected boolean createKeys(List<Person> list) {
        list.addAll(ftm.getAllPeople());
        logger.log(Level.FINER, "createKeys called: {0}", ftm.getAllPeople());
        return true;
    }

    @Override
    protected Node createNodeForKey(Person key) {
        logger.log(Level.FINER, "createNodeForKey: {0}", key);
        PersonNode node = new PersonNode(key);
       key.addPropertyChangeListener(WeakListeners.propertyChange(node, key));
        return node;
    }

    // PropertyChangeListener for FamilyTreeManager
    private final PropertyChangeListener familyTreeListener =
                                    (PropertyChangeEvent evt) -> {
       if (evt.getPropertyName().equals(FamilyTreeManager.PROP_PERSON_UPDATED)
                && evt.getNewValue() != null) {
            this.refresh(true);
        }
    };
}
```

In the constructor, we obtain a reference to the FamilyTreeManager service provider using the Global Lookup and add a property change listener. Recall that the Family-TreeManager service provider fires a property change event when it updates the underlying store of Person objects.

The `createKeys()` method specifies how the factory obtains the business objects for the child nodes this factory creates. Here we invoke the familiar `getAllPeople()` method to add the list of Person objects to the method's `List<Person> list`. The return value true means that the list is complete. To build the list with multiple invocations of `createKeys()`, you return false until the list is complete. This is useful when the list of business objects is extremely large and you want to return data in chunks.

The `createNodeForKey()` method builds each child node, here PersonNode, with the provided Person argument. We add a property change listener to the wrapped Person object with NetBeans Platform utility method `WeakListeners.propertyChange()`, as follows.

```
key.addPropertyChangeListener(WeakListeners.propertyChange(node, key));
```

A "weak" listener lets the Person object weakly reference PersonNode (which may have a shorter life span than the Person object). This technique avoids memory leaks since this listener is never explicitly removed.

Note that the node system invokes these methods for you as the Explorer View displays its content and nodes are dynamically expanded.

The PersonChildFactory property change listener reacts to changes in the FamilyTreeManager. When the user clicks the Update button in the PersonEditor UI, the edited Person object is updated with the FamilyTreeManager. This invokes the property change listener which calls `refresh()`.

The `refresh()` method is very powerful and efficient. When changes to the underlying data affect the node hierarchy, the `refresh()` method (and the listening Explorer View) handles the changes. Our simple hierarchy's structure never changes, so calling `refresh()` is not really needed. However, if the FamilyTreeManager update results in a re-ordering or restructuring of the node hierarchy, the call to `refresh()` becomes necessary. We'll show you this behavior in the next section.

## Create the Root Node

The final step in building the classes for this node hierarchy is to create the root node class. In this case, the root node's job is to use the ChildFactory to specify how to build its children. Note that you don't create the nodes directly (you don't call either method `createKeys()` or `createNodeForKey()`). Instead, the Nodes API coupled with the Explorer Manager and Explorer Views build the node hierarchy on demand. Listing 7.3 shows the code for the RootNode class, which also extends AbstractNode.

**Listing 7.3 RootNode.java**

```
@NbBundle.Messages({
    "HINT_RootNode=Show all people",
    "LBL_RootNode=People"
})
public class RootNode extends AbstractNode {

    public RootNode() {
        super(Children.create(new PersonChildFactory(), false));
        setIconBaseWithExtension(
            "com/asgteach/familytree/genderviewer/resources/personIcon.png");
        setDisplayName(Bundle.LBL_RootNode());
        setShortDescription(Bundle.HINT_RootNode());
    }
}
```

The constructor invokes `super()` with a PersonChildFactory instance and boolean false, which builds the nodes synchronously. Boolean true tells the Node system to build the child nodes on a background thread. This keeps the UI responsive when building the node hierarchy requires time-consuming calls.

Our root node uses the same icon that we use for PersonNode. If you run the application, you'll see how the icon changes as you expand and collapse the root node.

### Displaying the Node Hierarchy

With our node hierarchy defined, let's show you how to display the nodes in a TopComponent. This requires some plumbing code to connect the three parts of the Model View Controller elements as described in Figure 7.1 on page 292.

- Make the TopComponent class implement ExplorerManager.Provider and instantiate an ExplorerManager class field.
- Override abstract method `getExplorerManager()` and return the ExplorerManager object.
- Choose an appropriate Explorer View and add it to the TopComponent. Here, we use BeanTreeView. To use an alternate Explorer View, substitute its class name, such as OutlineView for example. Everything else will just work.
- Use `ExplorerUtils.createLookup()` to create a new Lookup that contains selected nodes and their Lookups. Associate the TopComponent's Lookup with this new Explorer Manager Lookup. This puts the Explorer View's selected node(s) in the TopComponent's Lookup. Other modules that listen for changes in the Global Selection Lookup can access these objects, as described in "Tracking Global Selection" on page 240 and further leveraged in "Creating a Selection History Feature" on page 332. The ActionMap holds actions associated with the nodes.
- Set the EntityManager's context root to the root of your node hierarchy.
- Activate the Entity Manager in `componentOpened()` and de-activate it in `componentClosed()`. This eliminates any Entity Manager processing while the window is closed.

Listing 7.4 lists the TopComponent code that displays the node hierarchy. We'll describe alternate Explorer Views later in this chapter.

**Listing 7.4 Displaying the Node Hierarchy**

```
public final class GenderTopComponent extends TopComponent
                              implements ExplorerManager.Provider {

    private final ExplorerManager em = new ExplorerManager();
```

```
    public GenderTopComponent() {
        initComponents();
        setName(Bundle.CTL_GenderTopComponent());
        setToolTipText(Bundle.HINT_GenderTopComponent());

        BeanTreeView view = new BeanTreeView();
        add(view, BorderLayout.CENTER);
        associateLookup(ExplorerUtils.createLookup(em, this.getActionMap()));
        em.setRootContext(new RootNode());
    }
. . . unchanged code omitted . . .

    @Override
    public void componentOpened() {
        ExplorerUtils.activateActions(em, true);
    }

    @Override
    public void componentClosed() {
        ExplorerUtils.activateActions(em, false);
    }

    @Override
    public ExplorerManager getExplorerManager() {
        return em;
    }
}
```

## A Multi-Level Node Hierarchy

Our node hierarchy has a root with a list of child nodes. These child nodes are all leaf nodes, so the hierarchy is only two levels: the root node and its children. In a more complex example, the node hierarchy can be many levels. In fact, a node hierarchy can be infinite. Since children nodes are created on demand, you can expand a potentially infinite hierarchy until you run out of resources.

Let's review the process for creating the classes you need to represent a node hierarchy, as shown in Figure 7.6. Each time you create a node class, you specify if that node is a leaf node or if it has Children nodes. If it has Children nodes, you build a ChildFactory specific to that type of child node. That child node, in turn, may have its own ChildFactory (quite possibly a different ChildFactory, depending on the structure of your business data).

Let's modify the node structure and create a set of Gender nodes for Male, Female, and Unknown. Under each Gender node you'll see the appropriate Person that matches its parent Gender node. Figure 7.7 shows this more complex node hierarchy

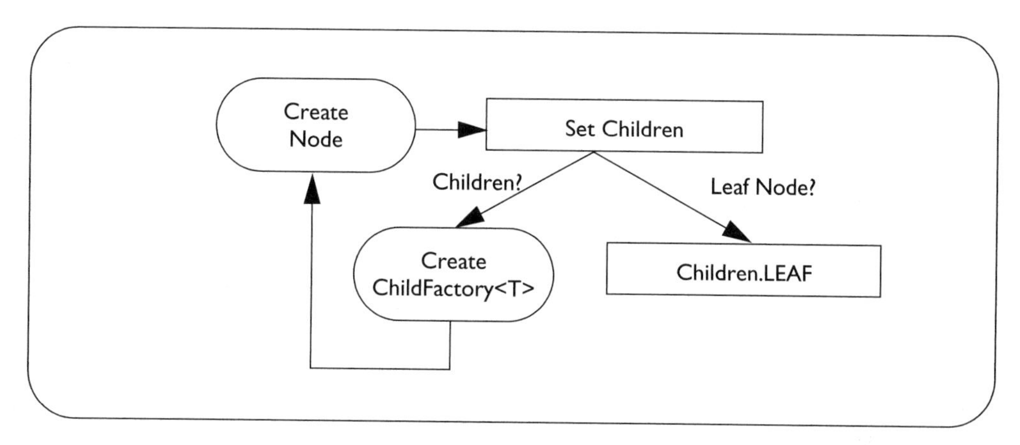


Figure 7.6 Node and ChildFactory relationship

in our running application. We also color code the PersonNode display name and use the same gender symbols as before.

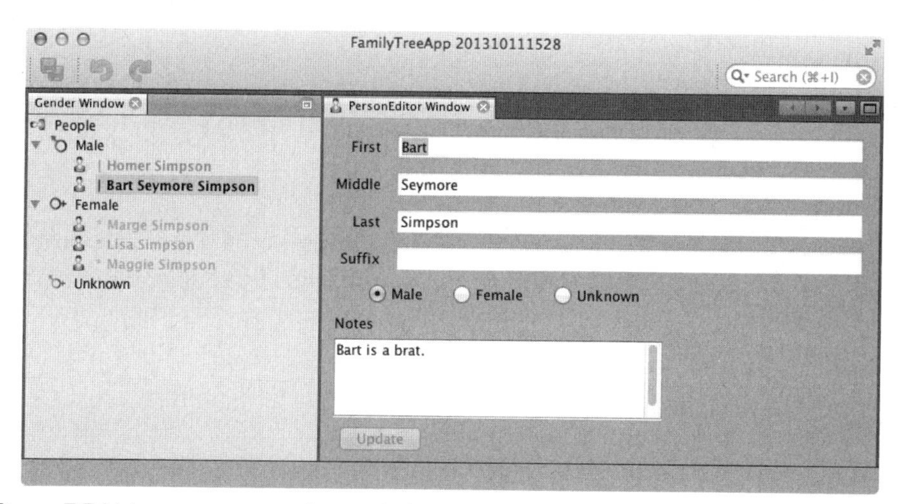


Figure 7.7 Using a more complex node hierarchy

Again, let's build the node classes we need from the bottom up.

## PersonNode and PersonChildFactory

PersonNode (the leaf node that displays a Person) has a slightly different `getHtmlDisplayName()` method, as shown in Listing 7.5.

**Listing 7.5 PersonNode**

```
public class PersonNode extends AbstractNode implements
                                    PropertyChangeListener {
. . . unchanged code omitted . . .

    @Override
    public String getHtmlDisplayName() {
        Person person = getLookup().lookup(Person.class);
        StringBuilder sb = new StringBuilder();
        if (person == null) {
            return null;
        }
        switch (person.getGender()) {
            case MALE:
                sb.append("<font color='#5588FF'><b>| ");
                break;
            case FEMALE:
                sb.append("<font color='#FF8855'><b>* ");
                break;
            case UNKNOWN:
                sb.append("<b>? ");
                break;
        }
        sb.append(person.toString()).append("</b></font>");
        return sb.toString();
    }
. . . unchanged code omitted . . .
}
```

Next, we'll modify PersonChildFactory so that it only builds PersonNodes that match the factory's gender. To do this, we set the Factory's gender in its constructor and modify the `createKeys()` method, as shown in Listing 7.6.

**Listing 7.6 PersonChildFactory**

```
public class PersonChildFactory extends ChildFactory<Person> {

    private final FamilyTreeManager ftm;
    private static final Logger logger = Logger.getLogger(
                        PersonChildFactory.class.getName());
    private final Person.Gender gender;

    public PersonChildFactory(Person.Gender gender) {
        this.gender = gender;
        this.ftm = Lookup.getDefault().lookup(FamilyTreeManager.class);
```

```
        if (ftm == null) {
            logger.log(Level.SEVERE, "Cannot get FamilyTreeManager object");
            LifecycleManager.getDefault().exit();
        }
        ftm.addPropertyChangeListener(familyTreeListener);
    }

    @Override
    protected boolean createKeys(List<Person> list) {
        ftm.getAllPeople().stream().forEach((Person p) -> {
            if (p.getGender().equals(gender)) {
                list.add(p);
            }
        });
        logger.log(Level.FINER, "createKeys called: {0}", list);
        return true;
    }

    @Override
    protected Node createNodeForKey(Person key) {
        . . . code unchanged . . .
    }

    // PropertyChangeListener for FamilyTreeManager
    private final PropertyChangeListener familyTreeListener =
                            (PropertyChangeEvent evt) -> {
      . . . code unchanged . . .
    };
}
```

## GenderNode and GenderChildFactory

Above the Person nodes in our node hierarchy is the GenderNode, a node that displays child nodes categorized by gender. Each of the different GenderNodes has its own icon and display name. The GenderNode uses PersonChildFactory to specify its children. Listing 7.7 shows this code. The icon, name, and display name all depend on the value of the gender argument passed in the constructor.

**Listing 7.7 GenderNode**

```
@Messages({
    "HINT_GenderNode=Gender Node"
})
public class GenderNode extends AbstractNode {

    public GenderNode(Gender gender) {
        super(Children.create(new PersonChildFactory(gender), false),
                                        Lookups.singleton(gender));
```

```
        setGenderStuff(gender);
        setShortDescription(Bundle.HINT_GenderNode());
    }

    private void setGenderStuff(Gender gender) {
        StringBuilder sb = new StringBuilder();
        StringBuilder iconString = new StringBuilder(
                "com/asgteach/familytree/genderviewer/resources/");
        switch (gender) {
            case MALE:
                sb.append("Male");
                iconString.append("maleIcon.png");
                break;
            case FEMALE:
                sb.append("Female");
                iconString.append("femaleIcon.png");
                break;
            case UNKNOWN:
                sb.append("Unknnown");
                iconString.append("unknownIcon.png");
                break;
        }
        setName(sb.toString());
        setDisplayName(sb.toString());
        setIconBaseWithExtension(iconString.toString());
    }
}
```

The GenderChildFactory creates one GenderNode for each of the possible Person.Gender enum values, as shown in Listing 7.8.

**Listing 7.8 GenderChildFactory**

```
public class GenderChildFactory extends ChildFactory<Gender> {

    private static final Logger logger =
                Logger.getLogger(GenderChildFactory.class.getName());

    @Override
    protected boolean createKeys(List<Gender> list) {
        list.addAll(Arrays.asList(Gender.values()));
        logger.log(Level.FINER, "createKeys called: {0}", list);
        return true;
    }
    @Override
    protected Node createNodeForKey(Gender key) {
        logger.log(Level.FINER, "createNodeForKey: {0}", key);
        return new GenderNode(key);
    }
}
```

### Modify the Root Node

Finally, the root node now invokes the GenderChildFactory (instead of PersonChildFactory) for its children. Modify the RootNode class to reflect this change, as shown in Listing 7.9.

**Listing 7.9 RootNode**

```
@NbBundle.Messages({
    "HINT_RootNode=Show all people",
    "LBL_RootNode=People"
})
public class RootNode extends AbstractNode {

    public RootNode() {
        super(Children.create(new GenderChildFactory(), false));
        setIconBaseWithExtension(
            "com/asgteach/familytree/genderviewer/resources/personIcon.png");
        setDisplayName(Bundle.LBL_RootNode());
        setShortDescription(Bundle.HINT_RootNode());
    }
}
```

Figure 7.8 shows the Gender window (detached) as it looks initially (on the left) and with its hierarchy expanded (on the right). Male gender nodes display in blue, female gender in red, and unknown gender in the default color.

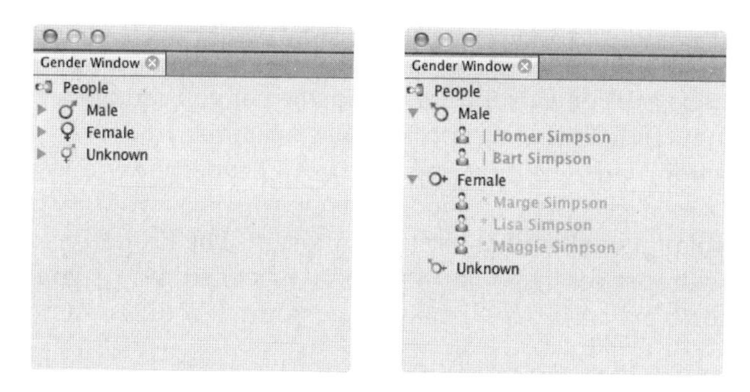


Figure 7.8 The Gender window at startup (left) and expanded (right)

### Expanding Nodes Programmatically

You expand a node by clicking its "open" handle in the UI (the small triangle shown in the left window in Figure 7.8). Explorer Views (that are based on trees) have two methods that expand a node hierarchy: `expandNode(Node node)` and `expandAll()`. Use the `expandAll()` method only when you know the size of the node hierarchy. To have the node hierarchy expand the gender nodes at startup, add the code in Listing 7.10 to the end of the GenderTopComponent constructor.

**Listing 7.10 Expand the Gender Nodes**

```
public GenderTopComponent() {
    . . .
    // expand the second level of nodes
    for (Node node : em.getRootContext().getChildren().getNodes()) {
        view.expandNode(node);
    }
}
```

Here we access the gender nodes through the Explorer Manager's root context and expand them using the Explorer View.

## Using BeanNode

**Selection and Editing**

*Selection is not a typical user experience case for displaying business objects in an editor. A better approach opens an editor with a context-sensitive menu item. In this section, we'll eliminate the PersonEditor module from our application and make changes to the business objects with property editors. In Chapter 9, we'll show you how to implement Open or Edit actions with editors.*

NetBeans Platform applications include a Properties window that you can open from the main menu with **Window | IDE Tools | Properties**. Because this window is hooked into the Global Selection, each selection appears in the Properties window when you select different nodes in the Gender window. The Properties window displays the node (using its display name) and its tooltip, if present. The Properties window also displays the node's properties in a default property sheet editor. As you can see from Figure 7.9, there are no properties to display when you select different nodes in the Gender window.

When PersonNode extends BeanNode rather than AbstractNode, a Person's properties appear in the Properties window. Furthermore, all writable properties can be modified in the BeanNode's default property sheet. Let's remove the PersonEditor module (aren't modules convenient?) and use a Properties window to update Person objects. We'll open the Properties window when the program starts and move the Gender window into the vacated editor position. The changes are quite straightforward.

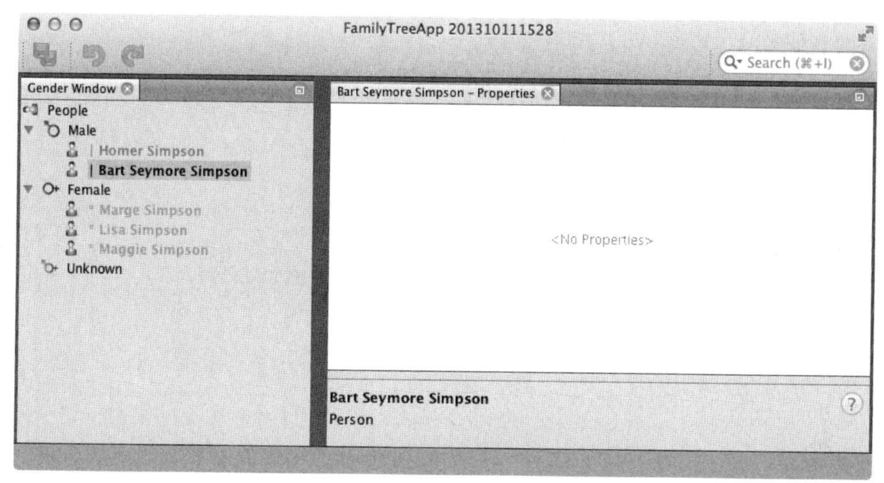


Figure 7.9 Including the Properties window

1. Remove module PersonEditor from the FamilyTreeApp application. Select the **Modules** node, right click, and choose **Remove** from the context menu.
2. In GenderTopComponent.java, change the **@TopComponent.Registration** annotation to window position (mode) "editor." (Removing the PersonEditor module vacated the editor position, so we'll put the GenderTopComponent into this central position.)
3. Include code to open the Properties window at startup.

These changes are shown in Listing 7.11.

#### Listing 7.11 GenderTopComponent Changes

```
@TopComponent.Registration(mode = "editor", openAtStartup = true)

. . . unchanged code omitted . . .

public final class GenderTopComponent extends TopComponent
        implements ExplorerManager.Provider {

    private final ExplorerManager em = new ExplorerManager();

    public GenderTopComponent() {
        initComponents();
        setName(Bundle.CTL_GenderTopComponent());
        setToolTipText(Bundle.HINT_GenderTopComponent());
```

```
        BeanTreeView view = new BeanTreeView();
        add(view, BorderLayout.CENTER);
        associateLookup(ExplorerUtils.createLookup(em, this.getActionMap()));
        em.setRootContext(new RootNode());
        // expand the second level of nodes
        for (Node node : em.getRootContext().getChildren().getNodes()) {
            view.expandNode(node);
        }
        // open the Properties window by default
        TopComponent tc = WindowManager.getDefault()
                                .findTopComponent("properties");
        if (tc != null) {
            tc.open();
        }
    }
. . .
}
```

Listing 7.12 shows the modified PersonNode. Note that we supply the Person object to the BeanNode constructor and add a throws clause to the PersonNode constructor. BeanNode uses introspection to determine the wrapped object's properties and automatically generates property support for each property in your object.

We also modify the PersonNode property change listener to update the FamilyTreeManager when the user updates a Person using the Properties window. The listening PersonChildFactory's event handler will update the node hierarchy as before.

**Listing 7.12 PersonNode Extending BeanNode**

```
@NbBundle.Messages({
    "HINT_PersonNode=Person"
})
public class PersonNode extends BeanNode<Person> implements
                                        PropertyChangeListener {

    public PersonNode(Person person) throws IntrospectionException {
        super(person, Children.LEAF, Lookups.singleton(person));
        setIconBaseWithExtension(
            "com/asgteach/familytree/genderviewer/resources/personIcon.png");
        setName(String.valueOf(person.getId()));
        setDisplayName(person.toString());
        setShortDescription(Bundle.HINT_PersonNode());
    }
   . . . unchanged code omitted . . .
    private final PropertyChangeListener propListener =
                    (PropertyChangeEvent evt) -> {
        Person person = (Person) evt.getSource();
        FamilyTreeManager ftm = Lookup.getDefault().lookup(
                                    FamilyTreeManager.class);
```

```
        if (ftm == null) {
            logger.log(Level.SEVERE, "Cannot get FamilyTreeManager object");
            LifecycleManager.getDefault().exit();
        } else {
            ftm.updatePerson(person);
            fireDisplayNameChange(null, getDisplayName());
        }
    };
}
```

Extending BeanNode affects the ChildFactory code as well. Listing 7.13 shows the modified PersonChildFactory class. Because of the throws clause in the constructor, the `createNodeForKey()` method must now wrap the PersonNode instantiation code in a try / catch block.

**Listing 7.13 PersonChildFactory with BeanNode Child**

```
public class PersonChildFactory extends ChildFactory<Person> {
. . . unchanged code omitted . . .

    @Override
    protected Node createNodeForKey(Person key) {
        logger.log(Level.FINER, "createNodeForKey: {0}", key);
        PersonNode node = null;
        try {
            node = new PersonNode(key);
            key.addPropertyChangeListener(
                        WeakListeners.propertyChange(node, key));
        } catch (IntrospectionException ex) {
            logger.log(Level.WARNING, "IntrospectionException: {0}", ex);
        }
        return node;
    }
}
```

Figure 7.10 shows the FamilyTreeApp running using `BeanNode<Person>` as the super class for PersonNode and the effect it has on the Properties window. Because of the property change listener, updates made in the Properties window are written to the FamilyTreeManager and reflected in the Gender node hierarchy in the left window.

**BeanNode Tip**

*BeanNode is a good option when you want to experiment with a node's property support, since it provides property support automatically. However, BeanNode has some overhead, since it builds the property support using introspection with each node you create. An alternative is to build your own property support, giving you much more control.*

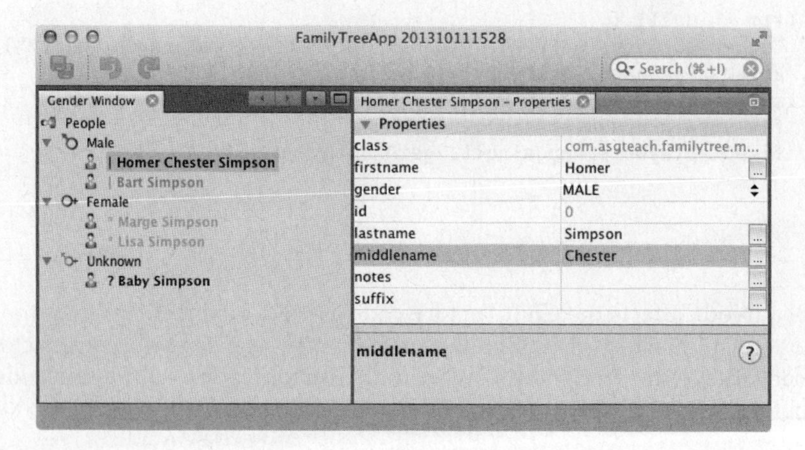


Figure 7.10 The default Properties window with BeanNode

## Creating Your Own Property Sheet

Now you can edit the selected Person and make changes to the wrapped Person object. However, the standard Properties window with BeanNode is not particularly user friendly. Properties appear in alphabetical order rather than grouped according to their use. When you want more control over the presentation of the Properties window, you can create your own property sheet.

What is a property sheet? A property sheet holds the properties (that you choose) from the node's wrapped object. You put properties into property sets. Furthermore, you can designate one or more sets to appear under separate tabs. And you can designate certain properties as read only.

Figure 7.11 shows the FamilyTreeApp running. In the left window you see the node hierarchy arranged by gender. In the right window you see an editable Properties window. Two property sets appear. The first is under heading Names that includes Person properties `firstname`, `middlename`, `lastname`, and `suffix`. The second set appears under heading Additional Information and includes the `gender` and `notes` properties.

The second tab (Id Info) includes a third property set with the read-only `id` property. This arrangement is a substantial improvement over the default BeanNode presentation.

To create a custom property sheet for a node's wrapped object, override the `createSheet()` method and return a Sheet object. Inside this method, create a Sheet and divide your object's properties into Sets. Create the sets, configure them with display

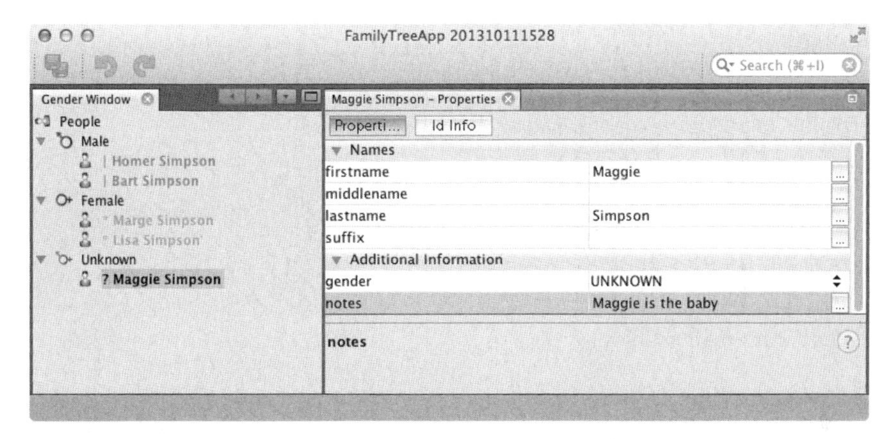


Figure 7.11 Using a custom property sheet

names, and add them to the Sheet. Finally, create PropertySupport objects for each property you want included in the sets and add the support objects to the appropriate set. Listing 7.14 shows how we built the property sheet displayed in Figure 7.11. Note that with custom property sheets, PersonNode extends AbstractNode, not BeanNode.

### Listing 7.14 Creating a Property Sheet

```
public class PersonNode extends AbstractNode implements
                                              PropertyChangeListener {
    private static final Logger logger = Logger.getLogger(
                PersonNode.class.getName());

    public PersonNode(Person person) {
        super(Children.LEAF, Lookups.singleton(person));
        setIconBaseWithExtension(
            "com/asgteach/familytree/genderviewer/resources/personIcon.png");
        setName(String.valueOf(person.getId()));
        setDisplayName(person.toString());
        setShortDescription(Bundle.HINT_PersonNode());
    }

. . . unchanged code omitted . . .

    @Override
    protected Sheet createSheet() {
        Sheet sheet = Sheet.createDefault();
        Person person = getLookup().lookup(Person.class);

        // create a property set for the names (first, middle, last, suffix)
        Sheet.Set setNames = Sheet.createPropertiesSet();
        setNames.setDisplayName("Names");
```

```
        // create a property set for read-only id
        Sheet.Set readOnlySet = new Sheet.Set();
        readOnlySet.setDisplayName("Identification");
        // put it under its own tab
        readOnlySet.setValue("tabName", " Id Info ");

        // create a property set for gender and notes
        Sheet.Set infoSet = new Sheet.Set();
        infoSet.setName("Additional Information");

        sheet.put(setNames);
        sheet.put(infoSet);
        sheet.put(readOnlySet);

        try {
            // create property support for the Names
            Property<String> firstnameProp = new PropertySupport
               .Reflection<String>(person, String.class, "firstname");
            Property<String> middlenameProp = new PropertySupport
               .Reflection<String>(person, String.class, "middlename");
            Property<String> lastnameProp = new PropertySupport
               .Reflection<String>(person, String.class, "lastname");
            Property<String> suffixProp = new PropertySupport
               .Reflection<String>(person, String.class, "suffix");

            setNames.put(firstnameProp);
            setNames.put(middlenameProp);
            setNames.put(lastnameProp);
            setNames.put(suffixProp);

            // create property support for gender and notes
            Property<Person.Gender> genderProp = new PropertySupport
            .Reflection<Person.Gender>(person, Person.Gender.class, "gender");
            Property<String> notesProp = new PropertySupport
               .Reflection<String>(person, String.class, "notes");

            infoSet.put(genderProp);
            infoSet.put(notesProp);

            // create read-only property support for id (the setter is null)
            Property<Long> idProp = new PropertySupport.Reflection<Long>(
                        person, Long.class, "getId", null);
            readOnlySet.put(idProp);
        } catch (NoSuchMethodException ex) {
            ErrorManager.getDefault();
        }
        return sheet;
    }
}
```

Property support enables a Properties context menu item for that node and brings up a popup Properties window, as shown in Figure 7.12. (This Properties context menu item is available with BeanNode, too.)

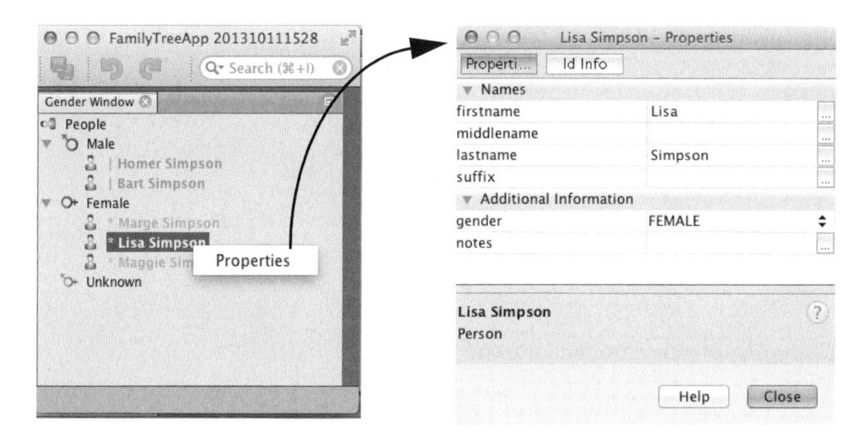


Figure 7.12 Node Properties popup window

## Using FilterNode

FilterNode lets you filter a node hierarchy using an arbitrary criterion. You create a filtered node hierarchy by having a delegate node with perhaps specialized behavior and a criterion upon which the original hierarchy's node is either included or not. In general, you implement the specialization by overriding methods that are also present in the original node. For example, if you'd like the filtered node to have a specialized display, then you can override either `getDisplayName()` or `getHtmlDisplayName()`, as we do in our example.

Note that when using FilterNode, you do not "replace" the original node or the original hierarchy. The original hierarchy remains intact and the filtered hierarchy affects which nodes are included.

For example, Figure 7.13 shows the Gender window with a filtered node hierarchy. You supply a search string in the provided text field followed by `<Return>` to display nodes with names that contain the search string (ignoring case). The filtered hierarchy uses italics in the display name instead of bold. To return to the "unfiltered" node hierarchy, you use an empty search String.

FilterNode is the "delegate" node. A special Children class extends FilterNode.Children to create the acceptance criterion. In our example we use a boolean `accept()` method that implements the decision logic. Let's show you how to implement the filtered node hierarchy that appears in Figure 7.13.

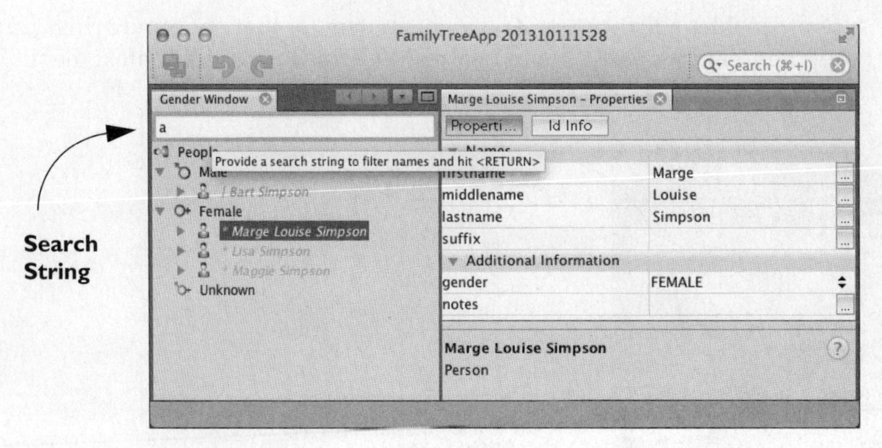


Figure 7.13 Displaying a filtered node hierarchy

## Update the Design View

First, you update the TopComponent's UI to include the text field control using these steps.

1. Bring up GenderTopComponent in the Design view. From the Swing Containers palette, select **Panel** and add it to the top of the design area. (The TopComponent should already use BorderLayout for its layout. Put the JPanel in BorderLayout.NORTH.)
2. Select the JPanel you just added in the Navigator window, right click, and change its layout to **GridLayout**.
3. From the Swing Controls palette, select **TextField** and add it to the JPanel component. The TextField will expand to the width of the Design view.
4. With the TextField selected, in the Properties window under the **Code** tab, change its **Variable Name** to **filterText**. Under the **Properties** tab, make its **text** property blank. Figure 7.14 shows the TopComponent Design and Navigator views.
5. Select the **TextField** in the Design view and double-click. This generates a Swing action event handler that is invoked when the user hits the `<Return>` key in the TextField. You'll add the event handling code after creating the FilterNode classes.

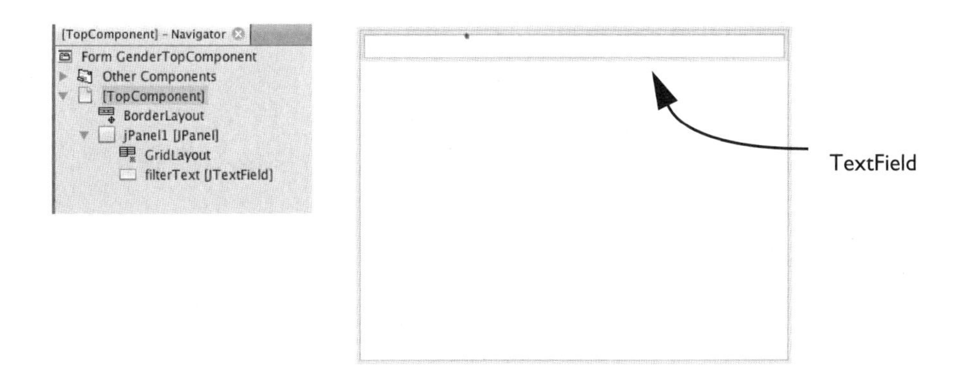


Figure 7.14 GenderTopComponent Design and Navigator views

With these Design view changes, you can run the program to test the new Gender window design, as shown in Figure 7.15. (The TextField doesn't do anything yet.)

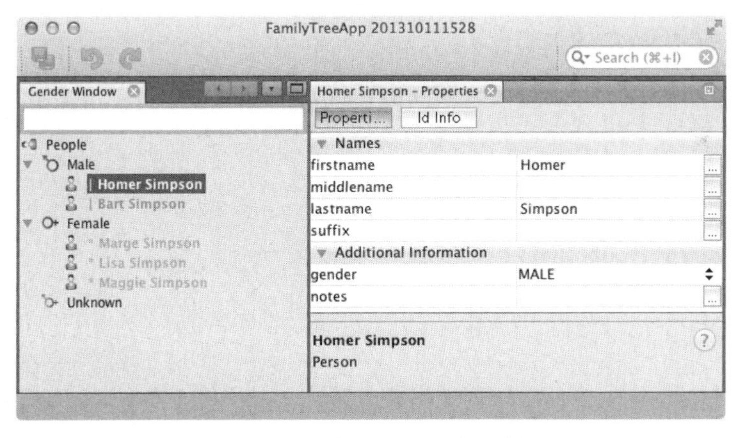


Figure 7.15 Testing out the new Gender window UI

## Create FilterNode Hierarchy Classes

With the Design view modifications made, let's now create the classes we need to filter the Gender node hierarchy. We'll start with PersonFilterNode, as shown in Listing 7.15.

**Listing 7.15 PersonFilterNode**

```
public class PersonFilterNode extends FilterNode {

    public PersonFilterNode(Node original, String searchString) {
        super(original, new PersonFilterChildren(original, searchString));
    }

    @Override
    public Node getOriginal() {
        return super.getOriginal();
    }

    @Override
    public String getHtmlDisplayName() {
        Person person = getOriginal().getLookup().lookup(Person.class);
        if (person == null) {
            return null;
        }
        StringBuilder sb = new StringBuilder();
        switch (person.getGender()) {
            case MALE:
                sb.append("<font color='#5588FF'><i>| ");
                break;
            case FEMALE:
                sb.append("<font color='#FF8855'><i>* ");
                break;
            case UNKNOWN:
                sb.append("<i>? ");
                break;
        }
        sb.append(person.toString()).append("</i></font>");
        return sb.toString();
    }
}
```

PersonFilterNode is a proxy or delegate node for every node in the original hierarchy (including the original root node, the GenderNodes, and the selected PersonNodes). The constructor includes the original node. FilterNodes are configured so that the node methods of the original node are invoked, unless the FilterNode specifically overrides them. That's how we can easily use a FilterNode to proxy all kinds of nodes.

PersonFilterNode overrides the `getHtmlDisplayName()` method to provide a special look for the filtered nodes. Note that `getHtmlDisplayName()` is invoked for the root node and each GenderNode. However, these nodes do not have a Person object in their Lookup, so `getHtmlDisplayName()` returns null and the original node's `getDisplayName()` is used instead.

PersonFilterNode creates its children with PersonFilterChildren, as shown in Listing 7.16. This is where we store the search string (which we convert to lowercase in the event handler). The `createNodes()` method selects the nodes from the original hierarchy. Here, the boolean `accept()` method accepts the node if either it has no Person object in its Lookup or the Person object's name contains the search string.

The `copyNode()` method builds the delegate node from the original one. The method is invoked as the filtered node hierarchy is built.

**Listing 7.16 PersonFilterChildren**

```
public class PersonFilterChildren extends FilterNode.Children {
    private final String searchString;

    public PersonFilterChildren(Node original, String searchString) {
        super(original);
        this.searchString = searchString;
    }

    @Override
    protected Node[] createNodes(Node key) {
        List<Node> result = new ArrayList<>();
        for (Node node : super.createNodes(key)) {
            if (accept(node)) {
                result.add(node);
            }
        }
        return result.toArray(new Node[0]);
    }

    @Override
    protected Node copyNode(Node original) {
        return new PersonFilterNode(original, this.searchString);
    }

    private boolean accept(Node node) {
        Person p = node.getLookup().lookup(Person.class);
        // make case insensitive
        return (p == null || p.toString().toLowerCase()
                                 .contains(searchString));
    }

}
```

### Display a Filtered Node Hierarchy

Listing 7.17 shows the TextField's event handler as well as other modifications made to GenderTopComponent. First, we add a tool tip to the TextField in the annotated

`@Messages` list. We also elevate BeanTreeView to a class field so that it is accessible in the event handler.

The event handler either restores the root context to the original root (if the search string is empty), or it builds a filtered node hierarchy based on the search string (converted to lowercase). When you invoke `setRootContext()`, the gender nodes collapse, so we include code to expand them.

**Listing 7.17 GenderTopComponent—Displaying a FilteredNode Hierarchy**

```
@Messages({
    "CTL_GenderAction=Gender",
    "CTL_GenderTopComponent=Gender window",
    "HINT_GenderTopComponent=This is a Gender window",
    "HINT_FilterTextField=Provide a search string to filter names and hit
<RETURN>"
})
public final class GenderTopComponent extends TopComponent
        implements ExplorerManager.Provider {
    private final ExplorerManager em = new ExplorerManager();
    private final BeanTreeView view;

    public GenderTopComponent() {
        initComponents();
        filterText.setToolTipText(Bundle.HINT_FilterTextField());
        setName(Bundle.CTL_GenderTopComponent());
        setToolTipText(Bundle.HINT_GenderTopComponent());

        view = new BeanTreeView();
        add(view, BorderLayout.CENTER);
        associateLookup(ExplorerUtils.createLookup(em, this.getActionMap()));
        em.setRootContext(new RootNode());
        // expand the second level of nodes
        for (Node node : em.getRootContext().getChildren().getNodes()) {
            view.expandNode(node);
        }
    }

    private void filterTextActionPerformed(java.awt.event.ActionEvent evt) {
        Node root = em.getRootContext();
        Node newRoot;
        if (root instanceof PersonFilterNode) {
            root = ((PersonFilterNode) root).getOriginal();
        }
        if (filterText.getText().isEmpty()) {
            // use the original root
            newRoot = root;
        } else {
            // make case insensitive
```

```
            newRoot = new PersonFilterNode(root,
                    filterText.getText().toLowerCase());
        }
        em.setRootContext(newRoot);
        for (Node node : em.getRootContext().getChildren().getNodes()) {
            view.expandNode(node);
        }
    }
}
```

## 7.3 Explorer Views

Explorer Views provide the View of a node hierarchy, as shown in Figure 7.1 on page 292. Explorer Views are not all inter-changeable, but they do all work with nodes. Explorer Views are useful for different presentation arrangements. The two most general Explorer Views are BeanTreeView (used in our TopComponent) and OutlineView. Both provide an expandable node tree structure. We briefly describe the Explorer Views in Table 7.1 and provide detailed examples of these in this section.

**TABLE 7.1 Explorer Views**

| Explorer View | Description |
|---|---|
| BeanTreeView | Displays a tree view of the node hierarchy |
| OutlineView | Displays a table view with the option of creating columns corresponding to a node's properties |
| ContextTreeView | Displays the top hierarchy of a node hierarchy; useful for the master view of a master-detail window |
| ListView | Displays child nodes in a list; useful for the detail view of a master-detail window |
| ChoiceView | Displays nodes in a ComboBox |
| MenuView | Provides a JMenu view of a node and its children |
| IconView | Displays nodes in a grid-like layout using a node's icon and display name |
| PropertySheetView | Provides a property sheet for editing a node's properties |

### Quick Search

Explorer Views have a built-in quick search feature. To see this, start typing in the window with an Explorer View, and a text field component will appear. The Explorer View selects the "next" node that matches the text you provide. Figure 7.16 shows this behavior. When you type the text "Bar" in a BeanTreeView, you see the Bart Simpson node is highlighted. In a master-detail window (see "Master-Detail View" on page 327), the quick search applies to whichever portion of the window has focus.

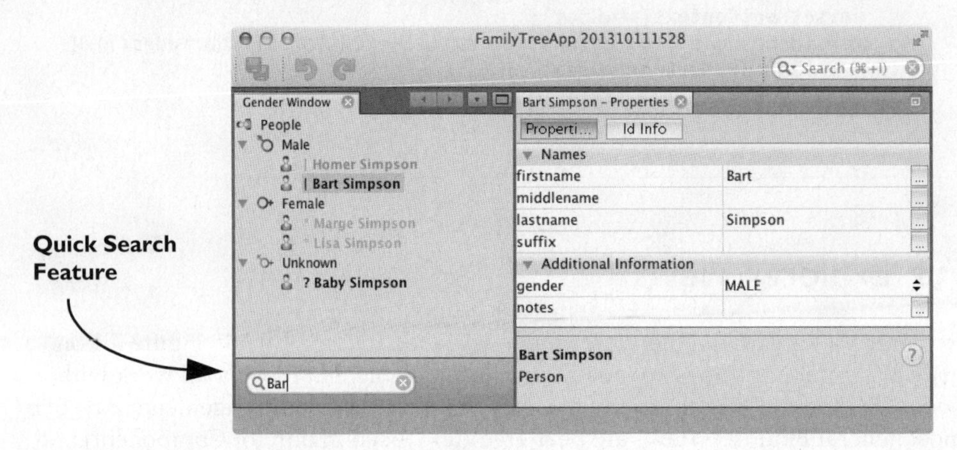


Figure 7.16 Explorer View quick search feature

## BeanTreeView

BeanTreeView displays the node hierarchy as a tree of all the nodes. This is the Explorer View we've used in our examples and is perhaps the most widely-used Explorer View. BeanTreeView uses a triangle icon pointed right to indicate an unexpanded node and pointed down to indicate an expanded (or opened) node. The default action (activated with double click) for a non-leaf node is to toggle between its expanded and unexpanded states.

## OutlineView

OutlineView is a powerful Explorer View that displays a node hierarchy in table form. The default configuration is similar to BeanTreeView. In our example, you see what's shown in Figure 7.17, with a single column (with heading "People"). Listing 7.18 shows the code to create this view in the GenderTopComponent.

**Listing 7.18 OutlineView Explorer View**

```
public final class GenderTopComponent extends TopComponent
        implements ExplorerManager.Provider {
    private final ExplorerManager em = new ExplorerManager();

    public GenderTopComponent() {
        initComponents();
        setName(Bundle.CTL_GenderTopComponent());
        setToolTipText(Bundle.HINT_GenderTopComponent());
```

```
        OutlineView view = new OutlineView("People");
        add(view, BorderLayout.CENTER);
        associateLookup(ExplorerUtils.createLookup(em, this.getActionMap()));
        em.setRootContext(new RootNode());
    }
. . . unchanged code omitted . . .
```

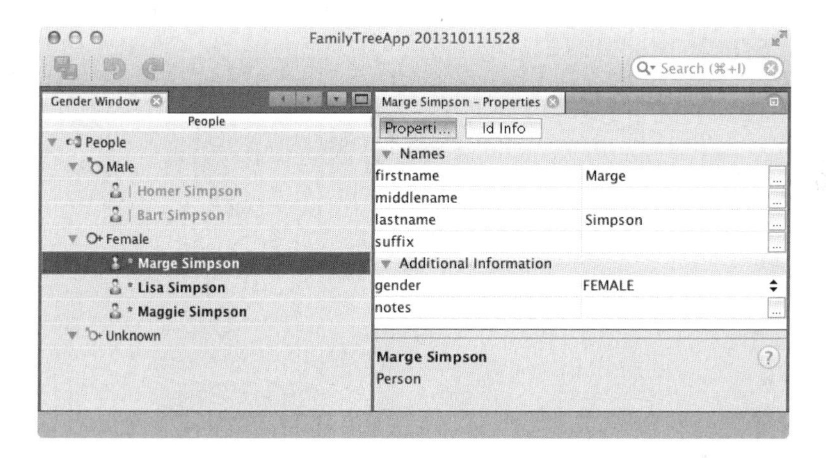


Figure 7.17 OutlineView with customized heading

OutlineView's columns are sortable (a click on the column header toggles between ascending / descending sort order). In our example, the default sorting behavior is to sort each Gender node, and within the Gender category, sort its children using the display name. Figure 7.18 shows the node hierarchy sorted in descending order.

With OutlineView, you can configure additional columns from a node's wrapped object's properties, as shown in Figure 7.19. When you configure OutlineView's columns, you must provide property support for the properties that you use. You can use either BeanNode or your own property sheet with AbstractNode (see Listing 7.14 on page 315) as we have done here. Listing 7.19 shows the code to create columns Gender and Notes.

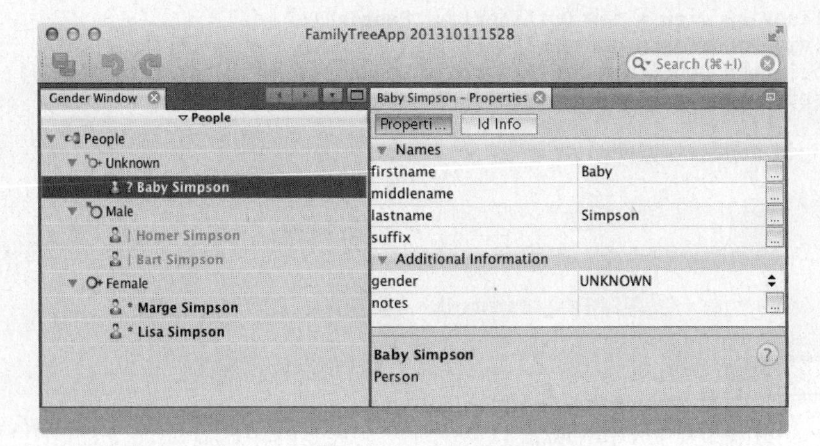


Figure 7.18 OutlineView with hierarchy sorted in descending order

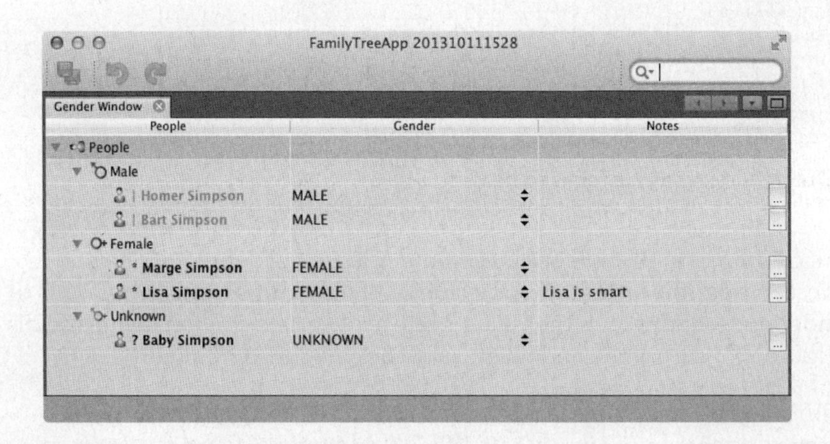


Figure 7.19 Using OutlineView's column feature

## Listing 7.19 OutlineView Property Columns

```
public GenderTopComponent() {
    initComponents();
    setName(Bundle.CTL_GenderTopComponent());
    setToolTipText(Bundle.HINT_GenderTopComponent());
```

```
    OutlineView view = new OutlineView("People");
    view.setPropertyColumns(
            "gender", "Gender",
            "notes", "Notes"
            );
    add(view, BorderLayout.CENTER);
    associateLookup(ExplorerUtils.createLookup(em, this.getActionMap()));
    em.setRootContext(new RootNode());

     . . . unchanged code omitted . . .
}
```

## Master-Detail View

You can easily implement a master-detail view using Explorer Views ContextTreeView for the master and ListView for the detail, as shown in Figure 7.20. These Explorer Views are designed to work together. Listing 7.20 shows you how to use these views when you add them to the same TopComponent. Both Explorer Views search the component tree to find the Entity Manager and hook into the node hierarchy. The master view displays the Gender nodes (which do not expand). When the user selects one of the "master" nodes, its children appear in the bottom area. As before, we open the Properties window so the user can edit a selected Person node.

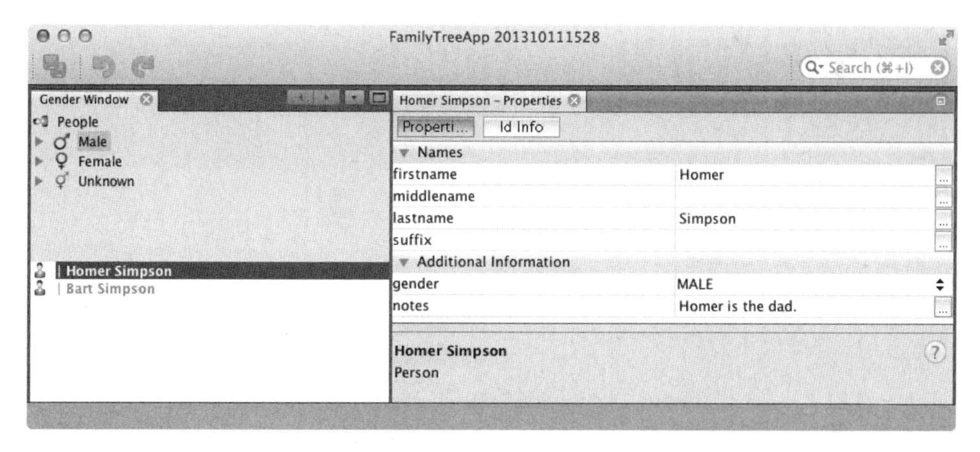


Figure 7.20 Creating a master-detail view

### Listing 7.20 Providing a Master-Detail View

```
public GenderTopComponent() {
    initComponents();
    setName(Bundle.CTL_GenderTopComponent());
    setToolTipText(Bundle.HINT_GenderTopComponent());
```

```
        ContextTreeView view = new ContextTreeView();
        ListView list = new ListView();
        add(view, BorderLayout.CENTER);
        add(list, BorderLayout.SOUTH);
        associateLookup(ExplorerUtils.createLookup(em, this.getActionMap()));
        em.setRootContext(new RootNode());
        // open the Properties window by default
        TopComponent tc = WindowManager.getDefault()
                           .findTopComponent("properties");
        if (tc != null) {
            tc.open();
        }
    }
```

## Master-Detail View with IconView

Instead of using ListView for the detail, you can also use IconView. This view displays node children in a grid-like layout similar to a Windows Explorer icon listing. Figure 7.21 shows the view when the user selects the root People node (left) and then when the Gender node Female is selected (right). Listing 7.21 shows the code that creates an IconView for the detail view in a master-detail window. Note that IconView uses a node's 32 x 32 icon file, if available (as shown in Figure 7.21).

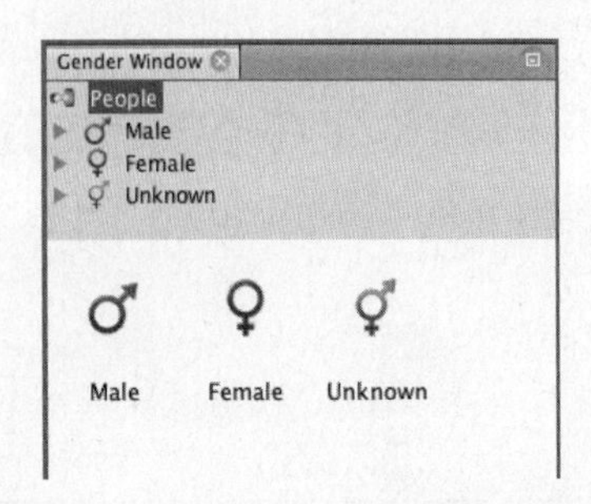


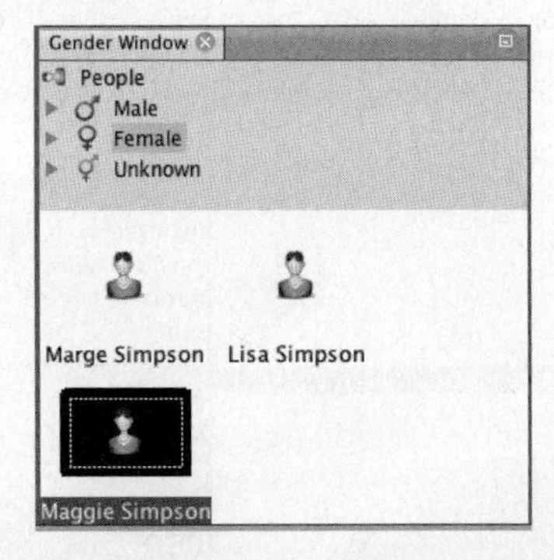


Figure 7.21 Creating a master-detail view with IconView instead of ListView

**Listing 7.21 Using IconView in a Master-Detail Window**

```
    public GenderTopComponent() {
        initComponents();
        setName(Bundle.CTL_GenderTopComponent());
        setToolTipText(Bundle.HINT_GenderTopComponent());
```

```
        ContextTreeView view = new ContextTreeView();
        IconView icon = new IconView();
        add(view, BorderLayout.CENTER);
        add(icon, BorderLayout.SOUTH);
        associateLookup(ExplorerUtils.createLookup(em, this.getActionMap()));
        em.setRootContext(new RootNode());
    }
```

### Master-Detail View with MenuView

An alternative to ContextTreeView in a master view window is MenuView, which provides two buttons to navigate your node hierarchy, as shown in Figure 7.22. The first button is "Browse from root" and provides a context selection mechanism for child nodes. Once a child node is selected, a second button, "Browse from current point," is enabled. (In our node hierarchy, the current point is a child node, so it will be empty.) Listing 7.22 shows the code to create a master-detail window with MenuView.

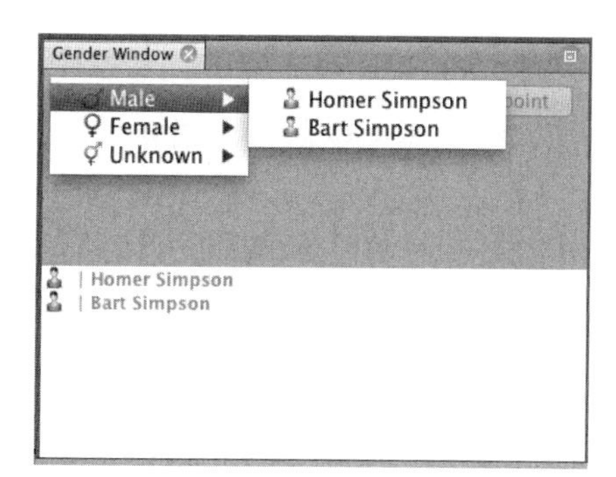


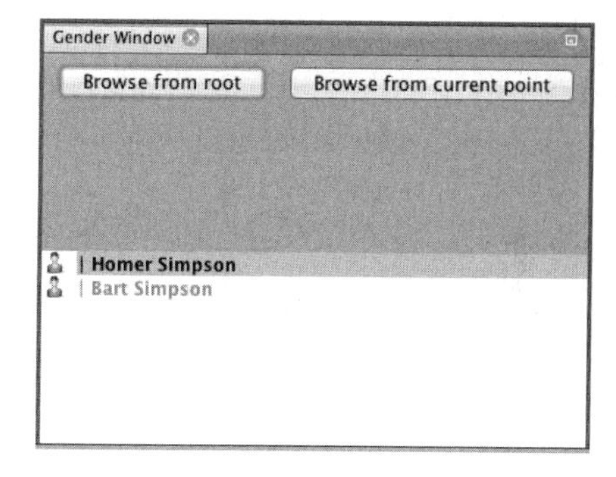


Figure 7.22 Creating a master-detail view with MenuView (top) and ListView

**Listing 7.22 Using MenuView in a Master-Detail Window**

```
    public GenderTopComponent() {
        initComponents();
        setName(Bundle.CTL_GenderTopComponent());
        setToolTipText(Bundle.HINT_GenderTopComponent());

        MenuView menu = new MenuView();
        ListView list = new ListView();
        add(menu, BorderLayout.CENTER);
        add(list, BorderLayout.SOUTH);
```

```
        associateLookup(ExplorerUtils.createLookup(em, this.getActionMap()));
        em.setRootContext(new RootNode());
    }
```

## Master-Detail View with ChoiceView

Finally, let's show you ChoiceView in a master-detail window for the detail view, as shown in Figure 7.23. ChoiceView provides a ComboBox with the children nodes of the selected Gender node in the master view. We provide ContextTreeView for the master view here. Listing 7.23 shows the code to create a master-detail window with ChoiceView.

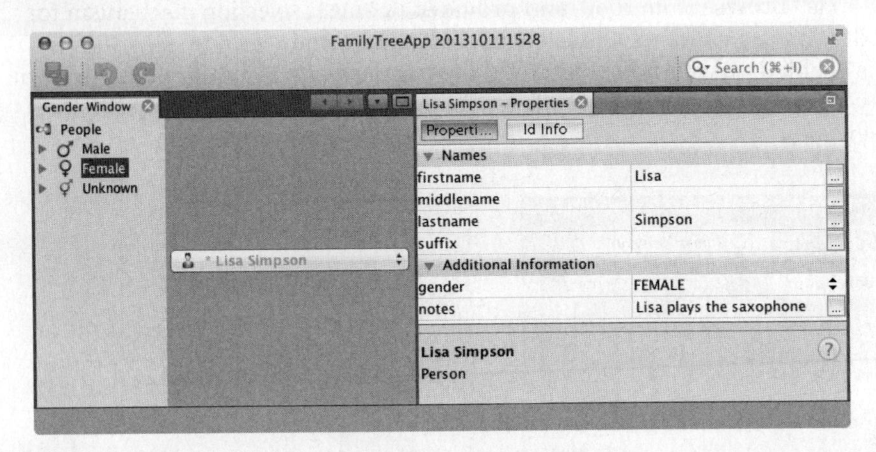


Figure 7.23 Creating a master-detail view with ChoiceView

**Listing 7.23 Using ChoiceView with a Master-Detail Window**

```
    public GenderTopComponent() {
        initComponents();
        setName(Bundle.CTL_GenderTopComponent());
        setToolTipText(Bundle.HINT_GenderTopComponent());

        ContextTreeView view = new ContextTreeView();
        ChoiceView choice = new ChoiceView();
        add(view, BorderLayout.CENTER);
        add(choice, BorderLayout.EAST);
        associateLookup(ExplorerUtils.createLookup(em, this.getActionMap()));
        em.setRootContext(new RootNode());
    }
```

## PropertySheetView

PropertySheetView is not really an Explorer View, but a view for presenting a node's properties. Like the built-in Properties window, PropertySheetView displays the selected node's properties when defined. Figure 7.24 shows a single window with a node hierarchy displayed with BeanTreeView (in BorderLayout.WEST). We define a PropertySheetView in BorderLayout.CENTER. You can use either BeanNode for your node's superclass or specify your own property sheet as shown earlier (see "Creating Your Own Property Sheet" on page 314). Listing 7.24 shows the code to display the selected node's properties with PropertySheetView. The GenderTopComponent window is in the "editor" position, which makes it easier to view the PropertySheetView at startup.

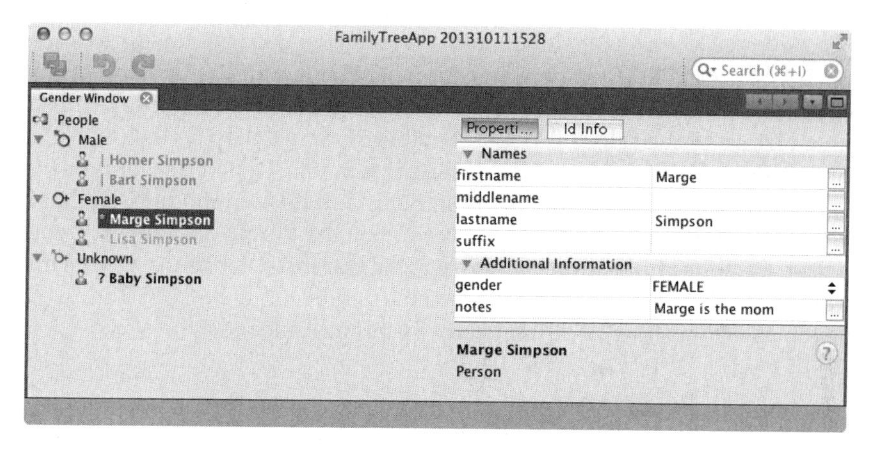


Figure 7.24 Using PropertySheetView to provide property editing

#### Listing 7.24 Using PropertySheetView

```
public GenderTopComponent() {
    initComponents();
    setName(Bundle.CTL_GenderTopComponent());
    setToolTipText(Bundle.HINT_GenderTopComponent());

    BeanTreeView view = new BeanTreeView();
    PropertySheetView propView = new PropertySheetView();
    add(view, BorderLayout.WEST);
    add(propView, BorderLayout.CENTER);
    associateLookup(ExplorerUtils.createLookup(em, this.getActionMap()));
    em.setRootContext(new RootNode());
```

```
        for (Node node : em.getRootContext().getChildren().getNodes()) {
            view.expandNode(node);
        }
    }
```

## 7.4 Creating a Selection History Feature

Let's pull together the concepts we've covered in this chapter and build a version of the FamilyTreeApp shown running in Figure 7.25. In this version, we'll make all the PersonNode properties read only except the `notes` property. We configure the Properties window for edits and use OutlineView as our Explorer View with a column defined for the `notes` property.

The FamilyTreeApp also includes a new Selection History window that is updated when the user makes a selection (and changes the Global Selection Lookup). This lets you maintain a history of the selected nodes. Furthermore, we display the user's current selection in the application status line, where it remains for just a second or two before being cleared. The new window is implemented in its own module, so that it can be added or removed. In addition, if you configure the Plugin Manager for your application, users of your application can dynamically uninstall or re-install this module (see "Application Updates" on page 857 for instructions on how to configure the Plugin Manager, as well as how to dynamically install modules).

### Modify PersonNode PropertySheet

We'll begin with the version of FamilyTreeApp used with the OutlineView (see "OutlineView" on page 324). We'll modify the PersonNode custom property sheet so that its properties are read only, except for the `notes` property.

1. In project GenderViewer, bring up PersonNode.java in the Java Editor.
2. Modify the `createSheet()` method for read-only PropertySupport, as shown in Listing 7.25. Note that you can create read-only PropertySupport using PropertySupport.Reflection and make the setter null, or you can use PropertySupport.ReadOnly as shown in Listing 7.25.

**Listing 7.25 Modified PersonNode createSheet() Method**

```
    @Override
    protected Sheet createSheet() {
        Sheet sheet = Sheet.createDefault();
        Person person = getLookup().lookup(Person.class);
```

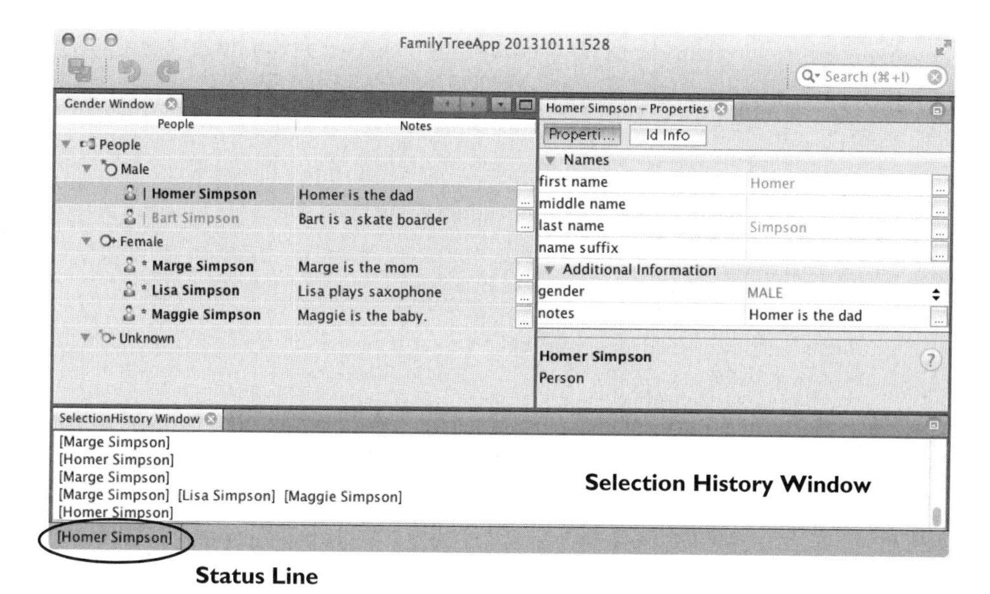


Figure 7.25 FamilyTreeApp with new SelectionHistory window

```
// create a property set for the names (first, middle, last, suffix)
Sheet.Set setNames = Sheet.createPropertiesSet();
setNames.setDisplayName("Names");

// create a property set read-only id
Sheet.Set readOnlySet = new Sheet.Set();
readOnlySet.setDisplayName("Identification");
// put it under its own tab
readOnlySet.setValue("tabName", " Id Info ");

// create a property set for gender and notes
Sheet.Set infoSet = new Sheet.Set();
infoSet.setName("Additional Information");
sheet.put(setNames);
sheet.put(infoSet);
sheet.put(readOnlySet);

try {
    // create read-only property support for the Names
    Property<String> firstnameProp = new PropertySupport
                                        .ReadOnly<String>(
            "firstname",                   // Name of the property
            String.class,                  // Type of property value
            "first name",                  // Display name
            "The person's first name") {   // Description
```

```
                @Override
                public String getValue() throws IllegalAccessException,
                                    InvocationTargetException {
                    return person.getFirstname();
                }
            };

        // make similar changes to property support for
        // middlenameProp
        // lastnameProp
        // suffixProp
        setNames.put(firstnameProp);
        setNames.put(middlenameProp);
        setNames.put(lastnameProp);
        setNames.put(suffixProp);

        // create read only property support for gender
        Property<Person.Gender> genderProp = new PropertySupport
                                .ReadOnly<Person.Gender>(
                "gender",
                Person.Gender.class,
                "gender",
                "The person's gender") {
                    @Override
                    public Person.Gender getValue() throws
                    IllegalAccessException, InvocationTargetException {
                        return person.getGender();
                    }
                };

        // use read-write property support for notes (unchanged)
        Property<String> notesProp = new PropertySupport
                    .Reflection<String>(person, String.class, "notes");

        infoSet.put(genderProp);
        infoSet.put(notesProp);

        // create read-only property support for id (the setter is null)
        Property<Long> idProp = new PropertySupport.Reflection<Long>(
                  person, Long.class, "getId", null);
        readOnlySet.put(idProp);
    } catch (NoSuchMethodException ex) {
        ErrorManager.getDefault();
    }
    return sheet;
}
```

### Modify OutlineView in GenderTopComponent

Modify the GenderTopComponent constructor so that the OutlineView is configured for property column Notes, as shown in Listing 7.26.

**Listing 7.26 Using OutlineView with Column Notes**

```
public GenderTopComponent() {
    initComponents();
    setName(Bundle.CTL_GenderTopComponent());
    setToolTipText(Bundle.HINT_GenderTopComponent());

    OutlineView view = new OutlineView("People");
    view.setPropertyColumns(
            "notes", "Notes"
            );
    add(view, BorderLayout.CENTER);
    associateLookup(ExplorerUtils.createLookup(em, this.getActionMap()));
    em.setRootContext(new RootNode());
    for (Node node : em.getRootContext().getChildren().getNodes()) {
        view.expandNode(node);
    }
    // open the Properties window by default
    TopComponent tc = WindowManager.getDefault()
                              .findTopComponent("properties");
    if (tc != null) {
        tc.open();
    }
}
```

## Add Features to Your Application

Now we are ready to add a brand new feature to the application—a Selection History window that tracks a user's selections. The concept is straightforward. By listening to the Global Selection Lookup, the new module displays a running list of the user's selections. To do this, we'll add a new module to the application.

### Create Module SelectionHistory

Add a new module to implement the SelectionHistory window.

1. Select the Modules node in the FamilyTreeApp project, right-click, and select **Add New . . .** from the context menu. NetBeans displays the Name and Location dialog for the New Project wizard.

2. For Project Name, specify **SelectionHistory** and accept the defaults for the remaining fields. Click **Next**.

3. NetBeans displays the Basic Module Configuration dialog. Specify **com.asgteach.familytree.selectionhistory** for the Code Name Base and accept the defaults for the remaining fields. Click **Finish**. NetBeans creates project SelectionHistory in the FamilyTreeApp application.
4. Expand project SelectionHistory, right click on node Libraries, and select **Add Module Dependency** from the context menu.
5. Select the **Nodes API** from the list of modules and click **OK**.

## Create and Configure SelectionHistoryTopComponent

The SelectionHistory module requires a TopComponent to display its content.

1. In the Projects view, expand project SelectionHistory Source node and right click on node **com.asgteach.familytree.selectionhistory**. Select **New | Window . . .** from its context menu.
2. NetBeans displays the Basic Settings dialog of the New Window wizard. Select **output** in the Window Position drop down menu and check **Open on Application Start**. Click **Next**. (This will position the window below the editor position.)
3. NetBeans displays the Name, Icon and Location dialog. Specify **SelectionHistory** for Class Name Prefix, leave the Icon field blank, and accept the defaults for the remaining fields. Click **Finish**.

NetBeans creates the SelectionHistoryTopComponent class and brings it up in the Design view. Create a BorderLayout and add a TextArea component.

1. In the Design view, select the TopComponent in the Navigator window.
2. Right click and select **Set Layout | BorderLayout** in the context menu.
3. In the Swing Controls palette, select **TextArea** and add it to the center of the TopComponent Design view. This adds both a JScrollPane and a JTextArea.
4. Select the TextArea and in its Properties window under the **Code** tab, change property Variable Name to **displayTextArea**.
5. Switch to the Source view and add code to the TopComponent, as shown in Listing 7.27 and described here.

Add class field `result` to hold the result of Global Selection Lookup. In the `componentOpened()` method, request Lookup for objects of Node.class and add the TopComponent as a Lookup listener.

In the `componentClosed()` method, remove the TopComponent as a Lookup listener.

Implement the `resultChanged()` Lookup listener, which fires when a Node.class object is added to or removed from the Global Selection Lookup. We store the Lookup contents in nodes. If the list is non-empty, we write the display names to the TextArea component and the status line (using StatusDisplay.getDefault().setStatus()). Note that if the user selects multiple nodes, these are all included in the SelectionHistory Window.

This implementation listens for all node objects, including RootNode, GenderNode, and PersonNode. If you want to limit the selection history to Person objects, then listen for Person.class instead. Since PersonNode objects carry a Person object in their Lookup, the SelectionHistory Lookup listener fires when the user selects one or more of the Person nodes.

**Listing 7.27 Listen for Changes to the Global Selection Lookup**

```
public final class SelectionHistoryTopComponent extends TopComponent
        implements LookupListener {

    private Lookup.Result<Node> result;

. . . unchanged code omitted . . .

    @Override
    public void componentOpened() {
        result = Utilities.actionsGlobalContext().lookupResult(Node.class);
        result.addLookupListener(this);
    }

    @Override
    public void componentClosed() {
        result.removeLookupListener(this);
    }

    @Override
    public void resultChanged(LookupEvent le) {
        Collection<? extends Node> nodes = result.allInstances();
        // only get the selection if there is one
        // otherwise leave the selection unchanged!
        if (!nodes.isEmpty()) {
            StringBuilder status = new StringBuilder();
            StringBuilder sb = new StringBuilder("\n");
            for (Node node : nodes) {
               sb.append("  [").append(node.getDisplayName()).append("] ");
               status.append("[").append(node.getDisplayName()).append("]");
            }
            StatusDisplayer.getDefault().setStatusText(status.toString());
            displayTextArea.setText(sb.insert(0,
                             displayTextArea.getText()).toString());
        }
    }
}
```

With this design, module SelectionHistory is not dependent on the FamilyTreeModel module or the GenderViewer module. Adding the SelectionHistory module also does not affect any of these modules (other than to consume space in the application's window frame). Yet the SelectionHistory module adds a distinct functionality to our application. Similarly, removing this module does not affect the remaining modules. This illustrates one of the major advantages of a modular system. You can add and remove functionality to your application without modifying the rest of the system!

## 7.5 Key Point Summary

When you use Nodes, Explorer Views, and the Explorer Manager, the NetBeans Platform provides a flexible system for displaying your business data. Together, these components handle selection events and let users dynamically expand and collapse trees of hierarchical data. Here are the key points in this chapter.

- Nodes, Explorer Views, and the Explorer Manager can be understood in the context of a Model View Controller pattern. Nodes are the Model, Explorer Views are the View, and the Explorer Manager is the Controller.
- Nodes wrap business objects and create a hierarchical structure for display.
- Nodes have a Lookup and place their wrapped business object in the Lookup.
- AbstractNode provides a general-purpose implementation of the Node class.
- To build a node hierarchy, create a root node and a ChildFactory for the root node's children. The ChildFactory is responsible for creating its Child nodes, which will also have a ChildFactory unless the node is a leaf node. Leaf nodes have the designation Children.Leaf for their child container.
- Nodes have names, display names, icons, and optional HTML display code.
- Nodes support the Java Event Model. NodeListener event handlers are invoked for events that change the node, such as children added, removed, or reordered and changes to the node's name, display name, icon, or tooltip. PropertyChangeListener event handlers are invoked for changes to the node's underlying property support objects.
- To display a node hierarchy in a TopComponent, implement ExplorerManager.Provider, instantiate an Explorer Manager and an Explorer View, and set the Explorer Manager's root context to the root node of your node hierarchy.
- BeanNode is an alternate implementation of the Node class that provides property support for its wrapped business object. The property support is used by the standard NetBeans Platform Properties window, as well as the PropertySheetView component and OutlineView Explorer View.

- Alternatively, you can create your own property sheet, which provides property support for its wrapped business object. A custom property sheet is also compatible with the Properties window, PropertySheetView, and the OutlineView Explorer View.
- Use FilterNode to create an alternate display for a node hierarchy. The FilterNode acts as a delegate for the original node. Whether or not a node is selected for display is controlled by the FilterNode.Children implementation.
- All Explorer Views work with Nodes and offer different types of presentation. BeanTreeView and OutlineView are both tree-based components. Other options include ContextTreeView and ListView to implement a master-detail window.
- Explorer Views provide a Quick Search feature for selection that is enabled by typing text into the view's window.
- Adding a feature to your application, such as a Selection History window, can be accomplished by creating a new module and adding it to your application. Because a NetBeans Platform application is modular, such added features frequently do not require existing modules to be modified.

# 8

# NetBeans Platform Window System

A typical desktop application requires top-level containers that are managed by a window system. What do we mean when we use the term "window system"? First, a window system includes a window manager that responds to user actions such as dragging, undocking, selecting, or minimizing windows to manage work space. Secondly, a window system should include a persistence mechanism so users aren't required to configure the application with each restart. Thirdly, a window system should provide a way to specify the window layout of an application and a way to group windows for common behavior. Finally, with a window system, you should be able to create multiple perspectives of an application so you can assign roles to different window configurations.

In this chapter you will explore the NetBeans Platform Window System. Significantly, the chapter includes many examples with various windows and operations on those windows. However, these windows, for the most part, lack any significant content.[1] In this chapter, we are concerned with window management—opening, closing, window layouts, groupings, floating, maximizing, and resizing. After you have explored the window system itself, subsequent chapters build on examples presented earlier and show you how to manipulate window content.

1. The NetBeans Platform has a powerful selection mechanism in which the Window System participates. When users select a window, for example, objects in the selected window's *Lookup* provide a global context for behaviors. We introduced Lookup and selection in "Lookup as an Object Repository" on page 225 and "Tracking Global Selection" on page 240. We further explore Lookup in "Actions and Lookup" on page 421.

### What You Will Learn

- Understand the window framework.
- Explore TopComponent basics, persistence, and client properties.
- Create non-singleton TopComponents.
- Understand the window system life cycle extension points.
- Explore window system modes.
- Use window groups in your application.
- Customize your application's window layout.
- Incorporate window layout roles in your application.

## 8.1 Window Framework Overview

Neither Swing nor JavaFX offers a framework with window management features. Developers can, of course, build a window management system themselves, but it takes a tremendous effort to create such a feature-rich system. The NetBeans Platform Window System provides this functionality. And, the window system is mostly configurable with Java annotations. Furthermore, you can specify many configuration parameters with the New Window wizard that NetBeans IDE provides.

Freed from having to provide such a sophisticated system (and re-inventing the wheel), developers can instead focus on building their business logic. In other words, they can concentrate on their domain issues and let the NetBeans Platform provide the window system.

We'll begin with a quick tour of the NetBeans Platform Window System and some of its terminology before delving into how to leverage its many features.

### Window Layout

Let's use the NetBeans IDE itself to examine the framework's window system. Figure 8.1 shows a typical window layout within the NetBeans IDE. The application framework includes a top-level menu bar and a toolbar, which are not part of the window system.

The remainder of the frame is the window layout. Here, a main editor-type window is surrounded by helper windows. In this example, the main editor window has three views with the Design view currently active. The Palette and Properties windows (on

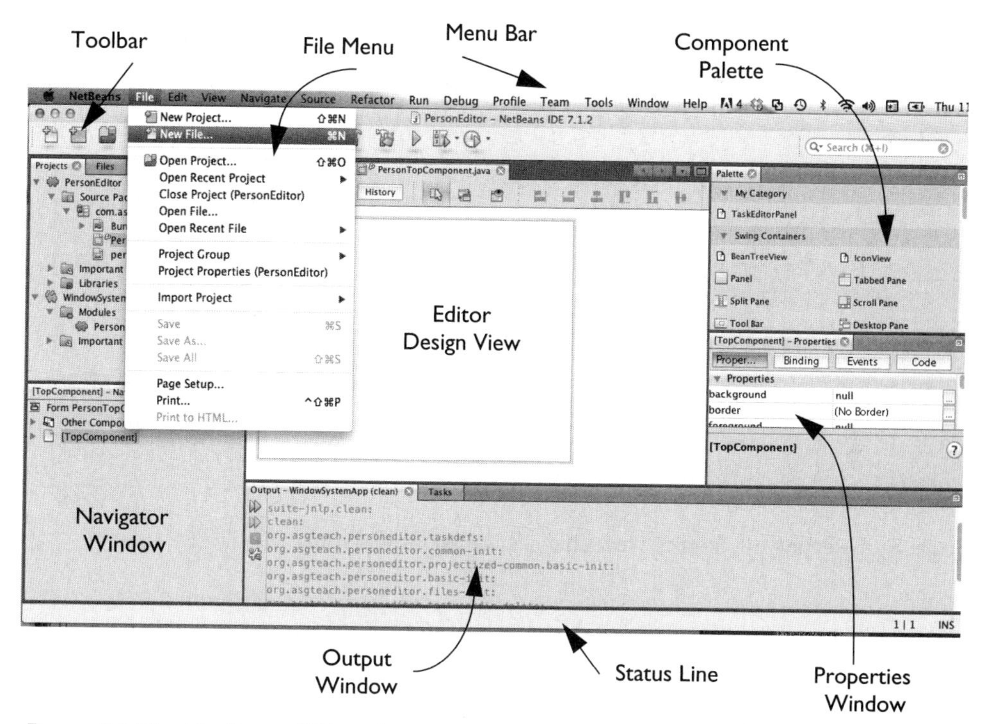


Figure 8.1 The NetBeans IDE application frame layout

the right) help a user select components to configure or add to the GUI. The Navigator window (lower left) displays a hierarchical view of the design window's components.

When you click the Source button and switch views to examine the source code, the Palette and Properties windows automatically close, leaving a larger work area for the Java source editor, as shown in Figure 8.2. The Palette and Properties windows form a *window group* with the Design view. That is, these three windows automatically open and close together. (Note that the Navigator window doesn't close, but its contents change when the view is switched to Source.)

On the left is the explorer area, currently containing three windows. The Projects window is visible and provides file-level information on each opened NetBeans project. You can make the other windows visible by clicking their tabs (Files and Services windows in Figure 8.2). All three windows occupy the same area (mode).

The Output and Tasks windows appear below the editor. Finally, a single status line (which is not a window) occupies the very bottom edge of the application.

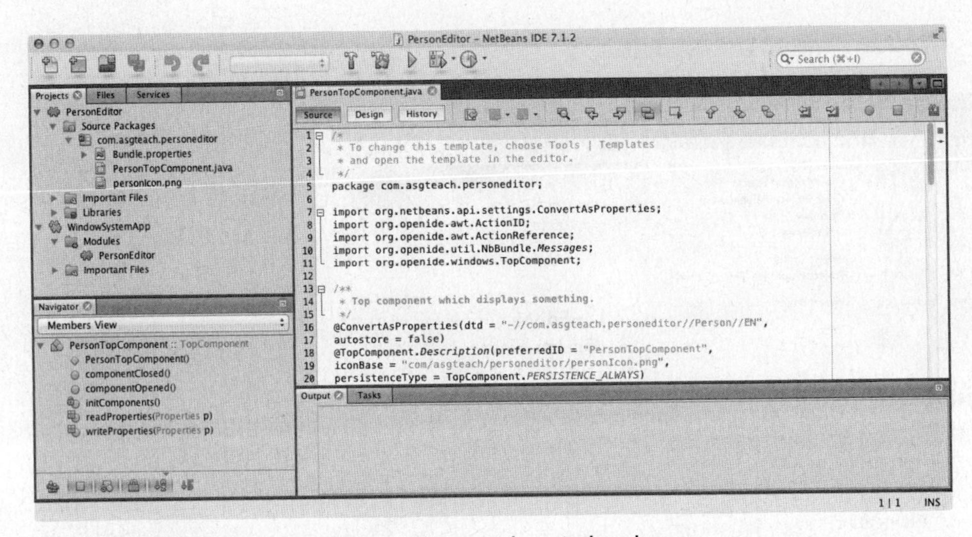


**Figure 8.2** Selecting the Source view changes the window layout

Figure 8.3 shows a detailed view of the editor window, which currently contains a Java source file with the Design view active (a GUI form editor). MultiView buttons let a user select among multiple views of the same file or other data.

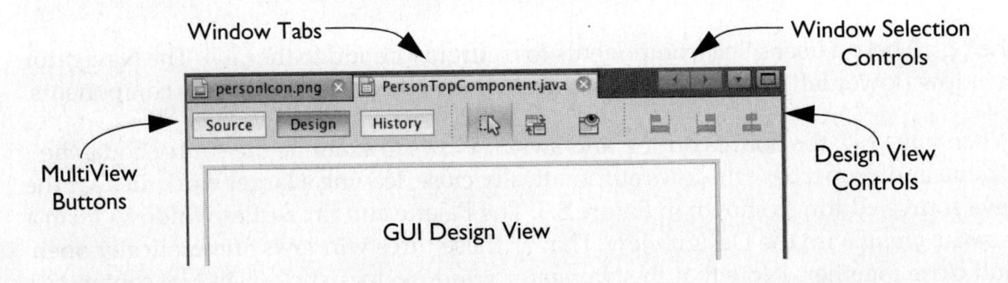


**Figure 8.3** Detailed view of editor window

**MultiView Windows**

*MultiView windows are used with editor windows, which we cover in Chapter 14 (see "Working with MultiView Windows" on page 697).*

Window tabs let a user select different windows in the same area (mode). Window selection controls in the editor area let the user cycle through window tabs when all the window tabs are not visible. The Design view controls are specific to the GUI form editors.

## Window Modes

The location and behavior of an application's window is defined by its window position, or mode, a container for windows. The NetBeans Platform Window System defines standard modes that you can use in your applications. Figure 8.4 shows these standard modes and their relative placement.

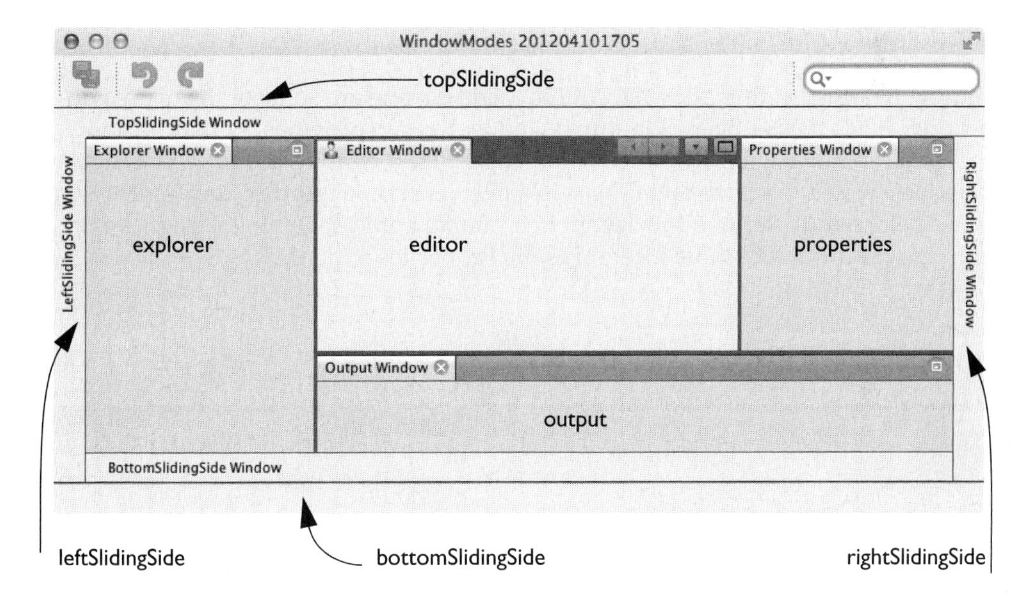


Figure 8.4 Window system default modes

There are three types of window modes: editor (typically for holding documents), view, and sliding. The editor mode is the default and provides specialized behaviors, such as window selection controls shown in Figure 8.3. By default, the editor mode always takes up at least part of the window frame. Editor mode windows cannot be minimized. The sliding modes are containers for holding minimized windows. The view modes hold helper windows and are generally placed around the main editor mode window.

The window system configures the standard (non-sliding) modes with XML configuration files. You can create your own modes or modify standard modes using these configuration files. We show you how to do this in "Window Layout" on page 387.

## TopComponents

The NetBeans Platform Window System manages windows that extend the TopComponent class. TopComponent, in turn, extends JComponent (a Swing-based container). With TopComponent, all application windows automatically integrate into the window system. That is, they are managed by the NetBeans Platform Window Manager and support a rich set of window operations.

## Window Operations

Docking, floating, sliding, moving, opening, and closing are some of the many window operations the NetBeans Platform Window System provides. With drag and drop, you can move windows around and customize a window layout. Click the mouse on the window's tab and drag it to a new location. Figure 8.5 and Figure 8.6 show a before and after window layout in a sample application. Here, we move the Explorer window to the same location as the Properties window.

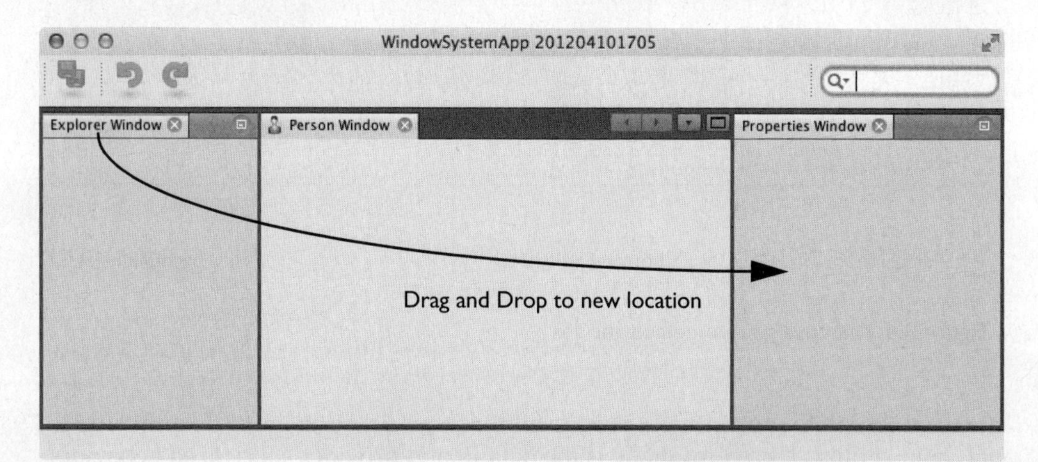


Figure 8.5 Before: Explorer window, Person window, and Properties window

The reconfiguration is automatically saved between application restarts during development unless you perform a clean and rebuild of your application.

A right click inside a window's tab displays a context menu for additional window operations. You can also access the context menu through the top-level menu

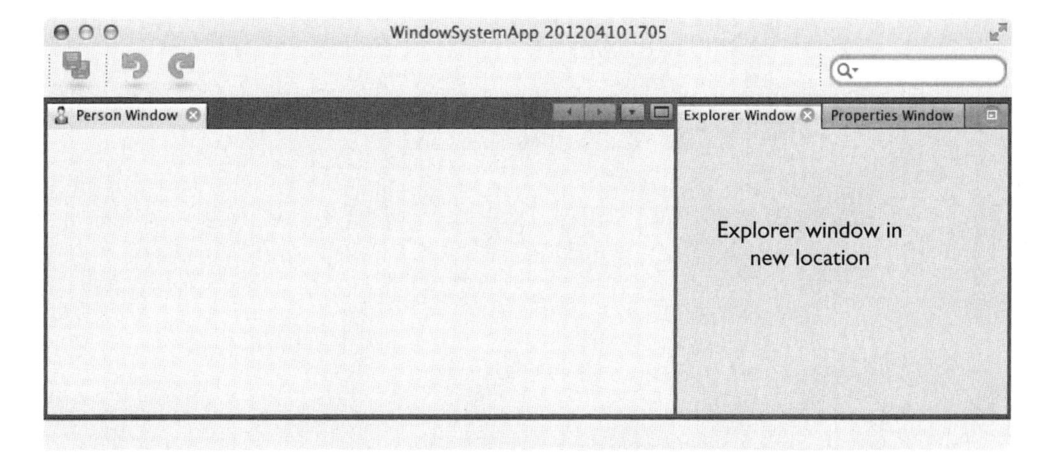


Figure 8.6 After: Person window with Explorer window and Properties window sharing the same mode

**Window | Configure Window**. Here are the available options. Note that the exact end result of a window operation would depend on the application's current window layout.

- **Float** detaches a window from the main window frame. This lets you move a window around independently of the application. You can float a single window or a window group. Once you float a window, you can then dock (reattach), resize, maximize, move, or close the window. Float is particularly useful when using multiple monitors. Figure 8.7 shows a floating Explorer window detached from the main window frame.
- **Minimize** hides a window or window group, creating a tab (or handle) at the nearest edge. This puts the window into one of the sliding modes at the edge of the application frame. You cannot minimize an editor window. With minimize, you can subsequently view a window by hovering over this tab. You can restore the window or window group by docking it or clicking the restore all button in the sidebar, which restores all windows in that group. Figure 8.8 shows two minimized windows, Explorer window and Properties window. The Explorer window is temporarily viewable by hovering the mouse over its tab.
- **Dock** reattaches a floating window or window group. It also restores a minimized window.
- **Maximize** is a toggle. If the window is docked, maximize enlarges the window so it takes up the entire application window frame. The other windows are then minimized along the nearest sides, but the status bar remains visible. If a window is floating, maximize enlarges the window so that it takes up the entire monitor

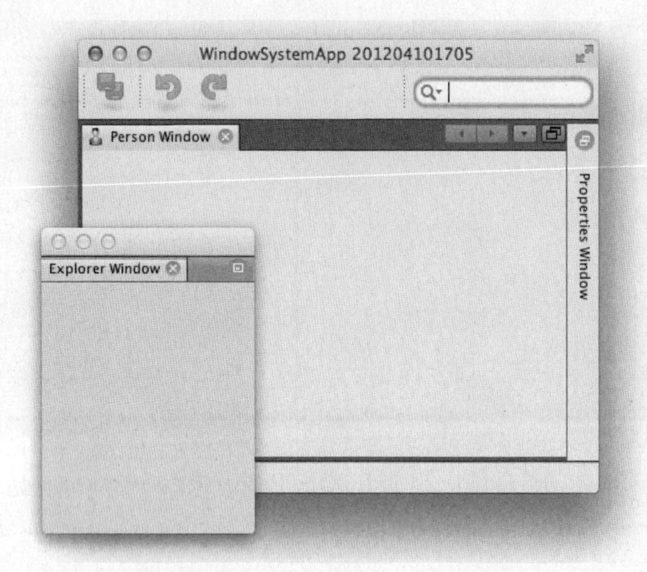


Figure 8.7 Floating a window

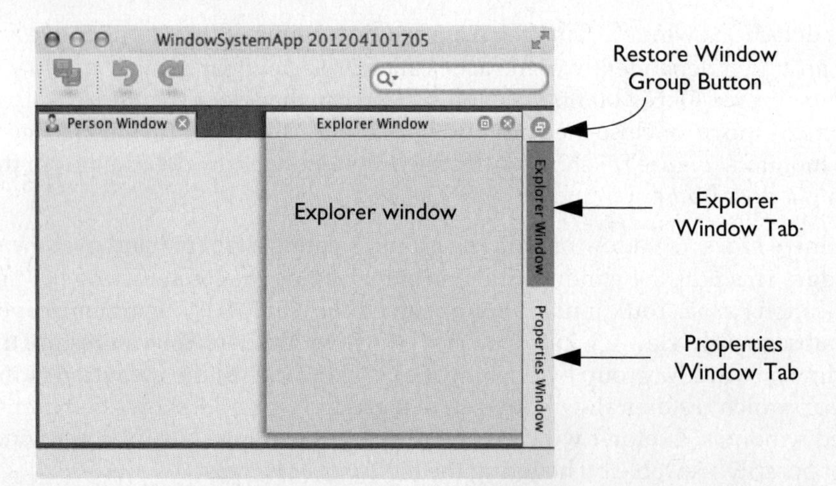


Figure 8.8 Viewing a minimized window

space (except for the top-level menu bar). When deselected, maximize restores the window to its previous size. To restore a floating maximized window to its docked size, re-dock the window.

You can also double click a window's tab to toggle the maximize operation.

- **Close** removes a window or window group from the window frame. Depending on the application, you may be prompted to save any unsaved data before the window closes. Again (if the window is configured with an open menu item), you can reopen a closed window by selecting **Window** in the top-level menu and selecting the window's name.
- **Size Group** lets you view the current dimensions of the selected window group.

*Documents* are TopComponents in the editor mode. Here are several window actions that apply exclusively to documents.

- **Clone** duplicates a window and its contents for viewing. That is, whatever changes you make to one copy are duplicated in the second copy. Only one copy of a document is persisted. You can make a window cloneable by extending CloneableTopComponent instead of TopComponent.
- **New Document Tab Group** creates a separate area or mode for the selected document or documents. This action can be applied when a document window contains at least two tabbed windows.
- **Collapse Document Tab Group** combines two or more documents into a single tabbed document area.

From the top level menu, **Window | Reset Windows** returns the window configuration to its default settings.

## Limiting the Window System's Behavior

You can limit the window system's behavior in your application through Branding Customization, as follows.

1. Select your NetBeans Platform application node in the Projects window, right click, and select **Branding . . . .**
2. When the Branding dialog appears, select the **Window System** tab.
3. By default, all behaviors are selected. De-select any standard behaviors that you want to remove and click **OK**, as shown in Figure 8.9.

You can also limit the behavior for any individual window (TopComponent) by selecting specific limitations during the New Window wizard, as shown in Figure 8.14 on page 354, or via client properties in the TopComponent constructor. See "TopComponent Client Properties" on page 363 for option details.

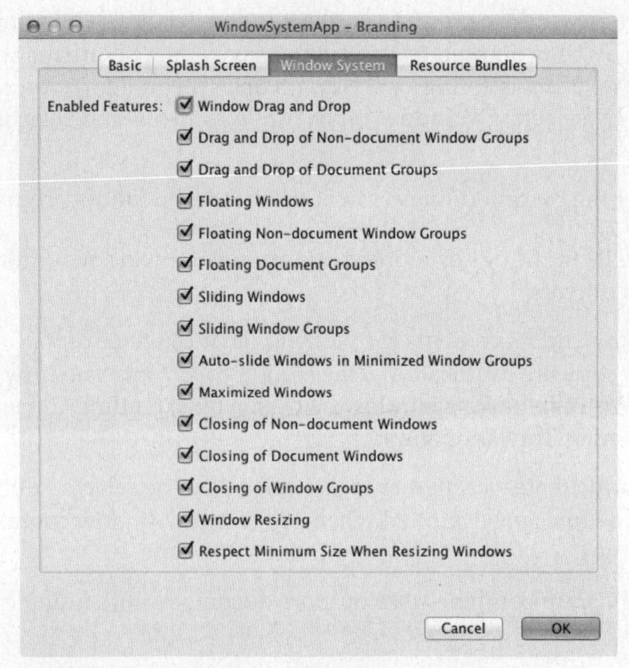


Figure 8.9 Limiting the window system's behavior

## Window Switching

At most one window is active (has focus) in a NetBeans Platform application. You can use the key stroke combination CTRL-TAB to cycle through all open windows to select a different open window, including non-document windows, as shown in Figure 8.10

## Window Tab Customization

You can configure editor tab placement in the Tools/Options (Windows) or NetBeans Preferences dialog (Mac OS X) under Miscellaneous/Windows, as shown in Figure 8.11. Select the desired Tabs placement radio button and/or the Multi-row tabs checkbox. (Note that the multi-row option doesn't provide multi-row behavior in the Mac OSX environment.)

## Window Manager

The NetBeans Platform Window System includes a window manager that keeps track of an application's windows, modes, window groups, and roles. Providing your own

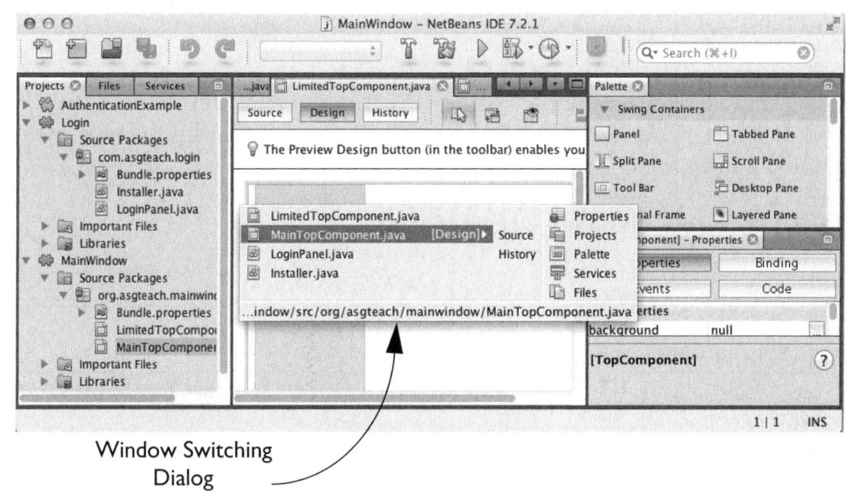

Figure 8.10 Switching active window with CTRL-TAB

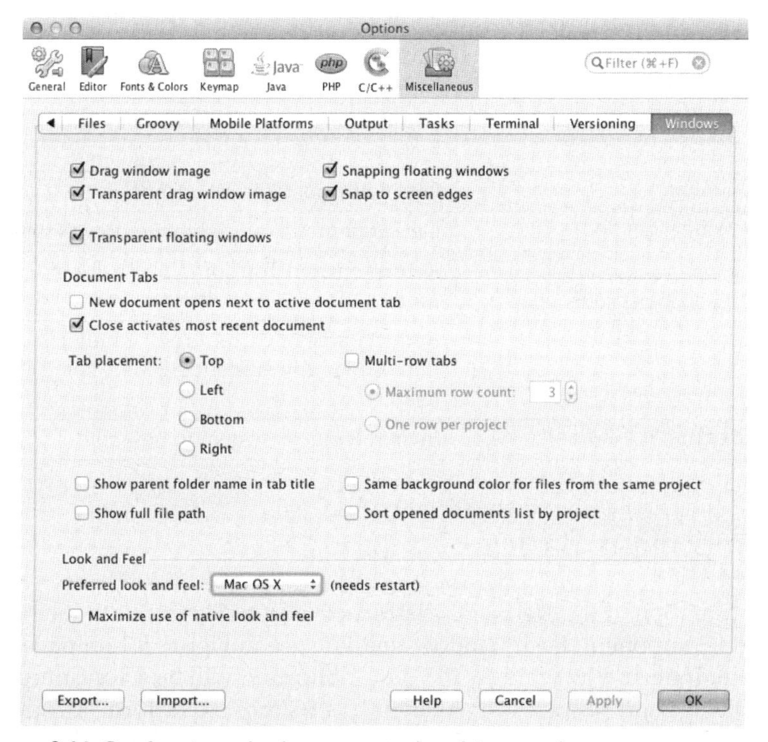
Figure 8.11 Configuring tab placement and multi-row tabs

window manager is possible, but most application developers use the standard window manager.

Table 8.1 lists several useful methods for finding modes, TopComponents, TopComponentGroups, and opened TopComponents. We'll show examples using some of these methods later in the chapter.

**TABLE 8.1 Window Manager Useful Methods**

| Method | Description |
|---|---|
| `Mode findMode(String name)` | Find mode name |
| `Mode findMode(TopComponent tc)` | Find mode that contains TopComponent |
| `TopComponent findTopComponent(String id)` | Find TopComponent with id |
| `TopComponentGroup findTopComponentGroup(String name)` | Find TopComponentGroup with name |
| `String findTopComponentID(TopComponent tc)` | Return specified TopComponent's ID |
| `TopComponent.Registry getRegistry()` | Return global component registry |
| `static WindowManager getDefault()` | Return singleton WindowManager instance |
| `Frame getMainWindow()` | Get NetBeans Main Window |
| `Set<? extends Mode> getModes()` | Get set of modes added to window system |
| `TopComponent[] getOpenedTopComponents(Mode mode)` | Return opened TopComponents for given mode |
| `String getRole()` | Return name of current role or null if default window system layout is being used |
| `void setRole(String roleName)` | Switch window system to new role |

## 8.2 TopComponent Basics

Let's begin our exploration of the NetBeans Platform Window System with its most basic unit—the TopComponent. Each window that you see in Figure 8.1 on page 343 is a TopComponent. Indeed, any window in your application will be a TopComponent (except for Dialogs and Wizard visual panels). At its most basic form, a TopComponent is straightforward to create and easy to use because most of the work of managing it is handled by the NetBeans Platform Window Manager.

### Build the Example

*To build the example for this and several other sections, create a new NetBeans Platform application called* ***WindowSystemApp****. Then create a new NetBeans module called* ***PersonEditor****, as shown in Figure 8.12.*

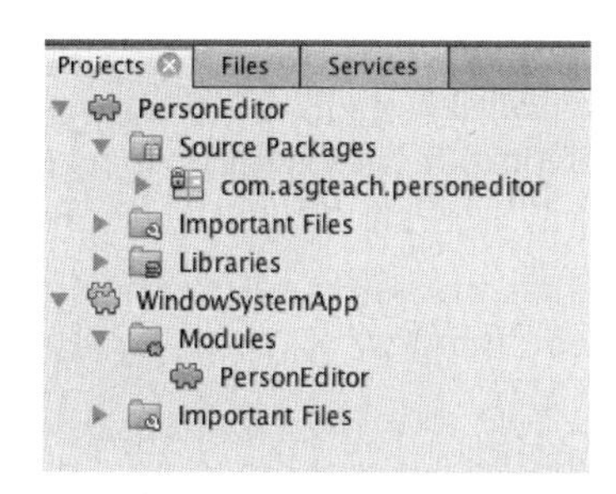


Figure 8.12 WindowSystemApp example application and PersonEditor module

Use the New Window wizard to create a TopComponent using the following steps.

1. Select the target module's source code package (`com.asgteach.personeditor` in our example), right click, and select **New | Other**.
2. The New File wizard displays the Choose File Type dialog. Under Categories select **Module Development** and under File Type select **Window**. Select **Next**, as shown in Figure 8.13.

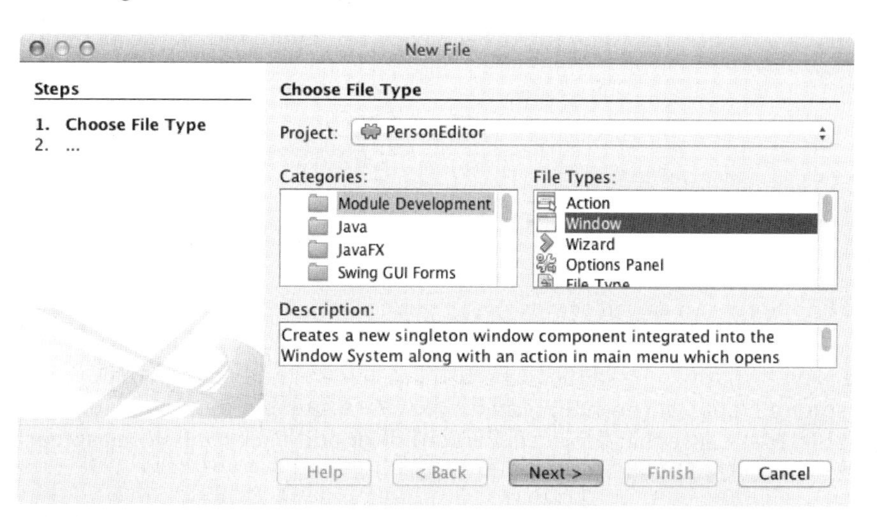


Figure 8.13 Create a new TopComponent with the New Window wizard

The New Window wizard next requires details on the basic characteristics of your window. The Window Position refers to its mode; choose from the available modes in the drop down selection. The Redefine button lets you create new modes and customize a layout design. We'll examine modes and layout design later in the chapter.

The remaining options let you specify your window's behaviors. You can choose to disable any number of these standard features, such as whether the window can be maximized, whether sliding is allowed, and other behaviors listed in the dialog. We discuss these features in more detail in "TopComponent Client Properties" on page 363.

3. For the Window Position, select mode **editor**. When you select editor, the options that refer to sliding are disabled, since editor mode windows cannot slide (be minimized).
4. For the remaining options, leave all of them unchecked except **Open on Application Start**, which should be checked, as shown in Figure 8.14. Click **Next**.

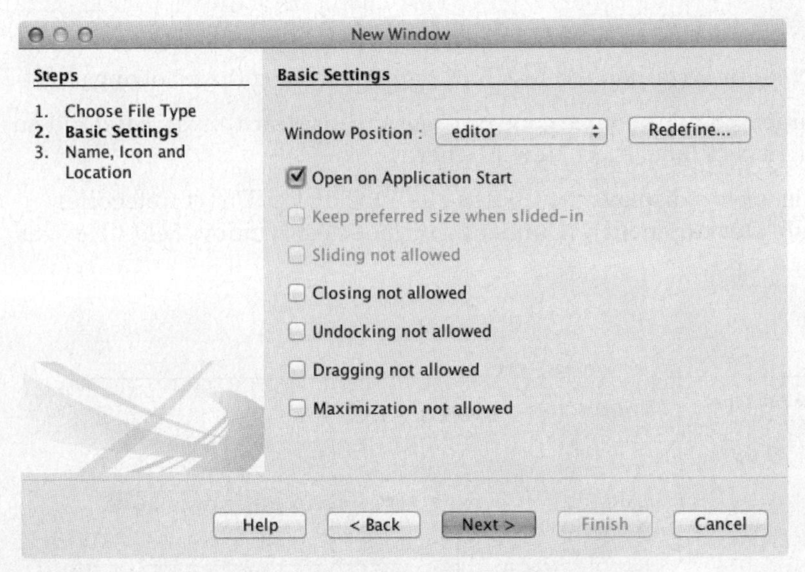


Figure 8.14 Specify a TopComponent's basic settings

5. The New Window wizard displays the Name, Icon and Location dialog. Specify **Person** for Name. For Icon, optionally provide a suitable 16 x 16 GIF or PNG graphic. Make sure that Project is **PersonEditor** and Package is **com.asgteach.personeditor**. Click **Finish**, as shown in Figure 8.15.

### TopComponent Tip

*You aren't restricted to a 16 x 16 graphic for the icon, but larger formats don't fit the size constraints of the component tab and menu item as well. Use file personIcon.png found in the download bundle for this book.*

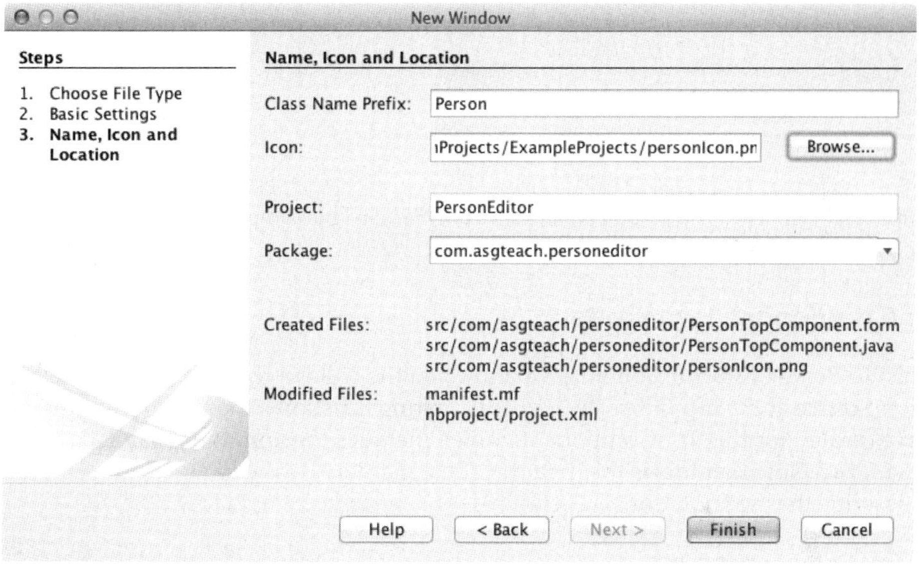

Figure 8.15 Name your TopComponent and optionally provide an icon

When the wizard completes, a new GUI component file PersonTopComponent.java appears in the project window of your module. This file opens in the Form Design editor.

Run the **WindowSystemApp** now and you'll see an application with a single window called Person window (with an icon on the tab), as shown in Figure 8.16. Open the top-level Window menu and you'll see the Person window (with its icon) included in the list of windows you can open.

Note that if you select Person from the Window menu now, nothing happens, since the Person window is already opened. By default, the New Window wizard creates a TopComponent singleton; that is, at most one window of that type will exist at any given time.

Close the Person window. Now select Person from the Window menu and you'll see that the Person window reopens in the window frame.

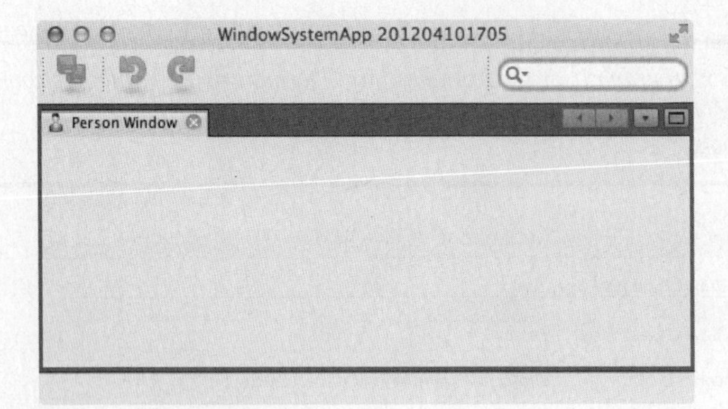


Figure 8.16 WindowSystemApp running showing PersonTopComponent window

## TopComponent Java Code

Return to **PersonTopComponent.java** and open the code in the Source view (select button **Source** at the top of the Java editor). Listing 8.1 shows the first part of the Java source created for this TopComponent, which includes the annotations that configure the window. Note that this is the default code generated by the New Window wizard. We describe these annotations in detail below.

### TopComponent Tip

*The New Window wizard creates a singleton TopComponent and the annotations assume a singleton TopComponent. To create a non-singleton TopComponent, see* *"Creating Non-Singleton TopComponents" on page 364.*

**Listing 8.1 PersonTopComonent.java—Part 1 (Annotations)**

```
import org.netbeans.api.settings.ConvertAsProperties;
import org.openide.awt.ActionID;
import org.openide.awt.ActionReference;
import org.openide.util.NbBundle.Messages;
import org.openide.windows.TopComponent;
@ConvertAsProperties(dtd = "-//com.asgteach.personeditor//Person//EN",
autostore = false)
@TopComponent.Description(preferredID = "PersonTopComponent",
iconBase = "com/asgteach/personeditor/personIcon.png",
persistenceType = TopComponent.PERSISTENCE_ALWAYS)
@TopComponent.Registration(mode = "editor", openAtStartup = true)
@ActionID(category = "Window",
      id = "com.asgteach.personeditor.PersonTopComponent")
```

```
@ActionReference(path = "Menu/Window", position = 333)
@TopComponent.OpenActionRegistration(displayName = "#CTL_PersonAction",
preferredID = "PersonTopComponent")
@Messages({
    "CTL_PersonAction=Person",
    "CTL_PersonTopComponent=Person Window",
    "HINT_PersonTopComponent=This is a Person window"
})
public final class PersonTopComponent extends TopComponent {

. . . class code, see Listing 8.2 . . .

}
```

The annotations provided by the New Window wizard configure the window. This includes specifying its persistence, assigning the window to a mode, providing an ID, and creating and registering an action to open the window. This configuration assumes that the TopComponent is a singleton.

### @ConvertAsProperties

The ConvertAsProperties annotation specifies that a TopComponent supports persisting TopComponent settings. Element `dtd` identifies a Document Type Definition (DTD) and must be a unique namespace. (You don't need to define the DTD.) With this annotation, you provide code for the `readProperties()` and `writeProperties()` methods (the New Window wizard generates these methods). Use the read/write methods to persist customized settings associated with this TopComponent. You should persist the information you need to properly reconstruct your component on a restart. "TopComponent Persistence" on page 361 includes a TopComponent persistence example.

The window manager invokes `writeProperties()` when the application shuts down and `readProperties()` when the application restarts.

When using ConvertAsProperties, be sure to set TopComponent.Description element `persistenceType` to `TopComponent.PERSISTENCE_ALWAYS` or `TopComponent.PERSISTENCE_ONLY_OPENED`, discussed next.

### @TopComponent.Description

The TopComponent.Description annotation includes required element `preferredID` and optional elements `iconBase` and `persistenceType`. Within the window manager, you can find or identify a TopComponent using its `preferredID`. Element `preferredID` (`String`) sets the TopComponent's ID. Element `iconBase` (`String`) provides the pathname for a TopComponent's icon. This graphic should be a 16 by 16 PNG or GIF file. Element `persistenceType` (`int`) specifies the TopComponent's persistence behavior.

If you always want persistence across restarts—even if the window is never opened—use `TopComponent.PERSISTENCE_ALWAYS`. This is the default setting and should only be used for singleton TopComponents. If you do not want any persistence, use `TopComponent.PERSISTENCE_NEVER`. With this setting, you should delete the annotation `@ConvertAsProperties` and methods `readProperties()` and `writeProperties()`. Finally, use `TopComponent.PERSISTENCE_ONLY_OPENED` to persist TopComponent settings across restarts when the window is open. A TopComponent should not change its persistence setting dynamically.

### @TopComponent.Registration

The TopComponent.Registration annotation registers the TopComponent into one of the existing window modes with elements `mode` (`String`) and `openAtStartup` (`boolean`). Optional element `position` (`int`) specifies the relative position of a window within a mode. That is, if more than one TopComponent opens in the same mode, use element `position` to control the window placement within the mode. A lower position value places the window on the left. Element `roles` (`String[]`) provides a comma separated list of roles. "Window Layout Roles" on page 401 includes an example with window layout roles.

### @ActionID

Annotations ActionID and ActionReference are not specific to TopComponents but are annotations that let you define actions within your application. In this case, the action defined is opening the window. Annotation TopComponent.OpenActionRegistration also relates to the action of opening the window. If you don't want your window opened via the top-level menu bar, remove these annotations from your TopComponent Java code.

Annotation ActionID requires element `category` ("Window") and `id`, which should be unique within the category.

### @ActionReference

The ActionReference annotation assigns an action identified by `@ActionID` using element `path` and optional element `position`. Element `path` is set to `"Menu/Window"` by the New Window wizard, meaning the Window menu of the top-level menu bar. Other possibilities are `"Toolbar/Edit"` or `"Shortcuts"` with `name="key_sequence"` to specify a keyboard shortcut (for example). Element `position` refers to the placement of the menu item in the specified window or toolbar. You can also specify menu item separators with optional elements `separatorBefore` and `separatorAfter`.

### @TopComponent.OpenActionRegistration

Annotation TopComponent.OpenActionRegistration is used along with `@ActionID` and `@TopComponent.Description` to create an action that opens a window. Required element `displayName` is the displayed action name (the menu item), and optional element `preferredID` should match element `preferredID` in `@TopComponent.Description`.

### @Messages

Use the Messages annotation when you have text to display to a user. This ensures that your application can be easily internationalized and localized. With TopComponent, `@Messages` are used for the menu item text, the window display name, and the tooltip text. You can customize these as needed.

**TopComponent Tip**

---

*If you make configuration changes to your TopComponent, perform a Clean All and Build All before running your application, since the Build process generates component configuration files. This ensures that your component is correctly configured. Alternatively, from the Files window, delete the directory* `build/testuserdir/config` *in your application's directory.*

---

Listing 8.2 shows the rest of the generated Java code for a TopComponent, discussed below.

**Listing 8.2 PersonTopComonent.java—Part II (TopComponent Java Code)**

```
. . . annotations omitted, see Listing 8.1 . . .
public final class PersonTopComponent extends TopComponent {

    public PersonTopComponent() {
        initComponents();
        setName(Bundle.CTL_PersonTopComponent());
        setToolTipText(Bundle.HINT_PersonTopComponent());
    }

    private void initComponents() {
         . . . code omitted . . .
    }
```

```
    @Override
    public void componentOpened() {
        // TODO add custom code on component opening
    }

    @Override
    public void componentClosed() {
        // TODO add custom code on component closing
    }

    void writeProperties(java.util.Properties p) {
        // better to version settings since initial version as advocated at
        // http://wiki.apidesign.org/wiki/PropertyFiles
        p.setProperty("version", "1.0");
        // TODO store your settings
    }

    void readProperties(java.util.Properties p) {
        String version = p.getProperty("version");
        // TODO read your settings according to their version
    }
}
```

Note that a TopComponent has a public default constructor, so that the system can create a TopComponent instance.

Method `initComponents()` is generated for any GUI component created with the Matisse design editor. This code cannot be edited in the Java editor, but you can configure components and provide other customization code using the GUI component palette and properties window.

Method `componentOpened()` and `componentClosed()` are two of the TopComponent life cycle methods. A common use for these is adding event listeners in `componentOpened()` and removing them in `componentClosed()`. Other life cycle methods are `componentActivated()`, `componentDeactivated()`, `componentHidden()`, and `componentShowing()`. We discuss these methods in detail in "Window System Life Cycle Management" on page 369.

Finally, methods `readProperties()` and `writeProperties()` persist your window's settings according to its configured persistence type, discussed next.

## Window Header Animated Notifications

A TopComponent's window header (its tab) contains an optional icon and the window's display name. You can display an animated notification that the window is currently busy (for example, window content is being loaded) with TopComponent method makeBusy(true). Use makeBusy(false) to turn off the animated notification. Figure 8.17 shows a TopComponent with an animated "wait" icon in its header.

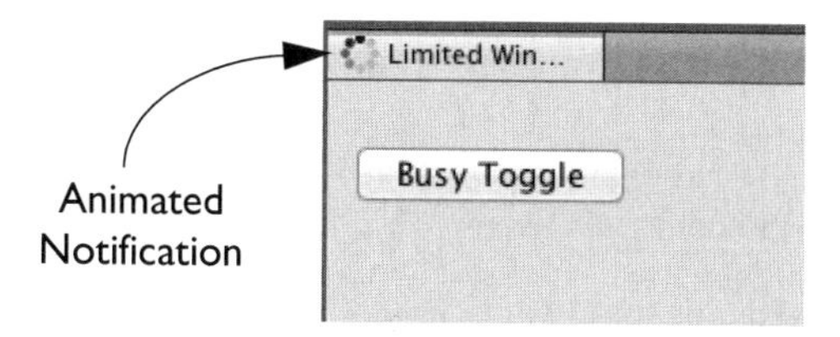


Figure 8.17 TopComponent animated notification appears in its window tab

## 8.3 TopComponent Persistence

Annotations control the persistence behavior of your TopComponent. For singleton TopComponents, define annotation @ConvertAsProperties and set the persistence type to either PERSISTENCE_ALWAYS or PERSISTENCE_ONLY_OPENED, as discussed in "@ConvertAsProperties" and "@TopComponent.Description" on page 357. With persistence, the NetBeans Platform saves your window configuration (its size, mode, and whether or not the window is opened). You can also persist additional String data specific to your TopComponent instance with methods writeProperties() and readProperties().

To demonstrate, let's add a label and textfield to the PersonTopComponent and persist the textfield's entered text. Whatever String a user enters in the textfield will now persist across restarts. Figure 8.18 shows the added JLabel and JTextField in the component's Design view.

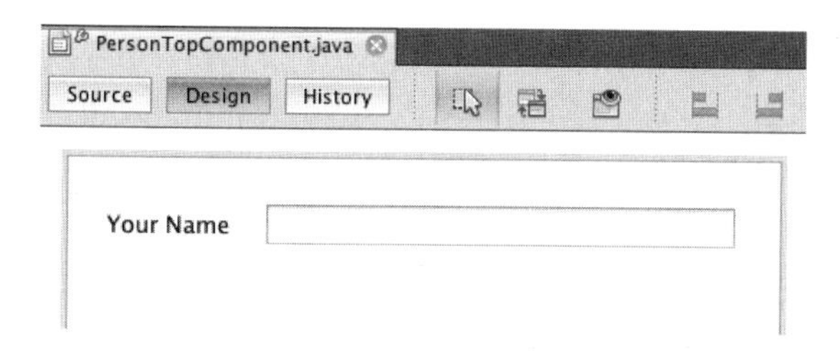


Figure 8.18 PersonTopComponent Design view

The text of the JTextField (whose variable name is nameTextField) is persisted as property "name" and subsequently restored, as shown in Listing 8.3. The added code is shown in bold.

**Listing 8.3 Methods writeProperties() and readProperties()**

```
public final class PersonTopComponent extends TopComponent {

  . . . omitted code . . .

    void writeProperties(java.util.Properties p) {
        // better to version settings since initial version as advocated at
        // http://wiki.apidesign.org/wiki/PropertyFiles
        p.setProperty("version", "1.0");
        p.setProperty("name", nameTextField.getText());
    }

    void readProperties(java.util.Properties p) {
        String version = p.getProperty("version");
        nameTextField.setText(p.getProperty("name"));
    }
}
```

Now on a restart, instead of being blank, the textfield will include the String entered previously by the user, as shown in Figure 8.19.

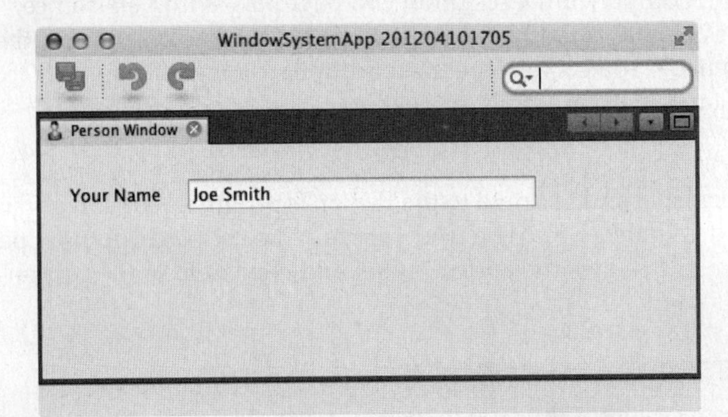


Figure 8.19 PersonTopComponent Design view

**TopComponent Tip**

*Note that methods* `writeProperties()` *and* `readProperties()` *manipulate a* `java.util.Properties` *stream. Each key and its corresponding value in the property list is a String.*

Where does NetBeans store user data? NetBeans stores component data in the application's user configuration file system in `config/Windows2Local/Components`. For our application, the window system creates XML file **PersonTopComponent.settings**.

Listing 8.4 shows its contents for our example. Here, property `"name"` has value `"Joe Smith"`.

**Listing 8.4 PersonTopComponent.settings**

```
<?xml version="1.0" encoding="UTF-8" ?>
<!DOCTYPE properties PUBLIC "-//com.asgteach.personeditor//Person//EN"
                    "http://www.netbeans.org/dtds/properties-1_0.dtd">
<properties>
    <property name="version" value="1.0"/>
    <property name="name" value="Joe Smith"/>
</properties>
```

### Windows2Local Folder

During development, configuration data is generated and stored in your project's build directory under `build/testuserdir/config`. Therefore, the **PersonTopComponent.settings** file is located at `Your_Application_Name/build/testuserdir/config/Windows2Local/Components`. However, when you package your application for distribution, the location of this user directory depends on the underlying operating system and the distribution method. On a Mac OS X using a zip file distribution, the user directory is at `User_Home_Directory/Library/Application Support/Your_Application_Name/dev/config`. On a Windows system using a zip file distribution, the user directory can be found at `User_Home_Directory/.Your_Application_Name/dev/config`. We discuss branding and application distribution in more detail in Chapter 17.

## 8.4 TopComponent Client Properties

When you create a new window using the New Window wizard, you can select behavior limitations that apply to that window. This generates client property settings in the window's TopComponent constructor, as shown in Listing 8.5. You can always edit the TopComponent constructor later and add or remove any client property settings.

**Listing 8.5 TopComponent Client Property Settings**

```
public final class LimitedTopComponent extends TopComponent {

    public LimitedTopComponent() {
        initComponents();
        setName(Bundle.CTL_LimitedTopComponent());
        setToolTipText(Bundle.HINT_LimitedTopComponent());
        putClientProperty(TopComponent.PROP_CLOSING_DISABLED, Boolean.TRUE);
```

```
        putClientProperty(TopComponent.PROP_DRAGGING_DISABLED, Boolean.TRUE);
        putClientProperty(TopComponent.PROP_MAXIMIZATION_DISABLED,
                Boolean.TRUE);
        putClientProperty(TopComponent.PROP_SLIDING_DISABLED, Boolean.TRUE);
        putClientProperty(TopComponent.PROP_UNDOCKING_DISABLED, Boolean.TRUE);
        putClientProperty(TopComponent.PROP_KEEP_PREFERRED_SIZE_WHEN_SLIDED_IN,
                Boolean.TRUE);

    }
    . . . omitted code . . .
}
```

Table 8.2 describe these configurable TopComponent behaviors.

**TABLE 8.2 TopComponent Behaviors That Can Be Configured**

| Behavior | Description |
|---|---|
| CLOSING_DISABLED | Prevents the user from closing the TopComponent. |
| DRAGGING_DISABLED | Prevents the user from dragging and dropping the TopComponent to a new location. |
| KEEP_PREFERRED_SIZE_WHEN_SLIDED_IN | The TopComponent is displayed in its original size instead of a modified size for the slided-in mode. (Only applies to non-editor TopComponents.) |
| MAXIMIZATION_DISABLED | Prevents the user from maximizing the TopComponent. |
| SLIDING_DISABLED | Prevents the user from minimizing the TopComponent. (Only applies to non-editor TopComponents.) |
| UNDOCKING_DISABLED | Prevents the user from floating the TopComponent. |
| "print.printable" | If true, enables Print for TopComponent content |

## 8.5 Creating Non-Singleton TopComponents

By default, the New Window wizard creates a TopComponent singleton, and the annotations that the wizard generates assume a singleton TopComponent. However, it is quite common for an application to require non-singleton TopComponents.

A common use case for non-singleton TopComponents is some sort of editor window where a user opens a file or domain object for editing. In this case, a user typically selects the domain object (or file), right clicks, and chooses Open from a context menu. Or, a user may double click the domain object (or file) and have the selected object open in an editor.

However, to properly illustrate this use case, we'll need several NetBeans Platform features we haven't discussed yet, such as conditionally-enabled Actions. So for now, let's show you how to create non-singleton windows with a simple example. (For a well-developed example of opening a domain object in an editor, see "Implementing Update" on page 488 in Chapter 10.)

Let's continue with the WindowSystemApp example that contains PersonTopComponent in module PersonEditor. In the previous section, we created a singleton TopComponent.

Listing 8.6 shows the changes that create a non-singleton TopComponent. When you decide to create a non-singleton TopComponent, you must also select a persistence behavior. You have two choices.

1. Specify `PERSISTENCE_NEVER` in annotation `@TopComponent.Description`. In this case, remove annotation `@ConvertAsProperties` and methods `writeProperties()` and `readProperties()`. With this persistence type, your window settings will not be saved across restarts.
2. Specify `PERSISTENCE_ONLY_OPENED` in annotation `@TopComponent.Description`. With this setting, you retain annotation `@ConvertAsProperties` as well as methods `writeProperties()` and `readProperties()`. Only the windows that are open when the application shuts down will be saved and restored across restarts. This means that if a window is closed before application shutdown, the window will not appear in the next restart, even if it was previously persisted.

**TopComponent Tip**

*Never specify* `PERSISTENCE_ALWAYS` *for non-singleton TopComponents. Otherwise, every instance of the TopComponent that is ever created will be persisted on shutdown, even if the associated domain object or file has been deleted. The saved windows accumulate over time, wasting disk space and slowing startup time.*

In Listing 8.6 we specify `PERSISTENCE_ONLY_OPENED` and therefore retain annotation `@ConvertAsProperties` as well as methods `writeProperties()` and `readProperties()`.

**Listing 8.6 PersonTopComponent.java—Non-Singleton Window**

```
@ConvertAsProperties(dtd = "-//com.asgteach.personeditor//Person//EN",
   autostore = false)
```

```
@TopComponent.Description(preferredID = "PersonTopComponent",
   iconBase = "com/asgteach/personeditor/personIcon.png",
persistenceType = TopComponent.PERSISTENCE_ONLY_OPENED)
@TopComponent.Registration(mode = "editor", openAtStartup = false)
@ActionID(category = "Window",
   id = "com.asgteach.personeditor.PersonTopComponent")
@ActionReference(path = "Menu/Window", position = 333)
@TopComponent.OpenActionRegistration(displayName = "#CTL_PersonAction"
//,preferredID = "PersonTopComponent"
      )
@Messages({
    "CTL_PersonAction=Person",
    "CTL_PersonTopComponent=Person Window",
    "HINT_PersonTopComponent=This is a Person window"
})
public final class PersonTopComponent extends TopComponent {
. . . code omitted . . .
}
```

Note that we changed attribute `openAtStartup` to `false` in annotation `@TopComponent.Registration`. You will normally specify this setting, since a non-singleton TopComponent typically opens in conjunction with a specific domain object or file action.

In Listing 8.6 we also kept the annotations to create the Windows menu item and action that opens the window. We did this so you could easily open multiple PersonTopComponent windows without writing code to specifically open the window. But, to enable opening multiple windows, you must remove attribute `preferredID` from annotation `@TopComponent.OpenActionRegistration`.

Figure 8.20 shows the non-singleton WindowSystemApp running with three open PersonTopComponent windows. Each window has a different textfield value, which persists across restarts. When the application restarts, not only will the same windows open, but they will have their previously specified text in the textfield component. However, once you close a window, its data will not be persisted and the window won't open with the next restart.

Since PersonTopComponent is no longer a singleton TopComponent, how does the window system persist each window's data? Recall that PersonTopComponent persistent data is stored in `Application/build/testuserdir/config/Windows2Local/Components/PersonTopComponent.settings` using the TopComponent's `preferredID` to generate the XML **.settings** file. With multiple instances of the same TopComponent, the persistent data is stored in **PersonTopComponent_1.settings**, **PersonTopComponent_2.settings**, and so on.

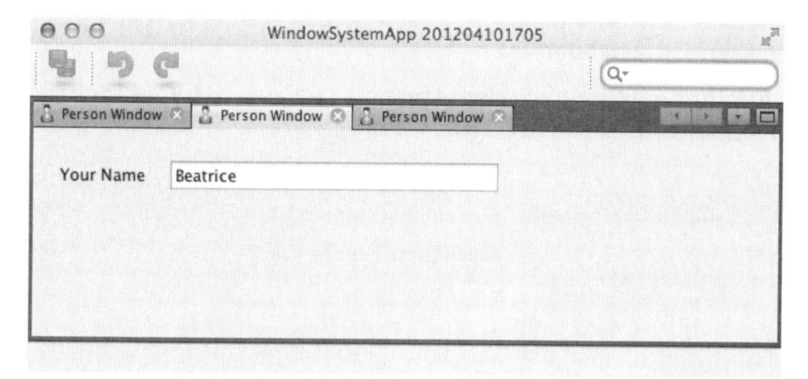


Figure 8.20 Non-singleton TopComponent

## Opening Windows from User Code

Now let's show you how to open the non-singleton TopComponent within your own code; that is, not from the top-level Windows menu. First, remove annotations `@ActionID`, `@ActionReference`, and `@TopComponent.OpenActionRegistration`, which all support the Open action in the top-level Windows menu. Listing 8.7 shows the updated PersonTopComponent code with these annotations removed.

**Listing 8.7 PersonTopComponent.java—Annotations for Open Removed**

```
@ConvertAsProperties(dtd = "-//com.asgteach.personeditor//Person//EN",
   autostore = false)
@TopComponent.Description(preferredID = "PersonTopComponent",
   iconBase = "com/asgteach/personeditor/personIcon.png",
   persistenceType = TopComponent.PERSISTENCE_ONLY_OPENED)
@TopComponent.Registration(mode = "editor", openAtStartup = false)
@Messages({
    "CTL_PersonAction=Person",
    "CTL_PersonTopComponent=Person Window",
    "HINT_PersonTopComponent=This is a Person window"
})
public final class PersonTopComponent extends TopComponent {
. . . code omitted . . .
}
```

Now let's create another (singleton) TopComponent with a button that opens a PersonTopComponent window. Follow these steps.

1. Create a new window with the New Window wizard. Specify Window Position **explorer**, select **Open on Application Start**, and click **Next**.

2. Specify **Open** for Class Name Prefix. Project should be **PersonEditor** and package should be **com.asgteach.personeditor**.
3. Click **Finish**. Application WindowSystemApp now contains two TopComponents in module PersonEditor as shown in Figure 8.21.

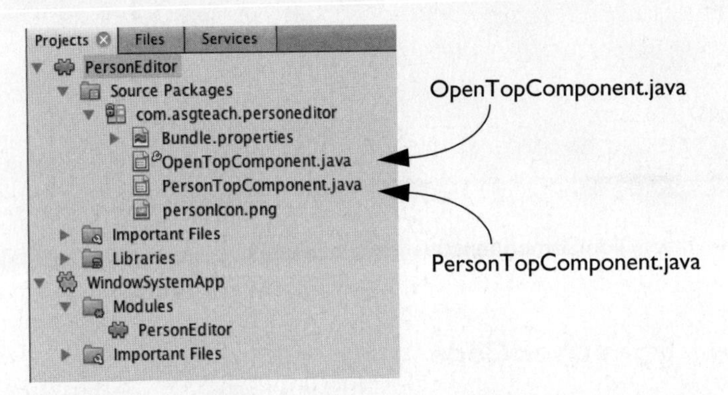


Figure 8.21 WindowSystemApp Projects window

4. Bring up OpenTopComponent in the Design view and drop a JButton component with label Open Person Window, as shown in Figure 8.22.

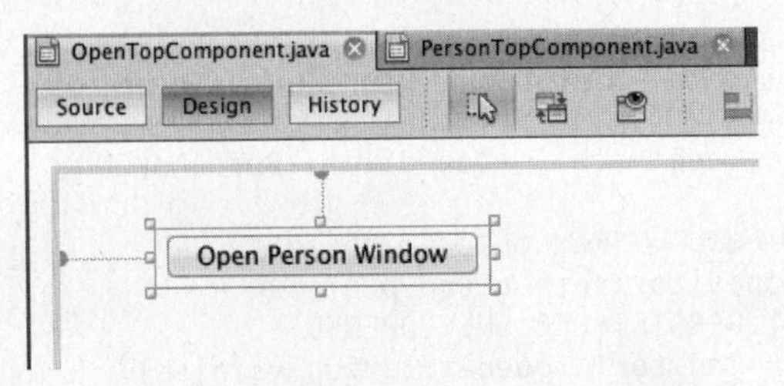


Figure 8.22 OpenTopComponent Design view with added JButton component

5. Select the button and click tab **Code** in the Properties window. This brings up the Code Generation tab for the button.
6. Change the button's **Variable Name** to **openPersonButton**.
7. Now double click the button, which creates method `openPersonButtonAction-Performed()` (this method will be invoked when a user clicks the button). NetBeans now switches to the Source view for OpenTopComponent.
8. Provide the following code for method `openPersonButtonActionPerformed()`, as shown in Listing 8.8.

**Listing 8.8 Method openPersonButtonActionPerformed**

```
private void openPersonButtonActionPerformed(
                            java.awt.event.ActionEvent evt) {
    TopComponent tc = new PersonTopComponent();
    tc.open();
    tc.requestActive();
}
```

Run application WindowSystemApp again. Click the Open Person Window button several times. Provide text in each window's textfield and then shut down the application. Run the application again and you'll see that the windows you previously created now reappear with the persisted textfield data. Figure 8.23 shows a sample run.

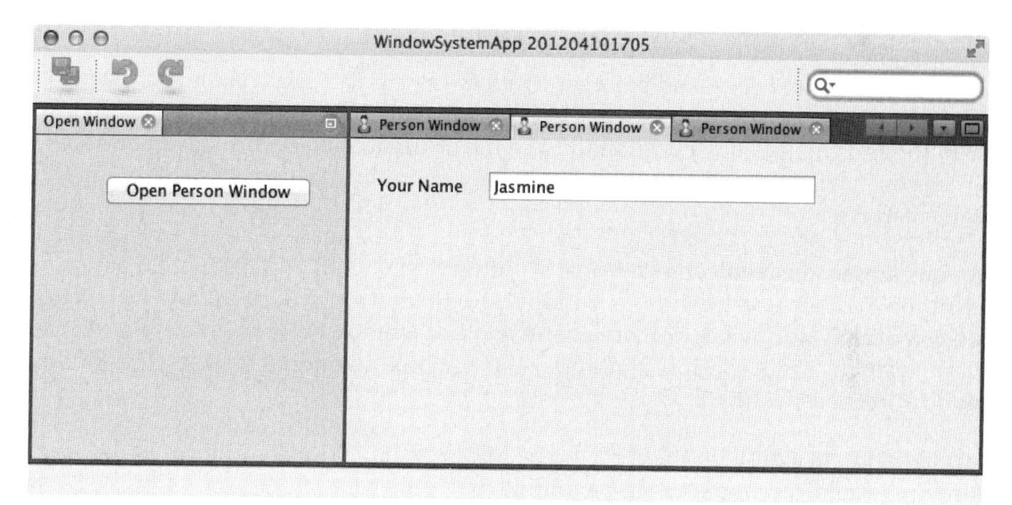


Figure 8.23 WindowSystemApp with button to open PersonTopComponent

## 8.6 Window System Life Cycle Management

Let's continue our exploration of the window system by looking at the TopComponent life cycle methods. Table 8.3 lists these life cycle methods, which you can override in your TopComponent Java code.

**TABLE 8.3 TopComponent Life Cycle Methods**

| Method | Called When |
|---|---|
| `public void componentOpened()` | Window is opened. |
| `public void componentClosed()` | Window is closed. |

**TABLE 8.3 TopComponent Life Cycle Methods** *(Continued)*

| Method | Called When |
|---|---|
| `public boolean canClose()` | Window is about to close. Return true if window is allowed to close. |
| `protected void componentActivated()` | Window is activated (has focus). |
| `protected void componentDeactivated()` | Window is deactivated (loses focus). |
| `protected void componentHidden()` | Window is hidden. |
| `protected void componentShowing()` | Window is showing (visible). |

The New Window wizard generates methods `componentOpened()` and `componentClosed()`. You typically place initialization/cleanup code here. (For example, include code that adds and removes event listeners.)

Method `canClose()` is invoked before a window closes. This is a convenient place for code that checks to see if it's okay to close a window. For example, if your window is an editor and changes have been made to a file or domain object but have not been saved, you can confirm closing with a user here and return true or false based on the user's response.

As you can see, the NetBeans Platform Window System makes a distinction between activation and hidden/showing. A window is activated when the window has focus. You can deactivate a window by selecting another window. When there are multiple windows in the same window container, you can hide a window by selecting another window in the same mode.

Let's experiment a bit with these methods. Modify PersonTopComponent in the same WindowSystemApp applications as follows.

1. Open PersonTopComponent in the Java editor and select **Source** to manipulate the Java code.
2. Place the cursor after method `componentClosed()`, right click, and select **Insert Code . . .** .
3. When the context menu appears, select **Generate Override Method . . .**
4. A dialog appears that lets you select which methods to override. Select methods `canClose()`, `componentActivated()`, `componentDeactivated()`, `componentHidden()`, and `componentShowing()`, as shown in Figure 8.24.
5. Click **Generate**. NetBeans will generate stub methods for the methods you select.
6. Provide code for these methods as well as methods `componentOpened()` and `componentClosed()`, as shown in Listing 8.9. Note that we retain calls to these methods' superclass with `super` when NetBeans generates the superclass calls.

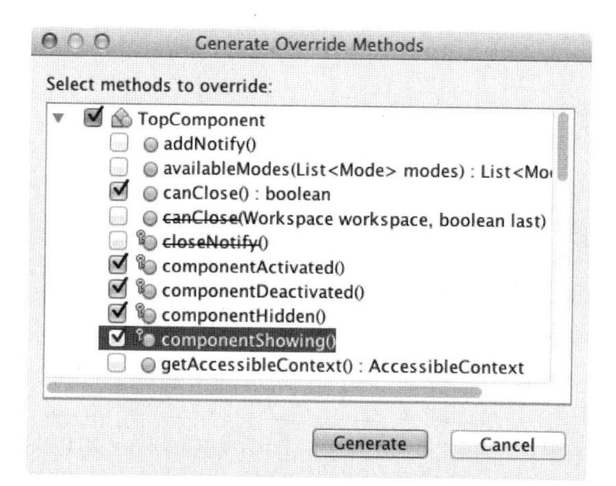


Figure 8.24 Generate selected override methods for PersonTopComponent

**Listing 8.9 Overriding TopComponent Methods**

```
@Override
public void componentOpened() {
    System.out.println(nameTextField.getText() + " opened");
}

@Override
public void componentClosed() {
    System.out.println(nameTextField.getText() + " closed");
}

@Override
public boolean canClose() {
    return !nameTextField.getText().toLowerCase().endsWith("guru");
}

@Override
protected void componentActivated() {
    super.componentActivated();
    System.out.println(nameTextField.getText() + " activated");
}

@Override
protected void componentDeactivated() {
    super.componentDeactivated();
    System.out.println(nameTextField.getText() + " deactivated");
}
```

```
@Override
protected void componentHidden() {
    super.componentHidden();
    System.out.println(nameTextField.getText() + " hidden");
}

@Override
protected void componentShowing() {
    super.componentShowing();
    System.out.println(nameTextField.getText() + " showing");
}
```

7. Clean All the application; then Run.

Experiment by running the application and examine the NetBeans IDE output window where the results of the `System.out.println` statements appear. For example, open several Person windows and provide names **Amy**, **Bob**, and **Charlie**. Figure 8.25 shows the application with Amy in the visible Person window.

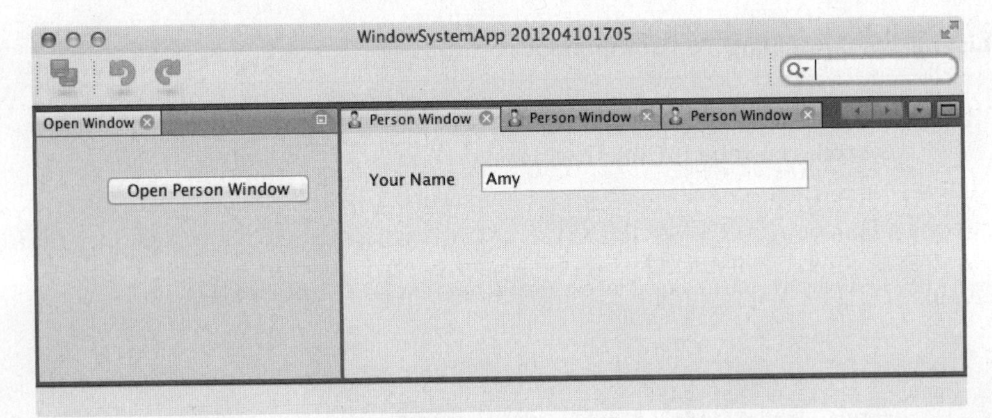


Figure 8.25 WindowSystemApp with TopComponent life cycle methods

Selecting different Person window tabs lets you see the order of the life cycle methods. Suppose the Person window with Charlie is activated and showing. Here is what happens when you then select the tab corresponding to Bob. First, `componentShowing()` is invoked for Bob followed by `componentHidden()` and `componentDeactivated()` for Charlie," and finally `componentActivated()` for Bob.

```
Charlie activated
Bob showing
Charlie hidden
Charlie deactivated
Bob activated
```

Now select the Open Window tab. Note that this deactivates the Person window but does not affect its hidden/showing status.

```
Charlie activated
Bob showing
Charlie hidden
Charlie deactivated
Bob activated
Bob deactivated
```

Close several Person windows and note that method `componentClosed()` is invoked. Now open a Person window with text **Component Guru**. Note that you cannot close this window because the code you provided in method `canClose()` disallows closing windows with a `nameTextField` text property that ends with String guru (converted to lowercase letters).

Finally, if you shut down the application and restart it, you'll see that the window manager opens the Person windows that were previously opened. In our example, a restart provided the following output.

```
Bob opened
Component Guru opened
Bob showing
Bob activated
```

## Using the Window Manager

Let's now show you some of the window manager methods that manipulate TopComponents. Follow these steps to add a second button to OpenTopComponent. This button lets a user close the top Person window shown in the editor mode.

1. Bring up OpenTopComponent in the Design view and drop a second JButton component with label **Close Top Person Window**, as shown in Figure 8.26.

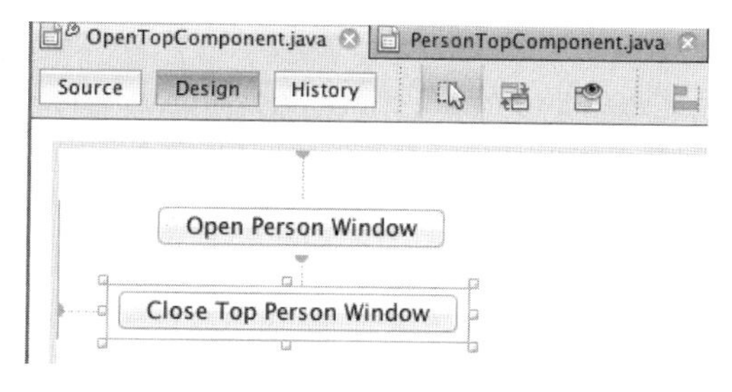


Figure 8.26 OpenTopComponent Design view with second JButton component

2. Select the button. In the Properties window, click tab **Code**. This brings up the Code Generation tab for the button.

3. Change the button's **Variable Name** to **closeTopPersonButton**.
4. Now double click the button, which creates method `closeTopPersonButtonAction-Performed()`. You are now switched to the Source view for OpenTopComponent.
5. Provide the following code for method `closeTopPersonButtonActionPerformed()`, as shown in Listing 8.10.

**Listing 8.10 Method closeTopPersonButtonActionPerformed**

```
private void closeTopPersonButtonActionPerformed(
                                java.awt.event.ActionEvent evt) {
    WindowManager wm = WindowManager.getDefault();
    Mode editorMode = wm.findMode("editor");
    for (TopComponent tc : wm.getOpenedTopComponents(editorMode)) {
        System.out.println("found " + tc.getName());
        if (tc.isShowing() ) {
            if (tc instanceof PersonTopComponent) {
                tc.close();
            }
            break;
        }
    }
}
```

Let's discuss how method `closeTopPersonButtonActionPerformed()` closes the top Person window.

The first step is to get a WindowManager instance by invoking the static WindowManager method `getDefault()`. Using the window manager, method `findMode()` returns the editor Mode object. The next step calls `getOpenedTopComponents()`, which provides a list of all opened TopComponents for that mode. The for loop looks for the one TopComponent in which `isShowing()` is true. When we find it, we close the TopComponent and exit the loop.

Note that this method also checks that the component that's showing is indeed a PersonTopComponent. A bit of defensive programming is not a bad idea here, just in case we later add another (different) TopComponent to the editor window position.

Now run application WindowSystemApp again and make sure you have several Person windows open. Click the Close Top Person Window button. You'll see that the top Person window closes. Figure 8.27 shows a sample run.

## Using @OnShowing

Similar to the Module System API `@OnStart` and `@OnStop` annotations (see "Module Life Cycle Annotations" on page 242), the Window System API provides the `@OnShow-`

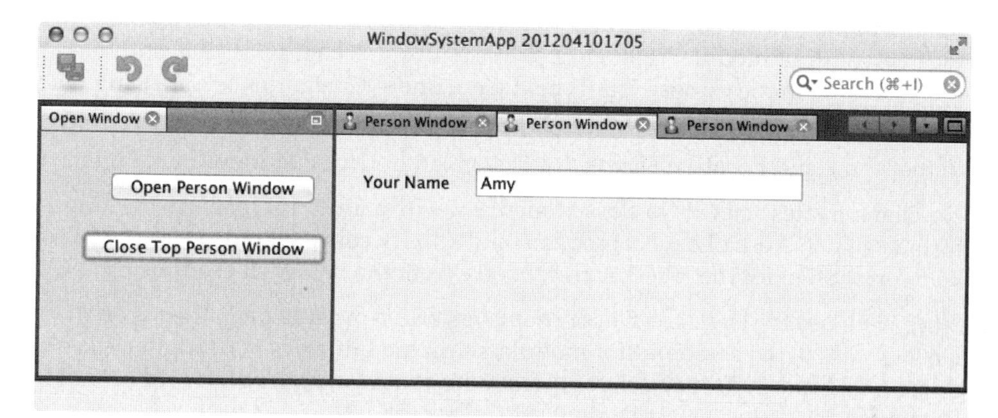


Figure 8.27 WindowSystemApp with button to close top Person window

`ing` annotation. You place the `@OnShowing` annotation on a class that implements Runnable and has a default constructor. You implement the `run()` method, which is invoked as soon as the window system is shown. Note that `@OnShowing` Runnables are invoked on the EDT. Therefore, if you configure more than one, they run consecutively.

Let's add a Runnable with `@Showing` to the WindowSystemApp. The Runnable displays a custom information dialog, which the user dismisses with either Cancel or OK. The dialog displays after the window system is showing, as shown in Figure 8.28. We can safely perform UI work, since the Runnable executes on the EDT.

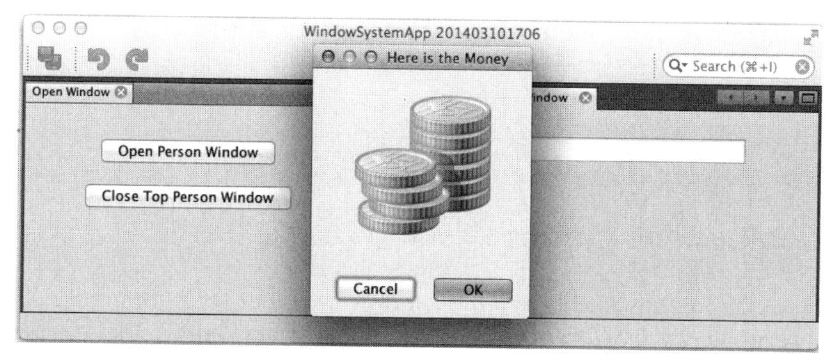


Figure 8.28 Using @OnShowing to display a dialog

Here are the steps.

1. Build a dialog with a custom inner panel (see "Custom Dialogs" on page 533). In the PersonEditor module, right click on the Source Packages package, and select **New | Other**. In the Choose File Type dialog, under Categories select **Swing GUI Form** and under File Types select **JPanel Form**. Click **Next**.
2. In the Name and Location Dialog, for Class Name specify **Money**. Click **Finish**.
3. NetBeans creates a new Java class Money.java with a top-level JPanel in the Matisse form designer. Add a Label component and specify **coins128.png** (or any .PNG or .GIF format file) for the label's icon property from the provided example code.
4. Since we'll use the standard DialogDisplayer, add a module dependency on the Dialogs API. In the PersonEditor module, select the **Libraries** node, right click, and select **Add Module Dependency . . .** from the context menu. In the Add Module Dependencies dialog, select **Dialogs API**. Click **OK**.
5. In the same package, create a new Java file called **ShowMeTheMoney**. Implement Runnable, provide annotation `@OnShowing`, and implement the `run()` method, as shown in Listing 8.11. Here we create and display a custom dialog. The dialog blocks until dismissed by the user.

**Listing 8.11 ShowMeTheMoney.java—Using @OnShowing**

```
package com.asgteach.personeditor;
. . . imports omitted . . .
@OnShowing
public final class ShowMeTheMoney implements Runnable {
    private final Money money = new Money();

    @Override
    public void run() {
        DialogDescriptor dd = new DialogDescriptor(money, "Here is the Money");
        DialogDisplayer.getDefault().notify(dd);
    }
}
```

## 8.7 TopComponent Modes

TopComponent modes define positions in the window layout of your application. These positions are basically window containers. The NetBeans Platform defines several default modes whose layout is shown in Figure 8.29. This layout is fluid, however. The window manager typically extends other windows to fill the window frame when you close a window.

**Layout Tip**

*Note that this layout includes two different TopComponents in editor mode, Editor Left and Editor Right. You control the relative position of different windows in the same mode with element* `position` *in the* `@TopComponent.Registration` *annotation, as described in "@TopComponent.Registration" on page 358.*

You can also use the resizing handles on the window frame to resize the entire window, resize individual windows, or change the window layout by dragging and dropping windows. Each mode affects how the overall window layout is resolved.

There are three basic mode types: editor, view, and sliding. Every window layout has a position of type editor, even when there are no editor windows opened. As you resize the window frame, the empty editor area is always present. (If you need to remove the editor area, see "A View-Only Window Layout" on page 395.)

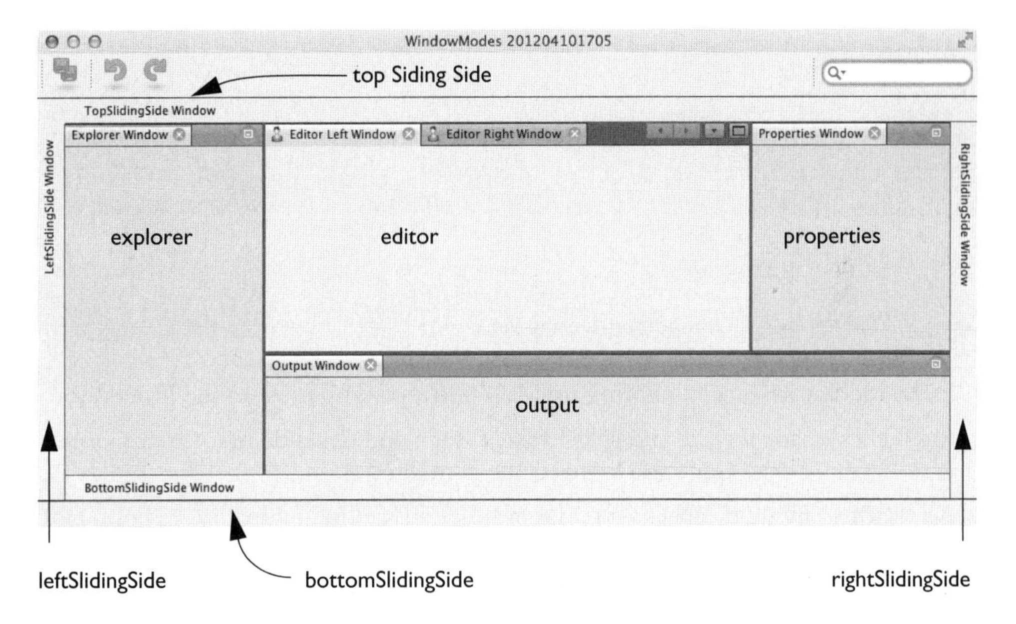


Figure 8.29 TopComponent default modes

Let's have some fun exploring modes. First, we create another window called MyMode. We make it a singleton (the default), and assign it to the explorer window position in application WindowSystemApp.

Next, we define another button in window OpenTopComponent that cycles window MyMode through all of the standard modes, re-docking the window in each mode and updating the status line with the old and new modes. MyModeTopComponent also updates its own label component with its current mode.

You may already have an idea of how to do this. If so, follow along with these steps. If not, use these steps as a guide to add the Change Mode functionality to this application.

1. Create and configure a new TopComponent with the WindowSystemApp we've built throughout this chapter (use **New | Window**).
2. Specify Window Position **explorer**, select **Open on Application Start**, and specify Class Name Prefix as **MyMode**.
3. NetBeans brings up the new TopComponent in the Design view. Add a JLabel component to the UI. Select tab **Code** in the Properties window and change property **Variable Name** to **title**.
4. Select tab **Properties** in the Properties window and set property **text** to **MyMode** as a placeholder. Figure 8.30 shows the configured MyModeTopComponent in the Design view.

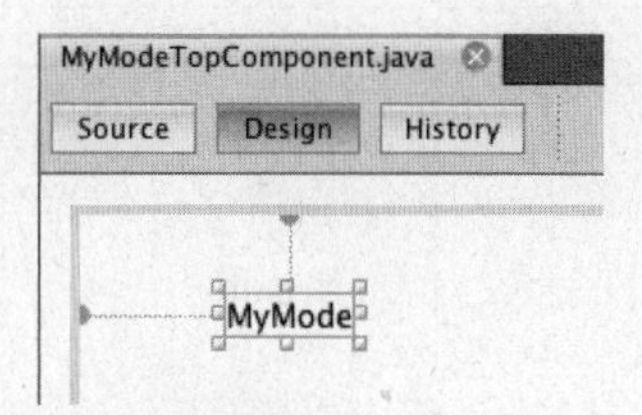


Figure 8.30 MyModeTopComponent Design view

5. Select the **Source** button to bring up MyModeTopComponent in the Java editor.
6. Right click inside the file and select **Insert Code** and override method `componentActivated()`. Select **Generate** to insert the generated code.
7. Add code to method `componentActivated()` as shown in Listing 8.12 in bold. Note that we use the system Window Manager to find this TopComponent's mode and set its label (variable name `title`) text to the mode's name.

   This added code updates MyModeTopComponent's label to display the current mode. As you'll see next in Listing 8.13, the code that implements the TopComponent's mode change invokes both `open()` and `requestActive()`. The window manager then invokes `componentActivated()`, making this method a logical place to update the label.

**Listing 8.12 MyModeTopComponent Method componentActivated()**

```
@Override
protected void componentActivated() {
    super.componentActivated();
    WindowManager wm = WindowManager.getDefault();
    title.setText(wm.findMode(this).getName());
}
```

Now let's add another button to OpenTopComponent that changes the mode of MyModeTopComponent. Follow these steps.

1. Bring up OpenTopComponent in the Design view and place a third JButton component with label **Change Mode**, as shown in Figure 8.31.

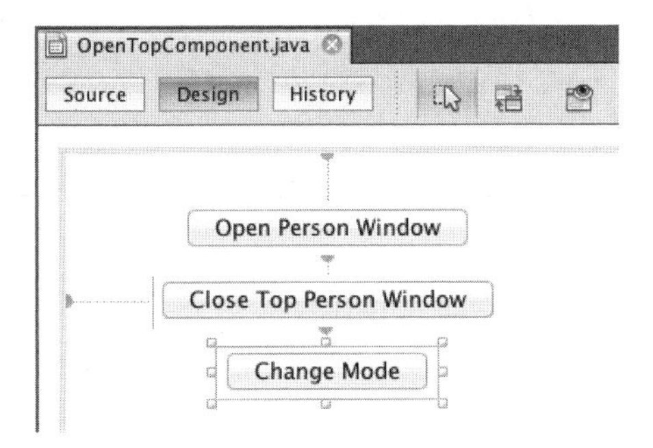


Figure 8.31 OpenTopComponent Design view with Change Mode button

2. Select the button. In the Properties window, click tab **Code**. This brings up the Code Generation tab for the button.
3. Change the button's **Variable Name** to **changeModeButton**.
4. Now double click the button, which creates method `changeModeButtonActionPerformed()`. This switches you to the Source view for OpenTopComponent.
5. Provide the following code for method `changeModeButtonActionPerformed()`, as shown in Listing 8.13.

**Listing 8.13 Method changeModeButtonActionPerformed()**

```
private void changeModeButtonActionPerformed(
              java.awt.event.ActionEvent evt) {

    WindowManager wm = WindowManager.getDefault();
    TopComponent tc = wm.findTopComponent("MyModeTopComponent");
```

```
    if (tc != null) {
        Mode currentMode = wm.findMode(tc);
        Set<? extends Mode> modes = wm.getModes();
        int nextModeIndex = 0;
        Mode[] modeArray = modes.toArray(new Mode[modes.size()]);
        for (int i = 0; i < modeArray.length; i++) {
            // find current mode
            if (currentMode == modeArray[i]) {
                nextModeIndex = i + 1;
                if (nextModeIndex == modeArray.length) {
                    nextModeIndex = 0;
                }
                break;
            }
        }

        Mode nextMode = modeArray[nextModeIndex];
        String nextModeName = nextMode.getName();
        String currentModeName = currentMode.getName();

        nextMode.dockInto(tc);
        tc.open();
        tc.requestActive();
        StatusDisplayer.getDefault().setStatusText("Docking from " +
                currentModeName + " into  " + nextModeName);
    }
```

Method `changeModeButtonActionPerformed()` obtains a WindowManager instance by invoking the static WindowManager method `getDefault()`. Using the window manager, we find TopComponent "MyModeTopComponent" (its `preferredID`) and this TopComponent's mode.

We then get a set of all the modes currently in the system and convert the set to an array. The method then searches the array to find the current mode and assigns the TopComponent to the next mode using the next array index value. We cycle back to the beginning of the array if we've reached the end.

With the current mode and the next mode determined, the next step is to dock the TopComponent into the next mode, open it, and invoke TopComponent method `requestActive()`. This is the usual sequence of methods you'll invoke for opening a window programmatically. Method `open()` opens the window (if not already opened), and `requestActive()` brings it to the front if hidden or shows the window if minimized (applicable to the sliding modes).

Since we invoke `requestActive()`, the window manager calls MyModeTopComponent method `componentActivated()`, which updates that component's label to display the current mode (see Listing 8.12 on page 379).

Finally, we display the old and new modes in the status line using the NetBeans Platform standard StatusDisplayer instance.

Figure 8.32 shows the application running. Here, MyModeTopComponent is docked into the output mode. Its label displays "output," and the status line displays "Docking from bottomSlidingSide into output."

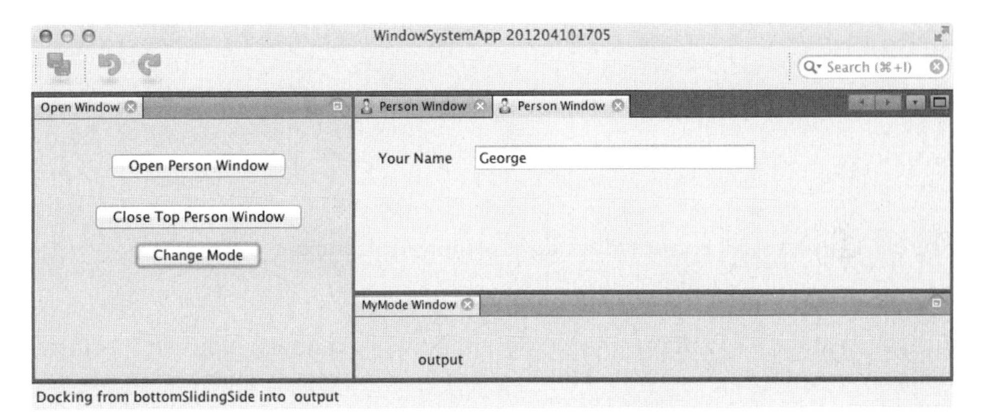


Figure 8.32 Window system modes demo

## 8.8 Window Groups

Window groups let you specify TopComponents that open and close as a group. You are familiar with this use case if you have ever used the NetBeans IDE to design a GUI component (such as a TopComponent). When the TopComponent is open in Design view, you see related helper windows open, including the component palette, the TopComponent properties window, and a TopComponent navigator window. As soon as you switch to Source mode, the component palette and properties windows disappear and the navigator window content relates to the Java source code instead of the visual components. Thus, you have a Design mode window group that opens and closes in conjunction with the TopComponent's Design mode. Figure 8.33 shows the Design view for PersonTopComponent.java in the NetBeans IDE and the related Palette and Properties windows. Switching to the PersonTopComponent.java Source view closes these windows.

However, window group opening and closing behavior is more nuanced. A TopComponent that belongs to a window group does not open the next time the group opens if it was specifically closed by a user when the group was last opened. Similarly, a TopComponent that belongs to the window group does not close the next time the group closes if the window was already open when the group opens.

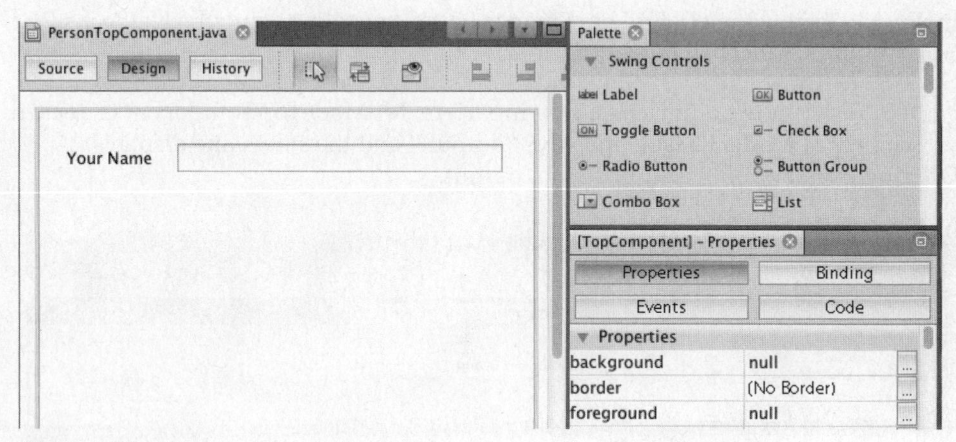


Figure 8.33 Palette and Properties windows form a TopComponent group

To further customize a window group TopComponent's behavior, you can specifically exclude a particular TopComponent from either opening or closing (or both) when the group opens and closes.

The good news is that you can use this window group feature in your NetBeans Platform applications with little effort. Once you create the TopComponents that comprise the window group, you specify XML configurations in your module, as shown in the following general steps.

1. Create a window system group definition file (.wsgrp) to define the window group.
2. For each TopComponent in the window group, create a Wstcgrp.xml file.
3. Add the group configuration information to the module's layer.xml file. If the layer.xml file doesn't exist, create it using a **New | Layer File** wizard.
4. Add Java code that opens and closes the window group.

We show an example in the next section.

## Window Group Example

Let's begin with the application WindowSystemApp from the previous section (shown running in Figure 8.32 on page 381). This application has a non-singleton PersonTopComponent that opens with an Open Person Window button. You close the window with either the built-in close button on the window or the Close Top Person Window button.

Two TopComponent helper windows open when a PersonTopComponent window becomes visible and close when the window is hidden or closes. Figure 8.34 shows the application running with two PersonTopComponent windows open and the unrelated hidden MyMode window docked in the editor mode. You see PersonProperty and PersonOutput windows open.

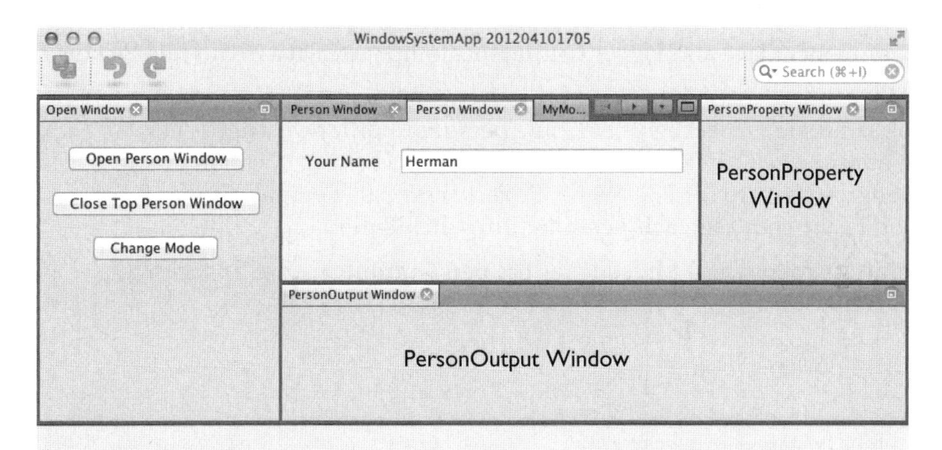


Figure 8.34 PersonProperty and PersonOutput windows form a group

When the visible PersonTopComponent with name "Herman" closes or is obscured, MyModeTopComponent becomes visible in the editor mode and both PersonProperty and PersonOutput windows close. The result is shown in Figure 8.35.

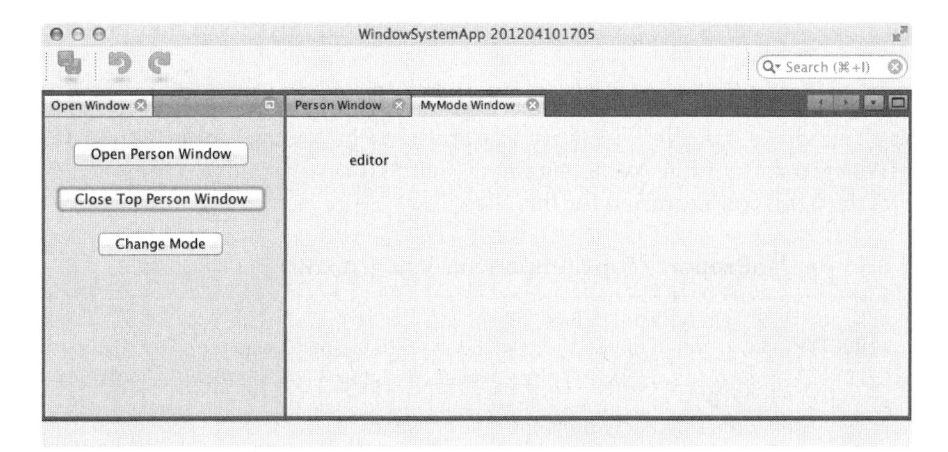


Figure 8.35 Person window group closes when PersonTopComponent closes or is hidden

Here are the steps to add a Person window group to the WindowSystemApp application.

1. In module PersonEditor, create two new TopComponents using the **New | Window** wizard. Select window position **properties** for PersonPropertyTopComponent and window position **output** for PersonOutputTopComponent. De-select **Open on Application Start** for both windows. This creates files PersonPropertyTopComponent.java and PersonOutputTopComponent.java in module PersonEditor source package.
2. In the same source package, create file **persongroup.wsgrp**. Right click the package name and select **New | Empty File**. In the Name and Location dialog, specify **persongroup.wsgrp** for File Name. Project should be **PersonEditor** and Folder should be **src/com/asgteach/personeditor**. Click **Finish**.
3. Provide the following XML code for file **persongroup.wsgrp**, as shown in Listing 8.14.

**Listing 8.14 persongroup.wsgrp**

```
<?xml version="1.0" encoding="UTF-8"?>
       <!DOCTYPE group PUBLIC
         "-//NetBeans//DTD Group Properties 2.0//EN"
         "http://www.netbeans.org/dtds/group-properties2_0.dtd">
         <group version="2.0">
         <name unique="persongroup" />
         <state opened="false" />
</group>
```

Element name with attribute unique must match the case sensitive filename. Element state with attribute opened="false" specifies that this group should not be open at application start.

4. Create a window system TopComponent group configuration file for each of the group's windows. Use **New | Empty File** and provide **PersonPropertyTopComponentWstcgrp.xml** for File Name (again, the name is case sensitive). Listing 8.15 shows the XML configuration for this file.

**Listing 8.15 PersonPropertyTopComponentWstcgrp.xml**

```
<?xml version="1.0" encoding="UTF-8" ?>
       <!DOCTYPE tc-group PUBLIC "-//NetBeans//DTD Top Component in Group
       Properties 2.0//EN" "http://www.netbeans.org/dtds/tc-group2_0.dtd">
<tc-group version="2.0">
    <module name="com.asgteach.personeditor" spec="1.0"/>
    <tc-id id="PersonPropertyTopComponent" />
    <open-close-behavior open="true" close="true" />
</tc-group>
```

The window system TopComponent group configuration file specifies the module that contains the TopComponent, the TopComponent ID (its `preferredID`), and the open and close default behavior for this TopComponent (normally these are both set to `true`).

5. Repeat this step and create window system TopComponent group configuration file for PersonOutputTopComponent, as shown in Listing 8.16.

**Listing 8.16 PersonOutputTopComponentWstcgrp.xml**

```
<?xml version="1.0" encoding="UTF-8" ?>
      <!DOCTYPE tc-group PUBLIC "-//NetBeans//DTD Top Component in Group
      Properties 2.0//EN" "http://www.netbeans.org/dtds/tc-group2_0.dtd">
<tc-group version="2.0">
    <module name="com.asgteach.personeditor" spec="1.0"/>
    <tc-id id="PersonOutputTopComponent" />
    <open-close-behavior open="true" close="true" />
</tc-group>
```

Note that the files are the same except for element `<tc-id>`, which matches each TopComponent's `preferredID`.

6. Create a Layer File for this module. Use **New | XML Layer . . . .** (If your module already has a Layer file, then you will instead edit the existing **layer.xml** file.)

**XML Layer File**

*Often you do not need a module Layer file since Java annotations help you specify many configuration options. During the build process, NetBeans generates layer.xml file for you. If you define a Layer file in your module (as you will here by using window groups), the build process will process and combine this configuration information with any annotations when generating the application's master layer.xml file.*

7. Add the following XML configuration to **layer.xml**, as shown in Listing 8.17.

**Listing 8.17 layer.xml**

```
<?xml version="1.0" encoding="UTF-8"?>
<!DOCTYPE filesystem PUBLIC "-//NetBeans//DTD Filesystem 1.2//EN" "http://
www.netbeans.org/dtds/filesystem-1_2.dtd">
<filesystem>
    <folder name="Windows2">
        <folder name="Groups">
            <file name="persongroup.wsgrp" url="persongroup.wsgrp"/>
            <folder name="persongroup">
                <file name="PersonOutputTopComponent.wstcgrp"
                      url="PersonOutputTopComponentWstcgrp.xml"/>
```

```
            <file name="PersonPropertyTopComponent.wstcgrp"
                  url="PersonPropertyTopComponentWstcgrp.xml"/>
        </folder>
    </folder>
  </folder>
</filesystem>
```

This Layer file registers the **persongroup** window group and specifies the TopComponent configuration files. If you create a new layer.xml file in the previous step, copy the entire XML code shown in Listing 8.17.

If your module already has a Layer file that includes folder **Windows2**, add the folder **Groups** to folder **Windows2**, leaving other subfolders intact.

8. The final steps add Java code to open and close the **persongroup** window group. In our previous description we open the window group when the PersonTopComponent is visible and close the window group when the PersonTopComponent is closed or hidden. Thus, we must add the code that opens the window group to the PersonTopComponent life cycle method `componentShowing()`, as shown in Listing 8.18.

**Listing 8.18 PersonTopComponent componentShowing() Method**

```
@Override
protected void componentShowing() {
    super.componentShowing();
    TopComponentGroup personGroup =
            WindowManager.getDefault().findTopComponentGroup("persongroup");
    if (personGroup != null) {
        personGroup.open();
    }
}
```

The window manager finds our TopComponentGroup **`persongroup`** and, if found, opens the group, which in turn, opens windows PersonPropertyTopComponent and PersonOutputTopComponent. The application should look something like Figure 8.34 on page 383.

9. Now comes the tricky part. Simply closing the group in method `componentHidden()` won't provide the desired behavior because of the order among the different PersonTopComponent life cycle methods. In other words, if the opening window's method `componentShowing()` is invoked *before* the closing window's method `componentHidden()`, then the window group closes incorrectly.

To handle this situation, we use the window manager TopComponent registry to find all open TopComponents. If one of them is a PersonTopComponent that is visible (`isShowing()` is `true`), we return and don't close the window group. If no

PersonTopComponent is visible (even if one is open), we can safely close the window group. Listing 8.19 shows the code.

**Listing 8.19 PersonTopComponent componentHidden() Method**

```
@Override
protected void componentHidden() {
    super.componentHidden();
    WindowManager wm = WindowManager.getDefault();
    TopComponentGroup personGroup =
            wm.findTopComponentGroup("persongroup");
    for (TopComponent tc : wm.getRegistry().getOpened()) {
        if (tc.isShowing() && tc instanceof PersonTopComponent) {
            return;
        }
    }
    if (personGroup != null) {
        personGroup.close();
    }
}
```

### Testing the Window Group Behaviors

You are now ready to fully test the behavior of the new persongroup window group. Be sure to Clean All before running the application. After creating several PersonTopComponent windows, use the Change Mode button to move window MyMode into the editor position. Experiment with activating and hiding several of the windows to see how window group persongroup correctly opens and closes, depending on whether a PersonTopComponent is visible.

You can also move (drag and drop) a PersonTopComponent to another window position. As long as a PersonTopComponent is visible, the persongroup window group remains open.

When you close one of the windows in the persongroup window group and the window group opens the next time, the closed window remains closed. Similarly, if you open one of the windows in persongroup window group when the group is closed (using the top menu **Windows | PersonOutput**, for example), the opened window remains open when the window group next closes.

## 8.9 Window Layout

You have a great idea for a NetBeans Platform application, but you don't want to use any of the standard window system modes (see Figure 8.29 on page 377). Rather, you want to create your own custom window layout and perhaps specify one or more new window positions (modes).

In previous versions of the NetBeans Platform, creating a new mode required customizing a module's Layer file. You also had to create a mode configuration file, which is an XML file with wsmode extension. Furthermore, determining the settings of the wsmode elements, especially the constraints and path elements, is challenging for the casual (and quite often the not-so-casual) NetBeans Platform developer. This is all still true, but NetBeans now has a Layout of Windows wizard to help customize a window layout. In this section we hope to dispel some of the mystery and challenge of creating custom window layouts.

Let's first show you the NetBeans Layout of Windows wizard, which we'll use to create a custom layout for a new application. This window layout will look like the application as shown in Figure 8.36. Here you see three windows: TopBanner (in mode topbanner), LeftSide, and RightSide.

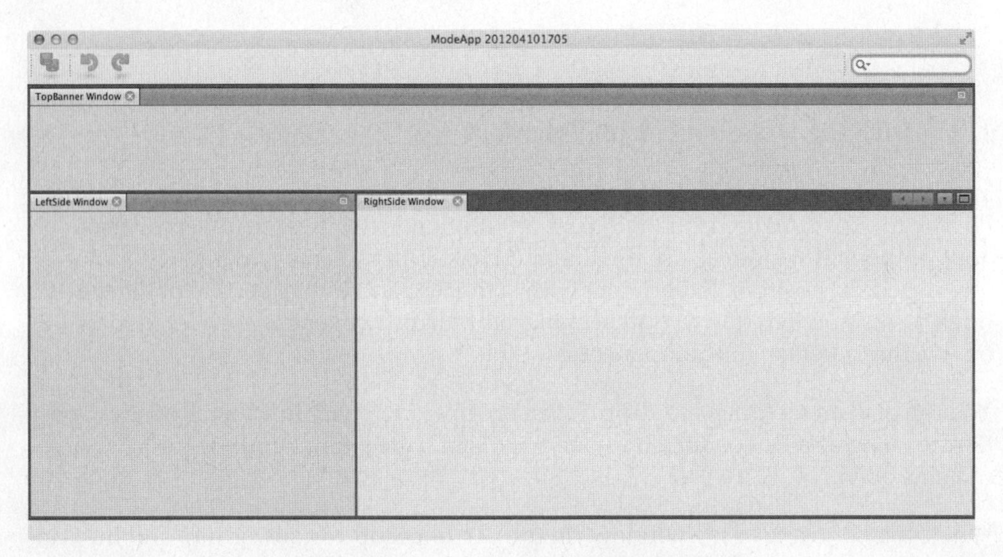


Figure 8.36 A customized window layout for application ModeApp

The TopBanner window spans the entire window frame and takes up about 25 percent of the vertical space. The remaining area is divided horizontally into two areas. The leftside mode consumes approximately 30 percent, and the rightside takes up the remaining 70 percent.

The rightside mode type is editor, whereas topbanner and leftside mode types are view. You can distinguish these types because the editor type mode has a darker line at the top and additional window control buttons at the top right of the window area. Furthermore, the window system treats an editor area differently than view-type modes. Even if no windows are open in your application, a small editor area remains, which grows if you resize your application. Depending on your own window layout, you may need to hide an empty editor area. We'll show you how to do this later in this section.

Here are the steps. To follow along, create a new NetBeans Platform application called **ModeApp** and create a new module called **Modes1**. We'll create our custom layout using module Modes1. The first step is to run the Layout of Windows wizard, as follows.

1. Expand project Modes1 and select the package name **com.asgteach.modes1**, right click, and select **New | Other**.
2. NetBeans displays the New File dialog. Under Categories, select **Module Development** and for File Types, select **Layout of Windows**. Click **Next** as shown in Figure 8.37.

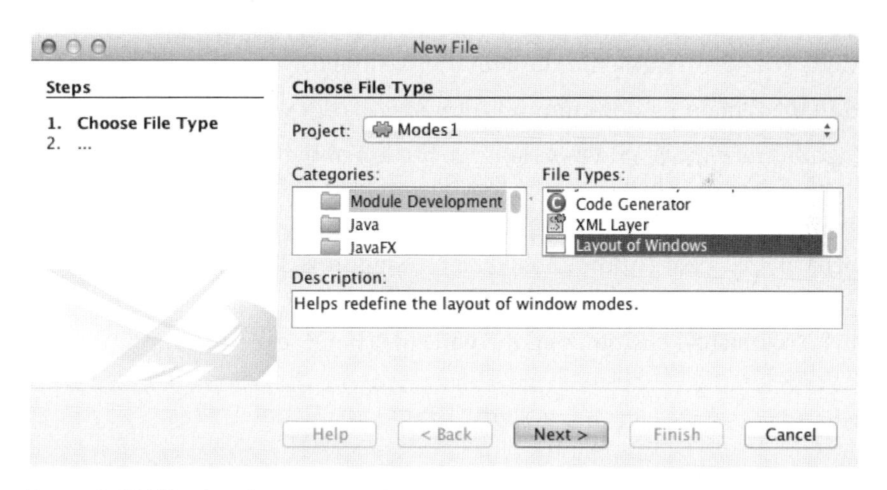


Figure 8.37 Window layout wizard

3. The Layout of Windows wizard lets you know that it will start your application in a special mode that lets you adjust the window layout. Click **Next** as shown in Figure 8.38.
4. Your application starts and displays a window layout with the default modes defined.
5. Click the **New Mode** icon (upper left below the application title). A new window that represents a mode is created in the editor position.

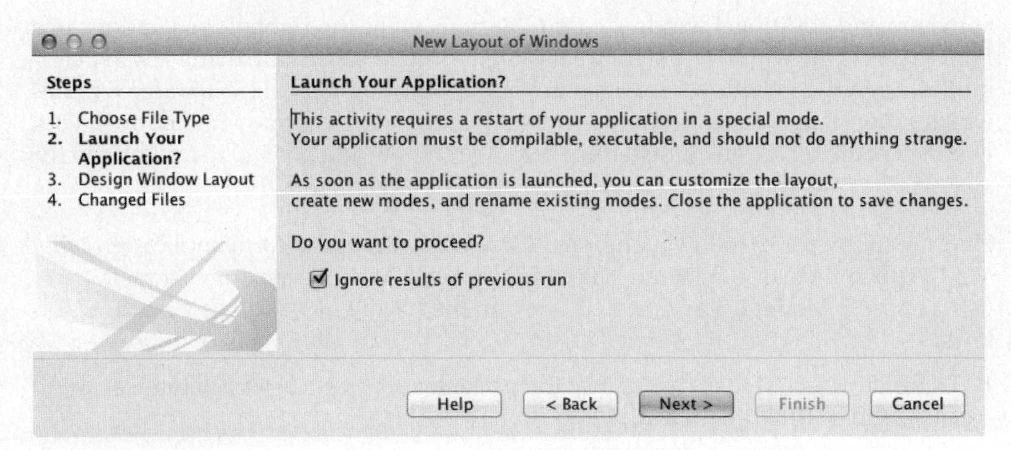


Figure 8.38 Window layout wizard—Launch Your Application

6. Reposition this window to the top of the application. Adjust the window until the red guidelines show a horizontal window that spans the application frame. Specify new Mode Name **topbanner** in the provided textfield.
7. Delete all the remaining non-minimized modes except the editor mode.
8. Now create a new mode and position it to the left of the editor mode. NetBeans will divide the area in half. Rename this new mode on the left to **leftside**.
9. Rename the editor mode to **rightside**. Resize the leftside and rightside modes so that their relative size is approximately 30-70. Figure 8.39 shows the new window layout with modes topbanner, leftside, and rightside.
10. When you're finished customizing the window layout, close the application. This takes you to the wizard's next step.

    Here are some tips for working with the Layout of Windows wizard.

**Window Layout Tip**

*You may find it difficult to place the new "banner" mode so it spans the entire application. By placing the cursor actually outside the top window, we were able to define the new mode so that it is truly a banner and not partitioned horizontally.*

**Window Layout Tip**

*Be sure to rename a new mode after you reposition it, not before.*

After you exit the launched application, the Layout of Windows wizard continues.

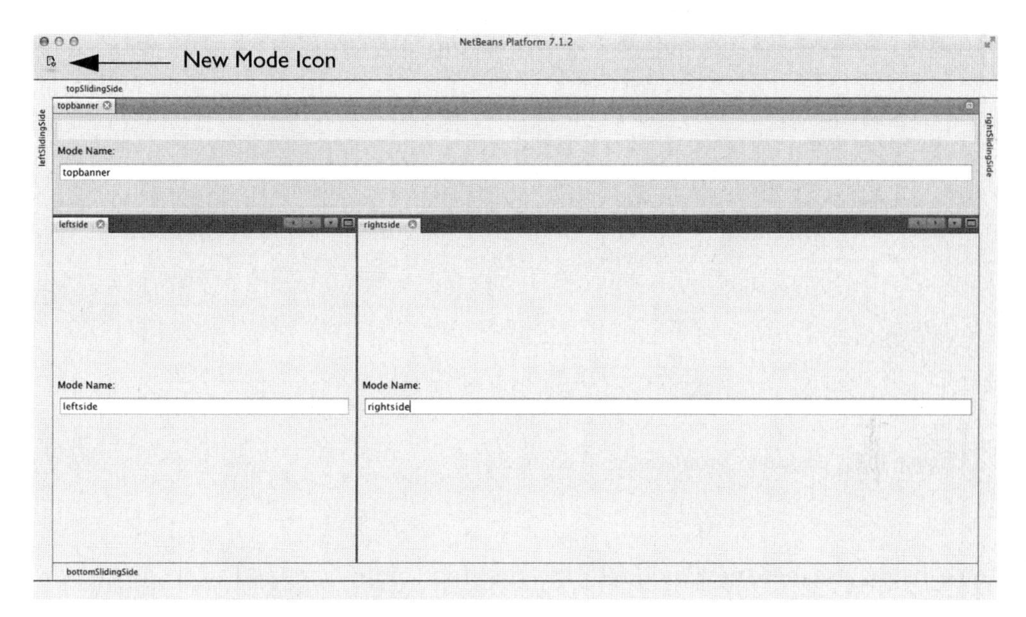


Figure 8.39 Window layout design view

11. The wizard displays the Found Modes list. Select only the new modes you created, as shown in Figure 8.40. Click **Next**.

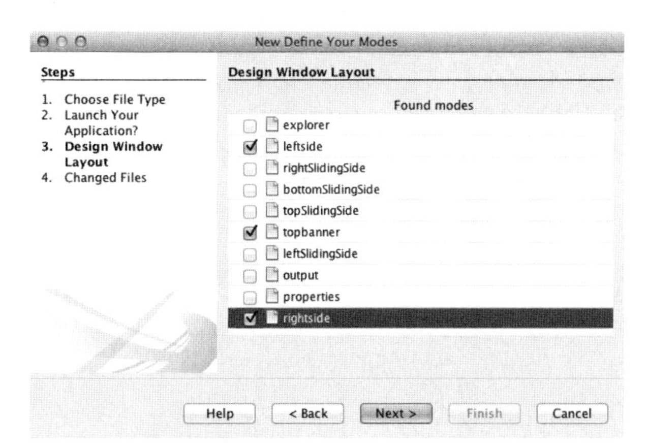


Figure 8.40 Window layout design—Found modes

12. NetBeans displays a list of created files. Here you see file layer.xml and Wsmode.xml files for each selected mode. Click **Finish** as shown in Figure 8.41.

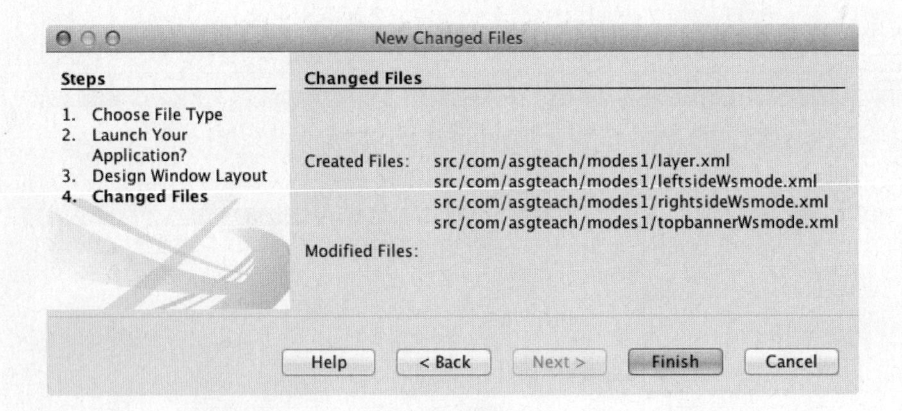


Figure 8.41 Window layout design—changed files

You can now use these new modes by creating TopComponents and selecting the new window position. However, let's first look at the configuration files. By familiarizing yourself with these files, you'll be able to tweak your window design and perhaps even add new modes without re-running the Layout of Windows wizard.

### Layout of Windows Wizard Tip

*Note that even though you did not select any of the default modes in Figure 8.40, the default modes are still present in the window system. If you plan on using any of the default modes and want their layout to conform to the new window layout that you specified in the Layout of Windows wizard, you should check these default modes along with any new modes you created.*

Listing 8.20 shows the Layer file. This file contains the declaration of the module's modes with a link to each mode's definition. The build process reads the Layer file and mode definition files and generates the Windows2 file structure that defines your application's modes.

**Listing 8.20 layer.xml**

```
<?xml version="1.0" encoding="UTF-8"?>
<!DOCTYPE filesystem PUBLIC "-//NetBeans//DTD Filesystem 1.2//EN" "http://
www.netbeans.org/dtds/filesystem-1_2.dtd">
<filesystem>
    <folder name="Windows2">
        <folder name="Modes">
            <file name="leftside.wsmode" url="leftsideWsmode.xml"/>
```

```
            <file name="rightside.wsmode" url="rightsideWsmode.xml"/>
            <file name="topbanner.wsmode" url="topbannerWsmode.xml"/>
        </folder>
    </folder>
</filesystem>
```

The mode definition file specifies a mode's configuration. Element `name` with attribute `unique` must match the mode.wsmode file as listed in layer.xml. Element `kind` with attribute `type` is `"view"`, `"editor"`, or `"sliding"`. (Attribute value `"sliding"` refers to minimized modes.) Element `state` with attribute `type` is `"joined"` (meaning docked into the main window frame as opposed to `"separated"`), and element `constraints` determine how the windows in the mode are sized in relation to other opened windows and modes.

The `constraints` element provides one or more `path` elements that split the window frame recursively. When attribute `orientation` is `"vertical"`, the area is split into rows (cells are defined from top to bottom). When attribute `orientation` is `"horizontal"`, the area is split into columns (cells are defined from left to right). Attribute `number` specifies the relative position of that mode in the split area, with 0 being the topmost or leftmost and the highest number used being the bottommost or rightmost.

If you use numbers such as 0, 20, 40, another module provider can specify a mode that appears in between any already-defined modes.

For a specific mode, attribute `weight` specifies the relative size each window should consume for a given cell within the frame. If all modes are weighted .5, then they will all take up the same space, even as the window frame is resized.

The simplest window layout contains a single frame and its `constraints` element is empty.

Listing 8.21 shows the mode definition file for **topbanner**. Here mode topbanner specifies one `path` element in position 0 (which will always be the first slot in a split cell). The mode consumes 25 percent of the vertical space. It does not share (split) space horizontally; thus it will take up the entire horizontal space providing the banner effect.

You should set element `empty-behavior` attribute `permanent` to `"true"`. Otherwise, if the mode is empty (because you floated a window for example), the window system will dynamically delete that mode.

**Listing 8.21 topbannerWsmode.xml**

```
<?xml version="1.0" encoding="UTF-8"?><mode version="2.4">
    <name unique="topbanner"/>
  <kind type="view"/>
  <state type="joined"/>
  <constraints>
    <path orientation="vertical" number="0" weight="0.25"/>
  </constraints>
  <bounds x="0" y="0" width="0" height="0"/>
  <frame state="0"/>
    <empty-behavior permanent="true"/>
</mode>
```

Listing 8.22 shows the mode definition file for mode **leftside**. It specifies a horizontal split (meaning columns), position number 0 (leftmost) and weight .3.

**Listing 8.22 leftsideWsmode.xml**

```
<?xml version="1.0" encoding="UTF-8"?><mode version="2.4">
    <name unique="leftside"/>
  <kind type="view"/>
  <state type="joined"/>
  <constraints>
    <path orientation="horizontal" number="0" weight="0.3"/>
  </constraints>
  <bounds x="0" y="0" width="0" height="0"/>
  <frame state="0"/>
    <empty-behavior permanent="true"/>
</mode>
```

Listing 8.23 also specifies a horizontal split, using position number 1 and weight .7. It will therefore be to the right of the previous mode and take up about .7 of the space. Mode **rightside** is of type `"editor"`, whereas the other two are of type `"view"`.

**Listing 8.23 rightsideWsmode.xml**

```
<?xml version="1.0" encoding="UTF-8"?><mode version="2.4">
    <name unique="rightside"/>
  <kind type="editor"/>
  <state type="joined"/>
  <constraints>
    <path orientation="horizontal" number="1" weight="0.7"/>
  </constraints>
  <bounds x="0" y="0" width="0" height="0"/>
  <frame state="0"/>
    <empty-behavior permanent="true"/>
</mode>
```

## Creating TopComponents

Let's test out the new window layout by creating TopComponents, one for each new mode.

1. Inside module Modes1, select the source package **com.asgteach.modes1** and select **New | Window**. NetBeans displays the Basic Settings dialog, as shown in Figure 8.42. The drop down corresponding to Window Position now contains the new modes. Select Window Position **topbanner** and check **Open on Application Start**. Click **Next**.

   Note that button Redefine lets you customize the Window Layout using the exact same procedure as the Window Layout wizard we just showed you.

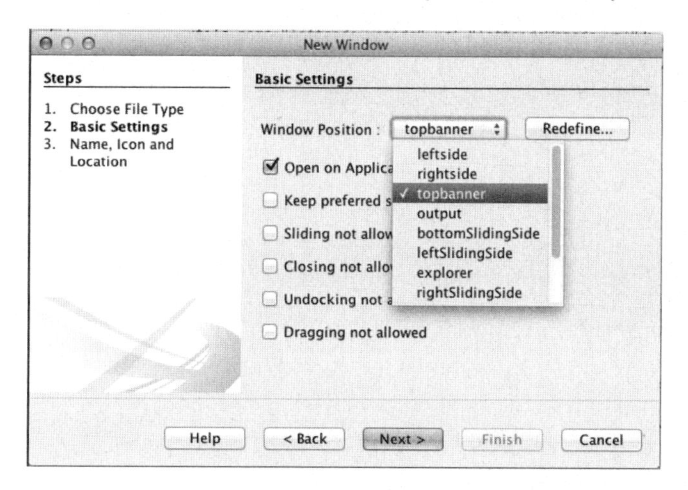


Figure 8.42 New Window Basic Settings dialog with new custom mode

2. NetBeans displays the Name, Icon and Location dialog. Specify **TopBanner** for Class Name Prefix and accept the defaults for Project and Package. Leave Icon blank. Click **Finish**.

3. Repeat these steps and add windows **LeftSideTopComonent** at window position **leftside** and **RightSideTopComponent** with window position **rightside**.

Run application ModeApp (be sure to Clean All first). Its layout should resemble Figure 8.36 on page 388. Perform several window operations (floating, maximizing, closing) to see how the layout resizes. The windows will retain their relative sizes.

## A View-Only Window Layout

We'll now go through a second custom window layout example. This example is from a document that describes the NetBeans Platform Window System API Changes (see `http://core.netbeans.org/windowsystem/changes.html`). This document contains an excellent explanation of the mode definition file elements.

The example defines four new modes, m1, m2, m3, and m4. All modes are type "view" and are shown in a running application in Figure 8.43.

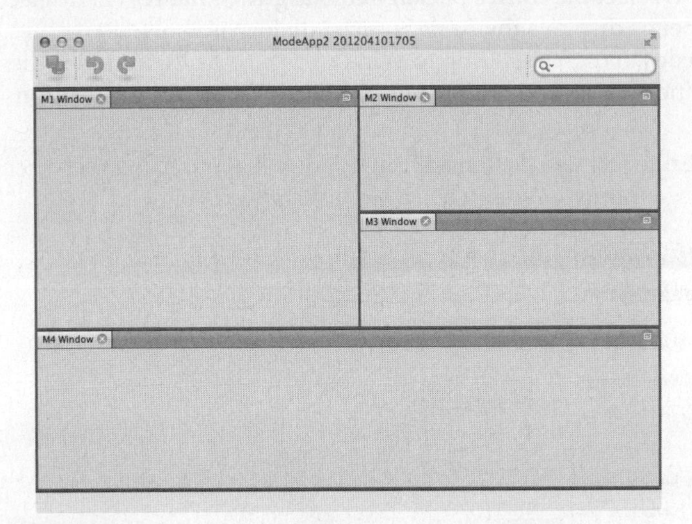


Figure 8.43 ModeApp2 running with custom window layout

Here are the steps to create the above custom window layout.

1. Create a new NetBeans Platform application called **ModeApp2**.
2. Create a new module in ModeApp2 called **Modes2** with package name **com.asgteach.modes2**.
3. Expand module Modes2 Source node. Right click on package name **com.asgteach.modes2** and select **New | Layout of Windows** from the context menu.
4. When the wizard launches the application, create four new modes (named **m1**, **m2**, **m3**, and **m4**) positioned as shown in Figure 8.44. Exit the application.
5. When the wizard displays the Found Modes dialog, select only the new modes: **m1**, **m2**, **m3**, and **m4** and complete the rest of the wizard.

The Layout of Windows wizard creates file layer.xml and a mode definition Wsmode.xml file for each mode, which we show in Listing 8.24 through Listing 8.27.

These mode definition files may look slightly different from yours, depending on how you sized the windows in the Window Layout Design view. Feel free to tweak your

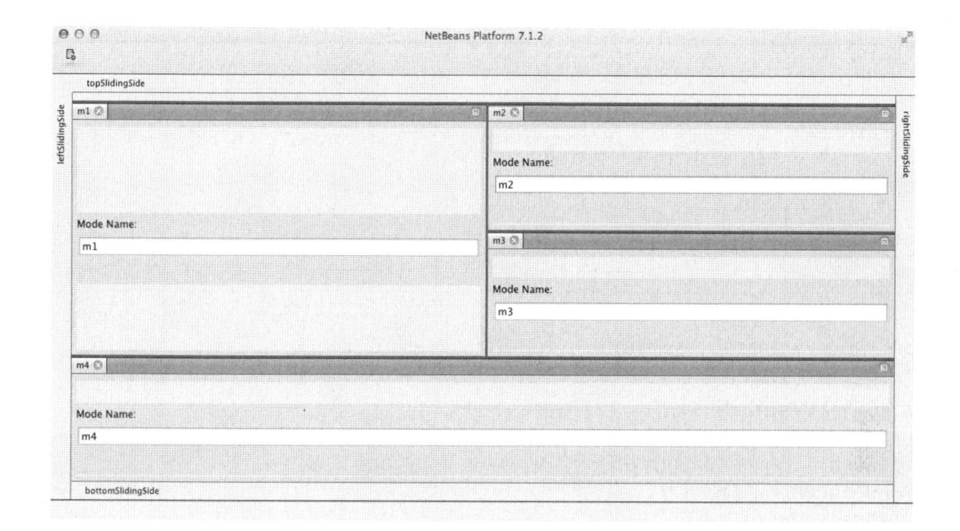


Figure 8.44 Window layout design view with four custom modes

files to match the following listings. Make sure that each mode is `type "view"` and element `empty-behavior` attribute `permanent` is set to `"true"`.

Look at element `constraints` for each mode. Note that modes m1, m2, and m3 all have the first `path` element set to `orientation="vertical"` and attribute `number="0"`. Mode m4 has `path` element set to `orientation="vertical"` and attribute `number="1"`. This splits the desktop into two vertical cells (rows) with the top cell accounting for .7 space and the bottom cell .3 space.

Next m1 and (m2 and m3) divide the top cell into two horizontally (two columns) with each part having equal space. Mode m1 has number `"0"` (the left side) of this horizontal division, and modes m2 and m3 are both positioned in the right side (with number `"1"`).

Finally, modes m2 and m3 divide the right column into two vertical spaces, giving each mode equal space.

Listing 8.24 shows the mode definition file for mode m1.

**Listing 8.24 m1Wsmode.xml**

```
<?xml version="1.0" encoding="UTF-8"?><mode version="2.4">
    <name unique="m1"/>
  <kind type="view"/>
```

```
  <state type="joined"/>
  <constraints>
    <path orientation="vertical" number="0" weight=".7" />
    <path orientation="horizontal" number="0" weight="0.5"/>
  </constraints>
  <bounds x="0" y="0" width="0" height="0"/>
  <frame state="0"/>

    <empty-behavior permanent="true"/>
</mode>
```

Listing 8.25 shows the mode definition file for mode m2.

**Listing 8.25 m2Wsmode.xml**

```
<?xml version="1.0" encoding="UTF-8"?><mode version="2.4">
    <name unique="m2"/>
  <kind type="view"/>
  <state type="joined"/>
  <constraints>
    <path orientation="vertical" number="0" weight=".7" />
    <path orientation="horizontal" number="1" weight="0.5"/>
    <path orientation="vertical" number="0" weight="0.5" />
  </constraints>
  <bounds x="0" y="0" width="0" height="0"/>
  <frame state="0"/>

    <empty-behavior permanent="true"/>
</mode>
```

Listing 8.26 shows the mode definition file for mode m3.

**Listing 8.26 m3Wsmode.xml**

```
<?xml version="1.0" encoding="UTF-8"?><mode version="2.4">
    <name unique="m3"/>
  <kind type="view"/>
  <state type="joined"/>
  <constraints>
    <path orientation="vertical" number="0" weight=".7" />
    <path orientation="horizontal" number="1" weight="0.5"/>
    <path orientation="vertical" number="1" weight="0.5" />
  </constraints>
  <bounds x="144" y="557" width="576" height="164"/>
  <frame state="0"/>
    <empty-behavior permanent="true"/>
</mode>
```

Finally, Listing 8.27 shows the mode definition file for mode m4.

**Listing 8.27 m4Wsmode.xml**

```
<?xml version="1.0" encoding="UTF-8"?><mode version="2.4">
    <name unique="m4"/>
  <kind type="view"/>
  <state type="joined"/>
  <constraints>
    <path orientation="vertical" number="1" weight="0.3"/>
  </constraints>
  <bounds x="0" y="0" width="0" height="0"/>
  <frame state="0"/>
    <empty-behavior permanent="true"/>
</mode>
```

Next, create four TopComponent windows, one for each new mode using code prefix M1, M2, M3, and M4. Clean All and Run the application. A small sliver will appear, which is the empty editor window. Resize the application (make it smaller and then larger). Figure 8.45 shows that the empty editor area has grown.

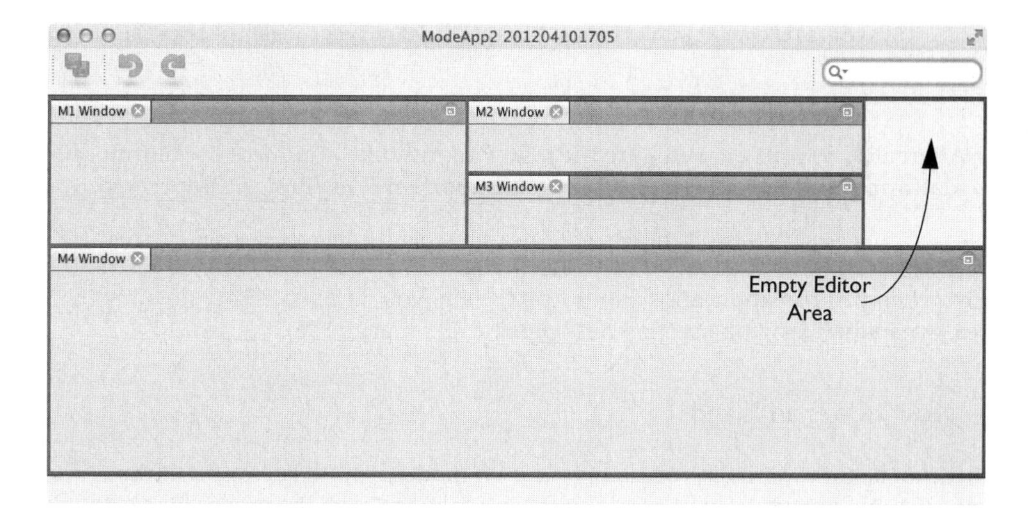


Figure 8.45 Window layout with four custom modes and an empty editor area

Follow these steps to hide an empty editor area. You'll add an `@OnStart` Runnable (see "Using @OnStart" on page 242). Note that you can still open a window in the editor area, but if the editor area is empty, other windows will completely fill in the space.

1. The `@OnStart` annotation requires a dependency on the Module System API. In the Modes2 module Libraries node, right click, and select **Add Module Dependency** .

. . from the context menu. In the Add Module Dependencies dialog, select **Module System API** from the list of modules. Click **OK**.

2. In the Modes2 module, right click on the package name **com.asgteach.modes2**, and select **New | Java Class . . .** from the context menu.
3. NetBeans displays the New Java Class dialog. For Class Name, specify **Installer** (any name is fine) and click **Finish**.
4. NetBeans adds the Installer.java class. Make the Installer class implement Runnable, add the `@OnStart` annotation, and implement the `run()` method, as shown in Listing 8.28.

**Listing 8.28 Installer.java—Provide Module Life Cycle Methods**

```
package com.asgteach.modes2;

import org.openide.modules.OnStart;
@OnStart
public class Installer implements Runnable {

    @Override
    public void run() {
        System.setProperty("netbeans.winsys.hideEmptyDocArea", "true");
    }
}
```

5. Alternatively, you can configure the following runtime argument in your modules **platform.properties** file (under **Modes2/Important Files/Project Properties**).

```
run.args.extra=-J-Dnetbeans.winsys.hideEmptyDocArea=true
```

Now when you run application ModeApp2 again, you'll see no empty document area, even when resizing (as shown in Figure 8.43 on page 396).

## No Mode Is an Island

Once you begin experimenting with your own modes, you'll discover that the window layout of your system depends on the interactions of all the modes in use and the actions of the user as the window frame is resized or windows are repositioned, floated, opened, and closed. Indeed, no mode is isolated from this behavior. Here are a few additional strategy hints you may find helpful as you experiment with your own window layout.

1. Use the Layout of Windows wizard first. Then fine tune your window layout if necessary by tweaking the generated wsmode files.
2. Try simplifying the `constraints` element as much as possible.

3. Make sure element `empty-behavior` attribute `permanent` is set to `"true"`.
4. We found it easier to create all new modes for a window layout instead of mixing new modes with default modes. If you do mix modes, retain the mode definition files of any default modes that you use (check them in the Found Modes dialog of the Layout of Windows wizard).
5. Experiment with window layouts by dragging and dropping windows into new positions and resizing. When you shut down the application, the most recent window layout will be preserved in directory **Windows2Local/Modes** under **build/testuserdir/config** directory in your application directory.

## 8.10 Window Layout Roles

The NetBeans Platform lets you define different window layouts based on roles. A common use case is to provide distinct role-based perspectives for an application. The Window Manager keeps track of roles that you define and persists a separate Windows2Local hierarchy under `build/testuserdir/config` in your application directory for each role that you use.

A role comes into existence by invoking WindowManager method `setRole("ModeName")`. TopComponents can be restricted to one or more named roles. Otherwise, any TopComponent can appear within any role.

If a TopComponent has one or more roles assigned to it, the TopComponent will only open if one of its roles is active. If a TopComponent has no roles assigned to it, it is eligible to open with any role.

When an application starts up, the default role is in effect. You can switch to the default role by invoking the WindowManager `setRole()` method with argument `null`. If you want your application to start up in a specific (non-default) role, then invoke the WindowManager method `setRole("MyRole")` in an `@OnStart` annotated Runnable.

Normally, when a user manipulates the window frame, resizes windows, or invokes other window operations, the window system saves these changes when the application shuts down. When using roles, the window system saves the window layout separately for each role. Thus, changes a user makes to the window layout in one role do not affect the window layout of any other roles.

Let's show you a role-based example with an application called RoleExample. This application has three roles: the default role, User, and Admin. The User and Admin roles each have TopComponents assigned specifically to these roles. When you run the application and the User role is active, you see one set of components. Similarly, when you run the application with the Admin role active, you see a distinct set of components.

Application RoleExample also has a LoginTopComponent that has no roles assigned to it. This means that LoginTopComponent can open in the default role and remain open when a new role becomes active.

The LoginTopComponent acts as a gatekeeper, requesting a username and password from a user. When the user clicks the Login button, an event handler looks up the username and password to find the corresponding role for that username. The role is then changed to either User or Admin depending on the username. No role change occurs if the login fails.

Figure 8.46 shows the RoleExample application running with the default role active. There is a single window open (LoginTopComponent) with the username and password fields filled in. As it turns out, Joe is in our data store with role User.

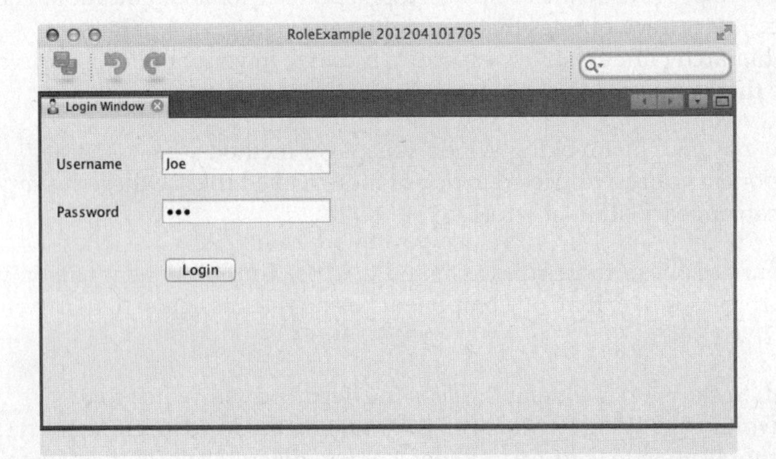


**Figure 8.46** RoleExample application with the default window layout (no role set)

When the Login button is clicked and Joe's credentials check out, the application invokes WindowManager method `setRole("User")`. The LoginTopComponent remains open and you see two additional windows: UserExplorer and UserEditor, as shown in Figure 8.47. These two TopComponents have role User assigned to them.

If at this point, Joe resizes the window frame, changes are persisted when the application switches roles or at application shutdown. The default role and Admin role are not affected by Joe's window operations.

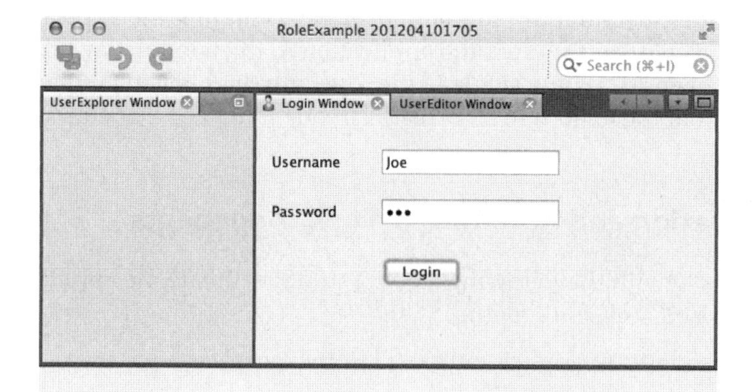


Figure 8.47 RoleExample application with role User

Since the LoginTopComponent is open, another user can log in. Let's suppose we have a second user Meg with role Admin. When Meg logs in, the application switches to role Admin, as shown in Figure 8.48. With this switch, the User-specific windows UserEditor and UserExplorer close and two different windows open: AdminEditor and AdminOutput. Again, LoginTopComponent remains open. Note that the Admin window layout is different from the User window layout, and its windows are docked into different modes.

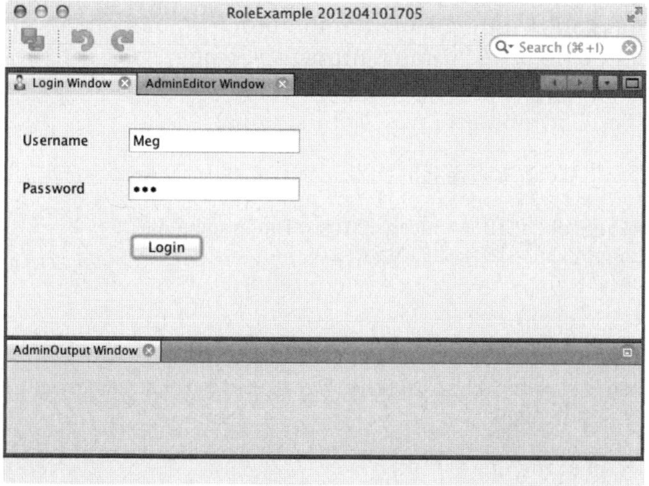

Figure 8.48 RoleExample application with role Admin

If at any time a user provides invalid information in the Login window, the application switches to the default role. This returns the application to the window layout you see in Figure 8.46 on page 402 with a single LoginTopComponent open (and an error message indicating that the login was incorrect). All other TopComponents are closed.

## RoleExample Application and Role-Based TopComponents

Let's build this example now with the following steps. You'll first create the application, modules, and role-based TopComponents.

1. Create a new NetBeans Platform application called RoleExample.
2. Create three new modules in RoleExample: AdminModule, UserModule, and RoleModel. Module RoleModel contains the User and UserRole classes that implement the credential checking and role assignments. Modules AdminModule and UserModule contain role-specific TopComponents.
3. Create two TopComponents inside module AdminModule called AdminEditorTopComponent and AdminOutputTopComponent. For AdminEditor, select window position **editor** and select **Open at Application Start**.
4. For AdminOutput, select window position **output** and select **Open at Application Start**. Assign role "Admin" to both windows by editing the `@TopComponent.Registration` annotation in the TopComponent source code using element `roles`.
5. Remove the Action annotations for both components.

   Listing 8.29 shows the annotation settings for AdminEditorTopComponent, and Listing 8.30 shows the annotations for AdminOutputTopComponent.

**Listing 8.29 AdminEditorTopComponent.java (Annotations)**

```
@ConvertAsProperties(dtd = "-//com.asgteach.adminmodule//AdminEditor//EN",
autostore = false)
@TopComponent.Description(preferredID = "AdminEditorTopComponent",
persistenceType = TopComponent.PERSISTENCE_ALWAYS)
@TopComponent.Registration(
        roles = {"Admin"},
        mode = "editor",
        openAtStartup = true)
@TopComponent.OpenActionRegistration(displayName = "#CTL_AdminEditorAction",
preferredID = "AdminEditorTopComponent")
@Messages({
    "CTL_AdminEdAction=AdminEditor",
    "CTL_AdminEdTopComponent=AdminEditor Window",
    "HINT_AdminEdTopComponent=This is a AdminEditor window"
})
```

```
public final class AdminEditorTopComponent extends TopComponent {
. . . code omitted . . .
}
```

**Listing 8.30 AdminOutputTopComponent.java (Annotations)**

```
@ConvertAsProperties(dtd = "-//com.asgteach.adminmodule//AdminOutput//EN",
autostore = false)
@TopComponent.Description(preferredID = "AdminOutputTopComponent",
persistenceType = TopComponent.PERSISTENCE_ALWAYS)
@TopComponent.Registration(
        roles = {"Admin"},
        mode = "output",
        openAtStartup = true)
@TopComponent.OpenActionRegistration(displayName = "#CTL_AdminOutputAction",
preferredID = "AdminOutputTopComponent")
@Messages({
    "CTL_AdminOutputAction=AdminOutput",
    "CTL_AdminOutputTopComponent=AdminOutput Window",
    "HINT_AdminOutputTopComponent=This is a AdminOutput window"
})
public final class AdminOutputTopComponent extends TopComponent {
. . . code omitted . . .
}
```

6. Add two TopComponents to module UserModule using code prefix UserEditor and UserExplorer. Specify window position **editor** and **explorer**, respectively. Select **Open at Application Start** for both TopComponents.
7. Assign role "User" to both windows by editing the `@TopComponent.Registration` annotation in the TopComponent source code using element `roles`. (Refer to Listing 8.29 and Listing 8.30 but specify role "User" instead of "Admin.")
8. Remove the Action annotations for both components.

## Credential Checking and Role Assignments

Now let's implement the credential checking and role assignments. We'll set up a bare-bones map-based collection to store users and roles.

1. In the RoleModel module, create Java interface UserRole in package `com.asgteach.rolemodel.api`, and provide the abstract methods, as shown in Listing 8.31.

**Listing 8.31 Interface UserRole**

```
package com.asgteach.rolemodel.api;

public interface UserRole {

    public User findUser(String username, String password);
    public User storeUser(User user);
    public String[] getRoles();
    public boolean storeRole(String role);

}
```

2. In the same package, create Java class User, as shown in Listing 8.32.

**Listing 8.32 User.java**

```
package com.asgteach.rolemodel.api;

public class User {
    private String username;
    private String password;
    private String role;

    public String getPassword() {
        return password;
    }

    public void setPassword(String password) {
        this.password = password;
    }

    public String getRole() {
        return role;
    }

    public void setRole(String role) {
        this.role = role;
    }

    public String getUsername() {
        return username;
    }

    public void setUsername(String username) {
        this.username = username;
    }

    @Override
    public String toString() {
        StringBuilder sb = new StringBuilder(this.getUsername()).append("-");
```

```
        sb.append(this.getPassword()).append("-");
        sb.append(this.getRole());
        return sb.toString();
    }
}
```

3. Add Lookup API dependency to module RoleModel and make package `com.asgteach.rolemodel.api` public under API Versioning. Create Java class SimpleUserRole in package `com.asgteach.rolemodel` with the implementation shown in Listing 8.33. Note that we use annotation `@ServiceProvider` with class UserRole.

   Besides providing a map-based lookup for username and password data, SimpleUserRole also initializes the map with user and role values. Here you see data for our test case Joe and Meg.

**Listing 8.33 SimpleUserRole**

```
@ServiceProvider(service = UserRole.class)
public class SimpleUserRole implements UserRole {

    private Map<String, User> userMap = new HashMap<>();
    private List<String> roles = new ArrayList<>();

    public SimpleUserRole() {
        initialize();
    }

    private void initialize() {
        User user1 = new User();
        user1.setUsername("Joe");
        user1.setPassword("Joe");
        user1.setRole("User");
        storeUser(user1);
        storeRole("Admin");
        User user2 = new User();
        user2.setUsername("Meg");
        user2.setPassword("Meg");
        user2.setRole("Admin");
        storeUser(user2);
    }

    @Override
    public User findUser(String username, String password) {
        User user = userMap.get(username);
        if (user != null && user.getPassword().equals(password)) {
            return user;
        }
        return null;
    }
```

```
    @Override
    public User storeUser(User user) {
        if (user.getRole() == null || user.getRole().isEmpty()) {
            user.setRole("User");
        }
        storeRole(user.getRole());
        return userMap.put(user.getUsername(), user);
    }

    @Override
    public String[] getRoles() {
        return roles.toArray(new String[roles.size()]);
    }

    @Override
    public boolean storeRole(String role) {
        if (!roles.contains(role)) {
            return roles.add(role);
        }
        else return false;
    }
}
```

## LoginTopComponent

Next, implement the Login process using these steps.

1. In module AdminModule, add dependencies to the Lookup API and to module RoleModel to access the service provider for UserRole.
2. Still in module AdminModule, create LoginTopComponent. Specify window position **editor** and select **Open at Application Start**.
3. Configure the GUI. Add three JLabels, a JTextField, a JPasswordField, and a JButton, arranged as shown in Figure 8.49. Rename the variable names for the components as listed in the figure.
4. From the Design view, double click the Login button and provide the following button event handling code. Add a new entry into the `@Messages` list for the incorrect login error message, as shown in Listing 8.34.

**Listing 8.34 LoginTopComponent loginButtonActionPerformed() Method**

```
@Messages({
    "CTL_LoginAction=Login",
    "CTL_LoginTopComponent=Login Window",
    "HINT_LoginTopComponent=This is a Login window",
    "ERROR_IncorrectLogin=Incorrect login for user "
})
. . . code omitted . . .
```

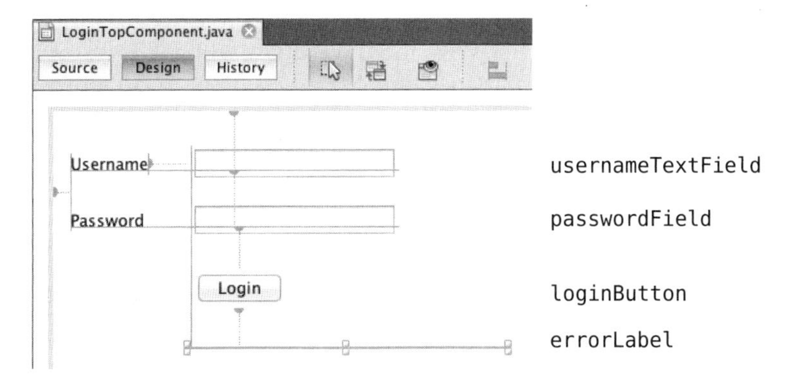


Figure 8.49 LoginTopComponent Design view

```
private void loginButtonActionPerformed(
                java.awt.event.ActionEvent evt) {
    errorLabel.setText("");
    UserRole userRole = Lookup.getDefault().lookup(UserRole.class);
    if (userRole != null) {
        User thisUser = userRole.findUser(usernameTextField.getText(),
                new String(passwordField.getPassword()));
        WindowManager wm = WindowManager.getDefault();
        if (thisUser != null) {
            // switch to new role
            wm.setRole(thisUser.getRole());
        } else {
            errorLabel.setText(Bundle.ERROR_IncorrectLogin()
                                  + usernameTextField.getText());
            if (wm.getRole() != null) {
                // put it back to the default role
                wm.setRole(null);
            }
        }
    }
}
```

The button event handler is invoked when the user clicks the Login button. The code first clears `errorLabel`. After instantiating `userRole` with a UserRole instance (obtained through the Lookup), the handler calls `findUser()` with the submitted username and password. If the return is not null, the login is valid and the handler switches roles by invoking WindowManager method `setRole()` with the user's assigned role.

The submitted username and password are not valid if the return from `findUser()` is null. In this case, the handler displays an error message and switches to the default role (unless the default role is already active).

Our application is now ready to build and run. Even though the role-specific TopComponents have attribute `openAtStart = true`, these windows will not open until their assigned roles are active in the window system.

By default, when the window system switches roles, it first hides the main window, persists the current window layout, loads the window layout of the new role, and then makes the main window visible. This hiding/showing may produce a flicker. To make the switch smoother, you can modify a branding property associated with the application, as follows.

1. Right click the RoleExample application node and select **Branding** from the context menu.
2. NetBeans displays the RoleExample Branding dialog. Select tab **Resource Bundles** and type **WinSys.Show** in the Search Box.
3. Change the value of property `WinSys.Show.Hide.MainWindow.While_Switching.Role` to **`false`** as shown in Figure 8.50. Click **OK**.

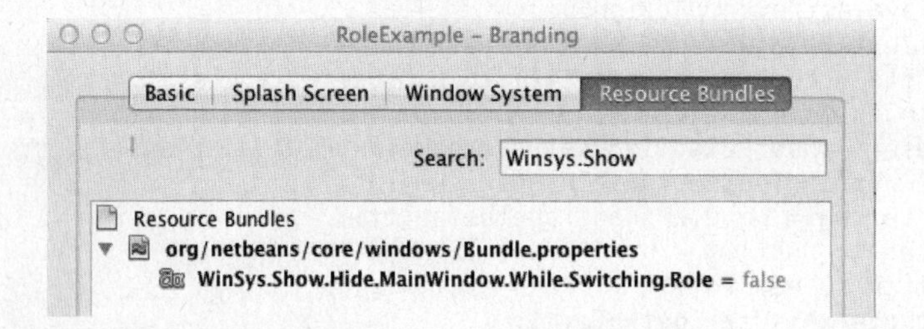


Figure 8.50 Property WinSys.Show.Hide.MainWindow.While_Switching.Role

Run the application again. You'll notice a smoother, flicker-free experience when switching roles.

See "Putting It All Together" on page 544 for an application Login dialog that sets the window system role via login at startup time.

## 8.11 Key Point Summary

The NetBeans Platform Window System provides standard window features for desktop applications. This includes drag-and-drop reconfiguration and window resizing, docking, maximizing, minimizing, opening, and closing. The window system also provides the following key features.

- Developers create windows by extending class TopComponent, allowing windows to automatically integrate into the NetBeans Platform Window System.

- The default configuration for a TopComponent provides a unique, singleton window, persistence between application restarts, and a registered action to open the window.
- Modes define window containers and specify a window's relative size and position as a user runs an application or resizes and reconfigures the window frame.
- The windows system provides default modes and you can also define new ones.
- A TopComponent is opened in a mode. The windows system opens a TopComponent in the editor mode if the TopComponent's mode is not defined or no mode has been assigned.
- There are three mode types: editor, view, and sliding. The editor mode type holds document windows that cannot be minimized. View type modes usually hold helper windows. Minimized windows are put into sliding modes.
- The window system defines TopComponent annotations that specify a window's configuration. This includes an assigned mode, persistence type, title and tooltip text, and an open action registration.
- TopComponents have three persistent options: `PERSISTENCE_ALWAYS`, `PERSISTENCE_ONLY_OPENED`, and `PERSISTENCE_NEVER`. You can also persist String data for your TopComponent by implementing methods `writeProperties()` and `readProperties()`.
- Create non-singleton TopComponents by removing element `preferredID` in annotation `@TopComponent.OpenActionRegistration`. With non-singleton TopComponents use persistence type `PERSISTENCE_NEVER` or `PERSISTENCE_ONLY_OPENED`.
- Override TopComponent methods to customize behavior at certain points in a TopComponent's life cycle. This includes at component opening, closing, activating, deactivating, hiding, and showing. You can also override method `canClose()` to dynamically allow or disallow TopComponent closing.
- Set client properties in a TopComponent's constructor to customize (that is, limit) a window's behavior.
- A window manager provides programmatic access to useful window operations, such as finding open windows, finding modes, finding TopComponent groups, setting roles, and accessing the current TopComponent registry. With access to a TopComponent instance or a Mode instance, you can open, close, activate, or hide a TopComponent and dock a TopComponent into different modes.
- Window groups let you specify TopComponents that should open and close as a group. Specify and configure groups with a window system group definition file (**.wsgrp**) and a window system TopComponent group file for each TopComponent in the group.

- NetBeans IDE provides a Layout of Windows wizard to customize window layouts for your applications. This wizard lets you define new modes, redefine standard modes, or rename standard modes.
- You can define different window layouts based on roles and specify TopComponents that belong to certain roles. The window manager keeps track of roles you define and persists a separate Windows2Local hierarchy for each role you use.
- TopComponents with no role configuration can open in any role.
- Switch roles with window manager method `setRole()` with a String role name. Use role name `null` for the default window layout, meaning no currently active role.

# 9

# Action Framework

Actions perform work within an application and users initiate this work by selecting menu items, clicking toolbar buttons, or issuing keyboard shortcuts. The NetBeans Platform has an Action framework that provides a configurable UI for action initiation. This framework also provides ways to dynamically enable and disable actions and customize behavior based on selection context. In this chapter we'll show you how to hook into the NetBeans Platform Action framework, create your own actions, and reuse some of the standard actions provided by the platform. We'll also introduce context-sensitive actions and capabilities in our continuing effort to create loosely-coupled, modular applications.

## What You Will Learn

- Create always-enabled, callback, and conditionally-enabled actions.
- Use annotations to register actions.
- Configure a TopComponent's ActionMap and a node's context menu.
- Use the capability pattern to dynamically enable and disable actions.
- Implement drag and drop, delete, cut, copy, and paste, and node reordering actions.
- Implement inter-window drag and drop behaviors.

## 9.1 Type of Actions

An application's UI has various ways for users to select actions. By default, a NetBeans Platform application includes a top-level menu bar, an icon-decorated toolbar, and individual context menus that pop up with a right mouse click on configured components. The action itself is identified in the menu item with a display name, an optional icon, and an optional shortcut key sequence. In the toolbar, a required icon identifies the action, and the display name and key shortcut appear in a tooltip.

Actions in menus and in the toolbar have state. They can be enabled or not and pressed or not. In addition, the icon in a menu item is a 16 x 16 PNG or GIF file. In the toolbar, the NetBeans Platform uses a 24 x 24 PNG or GIF file, if available.

You register an action in the menu and toolbar framework with annotations. These annotations also specify the action's display name, icon, shortcut key sequence, and whether or not separators appear either before or after the menu item (in menus) or icon (in the toolbar). The NetBeans Platform has a New Action wizard that lets you register actions easily. Because actions are configured, a module generally does not need to set a dependency on the module that defines the action. You connect to an action by referencing its key or "path," or by providing an implementation of a context that the action needs. We'll show you examples in this chapter.

**Menu System Configuration**

---

*A NetBeans Platform skeletal application includes a default top-level menu bar and an icon-decorated toolbar. See "Removing Layer Configuration Items" on page 659 to learn how to configure (or hide) the default menu and toolbar framework. Additionally, "Editing the Node Hierarchy" on page 444 shows you how to implement some of the pre-configured menu items, such as Copy, Cut, Paste, and others.*

---

### Always-Enabled Actions

We call an action that can be selected in any state of the application an *always-enabled action*. For example, in the NetBeans IDE top menu bar under menu item **NetBeans**, both **About NetBeans** and **Quit NetBeans** are menu items that are always enabled. These actions don't depend on the availability of objects, data, or files for their execution. They also don't depend on a user-selected item or items in any of the application's windows.

Let's show you how to create an always-enabled action by adding an action called Calendar to our FamilyTreeApp application. We'll start with the application previously created in Chapter 7 (see "Creating Your Own Property Sheet" on page 314).

This new action pops up a custom dialog with an image, text, and Cancel and OK buttons. Figure 9.1 shows you what it looks like.[1]

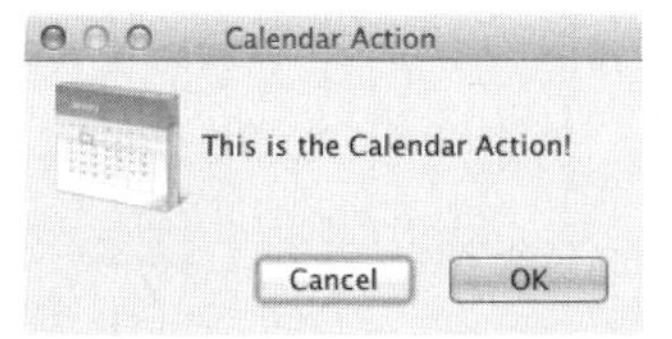


Figure 9.1 Invoking the Calendar action in the FamilyTreeApp application

## Add an Always-Enabled Action

Follow these steps to add an always-enabled action to an application.

1. Create a new module called **FamilyTreeActions** with code name base **com.asgteach.familytree.actions** (or use an already-existing module).
2. Expand the Source Packages node, right click on the package name, and select **New | Action . . .** from the context menu, as shown in Figure 9.2.

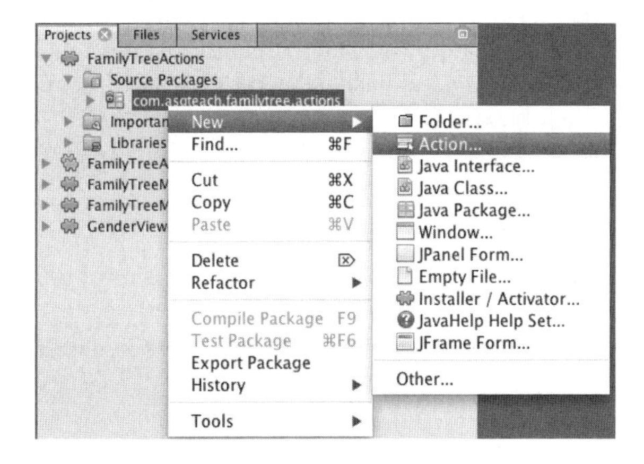


Figure 9.2 Create a new action

3. NetBeans displays New Action's Action Type dialog. Select **Always Enabled**, as shown in Figure 9.3 and click **Next**.

1. Icons for this chapter are from `http://www.visualpharm.com`.

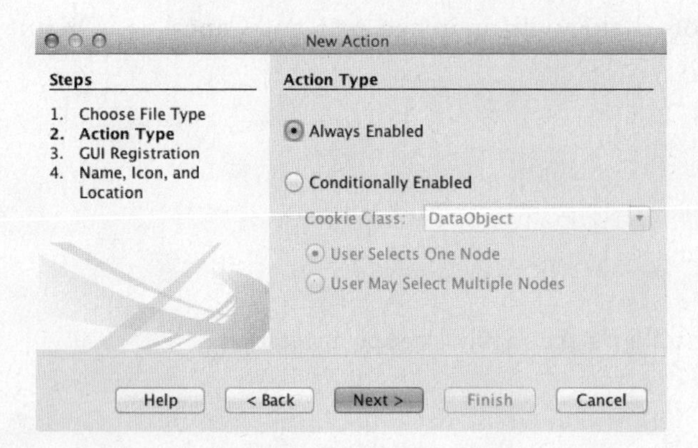


Figure 9.3 Specify Always Enabled for Action Type

4. NetBeans displays the GUI Registration dialog. Here you specify where your action should appear (under which menu in the top-level menu bar) and if it should appear in the toolbar.

   Actions in the toolbar require an icon. In menus, icons are optional. We register the action in Category **Tools** under Menu **Tools** and specify a Separator after the action. We also place the action in the **Toolbar** (before the Save All icon) and provide a shortcut key combination (Command-E on the Mac, which translates to Meta+E) to initiate the action directly from the keyboard. (E is for Calendar Event.) Figure 9.4 shows these selections. Click **Next**.

### New Action Category

*An action's category determines its "path" in the application's virtual file system. You can obtain a list of actions for a particular path. There are situations when you want to use a general category name (such as Tools) or a more refined name (such PersonNodeOpen).*

5. NetBeans displays the New Action's Name, Icon and Location dialog. Here, you specify the class file that implements this action, the action's display name, and the action's icon, as shown in Figure 9.5. NetBeans' naming convention for icon files is listed in Table 9.1. You specify a 16 x 16 PNG or GIF file, and NetBeans automatically includes other icon files as long as they're in the same directory. If you don't provide the other files, NetBeans provides default presenters for these (although the smaller 16 x 16 doesn't look very good on the toolbar). Click **Finish**.

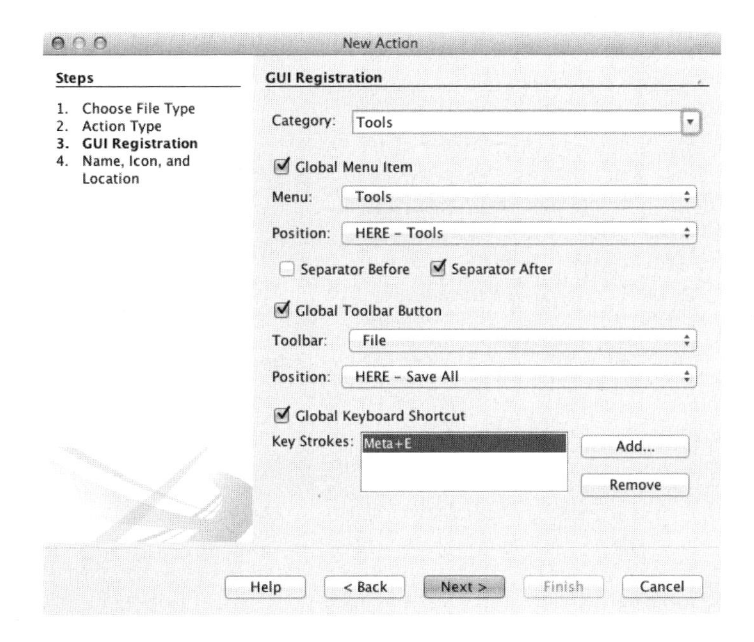


Figure 9.4 Specify the action's GUI Registration

**TABLE 9.1 Action Icon Naming Conventions**

| Filename Pattern | Description |
| --- | --- |
| icon.png (or .gif) | Base 16 x 16 icon file, used in menus |
| icon24.png | Larger icon 24 x 24, used in toolbar |
| icon_pressed.png | Base icon pressed condition |
| icon24_pressed.png | Larger icon pressed condition |
| icon_disabled.png | Base icon disabled condition |
| icon24_disabled.png | Larger icon disabled condition |

NetBeans creates the CalendarAction.java class in the FamilyTreeActions project and copies the icon files to the same directory. Listing 9.1 shows the generated annotations that define and register your action class with the application. Class CalendarAction implements the standard Java AWT ActionListener interface, which requires an implementation of the `actionPerformed()` method.

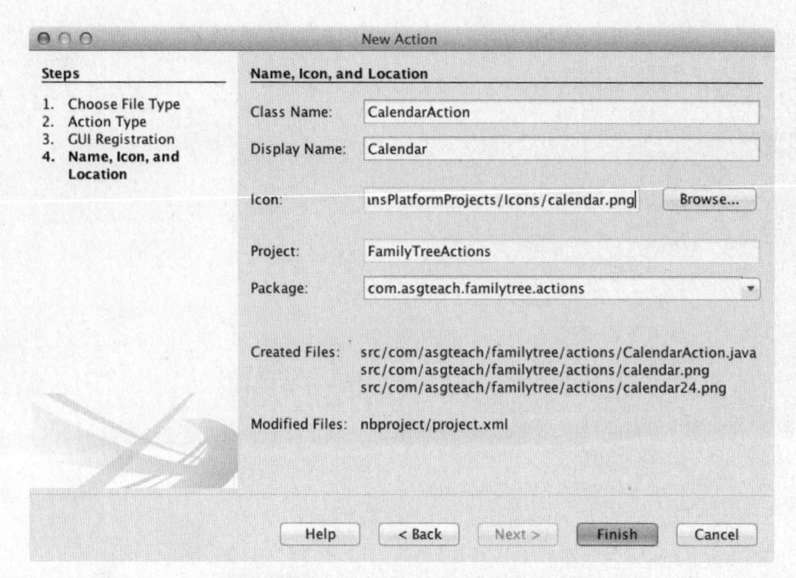


Figure 9.5 Specify the action's name, icon, and location

**Listing 9.1 CalendarAction.java**

```
@ActionID(
        category = "Tools",
        id = "com.asgteach.familytree.actions.CalendarAction"
)
@ActionRegistration(
        iconBase = "com/asgteach/familytree/actions/calendar.png",
        displayName = "#CTL_CalendarAction"
)
@ActionReferences({
    @ActionReference(path = "Menu/Tools", position = 0, separatorAfter = 50),
    @ActionReference(path = "Toolbars/File", position = 300),
    @ActionReference(path = "Shortcuts", name = "M-E")
})
@Messages("CTL_CalendarAction=Calendar")
public final class CalendarAction implements ActionListener {

    @Override
    public void actionPerformed(ActionEvent e) {
        // TODO implement action body
    }
}
```

While our action doesn't do anything yet, let's run the application to see how the new Calendar action is configured in the menu bar and toolbar. Figure 9.6 shows the top-level Tools menu open with the Calendar action, including its icon, display name, and shortcut key sequence.

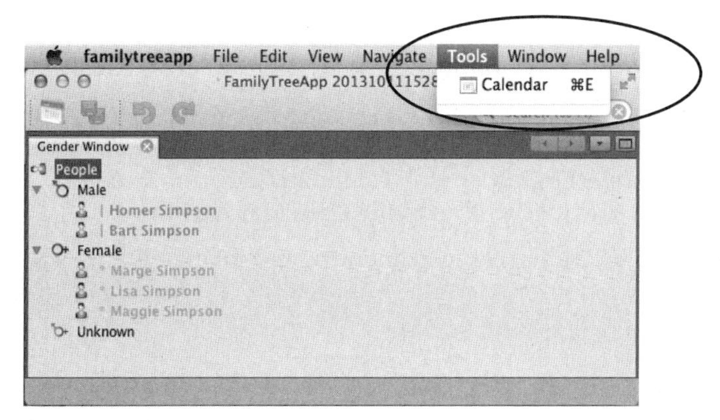


Figure 9.6 Calendar action and icon in the top-level Tools menu

Similarly, Figure 9.7 shows the Calendar action's icon (the 24 x 24 size) configured in the toolbar. A tooltip displays the action's name and shortcut key sequence.

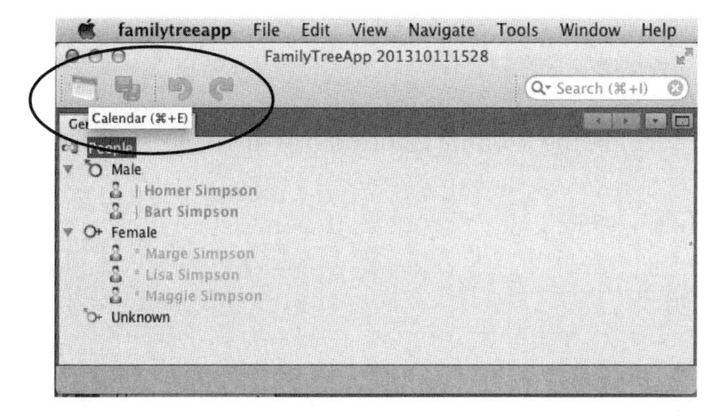


Figure 9.7 Calendar icon in the toolbar with display name and shortcut teletype

## Build a Custom JPanel Form

Now let's provide an implementation for our Calendar action, as shown in Figure 9.1 on page 415. First, we'll create a custom panel to hold an image with some text. We'll then use this custom panel in a NetBeans Platform dialog.[2] Build the custom panel with these steps.

1. Expand project **FamilyTreeActions** Source Packages node and right click on the package name. Select **New | JPanel Form . . .** from the context menu. In the dialog, specify **CalendarPanel** for the class name and click **Finish**.
2. NetBeans creates a new Java class CalendarPanel.java with a top-level JPanel and brings up the form designer.
3. From the Swing Controls palette, add a Label to the form in the upper left. In the Properties view under the Properties tab, specify **calendar64.png** for the **icon** property and change the **text** property to **This is the Calendar Action!**.
4. Resize the panel so that it holds the Label's icon and text, as shown in Figure 9.8.

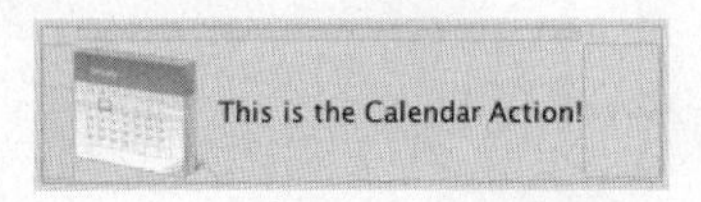


Figure 9.8 Custom Swing JPanel for the action's dialog

## Implement ActionListener

Dialogs require a dependency on the Dialogs API.

1. Expand the FamilyTreeActions project, right click on the **Libraries** node, and select **Add Module Dependency . . . .** In the Module Dependency dialog, select **Dialogs API** and click **OK**.
2. Provide code to implement the Calendar action, as shown in Listing 9.2.

**Listing 9.2 CalendarAction.java**

```
@Messages({
    "CTL_CalendarAction=Calendar",
    "CTL_CalendarTitle=Calendar Action"
})
public final class CalendarAction implements ActionListener {

    private CalendarPanel panel = null;
    private DialogDescriptor dd = null;
```

2. We discuss dialogs in detail in Chapter 11 and dialogs with custom panels in "Custom Dialogs" on page 533.

```
    @Override
    public void actionPerformed(ActionEvent e) {
        if (panel == null) {
            panel = new CalendarPanel();
        }
        if (dd == null) {
            dd = new DialogDescriptor(panel, Bundle.CTL_CalendarTitle());
        }
        // display & block
        if (DialogDisplayer.getDefault().notify(dd) ==
                                        NotifyDescriptor.OK_OPTION) {
            // User clicked OK . . .
        }
    }
}
```

The DialogDisplayer centers the dialog in the application and blocks until the user dismisses it by clicking either the Cancel or OK button. Figure 9.9 shows the application after clicking on the toolbar Calendar icon. (The toolbar icon remains "pressed" until the user dismisses the dialog.)

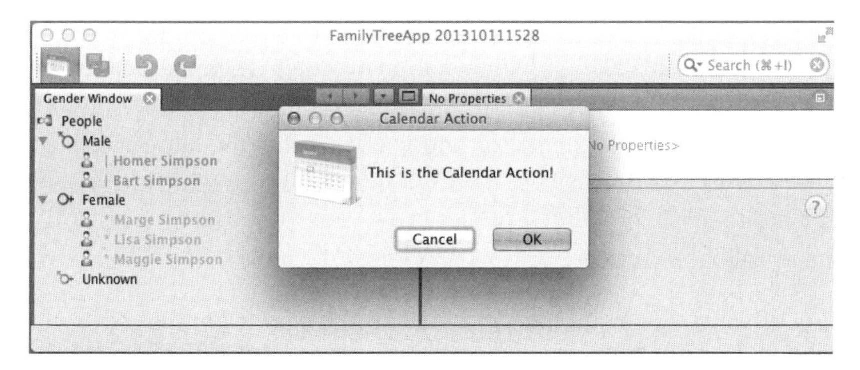


Figure 9.9 Clicking on the Calendar action icon in the toolbar

## 9.2 Actions and Lookup

Both TopComponents and nodes have Lookups that hold objects. These objects enable menu items (or toolbar icons) that apply specifically to the focused TopComponent or to the selected node or nodes. You'll see that the contents of the Global Selection Lookup affect the actions that are available for the user to select.

## Callback Actions

Callback actions are global actions with different behaviors depending on which component has focus. They are registered with a key, and you configure them in TopComponents by installing them in the TopComponent's ActionMap. An ActionMap is inherited by the TopComponent class from Swing JComponent and provides a mapping between a key String and an Action object. You can use the TopComponent's ActionMap to enable NetBeans Platform actions (such as cut, copy, paste) for your TopComponent.

Furthermore, a callback action can have a "fallback" implementation that is invoked when there isn't a version installed in the focused TopComponent's ActionMap. In this case, the action is always enabled, since the fallback version is accessed in the absence of a version referenced in the focused window.

Let's show you an example of a callback action and explore its behavior by changing the callback action's configuration, as follows.

1. First, register a Refresh callback action with a fallback implementation. Because the callback action has a fallback implementation, it is always enabled.
2. Next, install a version of this callback action in the Gender TopComponent's ActionMap. This locally installed implementation executes when the Gender TopComponent has focus. Otherwise, the fallback implementation executes.
3. Last, remove the fallback implementation and you'll see that the Refresh callback action is enabled only when the Gender TopComponent has focus.

### Creating the Fallback Action

Figure 9.10 shows the Refresh menu item and toolbar icon enabled in the application. Executing the Refresh action pops up a dialog that displays "This is the Fallback Refresh Action."

To build this callback action, create a Refresh action similar to an always-enabled action. The NetBeans Platform New Action wizard creates the annotations that register the action in the application. Here are the steps.

1. Add the Refresh action to the FamilyActions module. Expand the FamilyActions Source Packages node, right click on the source package name, and select **New | Action . . .** from the context menu.
2. In the Action Type dialog, select **Always Enabled** and click **Next**.
3. In the GUI Registration dialog, specify Category **File**, and put this action in the Global Menu under **File** at position **HERE - <separator>**. Also include this action in

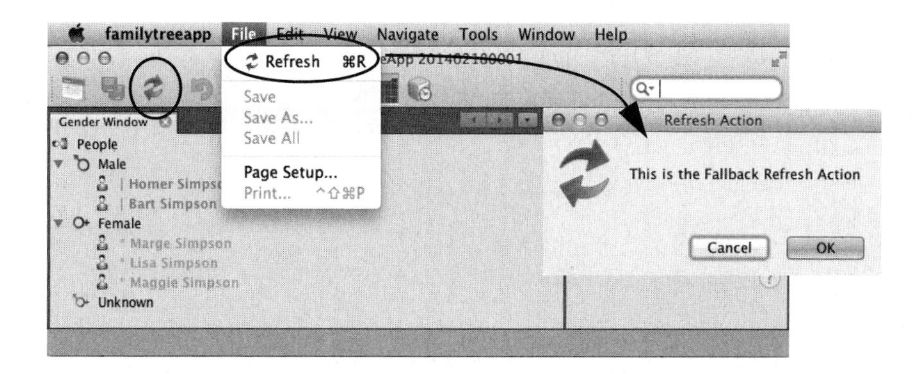


Figure 9.10 Refresh callback action enabled

the Global Toolbar under **File** after the **Save All** icon. Specify a Global Shortcut Key sequence (Command - R). Figure 9.11 shows these settings. Click **Next**.

New Action

Steps

1. Choose File Type
2. Action Type
3. **GUI Registration**
4. Name, Icon, and Location

GUI Registration

Category: File

Global Menu Item

Menu: File

Position: HERE - <separator>

Separator Before Separator After

Global Toolbar Button

Toolbar: File

Position: Save All - HERE

Global Keyboard Shortcut

Key Strokes: Meta+R

Add...

Remove

Help < Back Next > Finish Cancel

Figure 9.11 GUI Registration dialog

4. NetBeans displays the Name, Icon, and Location dialog as shown in Figure 9.12. Specify **RefreshAction** for the Class Name, **Refresh** for the Display Name, and **refresh-icon.png** for the Icon base name. Click **Finish**.

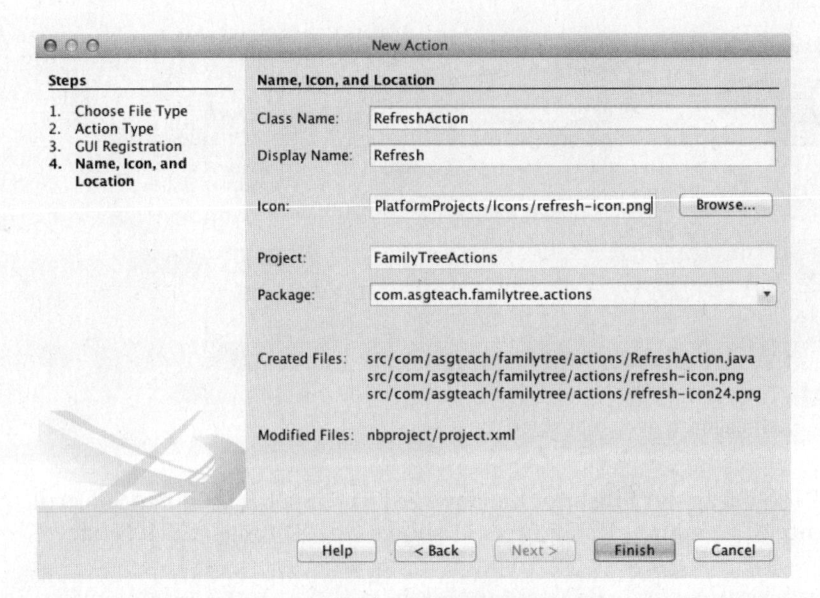


Figure 9.12 Name, Icon, and Location for Refresh action

NetBeans creates the RefreshAction class and generates the annotations. At this point, the Refresh action is an always-enabled action. To make Refresh a callback action, add a key to the `@ActionRegistration`, as shown in Listing 9.3. Here we use the key "MyCoolRefreshAction."

**Listing 9.3 RefreshAction.java**

```
@ActionID(
        category = "File",
        id = "com.asgteach.familytree.actions.RefreshAction"
)
@ActionRegistration(
        iconBase = "com/asgteach/familytree/actions/refresh-icon.png",
        displayName = "#CTL_RefreshAction",
        key = "MyCoolRefreshAction"
)
@ActionReferences({
    @ActionReference(path = "Menu/File", position = 1300),
    @ActionReference(path = "Toolbars/File", position = 500),
    @ActionReference(path = "Shortcuts", name = "M-R")
})
@Messages("CTL_RefreshAction=Refresh")
```

```
public final class RefreshAction implements ActionListener {

    @Override
    public void actionPerformed(ActionEvent e) {
      // Put fallback code here

    }
}
```

Add code to the actionPerformed() method to execute the fallback behavior, as shown in Listing 9.4. In our example, the fallback implementation displays a dialog, as shown in Figure 9.10 on page 423. (The DialogDescriptor uses RefreshPanel, which you build using the same steps used to build the CaldendarPanel. See "Build a Custom JPanel Form" on page 419.)

**Listing 9.4 RefreshAction.java—actionPerformed() Fallback Code**

```
      . . . Action annotations unchanged . . .
@Messages({
    "CTL_RefreshAction=Refresh",
    "CTL_RefreshTitle=Refresh Action"
})
public final class RefreshAction implements ActionListener {

    private RefreshPanel panel = null;
    private DialogDescriptor dd = null;

    @Override
    public void actionPerformed(ActionEvent e) {
        if (panel == null) {
            panel = new RefreshPanel();
        }
        if (dd == null) {
            dd = new DialogDescriptor(panel, Bundle.CTL_RefreshTitle());
        }
        // display & block
        if (DialogDisplayer.getDefault().notify(dd) ==
                                    NotifyDescriptor.OK_OPTION) {
            // User clicked OK . . .
        }
    }

}
```

### Create and Install a Callback Action Performer

Next, we'll define a version of Refresh callback action in the Gender window that is invoked when this window has focus. Recall that when a TopComponent has focus, its ActionMap is in the Global Selection Lookup and any defined actions become enabled.

The Refresh action is already registered in our application. Listing 9.5 shows how to install an implementation of "MyCoolRefreshAction" into the ActionMap of the Gender TopComponent. In the NetBeans Platform documentation, a callback action implementation is called an action "performer." Note that three steps are required for the TopComponent's version of RefreshAction to be invoked.

1. Include the ActionMap in the TopComponent's Lookup. This is accomplished with the `associateLookup()` method shown in Listing 9.5.
2. Add the action and its key to the TopComponent's ActionMap, as shown with the `getActionMap().put()` statement. The key must match the action's key attribute.
3. When running the application, the Gender window must have focus in order to invoke its version of RefreshAction.

**Listing 9.5 GenderTopComponent.java—Installing "MyCoolRefreshAction"**

```
public final class GenderTopComponent extends TopComponent
        implements ExplorerManager.Provider {
    private final ExplorerManager em = new ExplorerManager();

    public GenderTopComponent() {
        initComponents();
        setName(Bundle.CTL_GenderTopComponent());
        setToolTipText(Bundle.HINT_GenderTopComponent());

        BeanTreeView view = new BeanTreeView();
        add(view, BorderLayout.CENTER);
        associateLookup(ExplorerUtils.createLookup(em, this.getActionMap()));
        em.setRootContext(new RootNode());
        for (Node node : em.getRootContext().getChildren().getNodes()) {
            view.expandNode(node);
        }
        getActionMap().put("MyCoolRefreshAction", new AbstractAction() {

            @Override
            public void actionPerformed(ActionEvent e) {
                em.setRootContext(new RootNode());// Rebuild Node hierarchy
            }
        });
    }
```

Once an implementation of AbstractAction is installed in the Gender TopComponent's ActionMap with key "MyCoolRefreshAction" and the Gender TopComponent has focus, invoking the Refresh action executes the local implementation of the `actionPerformed()` method. Here, the installed, local implementation rebuilds the

Explorer View's node hierarchy (the RootNode is newly instantiated, rebuilding the entire hierarchy). If another window gains focus, the fallback implementation executes unless this other window installs a Refresh action performer as well. In this way, windows can implement their own versions of callback actions.

### Removing the Fallback Implementation

Sometimes it may not make sense for a callback action to have a fallback implementation. In this case, the action in the menu and toolbar should enable only if an implementation is installed in the focused component's ActionMap. To remove the fallback implementation, modify the RefreshAction class, as shown in Listing 9.6. Here are the steps.

1. Define a public `static final String` inside the class with the same value as the key.
2. Remove the `key` attribute from the `@ActionRegistration` annotation.
3. Move the action registration annotations inside the class so that they apply to the static String definition.
4. Remove the ActionListener implementation.

With these changes, the Refresh action is still registered in the top-level Menu and the toolbar, but now there is no fallback implementation.

**Listing 9.6 RefreshAction.java—Remove the Fallback Implementation**

```
@Messages({
    "CTL_RefreshAction=Refresh",
    "CTL_RefreshTitle=Refresh Action"
})
public final class RefreshAction {
    @ActionID(
        category = "File",
        id = "com.asgteach.familytree.actions.RefreshAction"
    )
    @ActionRegistration(
            iconBase = "com/asgteach/familytree/actions/refresh-icon.png",
            displayName = "#CTL_RefreshAction"
    )
    @ActionReferences({
        @ActionReference(path = "Menu/File", position = 1300),
        @ActionReference(path = "Toolbars/File", position = 500),
        @ActionReference(path = "Shortcuts", name = "M-R")
    })
    public static final String REFRESH_ACTION = "MyCoolRefreshAction";
}
```

With no fallback implementation, the Refresh action is only enabled if the Gender window has focus. Otherwise, Refresh is disabled on the toolbar as well as under the File menu, as shown in Figure 9.13.

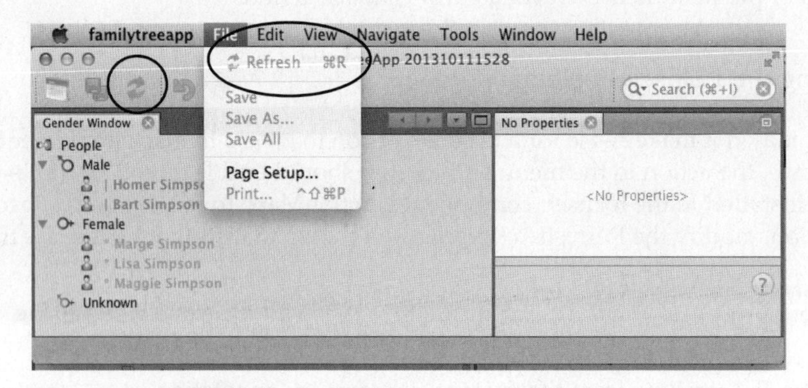


Figure 9.13 Refresh action is disabled

## Context-Aware Actions

The previous examples showed you how to register an always-enabled action (Calendar action) and a callback action that is enabled when the TopComponent in which it is registered has focus (Refresh action). Now let's show you how to create an action that is *context aware*. This action observes the current selection for a given type and enables itself if instances of the given type are present. Context-aware actions enable when their context is in the Lookup of a selected entity. Typically, the selected entity is one or more nodes, but it can also be a TopComponent.

### NetBeans Platform Capability Pattern

Nodes in the NetBeans Platform have context menus and Lookups. The NetBeans Platform builds a node's context menu from a list of actions provided by the node's `getActions()` method. Furthermore, a node's Lookup holds various "context" objects that enable an action when present in the selected node. Thus, we use a node's Lookup to install *capabilities*. In the NetBeans Platform, a capability is described generally by a Java interface or abstract class and realized by the implementation of the interface or concrete class added to the Lookup of an object. This arrangement lets objects dynamically configure their own capabilities that perform actions, such as reloading, storing (saving), opening, and deleting. Capabilities encourage loose coupling, since an unrelated entity can "look up" a capability and invoke it (if it exists) without being privy to the details of its implementation. This is similar to the Global Lookup, which makes Service Providers available to interested entities.

The NetBeans IDE, for example, uses this capability pattern. In the Java Editor, the Save All icon in the toolbar enables when you first make a change to your source code. How exactly does this happen?

When the editor detects an edit to the source code, it adds an implementation of AbstractSavable to its Lookup. The Action framework listens for the presence of an AbstractSavable object in the Global Lookup. When detected, the LookupListener event handler enables the Save All icon in the toolbar and the Save and Save All menu items in the File menu. When you click one of these menu items, the AbstractSavable `handleSave()` method is invoked. Your file is saved, the AbstractSavable is removed from the Java Editor's Lookup, and these menu items are once again disabled.[3]

The same principle applies to node selection. When you select a node that has a capability in its Lookup that corresponds to the context of a registered action, the action associated with that capability becomes enabled (available). Let's show you how this works with a different version of the Calendar action.

### Implementing a Context-Aware Action

Here's an overview of how we'll create a context-aware action and use it with PersonNodes in the GenderTopComponent.

- Remove the always-enabled CalendarAction from the application.
- Create a new Capabilities module and a CalendarCapability interface. Make its package public so that other modules can set a dependency on this module.
- Create a new conditionally-enabled action using the New Action wizard. Name this action Calendar and implement the action with context CalendarCapability.
- Modify PersonNode in module GenderViewer. Implement the CalendarCapability and add it to the PersonNode's Lookup. Reuse the CalendarPanel form and icons.
- Configure the PersonNode's list of actions so its context menu includes the Calendar action.

Initially, the Calendar action is disabled until the user selects a single PersonNode. Then, Calendar action is enabled in the File menu, toolbar, and the node's context menu. The action displays a dialog with the selected Person's name, as shown in Figure 9.14.

3. We show you how to do all this with the FamilyTreeApp in Chapter 10. See "Implementing Update" on page 488. We also have an example of dynamically enabling a capability later in this chapter. See "Add Drop Support to the Root Node" on page 465.

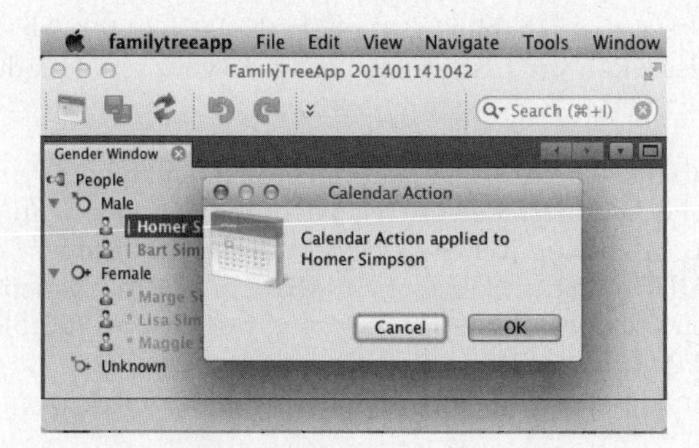


Figure 9.14 Invoking the context-aware Calendar action with node Homer Simpson

## Create the Capabilities Module

Let's first create a capability. Since capabilities are viewed as potentially application-wide definitions, we put CalendarCapability in a module (called Capabilities) and make its enclosing package public.

1. Select the Modules node in the FamilyTreeApp project, right-click, and select **Add New . . .** from the context menu. NetBeans displays the Name and Location dialog for the New Project wizard.
2. For Project Name, specify **Capabilities** and accept the defaults for the remaining fields. Click **Next**.
3. NetBeans displays the Basic Module Configuration dialog. Specify **com.asgteach.familytree.capabilities** for the Code Name Base and accept the defaults for the remaining fields. Click **Finish**. NetBeans creates project Capabilities in the FamilyTreeApp application.

## Create the Capability Interface

1. Expand the Capabilities project Source Packages node, right click on the package name, and select **New | Java Interface** from the context menu.
2. In the New Interface dialog, specify **CalendarCapability** for Class Name and click **Finish**.
3. NetBeans brings up CalendarCapability.java in the Java Editor. Provide the `doCalendar()` abstract method for the interface, as shown in Listing 9.7.

**Listing 9.7 CalendarCapability.java**

```
public interface CalendarCapability {

    public void doCalendar();

}
```

### Make the Capabilities Module's Package Public

1. Right click on the Capabilities project and select **Properties** from the context menu. NetBeans displays the Project Properties dialog.
2. Under Categories, select **API Versioning**.
3. Under Public Packages, select package **com.asgteach.familytree.capabilities** as shown in Figure 9.15. Click **OK** to close the dialog.

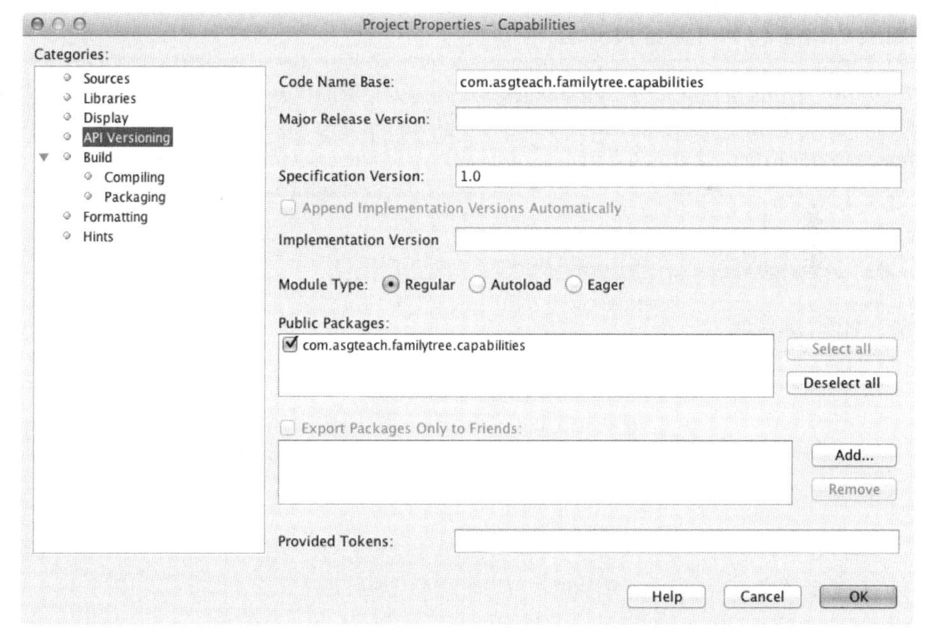


Figure 9.15 Making package com.asgteach.familytree.capabilities public

## Create a Context-Aware Action

Use the New Action wizard to create the Calendar action in the FamilyTreeActions module. Since the Calendar action will use the CalendarCapability, first set a dependency on the Capabilities module.

1. In the FamilyTreeActions project, select the **Libraries** node, right click, and select **Add Module Dependency . . .** from the context menu.
2. In the dialog, select the **Capabilities** module and click **OK**.
3. Now still in the FamilyTreeActions project, expand the Source Packages node, right click on the package name, and select **New | Action . . .** from the context menu.
4. NetBeans displays the Action Type dialog of the New Action wizard. Select **Conditionally Enabled** and specify **CalendarCapability** for the Cookie Class (the Cookie Class is the context). Select **User Selects One Node**, as shown in Figure 9.16. Click **Next**.

### One Node or Multiple Nodes

*We'll configure this action for single-node selection first. Then we'll show you how to make it work for multiple-node selections. Finally, we'll show you how to make the NodeCalendar-Action work for different kinds of nodes (both PersonNode and GenderNode).*

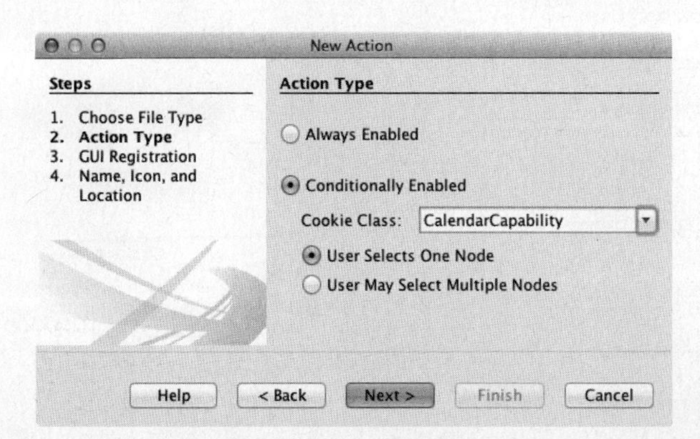


Figure 9.16 Creating a new context-aware action

5. NetBeans display the GUI Registration dialog. Register this new action in category Nodes, in the File menu and before the Save All icon in the toolbar. Leave the other options unselected, as shown in Figure 9.17. Click **Next**.

**Action Categories**

*The action's Category name lets you categorize actions and identify a set of actions to include in a node's context menu.*

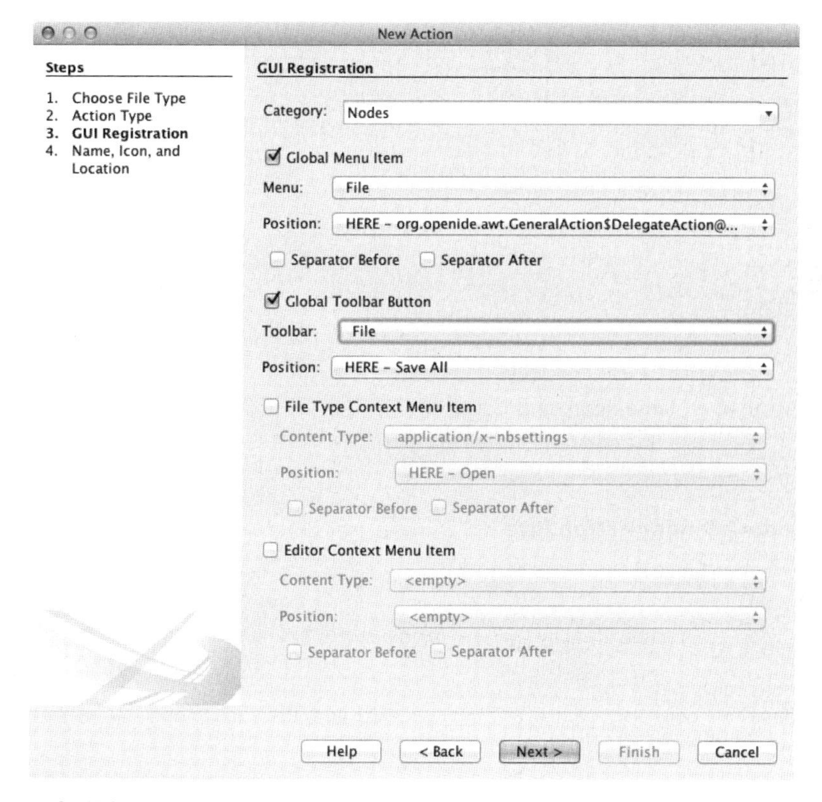


Figure 9.17 Register the context-aware action

6. NetBeans displays the Name, Icon, and Location dialog. Specify **NodeCalendar-Action** for the Class Name, **Calendar** for the Display Name, and **calendar.png** for the icon file, as shown in Figure 9.18. Click **Finish**.

7. NetBeans creates the NodeCalendarAction.java file, which uses Calendar-Capability for its context type. Implement the `actionPerformed()` method as shown in Listing 9.8. We also register the shortcut "Meta-E" (E for Event) to invoke the NodeCalendar action. Note that this shortcut is active only when a PersonNode is selected.

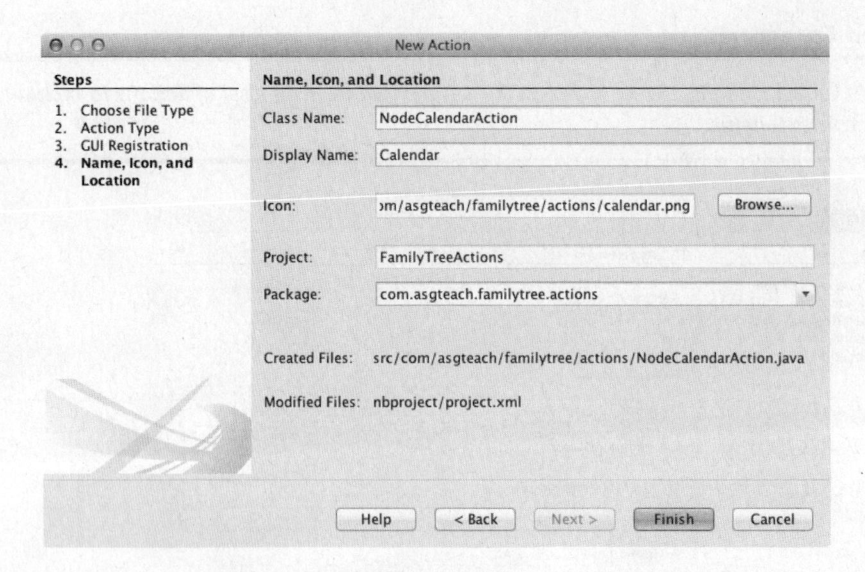


Figure 9.18 Specify the Name, Icon, and Location

**Listing 9.8 NodeCalendarAction.java**

```
@ActionID(
        category = "Nodes",
        id = "com.asgteach.familytree.actions.NodeCalendarAction"
)
@ActionRegistration(
        iconBase = "com/asgteach/familytree/actions/calendar.png",
        displayName = "#CTL_NodeCalendarAction"
)
@ActionReferences({
    @ActionReference(path = "Menu/File", position = 1200),
    @ActionReference(path = "Toolbars/File", position = 300),
    @ActionReference(path = "Shortcuts", name = "M-E")
})
@Messages("CTL_NodeCalendarAction=Calendar")
public final class NodeCalendarAction implements ActionListener {

    private final CalendarCapability context;

    public NodeCalendarAction(CalendarCapability context) {
        this.context = context;
    }
```

```
    @Override
    public void actionPerformed(ActionEvent ev) {
        context.doCalendar();
    }
}
```

## Make Changes to the GenderViewer Module

If you run the FamilyTreeApp application at this point, you will see a Calendar icon in the toolbar and a Calendar menu item in the File menu, but these actions are disabled. Furthermore, if you right click on a PersonNode, you will see only Properties in its context menu (because we configured a PropertiesSheet in PersonNode). To enable the Calendar action, we must provide an implementation of the Calendar action's context and add it to the PersonNode's Lookup. Here are the steps to set a dependency on both the Capabilities and the Dialogs API modules and copy the CalendarPanel and icon PNG file to the GenderViewer module.

1. Expand the GenderViewer project, right click on the **Libraries** node, and select **Add Module Dependency . . . .** In the Module Dependency dialog, select **Capabilities** and **Dialogs API**. Click **OK**.
2. Reuse the CalendarPanel created earlier (see "Build a Custom JPanel Form" on page 419). Expand the FamilyTreeActions project Source Packages and package name node. Select CalendarPanel.java and copy it into the GenderViewer Source Packages **com.asgteach.familytree.genderviewer** package.
3. Repeat the above step and copy file calendar64.png into the GenderViewer Source Packages **com.asgteach.familytree.genderviewer.resources** package.
4. Bring up CalendarPanel.java into the design view (click the **Design** tab). Make sure its JLabel component has Variable Name **myLabel**. Reset the icon property so that it uses the calendar64.png file in the **resources** package.
5. Bring up CalendarPanel.java in the Java Editor (click the **Source** tab). Add the `setText()` public method to the class, as shown in Listing 9.9.

**Listing 9.9 CalendarPanel.java**

```
public class CalendarPanel extends javax.swing.JPanel {
. . .
    public void setText(String text) {
        myLabel.setText(text);
    }
}
```

## Implement CalendarCapability in PersonNode

There are several modifications required to make PersonNode have the Calendar-Capability. Previously, the PersonNode Lookup contained a single object (Person), which was set in the constructor. Now, however, we want to add other objects to the Lookup. As previously discussed, class InstanceContent lets you dynamically add and remove objects to and from a Lookup (see "Lookup as an Object Repository" on page 225). We'll use InstanceContent here to give us a Lookup to which we can add objects. We use a private constructor, since a node's Lookup must be created in a constructor. Note that we now add the Person object to the Lookup in the constructor with `instanceContent.add()`.

Our second modification includes adding an implementation of CalendarCapability to the node's Lookup. We use an anonymous class and override the `doCalendar()` method. In it, we instantiate the CalendarPanel and invoke the `setText()` method to include the Person's name in the displayed dialog.

Finally, we override the `getActions()` method to include the Calendar action in the node's context menu. The `getActions()` method returns an array of actions. We call `super()` to include any actions already configured (Properties is already configured in this example). The NetBeans Platform provides the Utilities `actionsForPath()` method that returns a list of actions registered for a given path (that is, its location in the application's virtual file system, specified by its category). If you want to include a separator in the context menu, add a null to the List at the appropriate slot. Here, we add a separator before the Calendar menu item.

Listing 9.10 shows these modifications.

**Listing 9.10 PersonNode.java—Configuring Calendar Action**

```
@Messages({
    "HINT_PersonNode=Person",
    "CTL_CalendarTitle=Calendar Action"
})
public class PersonNode extends AbstractNode implements
                                        PropertyChangeListener {
    private static final Logger logger = Logger.getLogger(
                                PersonNode.class.getName());
    private final InstanceContent instanceContent;

    public PersonNode(Person person) {
        this(person, new InstanceContent());
    }
```

```
    private PersonNode(Person person, InstanceContent ic) {
        super(Children.LEAF, new AbstractLookup(ic));
        instanceContent = ic;
        instanceContent.add(person);

        setIconBaseWithExtension(
            "com/asgteach/familytree/genderviewer/resources/personIcon.png");
        setName(String.valueOf(person.getId()));
        setDisplayName(person.toString());
        setShortDescription(Bundle.HINT_PersonNode());

        // Add a Calendar Capability to this Node
        instanceContent.add(new CalendarCapability() {

            @Override
            public void doCalendar() {
                CalendarPanel panel = new CalendarPanel();
                panel.setText("<html>Calendar Action applied to<p/>"
                        + person + "</html>");
                DialogDescriptor dd = new DialogDescriptor(panel,
                        Bundle.CTL_CalendarTitle());
                DialogDisplayer.getDefault().notify(dd);  // display & block
            }
        });
    }

    @SuppressWarnings("unchecked")
    @Override
    public Action[] getActions(boolean context) {
        List<Action> personActions = new ArrayList<>(
                        Arrays.asList(super.getActions(context)));
        // add a separator
        personActions.add(null);
        personActions.addAll(Utilities.actionsForPath("Actions/Nodes"));
        return personActions.toArray(
                new Action[personActions.size()]);
    }
}
```

The code we added to PersonNode provides two distinct features.

- One, adding a CalendarCapability implementation to the PersonNode's Lookup enables the Calendar action when a user selects the node.
- Two, overriding the `getActions()` method and including the Calendar action in PersonNode's list of actions makes Calendar show up in PersonNode's context menu.

If you don't put the CalendarCapability context in the node's Lookup but you still override getActions(), then the action will never be enabled, but it will still show up disabled in the node's context menu.

Conversely, if you put the context in the Lookup but you don't override the getActions() method, the Calendar action is enabled in the File menu and in the toolbar when a user selects the node, but it does not appear in the node's context menu.

Figure 9.19 shows the application with the PersonNode's context menu and the Calendar action icon enabled in the toolbar.

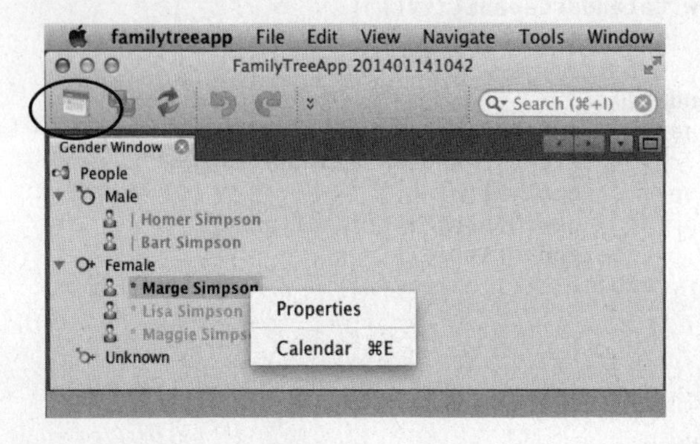


Figure 9.19 PersonNode context menu now includes Calendar action

## Configuring a Node's Preferred Action

Double clicking a node invokes a node's preferred action. To set a node's preferred action, override the getPreferredAction() method and return an action. To make Calendar action PersonNode's preferred action, we return the first (and only) action in the path "Actions/Nodes," as shown in Listing 9.11.

**Listing 9.11 PersonNode.java—getPreferredAction() Method**

```
@SuppressWarnings("unchecked")
@Override
public Action getPreferredAction() {
    List<Action> personActions = (List<Action>) Utilities.actionsForPath(
                                            "Actions/Nodes");
    if (!personActions.isEmpty()) {
        return personActions.get(0);
```

```
        } else {
            return super.getPreferredAction();
        }
    }
```

Note that you can override `getPreferredAction()` with or without also overriding `getActions()`. If you don't override `getActions()`, the node's context menu does not include the Calendar action, but you can still invoke the Calendar action with a double click.

## The Layer File

The NetBeans Platform Layer file is part of our discussion on window groups (see "Window Group Example" on page 382 in Chapter 8). Historically, you registered actions by editing a module's Layer file, an XML file used to configure NetBeans Platform applications. The build process in the NetBeans Platform still parses a module's Layer file (if it exists) and generates a single layer.xml file for the application.

Now, modules can be mostly configured with annotations and a per module Layer file is generally not needed for direct editing. Under the hood, however, Layer files still exist, and it can be helpful to examine them. When registering actions, for example, the category that you assign to an action affects its "path" (its location in the application's virtual file system).

Listing 9.12 shows the generated Layer file for the FamilyTreeActions module. The Layer file includes the registration information for the NodeCalendarAction and the RefreshAction from our examples. You can view a module's Layer file in the File view of the application's build directory, as follows.

```
build/cluster/modules/module-name.jar/META-INF/generated-layer.xml
```

where `module-name.jar` is the code name base-named jar file for a module. Not all modules will have a generated Layer file.

Looking at the Layer file, you can see that each action category has its own folder (here you see folder "Nodes" and folder "File"). Similarly, the top-level Menu has its own folder ("Menu"), as well as the Toolbar ("Toolbars"). This Layer file includes the registration information for the actions defined in this module. Other modules provide their own Layer file and action registrations, if any. The context-aware NodeCalendar action is registered for single node selection only (`"EXACTLY_ONE"`). (See "The File System API Overview" on page 624 for more details on the Layer file.)

**Listing 9.12 FamilyTreeActions Module—generated-layer.xml**

```
<?xml version="1.0" encoding="UTF-8"?>
<!DOCTYPE filesystem PUBLIC "-//NetBeans//DTD Filesystem 1.2//EN"
                           "http://www.netbeans.org/dtds/filesystem-1_2.dtd">
<filesystem>
    <folder name="Actions">
        <folder name="Nodes">
            <file name=
                "com-asgteach-familytree-actions-NodeCalendarAction.instance">
                <!--com.asgteach.familytree.actions.NodeCalendarAction-->
                <attr
                    bundlevalue=
    "com.asgteach.familytree.actions.Bundle#CTL_NodeCalendarAction"
    name="displayName"/>
                <attr methodvalue="org.openide.awt.Actions.context"
                     name="instanceCreate"/>
                <attr name="type" stringvalue=
                "com.asgteach.familytree.capabilities.CalendarCapability"/>
                <attr methodvalue="org.openide.awt.Actions.inject"
                name="delegate"/>
                <attr name="injectable" stringvalue=
                "com.asgteach.familytree.actions.NodeCalendarAction"/>
                <attr name="selectionType" stringvalue="EXACTLY_ONE"/>
                <attr name="iconBase" stringvalue=
                "com/asgteach/familytree/actions/calendar.png"/>
                <attr boolvalue="false" name="noIconInMenu"/>
            </file>
        </folder>
        <folder name="File">
            <file name=
                "com-asgteach-familytree-actions-RefreshAction.instance">
          <!--com.asgteach.familytree.actions.RefreshAction.REFRESH_ACTION-->
                <attr
                    bundlevalue="
                com.asgteach.familytree.actions.Bundle#CTL_RefreshAction"
                name="displayName"/>
                <attr methodvalue="org.openide.awt.Actions.callback"
                name="instanceCreate"/>
                <attr name="key" stringvalue="MyCoolRefreshAction"/>
                <attr name="iconBase" stringvalue=
                  "com/asgteach/familytree/actions/refresh-icon.png"/>
                <attr boolvalue="false" name="noIconInMenu"/>
            </file>
        </folder>
    </folder>
    <folder name="Menu">
        <folder name="File">
            <file name=
                "com-asgteach-familytree-actions-NodeCalendarAction.shadow">
```

```
                <!--com.asgteach.familytree.actions.NodeCalendarAction-->
                <attr name="originalFile" stringvalue="Actions/Nodes/
               com-asgteach-familytree-actions-NodeCalendarAction.instance"/>
                <attr intvalue="1200" name="position"/>
            </file>
            <file name="com-asgteach-familytree-actions-RefreshAction.shadow">
        <!--com.asgteach.familytree.actions.RefreshAction.REFRESH_ACTION-->
                <attr name="originalFile" stringvalue=
     "Actions/File/com-asgteach-familytree-actions-RefreshAction.instance"/>
                <attr intvalue="1300" name="position"/>
            </file>
        </folder>
    </folder>
    <folder name="Toolbars">
        <folder name="File">
            <file name=
        "com-asgteach-familytree-actions-NodeCalendarAction.shadow">
                <!--com.asgteach.familytree.actions.NodeCalendarAction-->
                <attr name="originalFile" stringvalue="Actions/Nodes/
               com-asgteach-familytree-actions-NodeCalendarAction.instance"/>
                <attr intvalue="300" name="position"/>
            </file>
            <file name="com-asgteach-familytree-actions-RefreshAction.shadow">
        <!--com.asgteach.familytree.actions.RefreshAction.REFRESH_ACTION-->
                <attr name="originalFile" stringvalue="Actions/File/
               com-asgteach-familytree-actions-RefreshAction.instance"/>
                <attr intvalue="500" name="position"/>
            </file>
        </folder>
    </folder>
    <folder name="Shortcuts">
        <file name="M-E.shadow">
            <!--com.asgteach.familytree.actions.NodeCalendarAction-->
            <attr name="originalFile" stringvalue="Actions/Nodes/
            com-asgteach-familytree-actions-NodeCalendarAction.instance"/>
        </file>
        <file name="M-R.shadow">
           <!--com.asgteach.familytree.actions.RefreshAction.REFRESH_ACTION-->
            <attr name="originalFile" stringvalue="Actions/File/
            com-asgteach-familytree-actions-RefreshAction.instance"/>
        </file>
    </folder>
</filesystem>
```

### Multi-Select Context-Aware Actions

When we built the NodeCalendarAction, we specified that the user selects one node (see Figure 9.16 on page 432). To build a context-aware action that allows users to select multiple nodes, you select the appropriate radio button in the New Action wizard. Then, the wizard generates a List in the action class for the appropriate context type.

If you decide that users can select multiple nodes after you have already created the context-aware action, you can easily modify the action class by converting the context type to a List, as shown in Listing 9.13 (compare this to the single-selection version in Listing 9.8 on page 434).

**Listing 9.13 NodeCalendarAction.java—Select Multiple Nodes**

```
. . . Annotations Unchanged . . .

public final class NodeCalendarAction implements ActionListener {

    private final List<CalendarCapability> context;

    public NodeCalendarAction(List<CalendarCapability> context) {
        this.context = context;
    }

    @Override
    public void actionPerformed(ActionEvent ev) {
        for (CalendarCapability calendarCapability : context) {
            calendarCapability.doCalendar();
        }
    }
}
```

Now, when you select multiple PersonNodes, the Calendar action is enabled, as shown in Figure 9.20. In this example, invoking the action results in a succession of dialogs displayed for each selected node. As each dialog is dismissed, the next one appears.

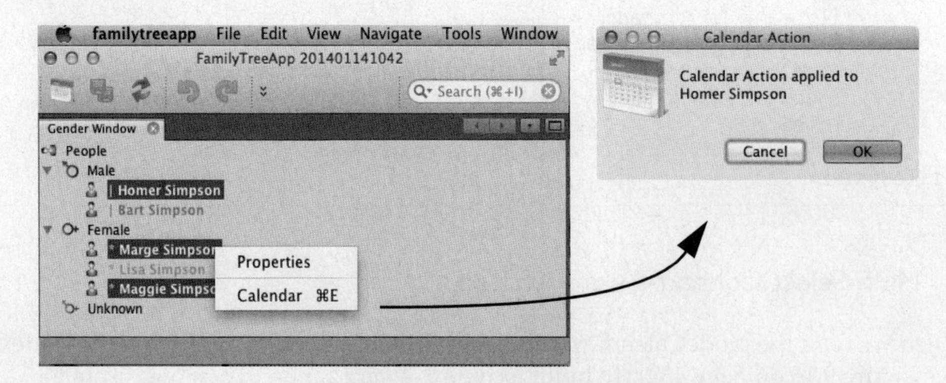


Figure 9.20 Calendar action allows a user to select multiple PersonNodes

To emphasize the flexibility and power of capabilities, let's add this Calendar-Capability to GenderNode by adding an implementation to its Lookup. Again, we restructure the GenderNode class to provide for an InstanceContent to which we can add things. Listing 9.14 shows the changes. We also override `getActions()` so that GenderNode context menu will also include the Calendar action. Note that this implementation of CalendarCapability is customized for GenderNode.

**Listing 9.14 GenderNode.java—with CalendarCapability**

```
public class GenderNode extends AbstractNode {
    private final InstanceContent instanceContent;

    public GenderNode(Gender gender) {
        this(gender, new InstanceContent());
    }

    private GenderNode(Gender gender, InstanceContent ic) {
        super(Children.create(new PersonChildFactory(gender), false),
                                     new AbstractLookup(ic));
        instanceContent = ic;
        instanceContent.add(gender);
        setGenderStuff(gender);
        setShortDescription(Bundle.HINT_GenderNode());

        // Add a Calendar capability to this Node
        instanceContent.add(new CalendarCapability() {

            @Override
            public void doCalendar() {
                CalendarPanel panel = new CalendarPanel();
                panel.setText("<html>Calendar Action applied to<p/>Gender "
                        + getDisplayName() + "</html>");
                DialogDescriptor dd = new DialogDescriptor(panel,
                        Bundle.CTL_CalendarTitle());
                DialogDisplayer.getDefault().notify(dd);  // display & block
            }
        });
    }

    @SuppressWarnings("unchecked")
    @Override
    public Action[] getActions(boolean context) {
        List<Action> nodeActions = new ArrayList<>(
                     Arrays.asList(super.getActions(context)));
        // add a separator
        nodeActions.add(null);
        nodeActions.addAll(Utilities.actionsForPath("Actions/Nodes"));
```

```
        return nodeActions.toArray(
                new Action[nodeActions.size()]);
    }
. . . unchanged code omitted . . .
}
```

Figure 9.21 shows that we can select both PersonNodes and GenderNodes and invoke the Calendar action, which executes according to the selected context.

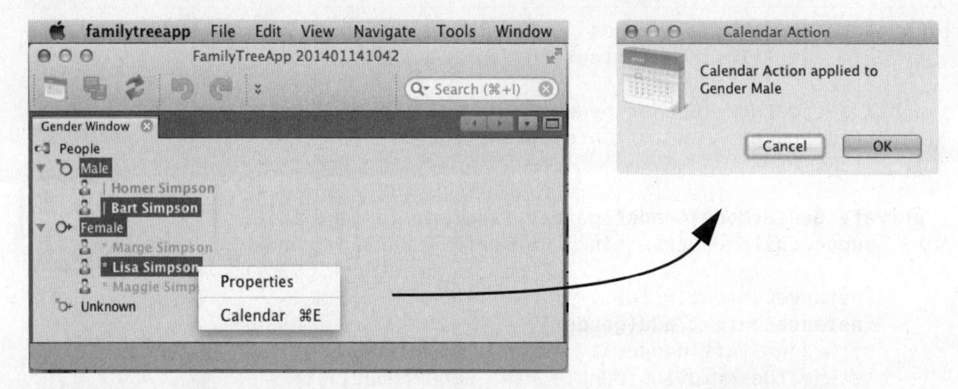


Figure 9.21 Calendar action implemented for GenderNodes and PersonNodes

## 9.3 Editing the Node Hierarchy

Applications may require modifying node hierarchies with drag and drop as well as cut, copy, paste, and delete. You may also want to reorder nodes within a node group. The NetBeans Platform provides actions and support for these tasks. To use these actions, you supply support code that hooks into the Action framework and the Explorer View/node hierarchy.[4]

Let's create a new node hierarchy so that users can move and reorder PersonNodes within three groups (implemented with a GroupNode). We call these groups Happy, Sad, and Undecided. We'll use the Simpson family from the FamilyTreeManager and let users Cut, Copy, Paste, Delete, Drag and Drop, as well as Reorder, Move Up, and Move Down. In this section, we'll show you how to implement all of these actions.

4. This example is adapted from blog posts and articles provided by Geertjan Wielenga (`https://blogs.oracle.com/geertjan/entry/node_cut_copy_paste_delete`) and Toni Epple (`http://netbeans.dzone.com/nb-how-to-drag-drop-with-nodes-api`).

## Group Window Node Actions

Let's first look at the Group window and its node structure. Figure 9.22 shows the FamilyTreeApp in its initial state. It includes a single window (Group window) with our favorite group of Person objects from the Simpson family. All family members appear under Group Undecided. You can move one or more Person objects among the three Groups (Happy, Sad, and Undecided) using Copy/Paste, Cut/Paste, or Drag and Drop, putting Person objects in different groups or moving them within the same group. In addition, you can reorder any group.

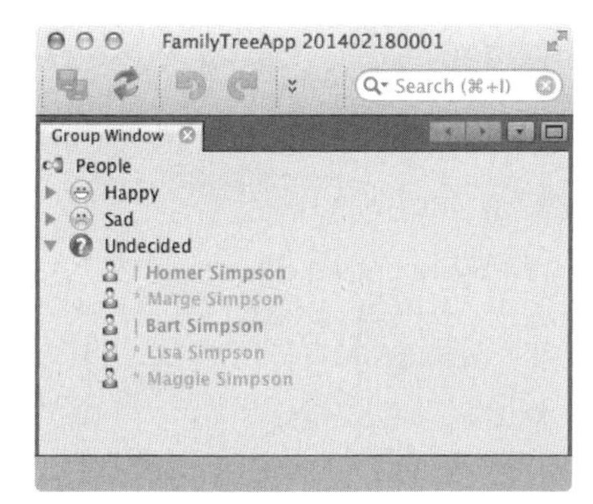


Figure 9.22 Group nodes let you recategorize people

The Group nodes include context menu item **Change Order ...**, as shown in Figure 9.23. Change Order pops up a separate dialog and lets you use Move Up and Move Down buttons to reorder the group. You dismiss the dialog with either OK to accept the changes or Cancel.

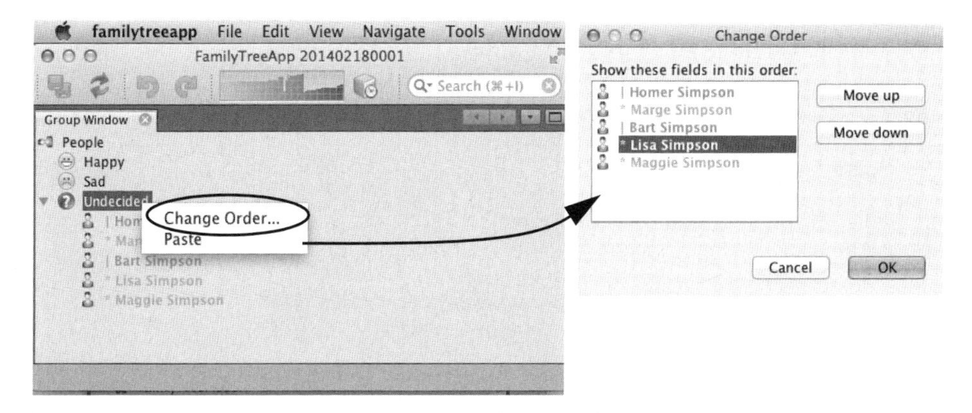


Figure 9.23 Group nodes let you reorder and receive pastes

Figure 9.24 shows node Bart Simpson selected and its context menu, which includes Cut, Copy, Delete, Move Up, and Move Down. The Move Up and Move Down actions move the selected node within its group.

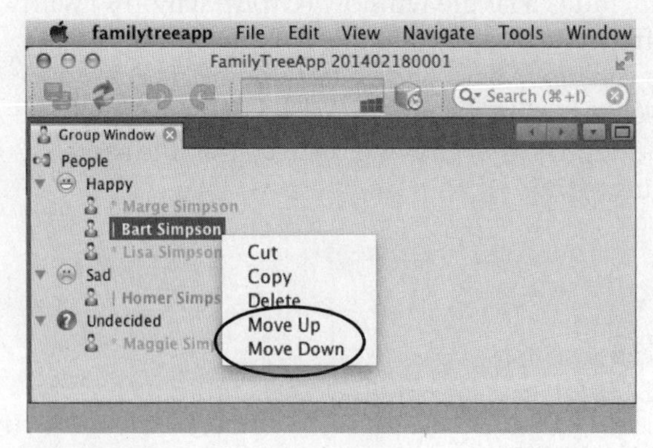


Figure 9.24 Person nodes let you cut, copy, delete, or move up and down

## Basic Node Hierarchy

Let's first examine the node hierarchy. From Figure 9.24 you see a root node labeled People, intermediate GroupNodes (Happy, Sad, and Undecided), and the familiar PersonNodes with their wrapped Simpson family Person objects.

Because we have a reordering capability, we create a model class (PersonModel) to manipulate the list of Person objects within a GroupNode. Each GroupNode, the PersonChildFactory, and all PersonNodes keep a reference to this model. Listing 9.15 shows the PersonModel class, which maintains an array list of Person objects for each GroupNode. The model also provides methods for adding, removing, and reordering objects as well as change support.

**Listing 9.15 PersonModel—Maintaining the GroupNode's List**

```
public class PersonModel {

    private final List<Person> persons;
    private final ChangeSupport cs = new ChangeSupport(this);

    public PersonModel(List<Person> persons) {
        this.persons = new ArrayList<>(persons);
    }

    public List<? extends Person> getPersons() {
        return persons;
    }
```

```
    public void add(Person p) {
        persons.add(p);
        cs.fireChange();
    }

    public void remove(Person p) {
        persons.remove(p);
        cs.fireChange();
    }

    public void reorder(int[] indexOrder) {
        Person[] reordered = new Person[persons.size()];
        for (int i = 0; i < indexOrder.length; i++) {
            int j = indexOrder[i];
            Person p = persons.get(i);
            reordered[j] = p;
        }
        persons.clear();
        persons.addAll(Arrays.asList(reordered));
        cs.fireChange();
    }

    public void addChangeListener(ChangeListener l) {
        cs.addChangeListener(l);
    }

    public void removeChangeListener(ChangeListener l) {
        cs.removeChangeListener(l);
    }
}
```

The hierarchy is built with GroupChildFactory, which creates each GroupNode. GroupNode in turn builds its children with PersonChildFactory, creating each PersonNode. Here are the responsibilities of each of these classes.

- GroupNodeChildFactory instantiates PersonModel for each GroupNode, as shown in Listing 9.16. It puts the Simpson family in the GroupNode Undecided when building the hierarchy. Otherwise, it builds an empty model.

**Listing 9.16 GroupChildFactory.java**

```
public class GroupChildFactory extends ChildFactory<PersonGroup> {

    private static final Logger logger = Logger.getLogger(
                        GroupChildFactory.class.getName());
    private final FamilyTreeManager ftm;
    private final List<Person> people = new ArrayList<>();
```

```
    GroupChildFactory() {
        ftm = Lookup.getDefault().lookup(FamilyTreeManager.class);
        if (ftm == null) {
            logger.log(Level.SEVERE, "Cannot get FamilyTreeManager object");
            LifecycleManager.getDefault().exit();
        }
        people.addAll(ftm.getAllPeople());
    }

    @Override
    protected boolean createKeys(List<PersonGroup> list) {
        list.addAll(Arrays.asList(GroupNode.PersonGroup.values()));
        return true;
    }

    @Override
    protected Node createNodeForKey(PersonGroup key) {
        // Put all people in group UNDECIDED to start
        if (key.equals(PersonGroup.UNDECIDED)) {
            return new GroupNode(key, new PersonModel(people));
        }
        return new GroupNode(key, new PersonModel(new ArrayList<>()));
    }
}
```

- GroupNode is one of Happy, Sad, or Undecided and receives a reference to its PersonModel in the constructor, as shown in Listing 9.17. The constructor passes this reference to its Children class (PersonChildFactory).

**Listing 9.17 GroupNode.java**

```
@NbBundle.Messages({
    "HINT_GroupNode=Group Node"
})
public class GroupNode extends AbstractNode {

    private static final Logger logger = Logger.getLogger(
                GroupNode.class.getName());
    private final PersonModel personModel;
    private final InstanceContent instanceContent;

    public enum PersonGroup {
        HAPPY, SAD, UNDECIDED
    }

    public GroupNode(PersonGroup group, final PersonModel personModel) {
        this(group, personModel, new InstanceContent());
    }
```

```
    private GroupNode(PersonGroup group,
                            final PersonModel personModel,InstanceContent ic) {
        super(Children.create(new PersonChildFactory(personModel), false),
                new AbstractLookup(ic));
        this.instanceContent = ic;
        this.personModel = personModel;
        this.instanceContent.add(group);
        setGroupStuff(group);
        setShortDescription(Bundle.HINT_GroupNode());
         . . .
    }

    private void setGroupStuff(PersonGroup group) {
        StringBuilder sb = new StringBuilder();
        StringBuilder iconString = new StringBuilder(
                  "com/asgteach/familytree/groupviewer/resources/");
        switch (group) {
            case HAPPY:
                sb.append("Happy");
                iconString.append("happy.png");
                break;
            case SAD:
                sb.append("Sad");
                iconString.append("sad.png");
                break;
            case UNDECIDED:
                sb.append("Undecided");
                iconString.append("undecided.png");
                break;
        }
        setName(sb.toString());
        setDisplayName(sb.toString());
        setIconBaseWithExtension(iconString.toString());
    }
}
```

- PersonChildFactory (Listing 9.18) extends `ChildFactory.Detachable<Person>`, which provides the life cycle methods `addNotify()` and `removeNotify()`. Here, PersonChildFactory adds/removes itself as a listener to the PersonModel object. PersonChildFactory receives a reference to its PersonModel in the constructor and is the "keeper" of the model, reacting to changes by invoking the `refresh()` method.

**Listing 9.18 PersonChildFactory.java**

```
public class PersonChildFactory extends ChildFactory.Detachable<Person>
        implements ChangeListener {

    private final PersonModel personModel;
```

```
    public PersonChildFactory(final PersonModel personModel) {
        this.personModel = personModel;
    }

    @Override
    protected boolean createKeys(List<Person> list) {
        list.addAll(personModel.getPersons());
        return true;
    }

    @Override
    protected Node createNodeForKey(Person key) {
        PersonNode node = new PersonNode(key, personModel);
        return node;
    }

    // Called immediately before the first call to createKeys().
    @Override
    protected void addNotify() {
        personModel.addChangeListener(this);
    }

    // Called when this child factory is no longer in use,
    // to dispose of resources, detach listeners, etc.
    @Override
    protected void removeNotify() {
        personModel.removeChangeListener(this);
    }

    @Override
    public void stateChanged(ChangeEvent e) {
        refresh(false);
    }

}
```

- Listing 9.19 shows PersonNode, which wraps the Person object. Its constructor receives the Person object and a reference to PersonModel. You'll see that PersonNode uses the PersonModel reference when it overrides the `destroy()` method for the delete-type actions Cut, Drag, and Delete (see Listing 9.23 on page 454).

**Listing 9.19 PersonNode.java**

```
@NbBundle.Messages({
    "HINT_PersonNode=Person"
})
public class PersonNode extends AbstractNode  {
    // This is the list that this PersonNode is part of!
    private final PersonModel personModel;
```

```
    public PersonNode(Person person, PersonModel personModel) {
        super(Children.LEAF, Lookups.singleton(person));
        this.personModel = personModel;
        setIconBaseWithExtension(
            "com/asgteach/familytree/groupviewer/resources/personIcon.png");
        setName(String.valueOf(person.getId()));
        setDisplayName(person.toString());
        setShortDescription(Bundle.HINT_PersonNode());
    }
      . . .
    @Override
    public String getHtmlDisplayName() {
      . . . unchanged code . . .
    }
}
```

## Reorder and Index.Support

You reorder a group in two ways. You can either select a GroupNode's **Change Order ...** context menu item (see Figure 9.23 on page 445) or you select a PersonNode's context menu Move Up or Move Down (see Figure 9.24 on page 446). Here are the steps to implement reorder with GroupNode and PersonNode.

1. In GroupNode, include ReorderAction in the `getActions()` method, as shown in Listing 9.20. This puts menu item Change Order . . . in the GroupNode's context menu.
2. Add an implementation of Index.Support to GroupNode's Lookup, overriding the `getNodes()`, `getNodeCount()`, and `reorder()` methods, as shown in Listing 9.20. This enables the Change Order . . . menu item. The `reorder()` method manipulates the model (PersonModel).

**Listing 9.20 GroupNode.java—Index.Support Implementation**

```
public class GroupNode extends AbstractNode {
              . . .

    private GroupNode(PersonGroup group, final PersonModel personModel,
                        InstanceContent ic) {
        super(Children.create(new PersonChildFactory(personModel), false),
                new AbstractLookup(ic));
              . . .
       // A support class that implements methods of Index.Support.
      // This class must be in the Node's Lookup to support the Reorder Action
       // and Move Up and Move Down in its children.
```

```
        instanceContent.add(new Index.Support() {
            @Override
            public Node[] getNodes() {
                return getChildren().getNodes(true);
            }

            @Override
            public int getNodesCount() {
                return getNodes().length;
            }

            // Reorder by permutation
            @Override
            public void reorder(int[] orderIndex) {
                personModel.reorder(orderIndex);
            }
        });
    }

    @Override
    public Action[] getActions(boolean context) {
        return new Action[]{
            ReorderAction.get(ReorderAction.class),
            PasteAction.get(PasteAction.class),};
    }
}
```

3. PersonNode includes MoveUpAction and MoveDownAction in the PersonNode's `getActions()` method, as shown in Listing 9.21. This puts menu items Move Up and Move Down in the PersonNode's context menu. These menu items are contextually enabled based on the Index.Support added to the parent GroupNode's Lookup and the PersonNode's current position in the group.

**Listing 9.21 PersonNode—Implementing MoveUp and MoveDown**

```
public class PersonNode extends AbstractNode {
    . . .

    @Override
    public Action[] getActions(boolean context) {
        return new Action[]{
                    CutAction.get(CutAction.class),
                    CopyAction.get(CopyAction.class),
                    DeleteAction.get(DeleteAction.class),
                    MoveUpAction.get(MoveUpAction.class),
                    MoveDownAction.get(MoveDownAction.class)
                };
    }
    . . .
}
```

## Implementing Drag and Drop

Drag and drop are closely related to cut, copy, and paste with shared support code. We'll look at drag and drop first, since these actions don't require menu items.

The drag and drop gesture executes the equivalent of a cut and paste without using menu items. You can select single or multiple PersonNodes. The target of a drop is a GroupNode, whose responsibility is to receive the dropped object (or objects). Figure 9.25 shows three PersonNodes being dragged to GroupNode Sad, with the target position indicated by a gray rectangle outline. The nodes are dropped into their new position and removed from their original position when the user releases the mouse.

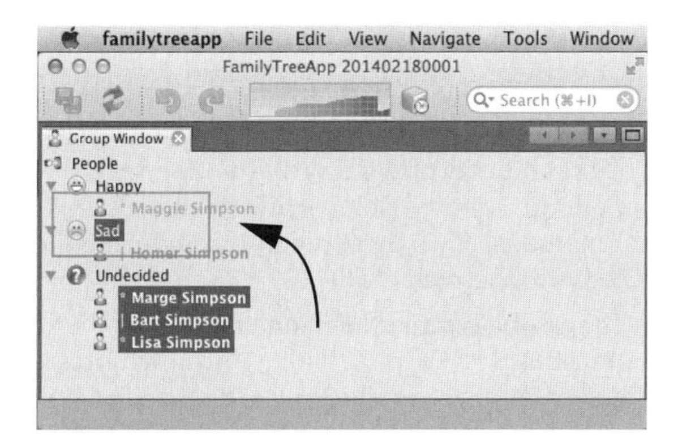


Figure 9.25 Drag and drop one or more PersonNodes to a GroupNode

Drag and drop requires building a Transferable object that contains the transferred data, as well as meta information associated with the Transferable (such as whether the transfer is a cut or copy). The Transferable data must be serializable. Transferable support is provided by Swing/AWT (many Swing components support drag and drop). The NetBeans Platform provides an extended Transferable object, called ExTransferable, that works with nodes.

Data integrity is maintained by setting the DataFlavor on a Transferable. DataFlavor encapsulates meta information about the data being transferred. This lets the drop target accept a Transferable of supported flavors (and reject unsupported flavors) and properly extract the data. Swing supports standard DataFlavors such as image (imageFlavor), String (stringFlavor), and a list of java.io.File objects (javaFileList). For this example, we create a new DataFlavor for Person objects.

Here are the steps to implement drag and drop in the Group window. Note that you don't configure any actions in a node's `getActions()` method for drag and drop.

1. Create a new DataFlavor for Person (PersonFlavor), as shown in Listing 9.22. Add this class to the FamilyTreeModel module public package so we can access it from multiple modules (which we access in a later example—see "Inter-Window Drag and Drop" on page 458).

**Listing 9.22 PersonFlavor.java**

```
public class PersonFlavor extends DataFlavor {

    public static final DataFlavor PERSON_FLAVOR = new PersonFlavor();

    public PersonFlavor() {
        super(Person.class, "Person");
    }
}
```

2. In PersonNode, override the `clipboardCut()` method, which builds an ExTransferable with PersonFlavor and adds it to the application clipboard. Put an ExTransferable.Single in the ExTransferable object and override the `getData()` method to return the Person object from this node. You must also override the node's `canDestroy()`, `canCut()`, and `destroy()` methods, since these are invoked during the drag and drop gesture. Listing 9.23 shows these methods.

   Note that the `destroy()` method removes the wrapped Person object from the underlying model (PersonModel in Listing 9.15 on page 446), which then fires a state change event processed by PersonChildFactory (Listing 9.18 on page 449).

**Listing 9.23 PersonNode—Implementing Drag and Drop**

```
public class PersonNode extends AbstractNode  {
  . . .
    @Override
    public Transferable clipboardCut() throws IOException {
        ExTransferable extrans = ExTransferable.create(super.clipboardCut());
        extrans.put(new ExTransferable.Single(PersonFlavor.PERSON_FLAVOR) {
            @Override
            protected Person getData() {
                return getLookup().lookup(Person.class);
            }
        });
        return extrans;
    }

    @Override
    public boolean canCut() {
        return true;                        // OK to cut this node
    }
```

```
    @Override
    public boolean canDestroy() {
        return true;                        // OK to destroy this node
    }

    @Override
    public void destroy() throws IOException {
        personModel.remove(getLookup().lookup(Person.class));
    }
}
```

3. In GroupNode, override the `getDropType()` method, as shown in Listing 9.24. This method receives the Transferable from either a cut, copy, or drag and creates a PasteType object if the Transferable is supported. The Person object is extracted from the Transferable and added to this group's model (`personModel`). If the transfer is either a cut or a drag and drop, the original node is destroyed.

   Note that here, the Person object is added to the GroupNode's model. Similar to the `destroy()` method, PersonModel fires a state change event processed by PersonChildFactory, and the ensuing `refresh()` builds the new PersonNode for the transferred Person object.

**Listing 9.24 GroupNode—Implementing Drag and Drop**

```
public class GroupNode extends AbstractNode {
    . . .
    // getDropType is required to support drop targets for drag and drop
    // as well as paste for cut/copy actions
    @Override
    public PasteType getDropType(Transferable t, int action, int index) {
        if (t.isDataFlavorSupported(PersonFlavor.PERSON_FLAVOR)) {
            return new PasteType() {
                @Override
                public Transferable paste() throws IOException {
                    try {
                        personModel.add((Person) t.getTransferData(
                              PersonFlavor.PERSON_FLAVOR));
                        final Node node = NodeTransfer.node(t,
                        NodeTransfer.DND_MOVE + NodeTransfer.CLIPBOARD_CUT);
                        // only destroy the original node for DND move or cut
                        if (node != null) {
                            node.destroy();
                        }
                    } catch (UnsupportedFlavorException ex) {
                        logger.log(Level.WARNING, null, ex);
                    }
                    return null;
                }
```

```
            };
        }
            return null;
        }
}
```

## Implementing Cut, Copy, Paste, Delete

PersonNode supports Cut, Copy, and Delete context menu items (see Figure 9.24 on page 446). In addition, Figure 9.26 shows the top-level Edit menu. PersonNode supports menu items Cut, Copy, and Delete and GroupNode supports Paste (after a PersonNode Cut or Copy action). (Figure 9.23 on page 445 shows the GroupNode Paste context menu item.)

Figure 9.26 Edit menu actions Cut, Copy, Paste, Delete and conditionally enabled

Follow these steps to implement these Edit menu actions.

1. Put the Copy, Cut, Paste, and Delete actions in the TopComponent's ActionMap, as shown in Listing 9.25. This enables these actions in the Edit menu (if the selected node supports the actions).

**Listing 9.25 GroupTopComponent—Implementing Edit Menu Actions**

```
public final class GroupTopComponent extends TopComponent
                              implements ExplorerManager.Provider {
    private final ExplorerManager em = new ExplorerManager();

    public GroupTopComponent() {
        initComponents();
        setName(Bundle.CTL_GroupTopComponent());
        setToolTipText(Bundle.HINT_GroupTopComponent());
         . . .
```

```
        ActionMap map = getActionMap();
        map.put(DefaultEditorKit.copyAction, ExplorerUtils.actionCopy(em));
        map.put(DefaultEditorKit.cutAction, ExplorerUtils.actionCut(em));
        map.put(DefaultEditorKit.pasteAction, ExplorerUtils.actionPaste(em));
        map.put("delete", ExplorerUtils.actionDelete(em, true));
        associateLookup(ExplorerUtils.createLookup(em, map));
    }
     . . .
}
```

2. In PersonNode, include CutAction, CopyAction, and DeleteAction in the `getActions()` method, as shown in Listing 9.21 on page 452. This puts Cut, Copy, and Delete in the node's context menu.
3. For Copy, override the `canCopy()` and `clipboardCopy()` methods, as shown in Listing 9.26. The `clipboardCopy()` method builds the ExTransferable that supports Copy with `PersonFlavor.PERSON_FLAVOR` data flavor. For Cut and Delete, the `canCut()`, `clipboardCut()`, `canDestroy()`, and `destroy()` methods were shown previously in Listing 9.23 on page 454.

**Listing 9.26 PersonNode—Implementing Edit Menu Actions**

```
public class PersonNode extends AbstractNode  {
   . . .

    @Override
    public Transferable clipboardCopy() throws IOException {
        ExTransferable extrans = ExTransferable.create(super.clipboardCopy());
        extrans.put(new ExTransferable.Single(PersonFlavor.PERSON_FLAVOR) {
            @Override
            protected Person getData() {
                return getLookup().lookup(Person.class);
            }
        });
        return extrans;
    }

    @Override
    public boolean canCopy() {
        return true;                // OK to copy this node
    }
}
```

4. In GroupNode, include PasteAction in the node's context menu and override the `createPasteTypes()` method, as shown in Listing 9.27. Note that `createPasteTypes()` invokes the `getDropType()` method, which is also used with drag and drop (see Listing 9.24 on page 455).

**Listing 9.27 GroupNode—Implementing Paste**

```
public class GroupNode extends AbstractNode {
   . . .
   @Override
   public Action[] getActions(boolean context) {
       return new Action[]{
           ReorderAction.get(ReorderAction.class),
           PasteAction.get(PasteAction.class),};
   }

   // This is required for cut and copy actions
   // It is not required for Drag and Drop
   @Override
   protected void createPasteTypes(Transferable t, List<PasteType> s) {
       super.createPasteTypes(t, s);
       PasteType p = getDropType(t, 0, 0);
       if (p != null) {
           s.add(p);
       }
   }
}
```

## 9.4 Inter-Window Drag and Drop

The Group window in the previous section illustrates drag and drop that occurs within the same window. You can also drag and drop objects between different windows, since the Transferable object contains all of the necessary information a receiving node needs to accept the transferred object.

### Trash Window Node Actions

Let's build on the previous section and implement a drag and drop Delete operation where the user drags a node to a special Trash window for later removal. The user can retrieve nodes from this Trash container, returning them to the Group window, or empty the Trash for their final removal. Let's also remove the previously implemented Delete action from the PersonNode context menu. We'll implement this "fancy delete" feature by creating a new module called TrashCan.

Figure 9.27 shows the Trash window with an empty trash icon, a disabled Empty Trash menu item, and no nodes under the Trash node.

In contrast, Figure 9.28 shows two nodes in the Trash window, the trash icon is "full," and the Empty Trash menu item is active.

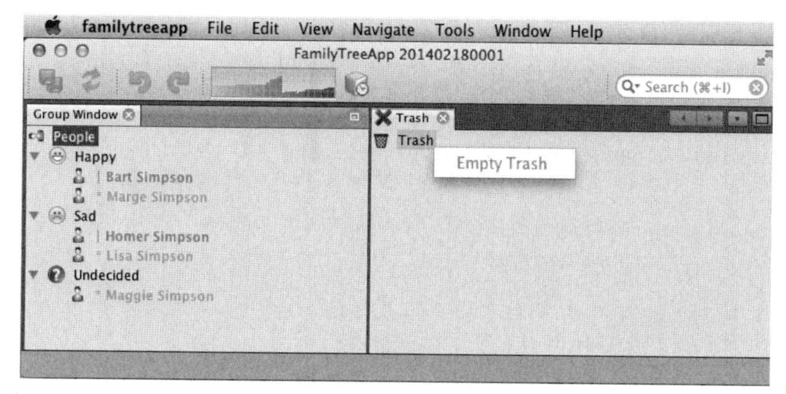


Figure 9.27 Trash is empty and Empty Trash menu item is disabled

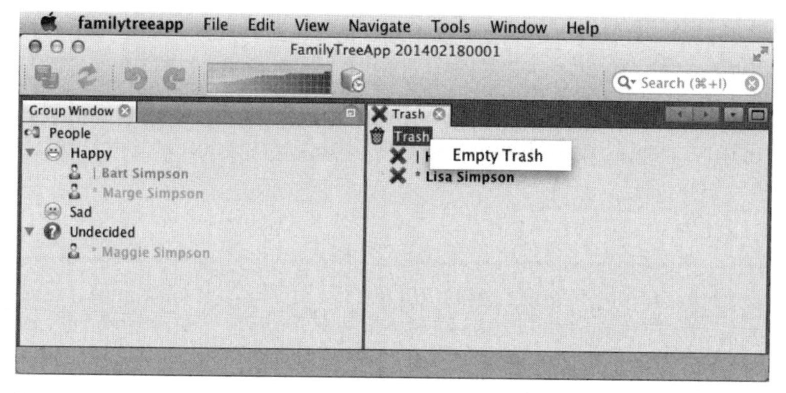


Figure 9.28 Trash is not empty and Empty Trash menu item is active

## Basic Node Hierarchy

Let's start with the basic classes for the root node (TrashNode), its Children class (PersonNodeContainer), and the node that wraps a Person object (RemovePersonNode). The Trash window root node is implemented by TrashNode, as shown in Listing 9.28. It uses InstanceContent so that capabilities can be added and removed from its Lookup.

**Listing 9.28 TrashNode.java**

```
public class TrashNode extends AbstractNode {

    private final InstanceContent instanceContent;
    private static final Logger logger = Logger.getLogger(
                                     TrashNode.class.getName());

    public TrashNode(String title) {
        this(title, new InstanceContent());
    }

    private TrashNode(String title, InstanceContent ic) {
        super(new PersonNodeContainer(), new AbstractLookup(ic));
        instanceContent = ic;
        setDisplayName(title);
        setIconBaseWithExtension(
         "com/asgteach/familytree/trashcan/resources/EmptyTrashicon.png");
    }
}
```

TrashNode's children are defined by PersonNodeContainer, which uses Index.ArrayChildren for its structure, as shown in Listing 9.29. Method `initCollection()` initializes an empty collection.

**Children**

*Note that since we aren't providing a reorder capability for TrashNode, we don't need a separate model to hold the children. Index.ArrayChildren supplies a simple ArrayList that contains the child nodes.*

**Listing 9.29 PersonNodeContainer**

```
public class PersonNodeContainer extends Index.ArrayChildren {
    private final List<Node> personList = new ArrayList<Node>();

    @Override
    protected List<Node> initCollection() {
        return personList;
    }
}
```

Each Person object is wrapped in a RemovePersonNode, as shown in Listing 9.30. RemovePersonNode overrides `getHtmlDisplayName()` to include the Person's gender. The node's icon is a delete symbol to emphasize its precarious condition "in the Trash" (see Figure 9.28 on page 459).

**Listing 9.30 RemovePersonNode.java**

```
@NbBundle.Messages({
    "HINT_RemoveNode=Person"
})
public class RemovePersonNode extends AbstractNode  {

    public RemovePersonNode(Person person) {
        super(Children.LEAF, Lookups.singleton(person));
        setIconBaseWithExtension(
                "com/asgteach/familytree/trashcan/resources/delete.png");
        setName(String.valueOf(person.getId()));
        setDisplayName(person.toString());
        setShortDescription(Bundle.HINT_RemoveNode());
    }

    @Override
    public String getHtmlDisplayName() {
        Person person = getLookup().lookup(Person.class);
        StringBuilder sb = new StringBuilder();
        if (person == null) {
            return null;
        }
        sb.append("<b>");
        switch (person.getGender()) {
            case MALE:
                sb.append("| ");
                break;
            case FEMALE:
                sb.append("* ");
                break;
            case UNKNOWN:
                sb.append("? ");
                break;
        }
        sb.append(person.toString()).append("</b>");
        return sb.toString();
    }
}
```

The TrashTopComponent uses familiar constructor code to initialize the node hierarchy and set the Explorer Manager's context root, as shown in Listing 9.31.

**Listing 9.31 TrashTopComponent.java**

```
@ConvertAsProperties(
        dtd = "-//com.asgteach.familytree.trashcan//Trash//EN",
        autostore = false
)
```

```
@TopComponent.Description(
        preferredID = "TrashTopComponent",
        iconBase = "com/asgteach/familytree/trashcan/resources/delete.png",
        persistenceType = TopComponent.PERSISTENCE_ALWAYS
)
@TopComponent.Registration(mode = "editor", openAtStartup = true)
@ActionID(category = "Window",
            id = "com.asgteach.familytree.trashcan.TrashTopComponent")
@ActionReference(path = "Menu/Window" /*, position = 333 */)
@TopComponent.OpenActionRegistration(
        displayName = "#CTL_TrashAction",
        preferredID = "TrashTopComponent"
)
@Messages({
    "CTL_TrashAction=Trash",
    "CTL_TrashTopComponent=Trash",
    "HINT_TrashTopComponent=This is a Trash window",
    "CTL_TrashTitle=Trash"
})
public final class TrashTopComponent extends TopComponent implements
                                    ExplorerManager.Provider {
    private final ExplorerManager em = new ExplorerManager();

    public TrashTopComponent() {
        initComponents();
        setName(Bundle.CTL_TrashTopComponent());
        setToolTipText(Bundle.HINT_TrashTopComponent());
        BeanTreeView view = new BeanTreeView();
        add(view, BorderLayout.CENTER);
        em.setRootContext(new TrashNode(Bundle.CTL_TrashTitle()));
        associateLookup(ExplorerUtils.createLookup(em, getActionMap()));
    }

    @Override
    public ExplorerManager getExplorerManager() {
        return em;
    }
. . .
}
```

The new "Fancy Delete" drag and drop replaces the Group window's Delete. Fortunately, only minor changes are required to the GroupViewer module to remove the original Delete capability.

1. Remove "delete" from the GroupTopComponent's ActionMap (see Listing 9.25 on page 456 and remove `ExplorerUtils.actionDelete()` from the map).
2. Remove DeleteAction from PersonNode's `getActions()` method (see Listing 9.21 on page 452).

The PersonNode and GroupNode in the GroupViewer module already provide the needed drag behavior, as well as the receiving drop behavior to work with the Trash window.

## Implementing Drag and Drop Delete

To implement the Trash window drag and drop Delete, you provide the same drag and drop support methods presented in the previous section. TrashNode is the drop target for the drag gesture originating with the Group window, and RemovePersonNode supports the returning drag gesture. Here are the general tasks.

- In TrashNode, override `getDropType()` in TrashNode to receive a Transferable.
- In RemovePersonNode, override methods `clipboardCut()`, `canCut()`, `canDestroy()`, and `destroy()` to support the drag gesture back to the Group window.
- Create a context-aware EmptyTrash action.

The EmptyTrash action is conditionally enabled when at least one RemovePersonNode exists in the node hierarchy. The action is disabled when the node hierarchy is empty. The TrashNode icon also changes depending on whether or not the EmptyTrash action is enabled.

Importantly, you'll see how to dynamically enable and disable actions by adding and removing capabilities to a node's Lookup. This is a central pattern with the NetBeans Platform. You will see this pattern again in the next chapter with the FamilyTreeApp Save and Save All actions (see "Implementing Update" on page 488).

Let's begin with the EmptyCapability interface and the EmptyTrash action.

### Create Capability and Context-Aware Action

Add interface EmptyCapability interface and its corresponding context-aware action, EmptyTrashAction to module TrashCan. Listing 9.32 shows the EmptyCapability interface.

**Listing 9.32 EmptyCapability.java**

```
public interface EmptyCapability {

    public void emptyTrash();

}
```

Listing 9.33 shows the EmptyTrashAction, created with the New Action wizard. You specify a conditionally enabled action type and **EmptyCapability** for the Cookie Class (the context type).

**Listing 9.33 EmptyTrashAction.java**

```
@ActionID(
        category = "TrashNode",
        id = "com.asgteach.familytree.trashcan.EmptyTrashAction"
)
@ActionRegistration(
        displayName = "#CTL_EmptyTrashAction"
)
@Messages("CTL_EmptyTrashAction=Empty Trash")
public final class EmptyTrashAction implements ActionListener {

    private final EmptyCapability context;

    public EmptyTrashAction(EmptyCapability context) {
        this.context = context;
    }

    @Override
    public void actionPerformed(ActionEvent ev) {
        context.emptyTrash();
    }
}
```

## Add Support for the Action and Implement Its Capability

Listing 9.34 shows the implementation code to support the EmptyTrashAction that is contextually enabled. First, we override the `getActions()` method to include the EmptyTrashAction in the TrashNode context menu.

The `enableEmptyAction()` method adds an EmptyCapability implementation to the Lookup and changes the node's icon. The `clearEmptyAction()` method removes the EmptyCapability object from the Lookup and changes the node's icon back to the original "empty trash." With these two methods, we dynamically enable and disable the EmptyTrashAction in TrashNode.

EmptyCapability's `emptyTrash()` method destroys the node's children. The `clearEmptyAction()` method is invoked from the `nodeDestroyed()` event handler shown in Listing 9.35 when the children node count is zero.

**Listing 9.34 TrashNode.java—EmptyAction Support**

```
public class TrashNode extends AbstractNode implements NodeListener {
    . . .
    @SuppressWarnings("unchecked")
    @Override
    public Action[] getActions(boolean context) {
        List<Action> actions = new ArrayList<>();
        actions.addAll(Utilities.actionsForPath("Actions/TrashNode"));
        return actions.toArray(new Action[actions.size()]);
    }

    private void enableEmptyAction() {
        EmptyCapability ec = getLookup().lookup(EmptyCapability.class);
        if (ec == null) {
            setIconBaseWithExtension(
            "com/asgteach/familytree/trashcan/resources/FullTrashicon.png");
            instanceContent.add(new EmptyCapability() {

                @Override
                public void emptyTrash() {
                    for (Node node : getChildren().getNodes()) {
                        try {
                            node.destroy();
                        } catch (IOException ex) {
                            logger.log(Level.WARNING, null, ex);
                        }
                    }
                }
            });
        }
    }

    // invoked from the NodeListener nodeDestroyed() method
    private void clearEmptyAction() {
        EmptyCapability ec = getLookup().lookup(EmptyCapability.class);
        if (ec != null) {
            instanceContent.remove(ec);
            setIconBaseWithExtension(
            "com/asgteach/familytree/trashcan/resources/EmptyTrashicon.png");
        }
    }
    . . .
}
```

## Add Drop Support to the Root Node

Listing 9.35 shows the all-important `getDropType()` method. This method returns a PasteType and overrides the `paste()` method, which performs several steps. First, the paste() method extracts the transferred node and disallows drag gestures from within the same hierarchy. Next, the method extracts the Person object, creates a RemovePersonNode, adds the TrashNode as a NodeListener, and adds the new node to the TrashNode hierarchy. Last, the method invokes the enableEmptyAction() method (see Listing 9.34) and deletes the transferred node from its original hierarchy.

TrashNode implements NodeListener, which requires overriding five methods. We're interested only in events that destroy nodes, handled by the nodeDestroyed() method. This method removes TrashNode as a listener and disables the EmptyTrashAction if the children node count is now zero.

**Listing 9.35 TrashNode.java—Handling Drop**

```
public class TrashNode extends AbstractNode implements NodeListener {
  . . .
    @Override
    public PasteType getDropType(Transferable t, int action, int index) {

        if (t.isDataFlavorSupported(PersonFlavor.PERSON_FLAVOR)) {
            return new PasteType() {
                @Override
                public Transferable paste() throws IOException {
                    final Node node = NodeTransfer.node(
                     t, NodeTransfer.DND_MOVE + NodeTransfer.CLIPBOARD_CUT);
                    if (node != null && !TrashNode.this.equals(
                              node.getParentNode())) {
                        try {
                            final Person person = ((Person) t.getTransferData(
                              PersonFlavor.PERSON_FLAVOR));
                            Node newNode = new RemovePersonNode(person);
                            newNode.addNodeListener(TrashNode.this);
                            getChildren().add(new Node[]{newNode});
                            // we have at least one RemovePersonNode
                            enableEmptyAction();
                            if ((action & DnDConstants.ACTION_MOVE) != 0) {
                                node.destroy();
                            }
                        } catch (UnsupportedFlavorException ex) {
                            logger.log(Level.WARNING, null, ex);
                        }
                    }
                    return null;
                }
            };
        }
        return null;
    }

    @Override
    public void childrenAdded(NodeMemberEvent nme) {}
```

```
    @Override
    public void childrenRemoved(NodeMemberEvent nme) {}

    @Override
    public void childrenReordered(NodeReorderEvent nre) {}

    @Override
    public void nodeDestroyed(NodeEvent ne) {
        ne.getNode().removeNodeListener(this);
        if (getChildren().getNodesCount() == 0) {
            clearEmptyAction();
        }
    }

    @Override
    public void propertyChange(PropertyChangeEvent evt) {}
}
```

## Add Drag Support to Child Nodes

To provide drag support back to the Group window, override the `canCut()`, `canDestroy()`, `destroy()`, and `clipboardCut()` methods in RemovePersonNode, as shown in Listing 9.36. The `clipboardCut()` method is the same code we used for PersonNode (see Listing 9.23 on page 454). The `destroy()` method fires a node destroyed event, which the TrashNode listens for.

**Listing 9.36 RemovePersonNode.java—Handling Drag**

```
public class RemovePersonNode extends AbstractNode  {
   . . .
    @Override
    public boolean canCut() {
        return true;
    }

    @Override
    public boolean canDestroy() {
        return true;
    }

    @Override
    public void destroy() throws IOException {
        getParentNode().getChildren().remove(new Node[] { this } );
        fireNodeDestroyed();
    }

    @Override
    public Transferable clipboardCut() throws IOException {
        ExTransferable extrans = ExTransferable.create(super.clipboardCut());
```

```
        extrans.put(new ExTransferable.Single(PersonFlavor.PERSON_FLAVOR) {
            @Override
            protected Person getData() {
                return getLookup().lookup(Person.class);
            }
        });
        return extrans;
    }
}
```

## 9.5 Key Point Summary

This chapter shows you how to hook into the NetBeans Platform Action framework. You learn how to create actions that are always enabled and actions that depend on the state of your application. We introduce the concept of capabilities and how to dynamically add and remove them to create loosely-coupled behaviors. Finally, we show you how to use the standard NetBeans Platform Edit actions to manipulate nodes in an Explorer View with Cut, Copy, Paste, Move Up, Move Down, Delete, and Drag and Drop. Here are the key points in this chapter.

- The NetBeans Platform New Action wizard lets you register actions with annotations.
- These annotations configure the top-level Menu and Toolbar as well as configure the action's display name, icon, shortcut key sequence, and action class.
- An action that can be selected in any state of the application is an always-enabled action. These actions do not depend on user-selected objects or the availability of objects, data, or files.
- NetBeans Platform actions implement ActionListener and override the `actionPerformed()` method.
- A TopComponent's ActionMap associates a key with a registered callback action.
- Callback actions perform different functions depending on which component has focus. Callback actions with a fallback implementation are always enabled. The fallback implementation is invoked if the focused TopComponent does not provide its own implementation in its ActionMap.
- Callback actions without a fallback implementation are only enabled when the TopComponent with focus has an implementation in its ActionMap.
- Context-aware actions are enabled when a particular context (Cookie class) becomes available through the Global Selection Lookup.

- Specify Conditionally Enabled in the New Action wizard to create context-aware actions.
- A capability is the implementation of an action context that can be dynamically added and removed from an object's Lookup. Capabilities encourage loose coupling, since an unrelated entity can look up a capability and invoke it without knowing about its implementation.
- The NetBeans Platform uses the capability pattern to implement the Save and Save All actions.
- You configure context-aware actions for either single or multiple node selection.
- Action categories let you classify actions and include them in a node's context menu.
- To add an action to a node's context menu, override the `getActions()` method and include the action's path.
- To enable a context-aware action for a node, include an implementation of the action's context in the node's Lookup.
- Override the `getPreferredAction()` method to set a node's preferred action. The action is invoked with a double click on the node.
- Implement node reordering by adding an implementation of Index.Support in the node's Lookup. Generally, you provide a model to maintain child node ordering. Include ReorderAction in the node's `getActions()` method.
- Include MoveUpAction and MoveDownAction in the context menu of child nodes when the parent node supports reordering.
- Implement drag and drop by configuring an ExTransferable object with a supported DataFlavor. Override the `getDropType()` method in the target node and the `clipboardCut()`, `canCut()`, `canDestroy()`, and `destroy()` methods in the draggable.
- Implement Cut, Copy, and Paste with `clipboardCut()` and `clipboardCopy()` in the source node and `createPasteTypes()` and `getDropType()` in the target node.
- Drag and Drop actions (as well as Cut/Copy and Paste) apply between windows since the ExTransferable object contains all the information the receiving node needs to accept or reject the transferred object.

# 10

# Building a CRUD Application

The FamilyTreeApp application has evolved considerably up to this point. Chapter 2 presents a loosely-coupled Swing application that lets you update Person objects. Chapter 5 shows you how to turn this example program into a modularized NetBeans Platform application. Chapter 7 improves the application with nodes and Explorer Views. And Chapter 9 introduces the Action framework and capabilities.

With these pieces in place, we can now turn our FamilyTreeApp application into a full CRUD-based system. For this enhancement, we'll use capabilities and the Action framework for the implementation and provide a back-end database for persistence. Finally, we make sure the application remains responsive by accessing the database asynchronously.

## What You Will Learn

- Apply capabilities and the Action framework to create context-aware actions.
- Use the NetBeans Platform DeleteAction and NewAction for deletes and object creation.
- Build context menus for application nodes.
- Integrate the Save and Save All menu items and Save All toolbar icon.
- Leverage `@ServiceProvider` to provide an alternate service implementation.
- Provide persistence with DerbyClient (JavaDB database) and EclipseLink (JPA).

- Use the Nodes API to build a node hierarchy asynchronously.
- Use SwingWorker to implement long-running tasks.

## 10.1 Create-Read-Update-Delete Application

Now that we've discussed the types of actions available with the NetBeans Platform Action framework in Chapter 9, we can show you how to create a CRUD-type application. CRUD is the well-known acronym for Create-Read-Update-Delete for database-type applications. Although the FamilyTreeApp is not a database application yet (we just store Person objects in a HashMap), the loosely-coupled design approach provided by the NetBeans Platform lets us easily migrate to a database implementation.

We'll use capabilities to implement the functions of a CRUD-based application, using the NetBeans Platform provided context where appropriate. We begin with a version of the FamilyTreeApp that includes a Person Viewer window (implemented by module PersonViewer). This window uses Explorer Views and nodes to display a hierarchy of the Person objects supplied by the FamilyTreeManager service provider.

The example application also includes the PersonEditor module you've seen before. However, we modify this module to remove the Update button. In its place, we use the NetBeans Platform Openable and AbstractSavable capabilities for editing. When a user opens a Person in a PersonEditor, the Person object receives a dedicated PersonEditor window. Thus, the user can have more than one Person open concurrently.

Figure 10.1 shows the old application and the starting point for our CRUD development. Figure 10.2 shows what the fully CRUD-based version looks like.

Before we begin, let's point out a few features in this new version (Figure 10.2). First, you'll see that we have three PersonEditor windows opened and the editor's tab displays the Person's name and icon. The Update button is gone from the editor window. Instead, when a user edits a Person, the toolbar's Save All icon becomes enabled as well as the Save and Save All menu items (as shown in Figure 10.2). These UI actions save changes to the underlying data store.

An Open icon appears on the toolbar, in the PersonNode's context menu, and under the File menu. Open is also the PersonNode's preferred action, so a double-click opens the selected Person in an editor window or gives the editor window focus when it's already open.

The root node (labeled People) has two context menu items: Refresh and Add New Person. Refresh provides the Read function in our CRUD application, and Add New

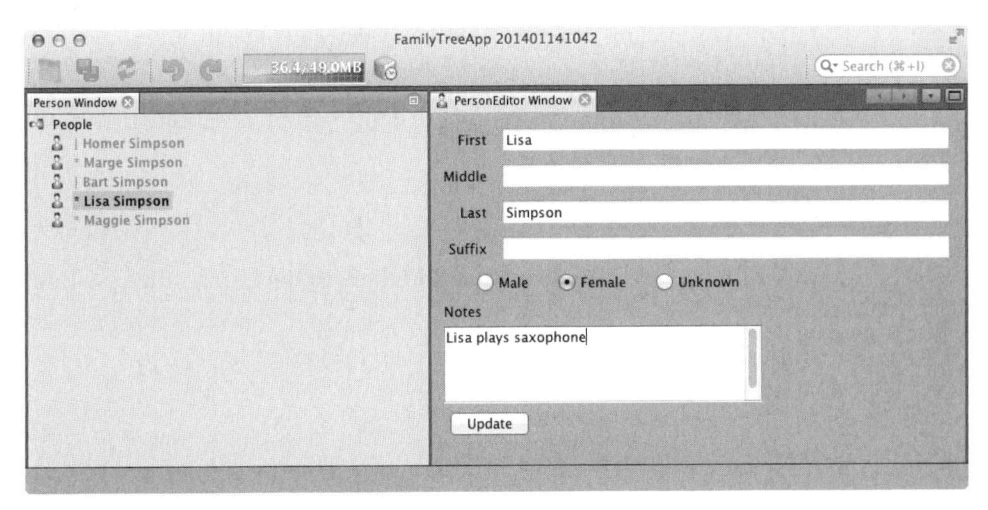


Figure 10.1 Old version of FamilyTreeApp BEFORE CRUD-functionality added

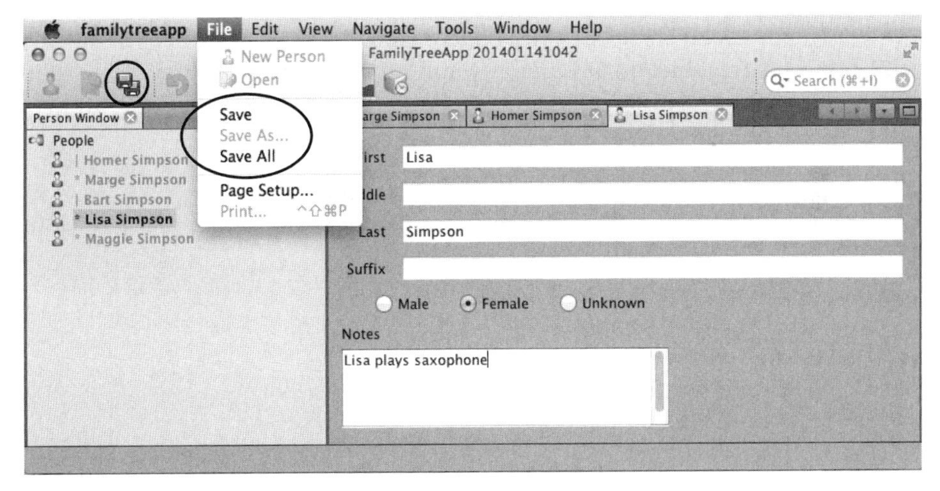


Figure 10.2 FamilyTreeApp AFTER CRUD-functionality added

Person (also available in the toolbar and under the File menu) provides the Create function.

A PersonNode has Open and Delete context menu items. Delete is enabled for both single and multiple node selection, but Open applies to single node selection only. In addition, the NetBeans Platform standard Delete menu item (under top-level Edit menu) is enabled when one or more PersonNodes are selected. Open (along with Save and Save All) provide the Update function in our CRUD application, and Delete provides the Delete function.

We'll show each CRUD implementation in detail. Let's begin by describing the capabilities that we need.

## Defining Capabilities

We define four capabilities (Java interfaces) and add them to the Capabilities module's public package, as follows.

- RefreshCapability—performs a read
- RemovablePersonCapability—performs a delete
- CreatablePersonCapability—performs a create
- SavablePersonCapability—performs an update

Listing 10.1 shows these interfaces (stored in separate class files in module Capabilities). They are implemented and used within the appropriate context, either in PersonNode (RemovablePersonCapability and SavablePersonCapability), in a PersonCapability object (CreatablePersonCapabilty and RefreshCapability), or in the RootNode (also RefreshCapability). The interfaces throw IOExceptions in anticipation of migrating to a database implementation.

**Listing 10.1 FamilyTreeApp Capabilities Defined**

```
public interface RefreshCapability {
    public void refresh() throws IOException;
}

public interface RemovablePersonCapability {
    public void remove(Person person) throws IOException;
}

public interface CreatablePersonCapability {
    public void create(Person person) throws IOException;
}

public interface SavablePersonCapability {
    public void save(Person person) throws IOException;
}
```

There are two NetBeans Platform defined capabilities that we also need.

- Openable—opens a Person in a PersonEditor

- AbstractSavable—enables the NetBeans Platform Save and Save All UI elements

## Implementing Read

RefreshCapability implements Read in our CRUD application. First, the RootNode context menu uses a context-aware Refresh action, which rebuilds the Person Viewer window's node hierarchy. Figure 10.3 shows the RefreshAction in the context menu of the root node.

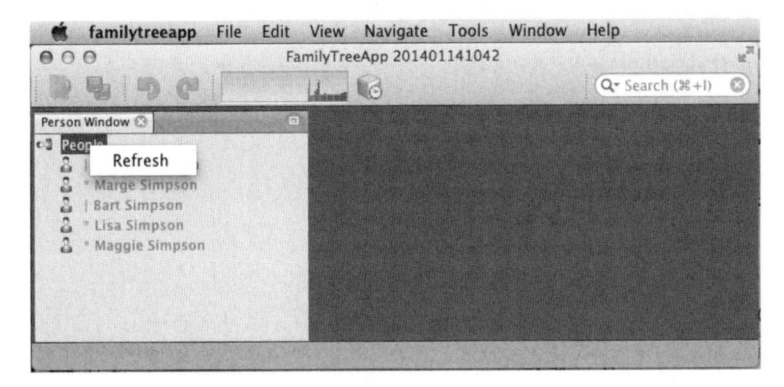


Figure 10.3 RootNode Refresh action rebuilds the node hierarchy

Second, the PersonChildFactory class uses the RefreshCapability to read Person objects from the FamilyTreeManager. We'll show you both of these "refresh" capabilities, starting with the root node RefreshAction.

### Create a Context-Aware Action

In module FamilyTreeActions, use the New Action wizard to create a conditionally enabled action called RefreshAction and use RefreshCapability for the Cookie Class. Put the action in category RootNode and do not select any Toolbar or Menu UI registrations. Make its display name "Refresh." (Optionally, to register this action with an icon on the toolbar or a menu item in the top-level menu, provide additional annotations in the RefreshAction class, as described in "Create a Context-Aware Action" on page 432.)

After NetBeans creates class RefreshAction.java, implement the `actionPerformed()` method to use the RefreshCapability, as shown in Listing 10.2.

**Listing 10.2 RefreshAction.java**

```
@ActionID(
    category = "RootNode",
    id = "com.asgteach.familytree.actions.RefreshAction"
)
@ActionRegistration(
    displayName = "#CTL_RefreshAction"
)
@Messages("CTL_RefreshAction=Refresh")
public final class RefreshAction implements ActionListener
{
    private final RefreshCapability context;

    public RefreshAction(RefreshCapability context) {
        this.context = context;
    }

    @Override
    public void actionPerformed(ActionEvent e) {
        try {
            context.refresh();
        } catch (IOException ex) {
            Exceptions.printStackTrace(ex);
        }
    }
}
```

### Implement the Capability

Implement the RefreshCapability in RootNode and put RefreshAction (included with path `"Actions/RootNode"`) in the `getActions()` method. Note that we use InstanceContent to add objects to the node's Lookup, as described in Chapter 9 (see "Implement CalendarCapability in PersonNode" on page 436). Listing 10.3 shows the changes to RootNode.

By adding an implementation of RefreshCapability to the node's Lookup, we enable the RefreshAction in the node's context menu. The call to `refresh()` happens through the RefreshAction's `actionPerformed()` method (Listing 10.2).

**Listing 10.3 RootNode.java**

```
@Messages({
    "HINT_RootNode=Show all people",
    "LBL_RootNode=People"
})
```

```
public class RootNode extends AbstractNode {

    private final InstanceContent instanceContent;
    public RootNode() {
        this(new InstanceContent());
    }

    private RootNode(InstanceContent ic) {
        super(Children.create(new PersonChildFactory(), false),
                  new AbstractLookup(ic));
        instanceContent = ic;
        setIconBaseWithExtension(
            "com/asgteach/familytree/personviewer/resources/personIcon.png");
        setDisplayName(Bundle.LBL_RootNode());
        setShortDescription(Bundle.HINT_RootNode());
        instanceContent.add(new RefreshCapability(){

            @Override
            public void refresh() throws IOException {
                setChildren(Children.create(new PersonChildFactory(), false));
            }
        });
    }

    @SuppressWarnings("unchecked")
    @Override
    public Action[] getActions(boolean context) {
        List<Action> actions = new ArrayList<>(Arrays.asList(
                    super.getActions(context)));
        actions.addAll(Utilities.actionsForPath("Actions/RootNode"));
        return actions.toArray(new Action[actions.size()]);
    }
}
```

**Using WeakListeners**

*Since Refresh rebuilds the node hierarchy each time, PersonChildFactory and PersonNode should use WeakListeners. This ensures that replaced node and ChildFactory objects are properly garbage collected. (We discuss WeakListeners in "Create ChildFactory for Person" on page 300.)*

## Using Refresh in the ChildFactory

Listing 10.4 shows PersonCapability.java, an object with its own Lookup. We store various capabilities in PersonCapability's Lookup that interact with the FamilyTreeManager routines. Capabilities help centralize implementations, yet they can also be customized. Here, we implement RefreshCapability. Note that RefreshCapability does not correspond to an action, but we invoke the capability directly to build children nodes (see the `createKeys()` method in Listing 10.5 on page 479).

PersonCapability includes property `personList`, providing access to the list of Person objects read from the FamilyTreeManager.

**Listing 10.4 PersonCapability.java**

```
public final class PersonCapability implements Lookup.Provider {

    private final Lookup lookup;
    private final InstanceContent instanceContent = new InstanceContent();
    private static final Logger logger = Logger.getLogger(
            PersonCapability.class.getName());
    private final List<Person> personList = new ArrayList<>();
    private FamilyTreeManager ftm = null;

    public PersonCapability() {
        lookup = new AbstractLookup(instanceContent);
        ftm = Lookup.getDefault().lookup(FamilyTreeManager.class);
        if (ftm == null) {
            logger.log(Level.SEVERE, "Cannot get FamilyTreeManager object");
            LifecycleManager.getDefault().exit();
        }
        instanceContent.add(new RefreshCapability() {

            @Override
            public void refresh() throws IOException {
                if (ftm != null) {
                    personList.clear();
                    personList.addAll(ftm.getAllPeople());
                } else {
                    logger.log(Level.SEVERE, "Cannot get FamilyTreeManager");
                }
            }
        });
      . . . other capabilities can be added . . .
    }

    public List<Person> getPersonList() {
        return personList;
    }

    @Override
    public Lookup getLookup() {
        return lookup;
    }

}
```

We modify PersonChildFactory to instantiate PersonCapability, look up the Refresh-Capability, and use this capability in its `createKeys()` method, as shown in Listing 10.5. Also note that PersonChildFactory has a property change listener. This listener calls its own `refresh()` method to rebuild child nodes as necessary when the underlying data store adds or removes Person objects.

**Listing 10.5 PersonChildFactory**

```
public class PersonChildFactory extends ChildFactory<Person> {

    private static final Logger logger = Logger.getLogger(
                     PersonChildFactory.class.getName());
    private final PersonCapability personCapability = new PersonCapability();
    private FamilyTreeManager ftm = null;

    public PersonChildFactory() {
        ftm = Lookup.getDefault().lookup(FamilyTreeManager.class);
        if (ftm == null) {
            logger.log(Level.SEVERE, "Cannot get FamilyTreeManager object");
            LifecycleManager.getDefault().exit();
        } else {
            ftm.addPropertyChangeListener(
                  WeakListeners.propertyChange(familytreelistener, ftm));
        }
    }

    @Override
    protected boolean createKeys(List<Person> list) {
        RefreshCapability refreshCapability =
               personCapability.getLookup().lookup(RefreshCapability.class);
        if (refreshCapability != null) {
            try {
                refreshCapability.refresh();
                list.addAll(personCapability.getPersonList());
                logger.log(Level.FINER, "createKeys called: {0}", list);
            } catch (IOException ex) {
                logger.log(Level.WARNING, null, ex);
            }
        }
        return true;
    }

    @Override
    protected Node createNodeForKey(Person key) {
        logger.log(Level.FINER, "createNodeForKey: {0}", key);
        PersonNode node = new PersonNode(key);
        return node;
    }
```

```
    // PropertyChangeListener for FamilyTreeManager
    private final PropertyChangeListener familytreelistener =
                                        (PropertyChangeEvent evt) -> {
        if (evt.getPropertyName().equals(FamilyTreeManager.PROP_PERSON_ADDED)
                || evt.getPropertyName().equals(
                FamilyTreeManager.PROP_PERSON_DESTROYED)) {
            this.refresh(true);
        }
    };
}
```

## Implementing Delete

The system DeleteAction implements the Delete capability for our nodes. The NetBeans Platform TopComponents and nodes are already set up to perform delete actions—you just need to configure them. We install a Delete context menu item in PersonNode and use the NetBeans Platform Delete menu item under the top-level Edit menu, as shown in Figure 10.4.

Figure 10.4 Delete action for PersonNode Maggie Simpson

Delete requires the following modifications. Note that Delete automatically works for multiple PersonNode selections.

- In the PersonViewer TopComponent constructor, create a DeleteAction and register it with the TopComponent's Explorer Manager. Helper function `ExplorerUtils.actionDelete()` includes a boolean to specify whether or not a confirmation dialog should appear before DeleteAction calls the node's `destroy()` method. Adding the DeleteAction to the TopComponent's ActionMap (and its Lookup) is required to enable the NetBeans Platform Delete menu items.

```
map.put("delete", ExplorerUtils.actionDelete(manager, true)); // or false
```

- In PersonNode, override the `canDestroy()` and `destroy()` methods. The `canDestroy()` method returns true and the `destroy()` method performs the delete. The system's DeleteAction invokes these methods.
- Add the NetBeans Platform DeleteAction to the PersonNode's `getActions()` method to include Delete in the node's context menu.

Listing 10.6 shows PersonNode.java. Here you see the `canDestroy()` and `destroy()` methods, the modified `getActions()` method, and the implementation of RemovablePersonCapability that is added to PersonNode's Lookup.

**Listing 10.6 PersonNode.java**

```
@NbBundle.Messages({
    "HINT_PersonNode=Person"
})
public class PersonNode extends AbstractNode {

    private final InstanceContent instanceContent;
    private static final Logger logger = Logger.getLogger(
            PersonNode.class.getName());

    public PersonNode(Person person) {
        this(person, new InstanceContent());
    }

    private PersonNode(Person person, InstanceContent ic) {
        super(Children.LEAF, new AbstractLookup(ic));
        instanceContent = ic;
        instanceContent.add(person);

         . . . other capabilities added to Lookup. . .

        // Add a RemovablePersonCapability to this Node
        instanceContent.add(new RemovablePersonCapability() {
            @Override
            public void remove(final Person p) throws IOException {
                if (ftm != null) {
                    ftm.deletePerson(p);
                }
            }
        });
    }
```

```
    @SuppressWarnings("unchecked")
    @Override
    public Action[] getActions(boolean context) {
        List<Action> personActions = new ArrayList<>(Arrays.asList(
                                super.getActions(context)));
        personActions.add(DeleteAction.get(DeleteAction.class));
        return personActions.toArray(
                new Action[personActions.size()]);
    }

    @Override
    public boolean canDestroy() {
        return true;
    }

    @Override
    public void destroy() throws IOException {
        final RemovablePersonCapability doRemove = getLookup().lookup(
                                RemovablePersonCapability.class);
        final Person person = getLookup().lookup(Person.class);
        if (doRemove != null && person != null) {
            doRemove.remove(person);
        }
    }
. . . code omitted . . .
}
```

Note that the Person Viewer window updates after the DeleteAction executes. That's because PersonChildFactory listens for `FamilyTreeManager.PROP_PERSON_DESTROYED` and invokes `refresh()` in the property change event handler (see Listing 10.5 on page 479).

## Implementing Create

To create new objects, the NetBeans Platform provides a NewType context as well as a standard NewAction that is responsive to context NewType. In the FamilyTreeApp, we implement the Create function with dialogs that prompt for a new Person's first and last names and a capability that adds the new Person to the FamilyTreeManager's data store.

A user can add a new Person through the context menu of the RootNode, as shown in Figure 10.5. Later, we'll show you how to configure NewAction in the top-level menu or toolbar.

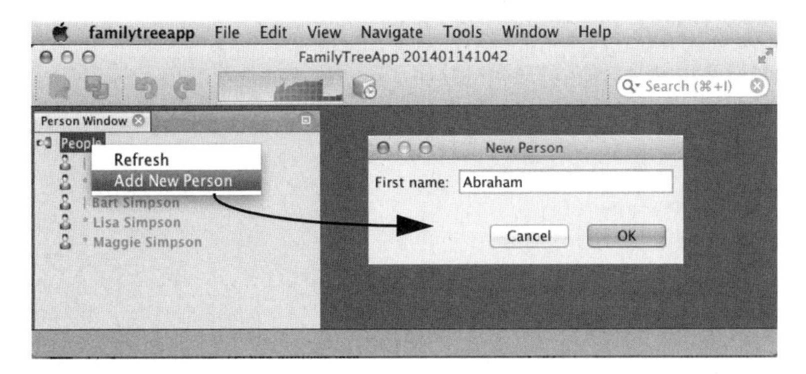


Figure 10.5 New Person action creates a new Person

## NewAction and NewType

The NetBeans Platform provides a built-in action called NewAction that enables creation-type actions for nodes. You provide an implementation of NewType and configure NewAction in the node's context menu, as follows.

- Override the node's `getActions()` method and include the system's NewAction in the returned array of actions.
- Override the node's `getNewTypes()` method and include an implementation of NewType in the returned array of NewTypes.

To add NewAction to the RootNode (the top-level node in the Person Viewer window), we configure methods `getActions()` and `getNewTypes()`, as shown in Listing 10.7.

**Listing 10.7 RootNode.java**

```
@Messages({
    "HINT_RootNode=Show all people",
    "LBL_RootNode=People"
})
public class RootNode extends AbstractNode {

. . . code omitted . . .

    private final PersonType personType = new PersonType();

    @Override
    public Action[] getActions(boolean context) {
        List<Action> actions = new ArrayList<>(
               Arrays.asList(super.getActions(context)));
```

```
        actions.addAll(Utilities.actionsForPath("Actions/RootNode"));
        // This puts the NewAction in the context menu
        actions.add(SystemAction.get(NewAction.class));
        return actions.toArray(new Action[actions.size()]);
    }

    @Override
    public NewType[] getNewTypes() {
        return new NewType[] { personType };
    }

}
```

## Create a Class That Extends NewType

Listing 10.8 shows PersonType.java, a class that extends NewType and overrides the `create()` method, which NewAction invokes. Here, we look up a CreatablePerson-Capability and use it to create a new Person.

**Listing 10.8 PersonType.java**

```
@Messages({
    "LBL_NewFirst_dialog=First name:",
    "LBL_NewLast_dialog=Last name:",
    "TITLE_NewPerson_dialog=New Person"
})
public class PersonType extends NewType {

    private final PersonCapability personCapability = new PersonCapability();
    private static final Logger logger = Logger.getLogger(
                PersonType.class.getName());
    @Override
    public String getName() {
        return Bundle.TITLE_NewPerson_dialog();
    }

    @Override
    public void create() throws IOException {
        NotifyDescriptor.InputLine msg = new NotifyDescriptor.InputLine(
                Bundle.LBL_NewFirst_dialog(), Bundle.TITLE_NewPerson_dialog());
        Object result = DialogDisplayer.getDefault().notify(msg);
        if (NotifyDescriptor.CANCEL_OPTION.equals(result)) {
            return;
        }
        String firstname = msg.getInputText();
        // check for a zero-length firstname
        if (firstname.equals("")) {
            return;
        }
```

```
        msg = new NotifyDescriptor.InputLine(Bundle.LBL_NewLast_dialog(),
                Bundle.TITLE_NewPerson_dialog());
        result = DialogDisplayer.getDefault().notify(msg);
        String lastname = msg.getInputText();
        if (NotifyDescriptor.YES_OPTION.equals(result)) {
            // Create a new Person object
            final Person person = new Person();
            person.setFirstname(firstname);
            person.setLastname(lastname);
            final CreatablePersonCapability cpc = personCapability
                    .getLookup().lookup(CreatablePersonCapability.class);
            if (cpc != null) {
                try {
                    cpc.create(person);
                    logger.log(Level.FINER, "Creating person {0}", person);
                } catch (IOException e) {
                    logger.log(Level.WARNING, e.getLocalizedMessage(), e);
                }
            }
        }
    }
}
```

### Implement the Capability

PersonType requires an implementation of interface CreatablePersonCapability (shown previously in Listing 10.1 on page 474). We implement CreatablePerson-Capability in PersonCapability, a class previously shown with RefreshCapability (see Listing 10.4 on page 478).

Listing 10.9 shows PersonCapability.java modified to include an implementation of CreatablePersonCapability.

**Listing 10.9 PersonCapability.java**

```
public final class PersonCapability implements Lookup.Provider {

    . . . code omitted . . .

    public PersonCapability() {
        lookup = new AbstractLookup(instanceContent);
        ftm = Lookup.getDefault().lookup(FamilyTreeManager.class);
        if (ftm == null) {
            logger.log(Level.SEVERE, "Cannot get FamilyTreeManager object");
            LifecycleManager.getDefault().exit();
        }
```

```
    . . . RefreshCapability implementation omitted . . .

        instanceContent.add(new CreatablePersonCapability() {
            @Override
            public void create(Person person) throws IOException {
                if (ftm != null) {
                    ftm.addPerson(person);
                }
            }
        });
    }
    . . . code omitted . . .
}
```

## Configuring NewAction in the Toolbar and Menu

With these changes, Add New Person now appears in the RootNode's context menu, as shown in Figure 10.5 on page 483. To configure NewAction for the toolbar and top-level menu, you first register the action. The easiest way to do this is to create a new context-aware action (call it NewPersonAction) and make its context NewType. Listing 10.10 shows this action, which we add to the FamilyTreeActions module.

**Listing 10.10 NewPersonAction.java**

```
@ActionID(
        category = "NewNode",
        id = "org.openide.actions.NewAction")
@ActionRegistration(
        iconBase = "com/asgteach/familytree/actions/personIcon.png",
        displayName = "#CTL_NewPersonAction")
@ActionReferences({
    @ActionReference(path = "Menu/File", position = 75),
    @ActionReference(path = "Toolbars/File", position = 50)
})
@Messages("CTL_NewPersonAction=New &Person")
public final class NewPersonAction implements ActionListener {

    private final NewType context;

    public NewPersonAction(NewType context) {
        this.context = context;
    }

    @Override
    public void actionPerformed(ActionEvent ev) {
        try {
            context.create();
```

```
        } catch (IOException ex) {
            Exceptions.printStackTrace(ex);
        }
    }
}
```

Now put the context (NewType) into the RootNode's Lookup to enable the toolbar and menu items. You can continue to use the NewAction in the context menu or use NewPersonAction instead, which is registered under `Actions/NewNode`. If you use NewPersonAction, then omit the `getNewTypes()` method, as shown in the modified RootNode in Listing 10.11.

**Listing 10.11 RootNode.java**

```
public class RootNode extends AbstractNode {

    private final InstanceContent instanceContent;
    private final PersonType personType = new PersonType();
    public RootNode() {
        this(new InstanceContent());
    }

    private RootNode(InstanceContent ic) {
        super(Children.create(new PersonChildFactory(), false),
                        new AbstractLookup(ic));
        instanceContent = ic;
        setIconBaseWithExtension(
            "com/asgteach/familytree/personviewer/resources/personIcon.png");
        setDisplayName(Bundle.LBL_RootNode());
        setShortDescription(Bundle.HINT_RootNode());
        // Required to enable New Person in context menu and Toolbar and Menus
        instanceContent.add(personType);
         . . .
    }

    @SuppressWarnings("unchecked")
    @Override
    public Action[] getActions(boolean context) {
        List<Action> actions = new ArrayList<>(Arrays.asList(
                        super.getActions(context)));
        actions.addAll(Utilities.actionsForPath("Actions/RootNode"));
        actions.addAll(Utilities.actionsForPath("Actions/NewNode"));
        return actions.toArray(new Action[actions.size()]);
    }

   // No longer necessary to override public NewType[] getNewTypes()
}
```

Figure 10.6 shows a New Person icon in the toolbar, as well as a New Person menu item under the top-level File menu.

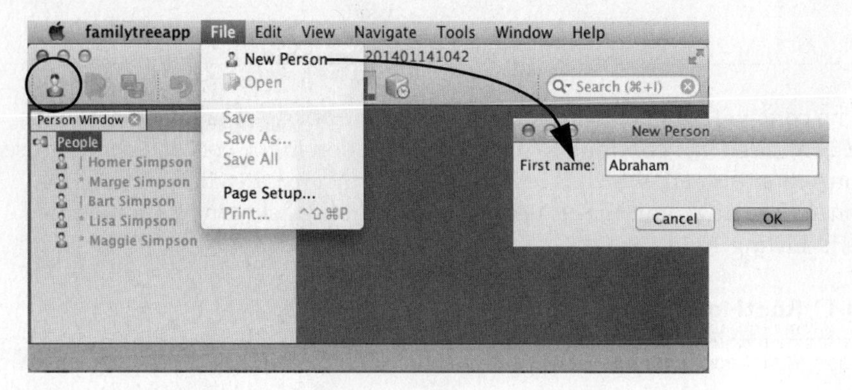


Figure 10.6 New Person action creates a new Person

## Implementing Update

The Update function occurs when a user opens the selected PersonNode in an editor, makes changes, and clicks the Save or Save All menu item. For updates, AbstractSavable enables and disables the Save and Save All menu items. We use Openable to implement opening a Person in an editor. Figure 10.2 on page 473 shows the Save / Save All menu items and the Save All icon enabled after a user makes changes in a PersonEditor. Figure 10.7 shows the built-in Show Opened Document List feature displaying the list of currently opened PersonEditor TopComponents.

Implementing Update requires several disparate modifications to the application, but the modifications all follow known guidelines in the NetBeans Platform Action framework. The result is a cohesive and cooperative feature. Here is a summary of the changes.

- Create a new module to hold the EditorManager service provider interface and make its package public.
- Implement the EditorManager service provider and add it to the PersonEditor module. (The PersonEditorTopComponent is already included in the PersonEditor module.)
- Use the standard NetBeans Platform context Openable to implement opening an editor. Put an implementation of Openable in PersonNode. The Openable implementation will look up the EditorManager service provider and acquire and open an editor for the selected PersonNode.

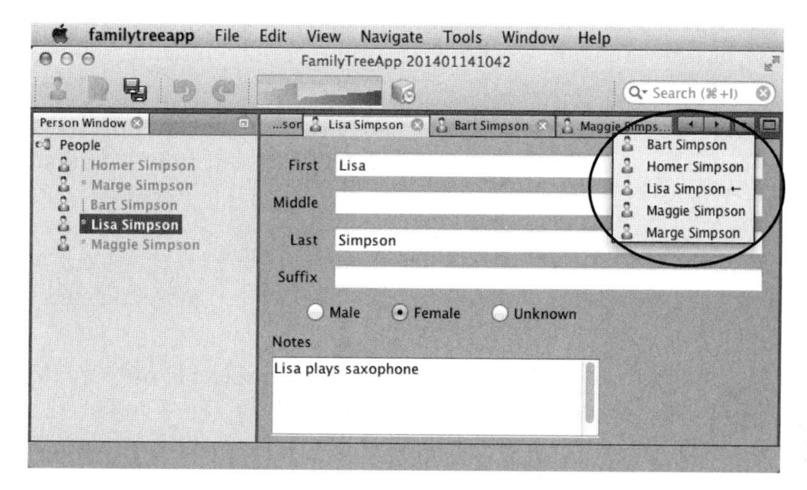


Figure 10.7 The built-in Show Opened Document List

- Create OpenAction as a context-aware action with context Openable. Make OpenAction the preferred action for PersonNode. This makes a double click open the node's Person in the editor.
- Each Person gets its own PersonEditor (a TopComponent), which is permanently associated with that Person. An EditorManager finds the TopComponent or creates it on demand, and opens the TopComponent with focus.
- In the editor, detect when a user makes changes to the domain object (Person) and put an implementation of AbstractSavable into the editor's Lookup. This enables Save All in the toolbar and Save and Save All in the File menu.
- Use a FamilyTreeManager property change listener to detect when the Person being edited has been deleted. When a delete occurs, unregister the editor (the TopComponent) and close it.
- The editor overrides the `canClose()` method and prompts the user to close if there are unsaved changes.

Let's start with the EditorManager service and its implementation.

## Create and Configure Module EditorManager

1. Expand the FamilyTreeApp, right click on the **Modules** node, and select **Add New...** from the context menu.

2. NetBeans displays the Add New Module Name and Location dialog. For Project Name, specify **EditorManager**. Accept the defaults for the remaining fields and click **Next**.
3. In the Basic Module Configuration dialog, specify **com.asgteach.familytree.editor.manager** for Code Name Base. Accept the defaults for the remaining fields and click **Finish**.

NetBeans creates project EditorManager. Now set dependencies.

1. Expand project EditorManager, right click on the **Libraries** node, and select **Add Module Dependency...** from the context menu.
2. In the Add Module Dependency dialog under Modules, select **FamilyTreeModel** and **Nodes API**. Click **OK** to add these dependencies.

Create the Java interface for the EditorManager service provider, as follows.

1. In project EditorManager, expand the Source Packages, right click on the package name, and select **New | Java Interface....**
2. In the New Java Interface dialog, specify Class Name **EditorManager** and click **Finish**.
3. In the Java Editor, provide abstract methods for EditorManager.java, as shown in Listing 10.12.

**Listing 10.12 EditorManager.java**

```
public interface EditorManager {
    public void openEditor(Node node);
    public void unRegisterEditor(Person person);
}
```

4. Using the Properties context menu of project EditorManager under API Versioning, make the package **com.asgteach.familytree.editor.manager** public so that other modules can set a dependency on this module.

### Implement the EditorManager Service Provider

Put the EditorManager service provider implementation in module PersonEditor. Here are the steps.

1. Expand project PersonEditor, right click on the **Libraries** node, and select **Add Module Dependency...** from the context menu.
2. In the Add Module Dependency dialog under Modules, select **EditorManager** and **Nodes API**. Click **OK** to add these dependencies.

3. In project PersonEditor, expand the Source Packages, right click on the package name, and select **New | Java Class....**
4. In the New Java Class dialog, specify Class Name **EditorManagerImpl** and click **Finish**.
5. In the Java Editor, provide the following code for EditorManagerImpl.java, as shown in Listing 10.13. Use annotation @ServiceProvider to register this class as a service provider for EditorManager.

The EditorManager service provider manages a HashMap of PersonEditorTopComponents using Person for the key. When the user opens a Person, the map is checked to see if a TopComponent for that Person exists. If one is found, it is opened and activated (request focus). If none exists, a TopComponent is created for that Person. The PersonEditorTopComponent `setPerson()` method configures the TopComponent with the Person and PersonNode. (The PersonNode includes needed capabilities in its Lookup.)

**Listing 10.13 EditorManagerImpl.java**

```
@ServiceProvider(service = EditorManager.class)
public class EditorManagerImpl implements EditorManager {

    private static final Logger logger = Logger.getLogger(
                                EditorManagerImpl.class.getName());
    Map<Person, PersonEditorTopComponent> tcMap = new HashMap<>();

    @Override
    public void openEditor(Node node) {
        Person person = node.getLookup().lookup(Person.class);
        if (person == null) {
            return;
        }
        PersonEditorTopComponent tc = tcMap.get(person);
        if (tc != null) {
            if (!tc.isOpened()) {
                tc.open();
            }
            tc.setPerson(node);
            tc.requestActive();
            return;
        }

        // Create a new TopComponent and open it...
        logger.log(Level.INFO, "Creating new Editor for {0}", person);
        tc = new PersonEditorTopComponent();
        tcMap.put(person, tc);
        tc.setPerson(node);
```

```
        tc.open();
        tc.requestActive();
    }

    @Override
    public void unRegisterEditor(Person person) {
        logger.log(Level.INFO, "Unregistering editor for {0}", person);
        tcMap.remove(person);
    }
}
```

## Configure PersonEditor to Work with AbstractSavable

The PersonEditor described in Chapter 5 (see "Configuring a Window with Form Editing" on page 231) lets a user edit a Person from the Global Selection Lookup. In that version, the TopComponent is a singleton. Now, each Person and PersonNode receive its own PersonEditorTopComponent.

To fulfill the Update portion of our CRUD application and use capabilities, we must make several changes to the PersonEditor. We'll show you these modifications in several parts. Note that much of the PersonEditorTopComponent is unchanged. This includes the components that let a user make changes, the listeners that detect edits, and the methods for updating the form.

Listing 10.14 shows the PersonEditorTopComponent code with the following updates.

- Change the annotations on the TopComponent so that it's no longer a singleton (see "Creating Non-Singleton TopComponents" on page 364 for a discussion).
- Add InstanceContent to the TopComponent so that you can add nodes and capabilities to its Lookup as needed.
- Implement a public `setPerson()` method so that the EditorManager can configure the Editor with the Person and its PersonNode (which has capabilities needed by the PersonEditor).
- Remove the Update button and its `actionPerformed()` event handler.
- Remove the LookupListener event handler code.
- Modify the window's name and tooltip to display the Person's name.
- Change the `modify()` method so that it puts an AbstractSavable implementation (SavableViewCapability) in the TopComponent's Lookup.
- Remove the AbstractSavable after a Save or when a Save is no longer needed.

**Listing 10.14 PersonEditorTopComponent.java—Modifications for CRUD**

```
@TopComponent.Description(
        preferredID = "PersonEditorTopComponent",
        iconBase =
            "com/asgteach/familytree/personeditor/personIcon.png",
        persistenceType = TopComponent.PERSISTENCE_NEVER
)
@TopComponent.Registration(mode = "editor", openAtStartup = false)
@Messages({
    "CTL_PersonEditorAction=PersonEditor",
    "CTL_PersonEditorTopComponent=PersonEditor Window",
    "CTL_PersonEditorSaveDialogTitle=Unsaved Data",
    "CTL_PersonEditorSave_Option=Save",
    "CTL_PersonEditorDiscard_Option=Discard",
    "CTL_PersonEditorCANCEL_Option=Cancel",
    "# {0} - person",
    "HINT_PersonEditorTopComponent=This is an Editor for {0}",
    "# {0} - person",
    "CTL_PersonEditorSaveDialogMsg=Person {0} has Unsaved Data. \nSave?"
})
public final class PersonEditorTopComponent extends TopComponent {
    /*
     TopComponents implement Lookup.Provider.
     In order to add objects to a TopComponents Lookup, instantiate
     InstanceContent and associate it with its Lookup using
     the associateLookup() method and create a Lookup with
     AbstractLookup.
     */

    private Person thePerson = null;
    private static final Logger logger = Logger.getLogger(
                PersonEditorTopComponent.class.getName());
    private boolean changeOK = false;
    private boolean noUpdate = true;
    private final InstanceContent instanceContent = new InstanceContent();
    private FamilyTreeManager ftm;

    public PersonEditorTopComponent() {
        initComponents();
        associateLookup(new AbstractLookup(instanceContent));
    }

    // The EditorManager must invoke the setPerson method with the Node
    // that contains the wrapped Person object in its Lookup
    public void setPerson(Node node) {
        thePerson = node.getLookup().lookup(Person.class);
        Node oldNode = getLookup().lookup(Node.class);
```

```
        if (oldNode != null) {
            instanceContent.remove(oldNode);
        }
        instanceContent.add(node);
    }

    private void updateModel() {
        if (noUpdate) {
            return;
        }
        thePerson.setFirstname(firstTextField.getText());
        thePerson.setMiddlename(middleTextField.getText());
        thePerson.setLastname(lastTextField.getText());
        thePerson.setSuffix(suffixTextField.getText());
        if (maleButton.isSelected()) {
            thePerson.setGender(Gender.MALE);
        } else if (femaleButton.isSelected()) {
            thePerson.setGender(Gender.FEMALE);
        } else if (unknownButton.isSelected()) {
            thePerson.setGender(Gender.UNKNOWN);
        }
        thePerson.setNotes(notesTextArea.getText());
        // Update the TopComponent's name and tooltip
        setName(thePerson.toString());
        setToolTipText(Bundle.HINT_PersonEditorTopComponent(
                thePerson.toString()));
    }

    private void modify() {
        // Add AbstractSavable to Lookup
        if (getLookup().lookup(SavableViewCapability.class) == null) {
            instanceContent.add(new SavableViewCapability());
        }
    }

    private void clearSaveCapability() {
        SavableViewCapability savable = getLookup().lookup(
                          SavableViewCapability.class);
        while (savable != null) {
            savable.removeSavable();
            instanceContent.remove(savable);
            savable = getLookup().lookup(SavableViewCapability.class);
        }
    }

    @Override
    public void componentOpened() {
        setName(thePerson.toString());
        setToolTipText(Bundle.HINT_PersonEditorTopComponent(
                        thePerson.toString()));
```

```
        configureComponentListeners();
        updateForm();
        ftm = Lookup.getDefault().lookup(FamilyTreeManager.class);
        if (ftm == null) {
            logger.log(Level.SEVERE, "Cannot get FamilyTreeManager object");
            LifecycleManager.getDefault().exit();
        } else {
            ftm.addPropertyChangeListener(familyListener);
        }
    }
```

- If the Person being edited in this PersonEditor is deleted, the TopComponent unregisters itself with the EditorManager and closes down. The delete is detected by the PropertyChangeListener, as shown in Listing 10.15. You must wrap the TopComponent `close()` in a Runnable and call it with `invokeWhenUIReady()`. This ensures the Window System modification is performed on the EDT.

**Listing 10.15 PersonEditorTopComponent—PropertyChangeListener**

```
    // PropertyChangeListener for FamilyTreeManager
    private final PropertyChangeListener familyListener =
                                 (PropertyChangeEvent pce) -> {
        if (pce.getPropertyName().equals(
                    FamilyTreeManager.PROP_PERSON_DESTROYED) &&
                                     pce.getNewValue() != null) {
            if (pce.getNewValue().equals(thePerson)) {
               // Our person has been removed from the FamilyTreeManager, so we
                // need to close!
                clearSaveCapability();
                EditorManager edManager = Lookup.getDefault().lookup(
                              EditorManager.class);
                if (edManager != null) {
                    edManager.unRegisterEditor(thePerson);
                    PersonEditorTopComponent.shutdown(this);
                }
            }
        }
    };

    private static void shutdown(final TopComponent tc) {
        WindowManager.getDefault().invokeWhenUIReady(() -> tc.close());
    }
```

- Override the TopComponent's `canClose()` method to prompt the user what to do with unsaved changes, as shown in Listing 10.16. Here, we customize a NetBeans Platform dialog so that the button labels are Cancel, Discard, and Save. (See "Customizing Standard Dialogs" on page 531 for more on dialogs.)

**Listing 10.16 PersonEditor.java—Method canClose()**

```
// Check to see if we have unsaved changes
// If so, ask the user if the changes should be saved or discarded
    @Override
    public boolean canClose() {
        SavableViewCapability savable = getLookup().lookup(
                        SavableViewCapability.class);
        if (savable == null) {
            // No modified data, so just close
            return true;
        }
        // Detected modified data, so ask user what to do
        String saveAnswer = Bundle.CTL_PersonEditorSave_Option();
        String discardAnswer = Bundle.CTL_PersonEditorDiscard_Option();
        String cancelAnswer = Bundle.CTL_PersonEditorCANCEL_Option();
        String[] options = {cancelAnswer, discardAnswer, saveAnswer};
        String msg = Bundle.CTL_PersonEditorSaveDialogMsg(
                                    thePerson.toString());
        NotifyDescriptor nd = new NotifyDescriptor(msg, // the question
                Bundle.CTL_PersonEditorSaveDialogTitle(), // the title
                NotifyDescriptor.YES_NO_CANCEL_OPTION, // the buttons provided
                NotifyDescriptor.QUESTION_MESSAGE, // the type of message
                options, // the button text
                saveAnswer // the default selection
        );
        Object result = DialogDisplayer.getDefault().notify(nd);
        if (result == cancelAnswer ||
                result == NotifyDescriptor.CLOSED_OPTION) {
            // Cancel the close
            return false;
        }
        if (result == discardAnswer) {
            // Don't save, just close!
            clearSaveCapability();
            return true;
        }
        try {
            // Yes, save the data, then close
            savable.handleSave();
            StatusDisplayer.getDefault().setStatusText(thePerson + " saved.");
            return true;
        } catch (IOException ex) {
            logger.log(Level.WARNING, null, ex);
            return false;
        }
    }
```

- In PersonEditor.java, extend AbstractSavable with private class SavableViewCapability to handle saves, as shown in Listing 10.17. With AbstractSavable, you override the `findDisplayName()`, `handleSave()`, `equals()`, and `hashcode()` methods.

Note that the `handleSave()` method looks up the node in the TopComponent's Lookup, then looks up SavablePersonCapability to perform the actual save. (We show you the implementation of SavablePersonCapability in the next section.) When the user clicks the Save menu item, the NetBeans Platform SaveAction invokes the AbstractSavable object's `handleSave()` method. Here, the `handleSave()` method makes a copy of the TopComponent's Person object after invoking `updateModel()`. This copy is required to safely add concurrency with the CRUD actions.

**Listing 10.17 SavableViewCapability Class**

```
private class SavableViewCapability extends AbstractSavable {

    SavableViewCapability() {
        register();
    }

    public void removeSavable() {
        unregister();
    }

    @Override
    protected String findDisplayName() {
        return thePerson.toString();
    }

    @Override
    protected void handleSave() throws IOException {
        final Node node = getLookup().lookup(Node.class);
        if (node != null) {
            final SavablePersonCapability savable
                  = node.getLookup().lookup(SavablePersonCapability.class);
            if (savable != null) {
                updateModel();
                final Person p = new Person(thePerson);
                clearSaveCapability();
                changeOK = true;
                try {
                    savable.save(p);
                } catch (IOException ex) {
                    logger.log(Level.WARNING, null, ex);
                }
            }
        }
    }
```

```
    @Override
    public boolean equals(Object other) {
        if (other instanceof SavableViewCapability) {
            SavableViewCapability sv = (SavableViewCapability) other;
            return tc() == sv.tc();
        }
        return false;
    }

    @Override
    public int hashCode() {
        return tc().hashCode();
    }

    PersonEditorTopComponent tc() {
        return PersonEditorTopComponent.this;
    }
}
```

Note that with AbstractSavable, you automatically get a confirmation dialog if there are unsaved changes and the user attempts to Quit the application, as shown in Figure 10.8.

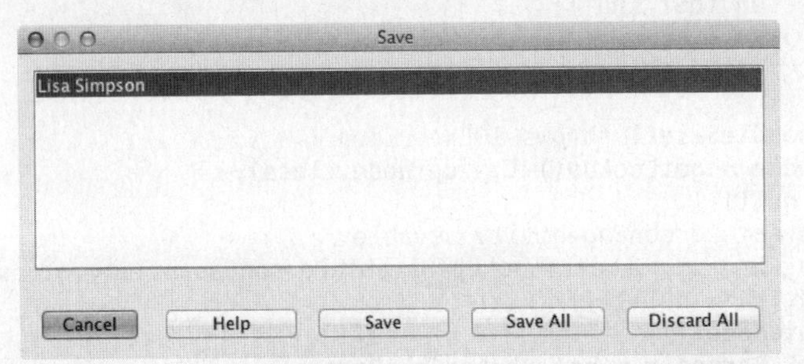


**Figure 10.8 NetBeans Platform Save dialog responds to AbstractSavable on a Quit**

## Create and Configure the OpenAction

A user initiates editing by executing an Open action on a PersonNode. Create a context-aware action (put the action in module FamilyTreeActions) and register it under category OpenNodes. This OpenAction (with an icon) is registered with the File menu and the toolbar. Make the context Openable, which is a standard NetBeans Platform capability. Figure 10.9 shows the Open icon in the toolbar and under the File menu. Listing 10.18 shows the code for OpenAction.java.

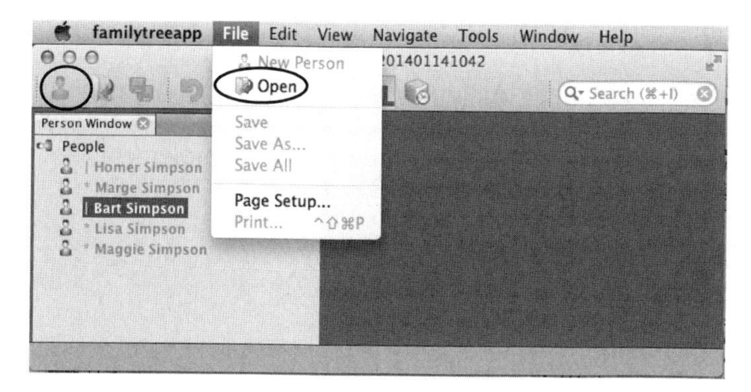


Figure 10.9 Open in the File menu and in the toolbar

**Listing 10.18 OpenAction.java**

```
@ActionID(
        category = "OpenNodes",
        id = "com.asgteach.familytree.actions.OpenAction"
)
@ActionRegistration(
        iconBase = "com/asgteach/familytree/actions/open.png",
        displayName = "#CTL_OpenAction"
)
@ActionReferences({
    @ActionReference(path = "Menu/File", position = 1100,
               separatorAfter = 1150),
    @ActionReference(path = "Toolbars/File", position = 200)
})
@Messages("CTL_OpenAction=Open")
public final class OpenAction implements ActionListener {

    private final Openable context;

    public OpenAction(Openable context) {
        this.context = context;
    }

    @Override
    public void actionPerformed(ActionEvent ev) {
        context.open();
    }
}
```

### Implement Openable and SavablePersonCapability

The Openable capability is used by OpenAction and the SavablePersonCapability capability is used in the PersonEditorTopComponent to save edits made by the user (see Listing 10.17 on page 497). Listing 10.19 shows the code that implements both of these capabilities and adds them to the PersonNode Lookup.

**Listing 10.19 PersonNode.java—Openable and SavablePersonCapability**

```
public class PersonNode extends AbstractNode {

   . . . code omitted . . .

   private PersonNode(Person person, InstanceContent ic) {
       super(Children.LEAF, new AbstractLookup(ic));
       instanceContent = ic;
       instanceContent.add(person);
     . . . code omitted . . .

       // Add an Openable object to this Node
       instanceContent.add(new Openable() {

           @Override
           public void open() {
               EditorManager edmanager = Lookup.getDefault().lookup(
                                EditorManager.class);
               if (edmanager != null) {
                   edmanager.openEditor(PersonNode.this);
               }
           }

       });
       // Add a SavablePersonCapability to this Node
       instanceContent.add(new SavablePersonCapability() {

           @Override
           public void save(final Person p) throws IOException {
               if (ftm != null) {
                   ftm.updatePerson(p);
               }
           }
       });
. . .
```

### Configure the Node's Actions

Add Open to the context menu of PersonNode and make it the preferred action, as shown in Listing 10.20. Note that OpenAction is registered under category OpenNodes and is the only action in that category.

**Listing 10.20 PersonNode.java—Configure Actions**

```
@SuppressWarnings("unchecked")
@Override
public Action[] getActions(boolean context) {
    List<Action> personActions = new ArrayList<>(
                    Arrays.asList(super.getActions(context)));
    personActions.addAll(Utilities.actionsForPath("Actions/OpenNodes"));
    personActions.add(DeleteAction.get(DeleteAction.class));
    return personActions.toArray(
            new Action[personActions.size()]);
}

@SuppressWarnings("unchecked")
@Override
public Action getPreferredAction() {
    // Make OpenAction the preferred action
    List<Action> actions = new ArrayList<>(
                         Utilities.actionsForPath("Actions/OpenNodes"));
    if (!actions.isEmpty()) {
        return actions.get(0);
    } else {
        return null;
    }
}
```

## 10.2 Using CRUD with a Database

At this point, we've built a FamilyTreeApp with a hashmap for its data store. With our simple example (Person objects with no relationships), a hashmap provides an adequate solution to illustrate many of the NetBeans Platform features. However, this is not a viable solution when your application requires a permanent data store. As we move to the next step, which includes using a database, the NetBeans Platform helps us with this migration in several ways.

- Database CRUD operations are a "black box" operation carried out by the FamilyTreeManager.
- Since the FamilyTreeManager is already a service provider, we can easily substitute a new one that uses a database.

In this section, we'll show you how to implement a FamilyTreeManager with JavaDB and JPA. JavaDB is a built-in database available with the NetBeans IDE. JPA (Java Persistence API) provides the middleware for persistence-based applications. Note that any JPA and database software is applicable here. We use JavaDB and EclipseLink JPA since they are bundled with the NetBeans IDE and JDK software.

When using a database (or a web service), you must ensure that the application remains responsive. The solution is to execute potentially long-running code in the background. We laid the groundwork for this approach in Chapter 2 (see "Swing Background Tasks" on page 73) and in Chapter 4 (see "JavaFX Background Tasks" on page 176). In the next section, we'll add concurrency to our application to keep the UI responsive.

Here's the approach we'll take to migrate the FamilyTreeApp application to a database.

- Create wrapped libraries for the database and JPA software. Wrapped libraries are NetBeans Platform modules that contain library JAR files configured with public packages.
- Start the JavaDB built-in database server and create a database to hold the application's data.
- Create a module to hold the persistence unit, entity classes, and FamilyTreeManager service provider to perform the JPA/database operations.
- Create an entity class corresponding to each table in the database (there is just one in this example).
- Create a Persistence Unit to describe the entity classes, database, and table generation strategy for JPA.
- Implement a FamilyTreeManager service provider that uses JPA.
- Modify Person.java so that it no longer auto-increments the `id` property, but instead gets an id generated from the database.

The improvements to the FamilyTreeApp for CRUD operations can be used with no further modifications (thanks to NetBeans Platform module system and service providers).

## Create Wrapped Libraries

The NetBeans Platform lets you use external libraries in applications by creating modules called *Library Wrapper Modules* or wrapped libraries. Wrapped libraries are modules that contain JAR files (that is, external library archive files). The JAR files' packages are public so that other modules can set dependencies as needed. You can bundle multiple JAR files into one module.

To implement database functionality, we'll create two wrapped libraries. The first library contains the JavaDB connection software (the Derby Client JAR file). The second library includes the EclipseLink JAR files that provide JPA. These library files are available with the NetBeans IDE distribution.

## Derby Client Module

First, create the Derby Client module, as follows.

1. Select the FamilyTreeApp **Modules** node, right click, and select **Add New Library ....** NetBeans initiates the New Library Wrapper Module Project wizard and displays the Select Library dialog.
2. Click the **Browse** button, navigate to the NetBeans Glassfish distribution subdirectory **javadb/lib**, and select **derbyclient.jar**, as shown in Figure 10.10. Click **Select** and then **Next** in the Select Library dialog.

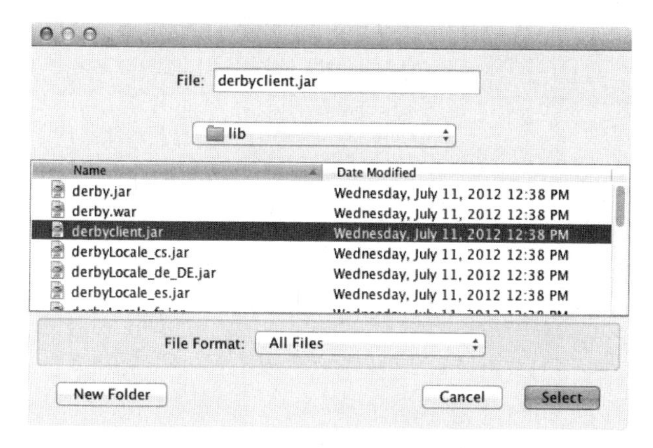


Figure 10.10 Select derbyclient.jar to include in Library Wrapper Module

3. In the Name and Location dialog, specify **DerbyClient** for Project Name, accept the default for the remaining fields, and click **Next**, as shown in Figure 10.11.
4. In the Basic Module Configuration dialog, specify **org.apache.derby** for Code Name Base, accept the default for the remaining fields, and click **Finish**, as shown in Figure 10.12.

NetBeans creates a new module named DerbyClient and makes all its packages public.

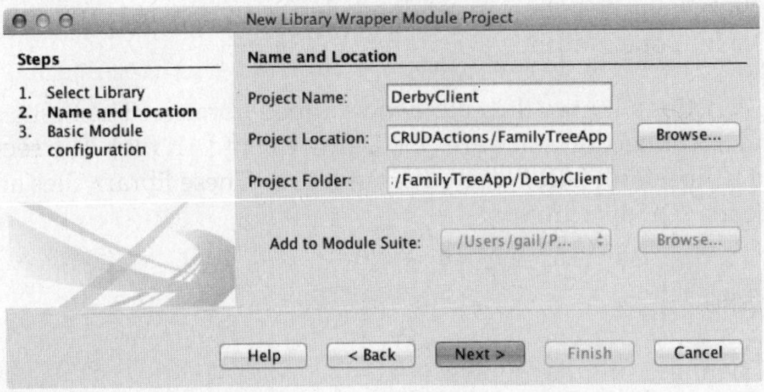

Figure 10.11 Specify DerbyClient for Project Name

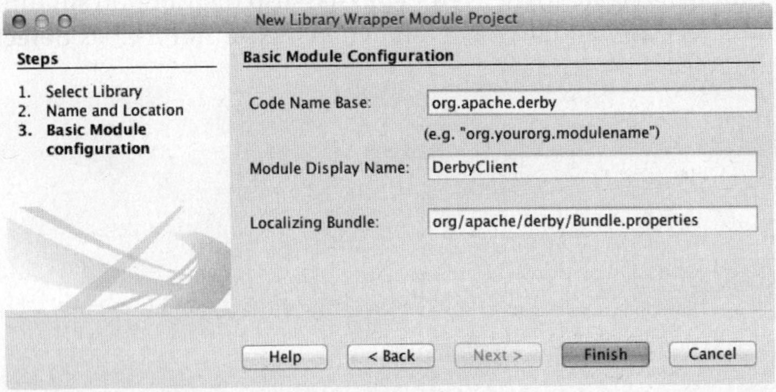

Figure 10.12 Specify Code Name Base for Library Wrapper module configuration

## EclipseLink Module

Follow the same steps to create a second Library Wrapper Module called EclipseLink. The EclipseLink library consists of four JAR files found in the NetBeans IDE distribution under `NetBeans/java/modules/ext/eclipselink` (the exact location depends on your operating system and the NetBeans distribution). The JAR files you need are as follows (xx refers to various version numbers). In the JAR file chooser dialog, Control-Click lets you select multiple JAR files.

```
eclipselink-xx.jar
javax.persistence_xx.jar
org.eclipse.persistence.jpa.jpql_xx.jar
org.eclipse.persistence.jpa.modelgen_xx.jar
```

Select all of the above JAR files. Use project name **EclipseLink** and code name base **org.eclipselink**. The two Library Wrapper Modules (DerbyClient and EclipseLink) appear as shown in Figure 10.13 in the Projects view with the Libraries node expanded.

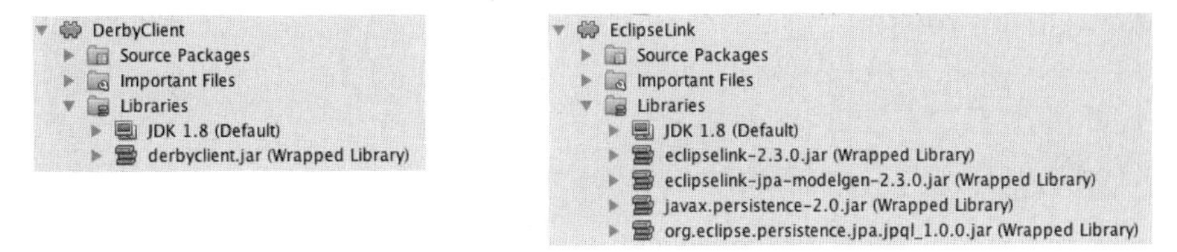


Figure 10.13 DerbyClient and EclipseLink wrapped library modules

## JavaDB Server and Database

The NetBeans IDE comes with a complete SQL database. To use it, you must start the JavaDB Server, as follows.

- In the NetBeans IDE Services tab, expand the Databases node, right click on **JavaDB**, and select **Start Server** from the context menu.

In the IDE Output window, you'll see a JavaDB Data Process tab with output similar to the following.

```
Tue Feb 18 16:02:47 PST 2014 : Apache Derby Network Server - 10.8.1.2 -
            (1095077) started and ready to accept connections on port 1527
```

**JavaDB Server Tip**

*Note that you must start the JavaDB Server before running the FamilyTreeApp once you add this database functionality to the application.*

### Create Database

With the JavaDB Server running, you can now create a database that holds the data managed by the FamilyTreeApp.

1. In the Services window, right click on JavaDB and select **Create Database ...** from the context menu.
2. NetBeans displays a Create Java DB Database dialog. Specify **personftm** for all fields (Database Name, User Name, Password, and Confirm Password), as shown in Figure 10.14. Click **OK**.

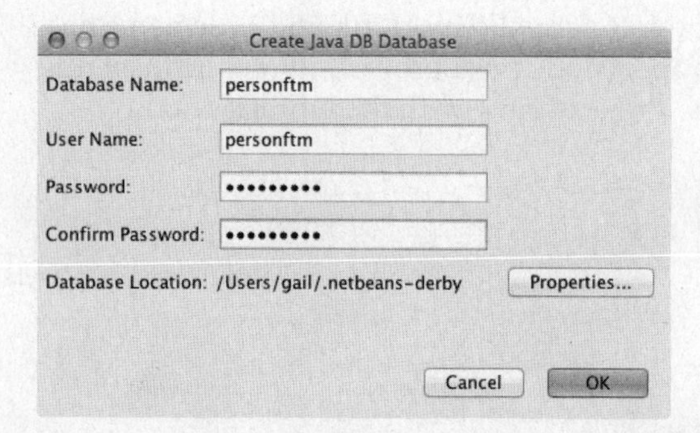


Figure 10.14 Create a Java DB Database

3. You'll now see **personftm** listed under JavaDB (expand it) as well as a JDBC-Derby URL. You can connect to this database, but it doesn't have any tables or structure yet. You'll provide the structure by defining a persistence unit and entity class.

## Implement FamilyTreeManager

Create a new module to implement the FamilyTreeManager that uses JPA.

### Create a New Module and Add Dependencies

1. In the FamilyTreeApp application, right click on the **Modules** node and select **Add New...** from the context menu.
2. Make the Project Name FamilyTreeManagerJPA and its code name base **com.asgteach.familytree.manager.jpa**.
3. This module requires some dependencies. Right click on the **Libraries** node and select **Add Module Dependencies...** in the context menu.
4. Set dependencies for modules **DerbyClient**, **EclipseLink**, **FamilyTreeModel**, **Lookup API**, and **Utilities API** and click **OK**.

### Create an Entity Class

JPA uses entity classes to persist data. Our entity class will be very similar to the Person class you've already seen with annotations that define its persistence behavior. We will keep the entity class (PersonEntity) isolated within this module and retain Person as an application-wide domain object that is not a persistent entity.

Create the class, as follows.

1. Right click on the FamilyTreeManagerJPA package name and select **New | Java Class** from the context menu.
2. Specify **PersonEntity** for the class name. Provide code, as shown in Listing 10.21.

There are a few important features worth discussing about this JPA entity class.

- PersonEntity uses @Entity to designate the class as a JPA entity class. The optional annotation @Table specifies its table name (otherwise, JPA uses the class name, PersonEntity, as the table name).
- Annotation @Id and @GeneratedValue specify that field `id` is the primary key and that its value is automatically generated. (This will require that we remove the auto-increment code in the Person class.)
- Annotation @Version is used by JPA to track the modifications made to the entity and maps to a column named VERSION in the table.
- The PersonEntity properties (`firstname`, `middlename`, `lastname`, `suffix`, `gender`, and `notes`) are mapped to equivalently named columns in the database.

**Listing 10.21 PersonEntity.java**

```
@Entity
@Table(name="Person")
public class PersonEntity implements Serializable {

    private static final long serialVersionUID = 1L;
    @Id
    @GeneratedValue(strategy = GenerationType.AUTO)
    private Long id;

    @Version
    private int version;

    private String firstname = "";
    private String middlename = "";
    private String lastname = "Unknown";
    private String suffix = "";
    private Person.Gender gender = Person.Gender.UNKNOWN;
    private String notes = "";

    public PersonEntity() {
    }

    public synchronized String getFirstname() {
        return firstname;
    }
```

```
    public synchronized void setFirstname(String firstname) {
        this.firstname = firstname;
    }

    public synchronized String getLastname() {
        return lastname;
    }

    public synchronized void setLastname(String lastname) {
        this.lastname = lastname;
    }

    public synchronized String getMiddlename() {
        return middlename;
    }

    public synchronized void setMiddlename(String middlename) {
        this.middlename = middlename;
    }

    public synchronized String getNotes() {
        return notes;
    }

    public synchronized void setNotes(String notes) {
        this.notes = notes;
    }

    public synchronized Person.Gender getGender() {
        return gender;
    }

    public synchronized void setGender(Person.Gender gender) {
        this.gender = gender;
    }

    public synchronized String getSuffix() {
        return suffix;
    }

    public synchronized void setSuffix(String suffix) {
        this.suffix = suffix;
    }

    public synchronized Long getId() {
        return id;
    }
```

```
    @Override
    public boolean equals(Object o) {
        if (o == null) {
            return false;
        }
        if (getClass() != o.getClass()) {
            return false;
        }
        return this.getId().equals(((PersonEntity) o).getId());
    }

    @Override
    public int hashCode() {
        int hash = 7;
        hash = 97 * hash + (this.id != null ? this.id.hashCode() : 0);
        return hash;
    }

    @Override
    public String toString() {
        StringBuilder sb = new StringBuilder();
        sb.append("[").append(getId()).append("] ");
        if (!this.getFirstname().isEmpty()) {
            sb.append(this.getFirstname());
        }
        if (!this.getMiddlename().isEmpty()) {
            sb.append(" ").append(this.getMiddlename());
        }
        if (!this.getLastname().isEmpty()) {
            sb.append(" ").append(this.getLastname());
        }
        if (!this.getSuffix().isEmpty()) {
            sb.append(" ").append(this.getSuffix());
        }
        return sb.toString();
    }
}
```

### Create a Persistence Unit

With an entity class and database created and the Java DB server running, you can now create a Persistence Unit for this module. The Persistence Unit is described by an XML file called persistence.xml. You add it to the META-INF directory of module FamilyTreeManagerJPA.

Listing 10.22 shows an example persistence.xml file. The Persistence Unit has a name (PersonFTMPU) and specifies a persistence provider (org.eclipse.persistence.jpa.PersistenceProvider). The persistence unit also describes how to connect to the database (here using JDBC/Derby) and (importantly) the table generation strategy. Here, we specify "drop-and-create-tables," which creates the database tables each time (deleting any data). If you want to keep the data between program executions, change the generation strategy to "create-tables" (which creates the tables only if needed) or "none" (which performs no table generation).

### Table Generation Strategy

*Note that if you change the generation strategy from "drop-and-create-tables," you'll need to remove the generation of test data in the FamilyTreeModel's Installer class, which creates the Simpson family test data each time.*

You can also change the default logging level for EclipseLink to FINE to see more detailed logging output from the persistence provider. (Warning: FINE produces many messages.)

**Listing 10.22 persistence.xml**

```
<?xml version="1.0" encoding="UTF-8"?>
<persistence version="2.0" xmlns="http://java.sun.com/xml/ns/persistence"
xmlns:xsi="http://www.w3.org/2001/XMLSchema-instance"
   xsi:schemaLocation=
   "http://java.sun.com/xml/ns/persistence
   http://java.sun.com/xml/ns/persistence/persistence_2_0.xsd">
  <persistence-unit name="PersonFTMPU" transaction-type="RESOURCE_LOCAL">
    <provider>org.eclipse.persistence.jpa.PersistenceProvider</provider>
    <class>com.asgteach.familytree.manager.jpa.PersonEntity</class>
    <properties>
      <property name="driverClass" value="org.apache.derby.jdbc.ClientDriver"/>
      <!--      <property name="eclipselink.logging.level" value="FINE"/>-->
      <property name="javax.persistence.jdbc.url"
            value="jdbc:derby://localhost:1527/personftm"/>
      <property name="javax.persistence.jdbc.user" value="personftm"/>
      <property name="javax.persistence.jdbc.driver"
            value="org.apache.derby.jdbc.ClientDriver"/>
      <property name="javax.persistence.jdbc.password" value="personftm"/>
      <property name="eclipselink.ddl-generation"
                        value="drop-and-create-tables"/>
    </properties>
  </persistence-unit>
</persistence>
```

### Database Configuration Options

*You can alternatively use a pre-existing database. In this case, the NetBeans IDE can generate the entity classes and the Persistence Unit for you. To do this, create a **Java Class Library Project**. Then, from the top-level menu, select **File | New File**. In the dialog specify category*

***Persistence**, then choose **Entity Classes from Database**. This will create the entity classes and the Persistence Unit you need based on the database connection you provide. Once you have these files, you can copy them into a module in your NetBeans Platform application.*

### Create a New FamilyTreeManager Service Provider

Now it's time to create a new class that implements FamilyTreeManager. Call this class FamilyTreeManagerJPA and make it a service provider (using @ServiceProvider) for FamilyTreeManager. Attribute `supersedes` specifies that this implementation takes precedence over the original FamilyTreeManager service provider. (You can also remove module FamilyTreeManagerImpl from the application.)

A static initializer initializes the EntityManagerFactory and creates an EntityManager. Creating the EntityManager fails if the JavaDB Database server is not running.

Similar to class FamilyTreeManagerImpl, this implementation provides property change support when Person objects are updated, added to, and removed from the database. We use SwingPropertyChangeSupport so that the property change events are fired on the EDT.

Private method `buildPerson()` creates a Person object with its database-generated `id` property. (Class Person in module FamilyTreeModel now requires a new constructor.) This replaces the auto-increment id in class Person used in the hashmap version.

With JPA, you execute database operations using the EntityManager, which provides the database management. Listing 10.23 shows class FamilyTreeManagerJPA.java.

**Listing 10.23 FamilyTreeManagerJPA.java**

```
@ServiceProvider
(service = com.asgteach.familytree.model.FamilyTreeManager.class,
   supersedes = {
      "com.asgteach.familytree.manager.impl.FamilyTreeManagerImpl"})
public class FamilyTreeManagerJPA implements FamilyTreeManager {

    // SwingPropertyChangeSupport is thread-safe
    // true means fire property change events on the EDT
    private SwingPropertyChangeSupport propChangeSupport = null;

    private static final EntityManagerFactory EMF;
    private static final Logger logger = Logger.getLogger(
            FamilyTreeManagerJPA.class.getName());
```

```
    static {
        try {
            EMF = Persistence.createEntityManagerFactory("PersonFTMPU");
            logger.log(Level.INFO, "Entity Manager Factory Created.");
           // Create/close entity manager to make sure JavaDB Server is running
            // This will fail if the JavaDB Server is not running
            EntityManager em = EMF.createEntityManager();
            em.close();
        } catch (Throwable ex) {
            logger.log(Level.SEVERE,
      "Make sure that the JavaDB Database Server has been started.", ex);
            throw new ExceptionInInitializerError(ex);
        }
    }

    private PropertyChangeSupport getPropertyChangeSupport() {
        if (this.propChangeSupport == null) {
           this.propChangeSupport = new SwingPropertyChangeSupport(this, true);
        }
        return this.propChangeSupport;
    }

    @Override
    public void addPropertyChangeListener(PropertyChangeListener listener) {
        getPropertyChangeSupport().addPropertyChangeListener(listener);
    }

    @Override
    public void removePropertyChangeListener(PropertyChangeListener listener) {
        getPropertyChangeSupport().removePropertyChangeListener(listener);
    }

    private Person buildPerson(PersonEntity pe) {
        Person person = new Person(pe.getId());
        person.setFirstname(pe.getFirstname());
        person.setGender(pe.getGender());
        person.setLastname(pe.getLastname());
        person.setMiddlename(pe.getMiddlename());
        person.setNotes(pe.getNotes());
        person.setSuffix(pe.getSuffix());
        return person;
    }

    @Override
    public void addPerson(final Person newPerson) {
        EntityManager em = EMF.createEntityManager();
        try {
            em.getTransaction().begin();
            PersonEntity person = new PersonEntity();
            person.setFirstname(newPerson.getFirstname());
            person.setLastname(newPerson.getLastname());
```

```
            person.setGender(newPerson.getGender());
            person.setMiddlename(newPerson.getMiddlename());
            person.setSuffix(newPerson.getSuffix());
            person.setNotes(newPerson.getNotes());
            em.persist(person);
            em.getTransaction().commit();
            logger.log(Level.INFO,
                        "New Person: {0} successfully added.",newPerson);
            getPropertyChangeSupport().firePropertyChange(
               FamilyTreeManager.PROP_PERSON_ADDED, null, buildPerson(person));
        } catch (Exception ex) {
            logger.log(Level.SEVERE, null, ex);
        } finally {
            em.close();
        }
    }

    @Override
    public void updatePerson(final Person p) {
        EntityManager em = EMF.createEntityManager();
        try {
            em.getTransaction().begin();
            PersonEntity target = em.find(PersonEntity.class, p.getId());
            if (target != null) {
                target.setFirstname(p.getFirstname());
                target.setGender(p.getGender());
                target.setLastname(p.getLastname());
                target.setMiddlename(p.getMiddlename());
                target.setNotes(p.getNotes());
                target.setSuffix(p.getSuffix());
                em.merge(target);
                em.getTransaction().commit();
                logger.log(Level.FINE, "Person {0} successfully updated.", p);
                getPropertyChangeSupport().firePropertyChange(
                FamilyTreeManager.PROP_PERSON_UPDATED, null,
                                             buildPerson(target));
            }
            logger.log(Level.WARNING, "No entity for Person {0}.", p);
        } catch (Exception ex) {
            logger.log(Level.SEVERE, null, ex);
        } finally {
            em.close();
        }
    }

    @Override
    public void deletePerson(Person p) {
        EntityManager em = EMF.createEntityManager();
        try {
            em.getTransaction().begin();
            PersonEntity target = em.find(PersonEntity.class, p.getId());
```

```
            if (target != null) {
                em.remove(target);
                em.getTransaction().commit();
                logger.log(Level.FINE, "Person {0} successfully removed.", p);
                getPropertyChangeSupport().firePropertyChange(
                    FamilyTreeManager.PROP_PERSON_DESTROYED, null, p);
            } else {
                logger.log(Level.WARNING, "No entity for Person {0}.", p);
            }
        } catch (Exception ex) {
            logger.log(Level.SEVERE, null, ex);
        } finally {
            em.close();
        }
    }

    @SuppressWarnings("unchecked")
    @Override
    public List<Person> getAllPeople() {
        EntityManager em = EMF.createEntityManager();
        try {
            List<Person> people = Collections.synchronizedList(
                                            new ArrayList<>());
            em.getTransaction().begin();
            Query q = em.createQuery(
      "select p from PersonEntity p order by p.lastname asc, p.firstname asc");
           List<PersonEntity> results = (List<PersonEntity>) q.getResultList();
            if (results != null && results.size() > 0) {
                results.stream().forEach((pe) -> {
                    people.add(buildPerson(pe));
                });
            }
            em.getTransaction().commit();
            return Collections.unmodifiableList(people);
        } catch (Exception ex) {
            logger.log(Level.SEVERE, null, ex);
            return null;
        }  finally {
            em.close();
        }
    }
}
```

## Updating Class Person

Listing 10.24 shows the modified Person class. The new constructor uses the id generated by the database.

**Listing 10.24 Person.java**

```
public final class Person implements Serializable {

    private long id;
    private String firstname;
    private String middlename;
    private String lastname;
    private String suffix;
    private Person.Gender gender;
    private String notes;

. . . code omitted . . .

    public Person() {
        this("", "", Gender.UNKNOWN);
    }

    public Person(long id) {
        this("", "", Gender.UNKNOWN);
        this.id = id;
    }

    public Person(String first, String last, Person.Gender gender) {
        this.firstname = first;
        this.middlename = "";
        this.lastname = last;
        this.suffix = "";
        this.gender = gender;
        this.notes = "";
    }

    public Person(Person person) {
        this.firstname = person.getFirstname();
        this.middlename = person.getMiddlename();
        this.lastname = person.getLastname();
        this.suffix = person.getSuffix();
        this.gender = person.getGender();
        this.notes = person.getNotes();
        this.id = person.getId();
    }
. . . code omitted . . .
}
```

### Running the Application

To run this application, start the JavaDB Database server and execute the Family-TreeApp. The first time you run the application, the Persistence Unit generates the database table. The FamilyTreeModel `@OnStart` class creates the sample data (see "Using @OnStart" on page 242).

Figure 10.15 shows the FamilyTreeApp running after the user makes changes (Person Abraham Simpson is added and several records have been updated). The full CRUD actions we implemented earlier work as before, except now the data is stored in a database.

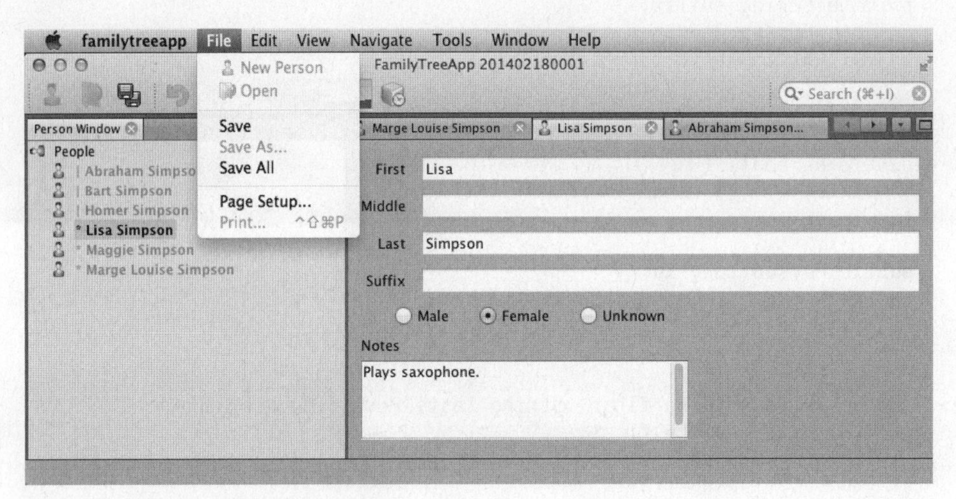


Figure 10.15 Running the application

## Viewing the Database

After running the application, you can view the database structure in the Services window of the NetBeans IDE. Expand the **Databases** node, right click on database **jdbc:derby://localhost:1527/personftm [personftm on PERSONFTM]**, and select **Connect**. After connecting, expand **PERSONFTM | Tables | PERSON** to view the database columns, as shown in Figure 10.16.

You can also view the data. In the Services window, right click on table **PERSON** and select **View Data** from the context menu. After executing the SQL, you see the data displayed in the IDE's window, as shown in Figure 10.17.

# 10.3 Concurrency in the FamilyTreeApp Application

Now that we've added database access to the FamilyTreeApp, we must make sure our application UI remains responsive. To that end, we'll execute database access code in

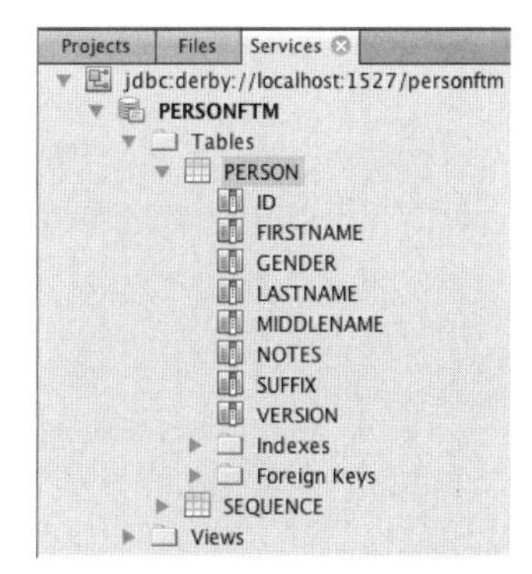


Figure 10.16 Viewing the database structure

Connection: jdbc:derby://localhost:1527/personftm [personftm on PER...

```
1    select * from PERSONFTM.PERSON;
```

select * from PERSONFTM.P...

Page Size: 20 Total Rows: 6 Page: 1 of 1

| # | ID | FIRSTNAME | GENDER | LASTNAME | MIDDLENAME | NOTES | SUFFIX |
|---|---|---|---|---|---|---|---|
| 1 | 1 | Homer | 0 | Simpson | | Doh | |
| 2 | 2 | Marge | 1 | Simpson | Louise | Marge is the mom. | |
| 3 | 3 | Bart | 0 | Simpson | | Bart is a skateboarder. | |
| 4 | 4 | Lisa | 1 | Simpson | | Plays saxophone. | |
| 5 | 5 | Maggie | 1 | Simpson | | Maggie is the baby. | |
| 6 | 6 | Abraham | 0 | Simpson | | Abe is Homer's dad. | |

Figure 10.17 Viewing the data after running the application

background threads. In general, SwingWorker provides the needed concurrency (see “Introducing SwingWorker” on page 73) . However, the NetBeans Platform also has built-in concurrency with the Nodes API that we can leverage.

## Concurrency with Read

Database reads occur when we build the node structures in the Person Viewer window. Class RootNode invokes `Children.create()` to build child nodes. The `Children.create()` method includes an asynchronous flag, which when set to true, builds the children nodes in a background thread and automatically includes a placeholder node with display name “Please wait ... ”. Modify RootNode.java to set the asynchronous flag to true, as shown in Listing 10.25.

**Listing 10.25 RootNode.java**

```
@Messages({
    "HINT_RootNode=Show all people",
    "LBL_RootNode=People"
})
public class RootNode extends AbstractNode {

    private final InstanceContent instanceContent;
    private final PersonType personType = new PersonType();
    public RootNode() {
        this(new InstanceContent());
    }

    private RootNode(InstanceContent ic) {
        // create children asynchronously
        super(Children.create(
            new PersonChildFactory(), true), new AbstractLookup(ic));
        instanceContent = ic;
        setIconBaseWithExtension(
         "com/asgteach/familytree/personviewer/resources/personIcon.png");
        setDisplayName(Bundle.LBL_RootNode());
        setShortDescription(Bundle.HINT_RootNode());
        // Required to enable New Person in context menu and Toolbar and Menus
        instanceContent.add(personType);
        instanceContent.add(new RefreshCapability(){

            @Override
            public void refresh() throws IOException {
                // create children asynchronously
                setChildren(Children.create(new PersonChildFactory(), true));
            }
        });
    }
   . . . code omitted . . .
}
```

When you invoke the ChildFactory with the asynchronous flag set to true, the factory's `createKeys()` and `refresh()` methods execute in a background thread (the `refresh()` method's boolean flag is ignored). No other changes are required in PersonChildFactory to achieve this concurrency.

## Progress Indicator

You can configure a progress indicator in the PersonChildFactory's `createKeys()` method. In this example, the database read is indeterminate. Figure 10.18 shows the progress indicator, as well as the node hierarchy display ("Please wait ... ") indicating a background thread is busy. You must add a module dependency on Progress API to use this progress indicator.

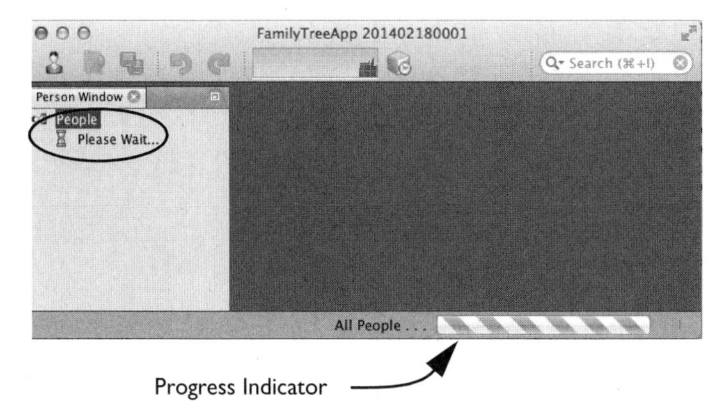


Figure 10.18 Using the NetBeans Platform progress indicator and node busy display

Listing 10.26 shows PersonChildFactory.java with the progress indicator configured. Note that a progress indicator does not appear if a background task is short lived. To make the progress indicator appear and test how a long-running background task affects the responsiveness of the application, we add a call to `Thread.sleep()` (for testing only) in the `createKeys()` method.

**Listing 10.26 PersonChildFactory—Using a Progress Indicator**

```
@NbBundle.Messages({
    "LBLPersonRead=All People . . . "
})
public class PersonChildFactory extends ChildFactory<Person> {

   . . . code omitted . . .

    @Override
    protected boolean createKeys(List<Person> list) {
        RefreshCapability refreshCapability =
            personCapability.getLookup().lookup(RefreshCapability.class);
        if (refreshCapability != null) {
            ProgressHandle handle = ProgressHandleFactory.createHandle(
                              Bundle.LBLPersonRead());
            try {
                handle.start();
                // testing only !!!
                Thread.sleep(1000);
                refreshCapability.refresh();
                list.addAll(personCapability.getPersonList());
                logger.log(Level.FINER, "createKeys called: {0}", list);
```

```
            } catch (IOException | InterruptedException ex) {
                logger.log(Level.WARNING, null, ex);
            } finally {
                handle.finish();
            }
        }
        return true;
    }
    . . . code omitted . . .
}
```

## Concurrency with Delete and Create

Both the delete and create functions of the FamilyTreeApp update the Person Viewer window. This invokes the `createKeys()` method in the background. However, we must perform the delete and create database functions in the background, too.

The delete function is performed by PersonNode's `destroy()` method, as shown in Listing 10.27. It looks up RemovablePersonCapability and Person from the Lookup and invokes the `remove()` method. Here, we use SwingWorker to execute this `remove()` method in a background task.

**Listing 10.27 PersonNode—Performing Destroy in the Background**

```
public class PersonNode extends AbstractNode {

   . . . code omitted . . .

    @Override
    public void destroy() throws IOException {
        final RemovablePersonCapability doRemove = getLookup().lookup(
                RemovablePersonCapability.class);
        final Person person = getLookup().lookup(Person.class);
        if (doRemove != null && person != null) {
            SwingWorker<Void, Void> worker = new SwingWorker<Void, Void>() {

                @Override
                protected Void doInBackground() {
                    try {
                        doRemove.remove(person);
                    } catch (IOException e) {
                        logger.log(Level.WARNING, null, e);
                    }
                    return null;
                }
            };
```

```
                worker.execute();
            }
        }
    }
```

Similarly, Listing 10.28 shows how class PersonType implements the create function. It looks up CreatablePersonCapability in the Lookup of PersonCapability and invokes the `create()` method in a background thread with SwingWorker. We configure a progress indicator (again, the indicator only appears if the background task is not short lived).

**Listing 10.28 PersonType—Performing Create in the Background**

```
public class PersonType extends NewType {

         . . . code omitted . . .

    @Override
    public void create() throws IOException {

              . . . code omitted . . .

        if (NotifyDescriptor.YES_OPTION.equals(result)) {
            // Create a new Person object
            final Person person = new Person();
            person.setFirstname(firstname);
            person.setLastname(lastname);
            final CreatablePersonCapability cpc = personCapability.getLookup()
                         .lookup(CreatablePersonCapability.class);
            if (cpc != null) {
               SwingWorker<Void, Void> worker = new SwingWorker<Void, Void>() {

                    @Override
                    protected Void doInBackground() throws Exception {
                        ProgressHandle handle = ProgressHandleFactory
                             .createHandle(Bundle.TITLE_NewPerson_dialog());
                        try {
                            handle.start();
                            cpc.create(person);
                            logger.log(Level.INFO,
                                   "Creating person {0}", person);
                        } catch (IOException e) {
                            logger.log(Level.WARNING,
                                   e.getLocalizedMessage(), e);
                        } finally {
                            handle.finish();
                        }
                        return null;
                    }
               };
```

```
                worker.execute();
            }
        }
    }
}
```

## Concurrency with Update

Updating occurs in the PersonEditorTopComponent when a user clicks the Save or SaveAll menu item, or when a user selects Save when closing the window with unsaved data. Listing 10.29 shows the `handleSave()` method. Here, the SavablePersonCapability `save()` method is invoked in a background thread with SwingWorker. We configure a progress indicator that includes the Person's name. Again, using the progress indicator requires a module dependency on the Progress API.

**Listing 10.29 SavableViewCapability—Performing Update in the Background**

```
private class SavableViewCapability extends AbstractSavable {

   . . . code omitted . . .

        @Override
        protected void handleSave() throws IOException {
            final Node node = getLookup().lookup(Node.class);
            if (node != null) {
                final SavablePersonCapability savable
                    = node.getLookup().lookup(SavablePersonCapability.class);
                if (savable != null) {
                    updateModel();
                    // make a copy of Person for the background thread
                    final Person p = new Person(thePerson);
                    clearSaveCapability();
                    changeOK = true;
                    // perform the save on a background thread
                    SwingWorker<Void, Void> worker =
                                   new SwingWorker<Void, Void>() {

                        @Override
                        protected Void doInBackground() throws Exception {
                            ProgressHandle handle = ProgressHandleFactory
                                .createHandle(Bundle.CTL_PersonUpdating(p));
                            try {
                                handle.start();
                                savable.save(p);
                            } catch (IOException ex) {
                                logger.log(Level.WARNING, "handleSave", ex);
```

```
                        } finally {
                            handle.finish();
                        }
                        return null;
                    }
                };
                worker.execute();
            }
        }
    }
}
```

Figure 10.19 shows the progress indicator during execution of the `handleSave()` method.

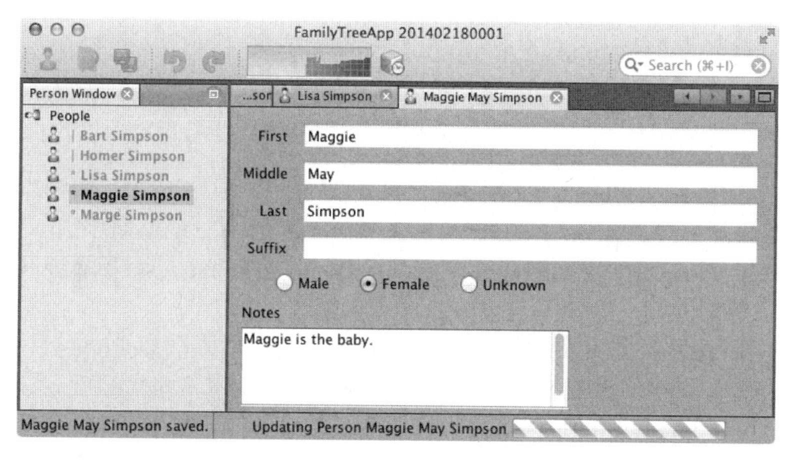


Figure 10.19 Saving the updated Person in a background thread

## 10.4 Key Point Summary

This chapter shows you how to apply capabilities and actions to implement CRUD operations for a NetBeans Platform application. You also learn how to implement a database for the persistent store and use concurrency to keep your application responsive. Here are the key points in this chapter.

- Adding capabilities to a Lookup (of a node or any object) is an effective way to customize actions. Capabilities and Lookup provide loose coupling between objects that invoke a capability's method and objects that own the capability.
- Read operations build node hierarchies in a CRUD application.

- The NetBeans Platform system DeleteAction lets you hook into the pre-configured Delete in the Edit menu. To use Delete with nodes, override a node's `canDestroy()` and `destroy()` methods.
- Add DeleteAction to a node's `getActions()` method to include Delete in the node's context menu.
- Use NewType and NewAction to configure Create operations. Override a node's `getNewTypes()` method and include an implementation of NewType. You can also register a create action for the top-level menu and toolbar.
- Implement Update operations with open/edit actions. Open an editor suitable for making changes to the domain object. A non-singleton TopComponent allows multiple editors to be opened concurrently.
- For Updates, use AbstractSavable to enable and disable the Save and Save All menu items and toolbar icon. Override TopComponent method `canClose()` to see if unsaved changes should be saved before closing an editor.
- Implement AbstractSavable to provide the save operation.
- Detect when an opened domain object has been deleted and gracefully close the editor.
- Migrating to a database implementation is straightforward when a service provider performs database actions.
- Create Library Wrapper Modules for library JAR files that your application requires. This integrates the libraries into the NetBeans module system.
- JavaDB provides a database that's built into the NetBeans Platform.
- EclipseLink provides an implementation of Java Persistence API (JPA) to interface with an underlying database.
- Create or use NetBeans to generate entity classes and a persistence unit that define the JPA/Database properties of your application.
- To keep NetBeans Platform applications responsive, use SwingWorker and the Nodes API asynchronous mode to execute database access in the background.
- Use the progress indicator to provide feedback to the user for long-running tasks.

# 11

# Dialogs

Chances are that at some point in your application, you'll need to display a dialog to communicate with the user. The NetBeans Platform has a Dialogs API that provides a collection of predefined dialogs and related utilities. Dialog types include simple messages, Yes-No confirmations, OK-Cancel confirmations, and dialogs that request input. The standard dialogs are also configurable, but if the standard fare is not flexible enough for you, you can always create a custom dialog.

In this chapter, we'll explore all of these offerings.

## What You Will Learn

- Create standard message, confirmation, and input line dialogs.
- Customize standard dialogs.
- Process user responses in dialogs.
- Customize dialogs.
- Provide error handling with custom dialogs.
- Use dialog notifications.
- Create a custom login dialog.

## 11.1 Dialog Overview

The Dialogs API provides several classes that help you create, display, and obtain input from dialogs. To use the Dialog framework, specify a dependency on the Dialogs API in your module.

**Dialogs, Windows, or Wizards?**

*Note that the Dialogs API provides separate, modal message boxes. Use TopComponents to create windows (see Chapter 8, "NetBeans Platform Window System," on page 341). For a multi-step sequence of input panels, refer to Chapter 12, "Wizards," on page 551.*

The NotifyDescriptor class has subclasses that let you create standard dialogs. You configure dialogs either with alternate constructors or NotifyDescriptor methods. After creating the dialog, you display it with DialogDisplayer methods. You can display the dialog immediately or asynchronously, and NotifyDescriptor provides constants to help you determine user responses.

You can also provide notifications within a dialog, either by defining the notification beforehand or as a response to user input.

For the most part, then, standard dialogs (perhaps with minor configuration) provide a rich selection of dialogs in the NetBeans Platform. For more customized uses, you can build your own panel component and give it to NotifyDescriptor or one of its subclasses. You can configure the dialog title or specify the set of option buttons. For advanced customizations, you build a dialog with DialogDescriptor. We'll show you how to create custom dialogs with DialogDescriptor later in the chapter.

The NetBeans dialog classes are similar to the Swing JOptionPane class except they provide the following features.

- NotifyDescriptor and DialogDescriptor are integrated into the NetBeans Platform window system and help system.
- Dialogs are automatically centered in the viewing area.
- You can use the ESC key to close a dialog.
- The DialogDisplayer class provides a standard look and feel for displaying dialogs and returning status.
- You can customize any dialog or notice, but many times customization is not necessary.
- You can optionally provide your own inner panel.

# 11.2 Standard Dialogs

Let's first look at the standard dialogs in their simplest forms. NotifyDescriptor includes several subclasses that define certain types of standard dialogs.

## NotifyDescriptor.Message

`NotifyDescriptor.Message` is meant to convey a message, as shown in Figure 11.1. The standard dialog includes the dialog title (Information), message text, and an OK button. Although you can access its return value, typically the user simply clicks OK to dismiss the dialog.

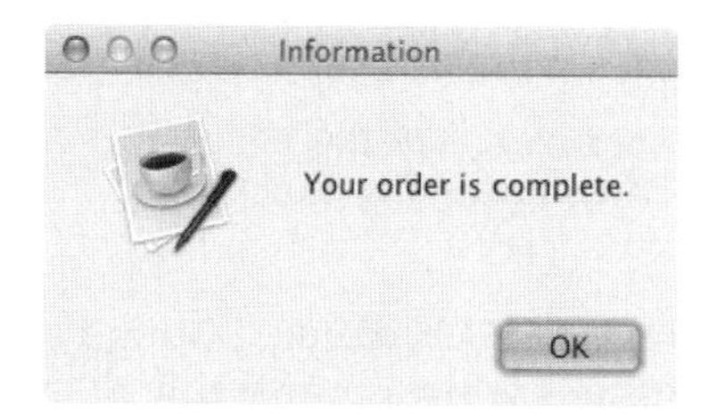


Figure 11.1 Standard Information dialog

Listing 11.1 creates the standard message dialog shown in Figure 11.1, displays the dialog, and blocks until the user closes the dialog (either by clicking the OK button or closing it explicitly).

**Listing 11.1 Standard Message Dialog**

```
NotifyDescriptor nd = new NotifyDescriptor.Message("Your order is complete.");
DialogDisplayer.getDefault().notify(nd);        // display and block
```

Variants of the `NotifyDescriptor.Message` include a Warning message and an Error message. Figure 11.2 shows a Warning message.

Listing 11.2 shows how to create this Warning message. Use constructor argument `NotifyDescriptor.WARNING_MESSAGE` to specify a warning icon and set the title to Warning.

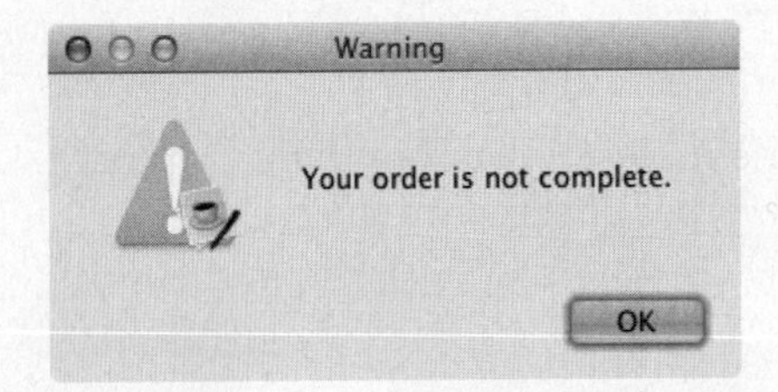


Figure 11.2 Standard Warning dialog

**Listing 11.2 Standard Warning Message Dialog**

```
NotifyDescriptor nd = new NotifyDescriptor.Message(
        "Your order is not complete.", NotifyDescriptor.WARNING_MESSAGE);
DialogDisplayer.getDefault().notify(nd);        // display and block
```

Similarly, Figure 11.3 shows the `NotifyDescriptor.ERROR_MESSAGE` dialog. Listing 11.3 shows how to build and display a standard Error message, which sets the title to Error and uses an error-type icon.

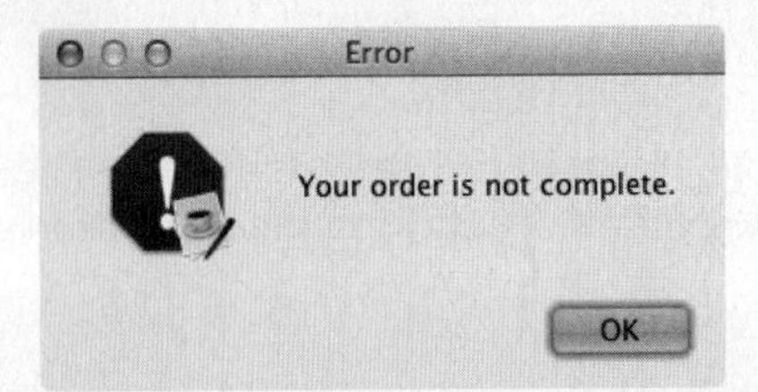


Figure 11.3 Standard Error message dialog

**Listing 11.3 Standard Error Message Dialog**

```
NotifyDescriptor nd = new NotifyDescriptor.Message(
        "Your order is not complete.", NotifyDescriptor.ERROR_MESSAGE);
DialogDisplayer.getDefault().notify(nd);        // display and block
```

Table 11.1 lists the available NotifyDescriptor message types. Note that `INFORMATION_MESSAGE` is the default for `NotifyDescriptor.Message` and `PLAIN_MESSAGE` displays no icon. `QUESTION_MESSAGE` is the default for `NotifyDescriptor.Confirmation` message, which we discuss next.

**TABLE 11.1 NotifyDescriptor Message Types**

| Type | Description/Icon | Default Title |
|---|---|---|
| `INFORMATION_MESSAGE` | Information Icon, default for `NotifyDescriptor.Message` | Information |
| `WARNING_MESSAGE` | Warning Symbol | Warning |
| `ERROR_MESSAGE` | Error Symbol | Error |
| `PLAIN_MESSAGE` | No Icon | Message |
| `QUESTION_MESSAGE` | Question Icon, default for `NotifyDescriptor.Confirmation` | Question |

## NotifyDescriptor.Confirmation

Confirming or verifying an action before proceeding is a common requirement in applications. The standard Confirmation dialog uses a Question title and supplies button options for Yes, No, and Cancel. You can check for a user's response (as well as `NotifyDescriptor.CLOSED_OPTION`) and react accordingly. Figure 11.4 shows the standard Confirmation dialog.

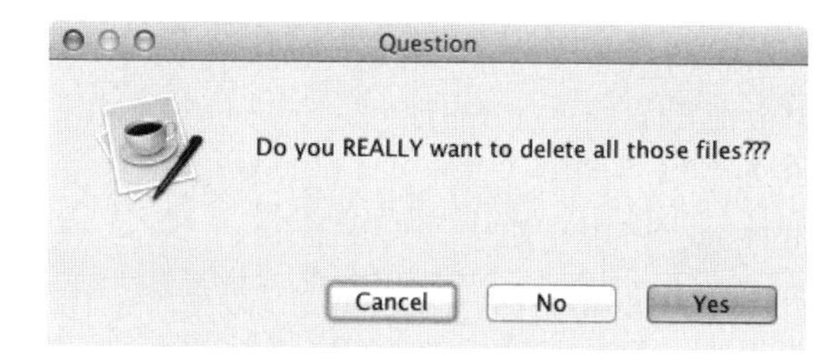


Figure 11.4 Standard Confirmation dialog

Listing 11.4 shows a typical usage with the standard Confirmation dialog. Here we check the return value against `NotifyDescriptor.YES_OPTION` (the user pressed the Yes button).

**Listing 11.4 Standard Confirmation Dialog**

```
NotifyDescriptor nd = new NotifyDescriptor.Confirmation(
        "Do you REALLY want to delete all those files???");

if (DialogDisplayer.getDefault().notify(nd) == NotifyDescriptor.YES_OPTION) {
        // Yes, really delete all those files.
}
```

Table 11.2 shows the possible return values for the standard dialogs.

**TABLE 11.2 NotifyDescriptor Return Values**

| Return Value Constant | Description |
|---|---|
| `YES_OPTION` | User pressed button YES. |
| `NO_OPTION` | User pressed button NO. |
| `OK_OPTION` | User pressed button OK. |
| `CANCEL_OPTION` | User pressed button Cancel. |
| `CLOSED_OPTION` | User closed the dialog without pressing any buttons. |

Although you typically check for a particular response result with a dialog, you might want to make a distinction among several possible return options, including `NotifyDescriptor.CLOSED_OPTION` (the user closed the dialog without pressing any buttons). The code in Listing 11.5 checks all possible user responses with a Confirmation dialog (such as the dialog shown in Figure 11.4).

**Listing 11.5 Checking the User's Response**

```
NotifyDescriptor nd = new NotifyDescriptor.Confirmation(
            "Do you REALLY want to delete all those files???");

Object status = DialogDisplayer.getDefault().notify(nd);
if (status == NotifyDescriptor.YES_OPTION) {
      // Yes
} else if (status == NotifyDescriptor.NO_OPTION) {
      // No
} else if (status == NotifyDescriptor.CANCEL_OPTION) {
      // Cancel
} else if (status == NotifyDescriptor.CLOSED_OPTION) {
      // Window explicitly closed
}
```

**Dialog Tip**

*Note that DialogDisplayer method* `notify()` *displays and blocks a dialog and returns the user input that closed it. If you need a dialog to remain open after the user clicks one or more of the option buttons, then you must supply an ActionListener with method* `actionPerformed()` *to process user input. We show you this technique in sections "Custom Login Dialog" on page 539 and "Putting It All Together" on page 544.*

### NotifyDescriptor.InputLine

Use `NotifyDescriptor.InputLine` to create dialogs that prompt for user input. Figure 11.5 shows the standard Input Line dialog with a preset text and after the user supplies an email address. InputLine dialogs include Cancel and OK button options.

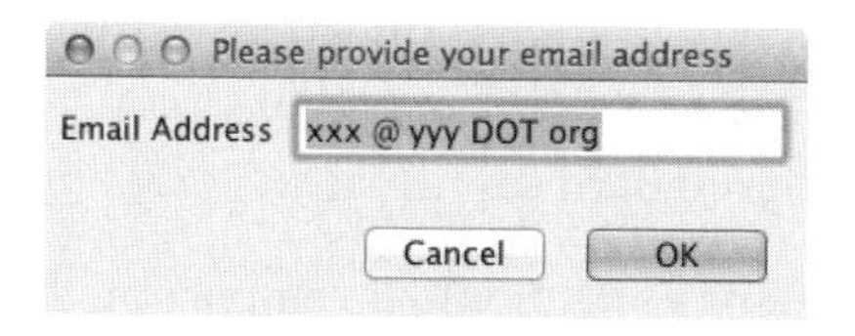


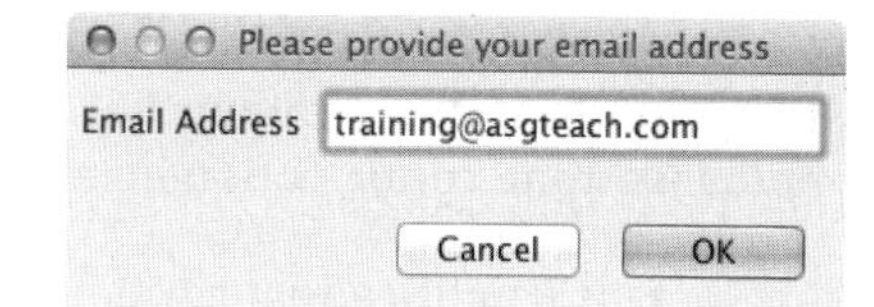


Figure 11.5 Standard InputLine dialog

Dialog `NotifyDescriptor.InputLine` constructor requires a prompt as the first argument and a dialog title as the second argument. Use `setInputText()` to optionally preset the text input and `getInputText()` to read user input after the dialog closes. Typically, you check to make sure the user clicks OK before reading the text, as shown in Listing 11.6.

**Listing 11.6 Standard Input Line Dialog**

```
NotifyDescriptor.InputLine nd = new NotifyDescriptor.InputLine(
      "Email Address", "Please provide your email address");

nd.setInputText("xxx @ yyy DOT org");
if (DialogDisplayer.getDefault().notify(nd) == NotifyDescriptor.OK_OPTION) {
      // OK, read the input
      doSomethingWithEmailAddress(nd.getInputText());
}
```

## 11.3 Customizing Standard Dialogs

You can easily customize any of the standard dialogs, although not all combinations of possible configurations make sense. Besides the various message types listed in Table 11.1, you can also configure the option buttons for a dialog, as shown in Table 11.3.

**TABLE 11.3 NotifyDescriptor Dialog Option Buttons**

| Option | Meaning |
|---|---|
| `DEFAULT_OPTION` | The default buttons according to the dialog type |
| `OK_CANCEL_OPTION` | Display OK and Cancel buttons |

**TABLE 11.3 NotifyDescriptor Dialog Option Buttons** *(Continued)*

| Option | Meaning |
|---|---|
| YES_NO_OPTION | Display Yes and No buttons |
| YES_NO_CANCEL_OPTION | Display Yes, No, and Cancel buttons |

Let's look at an example of customizing the Confirmation dialog. In Figure 11.6, you see a customized title, button options Yes and No (instead of the default Yes, No, and Cancel), and a warning confirmation instead of the standard confirmation.

In addition, there is a notification warning ("Please pay attention!") to emphasize the potential consequences of a wrong response. Listing 11.7 shows the code for this customized confirmation dialog.

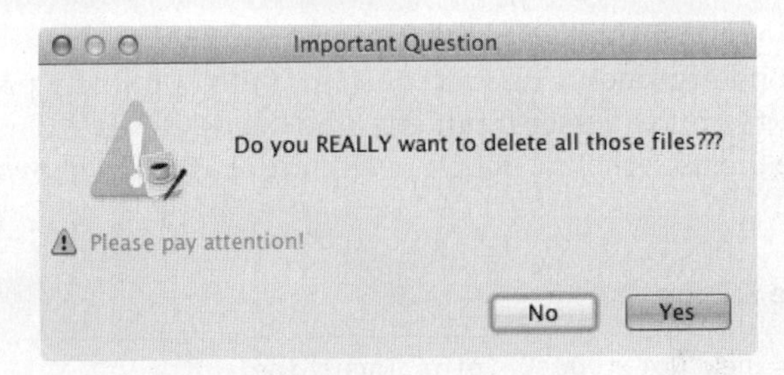


Figure 11.6 Customized Question dialog

**Listing 11.7 Customized Confirmation Dialog**

```
NotifyDescriptor nd = new NotifyDescriptor.Confirmation(
   "Do you REALLY want to delete all those files???",
   "Important Question",
   NotifyDescriptor.YES_NO_OPTION,
   NotifyDescriptor.WARNING_MESSAGE);

nd.createNotificationLineSupport();
nd.getNotificationLineSupport().setWarningMessage("Please pay attention!");

if (DialogDisplayer.getDefault().notify(nd) == NotifyDescriptor.YES_OPTION) {
         // Yes, really delete all those files.
}
```

# 11.4 Custom Dialogs

The Dialogs API lets you create custom dialogs with class DialogDescriptor, a class that extends NotifyDescriptor. DialogDescriptor offers several constructors that let you build custom dialogs. The main advantage of DialogDescriptor is that you can specify additional features, such as contextual help, button listeners, button alignment, and button text. You can also build your own inner panel for display inside a dialog, so that a dialog's view can hold any set of components that you need.

If you build a custom inner panel, you'll also need public methods that access user input. Let's build a simple custom dialog that asks for a person's first and last names. Later we'll enhance this dialog with error checking.

Figure 11.7 shows a Person Information dialog. We've configured the dialog with a title (Person Information), a notification line, and option buttons Cancel and OK.

Figure 11.7 Dialog with customized view

For the inner panel, we'll use a customized JPanel component that includes two labels (First Name and Last Name), two textfields, and an icon, as shown in Figure 11.8. To create this form, right-click on your module's package and select **New | JPanel Form**. Call the class **CustomPersonPanel**. NetBeans creates a new Java class with a top-level JPanel in the Matisse form designer. Now add the labels, textfields, and icon. (Use a JLabel component with a suitable image for the icon.)

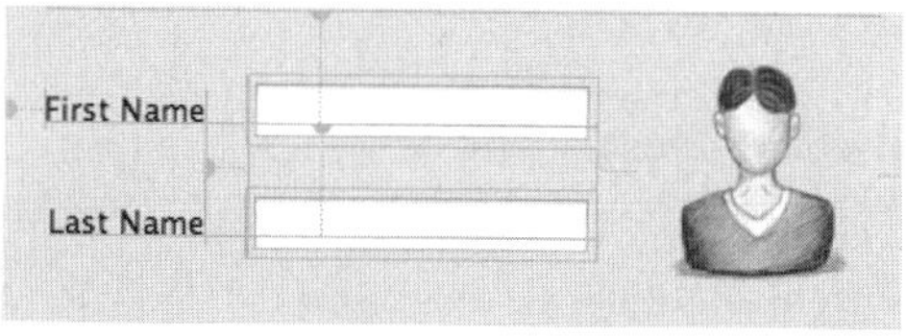

Figure 11.8 JPanel design view with labels, textfields, and an icon

**Dialog Tip**

*Note that you don't add the title, notification line, or option buttons to the JPanel. You configure these dialog artifacts with DialogDescriptor.*

Listing 11.8 shows the code for CustomPersonPanel.java. After the design is complete, add the public methods to access user input. Here we added methods `getFirstName()` and `getLastName()` (shown in bold).

### Listing 11.8 CustomPersonPanel—Customized JPanel Form

```
public class CustomPersonPanel extends javax.swing.JPanel {

    public CustomPersonPanel() {
        initComponents();
    }

    public String getFirstName() {
        return firstTextField.getText();
    }

    public String getLastName() {
        return lastTextField.getText();
    }

    // Generated Code

    . . . code omitted . . .

    // Variables declaration - do not modify
    private javax.swing.JTextField firstTextField;
    private javax.swing.JLabel imageLabel;
    private javax.swing.JLabel jLabel1;
    private javax.swing.JLabel jLabel2;
    private javax.swing.JTextField lastTextField;
    // End of variables declaration
}
```

With the JPanel complete, we can now build the custom dialog and configure it with DialogDescriptor, as shown in Listing 11.9.

### Listing 11.9 Build a Custom Dialog with DialogDescriptor

```
// Create the JPanel Form
CustomPersonPanel panel = new CustomPersonPanel();

// Create the dialog with CustomPersonaPanel panel
DialogDescriptor dd = new DialogDescriptor(panel, "Person Information");
```

```
// Configure a notification line
dd.createNotificationLineSupport();
// Specify the notification line; use Information-style
dd.getNotificationLineSupport().setInformationMessage(
      "Please provide your first and last names");

// Display the dialog and wait for the response
Object status = DialogDisplayer.getDefault().notify(dd);
if (status == NotifyDescriptor.OK_OPTION) {
   // Is there any input?
   if (panel.getFirstName().isEmpty() && panel.getLastName().isEmpty()) {
      // No, say hello to 'Anonymous'
      System.out.println("Welcome, Anonymous!");
   } else {
      // Supply a greeting using the person's name
      System.out.println("Welcome " + panel.getFirstName() + " "
                     + panel.getLastName() + "!");
   }
} else if (status == NotifyDescriptor.CANCEL_OPTION) {
   // Cancel
} else if (status == NotifyDescriptor.CLOSED_OPTION) {
   // User closed the dialog
}
```

Note that the above code does not specify any option buttons. As it turns out, the default provides Cancel and OK.

## Error Handling

Now let's modify the Person Information dialog to perform some error handling. Figure 11.9 shows the Person Information dialog with an error message for required input. Note that this dialog is currently marked invalid; that is, the OK button is disabled.

Person Information

First Name Homer

Last Name

Fields First Name and Last Name are required.

Cancel OK

Figure 11.9 Custom dialog with error handling and invalid status

Figure 11.10 shows the same dialog. This time both fields are filled in and the dialog's error message has been cleared. Also, the OK button is enabled, meaning that the dialog is currently valid.

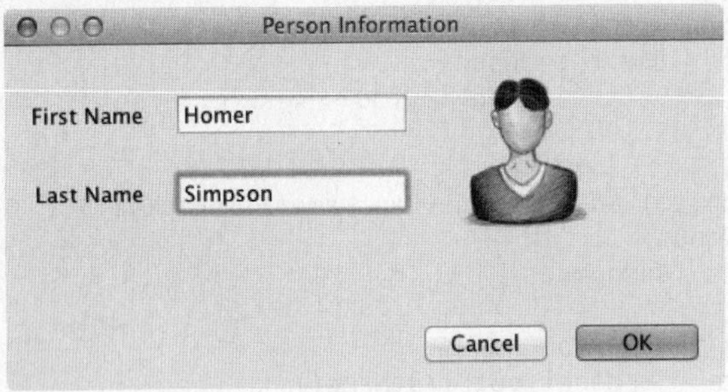

Figure 11.10 Custom dialog showing no errors and valid status

A powerful feature of NetBeans dialogs is that you can install property change listeners to detect input changes and update error messages and a dialog's valid status. This section shows you how to do this. You'll also see this technique used to validate panels when we build wizards (see "Wizard Validation" on page 565).

First, add DocumentListeners in the inner panel and have the inner panel fire property change events when user input changes. Then, the dialog code checks the input, provides feedback, and validates the dialog.

Let's begin by making the following modifications to the JPanel form in class CustomPersonPanel2. Here are the steps.

1. Make CustomPersonPanel2 implement DocumentListener and override methods `insertUpdate()`, `removeUpdate()`, and `changeUpdate()`.
2. Add public static String constants `PROP_FIRST_NAME` and `PROP_LAST_NAME` to identify the property change events.
3. Add document listeners to the first and last name textfield components.
4. Fire property change events when a user modifies a textfield's input.

Listing 11.10 shows these modifications to CustomPersonPanel2 in bold.

**Listing 11.10 CustomPersonPanel2—Implement Dialog Error Handling**

```
public class CustomPersonPanel2 extends javax.swing.JPanel implements
        DocumentListener {

    public static String PROP_FIRST_NAME = "firstName";
    public static String PROP_LAST_NAME = "lastName";
```

```
public CustomPersonPanel2() {
    initComponents();
    firstTextField.getDocument().addDocumentListener(this);
    lastTextField.getDocument().addDocumentListener(this);
}

public String getFirstName() {
    return firstTextField.getText();
}

public String getLastName() {
    return lastTextField.getText();
}

private void initComponents() {

  . . . generated code omitted . . .

}

// Variables declaration - do not modify
private javax.swing.JTextField firstTextField;
private javax.swing.JLabel imageLabel;
private javax.swing.JLabel jLabel1;
private javax.swing.JLabel jLabel2;
private javax.swing.JTextField lastTextField;
// End of variables declaration

@Override
public void insertUpdate(DocumentEvent de) {
    if (firstTextField.getDocument() == de.getDocument()) {
        firePropertyChange(PROP_FIRST_NAME, 0, 1);
    } else if (lastTextField.getDocument() == de.getDocument()) {
        firePropertyChange(PROP_LAST_NAME, 0, 1);
    }
}

@Override
public void removeUpdate(DocumentEvent de) {
    if (firstTextField.getDocument() == de.getDocument()) {
        firePropertyChange(PROP_FIRST_NAME, 0, 1);
    } else if (lastTextField.getDocument() == de.getDocument()) {
        firePropertyChange(PROP_LAST_NAME, 0, 1);
    }
}

@Override
public void changedUpdate(DocumentEvent de) {
    if (firstTextField.getDocument() == de.getDocument()) {
        firePropertyChange(PROP_FIRST_NAME, 0, 1);
```

```
        } else if (lastTextField.getDocument() == de.getDocument()) {
            firePropertyChange(PROP_LAST_NAME, 0, 1);
        }
    }
}
```

Now let's show you the code that creates, configures, and displays the dialog. This code implements the actual validation checking by listening for property change events, as shown in Listing 11.11. The code in bold marks the changes required to implement the error handling.

### Listing 11.11 Implement Dialog Error Handling

```
// Create the inner panel
private CustomPersonPanel2 panel2 = new CustomPersonPanel2();

// Create the Dialog and specify title
final DialogDescriptor dd = new DialogDescriptor(panel2,
               "Person Information");

// Configure a notification line
dd.createNotificationLineSupport();
// Specify the notification line; use Error-style
dd.getNotificationLineSupport().setErrorMessage(
               "Fields First Name and Last Name are required.");
// Specify that the dialog is not valid; this disables the OK button
dd.setValid(false);
// Create a property change listener anonymous class
panel2.addPropertyChangeListener(new PropertyChangeListener() {

            // Specify the class' propertyChange method
            // Look for PROP_FIRST_NAME and PROP_LAST_NAME property change
            // events and update valid status and error message
            @Override
            public void propertyChange(PropertyChangeEvent pce) {
                if (pce.getPropertyName().equals(
                     CustomPersonPanel2.PROP_FIRST_NAME)
                        || pce.getPropertyName().equals(
                           CustomPersonPanel2.PROP_LAST_NAME)) {
                    if (panel2.getFirstName().isEmpty() ||
                              panel2.getLastName().isEmpty()) {
                        dd.setValid(false);
                        dd.getNotificationLineSupport().setErrorMessage(
                              "Fields First Name and Last Name are required.");
```

```
                    } else {
                        dd.setValid(true);
                        dd.getNotificationLineSupport().clearMessages();
                    }
                }
            }
        });

// Display the dialog and wait for response
Object status = DialogDisplayer.getDefault().notify(dd);
if (status == NotifyDescriptor.OK_OPTION) {
   // Supply a greeting using the person's name
   System.out.println("Welcome " + panel.getFirstName() + " "
                        + panel.getLastName() + "!");
} else if (status == NotifyDescriptor.CANCEL_OPTION) {
   // Cancel
} else if (status == NotifyDescriptor.CLOSED_OPTION) {
   // Closed
}
```

Note that an anonymous class defines the property listener. Overridden method propertyChange() examines each property change event. If either of the panel's textfield components is empty, we mark the dialog invalid and display an error message using the notification message dialog feature. If both textfields contain input, we mark the dialog valid and clear the notification message.

## 11.5 Custom Login Dialog

In the previous section you see the makings of a Login process; that is, a dialog that requests a username and password and blocks the application until the user successfully completes the dialog.

We can implement such a login process using the @OnStart annotation with a Runnable to create and display a dialog. As discussed in "Module Life Cycle Annotations" on page 242, the @OnStart Runnable executes in a background thread during initialization. As you will soon see, we make the dialog display in the EDT by using the DialogDisplayer.notifyLater() method.

Let's examine the dialog first and then show you how to create, display, and process the login dialog.

Figure 11.11 shows a customized Login dialog. As before, we create an inner panel that contains two JLabels, a JTextField for the name, and a JPasswordField for the password.

The dialog itself includes a title ("Please Login") with the Cancel and OK buttons. Unlike the previous section, error handling for user input is not necessary. Once the user clicks OK, a login process authenticates the user.

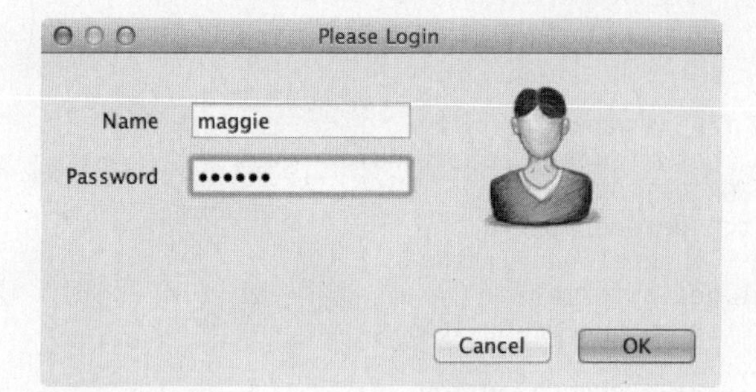


Figure 11.11 Login dialog with name, password, and icon

If the authentication process succeeds, the dialog closes and the application runs. If the user cancels or closes the dialog, the application exits. If the login fails, the dialog does not close. In this case, the login process displays an appropriate error message and the user attempts to log in again.

This login process must therefore carefully control a user's ability to dismiss or close the dialog. Any early dismissal without a successful login means the application exits.

Figure 11.12 shows an incorrect login scenario.

Figure 11.12 Login dialog when authentication fails

Listing 11.12 shows the Login dialog's inner panel, LoginPanel.java. Class LoginPanel extends JPanel and defines the Swing components that provide the dialog's user interface. LoginPanel also includes public methods `getUserName()` and `getPassword()` to access the user-provided login credentials.

**Listing 11.12 LoginPanel.java—Customized Login JPanel**

```
package com.asgteach.dialogs;

public class LoginPanel extends javax.swing.JPanel {

    public LoginPanel() {
        initComponents();
    }

    public String getUserName() {
        return nameTextField.getText();
    }

    public String getPassword() {
        return new String(passwordTextField.getPassword());
    }

    private void initComponents() {

      . . . generated code omitted . . .

    }
    // Variables declaration - do not modify
    private javax.swing.JLabel imageLabel;
    private javax.swing.JLabel jLabel1;
    private javax.swing.JLabel jLabel2;
    private javax.swing.JTextField nameTextField;
    private javax.swing.JPasswordField passwordTextField;
    // End of variables declaration
}
```

We'll use the Module System API `@OnStart` annotation with Runnable to create a class that is instantiated during an application's initialization process. We'll put the code to create, display, and process this Login dialog in the Runnable's `run()` method. (See "Module Life Cycle Annotations" on page 242 for more information on @OnStart.)

We add the `@OnStart` Runnable to the Dialogs module in its main source package using these steps.

1. The `@OnStart` annotation requires a dependency on the Module System API. In the Dialogs module, select the **Libraries** node, right click, and select **Add Module Dependency . . .** from the context menu. In the Add Module Dependencies dialog, select **Module System API** and click **OK**.
2. Right click on the **com.asgteach.dialogs** package and select **New | Java Class . . . .**
3. NetBeans displays the New Java Class dialog. For Class Name, specify **Login-Installer** and click **Finish**. NetBeans adds file LoginInstaller.java to package **com.asgteach.dialogs**.

Listing 11.13 shows the code for the LoginInstaller class, which we describe here.

- Add the `@OnStart` annotation to LoginInstaller, implement Runnable, and override the `run()` method.
- Instantiate the inner panel that contains the dialog's user input components.
- Implement the `login()` method, which determines whether a login is successful or not. In real-world applications, you would access a database or some other means to authenticate the user's credentials. Here, method `login()` returns true if the user name and password are the same.
- Use `@Messages` to create application text and error messages.
- Inside the `run()` method, create the dialog with DialogDescriptor. In the constructor specify the inner panel and the dialog title, make the dialog modal (which blocks the application until the dialog finishes), and specify a button ActionListener (a lambda expression, described below). You need an ActionListener because you'll display the dialog with `notifyLater()` instead of `notify()` and user responses won't be available in the return.
- Configure the dialog. Method `setClosingOptions()` invoked with an empty array prevents the dialog from closing after the user clicks OK. Otherwise, any input (whether valid or not) followed by OK closes the dialog. Method `createNotificationLineSupport()` provides a way to give the user feedback if the login fails.
- Configure a property change listener (also a lambda expression). Listen for the presence of the `DialogDescriptor.CLOSED_OPTION` and exit the application. This prevents the user from closing the dialog to bypass the login procedure.
- Process the user interaction with the dialog in the ActionEventListener. If the user cancels, exit the application. Otherwise, the user clicks OK. Read the values from the dialog panel and determine if the login is successful.

  If the login is successful, re-enable the normal closing options so that the dialog will close (and the application starts up).

  If the login fails, display an error message. Because the closing options are disabled, the dialog remains open and the user can attempt another login.
- Display the dialog with `DialogDisplayer.notifyLater()`. The dialog displays in the EDT after the NetBeans Platform splash screen and blocks the application until a user completes a successful login.

**Listing 11.13 LoginInstaller.java—Processing a Login**

```
@OnStart
public class LoginInstaller implements Runnable {

    private final LoginPanel panel = new LoginPanel();
    private DialogDescriptor dd = null;

    // stub method that says if the username and password
    // are the same then the login is good!
    private boolean login (String username, String password) {
        return username.equals(password) && !username.isEmpty();
    }

    @Messages({
        "LoginTitle=Please Login",
        "LoginError=Incorrect user name or password"
    })
    @Override
    public void run() {
        // @Onstart runs in a background thread by default
        // Here we use notifyLater to safely display the dialog.
        // Create a dialog using the LoginPanel and LoginTitle, make it modal,
        // and specify action listener
        dd = new DialogDescriptor(panel, Bundle.LoginTitle(), true,
                                            (ActionEvent ae) -> {
            // We need to listen for button pressed because we are using
            // notifyLater to display the dialog
            if (ae.getSource() == DialogDescriptor.CANCEL_OPTION) {
                // Adios
                System.out.println("Canceled!");
                LifecycleManager.getDefault().exit();
            } else {
                // Check login
                if (login(panel.getUserName(), panel.getPassword())) {
                    // Using null enables all options to close dialog
                    // (this is retroactive, so the dialog will close
                    // and the app will appear)
                    dd.setClosingOptions(null);
                } else {
                    // Bad login, try again
                    dd.getNotificationLineSupport().setErrorMessage(
                            Bundle.LoginError());
                }
            }
        });
        // Specify an empty array to prevent any option from closing the dialog
        dd.setClosingOptions(new Object[]{});
        dd.createNotificationLineSupport();
```

```
        // Define a property listener in case the dialog is closed
        dd.addPropertyChangeListener((PropertyChangeEvent pce) -> {
            // look for CLOSED_OPTION
            if (pce.getPropertyName().equals(DialogDescriptor.PROP_VALUE)
                    && pce.getNewValue() == DialogDescriptor.CLOSED_OPTION) {
                // Adios
                System.out.println("Closed!");
                LifecycleManager.getDefault().exit();
            }
        });
        // notifyLater will display the dialog in the EDT
        DialogDisplayer.getDefault().notifyLater(dd);
    }
}
```

## 11.6 Putting It All Together

Now that you've learned about dialogs in general and Login dialogs in particular, we're going to adapt application RoleExample (see "RoleExample Application and Role-Based TopComponents" on page 404) and use a Login dialog to set the application's role. We'll use the same technique we presented in the previous section with a Login dialog that we configure using the @OnStart annotation. Once the user successfully completes the Login dialog as shown in Figure 11.11 on page 540, the application sets the window system to the user's assigned role.

We'll also create an always-enabled action in this application that lets a user change roles with a Change Role dialog. This dialog processes a user's login credentials, but unlike the Login dialog, Cancel and Close do not exit the application. Also, the Change Role dialog does not close if a user login fails. This means we must supply an ActionListener to process user input instead of reading the return from method `notify()`. Figure 11.13 shows the Change Role dialog, which has a different title but otherwise looks the same as the Login dialog.

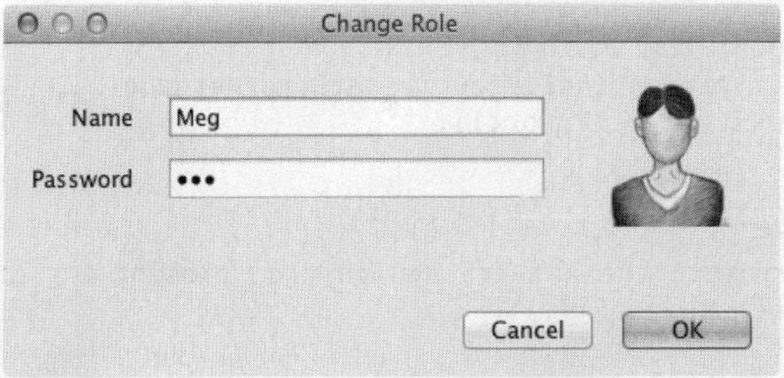

Figure 11.13 Change Role dialog

## RoleExample Application

Let's start with the RoleExample application from Chapter 8 (see "Window Layout Roles" on page 401). Follow these steps to add the Login dialog to the Runnable class, RoleLogin.java. Figure 11.14 shows the files in module AdminModule when you're finished adding the Login dialog and Change Role action to application RoleExample.

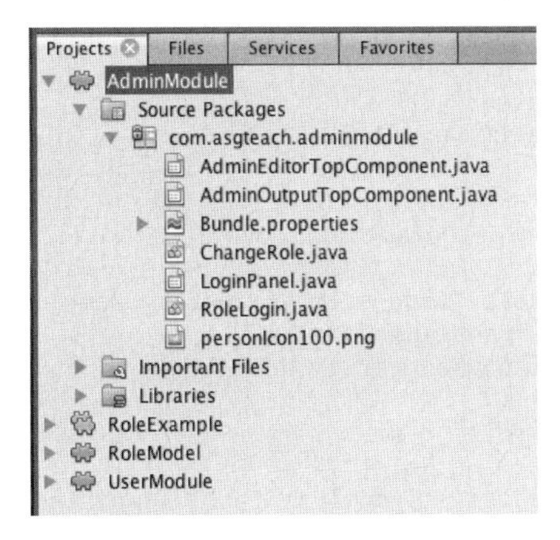


Figure 11.14 Module AdminModule with Login dialog and Change Role action

1. Open project RoleExample and expand project AdminModule.
2. In AdminModule, delete LoginTopComponent, since we'll replace the TopComponent with a dialog.
3. Create a LoginPanel form with **New | JPanel Form** to hold the Login/Change Role dialog GUI components, as shown in the previous section. Use personIcon100.png for the dialog's icon. Provide the same getter methods for LoginPanel.java as shown in Listing 11.12 on page 541.
4. In AdminModule, add Java class RoleLogin.java. Implement Runnable, override the `run()` method, and specify the `@OnStart` annotation. Provide code for the `run()` method as shown in Listing 11.14. This code is very similar to the LoginInstaller class in Listing 11.13 on page 543, except we use the UserRole module to authenticate the login process. Note that this code also prevents a user from canceling or closing the dialog to bypass authentication.

**Listing 11.14 RoleLogin.java—Processing a Role-Based Login**

```
@OnStart
public class RoleLogin implements Runnable {

    private final LoginPanel panel = new LoginPanel();
    private DialogDescriptor dd = null;
```

```
    @Override
    public void run() {
        // Create a dialog using the LoginPanel and LoginTitle, make it modal,
        // and specify action listener
        dd = new DialogDescriptor(panel, Bundle.LoginTitle(), true,
                                                    ((ActionEvent ae) -> {
            // We need to listen for button pressed because we are using
            // notifyLater to display the dialog
            if (ae.getSource() == DialogDescriptor.CANCEL_OPTION) {
                // Adios
                System.out.println("Canceled!");
                LifecycleManager.getDefault().exit();
            } else {
                // Check login
               UserRole userRole = Lookup.getDefault().lookup(UserRole.class);
                if (userRole != null) {
                    User thisUser = userRole.findUser(panel.getUserName(),
                                           panel.getPassword());
                    WindowManager wm = WindowManager.getDefault();
                    if (thisUser != null) {
                        // switch to new role
                        wm.setRole(thisUser.getRole());
                        // Using null enables all options to close dialog
                        // (this is retroactive, so the dialog will close
                        // and the app will appear)
                        dd.setClosingOptions(null);
                    } else {
                        // Bad login, try again
                        dd.getNotificationLineSupport().setErrorMessage(
                                Bundle.LoginError());
                    }
                } else {
                    // No UserRole instance, bail!
                    System.out.println("No UserRole!");
                    LifecycleManager.getDefault().exit();
                }
            }
        }));
        // Specify an empty array to prevent any option from closing the dialog
        dd.setClosingOptions(new Object[]{});
        dd.createNotificationLineSupport();
        // Define a property listener in case the dialog is closed
        dd.addPropertyChangeListener((PropertyChangeEvent pce) -> {
            // look for CLOSED_OPTION
            if (pce.getPropertyName().equals(DialogDescriptor.PROP_VALUE)
                    && pce.getNewValue() == DialogDescriptor.CLOSED_OPTION) {
                System.out.println("Closed!");
                LifecycleManager.getDefault().exit();
            }
        });
```

```
        // notifyLater will display the dialog on the EDT
        DialogDisplayer.getDefault().notifyLater(dd);
    }
}
```

5. Next, create an always-enabled Action called ChangeRole with **New | Action**. Put the action under Menu/Tools and use display text Change Role.
6. NetBeans generates class ChangeRole.java, which implements ActionListener. Provide code for the `actionPerformed()` method, as shown in Listing 11.15.

#### Listing 11.15 Action Class ChangeRole.java

```
@ActionID(category = "Tools",
id = "com.asgteach.adminmodule.ChangeRole")
@ActionRegistration(displayName = "#CTL_ChangeRole")
@ActionReferences({
    @ActionReference(path = "Menu/Tools", position = 0, separatorAfter = 50)
})
@Messages("CTL_ChangeRole=Change Role")
public final class ChangeRole implements ActionListener {

    private DialogDescriptor dd = null;

    @Override
    public void actionPerformed(ActionEvent e) {
        final LoginPanel panel = new LoginPanel();
        dd = new DialogDescriptor(panel, Bundle.CTL_ChangeRole(), true,
                                          (ActionEvent ae) -> {
            if (ae.getSource() == DialogDescriptor.OK_OPTION) {
                // Check login
                UserRole userRole = Lookup.getDefault().lookup(UserRole.class);
                if (userRole != null) {
                    User thisUser = userRole.findUser(
                            panel.getUserName(), panel.getPassword());
                    WindowManager wm = WindowManager.getDefault();
                    if (thisUser != null) {
                        // switch to new role
                        wm.setRole(thisUser.getRole());
                        // Using null enables all options to close dialog
                        dd.setClosingOptions(null);
                    } else {
                        // Bad login, try again
                        dd.getNotificationLineSupport().setErrorMessage(
                                Bundle.LoginError());
                    }
                }
            }
        });
```

```
        // Allow Cancel to close the dialog, but OK should not
        dd.setClosingOptions(new Object[]{DialogDescriptor.CANCEL_OPTION});
        dd.createNotificationLineSupport();
        DialogDisplayer.getDefault().notify(dd);      // display and block
    }
}
```

The ChangeRole class registers an always-enabled action with Java annotations `@ActionID`, `@ActionRegistration`, and `@ActionReferences`. Class ChangeRole implements ActionListener and overrides method `actionPerformed()`, which is invoked when a user selects the Change Role menu item.

Note that there are two `actionPerformed()` methods here. The outer `actionPerformed()` method instantiates the LoginPanel and dialog with DialogDescriptor. The inner `actionPerformed()` belongs to the ActionListener in the DialogDescriptor constructor. When DialogDescriptor method `notify()` returns, the dialog has already closed. The ActionListener lets you process user input without closing the dialog. The Change Roles dialog must stay open until we verify the UserRole credentials. If the credentials are bad, the dialog remains open and the user can try again.

The code in Listing 11.15 is subtly different than the application Login code in the RoleLogin class (Listing 11.14 on page 545). In Listing 11.15 we allow the user to either cancel or close the dialog, but specifically prohibit OK from closing the dialog. With the RoleLogin dialog, however, we detect both close and cancel, and exit the application.

## 11.7 Key Point Summary

The Dialogs API provides classes that help you create, display, and obtain input from dialogs. You specify a dependency on the Dialogs API to use dialogs in your application. You can use standard dialogs and notifications or customize these. Here are the main features of the Dialogs API.

- NotifyDescriptor provides several standard dialogs. `NotifyDescriptor.Message` provides an information dialog with text and OK button.
- Option `NotifyDescriptor.WARNING_MESSAGE` provides a warning dialog with text, OK button, and warning icon.
- Option `NotifyDescriptor.ERROR_MESSAGE` provides an error dialog with text, OK button, and error icon.
- `NotifyDescriptor.Confirmation` provides a question dialog with text and option buttons Cancel, No, and Yes.

- `NotifyDescriptor.InputLine` provides a dialog that prompts for user input with option buttons Cancel and OK. You include a prompt and dialog title with the constructor. Use method `getInputText()` to read user input.
- You can configure the option buttons for any of the dialog types.
- Use `DialogDisplayer.getDefault()` to obtain the NetBeans Platform default DialogDisplayer.
- DialogDisplayer method `notify()` displays a modal dialog (message box) and blocks until the dialog closes.
- Customize dialogs with DialogDescriptor, a class that extends NotifyDescriptor. DialogDescriptor provides flexibility in handling button clicks and blocking closure. You can also customize button alignment and button text.
- Customize a dialog's components by providing your own inner panel.
- DialogDisplayer method `notifyLater()` displays a modal dialog and may be called from any thread. This is useful, for example, for implementing a Login dialog with a Runnable class and the `@Onstart` annotation. With the `notifyLater()` method, you configure an ActionEventListener in the DialogDescriptor constructor to listen for and process user button events.
- To implement a Login dialog, override the `run()` method in an `@OnStart` Runnable class. With a dialog that implements both PropertyChangeListener and ActionListener, you can block an application until a user provides the necessary login credentials.

# 12

# Wizards

A common scenario in desktop applications is to gather user input to build an object—a new customer, file, Family Tree event, or number sequence, for example. When the building process has multiple steps with multiple options, you need a carefully crafted process to walk a user through the steps. A process that provides this sequence of input panels is called a *wizard*.

The NetBeans Platform wizard is a multi-class framework that lets you construct such a process. This wizard framework lets a developer specify the graphical components for user input, validate input, store each panel's state, and dynamically manipulate the wizard step sequence. When the wizard finishes, your application has access to the validated, user-provided input to then construct the target artifact (such as a file, a series of files, or one or more new data objects).

## What You Will Learn

- Create and configuring wizards.
- Register wizard actions.
- Store and retrieve wizard properties.
- Validate a wizard's user input.
- Coordinate validation between wizard steps.
- Use the Simple Validation API.

- Perform asynchronous validation.
- Use dynamic sequence wizards.
- Use instantiating iterators.
- Integrate a progress bar into a wizard.

## 12.1 Wizard Overview

Figure 12.1 shows the general architecture of a NetBeans Platform wizard example that has three steps. The WizardDescriptor class is the main controller, controlling wizard panels that are in turn controllers for each step that the wizard performs. The wizard panels instantiate visual panels (the views) that solicit input from users. Not shown here is the wizard action class, which starts the wizard process and creates wizard panels and the WizardDescriptor.

Our three-step wizard in Figure 12.1 is called Number. This wizard guides a user through the steps to create a number sequence. Each wizard panel controls a specific step and creates its own visual panel. The panel class extends JPanel and holds the user interface components needed for input.

To work with the WizardDescriptor, wizard panel classes override `WizardDescriptor.Panel` methods that the WizardDescriptor invokes. Table 12.1 lists these methods.

**TABLE 12.1 WizardDescriptor.Panel<WizardDescriptor> Methods**

| Method | Description |
|---|---|
| `public boolean isValid()` | Return the valid state of this panel. If valid state can change, implement the add/remove change listeners and fire state change events. |
| `public void readSettings (WizardDescriptor wiz)` | Retrieve panel state from WizardDescriptor. Use `wiz.getProperty(property_name)`. |
| `public void storeSettings (WizardDescriptor wiz)` | Store panel state to WizardDescriptor. Use `wiz.putProperty(property_name, value)`. |
| `public void addChangeListener (ChangeListener cl)` | Add listener interested in changes to `isValid`. |
| `public void removeChangeListener (ChangeListener cl)` | Remove listener interested in changes to `isValid`. |
| `public Component getComponent()` | Get component displayed by this panel. |
| `public HelpCtx getHelp()` | Provide help. |

The WizardDescriptor has three main responsibilities:

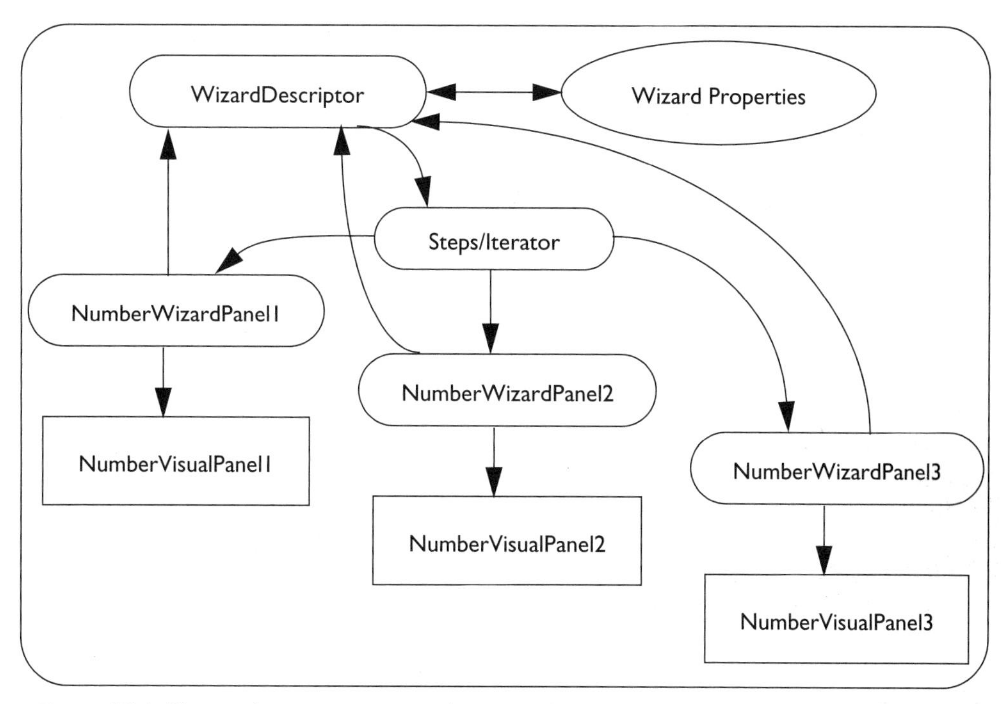


Figure 12.1 Classes that participate in the example wizard Number

1. The WizardDescriptor iterates through the collection of wizard panels, proceeding to the next panel when the user clicks Next (or Finish).
2. The WizardDescriptor stores properties needed by wizard panels. It invokes wizard panel methods `readSettings()` and `storeSettings()` at the beginning and ending, respectively, of each step.
3. The WizardDescriptor responds to change events fired from the wizard panel class. Typically, these events signal changes to the `isValid()` and `isFinishPanel()` methods, but the WizardDescriptor responds to changes in the step sequence as well. Depending on the return values of these methods, the WizardDescriptor enables or disables the Next and/or Finish buttons on the current visual panel.

**Wizard Tip**

*If a wizard panel is always valid, method* `isValid()` *returns true and there's no need to fire change events from the wizard panel. However, if a wizard panel's valid status depends on user input, the wizard panel must implement* `addChangeListener()` *and* `removeChangeListener()` *and fire state change events to its ChangeListeners. This makes the WizardDescriptor invoke* `isValid()` *and subsequently enable or disable Next and Finish. "Wizard Validation" on page 565 shows you how to do this.*

**Wizard Tip**

*Method* `isFinishPanel()` *is defined in class WizardDescriptor.FinishablePanel for panels that dynamically enable the Finish button. See "Finishing Early Option" on page 587 for an example of this option.*

You can see from Figure 12.1 that each wizard panel class is completely independent from the other wizard panel classes. The wizard panel creates the visual panel that it controls, gets user data from the visual panel components, and provides validation. The wizard panel also uses the WizardDescriptor to store state data. Other wizard panels and the wizard's action event handler can access this data to build the target artifact.

Let's look at the Number example now and show you how these wizard panels coordinate with visual panels and let the WizardDescriptor do its job.

## 12.2 The Wizard Wizard

The NetBeans IDE provides a Wizard wizard—that is, a wizard that helps you create wizards. Let's now create a wizard for something called New Number Sequence. This example wizard solicits a three-number sequence from the user in three separate steps.

**Build the Example**

*To build the example, create a new NetBeans Platform application called* ***WizardExample****. Then create a new NetBeans module called* ***Sequence****, as shown in Figure 12.2.*

To create a new wizard, select the target module (**Sequence** in our example). Right-click and select **New | Other**. Start with Figure 12.3. As you proceed through each step, pay attention to the panels with which you interact. The wizard has a title New File, and the steps are listed on the left. The main panel requests information.

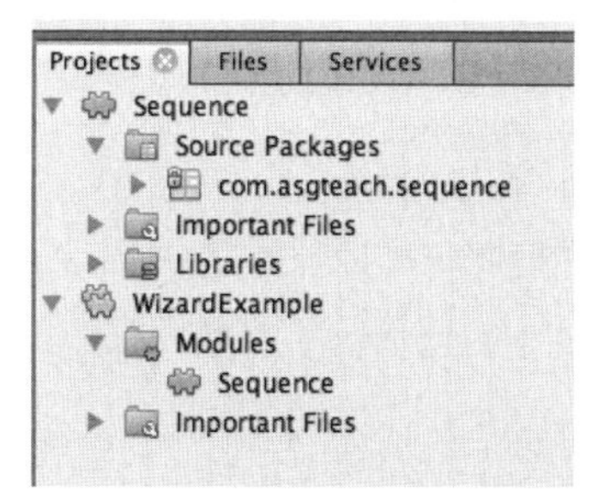


Figure 12.2 WizardExample application and Sequence module

## A Bare-Bones Wizard

In Figure 12.3, specify **Module Development** under Categories and **Wizard** under File Types. After you've made these selections, the Next button is enabled, and the Help, Back, and Finish buttons are all disabled.

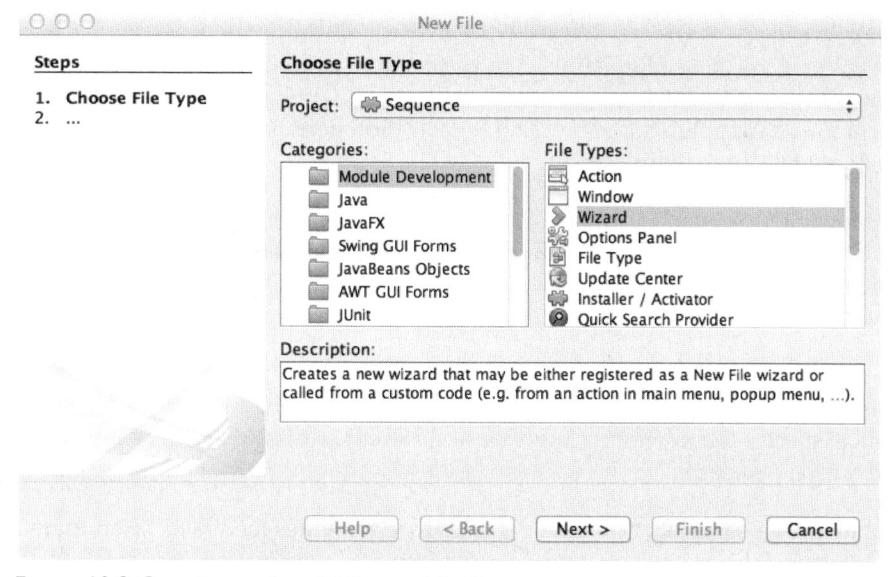


Figure 12.3 Creating a wizard: Choose File Type

After you select **Next**, the wizard proceeds to the next panel. Here you see Registration Type (Custom or New File), Wizard Step Sequence (Static or Dynamic), and Number of Wizard Panels. Select **Custom**, **Static**, and **3**, as shown in Figure 12.4.

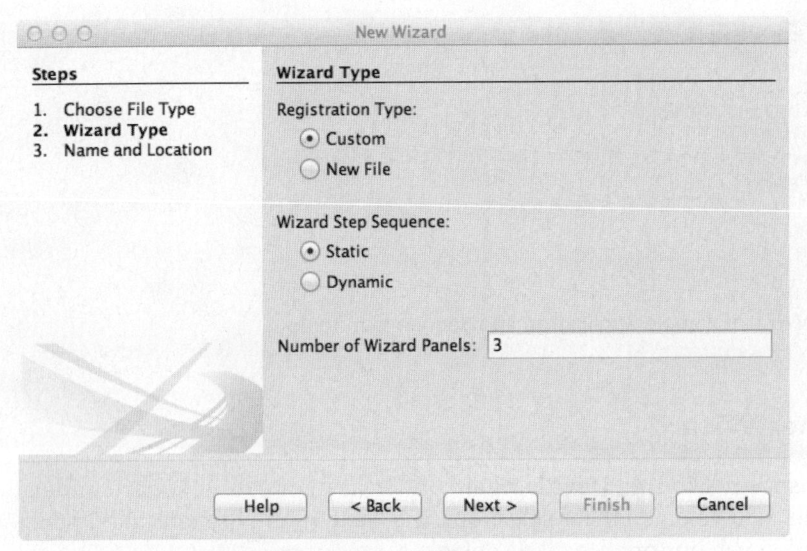


Figure 12.4 Creating a wizard: Specify Wizard Type

In this chapter, you'll use Registration Type **Custom**, the wizard registration type that creates arbitrary artifacts (such as domain objects or a directory structure with multiple files) for your application. New File Registration pertains to wizards that create files using a File Type template.

The Wizard Step Sequence provides two options. Static means your wizard always uses the same steps in the same order. Dynamic lets your wizard alter the sequence and the number of steps. We'll show you an example of a Dynamic Step Sequence wizard later in this chapter (see "Dynamic Sequence Wizards" on page 598).

The Number of Wizard Panels is where you specify the number of steps in your wizard. For Static Step Sequence, this is the total number of steps. For Dynamic Step Sequence, specify the maximum number of different panels your wizard requires, even if a given execution of the wizard uses less.

Note that as you complete this dialog, the wizard provides feedback when there are errors or omissions. When the input is error-free, the Next button is enabled. Again, select **Next.**

The wizard now displays the final panel: Name and Location, as shown in Figure 12.5. Specify **Number** for the Class Name Prefix. Make sure the selected Project is **Sequence** and the package name matches the selected project. NetBeans displays the files the wizard creates for your New Number Sequence wizard. Note that the Finish button is now enabled. Click **Finish** and the wizard is complete.

### Wizard Tip

*We won't rename the classes in this example, but you will typically provide more meaningful names for the wizard and visual panel classes in your wizard. To do this, select the Java source file in the Projects window and click* **Refactor | Rename** *in the NetBeans main menu (or select the Java source file and use key sequence* **Control-R***).*

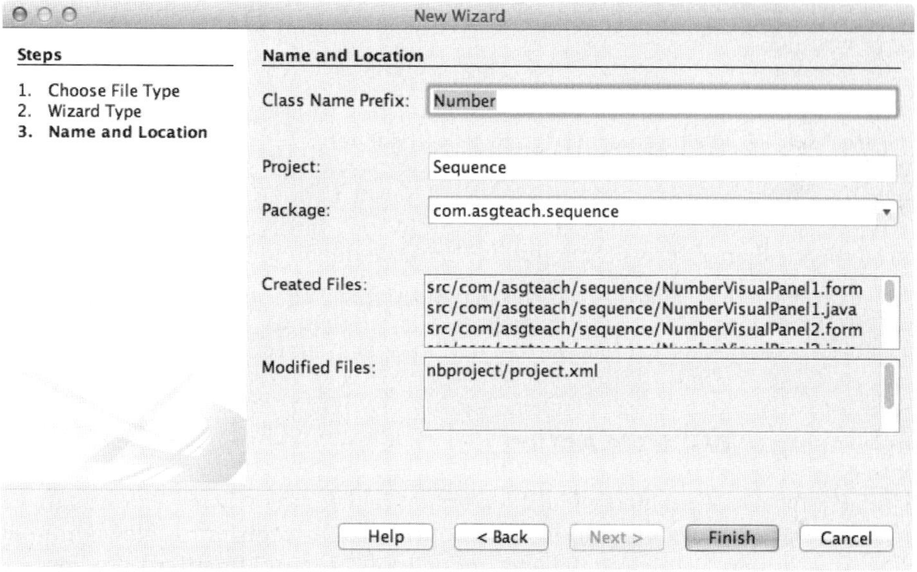

Figure 12.5 Creating a wizard: Specify Name and Location

You now have a bare-bones wizard consisting of three visual panels, three wizard controllers, and a wizard action class. NetBeans has created these seven files for you, as shown in Figure 12.6.

For each wizard panel that you specify in the wizard creation dialog, NetBeans creates a visual panel[1] (for building your graphical user interface) and a wizard panel (for validating the user input and saving state). NetBeans also creates a wizard action class (to initiate your wizard and build the wizard's target artifact).

1. The visual panel extends the JPanel Swing component. You can integrate JavaFX content using Swing JFXPanel. The Reference Application has an example of a NetBeans Platform wizard with JavaFX-integrated content. See "FamilyTreeApp Reference Application" on page 10.

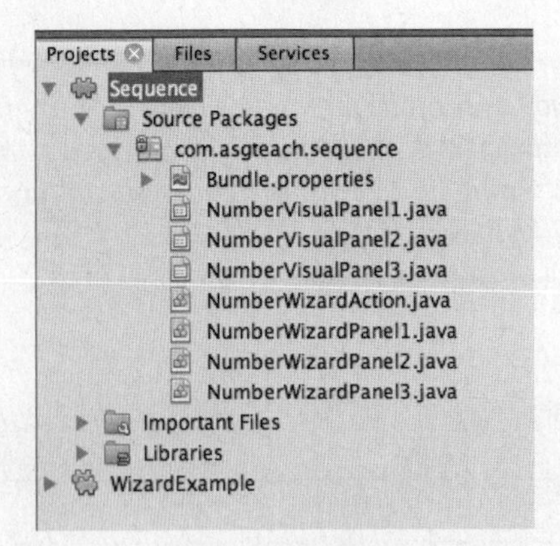


Figure 12.6 Files in a three-panel wizard called Number

The NetBeans Platform sets the following module dependencies for this project.

```
Dialogs API - Handles the dialog and wizard infrastructure
UI Utilities API - Helper methods for various UI related tasks
Utilities API - Various helper methods and basic concept definitions
```

## Registering a Wizard's Action

To invoke this newly created wizard, you must register the wizard action so that it appears either in the menu or toolbar, or both. Here, we register the New Number Sequence action in the top-level menu under Tools by providing the following action-based annotations, as shown in Listing 12.1. The modified code is in bold; the rest is generated by NetBeans. Chapter 9 discusses actions and how to register them (see "Always-Enabled Actions" on page 414).

As you examine this code, note that method `actionPerformed()` instantiates an ArrayList to hold the wizard panels, configures the visual panels (accessed through `getComponent()`), and instantiates WizardDescriptor. When WizardDescriptor finishes, the complete and validated user data is available.

### Wizard Tip

*Class WizardDescriptor is a subclass of DialogDescriptor. Like classes DialogDescriptor and NotifyDescriptor, you display the wizard and block the application with DialogDisplayer method* `notify()`*. We discuss dialogs in detail in Chapter 11.*

**Listing 12.1 NumberWizardAction.java**

```
@ActionID(category = "Tools",
   id = "org.asgteach.sequence.NumberWizardAction")
@ActionRegistration(
   displayName = "#CTL_NumberWizardAction")
@ActionReferences({
    @ActionReference(path = "Menu/Tools",
position = 0, separatorAfter = 50)
})
@NbBundle.Messages({
    "CTL_NumberWizardAction=New Number Sequence",
    "CTL_NumberDialogTitle=Create New Number Sequence"
})
public final class NumberWizardAction implements ActionListener {

    @Override
    public void actionPerformed(ActionEvent e) {
        List<WizardDescriptor.Panel<WizardDescriptor>> panels =
            new ArrayList<WizardDescriptor.Panel<WizardDescriptor>>();
        panels.add(new NumberWizardPanel1());
        panels.add(new NumberWizardPanel2());
        panels.add(new NumberWizardPanel3());
        String[] steps = new String[panels.size()];
        for (int i = 0; i < panels.size(); i++) {
            Component c = panels.get(i).getComponent();
            // Default step name to component name of panel.
            steps[i] = c.getName();
            if (c instanceof JComponent) { // assume Swing components
                JComponent jc = (JComponent) c;
                jc.putClientProperty(
                  WizardDescriptor.PROP_CONTENT_SELECTED_INDEX, i);
                jc.putClientProperty(
                  WizardDescriptor.PROP_CONTENT_DATA, steps);
                jc.putClientProperty(
                  WizardDescriptor.PROP_AUTO_WIZARD_STYLE, true);
                jc.putClientProperty(
                  WizardDescriptor.PROP_CONTENT_DISPLAYED, true);
                jc.putClientProperty(
                  WizardDescriptor.PROP_CONTENT_NUMBERED, true);
            }
        }
        WizardDescriptor wiz = new WizardDescriptor(
            new WizardDescriptor.ArrayIterator<WizardDescriptor>(panels));
       // {0} will be replaced by
       // WizardDesriptor.Panel.getComponent().getName()
        wiz.setTitleFormat(new MessageFormat("{0}"));
        wiz.setTitle(Bundle.CTL_NumberDialogTitle());
        if (DialogDisplayer.getDefault().notify(wiz) ==
                  WizardDescriptor.FINISH_OPTION) {
```

```
            // do something after the wizard has successfully finished
        }
    }
}
```

**Wizard Tip**

*The code inside the braces*

```
if (DialogDisplayer.getDefault().notify(wiz) ==
            WizardDescriptor.FINISH_OPTION) {
    // do something after the wizard has successfully finished
}
```

*only executes if the wizard finishes normally. It does not execute if the user clicks Cancel.*

Deploy and run the WizardExample application now. Note that with only minimal Java annotations, you can invoke our bare-bones wizard, accessed from **Menu | Tools**, as shown in Figure 12.7.

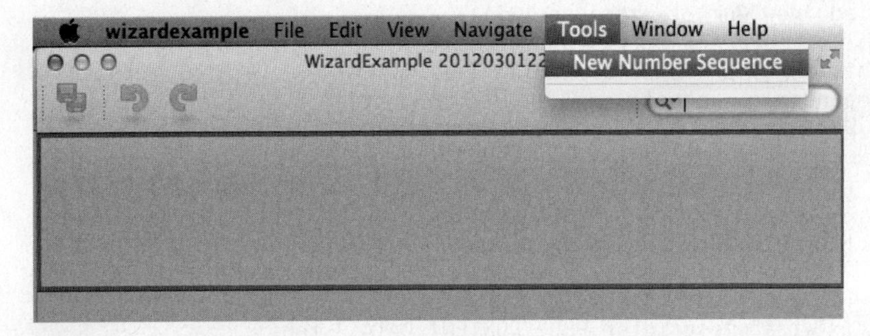


Figure 12.7 Invoking the New Number Sequence wizard

Initially, the wizard displays the first panel, as shown in Figure 12.8. Of course, there aren't any components yet, so you just see the standard elements that the NetBeans wizard defines: the title, a list of steps, the title of this panel (Step #1), and control buttons: Help, Back, Next, Finish, Cancel.

Help is not enabled because we haven't configured any Help, Back is not enabled since this is the first panel, and Finish is not enabled because we still have two more panels to work through. Interestingly, Next is enabled because the default behavior for a wizard panel is a valid status, allowing the user to proceed to the next panel.

Select **Next** and the wizard displays the second panel. The panel title now displays Step #2 (which is also in bold under the list of steps on the left). The Back button is now enabled, but Finish is still disabled.

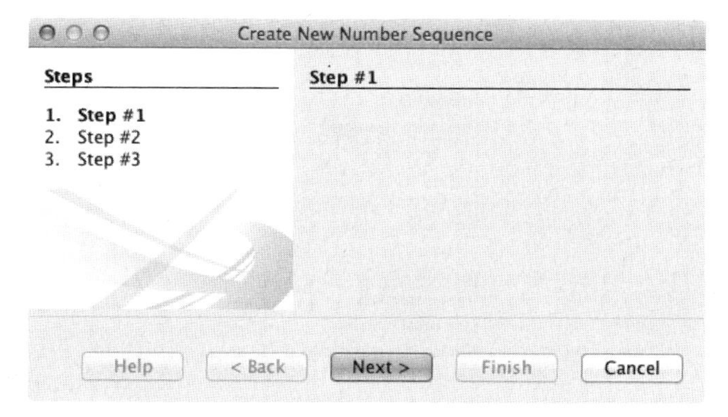


Figure 12.8 New Number Sequence wizard: Panel 1

Select **Next** again and Step #3 appears, the final and third panel. The Finish button is now enabled.

Select **Finish**. At this point the wizard is complete and control is returned to the `actionPerformed()` method, as shown here.

```
if (DialogDisplayer.getDefault().notify(wiz) ==
        WizardDescriptor.FINISH_OPTION) {
    // do something
}
```

The `actionPerformed()` method gathers any data that the wizard collects (there is no data yet!) and carries out its task (whatever it may be). That's all fine and good, but our New Number Sequence wizard should do more. Let's build a simple GUI next and show you how each panel's wizard gathers information from the user.

## 12.3 Wizard Input

Our wizard is simple. It prompts for a sequence of three numbers whose values are not important. In this first version, we don't even verify if the input is actually a number.

For each of the three visual panels, use the NetBeans Form designer to add a label and textfield to each panel. Name the JTextField components `firstNumber`, `secondNumber`, and `thirdNumber`, respectively. Figure 12.9 shows the Form designer for the first visual panel.

Now, run the application again and choose menu **Tools | New Number Sequence**. You will see a field in each panel where you can provide a number. At this point, there is no code that reads the value or determines if the input is actually a number.

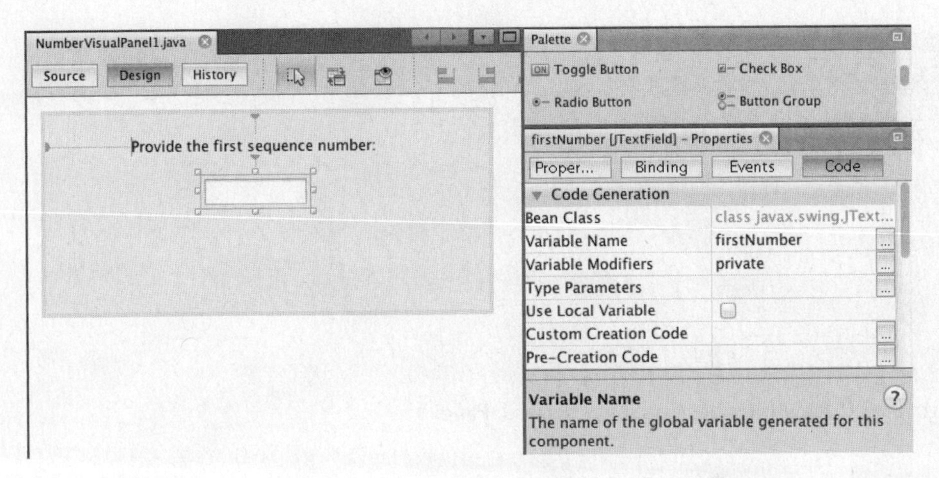


Figure 12.9 Adding components to the visual panel with the Form designer

Next, let's read each value and display the number sequence inside the `actionPerformed()` method using a predefined Information dialog provided by the NetBeans Platform (see "Standard Dialogs" on page 527). This important first step shows how to read user input and make the data accessible within the `actionPerformed()` method. Perform the following steps for each panel.

1. Create a property name for each value that you want to save. This will be a `public static final String` in the visual panel class.
2. Create a public getter to access the user input from each visual panel.
3. Store each property value with the WizardDescriptor to make the data accessible within the `actionPerformed()` method.

Listing 12.2 shows the changes for NumberVisualPanel1.java, shown in bold. You'll make comparable changes to NumberVisualPanel2.java and NumberVisualPanel3.java.

1. Define `public static final String` PROP_FIRST_NUMBER.
2. Define public method `getFirstNumber()` to return the text value of the JTextField component.

**Listing 12.2 NumberVisualPanel1.java**

```
public final class NumberVisualPanel1 extends JPanel {

    // Create property names for each piece of data that
    // we want to collect
    public static final String PROP_FIRST_NUMBER = "firstNumber";
```

```
    public NumberVisualPanel1() {
        initComponents();
    }

    @Override
    public String getName() {
        return "Step #1";
    }

    public String getFirstNumber() {
        return firstNumber.getText();
    }

    // Generated code
      . . .

    // Variables declaration - do not modify
    private javax.swing.JTextField firstNumber;
    private javax.swing.JLabel jLabel1;
    // End of variables declaration

}
```

Now, inside the wizard panel, save the property value in method `storeSettings()`. This stores the value in the WizardDescriptor's cache of properties. Listing 12.3 shows method `storeSettings()` for NumberWizardPanel1.java.

The WizardDescriptor invokes method `storeSettings()` when the wizard panel's step has finished. This is where you store property values in the WizardDescriptor's property cache. With the WizardDescriptor property cache, you can share data among any of your wizard panels and the wizard action class.

Similarly, the WizardDescriptor invokes method `readSettings()` at the beginning of a wizard panel's step. This is where you read properties from the WizardDescriptor's property cache. You can also put any "step initialization code" in method `readSettings()`—code that executes at the beginning of the wizard panel's step. As we continue to develop our Number wizard, you'll see why these two step life cycle methods are important.

**Listing 12.3 NumberWizardPanel1.java**

```
public class NumberWizardPanel1 implements
        WizardDescriptor.Panel<WizardDescriptor> {

    private NumberVisualPanel1 component;
```

```
    @Override
    public NumberVisualPanel1 getComponent() {
        if (component == null) {
            component = new NumberVisualPanel1();
        }
        return component;
    }

   . . . code omitted . . .

    @Override
    public void storeSettings(WizardDescriptor wiz) {
       // use wiz.putProperty to remember current panel state
        wiz.putProperty(NumberVisualPanel1.PROP_FIRST_NUMBER,
                getComponent().getFirstNumber());
    }
}
```

Make similar modifications to NumberWizardPanel2.java and NumberWizardPanel3.java to store values for properties `NumberVisualPanel2.PROP_SECOND_NUMBER` and `NumberVisualPanel3.PROP_THIRD_NUMBER`, respectively.

The `actionPerformed()` method in NumberWizardAction performs two steps. First, it displays a finish message in the status bar of the application with NetBeans Platform utility StatusDisplayer. Second, it displays the new number sequence using a NetBeans Platform predefined Information dialog. Note that the sequence numbers are available because we stored each one in the WizardDescriptor's property cache in `storeSettings()`. The WizardDescriptor method `getProperty()` retrieves each number.

All of the code in `actionPerformed()` (see Listing 12.4) is generated by NetBeans, except for the code in bold that performs these two tasks.

**Listing 12.4 Method actionPerformed—Version 1**

```
    @Override
    public void actionPerformed(ActionEvent e) {

   . . . code is unchanged . . .
          WizardDescriptor wiz = new WizardDescriptor(
              new WizardDescriptor.ArrayIterator<WizardDescriptor>(panels));
        // {0} will be replaced by
        // WizardDesriptor.Panel.getComponent().getName()
         wiz.setTitleFormat(new MessageFormat("{0}"));
         wiz.setTitle(Bundle.CTL_NumberDialogTitle());
```

```
        if (DialogDisplayer.getDefault().notify(wiz) ==
                WizardDescriptor.FINISH_OPTION) {
            StatusDisplayer.getDefault().setStatusText("Wizard Finished");
            // retrieve and display the numbers
           StringBuilder message = new StringBuilder("Number Sequence =  \n(");
            message.append(wiz.getProperty(
                NumberVisualPanel1.PROP_FIRST_NUMBER)).append(", ");
            message.append(wiz.getProperty(
                NumberVisualPanel2.PROP_SECOND_NUMBER)).append(", ");
            message.append(wiz.getProperty(
                NumberVisualPanel3.PROP_THIRD_NUMBER)).append(")");
            DialogDisplayer.getDefault().notify(
                    new NotifyDescriptor.Message(message.toString()));
        }
    }
```

Figure 12.10 shows the result when you run the New Number Sequence wizard again with the numbers 15, 25, and 44.

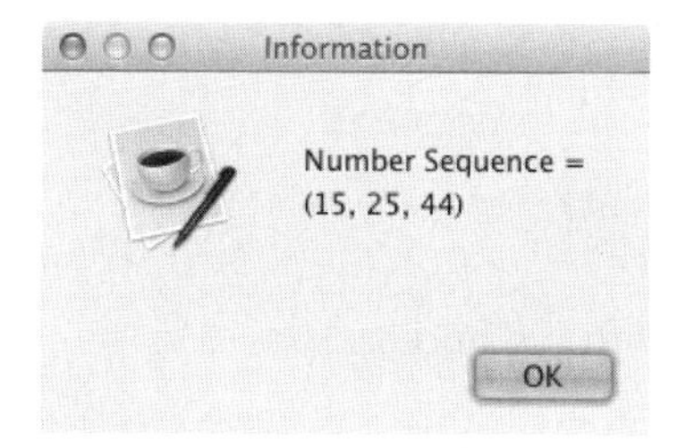


Figure 12.10 The New Number Sequence wizard completes

# 12.4 Wizard Validation

Now that you have learned how to read user input and make it available to the `actionPerformed()` method, let's add validation to the New Number Sequence wizard. For each panel input, we'll make sure the number field is not empty and that it is a non-negative integer.

To perform this validation, we install property listeners to inform the wizard panel of any updates from a user.

Note that validation occurs in the wizard panel and not in the visual panel. The WizardDescriptor oversees the wizard's progress and is responsible for maintaining the correct status of the Back, Next, Cancel, and Finish buttons in the visual panels, since these buttons are affected by the status of each panel. To maintain this visual status, the WizardDescriptor responds to state change events (from the wizard panel) by invoking wizard panel method `isValid()`.

Here are the general changes to the Number Sequence wizard for validation.

1. Implement document listeners in each visual panel to detect changes in the textfield and fire property change events when input changes.
2. Add property listeners to each wizard panel and react to property changes in the visual panel as user input changes.
3. Write a `propertyChange()` method in each wizard panel that validates input. When a change in validation occurs, fire state change events. The WizardDescriptor class updates the visual panel's wizard control buttons (Next, Finish) based on the panel's validation. That is, if the current panel is not valid, then its Next (or Finish) button is disabled.

Listing 12.5 shows the code changes in bold for the first visual panel, NumberVisualPanel1.java. Make similar changes to NumberVisualPanel2.java and NumberVisualPanel3.java.

1. Add DocumentListener to the `firstNumber` text field component.
2. Override document listener methods `insertUpdate()`, `removeUpdate()`, and `changedUpdate()`.
3. Provide a more descriptive name for the panel with method `getName()`.

**Listing 12.5 NumberVisualPanel1.java—Implementing Validation**

```
public final class NumberVisualPanel1 extends JPanel {

    // Create property names for each piece of data that
    // we want to collect
    public static final String PROP_FIRST_NUMBER = "firstNumber";

    public NumberVisualPanel1() {
        initComponents();
        // add a document listener to the textfield component
        firstNumber.getDocument().addDocumentListener(new DocumentListener() {

            @Override
            public void insertUpdate(DocumentEvent de) {
                fireChange(de);
            }
            @Override
            public void removeUpdate(DocumentEvent de) {
                fireChange(de);
            }
```

```
            @Override
            public void changedUpdate(DocumentEvent de) {
                fireChange(de);
            }

            private void fireChange(DocumentEvent de) {
                if (firstNumber.getDocument() == de.getDocument()) {
                    firePropertyChange(PROP_FIRST_NUMBER, 0, 1);
                }
            }
        });
    }

    // Create localized text for the panel
    @NbBundle.Messages({
      "CTL_Panel1Name=Provide Sequence Initial Value"
    })
    @Override
    public String getName() {
        return Bundle.CTL_Panel1Name();
    }

    public String getFirstNumber() {
        return firstNumber.getText();
    }

    private void initComponents() {

        jLabel1 = new javax.swing.JLabel();
        firstNumber = new javax.swing.JTextField();

      . . . code omitted . . .
    }
}
```

Now make related changes to the wizard panel. The wizard panel becomes a property change listener and validates user input when changes are detected. The wizard's valid status must initially be false since the wizard requires user input. Here are the changes, which are shown in Listing 12.6.

1. Implement PropertyChangeListener interface and override method `propertyChange()`.
2. Create an Integer field variable called `firstNumber` to store validated user input for the first number. Use `firstNumber` instead of `getComponent().getFirstNumber()` in method `storeSettings()`.
3. Create field variable `WizardDescriptor wizard`. Set its value inside method `readSettings()`.

4. Use EventListenerList to build ChangeListener support in the wizard panel and override methods `addChangeListener()` and `removeChangeListener()`. The WizardDescriptor invokes these to add itself as a ChangeListener; EventListenerList is a standard Swing class that manages listener lists.
5. Add a property change listener for the visual panel in `getComponent()`. Adding the listener in the conditional block that instantiates the visual panel guarantees that the listener is added just once.
6. Create method `checkValidity()` to implement any validation required of the user input. Create appropriate error messages for the WizardDescriptor to display.
7. In method `propertyChange()`, invoke `checkValidity()` and fire a state change event with method `fireChangeEvent()`. This notifies the WizardDescriptor (a ChangeListener) that the wizard panel's state has changed. The WizardDescriptor will invoke `isValid()` and update the control buttons Next and/or Finish.

**Listing 12.6 NumberWizardPanel1.java—Implementing Validation**

```
public class NumberWizardPanel1 implements
      WizardDescriptor.Panel<WizardDescriptor>, PropertyChangeListener {

    private NumberVisualPanel1 component;
    private WizardDescriptor wizard = null;
    private boolean isValid = false;
    private Integer firstNumber;
    . . .

    @Override
    public boolean isValid() {
        return isValid;
    }

    @Override
    public NumberVisualPanel1 getComponent() {
        if (component == null) {
            component = new NumberVisualPanel1();
            this.component.addPropertyChangeListener(this);
        }
        return component;
    }

    private final EventListenerList listeners = new EventListenerList();

    @Override
    public void addChangeListener(ChangeListener l) {
        listeners.add(ChangeListener.class, l);
    }
```

```
    @Override
    public void removeChangeListener(ChangeListener l) {
        listeners.remove(ChangeListener.class, l);
    }

    @Override
    public void readSettings(WizardDescriptor wiz) {
        this.wizard = wiz;
    }

    @Override
    public void storeSettings(WizardDescriptor wiz) {
        // use wiz.putProperty to remember current panel state
        // Method storeSettings() is called when the step finishes
        wiz.putProperty(NumberVisualPanel1.PROP_FIRST_NUMBER, firstNumber);
    }

    @Override
    public void propertyChange(PropertyChangeEvent event) {
        if (event.getPropertyName().equals(
                            NumberVisualPanel1.PROP_FIRST_NUMBER)) {
            boolean oldState = isValid;
            isValid = checkValidity();
            fireChangeEvent(this, oldState, isValid);
        }
    }

    private void setMessage(String message) {
        wizard.getNotificationLineSupport().setErrorMessage(message);
    }

    @NbBundle.Messages({
        "CTL_Panel1NegativeNumber= Number must be non-negative",
        "CTL_Panel1InputRequired= Number field input is required",
        "CTL_Panel1BadNumber= Bad number format"
    })
    private boolean checkValidity() {
        if (getComponent().getFirstNumber().isEmpty()) {
            setMessage(Bundle.CTL_Panel1InputRequired());
            return false;
        }
        try {
            firstNumber = Integer.parseInt(getComponent().getFirstNumber());
            if (firstNumber < 0) {
                setMessage(Bundle.CTL_Panel1NegativeNumber());
                return false;
            }
            setMessage(null);
            return true;
```

```
        } catch (NumberFormatException e) {
            setMessage(Bundle.CTL_Panel1BadNumber());
            return false;
        }
    }

    protected final void fireChangeEvent(Object source, boolean oldState,
                boolean newState) {
        if (oldState != newState) {
            ChangeEvent ev = new ChangeEvent(source);
            for (ChangeListener listener :
                        listeners.getListeners(ChangeListener.class)) {
                listener.stateChanged(ev);
            }
        }
    }
}
```

Make similar changes to the second and third panels, NumberWizardPanel2.java and NumberWizardPanel3.java.

Figure 12.11 shows how each visual panel fires a property change event when user input changes. The wizard panel, in turn, re-validates input when it receives the

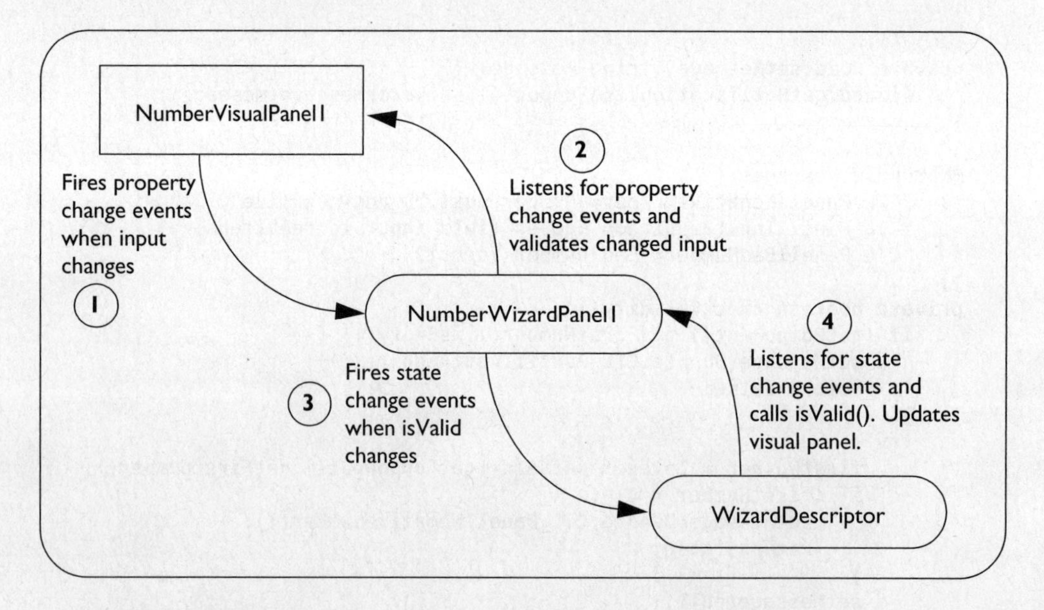


Figure 12.11 Property change events notify listeners to monitor and validate user input. Change events notify the WizardDescriptor when the isValid state changes.

property change event. If the `isValid` state of the panel changes, the wizard panel fires a state change event. The WizardDescriptor responds to state change events by invoking the wizard panel's `isValid()` method. This updates the Next and/or Final buttons on the visual panel accordingly.

Run the application again and invoke the New Number Sequence wizard. Figure 12.12 and Figure 12.13 show examples of error messages for missing input and negative numbers, respectively. An error message appears when input is required. Note that the Next button is disabled when there are errors.

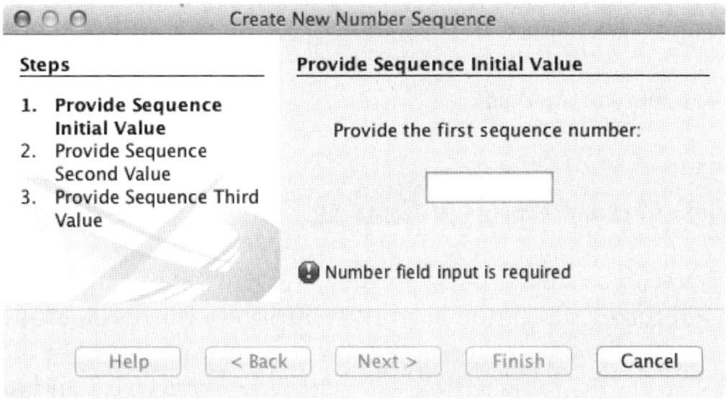

Figure 12.12 Input is required, Next button disabled

Likewise, an error message appears when the number is negative.

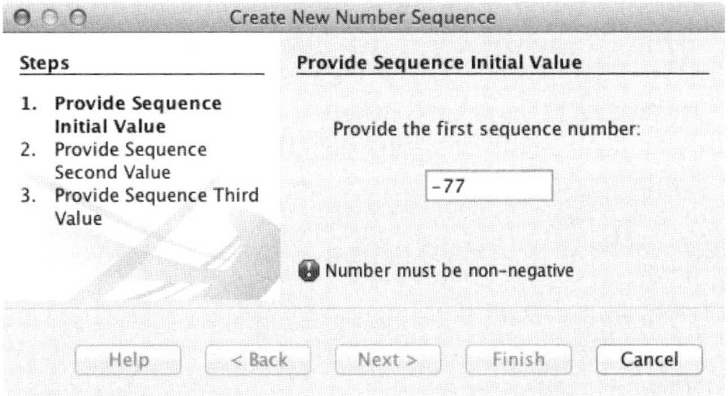

Figure 12.13 Negative numbers not valid, Next button disabled

When input is valid, the WizardDescriptor enables the Next button and no error message appears, as shown in Figure 12.14.

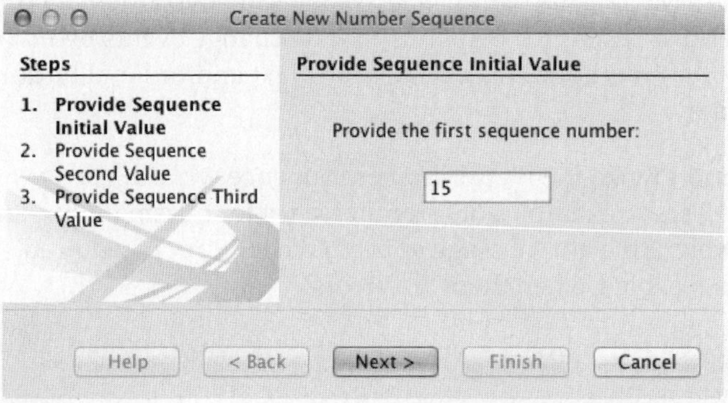

Figure 12.14 Input is valid, Next button enabled

## Coordinating Input with Other Panel Wizards

Once you make these changes to each visual panel and each wizard panel, all three sequence numbers will be well formed and non-negative. Suppose, however, that in addition to this validation, you'd also like to verify that each successive number is larger than the previous one. To do this, wizard panels 2 and 3 must access validated input from the previous panels.

Fortunately, this is straightforward. You read the previous panel's input value in method `readSettings()` and check its value with the current input value in the `checkValidity()` method. Helper method `updatePanel()` encapsulates the updating chores for input validation. (Remember, the WizardDescriptor invokes `readSettings()` at the beginning of a panel's step, so this is where you put step initialization code.)

You must validate the panel in `readSettings()` since the current input may be invalid. Using the Back button, a user can change the previous panel's value and, as a side effect, invalidate the current panel's number.

Listing 12.7 shows the changes (in bold) to wizard panel 2 to ensure that a user supplies a number greater than the value supplied in panel 1. Make similar changes to wizard panel 3, which checks the input provided in panel 2.

**Listing 12.7 NumberWizardPanel2—Modifications for Additional Validation**

```
public class NumberWizardPanel2 implements
        WizardDescriptor.Panel<WizardDescriptor>,
        PropertyChangeListener {

    private Integer firstNumber;
    private Integer secondNumber;
```

```
. . . code omitted . . .

@Override
public void readSettings(WizardDescriptor wiz) {
    // use wiz.getProperty to retrieve previous panel state
    this.wizard = wiz;
    firstNumber = (Integer) wizard.getProperty(
                        NumberVisualPanel1.PROP_FIRST_NUMBER);
    updatePanel();
}

@Override
public void propertyChange(PropertyChangeEvent event) {
    if (event.getPropertyName().equals(
                NumberVisualPanel2.PROP_SECOND_NUMBER)) {
        updatePanel();
    }
}

private void updatePanel() {
    boolean oldState = isValid;
    isValid = checkValidity();
    fireChangeEvent(this, oldState, isValid);
}

@NbBundle.Messages({
    "# {0} - previous sequence number",
    "CTL_Panel2BadSequence= Number must be greater than {0}."
})
private boolean checkValidity() {
    if (getComponent().getSecondNumber().isEmpty()) {
        setMessage(Bundle.CTL_Panel1InputRequired());
        return false;
    }
    try {
        secondNumber = Integer.parseInt(getComponent().getSecondNumber());
        if (secondNumber < 0) {
            setMessage(Bundle.CTL_Panel1NegativeNumber());
            return false;
        }
        if (secondNumber <= firstNumber) {
            setMessage(Bundle.CTL_Panel2BadSequence(firstNumber));
            return false;
        }
        setMessage(null);
        return true;
    } catch (NumberFormatException e) {
```

```
            setMessage(Bundle.CTL_Panel1BadNumber());
            return false;
        }
    }
}
```

Figure 12.15 shows the second panel when the first number is 25 and the user provides number 22.

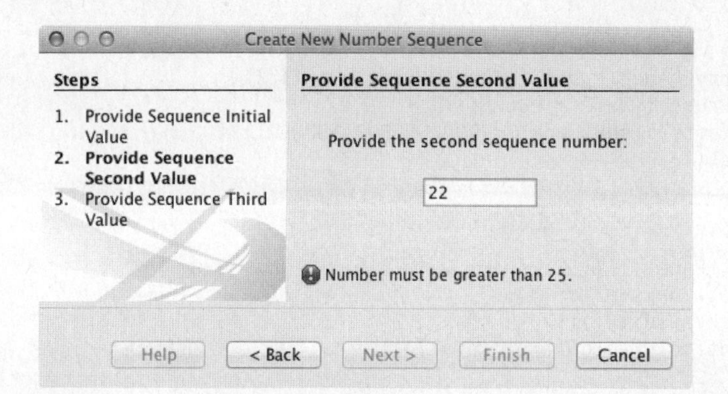


Figure 12.15 Validation of second number depends on value of first number

## Visual Panel Updates

Displaying data from previous panels on the current panel provides helpful visual feedback and shows how a wizard is progressing. Let's modify our New Number Sequence example to display the numbers from the previous panels. This shows users the minimum value required for the current panel.

To provide this visual feedback, modify visual panels 2 and 3. Add a JLabel, JTextArea, or JTextField component to display the data. We use a JLabel and place it below the JTextField component. We also provide a setter so that the wizard panel can update the JLabel component.

Here are the changes to visual panels 2 and 3.

1. Use the Form designer to add a JLabel component under the JTextField component. Change the JLabel variable name to `currentSequence`.
2. Provide public method `setCurrentSequence(String text)` to update the JLabel component.

Listing 12.8 shows the code with the changes in bold for visual panel 3.

**Listing 12.8 NumberVisualPanel3.java—Provide JLabel for Feedback**

```
public final class NumberVisualPanel3 extends JPanel {

    public static final String PROP_THIRD_NUMBER = "thirdNumber";

    . . . code omitted . . .

    public void setCurrentSequence(String text) {
        currentSequence.setText(text);
    }

    . . . code omitted . . .

    // Variables declaration - do not modify
    private javax.swing.JLabel currentSequence;
    private javax.swing.JLabel jLabel1;
    private javax.swing.JTextField thirdNumber;
    // End of variables declaration

. . . code omitted . . .

}
```

Next, update wizard panels 2 and 3, as follows.

1. Get all the previously supplied user data. This requires reading the value for the first number and the second number in wizard panel 3.
2. Invoke `setCurrentSequence()` to set the text of the JLabel component with the current sequence.
3. After invoking `checkValidity()`, update the current sequence. Include the current user input if the input is valid.

Listing 12.9 shows the added Message bundle to NumberWizardPanel2.java, and Listing 12.10 displays the changes to NumberWizardPanel3.java shown in bold. Make the corresponding changes to NumberVisualPanel2.java.

**Listing 12.9 NumberWizardPanel2.java—Providing Visual Feedback**

```
public class NumberWizardPanel2 implements
      WizardDescriptor.Panel<WizardDescriptor>, PropertyChangeListener {

. . . code omitted . . .

      @NbBundle.Messages({
         "# {0} - current sequence string",
         "CTL_Panel2CurrentSequence= Current Sequence: {0}."
         })
```

**Listing 12.10 NumberWizardPanel3.java—Providing Visual Feedback**

```
public class NumberWizardPanel3 implements
WizardDescriptor.Panel<WizardDescriptor>,
        PropertyChangeListener {

    private NumberVisualPanel3 component;
    private WizardDescriptor wizard = null;
    private boolean isValid = false;
    private Integer firstNumber;
    private Integer secondNumber;
    private Integer thirdNumber;

   . . . code omitted . . .

    @Override
    public void readSettings(WizardDescriptor wiz) {
        this.wizard = wiz;
        firstNumber = (Integer) wiz.getProperty(
                     NumberVisualPanel1.PROP_FIRST_NUMBER);
        secondNumber = (Integer) wiz.getProperty(
                     NumberVisualPanel2.PROP_SECOND_NUMBER);
        updatePanel();
    }

    private void updatePanel() {
        boolean oldState = isValid;
        isValid = checkValidity();
        if (isValid) {
            getComponent().setCurrentSequence(
                    Bundle.CTL_Panel2CurrentSequence(
                    firstNumber + ", " + secondNumber + ", " + thirdNumber));
        } else {
            getComponent().setCurrentSequence(
                    Bundle.CTL_Panel2CurrentSequence(
                    firstNumber + ", " + secondNumber));
        }
        fireChangeEvent(this, oldState, isValid);
    }
}
```

Now run the application again and invoke the New Number Sequence wizard. Figure 12.16 shows panel 3 when the user supplies invalid data.

When user input is valid, the current sequence includes the current panel's input number, as shown in Figure 12.17.

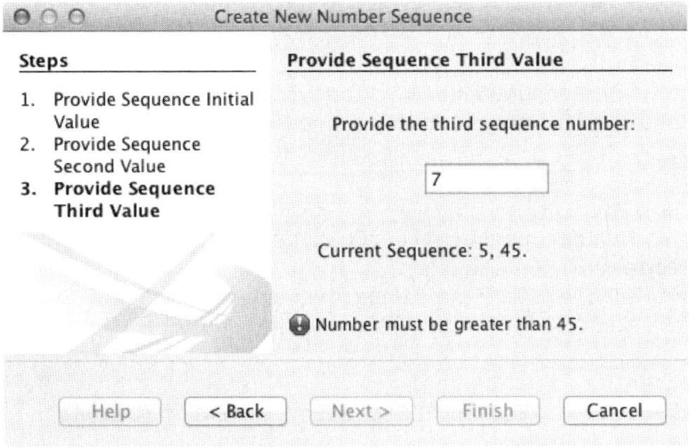

Figure 12.16 User sees current sequence

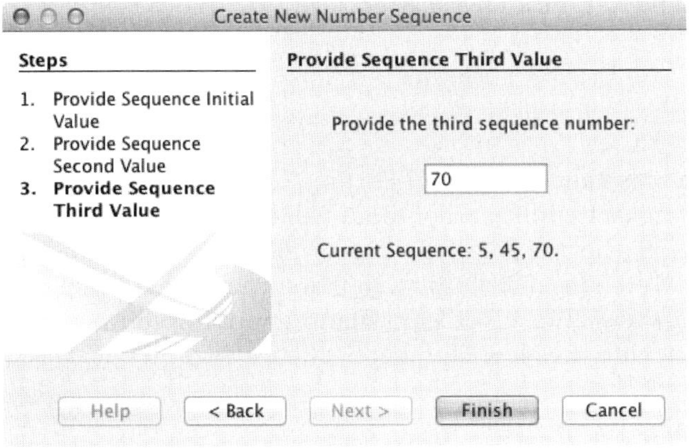

Figure 12.17 User input is valid and current sequence includes new input

# 12.5 Simple Validation API

Panels that have textfields (like those shown in the previous section) often require repetitive and tedious validation code. For example, in Listing 12.11 the `checkValidity()` method validates the second sequence number in NumberWizardPanel2 using several steps. First, the method verifies the input is not empty. Second, it converts the input to an integer (making sure the integer is well-formed), Third, it verifies the number is non-negative. And finally, it checks the input value against the first sequence number.

**Listing 12.11 Validate Second Sequence Number (NumberWizardPanel2)**

```
private boolean checkValidity() {
    if (getComponent().getSecondNumber().isEmpty()) {
        setMessage(Bundle.CTL_Panel1InputRequired());
        return false;
    }
    try {
        secondNumber = Integer.parseInt(getComponent().getSecondNumber());
        if (secondNumber < 0) {
            setMessage(Bundle.CTL_Panel1NegativeNumber());
            return false;
        }
        if (secondNumber <= firstNumber) {
            setMessage(Bundle.CTL_Panel2BadSequence(firstNumber));
            return false;
        }
        setMessage(null);
        return true;
    } catch (NumberFormatException e) {
        setMessage(Bundle.CTL_Panel1BadNumber());
        return false;
    }
}
```

Wouldn't it be nice to reduce this validation code? Fortunately, a general-purpose validation library is available for exactly this kind of input validation. Created by Tim Boudreau of NetBeans fame, this library is called Simple Validation API and is open-sourced and included in the NetBeans distribution. In this section, we'll show you how to use the validation library within a NetBeans Platform application. As an example, we'll use the library with the New Number Sequence wizard.

## Prepare to Use the Validation Library

To use the Simple Validation API in a NetBeans Platform application, you need to create a library wrapper for the JAR file. NetBeans will do this for you when you add the JAR file to your application, as follows.

1. In the Projects window, select application WizardExample, right-click, and choose **Add Existing Library . . . .**
2. In the Select Library dialog, click **Browse.** Navigate to **NetBeans/ide/modules/ext/ValidationAPI.jar** and click **Select**. Back in the Select Library dialog, click **Next** as shown in Figure 12.18.
3. In the Name and Location dialog, make sure the Project Name and directory locations are correct and click **Next**, as shown in Figure 12.19.

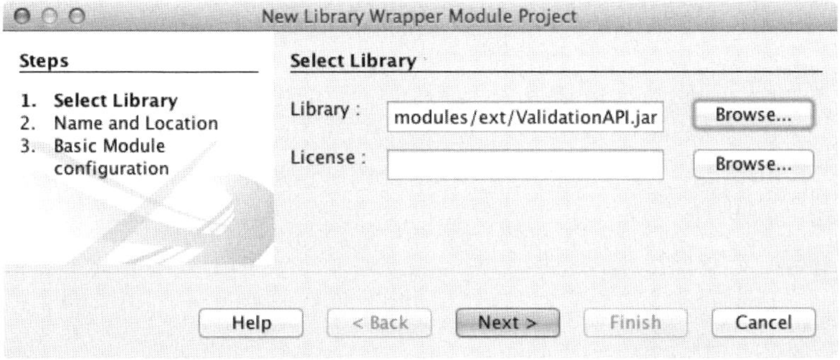

Figure 12.18 Creating a new library wrapper module project

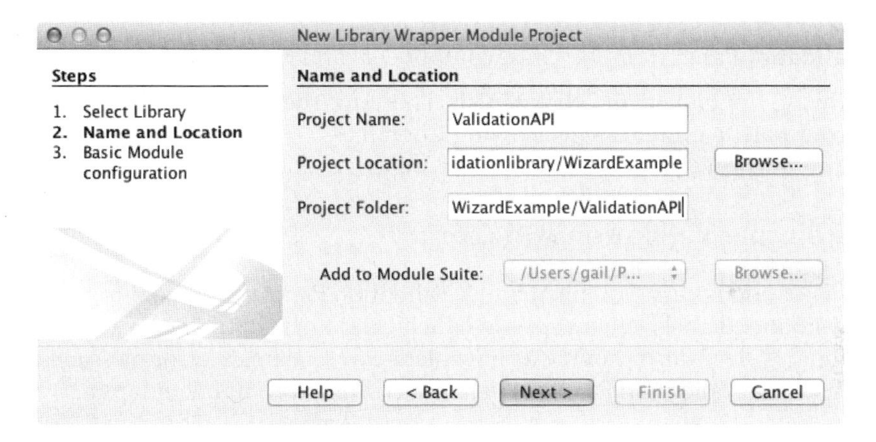


Figure 12.19 Name and Location dialog

4. Provide a Code Name Base in the Basic Module Configuration dialog and click **Finish**. NetBeans creates module ValidationAPI and adds it to your project, as shown in Figure 12.20.
5. Add a new dependency on the Validation API in module Sequence. Now you can use the library in this module.

Extend the Swing component palette, as follows.

1. In the NetBeans IDE, make sure the component design palette is open. Right-click inside the design palette and choose **Palette Manager** from the context menu.
2. Choose button **Add from JAR**, and browse to the same **ValidationAPI.jar**. Click **Next**.

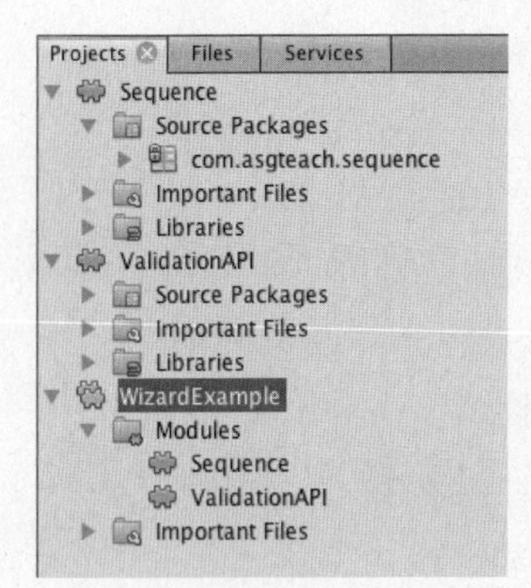


Figure 12.20 Module ValidationAPI is a wrapped JAR file

3. Select **ValidationPanel** from the list of components and click **Next**.
4. Choose Swing Containers and click **Finish**. This adds the Validation Panel component to your palette under category Swing Containers. With this extension, you can drag and drop Validation Panels to a Swing UI.

## Using the Simple Validation API Library

To use the Validation library, you must add a Validation Panel component to your Swing UI. Validation Panels let you specify which validators should apply to which input components. They also provide a convenient way to display error messages. Typically, you'll use Validation Panels to validate JTextField component input.

Table 12.2 shows ten useful validators from the Validation library (there are more). When you specify one or more validators for a specific component, validation proceeds in the order that you add them. For example, to validate input for an integer, you chain together `REQUIRE_NON_EMPTY_STRING`, `NO_WHITESPACE`, and `REQUIRE_VALID_INTEGER`. Note that the order is significant. Each validator is invoked until a problem occurs or the list is exhausted. Checking for empty strings first makes error messages clearer for the user.

**TABLE 12.2 Ten Useful Validators**

| Validator |
|---|
| `REQUIRE_NON_EMPTY_STRING` |
| `NO_WHITESPACE` |
| `REQUIRE_VALID_INTEGER` |
| `REQUIRE_NON_NEGATIVE_NUMBER` |
| `numberRange(minValue, maxValue)` |

**TABLE 12.2 Ten Useful Validators** *(Continued)*

| Validator |
|---|
| EMAIL_ADDRESS |
| FILE_MUST_EXIST |
| URL_MUST_BE_VALID |
| REQUIRE_JAVA_IDENTIFIER |
| REQUIRE_VALID_FILENAME |

In situations where these validators aren't suitable, you can build a custom validator. We'll show you how to do this shortly.

Let's begin by adding validation to the `firstNumber` textfield in the first visual panel, NumberVisualPanel1.

1. Open NumberVisualPanel1 in the Design view.
2. Select ValidationPanel from the palette and drag and drop it on the visual panel under the JTextField. This adds component `validationPanel1`.
3. Go to **Source** view and add the code as shown in Listing 12.12 to Number-VisualPanel1.java.

   Validation configuration starts with `validationPanel1`. From `validationPanel1` we first obtain a ValidationGroup object. We then assign a target component for validation and add validators. Here, we add validators to verify that input is not empty, contains no white space, is a valid integer, and is a non-negative number. We also make sure the integer is within the specified minimum and maximum values.

   We've modified the DocumentListener for `firstNumber` to invoke method `checkValidation()`, which includes a call to `group.validateAll()`.

   We also override method `isValid()` so that NumberWizardPanel1 knows if the input is valid. We still fire a property change event whenever input changes.

**Listing 12.12 Add Validation to NumberVisualPanel1**

```
public final class NumberVisualPanel1 extends JPanel {

    public static final String PROP_FIRST_NUMBER = "firstNumber";
    public static final Integer MAX_SEQUENCE_NUMBER = 10000; // arbitrary
    private ValidationGroup group = null;
    private boolean isValid = false;

    public NumberVisualPanel1() {
        initComponents();
        firstNumber.setName(Bundle.CTL_Panel1FieldName());
        group = validationPanel1.getValidationGroup();
```

```
        group.add(firstNumber,
                Validators.REQUIRE_NON_EMPTY_STRING,
                Validators.NO_WHITESPACE,
                Validators.REQUIRE_VALID_INTEGER,
                Validators.REQUIRE_NON_NEGATIVE_NUMBER,
                Validators.numberRange(0, MAX_SEQUENCE_NUMBER-2));

        firstNumber.getDocument().addDocumentListener(new DocumentListener() {

            @Override
            public void insertUpdate(DocumentEvent e) {
                checkValidation();
            }

            @Override
            public void removeUpdate(DocumentEvent e) {
                checkValidation();
            }

            @Override
            public void changedUpdate(DocumentEvent e) {
                checkValidation();
            }

            private void checkValidation() {
                Problem validateAll = group.validateAll();
                isValid = !validateAll.isFatal();
                firePropertyChange(PROP_FIRST_NUMBER, 0, 1);
            }
        });
    }

    @Override
    public boolean isValid() {
        return isValid;
    }
   . . . code omitted . . .
}
```

Since validation now takes place within the visual panel, the wizard panel no longer performs validation. However, the wizard panel must still store Integer `firstNumber` and keep the WizardDescriptor informed of the panel's valid status. (Remember, the WizardDescriptor must update the Next/Finish buttons as input changes.) Listing 12.13 shows the modified method `checkValidity()` in NumberWizardPanel1. Note that a NumberFormatException should not occur since the component returns already-validated text.

**Listing 12.13 NumberWizardPanel1: Method checkValidity()**

```
private boolean checkValidity() {
    if (getComponent().isValid()) {
        try {
           firstNumber = Integer.parseInt(getComponent().getFirstNumber());
            setMessage(null);
            return true;
        } catch (NumberFormatException e) {
            setMessage(Bundle.CTL_Panel1BadNumber());
            return false;
        }
    }
    return false;
}
```

## Using a Custom Validator

Now that we've implemented validation with the Validation API for the first panel, we can apply similar changes to the second and third panels. In this case, however, we must set the minimum value for the range validator through the wizard panel method `readSettings()`, since this minimum depends on the previous panel's number.

We must also be able to change the minimum range when a user clicks the Back button, changes the previous number, and returns to the second and third panels.

The general model for the built-in validators makes them immutable. In other words, you can't change a validator's parameters once you set them. While some might see this as less than ideal, mutable state validators are more complex. These validators are simple (hence the name) and easy to use.

The solution to the immutable validator restriction is to create a custom validator. To do this, implement the Validator interface and override method `validate()`. With a custom validator, we can delegate validation to a standard range validator created at validation time and thus achieve dynamic range validation.

With a bona fide motivation to create our own validator, let's do that now. Listing 12.14 shows CustomRangeValidator, a validator that lets you modify a validator's minimum and maximum range values.

Two setters configure the validator's range. In method `validate()`, we create a number range validator (using the built-in static `numberRange()` method) with range parameters `minVal` and `maxVal`. We then invoke `validate()` using the newly created delegate validator.

**Listing 12.14 CustomRangeValidator**

```
public class CustomRangeValidator implements Validator<String> {
    private Integer minVal = new Integer(0);
    private Integer maxVal= new Integer(0);

    public void setMaxVal(Integer maxVal) {
        this.maxVal = maxVal;
    }

    public void setMinVal(Integer minVal) {
        this.minVal = minVal;
    }

    @Override
    public boolean validate(Problems prblms, String string, String t) {
        Validator<String> rangeDelegate =
                            Validators.numberRange(minVal, maxVal);
        return rangeDelegate.validate(prblms, string, t);
    }
}
```

Listing 12.15 shows the corresponding changes to the visual panel. Note that we create a new class variable `customrange` for our CustomRangeValidator. Public method `setMinRange()` configures the minimum range value. The list of validators added to the ValidationGroup is the same, except we use the custom range validator instead of the built-in range validator.

We also define a public method `updateValidation()` that lets the wizard panel check validation from `readSettings()`. This is necessary to ensure correct behavior when the Back button is used to change the previous panel's value.

**Listing 12.15 Add Validation to NumberVisualPanel2**

```
public final class NumberVisualPanel2 extends JPanel {

    public static final String PROP_SECOND_NUMBER = "secondNumber";
    private boolean isValid = false;
    private CustomRangeValidator customrange = new CustomRangeValidator();
    private ValidationGroup group = null;

    public NumberVisualPanel2() {
        initComponents();
        secondNumber.setName(Bundle.CTL_Panel1FieldName());

        // setup validation
        group = validationPanel1.getValidationGroup();
        customrange.setMaxVal(NumberVisualPanel1.MAX_SEQUENCE_NUMBER - 1);
        customrange.setMinVal(0);
```

```
        group.add(secondNumber,
                Validators.REQUIRE_NON_EMPTY_STRING,
                Validators.NO_WHITESPACE,
                Validators.REQUIRE_VALID_INTEGER,
                Validators.REQUIRE_NON_NEGATIVE_NUMBER,
                customrange);
        secondNumber.getDocument().addDocumentListener(new DocumentListener() {

            @Override
            public void insertUpdate(DocumentEvent de) {
                checkValidation();
            }

            @Override
            public void removeUpdate(DocumentEvent de) {
                checkValidation();
            }

            @Override
            public void changedUpdate(DocumentEvent de) {
                checkValidation();
            }

            private void checkValidation() {
                updateValidation();
                firePropertyChange(PROP_SECOND_NUMBER, 0, 1);
            }
        });
    }

    public void setMinRange(Integer minNumber) {
        customrange.setMinVal(minNumber);
    }

    public void updateValidation() {
        Problem validateAll = group.validateAll();
        isValid = !validateAll.isFatal();
    }
. . . code omitted . . .
}
```

Listing 12.16 shows the changes required to NumberWizardPanel2 methods. Now, if a user clicks the Back button, changes the first sequence number, and then returns to the second panel, the range validator is configured with a new minimum range.

#### Listing 12.16 NumberWizardPanel2 methods

```
    @Override
    public void readSettings(WizardDescriptor wiz) {
        this.wizard = wiz;
```

```
        firstNumber = (Integer) wizard.getProperty(
                NumberVisualPanel1.PROP_FIRST_NUMBER);
        if (firstNumber == null) {
            firstNumber = 0;
        }
        getComponent().setMinRange(firstNumber + 1);
        updatePanel();
    }

  . . . code omitted . . .

    private void updatePanel() {
        boolean oldState = isValid;
        getComponent().updateValidation();
        isValid = checkValidity();
        if (isValid) {
            getComponent().setCurrentSequence(
                    Bundle.CTL_Panel2CurrentSequence(
                    firstNumber + ", " + secondNumber));
        } else {
            getComponent().setCurrentSequence(
                    Bundle.CTL_Panel2CurrentSequence(firstNumber));
        }
        fireChangeEvent(this, oldState, isValid);
    }
```

Make the corresponding changes to NumberVisualPanel3 and NumberWizardPanel3 to implement a dynamic range validator for the third panel. Figure 12.21 shows the error message when a number is outside the required range.

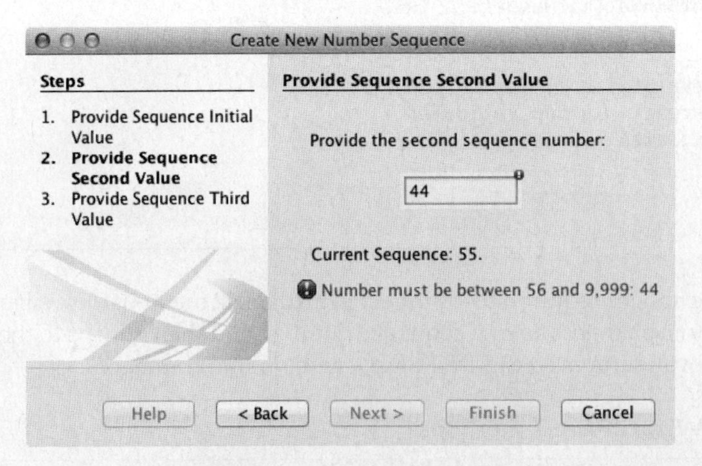


Figure 12.21 A custom number range validator

## 12.6 Finishing Early Option

The NetBeans Platform wizard lets you provide users with an option to finish a wizard early. Finishing early is always only an option, however, and not a requirement. The user is still able to proceed to the next panel by selecting Next.

This distinction is important. If you want to create a dynamic use case, where the user works through different panels depending on their selections, or the wizard ends early because of a user selection, then select the Dynamic Wizard Step Sequence instead of the Static Wizard Step Sequence when creating your wizard. (See "Dynamic Sequence Wizards" on page 598.)

Returning to our New Number Sequence wizard, let's say that if the second number is greater than 500, the user has the option of specifying only two numbers for the sequence instead of three. That is, in the second panel, we enable the Finish button so the user can optionally finish after providing valid input if the second number is greater than 500.

To implement this behavior, we store the number selections in an ArrayList, which simplifies the coding for sequences of different sizes. With an ArrayList, it's more convenient to retrieve all the numbers in the `actionPerformed()` method.

First, let's look at the modifications to store and retrieve the numbers using an ArrayList. Listing 12.17 shows the changes to NumberWizardPanel1 in bold.

Array `mynumbers` holds the numbers. In method `storeSettings()`, we put the ArrayList property into the WizardDescriptor's property cache.

**Listing 12.17 NumberWizardPanel1.java—Using ArrayList Property**

```
public class NumberWizardPanel1 implements
        WizardDescriptor.Panel<WizardDescriptor>,
        PropertyChangeListener {

    private NumberVisualPanel1 component;
    private WizardDescriptor wizard = null;
    private boolean isValid = false;
    private Integer firstNumber;
    private List<Integer> mynumbers = new ArrayList<Integer>();
    public final static String PROP_NUMBER_LIST = "mynumbers";

    @Override
    public void storeSettings(WizardDescriptor wiz) {
        wiz.putProperty(NumberVisualPanel1.PROP_FIRST_NUMBER, firstNumber);
        mynumbers.clear();
```

```
        mynumbers.add(firstNumber);
        wiz.putProperty(PROP_NUMBER_LIST, mynumbers);
    }
  . . . code omitted . . .
}
```

Make similar changes to NumberWizardPanel2 and NumberWizardPanel3. Listing 12.18 shows the code for NumberWizardPanel3. Note that here we must retrieve the `mynumbers` ArrayList in `readSettings()` as well as save it in `storeSettings()`.

**Listing 12.18 NumberWizardPanel3.java—Using ArrayList Property**

```
public class NumberWizardPanel3 implements
        WizardDescriptor.Panel<WizardDescriptor>,
        PropertyChangeListener {

    private NumberVisualPanel3 component;
    private WizardDescriptor wizard = null;
    private boolean isValid = false;
    private Integer firstNumber;
    private Integer secondNumber;
    private Integer thirdNumber;
    private List<Integer> mynumbers;

      . . . code omitted . . .

    @Override
    public void readSettings(WizardDescriptor wiz) {
        this.wizard = wiz;
        firstNumber = (Integer) wiz.getProperty(
                NumberVisualPanel1.PROP_FIRST_NUMBER);
        secondNumber = (Integer) wiz.getProperty(
                NumberVisualPanel2.PROP_SECOND_NUMBER);
        mynumbers = (List<Integer>) wizard.getProperty(
                NumberWizardPanel1.PROP_NUMBER_LIST);
        updatePanel();
    }

    @Override
    public void storeSettings(WizardDescriptor wiz) {
        wiz.putProperty(NumberVisualPanel3.PROP_THIRD_NUMBER, thirdNumber);
        mynumbers.clear();
        mynumbers.add(firstNumber);
        mynumbers.add(secondNumber);
```

```
            mynumbers.add(thirdNumber);
            wiz.putProperty(NumberWizardPanel1.PROP_NUMBER_LIST, mynumbers);
        }
      . . . code omitted . . .
}
```

Now in NumberWizardAction's method `actionPerformed()`, we retrieve the numbers from property `NumberWizardPanel1.PROP_NUMBER_LIST` to display the new sequence, as shown in Listing 12.19.

**Listing 12.19 Method actionPerformed—Version II**

```
    @Override
    public void actionPerformed(ActionEvent e) {

          . . . code omitted . . .

        if (DialogDisplayer.getDefault().notify(wiz) ==
                                    WizardDescriptor.FINISH_OPTION) {
            StatusDisplayer.getDefault().setStatusText("Wizard Finished");
            // retrieve and display the numbers
           StringBuilder message = new StringBuilder("Number Sequence =  \n(");
            List<Integer> numbers = (List<Integer>) wiz.getProperty(
                                    NumberWizardPanel1.PROP_NUMBER_LIST);
            for (int i = 0; i < numbers.size()-1; i++) {
                message.append(numbers.get(i)).append(", ");
            }
            message.append(numbers.get(numbers.size()-1)).append(")");
            DialogDisplayer.getDefault().notify(
                    new NotifyDescriptor.Message(message.toString()));
        }

    }
```

With that bit of housekeeping out of the way, let's return to NumberWizardPanel2. This is the panel we'll make "finishable."

To make a panel with a Finish button that is optionally enabled—finishable—the panel implements `WizardDescriptor.FinishablePanel<WizardDescriptor>` and overrides method `isFinishPanel()`. That's it. However, when the status of method `isFinishPanel()` changes, you must fire a state change event to the panel's listeners just like you do with method `isValid()`. This allows the WizardDescriptor to update the Finish button as the user input changes. Listing 12.20 shows how NumberWizardPanel2 implements FinishablePanel.

The boolean field `isFinishPanel` is updated whenever this class receives a property change event from the visual panel as the user provides input. After performing the normal validation check, we update `isFinishPanel`. If its status has changed, method `fireChangeEvent()` fires a state change event. This in turn causes the WizardDescriptor to invoke method `isFinishPanel()` and update the Finish button accordingly. Even if `isFinishPanel()` returns true, the Finish button is not enabled unless `isValid()` also returns true.

**Listing 12.20 NumberWizardPanel2.java—Implementing a Finish Early Option**

```
public class NumberWizardPanel2 implements
        WizardDescriptor.FinishablePanel<WizardDescriptor>,
        PropertyChangeListener {

    private NumberVisualPanel2 component;
    private WizardDescriptor wizard = null;
    private boolean isValid = false;
    private boolean isFinishPanel = false;
    private Integer firstNumber;
    private Integer secondNumber;
    private List<Integer> mynumbers;
    private static final int FINISH_LIMIT = 500;

      . . . code omitted . . .

    @Override
    public void propertyChange(PropertyChangeEvent event) {
        if (event.getPropertyName().equals(
                    NumberVisualPanel2.PROP_SECOND_NUMBER)) {
            updatePanel();
        }
    }

    private void updatePanel() {
        boolean oldState = isValid;
        isValid = checkValidity();
        if (isValid) {
            getComponent().setCurrentSequence(
                    Bundle.CTL_Panel2CurrentSequence(
                    firstNumber + ", " + secondNumber));
        } else {
            getComponent().setCurrentSequence(
                    Bundle.CTL_Panel2CurrentSequence(firstNumber));
        }
        fireChangeEvent(this, oldState, isValid);
        oldState = isFinishPanel;
        if (secondNumber != null) {
            isFinishPanel = secondNumber > FINISH_LIMIT;
            fireChangeEvent(this, oldState, isFinishPanel);
        }
    }
```

```
    @Override
    public boolean isFinishPanel() {
        return isFinishPanel;
    }
}
```

Run the WizardExample application again and invoke the New Number Sequence wizard. You'll see that if the second number is greater than 500, you can click Finish early and provide a number sequence of just two numbers, as shown in Figure 12.22. (Note that the Next button is also enabled.)

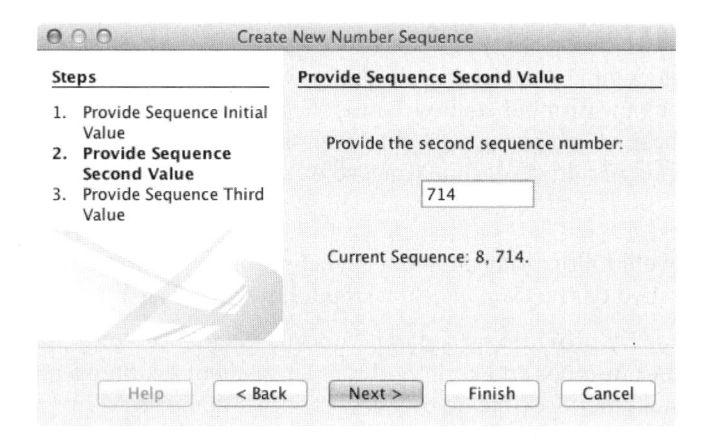


Figure 12.22 The second number is greater than 500, so the Finish button is enabled

After clicking Finish in the panel above, the new number sequence (consisting of only two numbers) shows in the Information window shown in Figure 12.23.

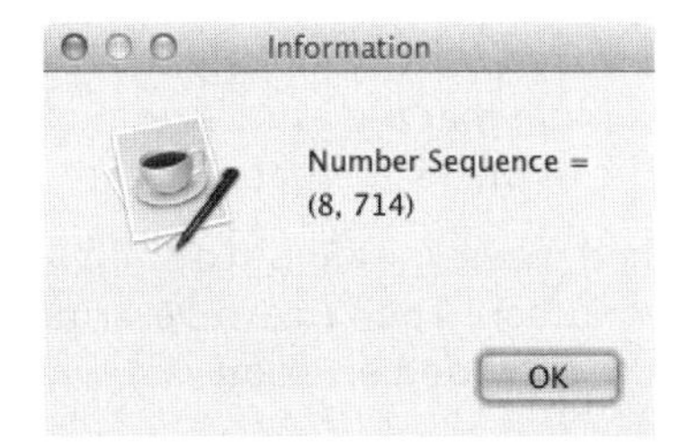


Figure 12.23 The new number sequence consists of only two numbers because the wizard finished early

## 12.7 Asynchronous Validation

The example you've seen so far includes validation that doesn't take much time—that is, the visual panel responds to a document change in the graphical user component. That in turn fires a property change event to the wizard panel which re-validates the input. What happens, however, if validation requires a longer process, such as a web service call or a database access? In this case, you don't want to block the user interface (and prevent the user from clicking the Cancel button). Instead, you provide *asynchronous* validation after the user clicks the Next button. This means the WizardDescriptor does not proceed to the next panel until the validation is complete, but the Cancel button is still active.

Let's show you how to implement asynchronous validation with a somewhat contrived example. Suppose the new number sequence must begin with a unique number; that is, a number that hasn't been previously used for the initial number. In our case, we assume that this check could take some time, so we want to perform the validation asynchronously.

Here are the general steps we'll follow to implement asynchronous validation in our example. We'll provide detailed descriptions of each step following this list.

1. Let's mimic a database call by providing a separate module (SequenceStore) that stores each initial sequence number and a method that lets a client validate a new number sequence. We must therefore create this new module, make its API package public, and add the module as a dependency to the Sequence module.
2. We add a JLabel component to the visual panel with public method `setStatus()` and make the JTextField component (the number input component) accessible from the wizard panel. (This is just to provide visual feedback to the user.)
3. The wizard panel implements `WizardDescriptor.AsynchronousValidatingPanel<WizardDescriptor>` instead of `WizardDescriptor.Panel<WizardDescriptor>`. In our example, we make this change to NumberWizardPanel1.
4. Override method `prepareValidation()`, which is invoked synchronously and performs any pre-validating access to the visual panel. Note that the asynchronous validation method should *not* access the components in the visual panel.
5. Override method `validate()`. This method is invoked in a separate thread. If validation fails, throw WizardValidationException (of course!). The WizardDescriptor handles the WizardValidationException, displays the provided error message, and prevents the user from proceeding to the next panel.
6. After the wizard finishes, store the initial sequence number in the SequenceStore module.

**Wizard Tip**

*Another option is to perform synchronous validation when between-panel validation is not time-critical. To do this, implement interface* `WizardDescriptor.ValidatingPanel<WizardDescriptor>` *and override method* `validate()`, *which the WizardDescriptor invokes synchronously. See Listing 12.28 on page 610 for an example.*

Let's begin our asynchronous validation example by creating a new module in the WizardExample application. Call the new module SequenceStore. In the SequenceStore module, create Java interface NumberStore in package `com.asgteach.sequencestore.api` and provide abstract methods `store()` and `isUnique()`, as shown in Listing 12.21.

**Listing 12.21 NumberStore.java**

```
package com.asgteach.sequencestore.api;

public interface NumberStore {

    public boolean isUnique(Integer num);

    public boolean store(Integer num);

}
```

Add Lookup API dependency to module SequenceStore and make package `com.asgteach.sequencestore.api` public in API Versioning. Now create new Java class SimpleNumberStore in package `com.asgteach.sequencestore` with the implementation shown in Listing 12.22. Note that we use annotation `@ServiceProvider` for class NumberStore.

**Listing 12.22 SimpleNumberStore.java—A NumberStore Service Provider**

```
package com.asgteach.sequencestore;

import com.asgteach.sequencestore.api.NumberStore;
import java.util.HashSet;
import java.util.Set;
import org.openide.util.lookup.ServiceProvider;

@ServiceProvider(service = NumberStore.class)
public class SimpleNumberStore implements NumberStore {

    private Set<Integer> numberSet = new HashSet<Integer>();
```

```
    @Override
    public boolean isUnique(Integer num) {
        return !numberSet.contains(num);
    }

    @Override
    public boolean store(Integer num) {
        // add returns true if the collection changed
        // (if num was not already present)
        return numberSet.add(num);
    }
}
```

Add a JLabel component to the Design view of NumberVisualPanel1 and change the JLabel's Variable Name property to **status**, as shown in Figure 12.24. (Remove the text from the label's text property.)

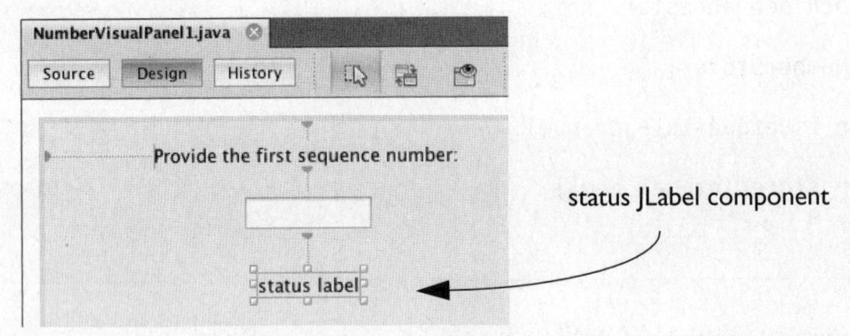


Figure 12.24 NumberVisualPanel1 with the added JLabel component

Listing 12.23 shows the changes required for the visual panel, NumberVisualPanel1.java. We add `getNumberComponent()` and `setStatus()` public methods, as shown in bold.

**Listing 12.23 NumberVisualPanel1.java**

```
public final class NumberVisualPanel1 extends JPanel {

   . . . code omitted . . .

    public JTextField getNumberComponent() {
        return firstNumber;
    }

    public void setStatus(String text) {
        status.setText(text);
    }
```

```
    . . . code omitted . . .

    // Variables declaration - do not modify
    private javax.swing.JTextField firstNumber;
    private javax.swing.JLabel jLabel1;
    private javax.swing.JLabel status;
    // End of variables declaration

    . . .
}
```

Now turn your attention to NumberWizardPanel1, the wizard panel that provides the asynchronous validation (see Listing 12.24). First, add dependencies to the Lookup API and module SequenceStore to access the service provider for NumberStore. Note that we still validate user input here to make sure the input is a valid, non-negative number. After this validation succeeds and the user clicks Next, the WizardDescriptor initiates the asynchronous validation by invoking `prepareValidation()` followed by `validate()`. These methods are required with interface `WizardDescriptor.AsynchronousValidatingPanel`, and we provide implementations of them in NumberWizardPanel1.

Method `prepareValidation()` performs any GUI-related functions required by the validation. Here, we write a status message to the visual panel and get a reference to the JTextField component. This component is needed for the WizardValidationException.

Method `validate()` performs the actual number sequence validation in a separate thread. First, we obtain a reference to the NumberStore service provider via the Global Lookup. We invoke method `isUnique()` to determine whether or not the initial number is unique. If it is, we return and the validation succeeds. If not, we throw WizardValidationException. The exception arguments include the input component from the visual panel that is responsible for the data and error messages that the WizardDescriptor displays.

**Listing 12.24 NumberWizardPanel1.java—Asynchronous Validation**

```
public class NumberWizardPanel1 implements
        WizardDescriptor.AsynchronousValidatingPanel<WizardDescriptor>,
        PropertyChangeListener {

    private NumberVisualPanel1 component;
    private WizardDescriptor wizard = null;
    private boolean isValid = false;
    private Integer firstNumber;
    private JComponent numberComponent = null;

   . . . Code unchanged . . .
```

```
    @Override
    public void prepareValidation() {
        getComponent().setStatus(Bundle.CTL_Panel1_CheckUnique(firstNumber));
        numberComponent = getComponent().getNumberComponent();
    }

    @NbBundle.Messages({
        "# {0} - current sequence number",
        "CTL_Panel1_DuplicateNumErr= {0} is not unique.",
        "CTL_Panel1_BadLookup=Can't get NumberStore",
        "# {0} - current sequence number",
        "CTL_Panel1_CheckUnique= Checking for {0} uniqueness . . ."
    })
    @Override
    public void validate() throws WizardValidationException {

        NumberStore numStore = Lookup.getDefault().lookup(NumberStore.class);
        if (numStore == null) {
            throw new WizardValidationException(numberComponent,
                    Bundle.CTL_Panel1_BadLookup(),
                    Bundle.CTL_Panel1_BadLookup());
        }
        // we don't store the first sequence number
        // until after the wizard finishes (so Back button doesn't bite us)
        if (!numStore.isUnique(firstNumber)) {
            throw new WizardValidationException(numberComponent,
                    Bundle.CTL_Panel1_DuplicateNumErr(firstNumber),
                    Bundle.CTL_Panel1_DuplicateNumErr(firstNumber));

        }
    }
}
```

When the asynchronous validation succeeds and the user proceeds through the remaining panels to complete the wizard, we store the new initial sequence number using the NumberStore service provider. Listing 12.25 shows the update to NumberWizardAction.java and method `actionPerformed()`. Once again, we get a reference to the NumberStore service provider through the Global Lookup and invoke `numStore.store()` to store the initial sequence number.

**Listing 12.25 NumberWizardAction.java—Store the Initial Sequence Number**

```
@ActionID(category = "Tools",
   id = "org.asgteach.sequence.NumberWizardAction")

      . . . code omitted . . .
```

```
public final class NumberWizardAction implements ActionListener {

    @Override
    public void actionPerformed(ActionEvent e) {
        List<WizardDescriptor.Panel<WizardDescriptor>> panels =
            new ArrayList<WizardDescriptor.Panel<WizardDescriptor>>();

         . . . code omitted . . .

        WizardDescriptor wiz = new WizardDescriptor(
               new WizardDescriptor.ArrayIterator<WizardDescriptor>(panels));
        wiz.setTitleFormat(new MessageFormat("{0}"));
        wiz.setTitle(Bundle.CTL_NumberDialogTitle());
        if (DialogDisplayer.getDefault().notify(wiz) ==
                                    WizardDescriptor.FINISH_OPTION) {
            // Store the number
            NumberStore numStore =
                  Lookup.getDefault().lookup(NumberStore.class);
            if (numStore != null) {
                numStore.store((Integer) wiz.getProperty(
                     NumberVisualPanel1.PROP_FIRST_NUMBER));
            }

            // Retrieve and display the numbers
           StringBuilder message = new StringBuilder("Number Sequence =  \n(");
            List<Integer> numbers = (List<Integer>) wiz.getProperty(
                     NumberWizardPanel1.PROP_NUMBER_LIST);
            for (int i = 0; i < numbers.size()-1; i++) {
                message.append(numbers.get(i)).append(", ");
            }
            message.append(numbers.get(numbers.size()-1)).append(")");
            DialogDisplayer.getDefault().notify(
                    new NotifyDescriptor.Message(message.toString()));
        }
    }
}
```

Figure 12.25 shows the first panel after it performs the asynchronous validation and finds a duplicate first sequence number. The user must now provide a new number and click Next again to validate the new input.

If the validation succeeds, the user automatically proceeds to the second panel. However, we don't store the first sequence number in NumberStore until after the wizard finishes. This lets a user click the Back button and use the same initial number without causing a validation error.

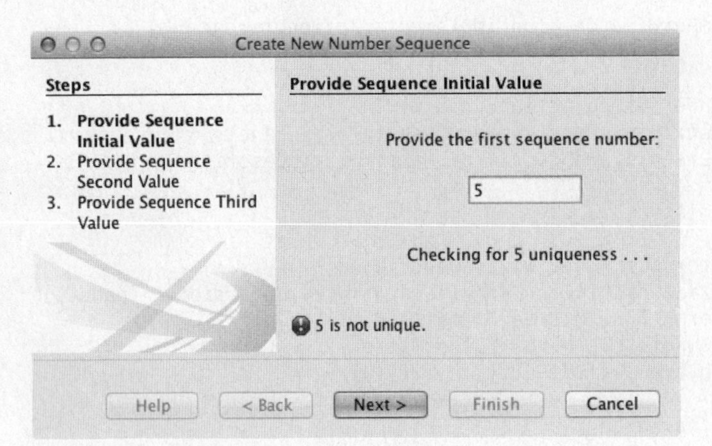


Figure 12.25 Performing asynchronous validation

## 12.8 Dynamic Sequence Wizards

With a NetBeans Platform wizard, the steps you take are not always the same. User input in one panel may affect the next panel you see. To handle this use case, you need a wizard with a dynamic step sequence.

To illustrate, let's create an example wizard that takes a user through a multi-step process to order a pizza. In the first step, the user provides a customer name. If the customer is new, the next panel asks for additional customer details. For returning customers, the user skips the new customer panel and goes directly to ordering a pizza. Here the customer selects a pizza size and toppings and whether the pizza is for pickup or delivery. If the user selects delivery, the next step requests an address, telephone number, and credit card number. If the user selects pickup, the user skips the delivery information panel and goes directly to the order confirmation panel.

Note that this wizard has five steps, but, depending on the input, the user sees either three, four, or five steps. Figure 12.26 shows an activity diagram depicting this pizza ordering sequence flow.

Figure 12.27 shows the PizzaWizard application. This application consists of two modules: Customer, which provides a very simplistic customer storage mechanism using a map, and NewPizza, the module that contains the OrderPizza wizard.

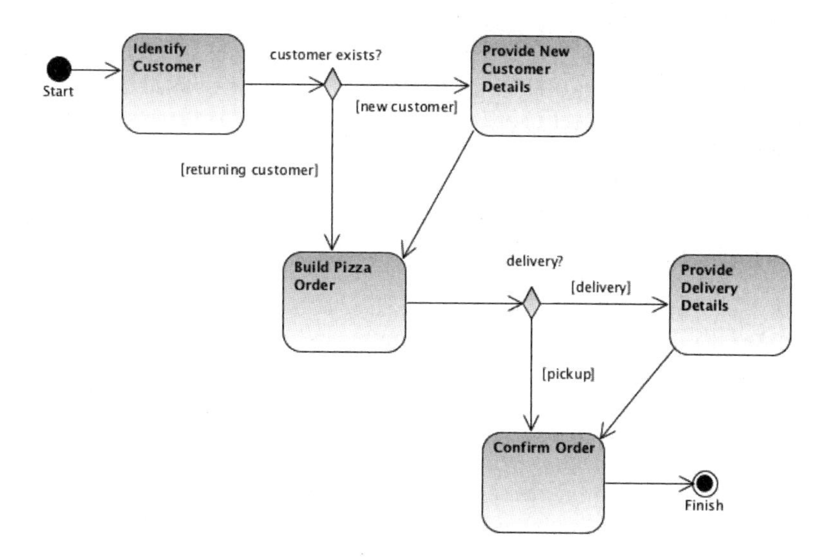


Figure 12.26 PizzaWizard activity diagram

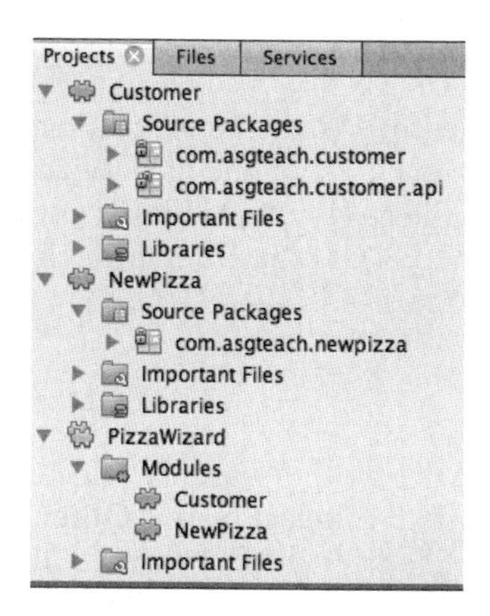


Figure 12.27 PizzaWizard application and NewPizza module

### PizzaWizard Example Application

*For this example that shows how to create a dynamic step wizard, we'll show you only partial code for each visual and wizard panel. You can obtain the complete source code for the Pizza-Wizard example application in the book's download bundle.*

In this application, the visual and wizard panel classes are very similar to the code we showed you with the New Number Sequence wizard. That is, the visual panels consist of graphical components that gather input. If the input requires validation, the visual panels set up listeners to detect user input changes and fire property change events. The wizard panels become property listeners for the visual panels and validate input when it changes. A change in validation status makes the wizard panels fire state change events to the listening WizardDescriptor. The WizardDescriptor then invokes the wizard panel's `isValid()` method and updates the Next and/or Finish buttons accordingly.

If the user selects Next, the WizardDescriptor increments the index value of the panels collection. If the user selects Back, the WizardDescriptor decrements the index value of the panels collection.

When you build a dynamic step wizard, the NetBeans Platform provides a WizardIterator class that includes iteration methods `current()` (provide the current panel), `hasNext()` (true if there are more panels), `hasPrevious()` (true if there are previous panels), `nextPanel()` (increment the panels index number), and `previousPanel()` (decrement the panels index number). The WizardDescriptor calls these methods to work its way through the wizard process. The WizardIterator maintains an ArrayList of panels and can dynamically add or remove panels (i.e., steps) from this ArrayList. It also maintains a separate String array that holds the name of each step.

Consistent with how NetBeans Platform wizards behave, the WizardIterator adjusts the `panels` ArrayList when it receives a property change event from one of its wizard panels. When the WizardIterator makes adjustments to the `panels` ArrayList, it notifies the WizardDescriptor. The WizardDescriptor then makes its adjustments (such as displaying a different panel when the user clicks Next).

## Building the Dynamic Step Wizard

Let's begin with the dynamic Pizza wizard. First, invoke the New Wizard by selecting the target module (**NewPizza** in this example), right-click, and select **New | Other**. Under Categories select **Module Development** and for File Type select **Wizard**. Click **Next**.

NetBeans displays the Wizard Type panel. For Registration Type, select **Custom**, for Wizard Step Sequence select **Dynamic**, and for Number of Wizard Panels specify **5**.

**Wizard Tip**

*When you select Dynamic for the Step Sequence, the number of panels is the maximum number of panels you need for your wizard, even if a given sequence uses fewer panels. You can always add more visual and wizard panel classes manually if you later determine that you need more steps.*

Click **Next**. Specify the Class Name Prefix (**Pizza**) and verify that the Project and Package names are correct. Click **Finish**.

As before, NetBeans creates two classes (a view and a controller) for each panel. Because you selected Dynamic Step Sequence, NetBeans also creates a WizardIterator class. Rename (refactor) the visual and wizard classes and give them meaningful class names. Note that NetBeans does not create the action class that invokes the wizard, but it does provide the code (with comments) to build your own action class.

**Wizard Tip**

*When specifying a Dynamic Step Sequence, don't give visual and wizard panel classes names with step numbers because the number will not be consistent. Instead, give descriptive names to these classes, as we have done in Table 12.3. Note that each class name corresponds to an activity in Figure 12.26 on page 599.*

**TABLE 12.3 Provide Meaningful Names for the NewPizza Wizard Classes**

| Step Order | Activity | Visual and Controller Names |
|---|---|---|
| 1 | Identify customer | `IdentifyCustomerVisual` |
| | | `IdentifyCustomerController` |
| 2 (optional) | Provide new customer details | `NewCustomerVisual` |
| | [*if customer is new*] | `NewCustomerController` |
| 3 | Build pizza order | `BuildPizzaVisual` |
| | (Size and Toppings) | `BuildPizzaController` |
| 4 (optional) | Provide delivery details | `DeliveryInfoVisual` |
| | [*if pizza is for delivery*] | `DeliveryInfoController` |
| 5 | Confirm order | `ConfirmOrderVisual` |
| | | `ConfirmOrderController` |

Let's show you the OrderPizza wizard in action now with sample input. We'll describe each panel in general terms and show partial code for each visual and wizard panel.

The wizard begins with the IdentifyCustomer panel. This panel asks for a customer name (Figure 12.28). The visual panel implements DocumentListener to detect changes in the name textfield. The wizard panel listens for property change events to make sure the textfield is not empty. The IdentifyCustomer wizard panel implements AsynchronousValidatingPanel. Therefore, when a user clicks Next, the wizard panel verifies if the provided name represents a new or returning customer. If the customer is returning, the next step is skipped. Otherwise, the user proceeds to the New Customer panel.

Figure 12.28 IdentifyCustomer panel in the OrderPizza wizard

The New Customer panel (Figure 12.29) asks for a phone number (the name is filled in from the previous panel). Again, a DocumentListener on the phone number textfield component notifies the New Customer wizard panel when the input changes. The wizard panel provides validation to make sure the textfield is not empty.

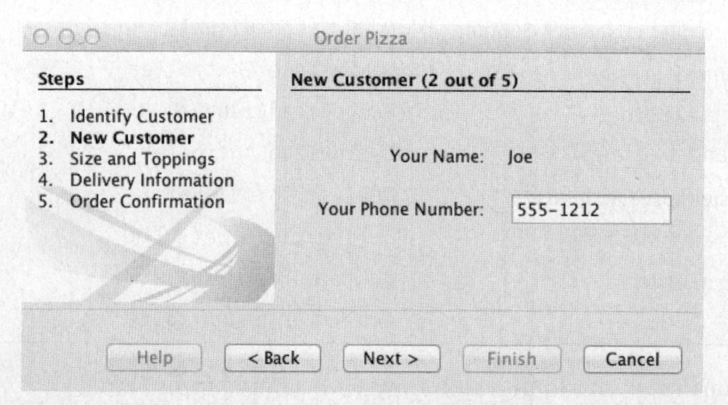


Figure 12.29 NewCustomer panel in the OrderPizza wizard

After clicking Next, the WizardDescriptor proceeds to the Size and Toppings panel (the BuildPizza step).

The Size and Toppings panel (Figure 12.30) has no validation, but the visual panel updates the Total field based on the size, toppings, and delivery selections. The BuildPizza visual panel therefore has change listeners for the various components, but it does not fire property change events. Instead, it simply updates Total. If the user selects Delivery, the wizard proceeds to the Delivery Information panel. The Pickup option skips this step and goes directly to the Order Confirmation step.

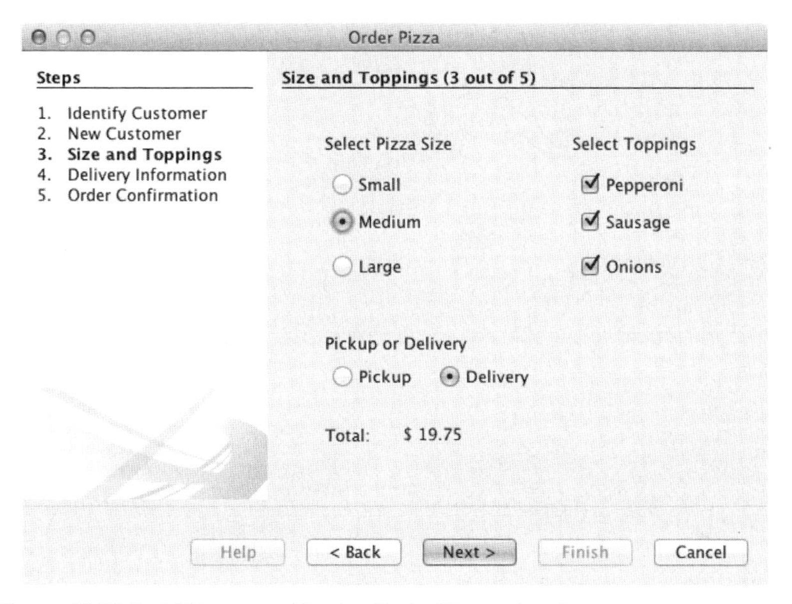


Figure 12.30 BuildPizza panel in the OrderPizza wizard

The Delivery Information panel (Figure 12.31) requests address, phone number, and credit card information from the user. Once again, this panel uses DocumentChangeListeners to monitor input and fires property change events to the listening wizard panel when input changes. Validation consists only of making sure the textfields are not empty. More realistic applications would likely provide phone and credit card number validation and make sure the address is within a certain proximity to the pizza shop.

The final panel is Order Confirmation (Figure 12.32). When the user checks the Order Is Confirmed checkbox, the Finish button is enabled. The ConfirmOrder visual panel listens for changes to the checkbox and fires a property change event. The wizard panel considers the panel valid if the checkbox is checked. Usually, panel component settings are maintained when the user clicks Back and then returns. In this case, the checkbox is reset each time, forcing the user to re-confirm the order.

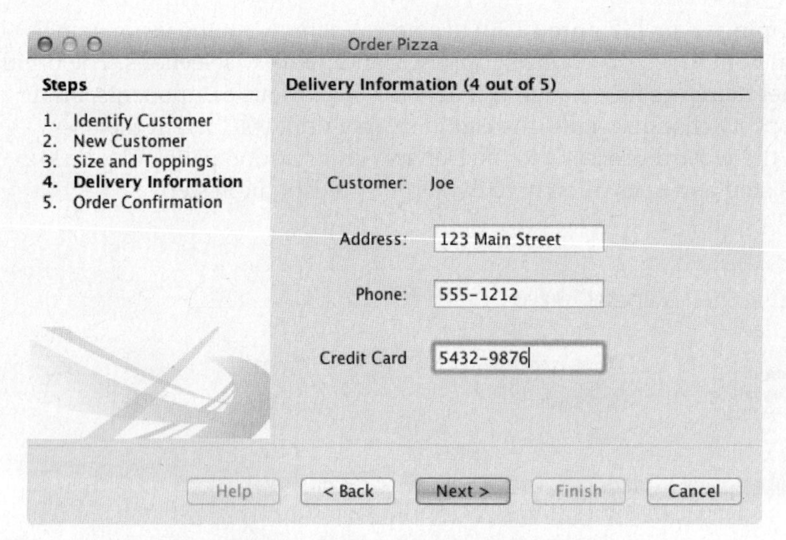


Figure 12.31 DeliveryInformation panel in the OrderPizza wizard

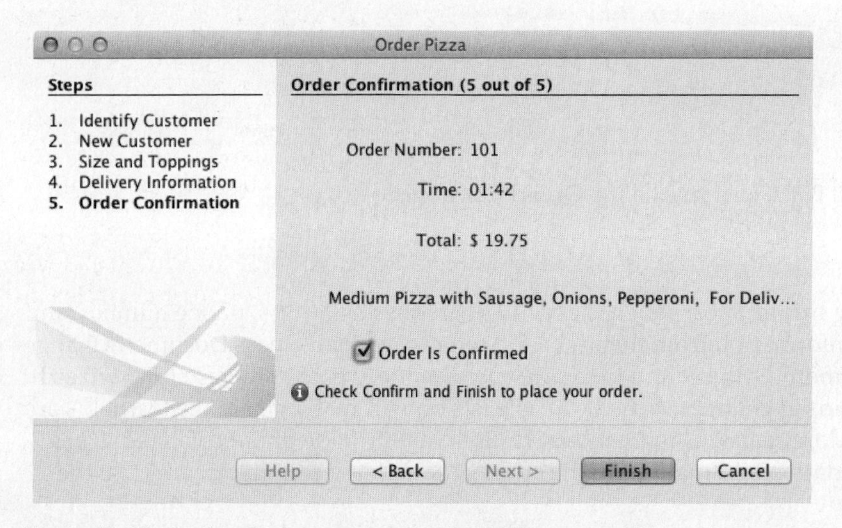


Figure 12.32 ConfirmOrder panel in the OrderPizza wizard

**Wizard Tip**

*Use the wizard panel's* `readSettings()` *method to reset a component's value. The Wizard-Descriptor invokes this method before it displays the visual panel.*

```
@Override
public void readSettings(WizardDescriptor wiz) {
    . . .
    // Reset the confirmCheckBox component each time
    getComponent().getConfirmCheckBox().setSelected(false);
}
```

## The PizzaWizardIterator

Now let's examine the PizzaWizardIterator, as shown in Listing 12.26. Recall that the NetBeans Platform wizard generates this class for you when you select Dynamic Steps. We show the modifications for the Order Pizza example in bold and describe these modifications here.

1. Class PizzaWizardIterator implements PropertyChangeListener and becomes a listener for wizard panels IdentifyCustomerController and BuildPizzaController. These panels collect input that affect the wizard's sequence flow.
2. Create wizard panel class fields for each wizard panel so that you can access them. Note that we add all panels to the ArrayList, but you could just add a subset, depending on how you want your "standard beginning list of steps" to appear.
3. Create method `updateSteps()`, which builds a `steps` String array containing each step name. All step names are displayed in the left hand portion of each panel. We extracted this code from method `getPanels()` so that we can invoke it separately as the step sequence changes.
4. Implement methods `addChangeListener()` and `removeChangeListener()` so that the WizardDescriptor is notified when a step sequence changes.
5. Implement method `propertyChange()`. If the source event property name is `IdentifyCustomerController.PROP_IS_NEW_CUSTOMER`, we either add or remove the New-Customer panel. If the source event property name is `BuildPizzaController.PROP_IS_PICKUP`, we either add or remove the DeliveryInformation panel. Note that method `add()` uses relative positioning for the Delivery-Information panel (it will always be the next to last panel). Thus, the ArrayList remains consistent without regard to which panels are currently in the collection when you add to the list.
6. Implement method `fireChangeEvent()`. This lets the WizardDescriptor know that the sequence list changed.

**Listing 12.26 PizzaWizardIterator.java—Control the Wizard's Steps**

```
public final class PizzaWizardIterator implements
        WizardDescriptor.Iterator<WizardDescriptor>,
        PropertyChangeListener {

    private int index;
    private List<WizardDescriptor.Panel<WizardDescriptor>> panels;

    // give panels variable names so we can add/remove them as needed
    IdentifyCustomerController icc = new IdentifyCustomerController();
    NewCustomerController ncc = new NewCustomerController();
    BuildPizzaController bpc = new BuildPizzaController();
    DeliveryInfoController delic = new DeliveryInfoController();
    ConfirmOrderController confoc = new ConfirmOrderController();

    private List<WizardDescriptor.Panel<WizardDescriptor>> getPanels() {
        if (panels == null) {
            panels = new ArrayList<WizardDescriptor.Panel<WizardDescriptor>>();
            panels.add(icc);
            panels.add(ncc);
            panels.add(bpc);
            panels.add(delic);
            panels.add(confoc);

            // Become a ChangeListener for IdentifyCustomerController and
            // BuildPizzaController
            icc.addPropertyChangeListener(this);
            bpc.addPropertyChangeListener(this);
            updateSteps();
        }
        return panels;
    }

    private void updateSteps() {
        String[] steps = new String[panels.size()];
            for (int i = 0; i < panels.size(); i++) {
                Component c = panels.get(i).getComponent();
                // Default step name to component name of panel.
                steps[i] = c.getName();
                if (c instanceof JComponent) { // assume Swing components
                    JComponent jc = (JComponent) c;
                    jc.putClientProperty(
                        WizardDescriptor.PROP_CONTENT_SELECTED_INDEX, i);
                    jc.putClientProperty(
                        WizardDescriptor.PROP_CONTENT_DATA, steps);
                    jc.putClientProperty(
                        WizardDescriptor.PROP_AUTO_WIZARD_STYLE, true);
                    jc.putClientProperty(
                        WizardDescriptor.PROP_CONTENT_DISPLAYED, true);
```

```
                jc.putClientProperty(
                    WizardDescriptor.PROP_CONTENT_NUMBERED, true);
            }
        }
}

@Override
public WizardDescriptor.Panel<WizardDescriptor> current() {
    return getPanels().get(index);
}

@Override
public String name() {
    return index + 1 + " out of " + getPanels().size();
}

@Override
public boolean hasNext() {
    return index < getPanels().size() - 1;
}

@Override
public boolean hasPrevious() {
    return index > 0;
}

@Override
public void nextPanel() {
    if (!hasNext()) {
        throw new NoSuchElementException();
    }
    index++;
}

@Override
public void previousPanel() {
    if (!hasPrevious()) {
        throw new NoSuchElementException();
    }
    index--;
}

private final EventListenerList listeners = new EventListenerList();

@Override
public void addChangeListener(ChangeListener l) {
    listeners.add(ChangeListener.class, l);
}
```

```
    @Override
    public void removeChangeListener(ChangeListener l) {
        listeners.remove(ChangeListener.class, l);
    }

    @Override
    public void propertyChange(PropertyChangeEvent pce) {
        if (pce.getPropertyName().equals(
                  IdentifyCustomerController.PROP_IS_NEW_CUSTOMER)) {
            if (icc.isIsNewCustomer()) {
                panels.add(1, ncc);
            } else {
                panels.remove(ncc);
            }
            updateSteps();
            fireChangeEvent(this, 0, 1);
        } else if (pce.getPropertyName().equals(
                  BuildPizzaController.PROP_IS_PICKUP)) {
            if (bpc.isIsPickup()) {
                panels.remove(delic);
            } else {
                panels.add(panels.size()-1, delic);
            }
            updateSteps();
            fireChangeEvent(this, 0, 1);
        }
    }

    protected final void fireChangeEvent(Object source, int oldState,
                                              int newState) {
        if (oldState != newState) {
            ChangeEvent ev = new ChangeEvent(source);
            for (ChangeListener listener : listeners.getListeners(
                                              ChangeListener.class)) {
                listener.stateChanged(ev);
            }
        }
    }
}
```

### Wizard Tip

*The code in the* `propertyChange()` *method (Listing 12.26) reflects the activity diagram in Figure 12.26 on page 599, where panels are added or removed based on user input. Your dynamic sequence wizard, however, may dictate a different flow, such as two or more completely separate collections of steps. In this case, define separate panel collections and activate the appropriate collection in* `propertyChange()`.

### IdentifyCustomer Panel

The IdentifyCustomer panel dynamically changes the step sequence. Let's show you how this controller class participates in the step sequence change.

Class IdentifyCustomerController implements `WizardDescriptor.AsynchronousValidatingPanel`. When the user clicks Next, method `validate()` determines whether or not the provided customer name represents a returning customer or a new customer. Since this affects the sequence, method `validate()` sends a property change event to the PizzaWizardIterator.

Listing 12.27 shows the code in IdentifyCustomerController that performs this check. Method `prepareValidation()` fetches the customer name from the visual panel. Method `validate()` then uses the Global Lookup to access the service provider for CustomerStore. CustomerStore method `findCustomer()` returns null if the customer does not exist. Method `setIsNewCustomer()` fires a property change event to the PizzaWizardIterator, which responds by adjusting the `panels` ArrayList.

**Listing 12.27 IdentifyCustomerController.java—New Customer?**

```
public class IdentifyCustomerController implements
        WizardDescriptor.AsynchronousValidatingPanel<WizardDescriptor>,
        PropertyChangeListener {

    private IdentifyCustomerVisual component;

   . . . code omitted . . .

    private String customerName;
    private Customer customer;
    public static final String PROP_CUSTOMER = "customer";
    private boolean isNewCustomer = true;
    private PropertyChangeSupport propChangeSupport;
    public static final String PROP_IS_NEW_CUSTOMER = "isNewCustomer";

   . . . code omitted . . .

    public void setIsNewCustomer(boolean isNewCustomer) {
        boolean oldValue = this.isNewCustomer;
        this.isNewCustomer = isNewCustomer;
        this.propChangeSupport.firePropertyChange(
            PROP_IS_NEW_CUSTOMER, oldValue, isNewCustomer);
    }

    @Override
    public void prepareValidation() {
        customerName = getComponent().getCustomerName();
    }
```

```
    @Override
    public void validate() throws WizardValidationException {
        CustomerStore custStore = Lookup.getDefault().lookup(
                            CustomerStore.class);
        if (custStore != null) {
            customer = custStore.findCustomer(customerName);
            wizard.putProperty(PROP_CUSTOMER, customer);
            setIsNewCustomer(customer == null);
        }
    }
}
```

## BuildPizza Panel

The BuildPizza step also affects the wizard's step sequence. Class BuildPizzaController collects the input required to create a PizzaOrder object. No validation is necessary since all input choices are either checkboxes or radio buttons. However, BuildPizzaController must determine if the pizza is for pickup or delivery. If the pizza is for delivery, the next panel is DeliveryInformation; otherwise the next panel is ConfirmOrder.

There are two approaches we can take here and the resulting wizard behavior is slightly different with each implementation. We'll show you both approaches. The first approach is to make BuildPizzaController implement `WizardDescriptor.ValidatingPanel` and override method `validate()`. In this case, the user doesn't see a change in the sequence flow until after clicking Next. This is the same behavior you see with the IdentifyCustomer panel. Listing 12.28 shows the code for this approach.

Recall that `WizardDescriptor.ValidatingPanel` provides *synchronous* validation after the user clicks Next. Synchronous validation is appropriate here because the code in method `validate()` does not take a long time. Method `validate()` gets PizzaOrder from the visual panel and invokes `setIsPickup()`, which fires a property change event if property `PROP_IS_PICKUP` has changed. Again, the PizzaWizardIterator listens for property change events, adjusts the `panels` ArrayList, and notifies the WizardDescriptor if the step sequence changes.

**Listing 12.28 BuildPizzaController—Pickup or Delivery? First Approach**

```
public class BuildPizzaController implements
        WizardDescriptor.ValidatingPanel<WizardDescriptor> {

    private BuildPizzaVisual component;
    private PizzaOrder pizzaOrder;
    private boolean isPickup;
    private PropertyChangeSupport propChangeSupport;

   . . . code omitted . . .
```

```
    public void setIsPickup(boolean isPickup) {
        boolean oldValue = this.isPickup;
        this.isPickup = isPickup;
        this.propChangeSupport.firePropertyChange(
            PROP_IS_PICKUP, oldValue, isPickup);
    }

    @Override
    public void validate() throws WizardValidationException {
        pizzaOrder = getComponent().getPizzaOrder();
        setIsPickup(pizzaOrder.isPickup());
    }
}
```

The second approach does not use `WizardDescriptor.ValidatingPanel` for class BuildPizzaController. Instead, BuildPizzaController detects changes to the Pickup / Delivery option. In its `propertyChange()` method, BuildPizzaController immediately fires a property change event to PizzaWizardIterator.

This approach makes the sequence change happen as soon as the user changes the Pickup / Delivery option, providing a more dynamic and immediate effect. Listing 12.29 shows the code to implement the second approach.

**Listing 12.29 BuildPizzaController—Pickup or Delivery? Second Approach**

```
public class BuildPizzaController implements
        WizardDescriptor.Panel<WizardDescriptor>, PropertyChangeListener {

    private BuildPizzaVisual component;
    private PizzaOrder pizzaOrder;
    private Customer customer;
    public static final String PROP_PIZZA_ORDER = "pizzaOrder";
    public static final String PROP_IS_PICKUP = "isPickup";
    private boolean isPickup;
    private PropertyChangeSupport propChangeSupport;

   . . . code omitted . . .

    @Override
    public BuildPizzaVisual getComponent() {
        if (component == null) {
            component = new BuildPizzaVisual();
            this.component.addPropertyChangeListener(this);
        }
        return component;
    }
```

```
    public void setIsPickup(boolean isPickup) {
        boolean oldValue = this.isPickup;
        this.isPickup = isPickup;
        this.propChangeSupport.firePropertyChange(
                    PROP_IS_PICKUP, oldValue, isPickup);
    }

    @Override
    public void propertyChange(PropertyChangeEvent pce) {
        if (pce.getPropertyName().equals(BuildPizzaVisual.PROP_IS_PICKUP)) {
            pizzaOrder = getComponent().getPizzaOrder();
            setIsPickup(pizzaOrder.isPickup());
        }
    }
}
```

**Wizard Tip**

*Having the WizardIterator fire a state change event (see Listing 12.26 on page 606) is only really necessary when the WizardDescriptor updates the step sequence as soon as the user modifies panel input. If all checks for panel changes occur when the user clicks Next, the WizardDescriptor will automatically grab the updated step panels. However, since the WizardIterator is not aware of when each wizard panel checks for changes, the safest approach is to have the WizardIterator always fire state change events, as we show in Listing 12.26.*

## Create the OrderPizzaAction

Our final step is to create the OrderPizzaAction to initiate the Order Pizza wizard. Listing 12.30 shows class OrderPizzaAction, an action registered under Tools in the main menu bar. Method `actionPerformed()` instantiates PizzaWizardIterator, which builds the five wizard panels and the WizardDescriptor. When the wizard completes, method `actionPerformed()` obtains the Customer and PizzaOrder objects from the WizardDescriptor property cache.

Method `actionPerformed()` also stores the Customer (using CustomerStore from the Global Lookup) and builds the Information message dialog.

**Listing 12.30 OrderPizzaAction.java—Always Enabled Action**

```
@ActionID(category = "Tools",
id = "com.asgteach.newpizza.OrderPizza")
@ActionRegistration(displayName = "#CTL_OrderPizza")
@ActionReferences({
    @ActionReference(path = "Menu/Tools", position = 150)
})
```

```
@Messages("CTL_OrderPizza=Order Pizza")
public final class OrderPizzaAction implements ActionListener {

    @Override
    public void actionPerformed(ActionEvent e) {
        WizardDescriptor wiz = new WizardDescriptor(new PizzaWizardIterator());
        wiz.setTitleFormat(new MessageFormat("{0} ({1})"));
        wiz.setTitle(Bundle.CTL_OrderPizza());
        if (DialogDisplayer.getDefault().notify(wiz) ==
                                        WizardDescriptor.FINISH_OPTION) {
            // Store the customer with module CustomerStore
            CustomerStore custStore = Lookup.getDefault().lookup(
                    CustomerStore.class);
            if (custStore != null) {
                Customer customer = (Customer) wiz.getProperty(
                     IdentifyCustomerController.PROP_CUSTOMER);
                custStore.storeCustomer(customer);
                PizzaOrder p = (PizzaOrder) wiz.getProperty(
                     BuildPizzaController.PROP_PIZZA_ORDER);
               // Access the PizzaOrder and build an Information Dialog
                StringBuilder sb = new StringBuilder();
                sb.append("Thank you, ").append(customer.getName()).append(
                           ", for your order!\n");
                sb.append(p.getPizzaSize());
                sb.append(" Pizza\n");
                if (!p.getToppings().isEmpty()) {
                    sb.append("With ");
                    for (String topping : p.getToppings()) {
                        sb.append(topping).append(", ");
                    }
                    sb.append("\n");
                }
                if (p.isPickup()) {
                    sb.append("For Pickup");
                } else {
                    sb.append("For Delivery");
                }
                DialogDisplayer.getDefault().notify(
                    new NotifyDescriptor.Message(sb.toString()));
            }
        }
    }
}
```

Figure 12.33 shows the Information dialog that the OrderPizza wizard displays upon completion.

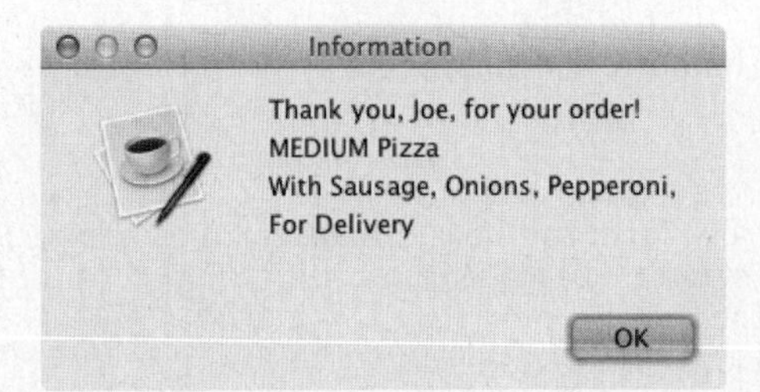


Figure 12.33 The OrderPizza wizard is complete

## 12.9 Wizard Instantiating Iterators

When you select Dynamic Step Sequence to build your wizard, as we did in the previous section, NetBeans provides a WizardIterator class for you that implements `WizardDescriptor.Iterator<WizardDescriptor>`. As you saw with PizzaWizard-Iterator, this class provides iterator methods and builds an ArrayList of your wizard panel objects. Property listeners adjust panel sequences as needed according to user input.

The NetBeans Platform has alternatives to this standard iterator class that let you build target artifacts when a wizard completes. Let's discuss these instantiating iterators and show you an example of how they work.

**Wizard Tip**

*You may want to use one of the instantiating iterators even if you don't dynamically alter your wizard step sequence. In this case, choose Dynamic Step Sequence during the New Wizard wizard and replace WizardDescriptor.Iterator with one of the instantiating iterators we discuss in this section.*

### WizardDescriptor.InstantiatingIterator

All the iterator classes are alternatives to WizardDescriptor.InstantiatingIterator, which extends WizardDescriptor.Iterator. To use them, replace WizardDescriptor.Iterator in your code with one of the alternative classes and override the necessary methods.

All instantiating iterator classes include method `instantiate()` that lets an iterator class build artifacts from the wizard process. The WizardDescriptor invokes `instantiate()` after the wizard successfully completes and (in most cases) blocks the wizard until this method completes.

Inside `instantiate()`, you build (instantiate) any objects that your wizard should create. A typical use case is the New Project wizard in the NetBeans IDE. Here, the IDE creates many files and directories in the target user directory according to the project type and the input provided by a user.

When the wizard completes with status `WizardDescriptor.FINISH_OPTION` in the invoking method, `instantiate()` has already executed. You can access the instantiated objects with WizardDescriptor method `getInstantiatedObjects()`.

If `instantiate()` fails for any reason, you should throw IOException. In this case, the WizardDescriptor keeps the wizard open and a user has a chance to change panel input. Method `instantiate()` is invoked again after the user clicks Finish. Reasons for failure typically fall outside normal validation, but include errors creating files or directories during instantiation, for example.

Method `initialize()` lets you initialize any objects required by the iterator. A typical use here is to store the WizardDescriptor object so the iterator has access to the WizardDescriptor property cache within `instantiate()`.

Method `uninitialize()` performs uninitialization tasks. This method is invoked when the wizard closes for *all* closing options (not just `FINISH_OPTION`).

Table 12.4 lists these additional methods that you override when using WizardDescriptor.InstantiatingIterator.

**TABLE 12.4 WizardDescriptor.InstantiatingIterator Methods**

| Method | Description |
| --- | --- |
| `void initialize( WizardDescriptor wizard)` | Called from WizardDescriptor constructor to initialize any needed objects. |
| `Set instantiate() throws IOException` | Called from WizardDescriptor after user clicks Finish. Returns a set of instantiated objects. IOException returns user to wizard to make changes. |
| `void uninitialize( WizardDescriptor wizard)` | Called after wizard finishes, even if user Cancels. |

### WizardDescriptor.AsynchronousInstantiatingIterator

The AsynchronousInstantiatingIterator is a subinterface of InstantiatingIterator. It has the same methods except that method `instantiate()` is invoked outside the Event Dispatch Thread (EDT). The wizard still remains open, however, which means you can handle errors as described above by throwing IOException within `instantiate()`.

Note that the user can't cancel or close the wizard while `instantiate()` is running.

## WizardDescriptor.ProgressInstantiatingIterator

ProgressInstantiatingIterator is a subinterface of AsynchronousInstantiatingIterator. It defines method `instantiate()` with a ProgressHandle parameter. To use this iterator, you must add a dependency on the Progress API. The WizardDescriptor instantiates the ProgressHandle object, but method `instantiate()` must start, update, and finish the progress bar. Like AsynchronousInstantiatingIterator, method `instantiate()` is invoked outside the EDT thread.

Let's modify the PizzaWizard to use ProgressInstantiatingIterator. Here are the steps.

1. Add a new dependency on the Progress API in module New Pizza.
2. Make PizzaWizardIterator implement `WizardDescriptor.ProgressInstantiatingIterator` and have NetBeans generate methods for `instantiate()`, `instantiate(ProgressHandle)`, `initialize()`, and `uninitialize()`.
3. Provide implementations for these methods, as shown in Listing 12.31. Note that the PizzaWizardIterator is unchanged except for the new methods.

   We initialize private class field `wizard` in method `initialize()`. This lets us access the WizardDescriptor's property cache so we can retrieve the required input provided by the user.

   Method `instantiate(ProgressHandle)` does the work that was previously performed in the Order Pizza `actionPerformed()` method. We grab the Customer and PizzaOrder objects from the property cache, build the pizza, store Customer in the CustomerStore, and return PizzaOrder in the `instantiate()` method's return object.

   We simulate a long-running process using `Thread.sleep()` and periodically update the progress bar with ProgressHandle method `progress()`.

   We also throw IOException if "JoeCriminal" is our customer. The WizardDescriptor catches this and returns focus to the wizard so the user can correct any problems. The WizardDescriptor invokes `instantiate()` again when the user clicks Finish.

   Finally, we override `instantiate()` to guard against WizardDescriptor invoking the no-argument version, which should not be invoked with ProgressInstantiatingIterator.

**Listing 12.31 PizzaWizardIterator—Using a Progress Bar**

```
public final class PizzaWizardIterator implements
        WizardDescriptor.ProgressInstantiatingIterator<WizardDescriptor>,
        PropertyChangeListener {
```

```
private int index;
private List<WizardDescriptor.Panel<WizardDescriptor>> panels;
private WizardDescriptor wizard = null;

  . . . Unchanged Code Omitted . . .

@Override
public Set<PizzaOrder> instantiate(ProgressHandle ph) throws IOException {
    Set<PizzaOrder> pizzaSet = new HashSet<>();
    PizzaOrder p = (PizzaOrder) wizard.getProperty(
        BuildPizzaController.PROP_PIZZA_ORDER);
    pizzaSet.add(p);
    Customer customer = (Customer) this.wizard.getProperty(
        IdentifyCustomerController.PROP_CUSTOMER);

     // Simulate a long-running multi-step task:
    ph.start(5);
    try {
        ph.progress("Storing customer  " + customer.getName(), 1);
        Thread.sleep(1500);
        if (customer.getName().contains("JoeCriminal")) {
            throw new IOException(" Cannot sell to JoeCriminal");
        }
        CustomerStore custStore = Lookup.getDefault().lookup(
           CustomerStore.class);
        if (custStore != null) {
            custStore.storeCustomer(customer);
        }
        ph.progress("Building " + p.getPizzaSize() + " pizza", 2);
        Thread.sleep(2000);
        ph.progress("Place toppings " + p.getToppings().toString(), 3);
        Thread.sleep(2000);
        ph.progress("Cooking pizza", 4);
        Thread.sleep(2000);
        ph.progress("Ready!", 5);
        Thread.sleep(2000);

    } catch (InterruptedException e) {
        Exceptions.printStackTrace(e);
    }
    ph.finish();
    return pizzaSet;
}

@Override
public Set instantiate() throws IOException {
    assert false : "This method cannot be called if the class implements
        WizardDescriptor.ProgressInstantiatingWizardIterator.";
    return null;
}
```

```
    @Override
    public void initialize(WizardDescriptor wd) {
        this.wizard = wd;
    }

    @Override
    public void uninitialize(WizardDescriptor wd) {
        this.panels = null;
        this.wizard = null;

    }
}
```

4. Make changes to OrderPizzaAction method `actionPerformed()`, as shown in Listing 12.32. Note that DialogDisplayer method `notify()` blocks until the user successfully completes and wizard *and* method `instantiate()` completes. This lets you access any objects created in method `instantiate()` with WizardDescriptor method `getInstantiatedObjects()`, as shown.

**Listing 12.32 OrderPizzaAction actionPerformed()—Using a Progress Bar**

```
    @Override
    public void actionPerformed(ActionEvent e) {
        WizardDescriptor wiz = new WizardDescriptor(new PizzaWizardIterator());
        wiz.setTitleFormat(new MessageFormat("{0} ({1})"));
        wiz.setTitle(Bundle.CTL_OrderPizza());
        if (DialogDisplayer.getDefault().notify(wiz) ==
                                WizardDescriptor.FINISH_OPTION) {
            // User clicked Finish and method instantiate() has finished
            Set<PizzaOrder> pizzaSet = wiz.getInstantiatedObjects();
            if (pizzaSet.iterator().hasNext()) {
                PizzaOrder p = pizzaSet.iterator().next();
                Customer customer = p.getCustomer();
                StringBuilder sb = new StringBuilder();
                sb.append("Thank you, ").append(customer.getName()).append(
                                ", for your order!\n");
                sb.append(p.getPizzaSize());
                sb.append(" Pizza\n");
                if (!p.getToppings().isEmpty()) {
                    sb.append("With ");
                    for (String topping : p.getToppings()) {
                        sb.append(topping).append(", ");
                    }
                    sb.append("\n");
                }
                if (p.isPickup()) {
                    sb.append("For Pickup");
                } else {
                    sb.append("For Delivery");
                }
```

```
                DialogDisplayer.getDefault().notify(
                        new NotifyDescriptor.Message(sb.toString()));
            }
        }
    }
```

Figure 12.34 shows the OrderPizza wizard running after the user clicks Finish. Note that the wizard is still running, even though the buttons are all disabled. The progress bar displays the completion percentage as well as the current task label.

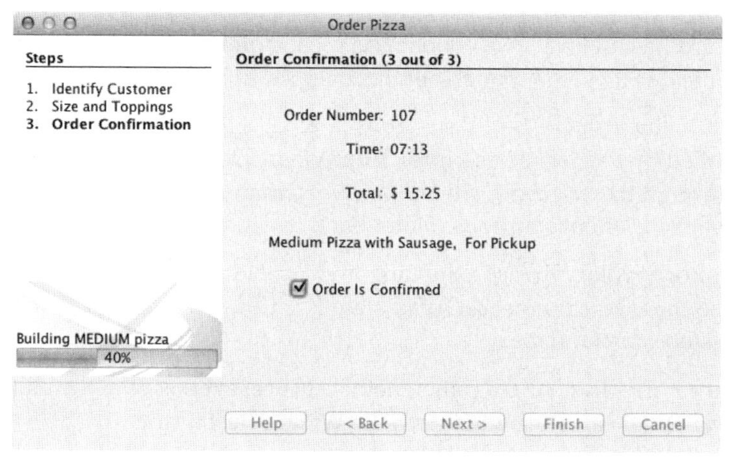


Figure 12.34 Showing a ProgressBar—40 percent complete

## WizardDescriptor.BackgroundInstantiatingIterator

BackgroundInstantiatingIterator is also a subinterface of AsynchronousInstantiating-Iterator, and you must override the same methods. For this iterator, the Wizard-Descriptor closes the wizard (when completed successfully) and then invokes the `instantiate()` method in a background thread. Because control returns to the invoking method, the instantiated objects are not available when the wizard completes. When using BackgroundInstantiatingIterator, you are responsible for handling GUI feedback and progress for the user as well as catching any exceptions thrown in method `instantiate()`.

BackgroundInstantiatingIterator is appropriate for an instantiation that is long-running or when it is not desirable to have the wizard remain open.

## 12.10 Key Point Summary

A process that guides users through multiple steps to create one or more artifacts is called a wizard. The NetBeans Platform provides a multi-class framework that lets you construct wizards for your application. The wizard framework has the following features.

- Classes that participate in a wizard include the WizardDescriptor, wizard panel classes (one for each step), visual panel classes, wizard iterators, and a wizard action class.
- Each step in a wizard has a visual component and a controller (a wizard panel). The wizard panel creates its visual panel, obtains user input, and updates panel state.
- A wizard is controlled by a WizardDescriptor. The WizardDescriptor is responsible for stepping through the wizard (using an iterator), maintaining state, and updating the visual component's buttons (Help, Back, Next, Cancel, and Finish).
- The WizardDescriptor invokes wizard panel method `readSettings()` at the beginning of each step so the wizard panel can read state from the WizardDescriptor and configure the step's visual panel.
- The WizardDescriptor invokes wizard panel method `storeSettings()` at the end of a step so the wizard panel can store state with the WizardDescriptor.
- Use Static step sequencing when the order and number of steps in a wizard is constant. Use Dynamic step sequencing when user input affects the order or number of steps.
- Use the standard DialogDisplayer method `notify()` to start a wizard. The return value `WizardDescriptor.FINISH_OPTION` means the wizard completed normally.
- Create public getter methods in the visual panel to obtain user input.
- Use listeners in the visual panel to respond to changes in user input. The wizard panels become property change listeners that respond to changes in user input.
- In general, the wizard panel implements user input validation and notifies the WizardDescriptor of changes in the validity of the current panel.
- Use the WizardDescriptor property cache to store state and coordinate input with other panels.
- The Simple Validation API provides validators suitable for visual panel input. This reduces tedious and redundant validation code in wizard panels.
- If a wizard panel can finish early, implement interface `WizardDescriptor.FinishablePanel` and override method `isFinishPanel()`. The wizard panel must fire a

state change event to notify the WizardDescriptor when a panel's finishable state changes.

- To validate user input asynchronously, implement interface `WizardDescriptor.AsynchronousValidatingPanel` in the wizard panel. Override the `prepareValidation()` method, which is accessed in the main thread, and the `validate()` method, which is invoked in a background thread. The WizardDescriptor invokes these methods after a user clicks Next. The Cancel button is active during asynchronous validation.
- Synchronous validation is appropriate when between-panel validation is not long running. Implement interface `WizardDescriptor.ValidatingPanel` and override method `validate()`.
- Dynamic sequence wizards include a Wizard Iterator class that lets you control a wizard sequence.
- Use property change events to communicate from wizard panels to the Wizard Iterator when user input causes changes to the wizard sequence.
- The Wizard framework includes several instantiating iterators. After a user completes a wizard, the WizardDescriptor invokes method `instantiate()` which creates one or more artifacts based on obtained input.
- The WizardDescriptor invokes method `instantiate()` synchronously, asynchronously, asynchronously with a ProgressBar, or as a background task, depending on which instantiating iterator you use.

# 13

# File System

The NetBeans Platform File System API provides an abstraction for standard Java files. With the File System API you can perform all the expected file operations that create, rename, and delete files and folders. You can read and write files with IOStreams and use convenience methods for reading. Furthermore, the NetBeans Platform enhances this abstraction by providing attributes for files and folders. You can also monitor changes to file system hierarchies with FileChangeListeners.

This chapter explores the File System API with several examples. You'll also learn about the Layer file, how it affects your application's configuration data, and how to access and contribute to this configuration information.

## What You Will Learn

- Use the File System API classes FileSystem, FileObject, and FileUtil to explore file-oriented operations.
- Use file attributes to store information about files and folders.
- Use FileChangeListener to monitor file and folder changes.
- Use the Output window to display status information.
- Include the Favorites window in your NetBeans Platform application to access the local file system within the UI.
- Install and access files in modules.

- Create and modify a module's Layer file.
- Access the System FileSystem programmatically.
- Use the Layer file for inter-module communication.

## 13.1 File System API

So far the applications we've built have persisted data in a database or in memory. The FamilyTree Application developed in Chapter 10 lets users manipulate data using the full CRUD operations of create, read, update, and delete. This application, however, does not perform any file-level operations.

In this chapter we examine the File System API that lets you manipulate files and folders on disk, in ZIP files, or in XML files. First, we'll explore the File System API with an application that creates and manipulates folders and files on the user's local file system. Next, we'll show you how to use the File System API's FileChangeListener to monitor changes to a file system hierarchy. You'll also learn how to include files in a NetBeans Platform application and how to access these files programmatically. Finally, we'll examine the Layer file, which is the gateway to a NetBeans Platform application's System FileSystem, and show you how to access this configuration file system programmatically. In the process of building these examples, you'll also learn how to use the Favorites window and write information to the Output window.

## 13.2 The File System API Overview

Let's begin with an overview of the File System API, the API that NetBeans uses to manipulate files and directories. The NetBeans Platform File System API provides support for virtual files. These files (or folders) may reside on disk, in memory, in a JAR or ZIP file, on a remote server, or even as elements in an XML document. The File System API provides this abstraction with the help of three main classes, FileSystem (a hierarchical collection of FileObjects), FileObject (an abstraction for `java.io.File`), and FileUtil, a utility class with many methods that manipulate FileSystems, FileObjects, and even standard java.io.File objects.

A FileSystem is a collection of FileObjects, which can be your computer's file system or a single JAR file, for example. A FileSystem is hierarchical and has a root. The FileSystem abstraction lets you view data from physically different sources in the same way.

A FileObject represents either a file or a directory (folder) in the FileSystem. A FileObject must exist in the FileSystem (unlike Java's java.io.File) and has a MIME type (which determines how the file is handled), but the data associated with a FileObject is just raw data. (The importance of MIME types will become clearer when we examine the Data System API in the next chapter.) If the FileObject represents a folder, you can delete, create, or obtain a list of its "children" (subfolders or files). You read FileObjects with InputStream and write to them with OutputStream. You can also read FileObjects with the convenience methods `asBytes()`, or in the case of text files, `asLines()` and `asText()`.

A FileObject also includes support for attributes. Attributes are arbitrary objects identified with a String and accessible with getters and setters. The File System API stores these String/serialized Object pairs according to the FileObject's path in an XML file called attributes.xml in the application's user directory.

With FileChangeListener, the FileSystem API supports notification for events such as file creation, folder creation, renaming, file modification, deletion, or attribute changing. You can add a FileChangeListener to a FileObject (file or folder) or to a java.io.File object using FileUtil.[1] You can also add a recursive listener to a folder, which receives file change events for all files and folders under the provided folder. Depending on the size of the hierarchy and the nature of the underlying file system, recursive listeners can be expensive in processing file change events.

In general, event notification works with file system modifications that occur within your application. Event notifications for modifications made outside of your application may not be received by your program.

## Exploring the FileSystem API

FileSystem, FileObject, and FileUtil all contain methods that manipulate files. Let's explore several of these methods by building a NetBeans Platform application that performs file operations and displays information in the Output window, as shown in Figure 13.1. This file system exploration is activated with an action called Explore File Actions, which we add to the toolbar and the top-level Tools menu.

The Explore File Actions menu item performs several operations. First, the action creates a folder and a text file in the user's local file system. Next, the action writes text to the file and reads the text back. Finally, the action renames the text file and then deletes it. Along the way, this action displays each step in the Output window.

---

1. Since JDK 7, Java also supports file change events with java.nio.FileSystem, Path, and WatchServices. Here, you register a WatchService to listen for key events. This is a low-level mechanism, necessary to account for differences in the underlying operating system. In contrast, the NetBeans Platform is able to provide event listener notification, since the NetBeans Platform File System API provides a level of abstraction above the traditional Java File class.

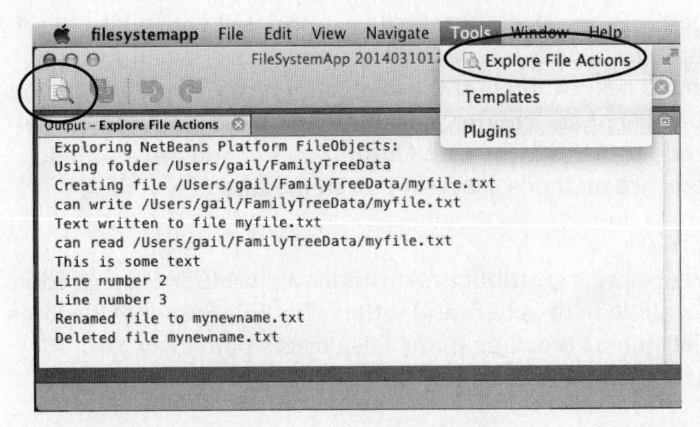


Figure 13.1 Exploring the File System APIs

Building this applications requires the following steps.

- Create a NetBeans Platform application called FileSystemApp.
- Create a module called FSExploration.
- Create and register a new action for the top-level Tools menu and the toolbar.
- Add module dependencies to the File System API, the I/O APIs, and the Lookup API.
- Implement the action.

## Create a NetBeans Platform Application and Module

Here are the steps to create the application and add the FSExploration module.

1. Create a new application called **FileSystemApp** using the NetBeans Platform New Project wizard.
2. Next, create a module and add it to the FileSystemApp application. Call the module **FSExploration** and provide package name **com.asgteach.fsexploration**. The application and module are shown in the Projects view in Figure 13.2.

## Create a New Action

Create and register an action to perform File System API operations.

1. In module FSExploration, expand Source Packages and right click on the package name. Select **New | Action** from the context menu.

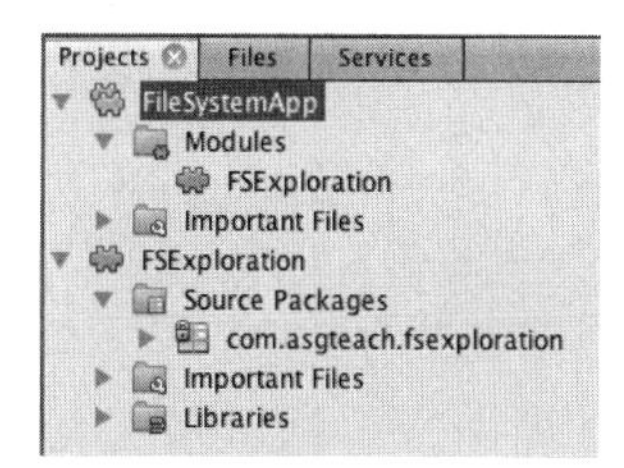


Figure 13.2 FileSystemApp and module FSExploration

2. NetBeans initiates the New Action wizard. In the Action Type dialog, select **Always Enabled** and click **Next**.
3. In the GUI Registration dialog, select Category **Tools**. Select the Global Menu Item checkbox. Specify Menu **Tools** with position **Here - Tools**, and **Separator After**. Select the **Global Toolbar Button** checkbox. Specify Toolbar **File** and Position **Here - Save All**. Click **Next**. Figure 13.3 shows this dialog.

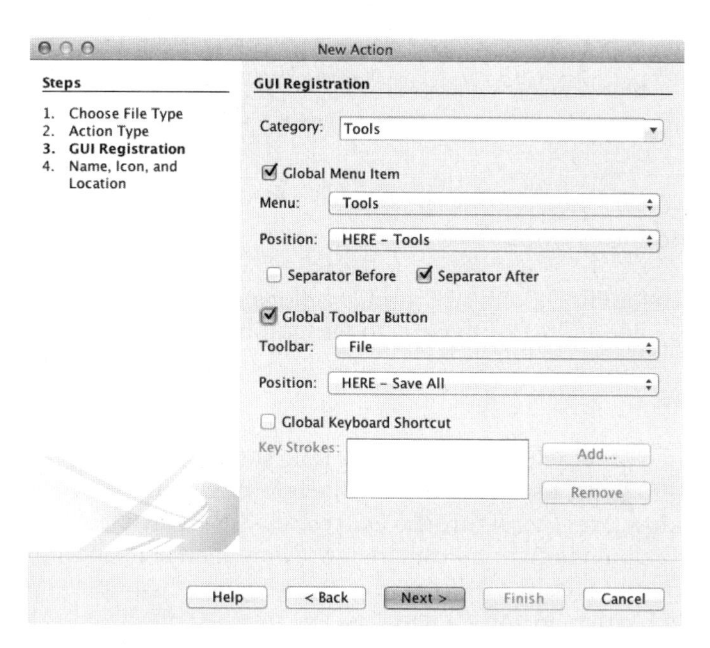


Figure 13.3 Register the File System Explorer action

4. NetBeans displays the Name, Icon, and Location dialog. For Class Name specify **ExploreFileAction**, for Display Name specify **Explore File Actions**, and click the **Browse** button and navigate to the provided icon file **ExploreFS.png**, as shown in Figure 13.4. Click **Finish**.

NetBeans creates **ExploreFileAction.java** and copies the icon files to the module's source package.

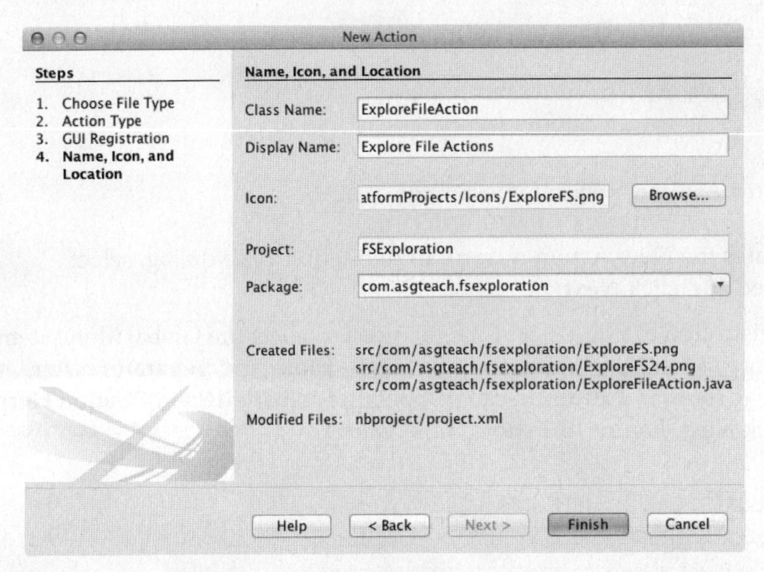


Figure 13.4 Specify the action class and icon

### Add Module Dependencies

Add module dependencies for File System API (for file actions), Lookup API (the File-Object class uses Lookups), and I/O APIs (to write to the Output window).

## The Output Window

The NetBeans IDE uses an Output window to communicate status and job progress (such as running a program) to the user. Let's display the information from our application to this Output window. We'll configure the Output window with a labeled tab and set up the I/O in the ExploreFileAction's constructor. (More than one module or process can write to the Output window, each having its own tabbed window.) We'll also create a helper method to display the content.

Listing 13.1 shows ExploreFileAction.java with the annotations that register the ExploreFileAction. We've included a label for the Output window's tab in the @Messages annotation and fields `io` and `writer` that write content to the window. The `displayMessage()` helper method writes a String to the Output window.

Static method `IOProvider.getDefault().getIO()` returns an InputOutput object for the Output window (field `io`), and method `io.getOut()` returns an OutputWriter. All of this configuration happens the first time the user invokes the Explore File Actions menu item.

#### Listing 13.1 ExploreFileAction—Configure Output Window

```
@ActionID(
        category = "Tools",
        id = "com.asgteach.fsexploration.ExploreFileAction"
)
@ActionRegistration(
        iconBase = "com/asgteach/fsexploration/ExploreFS.png",
        displayName = "#CTL_ExploreFileAction"
)
@ActionReferences({
    @ActionReference(path = "Menu/Tools", position = 0, separatorAfter = 50),
    @ActionReference(path = "Toolbars/File", position = 300)
})
@Messages({
    "CTL_ExploreFileAction=Explore File Actions",
    "CTL_FileActionTab=Explore File Actions"
})
public final class ExploreFileAction implements ActionListener {
    private final InputOutput io;
    private final OutputWriter writer;

    public ExploreFileAction() {
        io = IOProvider.getDefault().getIO(Bundle.CTL_FileActionTab(), false);
        writer = io.getOut();
    }

    private void displayMessage(String msg) {
        writer.println(msg);
    }

    @Override
    public void actionPerformed(ActionEvent e) {
        // TODO implement action body
    }
}
```

Now let's walk you through the different file manipulation activities that the Explore File Actions menu item performs in the overridden `actionPerformed()` method. We'll discuss the implementation code in separate sections.

### Clear and Select the Output Window

Each time a user invokes the Explore File Actions menu item, we clear the Output window and select its tab. (Since the Output window can be shared among multiple modules performing multiple tasks, selecting a tab with `io.select()` makes the contents associated with this InputOutput object visible.) Listing 13.2 shows this code. Note that the `reset()` method (invoked on the Output window's OutputWriter) requires catching IOException.

**Listing 13.2 Method actionPerformed—Clear and Select Output Window**

```
@Override
public void actionPerformed(ActionEvent e) {
    try {
        writer.reset();              // clear the window each time
    } catch (IOException ex) {
        Exceptions.printStackTrace(ex);
        return;
    }
    io.select();                     // select this tab
    displayMessage("Exploring NetBeans Platform FileObjects:");
     . . .
}
```

## Create a Folder

In the File System API, directories are referred to as "folders," so we will use this terminology. We first invoke the System property to find the user's home folder and create a standard Java `java.io.File` object for a subfolder under it. Creating the File object, however, does not necessarily mean the target folder **FamilyTreeData** exists.

Next, we create a FileObject from the file using the FileUtil `toFileObject()` method. If the folder doesn't exist, the FileUtil method returns null. We then create the folder with the FileUtil `createFolder()` method. Listing 13.3 shows this code.

**Listing 13.3 Method actionPerformed—Create a Folder**

```
@Override
public void actionPerformed(ActionEvent e) {
     . . .
    // Look in the User's home directory
    String home = System.getProperty("user.home");
    File dir = new File(home + "/FamilyTreeData");
    FileObject myfolder = FileUtil.toFileObject(dir);
    if (myfolder == null) {
        displayMessage("Creating folder " + dir.getPath());
```

```
            try {
                // Create folder
                myfolder = FileUtil.createFolder(dir);
            } catch (IOException ex) {
                Exceptions.printStackTrace(ex);
            }
        }
         . . .
    }
```

## Get or Create a File in a Folder

The next step is to see if file **myfile.txt** exists and if not, create it, as shown in Listing 13.4. Here, we use methods in the parent folder's FileObject instance. Object `myfolder` can return an individual entry with the `getFileObject()` method, which we use here to see if folder `myfolder` contains our target file. You can also return a folder's children as an array of FileObjects with the `getChildren()` method.

As before, a null return value indicates the file does not exist. In this case, we create the file in the `myfolder` folder using the FileObject method `createData()`. (The `createData()` method creates a file, and the `createFolder()` method creates a folder.)

Here are several FileObject methods that return a file or folder's name and/or path.

- `getpath()`—Return the FileObject's full path.
- `getName()`—Get the file or folder's name excluding the extension.
- `getExt()`—Get the file or folder's extension.
- `getNameExt()`—Get the file or folder's name and include the extension.

**Listing 13.4 Method actionPerformed—Create a File**

```
    @Override
    public void actionPerformed(ActionEvent e) {
         . . .
        if (myfolder != null) {
            displayMessage("Using folder " + myfolder.getPath());
            // Is there a file called myfile.txt in this folder?
            FileObject myfile = myfolder.getFileObject("myfile.txt");
            if (myfile == null) {
                // No, create the file
                displayMessage("Creating file " + myfolder.getPath()
                                 + "/myfile.txt");
                try {
                    // Create file
                    myfile = myfolder.createData("myfile.txt");
```

```
            } catch (IOException ex) {
                displayMessage("Can't create file "
                        + myfolder.getPath() + "/myfile.txt");
                Exceptions.printStackTrace(ex);
            }
        }
      . . .
  }
```

## Write to and Read from Files

We've created a text file. Now let's write some text to it, read it back, and display the text in the Output window. Listing 13.5 shows this code.

First, we make sure FileObject `myfile` is not null and check to see if we can perform write operations with the `canWrite()` method. Next, we use a try-with-resources statement to obtain resource PrintWriter from the file's output stream.[2] With a try-with-resources statement, PrintWriter closes automatically, so we don't need to invoke `close()` in a finally clause.

We write three lines of text to the file with the PrintWriter `println()` method and then read the text back. FileObject has several convenience methods for reading files, as follows (all methods throw IOException). We use the `asLines()` method and display each line to the Output window (as shown in Figure 13.1 on page 626).

- `asLines()`—Read the full text of a file line by line and return as a `List<String>`.
- `asLines(String encoding)`—Read the full text of a file line by line using the supplied encoding and return as a `List<String>`.
- `asText()`—Read the full text of a file and return as a String.
- `asText(String encoding)`—Read the full text of a file using the supplied encoding and return as a String.
- `asBytes()`—Read the file and return an array of bytes.

**Listing 13.5 Method actionPerformed—Write and Read Files**

```
  @Override
  public void actionPerformed(ActionEvent e) {
      . . .
          if (myfile != null) {
              // write some text to file
              if (myfile.canWrite()) {
```

2. The try-with-resources statement was introduced in JDK 7.

```
                displayMessage("can write " + myfile.getPath());
                try (PrintWriter output = new PrintWriter(
                                    myfile.getOutputStream())) {
                    output.println("This is some text");
                    for (int i = 0; i < 2; i++) {
                        output.println("Line number " + (i + 2));
                    }
                    displayMessage("Text written to file "
                                + myfile.getNameExt());
                } catch (IOException ex) {
                    displayMessage("Warning: problems writing file "
                                + myfile.getNameExt());
                    Exceptions.printStackTrace(ex);
                }
            }
            // read  file
            if (myfile.canRead()) {
                displayMessage("can read " + myfile.getPath());
                try {
                    for (String line : myfile.asLines()) {
                        displayMessage(line);
                    }
                } catch (IOException ex) {
                    displayMessage("Warning: problems reading file "
                                + myfile.getNameExt());
                    Exceptions.printStackTrace(ex);
                }

            }
        . . .
    }
```

You can also read FileObjects with streams using BufferedReader. Here is the equivalent code, as shown in Listing 13.6 (again, using a try-with resource statement).

**Listing 13.6 Read a File with Streams**

```
// read  file
if (myfile.canRead()) {
   displayMessage("can read " + myfile.getPath());
   try (BufferedReader input = new BufferedReader(
               new InputStreamReader(myfile.getInputStream()))) {
      String line;
      while ((line = input.readLine()) != null) {
         displayMessage(line);
      }
   } catch (IOException ex) {
      Exceptions.printStackTrace(ex);
   }
}
```

## Rename and Delete Files

Listing 13.7 shows the code for renaming and deleting files. Since we rename and delete our sample file, the user can invoke the Explore File Actions menu item multiple times.

Before renaming a folder or file, you must acquire a lock from the FileObject with the `lock()` method, which returns a FileLock object. Put the lock's `releaseLock()` call in a finally block. Rename will fail if the new name already exists. In our example, we rename the FileObject `myfile` (myfile.txt) to mynewname.txt.

Next, we delete our sample file (still referenced with FileObject `myfile`). The FileObject `delete()` method takes care of acquiring and releasing a lock. Alternatively, you can supply a FileLock object to the `delete()` method, which will be used instead of the one that's used implicitly.

Deleting a FileObject folder recursively deletes its contents.

**Listing 13.7 Method actionPerformed—Rename and Delete Files**

```
@Override
public void actionPerformed(ActionEvent e) {
     . . .
            // rename, requires a lock
            FileLock lock = null;
            try {
                lock = myfile.lock();
                myfile.rename(lock, "mynewname", myfile.getExt());
                displayMessage("Renamed file to " + myfile.getNameExt());

            } catch (IOException ex) {
                displayMessage("Warning: " + ex.getLocalizedMessage());
                Exceptions.printStackTrace(ex);

            } finally {
                if (lock != null) {
                    lock.releaseLock();
                }
            }
            try {
                // delete file
                myfile.delete();
                displayMessage("Deleted file " + myfile.getNameExt());
```

```
            } catch (IOException ex) {
                displayMessage("Warning: " + ex.getLocalizedMessage());
                Exceptions.printStackTrace(ex);
            }
        }
    }
```

## File System API Useful Methods

Table 13.1 provides a list of useful methods available with FileObject. (This is a partial list. The reader is encouraged to access the File System API documentation for a complete list.) In this table, **`fo`** represents a FileObject (file or folder), and **`folder`** represents a FileObject folder.

**TABLE 13.1 File System API Useful Methods with FileObject**

| Action | Method |
|---|---|
| Get Name | `fo.getName()` |
| Get Extension | `fo.getExt()` |
| Get Name + Extension | `fo.getNameExt()` |
| Get Path | `fo.getPath()` |
| Get Children | `folder.getChildren()` |
| Rename File | `fo.rename(lock, new_name, new_extension)`<br>`folder.rename(lock, new_name, new_extension)` |
| Create File | `folder.createData(newFileName)` |
| Create Folder | `folder.createFolder(newFolderName)` |
| Delete File | `fo.delete()`<br>`folder.delete() // recursive` |
| Move File | `fo.move(lock, dest_Folder, new_name, new_extension)` |
| Read File | `fo.asBytes(), fo.asText(), fo.asLines()` |
| Write File | `fo.getOutputStream(), use OutputStream` |

Table 13.2 provides a partial list of methods available with utility class FileUtil. These are all static methods. In this table, **`fo`** represents a FileObject (file or folder), **`file`** represents a java.io.File, and **`folder`** represents a FileObject folder.

**TABLE 13.2 File System API Useful Methods with FileUtil**

| Action | Method |
|---|---|
| File -> FileObject | `FileUtil.toFileObject(file);` |
| FileObject -> File | `FileUtil.toFile(fo)` |
| Copy streams | `FileUtil.copy(inputStream, outputStream)` |
| Copy file to folder | `FileUtil.copyFile(fo, destFolder, newName)`<br>`FileUtil.copyFile(fo, destFolder, newName, newExt)` |
| Create file if non-existent | `FileUtil.createData(file)`<br>`FileUtil.createData(folder, name)` |
| Create folder if non-existent | `FileUtil.createFolder(file)`<br>`FileUtil.createFolder(folder, name)` |
| Is FileObject an archive (ZIP or JAR file)? | `FileUtil.isArchiveFile(fo)` |
| Return archive's FileObject root (folder) | `FileUtil.getArchiveRoot(fo)` |
| Create a FileSystem in memory | `FileUtil.createMemoryFileSystem()` |
| Finds "brother" file with same base name but different extension | `FileUtil.findBrother()` |
| Get System FileSystem root | `FileUtil.getConfigRoot()` |
| Get a FileObject in the System FileSystem if it exists | `FileUtil.getConfigFile(path)` |
| Get a fo's extension | `FileUtil.getExtension(fo)` |
| Get a fo's name | `FileUtil.getFileDisplayName(fo)` |
| Get a fo's MIME type | `FileUtil.getMimeType(fo)` |
| Get relative resource path between folder and fo | `FileUtil.getRelativePath(folder, fo)` |

## 13.3 Monitoring File Changes

One of the big advantages with the NetBeans Platform File System API is that you can attach FileChangeListeners to FileObjects (either files or folders). You can also attach recursive FileChangeListeners to folders in a directory tree. In this section, we'll add a new module to the FileSystemApp we built in the previous section to show you how you can monitor changes to a file system.

### FileObject Attributes

For this file monitor, we'll use the FileObject attribute feature, which lets you associate arbitrary objects with FileObjects. These attributes persist through restarts of the application and are stored in the application's user directory (that is, they are not stored in the files themselves). During development, the **attributes.xml** file that stores the serialized attributes is deleted when you perform a Clean of the project.

We'll also introduce the Favorites window in this section. You enable this feature when you include the Favorites module from the **platform** cluster in your application. Here's a summary of the steps to create and configure this new module.

- Include the Favorites and Templates modules from cluster **platform**. (The Templates module lets you create empty files and folders from the Favorites window.)
- Add new module ChangeDetector to the FileSystemApp application.
- Add a new window (TopComponent) to module ChangeDetector.
- Add dependencies to the File System API and the I/O APIs in module ChangeDetector.
- Implement the TopComponent code to display a portion of the user's file system on the local disk. The display uses a FileObject's attributes to indicate its most recent modification to the file. The TopComponent uses a FileChangeListener to report event notification messages to a new tab in the Output window and refresh the TopComponent's display.

Figure 13.5 shows this application running with the Favorites window on the left and the ChangeDetector window in the editor position. The Output window appears below with two tabs, the previously built Explore File Actions tab, and a new tab entitled Watch Directory.

The application reports any changes made to the file system starting from directory FamilyTreeData under the user's home directory. After invoking the Explore File Actions menu item from the previous section, the Watch Directory Output window displays the changes that create, rename, and delete a text file.

Let's show you how to build these windows, starting with the Favorites window.

### Favorites Window

The Favorites window lets you view files in the your local file system, as well as create new empty files and folders (when you also add the Templates module).

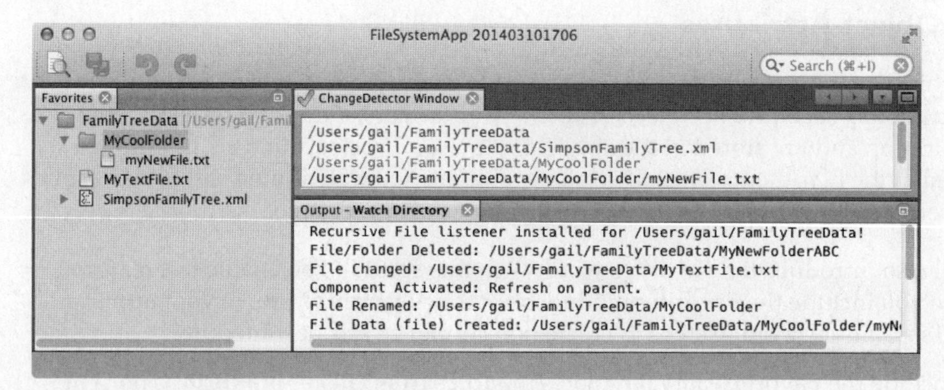


Figure 13.5 The FileSystemApp with the ChangeDetector window

Once the Favorite modules is installed, an action appears in the top-level Windows menu to open the Favorites window in the Explorer mode. Follow these steps to include both the Favorites and Templates modules in the FileSystemApp application.

1. Right click project FileSystemApp in the Projects view and select **Properties** from the context menu.
2. Under Categories, select **Libraries**. NetBeans lists all of the Platform Modules organized in clusters. Under cluster **platform**, select modules **Favorites** (as shown in Figure 13.6) and **Templates**. Select **OK**.

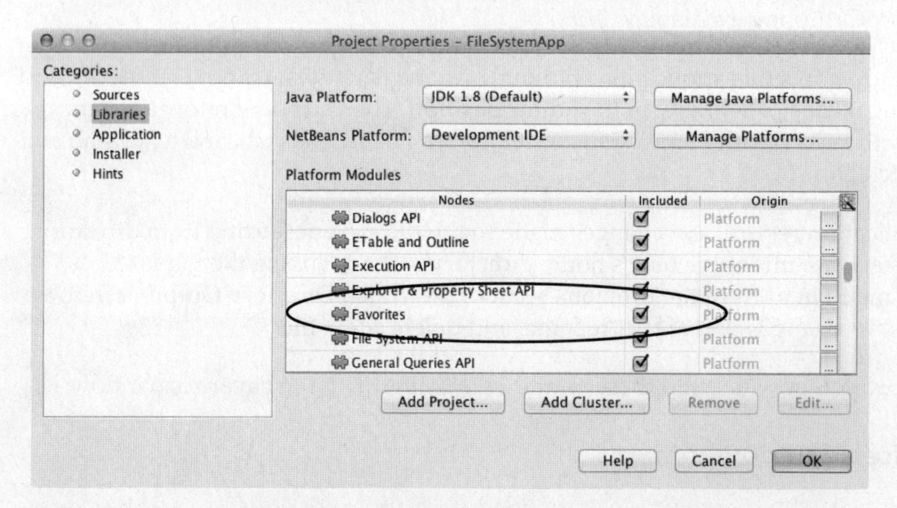


Figure 13.6 Select the Favorites and Templates modules in cluster platform

3. Now run the FileSystemApp application. When the application comes up, open the top-level Window menu and select **Favorites**. This opens the Favorites window in the Explorer view, as shown in Figure 13.7.

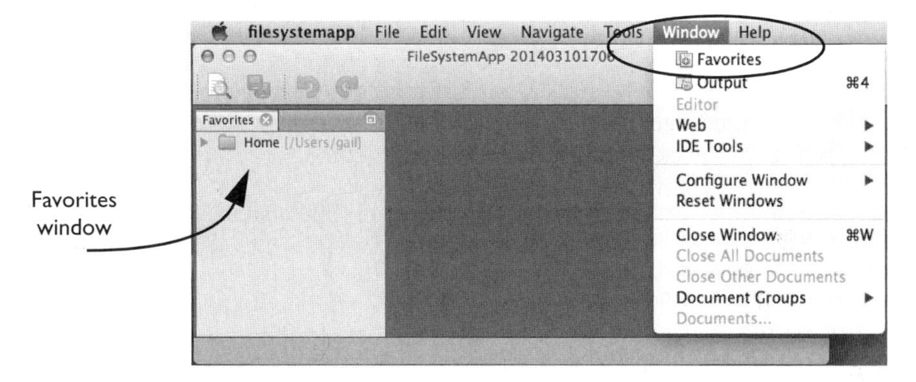


Figure 13.7 Select menu item Favorites to open the Favorites window

4. Expand the top-level directory (the home directory on your local file system). You can selectively add folders to and remove them from the Favorites window.
5. Experiment with different file manipulation actions. Create a new folder in a selected folder using right-click **New | All Templates**. In the Choose Template dialog, expand **Other** and select **Folder**. Click **Next**. Provide a new Folder Name and click **Finish**.
6. Create a new empty file with **New | All Templates**. Now expand **Other**, select **Empty File**, and click **Next**. In the New Object Name dialog, provide a file name. If the extension is recognized and corresponds to a text file (such as .txt or .xml), NetBeans will open the file in a plain Text Editor.

Use these file manipulation actions to test the FileChangeListener example in this section.

**Favorites Window Tip**

---

*You may find the Favorites window useful when working in the NetBeans IDE. Select the top-level Windows menu and select* ***Favorites****. With the Favorites window, you can open a file that does not belong to a NetBeans Platform project and edit the file depending on its MIME type: HTML, XML, FXML, or even Java, for example.*

---

### Add Module ChangeDetector

Use these steps to create module ChangeDetector in the FileSystemApp application.

1. Expand project FileSystemApp, select the **Modules** node, right-click, and select **New . . .** .
2. NetBeans initiates the New Module Project wizard. In the Name and Location dialog, specify **ChangeDetector** for Project Name and accept the defaults for the remaining fields. Click **Next**.
3. NetBeans displays the Basic Module Configuration dialog. Specify **com.asgteach.changedetector** for Code Name Base, accept the defaults for the remaining fields, and click **Finish**.

NetBeans creates module ChangeDetector in application FileSystemApp.

### Add the ChangeDetector Window

The ChangeDetector module displays a TopComponent (window) in the application. Follow these steps to create and register a TopComponent window in module ChangeDetector.

1. In the Projects view, expand module **ChangeDetector | Source Packages**. Select the package name, right click, and select **New | Window**. NetBeans initiates the New Window wizard.
2. In the Basic Settings dialog, select Window Position **editor** and **Open at Application Start**. Click **Next**.
3. NetBeans displays the Name, Icon, and Location dialog. For Class Name Prefix specify **ChangeDetector**. For the icon, click **Browse** and select the provided icon file **check.png**, and click **Finish**, as shown in Figure 13.8.

The ChangeDetector window is now registered. Next, we'll add code to the TopComponent.

### Add Module Dependencies

Add module dependencies in module ChangeDetector for the File System API (for file actions) and I/O APIs (to write content to the Output window).

### Configure the TopComponent

We use a Swing Text Panel to display information about the user's file system. The JTextPanel component lets you manipulate the text color. Here are the steps to configure the TopComponent's layout with a Text Panel.

1. Open ChangeDetectorTopComponent in the Design view.

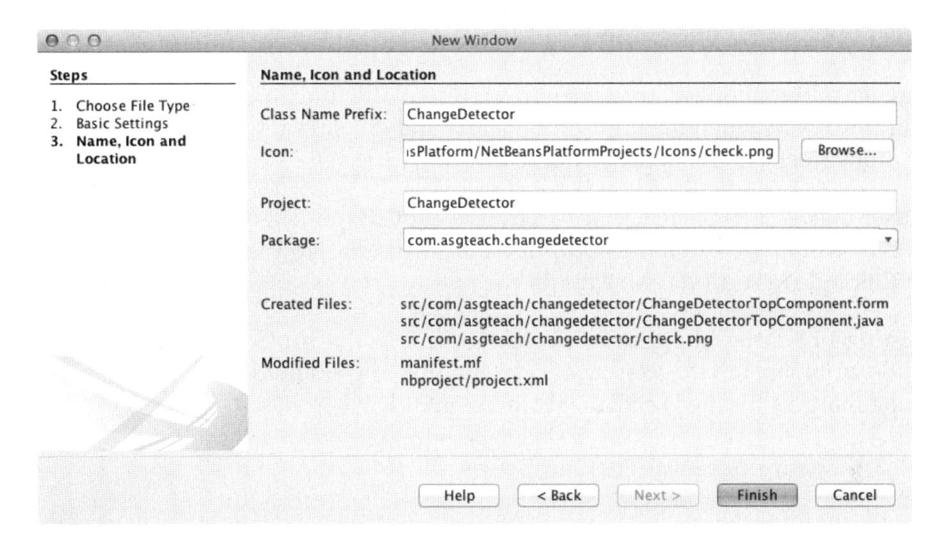


Figure 13.8 Creating the ChangeDetector window in module ChangeDetector

2. In the Palette under Swing Controls, select **Text Panel** and drop it onto the Design view.
3. NetBeans automatically encloses the JTextPanel with a JScrollPane. Expand the JScrollPane so that it covers the entire design area.
4. In the Navigator window, select the **JTextPane** component, right click, and select **Change Variable Name. . . .** In the dialog, provide new variable name **display** and click **OK**. Figure 13.9 shows the Navigator view for this TopComponent with the renamed JTextPanel component.

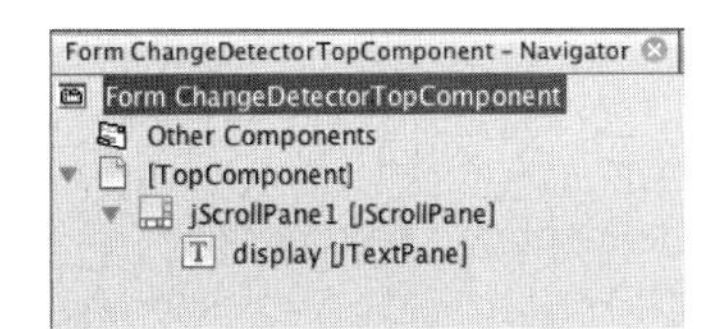


Figure 13.9 Navigator view of ChangeDetectorTopComponent

5. Click **Source** to return to the Source view and save your changes.

## Add TopComponent Code

The code we add to the TopComponent provides all the functionality of this module. This window opens when the application starts and displays the file hierarchy under folder FamilyTreeData in the user's home directory.

As the user makes changes to the hierarchy, the TopComponent refreshes and any file system events are reported in the Output window (under tab Watch Directory). We'll present this code in sections and explain each part.

First, Listing 13.8 shows the generated code to register the TopComponent. We add a Watch Directory label to the @Messages annotation and class fields to configure. We also create margins for the JTextPanel component.

**Listing 13.8 ChangeDetectorTopComponent**

```
@ConvertAsProperties(
        dtd = "-//com.asgteach.changedetector//ChangeDetector//EN",
        autostore = false
)
@TopComponent.Description(
        preferredID = "ChangeDetectorTopComponent",
        iconBase = "com/asgteach/changedetector/check.png",
        persistenceType = TopComponent.PERSISTENCE_ALWAYS
)
@TopComponent.Registration(mode = "editor", openAtStartup = true)
@ActionID(category = "Window",
         id = "com.asgteach.changedetector.ChangeDetectorTopComponent")
@ActionReference(path = "Menu/Window" /*, position = 333 */)
@TopComponent.OpenActionRegistration(
        displayName = "#CTL_ChangeDetectorAction",
        preferredID = "ChangeDetectorTopComponent"
)
@Messages({
    "CTL_ChangeDetectorAction=ChangeDetector",
    "CTL_ChangeDetectorTopComponent=ChangeDetector Window",
    "HINT_ChangeDetectorTopComponent=This is a ChangeDetector window",
    "CTL_ChangeLabel=Watch Directory"
})
public final class ChangeDetectorTopComponent extends TopComponent {

    private FileObject root;
    private OutputWriter writer;
    private boolean updateOK = true;
    public static final String FO_MODIFICATION_COLOR = "FOModificationColor";
```

```
    public ChangeDetectorTopComponent() {
        initComponents();
        setName(Bundle.CTL_ChangeDetectorTopComponent());
        setToolTipText(Bundle.HINT_ChangeDetectorTopComponent());
        display.setMargin(new Insets(5, 5, 5, 5));
    }
. . .
}
```

### Configure the TopComponent Life Cycle Methods

Listing 13.9 shows the code for the `componentOpened()`, `componentActivated()`, and `componentClosed()` life cycle methods (see "Window System Life Cycle Management" on page 369 for more on window life cycle methods). The `componentOpened()` method configures the Output window, adds a FileChangeListener (`fcl`) to the target folder in the user's home directory (class variable `root`), and updates the TopComponent's display with the `updateDisplay()` helper method (shown later).

We add a *recursive* FileChangeListener to the target folder. This potentially expensive arrangement (depending on how big the hierarchy is) fires change events for any of the files and folders below the target folder, including the target folder. Here, the hierarchy is small. We present the FileChangeListener implementation in an upcoming section.

The `componentActivated()` method is invoked when the user selects the ChangeDetector window. Here, we force a refresh on the parent of our target folder. This allows the FileChangeListener to detect changes made outside the FileSystemApp application.

The `componentClosed()` method removes the FileChangeListener from the target folder (`root`) so that the listener isn't active when the window is closed.

We also include the `displayMessage()` helper method that writes its String argument to the Output window using class field `writer` (OutputWriter).

**Listing 13.9 ChangeDetectorTopComponent—Life Cycle Methods**

```
public final class ChangeDetectorTopComponent extends TopComponent {
   . . .
    @Override
    public void componentOpened() {
        InputOutput io = IOProvider.getDefault().getIO(
                                       Bundle.CTL_ChangeLabel(), false);
        io.select();                   // tab is selected
        writer = io.getOut();
```

```
        String home = System.getProperty("user.home");
        File file = new File(home + "/FamilyTreeData");
        root = FileUtil.toFileObject(file);
        if (root == null) {
            displayMessage("Warning: File Object " + file.getPath()
                        + " does not exist.");
            displayMessage("Create " + file.getPath()
                        + ", close & reopen Window "
                        + Bundle.CTL_ChangeDetectorTopComponent());
            return;
        }
        root.addRecursiveListener(fcl);
        displayMessage("Recursive File listener installed for "
                  + root.getPath() + "!");
        updateDisplay();
    }

    @Override
    protected void componentActivated() {
        if (root != null) {
            try {
                root.getParent().getFileSystem().refresh(true);
                displayMessage("Component Activated: Refresh on parent.");
                updateDisplay();
            } catch (FileStateInvalidException ex) {
                Exceptions.printStackTrace(ex);
            }
        }
    }

    @Override
    public void componentClosed() {
        if (root != null) {
            root.removeFileChangeListener(fcl);
        }
    }

    private void displayMessage(String message) {
        writer.println(message); }

}
```

## Updating and Displaying the Hierarchy in the Window

Our TopComponent consists of a Swing JTextPanel added to a JScrollPane. Listing 13.10 shows how to write String messages to the window that are color coded and how to display the complete hierarchy that we are monitoring with the FileChangeListener.

Method `appendToDisplay()` writes a String with Color to the JTextPanel display. We temporarily make the Text Panel editable and set attributes that define the text color, font style, and alignment. We set the caret position at the end, add the String argument to the Text Panel, and return the Text Panel to non-editable.

The `updateDisplay()` method is invoked in `componentOpened()` and in the FileChangeListener code when a file change event is received. This method calls `displayFiles()` with the root (which then recursively calls itself for the entire hierarchy) so that each file and folder in the hierarchy is written to the window's Text Panel. The `displayFiles()` method handles archives by obtaining the archive's root and recursively displaying its contents (showing the power of the FileObject and FileSystem abstraction).

The `displayFiles()` method is invoked with a FileObject argument. If the FileObject has a Color attribute, this color is used to write the FileObject's path name. If the Color attribute is not present, then a default `Color.DARK_GRAY` color value is used.

Recall that a FileObject's attributes are stored in the user directory of the NetBeans Platform application. These attributes persist when the user reruns the FileSystemApp application.

**Listing 13.10 ChangeDetectorTopComponent—Updating the Text Panel**

```
private void appendToDisplay(String msg, Color c) {
    display.setEditable(true);
    StyleContext sc = StyleContext.getDefaultStyleContext();
    AttributeSet attrset = sc.addAttribute(SimpleAttributeSet.EMPTY,
           StyleConstants.Foreground, c);

    attrset = sc.addAttribute(attrset, StyleConstants.FontFamily,
           "Lucida Console");
    attrset = sc.addAttribute(attrset, StyleConstants.Alignment,
           StyleConstants.ALIGN_JUSTIFIED);

    display.setCaretPosition(display.getDocument().getLength());
    display.setCharacterAttributes(attrset, false);
    display.replaceSelection(msg);
    display.setEditable(false);
}

private void updateDisplay() {
    if (root == null || !updateOK) {
        return;
    }
    updateOK = false;
    display.setText("");
    displayFiles(root);
    updateOK = true;
}
```

```
    private void displayFiles(FileObject fo) {
        Color displayColor = (Color) fo.getAttribute(FO_MODIFICATION_COLOR);
        if (displayColor == null) {
            displayColor = Color.DARK_GRAY;
        }

        appendToDisplay(FileUtil.getFileDisplayName(fo) + "\n", displayColor);
        if (FileUtil.isArchiveFile(fo)) {
            FileObject arcRoot = FileUtil.getArchiveRoot(fo);
            displayFiles(arcRoot);
        } else if (fo.isFolder()) {
            for (FileObject childFileObject : fo.getChildren()) {
                displayFiles(childFileObject);
            }
        }
    }
```

## Implementing the FileChangeListener

The FileChangeListener interface has six methods to override, as listed in Table 13.3. (If it is not necessary to handle all the events in the FileChangeListener interface, you can use the FileChangeAdapter adapter class.)

**TABLE 13.3 FileChangeListener Interface Methods**

| Method | Description |
|---|---|
| `fileFolderCreated(FileEvent)` | Fired when the supervised folder contains a new folder |
| `fileDataCreated(FileEvent)` | Fired when the supervised folder contains a new file |
| `fileChanged(FileEvent)` | Fired when a file changes (e.g., edits are saved) |
| `fileDeleted(FileEvent)` | Fired when a file or folder is deleted |
| `fileRenamed(FileRenameEvent)` | Fired when a file or folder is renamed |
| `fileAttributeChanged(FileAttributeEvent)` | Fired when a file or folder's attribute has been added, updated, or removed |

Listing 13.11 shows the FileChangeListener implementation. For each method (except for the `fileAttributeChanged()` method, which is empty), we write the event name and affected file to the Output window and update the hierarchy in the TopComponent. We also set an attribute in the affected FileObject that color codes the event. (This attribute is read by the `displayFiles()` method shown previously in Listing 13.10 on page 645.) Green corresponds to a new folder, orange for a new file, blue for a changed file or folder, and magenta for a renamed file or folder. No attribute is set for a delete event, since that folder or file will no longer be displayed in the hierarchy.

**Listing 13.11 ChangeDetectorTopComponent—FileChangeListener**

```
private final FileChangeListener fcl = new FileChangeListener() {
    @Override
    public void fileFolderCreated(FileEvent fe) {
        displayMessage("File Folder Created: " + fe.getFile().getPath());
        try {
            fe.getFile().setAttribute(FO_MODIFICATION_COLOR, Color.GREEN);
            updateDisplay();
        } catch (IOException ex) {
            Exceptions.printStackTrace(ex);
        }
    }

    @Override
    public void fileDataCreated(FileEvent fe) {
        displayMessage("File Data (file) Created: "
                          + fe.getFile().getPath());
        try {
           fe.getFile().setAttribute(FO_MODIFICATION_COLOR, Color.ORANGE);
            updateDisplay();
        } catch (IOException ex) {
            Exceptions.printStackTrace(ex);
        }
    }

    @Override
    public void fileChanged(FileEvent fe) {
        displayMessage("File Changed: " + fe.getFile().getPath());
        try {
            fe.getFile().setAttribute(FO_MODIFICATION_COLOR, Color.BLUE);
            updateDisplay();
        } catch (IOException ex) {
            Exceptions.printStackTrace(ex);
        }
    }

    @Override
    public void fileDeleted(FileEvent fe) {
        displayMessage("File/Folder Deleted: " + fe.getFile().getPath());
        updateDisplay();
    }

    @Override
    public void fileRenamed(FileRenameEvent fre) {
        displayMessage("File Renamed: " + fre.getFile().getPath());
        try {
            fre.getFile().setAttribute(FO_MODIFICATION_COLOR,
                                      Color.MAGENTA);
```

```
                updateDisplay();
            } catch (IOException ex) {
                Exceptions.printStackTrace(ex);
            }
        }

        @Override
        public void fileAttributeChanged(FileAttributeEvent fae) { }
    };
```

## Trying Out the ChangeDetector Using the Favorites Window

With the TopComponent code in place, you can now use the Favorites window to create and rename files and folders and edit text files. You can also view how the hierarchy is updated in the ChangeDetector window. Figure 13.10 shows the FileSystemApp after several files and folders have been manipulated.

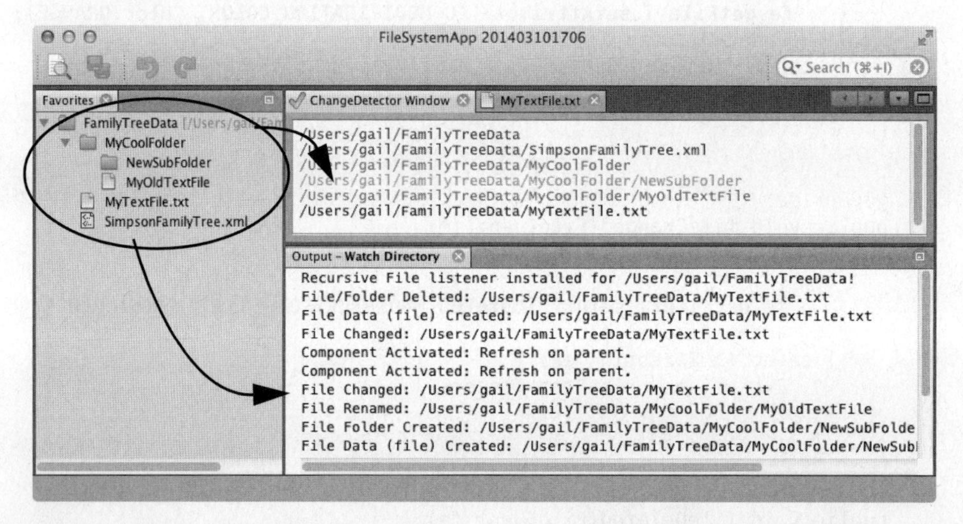


Figure 13.10 Running the FileSystemApp with the ChangeDetector window

Here, we add files and folders to folder FamilyTreeData (the target directory that module ChangeDetector watches). We also edit a text file and delete several files. The Output window (tab Watch Directory) lists the FileChange events and the Change-Directory window shows the most recent state of the hierarchy.[3]

3. You can also modify the target hierarchy using your native system file utility. The detected events might be different, however. For example, on our system a rename event is reported as a file create event followed by a file delete event.

## 13.4 Including a File with Your Application

Suppose you want to include a file in one of your modules and access the file programmatically. Let's show you how to do this in a new module called AppConfigFile. The file that we provide is **SimpsonFamilyTree.xml** and we'll install it in a folder called **configFile** within our module.

For testing, we'll create an action in the FileSystemApp application that locates the file and displays its contents in the Output window, as shown in Figure 13.11. (Note that we now have three independent tabs in the Output window: Watch Directory, Config File Contents, and Explore File Actions. The order of the tabs depends on the order that you invoke the actions associated with the tabs.)

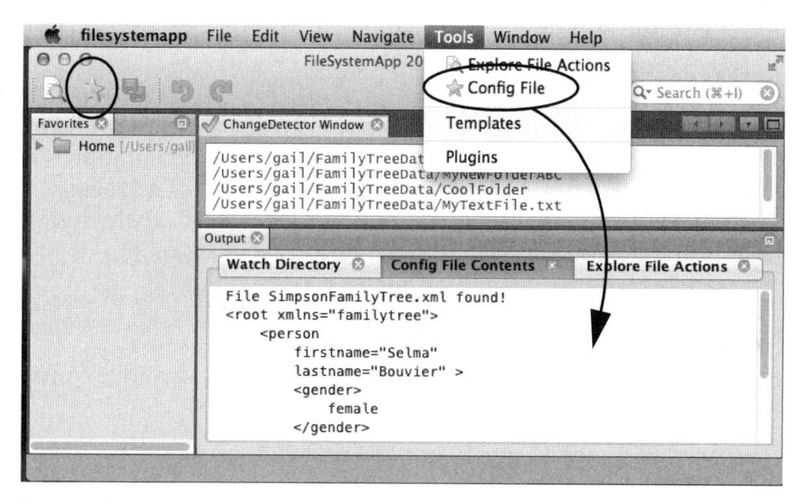


Figure 13.11 Locating and displaying the Config File

Here's a summary of the steps we'll perform to create and configure this module.

- Add new module AppConfigFile to the FileSystemApp application.
- Install file **configFile/SimpsonFamilyTree.xml** in module AppConfigFile's **release** directory.
- Register a new action in module AppConfigFile.
- Add module dependencies to the File System API, I/O APIs, Module System API, and Lookup API.
- Implement the action.

### Create Module AppConfigFile

Use these steps to create module AppConfigFile in the FileSystemApp application.

1. Expand project FileSystemApp, select the **Modules** node, right-click, and select **New . . . .**
2. NetBeans initiates the New Module Project wizard. In the Name and Location dialog, specify **AppConfigFile** for Project Name and accept the defaults for the remaining fields. Click **Next**.
3. NetBeans displays the Basic Module Configuration dialog. Specify **com.asgteach.appconfigfile** for Code Name Base, accept the defaults for the remaining fields, and click **Finish**.

NetBeans creates module AppConfigFile in application FileSystemApp.

## Install a File in a Module

To include a file (which could be a third-party library, a data file, documentation files, or a configuration file, for example), you place the file in a directory called **release** under the main directory of your module. The build process automatically includes any files or directories it finds in this specially-named directory. Here are the steps.

1. In the Files view, create a folder called **release** in the top-level directory of your module. (You must use name **release**.)
2. Next, create a containing folder (or folders) for your files. We create folder **configFile**. You can use any folder name here.
3. Copy any files you want included to this folder. We added file SimpsonFamilyTree.xml, as shown in Figure 13.12.

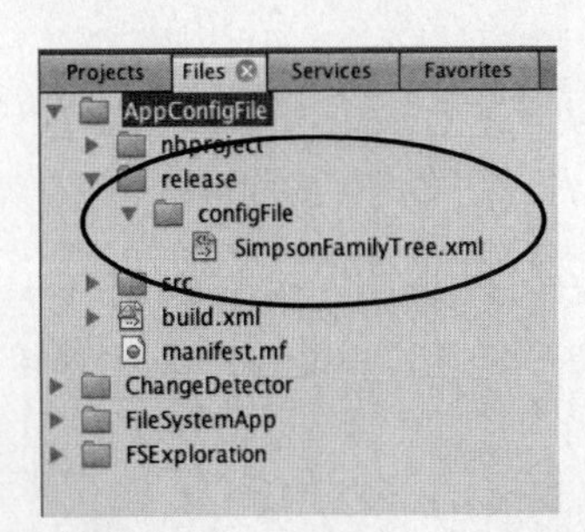


Figure 13.12 Adding files to the module's **release** directory

### Register an Action

Register a new action in module AppConfigFile using these steps.

1. In module AppConfigFile, expand Source Packages and right click on the package name. Select **New | Action** from the context menu.
2. NetBeans initiates the New Action wizard. In the Action Type dialog, select **Always Enabled** and click **Next**.
3. In the GUI Registration dialog, select Category **Tools**. Select the **Global Menu Item** checkbox. Specify Menu **Tools** with position **Here - Tools**, and **Separator After**. Select the **Global Toolbar Button** checkbox. Specify Toolbar **File** and Position **Here - Save All**. Click **Next**.
4. NetBeans displays the Name, Icon, and Location dialog. For Class Name specify **ConfigFileAction**, for Display Name specify **Config File**, and click the **Browse** button and navigate to the provided icon file **Favorites.png**. Click **Finish**.

NetBeans creates **ConfigFileAction.java** and copies the icon files to the module's source package.

### Add Module Dependencies

Add module dependencies for File System API (for file actions), I/O APIs (to write content to the Output window), and both Lookup API and Module System API (required by the InstalledFileLocator service).

### Implement the Action

We show the implementation of the ConfigFileAction in two parts. Listing 13.12 shows the action's registration annotations and the code that configures the Output window. This code is similar to Listing 13.1 on page 629 (see "The Output Window" on page 628 for a detailed description).

**Listing 13.12 ConfigFileAction—Registration Annotations**

```
@ActionID(
        category = "Tools",
        id = "com.asgteach.appuserfile.ConfigFileAction"
)
@ActionRegistration(
        iconBase = "com/asgteach/appconfigfile/Favorites.png",
        displayName = "#CTL_ConfigFile"
)
```

```
@ActionReferences({
    @ActionReference(path = "Menu/Tools", position = 25, separatorAfter = 37),
    @ActionReference(path = "Toolbars/File", position = 350)
})
@Messages({
    "CTL_ConfigFile=Config File",
    "CTL_configFileTab=Config File Contents"
})
public final class ConfigFileAction implements ActionListener {

    private final InputOutput io;
    private final OutputWriter writer;
    private static final String filename = "configFile/SimpsonFamilyTree.xml";

    public ConfigFileAction() {
        io = IOProvider.getDefault().getIO(Bundle.CTL_configFileTab(), false);
        writer = io.getOut();
    }

    private void displayMessage(String msg) {
        writer.println(msg);
    }
. . .
}
```

We implement the `actionPerformed()` method in Listing 13.13. First, we configure the Output window by resetting its content and activating the window with `io.select()`. Next, we get the default service provider for InstalledFileLocator and invoke the `locate()` method. This method looks for the provided file in the application and returns null if the file is not there.

We convert the File to FileObject and use the convenience method `asLines()` to read the file and display each line in the Output window.

**Listing 13.13 ConfigFileAction—actionPerformed() Method**

```
    @Override
    public void actionPerformed(ActionEvent e) {
        try {
            writer.reset();              // clear the window each time
        } catch (IOException ex) {
            Exceptions.printStackTrace(ex);
            return;
        }
        io.select();                     // select this tab
        File configFile = InstalledFileLocator.getDefault().locate(filename,
                "com.asgteach.appconfigfile", false);
        FileObject fo = null;
```

```
        if (configFile != null) {
            fo = FileUtil.toFileObject(configFile);
            if (fo != null) {
                displayMessage("File " + fo.getNameExt() + " found!");
                try {
                    for (String lines : fo.asLines()) {
                        displayMessage(lines);
                    }
                } catch (IOException ex) {
                    Exceptions.printStackTrace(ex);
                }
            }
        }
        if (fo == null || configFile == null) {
            displayMessage("Warning: File " + filename + " is missing!");
        }
    }
```

## Using the InstalledFileLocator Service

Let's take a closer look at the `locate()` method of the InstalledFileLocator service. The first argument is the path of the target file, including its enclosing directory but excluding the release directory. The second argument is the code name of the module that contains the file. This can be null and may (or may not) be used in the location service. However, providing the code name can speed up the location process. The third argument is a boolean indicating whether or not the file is localized. This is useful when the target file is a zip file containing localized documentation files, for example. In this case, you provide the "unlocalized" file name with `locate()` method, set the localized boolean to `true`, and install the localized file, as shown here.

```
docs/mydocs_es.zip   // installed in release directory of module MyModule

File file = locate("docs/mydocs.zip", "com.mymodule", true);
```

The InstalledFileLocator service also provides method `locateAll()`, which is useful when locating more than one file from a directory. The path should not include the trailing "/" and the return value is a (possibly empty) `Set<File>`.

```
Set<File> set = locateAll("docs", "com.mymodule", true);    // or false
```

The exact location of the file depends on the environment in which this module runs. In the development environment, the file is copied to the **cluster/configFile** directory of the application's **build** directory.

### Installing an NBM in NetBeans IDE

Now let's show you that you can use the InstalledFileLocator service in a module installed in the NetBeans IDE with no changes, although the file is physically located in a different place. You can install module AppConfigFile in your running NetBeans IDE as a PlugIn using the following steps.

1. First, create an NBM file (NBM stands for NetBeans Module). See "Create the Module NBM" on page 861. An NBM file can be installed in the IDE as a PlugIn.
2. From the NetBeans IDE top-level Tools menu, select **PlugIns**.
3. In the PlugIns window, click **Downloaded**.
4. Click the **Add PlugIns . . .** button.
5. Browse to the **build/updates** directory where you will see NBM files for each module in your application, as shown in Figure 13.13.

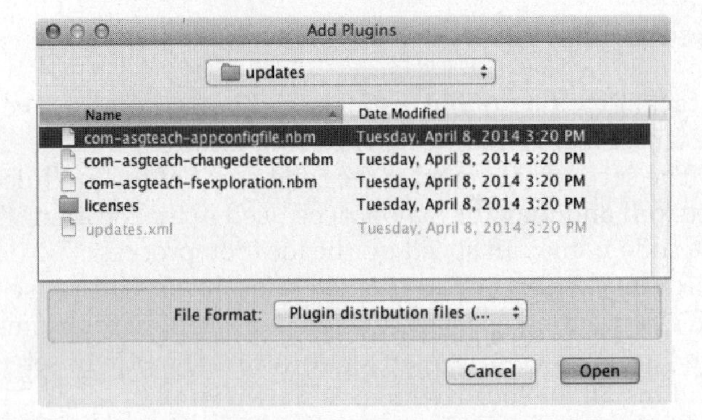


Figure 13.13 Adding module AppConfigFile to the NetBeans IDE as a PlugIn

6. Select **com-asgteach-appconfigfile.nbm**, then **Open** to install this module.

Figure 13.14 shows that the Config File action has been added to the NetBeans IDE and the installed file, SimpsonFamilyTree.xml, has been located within the running application. (We changed the Config File `actionPerformed()` method to display the file's complete path, which is shown in the screen shot.)

## 13.5 The Layer File and System FileSystem

Someday someone will write a book on the NetBeans Platform and not have to discuss the Layer file, that ubiquitous file that historically showed up regularly in your module's Projects view. Traditionally (and tediously) configured manually by the

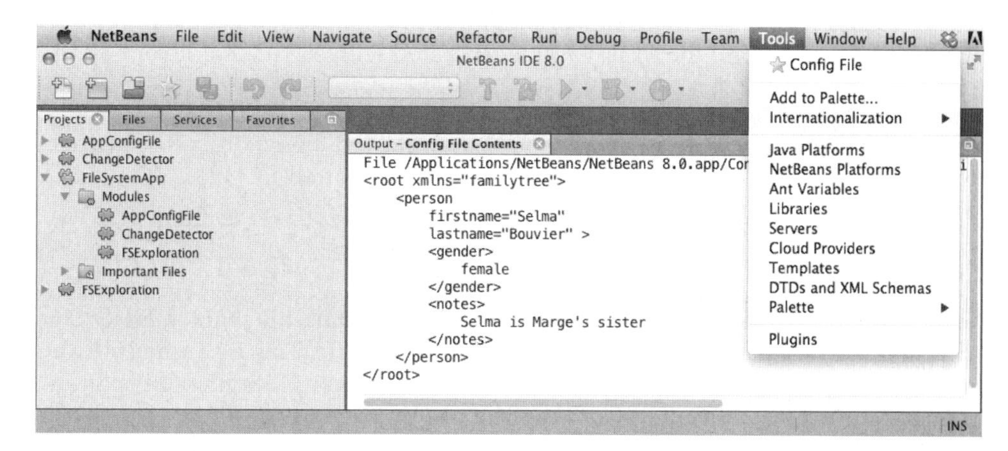


Figure 13.14 Module AppConfigFile has been added to the NetBeans IDE as a PlugIn

developer, the Layer file is now *mostly* generated by the various NetBeans IDE wizards. You can specify many configuration options with annotations (such as TopComponents, actions, menu and toolbar items, key bindings, and service providers, for example). Viewed from the Files window under the **build** directory as **classes/META-INF/generated-layer.xml**, a module now includes a generated Layer file if you've used any of these "configuration-type" annotations in your Java code.

But there are still occasions when creating a Layer file in a module is necessary (see, for example "Window Groups" on page 381). Furthermore, the Layer file is the gateway to your NetBeans Platform application's complete configuration data. From the information in each module's contributed Layer file, the Platform builds an actual writable file system on disk (called the System FileSystem) used to define all of the actions, menus, menu items, icons, key bindings, toolbars, and services available in your application. This configuration data tells the application how to configure menus and actions (for example) and even how to instantiate objects! Importantly, you can contribute to your application's configuration by specifying files and Java objects in a module's Layer file.

You can manipulate files and folders on the local disk file system with the File System API. The same File System API can also examine the System FileSystem and modify content. In this section, we'll examine both the Layer file and its relationship to the System FileSystem.

## Layer Files and Configuration

Let's examine Layer files now and see how a Layer file affects a NetBeans Platform application. First, most modules don't have an editable Layer file. Even when you create a Java class with annotations that affects registration information, the Layer file is quietly generated behind the scenes and regenerated with each build of your application.

But you can explicitly create a Layer file for a module and then modify its contents. Let's do that now and show you how a Layer file is structured.

## Create a Layer File

We'll continue to work with the application that was built in this chapter, **FileSystemApp**. First, we create a Layer file in module **AppConfigFile**. This is the module we created in the previous section that includes a file in our application's release directory (see "Including a File with Your Application" on page 649).

1. Select project **AppConfigFile**, right click, and select **New | Other** from the context menu.
2. NetBeans initiates the New File wizard and displays the Choose File Type dialog. Under Categories select **Module Development** and under File Types select **XML Layer**. Click **Next**.
3. NetBeans displays the Layer Location dialog and specifies AppConfigFile for the Project, as shown in Figure 13.15. Click **Finish**.

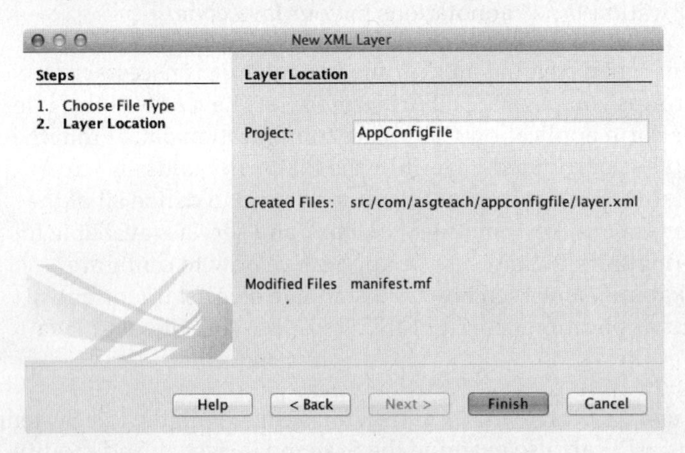


Figure 13.15 Creating a module's XML Layer file

NetBeans creates file **layer.xml** in the module's Source Package, brings up **layer.xml** in the XML text editor, and modifies the Module Manifest file (under Important Files) to include the entry describing its location in the module, as follows.

```
OpenIDE-Module-Layer: com/asgteach/appconfigfile/layer.xml
```

To add entries to this Layer file, break up the `<filesystem/>` tag into an open and close tag with `<filesystem></filesystem>` on separate lines, as shown in Listing 13.14.

**Listing 13.14 Layer.xml—Initial Contents**

```
<?xml version="1.0" encoding="UTF-8"?>
<!DOCTYPE filesystem PUBLIC "-//NetBeans//DTD Filesystem 1.2//EN"
                "http://www.netbeans.org/dtds/filesystem-1_2.dtd">
<filesystem>
</filesystem>
```

The Projects view is extremely useful for examining the concept of a Layer file. Once you've created a Layer file in a module (even one with no new content, as in Listing 13.14), build the application. You'll see two entries under **Important Files | XML Layer** called **<this layer>** and **<this layer in context>**. Entry **<this layer>** refers to configuration information in this module, and entry **<this layer in context>** refers to the entire application.

The AppConfigFile module also includes an Action that we registered previously via annotations. Because of this registration, our newly created XML Layer displayed in the Projects view under `<this layer>` contains this registration information, as shown in Figure 13.16 (even though the file layer.xml is empty). You see the Config File action is registered in three places: folders Actions/Tools, Menu/Tools, and Toolbars/File.

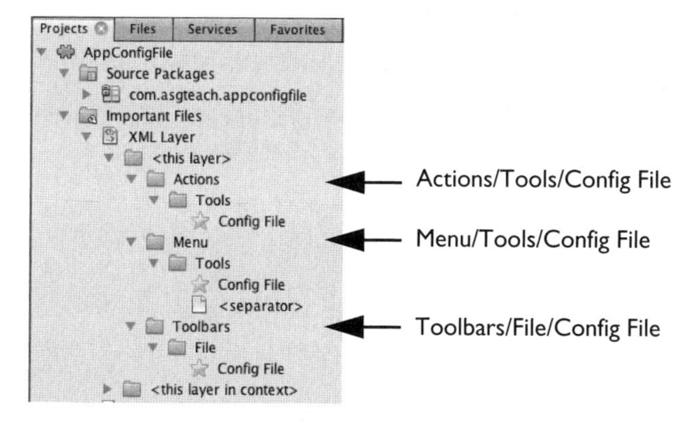


Figure 13.16 Examining a module's XML Layer file

## Dissecting the Layer File

Now let's look at the generated XML Layer file that corresponds to the Projects view displayed in Figure 13.16. Listing 13.15 shows the Actions folder and the Toolbars folder. (We omitted the Menu folder.)

The Layer file consists of four main tags: `<filesystem>`, `<folder>`, `<file>`, and `<attr>`.

- The `<filesystem>` tag defines the overall file system and is merged with an actual file system on disk, specifically the System FileSystem. You can use the File System API FileUtil class to access the root folder. (We'll show you how later in this chapter.)
- The `<folder>` tag defines folders (i.e., directories) within the file system. These are accessed with the File System API class FileObject, and the `isFolder()` method returns true for folders.
- The `<file>` tag refers to a file and can also be accessed with the FileObject class. In this case, `isFolder()` returns false.
- The `<attr>` tag defines attributes, arbitrary Objects identified by String names. Attributes are accessed with FileObject method `getAttribute(name)` shown previously (see "FileObject Attributes" on page 637). For examples that show attribute getters and setters, see Listing 13.10 on page 645 and Listing 13.11 on page 647.

**Listing 13.15 Folder "Actions" in Generated Layer File**

```
<filesystem>
    <folder name="Actions">
        <folder name="Tools">
            <file name="com-asgteach-appuserfile-ConfigFileAction.instance">
                <!--com.asgteach.appconfigfile.ConfigFileAction-->
                <attr
                    bundlevalue=
    "com.asgteach.appconfigfile.Bundle#CTL_ConfigFile" name="displayName"/>
                <attr
                    methodvalue=
    "org.openide.awt.Actions.alwaysEnabled" name="instanceCreate"/>
                <attr name="delegate" newvalue=
    "com.asgteach.appconfigfile.ConfigFileAction"/>
                <attr name="iconBase" stringvalue=
                    "com/asgteach/appconfigfile/Favorites.png"/>
                <attr boolvalue="false" name="noIconInMenu"/>
            </file>
        </folder>
    </folder>
    <folder name="Toolbars">
        <folder name="File">
            <file name="com-asgteach-appuserfile-ConfigFileAction.shadow">
```

```
            <!--com.asgteach.appconfigfile.ConfigFileAction-->
            <attr name="originalFile" stringvalue=
       "Actions/Tools/com-asgteach-appuserfile-ConfigFileAction.instance"/>
            <attr intvalue="350" name="position"/>
          </file>
        </folder>
    </folder>
</filesystem>
```

### Files as Objects

Instance files (file names ending in `.instance`) describe objects created either with a default constructor or a static method. Listing 13.15 shows the instance file for ConfigFileAction. This arrangement lets the application delay instantiating objects (for example, an Action) until it is actually needed. This optimizes startup time and system resources, such as memory.

Shadow files refer to previously referenced instance files and include attribute "originalFile" that references the instance file. The ConfigFileAction is defined in folder Action, where it is described as an instance file. ConfigFileAction is also defined in folder Toolbars, where it is a shadow file linked to the previously described instance file.

### Layer File in Context

Now let's examine the Layer file for the entire application, which you can view under `<this layer in context>`, as shown in Figure 13.17. Here, we've shown the Toolbars folder, which contains the File, Clipboard, and Undo/Redo subfolders. The Config File action appears under the File subfolder.

Other actions contributed by other modules also appear here. In the File subfolder, you see the AlwaysEnabledAction previously added and the Save All action, which is part of the NetBeans Platform.

Similarly, in subfolder Clipboard, you see the Cut, Copy, and Paste actions. The toolbar also includes Undo/Redo. This subfolder refers to the icons in the toolbar fragment in the FileSystemApp application shown in Figure 13.17.

### Removing Layer Configuration Items

In general, you can remove a menu item or other configuration object from your application by deleting its corresponding entry in the Layer file. These items are not actually deleted, however. Rather, their definition is modified in the Layer file to

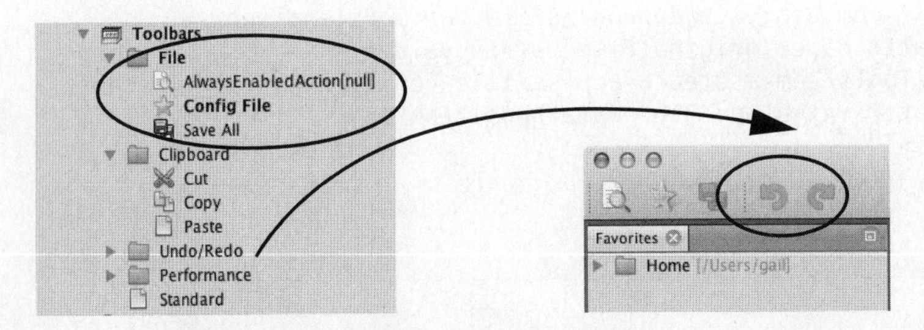


Figure 13.17 Examining a module's XML Layer file

include the suffix "_hidden," which effectively hides that menu item from the configuration. You can also hide individual files (actions or menu items, for example), or you can hide complete folders.

To remove the Undo/Redo folder from the toolbar, select the **Undo/Redo** folder in the Projects view, right click, and select **Delete** from the context menu. Figure 13.18 shows the Projects view Layer file before and after this folder is hidden. The next time you run the application, the Undo/Redo items will not appear in the toolbar, as shown in Figure 13.19.

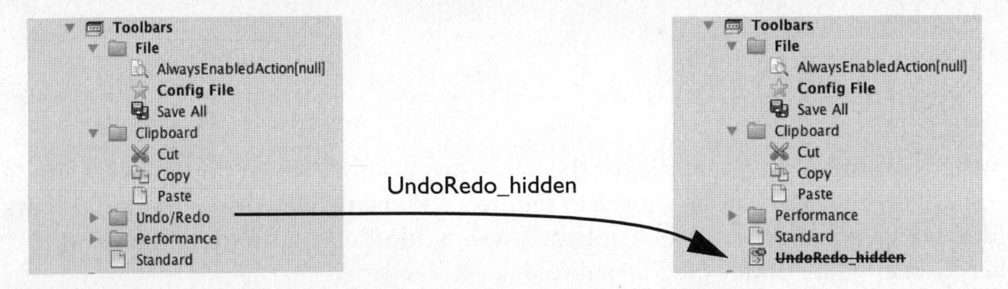


Figure 13.18 Hiding Layer file items

To restore this Layer file entry, right click on the **UndoRedo_hidden** item and select **Restore** from the context menu.

You can also remove items from the Layer file by directly editing their entry in any module's Layer file. For example, to remove the Undo/Redo toolbar items, provide the following modified entry for folder UndoRedo in the local Layer file, as shown in Listing 13.16.

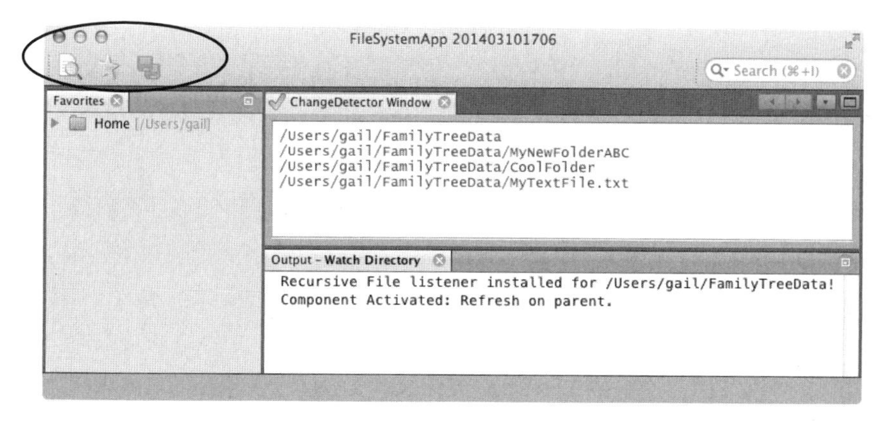


Figure 13.19 Hiding Layer file configuration items

**Listing 13.16 Hiding Undo/Redo Manually in Layer File**

```
<?xml version="1.0" encoding="UTF-8"?>
<!DOCTYPE filesystem PUBLIC "-//NetBeans//DTD Filesystem 1.2//EN" "http://
www.netbeans.org/dtds/filesystem-1_2.dtd">
<filesystem>
    <folder name="Toolbars">
        <folder name="UndoRedo_hidden"/>
    </folder>
</filesystem>
```

To restore this folder, remove the folder name with "_hidden" suffix in the Layer file.

## Exploring the System FileSystem

Let's apply what you've learned about Layer files and the File System API and display the contents of the System FileSystem to the Output window. We'll include all files and folders and color code them according to FileObject type (orange for folders and blue for Files). Furthermore, let's display the attributes for any of the files that have them defined. Figure 13.20 shows this application running.

Here's a summary of the steps we need to display the contents of the System FileSystem.

- Add a new module to the FileSystemApp application called FileSystemViewer.
- Create an Action called View System FileSystem to the Toolbar and under the top-level menu Tools.

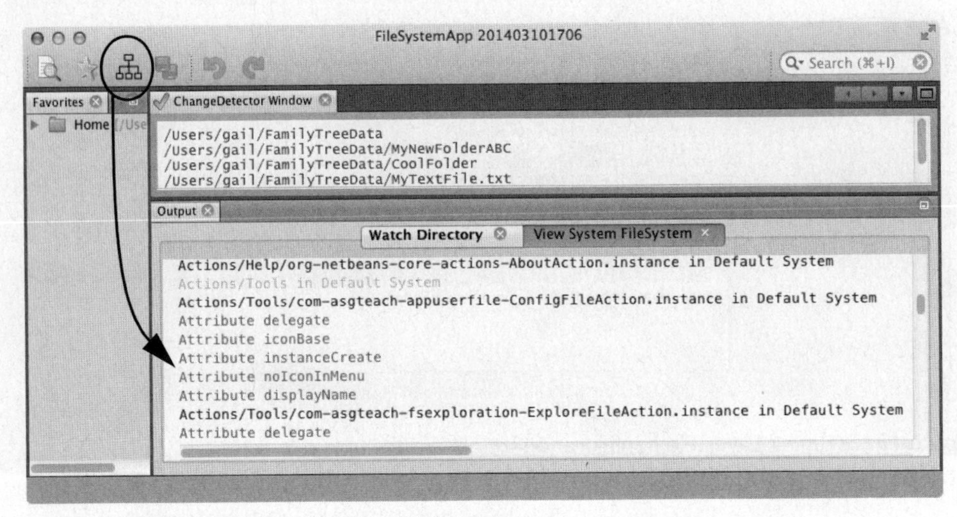


Figure 13.20 Displaying the System FileSystem

- Add dependencies to the File System API, Lookup API, and I/O APIs.
- Implement the action.

## Create Module FileSystemViewer

Use these steps to create module FileSystemViewer in the FileSystemApp application.

1. Expand project FileSystemApp, select the **Modules** node, right-click, and select **New . . . .**
2. NetBeans initiates the New Module Project wizard. In the Name and Location dialog, specify **FileSystemViewer** for Project Name and accept the defaults for the remaining fields. Click **Next**.
3. NetBeans displays the Basic Module Configuration dialog. Specify **com.asgteach.filesystem.viewer** for Code Name Base, accept the defaults for the remaining fields, and click **Finish**.

NetBeans creates module FileSystemViewer in application FileSystemApp.

## Create the View System FileSystem Action

Register a new action in module FileSystemViewer using these steps.

1. In module FileSystemViewer, expand Source Packages and right click on the package name. Select **New | Action** from the context menu.

2. NetBeans initiates the New Action wizard. In the Action Type dialog, select **Always Enabled** and click **Next**.
3. In the GUI Registration dialog, select Category **Tools**. Select the **Global Menu Item** checkbox. Specify Menu **Tools** with position **Here - Tools**, and **Separator After**. Select the **Global Toolbar Button** checkbox. Specify Toolbar **File** and Position **Config File - Here - Save All**. Click **Next**.
4. NetBeans displays the Name, Icon, and Location dialog. For Class Name specify **ViewSysFSAction**. For Display Name specify **View System File System**. Click the **Browse** button and navigate to icon file **fileSysIcon.png**. Click **Finish**.

NetBeans creates ViewSysFSAction.java and copies the icon files to the module's source package.

### Add Module Dependencies

Add module dependencies for File System API (for file actions), Lookup API (certain FileObject operations), and I/O APIs (to write content to the Output window).

### Implement the Action

We show the implementation of the ViewSysFSAction in two parts. Listing 13.17 includes the action's registration annotations and the code that configures the Output window. This code is similar to Listing 13.1 on page 629 (see "The Output Window" on page 628 for a detailed description).

**Listing 13.17 ViewSysFSAction—Registration Annotations**

```
@ActionID(
        category = "Tools",
        id = "com.asgteach.filesystem.viewer.ViewSysFSAction"
)
@ActionRegistration(
        iconBase = "com/asgteach/filesystem/viewer/fileSysIcon.png",
        displayName = "#CTL_ViewSysFSAction"
)
@ActionReferences({
    @ActionReference(path = "Menu/Tools", position = -100,
               separatorAfter = -50),
    @ActionReference(path = "Toolbars/File", position = 375)
})
@Messages("CTL_ViewSysFSAction=View System FileSystem")
public final class ViewSysFSAction implements ActionListener {
    private final InputOutput io;
    private final OutputWriter writer;
```

```
    public ViewSysFSAction() {
        io = IOProvider.getDefault().getIO(
                     Bundle.CTL_ViewSysFSAction(), false);
        writer = io.getOut();
    }
. . .
}
```

Listing 13.18 shows the implementation of the `actionPerformed()` method. Static FileUtil `getConfigRoot()` method returns the root folder of the System FileSystem. We then select the System FileSystem tab and clear the Output window. The file system is displayed by invoking the recursive `displayChildren()` method with the System FileSystem root folder (`root`). The root path is the application project's folder in directory **build/testuserdir/config**, as follows.

```
/[. . . local file system path . . .]/FileSystemApp/build/testuserdir/config
```

Note that some of the configuration information is in the NetBeans Platform distribution, which in our system is as follows.

```
/Applications/NetBeans/NetBeans 8.0.app/Contents/Resources/NetBeans/platform/
config/Modules
```

And some of the folders and files are displayed relative to the Default System, as follows.

```
Actions in Default System
Actions/Window in Default System
```

If the `displayChildren()` argument is a folder, each child returned from the `getChildren()` method is subsequently used as an argument with the `displayChildren()` method.

If the `displayChildren()` argument is a file, a different color is used with the display. The `getAttributes()` method is called for each file and each attribute name is displayed with color magenta.

#### Listing 13.18 ViewSysFSAction—actionPerformed() Method

```
@Override
    public void actionPerformed(ActionEvent e) {
        FileObject root = FileUtil.getConfigRoot();
        // "System FileSystem" tab is created in output window
        io.select();                     // select System FileSystem tab
        try {
            writer.reset();              // clear the output window
            displayChildren(root);
        } catch (IOException ex) {
            Exceptions.printStackTrace(ex);
```

```
        } finally {
            writer.flush();
            writer.close();
        }
    }

    private void displayChildren(FileObject fo) throws IOException {
        if (fo.isFolder()) {            // display folder (orange)
            writeMsg(FileUtil.getFileDisplayName(fo), Color.ORANGE);
            for (FileObject childFileObject : fo.getChildren()) {
                displayChildren(childFileObject);
            }
        } else {                        // display file (blue)
            writeMsg(FileUtil.getFileDisplayName(fo), Color.BLUE);
            Enumeration<String> attrNames = fo.getAttributes();
            while (attrNames.hasMoreElements()) {
                // display attributes (magenta)
              writeMsg("Attribute " + attrNames.nextElement(), Color.MAGENTA);
            }
        }
    }

    private void writeMsg(String str, Color color) {
        try {
            if (IOColorLines.isSupported(io)) {
                IOColorLines.println(io, str, color);
            } else {
                writer.println(str);
            }
        } catch (IOException ex) {
            Exceptions.printStackTrace(ex);
        }
    }
```

## Using the Layer File for Inter-Module Communication

You've seen how you use the Lookup API for inter-module communication. One module can implement a service provider that is available to other modules. The client modules must declare a dependency on the module that defines the interface, but not on the module that provides the implementation. You also use Lookup to manage selection and context sensitivity. This system helps create an application consisting of loosely-coupled modules.

The file system provides another type of inter-module communication. Using the Layer file, a module can register folders and files that another module can use. These folders and files affect the system file system and can be accessed to build any number of application artifacts.

Let's show you an example. Here, we'll modify the FamilyTreeApp we built in a previous chapter (see "Using CRUD with a Database" on page 501) and supply a customized application title using the Layer file. Figure 13.21 shows the application running. The module that implements the FamilyTreeManager using JPA and JavaDB also supplies text for a customized title identifying its persistence strategy.

The module that actually customizes the title, however, is not dependent on the module that provides the customized text. Instead, this information is accessed through the file system.

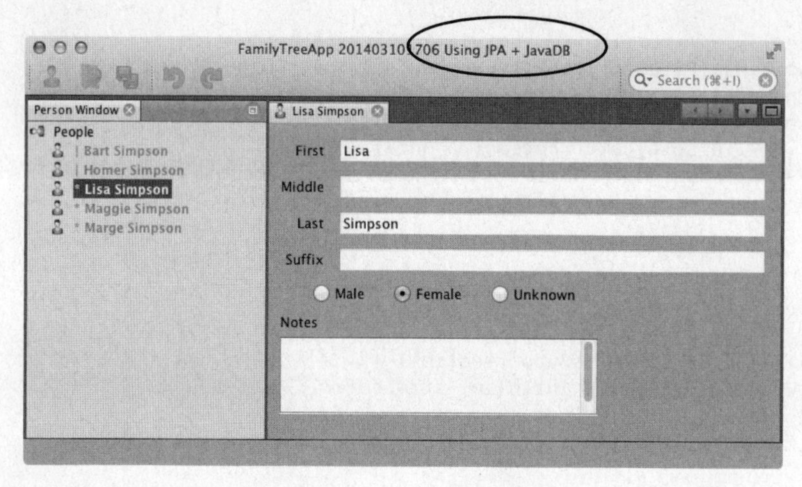


Figure 13.21 Customizing the application title through the Layer file

Here are the steps to build this customized title.

1. Open the **FamilyTreeApp** application in the NetBeans IDE. Expand the **FamilyTreeModel** project.
2. Add Module Dependencies to the **FileSystem API** and the **WindowSystem API**.
3. Under **Source Packages | com.asgteach.familytree.model.data** edit file Installer.java. This Java class is annotated with @OnStart to provide code that executes when the application starts and the module loads (see "Using @OnStart" on page 242).
4. Add code to the `run()` method to read the file system and possibly customize the application title, as shown in Listing 13.19. Note that we must use the `invokeWhenUIReady()` method because code that modifies the UI must run on the EDT. We check for null in case the target folder or attribute does not exist.

**Listing 13.19 Installer.java—Read for System File System to Customize**

```
@OnStart
public final class Installer implements Runnable {
. . .
    @Override
    public void run() {
        FamilyTreeManager ftm =
               Lookup.getDefault().lookup(FamilyTreeManager.class);
        . . .
        // Read configuration information from the system filesystem
        FileObject root = FileUtil.getConfigRoot();
        FileObject persistencetype = root.getFileObject("PersistenceType");
        if (persistencetype != null) {
            final String persistenceTypeName
                    = persistencetype.getAttribute("pTypeName").toString();
            if (persistenceTypeName != null) {
                WindowManager.getDefault().invokeWhenUIReady(() -> {
                    WindowManager.getDefault().getMainWindow().setTitle(
                         WindowManager.getDefault().getMainWindow().getTitle()
                           + " Using "
                           + persistenceTypeName);
                });
            }
        }

    }
```

5. Follow the steps in “Create a Layer File” on page 656 to create a Layer file for the **FamilyTreeManagerJPA** module. This is the module that provides the Family-TreeManager implementation using JPA and JavaDB.
6. Add a folder and attribute to the file system, as shown in Listing 13.20.

**Listing 13.20 Layer.xml—Adding Application Configuration**

```
<?xml version="1.0" encoding="UTF-8"?>
<!DOCTYPE filesystem PUBLIC "-//NetBeans//DTD Filesystem 1.2//EN" "http://
www.netbeans.org/dtds/filesystem-1_2.dtd">
<filesystem>
    <folder name="PersistenceType">
        <attr name="pTypeName" stringvalue="JPA + JavaDB" />
    </folder>
</filesystem>
```

When you run the FamilyTreeApp application, you’ll see the customized application title as shown in Figure 13.21. Another module providing a different persistence strategy could then supply its own “PersistenceType” folder and attribute and similarly affect the application title.

## 13.6 Key Point Summary

This chapter shows you how to use the NetBeans Platform File System API. You learn how to create folders and files in the local file system, how to read and write files, and how to rename and delete files and folders. You learn how to use FileObject attributes and monitor changes within a file system hierarchy, folder, or file with FileChange-Listener. You learn how to include files with your NetBeans Platform application and access them using the File System API. And, you learn about the System FileSystem and Layer file, which define the complete configuration data for a NetBeans Platform application. You see how to customize your application by creating folders, files, and attributes in a module's Layer file. Here are the key points in this chapter.

- The NetBeans Platform File System API lets you manipulate folders and files.
- A FileSystem is a collection of FileObjects. This collection is hierarchical and has a root. The FileSystem abstraction lets you view data from physically different sources in the same way.
- A FileObject represents either a file or folder and is an abstraction above the standard Java File. A FileObject supports file creation, deletion, reading, writing, and accessing attributes with getters and setters.
- FileObjects representing folders let you create subfolders and files. FileObjects also let you access their containing files and folders (children).
- Deleting a FileObject folder performs a recursive delete.
- FileUtil provides static methods for manipulating FileObjects.
- You can add a FileChangeListener to a FileObject (folder or file) and monitor changes to files and folders. You can also add a recursive FileChangeListener to folders in a directory tree.
- FileChangeListener receives events for folder creation, file creation, file (or folder) changes, file (or folder) delete, file (or folder) rename, and file (or folder) attribute changes. There are six methods to override in the FileChangeListener. Alternatively, you can use the FileChangeAdapter adapter class to override only the methods you need.
- The Output window is a predefined TopComponent that supports multiple tabs. This window is convenient for reporting status from different modules.
- The Favorites window lets you view files in your local file system. To add the Favorites window to a NetBeans Platform application, include module Favorites from the platform cluster.
- Add the Templates module to your NetBeans Platform application to let users create empty files and folders from the Favorites window.

- Create folder **release** in the top-level directory of your module to install one or more files in your NetBeans application.
- Access installed files with the `locate()` or `locateAll()` method from InstalledFile-Locator. These methods handle localized files as well.
- To install a module as a PlugIn in the NetBeans IDE, create an NBM file and install it with the PlugIns menu under Tools.
- The Layer file is the gateway to your NetBeans Platform application configuration data. This configuration data is written as a hierarchical file system to disk, called the System FileSystem.
- A module may contribute at most one Layer file. When your application runs, each module's Layer file is read and merged into a single application-wide Layer file.
- Typically, you contribute content to a generated Layer file with annotations. These annotations register services, actions, TopComponents, menu items, toolbar contents, and key bindings.
- You can create a Layer file and view it in context in the Projects view.
- To remove standard NetBeans Platform actions, menu items, and toolbar entries, append the suffix "_hidden" to the entry in a module's Layer file.
- Alternatively, use the context menu **delete** from the Projects view to remove items in the Layer file. Use context menu **restore** to subsequently restore any hidden items.
- You can access an application's System FileSystem programmatically with `FileUtil.getConfigRoot()`. This method returns a FileObject representing the System FileSystem root.
- Customize an application in a loosely-coupled way by having one module register folders and/or files in its Layer file that another module can access.

# 14

# Data System

This chapter explores the Data System API, which is an important bridge between files and nodes. You'll learn how to create file types that are recognized by the NetBeans Platform and how to manipulate these file types using both the File System API and Data System API.

DataObject and DataNode are the main classes in the Data System API. These important classes let you manage files within a NetBeans Platform application.

A MultiView editor lets users examine different views of the same file, typically a text-based view and a Visual view. You'll learn how to use DataObjects to build a MultiView editor. A Visual view creates a Swing JPanel, which lets you add Swing components, Visual Library API widgets (flexible graphical components), or JavaFX content.

Not all NetBeans Platform applications need to make use of the Data System API. If you do not need to integrate new types of files into your application, you probably do not need the Data System API.

## What You Will Learn

- Use the File System, the Data System, and the Nodes APIs to understand the relationship between file, FileObject, DataObject, and node objects.
- Create new file types and register their MIME types, DataLoader, Template File, and MultiView elements.

- Create a MultiView editor based on a text-based MIME type. Learn how to synchronize the underlying document among multiple views.
- Use both the Visual Library and JavaFX to build views in a MultiView editor.
- Build node hierarchies for DataObjects based on file contents.
- Create new XML-based file types with specific root elements.
- Parse XML files with the NetBeans Platform XMLUtil class.
- Incorporate the NetBeans Platform XML editor into a NetBeans Platform application.
- Create conditionally-enabled actions for specific file types.
- Create conditionally-enabled actions for specific MultiView windows.

## 14.1 Data System API Overview

The NetBeans Platform File System API lets you work with files and provides enhanced file manipulation functionality. You've seen how to add arbitrary attributes to files or monitor changes with a FileChangeListener. FileObjects, however, represent raw data. You can't do much with files other than read and write them with IOStream. (You can also read them as an array of bytes or as strings or lines with text files.)

The Data System API, in contrast, is the glue between the Nodes API and the File System API. Its main class, the DataObject, wraps a FileObject, and lets you perform tasks related to particular kinds of files. The nodes associated with a file let you visualize the file within Explorer Views. Nodes, DataObjects, and FileObjects each have a Lookup, which is important for accessing the capabilities associated with a file.

A FileObject has a MIME type. Registered DataLoaders exist for MIME types and create DataObjects subtypes that know something about the file (for example, how to open the file in an appropriate editor). Figure 14.1 shows the relationship between files, FileObject, DataObject, and nodes.

DataLoaders construct a single DataObject for a FileObject. However, sometimes more than one FileObject corresponds to a DataObject. For example, when you edit a Swing Design form using the NetBeans IDE Java editor, a pair of FileObjects correspond to the single DataObject (a .java file and a .form file).

The DataLoader recognizes the FileObject type via its MIME type, creating the DataObject associated with the FileObject. Typically you don't call methods directly on a DataObject. Rather, you ask for capabilities via the DataObject's Lookup and invoke methods on that capability. This is an application of the Capability Pattern

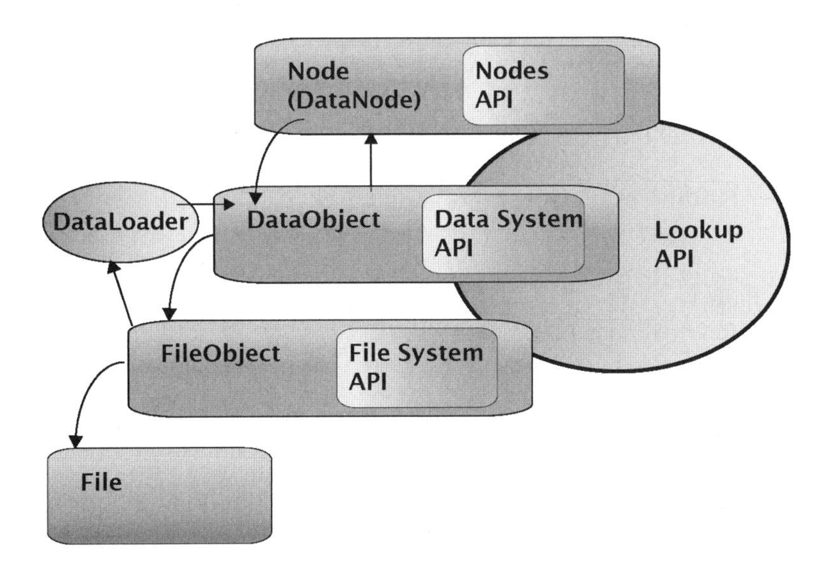


Figure 14.1 Relationship between files, FileObject, DataObject, and nodes

described earlier (see "NetBeans Platform Capability Pattern" on page 428). DataObjects provide programmatic access to files and create models from their contents.

Nodes wrap DataObjects and provide human-readable information in a presentation layer. For example, in the Favorites window, each file and folder is represented by a node. Different file types have different nodes with their own set of actions and icons.

DataLoaders are factories for DataObjects. A FileObject with a particular MIME type has an associated DataLoader that creates a DataObject for that file. A FileObject's MIME type is determined by a MIME type resolver. MIME resolvers are registered in the folder Services/MIMEResolver in a module's layer.

Typically MIME resolvers use a file's extension to determine its MIME type. For XML files, the MIME resolver also looks at the file's root element.

When you create new file types, the New File Type wizard registers a MIME resolver, DataLoader, file template, and DataObject for that file type.

## FileObject, DataObject, and Node

Let's now see how you access these related objects programmatically. To illustrate, we'll access a text file called **myfile.txt**. A file with extension **.txt** is an unknown MIME type and is treated as a generic text file in NetBeans. When you open the Favorites window, **myfile.txt** (if it exists) is shown with a generic document icon.

The code fragments in this section all use custom `displayMessage()` method to write information to the Output window. Furthermore, code is embedded in try blocks with catch handlers for IOException, as shown in Listing 14.1. (See "The Output Window" on page 628 for an introduction to the Output window.)

**Listing 14.1 Helper Method displayMessage() and try Block Code**

```
. . .
    private final InputOutput io;
    private final OutputWriter writer;
    private static final String FILENAME = "myfile.txt";

    public FileManipulations() {
        io = IOProvider.getDefault().getIO(Bundle.CTL_FileManipulations(),
                                    false);
        writer = io.getOut();
    }

    private void displayMessage(String msg) {
        writer.println(msg);
    }

. . .
   // Example code manipulating FileObject, DataObject, and Node
   try {
         . . .

      [See Listing 14.2, Listing 14.3, Listing 14.4,
         Listing 14.5, and Listing 14.6]
         . . .

    } catch (IOException ex) {
      Exceptions.printStackTrace(ex);
    }
```

## FileObject MIME Type and Lookup

Let's begin by accessing file **myfile.txt** as a FileObject. We use the `getFileObject()` method of its parent FileObject folder, as shown in Listing 14.2. The call to `getMIMEType()` returns "**content/unknown**."

FileObjects have a Lookup, which we access to open the file. Here, we look up an implementation of Openable and, if found, invoke its `open()` method to open the file in the NetBeans Platform plain text editor.

**Listing 14.2 FileObjects Have MIME Types and Lookup**

```
   . . .
   // Is there a file called myfile.txt in this folder?
   FileObject myfile = myfolder.getFileObject(FILENAME);
   . . .
   // Show that the FileObject has a MIME Type
   displayMessage(myfile.getNameExt() + " MIME Type: " + myfile.getMIMEType());

   // Show that the FileObject has a lookup
   Openable open_impl = myfile.getLookup().lookup(Openable.class);
   if (open_impl != null) {
      displayMessage("Openable found in fileobject");
      // Open the file (this opens the file in a plain text editor)
      open_impl.open();
   }
```

```
Output Window
myfile.txt MIME Type: content/unknown
Openable found in fileobject
```

## DataObject Factory and DataObject Lookup

The DataLoader lets you access a FileObject's DataObject. DataLoaders are factories for DataObjects and are registered in your application. You use the static DataObject `find()` method to access a FileObject's DataObject as shown in Listing 14.3.

DataObjects also have Lookups. Listing 14.3 shows the equivalent code for opening the file represented by this DataObject. As before, we invoke the Openable method `open()`. If the file is already opened, the plain text editor window receives focus.

**Listing 14.3 Factory Creates DataObject; DataObjects Have a Lookup**

```
   // Find the DataObject associated with the file
   // Use static DataObject method find()
   DataObject dob = DataObject.find(myfile);
   if (dob != null) {
      displayMessage("Found DataObject " + dob.getName() + " for "
                        + myfile.getNameExt());
      // Show that the DataObject also has a Lookup
      open_impl = dob.getLookup().lookup(Openable.class);
      if (open_impl != null) {
         displayMessage("Openable found in dataobject");
         // If already opened, focuses on the Editor Window
         open_impl.open();
      }
. . .
   }
```

```
Output Window
Found DataObject myfile.txt for myfile.txt
Openable found in dataobject
```

## Accessing FileObjects from DataObjects

In many cases, multiple FileObjects can be associated with a DataObject. However, one FileObject is designated as the primary file, which you access with the DataObject `getPrimaryFile()` method. Listing 14.4 shows how to access the FileObject from the DataObject and then read the file's contents using convenience method `asLines()`.

**Listing 14.4 Get FileObject from DataObject and Read Contents**

```
   // Get the FileObject from the DataObject
   FileObject myfob = dob.getPrimaryFile();
   if (myfob != null) {
      displayMessage("Got FileObject " + myfob.getNameExt()
                                         + " from DataObject");
      displayMessage("Display Contents:");
      // Use FileObject to read the contents
      for (String line : myfob.asLines()) {
         displayMessage(line);
      }
   }
```

```
Output Window
Got FileObject myfile.txt from DataObject
Display Contents:
testing
one
two
```

## DataObjects and Nodes

You've already seen how the NetBeans Platform Favorites window displays files and folders from your local file system in an Explorer View. As you may have surmised from Chapter 7 (see "Building a Node Hierarchy" on page 295 for details), each of these folders and files in the Explorer View is a node. Node is the presentation of your data and represents a DataObject, which in turn wraps a FileObject, representing a file on disk.

Nodes not only provide the human-friendly view but also offer a context menu of actions and capabilities stored in its Lookup. You're already familiar with nodes, but a specialized subclass of AbstractNode called *DataNode* wraps DataObjects (see Figure 7.3 on page 295 for a diagram of the Node class hierarchy).

DataObjects create node hierarchies. You invoke the `getNodeDelegate()` method, which returns the DataObject's node. With node, you can now access the familiar objects associated with nodes: actions, icons, and of course, the all-important Lookup.

Listing 14.5 shows how to access the node from the DataObject and access the node's icon and list of actions.

**Listing 14.5 Node from DataObject / Manipulate Node**

```
// Get the Node that represents the DataObject
Node node = dob.getNodeDelegate();
if (node != null) {
   displayMessage("Node is: " + node.getDisplayName());

   // See if the Node has an Icon (Image)
   Image image = node.getIcon(BeanInfo.ICON_COLOR_16x16);
   if (image != null) {
      displayMessage("Got the Node's Icon " + image.toString());
   }

   // Get the Node's Context-Menu Actions
   displayMessage("-------Node Context Menu Actions-------");
   for (Action action : node.getActions(true)) {
      if (action == null) {
         // separator
         displayMessage("-------");
      } else {
         displayMessage("Action " + action.toString());
      }
}
```

```
Output Window
Node is: myfile.txt
Got the Node's Icon BufferedImage@893049b: type = 3 DirectColorModel:
rmask=ff0000 gmask=ff00 bmask=ff amask=ff000000 IntegerInterleavedRaster:
width = 16 height = 16 #Bands = 4 xOff = 0 yOff = 0 dataOffset[0] 0
-------Node Context Menu Actions-------
. . . (output truncated)
```

## Using DataNode and Lookup

Now let's reverse direction and show you how to obtain the DataObject from a node. To use the node directly, you must cast node to DataNode and invoke the `getData-Object()` method. However, a cleaner approach is to use the node's Lookup and obtain its DataObject with the type-safe `lookup()` method. Listing 14.6 shows both approaches.

**Listing 14.6 Get the DataObject from the Node**

```
// Get the DataObject from the DataNode (cumbersome)
if (node instanceof DataNode) {
    // cast to DataNode
    DataNode dataNode = (DataNode) node;
    displayMessage("Node is a DataNode: " + dataNode.getDisplayName());
    DataObject mydob = dataNode.getDataObject();
    if (mydob != null) {
        displayMessage("Got the DataObject from the DataNode: "
                + mydob.getName());
    }
}

// Better to use Lookup (type-safe)
DataObject dob2 = node.getLookup().lookup(DataObject.class);
if (dob2 != null) {
    displayMessage("Got the DataObject from the Node's Lookup: "
                + dob2.getName());
}
```

```
Output Window
Node is a DataNode: myfile.txt
Got the DataObject from the DataNode: myfile.txt
Got the DataObject from the Node's Lookup: myfile.txt
```

## 14.2 Creating a New File Type

Now that you've learned about FileObject, DataObject, and DataNode, let's build an application with a new file type and register this file type in the application. This example shows you how to manipulate FileObjects, DataObjects, and nodes within the context of a NetBeans Platform application. You'll learn how to manipulate particular kinds of files within your program. With the New File Type wizard, you define a MIME type and register a DataLoader, which creates the necessary DataObjects when needed. The wizard also registers a File Template. The application then applies this File Template when a user creates a new file of this type.

Figure 14.2 shows the application running. You see that the Favorites window on the left includes several files with extension **ftr** (the new file type) identified with a special icon. Opening an FTR file brings up the file in a plain text editor in a MultiView window with two tabs labeled Text and Visual. For now, we'll work with just the Text window. We discuss adding functionality to the Visual tab in the next section (see "Working with MultiView Windows" on page 697).

When the user expands the file (clicks the expansion icon in the Favorites window), additional nodes appear based on the file's content. When the user edits the file and

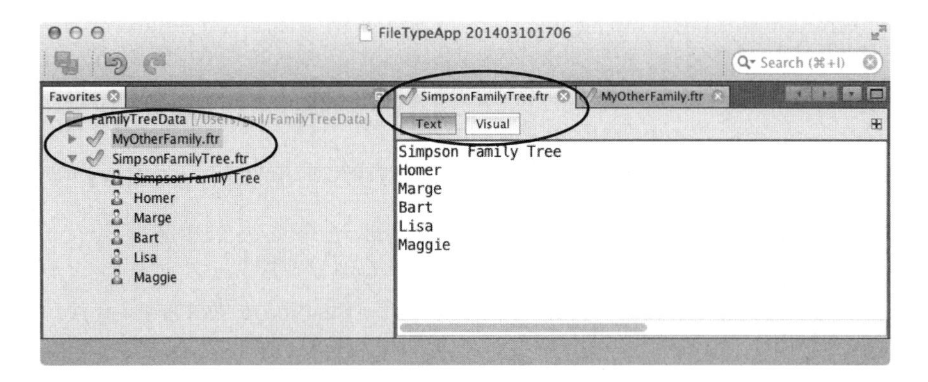


Figure 14.2 FileTypeApp with familytree (ftr) file defined

saves a new version, the Favorites window is synchronized with the new contents. This fairly simple example lets you see the relationship among file, FileObject, DataObject, DataNode, and node.

Because the Favorites window deals with displaying files, this new file type has the expected behaviors associated with files in general. Actions such as copy, delete, and rename are implemented by default. With the Templates module included, you can also create new FTR files, new empty files, and new folders. We also provide a context-sensitive action for this new file type that displays information about the file.

Here's a summary of the steps to build this application and create a new file type.[1]

- Create a new NetBeans Platform application called FileTypeApp.
- Create a new module called FamilyTreeSupport and add it to the FileTypeApp application.
- Add the Favorites and Templates modules to the FileTypeApp application.
- In module FamilyTreeSupport, create a new file type based on extension ftr or FTR (familytree).
- Create a new FTR file and open it for editing.
- Add a custom context-sensitive action to familytree files.

1. Alternatively you can build a NetBeans module *outside* of a NetBeans Platform application. Such a module runs inside a version of the NetBeans IDE, giving you access to all of the IDE's file-oriented features and editors. Here, we show you how to build a non-IDE based application and include just the NetBeans modules you need.

- Provide child nodes based on content. These nodes are displayed when the user expands the file's node in an Explorer View window. Respond to edit changes so the Favorites window is synchronized with the file's edited contents.

## Create a NetBeans Platform Application and Module

Let's begin with the steps to create the application and add the FamilyTreeSupport module.

1. Create a new application called FileTypeApp using the NetBeans Platform New Project wizard.
2. Next, create a Module and add it to the FileTypeApp application. Call the module FamilyTreeSupport and provide package name **com.asgteach.familytreesupport**. The application and module are shown in the Projects view in Figure 14.3.

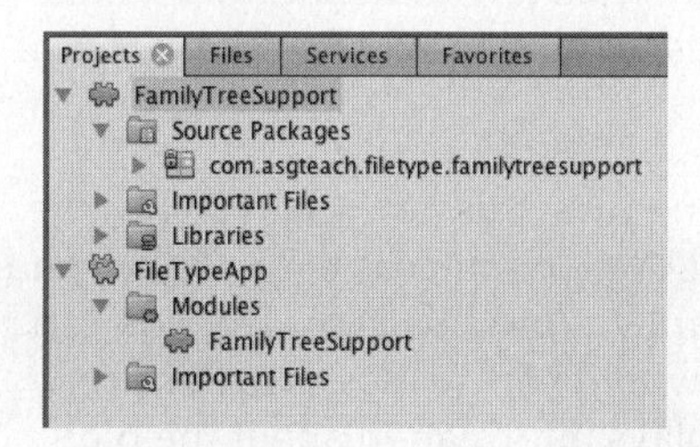


Figure 14.3 FileTypeApp and module FamilyTreeSupport

## Add the Favorites and Templates Modules

The Favorites window is a file viewer for your local disk. See "Favorites Window" on page 637 for a description of this useful module. The Templates module lets you create empty files and folders from the Favorites window. Follow these steps to include both the Favorites and Templates modules in the FamilyTreeApp application.

1. Right click project FileTypeApp in the Projects view and select **Properties** from the context menu.
2. Under Categories, select **Libraries**. NetBeans lists all of the Platform Modules organized in clusters. Under cluster **platform**, select modules **Favorites** and **Templates** and click **OK**.
3. When you run the FileTypeApp application, the Favorites window is now available in the top-level Window menu.

## Create a New File Type

Create a new file type that is recognized by your application. The result of running the New File Type wizard registers a MIME type resolver and a DataLoader that recognizes this MIME type. The wizard also creates and registers a template for this file type and instantiates a DataObject when the user opens a file of this type. The Favorites window displays this file's DataNode with its own icon. Furthermore, the DataNode includes menu items, actions, and properties (and if defined, child nodes).

Here are the steps.

1. In the Projects view, expand module **FamilyTreeSupport | Source Packages**, select the package name, right click, and select **New | Other** from the context menu.
2. In the Choose File Type dialog, under Categories select **Module Development** and under File Types select **File Type**. Click **Next**.
3. NetBeans displays the File Recognition dialog that lets you specify how your application will recognize this new file type. First, specify the MIME Type as **text/x-familytree**. This specifies that the file is a text-based file type called **familytree**. Select radio button **by Filename Extension** and provide one or more extensions. Use extension **ftr** and **FTR**[2], as shown in Figure 14.4. This defines a new MIME type that applies to files with extension **ftr** (or **FTR**). Click **Next**.

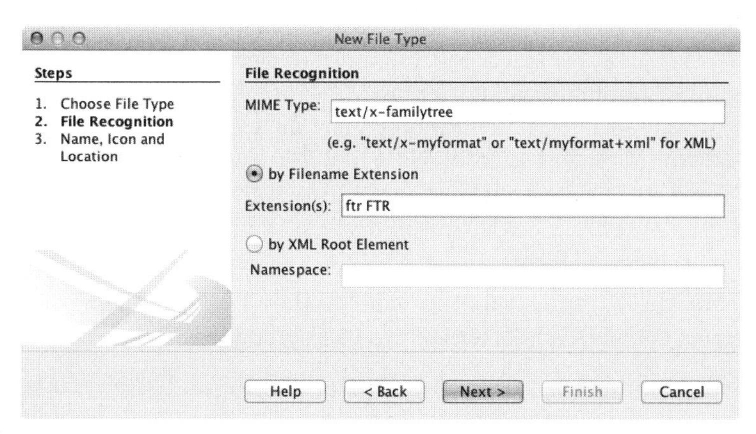


Figure 14.4 New File Type File Recognition dialog

4. NetBeans displays the Name, Icon, and Location dialog. For Class Name Prefix, specify **FamilyTree**. Click the **Browse** button and navigate to the provided icon file **check.png**. Make sure the **Use MultiView** checkbox is selected and accept the defaults for the remaining fields, as shown in Figure 14.5. Click **Finish**.

2. Do not include a "dot" preceding the file extension in the dialog.

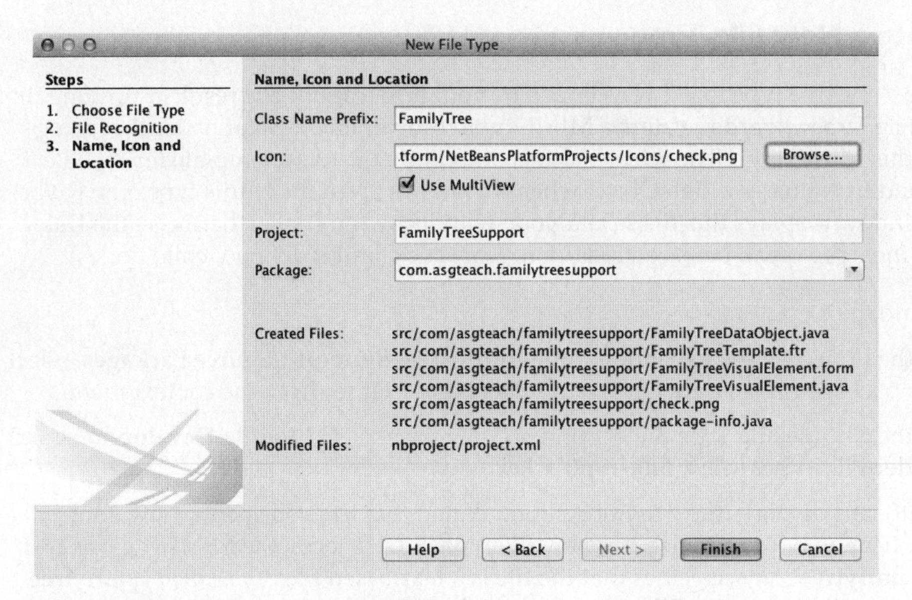


Figure 14.5 Name, Icon, and Location dialog

Now let's examine the files that NetBeans creates to support this new file type.

- **FamilyTreeDataObject.java**—This is a generated DataObject class that wraps a FileObject for FTR files. Annotations register the MIME type, the file's icon, an editor, and typical actions associated with Explorer View file elements: Open, Copy, Cut, Paste, Delete, Properties, and so forth. Note that this class extends MultiDataObject, which is a subclass of DataObject. MultiDataObjects are DataObjects that can handle more than one FileObject. Listing 14.7 on page 683 and Listing 14.8 on page 685 show this generated file.
- **FamilyTreeTemplate.ftr**—This file is the template used by the New File wizard when the user creates a new FTR file (see Listing 14.10 on page 687).
- **FamilyTreeVisualElement.java**—This Java file extends JPanel and implements MultiViewElement, which provides similar life cycle methods as TopComponents (see Listing 14.9 on page 685). MultiViewElement is one of perhaps several that provide different representations of the same file. This JPanel can hold Swing components, Visual Library elements, or even JavaFX components with the JFXPanel control.
- **check.png**—This is the 16 x 16 graphic icon attached to FTR files.
- **package-info.java**—This Java file registers FamilyTreeTemplate.ftr for the New File wizard (see Listing 14.11 on page 688).

Let's look at the FamilyTreeDataObject first. Listing 14.7 includes the annotations that register the MIME resolver and the actions available for this file type.

**Listing 14.7 FamilyTreeDataObject—Registration Information**

```
@Messages({
    "LBL_FamilyTree_LOADER=Files of FamilyTree"
})
@MIMEResolver.ExtensionRegistration(
        displayName = "#LBL_FamilyTree_LOADER",
        mimeType = "text/x-familytree",
        extension = {"ftr", "FTR"}
)
@DataObject.Registration(
        mimeType = "text/x-familytree",
        iconBase = "com/asgteach/familytreesupport/check.png",
        displayName = "#LBL_FamilyTree_LOADER",
        position = 300
)
@ActionReferences({
    @ActionReference(
            path = "Loaders/text/x-familytree/Actions",
            id = @ActionID(category = "System",
                           id = "org.openide.actions.OpenAction"),
            position = 100,
            separatorAfter = 200
    ),
    @ActionReference(
            path = "Loaders/text/x-familytree/Actions",
            id = @ActionID(category = "Edit",
                           id = "org.openide.actions.CutAction"),
            position = 300
    ),
    @ActionReference(
            path = "Loaders/text/x-familytree/Actions",
            id = @ActionID(category = "Edit",
                           id = "org.openide.actions.CopyAction"),
            position = 400,
            separatorAfter = 500
    ),
    @ActionReference(
            path = "Loaders/text/x-familytree/Actions",
            id = @ActionID(category = "Edit",
                           id = "org.openide.actions.DeleteAction"),
            position = 600
    ),
```

```
    @ActionReference(
            path = "Loaders/text/x-familytree/Actions",
            id = @ActionID(category = "System",
                           id = "org.openide.actions.RenameAction"),
            position = 700,
            separatorAfter = 800
    ),
    @ActionReference(
            path = "Loaders/text/x-familytree/Actions",
            id = @ActionID(category = "System",
                           id = "org.openide.actions.SaveAsTemplateAction"),
            position = 900,
            separatorAfter = 1000
    ),
    @ActionReference(
            path = "Loaders/text/x-familytree/Actions",
            id = @ActionID(category = "System",
                           id = "org.openide.actions.FileSystemAction"),
            position = 1100,
            separatorAfter = 1200
    ),
    @ActionReference(
            path = "Loaders/text/x-familytree/Actions",
            id = @ActionID(category = "System",
                           id = "org.openide.actions.ToolsAction"),
            position = 1300
    ),
    @ActionReference(
            path = "Loaders/text/x-familytree/Actions",
            id = @ActionID(category = "System",
                           id = "org.openide.actions.PropertiesAction"),
            position = 1400
    )
})
public class FamilyTreeDataObject extends MultiDataObject {
. . .
}
```

Listing 14.8 shows the remaining code for class FamilyTreeDataObject. The DataObject registers an editor for the appropriate MIME type and includes a static method to create a MultiViewEditorElement (see the related FamilyTreeVisualElement.java in Listing 14.9 on page 685). We also change the button's label for the plain text editor to **Text** from the default label **Source**.

Because we register a text editor here, the DataObject includes an EditorCookie in its Lookup. This makes it possible to access the editor's underlying model (a Swing text document) that reflects the current state of user edits.

**Listing 14.8 FamilyTreeDataObject—File Loader and MultiElement Registration**

```
. . .
public class FamilyTreeDataObject extends MultiDataObject {

    public FamilyTreeDataObject(FileObject pf, MultiFileLoader loader)
                        throws DataObjectExistsException, IOException {
        super(pf, loader);
        registerEditor("text/x-familytree", true);
    }

    @Override
    protected int associateLookup() {
        return 1;
    }

    @MultiViewElement.Registration(
            displayName = "#LBL_FamilyTree_EDITOR",
            iconBase = "com/asgteach/familytreesupport/check.png",
            mimeType = "text/x-familytree",
            persistenceType = TopComponent.PERSISTENCE_ONLY_OPENED,
            preferredID = "FamilyTree",
            position = 1000
    )
    @Messages("LBL_FamilyTree_EDITOR=Text")
    public static MultiViewEditorElement createEditor(Lookup lkp) {
        return new MultiViewEditorElement(lkp);
    }
}
```

Listing 14.9 shows the FamilyTreeVisualElement, which is similar in structure to TopComponent. The FamilyTreeVisualElement has a Lookup, a generated design section, actions that can be defined, and window life cycle methods. The MultiViewElement also includes field MultiViewElementCallback, which provides access to the enclosing TopComponent.

Method `getVisualRepresentation()` returns JComponent, the instance of the MultiViewElement, and is invoked whenever this view is activated. The default implementation returns **`this`**.

We'll return to this file when we add visual components.

**Listing 14.9 FamilyTreeVisualElement.java**

```
@MultiViewElement.Registration(
        displayName = "#LBL_FamilyTree_VISUAL",
        iconBase = "com/asgteach/familytreesupport/check.png",
```

```
        mimeType = "text/x-familytree",
        persistenceType = TopComponent.PERSISTENCE_NEVER,
        preferredID = "FamilyTreeVisual",
        position = 2000
)
@Messages("LBL_FamilyTree_VISUAL=Visual")
public final class FamilyTreeVisualElement extends JPanel
                              implements MultiViewElement {

    private FamilyTreeDataObject ftDataObject;
    private JToolBar toolbar = new JToolBar();
    private transient MultiViewElementCallback callback;

    public FamilyTreeVisualElement(Lookup lkp) {
        ftDataObject = lkp.lookup(FamilyTreeDataObject.class);
        assert obj != null;
        initComponents();
    }

    @Override
    public String getName() {
        return "FamilyTreeVisualElement";
    }
. . .
   **Generated Matisse Design Code***
. . .
    @Override
    public JComponent getVisualRepresentation() {
        return this;
    }

    @Override
    public JComponent getToolbarRepresentation() {
        return toolbar;
    }

    @Override
    public Action[] getActions() {
        return new Action[0];
    }

    @Override
    public Lookup getLookup() {
        return ftDataObject.getLookup();
    }
    @Override
    public void componentOpened() {
    }
```

```
    @Override
    public void componentClosed() {
    }

    @Override
    public void componentShowing() {
    }

    @Override
    public void componentHidden() {
    }

    @Override
    public void componentActivated() {
    }

    @Override
    public void componentDeactivated() {
    }

    @Override
    public UndoRedo getUndoRedo() {
        return UndoRedo.NONE;
    }

    @Override
    public void setMultiViewCallback(MultiViewElementCallback callback) {
        this.callback = callback;
    }

    @Override
    public CloseOperationState canCloseElement() {
        return CloseOperationState.STATE_OK;
    }

}
```

Listing 14.10 shows the Template file, which you customize for your application as we have here. NetBeans uses the Template file as a starting point when a user creates a new FTR file.

**Listing 14.10 FamilyTreeTemplate.ftr**

```
FAMILY Family Tree
```

Listing 14.11 shows how the Template file is registered with the generated package-info.java.

**Listing 14.11 package-info.java**

```
@TemplateRegistration(folder = "Other", content = "FamilyTreeTemplate.ftr")
package com.asgteach.familytreesupport;

import org.netbeans.api.templates.TemplateRegistration;
```

All of this registration information is included in the module's generated-layer.xml file when you build the module. The generated Layer file registers the FamilyTree FTR file type with `<folder>`, `<file>`, and `<attr>` tags that specify configuration information available through the System FileSystem (see "The Layer File and System FileSystem" on page 654).

The main folder names include editors to register the MultiView editor for text-based x-familytree type files, Services/MIMEResolvers to describe the MIME Resolver for FamilyTreeDataObject, loaders for both actions and factories with text/x-familytree files, and Templates to register FamilyTreeTemplate.ftr for creating new files of this type.

## Create and Edit a New FTR File

With the FamilyTree file type defined, let's run the application and create a new FTR file, as follows.

1. Run the FileTypeApp application and open the Favorites window.
2. From the Favorites window, select a folder, right click, and select **New | All Templates**. The application displays the Choose Template dialog. Select **FamilyTreeTemplate.ftr**, as shown in Figure 14.6. Click **Next**.

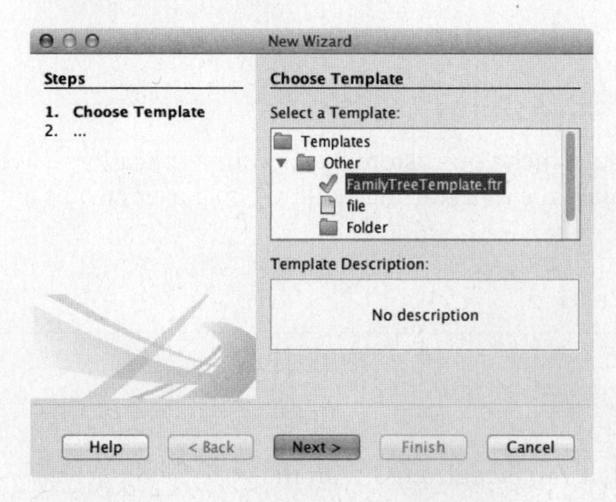


Figure 14.6 Choose Template dialog

3. The application now displays the New Object Name dialog. Specify a name for the new file, as shown in Figure 14.7. Click **Finish**.

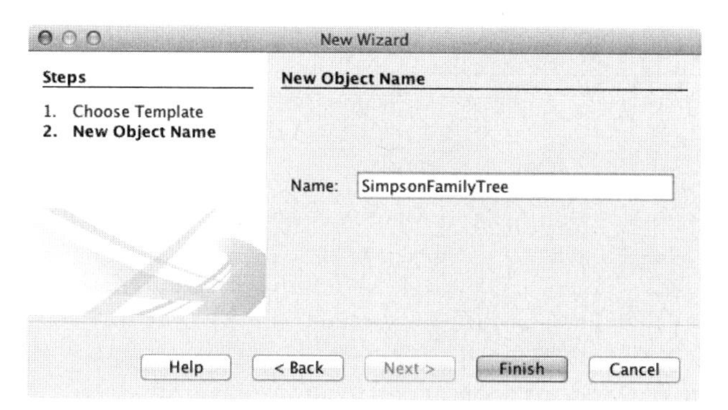


Figure 14.7 New Object Name dialog

4. Figure 14.8 shows the new file created (**SimpsonFamilyTree.ftr**) in the Favorites window and opened in the FamilyTree MultiView editor.

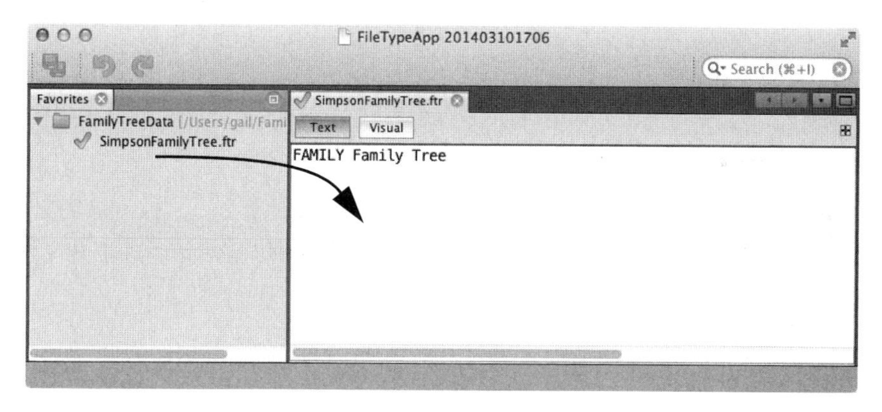


Figure 14.8 Editing file SimpsonFamilyTree.ftr

5. Edit the file and provide the Simpson Family names, as shown in Figure 14.9. Note that as you edit the file, the Save All icon is enabled. When you click the Save All icon, the changes are saved to the SimpsonFamilyTree.ftr file.

## Context-Sensitive Action

To add a context-sensitive action to your file as it's displayed in an Explorer View, you create a conditionally-enabled action (see "Context-Aware Actions" on page 428 in

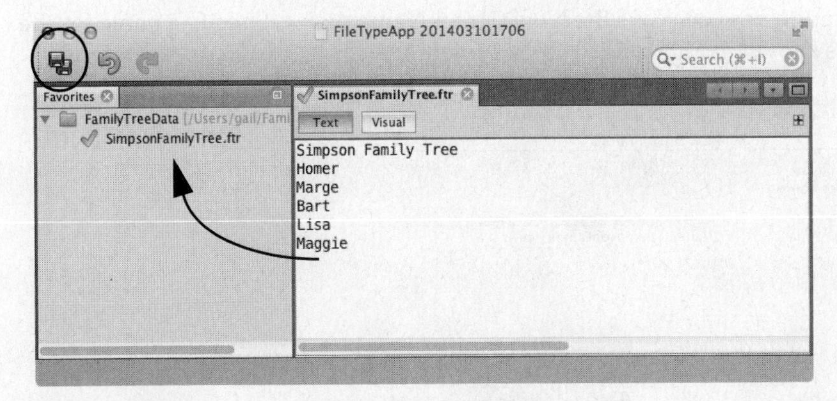


Figure 14.9 Plain text editor for FileTypeApp application

Chapter 9 for more information). Here, we add a Get Info action for our file type to the FamilyTreeSupport module, which displays an Information Dialog, as shown in Figure 14.10.

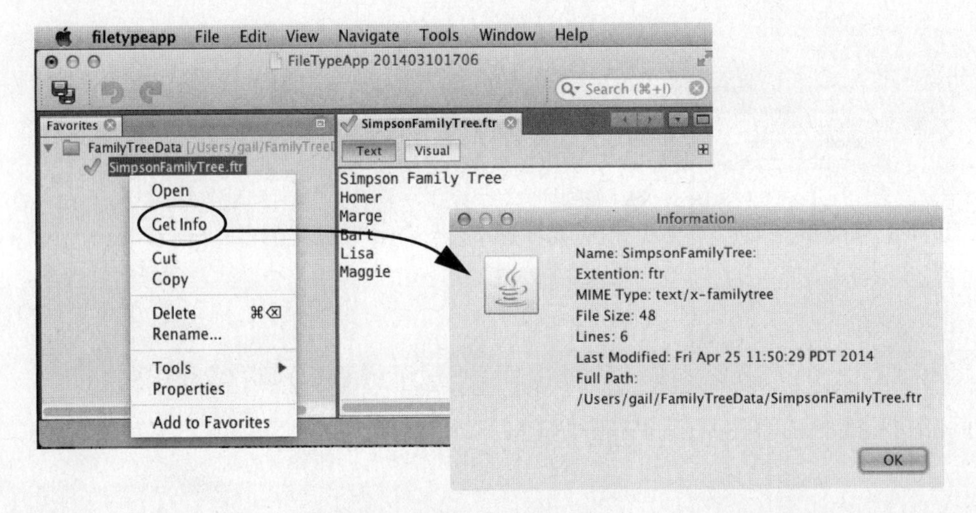


Figure 14.10 Get Info action added to file's context menu

Note that the file's context menu also includes typical file-type actions, such as Open, Cut, Copy, Delete, Rename, Tools, Properties, and Add to Favorites (because we're using the Favorites window).

Follow these steps to add this context-sensitive action to the `text/x-familytree` file type.

1. In the FamilyTreeSupport module Source Packages, right click on the package name and select **New | Action**.
2. In the Action Type dialog, select **Conditionally Enabled**. For the Cookie Class, specify **FamilyTreeDataObject**, which is the DataObject type for this file type. Select radio button **User Selects One Node** and click **Next**, as shown in Figure 14.11.

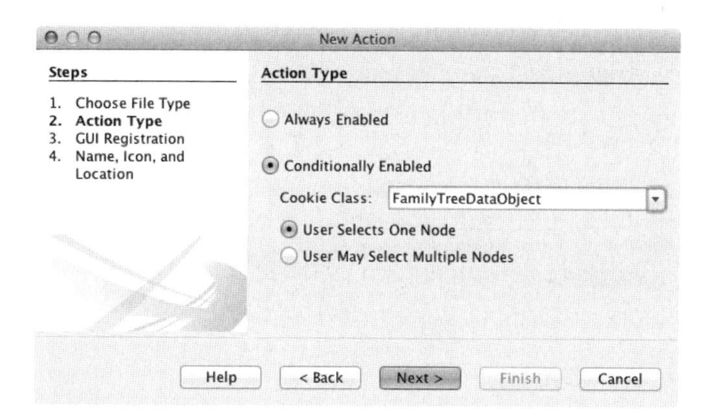


Figure 14.11 New Action Type dialog

3. Figure 14.12 shows the GUI Registration dialog. Register an action both in the top-level menu under File and in the context menu of this particular file type. Select **Global Menu File** and choose a position. Select **File Type Context Menu Item** and **text/x-familytree** from the drop down list for the context type. Click **Finish**. (Note that the Get Info action in the File menu will only be enabled if a file of type **text/x-familytree** is selected.)

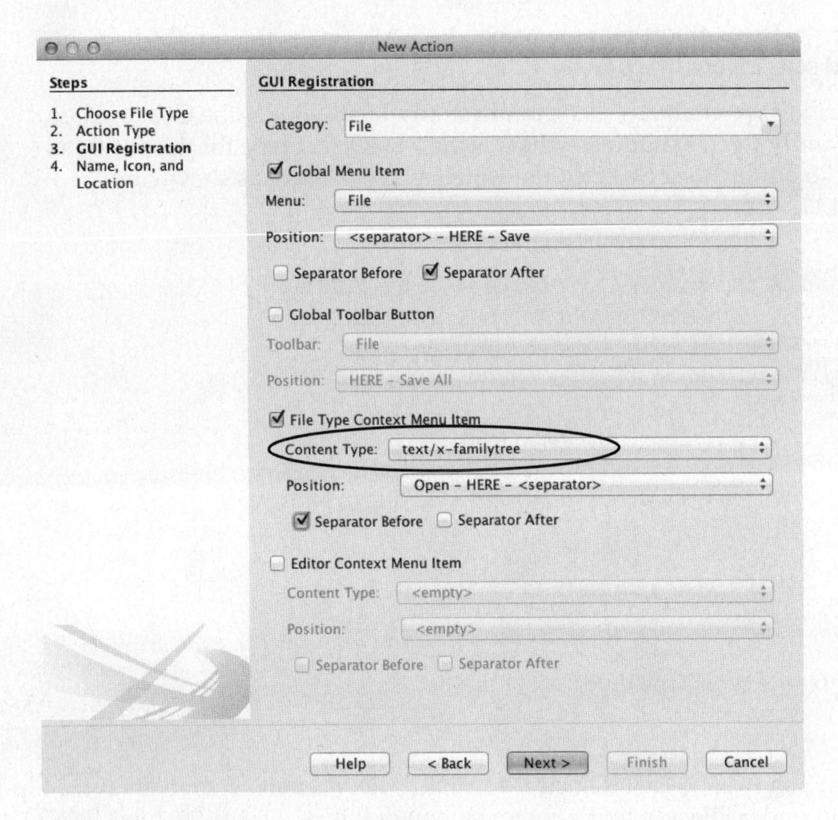


Figure 14.12 New Action GUI Registration for File Type Context Menu

4. NetBeans next displays the Name, Icon, and Location dialog shown in Figure 14.13. For Class Name specify **GetInfoAction** and for Display Name specify **Get Info**. Optionally provide an icon (for the top-level Menu item; context menus do not include icons). Accept the defaults for the remaining fields and click **Finish**.

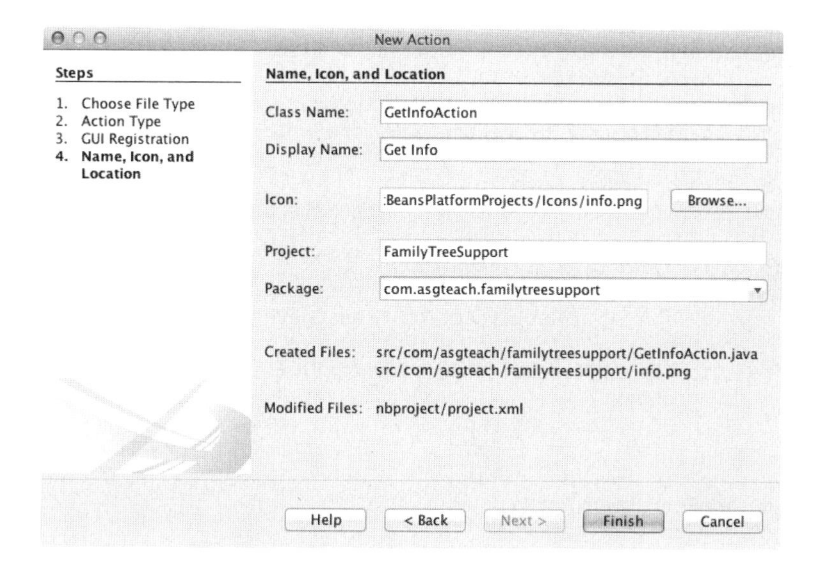


Figure 14.13 New Action Name, Icon and Location dialog

Listing 14.12 shows **GetInfoAction.java**, which includes annotations that register this action. We add code to the `actionPerformed()` method to pop up a dialog with information about the file. The Get Info action displays the selected file's name, extension, MIME type, the number of bytes, the number of lines, its last modification date, and its full path, as shown in Figure 14.10 on page 690.

Of interest is the @ActionReference with path `"Loaders/text/x-familytree/Actions,"` which adds this action to the context menu of these file types (identified by the appropriate DataLoader).

The context is type FamilyTreeDataObject, which we specified in the New Action wizard.

### Listing 14.12 GetInfoAction.java

```
@ActionID(
        category = "File",
        id = "com.asgteach.familytreesupport.GetInfoAction"
)
@ActionRegistration(
        iconBase = "com/asgteach/familytreesupport/info.png",
        displayName = "#CTL_GetInfoAction"
)
```

```
@ActionReferences({
    @ActionReference(path = "Menu/File", position = 1450,
                    separatorAfter = 1475),
    @ActionReference(path = "Loaders/text/x-familytree/Actions",
                    position = 150, separatorBefore = 125)
})
@Messages("CTL_GetInfoAction=Get Info")
public final class GetInfoAction implements ActionListener {

    private final FamilyTreeDataObject context;
    private static final Logger logger = Logger.getLogger(
                                GetInfoAction.class.getName());

    public GetInfoAction(FamilyTreeDataObject context) {
        this.context = context;
    }

    @Override
    public void actionPerformed(ActionEvent ev) {
        FileObject f = context.getPrimaryFile();
        String displayName = FileUtil.getFileDisplayName(f);
        String name = f.getName();
        StringBuilder sb = new StringBuilder("Name: ").append(name);
        sb.append(":\nExtension: ").append(FileUtil.getExtension(displayName));
        sb.append("\nMIME Type: ").append(FileUtil.getMIMEType(f));
        try {
            sb.append("\nFile Size: ").append(f.getSize());
            sb.append("\nLines: ").append(f.asLines().size());
            sb.append("\nLast Modified: ").append(f.lastModified());
            sb.append("\nFull Path:\n").append(f.getPath());
            NotifyDescriptor nd = new NotifyDescriptor.Message(sb.toString());
            DialogDisplayer.getDefault().notify(nd);
        } catch (IOException e) {
            logger.log(Level.WARNING, null, e);
        }
    }
}
```

The `actionPerformed()` method obtains the FileObject from the DataObject context. With the FileObject, we can display the file name, the extension, MIME type, length in bytes, number of lines, the last modification data, and the file's full path. The standard NotifyDescriptor and DialogDisplayer pop up an Information dialog and block until dismissed by the user. (See "NotifyDescriptor.Message" on page 527 for more on the NotifyDescriptor dialogs.)

## Provide Child Nodes Based on Content

The FamilyTreeDataObject (see Listing 14.8 on page 685) instantiates a MultiView editor when the user opens an FTR file. The generated code does not include the overloaded `createNodeDelegate()` method. Instead FamilyTreeDataObject relies on a default implementation inherited from DataObject. The `createNodeDelegate()` method returns a node (typically a DataNode) that represents this DataObject in an Explorer View. The default method sets the icon and display name and adds the DataObject to the node's Lookup.

To customize this default behavior, override the `createNodeDelegate()` method. For this example, we create a list of child nodes, one for each line in the FTR text file. The Favorites window automatically displays these child nodes when the user expands the file's node (see Figure 14.14 on page 697). The Favorites window must also be synchronized as users edit and save changes to the file.

As shown previously, a ChildFactory creates child nodes (for Person objects, see Listing 7.2 on page 300). Listing 14.13 shows the overridden `createNodeDelegate()` method, which likewise uses private class FamilyTreeChildFactory to create child nodes. Note that the FamilyTreeDataObject is included (`this`) in both the DataNode constructor and the FamilyTreeChildFactory constructor.

The FamilyTreeChildFactory has three tasks.

- Add a FileChangeListener to the underlying FileObject and refresh its data when receiving a file change event. This keeps the Favorites window synchronized when the user edits an FTR file. Here, we use the FileChangeAdapter class, since we only care about file change events. (We discuss FileChangeListeners in "Monitoring File Changes" on page 636.) The `refresh()` method rebuilds the child node hierarchy as needed.
- In the `createKeys()` method, parse the file, adding a String-based key to its underlying list of keys. (Blank lines are ignored.)
- In the `createNodeForKey()` method, create an AbstractNode based on the String `key` (line of text), using the personIcon.png graphic for the icon.

We discuss nodes, ChildFactory, and creating node hierarchies in detail in Chapter 7 (see "Building a Node Hierarchy" on page 295).

**Listing 14.13 FamilyTreeDataObject and FamilyTreeChildFactory**

```
public class FamilyTreeDataObject extends MultiDataObject {
   . . .
    @Override
    protected Node createNodeDelegate() {
        return new DataNode(this, Children.create(
                new FamilyTreeChildFactory(this), true), getLookup());
    }
```

```
    private static class FamilyTreeChildFactory extends ChildFactory<String> {

        private final FileObject fileObject;

        public FamilyTreeChildFactory(FamilyTreeDataObject dataObject) {
            fileObject = dataObject.getPrimaryFile();
            fileObject.addFileChangeListener(new FileChangeAdapter() {
                @Override
                public void fileChanged(FileEvent fe) {
                    refresh(true);
                }
            });
        }

        @Override
        protected boolean createKeys(List<String> list) {
            // create a String for each line in the file
            try {
                // skip blank lines
                for (String line : fileObject.asLines()) {
                    if (!line.isEmpty()) {
                        list.add(line);
                    }
                }
            } catch (IOException ex) {
                Exceptions.printStackTrace(ex);
            }
            return true;
        }

        @Override
        protected Node createNodeForKey(String key) {
            AbstractNode childNode = new AbstractNode(Children.LEAF);
            childNode.setDisplayName(key);
            childNode.setIconBaseWithExtension(
                    "com/asgteach/familytreesupport/personIcon.png");
            return childNode;
        }
    }
}
```

These changes create two enhancements. First, the Favorites window displays each line of text with a node. Second, as you edit an FTR file and save it (click **Save All** in the top-level toolbar), the Favorites window refreshes with the new file contents, as shown in Figure 14.14.

The NetBeans default text editor handles installing and subsequently removing a Savable in the TopComponent's Lookup as a user makes and saves changes. (See "Implement Openable and SavablePersonCapability" on page 500 for examples on working with Savable.)

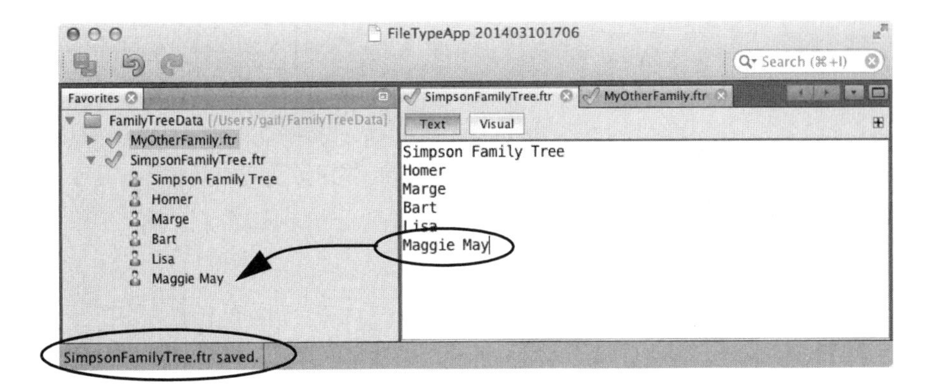


Figure 14.14 FileTypeApp synchronized Favorites window and text editor

## 14.3 Working with MultiView Windows

The FamilyTreeDataObject includes support for MultiView windows. A MultiView editor is a TopComponent with more than one embedded window, called a MultiViewElement. MultiViewElements are selectable with buttons in a toolbar that let you switch views. Our FileTypeApp has a window labeled Text that displays a plain text editor. The editor is completely supplied by the NetBeans Platform. The other window labeled Visual is currently empty (blank).

Let's add a Visual view of our file now so that users can switch between the text editor and the Visual view. As users make edits in the Visual view, these changes appear in the Text view and vice versa. Thus, both views access the same underlying document model that is synchronized as users edit the file. A change made through either view enables the Save All toolbar icon, and after saving, the Favorites window shows the updated contents.

Figure 14.15 shows the FileTypeApp with file **SimpsonFamilyTree.ftr** opened in the Visual view of the FTR editor. The Visual view uses the NetBeans Platform Visual Library to create movable widgets corresponding to each line in the FTR file. In this screenshot, the user is editing element Bart. The changes have not yet been saved to the file (so the Favorites window is not yet updated), and the Save All icon is enabled reflecting a modification to the underlying model.

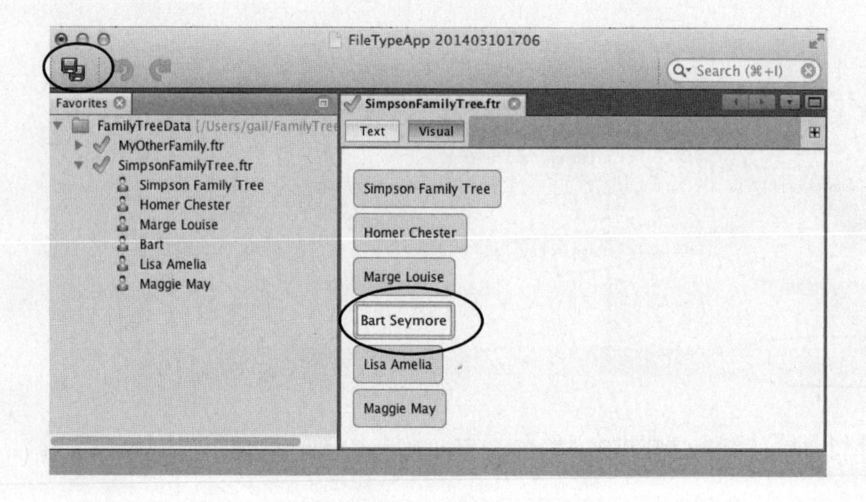


Figure 14.15 Editing with the FileTypeApp Visual view

At any time, users can select the Text button in the editor's toolbar to activate the Text view of this file, as shown in Figure 14.16. Here, you see the edited contents from the underlying document model.

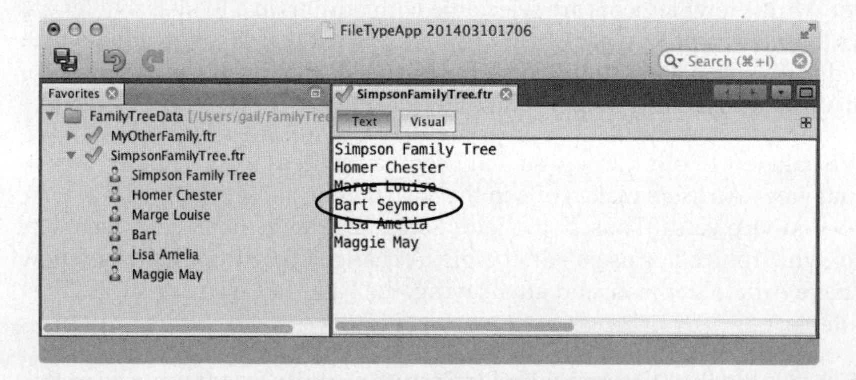


Figure 14.16 Keeping the Text and Visual views synchronized

When users click either the **Save All** icon or the **File | Save** menu item, the Favorites window shows the saved contents, as shown in Figure 14.17. The Save All icon is then disabled.

Now let's show you how to create a visual element with the Visual Library and keep the underlying document model consistent among multiple views.

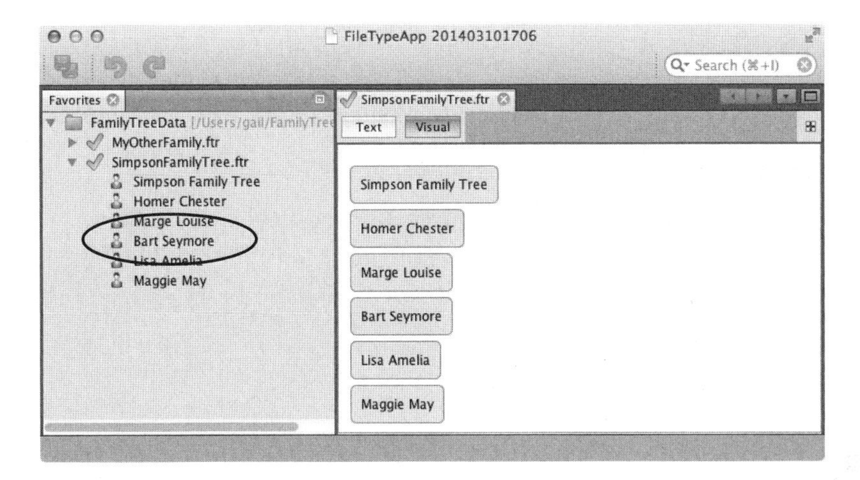


Figure 14.17 Saving refreshes the Favorites window

## Using the Visual Library

A complete description of the Visual Library is beyond the scope of this book, but we can provide a cursory outline to get you started. As its name implies, the Visual Library lets you create views with selectable, movable, and changeable graphical components called *widgets*. When you build a view with the Visual Library, you construct a Scene, which is a specialized widget that consists of a tree structure of widgets. The Scene is the root element and creates a Swing-compatible JComponent view that you can add to a Swing component.

To create actions for widgets, use ActionFactory and add them to the widgets with method `addAction()`. Some ActionFactory methods require a provider (such as the EditAction). Other actions have default providers (such as the MoveAction). In this application, we add both a MoveAction and an in-place editor action, using an implementation of TextFieldInplaceEditor.

A widget can be a container for additional widgets and also have a layout. Our example uses LayoutWidget (a transparent widget that has a layout and holds other widgets) and a LabelWidget (a widget that displays text).

A default NetBeans Platform application does not include the Visual Library API module. Therefore, before you can set a dependency on this module, you must first include the module in your application's build. Here are the steps.

1. In the Projects view, right click on the FileTypeApp project and select **Properties** from the context menu.

2. In the Project Properties dialog under Categories, select **Libraries**.
3. In the list of Platform Modules, scroll down and expand cluster **platform**.
4. Scroll to the end of the platform cluster, select **Visual Library API**, and click **OK**.

Now you can set a dependency on this module, as follows.

1. In the Projects view, expand project FamilyTreeSupport, right click on the **Libraries** node, and select **Add Module Dependency . . .** from the context menu.
2. In the list of modules, scroll down to the end, select **Visual Library API**, and click **OK**.

### Building a Scene and Adding Widgets

Let's now return to FamilyTreeVisualElement.java and build a Scene with widgets for each text line in the file. This requires a set of LabelWidgets (one for each non-empty text line) based on the opened document from the FTR file. Because the Family-TreeDataObject is configured with a file type and registered editor, we can access both the editor and the underlying document through the FamilyTreeDataObject Lookup.

Although this example is basic, you will see how the MultiViewElement's life cycle methods synchronize the underlying model when changes are made. Listing 14.14 shows the FamilyTreeVisualElement with added fields and a modified constructor, which now builds a Scene from the Visual Library.

The LayoutWidget field `layer` has a layout and is a container for other widgets. We use the default layout, which provides absolute positioning. We obtain the Editor-Cookie from the FamilyTreeDataObject Lookup and use it to access the underlying document model (StyledDocument). Field `scene` is the top-level Visual Library Scene object that creates a Swing-compatible view. Finally, `border` is a reusable Border element constructed through the Visual Library's BorderFactory and provides a rounded border with a yellow background in all of the LabelWidgets.

The constructor includes code to set the JPanel's layout (BorderLayout), instantiate the LayerWidget and add it to the Scene, and add the Scene's view to a Swing JScrollPane.

**Listing 14.14 FamilyTreeVisualElement—Adding Widgets**

```
@Messages("LBL_FamilyTree_VISUAL=Visual")
public final class FamilyTreeVisualElement extends JPanel
                                    implements MultiViewElement {

    private final FamilyTreeDataObject ftDataObject;
```

```
    private final JToolBar toolbar = new JToolBar();
    private transient MultiViewElementCallback callback;
    private final LayerWidget layer;
    private EditorCookie editCookie = null;
    private StyledDocument doc = null;
    private final Scene scene = new Scene();
    private final Border border = BorderFactory.createRoundedBorder(
                                    10, 10, Color.yellow, Color.gray);
    private static final Logger logger = Logger.getLogger(
                       FamilyTreeVisualElement.class.getName());

    public FamilyTreeVisualElement(Lookup lkp) {
        ftDataObject = lkp.lookup(FamilyTreeDataObject.class);
        assert ftDataObject != null;
        initComponents();
        setLayout(new BorderLayout());
        layer = new LayerWidget(scene);
        scene.addChild(layer);
        add(new JScrollPane(scene.createView()));
    }
. . .
}
```

Similar to TopComponents, MultiViewElements implement overridden life cycle methods that let you control how a MultiViewElement is initialized and refreshed. Here we use the `componentShowing()` method to initialize the widgets in the Scene from the open document. The `componentShowing()` method is invoked each time the user switches views and also when the application starts up with this view showing. (See "Window System Life Cycle Management" on page 369 for a description of these life cycle methods.) We use the DataObject's EditorCookie (from the Lookup) to make sure the editor is open and that the document has been initialized.

Opening an FTR file opens the file in the plain text editor by default. This open initializes the underlying document, making it available through the EditorCookie `getDocument()` method. If, however, the application last quit with the FTR file opened in the Visual view, then this visual element opens first with the underlying document not yet initialized. The `componentShowing()` method makes sure the document is properly initialized in this scenario.

The `refreshLines()` method parses the document and creates a LabelWidget for each line (ignoring empty lines). Since the `componentShowing()` method is invoked each time the user switches view from the Text to the Visual view, the Scene always displays the current edited document.

The `makeWidget()` method builds a LabelWidget (a widget that displays text) and sets its location, border, and text label. This method also configures the widget with two actions, an EditAction (that lets the user edit the widget's label) and a a MoveAction (that lets the user move the widget within the Scene). MoveAction has a default provider obtained from the ActionFactory. For EditAction, we configure a Provider, shown next.

Listing 14.15 shows the code for the `componentShowing()`, `refreshLines()`, and `makeWidget()` methods.

**Listing 14.15 FamilyTreeVisualElement—Adding the Widgets**

```
public final class FamilyTreeVisualElement extends JPanel
                                    implements MultiViewElement {
. . .
    @Override
    public void componentShowing() {
        editCookie = ftDataObject.getLookup().lookup(EditorCookie.class);
        if (editCookie != null) {
            doc = editCookie.getDocument();
            if (doc == null) {
                editCookie.open();                              // open
                try {
                    doc = editCookie.openDocument();            // get document
                } catch (IOException ex) {
                    Exceptions.printStackTrace(ex);
                    return;
                }
            }
            refreshLines();
        }
    }

    private void refreshLines() {
        layer.removeChildren();
        try {
            String docString = doc.getText(0, doc.getLength());
            int i = 1;
            for (String text : docString.split("\n")) {
                if (!text.isEmpty()) {
                    LabelWidget widget = makeWidget(text,
                                    new Point(20, 40 * i++));
                    layer.addChild(widget);
                }
            }
            scene.validate();
        } catch (BadLocationException ex) {
            Exceptions.printStackTrace(ex);
        }
    }

    private LabelWidget makeWidget(String text, Point point) {
        LabelWidget widget = new LabelWidget(scene, text);
        widget.getActions().addAction(editorAction);
```

```
        widget.getActions().addAction(ActionFactory.createMoveAction());
        widget.setPreferredLocation(point);
        widget.setBorder(border);
        return widget;
    }
. . .
}
```

The makeWidget() method adds a TextFieldInplaceEditor to the LabelWidget. Listing 14.16 shows the code that implements this in-place editor, which requires overriding the isEnabled(), getText(), and setText() methods. The setText() method updates both the LabelWidget and the underlying document. The NetBeans-provided plain text editor receives the resulting DocumentListener events and responds by adding a Savable implementation to the TopComponent's Lookup. This, in turn, enables the toolbar's Save All icon. If the user switches views, the Text view shows the updated text.

The updateDocument() method performs the actual update to the underlying document. Because we create widgets from non-empty lines only, we massage the document to remove any extra newline characters. This ensures that correct positions are provided when updating the document's text.

If the user sets the widget's label to an empty string, the method removes the widget from the scene by invoking refreshLines() (shown previously).

### Listing 14.16 FamilyTreeVisualElement—Implementing the LabelWidget Editor

```
    private final WidgetAction editorAction =
         ActionFactory.createInplaceEditorAction(new LabelTextFieldEditor());

    private class LabelTextFieldEditor implements TextFieldInplaceEditor {

        @Override
        public boolean isEnabled(Widget widget) {
            return true;
        }

        @Override
        public String getText(Widget widget) {
            return ((LabelWidget) widget).getLabel();
        }

        @Override
        public void setText(Widget widget, String text) {
            LabelWidget lw = (LabelWidget) widget;
            String oldText = lw.getLabel();
```

```
            lw.setLabel(text);
            updateDocument(lw, oldText.length());
        }
    }

    private void updateDocument(LabelWidget labelWidget, int oldTextSize) {
        if (editCookie != null) {
            doc = editCookie.getDocument();
            if (doc != null) {
                try {
                    //normalize the file--get rid of extra newlines
                    String docString = doc.getText(0, doc.getLength());
                    StringBuilder sb = new StringBuilder();
                    for (String text : docString.split("\n")) {
                        if (!text.isEmpty()) {
                            sb.append(text);
                            sb.append("\n");
                        }
                    }
                    // replace with normalized text
                    doc.remove(0, doc.getLength());
                    doc.insertString(0, sb.toString(), null);

                    // find the starting position in the document for the
                    // new String
                    int startPosition = 0;
                    for (Widget widget : layer.getChildren()) {
                        if (widget instanceof LabelWidget) {
                            LabelWidget lw = ((LabelWidget) widget);
                            if (lw.equals(labelWidget)) {
                                doc.remove(startPosition, oldTextSize + 1);
                                if (labelWidget.getLabel().isEmpty()) {
                                    // get rid of the widget if it's empty
                                    refreshLines();
                                } else {
                                    doc.insertString(startPosition,
                                       labelWidget.getLabel() + "\n", null);
                                }
                                break;
                            } else {
                                startPosition += lw.getLabel().length() + 1;
                            }
                        }
                    }
                } catch (BadLocationException ex) {
                    Exceptions.printStackTrace(ex);
                }
            }
        }
    }
}
```

## Create a Toolbar Action to Add a Widget to the View

The Visual view of the FTR editor lets users edit a widget's text label and remove the widget (by setting its label to an empty string). Let's now add an action to the application's toolbar and top-level File menu that lets users add widgets to the view (and a new line of text to the document). This action will be conditionally-enabled, available only when the Visual view has focus (is active).

We know that context is determined by the contents of the Global Lookup. Therefore, let's create a new capability and add an implementation to the FamilyTreeVisualElement's Lookup. We also create a new conditionally-enabled action that invokes a specific method in this capability. Here are the steps.

- Create a new capability called Droppable with abstract method `drop()`.
- Create a new conditionally-enabled Add Name action that invokes the `drop()` method.
- Implement Droppable with the code that builds a LabelWidget. Add this implementation to the FamilyTreeVisualElement's Lookup.

Figure 14.18 shows the FileTypeApp running. The Add Name action is enabled only when the Visual view of the FTR editor has focus. After clicking the Add Name icon in the toolbar, the action displays a dialog to prompt for the new name. When the user supplies a name and clicks OK, a new LabelWidget appears at the bottom of the Visual view. The Save All icon then becomes enabled.

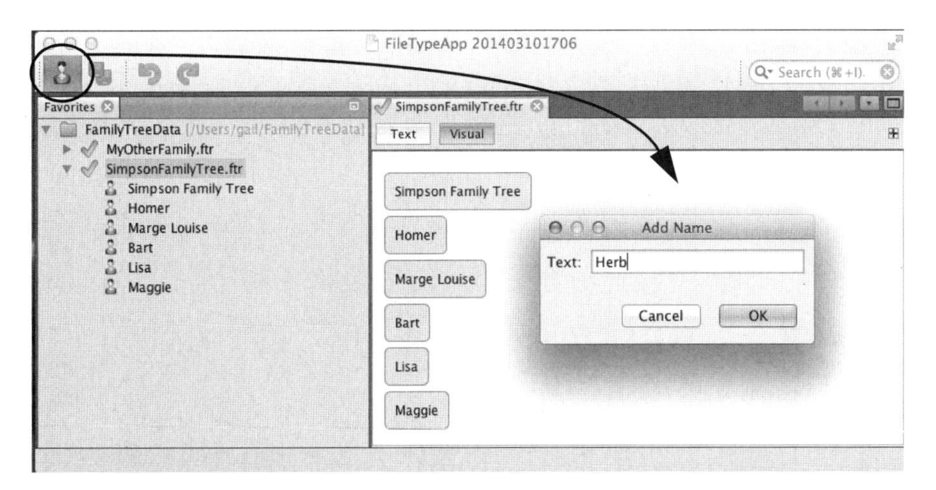


Figure 14.18 Invoking the Add Name action

Here are the steps.

1. Add Java Interface Droppable to module FamilyTreeSupport, as shown in Listing 14.17.

**Listing 14.17 Droppable.java**

```
public interface Droppable {
    public void drop(String text);
}
```

2. Add a new conditionally-enabled action to module FamilyTreeSupport called AddNameAction that requests a text String from the user and invokes the `drop()` method with the text. Specify **Droppable** as the Cookie Class (the context). Listing 14.18 shows the action implementation.

**Listing 14.18 AddNameAction.java**

```
@ActionID(
        category = "Edit",
        id = "com.asgteach.familytreesupport.AddNameAction"
)
@ActionRegistration(
        iconBase = "com/asgteach/familytreesupport/personIcon.png",
        displayName = "#CTL_AddNameAction"
)
@ActionReferences({
    @ActionReference(path = "Menu/File", position = 1300,
            separatorAfter = 1350),
    @ActionReference(path = "Toolbars/File", position = 300)
})
@Messages("CTL_AddNameAction=Add Name")
public final class AddNameAction implements ActionListener {

    private final Droppable context;

    public AddNameAction(Droppable context) {
        this.context = context;
    }

    @Override
    public void actionPerformed(ActionEvent ev) {
        NotifyDescriptor.InputLine inputLine =
                new NotifyDescriptor.InputLine("Text:", "Add Name");
        Object result = DialogDisplayer.getDefault().notify(inputLine);
        if (result == NotifyDescriptor.OK_OPTION) {
            String text = inputLine.getInputText();
```

```
            if (!text.isEmpty()) {
                context.drop(text);
            }
        }
    }
}
```

3. Listing 14.19 shows the changes to FamilyTreeVisualElement to support the AddNameAction. To add an object to the FamilyTreeVisualElement Lookup, you must instantiate InstanceContent and configure a proxy Lookup to include the FamilyTreeDataObject's Lookup. A proxy Lookup lets you combine Lookups from more than one source. (See "Lookup as an Object Repository" on page 225 for more on using InstanceContent with Lookups.) We re-implement the `getLookup()` method to return this proxy Lookup.

   Next, we implement Droppable, override the `drop()` method, and add the implementation to the Lookup. Adding the Droppable implementation to the FamilyTreeVisualElement's Lookup enables the AddNameAction in the application's toolbar when the Visual view has focus.

   The `drop()` method inserts the provided text into the underlying document and invokes `refreshLines()` to rebuild the view. (Listing 14.15 on page 702 shows the `refreshLines()` method.)

**Listing 14.19 FamilyTreeVisualElement—Implementing Droppable**

```
public final class FamilyTreeVisualElement extends JPanel
                                implements MultiViewElement {

    private final FamilyTreeDataObject ftDataObject;
    private final JToolBar toolbar = new JToolBar();
    private transient MultiViewElementCallback callback;
    private ProxyLookup proxyLookup = null;
    private final InstanceContent instanceContent = new InstanceContent();
. . .

    public FamilyTreeVisualElement(Lookup lkp) {
        proxyLookup = new ProxyLookup(
                          lkp, new AbstractLookup(instanceContent));
        ftDataObject = lkp.lookup(FamilyTreeDataObject.class);
        assert ftDataObject != null;
        initComponents();
        setLayout(new BorderLayout());
        layer = new LayerWidget(scene);
        scene.addChild(layer);
        add(new JScrollPane(scene.createView()));
        instanceContent.add(new Droppable() {
            @Override
            public void drop(String text) {
                // add text to end of document and call refreshLines()
```

```
                if (doc != null) {
                    try {
                        if (!(doc.getText(doc.getLength(), 1)).endsWith("\n")) {
                            doc.insertString(doc.getLength(), "\n", null);
                        }
                        doc.insertString(doc.getLength(), text + "\n", null);
                        refreshLines();
                    } catch (BadLocationException ex) {
                        Exceptions.printStackTrace(ex);
                    }
                }
            }
        });
    }

    @Override
    public Lookup getLookup() {
        return proxyLookup;
    }
. . .
}
```

## Using JavaFX

Let's continue our exploration of MultiView windows and add a Visual view with JavaFX content to our application. We'll provide the same functionality as the Visual view we just showed you. This VisualFX view includes synchronizing the underlying document among all the views, an in-place editor, a mouse drag of the visual elements, and a toolbar action to add elements. In addition, a fade-in transition plays when the user switches to the VisualFX view. And because we're using JavaFX, we style the elements with CSS.

Figure 14.19 shows the application running. The MultiView window now has three views: Text, Visual, and the VisualFX view shown. The user is editing the document and the toolbar's Save All icon is enabled. Similar to the MultiView window behavior you've already seen, changes made in the VisualFX view appear in both the Text and Visual views. Edits made in each of the other views similarly affect the VisualFX view.

The key strategy here is applying the same approach from Chapter 6 that integrates JavaFX content with NetBeans Platform applications. We use FXML for layout and an FXML controller class to manage and isolate JavaFX content. The VisualFX view uses all three types of communication strategies: self-contained events, one-way communication, and two-way communication (see "Communication Strategies" on page 261). In particular, note that property change support in the FXML controller class communicates user-initiated changes in the underlying document back to the enclosing MultiView element. We'll explain all of this as we show you how to build the VisualFX view.

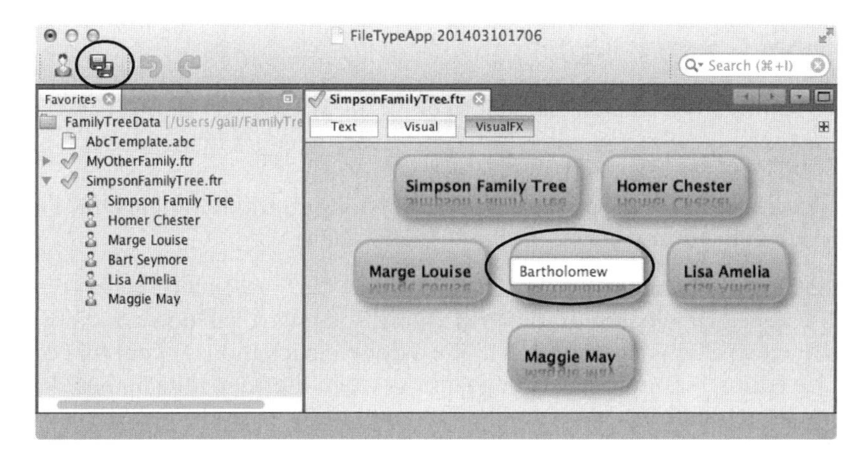


Figure 14.19 VisualFX view showing JavaFX content

Figure 14.20 shows the FileTypeApp application as the user clicks the VisualFX button. The text elements fade in, one by one. Also, note that the toolbar Add Name icon is enabled for both the Visual and VisualFX views.

Figure 14.20 VisualFX view fading in

Here's a summary of the steps required to add the VisualFX view to the FTR MultiView editor.

- Create the FamilyTreeVisualFXElement.java Java file by refactor copying FamilyTreeVisualElement.java.

- Create files FtrVisual.fxml, FtrVisualController.java, and FtrCSS.css for the JavaFX content.
- Configure FamilyTreeVisualFXElement to build the JavaFX scene graph and store a reference to the JavaFX controller. Build the JavaFX content in the `componentShowing()` life cycle method and when a property change event is received. Clear the JavaFX content in the `componentHidden()` life cycle method. Initiate a fade-in transition when the user switches to the VisualFX view.
- Configure the JavaFX controller class. Add a public `refresh()` method that builds the JavaFX scene graph based on the underlying document. Include drag mouse handlers to move elements around. Include a double-click mouse event that opens the in-place editor. Fire property change events when the user edits names. Add a public `doFadeIn()` method that plays the fade-in transitions and a public `clear()` method that clears the JavaFX content.

### Add FamilyTreeVisualFXElement.java

1. In module FamilyTreeSupport | Source Packages, right click **FamilyTreeVisualElement.java** and select **Copy** from the context menu.
2. Select the package name, right click, and select **Paste**. In the context menu, select **Refactor Copy**. In the dialog, specify **FamilyTreeVisualFXElement** for the new Java class name.

You will make changes to build the JavaFX Scene and instantiate the JavaFX controller class. First, create the JavaFX-related files.

### Create the JavaFX FXML, Controller Class, and CSS Files

Add files FtrVisualFX.fxml, FtrVisualFXController.java, and FtrCSS.css to the FamilyTreeSupport module.[3] We'll configure these files after we've made changes to the MultiView element file, FamilyTreeVisualFXElement.java.

### Configure FamilyTreeVisualFXElement.java

FamilyTreeVisualFXElement has a structure that is similar to the MultiView element you've already seen. Here, however, we construct the JavaFX scene and store a refer-

3. To create the FXML and JavaFX Controller files, build a new JavaFX FXML Application project in the NetBeans IDE and copy the resulting FXML document and FXML Controller class to the FamilyTreeSupport module Source Package.

ence to the JavaFX controller class. To safely store the reference, we use a countdown latch to wait for the `createScene()` method to complete.

As in the previous section, we also implement Droppable and add it to this element's Lookup. This implementation appends the provided String to the end of the document and then invokes the controller's `refresh()` method (using `Platform.runlater()` to execute on the JavaFX application Thread).

Listing 14.20 shows the code that registers the MultiView element, configures the proxy Lookup with InstanceContent and AbstractLookup, adds the Droppable to the Lookup, and creates the JavaFX content.

**Listing 14.20 FamilyTreeVisualFXElement—Initializing JavaFX Content**

```
@MultiViewElement.Registration(
        displayName = "#LBL_FamilyTreeFX_VISUAL",
        iconBase = "com/asgteach/familytreesupport/check.png",
        mimeType = "text/x-familytree",
        persistenceType = TopComponent.PERSISTENCE_NEVER,
        preferredID = "FamilyTreeFXVisual",
        position = 2000
)
@Messages("LBL_FamilyTreeFX_VISUAL=VisualFX")
public final class FamilyTreeVisualFXElement extends JPanel
                    implements MultiViewElement, PropertyChangeListener {

    private final FamilyTreeDataObject ftDataObject;
    private final JToolBar toolbar = new JToolBar();
    private transient MultiViewElementCallback callback;
    private ProxyLookup proxyLookup = null;
    private final InstanceContent instanceContent = new InstanceContent();
    private EditorCookie editCookie = null;
    private StyledDocument doc = null;
    private static JFXPanel fxPanel;
    private FtrVisualFXController controller;
    private static final Logger logger = Logger.getLogger(
                    FamilyTreeVisualFXElement.class.getName());

    public FamilyTreeVisualFXElement(Lookup lkp) {
        proxyLookup = new ProxyLookup(lkp,
                        new AbstractLookup(instanceContent));
        ftDataObject = lkp.lookup(FamilyTreeDataObject.class);
        assert ftDataObject != null;
        initComponents();
        setLayout(new BorderLayout());
        init();
        instanceContent.add(new Droppable() {
```

```
            @Override
            public void drop(String text) {
                // add the text to the end of the document, then refreshLines()
                if (doc != null) {
                    try {
                        if (!(doc.getText(doc.getLength(), 1)).endsWith("\n")) {
                              doc.insertString(doc.getLength(), "\n", null);
                        }
                        doc.insertString(doc.getLength(), text + "\n", null);
                        String docString = doc.getText(0, doc.getLength());
                        Platform.runLater(() -> controller.refresh(docString));
                    } catch (BadLocationException ex) {
                        Exceptions.printStackTrace(ex);
                    }
                }
            }
        });
    }

    private void init() {
        fxPanel = new JFXPanel();
        add(fxPanel, BorderLayout.CENTER);
        Platform.setImplicitExit(false);
        // need to wait for this to complete so that we can
        // safely add ourselves as a property change listener
        final CountDownLatch latch = new CountDownLatch(1);
        Platform.runLater(() -> {
            try {
                createScene();
            } finally {
                latch.countDown();
            }
        });
        try {
            latch.await();
        } catch (InterruptedException ex) {
            logger.log(Level.WARNING, null, ex);
        }
    }

    private void createScene() {
        try {
            URL location = getClass().getResource("FtrVisualFX.fxml");
            FXMLLoader fxmlLoader = new FXMLLoader();
            fxmlLoader.setLocation(location);
            fxmlLoader.setBuilderFactory(new JavaFXBuilderFactory());
            Parent root = (Parent) fxmlLoader.load(location.openStream());
            javafx.scene.Scene scene = new javafx.scene.Scene(root);
```

```
            fxPanel.setScene(scene);
            controller = (FtrVisualFXController) fxmlLoader.getController();
        } catch (IOException ex) {
            Exceptions.printStackTrace(ex);
        }
    }
. . .
}
```

Listing 14.21 shows the FamilyTreeVisualFXElement life cycle methods and the property change event handler. The `componentOpened()` method adds the class as a property change listener to the JavaFX controller class, and the `componentClosed()` method removes the listener.

The `componentShowing()` method (which is invoked when the user selects the VisualFX tab to make this element visible) accesses the underlying document from the DataObject EditorCookie. The `refresh()` method synchronizes the JavaFX content with the current state of the document.

The `doFadeIn()` method fades in the individual JavaFX scene graph elements with a sequential FadeTransition. A countdown latch makes sure this method executes after `refresh()` completes.

The `propertyChange()` method is invoked when the user makes a change to the text in the JavaFX scene graph. This event handler receives the updated String and replaces the underlying document with this new value. The updated document is detected in the NetBeans-provided Text editor, which responds by placing a Savable in its Lookup.

The `propertyChange()` event handler refreshes the JavaFX content after processing the document changes.

**Listing 14.21 FamilyTreeVisualFXElement—Life Cycle and Property Change**

```
public final class FamilyTreeVisualFXElement extends JPanel
                 implements MultiViewElement, PropertyChangeListener {
. . .
    @Override
    public void componentOpened() {
        // requires a countdown latch to make sure
        // controller is properly initialized
        controller.addPropertyChangeListener(this);
    }
```

```
@Override
public void componentClosed() {
    controller.removePropertyChangeListener(this);
}

@Override
public void componentShowing() {
    editCookie = ftDataObject.getLookup().lookup(EditorCookie.class);
    if (editCookie != null) {
        doc = editCookie.getDocument();
        if (doc == null) {
            editCookie.open();                    // open
            try {
                doc = editCookie.openDocument();  // get document
            } catch (IOException ex) {
                Exceptions.printStackTrace(ex);
                return;
            }
        }
        try {
            String docString = doc.getText(0, doc.getLength());
            final CountDownLatch latch = new CountDownLatch(1);
            Platform.runLater(() -> {
                try {
                    controller.refresh(docString);
                } finally {
                    latch.countDown();
                }
            });
            try {
                latch.await();
               // wait for refresh() to complete before calling the fade-in
                Platform.runLater(() -> controller.doFadeIn());
            } catch (InterruptedException ex) {
                logger.log(Level.WARNING, null, ex);
            }
        } catch (BadLocationException ex) {
            Exceptions.printStackTrace(ex);
        }
    }
}

@Override
public void componentHidden() {
    Platform.runLater(() -> controller.clear());
}

@Override
public void propertyChange(PropertyChangeEvent evt) {
    // the controller made changes; we have to update
    // the underlying document and refresh the JavaFX scene
```

```
        if (evt.getPropertyName().equals(
                FtrVisualFXController.PROP_DOCELEMENT_REMOVED) ||
            evt.getPropertyName().equals(
                FtrVisualFXController.PROP_DOCUMENT_UPDATED)) {
            // update the document
            if (doc != null) {
                try {
                    doc.remove(0, doc.getLength());
                    doc.insertString(0, (String) evt.getNewValue(), null);
                    Platform.runLater(() ->
                        controller.refresh((String) evt.getNewValue()));
                } catch (BadLocationException ex) {
                    Exceptions.printStackTrace(ex);
                }
            }
        }
    }
}
```

## Configure FXML, CSS, and Controller Class Files

Create the JavaFX content and controller code. Let's begin with the FXML file, shown in Listing 14.22. Here you see a FlowPane layout control with its alignment set to `TOP_CENTER` and padding insets of 10 pixels on all sides. The FlowPane control includes an assigned `fx:id` (**"mypane"**) that the controller class uses to reference this layout control. The FXML code also identifies the controller class (FtrVisualFXController) and specifies a CSS style sheet file.

Note that the FlowPane does not contain any child nodes. The controller class generates child nodes based on the underlying document (provided by the FamilyTreeVisualFXElement class).

**Listing 14.22 FtrVisualFX.fxml**

```
<?xml version="1.0" encoding="UTF-8"?>

<?import java.lang.*?>
<?import java.net.*?>
<?import java.util.*?>
<?import javafx.scene.*?>
<?import javafx.geometry.Insets?>
<?import javafx.scene.control.*?>
<?import javafx.scene.layout.*?>
<?import javafx.scene.shape.*?>
<?import javafx.scene.text.*?>
<?import javafx.scene.effect.*?>
```

```
<FlowPane
    hgap="20"
    vgap="20"
    alignment="TOP_CENTER"
    id="FlowPane"
    fx:id="mypane"
    xmlns:fx="http://javafx.com/fxml"
    fx:controller="com.asgteach.familytreesupport.FtrVisualFXController">
    <padding>
        <Insets bottom="10.0" left="10.0" right ="10.0" top="10.0"/>
    </padding>
    <stylesheets>
        <URL value="@FtrCSS.css" />
    </stylesheets>
    <children> </children>
</FlowPane>
```

Listing 14.23 shows the CSS file, which defines class-based styles for the Rectangle, Text, and FlowPane. The Rectangle style has a multi-element gradient for its fill and a drop shadow effect and the Text style specifies font, weight, and size. The FlowPane background color is a 3-part linear gradient.

**Listing 14.23 FtrCSS.css**

```
.ftr-rectangle {
   -fx-fill:
        linear-gradient(#ffd65b, #e68400),
        linear-gradient(#ffef84, #f2ba44),
        linear-gradient(#ffea6a, #efaa22),
        linear-gradient(#ffe657 0%, #f8c202 50%, #eea10b 100%),
        linear-gradient(from 0% 0% to 15% 50%, rgba(255,255,255,0.9),
               rgba(255,255,255,0));
   -fx-effect: dropshadow( three-pass-box , gray , 10 , 0 , 5.0 , 5.0 );
   -fx-stroke-width:3.0;
   -fx-stroke: goldenrod;
}
.ftr-text {
    -fx-font: Verdana;
    -fx-font-weight: bold;
    -fx-font-size: 14;
}
.ftr-pane {
    -fx-background-color: linear-gradient(lightblue, #c9d9e8, #ddeeeb);
}
```

Listing 14.24 shows the first part of the JavaFX controller class, FtrVisualFXController.java. Annotation `@FXML` identifies field `mypane` from the FXML file. The controller will use `mypane` to add nodes to the JavaFX scene graph. The controller also adds property change support with SwingPropertyChangeSupport so that the property change event fires on the EDT. The public static Strings define the monitored property names for property change support.

Event handlers `nodeOnMousePressedHandler` and `nodeOnMouseDraggedHandler` implement node dragging (move action) and use the `orgSceneX`, `orgSceneY`, `orgTranslateX`, and `orgTranslateY` fields to maintain node dragging.

#### Listing 14.24 FtrVisualFXController—Fields and Mouse Dragging

```
public class FtrVisualFXController implements Initializable {

    @FXML
    private FlowPane mypane;
    private SwingPropertyChangeSupport propChangeSupport = null;
    private final SequentialTransition seqTran = new SequentialTransition();

    public static final String PROP_DOCUMENT_UPDATED = "DocumentUpdated";
    public static final String PROP_DOCELEMENT_REMOVED = "DocElementRemoved";

    private double orgSceneX;
    private double orgSceneY;
    private double orgTranslateX;
    private double orgTranslateY;

    private static final Logger logger = Logger.getLogger(
                        FtrVisualFXController.class.getName());

    @Override
    public void initialize(URL url, ResourceBundle rb) {
        propChangeSupport = new SwingPropertyChangeSupport(this, true);
        mypane.getStyleClass().add("ftr-pane");
    }

    EventHandler<MouseEvent> nodeOnMousePressedEventHandler = ((event) -> {
        if (event.getButton().equals(MouseButton.PRIMARY)) {
            orgSceneX = event.getSceneX();
            orgSceneY = event.getSceneY();
            orgTranslateX = ((Node) (event.getSource())).getTranslateX();
            orgTranslateY = ((Node) (event.getSource())).getTranslateY();
        }
    });

    EventHandler<MouseEvent> nodeOnMouseDraggedEventHandler = ((event) -> {
        if (event.getButton().equals(MouseButton.PRIMARY)) {
            double offsetX = event.getSceneX() - orgSceneX;
            double offsetY = event.getSceneY() - orgSceneY;
            double newTranslateX = orgTranslateX + offsetX;
            double newTranslateY = orgTranslateY + offsetY;
```

```
            ((Node) (event.getSource())).setTranslateX(newTranslateX);
            ((Node) (event.getSource())).setTranslateY(newTranslateY);
        }
    });
. . .
}
```

Now let's look at the public methods that the MultiView element class invokes. Listing 14.25 shows the `doFadeIn()` method (which plays the sequential FadeTransitions), the `refresh()` method, and the `clear()` method.

The `refresh()` method receives a String argument and builds a multi-node element for each non-empty line in the String. The multi-node element consists of a StackPane layout control containing a Rectangle and Text element. There is also a hidden TextField control that becomes visible when the user double clicks the StackPane. This provides the in-place editor.

The TextField event handler invokes the `updateDocument()` method, which processes the user edits and fires a property change event.

Let's point out a few interesting JavaFX coding points.

- Variable `seqTran` is a SequentialTransition. This is cleared and rebuilt each time with each StackPane FadeTransition, fading in from opacity 0 to opacity 1.
- The MultiView element class invokes `clear()` from the `componentHidden()` method, which clears the FlowPane layout control. This makes sure that the JavaFX content doesn't flash but fades in smoothly when the user switches to the VisualFX view.
- The width of the Rectangle is determined by the bounds of the Text control, so that each Rectangle is only as wide as necessary to fit the Text node.
- The width of the hidden TextField is bound to the width of the Rectangle. This makes the TextField fit nicely over the underlying Rectangle when the TextField becomes visible.
- The TextField event handler is invoked when the user finishes editing with the Return key. The handler replaces the new text in the Text element, makes the TextField invisible again, adjusts the width of the underlying Rectangle, and invokes the `updateDocument()` method.
- The `updateDocument()` method processes the JavaFX node hierarchy and inserts the new text String into its proper place in the underlying document String. The `firePropertyChange()` method makes the edited String available to the listening MultiView element class.

**Listing 14.25 FtrVisualFXController—Build Content from String**

```
public class FtrVisualFXController implements Initializable {
. . .
    // Invoked by Swing visual element on the JavaFX Application Thread
    public void doFadeIn() {
        seqTran.playFromStart();
    }

    // Invoked by Swing visual element on the JavaFX Application Thread
    public void clear() {
        seqTran.getChildren().clear();
        mypane.getChildren().clear();
    }

    // Invoked by Swing visual element on the JavaFX Application Thread
    public void refresh(String docString) {
        clear();
        for (String line : docString.split("\n")) {
            if (!line.isEmpty()) {
                // Build the StackPane
                StackPane stack = new StackPane();

                // Build the Text
                final Text ftrText = new Text(line);
                ftrText.getStyleClass().add("ftr-text");
                ftrText.setEffect(new Reflection());

                // Build the Rectangle
                Rectangle ftrRectangle = new Rectangle(
                     ftrText.getBoundsInParent().getWidth() + 40, 55);
                ftrRectangle.setArcHeight(30);
                ftrRectangle.setArcWidth(30);
                ftrRectangle.getStyleClass().add("ftr-rectangle");

                // Build a TextField for editing
                TextField tf = new TextField();
                tf.prefWidthProperty().bind(ftrRectangle.widthProperty());
                tf.setVisible(false);
                tf.setOnAction(event -> {
                    String oldText = ftrText.getText();
                    ftrText.setText(tf.getText());
                    tf.setVisible(false);
                    updateDocument(ftrText, oldText.length(), docString);
                    ftrRectangle.setWidth(
                           ftrText.getBoundsInParent().getWidth() + 30);
                });

                // Add the Rectangle, Text, TextField to StackPane
                stack.getChildren().addAll(ftrRectangle, ftrText, tf);
```

```
                stack.setOnMouseClicked(event -> {
                    // enable editing on a double-click event
                    if (event.getClickCount() == 2 &&
                            event.getButton().equals(MouseButton.PRIMARY)) {
                        tf.setText(ftrText.getText());
                        tf.setVisible(true);
                    }
                });
                // Add the drag handlers
                stack.setOnMousePressed(nodeOnMousePressedEventHandler);
                stack.setOnMouseDragged(nodeOnMouseDraggedEventHandler);

                // Add the StackPane to the top-level Node (mypane)
                mypane.getChildren().add(stack);
                FadeTransition ft = new FadeTransition(
                                      Duration.millis(650), stack);
                ft.setFromValue(0);
                ft.setToValue(1);
                seqTran.getChildren().add(ft);
            }
        }
    }

    private void updateDocument(Text theText, int oldTextSize,
                                              String docString) {
        //normalize the file--get rid of extra newlines
        StringBuilder sb = new StringBuilder();
        for (String text : docString.split("\n")) {
            if (!text.isEmpty()) {
                sb.append(text);
                sb.append("\n");
            }
        }
        // find the starting position in the document for the new String
        int startPosition = 0;
        for (Node node : mypane.getChildren()) {
            if (node instanceof StackPane) {
                StackPane sp = (StackPane) node;
                for (Node childNode : sp.getChildren()) {
                    if (childNode instanceof Text) {
                        Text textNode = (Text) childNode;
                        if (textNode.equals(theText)) {
                          if (theText.getText().isEmpty()) {
                            sb.delete(startPosition,
                                 startPosition + oldTextSize + 1);
                            this.propChangeSupport.firePropertyChange(
                         PROP_DOCELEMENT_REMOVED, docString, sb.toString());
                          } else {
                            sb.replace(startPosition,
                           startPosition + oldTextSize, theText.getText());
                            this.propChangeSupport.firePropertyChange(
                         PROP_DOCUMENT_UPDATED, docString, sb.toString());
```

```
                              }
                              break;
                          } else {
                              // not our Text node, keep looking
                              startPosition += textNode.getText().length() + 1;
                          }
                      }
                  }
              }
          }
      }

      public void addPropertyChangeListener(
              PropertyChangeListener listener) {
          this.propChangeSupport.addPropertyChangeListener(listener);
      }

      public void removePropertyChangeListener(
              PropertyChangeListener listener) {
          this.propChangeSupport.removePropertyChangeListener(listener);
      }
}
```

## 14.4 Creating an XML-Based File Type

Now let's show you how to create an application with a new XML file type. This is an XML file with the expected XML extension, yet with a unique root element that includes a specific namespace. The New File Type wizard registers a MIME Resolver that recognizes an XML file root element with a specific namespace. We'll call this MIME type **`text/familytree+xml`** (that is, a text-based XML file with namespace **`familytree`**).

The New File Type wizard registers the file type, specifies a MIME resolver, and registers a DataLoader that recognizes this file type. We also provide an icon for this new file type. Like the previous example, the New File Type wizard creates a template for this file type, registers the template, and generates a DataObject. The wizard also creates a skeletal MultiView editor.

With an XML file type, you can incorporate the rich editing capabilities of the NetBeans Platform XML editor, including formatting, schema code completion, and XML verification. You enable this rich XML editor by including the required modules from the NetBeans Platform **`ide`** cluster in your application. We'll show you how to do this later in this section.

Figure 14.21 and Figure 14.22 show this application running. Let's point out a few features before we begin building this application.

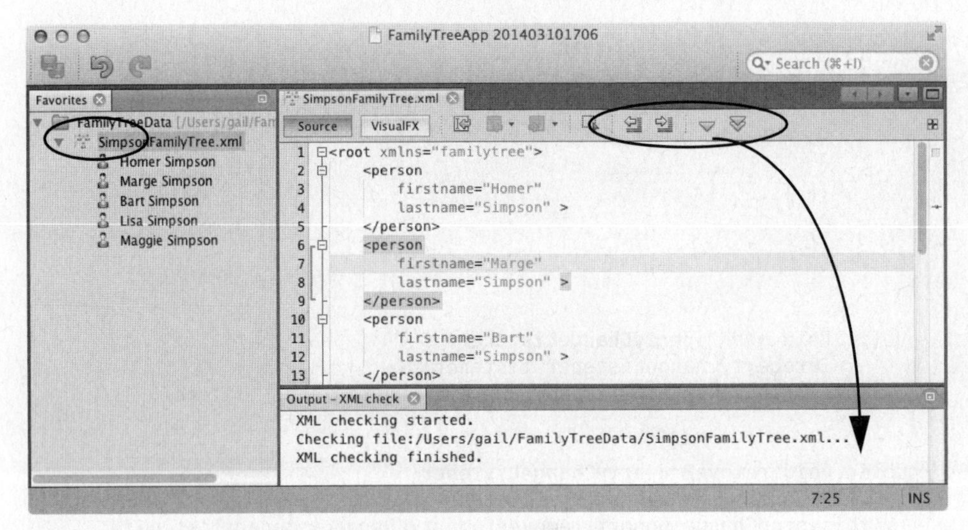


Figure 14.21 FamilyTreeApp with special XML file defined

- The XML file called SimpsonFamilyTree.xml shown in the Favorites window has a special icon that we assign to this particular XML file type.
- This file is opened in the XML editor, which provides color-coded XML element editing and a toolbar at the top of the editor for operations such as XML verification. The XML verification process appears in the Output window, shown below the editor window.
- When you right click the **SimpsonFamilyTree.xml** file, a context menu appears with expected operations such as Open, Cut, Copy, Delete, Rename, and others. These operations are automatically included when you create a new file type.
- The context menu also includes menu item **Show XML Structure**, a custom action built specifically for our new file type. The action parses the XML file and displays XML Elements and Attributes in the Output window, as shown in Figure 14.22.
- The MultiView editor includes two views. The Source view is the standard NetBeans Platform XML editor. The VisualFX view shows a JavaFX view of the XML file and displays contents only with no editing. It does, however, reflect any edits made to the Source view.
- You can expand the file node in the Favorites window and each child node displays the attributes and values of the `<person>` element tag.
- As in the previous example, the Save All icon and Save All and Save menu items are enabled when you edit the file. After saving the changes, the Favorites win-

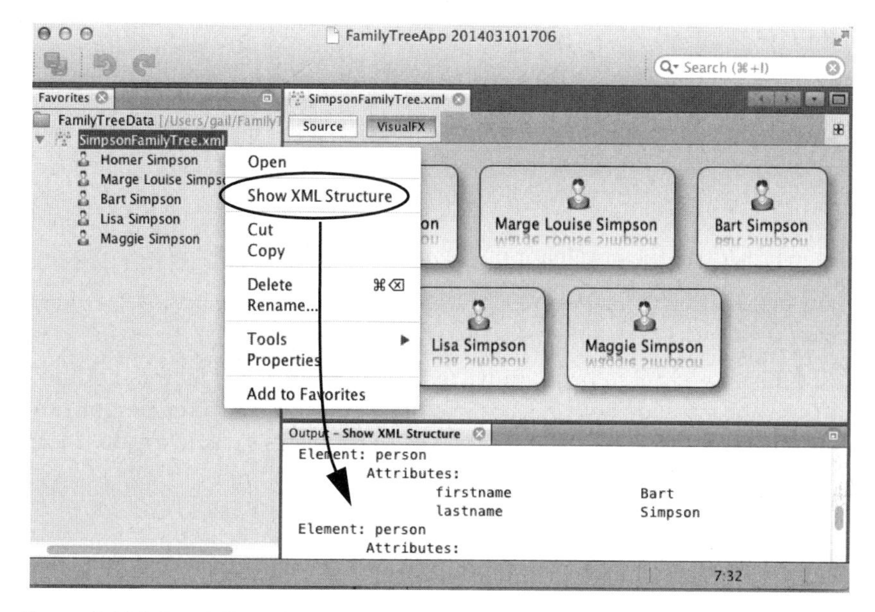


Figure 14.22 FamilyTree XML file action displays information about the file

dows shows the changes. When you switch between the Source and VisualFX views, the window always shows the current edited state of the file.

Note that you can optionally create this module as a NetBeans IDE plugin and have the full features of the NetBeans IDE available in your application.[4] However, we show you how to create a stand-alone NetBeans Platform application. This requires that you manually add the modules that provide XML file editing support.

Here's a summary of the steps to build the FamilyTreeApp application with an XML file type. We add a custom VisualFX view to the XML editor in a later section.

- Create a NetBeans Platform application called FamilyTreeApp.
- Create a module called PersonFileType.
- Add the Favorites and Template modules to the application.
- Create and register a new XML-based file type called FamilyTree.
- Add code to create child nodes for the FamilyTree DataNodes.

---

4. To create this as a NetBeans IDE plugin, do not create a NetBeans Platform Application project. Instead, create a Module Project for the PersonFileType module and Run the module. This installs the module into a version of the NetBeans IDE.

- Add the NetBeans IDE XML editor support.
- Add a context menu action to all FamilyTree XML files called Show XML Structure.

### Create a NetBeans Platform Application and Module

Here are the steps to create the application and add the PersonFileType module.

1. Create a new application called FamilyTreeApp using the NetBeans Platform New Project wizard.
2. Create a Module and add it to the FamilyTreeApp application. Call the module PersonFileType and provide package name **com.asgteach.familytree.personfiletype**. The application and module are shown in the Projects view in Figure 14.23.

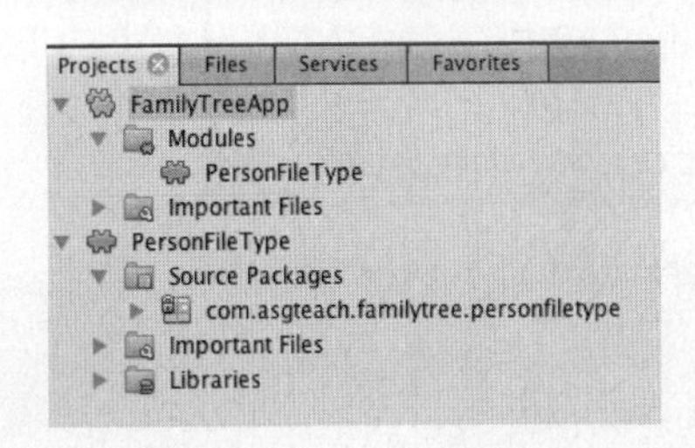


Figure 14.23 FamilyTreeApp and module PersonFileType in the Projects view

### Add the Favorites and Templates Modules

The Favorites window is a file viewer for your local disk. See "Favorites Window" on page 637 for a description of this useful module. The Templates module lets you create empty files and folders from the Favorites window. Follow these steps to include the Favorites and Templates modules in the FamilyTreeApp application.

1. Right click project FamilyTreeApp in the Projects view and select **Properties** from the context menu.
2. Under Categories, select **Libraries**. NetBeans lists all of the Platform Modules organized in clusters. Under cluster platform, select modules **Favorites** and **Templates** and click **OK**.
3. When you run the FamilyTreeApp application, the Favorites window will now appear in the top-level Window menu.

## Create a New XML File Type

Here are the steps to create a new file type for your application.

1. In the Projects view, expand module **PersonFileType | Source Packages**, select the package name, right click, and select **New | Other** from the context menu.
2. In the Choose File Type dialog under Categories, select **Module Development.** Under File Types select **File Type**. Click **Next**.
3. NetBeans displays the File Recognition dialog. Specify the MIME Type as **text/familytree+xml**. This defines a text-based XML file type called **familytree**. Select radio button **by XML Root Element** and provide **familytree** for Namespace, as shown in Figure 14.24. This new MIME type applies to XML files with root element **familytree**. Click **Next**.

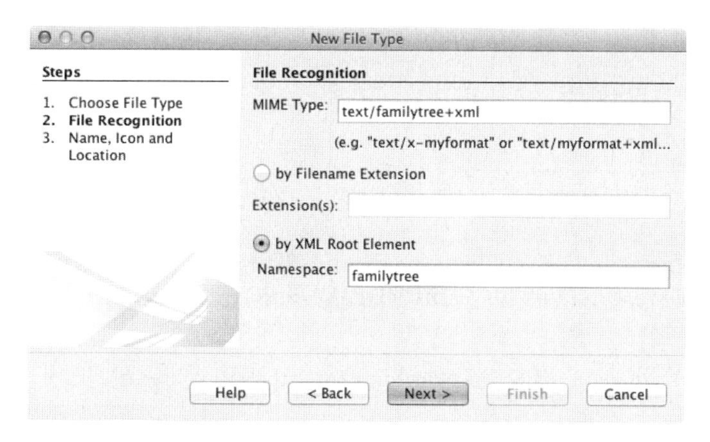


Figure 14.24 New File Type File Recognition dialog

4. NetBeans displays the Name, Icon, and Location dialog. For Class Name Prefix, specify **FamilyTree**. Click the **Browse** button and navigate to the provided icon file **FamilyTreeIcon.png**. Make sure the **Use MultiView** checkbox is selected and accept the defaults for the remaining fields, as shown in Figure 14.25. Click **Finish**.

NetBeans creates the following files to support this new file type. See "Create a New File Type" on page 681 for more details about these files.

- **FamilyTreeDataObject.java**—A DataObject that wraps a FileObject for FamilyTree XML files. Listing 14.28 on page 728 shows this file.
- **FamilyTreeTemplate.xml**—A template used by the New File wizard when the user creates a new Family Tree XML file.

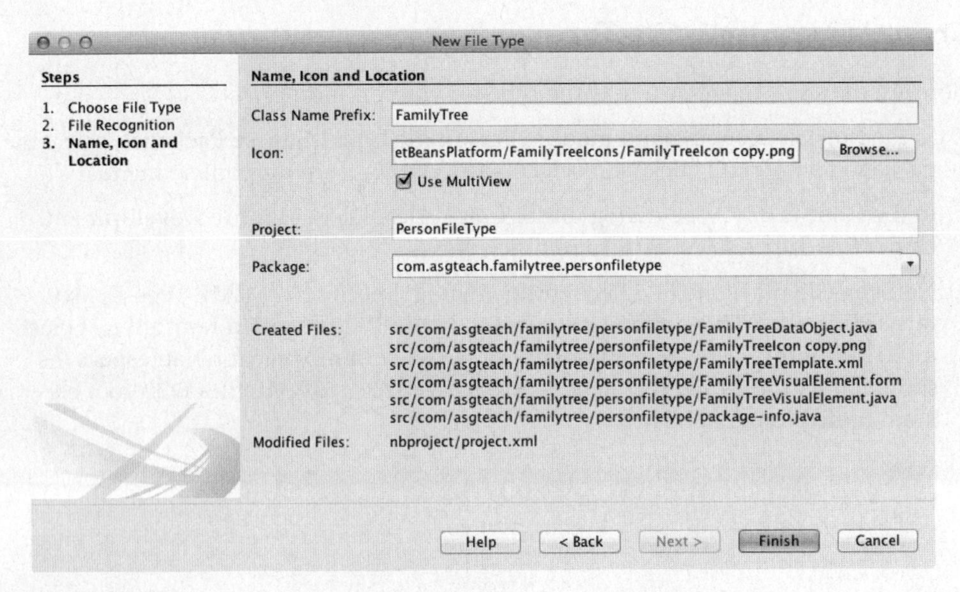


Figure 14.25 Name, Icon and Location dialog

- **FamilyTreeVisualElement.java**—This Java file extends JPanel and implements MultiViewElement. We rename this file **FamilyTreeVisualFXElement.java** and build JavaFX content (see Listing 14.31 on page 735).
- **FamilyTreeIcon.png**—This is the 16 x 16 graphic icon attached to Family Tree XML files.
- **package-info.java**—This Java file registers FamilyTreeTemplate.xml as a template for the New File wizard.

Your application will now recognize an XML file with namespace root of **familytree**. Listing 14.26 shows the template file that was created for this application.

**Listing 14.26 FamilyTreeTemplate.xml**

```
<root xmlns="familytree">
</root>
```

Next, we'll create test file SimpsonFamilyTree.xml with familytree root and place it in our file system. Listing 14.27 shows this test file.

**Listing 14.27 SimpsonFamilyTree.xml**

```
<root xmlns="familytree">
    <person
        firstname="Homer"
        lastname="Simpson" >
    </person>
    <person
        firstname="Marge"
        lastname="Simpson" >
    </person>
    <person
        firstname="Bart"
        lastname="Simpson" >
    </person>
    <person
        firstname="Lisa"
        lastname="Simpson" >
    </person>
    <person
        firstname="Maggie"
        lastname="Simpson" >
    </person>
</root>
```

### Add Child Nodes for the FamilyTreeDataObject DataNodes

Modify FamilyTreeDataObject.java and override the `createNodeDelegate()` method to build child nodes based on file content. This code is similar to Listing 14.13 on page 695. Here we parse the XML file and build the child nodes based on the `<person>` element tag. Listing 14.28 shows the code.

Class FamilyTreeChildFactory uses the NetBeans Platform XMLUtil `parse()` method to create a DOM document[5] from an XML file. With the DOM document, you can request a list of element tags by name and get attribute maps. The `getElementsByTagName()` method returns a list of `org.w3c.dom.Node` objects (*not* Node from the Nodes API). The `createKeys()` method uses this information to build its list of keys based on type Person. Person.java is shown in Listing 14.29 on page 730.

The ChildFactory also installs a FileChangeListener that performs a refresh when the underlying file is updated.

5. DOM stands for Document Object Model. The XMLUtil `parse()` method builds a DOM based on XML content. The DOM lets you build documents, navigate their structure, and add, modify, or delete elements and content. See `http://www.w3.org/DOM/` for further information.

**Listing 14.28 FamilyTreeDataObject**

```
@Messages({
    "LBL_FamilyTree_LOADER=Files of FamilyTree"
})
@MIMEResolver.NamespaceRegistration(
        displayName = "#LBL_FamilyTree_LOADER",
        mimeType = "text/familytree+xml",
        elementNS = {"familytree"},
        position = 0
)
@DataObject.Registration(
        mimeType = "text/familytree+xml",
        iconBase = "com/asgteach/familytree/personfiletype/FamilyTreeIcon.png",
        displayName = "#LBL_FamilyTree_LOADER",
        position = 0
)
@ActionReferences({
. . . code omitted . . .
})
public class FamilyTreeDataObject extends MultiDataObject {

    public FamilyTreeDataObject(FileObject pf, MultiFileLoader loader)
                        throws DataObjectExistsException, IOException {
        super(pf, loader);
        registerEditor("text/familytree+xml", true);
        InputSource inputSource = DataObjectAdapters.inputSource(this);
        CheckXMLCookie checkCookie = new CheckXMLSupport(inputSource);
        getCookieSet().add(checkCookie);
        ValidateXMLCookie validateXMLCookie = new ValidateXMLSupport(
                        inputSource);
        getCookieSet().add(validateXMLCookie);
    }

    @Override
    protected int associateLookup() {
        return 1;
    }

    @MultiViewElement.Registration(
            displayName = "#LBL_FamilyTree_EDITOR",
            iconBase =
               "com/asgteach/familytree/personfiletype/FamilyTreeIcon.png",
            mimeType = "text/familytree+xml",
            persistenceType = TopComponent.PERSISTENCE_ONLY_OPENED,
            preferredID = "FamilyTree",
            position = 1000
    )
    @Messages("LBL_FamilyTree_EDITOR=Source")
    public static MultiViewEditorElement createEditor(Lookup lkp) {
        return new MultiViewEditorElement(lkp);
    }
```

```
@Override
protected Node createNodeDelegate() {
    return new DataNode(this, Children.create(new
                FamilyTreeChildFactory(this), true), getLookup());
}

private static class FamilyTreeChildFactory extends ChildFactory<Person> {

    private final FileObject fileObject;
    private final FamilyTreeDataObject dataObject;

    public FamilyTreeChildFactory(FamilyTreeDataObject dataObject) {
        this.dataObject = dataObject;
        fileObject = dataObject.getPrimaryFile();
        fileObject.addFileChangeListener(new FileChangeAdapter() {
            @Override
            public void fileChanged(FileEvent fe) {
                refresh(true);
            }
        });
    }

    @Override
    protected boolean createKeys(List<Person> list) {
        try {
            EditorCookie editorCookie = dataObject.getLookup().lookup(
                       EditorCookie.class);
            // Get the InputStream from the EditorCookie
           try (InputStream is = ((org.openide.text.CloneableEditorSupport)
                                    editorCookie).getInputStream()) {
                // use XMLUtil to create a org.w3c.dom.Document
                Document doc = XMLUtil.parse(
                       new InputSource(is), true, true, null, null);
                NodeList nodeList = doc.getElementsByTagName("person");
                for (int i = 0; i < nodeList.getLength(); i++) {
                    //For each node in the list, get a org.w3c.dom.Node
                    org.w3c.dom.Node personNode = nodeList.item(i);
                    NamedNodeMap map = personNode.getAttributes();
                    Person person;
                    if (map != null) {
                        person = new Person();
                       person.setLastname("Unknown");
                        for (int j = 0; j < map.getLength(); j++) {
                            org.w3c.dom.Node attrNode = map.item(j);
                          if (attrNode.getNodeName().equals("firstname")) {
                              person.setFirstname(attrNode.getNodeValue());
                            }
                           if (attrNode.getNodeName().equals("lastname")) {
                               person.setLastname(attrNode.getNodeValue());
                            }
                        }
                        list.add(person);
```

```
                }
            }
        }
    } catch (SAXException | IOException ex) {
        Exceptions.printStackTrace(ex);
    }
    return true;
}

@Override
protected Node createNodeForKey(Person key) {
    AbstractNode childNode = new AbstractNode(Children.LEAF);
    childNode.setDisplayName(key.toString());
    childNode.setIconBaseWithExtension(
        "com/asgteach/familytree/personfiletype/personIcon.png");
    return childNode;
}
    }
}
```

Listing 14.29 is a simple Person class with properties `firstname` and `lastname`.

**Listing 14.29 Person.java**

```
public class Person {

    private String firstname = "";
    private String lastname = "";

    public String getFirstname() {
        return firstname;
    }

    public void setFirstname(String firstname) {
        this.firstname = firstname;
    }

    public String getLastname() {
        return lastname;
    }

    public void setLastname(String lastname) {
        this.lastname = lastname;
    }
```

```
    @Override
    public String toString() {
        return new StringBuilder(firstname).append(" ")
                                 .append(lastname).toString();
    }
}
```

## Add the XML Text Editor

The NetBeans Platform includes an XML Text editor that you can add to applications. This editor provides color-coding on XML elements, syntax checking, schema code completion, formatting, and many actions you would expect from a sophisticated XML editor. Here are the steps to add the XML Text editor to our application.

1. In the Projects view, right click the application name (FamilyTreeApp) and select **Properties**.
2. NetBeans displays the Project Properties dialog. Select category **Libraries**.
3. NetBeans displays all the modules available in the various clusters that form the NetBeans Platform.
4. In the Platform Modules window, expand node **ide** as shown in Figure 14.26 on page 733.
5. Select the modules from the **ide** cluster as listed in Table 14.1. These modules will configure a full-blown, fancy XML editor with color coding, formatting, and XML validation in your application.

**TABLE 14.1 XML Editing Modules**

| Cluster ide | Cluster ide |
|---|---|
| Abstract XML Instance Object Model (AXIOM) | Lexer |
| Apache Resolver Library 1.2 | Lexer to NetBeans Bridge |
| Classpath APIs | Lucene Integration |
| Common Scripting Language API (new) | Navigator API |
| Diff | Parsing API |
| Editor | Parsing Lucene Support |
| Editor Actions | Projects API |
| Editor Braces Matching | Projects Indexing Bridge |
| Editor Breadcrumbs | Projects UI API |
| Editor Code Completion | Refactoring API |
| Editor Code Folding | Schema Aware Code Completion |

**TABLE 14.1 XML Editing Modules** *(Continued)*

| **Cluster ide** | **Cluster ide** |
|---|---|
| Editor Code Folding UI | Schema-to-Beans Library |
| Editor Code Templates | Tags Based Editors Library |
| Editor Error Stripe | Task List API |
| Editor Error Stripe Impl | TAX Library |
| Editor Formatting Prior 6.5 Separation | User Utilities |
| Editor Guarded Sections | Xerces Integration |
| Editor Hints | XML Core |
| Editor Indentation | XML Document Model (XDM) |
| Editor Library | XML Lexer |
| Editor Library 2 | XML Multiview Editor |
| Editor Options | XML Productivity Tools |
| Editor Settings | XML Retriever |
| Editor Settings Storage | XML Schema API |
| Editor Utilities | XML Support |
| Extensible Abstract Model (XAM) | XML Text Editor |
| JSON Simple Library | XML Tools |
| Jump To | |

With the XML editor modules included and a new FileType installed, you can now edit a FamilyTree XML file in your application.

## Add a Context-Sensitive Action

Follow the steps in "Context-Sensitive Action" on page 689 to add a conditionally-enabled action to module PersonFileType. Call the action **ShowXMLStructureAction** and add it to the top-level File menu and the FamilyTree XML DataNode context menu. The Cookie Class is **FamilyTreeDataObject**. Listing 14.30 shows the code to implement this action.

Note that we use the same NetBeans XMLUtil method to parse the XML file and create a DOM document. The XML content information is displayed in the Output window (see Figure 14.22 on page 723). See "The Output Window" on page 628 for more details about the Output window.

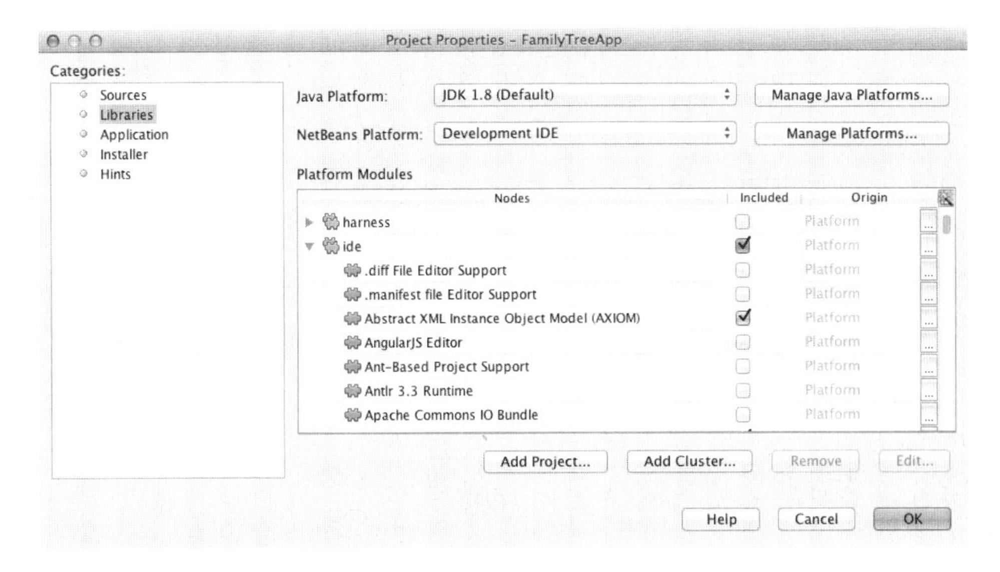


Figure 14.26 Adding modules for XML text editing support

**Listing 14.30 ShowXMLStructureAction.java**

```
@ActionID(
        category = "File",
        id = "com.asgteach.familytree.personfiletype.ShowXMLStructureAction"
)
@ActionRegistration(
        iconBase = "com/asgteach/familytree/personfiletype/info.png",
        displayName = "#CTL_ShowXMLAction"
)
@ActionReferences({
    @ActionReference(path = "Menu/File", position = 1465,
                                separatorAfter = 1482),
    @ActionReference(path = "Loaders/text/familytree+xml/Actions",
                                position = 150, separatorBefore = 125)
})
@Messages({
    "CTL_ShowXMLAction=Show XML Structure",
    "CTL_SHOWXMLStructureActionListener=Show XML Structure"})
public final class ShowXMLStructureAction implements ActionListener {

    private final FamilyTreeDataObject context;

    public ShowXMLStructureAction(FamilyTreeDataObject context) {
        this.context = context;
    }
```

```
    @Override
    public void actionPerformed(ActionEvent ev) {
        InputOutput io = IOProvider.getDefault().getIO(
                        Bundle.CTL_SHOWXMLStructureActionListener(), false);
        io.select();                    // "XML Structure" tab is selected
        try {
            EditorCookie editorCookie = context.getLookup().lookup(
                    EditorCookie.class);
            io.getOut().reset();
            try (InputStream is = (
               (org.openide.text.CloneableEditorSupport) editorCookie)
                        .getInputStream()) {
                Document doc = XMLUtil.parse(
                            new InputSource(is), true, true, null, null);
                parseDoc(doc, "root", io);
                parseDoc(doc, "person", io);
            }
        } catch (SAXException | IOException ex) {
            Exceptions.printStackTrace(ex);
        }
    }

    private void parseDoc(Document doc, String element, InputOutput io) {
        NodeList nodeList = doc.getElementsByTagName(element);
        io.getOut().println("Child Nodes, Size = " + nodeList.getLength());
        for (int i = 0; i < nodeList.getLength(); i++) {
            org.w3c.dom.Node personNode = nodeList.item(i);
            String nodeName = personNode.getNodeName();
            // Print the element and its attributes to the Output window
            io.getOut().println("Element: " + nodeName);
            // Create a map for Element's attributes
            NamedNodeMap map = personNode.getAttributes();
            if (map != null) {
                StringBuilder attrBuilder = new StringBuilder();
                // Iterate through map and display attribute name and value
                for (int j = 0; j < map.getLength(); j++) {
                    org.w3c.dom.Node attrNode = map.item(j);
                    String attrName = attrNode.getNodeName();
                    attrBuilder.append("\n\t\t").append(attrName);
                   attrBuilder.append("\t\t").append(attrNode.getNodeValue());
                }
                if (!attrBuilder.toString().isEmpty()) {
                    io.getOut().println(" \tAttributes:"
                                 + attrBuilder.toString());
                }
            }
        }
    }
}
```

## Add JavaFX Content

Now let's add JavaFX content to our renamed VisualFX view. The structure will be the same as the JavaFX content shown in the previous section (see "Using JavaFX" on page 708). Here, however, we have less work to do, since we only display content from the XML file. We've also changed the appearance with different CSS styles. To add JavaFX content, use the following files, which keeps the JavaFX and Swing code loosely coupled.

- **FamilyTreeVisualFXElement.java**—This Java file extends JPanel and implements MultiViewElement. The class stores a reference to the FamilyTreeFXController and invokes public methods in this controller class to build the JavaFX scene graph.
- **FamilyTree.css**—CSS style definitions to style the JavaFX scene.
- **FamilyTreeFX.fxml**—Declarative FXML code that defines the static part of the JavaFX scene graph.
- **FamilyTreeFXController.java**—The JavaFX controller class with public methods that the visual element class can invoke as needed.

Listing 14.31 shows the FamilyTreeVisualFXElement code. Because this element invokes the controller's `refresh()` method, a countdown latch is necessary to make sure the controller reference is safely initialized. We refresh the JavaFX content in the `componentShowing()` method, which updates the JavaFX scene graph each time the user switches to the VisualFX view. As before, we clear the JavaFX content in the `componentHidden()` method.

**Listing 14.31 FamilyTreeVisualFXElement.java**

```
@MultiViewElement.Registration(
        displayName = "#LBL_FamilyTree_VISUALFX",
        iconBase = "com/asgteach/familytree/personfiletype/FamilyTreeIcon.png",
        mimeType = "text/familytree+xml",
        persistenceType = TopComponent.PERSISTENCE_NEVER,
        preferredID = "FamilyTreeVisualFX",
        position = 2000
)
@Messages("LBL_FamilyTree_VISUALFX=VisualFX")
public final class FamilyTreeVisualFXElement extends JPanel
                                  implements MultiViewElement {

    private final FamilyTreeDataObject ftDataObject;
    private final JToolBar toolbar = new JToolBar();
    private transient MultiViewElementCallback callback;
    private EditorCookie editCookie = null;
    private Document doc = null;
    private static JFXPanel fxPanel;
    private FamilyTreeFXController controller;
```

```
    private static final Logger logger = Logger.getLogger(
                     FamilyTreeVisualFXElement.class.getName());

    public FamilyTreeVisualFXElement(Lookup lkp) {
        ftDataObject = lkp.lookup(FamilyTreeDataObject.class);
        assert ftDataObject != null;
        initComponents();
        setLayout(new BorderLayout());
        init();
    }

    private void init() {
      . . . see the init() method in Listing 14.20 on page 711 . . .
    }

    private void createScene() {
         . . . see the createScene() method in Listing 14.20 on page 711 . . .
    }
. . . code omitted . . .

    @Override
    public void componentShowing() {
        editCookie = ftDataObject.getLookup().lookup(EditorCookie.class);
        if (editCookie != null) {
            try (InputStream is = ((org.openide.text.CloneableEditorSupport)
                                    editCookie).getInputStream()) {
                doc = XMLUtil.parse(new InputSource(is),
                                    true, true, null, null);
                final CountDownLatch latch = new CountDownLatch(1);
                Platform.runLater(() -> {
                    try {
                        controller.refresh(doc);
                    } finally {
                        latch.countDown();
                    }
                });
                try {
                    latch.await();
                    // wait for refresh() to complete before initiating fade-in
                    Platform.runLater(() -> controller.doFadeIn());
                } catch (InterruptedException ex) {
                    logger.log(Level.WARNING, null, ex);
                }
            } catch (IOException | SAXException ex) {
                Exceptions.printStackTrace(ex);
            }
        }
    }
```

```
    @Override
    public void componentHidden() {
        Platform.runLater(() -> controller.clear());
    }
}
```

Listing 14.32 is the CSS to style our JavaFX content. Note that the Rectangles have a "leaner" look and the Text is no longer bold.

#### Listing 14.32 FamilyTree.css

```
.ftr-rectangle {
   -fx-fill: linear-gradient(#c9d9e8, #e7f7ff);
   -fx-effect: dropshadow( three-pass-box , gray , 10 , 0 , 5.0 , 5.0 );
   -fx-stroke-width:1.0;
   -fx-stroke: darkblue;
}
.ftr-text {
    -fx-font-size: 14;
}
.ftr-pane {
    -fx-background-color: linear-gradient(lightblue, #c9d9e8, #ddeeeb);
}
```

Listing 14.33 is the FXML for the JavaFX content. Again, a FlowPane control handles the scene's layout.

#### Listing 14.33 FamilyTreeFX.fxml

```
<FlowPane
    hgap="20"
    vgap="20"
    alignment="TOP_CENTER"
    id="FlowPane"
    fx:id="mypane"
    xmlns:fx="http://javafx.com/fxml"
    fx:controller=
         "com.asgteach.familytree.personfiletype.FamilyTreeFXController">
    <padding>
        <Insets bottom="10.0" left="10.0" right ="10.0" top="20.0"/>
    </padding>
    <stylesheets>
        <URL value="@FamilyTree.css" />
    </stylesheets>
    <children> </children>
</FlowPane>
```

Listing 14.34 shows the all-important FX controller class, **FamilyTreeFXController.java**. Here are a few interesting points about this JavaFX code.

- A double-click mouse event on the FlowPane control initiates the sequential transition that fades in the StackPane elements.
- The VisualFX MultiView element class invokes the public `refresh()`, `doFadeIn()`, and `clear()` methods on the JavaFX Application Thread. These methods implement one-way communication between Swing and the JavaFX controller.
- The private `makeElement()` method builds each StackPane element by parsing the editor's underlying document.
- Each StackPane element includes an ImageView control that displays the Image file **personIcon32.png**, a 32 x 32 PNG file.
- The StackPane groups a VBox control with an ImageView and Text on top of the Rectangle.

**Listing 14.34 FamilyTreeFXController.java**

```
public class FamilyTreeFXController implements Initializable {

    @FXML
    private FlowPane mypane;
    private final SequentialTransition seqTran = new SequentialTransition();
    private static final Logger logger = Logger.getLogger(
                                FamilyTreeFXController.class.getName());
    private final Image image = new Image(
      FamilyTreeFXController.class.getResourceAsStream("personIcon32.png"));

    @Override
    public void initialize(URL url, ResourceBundle rb) {
        mypane.getStyleClass().add("ftr-pane");
        mypane.setOnMouseClicked((event) -> {
            if (event.getClickCount() == 2) {
                doFadeIn();
            }
        });
    }

    // Invoked by Swing visual element on the JavaFX Application Thread
    public void doFadeIn() {
        seqTran.playFromStart();
    }
```

```
// Invoked by Swing visual element on the JavaFX Application Thread
public void clear() {
    seqTran.getChildren().clear();
    mypane.getChildren().clear();
}

// Invoked by Swing visual element on the JavaFX Application Thread
// Document is a parsed XML org.w3c.dom.Document
public void refresh(Document doc) {
    clear();
    NodeList nodeList = doc.getElementsByTagName("person");
    for (int i = 0; i < nodeList.getLength(); i++) {
        //For each node in the list, create a org.w3c.dom.Node
        org.w3c.dom.Node personNode = nodeList.item(i);
        NamedNodeMap map = personNode.getAttributes();
        Person person;
        if (map != null) {
            person = new Person();
            person.setLastname("Unknown");
            for (int j = 0; j < map.getLength(); j++) {
                org.w3c.dom.Node attrNode = map.item(j);
                if (attrNode.getNodeName().equals("firstname")) {
                    person.setFirstname(attrNode.getNodeValue());
                }
                if (attrNode.getNodeName().equals("lastname")) {
                    person.setLastname(attrNode.getNodeValue());
                }
            }
            StackPane stack = makeElement(person.toString());
            // Add the StackPane to the top-level Node (mypane)
            mypane.getChildren().add(stack);
            FadeTransition ft = new FadeTransition(
                        Duration.millis(650), stack);
            ft.setFromValue(0);
            ft.setToValue(1);
            seqTran.getChildren().add(ft);
        }
    }
}

private StackPane makeElement(String displayName) {
    // Build the StackPane
    StackPane stack = new StackPane();

    // Build the Text
    final Text ftrText = new Text(displayName);
    ftrText.getStyleClass().add("ftr-text");
    ftrText.setEffect(new Reflection());
```

```
        // Build the ImageView, put ImageView & Text in VBox
        ImageView iv = new ImageView(image);
        VBox vbox = new VBox(3, iv, ftrText);
        vbox.setAlignment(Pos.TOP_CENTER);
        vbox.setPadding(new Insets(10, 0, 0, 0));

        // Build the Rectangle
        Rectangle ftrRectangle = new Rectangle(
                    ftrText.getBoundsInParent().getWidth() + 40, 90);
        ftrRectangle.setArcHeight(20);
        ftrRectangle.setArcWidth(20);
        ftrRectangle.getStyleClass().add("ftr-rectangle");

        // Add the Rectangle, VBox to StackPane
        stack.getChildren().addAll(ftrRectangle, vbox);
        return stack;
    }
}
```

# 14.5 Key Point Summary

This chapter explores the Data System API, which provides handshaking between the Nodes API and the File System API. Here are the key points in this chapter.

- The DataObject class wraps a FileObject and creates a node that lets you visualize the file in an Explorer View.
- The DataObject's node may represent a multi-level node hierarchy, where child nodes depend on a file's contents.
- FileObjects have registered MIME types and DataLoaders, which are factories that create DataObjects.
- DataObjects have a Lookup that hold capabilities (such as editors) associated with a file.
- When you create a new file type, the New File Type wizard registers a MIME type resolver, DataLoader, file template, and DataObject subtype for that file type.
- In the New File Type wizard, use the MultiView checkbox to generate a MultiView editor associated with a file type. A MultiView window is a TopComponent with more than one window that is selectable with toolbar buttons. The default is Source (for text-based editors) and Visual (for Swing JComponent-based views).
- MultiViewElements have life cycle methods similar to TopComponent life cycle methods. You override these methods to control how views are initialized and refreshed.

- The New File Type wizard creates a default template that generates contents when creating a new file of that type. You can customize the template.
- Use the DataObject type associated with the file for the Cookie Class to create a conditionally-enabled action associated with a file type. To include the action in the file's Explorer View context menu, include checkbox File Type Context Menu Item and specify its MIME Type.
- Override a DataObject's `createNodeDelegate()` method to provide a custom node hierarchy. Install a FileChangeListener to keep the node hierarchy synchronized with the underlying file.
- Use Swing, the Visual Library, or JavaFX to create content for MultiView visual windows.
- Keep the views synchronized by updating the underlying document with any edits. You access the document through the DataObject's EditorCookie, available through its Lookup.
- The Visual Library lets you build Scenes with selectable, movable, and modifiable graphical components called widgets. The Scene is the root element and creates a Swing-compatible JComponent view that you can add to a Swing JPanel.
- Add actions to widgets to provide new behaviors, such as editing content.
- To add an action that is enabled when a particular visual element has focus, create a capability and add its implementation to the visual element's Lookup. The conditionally-enabled action depends on this capability. Use InstanceContent, AbstractLookup, and ProxyLookup to properly configure the visual element's Lookup.
- To build visual elements with JavaFX content, use the JavaFX integration strategies that keep JavaFX and Swing code loosely coupled.
- One-way communication between Swing visual elements and JavaFX controllers invoke public JavaFX controller methods on the JavaFX Application Thread. Use property change events to communicate user-initiated changes in the JavaFX scene graph back to the visual element.
- Create new XML file types with specific root elements.
- The NetBeans Platform is bundled with a full-featured XML editor. To use it in your NetBeans Platform application, include modules from the **ide** cluster.
- Use the NetBeans Platform XMLUtil class to manipulate XML content. The XMLUtil `parse()` method builds DOM documents from XML files.
- Build node hierarchies based on XML content by parsing the file and obtaining a DOM NodeList for specific tag names.

# 15

# JavaFX Charts

Before JavaFX, Swing developers had to rely on third-party libraries for chart components. Now that JavaFX is part of the JDK, developers can use the JavaFX Charts API to visualize data in their applications. And with the NetBeans Platform, you have the beauty of JavaFX charts and the architectural advantages of a sophisticated framework that lets you build applications with integrated JavaFX and Swing content.

This chapter shows you how to use the JavaFX Charts API with the NetBeans Platform. You'll learn how to create modular, loosely-coupled applications that display data with a wide variety of chart types in separate windows. You'll also learn how to apply JavaFX features such as animation, effects, and event handling to enhance your application.

## What You Will Learn

- Use JavaFX charts in a NetBeans Platform application.
- Structure modules that display chart data.
- Structure a NetBeans Platform application with multiple chart windows, keeping chart modules and data loosely coupled.
- Create a service provider for modules to access chart data from the Global Services Lookup.
- Explore each JavaFX chart.
- Style JavaFX charts with CSS.

- Add effects, animations, and event handlers to charts or individual display artifacts within a chart.
- Enable data editing in a Swing JTable or JavaFX chart window, and propagate these data changes throughout the application.
- Use binding to keep JavaFX controls synchronized.
- Create a NetBeans Platform conditionally-enabled action that applies to JavaFX chart windows.
- Save a chart window (or any window with JavaFX content) to a PNG-format file.
- Print a TopComponent window.

## 15.1 JavaFX Charts and the NetBeans Platform

Let's begin by showing you JavaFX charts in the context of a NetBeans Platform application. The JavaFX Chart package currently provides eight different charts to visualize data. Our example, the SmartPhone Data application, provides a set of sales data for smartphone companies over a four-year period. Each company's data is a series represented by a row in a table, and each year of data corresponds to a table column.

Before we discuss how JavaFX handles chart data, let's describe the application and its features.

Figure 15.1 shows the SmartPhone Data application (called the SDA) running. There are ten windows in total. Nine windows contain JavaFX charts, and the tenth window displays the raw data in table form (the lower-right window). You can edit the data in the table, and edits are propagated to the other chart windows. When you change JavaFX chart data, the charts use animation to redraw their contents. These changes may also reposition the chart legend and rescale the chart.

Visible chart windows in Figure 15.1 include the Pie Chart (on the left), Bar Chart (top center), and Line Chart (top right).

JavaFX charts are rendered as nodes in the scene graph. This means you can apply effects and add animations to charts. You can also manipulate the scene graph. Figure 15.2 shows two examples with Pie Chart windows. The left window depicts a selected wedge animating outward. The percentage represented by the selected wedge is shown in a label that fades in during the wedge animation. The right window shows a JavaFX TextField that displays the value of the selected wedge. The TextField appears with a control mouse-click event over a pie slice. When the user provides a new number, the change updates the other charts and the table.

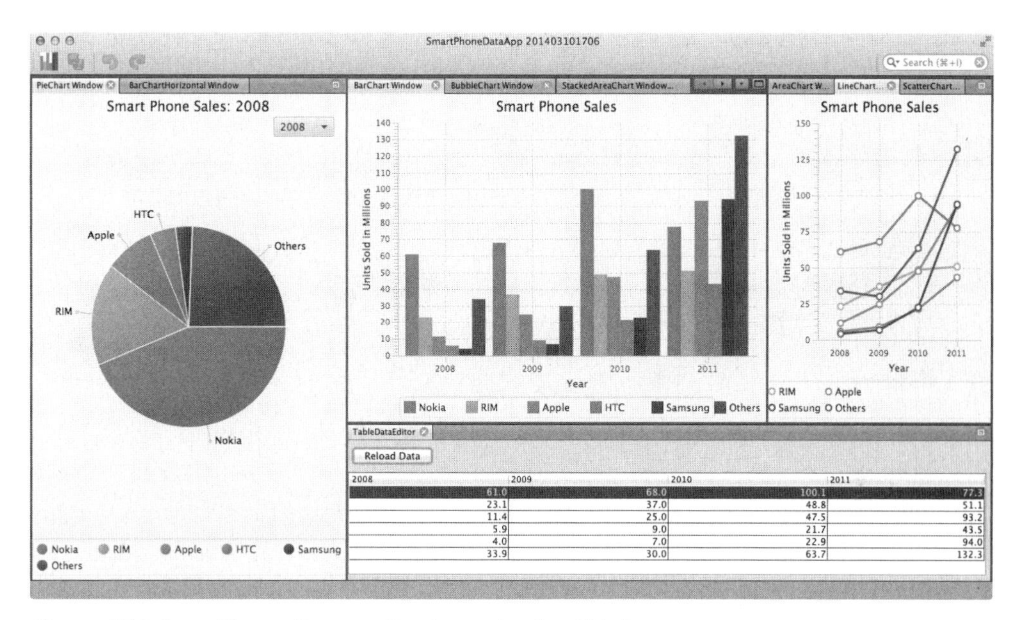


Figure 15.1 SmartPhone Data application: using JavaFX charts

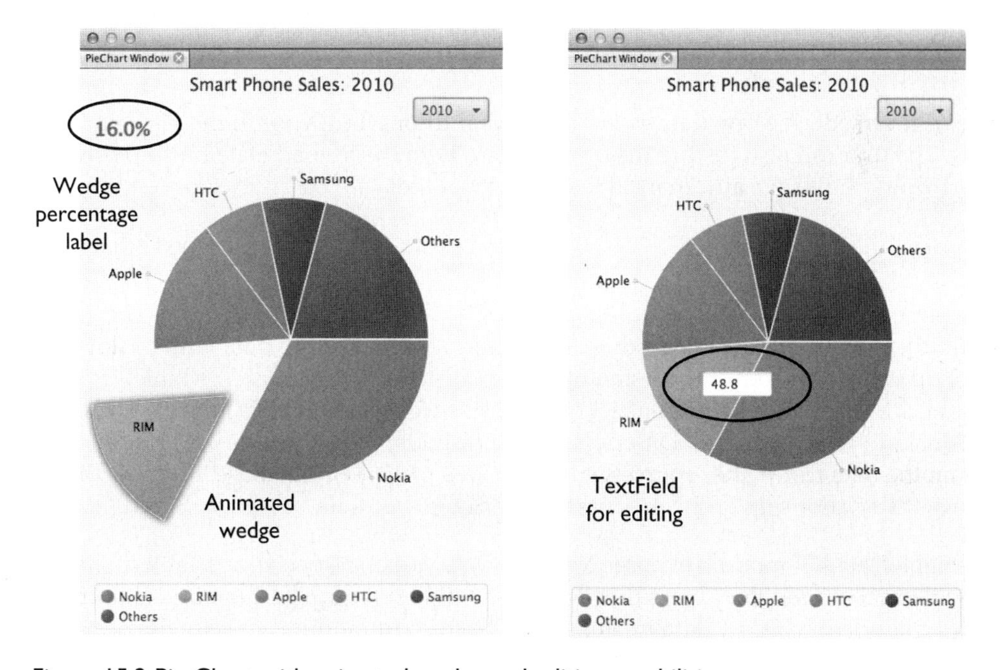


Figure 15.2 Pie Chart with animated wedge and editing capabilities

Figure 15.3 shows another set of windows, including a horizontal Bar Chart on the left, a Bubble Chart in the center, and an Area Chart in the top-right window.

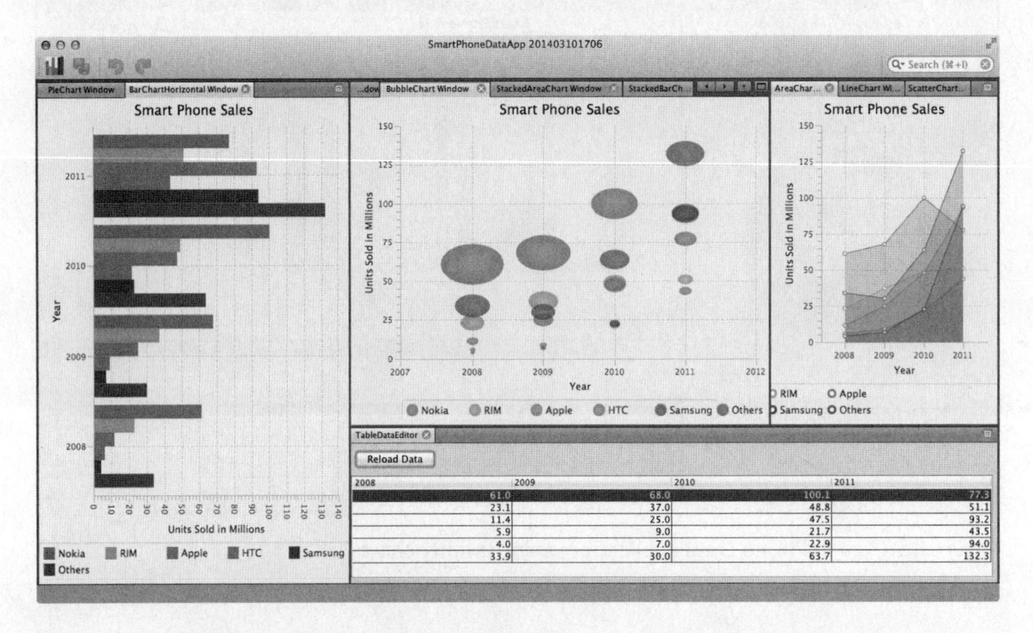


Figure 15.3 SmartPhone Data application with different charts visible

The user can edit the raw data in the TableDataEditor window or in the PieChart window. The user can also restore the original data with the Reload Data button, print a chart window, or save any chart to disk as a PNG file.

## Application Overview

The SDA is organized into modules, with each chart in a separate module. The TableDataEditor is also in its own module. Each module accesses the data with a Global Lookup using a customized version of Swing AbstractTableModel (MyTableDataModel). To work with a different set of data, you would extend MyTableDataModel and include your own data. Different service providers for MyTableDataModel can obtain the data from other sources, such as a web service or database. Figure 15.4 shows the relationship of the modules in the SDA.

The TableDataAPI module exposes MyTableDataModel, a specialized TableModel class that other modules access through the Global Lookup. The TableDataEditor displays a window with the data in table form. Each chart module accesses the data by obtaining the service provider for MyTableDataModel through the Global Lookup.

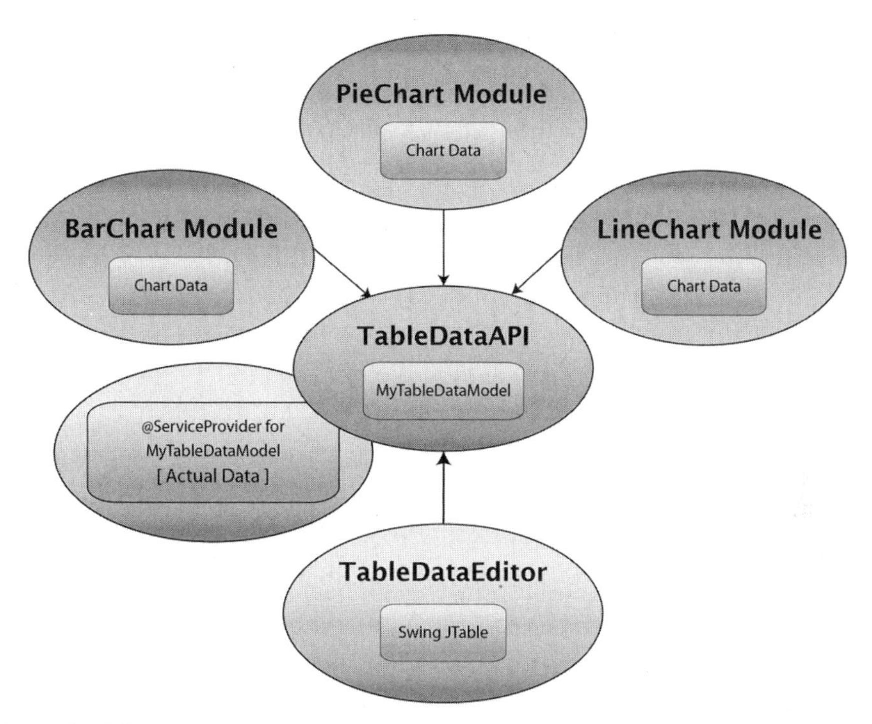


Figure 15.4 SmartPhone Data application module organization

The JavaFX chart modules all use FXML for chart controls and a corresponding JavaFX controller class that builds the chart data. When the data changes, the table model implementation fires a Swing TableModelEvent, allowing registered listeners to respond. Each JavaFX controller class implements a TableModelListener to respond to user edits of the table data.

### Steps to Build the SmartPhone Data Application

Let's summarize the steps required to build the SmartPhone Data application. The summarized application structure shows you how a NetBeans Platform application can effectively use the JavaFX chart controls to visualize data. We'll discuss the individual modules in more detail throughout this chapter.

- Create a new NetBeans Platform application called **SmartPhoneDataApp**.
- Create a **TableDataAPI** module and add it to the SmartPhoneDataApp application. Create abstract Java class MyTableDataModel to extend AbstractTableModel. Make MyTableDataModel's enclosing package public so that other modules can add a module dependency on the TableDataAPI module.

- Create a **SmartPhoneDataImpl** module and set a module dependency on the TableDataAPI module. Create concrete Java class SmartPhoneDataImpl that extends MyTableDataModel. Install the data and provide implementations for the methods in AbstractTableData and MyTableDataModel. Register SmartPhone-DataImpl as a @ServiceProvider for MyTableDataModel.
- Create a **TableDataEditor** module and set a module dependency on the Table-DataAPI module. Create a TopComponent window. Add a JTable and a Reload Data button. Initialize the JTable using the Global Lookup to access the data.
- Create modules for each of the JavaFX charts. Include separate modules for a Bar Chart displayed vertically and horizontally. Set module dependencies on the TableDataAPI module. Create TopComponent windows, FXML files, and JavaFX controller classes for each module. Initialize the JavaFX chart controls using the Global Lookup to access the data. Enable printing for the TopComponents.
- Add special behaviors to the JavaFX chart controller classes as you like. We discuss features added to the PieChart module.
- Create a **ChartUtilities** module and add a conditionally-enabled action that saves the selected chart window to a file on disk. Implement the ChartSaveCapability in each TopComponent to provide the support code for saving a chart.

## Working with AbstractTableModel

Access to table data in Swing requires the TableModel interface, which provides methods for manipulating table data. The AbstractTableModel class provides default implementations for most of the methods in the TableModel interface. This abstract class manages listeners and provides methods for generating TableModelEvents, which are then dispatched to registered listeners. With AbstractTableModel you must provide implementations minimally for the `getRowCount()`, `getColumnCount()`, and `getValueAt()` methods.

The MyTableDataModel abstract class has methods for extracting additional information to decorate JavaFX charts. The information includes a title, category names (names assigned to each data series), and descriptive labels for the data. Additionally, the `getOriginalData()` method restores the data to the original values, which lets users experiment with different data values.

The MyTableDataModel class extends AbstractTableModel and is the service provider target class for accessing the application's data. We add this class, shown in Listing 15.1, to the TableDataAPI module's public package.

**Listing 15.1 MyTableDataModel.java**

```
public abstract class MyTableDataModel extends AbstractTableModel {

    public abstract Object[][] getOriginalData();
    public abstract double getTickUnit();
    public abstract List<String> getColumnNames();

    public abstract List<String> getCategoryNames();
    public abstract int getCategoryCount();
    public abstract String getCategoryName(int row);
    public abstract String getDataDescription();
    public abstract String getNameDescription();
    public abstract String getTitle();

}
```

Listing 15.2 shows the SmartPhoneDataImpl class, which provides a concrete extension of the MyTableDataModel abstract class. We install this class in the SmartPhone-DataImpl module and register the class as a service provider for MyTableDataModel.

The `names` and `categories` String arrays provide labels for the data columns and category names. Similarly, the `dataDescription` and `nameDescription` Strings provide legend labels. The `title` String provides the title text.

The actual data is a two-dimensional Object array used by TableModel. The `clone()` method makes a deep copy of the original data for later retrieval.

The SmartPhoneDataImpl class implements the public methods from MyTableData-Model (see Listing 15.1) and the methods required by AbstractTableModel. The `isCellEditable()` method returns true, allowing user updates. The `setValueAt()` method updates the data and fires a table cell updated event. (The Abstract-TableModel class handles listener registration and event dispatching.)

Since the data is configured with the Swing TableModel, the Swing JTable component can use this class directly. The JavaFX charts, however, need to extract the data and inject them into the required JavaFX charts observable collections.[1]

1. SmartPhone sales data sources: Year 2008: Gartner (March 2009); Year 2009: Tomi Ahonen (April 2010); Years 2010 and 2011: IDC (February 2012).

**Listing 15.2 SmartPhoneDataImpl.java**

```
@ServiceProvider(service = MyTableDataModel.class)
public class SmartPhoneDataImpl extends MyTableDataModel {

    private final String[] names = {"2008", "2009", "2010", "2011"};
    private final String[] categories =
            {"Nokia", "RIM", "Apple", "HTC", "Samsung", "Others"};
    private final String dataDescription = "Units Sold in Millions";
    private final String nameDescription = "Year";
    private final String title = "Smart Phone Sales";
    private final Object[][] data = {
        // Sources:
        // 2008: Gartner (March 2009)
        // 2009: Tomi Ahonen (April 2010)
        // 2010, 2011: IDC (February 2012)
            // Nokia
            {61.0, 68.0, 100.1, 77.3},

            // ResearchInMotion
            {23.1, 37.0, 48.8, 51.1},

            // Apple
            {11.4, 25.0, 47.5, 93.2},

            // HTC
            {5.9, 9.0, 21.7, 43.5},

            // Samsung
            {4.0, 7.0, 22.9, 94.0},

            // Others
            {33.9, 30.0, 63.7, 132.3}
        };

    private final Object[][] orig = clone(data);

    // provide deep copy semantics
    private static Object[][] clone(Object[][] g) {
        Object[][] newArray = new Object[g.length][];
        for (int i = 0; i < g.length; i++) {
            newArray[i] = new Object[g[i].length];
            System.arraycopy(g[i], 0, newArray[i], 0, g[i].length);
        }
        return newArray;
    }

    @Override
    public final Object[][] getOriginalData() {
        return orig;
    }
```

```
@Override
public double getTickUnit() {
    return 1000;
}

@Override
public List<String> getColumnNames() {
    return Arrays.asList(names);
}

// Add support for Category Names
@Override
public List<String> getCategoryNames() {
    return Arrays.asList(categories);
}
@Override
public int getCategoryCount() {
    return getRowCount();
}
@Override
public String getCategoryName(int row) {
    return categories[row];
}

@Override
public String getDataDescription() {
    return dataDescription;
}

@Override
public String getNameDescription() {
    return nameDescription;
}

@Override
public String getTitle() {
    return title;
}

@Override
public int getRowCount() {
    return data.length;
}

@Override
public int getColumnCount() {
    return names.length;
}
```

```
    @Override
    public Object getValueAt(int row, int column) {
        return data[row][column];
    }

    @Override
    public String getColumnName(int column) {
        return names[column];
    }

    @Override
    public Class<?> getColumnClass(int columnIndex) {
        return getValueAt(0, columnIndex).getClass();
    }

    @Override
    public boolean isCellEditable(int row, int column) {
        return true;
    }

    @Override
    public void setValueAt(Object value, int row, int column) {
        if (value instanceof Double) {
            data[row][column] = (Double) value;
        }
        fireTableCellUpdated(row, column);
    }
}
```

## Working with Swing JTable

The TableDataEditor module includes a TopComponent configured in the output mode. This window appears in the lower-right location as shown in Figure 15.1 on page 745. The TopComponent has a Swing JTable that displays the raw data and a Data Reload button to restore the original data values from the clone array.

Listing 15.3 shows the TopComponent registration and initialization code for the TableDataEditorTopComponent class. The constructor initializes the `tableModel` field with the MyTableModelData service provider from the Global Lookup. The TopComponent includes custom initialization code to set the JTable component model property with this data.

**Listing 15.3 TableDataEditorTopComponent.java—Initialization Code**

```
@ConvertAsProperties(
        dtd = "-//org.smartphone.data.editor//TableDataEditor//EN",
        autostore = false
)
```

```
@TopComponent.Description(
        preferredID = "TableDataEditorTopComponent",
        iconBase = "org/smartphone/tabledata/editor/line_chart.png",
        persistenceType = TopComponent.PERSISTENCE_ALWAYS
)
@TopComponent.Registration(mode = "output", openAtStartup = true)
@ActionID(category = "Window",
         id = "org.smartphone.tabledata.editor.TableDataEditorTopComponent")
@ActionReference(path = "Menu/Window" /*, position = 333 */)
@TopComponent.OpenActionRegistration(
        displayName = "#CTL_TableDataEditorAction",
        preferredID = "TableDataEditorTopComponent"
)
@Messages({
    "CTL_TableDataEditorAction=TableDataEditor",
    "CTL_TableDataEditorTopComponent=TableDataEditor",
    "HINT_TableDataEditorTopComponent=This is a TableDataEditor window"
})
public final class TableDataEditorTopComponent extends TopComponent {

    private static MyTableDataModel tableModel;
    private static final Logger logger = Logger.getLogger(
                    TableDataEditorTopComponent.class.getName());

    public TableDataEditorTopComponent() {
        // initialize tableModel before invoking initComponents()
        tableModel = Lookup.getDefault().lookup(MyTableDataModel.class);
        if (tableModel == null ) {
            logger.log(Level.SEVERE, "Cannot get TableModel object");
            LifecycleManager.getDefault().exit();
        }
        initComponents();
        setName(Bundle.CTL_TableDataEditorTopComponent());
        setToolTipText(Bundle.HINT_TableDataEditorTopComponent());
        // setup the JTable
        init();
    }

      // Generated code to initialize the components
    private void initComponents() {

        reloadButton = new javax.swing.JButton();
        jScrollPane1 = new javax.swing.JScrollPane();
        table = new javax.swing.JTable();
         . . .

        table.setModel(tableModel);       // custom code
            . . .
    }
. . .
}
```

The JTable table component uses a custom cell renderer to format the numbers and provide cell editing. Listing 15.4 shows the init() method that the TopComponent constructor calls. This method sets the JTable's row sorter, grid color, and installs a custom renderer for each cell.

**Listing 15.4 TableDataEditorTopComponent.java—Table Configuration**

```
public final class TableDataEditorTopComponent extends TopComponent {
. . .
    public void init() {
        table.setAutoCreateRowSorter(true);
        table.setGridColor(Color.DARK_GRAY);

        TableDataEditorTopComponent.DecimalFormatRenderer renderer =
               new TableDataEditorTopComponent.DecimalFormatRenderer();
        renderer.setHorizontalAlignment(JLabel.RIGHT);
        for (int i = 0; i < table.getColumnCount(); i++) {
            table.getColumnModel().getColumn(i).setCellRenderer(renderer);
        }
    }

    private static class DecimalFormatRenderer extends
                                    DefaultTableCellRenderer {

       private static final DecimalFormat formatter = new DecimalFormat("#.0");

        @Override
        public Component getTableCellRendererComponent(
                JTable table, Object value,
                boolean isSelected,
                boolean hasFocus,
                int row,
                int column) {
            value = formatter.format((Number) value);
            return super.getTableCellRendererComponent(
               table, value, isSelected, hasFocus, row, column);
        }
    }
. . .
}
```

Listing 15.5 shows the Reload Data button event handler. The handler invokes MyTableDataModel method getOriginalData() to load the original data into the JTable table component. The JTable setValueAt() method invokes the model's setValueAt() method, which fires table cell updated events for registered listeners. This in turn updates the chart windows.

**Listing 15.5 TableDataEditorTopComponent.java—Reload Data Event Handler**

```
public final class TableDataEditorTopComponent extends TopComponent {
. . .
    private void reloadButtonActionPerformed(
                                ActionEvent evt) {
        // Get the original data
        Object[][] orig = tableModel.getOriginalData();
        for (int row = 0; row < orig.length; row++) {
            for (int col = 0; col < orig[row].length; col++) {
                Double current = (Double)orig[row][col];
                table.setValueAt(current, row, col);
            }
        }
    }
. . .
}
```

## Integrating JavaFX Charts

In a NetBeans Platform application with JavaFX charts, you configure the JavaFX content as described in Chapter 6 (see "JavaFX and the NetBeans Platform" on page 250). Our SDA application has a module for each chart, giving maximum flexibility for window layout. Each module includes the window (TopComponent), FXML markup for the JavaFX controls, and the JavaFX controller class. All JavaFX modules have the same structure, which we'll describe next using the Line Chart as an example. We'll discuss the other charts in the following sections.

### Create Chart Module

Create a new module named **Chart - Line** and add it to the SDA application. Use package name **org.smartphone.chart.line**.

### Chart FXML

Add FXML file **linechart.fxml** to the Source Package in module Chart - Line, as shown in Listing 15.6. We place the chart in a StackPane control since StackPane automatically centers its content, even with window resizing.

The FXML markup specifies the controller class with the `fx:controller` attribute. The StackPane and LineChart both specify `fx:id` attributes that let the controller class access these controls. LineChart is an XYChart, which requires xAxis and yAxis elements. These also have `fx:id` definitions. The axis element type (CategoryAxis or NumberAxis) depends on the data, chart, and chart layout.

**Listing 15.6 linechart.fxml**

```
<?xml version="1.0" encoding="UTF-8"?>

<?import java.lang.*?>
<?import java.util.*?>
<?import javafx.geometry.*?>
<?import javafx.scene.*?>
<?import javafx.scene.control.*?>
<?import javafx.scene.layout.*?>
<?import javafx.scene.chart.*?>

<StackPane id="StackPane" fx:id="stackpane"
           xmlns:fx="http://javafx.com/fxml"
           fx:controller="org.smartphone.chart.line.LineChartController">

    <LineChart fx:id="chart" >
        <xAxis>
            <CategoryAxis fx:id="xAxis"/>
        </xAxis>
        <yAxis>
            <NumberAxis fx:id="yAxis"/>
        </yAxis>
    </LineChart>
</StackPane>
```

## Chart Controller

Listing 15.7 shows the chart controller code. All chart controllers have `@FXML` annotations that identify the FXML file controls. The Global Lookup returns the MyTableDataModel service provider (the `tableModel` field) to access the data. The JavaFX controller configures each chart (shown in the next section) and defines a public `getImage()` method that returns a Swing-compatible snapshot of the JavaFX scene graph.[2] The TopComponent invokes the `getImage()` method to implement the Save Chart action. (See “Saving Charts” on page 789 for the Save Chart action implementation.)

**Listing 15.7 LineChartController.java**

```
public class LineChartController implements Initializable {

    @FXML
    private StackPane stackpane;
    @FXML
    private CategoryAxis xAxis;
```

2. Note that a “snapshot” reflects the scene graph as it is configured within the enclosing TopComponent; resizing a window affects the resulting image.

```
    @FXML
    private NumberAxis yAxis;
    @FXML
    private LineChart<String, Number> chart;

    private ObservableList<XYChart.Series<String, Number>> lcData;
    private MyTableDataModel tableModel;
    private static final Logger logger = Logger.getLogger(
            LineChartController.class.getName());

    @Override
    public void initialize(URL url, ResourceBundle rb) {
        createLineChart();
    }

    private void createLineChart() {
        tableModel = Lookup.getDefault().lookup(MyTableDataModel.class);
        if (tableModel == null) {
            logger.log(Level.SEVERE, "Cannot get TableModel object");
            LifecycleManager.getDefault().exit();
        }
      . . . code to setup and configure JavaFX Chart using tableModel data . . .
    }

    public BufferedImage getImage() {
        // must be in JavaFX Application Thread
        SnapshotParameters params = new SnapshotParameters();
        Image jfximage = stackpane.snapshot(params, null);
        return SwingFXUtils.fromFXImage(jfximage, null);
    }
}
```

### Chart TopComponent

Add a LineChartTopComponent window to the Chart - Line module, as shown in Listing 15.8. The constructor uses JFXPanel to initialize the JavaFX content in the scene graph. Build the JavaFX content on the JavaFX Application Thread by loading the FXML and instantiating the JavaFX controller class.

A single line of code provides the print capabilities for the window, which sets the `print.printable` property to true. InstanceContent (see "Lookup as an Object Repository" on page 225) lets you add objects to the TopComponent's Lookup. We'll use InstanceContent to implement the Save Chart capability.

**Listing 15.8 LineChartTopComponent.java**

```
@ConvertAsProperties(
    dtd = "-//org.smartphone.chart.line//LineChart//EN",
   autostore = false)
@TopComponent.Description(
    preferredID = "LineChartTopComponent",
   //iconBase="SET/PATH/TO/ICON/HERE",
   persistenceType = TopComponent.PERSISTENCE_ALWAYS)
@TopComponent.Registration(mode = "properties", openAtStartup = true)
@ActionID(category = "Window",
      id = "org.smartphone.chart.line.LineChartTopComponent")
@ActionReference(path = "Menu/Window" /*, position = 333 */)
@TopComponent.OpenActionRegistration(
      displayName = "#CTL_LineChartAction",
      preferredID = "LineChartTopComponent")
@Messages({
    "CTL_LineChartAction=LineChart",
    "CTL_LineChartTopComponent=LineChart Window",
    "HINT_LineChartTopComponent=This is a LineChart window"
})
public final class LineChartTopComponent extends TopComponent {

    private static JFXPanel chartFxPanel;
    private LineChartController controller;
    private final InstanceContent content = new InstanceContent();

    public LineChartTopComponent() {
        initComponents();
        setName(Bundle.CTL_LineChartTopComponent());
        setToolTipText(Bundle.HINT_LineChartTopComponent());
        associateLookup(new AbstractLookup(content));

        setLayout(new BorderLayout());
        // Enable the Print action for the TopComponent:
        putClientProperty("print.printable", true);
        init();
    }

    public void init() {
        chartFxPanel = new JFXPanel();
        add(chartFxPanel, BorderLayout.CENTER);
        Platform.setImplicitExit(false);
        Platform.runLater(() -> createScene());
    }

    private void createScene() {
        try {
            URL location = getClass().getResource("linechart.fxml");
            FXMLLoader fxmlLoader = new FXMLLoader();
            fxmlLoader.setLocation(location);
            fxmlLoader.setBuilderFactory(new JavaFXBuilderFactory());
```

```
            Parent root = (Parent) fxmlLoader.load(location.openStream());
            chartFxPanel.setScene(new Scene(root));
            controller = (LineChartController) fxmlLoader.getController();

        } catch (IOException ex) {
            Exceptions.printStackTrace(ex);
        }
    }
    . . .
}
```

## 15.2 Introducing JavaFX Charts

The JavaFX Chart API is an important feature for applications that visualize data. Fortunately, you can easily integrate JavaFX charts into your NetBeans Platform applications. Depending on your data's characteristics and the type of visualization that you require, you can choose one or more charts. In the SmartPhone Data application, we use all charts with the same data, which shows each chart's visualization strengths.

You'll discover the JavaFX charts are straightforward to use. Although the charts are highly configurable, default settings fit most requirements. You can also alter any chart's appearance with custom CSS styling. Let's begin with an overview of the JavaFX Chart API.

### JavaFX Chart Overview

Figure 15.5 shows the JavaFX chart class hierarchy. Abstract class Chart extends Node, Parent, and Region, and therefore inherits all the features of these superclasses, including animation, effects, and CSS styling. All charts have an XY axis except Pie Chart.

Chart is the base class for all charts and defines the title, legend, and content for each chart. The chart content is populated by the specific subclass of Chart. For example, Figure 15.6 shows a Line Chart, which is responsible for creating its chart contents. In this example, the contents include the X axis with a label, Y axis with a label, and plotted lines and tick marks.

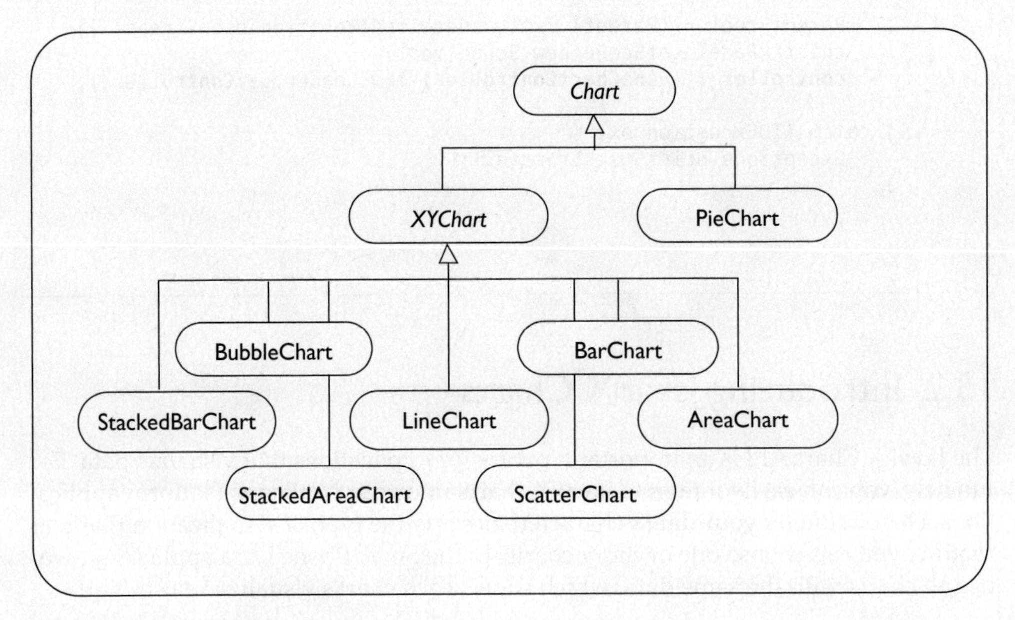


Figure 15.5 JavaFX Chart class hierarchy

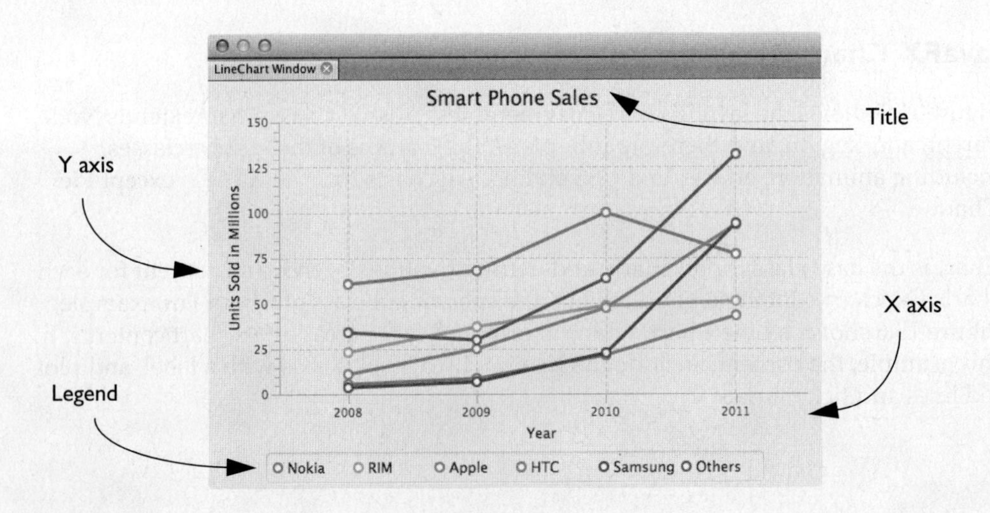


Figure 15.6 Parts of a chart

## Chart Properties

Table 15.1 lists the properties common to all charts. Note that these JavaFX properties can participate in binding expressions. Typically, the only property you'll need to set is the `title` property.

By default, charts animate changes to their data. For example, in Figure 15.6, if a LineChart value changes in one of the series for 2008, the line angle moves as the data point travels to its new plot location. Similarly, in a PieChart, a new value affects the entire wedge layout. The content is not re-drawn from scratch. Rather, all wedges dynamically resize as their relative shapes adjust to the new values. You can disable this feature by setting the `animated` property to false.

As shown in Table 15.1, you can also configure the legend location, the title and its location, and whether or not the legend is visible.The legend property itself is protected and configured by chart subclasses.

**TABLE 15.1 Properties Common to All Charts**

| Property | Type | Description |
|---|---|---|
| animated | BooleanProperty | Animate data changes |
| legend | ObjectProperty<Node> | Node that contains the legend |
| legendSide | ObjectProperty<Side> | Chart side location of the legend |
| legendVisible | BooleanProperty | Display legend |
| title | StringProperty | Chart title |
| titleSide | ObjectProperty<Side> | Chart side location of title |

## XY Charts

The XYChart abstract class is the base class for all two-axis charts and is responsible for drawing the axes and plot contents. Subclasses of XYChart are shown in Figure 15.5 on page 760. Properties for the XYChart class include controlling grid line visibility and whether alternating columns and rows have a visible fill. The most important property for XYChart is the data, whose type is as follows.

```
ObjectProperty<ObservableList<XYChart.Series<X,Y>>>
```

A chart's data is stored in an ObservableList (see "Observable Collections" on page 148). The list type is `XYChart.Series<X,Y>`, which is a named series of data items (XYCharts manipulate a list of lists). Data items are type `XYChart.Data<X,Y>`, a generic type where X represents the X axis type and Y represents the Y axis type. Data items also include an extra value (`extraValue` property) that can be used in any way the subclassed chart needs.

For example, the LineChart in Figure 15.6 on page 760, has six series (Nokia, RIM, Apple, HTC, Samsung, and Others) whose names are displayed in the chart's legend. Each series has four data points, and each data point has an X value String for the year and a Y value Number for the sales in millions of units. (You can review the raw data in Listing 15.2 on page 750.) Thus, the LineChart's ObservableList is type

```
ObservableList<XYChart.Series<String, Number>>
```

where the X axis is a String type and the Y axis is a Number type. The data item for this series is

```
XYChart.Data<String, Number>
```

where the X axis value is a String (the year) and the Y axis value is a Number (units sold in millions).

Table 15.2 shows the properties of the XYChart.Series<X,Y> type. Table 15.3 shows useful properties of the XYChart.Data<X,Y> type. For example, to get the node that represents the series, use getNode() for the node or nodeProperty() for the JavaFX property getter. To set the XValue and YValue of a data item, use

```
XYChart.Data<String, Number> myData;
. . .
myData.setXValue("2009");
myData.setYValue(25.5);
```

**TABLE 15.2 XYChart.Series<X, Y> Useful Properties**

| Property | Type | Description |
|---|---|---|
| data | ObjectProperty<ObservableList<XYChart.Data<X,Y>>> | The data contained in this series |
| chart | ReadOnlyObjectProperty<XYChart<X,Y>> | Chart this series belongs to |
| node | ObjectProperty<Node> | Node represented by this series |
| name | StringProperty | The name of this series |

**TABLE 15.3 XYChart.Data<X, Y> Useful Properties**

| Property | Type | Description |
|---|---|---|
| XValue | ObjectProperty<X> | Data value for the X axis |
| YVaue | ObjectProperty<Y> | Data value for the Y axis |
| extraValue | ObjectProperty<Object> | Data corresponding to an extra value |
| node | ObjectProperty<Node> | Node represented by plot point |

Because charts manage observable lists, chart objects respond to data changes automatically, updating their content with animation (and redrawing the legend and axes as necessary). Charts also respond to resizing events. For example, the Line Chart in Figure 15.7 appears in a floating window that has been reduced in size. The StackPane layout control keeps the chart centered, and the LineChart adjusts the contents. Here, the legend is no longer visible, the Y axis description is shortened, and the Y axis labels are reduced. The plot points have also been adjusted to appropriately fill the chart space.

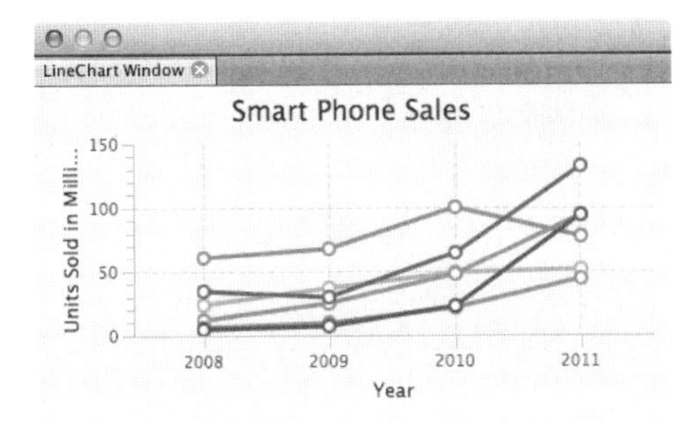


Figure 15.7 Automatic adjustments after resizing a chart

Ultimately, the chart's data items are represented by nodes in a scene graph. You can access a data item's node, the chart's node, and the data series' node. You can therefore configure these nodes with event listeners (such as mouse clicks), effects, and animations. We'll show you how to do this in "Accessing JavaFX Chart Nodes" on page 782.

## Chart Styling

Charts use CSS for styling. You can configure the padding, text sizes, and fonts, and define legend and plot data symbols. CSS styles also define default colors for pie wedges and series data. The JavaFX charts have been restyled in JavaFX 8 to use the Modena theme. You can customize chart styles by providing your own values for the CSS chart styles. See "CSS Files" on page 98 for locating the default Modena CSS file.

For example, Figure 15.8 shows a restyled Line Chart. Three series colors are customized, along with their corresponding legend colors. In addition, we increase the Line Chart's line stroke width (a change you can actually discern in the black and white screenshot).

Listing 15.9 shows the CSS styles used. Each chart type has its own styles. To load the CSS file, add attribute `stylesheets="org/smartphone/chart/line/lineChartStyle.css"` to the top-level StackPane in the Line Chart module's FXML file, **linechart.fxml**.

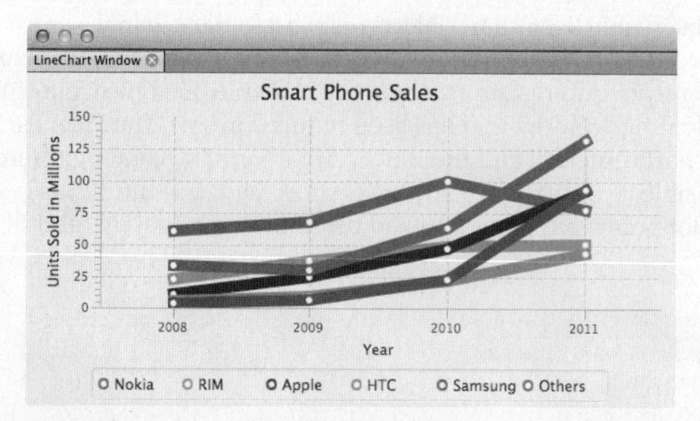


Figure 15.8 Customize styling with CSS

**Listing 15.9 lineChartStyle.css**

```
.chart-series-line {
    -fx-stroke-width: 10px;
    -fx-effect: null;
}

.default-color0.chart-series-line { -fx-stroke: #ff3300; }
.default-color1.chart-series-line { -fx-stroke: #00ff00; }
.default-color2.chart-series-line { -fx-stroke: #0033ff; }

.default-color0.chart-line-symbol { -fx-background-color: #ff3300, white; }
.default-color1.chart-line-symbol { -fx-background-color: #00ff00, white; }
.default-color2.chart-line-symbol { -fx-background-color: #0033ff, white; }
```

## 15.3 Data Visualization with JavaFX Charts

Each chart emphasizes different aspects of the same data. In this section, we'll summarize the features of the JavaFX charts. First, let's build charts from what we know about charts, series, and data items. We'll start with the Line Chart. Unless otherwise indicated, all charts are built exactly how we describe in the following section for Line Chart.

### Line Chart

Line Charts (see Figure 15.6 on page 760 and Figure 15.8) show you comparative trends with plotted data series. Because the chart draws lines connecting plot points, you can visualize trends within a series and comparative trends when there is more than one series. Plotting stock prices over time is a common application for Line Charts.

Listing 15.10 shows how to build the LineChart's data. The LineChartController class configures and sets the data for the Line Chart.

First, the declarations for the `xAxis`, `yAxis`, `chart`, and `lcdata` fields show that `chart` is a LineChart with a String value for the X Axis and a Number value for the Y Axis. The `xAxis` field is therefore a CategoryAxis type (String label), and `yAxis` is a NumberAxis type (Number value). The `lcData` LineChart data field type is an `ObservableList<XYChart.Series<String, Number>>`.

The `createLineChart()` method configures the LineChart. The methods we added to the MyTableDataModel abstract class define the labels and descriptive values of the axes. X axis is a CategoryAxis with an observable list of Strings for the category names. These are the MyTableDataModel column names (the years in String form). The X Axis label is set from the MyTableDataModel name description.

The Y Axis also has a label. Because the Y Axis is a NumberAxis type, we set the tick unit. Lastly, we set the chart's title and its data with the `getLineChartData()` method (shown in Listing 15.11 on page 766).

#### Listing 15.10 LineChartController.java—Configure the LineChart

```
public class LineChartController implements Initializable {

    @FXML
    private StackPane stackpane;
    @FXML
    private CategoryAxis xAxis;
    @FXML
    private NumberAxis yAxis;
    @FXML
    private LineChart<String, Number> chart;
    private ObservableList<XYChart.Series<String, Number>> lcData;
    private MyTableDataModel tableModel;
    private static final Logger logger = Logger.getLogger(
                    LineChartController.class.getName());

    @Override
    public void initialize(URL url, ResourceBundle rb) {
        createLineChart();
    }
```

```
    private void createLineChart() {
        tableModel = Lookup.getDefault().lookup(MyTableDataModel.class);
        if (tableModel == null) {
            logger.log(Level.SEVERE, "Cannot get TableModel object");
            LifecycleManager.getDefault().exit();
        }
        xAxis.setCategories(FXCollections.observableArrayList(
                tableModel.getColumnNames()));
        xAxis.setLabel(tableModel.getNameDescription());
        yAxis.setTickUnit(tableModel.getTickUnit());
        yAxis.setLabel(tableModel.getDataDescription());

        chart.setTitle(tableModel.getTitle());
        chart.setData(getLineChartData());

. . . Add TableModelListener to tableModel, see Listing 15.12 on page 767 . . .
    }
. . .
}
```

Listing 15.11 shows the `getLineChartData()` method, which builds an observable collection containing the XYChart.Series for each row in the table data. Each Series, in turn, has a list of data items set by the appropriate row and column data from the table model. The table model `getColumnName()` method returns the column's String name (the year in String form).

#### Listing 15.11 LineChartController.java—getLineChartData()

```
public class LineChartController implements Initializable {
    . . .

    private ObservableList<XYChart.Series<String, Number>>
                                                    getLineChartData() {
        if (lcData == null) {
            lcData = FXCollections.observableArrayList();
            for (int row = 0; row < tableModel.getRowCount(); row++) {
                XYChart.Series<String, Number> series = new XYChart.Series<>();
                series.setName(tableModel.getCategoryName(row));
                for (int column = 0;
                        column < tableModel.getColumnCount(); column++) {
                    series.getData().add(new XYChart.Data<>(
                            tableModel.getColumnName(column),
                            (Number) tableModel.getValueAt(row, column)));
                }
```

```
                lcData.add(series);
            }
        }
        return lcData;
    }
}
```

Listing 15.12 shows the TableModelListener that we add to the `tableModel` field. Recall that `tableModel` extends AbstractTableModel, which provides support for adding listeners. The event handler obtains the row and column number of the changed value and gets the new value from the event source. In the JavaFX Application Thread, the handler gets the series that corresponds to the changed row, and `data.setYValue()` updates the corresponding data item.

**Listing 15.12 LineChartController.java—TableModelListener**

```
public class LineChartController implements Initializable {
   . . .
    private void createLineChart() {
   . . . code omitted . . . (see Listing 15.10) . . .

        // set up the event handler to respond to changes in the table data
        // This is a Swing event, so we must use Platform.runLater()
        // to update JavaFX components
        tableModel.addTableModelListener((TableModelEvent e) -> {
            if (e.getType() == TableModelEvent.UPDATE) {
                final int row = e.getFirstRow();
                final int column = e.getColumn();
                final Number value = (Number)((MyTableDataModel)
                                    e.getSource()).getValueAt(row, column);
                Platform.runLater(() -> {
                   XYChart.Series<String, Number> s = chart.getData().get(row);
                    LineChart.Data<String, Number> data =
                           s.getData().get(column);
                    data.setYValue(value);
                });
            }
        });
    }
. . .
}
```

## Scatter Chart

Figure 15.9 shows the Scatter Chart (also called an XY Plot) for the SDA. Scatter Charts excel at displaying large sets of data and possibly showing correlations between X Axis and Y Axis values. For the SmartPhone sales data, we see a slight positive correlation between the sales year and the number of units sold. That is, each year, more and more units were sold.

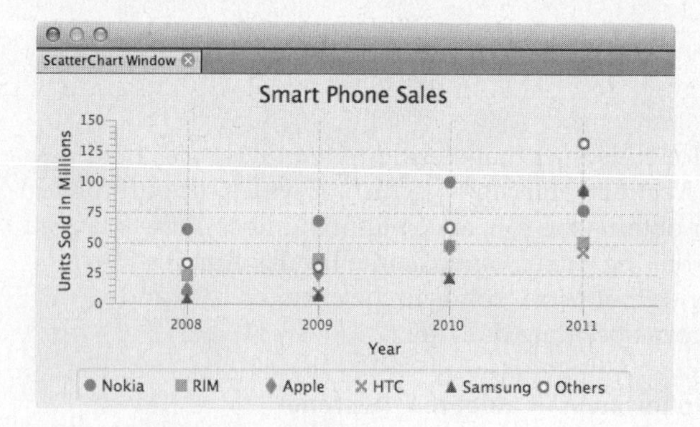


Figure 15.9 Scatter Chart

You build the Scatter Chart with the SmartPhone sales data exactly like the Line Chart. First, create a module for the Scatter Chart and create a window (ScatterChart-TopComponent). Next, add the **scatterchart.fxml** FXML file and the JavaFX controller class, **ScatterChartController.java**.

In **scatterchart.fxml**, use the `<ScatterChart>` element for the chart control. The JavaFX controller class builds the data and configures the chart. The code is unchanged from the Line Chart code shown in the previous section, except you use ScatterChart in place of LineChart.

You can change the Scatter Chart symbols with CSS styling, as explained in "Chart Styling" on page 763.

## Bar Chart

The JavaFX Bar Chart is an XY Chart that draws bars for values. Bar Charts help visualize change over time. You can also compare multiple series within each time frame. The horizontal Bar Chart emphasizes maximum values as your eye follows the chart from left to right. The vertical Bar Chart emphasizes changes over time.

In the JavaFX BarChart, the bar orientation depends on which axis is the CategoryAxis and which axis is the NumberAxis. In Figure 15.10, the left chart is a vertical Bar Chart, defining the X axis as the CategoryAxis and the Y axis as the NumberAxis. The right-side chart is a horizontal Bar Chart that switches the Number and Category axes.

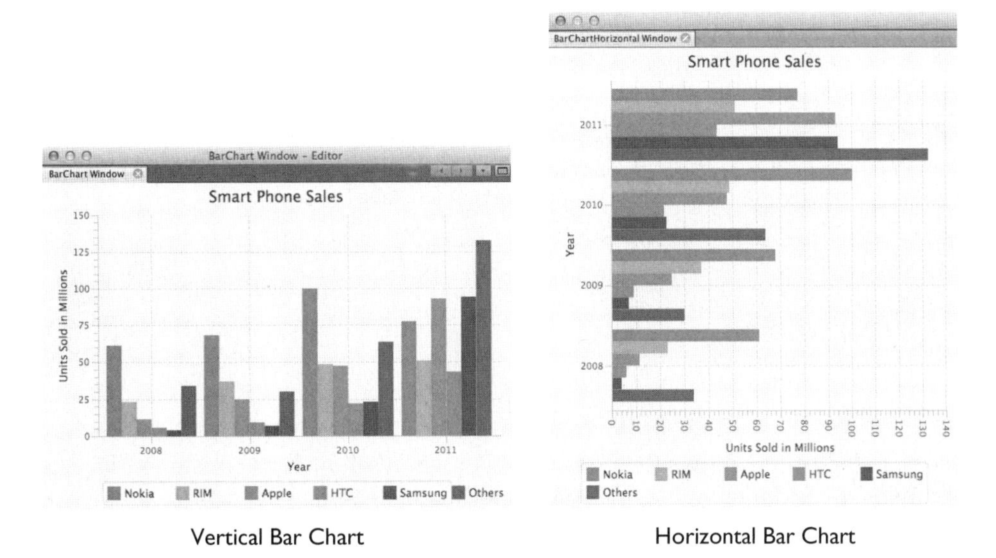


Vertical Bar Chart                Horizontal Bar Chart

Figure 15.10 Vertical and Horizontal Bar Charts

Building the vertical Bar Chart and defining the TableModelListener is unchanged from the Line Chart. For the horizontal Bar Chart, Listing 15.13 shows the `createBarChartData()` method, which switches the axes.

**Listing 15.13 BarChartHorizontalController.java—getBarChartData()**

```
public class BarChartHorizontalController implements Initializable {

    @FXML
    private StackPane stackpane;
    @FXML
    private CategoryAxis catAxis;
    @FXML
    private NumberAxis numAxis;
    @FXML
    private BarChart<Number, String> chart;
    private ObservableList<BarChart.Series<Number, String>> bcData;
    private MyTableDataModel tableModel;

      . . .

    private ObservableList<XYChart.Series<Number, String>> getBarChartData() {
        if (bcData == null) {
            bcData = FXCollections.observableArrayList();
```

```
            for (int row = 0; row < tableModel.getRowCount(); row++) {
                XYChart.Series<Number, String> series = new XYChart.Series<>();
                series.setName(tableModel.getCategoryName(row));
                for (int column = 0;
                        column < tableModel.getColumnCount(); column++) {
                    series.getData().add(new BarChart.Data<>(
                            (Number) tableModel.getValueAt(row, column),
                            tableModel.getColumnName(column)));
                }
                bcData.add(series);
            }
        }
        return bcData;
    }
}
```

Similarly, Listing 15.14 shows the horizontal Bar Chart's TableModelListener. This listener must use the data item's `setXValue()` method instead of `setYValue()` when updating the modified data item.

**Listing 15.14 BarChartHorizontalController.java—TableModelListener**

```
public class BarChartHorizontalController implements Initializable {
  . . .
        // set up the event handler to respond to changes in the table data
        // This is a swing event, so we must use Platform.runLater()
        // to update JavaFX components
        tableModel.addTableModelListener((TableModelEvent e) -> {
            if (e.getType() == TableModelEvent.UPDATE) {
                final int row = e.getFirstRow();
                final int column = e.getColumn();
                final Number value = (Number) ((MyTableDataModel)
                        e.getSource()).getValueAt(row, column);
                Platform.runLater(() -> {
                   XYChart.Series<Number, String> s = chart.getData().get(row);
                   XYChart.Data<Number, String> data = s.getData().get(column);
                    data.setXValue(value);
                });
            }
        });
. . .
```

## Area Chart

Figure 15.11 shows an Area Chart for the SDA. Area Charts are similar to Line Charts. However, Area Charts shade the area below lines that connect data points. Recall that each line represents a named series. Because Area Charts create overlapping shaded areas, a reduced opacity makes the obscured areas visible.

You build the Area Chart with the SmartPhone sales data exactly like the Line Chart. Create a module for the Area Chart and create a window (AreaChartTopComponent). Next, add the **areachart.fxml** FXML file and the JavaFX controller class, **AreaChart-Controller.java**.

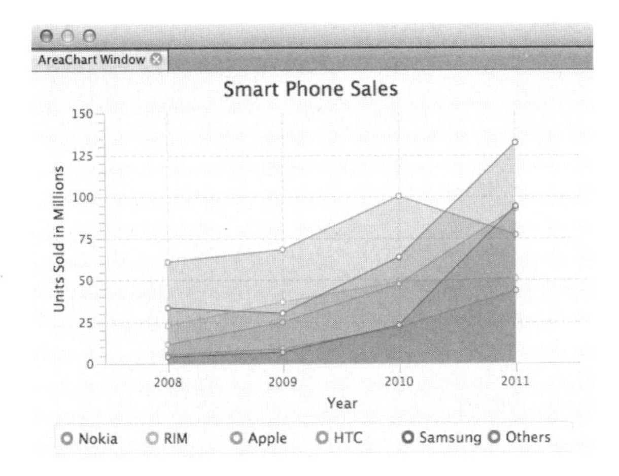


Figure 15.11 Area Chart

## Stacked Area Chart

Figure 15.12 shows a Stacked Area Chart for the SDA. As its name implies, a Stacked Area Chart stacks plotted areas on top of each other instead of plotting the Y values for each series from 0. This chart provides a more obvious view of the change in the total amount for each time frame. Stacked Area Charts also emphasize relative shapes of each named series, showing how a series changes over time. For example, the Nokia and RIM series have relatively "flat" shapes, whereas the remaining four series have shapes that "expand."

You build the Stacked Area Chart exactly like the Line Chart. Here, the X axis is CategoryAxis and the Y axis is NumberAxis. Create a module for the Stacked Area Chart and create a window (StackedAreaChartTopComponent). Next, add the **stackedareachart.fxml** FXML file and the JavaFX controller class, **StackedAreaChart-Controller.java**.

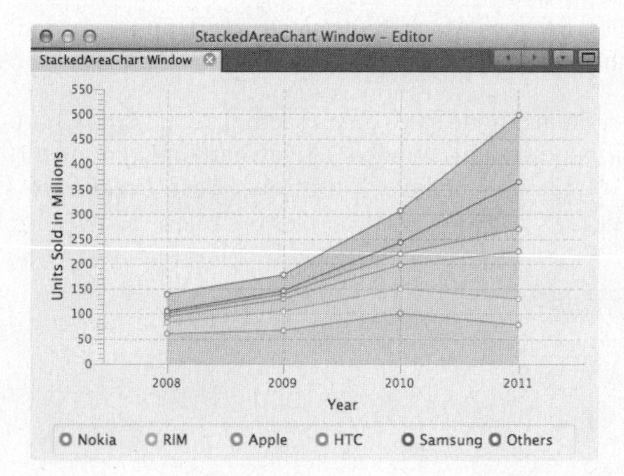


Figure 15.12 Stacked Area Chart

## Stacked Bar Chart

Figure 15.13 shows a Stacked Bar Chart for the SDA. A Stacked Bar Chart stacks each series' bar on top of each other instead of rendering the bars next to each other from 0. This emphasizes changes in the total amount for each time frame. In Figure 15.13, you can see how each bar is larger than the bar from the preceding time frame, indicating an obvious growth in total sales.

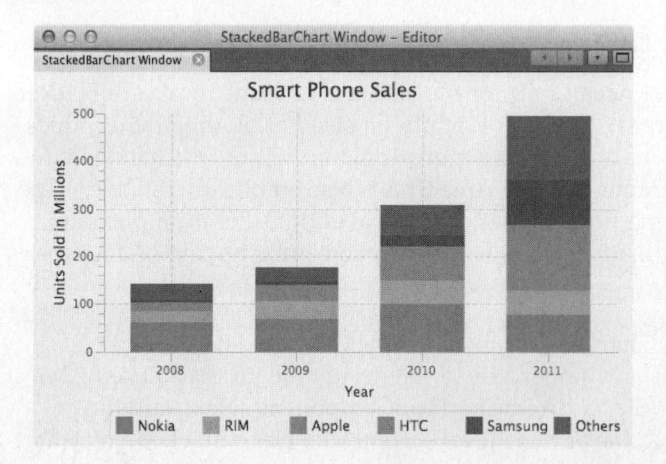


Figure 15.13 Stacked Bar Chart

You build the Stacked Bar Chart exactly like the Line Chart. Again, the X axis is CategoryAxis and the Y axis is NumberAxis. Create a module for the Stacked Bar Chart and create a window (StackedBarChartTopComponent). Add the **stackedbar-chart.fxml** FXML file and the JavaFX controller class, **StackedBarChart-Controller.java**

## Bubble Chart

Figure 15.14 shows a Bubble Chart for the SDA, which uses both the relative size and location of the plotted "bubbles" to visualize a data item's value. With Bubble Charts, you can optionally provide a third data value (besides the X and Y plot point values) to indicate the radius of the bubble. Here, we configure this extra value to show the relative percentage of a data item's value compared to the total for that time frame. Thus, a larger bubble indicates a bigger market share for that time frame, and a smaller bubble represents a smaller market share. If you don't provide an extra value, the bubbles are all the same size.[3]

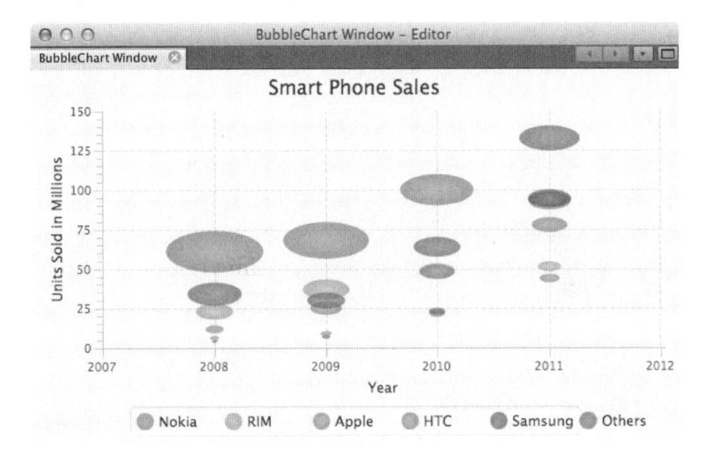


Figure 15.14 Bubble Chart

BubbleCharts do not use CategoryAxis. Both X and Y axis types are NumberAxis. To make the chart more visually appealing, we provide a String formatter for the X axis year values. Because both axes use NumberAxis types, the chart, observable list, and data item specify Number for their generic types.

Now let's show you the BubbleChartController class that configures the chart and builds the chart's data. We also show you the custom formatter for the X axis and the

3. Note that as you resize a Bubble Chart, the relative size of the plot bubbles is constant. However, the shape of the bubbles can change as you expand or shrink either the vertical or horizontal axis of the chart.

TableModelListener code, since these are all slightly different than the XY Charts you've seen so far.

Listing 15.15 shows the `@FXML` declarations and the `createBubbleChartData()` method, which computes an extra value for the data item. This value is based on the total for that time frame (column in the table data model).

Constant `XFACTOR` is an integer that scales the X Axis. This makes the X and Y axes scales similar and keeps the bubble shapes proportional to the chart.

**Listing 15.15 BubbleChartController.java—getBubbleChartData()**

```
public class BubbleChartController implements Initializable {

    @FXML
    private StackPane stackpane;
    @FXML
    private NumberAxis xAxis;
    @FXML
    private NumberAxis yAxis;
    @FXML
    private BubbleChart<Number, Number> chart;

      . . .


    private ObservableList<BubbleChart.Series<Number, Number>>
                                        getBubbleChartData() {
        if (bcData == null) {
            bcData = FXCollections.observableArrayList();
            // Find totals for each column
            double[] totals = new double[tableModel.getColumnCount()];
            for (int column = 0; column < tableModel.getColumnCount();
                                                      column++) {
                for (int row = 0; row < tableModel.getRowCount(); row++) {
                    totals[column] +=
                        (double)tableModel.getValueAt(row, column);
                }
            }
            for (int row = 0; row < tableModel.getRowCount(); row++) {
                XYChart.Series<Number, Number> series = new XYChart.Series<>();
                series.setName(tableModel.getCategoryName(row));

                for (int column = 0; column < tableModel.getColumnCount();
                                                          column++) {
                    Integer year = Integer.valueOf(
                                tableModel.getColumnName(column));
                   Number units = (Number) tableModel.getValueAt(row, column);
```

```
                    series.getData().add(new XYChart.Data<Number, Number>(
                            year * XFACTOR,
                            units,
                            (units.doubleValue() / totals[column]) * XFACTOR));
                }
                bcData.add(series);
            }
        }
        return bcData;
    }
}
```

Similarly, Listing 15.16 shows the Bubble Chart's TableModelListener. This listener must not only update the new YValue for the changed data item but also recompute the percentage of the total for all data items in that time frame (column).

**Listing 15.16 BubbleChartController.java—TableModelListener**

```
public class BubbleChartController implements Initializable {
    . . .

        // set up the event handler to respond to changes in the table data
        // This is a swing event, so we must use Platform.runLater()
        // to update JavaFX components
        tableModel.addTableModelListener((TableModelEvent e) -> {
            if (e.getType() == TableModelEvent.UPDATE) {
                final int row = e.getFirstRow();
                final int column = e.getColumn();
                final Number value = (Number) ((MyTableDataModel)
                            e.getSource()).getValueAt(row, column);
                // Get new total for column
                double total = 0;
                for (int r = 0; r < tableModel.getCategoryCount(); r++) {
                    total += (double) tableModel.getValueAt(r, column);
                }
                final double newTotal = total;

                Platform.runLater(() -> {
                   XYChart.Series<Number, Number> s = chart.getData().get(row);
                    BubbleChart.Data<Number, Number> data =
                                    s.getData().get(column);
                    data.setYValue(value);
                    // update extra value for the entire column
                    for (int r = 0; r < tableModel.getCategoryCount(); r++) {
                        XYChart.Series<Number, Number> ss =
                                    chart.getData().get(r);
                        BubbleChart.Data<Number, Number> data1 =
                                    ss.getData().get(column);
```

```
                    data1.setExtraValue(((double) tableModel.getValueAt(
                                            r, column) / newTotal) * XFACTOR);
                }
            });
        }
    });
. . .
```

Finally, Listing 15.17 shows the custom formatter we use for the X axis, which is a Number value. The StringConverter overrides the `toString()` and `fromString()` methods. These methods provide the conversion between the data item Number and the displayed String representing the year.

Constant `XFactor` makes the X axis and Y axis proportional so that the bubble shape is within an appealing range.

**Listing 15.17 BubbleChartController.java—Customize X Axis**

```
public class BubbleChartController implements Initializable {
   . . .

        xAxis.setAutoRanging(false);
        xAxis.setLowerBound((Integer.valueOf(
                tableModel.getColumnName(0)) - 1) * XFACTOR);
        xAxis.setUpperBound(((Integer.valueOf(tableModel.getColumnName(
                tableModel.getColumnCount() - 1)) + 1) * XFACTOR) + 1);

        xAxis.setTickLabelFormatter(new StringConverter<Number>() {
            @Override
            public String toString(Number t) {
                return String.valueOf(t.intValue() / XFACTOR);
            }

            @Override
            public Number fromString(String string) {
                return Integer.valueOf(string) * XFACTOR;
            }
        });
        xAxis.setTickUnit(XFACTOR);
        xAxis.setMinorTickCount(0);
        xAxis.setLabel(tableModel.getNameDescription());
. . .
```

## Pie Chart

Figure 15.15 shows a Pie Chart window. Because PieChart is not an XY Chart and cannot display two-axes data, we must apply the table data differently. Pie Charts are suitable for visualizing product market share, since they show you relative percentages of a whole. In Figure 15.15, the Pie Chart visualizes a single column in the table data. Each pie wedge represents the company's sales for a specific year. Since the total of each column represents the total product sold for a given year, the Pie Chart reflects each company's market share for that year.

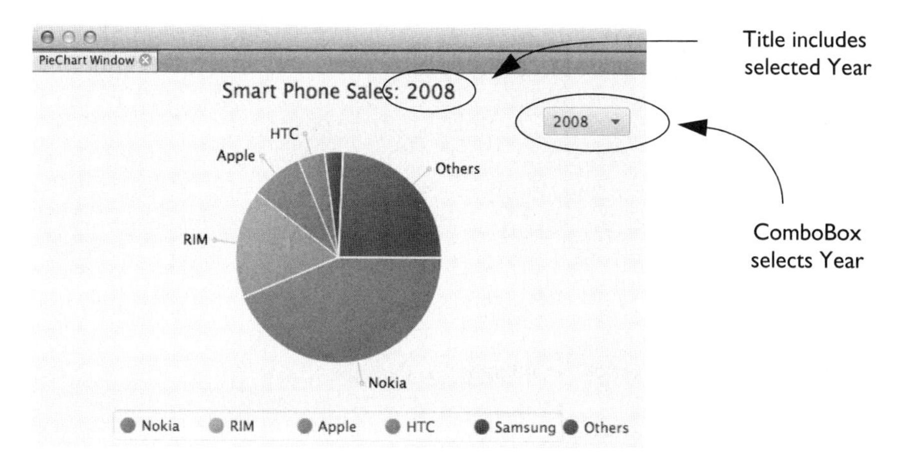


Figure 15.15 Pie Chart

PieChart data is stored in an `ObservableList<PieChart.Data>` type. `PieChart.Data` includes a read-only reference to its chart, a `name` StringProperty (used as a wedge label), and a `pieValue` DoubleProperty.

In addition to the chart properties inherited from Chart, PieChart includes the properties shown in Table 15.4.

**TABLE 15.4 PieChart Properties**

| Property | Type | Description |
|---|---|---|
| `clockwise` | `BooleanProperty` | If true, start placing wedges clockwise from the start angle. |
| `data` | `ObjectProperty<ObservableList<PieChart.Data>>` | PieChart's data. |
| `labelLineLength` | `DoubleProperty` | The length of the line from the outside of the pie to the wedge labels. |
| `labelsVisible` | `BooleanProperty` | If true, draw the pie wedge labels. |
| `startAngle` | `DoubleProperty` | The starting angle of the first wedge. |

In the SDA PieChart window, a JavaFX ComboBox control lets users select a year. The chart title includes the selected year for clarity.

Let's examine the FXML and JavaFX controller class for the PieChart window. Listing 15.18 shows **piechart.fxml**. The StackPane has two child nodes, PieChart and ComboBox, and all three elements include `fx:id` attributes. StackPane normally stacks child nodes on top of each other, but in the controller we reposition the ComboBox.

**Listing 15.18 piechart.fxml**

```
<?import java.lang.*?>
<?import java.util.*?>
<?import javafx.scene.*?>
<?import javafx.scene.control.*?>
<?import javafx.scene.layout.*?>
<?import javafx.scene.chart.*?>

<StackPane id="StackPane" fx:id="stackpane"
   xmlns:fx="http://javafx.com/fxml/1"
   fx:controller="org.smartphone.chart.pie.PieChartController">
    <children>
        <PieChart fx:id="chart"  />
        <ComboBox fx:id="yearChoice" />
    </children>
</StackPane>
```

Listing 15.19 shows the class fields for the PieChartController class and the code that configures the Pie Chart. We'll present this code in several listings. Here you see the `stackpane`, `chart`, and `yearChoice` fields from the FXML file. We also define a `tableModel` field to hold the data and the Pie Chart data's observable list.

The `createPieChart()` method builds and configures the pie chart data. First, we obtain the `tableModel` field from the Global Lookup. Next, we position the ComboBox in the upper right area of the StackPane with margins.

The next step configures the `ComboBox<String>`. The ComboBox `itemsProperty` is an observable list of Strings that we initialize from the list of column names (the years). We invoke the ComboBox selection model `selectFirst()` method to select year "2008" initially. We also add an invalidation listener to the ComboBox selection model's `selectedIndexProperty` (see "Using Listeners with Observable Properties" on page 105). The handler uses a lambda expression to reset the Pie Chart data from the `tableModel` field based on the selected year.

The last step configures the Pie Chart. We invoke the `getPieChartData()` method (shown Listing 15.20 on page 780) with the selected index value of the ComboBox.

This integer value is the column number index from the table model data. A binding expression concatenates the chart's title with the selected year.

This binding expression uses static Bindings methods. The `Bindings.concat()` method concatenates two String expressions. The first expression is the table model's title followed by a : and <space>.

```
Bindings.concat(tableModel.getTitle() + ": ",
```

The second expression returns the selected String item from the ComboBox.

```
Bindings.stringValueAt(yearChoice.itemsProperty().get(),
        yearChoice.getSelectionModel().selectedIndexProperty()))
```

The `Bindings.stringValueAt()` method takes two arguments, an observable list and an index into the list. The list is the ComboBox selection model (the list of items). The index corresponds to the selected value.

Note that the invalidation handler could have updated the chart's `titleProperty`. However, property binding is better because bindings always perform *implicit assignments*. This avoids the extra step of separately initializing the `titleProperty` value.

**Listing 15.19 PieChartController.java—Set Up PieChart Data**

```
public class PieChartController implements Initializable {

    @FXML
    private StackPane stackpane;
    @FXML
    private PieChart chart;
    @FXML
    private ComboBox<String> yearChoice;
    private MyTableDataModel tableModel;
    private ObservableList<PieChart.Data> pcData;

    private static final Logger logger = Logger.getLogger(
            PieChartController.class.getName());

    @Override
    public void initialize(URL url, ResourceBundle rb) {
        createPieChart();
    }

    private void createPieChart() {
        // set up the tableModel data
        tableModel = Lookup.getDefault().lookup(MyTableDataModel.class);
        if (tableModel == null) {
            logger.log(Level.SEVERE, "Cannot get TableModel object");
            LifecycleManager.getDefault().exit();
        }
```

```
        // position the combobox within the stackpane
        StackPane.setAlignment(yearChoice, Pos.TOP_RIGHT);
        StackPane.setMargin(yearChoice, new Insets(30, 15, 8, 8));

        // set up the combobox
        yearChoice.setItems(FXCollections.observableArrayList(
                tableModel.getColumnNames()));
        yearChoice.getSelectionModel().selectFirst();
        yearChoice.setTooltip(new Tooltip("Select the sales data year"));
       yearChoice.getSelectionModel().selectedIndexProperty().addListener(o->{
            getPieChartData(yearChoice.getSelectionModel().getSelectedIndex());
        });

        // configure the pie chart
        chart.setData(getPieChartData(yearChoice.getSelectionModel()
                                                .getSelectedIndex()));
        chart.titleProperty().bind(
                Bindings.concat(tableModel.getTitle() + ": ",
                Bindings.stringValueAt(yearChoice.itemsProperty().get(),
                yearChoice.getSelectionModel().selectedIndexProperty())));
        . . .
    }
}
```

Listing 15.20 shows the `getPieChartData()` method. Here we set the Pie Chart's data using the provided column number to index into the table model's column. The first time this method is invoked, we instantiate an observable arraylist for the `pcData` field and the `PieData.Data` values. Subsequent calls use the `setPieValue()` method to update existing `PieData.Data` elements. The update is registered as a change to the Pie Chart data. The chart responds by resizing the existing wedges with animation.

**Listing 15.20 PieChartController.java—getPieChartData()**

```
    // Return the data corresponding to the column number (year)
    private ObservableList<PieChart.Data> getPieChartData(int column) {
        if (pcData == null) {
            pcData = FXCollections.observableArrayList();
            for (int row = 0; row < tableModel.getRowCount(); row++) {
                pcData.add(new PieChart.Data(tableModel.getCategoryName(row),
                        (Double) tableModel.getValueAt(row, column)));
            }
        } else {
            for (int row = 0; row < tableModel.getRowCount(); row++) {
                PieChart.Data data = chart.getData().get(row);
                data.setPieValue((Double) tableModel.getValueAt(row, column));
            }
        }
        return pcData;
    }
```

Listing 15.21 shows the TableModelListener added to the `tableModel` field. First, we make sure the changed table data refers to the currently displayed year. After accessing the changed data, we update the Pie Chart data item with the `setPieValue()` method in the JavaFX Application Thread.

**Listing 15.21 PieChartController.java—TableModelListener**

```
public class PieChartController implements Initializable {
        . . .
    private void createPieChart() {
        . . .
        tableModel.addTableModelListener((TableModelEvent e) -> {
            if (e.getType() == TableModelEvent.UPDATE) {
                final int row = e.getFirstRow();
                final int column = e.getColumn();
                if (column != yearChoice.getSelectionModel()
                                      .getSelectedIndex()) {
                    return;
                }
                final Double value = (Double) ((MyTableDataModel)
                     e.getSource()).getValueAt(row, column);
                Platform.runLater(() -> {
                    // Update JavaFX scene in JavaFX Application Thread
                    PieChart.Data data = chart.getData().get(row);
                    data.setPieValue(value);
                });
            }
        });
    }
. . .
}
```

# 15.4 Adding Behaviors to JavaFX Charts

All displayed parts of a chart are JavaFX nodes. This means you can attach mouse event handlers, set effects, and have chart nodes participate in transitions. In this section, we add a transition that animates a selected Pie Chart wedge. During the wedge animation, a label that displays the wedge's percentage of the total will fade in. We also add an in-place editor that is invoked with a right-mouse click on the selected pie wedge. So far, all of the JavaFX charts have been read-only displays, so this in-place editor shows you how to add editing capabilities to JavaFX charts.

Figure 15.16 is a snapshot of a Pie Chart wedge animating outward, initiated with a mouse click inside the wedge. The wedge has a drop shadow effect. The label in the upper left corner displays the percentage value, which is dynamically updated when the value changes. Furthermore, when the user clicks anywhere in the background of the window, the wedge loses the drop shadow and the label gradually fades out. With JavaFX, we can easily add these user-initiated effects to charts.

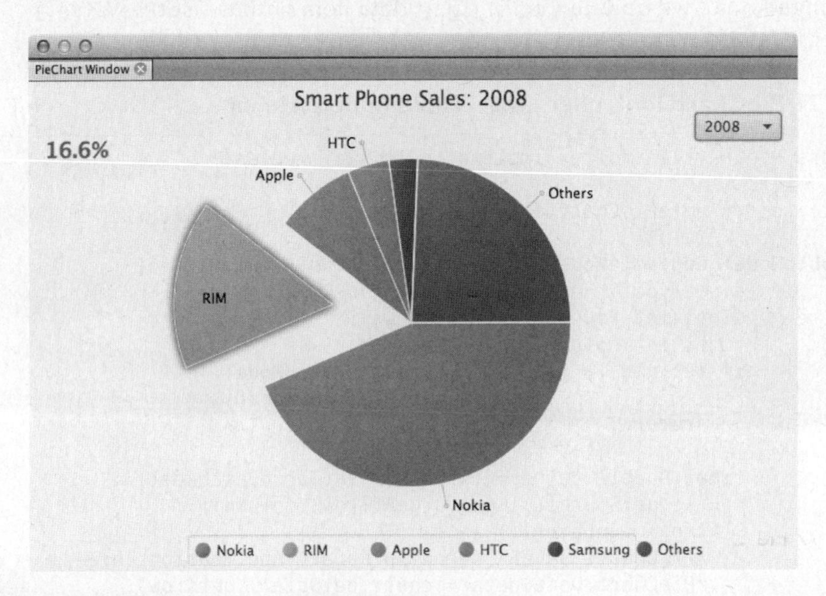


Figure 15.16 Pie Chart wedge animation

Figure 15.17 shows an in-place text editor. Invoked with a right click or a control click, this editor lets users change selected pie wedge values. The user hits the Enter or Return key to finish editing, which makes the TextField control fade out. New values propagate to the table model and update the entire application (including the JTable that displays the raw table data).

These two features require new controls in the FXML file, binding to keep the controls synchronized, and mouse click event handlers for the individual nodes that represent the pie wedges. The event handler builds transitions to perform wedge animation and fade in/out the label and textfield.

Before we show you this code, let's review how to access chart nodes so that you can add features and special effects.

## Accessing JavaFX Chart Nodes

JavaFX makes it easy to attach event handlers to JavaFX charts or to individual data items. To attach an event handler to the background area of a chart, for example, use the chart object directly (since Chart extends Node and is part of the scene graph).

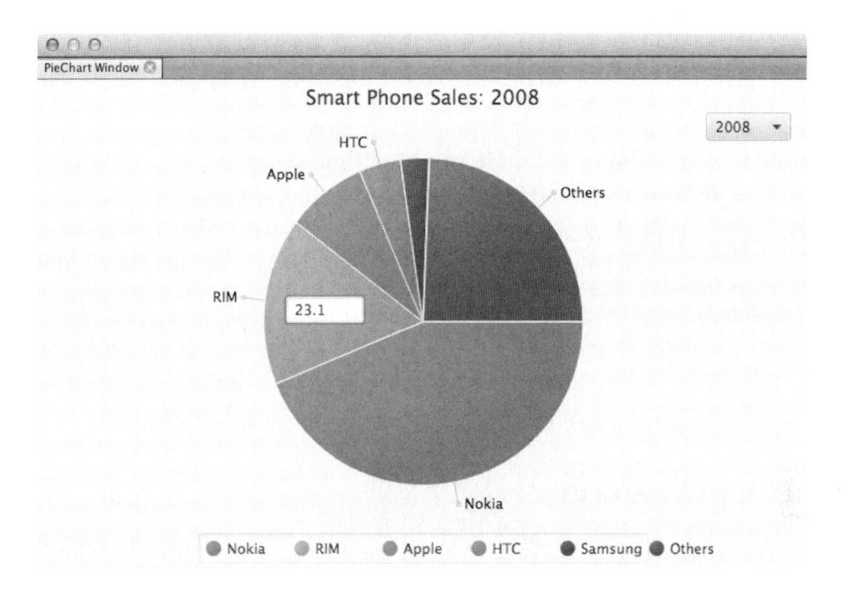


Figure 15.17 Pie Chart editing

```
Chart myChart;
. . .
myChart.addEventHandler(MouseEvent.MOUSE_CLICKED, (MouseEvent t) -> {
     . . . event handler code here . . .
});
```

Similarly, to apply an effect to a chart, use `setEffec()` as follows.

```
myChart.setEffect(new DropShadow());
```

You can also manipulate a chart's individual data items using the `getNode()` method of the data item. Here, we get the first element of a Pie Chart data list and add an event handler to the data item's node.

```
PieChart chart;
. . .
chart.getData().get(0).getNode().addEventHandler(
     MouseEvent.MOUSE_CLICKED, (MouseEvent t) -> {
     . . . event handler code . . .
     });
```

With XYCharts, data access requires slightly different code. For example, here's how to access the node representing the first series of a Line Chart, to which we apply a drop shadow effect.

```
LineChart<String, Number> chart;
   . . .
XYChart.Series series = chart.getData().get(0);    // get first series
series.getNode().setEffect(new DropShadow());
```

And here's how to access the first data item of the first series and add a mouse event handler for a data item with type `XYChart.Data<String, Number>`.

```
XYChart.Data<String, Number> dataItem =
         chart.getData().get(0).getData().get(0);  // get first data item
dataItem.getNode().addEventHandler(
   MouseEvent.MOUSE_CLICKED, (MouseEvent t) -> {
         . . . event handler code . . .
   });
```

Let's apply these concepts to add new features to the PieChart window.

## Adding PieChart Features

We begin with **piechart.fxml**, the FXML file for the PieChart window. Listing 15.22 shows the added `<TextField>` and `<Label>` elements. Both include `fx:id` attributes so the JavaFX controller class can access them. These added controls have their `opacity` properties set to zero. This makes them invisible initially, but the controls will fade in and out as needed.

The TextField control sets its `maxWidth` property, and the Label control configures its `textFill` and `style` properties.

**Listing 15.22 piechart.fxml**

```
<StackPane id="StackPane" fx:id="stackpane"
           xmlns:fx="http://javafx.com/fxml/1"
         fx:controller="org.smartphone.chart.pie.PieChartController">
    <children>
        <PieChart fx:id="chart"  />
        <ComboBox fx:id="yearChoice" />
        <TextField fx:id="textField"
                   maxWidth="75"
                   opacity="0.0" />
        <Label fx:id="label"
                   textFill="RoyalBlue"
                   opacity="0.0"
                   style="-fx-font-size: 20 ; -fx-font-weight: bold; "/>
    </children>
</StackPane>
```

Listing 15.23 shows the class fields added to PieChartController class. The `@FXML` annotations identify the controls defined in the FXML file. We also add a JavaFX Node field called `lastNode` that is set to the most recent node that takes on effects and animation.

### Listing 15.23 PieChartController.java—Add Class Fields

```
public class PieChartController implements Initializable {

    @FXML
    private Label label;
    @FXML
    private StackPane stackpane;
    @FXML
    private PieChart chart;
    @FXML
    private ComboBox<String> yearChoice;
    @FXML
    private TextField textField;
    private MyTableDataModel tableModel;
    private ObservableList<PieChart.Data> pcData;
    private Node lastNode = null;
. . .
```

Now let's show you the PieChartController code that configures the event handlers. These handlers create the animation and in-place editing and restore the wedges to normal. We'll show this code in several parts. First, Listing 15.24 shows the `resetTextField()` method that fades out the TextField control and returns the TextField to its original location at the bottom of the window.

Next, we define a background mouse click event handler that invokes this `resetTextField()` method, fades out the label, restores the pie wedge to its normal location, and removes the drop shadow effect from the pie wedge.

### Listing 15.24 PieChartController.java—Event Handler Code Part 1

```
    private void resetTextField() {
        FadeTransition ft = new FadeTransition(Duration.millis(1000),
                        textField);
        ft.setToValue(0.0);
        ft.playFromStart();
        ft.setOnFinished((event) -> {
            textField.setTranslateX(0);
            textField.setTranslateY(0);
        });
    }

    private void setupEventHandlers() {
        final DropShadow dropShadow = new DropShadow();
        // add a MOUSE_CLICKED handler to the background chart
```

```
        // to turn off any dropshadow effects
        // and make the Label/TextField fade out
        chart.addEventHandler(MouseEvent.MOUSE_CLICKED, (MouseEvent t) -> {
            resetTextField();
            FadeTransition ft = new FadeTransition(Duration.millis(1500),
                                label);
            ft.setToValue(0.0);
            ft.playFromStart();
            if (lastNode != null) {
                lastNode.setEffect(null);
                lastNode.setTranslateX(0);
                lastNode.setTranslateY(0);
            }
            t.consume();
        });
. . . method setupEventHandlers() continues in Listing 15.25 . . .
```

Listing 15.25 continues with the `setupEventHandlers()` method. First, we have a for loop that invokes `chart.getData()` to access each PieChart data item. An integer `row` counter keeps track of the current row number, which we assign to `currentRow` for access within the event handler. The `row` variable updates at the end of the for loop.

Next, we define a StringBinding `percentBinding` object. This custom binding object (see "Custom Binding" on page 116 for more information) returns the percentage of the whole for the selected wedge. Note that binding makes this value always correct, even if the user selects a different pie wedge or different year, or if the user updates the table data.

**Listing 15.25 PieChartController.java—Event Handler Code Part II**

```
    private void setupEventHandlers() {
      . . .

        // set up bindings and event handlers for piechart nodes
        int row = 0;
        for (final PieChart.Data data : chart.getData()) {
            final int currentRow = row;
            final StringBinding percentBinding = new StringBinding() {
                {
                    pcData.stream().forEach((data) -> {
                        super.bind(data.pieValueProperty());
                    });
                }

                @Override
                protected String computeValue() {
                    double total = 0;
```

```
                for (final PieChart.Data thisdata : pcData) {
                    total += thisdata.getPieValue();
                }
                return String.format("%.1f%%", data.getPieValue()
                        / total * 100);
            }
        };
. . . method setupEventHandlers() continues in Listing 15.26 . . .
```

Listing 15.26 shows the continuation of the `for` loop from Listing 15.25. Here we invoke `data.getNode()` to add mouse click event handlers to each PieChart data node. Each handler is divided into two parts. We process the in-place editor if the mouse event `isMetaDown()` method returns true. Otherwise, the handler initiates the pie wedge animation.

The `lastNode` field is set so that the background mouse click handler can reset the most recently selected pie wedge node (see Listing 15.24 on page 785).

The in-place editor places the TextField at the mouse click location, makes the TextField visible, and initializes the TextField `text` property to the node's `pieValue` property. The TextField action event handler (the `setOnAction()` method) reads the value from the TextField, updates the PieChart data `pieValue` property, resets the TextField, and updates the corresponding table data value in the Swing EDT. This update propagates to the other charts and the TableDataEditor window.

If the `isMetaDown()` method returns false then we animate the pie wedge. Here, the selected node's `getBoundsInLocal()` method helps calculate X and Y values for the TranslateTransition (the animation that moves the node). We bind the label's `textProperty` to the `percentBinding` object defined earlier (see Listing 15.25 on page 786) and place a drop shadow effect on the selected node. We then build both the TranslateTransition to move the wedge and the FadeTransition to fade in the label. A ParallelTransition plays them at the same time.

#### Listing 15.26 PieChartController.java—Event Handler Code Part III

```
    private void setupEventHandlers() {
        . . .
        // Still inside the chart.getData() for loop
        for (final PieChart.Data data : chart.getData()) {
         . . .
            data.getNode().addEventHandler(
                        MouseEvent.MOUSE_CLICKED, (MouseEvent t) -> {
                if (lastNode != null) {
                    lastNode.setEffect(null);
                }
                lastNode = data.getNode();
```

```
            if (t.isMetaDown()) {           // In-Place Editor
                // Move the textfield to where the mouse click is
                textField.setTranslateX(
                        t.getSceneX() - textField.getLayoutX());
                textField.setTranslateY(
                        t.getSceneY() - textField.getLayoutY());
                textField.setText(data.getPieValue() + "");
                textField.setOpacity(1.0);
                textField.setOnAction((event) -> {   // User edit complete
                    try {
                        final Double num = Double.valueOf(
                                            textField.getText());
                        data.setPieValue(num);
                        resetTextField();
                        final int currentColumn = yearChoice
                                 .getSelectionModel().getSelectedIndex();
                        SwingUtilities.invokeLater(() -> {
                            tableModel.setValueAt(num,
                                        currentRow,
                                        currentColumn);
                        });
                    } catch (NumberFormatException e) {
                      // Just use the original number if the format is bad
                        textField.setText(data.getPieValue() + "");
                    }
                });
            } else {                              // Do the Pie Wedge animation
                resetTextField();
                Bounds b1 = data.getNode().getBoundsInLocal();
                double newX = (b1.getWidth()) / 2 + b1.getMinX();
                double newY = (b1.getHeight()) / 2 + b1.getMinY();
                label.setOpacity(0);
                label.textProperty().bind(percentBinding);
                data.getNode().setEffect(dropShadow);
                TranslateTransition tt = new TranslateTransition(
                            Duration.millis(1500), data.getNode());
                tt.setByX(newX);
                tt.setByY(newY);
                tt.setAutoReverse(true);
                tt.setCycleCount(2);

                FadeTransition ft = new FadeTransition(
                        Duration.millis(1500), label);
                ft.setToValue(1.0);
                ParallelTransition pt = new ParallelTransition(
                        tt, ft);
                pt.play();
            }
            t.consume();
        });
```

```
            row++;
        }               // end of for loop
    }                   // end of setupEventHandlers() method
}
```

### Special Behaviors for Other Charts

In addition to the animation and editing added to the Pie Chart, we also added behaviors to the Bubble Chart (selected bubbles rotate using a ScaleTransition) and Bar Charts (selected bars fade in a label displaying the bar's value). Since we use the same techniques for accessing the chart's nodes and building transitions based on mouse click events, we leave it to the reader to peruse this code from the book's download bundle.

## 15.5 Saving Charts

The SDA application also includes the ability to save any JavaFX chart window to a PNG file. This feature uses a NetBeans Platform conditionally-enabled action and the communication strategies discussed in integrating JavaFX (see "Communication Strategies" on page 261).

Figure 15.18 shows the Save Chart icon on the toolbar and the Save Chart menu item under the top-level File menu. These icons and menu items are enabled when any JavaFX chart window has focus. The chart image saved corresponds to the specific window that has focus. Selecting a non-JavaFX chart window (such as the TableDataEditor window) disables the Save Chart menu selections.

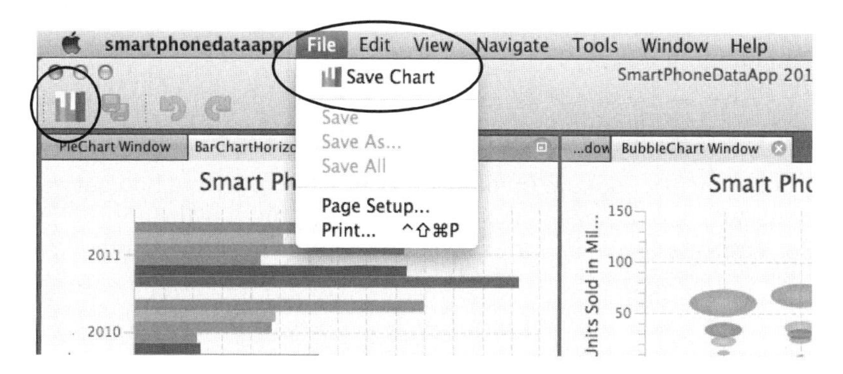


Figure 15.18 Saving charts

Selecting the Save Chart icon or menu item displays a File Chooser dialog with the name of the chart window to be saved. For example, Figure 15.19 shows a File Chooser for the LineChart window. The File Chooser lets the user select the enclosing folder and file name for the resulting PNG file to be saved to disk.

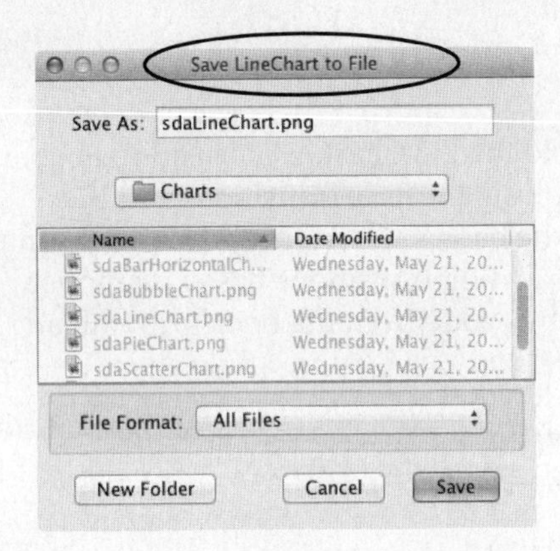


Figure 15.19 Invoking the FileChooser window

Here's a summary of the steps to implement the Save Chart feature.

- Create a module called **ChartUtilities** with package name **org.smart-phone.chart.utilities**. Make its package public so that other modules can set a module dependency on this module.
- Create **ChartSaveCapability** and add this interface to the ChartUtilities public package.
- Create conditionally-enabled action **ChartSaveAction** and specify **ChartSaveCapability** for its Cookie class.
- Implement the ChartSaveAction using context ChartSaveCapability.
- In each module with a JavaFX chart, add an implementation of ChartSaveCapability to the TopComponent's Lookup. Invoke the JavaFX controller method `getImage()` to obtain a BufferedImage of the JavaFX scene graph. Use the appropriate communication strategies between the Swing TopComponent and the JavaFX controller.

## ChartSaveCapability

Listing 15.27 shows the ChartSaveCapability interface in the ChartUtilities public package.

**Listing 15.27 ChartSaveCapability.jave**

```
package org.smartphone.chart.utilities;

import java.awt.image.BufferedImage;

public interface ChartSaveCapability {

    public String getChartName();
    public BufferedImage getImage();

}
```

### ChartSaveAction

In module ChartUtilities, add a new conditionally-enabled action called **ChartSave-Action**. Use ChartSaveCapability as the action's Cookie class (see "Context-Aware Actions" on page 428 for a discussion of context-aware actions). Implement the `actionPerformed()` method, as shown in Listing 15.28.

The ChartSaveAction class includes annotations to configure the action in the toolbar and the top-level menu system. The ChartSaveAction constructor defines the Chart-SaveCapability as its context. This context is provided by the selected TopComponent through the Global Selection Lookup.

To save the PNG file, the `actionPerformed()` method invokes the context `getChart-Name()` method for the chart name and the `getImage()` method for the BufferedImage.

The FileChooserBuilder (discussed next) provides a popup dialog that lets users choose a file. The Save Chart action creates the file if it doesn't exist and prompts if overwriting is okay when the file does exist. Both DialogDisplayer and Notify-Descriptor configure these additional popup dialogs (see Chapter 11 for details on using the Dialogs API).

**Listing 15.28 ChartSaveAction.java**

```
@ActionID(
        category = "File",
        id = "org.smartphone.chart.utilities.ChartSaveAction"
)
@ActionRegistration(
        iconBase = "org/smartphone/chart/utilities/saveChartIcon.png",
        displayName = "#CTL_ChartSaveAction"
)
```

```
@ActionReferences({
    @ActionReference(path = "Menu/File", position = 1300),
    @ActionReference(path = "Toolbars/File", position = 200)
})
@Messages({
    "CTL_ChartSaveAction=Save Chart",
    "# {0} - windowname",
    "MSG_SAVE_DIALOG=Save {0}",
    "# {0} - Filename",
    "MSG_SaveFailed=Could not write to file {0}",
    "# {0} - Filename",
    "MSG_Overwrite=File {0} exists. Overwrite?"
})
public final class ChartSaveAction implements ActionListener {

    private final ChartSaveCapability context;
    private static final Logger logger = Logger.getLogger(
                                ChartSaveAction.class.getName());

    public ChartSaveAction(ChartSaveCapability context) {
        this.context = context;
    }

    @Override
    public void actionPerformed(ActionEvent ev) {
        // use a FileChooser to get a user-supplied filename
        String title = "Save " + context.getChartName() + " to File";
        File f = new FileChooserBuilder(
                ChartSaveAction.class).setTitle(title).showSaveDialog();
        if (f != null) {
            if (!f.getAbsolutePath().endsWith(".png")) {
                f = new File(f.getAbsolutePath() + ".png");
            }
            try {
                if (!f.exists()) {
                    // the file doesn't exist; create it
                    if (!f.createNewFile()) {
                        DialogDisplayer.getDefault().notify(
                                new NotifyDescriptor.Message(
                                        Bundle.MSG_SaveFailed(f.getName())));
                        return;
                    }
                } else {
                    // the file exists; asks if it's okay to overwrite
                    Object userChose = DialogDisplayer.getDefault().notify(
                            new NotifyDescriptor.Confirmation(
                                    Bundle.MSG_Overwrite(f.getName())));
                    if (NotifyDescriptor.CANCEL_OPTION.equals(userChose)) {
                        return;
                    }
                }
```

```
                // Need getAbsoluteFile(),
                // or X.png and x.png are different on windows
                BufferedImage image = context.getImage();
                if (image != null) {
                    ImageIO.write(image, "png", f.getAbsoluteFile());
                    logger.log(Level.INFO, "Image saved to file {0}",
                           f.getName());
                } else {
                    logger.log(Level.WARNING, "Could not get Image from {0}",
                           context.getChartName());
                }
            } catch (IOException ioe) {
                Exceptions.printStackTrace(ioe);
            }
        }
    }
}
```

### FileChooserBuilder

FileChooserBuilder is a utility class in the File System API that works with JFile-Chooser. One nice feature is the ability to remember the last-used directory for a given file. You pass a string key or a class type (here we use the ChartSaveAction class type) to the constructor. The key is used to look up the most recently-used directory from any previous invocations with the same key.

FileChooserBuilder is structured using the "Builder" pattern (like StringBuilder, for example), so it's possible to chain invocations that simplify the setup of a file chooser. We use the `setTitle()` method (to provide a title for the dialog) and, to complete the configuration, the `showSaveDialog()`, which returns the user-selected file as `File`. Other show dialog methods include `showOpenDialog()`, which also returns `File`, and `showMultiOpenDialog()`, which returns a `File[]` array and lets users select more than one file.

The return from any show dialog method is null if the user clicked Cancel or closed the dialog without selecting OK.

### BufferedImage

BufferedImage is a subclass of AWT's Image class, and ImageIO is a class containing static convenience methods that encode and decode image data. The following statements write the BufferedImage (an encoding of the JavaFX scene graph) to a file with a PNG format.

```
BufferedImage image = context.getImage();
    . . .
ImageIO.write(image, "png", f.getAbsoluteFile());
```

### Implementing the ChartSaveCapability

Each module with a JavaFX chart TopComponent sets a module dependency on the ChartUtilities module and implements ChartSaveCapability. Listing 15.29 shows how we do this for the LineChartTopComponent. The other JavaFX Chart modules implement ChartSaveCapability the same way.

First, we use InstanceContent and AbstractLookup to add objects to the TopComponent's Lookup. These objects are exposed to the Global Selection Lookup when the TopComponent has focus. ("Lookup as an Object Repository" on page 225 discusses the Global Selection Lookup.) We then add an implementation of ChartSaveCapability to the TopComponent Lookup.

The implementation of ChartSaveCapability requires overriding two methods. The `getChartName()` method returns "LineChart" here. The `getImage()` method invokes the JavaFX controller `getImage()` method. Here, we must use a countdown latch to wait for the `getImage()` method to finish executing, since the TopComponent invokes this method on the JavaFX Application Thread. When the method finishes executing, we return the BufferedImage object to the caller. (See Listing 15.7 on page 756 for the JavaFX controller's `getImage()` method.)

**Listing 15.29 LineChartTopComponent.java—Implement ChartSaveCapability**

```
public final class LineChartTopComponent extends TopComponent {

    private static JFXPanel chartFxPanel;
    private LineChartController controller;
    private BufferedImage image = null;
    private final InstanceContent content = new InstanceContent();

    public LineChartTopComponent() {
        initComponents();
        setName(Bundle.CTL_LineChartTopComponent());
        setToolTipText(Bundle.HINT_LineChartTopComponent());
        // Connect our lookup to the rest of the system, so that
        // Save Chart action can access the image
        associateLookup(new AbstractLookup(content));
        setLayout(new BorderLayout());
        //Enable the Print action for the TopComponent:
        putClientProperty("print.printable", true);
        init();
        content.add(new ChartSaveCapabilityImpl());
    }
  . . .
```

```
    private class ChartSaveCapabilityImpl implements ChartSaveCapability {

        @Override
        public String getChartName() {
            return Bundle.CTL_LineChartAction();
        }

        @Override
        public BufferedImage getImage() {
            if (controller == null) {
                return null;
            }
            final CountDownLatch latch = new CountDownLatch(1);
            Platform.runLater(() -> {
                // get the JavaFX image from the controller
                // must be in JavaFX Application Thread
                try {
                    image = controller.getImage();
                } finally {
                    latch.countDown();
                }
            });
            try {
                latch.await();
                return image;
            } catch (InterruptedException ex) {
                Exceptions.printStackTrace(ex);
                return null;
            }
        }
    }
  . . .
}
```

# 15.6 Key Point Summary

This chapter explores the JavaFX Charts API, which lets you visualize data within a NetBeans Platform application. The chapter shows how to use all of the JavaFX charts in the context of a modular system. Here are the key points in this chapter.

- The NetBeans Platform is well suited for a data visualization application with JavaFX charts. The NetBeans Platform modular architecture coupled with the flexibility of the JavaFX charts create compelling charting applications.
- The SmartPhone Data application presents sales data for smartphone companies over a four-year period and uses JavaFX charts to visualize the data. Each chart is configured in a separate module. The application integrates JavaFX charts with a Swing JTable presentation.

- The SmartPhone Data application uses the Global Lookup to access the chart data. This provides flexibility in obtaining alternate sources of data.
- The application extends Swing AbstractTableModel to provide additional methods applicable to JavaFX charts.
- Each chart module includes a TopComponent for display, an FXML file for JavaFX controls, and a JavaFX controller class.
- The chart modules use the communication strategies discussed in Chapter 6 to keep the Swing EDT and JavaFX Application threads properly managed.
- The JavaFX controller class is responsible for building the chart contents, legend, and title.
- The JavaFX controller class supplies a snapshot of the chart window with the scene graph's root node `snapshot()` method. This returns a JavaFX Image object. The JavaFX Image is then converted to a BufferedImage with the static SwingFXUtils `fromFXImage()` method.
- The JavaFX controller class implements a TableModelListener that responds to changes in the displayed data. By default, JavaFX charts update their rendered chart display with animation.
- The JavaFX Chart class hierarchy includes an abstract Chart superclass, an abstract XYChart class for all two-axes charts, and a PieChart class. XYCharts include BarChart, AreaChart, LineChart, ScatterChart, StackedBarChart, StackedAreaChart, and BubbleChart.
- All XYCharts include an X Axis and Y Axis, which is either NumberAxis (numerical values) or CategoryAxis (String values). BubbleCharts require both axes to be NumberAxis types.
- The data type for XYCharts is an ObservableList of Series. Each Series, in turn, is an ObservableList of data items. A data item is an `XYChart.Data<X, Y>` generic type, where X corresponds to the X axis type (Number or String) and Y corresponds to the Y axis type (Number or String).
- The BubbleChart uses the data item's `extraValue` property to set the radius of the rendered bubble.
- A chart's displayed parts are JavaFX nodes. You can add effects, animations, and event handlers to these nodes.
- Charts use CSS for styling, and you can provide your own chart-specific style classes.
- LineChart, ScatterChart, AreaChart, BarChart, StackedBarChart, and StackedAreaChart are all configured the same way.

- Switch the X and Y axes types to convert a vertical BarChart to a horizontal BarChart.
- The PieChart data is an ObservableList of PieChart.Data items. Each data item represents a portion of a whole and includes a `name` StringProperty and a `pieValue` DoubleProperty.
- The SmartPhone Data application lets users select years with a JavaFX ComboBox control in the PieChart window. The selected year corresponds to a column in the TableModel.
- The SmartPhone Data application includes animation effects added for Pie Chart wedges and an in-place editor for changing the selected Pie wedge value.
- Each chart window implements a ChartSaveCapability and installs it in the TopComponent Lookup. This enables the Save Chart menu items when one of the chart windows has focus. The Save Chart feature saves the selected chart window to a PNG file.

# 16

# Using Web Services

A RESTful web service is a common technology that lets remote clients interact with services. In this chapter, we'll show you the steps to create and test RESTful web services and how to build a RESTful web service client in a NetBeans Platform application. Since web services should be accessed in background threads, we'll show you how to build several JavaFX Service objects to handle multi-threading.

We'll build JavaFX-integrated content with the JavaFX TableView control and provide another look at the JavaFX LineChart. We'll also show you how to add JavaFX properties to JPA entity classes.

## What You Will Learn

- Create RESTful web services from a database.
- Add JavaFX properties to JPA entity classes.
- Create a Java Application RESTful web service client for testing.
- Configure a Jersey client in a NetBeans Platform module.
- Use the JavaFX Service class for re-usable background tasks.
- Create JavaFX-integrated modules as web service clients.

## 16.1 RESTful Web Services and the NetBeans Platform

REST is an architectural style based on web standards and the HTTP protocol. Access to a RESTful web service is provided by resources. A RESTFul web service typically defines the base URI (resource) for the service and a set of operations (POST, GET, PUT, DELETE). Resources can have different representations, such as text, XML, JSON, or even user-defined.

Java supports RESTful web services with JAX-RS (Java API for RESTful Web Services), defined with the JSR 311 specification. Jersey is the reference implementation for JSR 311. The NetBEans IDE bundles Jersey with the Java EE download.

RESTful web services are scalable and flexible. The HTTP protocol is stateless, cacheable, and layered. The NetBeans IDE lets you build both RESTful web services and web service clients. Furthermore, the IDE includes registered RESTful web services from Amazon, Delicious, Flickr, Google, StrikeIron, Weatherbug, Zillow, and Zevents.

In this chapter, we'll build a RESTful web service client in a NetBeans Platform application. Such a client must include the RESTful client code, support libraries, and any applicable entity classes. Furthermore, you'll want to invoke web service calls within a background thread to keep the UI responsive.

The RESTful client application in this chapter is similar to our JavaFX Charts application that displays smartphone sales data (see "JavaFX Charts and the NetBeans Platform" on page 744). With this example, we'll focus on the support that consumes sales data from the web service.

The SmartPhoneDataApp consists of two windows, as shown in Figure 16.1. The TableView window displays smartphone data with a JavaFX TableView control. The second window visualizes the same data with a JavaFX LineChart. The windows are in separate modules and have no dependencies on each other. They both form dependencies on the modules that provide access to the data via web services.

The TableView window supports data filtering using the JavaFX FilteredList class. Figure 16.2 shows a user-supplied filter text String "apple" that limits the TableView window to Company names matching this text. You can filter by year as well.

TableView also supports column sorting by default. Our application disables this feature and instead pre-sorts the data by Company then Year using the JavaFX SortedList class.

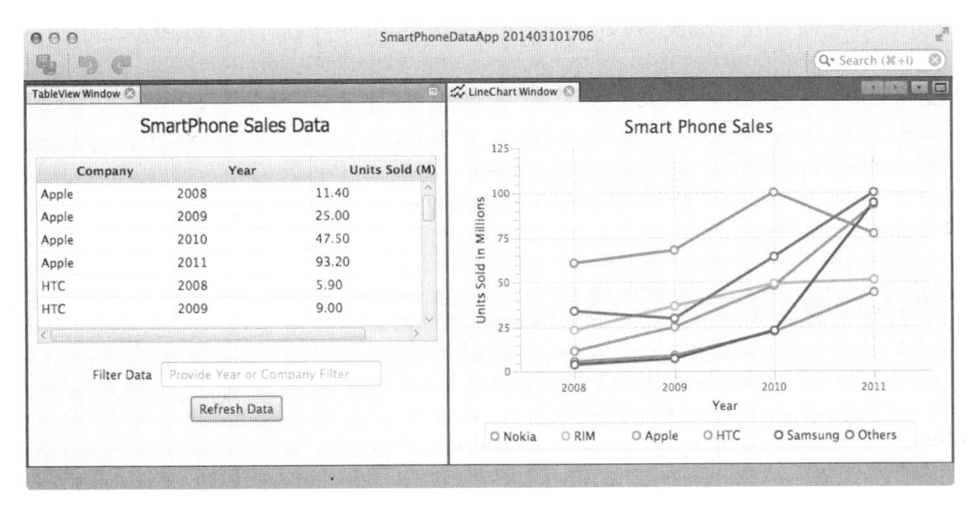


Figure 16.1 Smartphone Data application using web services

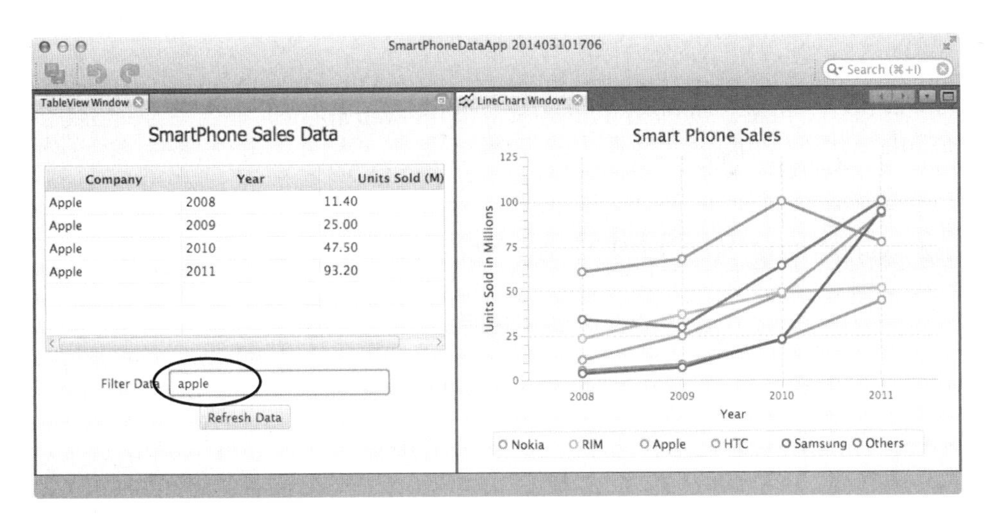


Figure 16.2 JavaFX TableView with sorting and filtering

The TableView window configures the Units Sold column to support editing, as shown in Figure 16.3. When the user supplies a new value and presses the Return or Enter key, the Update Salesdata web service is invoked in the background. Here, you see the new value 75.0 for year 2009. A progress indicator shows the background thread is active. Upon completion, the LineChart reflects the new value by animating the updated plot point to its new position on the chart.[1]

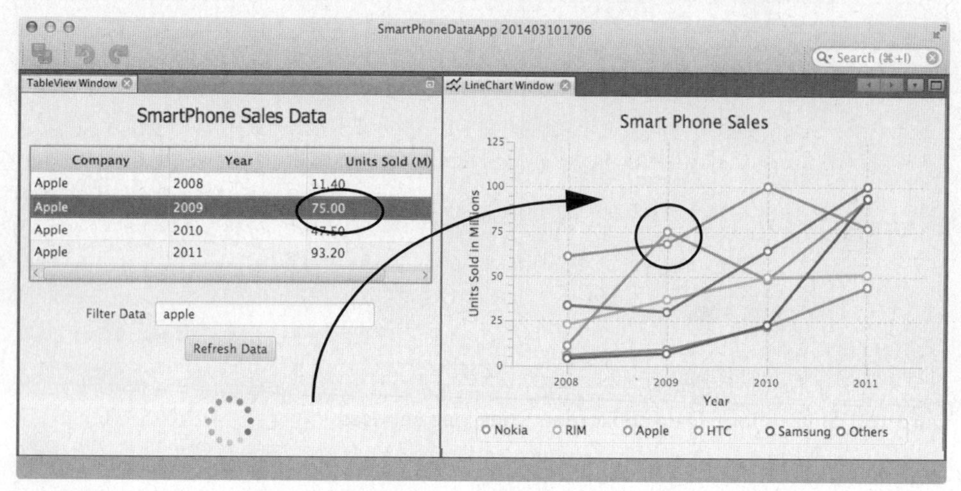


Figure 16.3 Updating using the underlying web service

Before we build this application, let's take you through the steps to create the underlying database. We'll also show you how to build the web application that provides the RESTful smartphone sales data web services.

## 16.2 Creating RESTful Web Services

In this section, you'll create a database, populate the database with data, and create a web application with RESTful web services to manipulate the data. Fortunately, the NetBeans IDE generates much of this code for you.

### Create Database

Using the NetBeans IDE built-in database server JavaDB, create a database with these steps.

1. Follow the steps in Chapter 10 to start the JavaDB Server and create a database. See "JavaDB Server and Database" on page 505 and "Create Database" on page 505.

---

1. Despite the image in Figure 16.3, the chart doesn't actually update until after the web service successfully completes.

2. In the Create Java DB Database dialog, specify **phonedata** for all the fields. JavaDB creates a database listed under the Databases node as

```
jdbc:derby://localhost:1527/phonedata [phonedata on PHONEDATA]
```

3. Right-click on this **phonedata** database node and select **Connect**.
4. Open the **SmartPhoneDataSales.sql** file in the book's download bundle and connect to the PhoneData database as shown in Figure 16.4. Click the **Run SQL** icon in the SQL Editor window to execute the SQL. These SQL statements create the Salesdata and Company tables and populate them with data. Disregard any errors that say "'DROP TABLE' cannot be performed."

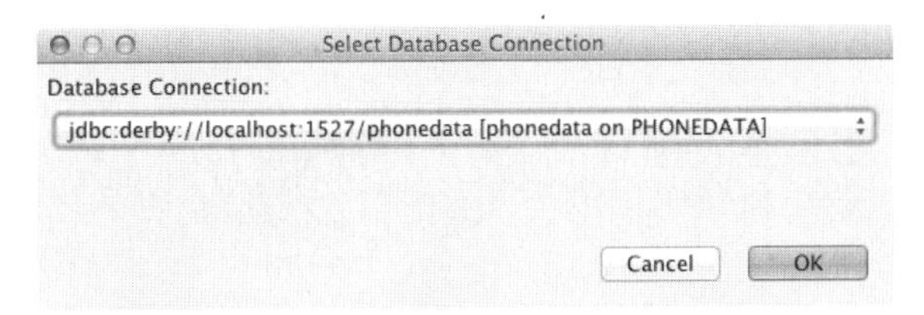


Figure 16.4 Select Database Connection dialog

5. You can re-execute this SQL file any time to restore the data. The 'DROP TABLE' errors do not appear with subsequent executions of this SQL file.

## Create RESTful Web Service Application

You'll now create a RESTful web service application.

### NetBeans IDE Configuration

*This project uses Java EE technologies and a bundled server (GlassFish), optionally included with the NetBeans IDE. Download and install these technologies if your configuration does not include them. You can add these modules with the IDE's Plugin Manager (Tools | Plugins).*

1. In the Projects window, select **File | New Project**. In the Choose Project dialog, under Categories, select **Java Web** and under Projects select **Web Application**.
2. NetBeans displays the Name and Location dialog. Specify **SmartPhoneDataServer** for the Project Name. Click the **Browse** button to choose the appropriate Project Location and click **Next**.
3. Figure 16.5 shows the Server and Settings dialog. Specify the Server (**GlassFish Server**). If you haven't yet added a Server to the IDE, click the **Add** button to do

that. Select **Java EE 7 Web** for the Java EE Version. Accept the default for the web application Context Path and click **Finish**.

(Note that if you click Next, you'll be asked to specify a framework. Leave the frameworks unchecked and click Finish.)

Figure 16.5 Specify the web application's server and settings

With the SmartPhoneDataServer web application project created, you can now use the RESTful Services from Database wizard to generate entity classes and the RESTful web services. This wizard also generates the persistence unit.

## RESTful Services from Database

Create the RESTful services with the NetBeans IDE wizard using these steps.

1. In the Projects window, right click on the SmartPhoneDataServer project and select **New | Other**. In the Choose File Type dialog, select **Web Services** under Categories and **RESTful Web Services from Database** under File Types, as shown in Figure 16.6. Click **Next**.
2. NetBeans prompts you to configure the connection to the PhoneData database. After the database data source is configured, you'll see the tables in the selection list. Choose both **Company** and **Salesdata** and click **Add**. The selected tables then move to the right side, as shown in Figure 16.7. Click **Next**.

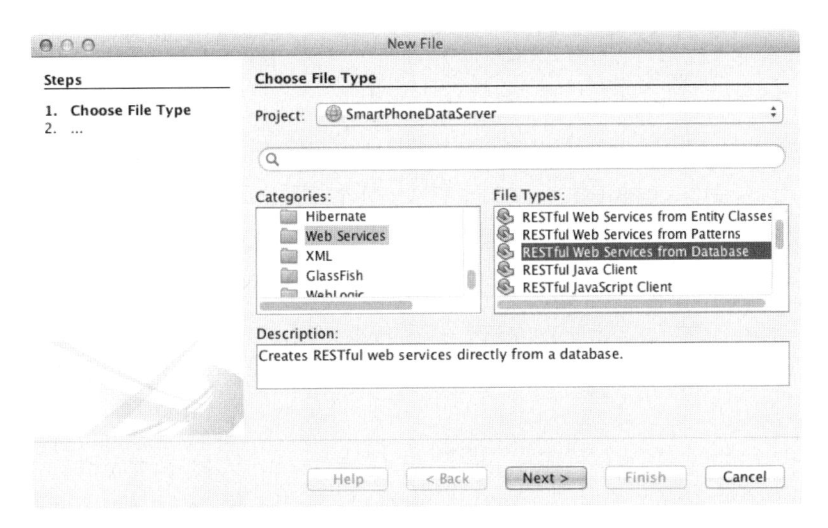


Figure 16.6 Create RESTful web services from database wizard

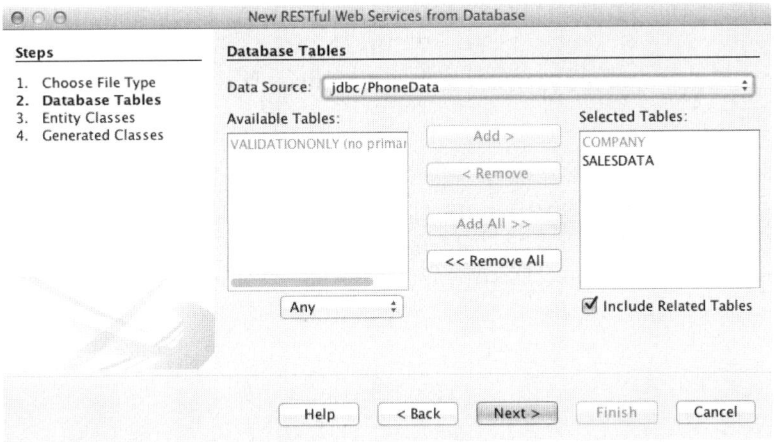

Figure 16.7 Select database tables

3. Supply a package name for the entity classes that NetBeans will generate. Here we use package **com.server.smartphonedata.entities**, as shown in Figure 16.8. Click **Next**.

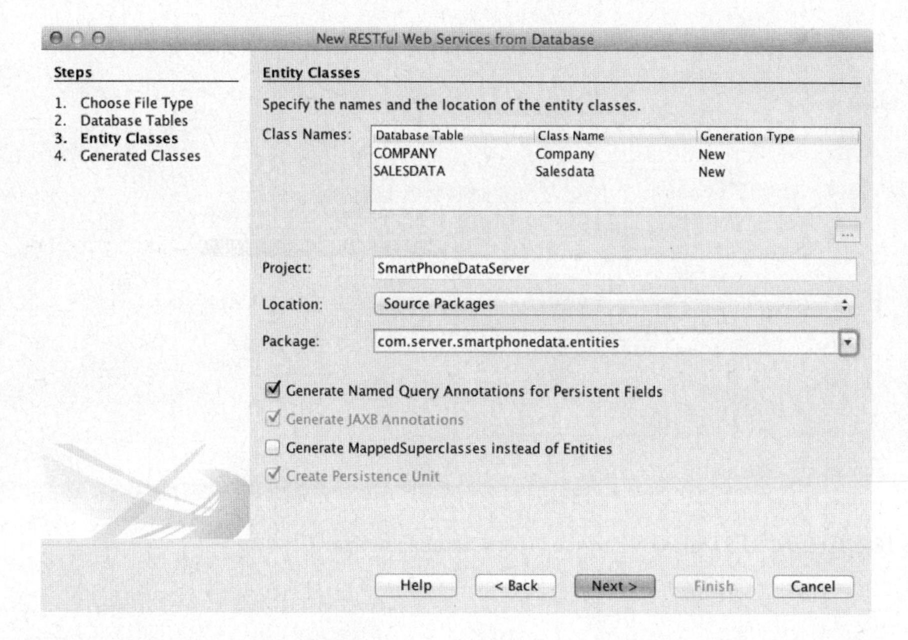


Figure 16.8 Configure entity classes

4. Review the configuration information for the generated classes and click **Finish**, as shown in Figure 16.9.

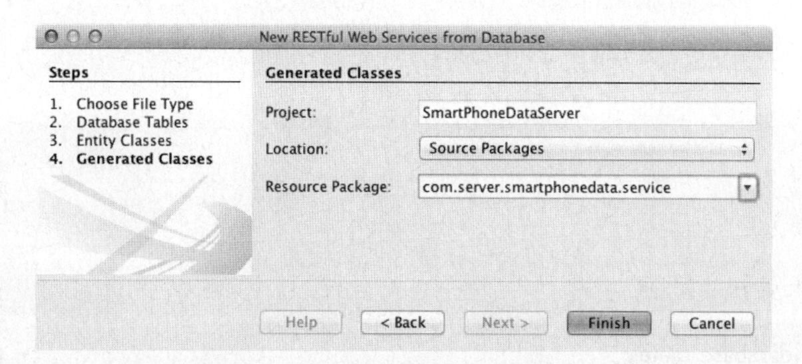


Figure 16.9 Review generated classes configuration

5. NetBeans generates both the services and entity classes. Now deploy the application. In the Services window, expand **Servers | GlassFish Server | Applications**. You should see the web application **SmartPhoneDataServer** listed.

### Entity Classes and JavaFX Properties

The RESTful services wizard generates the Company and Salesdata entity classes. These are Plain Old Java Objects (POJOs) with Java Persistence API (JPA) annotations. By default, the wizard annotates the POJO's class fields. Thus, JPA uses the class fields to synchronize the entity's state with the database.

Although JPA is not aware of JavaFX properties, you can implement JavaFX properties in entity classes and still maintain compatibility with JPA. Instead of using class fields to synchronize the entity's state with the database, you tell JPA to use the Java property getters and setters. To do this, move the annotations from the class fields to the property getters. Since entity classes must define a consistent JPA access strategy, you can annotate either class fields or property getters (but you can't mix the access strategy).

Once you move the annotations to the property getters, replace the class fields with corresponding JavaFX properties. You'll then modify the accessors to use the JavaFX property and add a JavaFX property getter. Listing 16.1 shows these modifications for the Salesdata.java entity class in bold. Perform similar modifications to the Company.java entity class.

#### Listing 16.1 Salesdata.java—Entity Class and JavaFX Properties

```
@Entity
@Table(name = "SALESDATA")
@XmlRootElement
@NamedQueries({ . . . })
public class Salesdata implements Serializable {

    private static final long serialVersionUID = 1L;

    private final IntegerProperty salesidProperty =
                        new SimpleIntegerProperty();
    private final StringProperty salesyearProperty =
                        new SimpleStringProperty();
    private final ObjectProperty<BigDecimal> unitsinmillionsProperty =
                        new SimpleObjectProperty<>();
    private final ObjectProperty<Company>  companyidProperty =
                        new SimpleObjectProperty<>();

    public Salesdata() {
    }

    public Salesdata(Integer salesid) {
        salesidProperty.set(salesid);
    }
```

```
    @Id
    @GeneratedValue(strategy = GenerationType.IDENTITY)
    @Basic(optional = false)
    @Column(name = "SALESID")
    public Integer getSalesid() {
        return salesidProperty.get();
    }

    public void setSalesid(Integer salesid) {
        salesidProperty.set(salesid);
    }

    public IntegerProperty salesidProperty() {
        return salesidProperty;
    }

    @Size(max = 10)
    @Column(name = "SALESYEAR")
    public String getSalesyear() {
        return salesyearProperty.get();
    }

    public void setSalesyear(String salesyear) {
        salesyearProperty.set(salesyear);
    }

    public StringProperty salesyearProperty() {
        return salesyearProperty;
    }

    @Column(name = "UNITSINMILLIONS")
    public BigDecimal getUnitsinmillions() {
        return unitsinmillionsProperty.get();
    }

    public void setUnitsinmillions(BigDecimal unitsinmillions) {
        unitsinmillionsProperty.set(unitsinmillions);
    }

    public ObjectProperty<BigDecimal> unitsinmillionsProperty() {
        return unitsinmillionsProperty;
    }

    @JoinColumn(name = "COMPANYID", referencedColumnName = "COMPANYID")
    @ManyToOne
    public Company getCompanyid() {
        return companyidProperty.get();
    }

    public void setCompanyid(Company companyid) {
        companyidProperty.set(companyid);
    }
```

```
    public ObjectProperty<Company> companyidProperty() {
        return companyidProperty;
    }

    @Override
    public int hashCode() {
        int hash = 0;
        hash += (getSalesid() != null ? getSalesid().hashCode() : 0);
        return hash;
    }

    @Override
    public boolean equals(Object object) {
        if (!(object instanceof Salesdata)) {
            return false;
        }
        Salesdata other = (Salesdata) object;
        return (getSalesid() != null || other.getSalesid() == null)
                && (getSalesid() == null
                || getSalesid().equals(other.getSalesid()));
    }

    @Override
    public String toString() {
        return "com.server.smartphonedata.entities.Salesdata[ salesid="
                        + getSalesid() + " ]";
    }
}
```

## Test the Web Services

Test your newly-created web services using the following steps.

1. In the Projects view, right click on the SmartPhoneDataServer project and select **Test RESTful Web Services**. NetBeans displays a dialog to configure the Test Client. Select the **Web Test Client in Project** radio button and click **Browse**.
2. Select the **SmartPhoneDataServer** project. NetBeans supplies the Target Folder path, as shown in Figure 16.10. Click **OK**.
3. NetBeans brings up a browser and provides a testing menu for either Company or Salesdata. Here, we select the Salesdata service for `GET()` and select **Test**. Figure 16.11 shows a portion of the (successful) response displaying raw XML-formatted data.

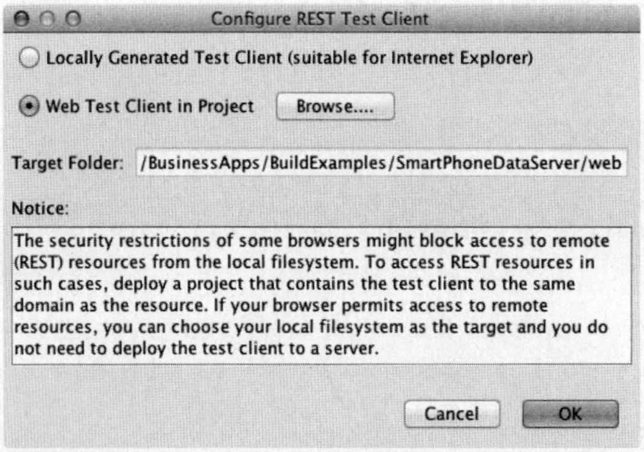

Configure REST Test Client

○ Locally Generated Test Client (suitable for Internet Explorer)

◉ Web Test Client in Project [Browse....]

Target Folder: /BusinessApps/BuildExamples/SmartPhoneDataServer/web

Notice:

The security restrictions of some browsers might block access to remote (REST) resources from the local filesystem. To access REST resources in such cases, deploy a project that contains the test client to the same domain as the resource. If your browser permits access to remote resources, you can choose your local filesystem as the target and you do not need to deploy the test client to a server.

[Cancel] [OK]

Figure 16.10 Configure the REST test client.

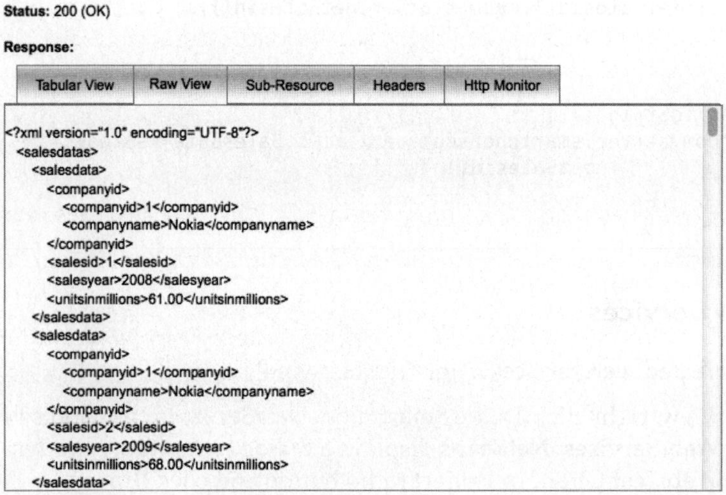

**Status:** 200 (OK)

**Response:**

Tabular View | Raw View | Sub-Resource | Headers | Http Monitor

```
<?xml version="1.0" encoding="UTF-8"?>
  <salesdatas>
    <salesdata>
      <companyid>
        <companyid>1</companyid>
        <companyname>Nokia</companyname>
      </companyid>
      <salesid>1</salesid>
      <salesyear>2008</salesyear>
      <unitsinmillions>61.00</unitsinmillions>
    </salesdata>
    <salesdata>
      <companyid>
        <companyid>1</companyid>
        <companyname>Nokia</companyname>
      </companyid>
      <salesid>2</salesid>
      <salesyear>2009</salesyear>
      <unitsinmillions>68.00</unitsinmillions>
    </salesdata>
```

Figure 16.11 Testing the web service

## 16.3 A Java Application Web Service Client

Next, let's build a RESTful web service client as a regular Java application. While it is not necessary to create this web service client, we recommend this step if you're unfamiliar with working with RESTful web services. Once you're able to successfully execute a Java application web service client, moving the pieces to a NetBeans Platform application is straightforward.

To successfully execute client code you must do the following.

- Deploy a web application and start its required database and enterprise servers.
- Include libraries to access RESTful resources.
- Include libraries to convert XML and/or JSON responses to POJOs.
- Include access to entity classes (POJOs).

### Create Java Application

Create a Java application client to test the web services with these steps.

1. In the Projects view, select **File | New Project**. Under Categories select **Java** and under Projects select **Java Application**. Click **Next**.
2. In the Name and Location dialog, specify **SmartPhoneDataClient** for Project Name. Click the **Browse** button to choose an appropriate location for the project. Accept the defaults for the remaining fields and make sure option **Create Main Class** is selected. Click **Finish**.

### Add RESTful Java Client

Generate RESTful Java client code and add the necessary libraries with these steps.

1. In the Projects view, expand SmartPhoneDataClient, right click on the Source Packages node, and select **New | Other**.
2. In the Choose File Type dialog, select **Web Services** under Categories and **RESTful Java Client** under File Types, as shown in Figure 16.12. Click **Next**.
3. In the Name and Location dialog, specify **CompanyJerseyClient** for Class Name and select the **smartphoneclient** package (or provide another package name), as shown in Figure 16.13.

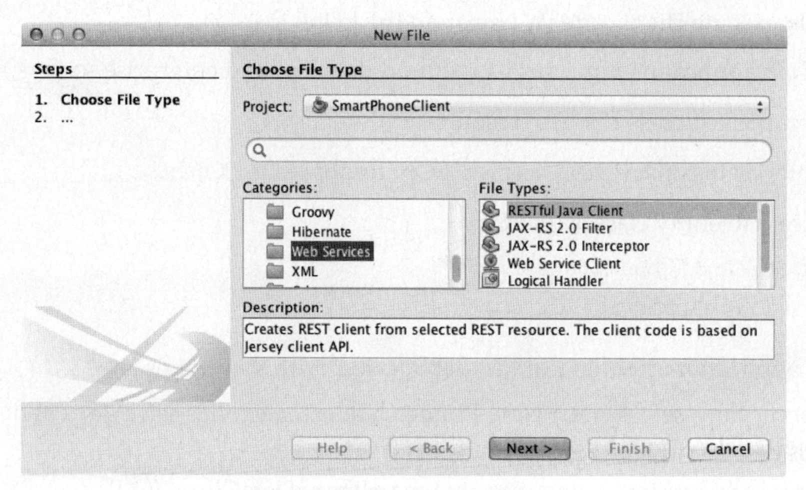


Figure 16.12 Generate RESTful a Java client

New RESTful Java Client

Steps

1. Choose File Type
2. Name and Location

Name and Location

Class Name: CompanyJerseyClient

Project: SmartPhoneClient

Location: Source Packages

Package: smartphoneclient

Created File: SmartPhoneClient/src/smartphoneclient/CompanyJerseyClient.java

Select the REST resource:

From Project IDE Registered Browse...

REST Resource Name:

CompanyFacadeREST [com.server.smartphonedata.entities.company]

Authentication: NONE SSL

Help < Back Next > Finish Cancel

Figure 16.13 Configure the RESTful Java client

4. Still in the same dialog, click **Browse** to select the REST resource. In the Select REST Resource dialog, expand the SmartPhoneDataServer node and select **CompanyFacadeREST** from the available choices, as shown in Figure 16.14 (the SmartPhoneDataServer web application must be deployed). Click **OK**.

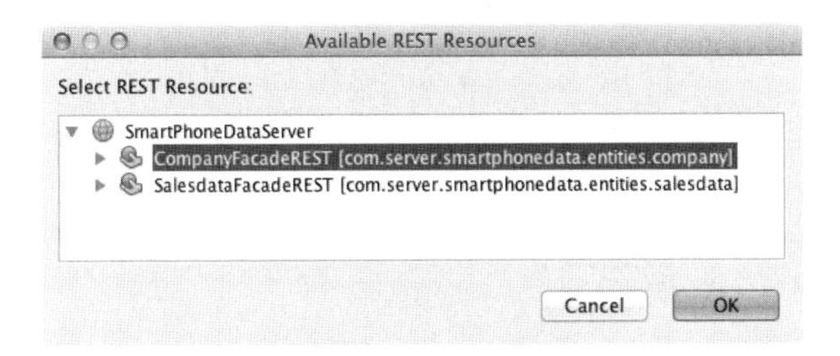


Figure 16.14 Select the REST resource

5. Now with the RESTful Java client configured, click **Finish**. NetBeans generates file CompanyJerseyClient.java in your Java Application project and adds support libraries to the project.
6. Repeat the above steps and add a RESTful Java client called **SalesdataJerseyClient** for the REST resource **SalesdataFacadeREST**.

## Add JAR Files to Project

The client code (shown in Listing 16.2 on page 814) references entity classes. You can either copy these from the SmartPhoneDataServer project or include the SmartPhone-DataServer WAR file in the Java application web service client's build. Here are the steps to include the WAR file.

1. In the Projects view, right click on **SmartPhoneDataClient | Libraries** and select **Add JAR/Folder** from the context menu.
2. In the dialog, navigate to the **dist** folder in project SmartPhoneDataServer and select the WAR file, as shown in Figure 16.15. Click **Choose**. NetBeans adds **Smart-PhoneDataServer.war** to the list of Libraries.

The test program also invokes JSON resources. When you generate a RESTful Java client, the libraries do not include a JSON MessageBodyReader provider. For JSON, use the third-party Genson Library available at **`http://owlike.github.io/genson/`**.

1. Click the **Download** link on the **`owlike.gethub.io/genson/`** page and download the Genson library JAR file.
2. Follow the above steps and add the Genson library to your project.

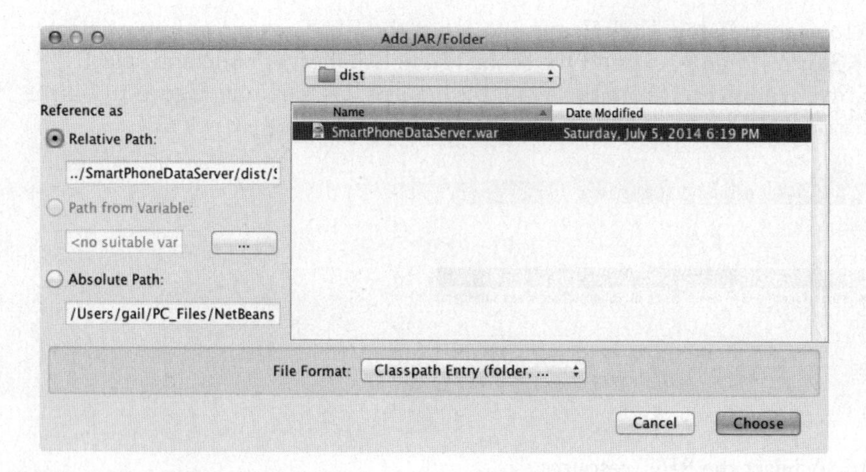


Figure 16.15 Select the WAR file

## Add Client Code to Main Program

Next, add the following code to the `main()` method in SmartPhoneClient.java, as shown in Listing 16.2. Right-click and select **Fix Imports** to resolve any errors.[2]

**Listing 16.2 SmartPhoneClient.java—main() Method**

```
import com.server.smartphonedata.entities.Company;
import com.server.smartphonedata.entities.Salesdata;
import java.util.List;
import javax.ws.rs.core.GenericType;
import javax.ws.rs.core.Response;

public class SmartPhoneClient {

    public static void main(String[] args) {
        CompanyJerseyClient client = new CompanyJerseyClient();
        Company company = client.find_XML(Company.class, "2");
        System.out.println("Company = " + company.getCompanyname());

        Response response = client.find_XML(Response.class, "1");
        company = response.readEntity(Company.class);
        System.out.println("Company = " + company.getCompanyname());
```

2. Note that NetBeans currently bundles Jersey 2.x, which provides different classes than Jersey 1.x.

```
company = client.find_JSON(Company.class, "2");
System.out.println("Company = " + company.getCompanyname());

GenericType<List<Company>> gType1 =
             new GenericType<List<Company>>() {};
response = client.findAll_XML(Response.class);
List<Company> companies = response.readEntity(gType1);
System.out.println("Companies = " + companies);

SalesdataJerseyClient client2 = new SalesdataJerseyClient();
Salesdata data = client2.find_XML(Salesdata.class, "1");
System.out.println("Salesdata = " + data.getSalesyear() + ", "
        + data.getCompanyid() + ", "
        + data.getUnitsinmillions());

GenericType<List<Salesdata>> gType2 =
       new GenericType<List<Salesdata>>() {};
response = client2.findAll_XML(Response.class);
List<Salesdata> dataList = response.readEntity(gType2);
System.out.println("Data List = " + dataList);

// print out all the data
for(Company c  : companies) {
    System.out.println("Data for Company: " + c.getCompanyname());
    for (Salesdata dataItem : dataList) {
        if (dataItem.getCompanyid().getCompanyid().equals(
                                     c.getCompanyid())) {
            System.out.println("Year=" + dataItem.getSalesyear()
                + ", " + "Units Sold in Millions = "
                + dataItem.getUnitsinmillions());
        }
    }
}

// test JSON
System.out.println("Testing JSON");
response = client2.findAll_JSON(Response.class);
List<Salesdata> dataList2 = response.readEntity(gType2);
System.out.println("Data List = " + dataList2);

// print out all the data
for(Company c  : companies) {
    System.out.println("Data for Company: " + c.getCompanyname());
    for (Salesdata dataItem : dataList2) {
        if (dataItem.getCompanyid().getCompanyid().equals(
                                  c.getCompanyid())) {
```

```
                    System.out.println("Year=" + dataItem.getSalesyear()
                        + ", " + "Units Sold in Millions = "
                        + dataItem.getUnitsinmillions());
                }
            }
        }
    }
}
```

**Run** this Java RESTful client application. Listing 16.3 shows the truncated output.

### Listing 16.3 SmartPhoneClient—Output

```
Company = RIM
Company = Nokia
Company = RIM
Companies = [com.server.smartphonedata.entities.Company[ companyid=1 ],
com.server.smartphonedata.entities.Company[ companyid=2 ],
com.server.smartphonedata.entities.Company[ companyid=3 ],
com.server.smartphonedata.entities.Company[ companyid=4 ],
. . . truncated . . .
Salesdata = 2008,
com.server.smartphonedata.entities.Company[ companyid=1 ], 61.00
Data List = [com.server.smartphonedata.entities.Salesdata[ salesid=1 ],
com.server.smartphonedata.entities.Salesdata[ salesid=2 ],
com.server.smartphonedata.entities.Salesdata[ salesid=3 ],
com.server.smartphonedata.entities.Salesdata[ salesid=4 ],
. . . truncated . . .
Data for Company: Nokia
Year=2008, Units Sold in Millions = 61.00
Year=2009, Units Sold in Millions = 68.00
Year=2010, Units Sold in Millions = 100.10
Year=2011, Units Sold in Millions = 77.30
Data for Company: RIM
Year=2008, Units Sold in Millions = 23.10
Year=2009, Units Sold in Millions = 37.00
Year=2010, Units Sold in Millions = 48.80
Year=2011, Units Sold in Millions = 51.10
Data for Company: Apple
Year=2008, Units Sold in Millions = 11.40
Year=2009, Units Sold in Millions = 25.00
Year=2010, Units Sold in Millions = 47.50
Year=2011, Units Sold in Millions = 93.20
. . . truncated . . .
Testing JSON
Data List = [com.server.smartphonedata.entities.Salesdata[ salesid=1 ],
com.server.smartphonedata.entities.Salesdata[ salesid=2 ],
com.server.smartphonedata.entities.Salesdata[ salesid=3 ],
. . . truncated . . .
```

```
Data for Company: Nokia
Year=2008, Units Sold in Millions = 61.0
Year=2009, Units Sold in Millions = 68.0
Year=2010, Units Sold in Millions = 100.1
Year=2011, Units Sold in Millions = 77.3
. . . truncated . . .
```

## 16.4 RESTful Web Services in a NetBeans Platform Application

Let's now show you how to build a NetBeans Platform application that consumes our two RESTful web services. You'll create this application with the following steps.

1. Build a new NetBeans Platform application called **SmartPhoneDataApp** and a new module for the RESTful web services clients with the name **PhoneDataWebService**.
2. Use the NetBeans IDE to generate the RESTful web service clients and add JAR files to the module. Create an `@OnStart` Runnable to test the client.
3. Create JavaFX Services to invoke the RESTful web service clients in a background thread. Create a service provider so that other modules can access these services in a loosely-coupled way.
4. Build a new module that displays the data using a JavaFX TableView control. Let the user edit and update the sales amount field.
5. Build a new module that displays the data using a JavaFX LineChart control. Update the chart with any changes in the underlying data.

#### Create a NetBeans Platform Application and Module

First, let's create the application and the **PhoneDataWebService** module.

1. Create a new application called **SmartPhoneDataApp** using the NetBeans Platform New Project wizard.
2. Create a module and add it to the SmartPhoneDataApp application. Call the module **PhoneDataWebService** and provide code name **com.asgteach.phonedata.webservice**.

### Generate RESTful Web Service Clients

Use the NetBeans IDE to generate RESTful Java clients as follows.

1. Expand **PhoneDataWebService | Source Packages**, right click and select **New | RESTful Java Client**.
2. Use the same steps to complete the wizard (see "Add RESTful Java Client" on page 811) to add the RESTful Java client to the PhoneDataWebService module. Figure 16.16 shows the Project View with the CompanyJerseyClient.java and SalesdataJerseyClient.java files added. Note that you must manually add JAR files to the module to resolve the source code errors.

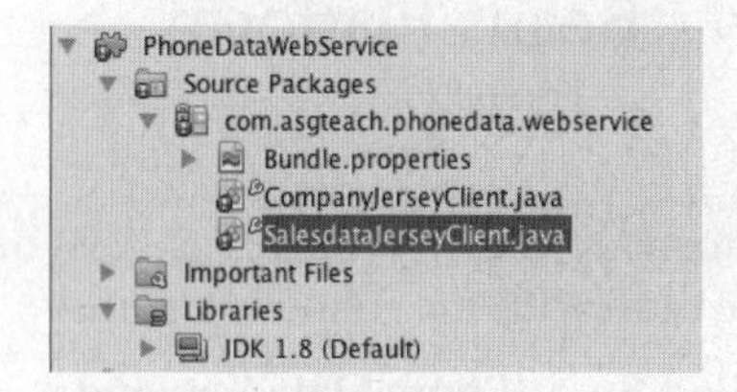


Figure 16.16 PhoneDataWebService module Projects view

### Add Libraries to the Module

Add the JAR files to the PhoneDataWebService module as listed in Table 16.1.[3] Right click the module name and select **Properties** then **Libraries**. In the dialog, select the **Wrapped JARs** tab and click **Add JAR**. You can add more than one JAR file at once. Figure 16.17 shows several JARs. Click **OK** to complete the process.

#### Adding a Library to a Module vs. Wrapped Library Modules

*Note that we add libraries directly to a module here instead of creating Wrapped Library Modules (see "Create Wrapped Libraries" on page 502). Wrapped Library Modules allow other modules to add dependencies on these libraries. The packages of the added libraries are not exposed and therefore can only be used by a specific module (here, the PhoneDataWebService module). In general, use Wrapped Library Modules. However, when you know that libraries will be used exclusively by a single module, you can add them directly. This avoids cluttering your application with additional modules.*

3. These JAR files may not always be in the listed locations, and the version numbers will certainly change as new releases of these libraries are distributed. (On Mac OS X, create a symbolic link to the directory that contains the NetBeans application to view the directory contents from the NetBeans IDE dialogs.)

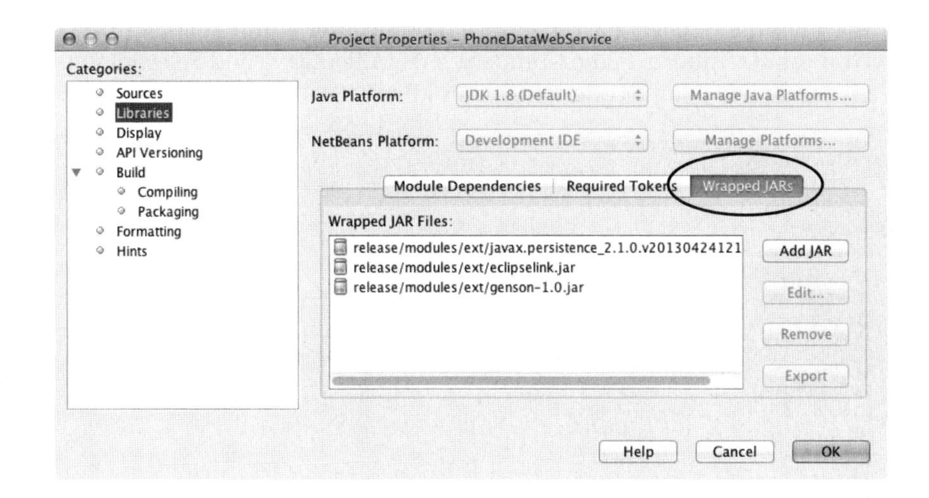


Figure 16.17 PhoneDataWebService module's added JARs

**TABLE 16.1 RESTful Java Client Support Libraries**

| JAR File | Location |
|---|---|
| cglib-2.1.88.jar | `NetBeans/enterprise/modules/ext/jersey2/ext` |
| eclipselink.jar | `NetBeans/java/modules/ext/eclipselink` |
| genson-1.0.jar | `Download http://owlike.github.io/genson/` |
| guava-14.0.1.jar | `NetBeans/enterprise/modules/ext/jersey2/ext` |
| hk2-api-2.1.88.jar | `NetBeans/enterprise/modules/ext/jersey2/ext` |
| hk2-locator-2.1.88.jar | `NetBeans/enterprise/modules/ext/jersey2/ext` |
| hk2-utils-2.1.88.jar | `NetBeans/enterprise/modules/ext/jersey2/ext` |
| javax.inject-2.1.88.jar | `NetBeans/enterprise/modules/ext/jersey2/ext` |
| javax.persistence-2.1.0.vxx.jar | `NetBeans/java/modules/ext/eclipselink` |
| javax.ws.rs-api.2.0.jar | `NetBeans/enterprise/modules/ext/jaxrs-2.0` |
| jersey-client.jar | `NetBeans/enterprise/modules/ext/jersey2` |
| jersey-common.jar | `NetBeans/enterprise/modules/ext/jersey2` |
| osgi-resource-locator-1.0.1.jar | `NetBeans/enterprise/modules/ext/jersey2/ext` |

Figure 16.18 shows the PhoneDataWebService module after adding the required JAR files. Now you can fix imports in the CompanyJerseyClient.java and SalesdataJersey-Client.java files and any source code errors should resolve.

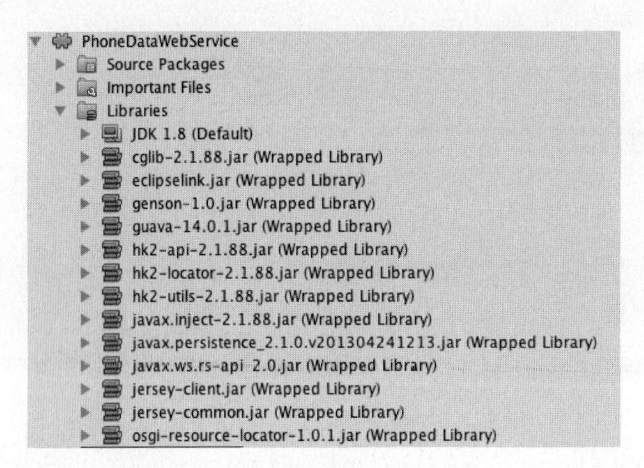


Figure 16.18 PhoneDataWebService module's added JARs

## Create the @OnStart Runnable for Testing

You're almost ready to test the application. Here are the steps to create a Java class for testing.

1. In the PhoneDataWebService module, add a module dependency on the Module System API.
2. In the PhoneDataWebService module Source Packages node, create a new Java package called **com.asgteach.phonedata.entities**.
3. Copy and **Refactor | Paste** classes Salesdata.java and Company.java from the **SmartPhoneDataServer** web application. (You can disregard the warnings associated with the @Entity annotation.)
4. Create a new Java class called **ClientTest.java** that implements Runnable. Add the **@OnStart** annotation and implement the `run()` method as shown in Listing 16.4. Include the test code from the SmartPhoneClient project's `main()` method (Listing 16.2 on page 814).

**Listing 16.4 ClientTest—run() Method**

```
package com.asgteach.phonedata.webservice;

import com.asgteach.phonedata.entities.Company;
import com.asgteach.phonedata.entities.Salesdata;
```

```
import java.util.List;
import javax.ws.rs.core.GenericType;
import javax.ws.rs.core.Response;
import org.openide.modules.OnStart;

@OnStart
public final class ClientTest implements Runnable {

    @Override
    public void run() {
        CompanyJerseyClient client = new CompanyJerseyClient();
        Company company = client.find_XML(Company.class, "2");
        System.out.println("Company = " + company.getCompanyname());

      . . . remaining test code omitted, see Listing 16.2 on page 814 . . .

    }
}
```

5. Run the **SmartPhoneDataApp**. The application will execute and create an empty window frame. In the NetBeans IDE Output window, the same test output should appear as shown in Listing 16.3 on page 816.

Now that you have a working NetBeans Platform application client module, you can add JavaFX services and windows with integrated JavaFX content.

## Application Overview

Figure 16.19 shows the modules in the SmartPhoneDataApp. The PhoneDataWeb-Service module contains the entity classes and the RESTful web service client code. This module also contains a Java interface called PhoneDataShare, which defines how other modules can access the smartphone data. In the next section, you'll add JavaFX Services to this module. These classes provide access to the RESTful services in a background thread.

The CoreTableView module implements the JavaFX TableView window (see Figure 16.1 on page 801) and the LineChart module implements the JavaFX LineChart window. Finally, the @ServiceProvider module implements the PhoneDataShare interface.

## Using JavaFX Services

Chapter 4 describes the JavaFX Worker interface, which lets you create background tasks and services (see "JavaFX Background Tasks" on page 176). Here we'll use the Service class to create a reusable implementation of the Worker interface for background execution.

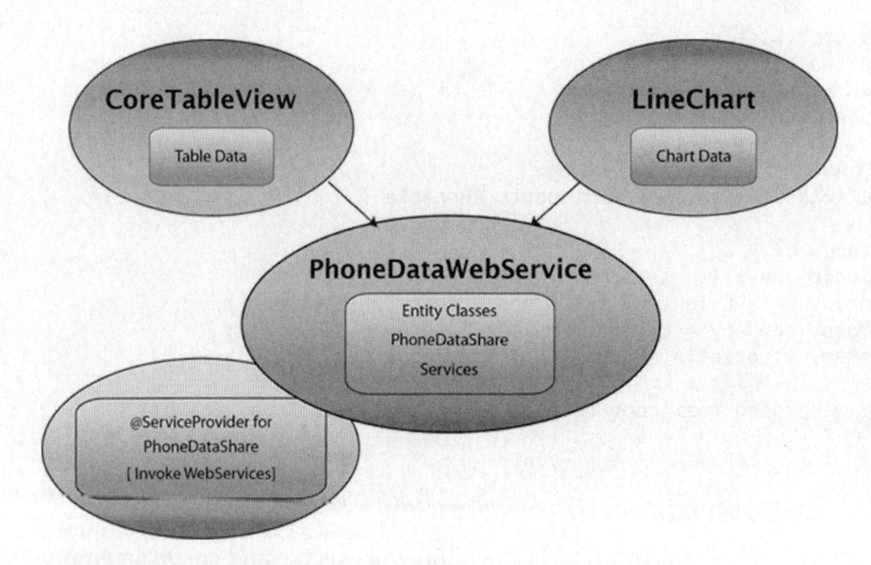


Figure 16.19 SmartPhoneDataApp modules

Recall that Service (like Task) is aware of the JavaFX Application Thread. Therefore, all Service methods and state must be invoked from the JavaFX Application Thread. However, you can initially configure and start a service from any thread.

Service includes the same Worker.State values as Task (see Table 4.1 on page 176) as well as the Worker JavaFX Properties and Task Update Methods (see Table 4.2 on page 177 and Table 4.3 on page 178).

Let's show you how to define a Service first. Then we'll show you code that uses it.

Listing 16.5 shows the GetSmartPhoneSalesService class, which extends Service. Here, the generic type for Service is `ObservableList<Salesdata>`, which is also the return type for a successful completion of this Service.

When you extend Service, you must override the protected `createTask()` method. This method builds a Task object and overrides the `call()` method. Here, `call()` invokes the `findAll_XML()` method in the SalesdataJerseyClient RESTful Java client. By providing GenericType, we transform the Response object with `readEntity()` into a `List<Salesdata>`. We then create the ObservableList with the FXCollections `observableArrayList()` method.

**Listing 16.5 GetSmartPhoneSalesService.java**

```
public class GetSmartPhoneSalesService extends
                              Service<ObservableList<Salesdata>> {
```

```
    private static final Logger logger =
                Logger.getLogger(GetSmartPhoneSalesService.class.getName());
    private ObservableList<Salesdata> salesdata =
                      FXCollections.observableArrayList();

    @Override
    protected Task<ObservableList<Salesdata>> createTask() {

        return new Task<ObservableList<Salesdata>>() {
            private final SalesdataJerseyClient client1 =
                                        new SalesdataJerseyClient();

            @Override
            protected ObservableList<Salesdata> call() throws Exception {
                logger.log(Level.INFO, "GetSmartPhoneSalesTask called.");
                Response response = client1.findAll_XML(Response.class);
                GenericType<List<Salesdata>> genericType =
                     new GenericType<List<Salesdata>>() {};
                int status = response.getStatus();
                if (status != Response.Status.OK.getStatusCode()) {
                    logger.log(Level.WARNING, "Bad status {0}",
                        response.getStatusInfo().getReasonPhrase());
                    throw new Exception("Bad status: " + status
                        + " for web service call");
                }
                // Returns an ArrayList of SalesData from the web service
                List<Salesdata> data = (response.readEntity(genericType));
                salesdata = FXCollections.observableArrayList(data);
                return salesdata;
            }
        };
    }
}
```

Listing 16.6 shows how to use this service. The UseService class instantiates the GetSmartPhoneSalesService service (`salesService`) and defines public method `refreshData()` with an optional ProgressIndicator control. The `refreshData()` method, in turn, invokes the private `getDataInBackground()` method. Inside this method, the `salesService` service is started. Note that you must reset the service each time it completes in order to reuse the service.

UseService also defines two event handlers, `setOnSucceeded()` and `setOnFailed()`. The `setOnSucceeded()` event handler provides access to the underlying Task's return object with `t.getSource().getValue()`, where `t` is WorkerStateEvent.

Note that the event handlers run in the JavaFX Application Thread. Therefore, we can safely update visual controls (such as the ProgressIndicator) and safely manipulate JavaFX properties. Here, the `setOnSucceeded()` event handler sets the `underlyingData` ListProperty. A JavaFX TableView control can safely bind to this property.

**Listing 16.6 UseService Example**

```
public class UseService {

    private final ListProperty<Salesdata> underlyingData = new
         SimpleListProperty<Salesdata>(FXCollections.observableArrayList());

    private final GetSmartPhoneSalesService salesService = new
         GetSmartPhoneSalesService();

    public void refreshData(ProgressIndicator progressIndicator) {
        getDataInBackground(progressIndicator);
    }

    @SuppressWarnings("unchecked")
    private void getDataInBackground(ProgressIndicator progressIndicator) {
        // This service can be invoked multiple times
        salesService.setOnSucceeded((WorkerStateEvent t) -> {
                logger.log(Level.INFO, "sales data Done.");
                if (progressIndicator != null) {
                    progressIndicator.setVisible(false);
                }
                underlyingData.set((ObservableList<Salesdata>)
                        t.getSource().getValue());
                }
        });
        salesService.setOnFailed((WorkerStateEvent t) -> {
                if (progressIndicator != null) {
                    progressIndicator.setVisible(false);
                }
                logger.log(Level.WARNING, "Failed: Read Salesdata");
        });
        // only start the service if it's ready
        if (salesService.getState() == Worker.State.SUCCEEDED) {
            salesService.reset();
        }
        if (salesService.getState() == Worker.State.READY) {
            if (progressIndicator != null) {
                progressIndicator.setVisible(true);
            }
            salesService.start();
        }
    }
}
```

## Add JavaFX Service Classes to the Module

Here are the steps to add the JavaFX Service classes to the PhoneDataWebService module.

1. Create a new Java package in the PhoneDataWebService module called **com.asgteach.phonedata.services** and add the following Service classes to the package.

- **GetSmartPhoneSalesService.java**—a service that accesses the smartphone sales data via a RESTful web service client
- **GetCompanyDataService.java**—a service that accesses the smartphone companies via a RESTful web service client
- **UpdateSalesItemService.java**—a service that updates a single Salesdata item via a RESTful web service client

2. Make the **com.asgteach.com.phonedata.services** package public.

Listing 16.5 on page 822 shows the code for GetSmartPhoneSalesService. Using a similar approach, Listing 16.7 shows GetCompanyDataService.java. Here, the Task's `call()` method invokes the `findAll_XML()` method of the RESTful Java client, CompanyJerseyClient.

#### Listing 16.7 GetCompanyDataService.java

```
public class GetCompanyDataService extends Service<ObservableList<Company>> {
    private static final Logger logger =
                Logger.getLogger(GetCompanyDataService.class.getName());

    @Override
    protected Task<ObservableList<Company>> createTask() {
        return new Task<ObservableList<Company>>() {

            private final CompanyJerseyClient client1 =
                                        new CompanyJerseyClient();

            @Override
           protected ObservableList<Company> call() throws Exception {
                Response response = client1.findAll_XML(Response.class);
                GenericType<List<Company>> genericType =
                            new GenericType<List<Company>>() {};
                int status = response.getStatus();
                if (status != Response.Status.OK.getStatusCode()) {
                    logger.log(Level.WARNING, "Bad status {0}",
                            response.getStatusInfo().getReasonPhrase());
                    throw new Exception("Bad status: " + status
                            + " for web service call");
                }

                // Returns an ArrayList of Companies from the web service
                List<Company> data = (response.readEntity(genericType));
```

```
                ObservableList<Company> companyList =
                        FXCollections.observableArrayList(data);
                return companyList;
            }
        };
    }
}
```

Listing 16.8 shows the code for UpdateSalesItemService, which invokes the Salesdata web service for edit (update) using the data stored in the `salesdata` class variable. The `createTask()` method accesses the salesdata variable in the JavaFX Application Thread before creating the Task. The `call()` method invokes the `edit_XML()` Salesdata-JerseyClient method. To reuse this service, the caller invokes the `setSalesdata()` method with the new data before calling the UpdateSalesItemService `start()` method.

**Listing 16.8 UpdateSalesItemService.java**

```
public class UpdateSalesItemService extends Service<Salesdata> {

    private Salesdata salesdata;

    public Salesdata getSalesdata() {
        return salesdata;
    }

    public void setSalesdata(Salesdata salesdata) {
        this.salesdata = salesdata;
    }

    @Override
    protected Task<Salesdata> createTask() {
        final Salesdata _salesdata = getSalesdata();
        return new Task<Salesdata>() {
            private final SalesdataJerseyClient client1 =
                        new SalesdataJerseyClient();

            @Override
            protected Salesdata call() throws Exception {
                client1.edit_XML(_salesdata,
                                _salesdata.getSalesid().toString());
                return _salesdata;
            }
        };
    }
}
```

## Implementing a RESTful Client Service Provider

The windows in the SmartPhoneDataApp display the data with a TableView control and in a JavaFX Line Chart. These modules use a Service Provider to access the data. In this section, you'll perform the steps to configure this Service Provider.

- Create package **com.asgteach.phonedata.share** in the PhoneDataWebService module and make this package public.
- Create the **PhoneDataShare** interface in package com.asgteach.phonedata.share.
- Create the **PhoneDataShareImpl** module. Add a dependency to the PhoneDataWebService module and the Lookup API.
- Create class **PhoneDataShareImpl** and implement PhoneDataShare.

Listing 16.9 shows the PhoneDataShare interface, which you add to the PhoneDataWebService module.

The `refreshData()` and `updateSales()` methods include a ProgressIndicator control. This is useful for keeping the user informed when a background task is currently executing. Note that a caller can supply a `null` value when not using a ProgressIndicator. The implementation code must therefore check for a `null`-value ProgressIndicator.

**Listing 16.9 PhoneDataShare Interface**

```
public interface PhoneDataShare {
    // Salesdata
    public abstract ListProperty<Salesdata> theDataProperty();
    // Company
    public abstract ListProperty<Company> companyNamesProperty();
    // year as a String
    public abstract ListProperty<String> categoryListProperty();
    public abstract String getDataDescription();
    public abstract String getNameDescription();
    public abstract String getTitle();
    public abstract double getTickUnit();
    public abstract void refreshData(ProgressIndicator progressIndicator);
    public abstract void updateSales(Salesdata salesdata,
            ProgressIndicator progressIndicator);
}
```

Listing 16.10 shows the PhoneDataShareImpl class, which you add to the PhoneDataShareImpl module. This class creates several JavaFX ListProperty objects to manage the ObservableLists for the Salesdata, Company names, and Category names.

The class also instantiates the JavaFX Service classes we described in the previous section: GetSmartPhoneSalesService, GetCompanyDataService, and UpdateSalesItemService. The services manipulate the ListProperty objects.

**Listing 16.10 PhoneDataShareImpl—Implement PhoneDataShare**

```
@ServiceProvider(service = PhoneDataShare.class)
public class PhoneDataShareImpl implements PhoneDataShare {

    private final ListProperty<Salesdata> underlyingData = new
             SimpleListProperty<>(FXCollections.observableArrayList());
    private final ListProperty<Company> companyDataNames = new
             SimpleListProperty<>(FXCollections.observableArrayList());
    private final ListProperty<String> categoryDataNames = new
             SimpleListProperty<>(FXCollections.observableArrayList());
    private static final String dataDescription = "Units Sold in Millions";
    private final String nameDescription = "Year";
    private final String title = "Smart Phone Sales";

    private final GetSmartPhoneSalesService salesService =
                                 new GetSmartPhoneSalesService();
    private final GetCompanyDataService companyService =
                                 new GetCompanyDataService();
    private final UpdateSalesItemService update = new UpdateSalesItemService();

    private static final Logger logger
            = Logger.getLogger(PhoneDataShareImpl.class.getName());

    public PhoneDataShareImpl() {
        getDataInBackground(null);
        getCompanyDataInBackground();
    }

    @Override
    public ListProperty<Company> companyNamesProperty() {
        return companyDataNames;
    }

    @Override
    public ListProperty<String> categoryListProperty() {
        return categoryDataNames;
    }

    @Override
    public String getDataDescription() {
        return dataDescription;
    }
```

```
@Override
public String getNameDescription() {
    return nameDescription;
}

@Override
public String getTitle() {
    return title;
}

@Override
public double getTickUnit() {
    return 1000;
}

@Override
public void refreshData(ProgressIndicator progressIndicator) {
    getDataInBackground(progressIndicator);
}

@Override
public void updateSales(Salesdata salesdata,
                        ProgressIndicator progressIndicator) {
    updateSalesDataInBackground(salesdata, progressIndicator);
}

@Override
public ListProperty<Salesdata> theDataProperty() {
    return underlyingData;
}

@SuppressWarnings("unchecked")
private void getCompanyDataInBackground() {
    // This service is only invoked once
    companyService.setOnSucceeded((WorkerStateEvent t) -> {
        companyDataNames.set(
              (ObservableList<Company>) t.getSource().getValue());
    });
    companyService.setOnFailed((WorkerStateEvent t) -> {
        logger.log(Level.WARNING, "Failed: Read Company data.");
    });
    companyService.start();
}

private void updateSalesDataInBackground(final Salesdata newSalesdata,
                          ProgressIndicator progress) {
    // This service can be invoked multiple times
    update.setOnSucceeded((WorkerStateEvent t) -> {
        if (progress != null) {
            progress.setVisible(false);
        }
```

```
                // this will cause 2 separate change events: a remove and then an add
                underlyingData.remove(newSalesdata);
                underlyingData.add(newSalesdata);
            });
            update.setOnFailed((WorkerStateEvent t) -> {
                logger.log(Level.WARNING, "Failed: Salesdata UPDATED for {0}",
                        newSalesdata.getCompanyid().getCompanyname());
                if (progress != null) {
                    progress.setVisible(false);
                }
            });
            // only start the service if it's ready
            if (update.getState() == Worker.State.SUCCEEDED) {
                update.reset();
            }
            if (update.getState() == Worker.State.READY) {
                if (progress != null) {
                    progress.setVisible(true);
                }
                update.setSalesdata(newSalesdata);
                update.start();
            }
        }

        @SuppressWarnings("unchecked")
        private void getDataInBackground(ProgressIndicator progressIndicator) {
            // This service can be invoked multiple times
            salesService.setOnSucceeded((WorkerStateEvent t) -> {
                if (progressIndicator != null) {
                    progressIndicator.setVisible(false);
                }
                underlyingData.set(
                   (ObservableList<Salesdata>) t.getSource().getValue());
                for (Salesdata sales : underlyingData.get()) {
                    if (!categoryDataNames.contains(sales.getSalesyear())) {
                        categoryDataNames.add(sales.getSalesyear());
                    }
                }
            });
            salesService.setOnFailed((WorkerStateEvent t) -> {
                if (progressIndicator != null) {
                    progressIndicator.setVisible(false);
                }
                logger.log(Level.WARNING, "Failed: Read Salesdata");
            });
            // only start the service if it's ready
            if (salesService.getState() == Worker.State.SUCCEEDED) {
                salesService.reset();
            }
```

```
        if (salesService.getState() == Worker.State.READY) {
            if (progressIndicator != null) {
                progressIndicator.setVisible(true);
            }
            salesService.start();
        }
    }
}
```

There is a subtle relationship between the Services and the JavaFX ListProperty objects. When a client looks up PhoneDataShare, the PhoneDataShareImpl constructor code (invoked once, since this class is a singleton) calls the `getDataInBackground()` method. Because this method invokes the web services in a background thread, the data may not yet be installed in the ListProperty object returned by `theDataProperty()` method. However, since we use JavaFX properties, the client will be notified with either a bind expression or a listener when the ListProperty changes. We'll show you how to do this with JavaFX UI code in the upcoming sections.

## JavaFX TableView

The SmartPhoneDataApp includes a TableView window implemented with the CoreTableView module (see Figure 16.19 on page 822 for a diagram of the applications modules). Here is a summary of the steps you'll follow to build this module.

- Create module **CoreTableView** with code name **com.asgteach.coretableview**.
- Add a new window (TopComponent) to the module in the Explorer position with name **TableView**. This creates file TableViewTopComponent.java.
- Set a dependency on the **PhoneDataWebService** module and the **Lookup API**.
- This module includes integrated JavaFX content, which you structure using FXML and JavaFX as described in "Integrating with the NetBeans Platform" on page 265. Add the FXML markup with file TableView.fxml and its controller class with file TableViewController.java.

Let's first explore the JavaFX TableView control and then we'll examine the **TableView.fxml** and **TableViewController.java** files in detail.

### JavaFX TableView Control

Figure 16.20 shows the TableView window, which includes a JavaFX TableView control, a title, a TextField control for filtering table data, and a Button control to refresh the data.

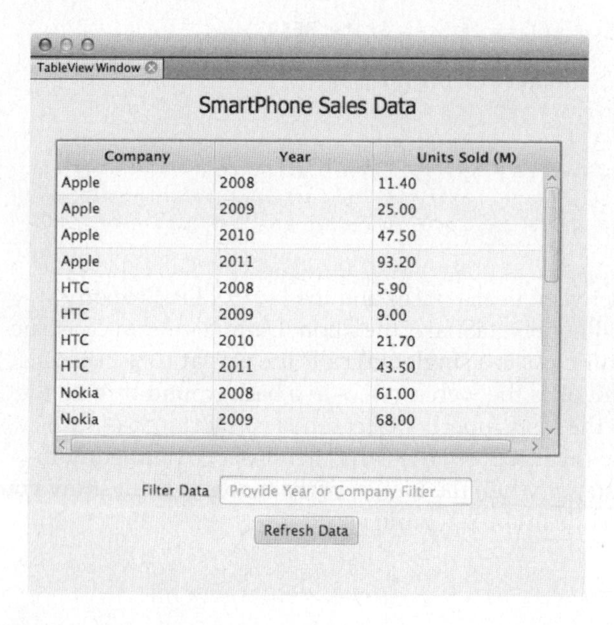


Figure 16.20 TableView window

The JavaFX TableView control is a general purpose visualization of tabular data. Minimally, you instantiate the control with an ObservableList. The generic type of the ObservableList matches the generic type for the TableView. For example, the following code instantiates a TableView of Salesdata objects and invokes the TableView `setItems()` method to set its data. Note that when data in the ObservableList changes, the TableView automatically updates.

```
TableView<Salesdata> tableview = new TableView<>();
ObservableList<Salesdat> theList = getTheListSomeHow();
tableview.setItems(theList);
```

To define columns in a TableView control, use the TableColumn class. If the data matches a JavaFX property in the TableView's generic type, the TableColumn configuration is straightforward. For example, here we define a String TableColumn for year data and set the heading to "Year." We specify that the value is from the `salesyear` property using the `setCellValueFactory()` method.

```
TableColumn<Salesdata, String> colYear = new TableColumn<>("Year");
colYear.setCellValueFactory(
        new PropertyValueFactory<Salesdata, String>("salesyear"));
```

The Company column is trickier, since a company name is not a direct property. Instead, we get the company name from the `companyid` property with the `get-CompanynameProperty()` method in a JavaFX Callback construct, as follows.

```
TableColumn<Salesdata, String> colCompany = new TableColumn<>("Company");
colCompany.setCellValueFactory(new Callback<CellDataFeatures<Salesdata,
                              String>, ObservableValue<String>>() {
        @Override
        public ObservableValue<String> call(CellDataFeatures<Salesdata,
                              String> p) {
            // p.getValue() returns the Salesdata instance for a row
            return p.getValue().getCompanyid().companynameProperty();
        }
    });
```

Since Callback is a functional interface, we can use a lambda expression, as follows (the return statement is implied).

```
colCompany.setCellValueFactory((TableColumn.CellDataFeatures
                              <Salesdata, String> p) ->
        p.getValue().getCompanyid().companynameProperty());
```

Similarly, we define the `colUnitsSold` TableColumn with a BigDecimal type set from the `unitsinmillions` property in a JavaFX Callback construct, as follows.

```
TableColumn<Salesdata, BigDecimal> colUnitsSold
                    = new TableColumn<>("Units Sold");
colUnitsSold.setCellValueFactory((TableColumn.CellDataFeatures
                              <Salesdata, BigDecimal> cell) ->
        cell.getValue().unitsinmillionsProperty());
```

Finally, here's how you add columns to the TableView control.

```
tableview.getColumns().setAll(colCompany, colYear, colUnitsSold);
```

## Build the JavaFX TableView UI

With the basics of TableView explored, let's show you how to use TableView to display and edit the Salesdata obtained from the RESTful web services client. We'll examine the FXML markup first.

Listing 16.11 shows **TableView.fxml**, the FXML for this window. Let's point out a few interesting constructs.

- The `"%key"` notation references a key in a Resource file (a properties file) containing key value pairs for text. This makes internationalizing applications straightforward. (See "Application Internationalization" on page 868 for how to adapt a NetBeans Platform application to different languages and locales.)

- We define all our JavaFX controls in this FXML file. This means you don't need to create the controls in Java code. You also don't need to add the TableColumns to the TableView, since the FXML Loader performs this step.
- Although FXML definitions do not include generic notation, you still use generics with the Java object declaration in the controller class (for example, see the TableView declaration in Listing 16.12 on page 836).
- Each TableColumn disables sorting, and the `colUnitsSold` TableColumn enables editing.
- The `"#refreshData"` notation defines the Button's `onAction` event handler. This references the `refreshData()` method in the TableViewController class.
- The ProgressIndicator control is set to indeterminate (`-1`) and initially not visible. Its visibility is controlled by the JavaFX Service classes.

**Listing 16.11 TableView.fxml**

```
<?xml version="1.0" encoding="UTF-8"?>

<?import java.lang.*?>
<?import java.util.*?>
<?import javafx.geometry.Insets?>
<?import javafx.scene.*?>
<?import javafx.scene.control.*?>
<?import javafx.scene.layout.*?>
<?import javafx.collections.*?>

<BorderPane  fx:controller="com.asgteach.coretableview.TableViewController"
             xmlns:fx="http://javafx.com/fxml">
    <top>
        <GridPane alignment="center" hgap="10" vgap="15">
            <padding>
                <Insets top="10" right="10" bottom="10" left="10"/>
            </padding>
            <Label text="%smartphonetitle"
                   GridPane.columnIndex="0"
                   GridPane.rowIndex="0"
                   GridPane.halignment="center"
                   style="-fx-font: NORMAL 20 Tahoma;"/>
        </GridPane>
    </top>
    <center>
        <GridPane alignment="center" hgap="10" vgap="15">
            <padding>
                <Insets top="10" right="10" bottom="10" left="10"/>
            </padding>
```

```
            <TableView fx:id="tableview"
                       editable="true"
                       GridPane.columnIndex="0"
                       GridPane.rowIndex="0" >
                <columns>
                    <TableColumn fx:id="colCompany" text="%company"
                                 sortable="false" minWidth="150" />
                    <TableColumn fx:id="colYear" text="%year"
                                 sortable="false" minWidth="150" />
                    <TableColumn fx:id="colUnitsSold" text="%unitsSold"
                                 editable="true" sortable="false"
                                 minWidth="175" />
                </columns>
            </TableView>
        </GridPane>
    </center>
    <bottom>
        <GridPane alignment="center" hgap="10" vgap="15">
            <padding>
                <Insets top="10" right="10" bottom="10" left="10"/>
            </padding>
            <VBox spacing="10" alignment="BOTTOM_CENTER"
                  GridPane.columnIndex="0"
                  GridPane.rowIndex="0">
                <HBox spacing="10" alignment="CENTER" >
                    <Label text="Filter Data" />
                    <TextField  fx:id="filterText" prefColumnCount="20"
                                promptText="%filterPrompt" />
                </HBox>
                <Button text="%refreshData" onAction="#refreshData" />
                <Label fx:id="displayMessage" />
                <ProgressIndicator fx:id="progress"
                                   visible="false"
                                   progress="-1" />
            </VBox>
        </GridPane>
    </bottom>
</BorderPane>
```

### TableViewController Class

Now let's show you the TableViewController class, which we'll present in several parts. Listing 16.12 shows the `@FXML` annotations and class fields. Note that the TableView and TableColumn fields have generic types.

The other fields include a logger and a PhoneDataShare reference (which is instantiated via the Global Lookup). To both filter and sort the data, we also define a FilteredList, SortedList, and Comparator. These are all initialized in the `initialize()` method.

**Listing 16.12 TableViewController—Class Fields**

```
public class TableViewController implements Initializable {

    @FXML
    private TableView<Salesdata> tableview;
    // Columns
    @FXML
    private TableColumn<Salesdata, String> colCompany;
    @FXML
    private TableColumn<Salesdata, String> colYear;
    @FXML
    private TableColumn<Salesdata, BigDecimal> colUnitsSold;
    @FXML
    private ProgressIndicator progress;
    @FXML
    private Label displayMessage;
    @FXML
    private TextField filterText;

    private static final Logger logger
            = Logger.getLogger(TableViewController.class.getName());
    private PhoneDataShare share = null;
    FilteredList<Salesdata> filteredData = null;
    SortedList<Salesdata> sortedData = null;
    Comparator<? super Salesdata> comparatorSalesdata = null;
. . .
}
```

Listing 16.13 shows the first part of the `initialize()` method. Recall that the FXML Loader invokes this method after instantiating all the declared objects in the FXML markup and the controller class.

First, we look up a Service Provider for PhoneDataShare. This is how we invoke the web service calls to access the data and update the persistent store when the user edits the table.

Next, we configure the TableColumns using the `setCellValueFactory()` method to configure all three columns. For the Units Sold column, we invoke the `setCellFactory()` method to create a TextField control for editing. We also define a converter to convert values between BigDecimal and String during edits.

The `onEditCommit()` event handler (defined for the Units Sold column) updates the edited data in the table and also invokes the PhoneDataShare service provider `updateSales()` method. This method eventually invokes the JavaFX Service previously defined with the new data and the ProgressIndicator control (`progress`). The updated Salesdata value is available through the CellEditEvent object `t`.

If the conversion between String and BigDecimal fails, the converter returns null. In this case, the handler leaves the old data intact and displays an error message.

**Listing 16.13 TableViewController—initialize() Method Part I**

```
    @Override
    public void initialize(final URL url, final ResourceBundle resources) {
        share = Lookup.getDefault().lookup(PhoneDataShare.class);
        if (share == null) {
            logger.log(Level.SEVERE, "Cannot get PhoneDataShare object");
            LifecycleManager.getDefault().exit();
        }

        // Configure the Columns
        colCompany.setCellValueFactory((TableColumn.CellDataFeatures
                                        <Salesdata, String> p) ->
            p.getValue().getCompanyid().companynameProperty());

        colYear.setCellValueFactory(new PropertyValueFactory<Salesdata,
                    String>("salesyear"));

        colUnitsSold.setCellValueFactory((TableColumn.CellDataFeatures
                                    <Salesdata, BigDecimal> cell) ->
            cell.getValue().unitsinmillionsProperty());
        colUnitsSold.setCellFactory(TextFieldTableCell.
                <Salesdata, BigDecimal>forTableColumn(
                        new DecimalConverter()));

        // Configure editing for the UnitsSold column
        colUnitsSold.setOnEditCommit(
                (TableColumn.CellEditEvent<Salesdata, BigDecimal> t) -> {
                    // If the new value is null, use the old value
                    BigDecimal bd;
                    if (t.getNewValue() != null) {       // good value
                        bd = t.getNewValue();
                        t.getRowValue().setUnitsinmillions(bd);
                        displayMessage.setText("");
                        displayMessage.setStyle("-fx-text-fill: black;");
                        share.updateSales(t.getRowValue(), progress);
                    } else {                             // bad conversion
                        bd = t.getOldValue();
                        t.getRowValue().setUnitsinmillions(bd);
                        // force a refresh
                        t.getTableColumn().setVisible(false);
                        t.getTableColumn().setVisible(true);
                        displayMessage.setStyle("-fx-text-fill: red;");
                        displayMessage.setText(Bundle.salesAmountBadFormat());
                    }
                });
. . .
```

Listing 16.14 shows you how to filter and sort the ObservableList displayed in the TableView control. First, we define a comparator for sorting. The Salesdata list is sorted first by company name and then by year.

Next, we define a change listener for the ListProperty returned by the PhoneDataShare `theDataProperty()` method. The change listener builds a FilteredList based on the user-provided text String and a SortedList based on the previously defined comparator. The FilteredList predicate converts the filter target to lowercase and compares first the company name, then the year for a match. The predicate returns true for a match (or if the filter TextField text is empty).

Next, we define a change listener for the `filterText` TextField's `textProperty`. This change listener is invoked for each key stroke and dynamically reapplies the filter.

**Listing 16.14 TableViewController—initialize() Method Part II**

```
@Override
    public void initialize(final URL url, final ResourceBundle resources) {
        . . .

        // Define the Comparator for Sorting
        comparatorSalesdata = (Salesdata o1, Salesdata o2) -> {
            // First compare the company name, then compare the year
           int result = o1.getCompanyid().getCompanyname().compareToIgnoreCase(
                    o2.getCompanyid().getCompanyname());
            if (result == 0) {
                return o1.getSalesyear().compareTo(o2.getSalesyear());
            }
            return result;
        };

        // When the underlying data change, reset the filtering and sorting
        share.theDataProperty().addListener(
                (ListChangeListener.Change<? extends Salesdata> change) -> {
            filteredData = new FilteredList<>(
                        share.theDataProperty().get(), salesdata -> {
                // Reapply filter when data changes
                String newValue = filterText.getText();
                // If filter text is empty, display all data
                if (newValue == null || newValue.isEmpty()) {
                    return true;
                }
                // Compare company name and year with filter text
                String lowerCaseFilter = newValue.toLowerCase();
                if (salesdata.getCompanyid().getCompanyname().toLowerCase()
                                        .contains(lowerCaseFilter)) {
                    return true;                    // Filter matches company
               } else if (salesdata.getSalesyear().contains(lowerCaseFilter)) {
                    return true;                    // Filter matches sales year
```

```
            }
            return false;                    // No match
        });
        sortedData = new SortedList<>(filteredData);
        sortedData.setComparator(comparatorSalesdata);
        tableview.setItems(sortedData);
    });

    // Reapply the filter when the user supplies a new filter text
    filterText.textProperty().addListener(
                            (observable, oldValue, newValue) -> {
        filteredData.setPredicate(salesdata -> {
            // If filter text is empty, display all data.
            if (newValue == null || newValue.isEmpty()) {
                return true;
            }
            // Compare company name and year with filter text.
            String lowerCaseFilter = newValue.toLowerCase();

            if (salesdata.getCompanyid().getCompanyname().toLowerCase()
                                  .contains(lowerCaseFilter)) {
                return true;
           } else if (salesdata.getSalesyear().contains(lowerCaseFilter)) {
                return true;
            }
            return false;
        });
    });
}
```

Listing 16.15 shows the DecimalConverter that performs conversions for String and BigDecimal in the TableColumn's in-place editor. You override both the `toString()` and `fromString()` methods. The NumberFormat class is sensitive to the locale because we invoke `Locale.getDefault()` with the `getInstance()` method.

### Listing 16.15 TableViewController—DecimalConverter

```
private class DecimalConverter extends StringConverter<BigDecimal> {

    NumberFormat nf = NumberFormat.getInstance(Locale.getDefault());

    public DecimalConverter() {
        nf.setMaximumFractionDigits(2);
        nf.setMinimumFractionDigits(1);
    }
```

```
        @Override
        public String toString(BigDecimal t) {
            try {
                return nf.format(t);
            } catch (Exception e) {
                return null;
            }
        }

        @Override
        public BigDecimal fromString(String string) {
            try {
                Number newValue = nf.parse(string);
                BigDecimal result = new BigDecimal(newValue.doubleValue());
                return result.setScale(2, BigDecimal.ROUND_HALF_EVEN);
            } catch (ParseException e) {
                return null;
            }
        }
    }
```

## JavaFX Chart Module

The SmartPhoneDataApp also includes a LineChart window, shown in Figure 16.21. This chart is implemented with the LineChart module. (See Figure 16.19 on page 822 for a diagram of the application's modules.)

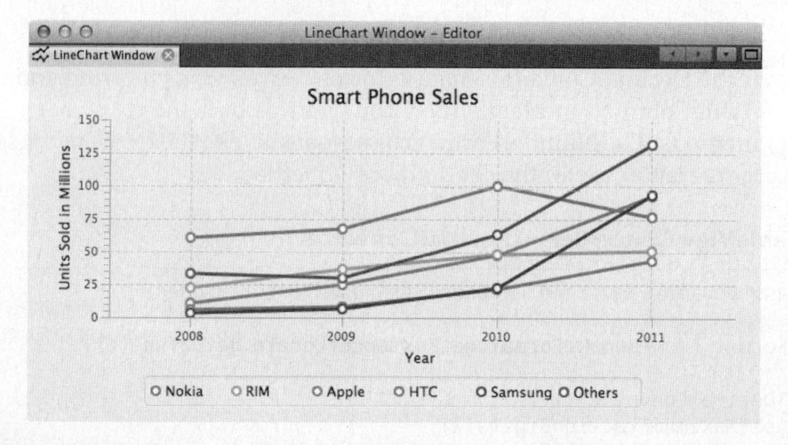


Figure 16.21 LineChart Window

Here is a summary of the steps you'll follow to build this module.

- Create the **LineChart** module with code name **com.asgteach.linechart**.

- Add a new window (TopComponent) to the module in the Editor position with name **LineChart**. This creates file LineChartTopComponent.java.
- Set a dependency on the **PhoneDataWebService** module and the **Lookup API**.
- This module includes integrated JavaFX content, which you structure using FXML and JavaFX as described in "Integrating with the NetBeans Platform" on page 265. Add the FXML markup with file **LineChart.fxml** and its controller class with file **LineChartController.java**. Refer to the description of the JavaFX Chart package in Chapter 15, especially "Line Chart" on page 764.

### Build the JavaFX LineChart UI

Let's examine the FXML markup and then show you the LineChartController code.

Listing 16.16 is LineChart.fxml, the FXML for this window. We define a LineChart control inside of a StackPane. The LineChart has a CategoryAxis for its X-axis and a NumberAxis for its Y-axis. The `fx:id` attributes allow the controller class to access these controls.

**Listing 16.16 LineChart.fxml**

```
<?xml version="1.0" encoding="UTF-8"?>
<?import java.lang.*?>
<?import java.util.*?>
<?import javafx.geometry.*?>
<?import javafx.scene.*?>
<?import javafx.scene.control.*?>
<?import javafx.scene.layout.*?>
<?import javafx.scene.chart.*?>

<StackPane id="StackPane" fx:id="stackpane"
           xmlns:fx="http://javafx.com/fxml"
           fx:controller="com.asgteach.linechart.LineChartController">
    <padding>
        <Insets top="10" right="10" bottom="10" left="10"/>
    </padding>

    <LineChart fx:id="chart" >
        <xAxis>
            <CategoryAxis fx:id="xAxis"/>
        </xAxis>
        <yAxis>
            <NumberAxis fx:id="yAxis"/>
        </yAxis>
    </LineChart>
</StackPane>
```

The controller class, **LineChartController**, initializes the LineChart's data and keeps the data current when changes are detected. Since the user can edit data in the TableView window, the LineChart must react to these updates. We'll present the LineChartController class in several parts.

Listing 16.17 shows the LineChartController class fields, including the controls defined in the FXML file. These class fields include the LineChart data (`lcdata`) and a logger. The `data` field is the PhoneDataShare service provider. Finally, we have a SortedList and a comparator that sorts sales data before initializing and/or updating the chart.

**Listing 16.17 LineChartController—Class Fields**

```
public class LineChartController implements Initializable {

    @FXML
    private StackPane stackpane;
    @FXML
    private CategoryAxis xAxis;
    @FXML
    private NumberAxis yAxis;
    @FXML
    private LineChart<String, Number> chart;
    private ObservableList<XYChart.Series<String, Number>> lcData
            = FXCollections.observableArrayList();
    private static final Logger logger
            = Logger.getLogger(LineChartController.class.getName());
    private PhoneDataShare data = null;
    SortedList<Salesdata> sortedData = null;
    Comparator<? super Salesdata> comparatorSalesdata = null;
```

Listing 16.18 shows the LineChartController's `initialize()` method. Although this code is similar to the LineChartController presented in Chapter 15, here we use data from an ObservableList instead of the Swing TableModel's two-dimensional array.

First, we look up the PhoneDataShare service provider from the Global Lookup, which provides the label text for the chart axes and the Y-axis tick unit.

Next, we define the comparator for sorting. We sort by company name, then year. Sorting the data by year makes LineChart plot points always appear in increasing year order. We then set the chart's title and its data.

Last, we add ListChangeListeners to both the data list (`theDataProperty()`) and the company names list (`companyNamesList()`). Because these lists are populated after web service calls complete in a background thread, these lists may not yet contain data. Adding a ListChangeListener to these properties notifies the LineChartController code when the lists are complete. Changes make the handlers invoke the `getLineChartData()` method, shown next.

**Listing 16.18 LineChartController—initialize() Method**

```
@Override
public void initialize(URL url, ResourceBundle rb) {
    data = Lookup.getDefault().lookup(PhoneDataShare.class);
    if (data == null) {
        logger.log(Level.SEVERE, "Cannot get PhoneDataShare object");
        LifecycleManager.getDefault().exit();
    }
    xAxis.setCategories(data.categoryListProperty());
    xAxis.setLabel(data.getNameDescription());
    yAxis.setTickUnit(data.getTickUnit());
    yAxis.setLabel(data.getDataDescription());
    logger.log(Level.INFO, "yAxis label = {0}", data.getDataDescription());
    logger.log(Level.INFO, "xAxis label = {0}", data.getNameDescription());
    comparatorSalesdata = (Salesdata o1, Salesdata o2) -> {
        // First compare the company name, then compare the year
       int result = o1.getCompanyid().getCompanyname().compareToIgnoreCase(
                o2.getCompanyid().getCompanyname());
        if (result == 0) {
            return o1.getSalesyear().compareTo(o2.getSalesyear());
        }
        return result;
    };
    chart.setTitle(data.getTitle());
    chart.setData(lcData);

    data.theDataProperty().addListener(
            (ListChangeListener.Change<? extends Salesdata> c) -> {
                while (c.next()) {
                    if (c.wasAdded()) {
                        logger.log(Level.INFO, "was added");
                        getLineChartData();
                    }
                }
            });
    data.companyNamesProperty().addListener(
            (ListChangeListener.Change<? extends Company> change) -> {
                getLineChartData();
            });
}
```

Listing 16.19 shows the `getLineChartData()` method, which builds the XYChart.Series for each company. After sorting the data, this method installs the data into the appropriate series. Note that the processing code only creates new XYChart.Data objects if necessary. This avoids completely redrawing the LineChart when changes are detected. Instead, changed plot points animate to new plot point locations.

**Listing 16.19 LineChartController—getLineChartData() Method**

```
    private void getLineChartData() {
        // create all the series if necessary
        if (data.companyNamesProperty().getSize() != lcData.size()) {
            for (int i = 0; i < lcData.size(); i++) {
                lcData.clear();
            }
            for (int row = 0; row < data.companyNamesProperty().getSize();
                                                                row++) {
                XYChart.Series<String, Number> series = new XYChart.Series<>();
                series.setName(data.companyNamesProperty().get(row)
                                                .getCompanyname());
                lcData.add(series);
            }
        }

        // Sort the data so that the Chart looks nice
        sortedData = new SortedList<>(data.theDataProperty().get());
        sortedData.setComparator(comparatorSalesdata);

        // install each datum in the correct series if necessary
        for (Salesdata sales : sortedData) {
            boolean processed = false;
            for (XYChart.Series<String, Number> series : lcData) {
                if (sales.getCompanyid().getCompanyname().equals(
                                series.getName())) {
                    // correct series
                    for (XYChart.Data<String, Number> currentDatum :
                                                series.getData()) {
                        // correct year
                        if (currentDatum.getXValue().equals(
                                            sales.getSalesyear())) {
                            processed = true;
                            if (!currentDatum.getYValue().equals(
                                            sales.getUnitsinmillions())) {
                                // replace
                                currentDatum.setYValue(
                                            sales.getUnitsinmillions());
                            }
                            break;
                        }
                    }
                    // need new data point
                    if (!processed) {
                      XYChart.Data<String, Number> datum = new XYChart.Data<>(
                           sales.getSalesyear(), sales.getUnitsinmillions());
                        series.getData().add(datum);
                    }
```

```
                    break;
                }
            }
        }
    }
```

## 16.5 Key Point Summary

This chapter shows you how to use RESTful web services in a NetBeans Platform application. Here are the key points in this chapter.

- You can create RESTful web services from a database with the NetBeans IDE RESTful Services from Database wizard. This generates the web services, entity classes, and database persistence unit.
- You can add JavaFX property support to JPA entity classes by moving generated annotations. This approach synchronizes the entity class with the database using accessor methods instead of class fields. JavaFX properties replace the class fields. Accessor methods then use the JavaFX properties to get and set the data.
- When you deploy a web application that implements web services, you can test the RESTful web services with the NetBeans IDE.
- A Java application web service client helps you correctly configure libraries for a RESTful web service client.
- A NetBeans IDE wizard generates RESTful web service clients for a NetBeans Platform module. You can then add the required libraries to the module.
- Adding Wrapped JARs lets you add libraries to a module without creating wrapped library modules.
- The SmartPhoneDataApp consists of a PhoneDataWebService module that includes Jersey clients, entity classes, and a service provider interface.
- Our application includes two windows: a TableView window with a JavaFX TableView control and a LineChart window with a JavaFX LineChart. Both windows access the data through RESTful clients.
- The JavaFX Service class lets you build re-usable Worker objects that manage their execution in a background thread.
- A Service object lets you safely access setup and return objects on the JavaFX Application Thread. Service objects are suitable for RESTful web service clients.

- The JavaFX TableView is a general-purpose control with TableColumns for visualizing tabular data. Use the `setCellValueFactory()` method to configure TableColumns.
- Configure a TableColumn with TextFieldTableCell to create a TextField component for editing. Use the `setOnEditCommit()` method to configure an event handler to handle edits.
- The TableView control supports an ObservableList. Use SortedList with a comparator for sorting and FilteredList with a filter predicate for filtering.
- When configuring JavaFX Charts, sort the data before you create the XYChart.Data objects. This makes the chart's plot points appear in a consistent order.

# 17

# Branding, Distribution, and Internationalization

NetBeans Platform applications should be customized to fit the distributor and the users of the application. By customizing the splash screen, application title, and text, you can control the look and usefulness of your application.

This chapter shows you how to brand your application so that it correctly reflects what the application does and who its users are. You'll learn how to configure applications for dynamic updates, create distribution files, and build localized versions for international users.

## What You Will Learn

- Customize an application name and title.
- Provide version numbers in an application title.
- Customize the splash screen.
- Customize text in Resource Bundles.
- Enable updates of your application.
- Build an update center.
- Create distribution files for your application.
- Internationalize and localize your application.

# 17.1 What Is Branding?

Branding lets you customize your application with a display name, splash screen, and text that your users see. You can also customize Resource Bundles or modify Window System behavior. (See "Limiting the Window System's Behavior" on page 349 for modifications to the Window System.)

In this section we'll show you how to modify an application's display name (its title) and the name in the top-level menu bar. You'll also learn how to customize the application "branding name" and change the splash screen.

Figure 17.1 shows an application from Chapter 5 running. By default, an application's branding name appears in the top-level menu (familytreeapp). The application's title (FamilyTreeApp) appears in the top JFrame title bar with a build number. Let's first show you how to change the project name, application title, and branding name.

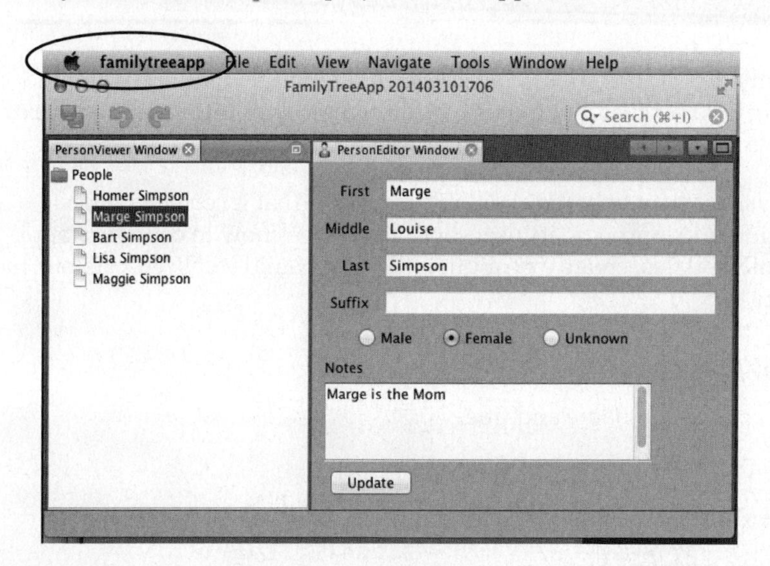


Figure 17.1 FamilyTreeApp running

## Using the Branding Menu

Here are the steps to change the project name and application title using the project's Branding menu.

1. Right click the project name in the Projects view window and select **Branding . . .** from the context menu. NetBeans displays the Branding dialog with the **Basic** tab selected.

2. Supply another title in the **Application Title** text field, as shown in Figure 17.2. This menu item changes the title and project name. (Note that the project's directory name does not change.)

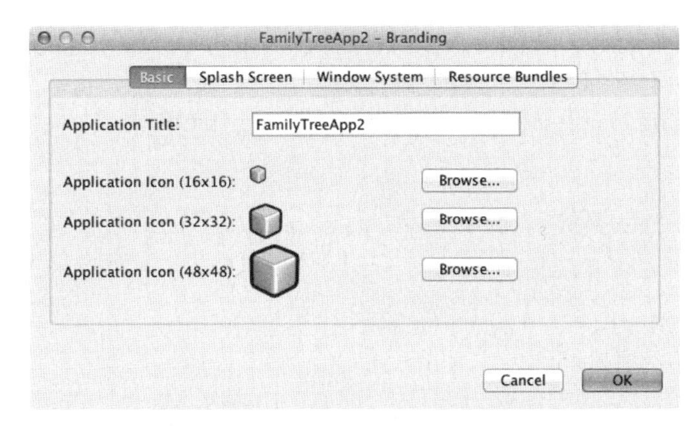


Figure 17.2 Branding: Basic dialog used to change the application title.

3. Click **OK** to accept the name change and rerun the application.

The application's title and project name change, but not its branding name, which remains **familytreeapp**, as shown in Figure 17.3.

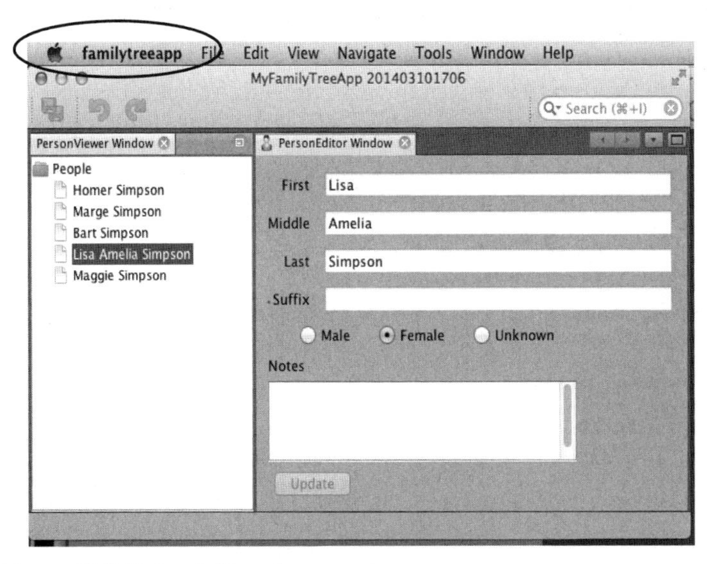


Figure 17.3 MyFamilyTreeApp running

## Rename Branding Token

Use these steps to customize the branding token.

1. In the Projects view, select the application project name, right click, and select **Properties** from the context menu. In the Project Properties dialog under Categories, select **Application**.
2. Change property Branding Name to **myfamilytreeapp** and click **OK**, as shown in Figure 17.4.

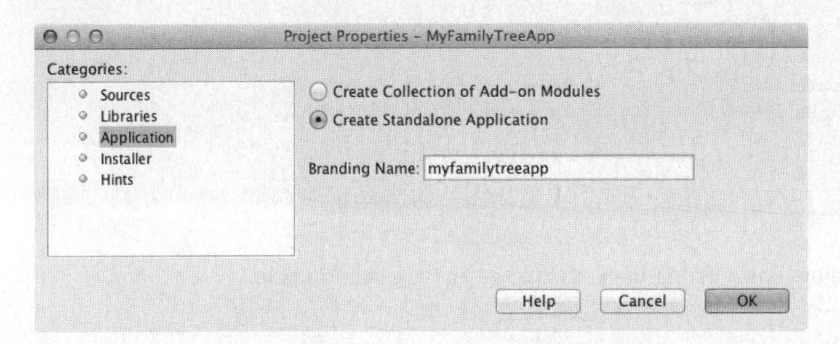


Figure 17.4 Project Properties dialog, category Application

Figure 17.5 shows the MyFamilyTreeApp application running with the top-level menu title changed to **myfamilytreeapp**.

When you modify the application's title and branding name, this affects the application's **Project Properties** file (**project.properties**) and **NetBeans Platform Config** file (**platform.properties**). In the Project Properties file, the `app.title` property is set to MyFamilyTreeApp. The `app.name` property is `${branding.token}`.

```
app.name=${branding.token}
app.title=MyFamilyTreeApp
```

The **platform.properties** file defines property `branding.token`, as follows.

```
branding.token=myfamilytreeapp
```

**Branding Token Tip**

*Note that the branding token is for internal code use and is not intended for display to the user.*

You can change the branding token, but it must begin with a lowercase letter and exclude special characters. Here are the rules for `branding.token` names.

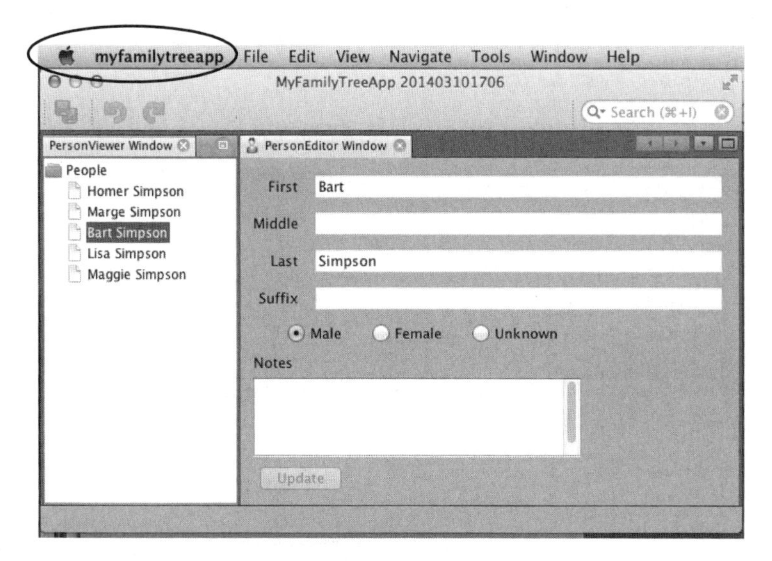


Figure 17.5 Top-level menu title changed

1. Only lowercase letters, numbers, and the _ character (under bar) are allowed.
2. The branding token must begin with a lowercase letter.
3. At least one lowercase letter must follow an _ character (under bar).

If you supply an illegal name, the Branding Token dialog lets you know.

By default, NetBeans Platform applications use the `branding.token` property to create the name that appears in the top-level menu and in the operating system's task manager (property `app.name`). If you want this name to match the application title (property `app.title`), change these properties so that they are the same, as follows.

```
app.name=MyFamilyTreeApp
app.title=${app.name}
```

Figure 17.6 shows the application running with its application name and title both set to MyFamilyTreeApp (with mixed case letters). Figure 17.6 also shows the Mac OS X Force Quit applications list with application name MyFamilyTreeApp.

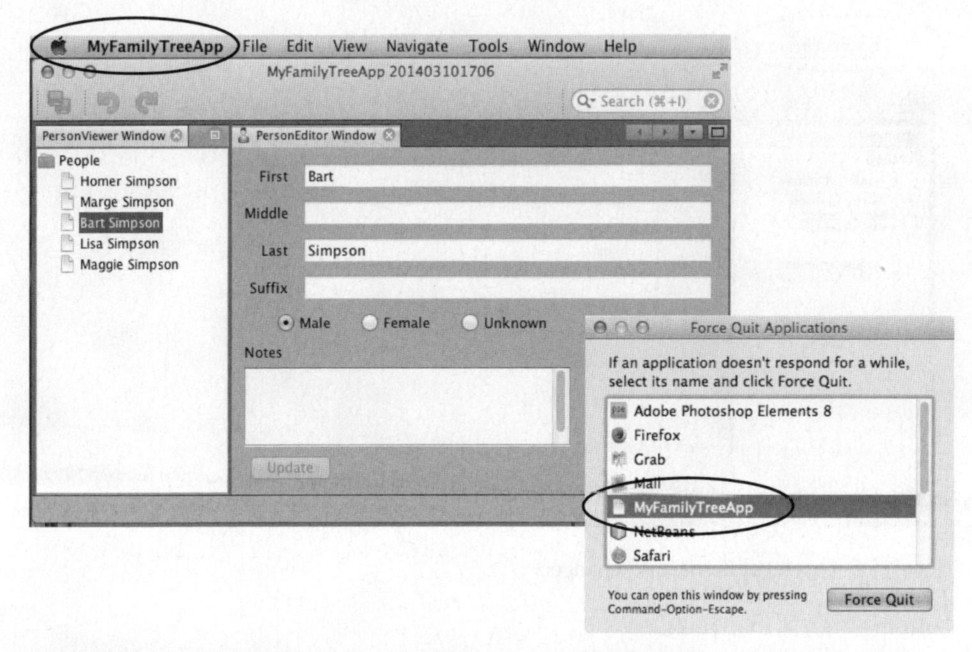


Figure 17.6 MyFamilyTreeApp running and Force Quit Applications running (Mac OS X)

## Customizing the Application Title

By default, NetBeans includes a NetBeans IDE build number with your application title. You might prefer to include a version number for your application instead of the build number from NetBeans IDE in the title. One way to do this is to modify the Build Script in the Important Files folder of your application. Here are the steps.

1. In the Projects view, expand the **Important Files** node under your application project.

2. Add an `app.version` property to the **project.properties** file. Set it to the desired version number for your application. Here we use 3.2, as shown in Listing 17.1.

**Listing 17.1 Project Properties—Add app.version Property**

```
app.name=MyFamilyTreeApp
app.title=${app.name}
app.version=3.2
modules=\
    ${project.com.asgteach.familytree.model}:\
    ${project.com.asgteach.familytree.personviewer}:\
    ${project.com.asgteach.familtree.personeditor}:\
    ${project.com.asgteach.familytree.manager.impl}
```

```
project.com.asgteach.familtree.personeditor=PersonEditor
project.com.asgteach.familytree.manager.impl=FamilyTreeManagerImpl
project.com.asgteach.familytree.model=FamilyTreeModel
project.com.asgteach.familytree.personviewer=PersonViewer
```

3. Double click the **Build Script** node to bring the build.xml file up into the XML editor. (The Build Script lets you make changes to the ANT-based build system provided by the NetBeans IDE.)

4. Add the XML code as shown in bold in Listing 17.2.[1]

**Listing 17.2 Build Script—Show Application Build Information in Title**

```
<?xml version="1.0" encoding="UTF-8"?>
<!-- You may freely edit this file. -->
<!-- See harness/README in the NetBeans platform -->
<!-- for some information on what you could do (e.g. targets to override). -->
<!-- If you delete this file and reopen the project it will be recreated. -->
<project name="FamilyTreeApp" basedir=".">
    <description>Builds the module suite FamilyTreeApp.</description>
    <!-- override build to add update branding -->
    <target name="build" depends="build-brand,suite.build"/>
    <target name="build-brand" depends="-init">
        <propertyfile
            file="${basedir}/branding/core/core.jar/org/netbeans/core/startup/
                                 Bundle.properties"
            comment="Updated by build script">
            <entry key="currentVersion" value="${app.title} ${app.version} " />
        </propertyfile>

        <propertyfile
            file="${basedir}/branding/modules/org-netbeans-core-windows.jar/
                       org/netbeans/core/windows/view/ui/Bundle.properties"
            comment="Updated by build script">
            <entry key="CTL_MainWindow_Title"
                                 value="${app.title} ${app.version}" />
            <entry key="CTL_MainWindow_Title_No_Project"
                                 value="${app.title} ${app.version}" />
        </propertyfile>
    </target>
    <import file="nbproject/build-impl.xml"/>
</project>
```

Figure 17.7 shows the customized version number displayed with the application's title.

1. This build script is adapted from a blog by Tonny Kohar at http://blogs.kiyut.com/tonny/2007/08/06/netbeans-platform-branding-and-version-info/.

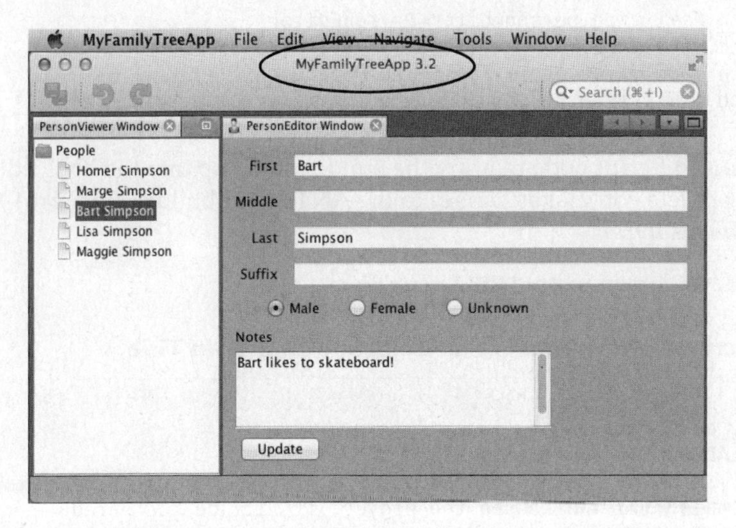


Figure 17.7 Displaying a customized version number with the application title

## Branding and Resource Bundles

Now let's show you how to remove version and build information from the application title. (If you added the code in Listing 17.1 and Listing 17.2, you should remove it first.)[2]

1. Bring up the **Branding** dialog.
2. Click the **Resource Bundles** tab.
3. In the search window, specify **MainWindow_Title** for the search string. NetBeans displays two entries as shown in Figure 17.8.
4. For both entries, right click on the property entry and select **Add to Branding**. NetBeans displays an editing dialog. Remove the **{0}** argument placeholder, which removes the build number from the title. Click **OK** to accept the change. In the Branding dialog, click **OK** to complete the process.
5. In the Files view, expand the branding folder as shown in Figure 17.9, and open the modified **.properties** file shown in the Editor.

---

2. Note that you can use these steps to modify menus or dialog text in any NetBeans Platform module.

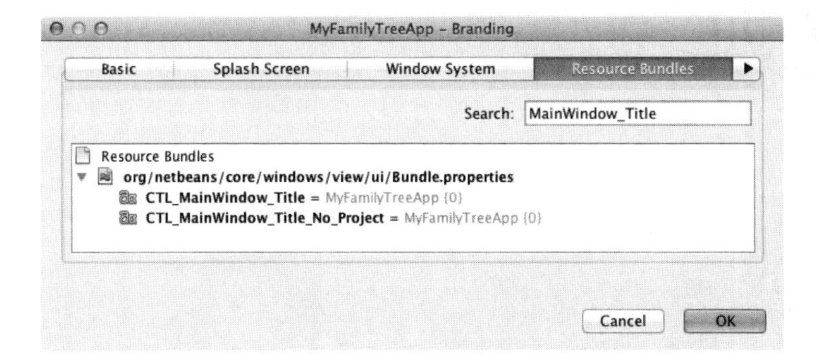


Figure 17.8 Change how the title is displayed for your application

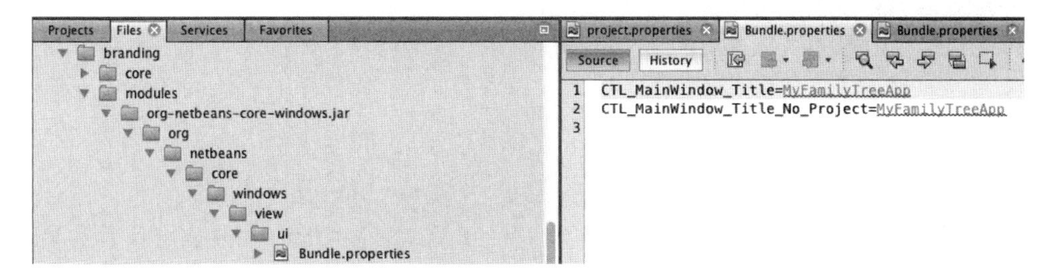


Figure 17.9 Modified Bundle.properties file

With this change, your application JFrame will include a title without any version information.

## Customizing the Splash Screen

Your application will display a standard NetBeans Platform splash screen unless you provide your own. We've created a custom PNG splash screen for the FamilyTreeApp application. Here's how to incorporate this custom splash screen into the application.

1. In the Projects view, right click the application name and select **Branding . . .** from the context menu.
2. Select the **Splash Screen** tab and click **Browse** to select a .gif or .png graphic file.
3. Adjust the color and placement of the progress bar and the size, color, and placement of the running text. Figure 17.10 shows the dialog with the adjustable options for the splash screen.

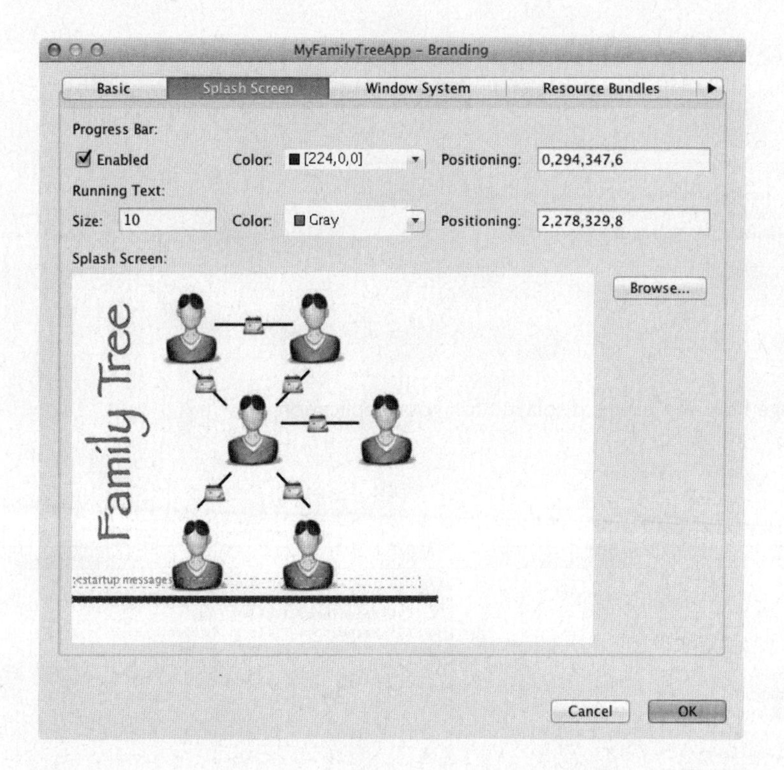


Figure 17.10 Customize the splash screen

4. Click **OK** to accept the settings.

When you customize the splash screen, NetBeans adds the following entry to the Project Properties file.

```
app.icon=branding/core/core.jar/org/netbeans/core/startup/frame48.gif
```

## Removing the Splash Screen

Add the following line to the application's Project Properties file to eliminate the splash screen in your application.

```
run.args.extra=--nosplash
```

# 17.2 Application Updates

Two important events occur with a released application: distribution and updates. You can generate an Installer for your NetBeans Platform application, and you can configure your application for dynamic updates. For updates to work, however, you must first include two modules in your application. With these modules installed, users can update applications by accessing an Update Center or by installing downloaded modules individually. We'll discuss application updates first and then cover creating application installers in the next section. To show you these features, we'll use the FamilyTreeApp we created in Chapter 7 (see "Creating a Selection History Feature" on page 332).

## Enable Updates of Your Application

To let users dynamically update your NetBeans Platform application, you must include the AutoUpdate Services and AutoUpdate UI modules in the *platform* cluster, as follows.

1. In the Projects view window, right click **FamilyTreeApp** and select **Properties** from the context menu. NetBeans displays the Project Properties window.
2. Under Categories, select **Libraries**. Under Nodes, scroll down and expand the **platform** cluster.
3. Select modules **AutoUpdate Services** and **AutoUpdate UI** as shown in Figure 17.11. Click **OK**.

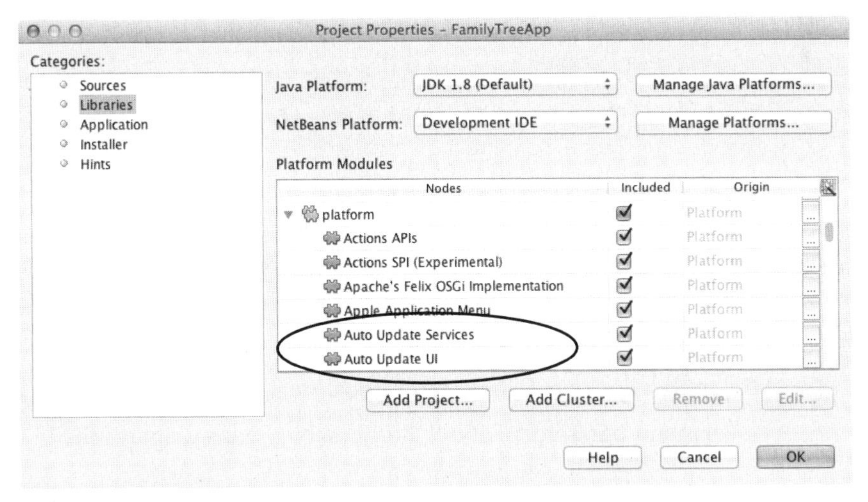


Figure 17.11 Adding Auto Update Services and UI to FamilyTreeApp

4. Run the FamilyTreeApp. (Note that you must perform a **Clean and Build** to see the Plugins menu item.) You will now have a Plugin Manager that you access through the top-level menu item **Tools | Plugins**.

## Create an Update Center

This section shows you how to create an Update Center for your application and activate it through your application's Plugin Manager.

An Update Center consists of a URL that contains an **updates.xml** file and the most up-to-date versions of all of your application's modules. Fortunately, NetBeans will build these files for you through your application's context menu.

For the FamilyTreeApp, follow these steps to create the Update Center contents.

- In the Projects view window of the NetBeans IDE, right click the **FamilyTreeApp** project and select **Package As | NBMs** from the context menu.

NetBeans creates directory **build/updates** and includes the **updates.xml** file and your application module NBM files, as shown in Figure 17.12. The XML file contains descriptions for each module with required dependencies and build and version information.

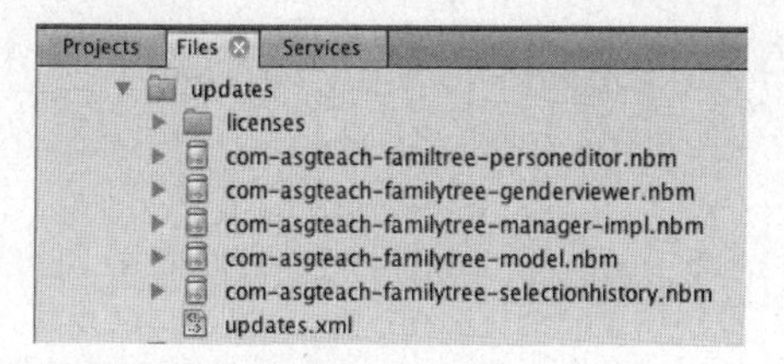


Figure 17.12 Create Update Center content

This is the content you need for an Update Center. The Update Center itself resides at a publicly accessible URL or in a directory on the local file system (for testing or local use only). Here we use the local file system.

Now you need to configure an Update Center inside your application. To do this, run the FamilyTreeApp application and follow these steps.

1. From the top-level menu bar, select **Tools | Plugins**. NetBeans displays the Plugin Manager.
2. In the Plugin Manager, select **Settings**. Click **Add** to add an Update Center.

3. In the Update Center Customizer, supply an Update Center name and URL. You can use the location of the updates directory you created in the previous steps with URL resource `file://`, as shown in Figure 17.13 (or the appropriate URL with the required files). Click **OK**.

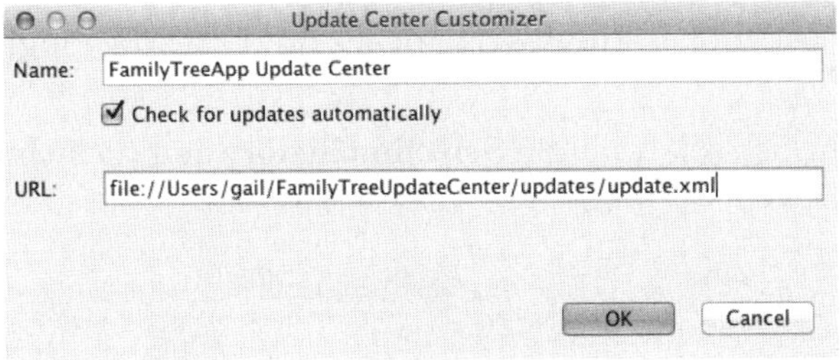

Figure 17.13 Update Center Customizer

Figure 17.14 shows the newly customized FamilyTreeApp Update Center. Note that the Plugin Manager now shows six Installed plugins under tab Installed.

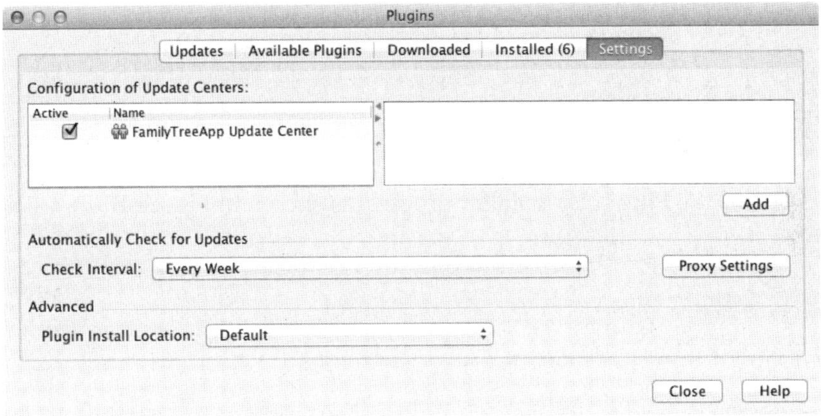

Figure 17.14 Customizing the FamiilyTreeApp Update Center

With the Plugin Manager configured in your application, let's now show you how to dynamically remove a plugin as well as a few options for re-installing a plugin.

## Dynamically Uninstall a Module (Plugin)

Let's remove the SelectionHistory module from the FamilyTreeApp. Recall from Chapter 7 that the FamilyTreeApp runs just fine without this module (plugin) installed. To remove the plugin, run the FamilyTreeApp and follow these steps.

1. From the top-level menu, select **Tools | Plugins**. NetBeans brings up the Plugin Manager.
2. Select the **Installed** tab. In the list, select plugin **SelectionHistory** and click **Uninstall**, as shown in Figure 17.15.

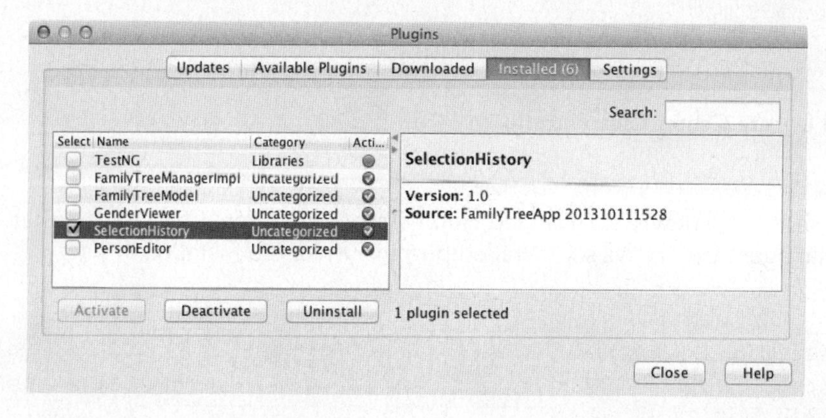


Figure 17.15 Uninstall a plugin

3. NetBeans begins the Plugin Uninstaller process, as shown in Figure 17.16. Click **Uninstall**.

Figure 17.16 The Plugin Uninstaller process

4. NetBeans removes the SelectionHistory module from the FamilyTreeApp. You can choose to restart the application now or later. Click **Finish**, as shown in Figure 17.17.

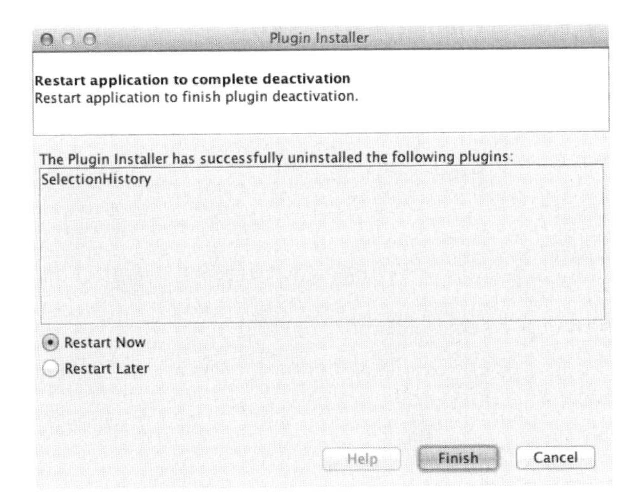


Figure 17.17 Restart now or later and Finish the uninstall process

## Adding Modules to an Application

You can add modules to an application with either your application's Update Center or by installing a downloaded NetBeans Module (NBM). Both options require an application with a Plugin Manager.

Let's first show you how you might add a new NBM to a running application by adding the SelectionHistory module to the FamilyTreeApp. This scenario applies when you've downloaded an NBM file and now wish to install it in your running application. You use the Plugin Manager, but you do not need to access the Update Center.

### Create the Module NBM

To add the SelectionHistory module to a running application as an NBM, you first must create the NBM file (if you haven't done this previously) and somehow send to your user.

1. In the Projects view, right click project **SelectionHistory** and select **Create NBM** from the context menu.
2. NetBeans builds the module and places the NBM file under the modules build directory with the name `com-asgteach-familytree-selectionhistory.nbm`. You can view the NBM using the Files window as shown in Figure 17.18.

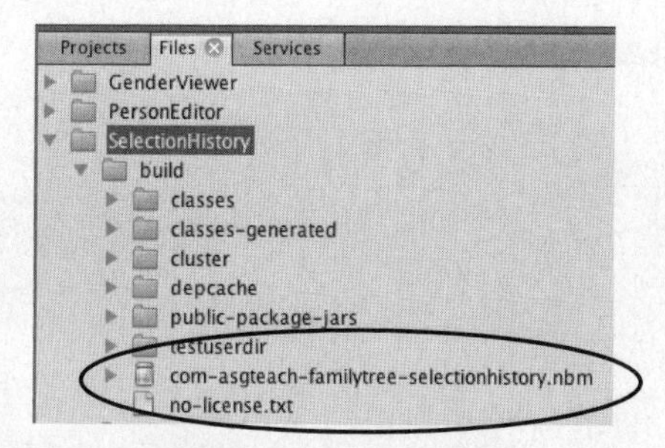


Figure 17.18 Creating an NBM for module SelectionHistory

## Install a Downloaded NBM

You'll now add the module to the FamilyTreeApp using the following steps.

1. Run the FamilyTreeApp and from the top menu, select **Tools | Plugins**. The application displays the Plugin Manager.
2. Select the **Downloaded** tab, then click **Add Plugins . . .** as shown in Figure 17.19.

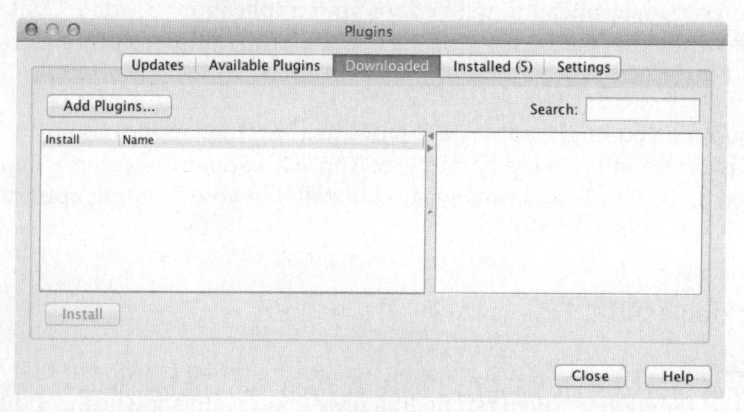


Figure 17.19 Add a plugin to an application

3. NetBeans displays a file chooser window. Browse to the directory that contains the NBM file (here we browse to the **build** directory under project SelectionHistory) and select the NBM file, as shown in Figure 17.20. Click **Open**.

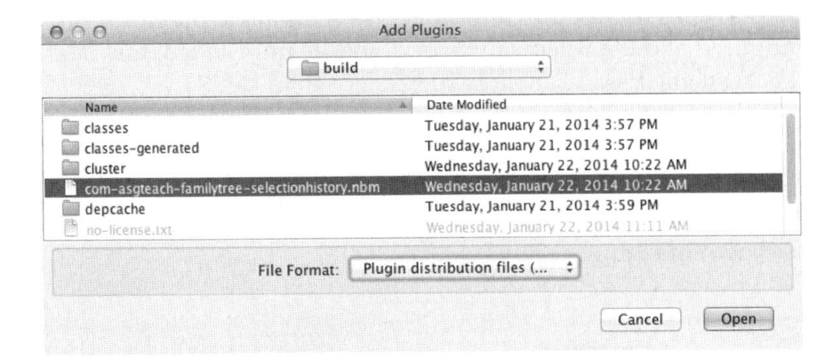


Figure 17.20 Choose the NBM file

4. NetBeans displays the Plugin in the Downloaded window. Select plugin **SelectionHistory** and click **Install**, as shown in Figure 17.21.

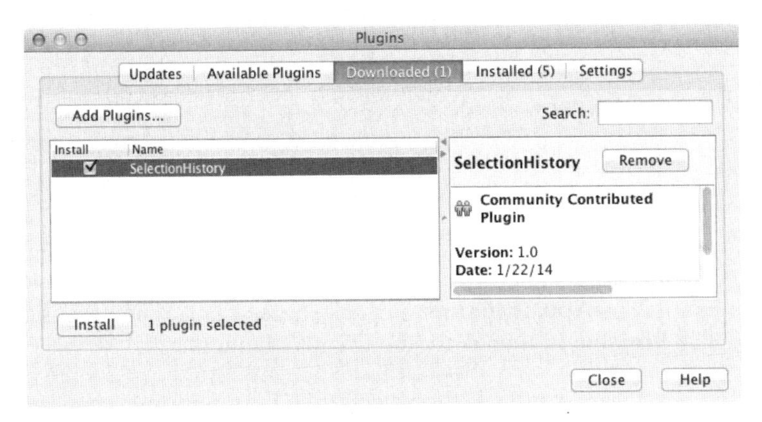


Figure 17.21 Install the SelectionHistory plugin

5. NetBeans initiates the Plugin Installer, which takes you through the steps to install the NBM into the FamilyTreeApp, including a license agreement. When the installation completes, click **Finish** and then close the Plugin Manager.

When the Plugin Manager closes, you'll see the SelectionHistory window open in your application.

## Install a Plugin

When you create and configure an Update Center with your application's modules, new and updated modules become available for installation through the Update Center. A Plugin Manager checks for updates and categorizes available plugins. With an Update Center configured and the SelectionHistory module uninstalled, this module shows up under tab Available Plugins. Follow these steps to install it.

1. From the top-level menu bar, select **Tools | Plugins**. NetBeans displays the Plugin Manager.
2. Click **Available Plugins** and select the **SelectionHistory** plugin.
3. Click **Install**, as shown in Figure 17.22.

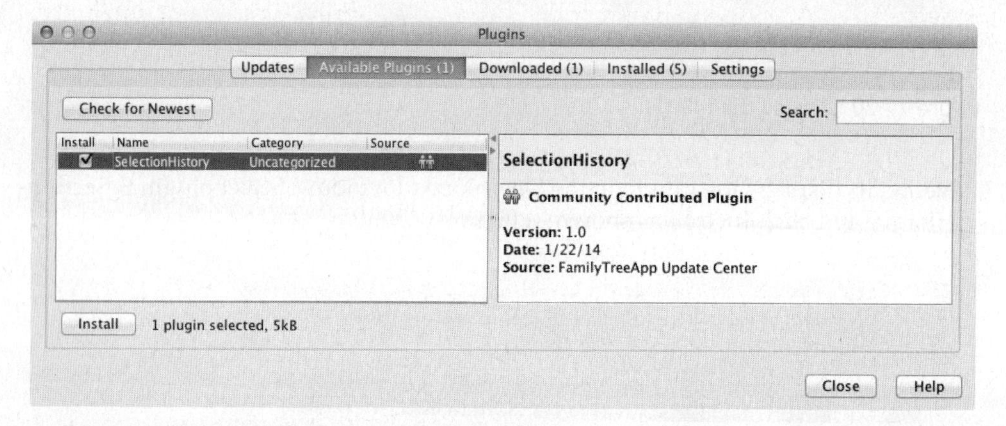


Figure 17.22 Install a plug using the Update Center

4. NetBeans initiates the Plugin Installer, which takes you through the steps to install the NBM into the FamilyTreeApp, including a license agreement. When the installation completes, click **Finish** and then close the Plugin Manager.

When the Plugin Manager closes, you'll see the SelectionHistory window open in your application.

## 17.3 Application Distribution

The NetBeans IDE lets you create distribution files for users to install your application. You can create an installation that is compatible with Windows, Linux, Mac OS X, or Solaris. As part of the process for creating a distribution, you can include a custom License Agreement.

#### Enabling the Plugin Manager

*Prior to creating a distribution for your application, if you want to provide updates either through an Update Center or with individual NBM files, you must enable the Plugin Manager, as described in "Enable Updates of Your Application" on page 857.*

### Create an Installer

By default, NetBeans assumes you want to create an Installer that is compatible with your development system. To create Installers for other systems, use the Properties menu, as follows.

1. Right click on the **FamilyTreeApp** application project and select **Properties** from the context menu. Under Categories, select **Installer**, as shown in Figure 17.23.

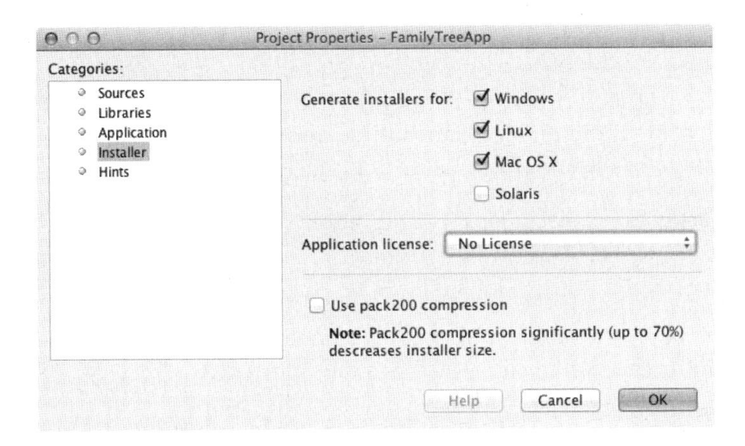


Figure 17.23 Choosing Installer targets

2. Options include Windows, Linux, Mac OS X, and Solaris. Check all that apply.
3. For Application license, select the option that applies to your application from the drop down menu, as shown in Figure 17.24. If you want to supply your own license, choose **Select license file . . .** and a File Chooser lets you select a text file that contains the license wording. This license text will then be used during application installation.
4. Specify **Use pack200 compression** if you want to reduce the installer size.
5. Click **OK** to set the Installer properties.

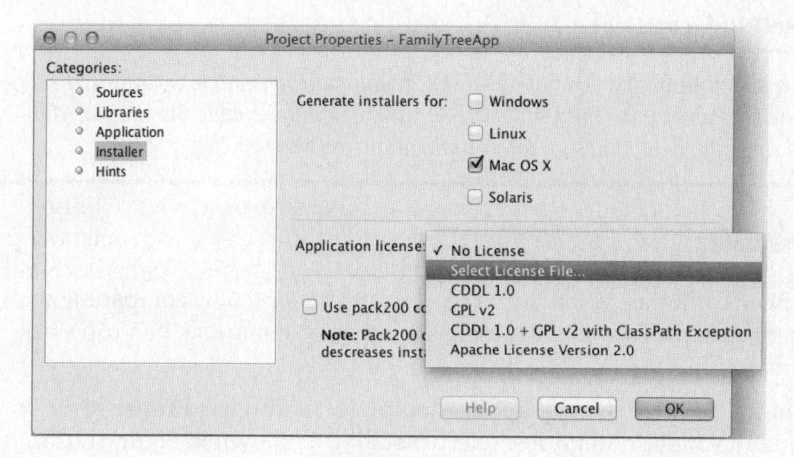


Figure 17.24 Choosing Installer targets

6. To create the Installers, right click project **FamilyTreeApp** and select **Package as ... | Installers** from the context menu. NetBeans builds installers in the application's **`dist`** directory (as shown in Figure 17.25) for each target specified, as follows.

```
Installer(s) for [windows linux macosx] are available
      at <full path>/FamilyTreeApp/dist
```

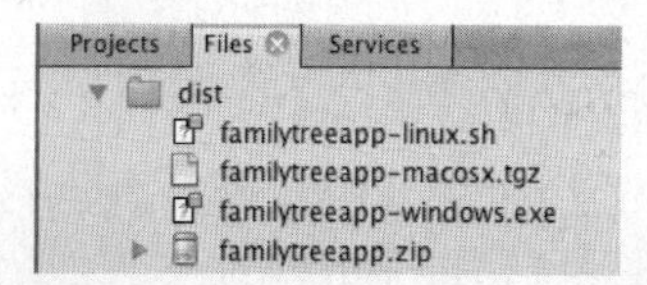


Figure 17.25 Installers are created in the project's **dist** directory

### Installer Tip

---

*Creating Installers can take a long time. Monitor the process in the NetBeans IDE Output window.*

---

## Installing the Application

Let's show you the installation process on a Mac. Other target systems have similar installation processes.

On a Mac, once you double-click the **.zip** or **.tgz** file, you'll see an executable Installer. When you run the Installer, an Installer wizard takes you through the installation. Figure 17.26 shows the first panel. Click **Next** to continue to successive panels, which include a License Agreement, installation directory and icon creation, and a summary panel that recaps the install features.

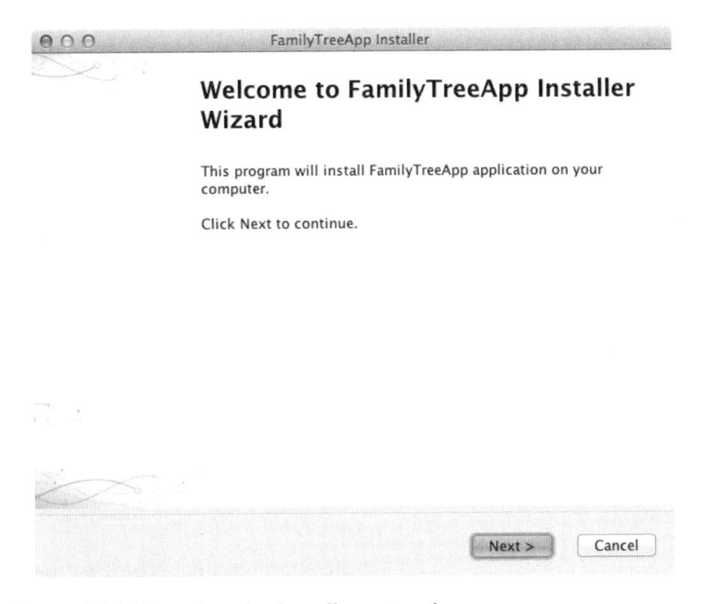


Figure 17.26 Running the Installer wizard

Figure 17.27 shows the last panel after the installation completes. You can optionally launch the application when you click **Finish** to end the Installer wizard.

## Customizing the Installer Images

The default Installer uses standard images for the Installer wizard. You can customize these images by modifying image files found in the standard NetBeans Installation (nbi) hierarchy in your NetBeans installation directory, located at **<Your NetBeans Installation>/harness/nbi**.

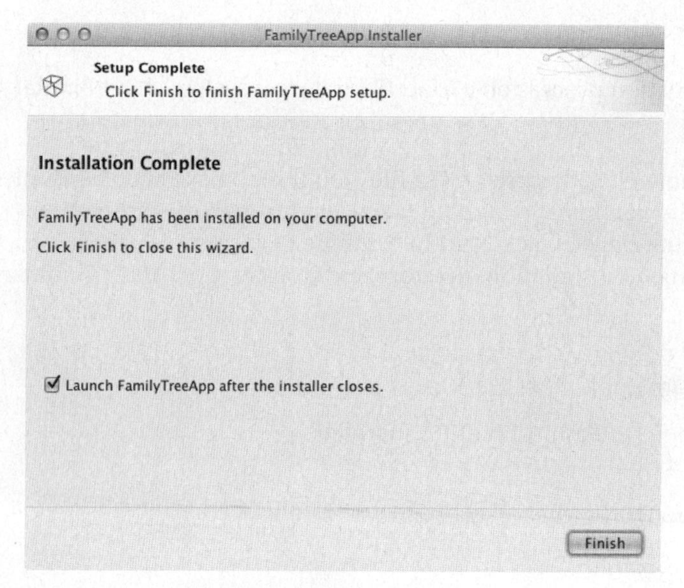


Figure 17.27 Installation Complete panel

Table 17.1 shows the images used in the standard Installer wizard and their locations. You can replace these files with your own. After regenerating the Installer, you'll see the new images.

**TABLE 17.1 Location and Name of Default Installer Images**

| Directory under nbi | File name |
|---|---|
| stub/ext/engine/src/org/mycompany/installer/wizard | wizard-description-background-left.png<br>wizard-description-background-right.png<br>wizard-icon.png |
| stub/ext/engine/src/org/mycompany/installer/wizard/components/panels/resources | welcome-left-bottom.png<br>welcome-left-top.png |

# 17.4 Application Internationalization

Internationalizing an application configures the application for one or more locales. Internationalization includes target language translations and localizing the look and feel, such as number formatting and currency symbols. Internationalization is a big topic, but with an example, you'll gain a good understanding of the issues.

We have internationalized the SmartPhoneDataApp presented in the previous chapter and localized the application for English, Spanish, and Portuguese. (See "RESTful Web Services and the NetBeans Platform" on page 800 for a description of this application.)[3]

Figure 17.28 shows the TableView window of the SmartPhoneDataApp. The left window is localized for Spanish, and the right window is localized for Brazilian Portuguese. Localization includes text for the window names, titles, labels, and buttons, as well as localized number formatting.

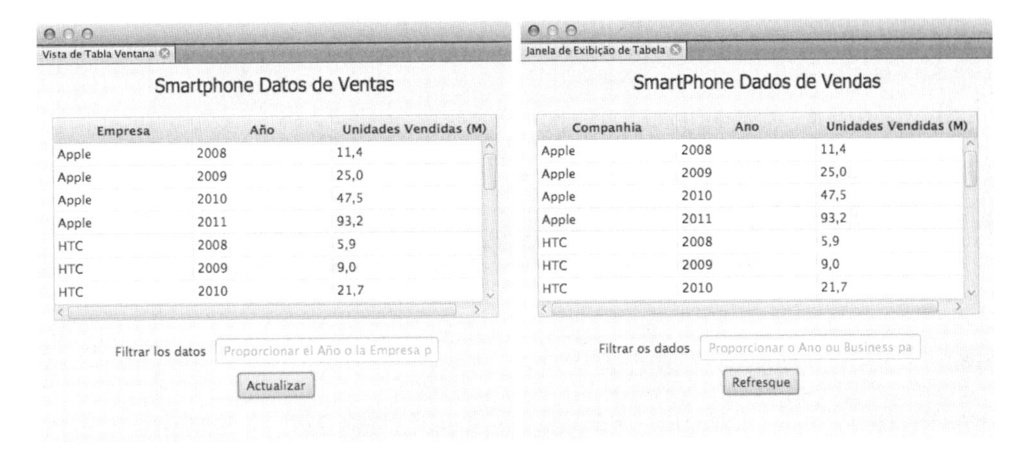


Figure 17.28 Localized TableView window

Similarly, Figure 17.29 shows localized versions of the LineChart window from the same application.

## Internationalization and Java

Java and the NetBeans Platform have long supported application internationalization. You can find helpful documentation and tutorials at the following URLs.

- `http://docs.oracle.com/javase/tutorial/i18n/`—Internationalization Learning Trail
- `http://docs.oracle.com/javase/7/docs/technotes/guides/intl/`—Internationalization Technical Guide

3. With apologies to native speakers of Spanish and Portuguese, we have mainly relied on web-based translation services.

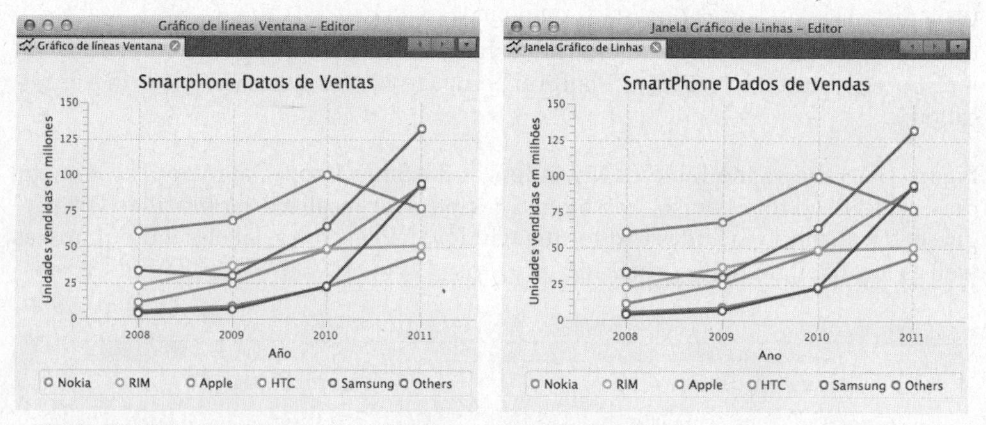


Figure 17.29 Localized LineChart window

- `http://bits.netbeans.org/dev/javadoc/org-openide-modules/org/openide/modules/doc-files/i18n-branding.html`—Internationalization and Branding Guide for NetBeans

## Internationalization and the NetBeans Platform

Let's describe how to internationalize your application and provide examples with the SmartPhoneDataApp. In general, the process includes the following steps.

1. Identify all text that should be localized and assign a key, unique within the Java package where the text appears.
2. Provide translations of these text strings in the target language or languages in locale-specific `.properties` files.
3. Use the `@Messages` annotation (described below) to define key-value properties for the text.
4. Provide localized JAR files for the NetBeans Platform modules' localized text (discussed in the next section).

The NetBeans Platform provides the `@Messages` annotation to isolate text for localization. You put all of the key-value text Strings directly in the Java source file. This annotation generates a **Bundle.properties** file and creates static methods based on the message key. Keys must be unique within the same package. You can have multiple `@Messages` annotations within a Java file. For example, when you create a TopComponent, NetBeans generates an initial `@Messages` annotation for you.

```
@Messages({
    "HINT_TableViewTopComponent=This is a TableView window",
    "CTL_TableViewAction=TableView",
    "CTL_TableViewTopComponent=TableView Window"
})
. . .
        setName(Bundle.CTL_TableViewTopComponent());
        setToolTipText(Bundle.HINT_TableViewTopComponent());
```

The `@Messages` annotation generates static methods as follows.

- A Bundle.java file is generated in your module's directory `build/classes-generated/your_package_name` with the static methods.

```
package com.asgteach.coretableview;
/** Localizable strings for {@link com.asgteach.coretableview}. */
@javax.annotation.Generated(value=
           "org.netbeans.modules.openide.util.NbBundleProcessor")
class Bundle {
    /**
     * @return <i>TableView</i>
     * @see TableViewTopComponent
     */
    static String CTL_TableViewAction() {
        return org.openide.util.NbBundle.getMessage(Bundle.class,
                              "CTL_TableViewAction");
    }
    /**
     * @return <i>TableView Window</i>
     * @see TableViewTopComponent
     */
    static String CTL_TableViewTopComponent() {
        return org.openide.util.NbBundle.getMessage(Bundle.class,
                          "CTL_TableViewTopComponent");
    }
. . .
}
```

- This file updates as you save your Java source file, giving you edit-time source code checks for static methods with localized Strings. This edit-time source code checking avoids run-time MissingResourceException errors.

- The build system then compiles your Java classes, including Bundle.java, and generates the proper Bundle.properties file in directory `build/classes/your_package_name`. (Resource properties files are loaded by classloader.)

- The key-value pairs configured in the `@Messages` annotation create the default message bundle for that package.

You build alternate **Bundle.properties** files as needed when internationalizing an application, as follows.

- To create message bundles for other locales, create **Bundle_xx.properties** files for each locale that you support. Use either a two-character language code or a combined four character language_region code with a separator. For example, a properties file that supports Portuguese uses suffix `_pt` and Portuguese localized for Brazil is suffix `pt_BR`, as follows.

```
Bundle_pt.properties
Bundle_pt_BR.properties
```

- When users run your application, the user's default Locale applies. If the user's Locale does not match any of the provided `.properties` files, then the default message bundle applies.

## Number Formatting

The Java NumberFormat class supports Locales. Thus, if your application displays numbers, you can format them with NumberFormat using the default locale. For example, the DecimalFormat class in the SmartPhoneDataApp shown in Listing 17.3 instantiates a NumberFormat object with the default Locale. The `toString()` method invokes the NumberFormat `format()` method for locale-sensitive formatting. Similarly, the `fromString()` method accepts the locale-specific decimal and number separator characters used with the in-place editor. Note that the decimal separator in both the Spanish and Portuguese TableView windows shown in Figure 17.28 on page 869 is a comma.

**Listing 17.3 DecimalFormat.java**

```
private class DecimalConverter extends StringConverter<BigDecimal> {

    NumberFormat nf = NumberFormat.getInstance(Locale.getDefault());

    public DecimalConverter() {
        nf.setMaximumFractionDigits(2);
        nf.setMinimumFractionDigits(1);
    }

    @Override
    public String toString(BigDecimal t) {
        try {
            return nf.format(t);
        } catch (Exception e) {
            return null;
        }
    }
```

```
        @Override
        public BigDecimal fromString(String string) {
            try {
                Number newValue = nf.parse(string);
                BigDecimal result = new BigDecimal(newValue.doubleValue());
                return result.setScale(2, BigDecimal.ROUND_HALF_EVEN);
            } catch (ParseException e) {
                return null;
            }
        }
    }
```

## Editing Properties Files

The `@Messages` annotation generates a default **Bundle.properties** file. To support additional locales, you must create the **Bundle.properties** file for each supported locale. You can either edit these files individually or edit them together. Figure 17.30 shows the NetBeans IDE simultaneous edit capability with the Bundle.properties file for `en`, `es`, and `pt_BR` locales. The default language is empty, since these Strings are generated from the `@Messages` annotation.

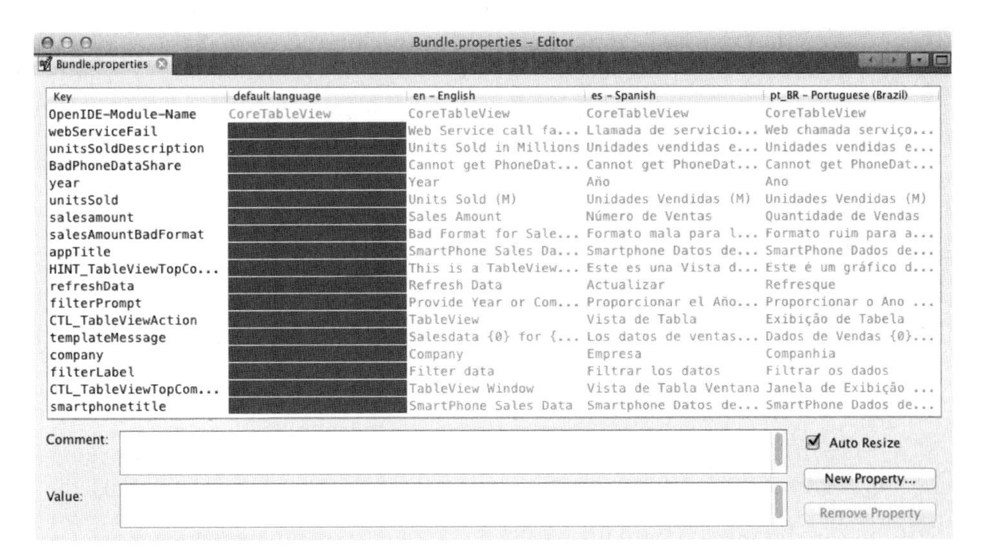


Figure 17.30 Editing Properties files

## Internationalization and JavaFX

The SmartPhoneDataApp windows also include JavaFX content. You can specify a ResourceBundle when you build the JavaFX scene graph, typically in TopComponent code. The JavaFX controller class (Java code) uses the `@Messages` static methods and can define additional key-value pairs with the `@Messages` annotation. Listing 17.4 shows you how to invoke the FXMLLoader to set the resources for the scene graph described by TableView.fxml inside the TopComponent code.

**Listing 17.4 TableViewTopComponent.java—Initializing ResourceBundle**

```
public final class TableViewTopComponent extends TopComponent {

    private static JFXPanel fxPanel;
    private TableViewController controller;
    private final ResourceBundle resources;

    public TableViewTopComponent() {
        initComponents();
        resources = ResourceBundle.getBundle(
                "com.asgteach.coretableview.Bundle", Locale.getDefault());
        setName(Bundle.CTL_TableViewTopComponent());
        setToolTipText(Bundle.HINT_TableViewTopComponent());

        setLayout(new BorderLayout());
        init();
    }

    public void init() {
        fxPanel = new JFXPanel();
        add(fxPanel, BorderLayout.CENTER);
        Platform.setImplicitExit(false);
        Platform.runLater(() -> createScene());
    }

    private void createScene() {
        try {
            URL location = getClass().getResource("TableView.fxml");
            FXMLLoader fxmlLoader = new FXMLLoader();

            fxmlLoader.setResources(resources);
            fxmlLoader.setLocation(location);
            fxmlLoader.setBuilderFactory(new JavaFXBuilderFactory());

            Parent root = (Parent) fxmlLoader.load(location.openStream());
            fxPanel.setScene(new Scene(root));
            controller = (TableViewController) fxmlLoader.getController();
        } catch (IOException ex) {
            Exceptions.printStackTrace(ex);
        }
    }
. . .
}
```

With the ResourceBundle defined, you can use the `%key` notation in FXML, as shown in Listing 17.5. Here is a portion of TableView.fxml that defines the TableView control and its embedded TableColumns. We define each TableColumn `text` property with the `%key` notation.

**Listing 17.5 TableView.fxml—Using Resource Keys**

```
<TableView fx:id="tableview"
           editable="true"
           GridPane.columnIndex="0"
           GridPane.rowIndex="0" >
    <columns>
        <TableColumn fx:id="colCompany" text="%company"
                     sortable="false" minWidth="150" />
        <TableColumn fx:id="colYear" text="%year"
                     sortable="false" minWidth="150" />
        <TableColumn fx:id="colUnitsSold" text="%unitsSold"
                     editable="true" sortable="false"
                     minWidth="175" />
    </columns>
</TableView>
```

Note that `%key` bypasses compile-time checking for valid keys, however. Here is the exception you get when using a key that doesn't exist.

```
SEVERE [org.openide.util.Exceptions]
javafx.fxml.LoadException: Resource "blahblah" not found.
```

### @Messages and FXML

*To retain the compile-time safeguards of* `@Messages`*, move the FXML text property initializations into the controller code, as follows. Here we invoke the* `setText()` *method with the static Bundle methods for the appropriate keys.*

```
@Override
public void initialize(final URL url, final ResourceBundle resources) {
     . . .
    colCompany.setText(Bundle.company());
    colYear.setText(Bundle.year());
    colUnitsSold.setText(Bundle.unitsSold());
     . . .
```

## Testing Target Locales

Test your application for different locales by defining the run.args.extra property with the target locale in the application's **project.properties** file, as shown in Listing 17.6. Here the default locale changes to pt_BR for the Portuguese language (Brazil). The **project.properties** file appears in the Projects view under node **Important Files** of your NetBeans Platform Application project.

**Listing 17.6 Application's project.properties File**

```
app.name=${branding.token}
app.title=SmartPhoneDataApp
# to test a new locale, uncomment the following line
# and specify your target locale
run.args.extra=run.args.extra=-J-Duser.language=pt -J-Duser.region=BR
modules=\
    ${project.com.asgteach.coretableview}:\
    ${project.com.asgteach.phonedata.webservice}:\
    ${project.com.asgteach.linechart}:\
    ${project.com.asgteach.phonedatashareimpl}
project.com.asgteach.coretableview=CoreTableView
project.com.asgteach.linechart=LineChart
project.com.asgteach.phonedata.webservice=PhoneDataWebService
project.com.asgteach.phonedatashareimpl=PhoneDataShareImpl
```

## NetBeans Platform Application Internationalization

The preceding steps show how to internationalize/localize text that you provide in your application. However, since you are building on top of the NetBeans Platform, there are still menus, tooltips, error messages, and other text that originate from the NetBeans Platform modules. These will still be in English unless you provide the JAR files containing localized property bundles.[4]

The NetBeans IDE (and therefore, the NetBeans Platform) supports the following languages.

- Brazilian Portuguese (locale pt_BR)
- Russian (locale ru)
- Japanese (locale ja)
- Simplified Chinese (locale zh_CN)

4. Geertjan Wielenga provided guidance for this approach to localization.

If you specify one of these languages on the NetBeans IDE Download page (`https://netbeans.org/downloads/`), you can install an international version of the IDE. (This version includes English as well.) With the international version installed, you can use localized JAR files in your own NetBeans Platform application. Here are the steps to add support for Brazilian Portuguese. We'll continue to use the SmartPhoneDataApp described in this chapter.

1. Download and install the international version of the NetBeans IDE.
2. Open up the SmartPhoneDataApp in the international version of the IDE.
3. Specify the target locale in the application's **project.properties** file for testing, as shown in Listing 17.6 on page 876.
4. Run the application using the international version of the NetBeans IDE. You will see Brazilian Portuguese for the NetBeans Platform modules.

### Creating a Localized Application Bundle

The previous steps test the application using the localized bundles from the international version of the NetBeans IDE. These next steps are necessary to run a localized version of your application as a stand-alone application outside the environment of the NetBeans IDE.

For this, you must copy the localized JAR files (which are included in the international version of the IDE) from the NetBeans distribution into your application. Furthermore, to create a modularized structure for localization support, create a module for each target locale. As an example, here are the steps to add support for Brazilian Portuguese.

1. Create a new module in the SmartPhoneDataApp called **Locale_PT_BR** with code name **com.asgteach.localeptbr**.
2. Switch to the File view and create the following folders at the top level. These folders will be at the same level as **nbproject** and **src**.

- **release/core/locale**
- **release/lib/locale**
- **release/modules/locale**

3. Now browse to the NetBeans IDE installation and find the corresponding **platform/core/locale**, **platform/lib/locale**, and **platform/modules/locale** folders. For Brazilian Portuguese support, copy all JAR files with names ending in **pt_BR.jar** to the corresponding folders in the **Locale_PT_BR** module under the **release** directory, as shown in Figure 17.31 (the list of JAR files under **release/modules/locale** is truncated).

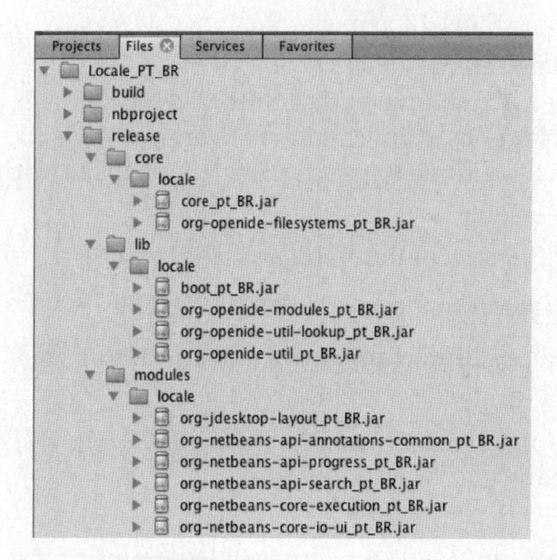


Figure 17.31 Adding localized property bundles for the NetBeans Platform

4. For each supported language, create a module with these release folders to hold the NetBeans Platform locale JAR files as shown in the above steps.

Using this modular approach, users can dynamically add or remove language support for the NetBeans Platform modules (see "Dynamically Uninstall a Module (Plugin)" on page 860 and "Adding Modules to an Application" on page 861).

Figure 17.32 shows the SmartPhoneDataApp with localized top-level menus and menu items from the NetBeans Platform module localized bundles in Portuguese.

Note that your application probably doesn't require the full complement of locale JAR files. However, the entire group of JAR files for Brazilian Portuguese, for example, does not consume much space.

## Localization Support for Additional Languages[5]

Although the NetBeans IDE gives you the localized bundles for languages that NetBeans officially supports, you may want to support other languages. Fortunately, a community project exists that provides localized bundles for additional languages.

5. Besides the information presented here, NetBeans.org has created a NetBeans localization project. See the following Blog Entry by Geertjan Wielenga at `https://blogs.oracle.com/geertjan/entry/lightweight_process_for_translating_netbeans`.

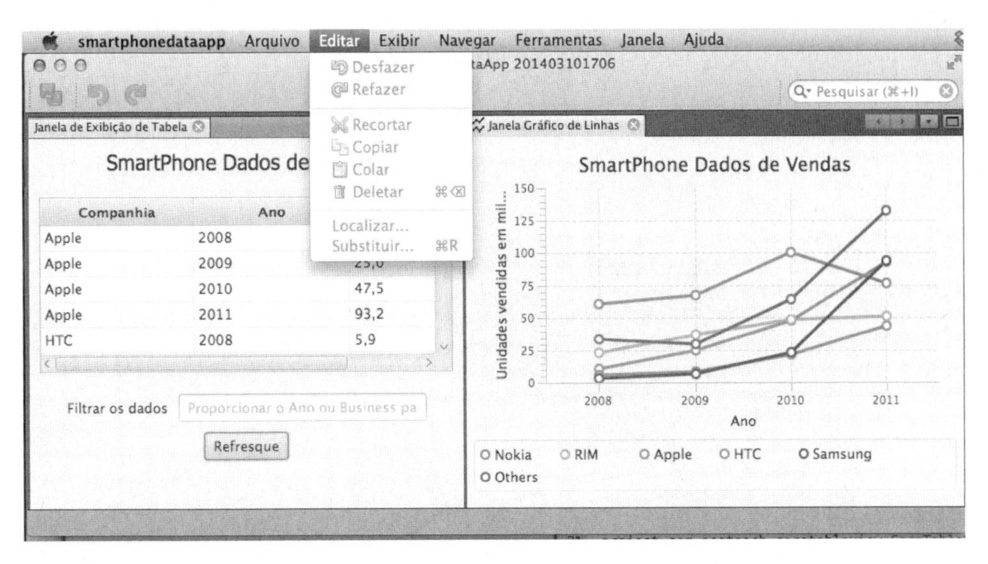


Figure 17.32 SmartPhoneDataApp with localized NetBeans Platform modules

The AgroSense[6] team led by Timon Veenstra has published community translations for additional languages. These localized JARs are from the NetBeans Platform 7.2 release. Fortunately, most changes to the NetBeans Platform modules since then do not affect UI components and other text-sensitive behaviors.

Let's now access this resource that includes localized JAR files to support Spanish. Here are the steps using the same modularized approach.

1. Create a new module in the SmartPhoneDataApp called **Locale_ES** with code name **com.asgteach.localees**.
2. Switch to the File view and create the same folders at the top level that you created for the Portuguese localization: **release/core/locale**, **release/lib/locale**, and **release/modules/locale**.
3. Go to `https://java.net/projects/nb-library-wrappers/sources/core/show/lib-platform-l10n/nb72_platform_l10n/platform` and download the JARs you need for your target language. For Spanish, download the JAR files ending in **_es.jar**.[7]

6. See `http://agrosense.eu/`.
7. Alternatively, check out the entire project to access all of the localized JAR files.

4. Populate the **locale** folders in the Locale_ES module, as shown in Figure 17.33 (the list of JAR files under **modules/locale** is truncated).

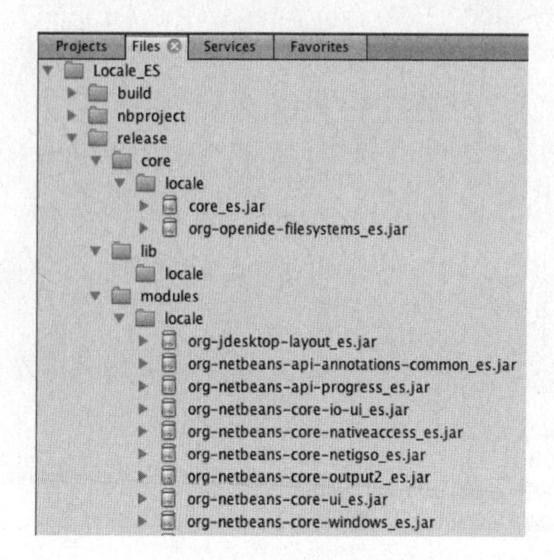


Figure 17.33 Add the localized JAR files to the Locale_ES module

Figure 17.34 shows the SmartPhoneDataApp with localized top-level menus and menu items for Spanish.

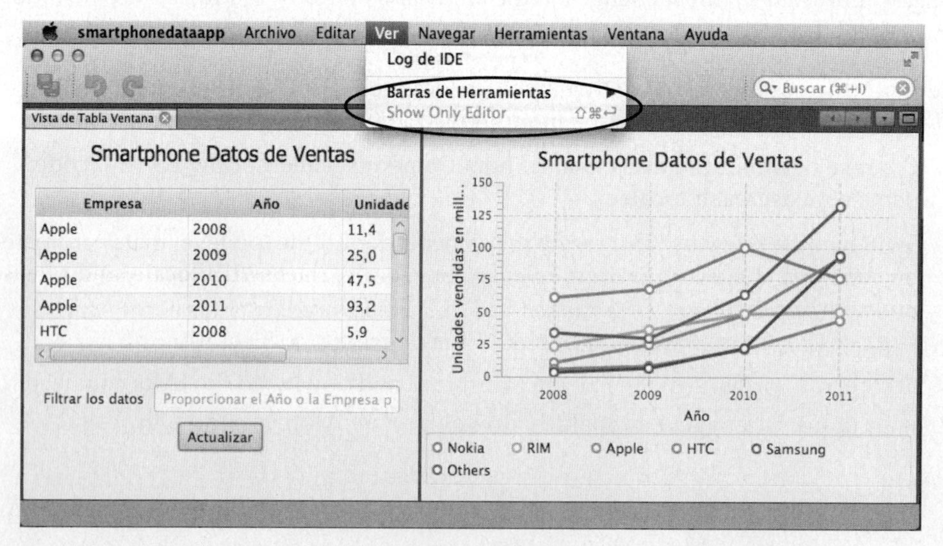


Figure 17.34 SmartPhoneDataApp with localized NetBeans Platform modules

## Customizing Resource Bundles

The JAR files that you add to your module's locale directories are Resource Bundles. You can customize these if the translations are incomplete or if you'd like to modify a particular translation.

For example, in the Spanish version we acquired, Figure 17.34 shows that there isn't a translation for the **Show Only Editor** menu item under View (**Ver**). Here's how to fix this omission.

1. In the SmartPhoneDataApp Projects view, right click on the application name and select **Branding . . .** from the context menu.
2. Select the **Internationalization Resource Bundles** tab and choose the locale you want to modify. Here, we specify the locale "**es**" for Spanish.
3. Use the Search field to look for the target text as shown in Figure 17.35 (here, we search for "**Only Editor**").

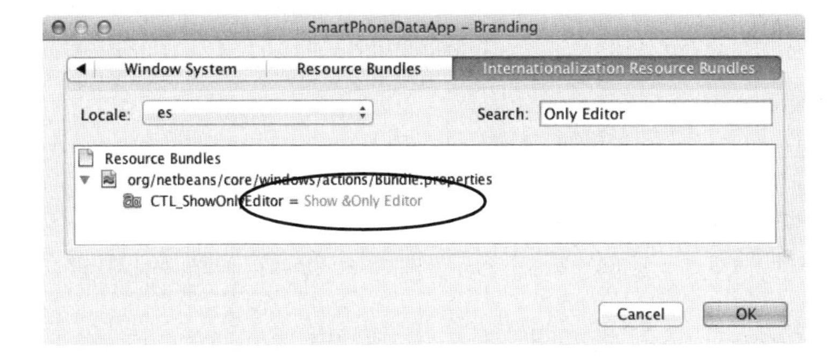


Figure 17.35 Select target locale and provide search String

### Search Tip

*If your target search string is a menu item with an attached accelerator (as in our example), then include an ampersand before the accelerator letter when searching. Alternatively, try limiting the search term.*

4. Right click the target text and select **Add to Branding**. In the dialog, provide the translated text and click **OK**. NetBeans changes the value associated with this key for the **es** resource bundle, as shown in Figure 17.36. Click **OK** to close the Branding dialog.
5. The Files view shows that NetBeans created file **Bundle_es.properties** under folders **branding/modules** (expand the directory hierarchy under the JAR file).

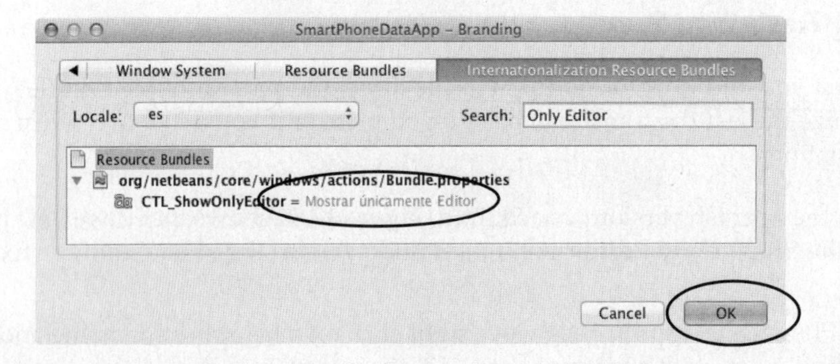


Figure 17.36 Modifying selected key-value pairs for localization

Figure 17.37 shows the directory hierarchy and the corresponding **.properties** file in the Editor.

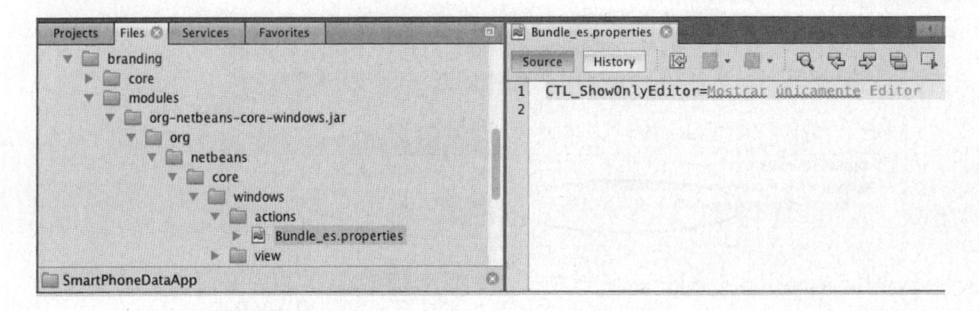


Figure 17.37 Add to Branding creates a Bundle_es.properties file

And now, when you re-run the SmartPhoneDataApp, the Show Only Editor menu item has a Spanish translation, as shown in Figure 17.38.

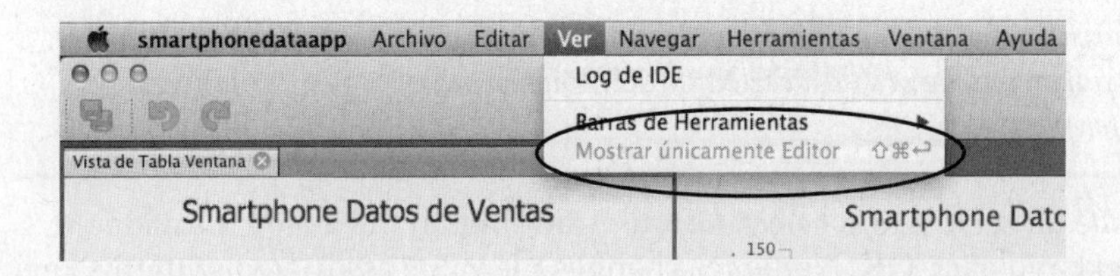


Figure 17.38 SmartPhoneDataApp with localized menu item included

# 17.5 Key Point Summary

This chapter shows you how to brand your application, provide distribution files and updates to your users, and internationalize and localize your application. Here are the key points in this chapter.

- Branding lets you customize your application's name and title, splash screen, as well as any text found in the application's resource bundles.
- Use the Branding dialog to change an application's title.
- Use the Properties dialog to change an application's branding name. The branding name is mainly for internal use and has restrictions on its form.
- Modify the `app.name` property in the application's Project Properties file to customize the application's name as it appears in the top-level menu and your operating system's task manager.
- You can customize an application's title to include your own version number (instead of the NetBeans IDE build number). You can also remove any version information from the title.
- Use the Branding dialog to customize your application's splash screen. You can also modify how the progress bar appears and the position, font size, and color of the running text.
- In order for users to dynamically update a NetBeans Platform application, include the AutoUpdate Services and AutoUpdate UI modules.
- Create content for an Update Center using the application's **Package As | NBMs** menu.
- Configure an Update Center for your application using the Plugin Manager.
- Use the Plugin Manager to dynamically install and uninstall modules in your application.
- You can create distribution files so that users can install your application. NetBeans supports Windows, Linux, Mac OS X, and Solaris.
- You can customize an installer by providing your own License Agreement and installer images.
- Internationalizing an application means configuring the application for one or more locales.
- The first step to internationalize an application is to isolate its text.

- The NetBeans Platform `@Messages` annotation provides edit-time checking for key-value properties stored in resource bundles.
- The Java NumberFormat class is locale-sensitive, and any numbers used in your application can be localized.
- The NetBeans IDE lets you simultaneously edit multiple **.properties** files.
- You can easily internationalize your JavaFX code. We recommend using the `@Messages` annotation to retain edit-time checking for the key-value properties.
- Add the `-J-Duser.language` and `-J-Duser.region` properties to the application's Project Properties file to test target locales.
- The NetBeans Platform officially supports English, Brazilian Portuguese, Russian, Japanese, and simplified Chinese. Download the international version of the IDE to access the localized JAR files for these locales and add them to your application.
- You can access the AgroSense community project that supports localizing bundles for other languages. See also the NetBeans Localization project at `java.net` described at `https://blogs.oracle.com/geertjan/entry/lightweight_process_for_translating_netbeans`.
- Use the Internationalization Resource Bundles tab in the Branding dialog to customize any localized JAR files in your application.

# Index

## A

## B



## C

# D



# E

# L

# M



# N

# O



# P



# Q



# R

## S

# T



# U



# V

## W



## X



## Y